Breathing-Related Sleep Disorders
Obstructive Sleep Apnea Hypopnea/
Central Sleep Apnea/Sleep-Related
Hypoventilation/Circadian Rhythm
Sleep-Wake Disorders

Parasomnias
Non-Rapid Eye Movement Sleep Arousal
Disorders/Nightmare Disorder/
Rapid Eye Movement Sleep Behavior
Disorder/Restless Legs Syndrome/
Substance/Medication-Induced
Sleep Disorder/Other Specified
Insomnia Disorder/Unspecified
Insomnia Disorder/Other Specified
Hypersomnolence Disorder/
Unspecified Hypersomnolence
Disorder/Other Specified Sleep-Wake
Disorder/Unspecified Sleep-Wake
Disorder

Sexual Dysfunctions
Delayed Ejaculation/Erectile Disorder/
Female Orgasmic Disorder/Female
Sexual Interest/Arousal Disorder/
Genito-Pelvic Pain/Penetration
Disorder/Male Hypoactive Sexual
Desire Disorder/Premature (Early)
Ejaculation/Substance/Medication-
Induced Sexual Dysfunction/Other
Specified Sexual Dysfunction/
Unspecified Sexual Dysfunction

Gender Dysphoria
Gender Dysphoria/Other Specified
Gender Dysphoria/Unspecified
Gender Dysphoria

Disruptive, Impulse-Control, and Conduct Disorders
Oppositional Defiant Disorder/
Intermittent Explosive Disorder/
Conduct Disorder/Antisocial
Personality Disorder/Pyromania/
Kleptomania/Other Specified
Disruptive, Impulse-Control, and
Conduct Disorder/Unspecified
Disruptive, Impulse-Control, and
Conduct Disorder

Substance-Related and Addictive Disorders
Substance-Related Disorders
Alcohol-Related Disorders: Alcohol Use
Disorder/Alcohol Intoxication/Alcohol
Withdrawal/Other Alcohol-Induced
Disorders/Unspecified Alcohol-Related
Disorder
Caffeine-Related Disorders: Caffeine
Intoxication/Caffeine Withdrawal/
Other Caffeine-Induced Disorders/
Unspecified Caffeine-Related Disorder
Cannabis-Related Disorders: Cannabis
Use Disorder/Cannabis Intoxication/
Cannabis Withdrawal/Other Cannabis-
Induced Disorders/Unspecified
Cannabis-Related Disorder
Hallucinogen-Related Disorders:
Phencyclidine Use Disorders/
Other Hallucinogen Use Disorder/
Phencyclidine Intoxication/
Other Hallucinogen Intoxication/
Hallucinogen Persisting Perception
Disorder/Other Phencyclidine-Induced
Disorders/Other Hallucinogen-Induced
Disorders/Unspecified Phencyclidine-
Related Disorders/Unspecified
Hallucinogen-Related Disorders
Inhalant-Related Disorders: Inhalant
Use Disorder/Inhalant Intoxication/
Other Inhalant-Induced Disorders/
Unspecified Inhalant-Related Disorders
Opioid-Related Disorders: Opioid Use
Disorder/Opioid Intoxication/Opioid
Withdrawal/Other Opioid-Induced
Disorders/Unspecified Opioid-Related
Disorder
Sedative-, Hypnotic-, or Anxiolytic-
Related Disorders: Sedative, Hypnotic,
or Anxiolytic Use Disorder/Sedative,
Hypnotic, or Anxiolytic Intoxication/
Sedative, Hypnotic, or Anxiolytic
Withdrawal/Other Sedative-, Hypnotic-,
or Anxiolytic-Induced Disorders/
Unspecified Sedative-, Hypnotic-, or
Anxiolytic-Related Disorder
Stimulant-Related Disorders: Stimulant
Use Disorder/Stimulant Intoxication/
Stimulant Withdrawal/Other
Stimulant-Induced Disorders/
Unspecified Stimulant-Related Disorder
Tobacco-Related Disorders: Tobacco
Use Disorder/Tobacco Withdrawal/
Other Tobacco-Induced Disorders/
Unspecified Tobacco-Related Disorder
Other (or Unknown) Substance-Related
Disorders: Other (or Unknown)
Substance Use Disorder/Other (or
Unknown) Substance Intoxication/
Other (or Unknown) Substance
Withdrawal/Other (or Unknown)
Substance-Induced Disorders/
Unspecified Other (or Unknown)
Substance-Related Disorder

Non-Substance-Related Disorders
Gambling Disorder

Neurocognitive Disorders
Delirium

Major and Mild Neurocognitive Disorders
Major or Mild Neurocognitive Disorder
Due to Alzheimer's Disease
Major or Mild Frontotemporal
Neurocognitive Disorder
Major or Mild Neurocognitive Disorder
with Lewy Bodies
Major or Mild Vascular Neurocognitive
Disorder
Major or Mild N— — — — — — Disorder

— — — — — Major or
— — — — — isorder
Major or Mild Neurocognitive Disorder
Due to Prion Disease
Major or Mild Neurocognitive Disorder
Due to Parkinson's Disease
Major or Mild Neurocognitive Disorder
Due to Huntington's Disease
Major or Mild Neurocognitive Disorder
Due to Another Medical Condition
Major and Mild Neurocognitive
Disorders Due to Multiple Etiologies
Unspecified Neurocognitive Disorder

Personality Disorders
Cluster A Personality Disorders
Paranoid Personality Disorder/Schizoid
Personality Disorder/Schizotypal
Personality Disorder

Cluster B Personality Disorders
Antisocial Personality Disorder/
Borderline Personality Disorder/
Histrionic Personality Disorder/
Narcissistic Personality Disorder

Cluster C Personality Disorders
Avoidant Personality Disorder/
Dependent Personality Disorder/
Obsessive-Compulsive Personality
Disorder

Other Personality Disorders
Personality Change Due to Another
Medical Condition/Other Specified
Personality Disorder/Unspecified
Personality Disorder

Paraphilic Disorders

Voyeuristic Disorder/Exhibitionist Disorder/Frotteuristic Disorder/Sexual Masochism Disorder/Sexual Sadism Disorder/Pedophilic Disorder/Fetishistic Disorder/Transvestic Disorder/Other Specified Paraphilic Disorder/Unspecified Paraphilic Disorder

Other Mental Disorders

Other Specified Mental Disorder Due to Another Medical Condition/Unspecified Mental Disorder Due to Another Medical Condition/Other Specified Mental Disorder/Unspecified Mental Disorder

Medication-Induced Movement Disorders and Other Adverse Effects of Medication

Neuroleptic-Induced Parkinsonism/Other Medication-Induced Parkinsonism/Neuroleptic Malignant Syndrome/

Medication-Induced Acute Dystonia/Medication-Induced Acute Akathisia/Tardive Dyskinesia/Tardive Dystonia/Tardive Akathisia/Medication-Induced Postural Tremor/Other Medication-Induced Movement Disorder/Antidepressant Discontinuation Syndrome/Other Adverse Effect of Medication

Other Conditions That May Be a Focus of Clinical Attention

Relational Problems
Problems Related to Family Upbringing
Other Problems Related to Primary Support Group

Abuse and Neglect
Child Maltreatment and Neglect Problems
Adult Maltreatment and Neglect Problems

Educational and Occupational Problems
Educational Problems
Occupational Problems

Housing and Economic Problems
Housing Problems
Economic Problems

Other Problems Related to the Social Environment

Problems Related to Crime or Interaction with the Legal System

Other Health Service Encounters for Counseling and Medical Advice

Problems Related to Other Psychosocial, Personal, and Environment Circumstances

Other Circumstances of Personal History
Problems Related to Access to Medical and Other Health Care
Nonadherence to Medical Treatment

DSM-5 DISORDERS FOR FURTHER STUDY

The *DSM-5* Task Force judged that these disorders do not currently have sufficient supporting data for inclusion in *DSM-5* and therefore require further study. In fact, only a few of these proposed disorders will ultimately meet criteria, and others will be excluded from further consideration. Many of the more interesting disorders are discussed in one or more appropriate chapters.

Attenuated Psychosis Syndrome
Key features include delusions, hallucinations, or disorganized speech that distresses and disables the individual; the symptoms are like psychosis but not extreme enough to be considered a full psychotic disorder.

Depressive Episodes with Short-Duration Hypomania
Key features of this disorder are depressive episodes and episodes resembling hypomanic episodes but having a shorter duration (at least 2 days but below the 4-day minimum for hypomanic episodes).

Persistent Complex Bereavement Disorder
Key feature is intense grief for a year or more after the death of someone close to the bereaved individual.

Caffeine Use Disorder
Key features of this disorder are constant caffeine use and an inability to control use.

Internet Gaming Disorder
Key features of this disorder are the fixation on Internet games and continually playing them, at the expense of school, work, and/or social interactions.

Neurobehavioral Disorder Associated with Prenatal Alcohol Exposure
The key feature is diminished behavioral, cognitive, or adaptive functioning due to prenatal alcohol exposure.

Suicidal Behavior Disorder
Key feature is a suicide attempt within the past 2 years that is not related to confusion or delirium.

Nonsuicidal Self-Injury
Key feature is repeated, yet nonserious, self-inflicted bodily damage. The individual engages in these acts due to interpersonal problems, negative feelings, or uncontrollable and/or intense thoughts about the act of injuring themselves.

Source: American Psychiatric Association. (2013). *Diagnostic and statistical manual of mental disorders* (5th ed.). Arlington, VA: American Psychiatric Association.

Abnormal Child Psychology

Preliminary Edition

Sixth Edition

Eric J. Mash | David A. Wolfe

CENGAGE
Learning·

Australia • Brazil • Japan • Korea • Mexico • Singapore • Spain • United Kingdom • United States

Abnormal Psychology: Sixth Edition
Preliminary Edition

Senior Manager, Student Engagement:

Linda deStefano

Janey Moeller

Manager, Student Engagement:

Julie Dierig

Marketing Manager:

Rachael Kloos

Manager, Production Editorial:

Kim Fry

Manager, Intellectual Property Project Manager:

Brian Methe

Senior Manager, Production and Manufacturing:

Donna M. Brown

Manager, Production:

Terri Daley

Printed in the United States of America

Abnormal Psychology, Sixth Edition
Eric J. Mash | David A. Wolfe

For product information and technology assistance, contact us at
Cengage Learning Customer & Sales Support, 1-800-354-9706
For permission to use material from this text or product,
submit all requests online at **cengage.com/permissions**
Further permissions questions can be emailed to
permissionrequest@cengage.com

This book contains select works from existing Cengage Learning resources and was produced by Cengage Learning Custom Solutions for collegiate use. As such, those adopting and/or contributing to this work are responsible for editorial content accuracy, continuity and completeness.

Compilation © 2014 Cengage Learning

ISBN-13: 9781305288218

ISBN-10: 1305288211

WCN: 01-100-101

Cengage Learning

5191 Natorp Boulevard
Mason, Ohio 45040
USA

Cengage Learning is a leading provider of customized learning solutions with office locations around the globe, including Singapore, the United Kingdom, Australia, Mexico, Brazil, and Japan. Locate your local office at:
international.cengage.com/region.

Cengage Learning products are represented in Canada by Nelson Education, Ltd.
For your lifelong learning solutions, visit **www.cengage.com/custom.**
Visit our corporate website at **www.cengage.com.**

Brief Contents

1

Introduction to Normal and Abnormal Behavior in Children and Adolescents

Mankind owes to the child the best it has to give.

—UN Convention on the Rights of the Child (1989)

CHAPTER PREVIEW

AFTER CENTURIES OF SILENCE, misunderstanding, and outright abuse, children's mental health problems and needs now receive greater attention, which corresponds to society's recent concern about children's well-being. Fortunately, today more people like you want to understand and address the needs of children and adolescents. Perhaps you have begun to recognize that children's mental health problems differ in many ways from those of adults, so you have chosen to take a closer look. Maybe you are planning a career in teaching, counseling, medicine, law, rehabilitation, or psychology—all of which rely somewhat on knowledge of children's special needs to shape their focus and practice. Whatever your reason is for reading this book, we are pleased to welcome you to an exciting and active field of study, one that we believe will expose you to concepts and issues that will have a profound and lasting influence. Child and adolescent mental health issues are becoming relevant to many of us in our current and future roles as professionals, community members, and parents, and the needs for trained personnel are increasing (McLearn, Knitzer, & Carter, 2007).

Let's begin by considering Georgina's problems, which raise several fundamental questions that guide our current understanding of children's **psychological disorders**. Ask yourself: Does Georgina's behavior seem abnormal, or are aspects of her behavior normal under certain circumstances?

How would you describe Georgina's problem? Is it an emotional problem? A learning problem? A developmental disability? Could something in her environment cause these strange rituals, or is she more likely responding to internal cues we do not know about? Would Georgina's behavior be viewed differently if she were a boy, or African American or Hispanic? Will she continue to display these behaviors and, if so, what can we do to help?

GEORGINA

Counting for Safety

At age 10, Georgina's strange symptoms had reached the point where her mother needed answers—and fast. Her behavior first became a concern about 2 years ago, when she started talking about harm befalling herself or her family. Her mother recalled how Georgina would come home from the third grade and complain that "I need to finish stuff but I can't seem to," and "I know I'm gonna forget something so I have to keep thinking about it." Her mother expressed her own frustration and worry: "As early as age 5, I remember Georgina would touch and arrange things a certain way, such as brushing her teeth in a certain sequence. Sometimes I'd notice that she would walk through doorways over and over, and she seemed to need to check and arrange things her way before she could leave a room." Georgina's mother had spoken to their family doctor about it back then and was told, "It's probably a phase she's going through, like stepping on cracks will break your mother's back. Ignore it and it'll stop."

But it didn't stop. Georgina developed more elaborate rituals for counting words and objects, primarily in groups of four. She told her mom, "I need to count things out and group them a certain way—only I know the rules how to do it." When she came to my office, Georgina told me, "When someone says something to me or I read something, I have to count the words in groups of four and then organize these groups into larger and larger groups of four." She looked at the pile of magazines in my office and the books on my shelf and explained, matter-of-factly, that she was counting and grouping these things while we talked! Georgina was constantly terrified of forgetting a passage or objects or being interrupted. She believed that if she could not complete her counting, some horrible

Even at age 5, Georgina's strange counting ritual was a symptom of her obsessive–compulsive disorder.

tragedy would befall her parents or herself. Nighttime was the worst, she explained, because "I can't go to sleep until my counting is complete, and this can take a long time." (In fact, it took up to several hours, her mother confirmed.) Understandably, her daytime counting rituals had led to decline in her schoolwork and friendships. Her mother showed me her report cards: Georgina's grades had gone from above average to near failing in several subjects. (Based on Piacentini & Graae, 1997)

When seeking assistance or advice, parents often ask questions similar to these about their child's behavior, and understandably they need to know the probable course and outcome. These questions also exemplify the following issues that research studies in abnormal child psychology seek to address:

▶ Defining what constitutes normal and abnormal behavior for children of different ages, sexes, and ethnic and cultural backgrounds

▶ Identifying the causes and correlates of abnormal child behavior

▶ Making predictions about long-term outcomes

▶ Developing and evaluating methods for treatment and/or prevention

How you choose to describe the problems that children show, and what harm or impairments such problems may lead to, is often the first step toward understanding the nature of their problems. As we discuss in Chapter 11, Georgina's symptoms fit the diagnostic criteria for obsessive–compulsive disorder. This diagnostic label, although far from perfect, tells a great deal about the nature of her disorder, the course it may follow, and the possible treatments.

Georgina's problems also illustrate important features that distinguish most child and adolescent disorders:

▶ *When adults seek services for children, it often is not clear whose "problem" it is.* Children usually enter the mental health system as a result of concerns raised by adults—parents, pediatricians, teachers, or school counselors—and the children themselves may have little choice in the matter. Children do not refer themselves for treatment. This has important implications for how we detect children's problems and how we respond to them.

▶ *Many child and adolescent problems involve failure to show expected developmental progress.* The problem may be transitory, like most types of bed-wetting, or it may be an initial indication of more severe problems ahead, as we see in Georgina's case. Determining the problem requires familiarity with normal, as well as abnormal, development.

▶ *Many problem behaviors shown by children and youths are not entirely abnormal.* To some extent, most children and youth commonly exhibit certain problem behaviors. For instance, worrying from time to time about forgetting things or losing track of thoughts is common; Georgina's behavior, however, seems to involve more than these normal concerns. Thus, decisions about what to do also require familiarity with known psychological disorders and troublesome problem behaviors.

▶ *Interventions for children and adolescents often are intended to promote further development, rather than merely to restore a previous level of functioning.* Unlike interventions for most adult disorders, the goal for many children is to boost their abilities and skills, as well as to eliminate distress.

Before we look at today's definitions of abnormal behavior in children and adolescents, it is valuable to discover how society's interests and approaches to these problems during previous generations have improved the quality of life and mental health of children and youths. Many children, especially those with special needs, fared poorly in the past because they were forced to work as coal miners, field hands, or beggars. Concern for children's needs, rights, and care requires a prominent and consistent social sensitivity and awareness that simply did not exist prior to the twentieth century (Aries, 1962). As you read the following historical synopsis, note how the relatively short history of abnormal child psychology has been strongly influenced by philosophical and societal changes in how adults view and treat children in general (Borstelmann, 1983; V. French, 1977).

HISTORICAL VIEWS AND BREAKTHROUGHS

These were feverish, melancholy times; I cannot remember to have raised my head or seen the moon or any of the heavenly bodies; my eyes were turned downward to the broad lamplit streets and to where the trees of the garden rustled together all night in undecipherable blackness; . . .

—Robert Louis Stevenson, describing memories of childhood illness and depression (quoted in Calder, 1980)

We must recognize children as valuable, independent of any other purpose, to help them develop normal lives and competencies. Although this view of children should seem self-evident to us today, valuing children as persons in their own right—and providing medical, educational, and psychological resources to encourage their progress—has not been a priority of previous societies. Early writings suggest that children were considered servants of the state in the city-states of early Greece. Ancient Greek and Roman societies believed that any person—young or old—with a physical or mental handicap, disability, or deformity was an economic burden and a social embarrassment, and thus was to be scorned, abandoned, or put to death (V. French, 1977).

Prior to the eighteenth century, children's mental health problems—unlike adult disorders—were seldom mentioned in professional or other forms of communication. Some of the earliest historical interest in abnormal child behavior surfaced near the end of the eighteenth century. The Church used its strong influence to attribute children's unusual or disturbing behaviors to their inherently uncivilized and provocative nature (Kanner, 1962). In fact, during this period, nonreligious explanations for disordered behavior in children were rarely given serious consideration because possession by the devil and similar forces of evil was the only explanation anyone needed (Rie, 1971). No one was eager to challenge this view, given that they too could be seen as possessed and dealt with accordingly.

Sadly, during the seventeenth and eighteenth centuries, as many as two-thirds of children died before their fifth birthday, often because there were no antibiotics or similar medications to treat deadly diseases (Zelizer, 1994). Many children were treated harshly or indifferently by their parents. Cruel acts ranging from extreme parental indifference and neglect to physical and sexual abuse of children went unnoticed or were considered an adult's right in the education or disciplining of a child (Radbill, 1968). For many generations, the implied view of society that children are the exclusive property and responsibility of their parents was unchallenged by any countermovement to seek more humane treatment for children. A parent's prerogative to enforce child obedience, for example, was formalized by Massachusetts' Stubborn Child Act of 1654, which permitted parents to put "stubborn" children to death for misbehaving. (Fortunately, no one met this ultimate fate.) Into the mid-1800s, specific laws allowed children with severe developmental disabilities to be kept in cages and cellars (Donohue, Hersen, & Ammerman, 2000).

The Emergence of Social Conscience

"It is easier to build strong children than to fix broken men."

—Attributed to Frederick Douglass

Fortunately, the situation gradually improved for children and youths throughout the nineteenth century and progressed significantly during the latter part of the twentieth century. However, until very recent changes in laws and attitudes, children (along with women, members of minority groups, and persons with special needs) were often the last to benefit from society's prosperity and were the primary victims of its shortcomings. With the acuity of hindsight, we now know that before any real change occurs, it requires a philosophy of humane understanding in how society recognizes and addresses the special needs of some of its members. In addition to humane beliefs, each society must develop ways and means to recognize and protect the rights of individuals, especially children, in the broadest sense (UN Convention on the Rights of the Child, 1989). An overview of some of these major developments provides important background for understanding today's approaches to children's mental health issues.

In Western society, an inkling of the prerequisites for a social conscience first occurred during the seventeenth century, when both a philosophy of humane care and institutions of social protection began to take root. One individual at the forefront of these changes was John Locke (1632–1704), a noted English philosopher and physician who influenced present-day attitudes and practices of childbirth and child-rearing. Locke believed in individual rights, and he expressed the novel opinion that children should be raised with thought and care instead of indifference and harsh treatment. Rather than seeing children as uncivilized tyrants, he saw them as emotionally sensitive beings who should be treated with kindness and understanding and given proper educational opportunities (Illick, 1974). In his words, "the only fence [archaic use, meaning "defense"] against the world is a thorough knowledge of it."

Then, at the turn of the nineteenth century, one of the first documented efforts to work with a special child was undertaken by Jean Marc Itard (1774–1838). A Closer Look 1.1 explains how Itard treated Victor (discovered living in the woods outside Paris) for his severe developmental delays rather than sending him to an asylum. Symbolically, this undertaking launched a new era of a helping orientation toward special children, which initially focused on the care, treatment, and training of the people then termed "mental defectives."

As the influence of Locke and others fostered the expansion of universal education throughout Europe and North America during the latter half of the nineteenth century, children unable to handle the demands of school became a visible and troubling group. Psychologists such as Leta Hollingworth (1886–1939) argued that many mentally defective children were actually suffering from emotional and behavioral problems primarily due to inept treatment by adults and lack of appropriate intellectual challenge (Benjamin & Shields, 1990). This view led to an important and basic distinction between persons with intellectual disability ("imbeciles") and those with psychiatric or mental disorders ("lunatics"), although this distinction was far from clear at the time. Essentially, local governments needed to know who was responsible for helping children whose cognitive development appeared normal but who showed serious emotional or behavioral problems. The only guidance they had previously had in distinguishing children with intellectual deficits

Victor of Aveyron

Victor, often referred to as the "wild boy of Aveyron," was discovered in France by hunters when he was about 11 or 12 years old, having lived alone in the woods presumably all of his life. Jean Marc Itard, a young physician at the time, believed the boy was "mentally arrested" because of social and educational neglect, and set about demonstrating whether such retardation could be reversed. Victor—who initially was mute, walked on all fours, drank water while lying flat on the ground, and bit and scratched—became the object of popular attention as rumors spread that he had been raised by animals. He was dirty, nonverbal, incapable of attention, and insensitive to basic sensations of hot and cold. Despite the child's appearance and behavior, Itard believed that environmental stimulation could humanize him. Itard's account of his efforts poignantly reveals the optimism, frustration, anger, hope, and despair that he experienced in working with this special child.

Itard used a variety of methods to bring Victor to an awareness of his sensory experiences: hot baths, massages, tickling, emotional excitement, even electric shocks. After 5 years of training by Dr. Itard, Victor had learned to identify objects, identify letters of the alphabet, comprehend many words, and apply names to objects and parts of objects. Victor also showed a preference for social life over the isolation of the wild. Despite his achievements, Itard felt his efforts had failed, because his goals of socializing the boy to make him normal were never reached. Nevertheless, the case of Victor was a landmark in the effort to assist children with special needs. For the first time an adult had tried to really understand—to feel and know—the

SAVAGE OF AVEYRON.
© Mary Evans Picture Library/Alamy

mind and emotions of a special child, and had proved that a child with severe impairments could improve through appropriate training. This deep investment on the part of an individual in the needs and feelings of another person's child remains a key aspect of the helping orientation to this day.

Source: From A History of the Care and Study of the Mentally Retarded, by L. Kanner, 1964, p. 15. Courtesy of Charles C Thomas, Publisher, Springfield, Illinois.

---

from children with behavioral and emotional problems was derived from religious views of immoral behavior: children who had normal cognitive abilities but who were disturbed were thought to suffer from moral insanity, which implied a disturbance in personality or character (Pritchard, 1837). Benjamin Rush (1745–1813), a pioneer in psychiatry, argued that children were incapable of true adult-like insanity, because the immaturity of their developing brains prevented them from retaining the mental events that caused insanity (Rie, 1971). Consequently, the term *moral insanity* grew in acceptance as a means of accounting for nonintellectual forms of abnormal child behavior.

The implications of this basic distinction created a brief yet significant burst of optimism among professionals. Concern for the plight and welfare of children with mental and behavioral disturbances began to rise in conjunction with two important influences. First, with advances in general medicine, physiology, and neurology, the moral insanity view of psychological disorders was replaced by the organic disease model,

which emphasized more humane forms of treatment. This advancement was furthered by advocates such as Dorothea Dix (1802–1887), who in the mid-nineteenth century established 32 humane mental hospitals for the treatment of troubled youths previously relegated to cellars and cages (Achenbach, 1982). Second, the growing influence of the philosophies of Locke and others led to the view that children needed moral guidance and support. With these changing views came an increased concern for moral education, compulsory education, and improved health practices. These early efforts to assist children provided the foundation for evolving views of abnormal child behavior as the result of combinations of biological, environmental, psychological, and cultural influences.

Early Biological Attributions

The successful treatment of infectious diseases during the latter part of the nineteenth century strengthened the emerging belief that illness and disease, including

Masturbatory Insanity

Today, most parents hardly balk at discovering their child engaging in some form of self-stimulation—it is considered a normal part of self-discovery and pleasant-sensation seeking. Such tolerance was not always the case. In fact, children's masturbation is historically significant because it was the first "disorder" unique to children and adolescents (Rie, 1971). Just over a hundred years ago, *masturbatory insanity* was a form of mental illness and, in keeping with the contemporaneous view that such problems resided within the individual, it was believed to be a very worrisome problem (Rie, 1971; Szasz, 1970).

By the eighteenth century, society's objections to masturbation originated from religious views that were augmented by the growing influence of science (Rie, 1971; Szasz, 1970). Moral convictions regarding the wrongfulness of masturbation led to a physiological explanation with severe medical ramifications, based on pseudoscientific papers such as *Onania, or the Heinous Sin of Self-Pollution* (circa 1710) (Szasz, 1970). The medical view of masturbation focused initially on adverse effects on physical health, but by the mid-nineteenth century the dominant thought shifted to a focus on the presumed negative effects on mental health and nervous system functioning. With amazing speed, masturbation became the most frequently mentioned "cause" of psychopathology in children.

Interest in masturbatory insanity gradually waned toward the end of the nineteenth century, but the argument still remained tenable as psychoanalytic theory gained acceptance. Eventually, the notion of masturbatory insanity gave way to the concept of neurosis. It was not until much later in the twentieth century that the misguided and illusory belief in a relationship between masturbation and mental illness was dispelled. Let this example remind us of the importance of scientific skepticism in confirming or disconfirming new theories and explanations for abnormal behavior.

Source: Based on author's case material.

mental illness, were biological problems. However, early attempts at biological explanations for deviant or abnormal behavior were highly biased in favor of the cause being the person's fault. The public generally distrusted and scorned anyone who appeared "mad" or "possessed by the devil" or similar evil forces. A Closer Look 1.2 describes masturbatory insanity, a good illustration of how such thinking can lead to an explanation of abnormal behavior without consideration of objective scientific findings and the base rate of masturbation in the general population. The notion of masturbatory insanity also illustrates how the prevailing political and social climates influence definitions of child psychopathology, which is as true today as it was in the past. Views on masturbation evolved from the moral judgment that it was a sin of the flesh, to the medical opinion that it was harmful to one's physical health, to the psychiatric assertion that sexual overindulgence caused insanity.

In contrast to the public's general ignorance and avoidance of issues concerning persons with mental disorders that continued during the late nineteenth century, the mental hygiene movement provides a benchmark of changing attitudes toward children and adults with mental disorders. In 1909, Clifford Beers, a layperson who had recovered from a severe psychosis, spearheaded efforts to change the plight of others also afflicted. Believing that mental disorders were a form of disease, he criticized society's ignorance and indifference and sought to prevent mental disease by raising the standards of care and disseminating reliable information (M. Levine & Levine, 1992). As a result, detection and intervention methods began to flourish, based on a more tempered—yet still quite frightened and ill-informed—view of afflicted individuals.

Unfortunately, because this paradigm was based on a biological disease model, intervention was limited to persons with the most visible and prominent disorders, such as psychoses or severe intellectual disability. Although developmental explanations were a part of this early view of psychopathology, they were quite narrow. The development of the disease was considered progressive and irreversible, tied to the development of the child only in that it manifested itself differently as the child grew, but remained impervious to other influences such as treatment or learning. All one could do was to prevent the most extreme manifestations by strict punishment and to protect those not affected.

Sadly, this early educational and humane model for assisting persons with mental disorders soon reverted to a custodial model during the early part of the twentieth century. Once again, attitudes toward anyone with mental or intellectual disabilities turned from cautious optimism to dire pessimism, hostility, and disdain. Particularly children, youths, and adults with intellectual disability were blamed for crimes and social ills during the ensuing alarmist period (Achenbach, 1982). Rather than viewing knowledge as a form of protection, as Locke had argued, society returned to the view that mental illness and retardation were diseases that could spread if left unchecked. For the next two decades, many communities opted to segregate or institutionalize people with mental disabilities and to prevent them from procreating (eugenics). We will return to these important developments in our discussion of the history of intellectual disability (formerly known as mental retardation) in Chapter 5.

Early Psychological Attributions

To conceptualize and understand abnormal child psychology, biological influences must be balanced with important developmental and cultural factors, including the family, peer group, and school. Of course, this perception was not always the case. The long-standing, medically based view that abnormal behavior is a disorder or disease residing within the person unfortunately led to neglect of the essential role of a person's surroundings, context, and relations, and of the interactions among these variables.

The recognition of psychological influences emerged early in the twentieth century, when attention was drawn to the importance of major psychological disorders and to formulating a taxonomy of illnesses. Such recognition allowed researchers to organize and categorize ways of differentiating among various psychological problems, resulting in some semblance of understanding and control. At the same time, there was concern that attempts to recognize the wide range of mental health needs of children and adults could easily backfire and lead to the neglect of persons with more severe disorders. This shift in perspective and increase in knowledge also prompted the development of diagnostic categories and new criminal offenses, the expansion of descriptions of deviant behavior, and the addition of more comprehensive monitoring procedures for identified individuals (Costello & Angold, 2006). Two major theoretical paradigms helped shape these emerging psychological and environmental influences: psychoanalytic theory and behaviorism. We'll limit our discussion here to their historical importance, but additional content concerning their contemporary influence appears in the Chapter 2 discussion of theories and causes.

Psychoanalytic Theory

In Sigmund Freud's day, near the beginning of the twentieth century, many child psychiatrists and psychologists had grown pessimistic about their ability to treat children's mental disorders other than with custodial or palliative care. Freud was one of the first to reject such pessimism and raise new possibilities for treatment as the roots of these disorders were traced to early childhood (Fonagy, Target, & Gergely, 2006).

Although he believed that individuals have inborn drives and predispositions that strongly affect their development, he also believed that experiences play a necessary role in psychopathology. For perhaps the first time, the course of mental disorders was not viewed as inevitable; children and adults could be helped if provided with the proper environment, therapy, or both.

Psychoanalytic theory significantly influenced advances in our ways of thinking about the causes and treatment of mental disorders. Perhaps the most important of these advances from the perspective of abnormal child psychology was that Freud was the first to give meaning to the concept of mental disorder by linking it to childhood experiences (Rilling, 2000). His radical theory incorporated developmental concepts into an understanding of psychopathology at a time when early childhood development was virtually ignored by mainstream child psychiatry and psychology. Rather than focusing on singular, specific causes (a hallmark of the disease model in vogue at the time), psychoanalytic theory emphasized that personality and mental health outcomes had multiple roots. Outcomes depended to a large degree on the interaction of developmental and situational processes that change over time in unique ways (Fonagy et al., 2006). In effect, Freud's writings shifted the view from one of children as innocent or insignificant to one of human beings in turmoil, struggling to achieve control over biological needs and to make themselves acceptable to society through the microcosm of the family (Freud, 1909/1953).

Contributions based on Freud's theory continued to expand throughout the early part of the twentieth century, as clinicians and theorists broke from some of his earlier teachings and brought new insights to the field. His daughter, Anna Freud (1895–1982), was instrumental in expanding his ideas to understanding children, in particular by noting how children's symptoms were related more to developmental stages than were those of adults. Anna Freud's contemporary, Melanie Klein (1882–1960), also took an interest in the meaning of children's play, arguing that all actions could be interpreted in terms of unconscious fantasy. The work of both women made possible the analysis of younger children and the recognition of nonverbal communication for patients of all ages (Mason, 2003).

In recent years, psychoanalytic theory's approach to abnormal child psychology has had less influence on clinical practice and teaching, largely because of the popularity of the phenomenological (descriptive) approach to psychopathology (Costello & Angold, 2006). Nevertheless, it is important to remember that current **nosologies** (the efforts to classify psychiatric disorders into descriptive categories) are essentially nondevelopmental in their approaches. Rather than attempting, as the Freudian approach does, to describe the development of the disease in the context of the development of the individual, nosologies such as those in the *Diagnostic and Statistical Manual of Mental Disorders* (DSM-5; American Psychiatric Association, 2013) attempt to find common denominators that describe the manifestations of a disorder at any age (Achenbach & Rescorla, 2006). Despite valid criticism and a lack of empirical validation of the content of psychoanalytic theory and its many derivatives, the idea of emphasizing the interconnection between children's normal and abnormal development retains considerable attraction as a model for abnormal child psychology.

Behaviorism

The development of evidence-based treatments for children, youths, and families can be traced to the rise of behaviorism in the early 1900s, as reflected in Pavlov's experimental research that established the foundations for classical conditioning, and in the classic studies on the conditioning and elimination of children's fears (Jones, 1924; J. B. Watson & Rayner, 1920). Initially, John Watson (1878–1958), the "Father of Behaviorism," intended to explain Freud's concepts in more scientific terms, based on the new learning theory of classical conditioning.

Ironically, Watson was perhaps more psychoanalytically inspired by Freud's theories than he intended. As he attempted to explain terms such as *unconscious* and *transference* using the language of conditioned emotional responses (and thereby discredit Freud's theory of emotions), he in fact pioneered the scientific investigation of some of Freud's ideas (Rilling, 2000). A Closer Look 1.3 highlights some of Watson's scientific ambitions and his famous study with Little Albert, as well as some of the controversy surrounding his career.

Watson is known for his theory of emotions, which he extrapolated from normal to abnormal behavior. His infamous words exemplify the faith some early researchers—and the public—placed in laboratory-based research on learning and behavior: "Give me a dozen healthy infants ... and I'll guarantee to take any one at random and train him to become any type of specialist I might select—doctor, lawyer, artist, merchant-chief and, yes, even beggar-man and thief, regardless of his talents, penchants, tendencies, abilities, vocations, and race of his ancestors." (J. B. Watson, 1925, p. 82)

Beyond the work in their lab, the Watson household must have been an interesting place. Consider the following contrasting views and advice on raising children from one of America's first "child experts" and his wife:

John Watson (1925): Never hug and kiss them, never let them sit in your lap. If you must, kiss them once on the forehead when they say goodnight. Shake hands with them in the morning.

Rosalie Rayner Watson (1930): I cannot restrain my affection for the children completely. ... I like being merry and gay and having the giggles. The behaviorists think giggling is a sign of maladjustment, so when the children want to giggle I have to keep a straight face or rush them off to their rooms.

This example and the study of Little Albert illustrate the importance of keeping in perspective any new advances and insights that at first may seem like panaceas for age-old problems. As any soiled veteran of parenting would attest, no child-rearing shortcuts or uniform solutions guide us in dealing with children's problems—raising children is part skill, part wisdom, and part luck. Nonetheless, families, communities, and societal and cultural values play a strong role in determining how successful current child-rearing philosophies are at benefiting children.

Evolving Forms of Treatment

Compared with the times that followed, the period from 1930 to 1950 was a quiet time for research and treatment in abnormal child psychology. A few reports in the 1930s described the behavioral treatment of isolated problems such as bed-wetting (O. H. Mowrer & Mowrer, 1938), stuttering (Dunlap, 1932), and fears (F. B. Holmes, 1936). Other than these reports, psychodynamic approaches were the dominant form of treatment during this period. As a carryover from the 1800s, most children with intellectual or mental disorders were still institutionalized. This practice had come under mounting criticism by the late 1940s, when studies by René Spitz raised serious questions about the harmful impact of institutional life on children's growth and development (R. Spitz, 1945). He discovered that infants raised in institutions without adult physical contact and stimulation developed severe physical and emotional problems. Efforts were undertaken to close institutions and place dependent and difficult children in foster family homes or group homes. Within a 20-year period, from 1945 to 1965, there was a rapid decline in the number of children in institutions, while the number of children in foster family homes and group homes increased.

During the 1950s and early 1960s, behavior therapy emerged as a systematic approach to the treatment of child and family disorders. The therapy was originally based on operant and classical conditioning principles established through laboratory work with animals. In their early form, these laboratory-based techniques to modify undesirable behaviors and shape adaptive

Little Albert, Big Fears, and Sex in Advertising

Most of us are familiar with the story of Little Albert and his fear of white rats and other white furry objects, thanks to the work of John Watson and his graduate assistant (and then wife) Rosalie Rayner. However, understanding the times and background of John Watson helps put these pioneering efforts into a broader historical perspective, and highlights the limited concern for ethics in research that existed in his day.

Watson's fascination with and life dedication to the study of fears may have stemmed from his own acknowledged fear of the dark, which afflicted him throughout his adult life. His career break arrived when he was given an opportunity to create a research laboratory at Johns Hopkins University for the study of child development. Instead of conditioning rats, he could now use humans to test his emerging theories of fear conditioning. However, at that time the only source of human subjects was persons whose rights were considered insignificant or who had less than adequate power to protect themselves, such as orphans, mental patients, and prisoners. Just as he had studied rats in their cages, Watson now studied babies in their cribs.

Clearly, his method of obtaining research subjects and experimenting with them would be considered highly unethical today. To demonstrate how fear might be conditioned in a baby, Watson and Rayner set out to condition fear in an 11-month-old orphan baby they named Albert B., who was given a small white rat to touch, toward which he showed no fear. After this warm-up, every time the infant reached to touch the rat, Watson would strike a steel bar with a hammer. After repeated attempts to touch the rat brought on the same shocking sounds, "the infant jumped violently, fell forward and began to whimper." The process was repeated intermittently, enough times that eventually Albert B. would break down and cry, desperately trying to crawl away, whenever he saw the rat. Watson and Rayner had successfully conditioned the child to fear rats. They then conditioned him to fear rabbits, dogs, fur coats, and—believe it or not—Santa Claus masks (Karier, 1986).

It is disconcerting that Albert B. moved away before any deconditioning was attempted, resulting in decades of speculation as to his identity and the strange set of fears he might have suffered. In 2009 a team of psychologists tracked down Little Albert's identity and fate: he was identified as Douglas

Source: Neurobiology of Pavlovian Fear Conditioning Annual Review of Neuroscience Vol. 24: 897–931, by Stephen Maren; Annual Review of Neuroscience ©2011 Annual Reviews. All rights reserved.

Merritte, whose mother worked at the campus hospital and was paid $1 for her baby's research participation. Sadly, the team discovered that Douglas died at age 6 of acquired hydrocephalus (Beck, Levinson, & Irons, 2009).

It is ironic, moreover, that Watson went on to develop a career in advertising after he was ousted from the university (presumably as a result of concerns over his extramarital relationship with his graduate student; Benjamin et al., 2007). His brand of behaviorism, with its emphasis on the prediction and control of human behavior, met with unqualified success on Madison Avenue. As he explained, "No matter what it is, like the good naturalist you are, you must never lose sight of your experimental animal—the consumer." We can thank John B. Watson for advertising's dramatic shift in the 1930s toward creating images around any given product that exploited whenever possible the sexual desires of both men and women.

Source: Based on Karier, 1986.

abilities stood in stark contrast to the dominant psychoanalytic approaches, which stressed resolution of internal conflicts and unconscious motives. Behavior therapy focused initially on children with intellectual disability or severe disturbances. Psychoanalytic practices for these children were perceived as ineffective or inappropriate. Much of this early work took place in institutions or classroom settings that were thought to provide the kind of environmental control needed to change behavior effectively. Since that time, behavior therapy has continued to expand in scope, and has emerged as a prominent form of therapy for a wide range of children's disorders (Ollendick, King, & Chorpita, 2006; Weisz & Kazdin, 2010).

Progressive Legislation

Just how far some countries have advanced in the humane and egalitarian treatment of children and youths is exemplified by the various laws enacted in the past few decades to protect the rights of those with special needs. For example, in the United States the Individuals with Disabilities Education Act (IDEA; Public Law 104–446) mandates:

▶ free and appropriate public education for any child with special needs in the least restrictive environment for that child;

▶ each child with special needs, regardless of age, must be assessed with culturally appropriate tests;

▶ each of these children must have an individualized education program (IEP) tailored to his or her needs, and must be re-assessed.

Similar legislation for protecting the rights of children with disabilities (and ensuring their access to appropriate resources) exists in Canada, the United Kingdom, and many other nations.

In 2007, the United Nations General Assembly adopted a new convention to protect the rights of persons with disabilities around the world. This convention represents an important shift from addressing the "special needs" of children to realizing their rights and removing the physical, linguistic, social, and cultural barriers that remain. Countries that ratify the convention agree to enact laws and other measures to improve disability rights, and also to abolish legislation, customs, and practices that discriminate against persons with disabilities. These efforts signify a paradigm shift in attitudes toward and treatment of people with disabilities—from seeing persons with disabilities as objects of charity to considering them as individuals with human rights. Specific principles addressing the needs of children with disabilities are shown in A Closer Look 1.4.

Section Summary

Historical Views and Breakthroughs

● Early biological explanations for abnormal child behavior favored locating the cause of the problem within the individual, which sometimes led to simplistic or inaccurate beliefs about causes of the behavior.

● Early psychological approaches attempted to integrate basic knowledge of inborn processes with environmental conditions that shape behavior, emotions, and cognitions.

● Greater attention to the problems of children and youths in recent years has improved their quality of life and mental health. This improvement resulted from greater societal recognition of and sensitivity to children's special status and needs since the turn of the twentieth century.

WHAT IS ABNORMAL BEHAVIOR IN CHILDREN AND ADOLESCENTS?

A CLOSER LOOK 1.4

UN Convention on the Rights of Persons with Disabilities (2007)

[Article 7, pertaining to children's rights]:

1. States Parties shall take all necessary measures to ensure the full enjoyment by children with disabilities of all human rights and fundamental freedoms on an equal basis with other children.

2. In all actions concerning children with disabilities, the best interests of the child shall be a primary consideration.

3. States Parties shall ensure that children with disabilities have the right to express their views freely on all matters affecting them, their views being given due weight in accordance with their age and maturity, on an equal basis with other children, and to be provided with disability and age-appropriate assistance to realize that right.

Source: UN Convention on the Rights of Persons with Disabilities (2007). Office of the United Nations High Commissioner for Human Rights.

ADAM LANZA

Early Troubles

"You could tell that he felt so uncomfortable about being put on the spot, I think that maybe he wasn't given the right kind of attention or help. I think he went so unnoticed that people didn't even stop to realize that maybe there's actually something else going on here—that maybe he needs to be talking or getting some kind of mental help. In high school, no one really takes the time to look and think, 'Why is he acting this way?' " (Halbfinger, 2012)

"It's easy to understand why Adam Lanza felt at war with reality. Living was torture for the young boy—bright lights, loud sounds, even a touch could cause him to withdraw and become nonverbal. He became obsessed with violence to a degree that was abnormal even in today's desensitized society. Violent pictures. Violent writings. Violent poetry. Hours spent playing violent video games and researching weapons and serial killers on the Internet. Adam Lanza created a world in which he was surrounded by death."

Lysaik (2013, December 6). Newtown massacre. Inside. Out. *Newsweek*. Available T: http://mag.newsweek.com/2013/12/06/newtown-massacre-inside-out.html

Kateleen Foy/Getty Images

Were there any clues in Adam Lanza's childhood that might suggest his violent behavior later on?

These comments were made by Olivia DeVivo reflecting on her time as a former student at Sandy Hook Elementary School with a boy named Adam Lanza. As she and other classmates noted, Lanza was considered a "loner," an odd character who was very uncomfortable around others and made no effort to connect. Despite living in the same house, he communicated with his mother by e-mail. This example reveals how children's behavior can be difficult to classify into its causes, expression, and contributing factors. It also raises several key questions: First, how do we judge what is normal? A lot of kids are "loners" during adolescence and have difficulty connecting to peers. Second, when does an issue become a problem? In this instance, did anyone sense that Lanza's social isolation might lead to or be due to potentially serious social and mental problems? Finally, why are some children's abnormal patterns of behavior relatively continuous from early childhood through adolescence and into adulthood, whereas other children show more variable (discontinuous) patterns of development and adaptation? Was there anything about Lanza's behavior in childhood that indicated that he would kill innocent children and teachers at Sandy Hook Elementary years later?

Although these questions are central to defining and understanding abnormal child behavior and warrant thoughtful consideration, no simple, straightforward answers exist. (This should be familiar ground to those of you who are psychology majors.) More often than not, childhood disorders are accompanied by various layers of abnormal behavior or development, ranging from the more visible and alarming (such as delinquent acts or physical assault), to the more subtle yet critical (such as teasing and peer rejection), to the more hidden and systemic (such as depression or parental rejection).

Moreover, mental health professionals, while attempting to understand children's weaknesses, too often unintentionally overlook their strengths. Yet, many children cope effectively in other areas of their lives, despite the limitations imposed by specific psychological disorders. An understanding of children's individual strengths and abilities can lead to ways to assist them in healthy adaptation. Also, some children may show less extreme forms of difficulty or only the early signs of an emerging problem rather than a full-blown disorder. Therefore, to judge what is abnormal, we need to be sensitive to each child's stage of development and consider each child's unique methods of coping and ways of compensating for difficulties (Achenbach, 2010).

Childhood disorders, like adult disorders, have commonly been viewed in terms of deviancies from normal, yet disagreement remains as to what constitutes normal and abnormal. While reading the following discussion, keep in mind that attempting to establish boundaries between abnormal and normal functioning is an arbitrary process at best, and current guidelines are constantly being reviewed for their accuracy, completeness, and usefulness.

Defining Psychological Disorders

The study of abnormal behavior often makes us more sensitive to and wary of the ways used to describe the behavior of others. Whose standard of "normal" do we adopt, and who decides whether this arbitrary standard has been breached? Does abnormal behavior or performance in one area, such as mood, have implications for the whole person?

Although there are no easy answers to these questions, Georgina's real-life problems require an agreement on how to define a psychological (or mental) disorder. A **psychological disorder** traditionally has been defined as a pattern of behavioral, cognitive, emotional, or physical symptoms shown by an individual. Such a pattern is associated with one or more of the following three prominent features:

▶ The person shows some degree of distress, such as fear or sadness.

▶ His or her behavior indicates some degree of disability, such as impairment that substantially interferes with or limits activity in one or more important areas of functioning, including physical, emotional, cognitive, and behavioral areas.

▶ Such distress and disability increase the risk of further suffering or harm, such as death, pain, disability, or an important loss of freedom (American Psychiatric Association [APA], 2013).

To account for the fact that we sometimes show transitory signs of distress, disability, or risk under unusual circumstances (such as the loss of a loved one), this definition of a psychological disorder excludes circumstances in which such reactions are expected and appropriate as defined by one's cultural background. Furthermore, these three primary features of psychological disorders only describe what a person does or does not do in certain circumstances. The features do not attempt to attribute causes or reasons for abnormal behavior to the individual alone. On the contrary, understanding particular impairments should be balanced with recognizing individual and situational circumstances.

Labels Describe Behavior, Not People

It is important to keep in mind that terms used to describe abnormal behavior do not describe people; they only describe patterns of behavior that may or may not occur in certain circumstances. We must be careful to avoid the common mistake of identifying the person with the disorder, as reflected in expressions such as "anxious child" or "autistic child." The field of child and adult mental health is often challenged by **stigma**, which refers to a cluster of negative attitudes and beliefs that motivates fear, rejection, avoidance, and discrimination with respect to people with mental illnesses (Heflinger & Hinshaw, 2010). Stigma leads to prejudice and discrimination against others on the basis of race, ethnicity, disabilities, sexual orientation, body size, biological sex, language, and religious beliefs. Because of stigma, persons with mental disorders may also suffer from low self-esteem, isolation, and hopelessness, and they may become so embarrassed or ashamed that they conceal symptoms and fail to seek treatment (Puhl & Latner, 2007). Accordingly, throughout this text we separate the child from the disorder by using language such as "Ramon is a child with an anxiety disorder," rather than "Ramon is an anxious child." Children like Ramon have many other attributes that should not be overshadowed by global descriptive or negative labels.

In addition, the problems shown by some children may be the result of their attempts to adapt to abnormal or unusual circumstances. Children with chronic health problems must adapt to their medical regimens and to negative reactions from peers; children raised in abusive or neglectful environments must learn how to relate to others adaptively and to regulate emotions that may, at times, be overwhelming. Therefore, the primary purpose of using terms such as *disorder* and *abnormal behavior* for describing the psychological

status of children and adolescents is to aid clinicians and researchers in describing, organizing, and expressing the complex features often associated with various patterns of behavior. By no means do the terms imply a common cause, since the causes of abnormal behavior are almost always multifaceted and interactive.

This approach to defining abnormal behavior is similar to the one most often used to classify and diagnose mental disorders, according to the guidelines in the DSM-5 (APA, 2013). We use this approach in guiding the thinking and structure of this book because of its clinical and descriptive utility. Yet, despite advances in defining abnormality and vast improvements in the diagnostic and classification systems, ambiguity remains, especially in defining a particular child's maladaptive dysfunction (Rutter, 2010; Zachar & Kendler, 2007). Boundaries between what constitute normal and abnormal conditions or distinctions among different abnormal conditions are not easily drawn. At present, the DSM-5 approach has achieved some consensus supporting its value in facilitating greater communication and increased standardization of research and clinical knowledge concerning abnormal child psychology. We consider the DSM-5 and current alternatives to classification of childhood disorders in Chapter 4.

Competence

Definitions of abnormal child behavior must take into account the child's **competence**—that is, the ability to successfully adapt in the environment. Developmental competence is reflected in the child's ability to use internal and external resources to achieve a successful adaptation (Masten, 2011). Of course, this prompts the question "What is successful?" Successful adaptation varies across culture and ethnicity, so it is important that the traditions, beliefs, languages, and value systems of a particular culture be taken into account when defining a child's competence. Similarly, some children face greater obstacles than others in their efforts to adapt to their environment. Minority children and families, as well as those with socioeconomic disadvantages, must cope with multiple forms of racism, prejudice, discrimination, oppression, and segregation, all of which significantly influence a child's adaptation and development (Children's Defense Fund, 2007).

Judgments of deviancy also require knowledge of a child's performance relative to that of same-age peers, as well as knowledge of the child's course of development and cultural context. In effect, the study of abnormal child psychology considers not only the degree of maladaptive behavior children show but also the extent to which they achieve normal developmental milestones. As with deviancy, the criteria for defining competence can be very specific and narrow in focus, or they can be as plentiful and as broad as we wish (Masten & Wright, 2010).

How do we know whether a particular child is doing well, and how do we, as parents, teachers, or professionals, guide our expectations? **Developmental tasks**, which include broad domains of competence such as conduct and academic achievement, tell how children typically progress within each domain as they grow. Knowledge of the developmental tasks provides an important backdrop for considering a child or adolescent's developmental progress and impairments. Examples of several important developmental tasks are shown in Table 1.1.

TABLE 1.1 | Examples of Developmental Tasks

Age Period	Task
Infancy to preschool	• Attachment to caregiver(s) • Language • Differentiation of self from environment
Middle childhood	• Self-control and compliance • School adjustment (attendance, appropriate conduct) • Academic achievement (e.g., learning to read, do arithmetic) • Getting along with peers (acceptance, making friends) • Rule-governed conduct (following rules of society for moral behavior and prosocial conduct)
Adolescence	• Successful transition to secondary schooling • Academic achievement (learning skills needed for higher education or work) • Involvement in extracurricular activities (e.g., athletics, clubs) • Forming close friendships within and across gender • Forming a cohesive sense of self-identity

Source: From *The Development of Competence in Favorable and Unfavorable Environments: Lessons from Research on Successful Children*, by A. S. Masten and J. D. Coatsworth, 1998, American Psychologist, 53, 205–220. Copyright © 1998 by the American Psychological Association. The APA is not responsible for the accuracy of this translation.

Photo Credits (top to bottom): ©Flashon Studio/Shutterstock.com; ©Gelpi JM/Shutterstock.com; ©OLJ Studio/Shutterstock.com.

Conduct is one of the fundamental domains in Table 1.1; it indicates how well a person follows the rules of a particular society. From a young age, children are expected to begin controlling their behavior and to comply with their parents' requests. (This doesn't mean they always do so. . . .) By the time children enter school, they are expected to follow the rules for classroom conduct and to refrain from harming others. Then, by adolescence, they are expected to follow the rules set by school, home, and society without direct supervision. Similar developmental progression occurs in the self-domain, where children initially learn to differentiate themselves from the environment, and to gradually develop self-identity and autonomy. In the discussion of disorders in the chapters to follow, we attempt whenever possible to balance the information on abnormal behavior with the growing awareness of children's competencies and strengths.

Developmental Pathways

Why don't children with similar early experiences have similar problems later in life? Conversely, why do children and adolescents with the same disorder sometimes have very different early experiences or family characteristics? Another aspect of judging deviancy involves deciding when a concern or issue about a child's behavior starts to become a more recognizable pattern, especially since behavior fluctuates and changes considerably as a child develops. Therefore, in addition to distinguishing between normal and abnormal adaptation, we must consider the temporal relationship between emerging concerns in early childhood and the likelihood that they will lead to problems later on.

A **developmental pathway** refers to the sequence and timing of particular behaviors and possible relationships between behaviors over time. The concept allows us to visualize development as an active, dynamic process that can account for very different beginnings and outcomes (Pickles & Hill, 2006). It helps us to understand the course and nature of normal and abnormal development. Two examples of developmental pathways are shown in ● Figure 1.1. The child in Figure 1.1(a) has experienced maltreatment at a young age. Maltreatment can significantly alter the child's initial course of development, resulting in diverse and often unpredictable outcomes, such as eating, mood, or conduct disorders. This example illustrates **multifinality**, the concept that various outcomes may stem from similar beginnings (in this case, child maltreatment).

A Multifinality

Early childhood maltreatment

Eating disorder	Mood disorder	Conduct disorder	Normal adjustment
Possible outcomes			

B Equifinality

Possible beginnings		
Genetic pattern	Familial characteristics	Environmental features

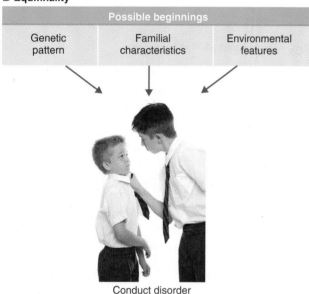

Conduct disorder

● **FIGURE 1.1** | (a) Multifinality: Similar early experiences lead to different outcomes; (b) Equifinality: Different factors lead to a similar outcome.

Photo Credits: (a) SW Productions/Jupiter Images; (b) ©iStockphoto.com/yellowsarah.

In contrast, other children might set out on their developmental journeys with very different strengths and weaknesses, but later have a similar disorder. As illustrated in Figure 1.1(b), genetic patterns, familial characteristics, and features of each child's environment represent different pathways leading to a similar outcome (conduct disorder). This example illustrates **equifinality**, the concept that similar outcomes stem from different early experiences and developmental

pathways. As we will learn in Chapter 9, children with conduct problems may have very diverse early experiences and risk factors but later show similar patterns of behavior. By looking at possible developmental pathways, we gain a better understanding of the ways in which children's problems may change or remain the same over time.

In summary, diversity in how children acquire psychological strengths and weaknesses is a hallmark of abnormal child psychology. Because no clear cause-and-effect relationship exists for each child and adolescent disorder, the following assumptions need to be kept firmly in mind (Hayden & Mash, 2014):

▸ There are many contributors to disordered outcomes in each individual.

▸ Contributors vary among individuals who have the disorder.

▸ Individuals with the same specific disorder express the features of their disturbance in different ways (e.g., some children with a conduct disorder are aggressive, whereas others may be destructive to property or engage in theft or deceit).

▸ The pathways leading to any particular disorder are numerous and interactive, as opposed to unidimensional and static.

Section Summary

What Is Abnormal Behavior in Children and Adolescents?

● Defining a psychological disorder involves agreement about particular patterns of behavioral, cognitive, and physical symptoms shown by an individual.

● Terms used to describe abnormal behavior are meant to define behavior, not to be used as labels to describe individuals.

● Defining abnormal behavior requires judgment concerning the degree to which a person's behavior is maladaptive or harmful as well as dysfunctional or impaired.

● Diversity in how children acquire psychological strengths and weaknesses is a hallmark of abnormal child psychology. The many contributors to abnormal behavior may vary within and between individuals with similar disorders.

● The study of psychological disorders involves attempts to describe the presenting problems and abilities, to understand contributing causes, and to treat or prevent them.

● Developmental pathways help to describe the course and nature of normal and abnormal development; multifinality means that various outcomes may stem from similar beginnings, whereas equifinality means that similar outcomes stem from different early experiences.

RISK AND RESILIENCE

I am convinced that, except in a few extraordinary cases, one form or another of an unhappy childhood is essential to the formation of exceptional gifts.

—Thornton Wilder (1897–1975)

RAOUL AND JESSE

Why the Differences?

Raoul and Jesse were childhood friends who grew up in the same rundown housing project, in a neighborhood plagued by drugs and crime. By the time they were 10 years old they were both familiar with domestic and community violence, and each lived with his mother and an older sibling after his parents divorced. The boys rarely saw their fathers, and when they did it usually wasn't a pleasant experience. By the time they reached grade 6 they were falling behind at school, and started to get into trouble with the police for staying out too late, hassling kids at school, and breaking into cars. Despite these problems and a struggle to keep up, Raoul finished high school and received 2 years of training in a local trade school. He is now 30 years old, works at a local factory, and lives with his wife and two children. Raoul sums up his life thus far as "dodging bullets to reach where I want to go," but he's happy to be living in a safe neighborhood and to have the hope of sending his children to college.

His friend Jesse never graduated from high school. He dropped out after being expelled for bringing a weapon to school, and has been in and out of prison several times. At age 30, Jesse drinks too much and has a poor record of finding and keeping a job. He has had several short-term relationships and fathered two children, but he rarely visits them and never married either mother. Jesse has lived in several locations over the years, mostly in his old, unchanged neighborhood. (Based on Zimmerman & Arunkumar, 1994)

These brief life histories illustrate two very different developmental paths that started out at the same place. Jesse's troubles might have been predicted based on present knowledge of abnormal development, but it is more difficult to explain how some children, like Raoul, seem to escape harm despite stress and adversity. Perhaps you are familiar with someone—from a novel, the entertainment field, or personal friendship—who seems to come out on top despite adversity and limited resources. How do you suppose individuals such as Jay Z (see Box 1.5) escape the odds and achieve their life goals?

Overcoming the Odds

Sometimes we can learn a lot from the personal stories of individuals who are famous. In some cases, like that of Shawn Corey "Jay Z" Carter, the popular rap artist, music producer, fashion designer, publisher, entertainer, and basketball team and restaurant owner, the stories reveal early experiences of adversity or loss that were instrumental in setting them on a life course.

In Brooklyn during the 1980s, Carter grew up in a difficult living situation. His father left him, along with his mother, two sisters and a brother, when he was only 12. Without a father figure and role model in his life, the young rapper turned to the streets of Brooklyn. A friend showed him how to make money in the drug trade and other activities. As Jay Z remembers, "No one hired a skywriter and announced crack's arrival. But when it landed in your hood, it was a total takeover." But Carter had a way to escape this new reality. When his mother gave him a boom box for Christmas, his life changed. The artist began rapping in the streets of Brooklyn, and a local DJ convinced him to stop selling crack and focus on his career. In 1996, at the age of 26, he came out with his debut album. By 1998, his album *Vol. 2… Hard Knock Life* had won him a Grammy award.

Throughout his career, Carter channeled his early experiences into a driven ambition to succeed both financially and socially. He has advocated for rights for African Americans and rappers, negating the premise that because you are involved with rap culture means that you are a criminal. He has helped bring more black voters to the polls with his free concerts and his speech on behalf of President Obama. His story shows that with resilience one can adapt and change life circumstances for the better.

Source: Amy Legate-Wolfe, 2013 (personal communication).

Shawn Corey "Jay Z" Carter's life exemplifies resiliency.

The answer to this complicated question is coming into focus, thanks to studies that look at risk as well as protective factors affecting children's courses of development (Compas & Andreotti, 2013). A **risk factor** is a variable that precedes a negative outcome of interest and increases the chances that the outcome will occur. In contrast, a **protective factor** is a personal or situational variable that reduces the chances for a child to develop a disorder. As you might suspect, children like Raoul and Jesse, who face many known risk factors such as community violence and parental divorce, are vulnerable to abnormal development. Acute, stressful situations as well as chronic adversity put children's successful development at risk. Chronic poverty, serious caregiving deficits, parental mental illness, divorce, homelessness, and racial prejudice are known risk factors that increase children's vulnerability to psychopathology—especially in the absence of compensatory strengths and resources (Evans, Li, & Whipple, 2013; Kim-Cohen & Gold, 2009).

Yet, like Raoul, some vulnerable children do not develop problems later. Instead, they seem resilient despite their stress-filled environments, managing to achieve positive outcomes despite being at significant risk for psychopathology. Children who survive risky environments by using their strong self-confidence, coping skills, and abilities to avoid risk situations may be considered resilient—they seem able to fight off or recover from their misfortune (Luthar, 2006). These children are also most likely to show sustained competence while under stress, or to rebound to a previously healthy level of competence following traumatic or stressful experiences (Kim-Cohen & Gold, 2009). **Resilience** is not a universal, categorical, or fixed attribute of the child; rather, it varies according to the type of stress, its context, and similar factors (Rutter, 2012). Individual children may be resilient with respect to some specific stressors but not others, and resilience may vary over time and across situations. Resilience is seen in children across cultures, despite the extraordinary circumstances that some may face (Kirmayer et al., 2011; Ungar, 2010).

The concept of resilience reminds us that a direct causal pathway rarely leads to a particular outcome. Ongoing interactions exist between protective and risk factors within the child, between the child and his or her surroundings, and among risk factors themselves. Protective factors are personal or situational variables that reduce the chances for a child to develop a disorder. Risk factors do the exact opposite—they increase the child's likelihood of developing a problem. Risk factors and protective factors should be thought of as processes rather than absolutes, since the same event or condition can function as either type of factor, depending on the overall context in which it occurs(Rutter, 2007a). For example, placing young children with another family may serve to protect them if they were being severely mistreated. However, for some children out-of-home placement could increase their vulnerability if it creates more stress due to being removed from their mother or father. Throughout each chapter, we offer similar examples of children's vulnerability and resilience in relation to particular circumstances and disorders.

● Figure 1.2 illustrates some of the better-known characteristics of children and adolescents who display resilience, which are sometimes overlooked in attempts to explain abnormal development. These characteristics constitute a protective triad of resources and health-promoting events: the strengths of the individual, the family, and the school and community (Luthar, 2006). Protective factors vary tremendously in magnitude and scope, and not all three resources are necessary. For some children, merely the availability of a supportive grandparent or teacher can effectively change the course and direction of their development. Other children may need additional or different protective factors, such as a better learning environment, community safety, or sufficient family resources.

Source	Characteristics
Individual	Good intellectual functioning
	Appealing, sociable, easygoing disposition
	Self-efficacy, self-confidence, high self-esteem
	Talents
	Faith
Family	Close relationship to caring parent figure
	Authoritative parenting, warmth, structure, high expectations
	Socioeconomic advantages
	Connections to extended supportive family networks
School and community	Adults outside the family who take an interest in promoting the child's welfare
	Connections to social organizations
	Attendance at effective schools

● **FIGURE 1.2** | Characteristics of children and adolescents who display resilience in face of adversity.

Photo Credits (top to bottom): ©Odua Images/Shutterstock.com; ©Apollofoto/Shutterstock.com; ©iofoto/Shutterstock.com.

Section Summary

Risk and Resilience

- Children's normal development may be put in jeopardy because of risk factors, which can include acute, stressful situations and chronic adversity.

- Some children seem to be more resilient in the face of risk factors. Resiliency is related to strong self-confidence, coping skills, and the ability to avoid risk situations, as well as the ability to fight off or recover from misfortune.

- Children's resilience is connected to a protective triad of resources and health-promoting events that include individual opportunities, close family ties, and opportunities for individual and family support from community resources.

THE SIGNIFICANCE OF MENTAL HEALTH PROBLEMS AMONG CHILDREN AND YOUTHS

It's up to each of us to help create a better world for our children.

—Dr. Benjamin Spock

Until very recently, children's mental health problems were the domain of folklore and unsubstantiated theories in both the popular and scientific literatures. Only a few generations ago, in the mid-nineteenth century, overstimulation in schools was seen as a cause of insanity (Makari, 1993), and only one generation ago, in the mid-twentieth century, autism was believed to be caused by inadequate, uncaring parents (Bettelheim, 1967).

We now recognize that mental health problems of children and adolescents are a frequently occurring and significant societal concern worldwide. For example, by 2020 behavioral health disorders will surpass all physical diseases as a major cause of disability throughout the world (Substance Abuse and Mental Health Services Administration [SAMHSA], 2011; World Health Organization [WHO], 2007). Perhaps most telling of all is the mounting evidence that *"many, if not most, lifetime psychiatric disorders will first appear in childhood or adolescence"* (Costello, Egger, & Angold, 2005a, p. 972, italics added; Kessler et al., 2009).

Surveys conducted in North America and elsewhere find that about one child in eight has a mental health problem that significantly impairs functioning (Costello et al., 2005a), a finding that extends even to infants and toddlers (Skovgaard et al., 2007). Many other children have emerging problems that place them at risk for later development of a psychological disorder. As surprising as it may sound, recent longitudinal studies have found that by their 21st birthday, three out of five young

In the United States, the richest country in the world, nearly one in four children (23.1%) live in poverty, ranking the United States second out of 35 developed countries in terms of child poverty (UNICEF Innocenti Research Centre, 2012).

adults meet criteria for a well-specified psychiatric disorder (Copeland et al., 2011). Some children have difficulties adapting to school or to family circumstances, so they behave in ways that are developmentally or situationally inappropriate. Others show more pronounced patterns of poor development and maladjustment that suggest one or more specific disorders of childhood or adolescence. The process of deciding which problems merit professional attention and which ones might be outgrown involves a good understanding of both normal and abnormal child development and behavior.

Despite the magnitude of children's mental health needs today, the youngest one-fourth of the population (those under age 18) have very few treatment options, and the options that are available are woefully underfunded (Weisz & Kazdin, 2010). Sadly, the majority of children and youths needing mental health services do not receive them, due largely to poor understanding of mental disorders and limited access to intervention (Mark et al., 2008; McEwan, Waddell, & Barker, 2007). The demand for children's mental health services is expected to double over the next decade because the number of child and adolescent mental health professionals is not expected to increase at the required rate (Health Resources and Services Administration, 2010). A career in children's mental health, anyone?

The chapters that follow explain that a significant proportion of children do not grow out of their childhood difficulties, although the ways in which children express difficulties are likely to change in both form and severity over time. Children's developmental impairments may have a lasting negative impact on later family life, occupations, and social adjustment, even when they no longer have the disorder.

© iStockphoto.com/Brandy Taylor

PRELIMINARY EDITION

The Changing Picture of Children's Mental Health

If all children and adolescents with known psychological disorders could be captured in a photograph, the current picture would be much clearer than that of only a generation ago. The improved focus and detail are the result of efforts to increase recognition and assessment of children's psychological disorders. In the past, children with various mental health and educational needs were too often described in global terms such as *maladjusted*, because assessment devices were not sensitive to different syndromes and diagnostic clusters of symptoms (Achenbach & Rescorla, 2007). Today, we have a better ability to distinguish among the various disorders. This ability has given rise to increased and earlier recognition of previously poorly understood or undetected problems—learning disorders, depression, teen suicide, eating disorders, conduct disorders, and problems stemming from chronic health conditions and from abuse and neglect.

Another difference in today's portrait would be the group's composition. Younger children (Skovgaard et al., 2007) and teens (Wolfe & Mash, 2006) would appear more often in the photo, reflecting greater awareness of their unique mental health issues. Specific communication and learning disorders, for example, have only recently been recognized as significant concerns among preschoolers and young school-age children. Similarly, emotional problems, such as anxiety and depression, which increase dramatically during adolescence (Rudolph, Hammen, & Daley, 2006), were previously overlooked because the symptoms are often less visible or disturbing to others than are the symptoms of behavior or learning problems.

What would not have changed in our photo is the proportion of children who are receiving proper services. Fewer than 10% of children with mental health problems receive proper services to address impairments related to personal, family, or situational factors (Costello et al., 2005a). Limited and fragmented resources mean that children do not receive appropriate

Surveys estimate that about 1 child in 8 has a mental health problem that interferes with his or her development, and 1 in 10 has a specific psychological disorder.

mental health services at the appropriate time. Fortunately, this situation is beginning to change, with greater attention paid to evidence-based prevention and treatment programs for many childhood disorders and calls for more integrated services for children within school systems (Kirby & Keon, 2006; Weisz & Kazdin, 2010).

The children and teens in the picture would not reflect a random cross section of all children because mental health problems are unevenly distributed. Those disproportionately afflicted with mental health problems are:

▶ Children from disadvantaged families and neighborhoods (Brooks-Gunn, Schneider, & Waldfogel, 2013)

▶ Children from abusive or neglectful families (Cicchetti et al., 2010; Wekerle et al., 2006)

▶ Children receiving inadequate child care (Pollak et al., 2010)

▶ Children born with very low birth weight due to maternal smoking, diet, or abuse of alcohol and drugs (D'Onofrio et al., 2010)

▶ Children born to parents with mental illness or substance abuse problems (Davis et al., 2011; Mellin, 2010)

Also, the children in the picture could not easily be grouped according to these categories because children often face combinations of environmental stressors and psychosocial deprivations. Such children are especially at risk of having their healthy development compromised to the degree that they are said to show abnormal behavior or to suffer from a mental disorder.

WHAT AFFECTS RATES AND EXPRESSION OF MENTAL DISORDERS? A LOOK AT SOME KEY FACTORS

New pressures and social changes may place children at increasing risk for the development of disorders at younger ages (Obradovic et al., 2010). Many stressors today are quite different from those faced by our parents and grandparents. Some have been around for generations: chronic poverty, inequality, family breakup, single parenting, and so on. Others are more recent or are now more visible: homelessness, adjustment problems of children in immigrant families, inadequate child care available to working parents, and conditions associated with the impact of prematurity, parental HIV, and cocaine or alcohol abuse on children's growth and development (Chapman, Dube, & Anda, 2007). Even welcome medical advances can have a negative effect. Higher rates of fetal survival have contributed to a greater number of children with behavior and learning difficulties who require specialized services at a younger age.

It is important to remember that the manner in which one's circumstances affect the course (e.g., progression) of a disorder should be distinguished from how they may initially contribute to the problem. That is, environmental stressors, such as poverty, child abuse, or lack of safety, may act as nonspecific stressors that bring about poor adaptation or even the onset of a disorder in some vulnerable children. In contrast, these same environmental influences may affect the course of the disorder in other children by affecting the extent to which the child's problems are attenuated or exacerbated (Schreier & Chen, 2013; Williams & Steinberg, 2011). Examples of major factors in the development and expression of child psychopathology are noted next, and they resurface throughout our subsequent discussions of each disorder.

Poverty and Socioeconomic Disadvantage

The most dangerous place for a child to try to grow up in America is at the intersection of race and poverty.

—Children's Defense Fund (2007)

If you looked beyond the faces of the children in our hypothetical photo, you would note that in many cases, the background and circumstances of children and youths with mental health problems provide obvious clues to their origins. Some of the most telling clues are the experiences of poverty, disadvantage, and violence faced by many, which can have a cumulative effect on mental health.

Childhood poverty is a daily reality for about 1 in 4 children in the United States (U.S. Census Bureau, 2011a) and 1 in 7 in Canada (Statistics Canada, 2011); it is especially pronounced among Native American/ First Nations and African American children (Spicer & Sarche, 2006). Growing up with poverty has a substantial effect on the well-being of children and adolescents, especially in terms of impairments in learning ability and school achievement. Moreover, low income is tied to many other forms of disadvantage: less education, low-paying jobs, inadequate health care, single-parent status, limited resources, poor nutrition, and greater exposure to violence. Any one disadvantage can impair children's developmental progress significantly (Razza, Martin, & Brooks-Gunn, 2010).

The impact of childhood poverty is telling. Children from poor and disadvantaged families suffer more conduct disorders, chronic illness, school problems, emotional disorders, and cognitive/learning problems than children who are not poor (McMahon & Luthar, 2007). These impairments may be due to the pronounced effect on prefrontal cortex development stemming from the social inequalities of chronic poverty (Kishiyama et al., 2009; Luby et al., 2013). Economic

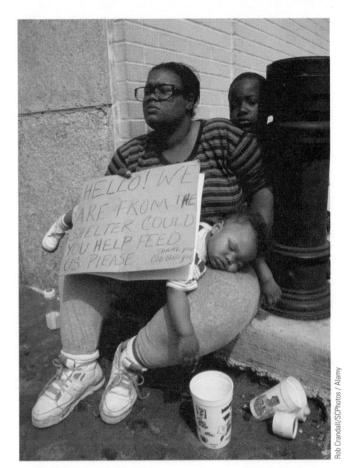

Eighty-eight percent of homeless families in the United States are headed by women.

deprivation alone is not responsible for these higher rates because many children do succeed under harsh circumstances. Nevertheless, the greater the degree of inequality, powerlessness, and lack of control over their lives, the more children's physical and mental health are undermined (Aber, Jones, & Raver, 2007).

Poverty has a significant, yet indirect, effect on children's adjustment, most likely because of its association with negative influences—particularly harsh, inconsistent parenting and elevated exposure to acute and chronic stressors—that define the day-to-day experiences of children in poverty. For example, youths who live in inner-city areas and witness community violence are most likely to develop post-traumatic stress disorder (Kiser, 2007) as well as cognitive delays and impairments that affect both learning and mental health (Farah et al., 2006).

Sex Differences

We have known for some time that boys and girls express their problems in different ways (Zahn-Waxler et al., 2006). For example, hyperactivity, autism, childhood disruptive behavior disorders, and learning and communication disorders are more common in boys than in girls; the opposite is true for most anxiety disorders, adolescent depression, and eating disorders. What we don't understand is whether these differences are caused by definitions, reporting biases (the more "disturbing" problems are most likely to come to the attention of mental health agencies), or differences in the expression of the disorder (Martel, 2013). For example, aggressive behavior may be expressed more directly by boys (fighting) and more indirectly by girls (spreading rumors). Although mental health problems for girls have been understudied, this situation is changing; therefore, we consider the expression of problems for boys and girls in each chapter.

Sex differences in problem behaviors are negligible in children under the age of 3 but increase with age (Achenbach & Rescorla, 2006). Boys show higher rates of early-onset disorders that involve some form of neurodevelopmental impairment, and girls show more emotional disorders, with a peak age of onset in adolescence. For example, boys generally have higher rates of reading disorders, autism spectrum disorders, attention-deficit/hyperactivity disorder (ADHD), and early-onset persistent conduct problems, whereas girls have higher rates of depression and eating disorders (Copeland et al., 2011; Rutter et al., 2004).

● Figure 1.3 depicts the normal developmental trajectories for girls and boys across the two major dimensions of internalizing and externalizing behaviors.

Internalizing problems include anxiety, depression, somatic symptoms, and withdrawn behavior; **externalizing problems** encompass more acting-out behaviors, such as aggression and delinquent behavior. You'll notice from Figure 1.3(A) that externalizing problems for boys start out higher than for girls in preschool and early elementary years, and that these problems decrease gradually for both boys and girls until the rates almost converge by age 18. The opposite pattern emerges for internalizing problems. Parents report similar rates of internalizing problems for boys and girls in early childhood, but girls outpace boys in these problems over time (Bongers et al., 2003). These developmental trajectories of problem behaviors provide a useful basis for identifying deviations from the normal course, although these overall trends need to be considered in relation to a number of additional factors that we discuss throughout the text.

Finally, it is interesting to note that the types of child-rearing environments predicting resilience in the face of adversity also differ for boys and girls. Resilience in boys is associated with households in which there is a male role model (such as a father, grandfather, or older brother); structure; rules; and some encouragement of emotional expressiveness. In contrast, girls who display resilience come from households that combine risk taking and independence with support from a female caregiver (such as a mother, grandmother, or older sister; Werner, 2005).

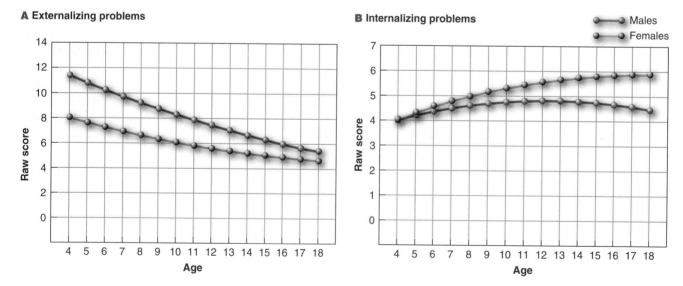

● **FIGURE 1.3** | Normative developmental trajectories of externalizing problems (A) and internalizing problems (B) from the child behavior checklist. Ages are shown on the *x* axis. The *y* axis shows the raw scores (higher score means more problems).

Adapted from "The normative development of child and adolescent problem behavior," by Bongers, I. L., Koot, H. M., van der Ende, J., & Verhulst, F. C., 2003, *Journal of Abnormal Psychology*, 112, 179–192. Copyright © 2003 by the American Psychological Association. Reprinted with permission. The APA is not responsible for the accuracy of this translation.

Race and Ethnicity

Physical variations in the human species have no meaning except the social ones that humans put on them.

—American Anthropological Association, 1998

People who are from racial or ethnic minority groups comprise a substantial and vibrant segment of many countries, enriching each society with many unique strengths, cultural traditions, and important contributions. In the United States, the number of people who are ethnic minorities is growing rapidly—by 2050, the nation's population of children is expected to be 62% minority, up from 44% today (U.S. Census Bureau, 2011b).

As reflected in the quote above, the majority of cultural anthropologists today believe that race is a socially constructed concept, not a biological one (Crisp & Turner, 2011; Sternberg, Grigorenko, & Kidd, 2005). This helps explain why very few emotional and behavioral disorders of childhood occur at different rates for different racial groups. Children from certain ethnic and racial groups in the United States are overrepresented in rates of some disorders, such as substance abuse, delinquency, and teen suicide (Nguyen et al., 2007). However, once the effects of socioeconomic status (SES), sex, age, and referral status are controlled for (i.e., the unique contributions of these factors are removed or accounted for), few differences in the rate of children's psychological disorders emerge in relation to race or ethnicity (Roberts, Roberts, & Xing, 2006). Some minority groups, in fact, show less psychopathology after controlling for SES (Nguyen et al., 2007; Roberts et al., 2006).

Even though rates of problems are similar, significant barriers remain in access to, and quality and outcomes of, care for minority children (Alegria, Vallas, & Pumariega, 2010). As a result, American Indians, Alaska Natives, African Americans, Asian Americans, Pacific Islanders, and Hispanic Americans bear a disproportionately high burden of disability from mental disorders (Agency for Healthcare Research and Quality, 2011). Specifically, the majority culture has neglected to incorporate respect for or understanding of the histories, traditions, beliefs, languages, and value systems of culturally diverse groups. Misunderstanding and misinterpreting behaviors have led to tragic consequences, including inappropriately placing minorities in the criminal and juvenile justice systems (Pumariega, Rothe, Song, & Lu, 2010).

Minority children and youths face multiple disadvantages, such as poverty and exclusion from society's benefits. This exclusion is often referred to as marginalization, and it can result in a sense of alienation, loss of social cohesion, and rejection of the norms of the larger society. Resisting the combined effects of poverty and marginalization takes unusual personal strength and family support. Since children from ethnic and racial minority groups are overrepresented in low-SES groups, we must interpret with caution the relationships among SES, ethnicity, and behavior problems that often emerge while discussing childhood disorders. We also have to keep in mind that, despite the growing ethnic diversity of the North American population, ethnic representation in research studies and the study of ethnicity-related issues receive relatively little attention in studies of child psychopathology and treatment (Coll, Akerman, & Cicchetti, 2000; Schwartz et al., 2010).

As was the case for SES and sex differences, global comparisons of the prevalence of different types of problems for different ethnic groups are not likely to be very revealing. On the other hand, investigations into the processes affecting the form, associated factors, and outcomes of different disorders for various ethnic groups hold promise for increasing our understanding of the relationship between ethnicity and abnormal child behavior.

Cultural Issues

The values, beliefs, and practices that characterize a particular ethnocultural group contribute to the development and expression of children's disorders, and affect how people and institutions react to a child's problem (Rescorla et al., 2011). Because the meaning of children's social behavior is influenced by cultural beliefs and values, it is not surprising that children express their problems somewhat differently across cultures. For example, shyness and oversensitivity in children have been found to be associated with peer rejection and social maladjustment in Western cultures, but to be associated with leadership, school competence, and academic achievement in Chinese children in Shanghai (Chen, Rubin, & Li, 1995; Rubin et al., 2006).

Because of cultural influences, it is important that research on abnormal child behavior not be generalized from one culture to another unless there is support for doing so. Some underlying processes, such as regulating emotion and its relationship to social competence, may be similar across diverse cultures (Eisenberg, Smith, & Spinrad, 2011). Similarly, some disorders, particularly those with a strong neurobiological basis (e.g., ADHD, autism spectrum disorder), may be less susceptible to cultural influences. Nonetheless, social and cultural beliefs and values are likely to influence the meaning

PRELIMINARY EDITION

given to these behaviors, the ways in which they are responded to, their forms of expression, and their outcomes (APA, 2013). Few studies have compared the attitudes, behaviors, and biological and psychological processes of children with mental disorders across different cultures. However, in this text, we will indicate where this situation is beginning to change.

Child Maltreatment and Non-Accidental Trauma

Children and adolescents are being neglected and abused at an alarming rate worldwide (WHO, 2010). Each year nearly 1 million verified cases of child abuse and neglect (a rate of 10 per 1,000 children) occur in the United States (U.S. Department of Health and Human Services, 2010), and more than 80,000 in Canada (Public Health Agency of Canada, 2010). U.S. phone surveys of children and youths between 10 and 16 years old estimate that more than one-third of U.S. children (6 million) in that age bracket experience physical and/or sexual assaults during these ages, not only by family members but also by persons they may know from their communities and schools (Finkelhor, 2011).

These related forms of non-accidental trauma—being the victim of violence at school or being exposed to violent acts in their homes or neighborhoods—lead to significant mental health problems in children and youths.

In a telephone survey of more than 4,000 youths between 12 and 17 years of age, 16% of boys and 19% of girls met the criteria for either post-traumatic stress disorder, major depressive episode, or substance abuse/dependence in relation to acts of violence (Kilpatrick et al., 2003). Tragically, these acts of abuse and trauma are estimated to cost $124 billion per year in the United States as a result of direct and indirect harm over the lifetime of these children (Fang, Brown, Florence, & Mercy, 2012). Because of the increasing significance of these acts, more attention is being given to developing ways to prevent maltreatment, and help youngsters exposed to maltreatment and trauma. We devote discussion to this concern in Chapter 12: Trauma- and Stressor-Related Disorders.

Special Issues Concerning Adolescents and Sexual Minority Youths

Early to mid-adolescence is a particularly important transitional period for healthy versus problematic adjustment (Cicchetti & Rogosch, 2002; Wolfe & Mash, 2006). Substance use, risky sexual behavior, violence, accidental injuries, and mental health problems are only a few of the major issues that make adolescence a particularly vulnerable period. Disturbingly, mortality rates more than triple between late childhood and early adulthood, primarily as the result of risk-taking behaviors (Centers for Disease Control and Prevention, 2010).

Late childhood and early adolescence is also a time during which youths who are lesbian, gay, bisexual, and transgendered (LGBT) face multiple challenges that can affect their health and well-being. Growing up in a society that is predominantly heterosexual—and largely biased against other sexual identities—makes adolescence a particularly difficult time for those who are not heterosexual. According to several large surveys of LGBT youths in middle and high schools, they are more likely to be victimized by their peers as well as by family members, and they report more bullying, teasing, harassment, and physical assault than other students (Kosciw, Greytak, & Diaz, 2009). For example, 81% report experiencing verbal abuse related to being LGBT, 38% have been threatened with physical attacks, 22% have had objects thrown at them, 15% have been physically assaulted, and 16% have been sexually assaulted (D'Augelli, 2006). Given the stigma and prejudice that exist in many parts of society, it is not surprising that young people who are LGBT have higher rates of mental health problems, including depression and suicidal behavior, substance abuse, and risky sexual behavior, as compared with their heterosexual counterparts (Coker, Austin, & Schuster, 2010).

In response to mounting concerns, the special needs and problems of adolescents are receiving greater attention, especially because serious consequences are preventable. For example, various health organizations and government agencies implemented campaigns in schools, community programs, and health-care settings to reduce adolescent risk taking and experimentation (Beardslee, Chien, & Bell, 2011). Because the problems of adolescents have been neglected as compared with those of children, throughout this text we will look at the expression of each disorder in both childhood and adolescence as much as possible.

Lifespan Implications

Over the long term, the impact of children's mental health problems is most severe when the problems continue untreated for months or years. The developmental tasks of childhood are challenging enough without the added burden of emotional or behavioral disturbances that interfere with the progress and course of development. About 20% of the children with the most chronic and serious disorders face sizable difficulties throughout their lives (Costello & Angold, 2006). They are least likely to finish school and most likely to have social problems or psychiatric disorders that affect many aspects of their lives throughout adulthood.

The lifelong consequences associated with child psychopathology are exceedingly costly in terms of economic impact and human suffering. The costs are enormous with respect to demands on community resources such as health, education, mental health, and criminal justice systems; loss in productivity; the need for repeated and long-term interventions; and the human suffering of both the afflicted children and the family and community members they encounter. Fortunately, children and youths can overcome major impediments when circumstances and opportunities promote healthy adaptation and competence.

The growing recognition of the concerns presented in this chapter has led to a number of major initiatives to achieve the goals of prevention and help. These initiatives are summarized in a number of government reports that include recommendations as to how these goals can be achieved. Many of these important reports are available on the Internet (see A Closer Look 1.6), and we recommend that you familiarize yourself with these developments.

Section Summary

What Affects the Rates and Expression of Mental Disorders? A Look at Some Key Factors

- Clear understanding of both normal and abnormal child development and behavior is needed to decide which problems are likely to continue and which might be outgrown.
- About one child in eight has a mental health problem that significantly impairs functioning.
- A significant proportion of children do not grow out of their childhood difficulties, although the ways in which these difficulties are expressed are likely to change in both form and severity over time.
- Mental health problems are unevenly distributed. Children who experience more social and economic disadvantage or inequality and children exposed to more violent, inadequate, or toxic environments are disproportionately afflicted with mental health problems.
- A child's biological sex, ethnic background, and cultural surroundings are all important contributors to the manner in which his or her behavioral and emotional problems are expressed to and recognized by others.
- Many childhood problems can have lifelong consequences for the child and for society.

A CLOSER **LOOK** **1.6**

Current Reports on Mental Health Issues Pertaining to Children and Youths

Since release of the U.S. Surgeon General's Report on Mental Health in 1999, there have been many important national and international initiatives and reports about understanding and helping children and adolescents with mental health problems. The wonders of the information age provide free access to this wealth of information (as if reading your textbook were not enough!). Below is a list of some (but by no means all) of the more important documents that are shaping the field. Your Psychology CourseMate provides live links to most of these documents.

Mental Health
U.S. Public Health Service Office of the Surgeon General. (1999). *Mental health: A report of the Surgeon General.* Rockville, MD: Department of Health and Human Services, U.S. Public Health Service.

Development and Psychopathology
Institute of Medicine. (2000). *From neurons to neighborhoods: The science of early childhood development.* Washington, DC: National Academies Press.

Children's Rights
UNICEF (2013): Convention on the Rights of the Child. Protecting and realizing children's rights. Available at: http://www.unicef.org/crc/index_protecting.html.

Culture, Race, and Ethnicity
U.S. Public Health Service Office of the Surgeon General. (2001). *Mental health: Culture, race, and ethnicity: A supplement to Mental health: A report of the Surgeon General.* Rockville, MD: Department of Health and Human Services, U.S. Public Health Service.

Children's Mental Health
Report of *Healthy Development: A Summit on Young Children's Mental Health* (2009). Partnering with communication scientists, collaborating across disciplines, and leveraging impact to promote children's mental health. Washington, DC: Society for Research in Child Development. Available at: www.apa.org/pi/families/summit-report.pdf

(continues)

PRELIMINARY EDITION

(continued)

Research on Children's Mental Health

Children's Health Policy Centre: Children's Mental Health Research Quarterly. Available at: http://childhealthpolicy.ca/the-quarterly

Mental Health: International Perspective

World Health Organization. (2007). *The world health report 2007.* Geneva: World Health Organization.

Transforming Mental Health Care

Transforming mental health care in America. Rockville, MD: Substance Abuse and Mental Health Services Administration (SAMHSA). Available at: http://www.samhsa.gov/federalactionagenda/NFC_TOC.aspx.

Out of the Shadows At Last: Transforming Mental Health, Mental Illness and Addiction Services in Canada. The Standing Senate Committee on Social Affairs, Science and Technology. Available at: http://www.parl.gc.ca/Content/SEN/Committee/391/soci/rep/rep02may06-e.htm

Substance Abuse

Substance Abuse and Mental Health Services Administration. (2011). *Results from the 2010 National Survey on Drug Use and Health: Summary of National Findings* (NSDUH Series H-41, HHS Publication No. (SMA) 11-4658. Rockville, MD. Available at: http://oas.samhsa.gov/nsduhlatest.htm

Suicide Prevention

U.S. Department of Health and Human Services. *Suicide Prevention: Resources and Publications.* Substance Abuse and Mental Health Services Administration. Available at: http://www.samhsa.gov/prevention/suicide.aspx

National Strategy for Suicide Prevention: Goals and Objectives for Action. A Report of the U.S. Surgeon General and of the National Action Alliance for Suicide Prevention (2012). Available at: http://www.surgeongeneral.gov/library/reports/national-strategy-suicide-prevention/index.html

Youth Violence

U.S. Public Health Service Office of the Surgeon General. (2001). *Youth violence: A report of the Surgeon General.* Rockville, MD: Department of Health and Human Services, U.S. Public Health Service.

Centers for Disease Control and Prevention. *Injury Prevention and Control: Youth Violence.* Available at: http://www.cdc.gov/ViolencePrevention/youthviolence/index.html

Reducing Health Risks

World Health Organization. (2012, September). *What are the key health dangers for children?* Available at: http://www.who.int/features/qa/13/en/index.html

Violence and Health

World Health Organization. (2002). *World report on violence and health.* Geneva: World Health Organization. Also see: *WHO Violence and Injury Prevention.* Available at: http://www.who.int/violence_injury_prevention/violence/en

Sexual Minority Youths

Centers for Disease Control and Prevention. (2011, June). *MMWR: Sexual Identity, Sex of Sexual Contacts, and Health-Risk Behaviors Among Students in Grades 9–12—Youth Risk Behavior Surveillance, Selected Sites, United States, 2001–2009.* Available at: http://www.cdc.gov/healthyyouth/disparities/smy.htm

LOOKING AHEAD

The significance of children's mental health problems emerges over and over again throughout this text, as we consider the many different individual, family, social, and cultural influences that define abnormal child psychology. Because children cannot advocate on their own behalf, and because their mental health needs and developmental issues differ markedly from those of adults, it is important that we keep these concerns in mind. Moreover, children's problems don't come in neat packages. Many disorders discussed in the text overlap with other disorders in terms of symptoms, characteristics, and treatment needs. Once again, the importance of viewing the whole child in relation to his or her difficulties emerges as the best strategy in understanding abnormal child and adolescent psychology,

using diagnostic criteria as guideposts rather than as firm rules.

The next three chapters discuss theories, causes, research, and clinical issues. Chapter 2 looks at current ways of viewing child and adolescent disorders. It includes the exciting advances made possible by new discoveries about the brain, and notes how these discoveries have become more integrated with knowledge of the biological and psychological processes affecting children's development and disorders. Chapter 3 reviews research methods with children, youths, and families that help us understand features, causes, course, and treatment methods. Chapter 4 discusses clinical issues pertaining to children's mental health, especially current approaches to assessment, diagnosis, and treatment. Because psychological interventions vary considerably in relation to each disorder, we will describe the most recent and effective treatments for specific disorders in the context of the disorders to which they apply. This allows information on treatments and their effectiveness to be woven into our knowledge about the description and causes of the disorder.

Chapters 5 through 14 examine specific disorders and conditions affecting children and adolescents. We organize these disorders and conditions into three general categories:

▸ *Neurodevelopmental disorders.* Chapters 5 through 8 examine a broad range of disorders that appear early in development and lead to a range of impairments in personal, social, and academic functioning. These developmental deficits are often chronic and affect children's ability to learn or perform normally, including intellectual disability, autism spectrum disorder, communication and learning disorders, and attention-deficit/hyperactivity disorder (ADHD).

▸ *Behavioral and emotional disorders.* Chapters 9 through 12 cover behavioral and emotional conditions that typically emerge in mid-childhood to late childhood and adolescence. These include disruptive and conduct disorders (sometimes referred to as externalizing problems because they involve conflicts with the environment), mood and anxiety disorders (sometimes referred to as "internalizing problems" because they involve conflicts within the child that are less visible to others), and trauma- and stressor-related disorders. We also discuss child maltreatment in the chapter on trauma- and stressor-related disorders because of the significance of abuse and other forms of non-accidental trauma on children's developmental progress and course.

▸ *Problems related to physical and mental health.* Chapters 13 and 14 discuss child and adolescent disorders stemming from medical or physical conditions that may affect children's overall psychological functioning, and vice versa, such as chronic illness, substance abuse, and eating disorders and related conditions.

Far greater attention has been devoted to the description and classification of abnormality in children than to healthy child functioning and how children adapt to the challenges of growing up. In light of this imbalance, throughout this text we introduce each disorder with a discussion of normal developmental processes, such as children's normal intellectual development (in relation to intellectual disability) and the normal range of misbehavior and acting out (in reference to conduct problems). We also consider children's strengths and adaptive abilities, regardless of the presence of a particular disorder, and factors that are believed to encourage healthy adaptation regardless of other impairments. We then present the core features of each disorder (such as hyperactivity–impulsivity, sad mood, or antisocial behavior), followed by significant associated features (such as problems in self-esteem, peer relations, or substance abuse).

As you begin your journey into the field of abnormal child psychology, keep in mind that the threats facing children today—child poverty, chronic illness, maltreatment, and indifference—are no less significant than those of the past, although they sometimes fail to arouse the indignation of society to the extent that major changes are implemented and maintained. Even countries that have outlawed child labor, child abuse, and many other forms of actual and potential harm have only recently begun to recognize the profound importance of the quality of the early childhood environment for children's health, well-being, and competence. Fortunately, it is unlikely that children and youths will ever again be seen as insignificant, costly burdens on society. As each chapter in this text indicates, efforts aimed at change in policies and programs directed toward children and youths are gaining momentum.

Study Resources

SECTION SUMMARIES

KEY TERMS

PRELIMINARY EDITION

2

Theories and Causes

Everything should be made as simple as possible, but not simpler.

—Albert Einstein

PRELIMINARY EDITION

A T THE RISK OF sounding vague, we must acknowledge that nearly all child and family disturbances result from multiple, interacting risk factors and processes. Contextual events in the family or school environment exert considerable influence over an individual's course of development (see the Chapter 1 discussion of risk and resilience). Therefore, a given child's problems must be considered in relation to multiple levels of influence—individual, family, community, and culture—rather than be attributed to any one factor. Since the causes of psychological disorders are significant, in this chapter we describe the primary biological and psychological influences.

In this chapter, we consider theories and research findings regarding influences that shape the child's ongoing development in many different ways. Some influences (such as biological factors and the effects of environmental factors) are contained within the child, whereas many others (such as family patterns and cultural norms) lie at various distances from the child's immediate surroundings. We will see how examining these various causal influences contribute to a better understanding of abnormal child development and how they are conceptually related to one another.

Let's begin by considering Jorge's situation and his parents' complaints, which raise important issues. Could Jorge have mild intellectual disability that impairs his learning? Is Jorge's mother right about his having a learning disability? Does Jorge have a specific communication or learning problem unrelated to intellectual disability that affects his schoolwork? Perhaps his school and family environments have contributed to his learning difficulties and fear of school. Did his parents and teachers expect him to fail? Has he been given much assistance? Has he been abused or neglected at home?

WHAT IS CAUSING JORGE'S PROBLEMS?

Suppose you were asked to interview Jorge, his teachers, and his parents to find out why schoolwork is difficult for him. How would you go about this task? What information do you feel would be essential to know, and what plan might you follow to organize and explore the many possible reasons for his problem? Most likely, you would form a working theory to help you in determining what to ask and why. At first, your theory might be very basic and unrefined. Jorge's problem in school might be connected to the negative comments and pressure he is getting from his parents and teacher. As you proceed, your theory about Jorge's problem would likely expand and become more detailed, allowing you to probe with more precise questions.

Let's briefly consider possible interrelated causes of Jorge's behavior:

1. *Biological influences.* Because we know little about Jorge's early development, we might ask his mother about her prenatal history, including major illnesses, injuries, or perhaps marital problems or undue stresses that might have affected her pregnancy. Jorge's problems also reflect a tendency toward behavioral inhibition; he may approach new or challenging situations with greater apprehension and fear than other children (Gleason et al., 2011).

Children with fears and anxiety—which are affected by levels of stress hormones circulating in the body—are more likely to have parents who had similar problems during childhood (Micco et al., 2009). Jorge may have inherited a tendency to respond to his environment with heightened arousal or sensitivity. Alternatively, his early neurological development and the patterns of connections established within his brain may have been influenced by the child-rearing styles his parents used when he was an infant. These early patterns, in turn, can influence how Jorge approaches new tasks, reacts to criticism, or relates to others (Belsky & de Haan, 2011). Another possibility is that Jorge may have inherited one or more genes that influence his phonological awareness. He may not be able to recognize and process all the English language phonemes (individual sounds) and thus suffers from a reading disorder (Scerri & Schulte-Körne, 2010).

2. *Emotional influences.* Children like Jorge not only think and behave in ways that provide clues to their distress, but also show various emotional signals that are not obvious at first. Emotional expression offers another unique window for viewing Jorge's inner world, especially his emotional reactions to challenges such as reading. Consider this possibility: As Jorge approaches his reading assignment or thinks about returning to school the next morning, he is overwhelmed by fear, bordering on panic. His heart races, his breathing quickens, and his thoughts turn to ways to escape from this dreaded situation as quickly as possible. As he is preoccupied by such feelings and worry, his concentration declines further.

Jorge's inability to regulate feelings of arousal, distress, or agitation that may surface without warning is a key element in describing his problem, but we still have not determined how it might have originated. Emotional reactivity and expression are the ways infants and young children first communicate with the world around them, and their ability to regulate these emotions as they adapt is a critical aspect of their early relationships with caregivers (Eisenberg, Smith, & Spinrad, 2011). Emotions can be powerful events,

Not Keeping Up

Jorge was almost 14 years old when he was referred to me because of his academic problems. Since grade 4 he had been performing well below average in his classes, had difficulty concentrating, and was considered to be "too quiet and nervous." For the past four summers he had taken extra classes to improve his reading, but was currently reading at the third-grade level. As a result, his parents received a letter from the school saying he likely would not be promoted to the next grade if his work didn't improve. Everyone seemed angry at Jorge for not keeping up.

When I met with Jorge, his version of his school problems was short and to the point: "It's the teachers," he said, as he looked at the floor and squirmed in his seat. "How am I expected to learn anything when they yell at you? When I told my English teacher that I hadn't finished reading my book for class, he said I take too long 'cuz my mind wanders too much. How am I expected to learn when they think I'm dumb?" After further discussion, Jorge summed up his view of the problem in a quiet, sullen voice: "I know I'll never get anywhere with the brain I've got. I can't figure stuff out very fast, and the teachers aren't much help. Just thinking about school makes me jittery. I'm afraid I'll say something stupid in class and everyone will laugh at me."

Jorge's mother and father met with me separately and were quick to add their own opinions about why their son didn't do well in school. They had moved from their Spanish-speaking neighborhood when Jorge was in grade 2, and he struggled to learn English in school because his parents did not speak it at home. His mother admitted that she becomes aggravated and starts to yell when Jorge says he doesn't want to go to school or can't do his schoolwork,

Everyone seemed to be angry with Jorge

but she didn't think this was an issue. She quickly added, "I've read about learning disabilities and I think he's got one. He can't control his mind enough to center on anything. He's scared to go to school, and avoids homework as if his life depended on it." By the end of the interview it was evident that Jorge's parents were angry at him. They felt Jorge blamed his teachers for his own lack of effort, and that he should be in a special classroom and maybe given medications to calm him down so he wouldn't worry so much about school. (Based on authors' case material)

---

demanding that the child find ways to reduce or regulate their force. The most adaptive way is to seek comfort from a caregiver, which gradually helps the child learn ways to self-regulate. By extension, Jorge's school refusal or phobia could have emerged at a younger age from anxiety about his mother's availability, which grew to a more pronounced and generalized insecurity (Bernstein & Victor, 2010).

3. *Behavioral and cognitive influences.* Jorge has been performing below average in reading for some time. Using our knowledge of learning principles, we might investigate Jorge's current situation from the perspective of events that elicit fear or avoidance, and events that maintain such avoidance by reducing unpleasant reactions. Jorge's lack of progress may be a function of punitive events when he is criticized by his parents or singled out by his teacher.

A behavioral approach to Jorge's problem might be to try to change aspects of his environment—such as the attention he receives from his teacher or parents for his gradual, slow efforts to do his schoolwork—to see what effect this approach has on his school performance and avoidance. We might also consider the teasing or rejection by peers in his school environment that may make him fearful. By observing Jorge at school and narrowing the list of possible events that may contribute to his fears, we can begin to develop hypotheses about Jorge's learning history and, most importantly, possible ways to remedy the problem. One possibility might be to increase the likelihood of reinforcement that is contingent on Jorge's efforts to complete his schoolwork (Little, Akin-Little, & Newman-Eig, 2010).

Cognitive influences, such as a person's interpretation of events, are also important to consider. How does Jorge view the situation, and does his view accurately reflect the situation? Children with fears and worries sometimes develop a belief system that can be self-defeating, leading them to believe that they will fail at everything (Beidel & Turner, 2007). Jorge has failed in reading and other events at school, and it is plausible that he anticipates further struggles with schoolwork and with other children. His own words are quite clear in this respect: "How am I expected to learn when they think I'm dumb?" "I know I'll never get anywhere with the brain I've got." "Just thinking about school makes me jittery." Such thoughts only tend to make him more anxious and more likely to avoid school as much as possible. In short, Jorge expects to fail and be ridiculed at school, issues that certainly warrant attention. Children's self-expressions and other cognitions offer a window on their inner world, which may provide clues that we miss when observing their actions.

4. *Family, cultural, and ethnic influences.* An understanding of the possible causes of Jorge's difficulties would be incomplete without considering his family and peer relationships, his social setting, and his larger cultural and ethnic identity (Marks, Patton, & Coll, 2011). His early relationship with his parents may have contributed to a lessened ability to regulate his emotions adaptively; his current relationships with his teachers, peers, and family members offer further clues. At the family level, how sensitive are his parents to recognizing his special limitations, and how willing are they to teach him alternative strategies? His mother has high hopes and expectations for her child, as well as a life and problems of her own (including a job). Even though she wants only what's best for Jorge, and her behavior is understandable, her lack of sensitivity may still be a problem. Her pointed statement, "I've read about learning disabilities and I think he's got one," suggests that she dismisses the problem by labeling it as "his" problem. Neither parent appears to be open to considering other possible explanations. Furthermore, his mother admits to becoming exasperated and yelling at Jorge. What effect might this have on his tenuous self-concept and his attempts to regulate his fear and arousal?

All children, not only those with problems, require a parenting style that is sensitive to their unique needs and abilities and that places appropriate limits on them to help them develop self-control (Morris et al., 2011). Significant adults both within Jorge's family and at school have not been responding to him with sensitivity, so it's not surprising that Jorge's behavior has grown worse over time.

Along these same lines, it is important to consider how Jorge's behavior might be affected by culturally specific norms and standards. That is, his family's expectations for how he should behave at school and at home may be at odds with those of his non-Hispanic peers (Trommsdorff & Cole, 2011). Children from cultural minority groups face challenges in adapting to their receiving culture—a process known as "acculturation"—and Jorge may be caught between the two. Over time, he may learn to balance these opposing demands and expectations, especially if he lives in a bicultural environment. There is growing evidence that biculturalism, in which the child or adolescent strives to adapt to both their heritage and their receiving cultures, is the most adaptive approach to acculturation (Schwartz et al., 2013).

Finally, for proper development, children require a basic quality of life that includes a safe community, good schools, proper health and nutrition, access to friends their own age, and opportunities to develop close relationships with extended family and members of their community. These opportunities and necessities are in the background of every child's developmental profile and can emerge as very significant issues for children undergoing parental divorce or living in poverty (Fabricius & Luecken, 2007; Rutter, 2003a).

Several important factors that need to be considered in addressing Jorge's problems are shown in ● Figure 2.1. There are many "strikes against Jorge" that need to be considered; clinicians and researchers often attempt to visualize the multiple causes to allow assessment and intervention to address them properly.

● **FIGURE 2.1** | Jorge's concerns: where do we intervene?

Photo Credit: Kin Images/Photodics/Jupiter Images

Section Summary

What Is Causing Jorge's Problems?

- Jorge's case exemplifies many interconnected factors that cause or contribute to psychological problems in children.
- The study of causes of abnormal child behavior involves theory and findings on biological, psychological, social, and cultural/ethnic factors.
- Biological factors include genetic and neurobiological contributors, among others.
- Psychological influences include the role of behavioral and cognitive processes, as well as emotional and relationship influences.
- Major social contributors to child problems involve family patterns, peer relations, community factors, and cultural expectations.
- Factors in each one of these areas impact and interact with the other areas.

THEORETICAL FOUNDATIONS

Defining what is abnormal within the context of children's ongoing adaptation and development, and sorting out the most probable causes of identified problems, is a complicated process. Very few simple or direct cause-and-effect relationships exist. The study of abnormal child behavior requires an appreciation of developmental processes as well as individual and situational events that can have a major bearing on the course and direction of a particular child's life. Studying normal development informs our theories of abnormal development, and vice versa.

Most clinical and research activity begins with a theoretical formulation for guidance and information. Theory is essentially a language of science that allows us to assemble and communicate existing knowledge more comprehensively. A theory permits us to make educated guesses and predictions about behavior based on samples of knowledge, moving us forward to explore possible explanations. Like a treasure map that provides clues and signposts, a theory offers guidance for our pursuit of causal explanations. Knowledge, skill, and evidence must be added to bring these theoretical clues to life.

The study of the causes of childhood disorders is known as **etiology**, which considers how biological, psychological, and environmental processes interact to produce the outcomes that are observed over time. Research into biological determinants has focused on possible causes such as structural brain damage or dysfunction, neurotransmitter imbalances, and genetic influences. Psychological and environmental models emphasize the role of environmental toxins, early experiences, learning opportunities, disciplinary practices, family systems, and sociocultural contexts. Although these factors are often described as possible "causes," they are, in fact, primarily risk factors and correlates associated with certain disorders—their causal role is not always clear.

Numerous theoretical models have been proposed to explain and suggest treatment for children's psychological disorders, although many of the theories have not been substantiated or even tested (Weisz & Kazdin, 2010). Until recently, most models focused on single explanations that failed to consider other influences and their interactions. One-dimensional models do not capture the complexities of abnormal child behavior that are increasingly evident from research (Kazdin & Whitley, 2006). The alternative to single-factor explanations is much more complex and informative. It considers multiple causes that can interact in various ways over time to affect normal and abnormal development. Keeping in mind this central theme of multiple, interactive causes will help you grasp the complexity of each disorder discussed within this text.

Developmental Psychopathology Perspective

Developmental psychopathology is an approach to describing and studying disorders of childhood, adolescence, and beyond in a manner that emphasizes the importance of developmental processes and tasks. This approach provides a useful framework for organizing the study of abnormal child psychology around milestones and sequences in physical, cognitive, social–emotional, and educational development. It also uses abnormal development to inform normal development, and vice versa (Cicchetti, 2006; Hinshaw, 2013). Simply stated, developmental psychopathology emphasizes the role of developmental processes, the importance of context, and the influence of multiple and interacting events in shaping adaptive and maladaptive development. We adopt this perspective as an organizing framework to describe the dynamic, multidimensional process leading to normal or abnormal outcomes in development (Hayden & Mash, 2014).

A central belief of developmental psychopathology is that to understand maladaptive behavior adequately, one must view it in relation to what is normative for a given period of development (Cicchetti, 2006). The main focus is on highlighting developmental processes, such as language and peer relations and how they function, by looking at extremes and variations in developmental outcomes. In so doing, this perspective emphasizes the importance and complexity of biological, familial, and sociocultural factors in predicting and understanding developmental changes. It draws on knowledge from several disciplines, including psychology, psychiatry, sociology, and neuroscience, and integrates this knowledge within a developmental framework (Hinshaw, 2013).

The value of theory lies not only in providing answers but also in raising new questions and looking at familiar problems in different ways. Theory, research, and practice in abnormal child psychology all require an understanding of the assumptions underlying work in this area. Let's look at three prominent assumptions derived from a developmental psychopathology perspective and how they have shaped our approach to abnormal child psychology.

Children's comfort with their environment is shown by their actions

Abnormal Development Is Multiply Determined

Our first underlying assumption is that abnormal child behavior is *multiply determined*. Thus, we have to look beyond the child's current symptoms and consider developmental pathways and interacting events that, over time, contribute to the expression of a particular disorder.

To illustrate this assumption, let's return to Jorge's problems. One way to look at Jorge's problems is to say that he lacks motivation. Although it is a reasonable explanation, this one-dimensional causal model, which attempts to trace the origins of Jorge's reading difficulty to a single underlying cause, is probably too simplistic. Scientific method emphasizes the need to simplify variables to those of the most importance, but focusing on one primary explanation rather than identifying and allowing for several possible explanations (e.g., genetic factors, reinforcement history, and peer problems) fails to consider the concept of developmental pathways (discussed in Chapter 1). A particular problem or disorder may stem from a variety of causes, and similar risk factors may lead to very different outcomes.

Another way to view Jorge's difficulties—the way we emphasize here—considers multiple influences, including his developmental profile and abilities, his home and school environment, and the ongoing, dynamic interactions among these factors. To address Jorge's reading problem from a multidimensional perspective, we would first assess his current abilities by using multiple sources of data on his ability to function in different settings. Even if we were interested only in his reading ability, we would consider a wide range of characteristics besides those we initially believed to be signs of reading problems. Otherwise, our assumptions about the nature of reading problems might prevent us from considering other explanations. Could criticism and yelling from Jorge's mother affect his concentration or self-esteem? Is Jorge different from other children in terms of his ability to recognize language sounds from written words? These are some of the questions we would want to answer through careful observation and assessment, using a theoretically guided decision-making strategy.

Child and Environment Are Interdependent

Our second assumption extends the influence of multiple causes by stressing how the child and environment are **interdependent**—how they influence each other. This concept departs from the tradition of viewing the environment as acting on the child to cause changes in development, and instead argues that children also influence their own environment. In simple terms, the concept of interdependence appreciates how nature and nurture work together and are, in fact, interconnected (Rutter, 2011a). Thus, children elicit different reactions from the same environment; different environments, such as home or school, elicit different reactions from the same child.

The dynamic interaction of child and environment is referred to as a **transaction** (Sameroff, 2010; Sameroff & MacKenzie, 2003). The child and the environment both contribute to the expression of a disorder, and one cannot be separated from the other. A transactional view regards both children and the environment as *active contributors* to adaptive and maladaptive behavior. Most persons who know children best—parents, teachers, child care workers, and others—would probably agree that this view makes the most sense: Children act on their environment, and their environment acts on them, as in the example of Jorge. According to this transactional perspective, children's psychological disorders do not reside within the child, nor are they due solely to environmental causes. They most often emerge from a combination

"The title of my science project is 'My Little Brother: Nature or Nurture.'"

Michael Shaw/The New Yorker Collection/The Cartoon Bank

of factors, which interact in ways that follow general laws of organized development.

Although a transactional view considers general principles of development that apply to all children, it is also sensitive to individual circumstances—in the child's family or biological makeup—that influence or alter typical outcomes. Learning about such deviations from the norm is what this textbook is all about.

Abnormal Development Involves Continuities and Discontinuities

Think for a moment about how Jorge's various problems might have begun and how they might change or even disappear over time. Might his current problems of avoiding school and homework be connected to his earlier difficulties in reading? Are these qualitatively different problems, or are they different manifestations of the same problem? Are his current problems qualitatively different from those he had at a younger age because his problems today include avoiding school and homework?

Few psychological disorders or impairments suddenly emerge without at least some warning signs or connections to earlier developmental issues. This connection is apparent, for example, in early-onset and persistent conduct disorders, with which parents and other adults often see troublesome behaviors at a young age that continue in some form into adolescence and adulthood (Reef, van Meurs, Verhulst, & van der Ende, 2010). However, it is critical to note that some forms of abnormal child development may be continuous or discontinuous across childhood, adolescence, and adulthood, in either a consistent or a transformed manner (Schulenberg, Sameroff, & Cicchetti, 2006).

Continuity implies that developmental changes are gradual and quantitative (i.e., expressed as amounts that can be measured numerically, such as weight and height changes) and that future behavior patterns can be predicted from earlier patterns. **Discontinuity**, in contrast, implies that developmental changes are abrupt and qualitative (i.e., expressed as qualities that cannot be measured numerically, such as changes in mood or expression) and that future behavior is poorly predicted by earlier patterns.

As an example, consider a preschool child who uses physical aggression with peers. What would you expect that child to be like 10 years later? According to the notion of continuity, he or she would be more likely to engage in antisocial and delinquent behaviors as an adolescent and adult. That is, the pattern of problem behavior (in this case, physical aggression) is continuous across developmental periods, although it gradually changes in form and intensity. Pushing a peer may turn into striking someone with a fist or object. Importantly, continuity refers to patterns of behavior, rather than specific symptoms that remain over time. Continuity is well supported for early-onset and persistent conduct disorders, which have a significant likelihood of later evolving into serious antisocial acts (Lynam et al., 2009).

Other problem behaviors, such as eating disorders, seem to follow a more discontinuous pattern; they occur more suddenly and without much prior warning. In these cases, there are few good behavioral predictors from early childhood as to why a particular child begins to restrict eating or to purge food during early adolescence (see Chapter 14). Sometimes discontinuity can refer to an unexpected or atypical outcome, such as a child who shows normal development until about 18 months of age and then displays loss of language and reduced social engagement (characteristics of some children with autism). In such circumstances, the connection between early and later patterns seems abrupt and discontinuous, which is very baffling to parents.

As we will see throughout our discussion of each disorder, positive factors such as individual competence or social intervention, as well as negative factors such as poverty or discrimination, can influence the continuity or discontinuity of development over time (Rutter, Kim-Cohen, & Maughan, 2006). Returning to Jorge, can you think which of his behavior patterns (if any) were continuous and which seemed to be more discontinuous? Like many problems in abnormal child psychology, Jorge's current behavior pattern involves *both* continuities and discontinuities. Some of his troubles, such as school and homework avoidance, seem qualitatively different (discontinuity) from his reading disorder. His other behaviors, such as slow reading and comprehension, seem to follow (continuity) from his earlier academic problems.

Remember that the concepts of continuity and discontinuity apply to the understanding of abnormal and normal development. However, even with wide fluctuations in the way problems are expressed over time, children show some degree of consistency in organizing their experiences and interacting with their environment, whether that consistency is adaptive or maladaptive (Sroufe, Coffino, & Carlson, 2010). The degree of continuity or discontinuity will vary as a function of changing environmental circumstances and transactions between the child and the environment. These continual changes, in turn, will affect the child's developmental course and direction.

In sum, a central theme of our basic assumptions is that the study of abnormal child psychology must consider abnormality in relation to multiple, interdependent causes and major developmental changes that typically occur across the life cycle. Until recently, developmental aspects of abnormal child behavior were often overlooked in relation to children's behavioral and emotional problems (Cicchetti, 2006). To redress this imbalance, throughout this text we discuss developmental issues pertaining to the nature, symptoms, and course of each disorder.

Changes, Typical and Atypical

● Figure 2.2 presents an overview of developmental periods by age. It gives examples of normal achievements for each period, as well as behavior problems most often reported in general population samples and the clinical disorders that typically become evident at each period. Guidelines for the typical sequence of development across several important dimensions are helpful, but we must keep in mind that age in years is an arbitrary way to segment continuous sequences of development. You may find yourself turning back to this table to reorient yourself to children's normal and abnormal development.

Children's behaviors—both adaptive and maladaptive—are interconnected with their environment and influenced by their biological makeup. Recently, the field of developmental psychopathology has taken an interest in developmental cascades to help explain why some problems in childhood go on to become major problems later on, whereas others do not (Masten & Cicchetti, 2010). **Developmental cascades** refer to the process by which a child's previous interactions and experiences may spread across other systems and alter his or her course of development, somewhat like a chain reaction (Masten & Cicchetti, 2010). This concept helps to explain how processes that function at one level or domain of behavior (such as curiosity) can affect how the child adapts to other challenges later on (such as academic performance) (Cox et al., 2010). Throughout this book, the developmental psychopathology perspective adds developmental relevance and richness to categorically based DSM-5 disorders and to early intervention possibilities.

Approximate age (years)	Normal achievements	Common behavior problems	Clinical disorders
0–2	Eating, sleeping, attachment	Stubbornness, temper, toileting difficulties	Mental retardation, feeding disorders, autistic disorder
2–5	Language, toileting, self-care skills, self-control, peer relationships	Arguing, demanding attention, disobedience, fears, overactivity, resisting bedtime	Speech and language disorders, problems stemming from child abuse and neglect, some anxiety disorders, such as phobias
6–11	Academic skills and rules, rule-governed games, simple responsibilities	Arguing, inability to concentrate, self-consciousness, showing off	ADHD, learning disorders, school refusal behavior, conduct problems
12–20	Relations with opposite sex, personal identity, separation from family, increased responsibilities	Arguing, bragging, anger outbursts, risk-taking	Anorexia, bulimia, delinquency, suicide attempts, drug and alcohol abuse, schizophrenia, depression

● **FIGURE 2.2** | A developmental overview.

Photo Credits (top to bottom): © Michael Pettigrew/Shutterstock.com; © YUYI /Shutterstock.com; © iStockphoto.com/aabejon; © iStockphoto.com/bmcent1. Based on Achenbach, 1982; Tully & Goodman, 2007

An Integrative Approach

How do we attempt to make sense of the many environmental and individual factors that influence child behavior? Since no single theoretical orientation can explain various behaviors or disorders, we must be familiar with many theories and conceptual models—each contributes important insights into normal and abnormal development.

Even models that consider more than one primary cause can be limited by the boundaries of their discipline or orientation. Biological explanations, for instance, emphasize genetic mutations, neuroanatomy, and neurobiological mechanisms as factors contributing to psychopathology. Similarly, psychological explanations emphasize causal factors such as insecure attachments, cognitive distortions, or maladaptive reinforcement and/or learning histories. Biological and psychological models are both multicausal and distinctive in terms of the relative importance each attaches to certain events and processes. Each model is restricted in its ability to explain abnormal behavior to the extent that it fails to incorporate important components of other models. Fortunately, such disciplinary boundaries are gradually diminishing as different perspectives take into account important variables derived from other models. For example, biological influences are often taken into account when explaining how psychological factors, such as behavior or cognition, interact over time and result in a psychological disorder (Cicchetti & Curtis, 2006; Sameroff, 2010).

Over time, major theories of abnormal child psychology have become compatible with one another. Rather than offering contradictory views, each theory contributes one or more pieces of the puzzle of atypical development. As all the available pieces are assembled, the picture of a particular child or adolescent disorder becomes more and more distinct. Psychological theories are merely tools to study human behavior; the more you learn what these tools can and cannot do and which tool to use for which purpose, the more knowledgeable and skilled you will become. Remember that no single integrative theory fully captures the diversity of perspectives and findings represented by current research in abnormal child psychology.

Section Summary

Theoretical Foundations

- A theory allows us to make educated guesses and predictions about behavior that are based on existing knowledge, and it allows us to explore these possible explanations empirically.

- Developmental psychopathology provides a useful framework for organizing the study of abnormal child psychology around milestones and sequences in physical, cognitive, social–emotional, and educational development.

- A central theme of this text is the importance of considering multiple, interactive causes for abnormal behavior, in conjunction with the major developmental changes that typically occur.

- Three underlying assumptions about abnormal development are stressed: It is multiply determined, the child and the environment are interdependent, and abnormal development involves continuities and discontinuities of behavior patterns over time.

- The complexity of abnormal child behavior requires consideration of the full range of biological, psychological, and sociocultural factors that influence children's development.

DEVELOPMENTAL CONSIDERATIONS

Even though children's psychological disorders have very different symptoms and causes, they share common ground: They are an indication of adaptational failure in one or more areas of development (Rutter & Sroufe, 2000). **Adaptational failure** is the failure to master or progress in accomplishing developmental milestones. In other words, at the broadest level, children with psychological disorders differ from children their own age in some aspect of normal development. Again, such failure or deviation is rarely due to a single cause, but typically results from an ongoing interaction between individual development and environmental conditions.

The causes and outcomes of abnormal child behavior operate in dynamic and interactive ways over time, making them a challenge to disentangle. Designating a specific factor, such as Jorge's reading problem, either as a cause or as an outcome of a particular disorder usually reflects the point at which we take note of the problem.

Children's development follows an organized pattern that is nurtured through positive experiences with their caregivers

His reading problem, for example, may be viewed as a disorder in its own right (such as a learning disorder in reading), the cause of his other difficulties (such as poor study habits and oppositional behavior), or the outcome of some other condition or disorder (such as a communication disorder). As you read the following chapters and gain a better understanding of the causes of abnormal child behavior, remember that children's behavior and their environment are interconnected.

Organization of Development

Change and reorganization are fundamental aspects of biological and behavioral systems (Sameroff, 2010). An organizational viewpoint looks closely at the psychological processes that may explain how these systems influence each other. In an attempt to understand abnormal development, we may choose to focus on any or all aspects of this organizational process. In the **organization of development** perspective, early patterns of adaptation, such as infant eye contact and speech sounds, evolve with structure over time and transform into higher-order functions such as speech and language. Prior patterns of adaptation are incorporated into successive reorganizations at subsequent periods of development, much as toddlers learn to make certain speech sounds before they develop the ability to use language.

An organizational view of development implies an active, dynamic process of continual change and transformation. As the child's biological abilities unfold during each new stage of development, they interact with environmental factors to direct and redirect the course of development. Because development is organized, sensitive periods play a meaningful role in any discussion of normal and abnormal behavior. **Sensitive periods** are windows of time during which environmental influences on development, both good and bad, are enhanced (Roth & Sweatt, 2011a). Infants, for example, are highly sensitive to emotional cues and proximity to their caregivers, which assists them in developing secure attachments (R. A. Thompson & Meyer, 2007). Toddlers are sensitive to the basic sounds of language, which helps them distinguish sounds and combine them to form words (Shafer & Garrido-Nag, 2007). Sensitive periods can be enhanced opportunities for learning but are not the only opportunities; change can take place at other times. For example, children adopted from orphanages show a number of negative developmental outcomes as a result of their early institutional deprivation. However, their outcome is also affected by later experiences in the post-institutional environment (Reeb et al., 2009). Human development is a process of increasing differentiation and integration, more like a network of interconnecting pathways than one straight line.

Understanding the seemingly endless list of possible causes that influence children's normal and abnormal development is made easier by the fact that development generally proceeds in an organized, hierarchical manner (Sameroff, 2010). Simply stated, a child's current abilities or limitations are influenced by prior accomplishments, just as your progress through trigonometry or calculus depends on the command of arithmetic you acquired in elementary school. As children develop greater abilities or show signs of adaptational failure, these changes influence their further developmental success or failure. Studying abnormal child behavior within a developmental psychopathology perspective, as described previously, fosters an understanding of the interactive, progressive nature of children's abilities and difficulties.

Section Summary

Developmental Considerations

- Children's development is organized, which means that early patterns of adaptation evolve over time and transform into higher-order functions in a structured, predictable manner.

We turn now to three major perspectives on abnormal child development: (1) biological perspectives, which include both genetic and neurobiological factors that are often established (but by no means fixed) at birth or soon thereafter; (2) psychological perspectives, such as emotions, relationships, and thought processes; and (3) familial, social, and cultural influences, which set additional parameters on normal and abnormal development.

BIOLOGICAL PERSPECTIVES

Broadly speaking, a neurobiological perspective considers brain and nervous system functions as underlying causes of psychological disorders in children and adults. Biological influences on a very young child's brain development include genetic and constitutional factors, neuroanatomy, and rates of maturation. Regions of the brain are highly influenced by the availability of various biochemicals and neurohormones, which interact differently to affect an individual's psychological experiences (Cicchetti & Cannon, 1999). This process depends on environmental factors that direct or reroute ongoing brain processes. Remember that a neurobiological perspective acknowledges and recognizes the need to incorporate environmental influences in accounting for disorders.

The developing brain has long been a mystery, but its secrets are gradually being revealed. The examination of biological influences begins with the amazing process of neuronal growth and differentiation. During pregnancy, the fetal brain develops from a few all-purpose cells into a complex organ made up of billions of specialized, interconnected neurons (Johnson & de Haan, 2006). The speed and distance these emerging neurons travel is astonishing as they multiply to form various brain structures and functions. The brain stem commands heartbeat and breathing, the cerebellum controls and coordinates sensorimotor integration, and the cortex is where thought and perception originate.

Embryonic development generates an initial overabundance of neurons (Innocenti, 1982). At first these cells are largely undifferentiated, but as they reach their destinations, they become neurons with axons that carry electrical signals to other parts of the brain. These axonal connections, or synapses, form the brain's circuits and lay the foundation for further growth and differentiation. Notably, genes determine the main highways along which axons travel to make their connection; but to reach particular target cells, axons follow chemical cues strewn along their path that tell them the direction to various destinations.

By the fifth month of prenatal development, most axons have reached their general destination, although there are far more axons than the target cells can accommodate. Thus, during early childhood, synapses multiply; then selective *pruning* reduces the number of connections in a way that gradually shapes and differentiates important brain functions (Johnson & de Haan, 2006). The nervous system seems to prepare itself for new growth and demands by sending in reinforcements and then cutting back once the environment has signaled it has everything it needs. Throughout life we undergo cycles that narrow the gap between structure and function. At the level of the nervous system, the microanatomy of the brain is constantly redefined to meet the demands and requirements of an adult world. Like the pruning of a tree, this process fosters healthy growth of different areas of the brain according to individual needs and environmental demands, and eliminates connections that serve to restrict healthy growth.

How permanent are these early brain connections? This question has provoked different theories and agonized many parents who are concerned about their children's early development. For instance, if early brain functions are unlikely to change, this implies that early experiences set the course for lifetime development. Freud's similar contention implied that an individual's core personality is formed from an early age, which sets the pace and boundaries for further personality formation. To the contrary, scientists now believe that brain functions undergo continual changes as they adapt to environmental demands (Fox, Levitt, & Nelson, 2010).

Neural Plasticity and the Role of Experience

Many early neural connections are not stable; some are strengthened and become more established through use, while many others regress or disappear. Thus, the answer to the question about the permanence of early connections is that the brain shows neural plasticity throughout the course of development (Nelson, 2011). **Neural plasticity**, or malleability, means the brain's anatomical differentiation is use-dependent: Nature provides the basic processes, whereas nurture provides the experiences needed to select the most adaptive network of connections, based on the use and function of each. It is truly fascinating how nature and nurture work together to create such highly specific, extremely adaptive central nervous system functions.

Think of the developing brain as a work in progress, one in which the environment plays an essential role as supervisor of this dynamic rewiring project (see ● Figure 2.3). In fact, environmental experience is now recognized to be critical to the differentiation of brain tissue itself. Although nature has a plan for creating the human brain and central nervous system, environmental opportunities and limitations significantly influence this plan from the beginning. Thus, a transactional model explains normal and abnormal development. A

TOM BARRICK, CHRIS CLARK, SGHMS/Science Source

● **FIGURE 2.3** | Colored 3-dimensional magnetic resonance imaging (MRI) scan of the white matter pathways of the brain, side view. White matter is composed of myelin-coated nerve cell fibers that carry information between nerve cells in the cerebrum of the brain (top half of image) and the brain stem (bottom center). Blue represents neural pathways from the top to the bottom of the brain, green represents pathways from the front (left) to the back (right), and red shows pathways between the right and left hemispheres of the brain.

child's brain structure remains surprisingly malleable for months and even years after birth; therefore, transaction occurs between ongoing brain development and environmental experiences; neither nature nor nurture is sufficient to explain the complexity of the developing brain (Fox et al., 2010).

Experience, of course, comes in all shapes and sizes. The prenatal environment as well as childhood illness and diet count as experience, as do maltreatment and inadequate stimulation. Children's early caregiving experiences play an especially important role in designing the parts of the brain involved in emotion, personality, and behavior (O'Connor, 2006). Normal, healthy methods of child rearing, for instance, may increase children's ability to learn and cope with stress (Belsky & de Haan, 2011). In contrast, abuse and neglect can prime the brain for a lifetime of struggle with handling stress or forming healthy relationships (De Bellis, Woolley, & Hooper, 2013).

Brain maturation is an organized, hierarchical process that builds on earlier function, with brain structures restructuring and growing throughout the life span. Primitive areas of the brain, which govern basic sensory and motor skills, mature first and undergo the most dramatic restructuring, during the first 3 years of life. Moreover, these perceptual centers, along with instinctive centers such as the limbic system, are strongly affected by early childhood experiences and set the foundation for further development (Nelson, 2011). The prefrontal cortex, which governs planning and decision making, and the cerebellum, a center for motor skills, are not rewired until a person is 5 to 7 years old. Major restructuring of the brain occurs between ages 9 and 11 in relation to pubertal development, and then throughout adolescence the brain once again prunes unnecessary synaptic connections. Thus, the brain certainly does not stop changing after 3 years. For some functions, the windows of influence are only beginning to close at that age, while for others they are only beginning to open. Our brain functions undergo lifelong

renovation, with restructuring being a natural by-product of growth.

Because the brain is intrinsically shaped by the effects of early experience, the consequences of inadequate or traumatic experience may be enduring and extremely difficult to change (Glover, 2011). During this evolution of brain growth and differentiation many things can go wrong, thereby altering how neurons form or interconnect. Problems or disruptions at a younger age are typically associated with more severe organic disorders and central nervous system complications. Proper prenatal care, proper nutrition, and avoidance of tobacco or alcohol during pregnancy can go a long way in reducing the risk of such complications and lifelong disabilities.

Genetic Contributions

Genetics explains why you look like your father, and if you don't, why you should.

—Tammy, age 8

To understand genetic influences, we first must understand the nature of genes, bearing in mind that virtually any trait results from the interaction of environmental and genetic factors (Rutter, 2011a). A review of genetics terminology and function may assist our understanding of some causes of abnormal child behavior.

Each person's unique genome is established at conception and consists of approximately 20,000 to 25,000 genes (International Human Genome Sequencing Consortium, 2004). Genes contain genetic information from each parent, and they are distributed on 22 matched pairs of chromosomes and a single pair of sex chromosomes. In males, the sex chromosome pair consists of an X and a Y chromosome (XY), and in females, the sex chromosome pair consists of two X chromosomes (XX).

Genetic factors are implicated in all of the childhood disorders discussed in this text. Some genetic influences are expressed early in development, such as

ZITS © 2008 Zits Partnership, Dist. By King Features

behavioral inhibition or shyness (Nigg, 2006), whereas others show up years later, such as a depressive cognitive style (Garber & Flynn, 2001). Moreover, the expression of genetic influences is malleable and responsive to the social environment. Positive environmental circumstances can help a child "beat the odds" of developing a significant disorder, despite genetic predisposition (Masten & Wright, 2010).

The Nature of Genes

A gene is basically a stretch of DNA and, by itself, it does not produce a behavior, an emotion, or even a passing thought. Rather, it produces a protein. Although these proteins are vital for the brain to function, very rarely do they cause a behavior to happen. Instead, they produce tendencies to respond to the environment in certain ways (Sapolsky, 1997). Each of us has genetic vulnerabilities, tendencies, and predispositions, but rarely are the outcomes inevitable. The lesson in all of this is simple, yet important. The false notion that genes determine behavior should be replaced with the more accurate statement: Genes influence how we respond to the environment, and the environment influences our genes. Today, researchers are highly interested in this **gene–environment interaction (G×E)**, as discussed in A Closer Look 2.1.

A CLOSER **LOOK** 2.1

Gene–Environment Interactions in Abnormal Child Psychology

Normal and abnormal child development are the result of complex interchanges between nature and nurture and are affected not only by genetic and environmental influences, but also by the timing of when they meet (Lenroot & Giedd, 2011). Researchers refer to this interplay of nature and nurture as *gene–environment interactions*, or G×E. The underlying biological changes to genetic structure result from **epigenetic** mechanisms, which involve changes in gene activity resulting from a variety of environmental factors, such as toxins, diet, stress, and many others; in other words, the environment can turn genes on and off (Roth & Sweatt, 2011b). The growing field of developmental neuroscience has shown that epigenetic changes may play a central role in the long-term impact of early life experiences, as these experiences become biologically embedded in the development of our organ systems, especially the brain (Shonkoff, 2010).

G×E helps explain why some people exhibit disorders and others do not, in the face of similar environmental events. For example, as shown in the top of the diagram below (A), children may be exposed to domestic violence or abuse in their family (a high environmental stressor), but only those who possess a particular genotype may end of showing significant problems later on. Alternatively (B), children who carry a genotype known to increase susceptibility for a particular disorder may only develop that disorder if they are exposed to specific environmental risks (i.e., a toxic prenatal or postnatal environment) (Wermter et al., 2010).

There's more to the story—epigenetic alterations may be reversible through pharmacological and behavioral interventions. Research on gene–environment interactions is opening new windows of opportunity—targeting children with particular risk factors (either genetic, environmental, or both)—that determine the best timing and strategies for early intervention (Bakermans-Kranenburg & Van IJzendoorn, 2011; Ellis et al., 2011).

A Environmental factors, such as abuse or social isolation, only lead to a psychological disorder if the person has a specific genetic makeup.

B A person who has a susceptible genetic makeup will only develop a psychological disorder if additional environmental risk factors exist.

©iStockphoto.com/nkbimages

Calvin and Hobbes   by Bill Watterson

Behavioral Genetics

Sorting out the interactive influences of nature and nurture is the not-so-easy task of **behavioral genetics**, a branch of genetics that investigates possible connections between a genetic predisposition and observed behavior, taking into account environmental and genetic influences. Behavioral genetics researchers often begin their investigations by conducting familial aggregation studies. They look for a nonrandom clustering of disorders or characteristics within a given family and compare these results with the random distribution of the disorders or characteristics in the general population (Rende & Waldman, 2006). For example, parents of children with childhood-onset schizophrenia tend to have higher rates of schizophrenia spectrum disorders relative to normative prevalence rates.

Family aggregation studies cannot control for environmental variables that may also contribute to a particular outcome. For example, a child may be anxious because of his parents' child-rearing methods rather than their genetic contributions. To increase scientific rigor following suggestive familial aggregation studies, researchers may conduct twin studies to control for the contribution of genetic factors (Ehringer et al., 2006). Twin studies may compare identical—or monozygotic (MZ)—twins, who have the same set of genes, to fraternal—or dizygotic (DZ)—twins, who share about half of each other's genes (the same as all first-degree relatives). The crucial scientific question is whether identical twins share the same trait—say, reading difficulties—more than fraternal twins do. Studies of twins provide a powerful research strategy for examining the role of genetic influences in both psychiatric and nonpsychiatric disorders. However, the shared environment presents a potential confounding element in any twin study unless the twins are reared apart (Ehringer et al., 2006).

Molecular Genetics

No twisted thought without a twisted molecule.

—Ralph Waldo Gerard (1900–1974)

Compared to behavioral genetics, molecular genetics more directly supports the influence of genes on child psychopathology. **Molecular genetics** research methods directly assess the association between variations in DNA sequences and variations in a particular trait or traits. More than an association, variations in genetic sequences are thought to cause the variations in the trait(s) (Rutter & Dodge, 2011). As we will discuss throughout this book, molecular genetics research methods have been used to search for specific genes for many childhood disorders, including autism, attention-deficit/hyperactivity disorder, and learning disability (however, no specific gene has been identified for most of the disorders discussed in the book). Discovering that mutations in one gene or another may causally influence a particular form of child psychopathology is only the beginning. The longer-term goal is to determine how genetic mutations alter how the genes function in the development of the brain and behavior for different psychopathologies (Rende & Waldman, 2006).

The identification of specific genes has the potential to greatly enhance our understanding of a disorder and its specific components. However, identifying a specific gene for any disorder addresses only a small part of genetic risk. Similar and multiple interactive genes are a far more likely cause than a single gene. Moreover, genetic influences are probabilistic rather than deterministic; environmental and genetic factors generally have equal importance (Rutter & Dodge, 2011). Most forms of abnormal child behavior are polygenic, involving a number of susceptibility genes that interact with one another and with environmental influences, to result in observed levels of impairment (Rende & Waldman, 2006).

Neurobiological Contributions

The study of abnormal child psychology requires a working familiarity with brain structures, as shown in ● Figures 2.4, 2.5, and 2.6. This section provides an overview of major structures mentioned later in the context of specific disorders. Once you are familiar with the various areas and functions of the brain, you will have the basic vocabulary needed to understand exciting research in childhood psychopathology.

Brain Structure and Function

The brain is often divided into the *brain stem* and the *forebrain* (telencephalon) because of their separate functions. The brain stem (see Figure 2.5), located at the base of the brain, handles most of the autonomic functions necessary to stay alive. The lowest part of the brain stem, called the *hindbrain*, contains the *medulla*, the *pons*, and the *cerebellum*. The hindbrain provides essential regulation of autonomic activities such as breathing, heartbeat, and digestion, and the cerebellum controls motor coordination. The brain stem also contains the *midbrain*, which coordinates movement with sensory input. The midbrain houses the

reticular activating system (RAS), which contributes to processes of arousal and tension.

At the very top of the brain stem is the *diencephalon*, located just below the forebrain. The diencephalon contains the *thalamus* and *hypothalamus*, which are both essential to the regulation of behavior and emotion. The diencephalon functions primarily as a relay between the forebrain and the lower areas of the brain stem.

Next is the forebrain, which has evolved in humans into highly specialized functions. At the base of the forebrain is an area known as the *limbic*, or border, *system* (see Figure 2.6). It contains a number of structures that are suspected causes of psychopathology, such as the *hippocampus, cingulate gyrus, septum,* and *amygdala.* These important structures regulate emotional experiences and expressions and play a significant role in learning and impulse control. The limbic system also regulates the basic drives of sex, aggression, hunger, and thirst.

Also at the base of the forebrain lay the *basal ganglia,* which include the *caudate nucleus.* Researchers are discovering that this area regulates, organizes, and filters information related to cognition, emotions, mood, and motor function, and that it has been implicated

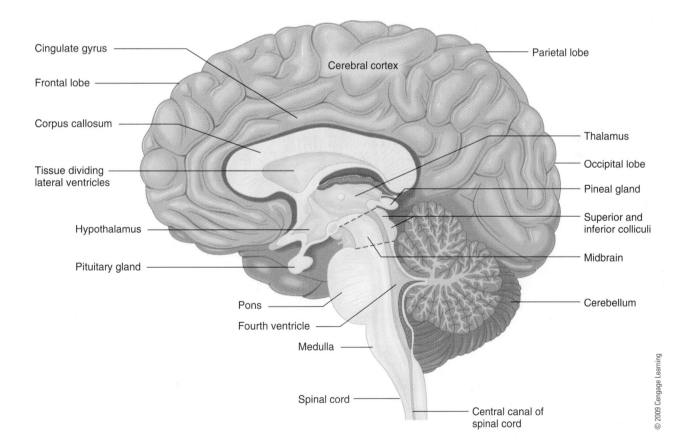

● **FIGURE 2.4** | Structures of the human brain.

Based on Kalat, *Biological Psychology*, 10E.

● FIGURE 2.5 | The brain stem (cerebellum removed to reveal other structures).

Based on Kalat, *Biological Psychology*, 10E.

in attention-deficit/hyperactivity disorder (ADHD, discussed in Chapter 8); disorders affecting motor behavior, such as tics and tremors; and obsessive–compulsive disorder (OCD, discussed in Chapter 11).

The cerebral cortex, the largest part of the forebrain, gives us our distinctly human qualities and allows us to plan as well as to reason and to create. The cerebral cortex is divided into two hemispheres that look very much alike but have different functions. The left hemisphere plays a chief role in verbal and other cognitive processes. The right hemisphere is better at social perception

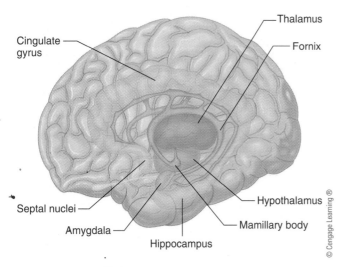

● FIGURE 2.6 | Structures of the limbic system.

and creativity. Researchers believe that each hemisphere plays a different role in certain psychological disorders, such as communication and learning disorders.

Around puberty, the brain develops new brain cells and neural connections, and then once again begins to reorganize and consolidate (Benes, 2006). This new growth and restructuring results in further maturation of the lobes of the brain. ● Figure 2.7 shows the *temporal, parietal*, and *frontal lobes* of the brain and their important functions. The **frontal lobes** are discussed most often in subsequent chapters on disorders and are worth special attention. The frontal lobes contain the functions underlying most of our thinking and reasoning abilities, including memory. These functions enable us to make sense of social relationships and customs and to relate to the world and the people around us, which is why they have considerable relevance in the study of abnormal child psychology. Fortunately, all of these functions continue to mature well into late adolescence and early adulthood. By implication, the brain you had when you reached adolescence is not the one you have now.

Remarkably, these critical brain areas perform their functions in an integrated, harmonious fashion—aided by important regulatory systems and neurotransmitters—that permits the whole to be much larger than the sum of its parts. However, for many disorders defined in this text, one or more of these brain areas are not performing

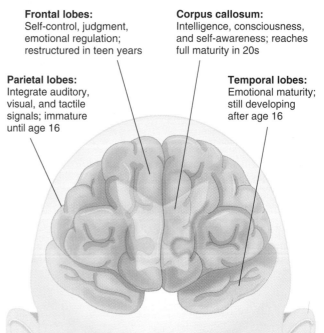

● FIGURE 2.7 | The lobes of the brain and their functions.

their functions as they should, either as a result of other problems or as a primary cause of the disorder.

The Endocrine System

The endocrine system is an important regulatory system that has been linked to specific psychological disorders, such as anxiety and mood disorders, in both children and adults. There are several endocrine glands, and each produces a particular hormone that it releases into the bloodstream. The *adrenal* glands (located on top of the kidneys) are most familiar because they produce **epinephrine** (also known as adrenaline) in response to stress. Epinephrine energizes us and prepares our bodies for possible threats or challenges. The *thyroid* gland produces the hormone thyroxine, which is needed for proper energy metabolism and growth and is implicated in certain eating disorders of children and youths (discussed in Chapter 14). Finally, the *pituitary* gland, located deep within the brain, orchestrates the body's functions by regulating a variety of hormones, including estrogen and testosterone. Because the endocrine system is closely related to the immune system, which protects us from disease and many other biological threats, it is not surprising that it is implicated in a variety of disorders, particularly health- and stress-related disorders (discussed in Chapter 13).

One brain connection that is implicated in some psychological disorders involves the hypothalamus and the endocrine system. The hypothalamus carries out the commands it receives from the adjacent pituitary gland and other hormones, such as those regulating hunger and thirst. The pituitary gland in turn stimulates the adrenal glands to produce epinephrine and the stress hormone known as **cortisol**. The hypothalamus control center, coupled with the pituitary and adrenal glands, make up a regulatory system in the brain known as the **hypothalamic–pituitary–adrenal (HPA) axis**. A Closer Look 2.2 explains how this axis has been implicated in several psychological disorders, especially those connected to a person's response to stress and ability to regulate emotions, such as anxiety and mood disorders.

Neurotransmitters

Neurotransmitters are similar to biochemical currents in the brain. These currents develop in an organized fashion to make meaningful connections that serve larger functions such as thinking and feeling. Neurons that are more sensitive to one type of neurotransmitter, such as serotonin, tend to cluster together and form **brain circuits**, which are paths from one part of the brain to another (R. R. Dean et al., 1993). Tens of thousands of these circuits operate in our brains. Brain

---

A CLOSER **LOOK** 2.2

The HPA Axis and Stress Regulation

The HPA axis is a central component of the brain's neuro-endocrine response to stress. The hypothalamus, when stimulated, secretes the corticotropin-releasing hormone (CRH), which stimulates the pituitary gland to secrete the andrenocorticotropic hormone (ACTH) into the bloodstream. ACTH then causes the adrenal glands to release cortisol, the familiar stress hormone that arouses the body to meet a challenging situation. This system, like many others, works on a feedback loop: Cortisol modulates the stress response by acting on the hypothalamus to inhibit the continued release of CRH (Sternberg & Gold, 1997). Researchers are discovering that this important feedback loop, which regulates our level of arousal and apprehension, can be seriously disrupted or damaged by various traumatic and uncontrollable events. These events can cause a child or adolescent to maintain a state of fear or alertness that becomes toxic over prolonged periods of time (Bremner, 2007).

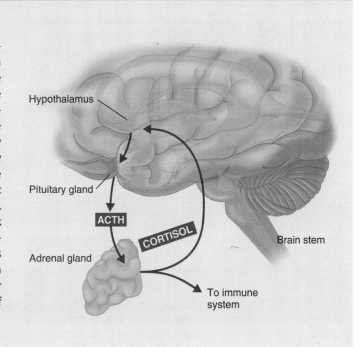

circuits and neurotransmitters relate to particular psychological disorders, permitting more targeted treatments. Psychoactive drugs work by either increasing or decreasing the flow of various neurotransmitters—for example, increasing dopamine in the case of stimulant medications for ADHD (Vitiello, 2007). However, changes in neurotransmitter activity may make people *more likely* or *less likely* to exhibit certain kinds of behavior in certain situations, but they do not cause the behavior directly. Table 2.1 summarizes the four neurotransmitter systems most often mentioned in connection with psychological disorders.

Section Summary

Biological Perspectives

- Brain functions undergo continual changes, described as neural plasticity, as they adapt to environmental demands.
- Genetic influences depend on the environment. Genetic endowment influences behavior, emotions, and thoughts; environmental events are necessary for this influence to be expressed.
- Gene–environment interactions (GxE) explain how the environment shapes our genotype through a process known as "epigenetics."

- Neurobiological contributions to abnormal child behavior include knowledge of brain structures, the endocrine system, and neurotransmitters, all of which perform their functions in an integrated, harmonious fashion.

PSYCHOLOGICAL PERSPECTIVES

Each psychological perspective described in this section has value in explaining the development of psychopathology. At the same time, each perspective has certain limitations and may be more, or less, applicable to a particular disorder or situation. Remember, transactions between environmental and individual influences cause abnormal behavior. Children's inherited characteristics coupled with the experiences and influences in their environment make them the way they are today. Also, some seemingly maladaptive behaviors, such as excessive fearfulness or watchfulness, may in fact be understandable when considered in the context of the child's environment if it involves parental abuse or school violence.

Our interest in psychological bases for abnormal behavior begins with a focus on the role of emotions in establishing an infant's ability to adapt to new surroundings. Infants use emotion to organize new information

TABLE 2.1 | Major Neurotransmitters and Their Implicated Roles in Psychopathology

Neurotransmitter	Normal Functions	Implicated Role in Psychopathology
Benzodiazepine-GABA	Reduces arousal and moderates emotional responses, such as anger, hostility, and aggression Is linked to feelings of anxiety and discomfort	Anxiety disorder
Dopamine	May act as a *switch* that turns on various brain circuits, allowing other neurotransmitters to inhibit or facilitate emotions or behavior Is involved in exploratory, extroverted, and pleasure-seeking activity	Schizophrenia Mood disorders Attention-deficit/hyperactivity disorder (ADHD)
Norepinephrine	Facilitates or controls emergency reactions and alarm responses Plays a role in emotional and behavioral regulation	Not *directly* involved in specific disorders (acts generally to regulate or modulate behavioral tendencies)
Serotonin	Plays a role in information and motor coordination Inhibits children's tendency to explore their surroundings Moderates and regulates a number of critical behaviors, such as eating, sleeping, and expressing wanger	Regulatory problems, such as eating and sleep disorders Obsessive–compulsive disorder Schizophrenia and mood disorders

Source: © Cengage Learning ®

and avoid potential harm. Early relationships between infants and caregivers further provide structure and regulation for these emotional responses. As the child develops, cognitive processes such as self-efficacy play a larger role in assisting the young child to make sense of the world and to reorganize earlier functions that may be unnecessary or even maladaptive for new challenges involving language development, peer interactions, and similar skills. As with brain development, things can go wrong at any point along this continuum of emotional and cognitive development as a function of the child's interaction with the environment.

Emotional Influences

Emotions and affective expression are core elements of human psychological experience. From birth, they are a central feature of infant activity and regulation (Sroufe, 2005). Throughout our lives, emotional reactions assist us in our fight-or-flight response. From an evolutionary perspective, emotions give special value to events and make particular actions most likely to occur. In effect, emotions tell us what to pay attention to and what to ignore, what to approach and what to avoid. Given their important job, and backed up by powerful stress-regulating hormones such as cortisol, emotions are critical to healthy adaptation.

Interest in emotional processes and their relation to abnormal child behavior has grown considerably in recent years (Arsenio & Lemerise, 2010). Children's emotional experiences, expressions, and regulation affect the quality of their social interactions and relationships and thus are at the foundation of early personality development. Researchers are discovering a wealth of information demonstrating the influential role of emotion in children's lives. Emotions not only serve as important internal monitoring and guidance systems designed to appraise events as either beneficial or dangerous, but they also provide motivation for action (Hastings, Zahn-Waxler, & Usher, 2007).

Children have a natural tendency to attend to emotional cues from others, which helps them learn to interpret and regulate their own emotions. They learn, from a very young age, through the emotional expressions of others (Bretherton & Munholland, 2008). Within the first year of life, infants learn the importance of emotions for communication and regulation; by their second year, they have some ability to attribute cause to emotional expression. Of particular interest to abnormal child psychology is the finding that children look to the emotional expression and cues of their caregivers to provide them with the information needed to formulate a basic understanding

The ability to infer another's emotional state by reading facial, gestural, postural, and vocal cues has an important adaptive function, especially for infants and toddlers

of what's going on. To young children, emotions are a primary form of communication that permits them to explore their world with increasing independence (LaFreniere, 2000).

Emotion Reactivity and Regulation

We can divide emotional processes into two dimensions: emotion reactivity and emotion regulation. **Emotion reactivity** refers to individual differences in the threshold and intensity of emotional experience, which provide clues to an individual's level of distress and sensitivity to the environment. **Emotion regulation**, on the other hand, involves enhancing, maintaining, or inhibiting emotional arousal, which is usually done for a specific purpose or goal (Perlman & Pelphrey, 2011; Southam-Gerow & Kendall, 2002). Jorge, for example, was emotionally reactive to certain academic tasks; he became upset and couldn't concentrate. This emotional reaction could lead to poor regulation, resulting in Jorge becoming distraught and difficult to manage at times. Once again, a transactional process is at work, whereby emotional reactions prompt the need for regulation, which influences further emotional expression.

A further distinction can be made between problems in *regulation* and problems in *dysregulation*. Regulation problems involve weak or absent control structures, such as Jorge's trouble concentrating in class; dysregulation means that existing control structures operate maladaptively (Izard et al., 2006). For example, a child may be fearful even when there is no reason in the environment to be fearful or anxious.

Children's emotion regulation abilities, as often shown by their emotion reactivity and expression, are important signals of normal and abnormal development. Emotions also help young children learn more about themselves and their surroundings, as part of learning to identify and monitor their feelings and behavior. The child–caregiver relationship plays a critical role in this process because it provides the basic setting for children to express emotions and to experience caring guidance and have limits placed on them. *Authoritative* parents establish limits that are both sensitive to the child's individual development and needs and demanding of the child to foster self-control and healthy regulation (Maccoby & Martin, 1983). Because of its vital role in emotional development, the child–caregiver relationship will surface again and again when we discuss childhood disorders.

Some forms of emotion dysregulation may be adaptive in one environment or at one time but maladaptive in other situations. Children who have been emotionally and sexually abused may show shallow emotions, known as "numbing," which is a symptom of a posttraumatic stress reaction that serves to protect the child from overwhelming pain and trauma (described in Chapter 12). If numbing becomes a characteristic way of coping with stressors later in life, however, it may interfere with adaptive functioning and long-term goals.

Temperament and Early Personality Styles

You hear it all the time: "She was an easy baby, right from the first day I brought her home from the hospital," or "Sleep? What's that? Since little Freddy was born, we are up all hours of the night, feeding, changing, and trying to soothe him." Unmistakably, some infants are more placid than others, some are more active, and some are more high-strung, and these differences are often recognizable in the first few days or weeks of life (Thomas & Chess, 1977). What relevance does this have to abnormal development?

The development of emotion regulation or dysregulation is thought to derive from both socialization and innate predispositions, or temperament. **Temperament** refers to the child's organized style of behavior that appears early in development, such as fussiness or fearfulness, which shapes the child's approach to his or her environment, and vice versa. Temperament is a subset of the broader domain of personality, so it is often considered an early building block of personality (Kagan, 2013). Three primary dimensions of temperament are linked to normal and abnormal child development (Rothbart & Posner, 2006):

1. *Positive affect and approach.* This dimension describes the "easy child," who is generally approachable and adaptive to his or her environment and possesses the ability to regulate basic functions of eating, sleeping, and elimination relatively smoothly.

2. *Fearful or inhibited.* This dimension describes the "slow-to-warm-up child," who is cautious in his or her approach to novel or challenging situations. Such children are more variable in self-regulation and adaptability and may show distress or negativity toward some situations.

3. *Negative affect or irritability.* This dimension describes the "difficult child," who is predominantly negative or intense in mood, not very adaptable, and arrhythmic. Some children with this temperament show distress when faced with novel or challenging situations, and others are prone to general distress or irritability, including when limitations are placed on them.

These temperament dimensions, or early self-regulatory styles, have been linked to distinct brain activity that underlies a child's cautious versus more eager approach to novel situations, which supports the conclusion that temperament is established during early brain development (Berger & Berger, 2011; Perlman & Pelphrey, 2010). Early infant temperament may be linked to psychopathology or risk conditions in several ways. In some instances, a temperamental style may be highly related to a particular disorder, such as anxiety. In other instances, the condition may develop from the features closely related to temperament, but the condition itself may appear unrelated (Rothbart & Posner, 2006). For example, an infant's extreme sensitivity to emotional stimuli may contribute to a tendency to withdraw from others as a toddler or preschooler; over time, this tendency may transform into an interpersonal style characterized by a self-reported lack of feeling toward others and, consequently, peer rejection or other risk conditions. Also, infant negative affect can contribute to maternal withdrawal or indifference, leading to insecure attachment and its associated risk conditions.

Courtesy of David Wolfe

Young children with an irritable temperament may show distress when demands are placed on them

Temperament may influence later development by affecting a child's development of self-control. Notably, a fearful or cautious temperament style at a young age is linked to better self-control, presumably because the child is less impulsive and takes his or her time before making choices (Tarullo, Obradovic, & Gunnar, 2009). But like most aspects of child psychology, temperament and self-control have to achieve a reasonable balance—a high degree of self-control is a positive thing for the more exuberant toddlers, but can be problematic for more shy youngsters because others view them as socially withdrawn (White et al., 2011). Thus, a balance between emotional reactivity and self-control, known as *self-regulation*, is the best formula for healthy, normal adjustment.

Personality disorders are rarely diagnosed until late adolescence or early adulthood, by which time it is evident that the person's pattern of behavior or inner experience is enduring and problematic (Shiner, 2007). For this reason, personality disorders are not discussed in the following abnormal child psychology chapters. A brief overview is provided below to assist students in gaining familiarity with the concept of personality disorders as they may apply to children and adolescents.

As described in the DSM-5 (APA, 2013), personality disorders include antisocial, borderline, histrionic, paranoid, schizoid, schizotypal, narcissistic, avoidant, dependent, and obsessive–compulsive. These 10 types share a common set of criteria:

▶ An enduring pattern of inner experience and behavior that deviates noticeably from the expectations of the individual's culture. For example, one individual may show very different ways of thinking, feeling, and behaving as compared with others in his or her culture.

▶ This enduring pattern of unusual thinking, feeling, or behaving is inflexible and pervasive across a wide range of situations, and results in clinically significant distress or impairment in functioning.

Additional considerations should be used in diagnosing those rare cases of personality disorders among children and adolescents (APA, 2013, p. 647):

▶ Personality disorder categories may be applied to children or adolescents in those relatively unusual instances when the individual's particular maladaptive personality traits appear to be pervasive, persistent, and unlikely to be limited to a particular developmental stage or another mental disorder.

▶ To diagnose a personality disorder in an individual under age 18, the features must have been present for at least 1 year. The one exception to this is antisocial personality disorder, which cannot be diagnosed in individuals under the age of 18 years.

Remember, some personality traits that may be regarded as pathological during adulthood are considered relatively normal during adolescence (such as mood swings and impulsivity!). For this reason, the diagnostic criteria emphasize that a personality trait must *deviate markedly* from cultural expectations to be considered symptomatic of a personality disorder.

The lifelong significance of emotion reactivity and regulation is backed up by strong empirical evidence linking early behavioral styles to adult personality characteristics 30 years later, as described in A Closer Look 2.3.

Behavioral and Cognitive Influences

Behavioral and cognitive explanations for abnormal child behavior emphasize principles of learning and cognition, which shape children's behavior and their interpretation of things around them. Behavioral and cognitive approaches differ essentially in the extent to which they apply cognitive concepts and procedures to the understanding of behavior. Applied behavior analysis, at one end of this continuum, focuses primarily on observable behavior and rejects the notion that cognitive mediation is necessary for explaining behavior. At the other end is social learning theory, which relies more broadly on cognitive processes and explanations.

Most behavioral explanations assume that the child is best understood and described by behavior in a particular situation rather than in terms of stable traits. Although a child's particular learning history is of interest, behavioral methods focus on the most pragmatic, parsimonious explanation for a particular problem behavior. By the same reasoning, this approach recognizes that successfully changing a problem behavior does not imply knowledge about its origin, but rather emphasizes contemporaneous causes, referred to as *controlling variables*. Cognitive theorists, on the other hand, are interested in how certain thought patterns develop over time and how they relate to particular behavioral strategies, such as problem solving. Following is a refresher on some of the major behavioral and cognitive theories.

Applied Behavior Analysis (ABA)

Based on B. F. Skinner's classic studies, ABA examines the relationships between behavior and its antecedents and consequences, which is known as a *functional approach* to behavior. No implicit assumptions are made about underlying needs or motives that contribute to abnormal behavior; ABA describes and tests

Similarities in Children's Early Behavioral Styles and Adult Personality and Well-Being

Caspi et al. (2003) conducted a landmark study of the connection between early temperament style in children and their later personality traits as adults. These researchers observed more than 1,000 children at age 3 and evaluated their temperament along five dimensions: undercontrolled, inhibited, confident, reserved, and well-adjusted. Twenty-three years later they conducted an assessment of these same individuals as adults, and found some interesting consistencies in "personality style" over this length of time.

When observed at age 3, children classified as undercontrolled (10% of the sample) were rated as irritable, impulsive, and restless. At age 26, these same individuals scored high on personality traits linked to "negative emotionality." They were easily upset and most likely to overreact to minor events, and they reported feeling mistreated, deceived, and betrayed by others. Children classified as inhibited (8% of the sample) were considered a bit fearful and easily upset, and by age 26 they were described as unassertive and took little pleasure in life. The researchers found that the remaining three temperament groups did not display such dramatic personality profiles as adults, but a considerable amount of continuity in style did occur over time. Confident children (28% of the sample) were seen as friendly and eager to explore, and they were the least conventional and most extroverted as adults. Reserved children (15% of the sample) were described as timid and somewhat uncomfortable, and by adulthood they described themselves as unassertive and were seen by others as being introverted. Finally, the well-adjusted children (40% of the sample), who behaved in an age- and situation-appropriate manner at age 3, showed adult personality traits that closely resembled the average, well-adjusted adult.

The story doesn't end there. The researchers have continued to follow this sample and have determined that their degree of self-control as children predicted their adult health, substance use problems, personal finances, and criminal offenses in their early 30s (Moffitt et al., 2011). These findings provide the strongest evidence to date that children's early behavioral styles forecast how they will typically behave, think, and feel as adults. They also imply that tremendous benefits to individuals and society could result if large-scale programs to teach children self-control skills were offered at an early age.

© Cengage Learning ®

©Zdenek Rosenthaler/Shutterstock.com   ©Yuri Arcurs /Shutterstock.com   ©Yuri Arcurs /Shutterstock.com

PRELIMINARY EDITION

functional relationships between stimuli, responses, and consequences. ABA is based on four primary operant learning principles, which explain how behaviors are acquired or changed as a result of particular consequences. These four principles are probably familiar to you: *Positive* and *negative reinforcement* are any actions that increase the target response; *extinction* and *punishment* decrease a response. Children are quite accomplished at learning the contingencies between their behavior and its consequences, and have an uncanny ability to apply some of their own! These principles of operant conditioning remain influential across a variety of applied areas—from basic experimental research to clinical treatment (DeGrandpre, 2000).

Classical Conditioning

Based on the extension of Pavlov's famous learning trials and Watson's experiments with Little Albert (see Chapter 1), classical conditioning explains the acquisition of deviant behavior on the basis of paired associations between previously neutral stimuli (such as math problems) and unconditioned stimuli (such as food or criticism). Any neutral event can become a *conditioned stimulus* if it is paired enough times with an event that already elicits a certain response. Paired associations can help explain many adjustment problems in children and adolescents, although we do not typically know what the original association may have been. In addition, more than one learning paradigm may occur at the same time. For this reason, dual learning explanations for undesirable behavior are common (that is, combinations of features of both operant and classical conditioning).

Returning to Jorge's problem, imagine that he associates reading (a neutral event) with humiliation or anxiety (unconditioned stimuli), which prompts him to escape or avoid the activity. His avoidance, in turn, is negatively reinforced by its consequences: His anxiety decreases and he avoids feelings of humiliation. This analysis considers both instrumental (operant) and respondent (classical) conditioning as part of his learning history. Can you think of possible environmental changes or contingencies that might modify Jorge's behavior in a desirable fashion?

Social Learning and Cognition

Social learning explanations consider not only overt behaviors such as Jorge's school problems, but also the role of possible *cognitive mediators* that may influence the behaviors directly or indirectly. According to Albert Bandura's (1977, 1986) social learning explanation, behavior may be learned not only by operant and classical conditioning, but also indirectly through *observational* (vicarious) learning. Children can learn a new behavior merely by watching another person model the behavior, without apparent reinforcement or practice.

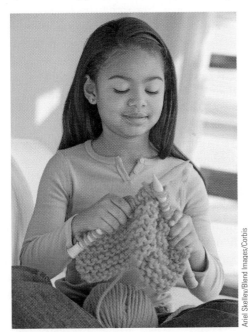

Children's increasing cognitive abilities play a role in both normal and abnormal development

Social learning also incorporates the role of social cognition in acquiring desirable and undesirable behavior. **Social cognition** relates to how children think about themselves and others, resulting in the formation of mental representations of themselves, their relationships, and their social world. These representations are not fixed, but are continually updated on the basis of maturation and social interaction (Herrmann et al., 2007). Children's ongoing cognitive development in reasoning, problem solving, and making attributions helps them make sense of who they are and how they relate to their surroundings. Moreover, social learning and social–cognitive viewpoints also consider the role of affect and the importance of contextual variables, such as family and peers, in both the origins and maintenance of problem behaviors (Arsenio & Lemerise, 2010).

Like individual differences in temperament and emotion regulation, crucial differences exist in how children process information and make sense of their social worlds. Like adults, children have a natural desire to evaluate their behavior in various circumstances, especially those involving some element of possible failure, harm, or personal risk. For some children, teens, and adults, these self-appraisals may be based on faulty beliefs or distortions; for others, an attributional bias about their ability or the intentions of others leads them to reinterpret the event in a way that fits their preexisting belief ("I got a good grade in math because the exam was too easy"; "He's a jerk, so who cares if I tease him?") (Lansford et al., 2010).

Since the first description of observational learning in the early 1960s, cognitive models have grown in both richness and complexity, and their constructs appear quite often throughout this text. Cognitive distortions, insufficient cognitive mediation, and attributional styles and expectations are important determinants in the development and treatment of behavioral and emotional problems in children and adolescents (Bierman et al., 2010).

Section Summary

Psychological Perspectives

- Emotion reactivity and regulation are critical aspects of early and subsequent development, affecting the quality of children's social interactions and relationships throughout their life span.

- Three major approaches to abnormal behavior, based on principles of learning, are applied behavior analysis, principles of classical conditioning, and social learning and social cognition theories. Social learning and social cognition theories place more significance on cognitive processes than overt behavior.

PRELIMINARY EDITION

Ariel Skelley/Blend Images/Corbis

FAMILY, SOCIAL, AND CULTURAL PERSPECTIVES

In addition to biological and psychological influences, children's normal and abnormal development depends on social and environmental contexts. Understanding context requires a consideration of both *proximal* (close-by) and *distal* (further-removed) events, as well as those that impinge directly on the child in a particular situation at a particular time. We consider these wide-ranging environmental conditions and learning experiences in relation to the family and peer context and the social and cultural context.

What exactly do we mean when we refer to a child's environment? Family? Peer groups? Clean air? A child's environment is constantly changing in relation to its many components, much as a lake or stream is affected by a proximal event, such as a rainstorm, as well as more distal events, such as the seasons.

Environmental influences include shared and nonshared types. **Shared environment** refers to environmental factors that produce similarities in developmental outcomes among siblings in the same family. For example, if siblings are more similar than expected from only their shared genetics, this implies an effect of the environment they share, such as being exposed to marital conflict or poverty, or being parented in a similar manner. In the example of identical twins, shared environmental influence is estimated indirectly from correlations between twins by subtracting the heritability estimate from the MZ twin correlation. **Nonshared environment**, which refers to environmental factors that produce behavioral differences among siblings, can then be calculated by subtracting the MZ twin correlation from 1.0 (Pike & Kretschmer, 2009; Pike & Plomin, 1996).

Interestingly, it is nonshared environmental factors that create differences among siblings that seem to contribute to a large portion of the variation. Environmental factors that have been postulated as nonshared include differential treatment by parents, peer influences, and school environment (Eley & Lau, 2005).

● Figure 2.8 depicts Bronfenbrenner's (1977) ecological model, which shows the richness and depth of the various layers of a child's environment by portraying it as a series of nested and interconnected structures. Note that the child is at the center of this sphere of influence, which contains various levels interconnected in meaningful ways. The child's immediate environment begins with family members and home surroundings, but it quickly grows more complex as the child enters preschool, visits neighborhood parks, and makes friends.

Social settings also affect the child even when the child does not directly experience these influences. Parents' friends and jobs, the availability of family support services such as health and welfare programs, and similar community resources and activities that are positive and negative make up the child's larger social framework (Sameroff, 2010). Finally, though far removed from the child's day-to-day activities, cultural ideology or identity governs how children should be treated (the sanctioning of corporal punishment), what they should be taught, and what goals are important to achieve (Achenbach & Rescorla, 2007). These levels of environmental influences and their reciprocal connections (they affect the child, and the child affects them) are key elements in understanding the nature of child abuse and neglect and many child and adolescent disorders.

Infant–Caregiver Attachment

The study of abnormal development has profited from extensive work on child–caregiver relationships; this has painted a dramatic picture of the importance of early caregiver attachment to a child's emotional health (Sweeney, 2007). British child psychiatrist John Bowlby (1973, 1988) integrated aspects of evolutionary biology with existing psychodynamic conceptions of early experiences to derive his theory of attachment. **Attachment** refers to the process of establishing and maintaining an emotional bond with parents or other significant individuals. This process is ongoing, typically beginning between 6 and 12 months of age, and provides infants with a secure, consistent base from which to explore and learn about their world (Sroufe, 2005).

In attachment theory, instinctive behaviors are not rigidly predetermined but rather become organized into flexible, goal-oriented systems through learning and goal-corrected feedback. Bowlby reasoned that infants are "preadapted" to engage in relationship-enhancing behaviors such as orienting, smiling, crying, clinging, signaling, and, as they learn to move about, proximity seeking. In order to survive, however, infants must become attached to a specific person (or persons) who is available and responsive to their needs. Adults are similarly equipped with attachment-promoting behaviors to respond to an infant's needs, which are complementary to the needs of the infant—smiling, touching, holding, and rocking.

The evolving infant–caregiver relationship helps the infant regulate her or his behavior and emotions, especially under conditions of threat or stress. Accordingly, attachment serves an important stress-reduction function. The infant is motivated to maintain a balance between the desire to preserve the familiar and the desire to seek and explore new information. Self-reliance develops when the attachment figure provides a secure base for exploration (Bretherton & Munholland, 2008). Moreover, a child's *internal working model* of relationships—what he or she expects

● FIGURE 2.8 | An ecological model of environmental influences.

Photo Credits (clockwise from center and top): ©glenda/Shutterstock.com; ©Pressmaster/Shutterstock.com; ©iStockphoto.com/ lostinbids; © iStockphoto.com/Sean Locke; ©Goodluz/Shutterstock.com

from others and how he or she relates to others—emerges from this first crucial relationship and is carried forward into later relationships. The three major organized patterns of attachment (and one disorganized pattern) are summarized in Table 2.2, along with their theoretical and empirical links to various forms of psychopathology. Keep in mind, however, that attachment features constitute only one aspect of human relationships. Insecure attachments have been implicated

in a number of childhood disorders, but no one-to-one correspondence exists between specific patterns of attachment and particular disorders (Sroufe, 2005).

The Family and Peer Context

Child psychopathology research has increasingly focused on the role of the family system, the complex relationships within families, and the reciprocal influences among

TABLE 2.2 | Types of Attachment and Their Relation to Disordered Outcomes

Type of Attachment	Description during Strange Situation[1]	Possible Influence on Relationships	Possible Disordered Outcomes
Secure	Infant readily separates from caregiver and likes to explore. When wary of a stranger or distressed by separation, the infant seeks contact and proximity with caregiver; the infant then returns to exploration and play after contact.	Individuals with secure attachment histories tend to seek out and make effective use of supportive relationships.	Although individuals with secure attachments may suffer psychological distress, their relationship strategy serves a protective function against disordered outcomes.
Insecure *Anxious, avoidant type*	Infant engages in exploration, but with little affective interaction with caregiver. Infant shows little wariness of strangers, and generally is upset only if left alone. As stress increases, avoidance increases.	As children and adults, individuals with an insecure, *avoidant pattern of early* attachment tend to mask emotional expression. They often believe they are vulnerable to hurt, and others are not to be trusted.	Conduct disorders; aggressive behavior; depressive symptoms (usually as a result of failure of self-reliant image).
Insecure *Anxious, resistant type*	Infant shows disinterest in or resistance to exploration and play, and is wary of novel situations or strangers. Infant has difficulty settling when reunited with caregiver, and may mix active contact-seeking with crying and fussiness.	As children and adults, individuals with an *insecure, resistant* pattern of early attachment have difficulties managing anxiety. They tend to exaggerate emotions and maintain negative beliefs about the self.	Phobias; anxiety; psychosomatic symptoms; depression.
Disorganized, disoriented type (not an organized strategy)	Infant lacks a coherent strategy of attachment. Appears disorganized when faced with a novel situation and has no consistent pattern of regulating emotions.	Individuals with disorganized, disoriented style show an inability to form close attachments to others; may show indiscriminate friendliness (little selective attachment).	No consensus, but generally a wide range of personality disorders (van Ijzendoorn et al., 1999).

[1]The Strange Situation is a method of assessing infant–caregiver attachment. It involves a series of increasingly stressful separations and reunions that resemble typical daily occurrences, such as meeting strangers and being left alone (Ainsworth et al., 1978).

Note: The relationships between attachment styles and abnormal development are based on both theoretical and empirical findings, summarized in E. A. Carlson and Sroufe (1995). (Sroufe et al., 1999)

Source: © Cengage Learning ®

various family subsystems. There is a need to consider the processes occurring within disturbed families, and the common and unique ways these processes affect both individual family members and subsystems. Within the family, the roles of the mother–child and marital subsystems have received the most research attention, with less attention being given to the role of siblings (Defoe et al., 2013) or fathers (Smith et al., 2012).

Family systems theorists argue that it is difficult to understand or predict the behavior of a particular family member, such as a child, in isolation from other family members (P. A. Cowan & C. P. Cowan, 2006). This view is in line with our earlier discussion of underlying assumptions about children's abnormal development—*relationships*, not individual children or teens, are often the crucial focus. This view, however, is often at odds with mainstream psychological and psychiatric approaches to psychopathology, yet it is compatible with developmental processes.

More and more, the study of individual factors and the study of the child's context are being seen as mutually compatible and beneficial to both theory and intervention. Furthermore, the manner in which the family, as a unit, deals with typical and atypical stress plays an instrumental role in children's adjustment and adaptation. The outcome of stressful events depends in part on the nature and severity of the stress, the level of family functioning prior to the stress, and the family's coping skills and resources. Stress that is positive or tolerable, such as changing schools or a decline in family income, often brings about change, growth, and reorganization of families and is not usually harmful to children's development (Masten & Wright, 2010; Rutter, 2011a). However, some forms of stress are considered "toxic" to child development because they cause strong, frequent, and/or prolonged activation of the child's stress response in the absence of adult protection and support (Shonkoff, 2010). Some of the more influential family-related issues raised in

The "Core Story" of Development

For several years a group of neuroscientists, developmental psychologists, pediatricians, and others have been working on a "core story" of child development in an effort to translate complex ideas and findings into actions that reduce social problems and improve children's chances at successful development. We thought a brief list of their core story themes would provide a nice summary of the important issues you have read about in this chapter:

1. Child development is a foundation for community development and economic development because capable children become the foundation of a prosperous and sustainable society.
2. Brain architecture is constructed through an ongoing process that begins before birth and continues into adulthood. The quality of that architecture establishes either a sturdy or a fragile foundation for all the capabilities and behavior that follow.
3. Skill begets skill as brains are built in a hierarchical fashion, from the bottom up. Increasingly complex circuits and skills build on simpler circuits and skills over time.
4. The interaction of genes and experience shapes the circuitry of the developing brain. Young children serve up frequent invitations to engage with adults, who are either responsive or unresponsive to their needs. This "serve and return" process is fundamental to the wiring of the brain, especially in the early years.
5. Cognitive, emotional, and social capacities are intertwined. Learning, behavior, and both physical and mental health are highly interrelated over the life course. You cannot address one domain without affecting the others.
6. Although manageable levels of stress are normative and growth promoting, toxic stress in the early years (e.g., from severe poverty, serious parental mental health impairment such as maternal depression, child maltreatment, and/or family violence) can damage developing brain architecture and lead to problems in learning and behavior, as well as increased susceptibility to physical and mental illness.
7. Brain plasticity and the ability to change behavior decrease over time. Consequently, getting it right early leads to better outcomes and is less costly, both to society and to individuals, than trying to fix it later.

Source: Based on Shonkoff & Bales, 2011.

Supported by the National Scientific Council on the Developing Child and the FrameWorks Institute.

---

discussions of childhood disorders throughout this book are parental depression, child abuse, parental substance abuse, divorce, marital violence, poverty, and parental criminality.

Although quite distinct, these major family and individual issues share a common thread in terms of their impact on child development: They disrupt, disturb, or interfere with consistent and predictable child care and basic necessities. Such disruption or impairment, in turn, interferes with children's ongoing development to such an extent that their ability to manage stress and form satisfactory relationships with peers, teachers, and other adults cascade into lifelong psychological difficulties (Cox et al., 2010; Obradović, Burt, & Masten, 2010).

A Closer Look 2.4 provides a useful summary of the concepts discussed throughout this chapter to assist readers in understanding the major processes affecting normal and abnormal development.

Section Summary

Family, Social, and Cultural Perspectives

- Attachment approaches to abnormal child behavior emphasize the evolving infant–caregiver relationship, which helps the infant regulate behavior and emotions, especially under conditions of threat or stress.
- Children's normal and abnormal development depends on a variety of social and environmental settings, including the child's family and peer system and the larger social and cultural context.

LOOKING AHEAD

Society's understanding of children's and adolescents' healthy, normal development has been gradually evolving toward a more holistic, health-promoting orientation, which is impacting the definitions and services related to children's mental health (Barry, 2009; Lewin-Bizan, Bowers, & Lerner, 2010). This emerging dynamic, interactive view of health recognizes the importance of both individual and environmental factors in achieving positive development. The neuroscience and ecological perspectives on human health and behavior add momentum to this growing view because they consider human adaptation within its normal context.

Health and successful adaptation are today seen as worthy and appropriate aspects of the study of abnormal child and adolescent psychology. Along with an increased emphasis on **health promotion**, today's research and thinking accept the notion that various childhood disorders share many clinical features and causes. Health promotion encourages changes, opportunities, and competence to achieve one's health potential (R. M. Kaplan, 2000; Ungar, 2010). When applied to children, this view recognizes the multicausal and interactive nature of many child and adolescent psychological disorders and the importance of contextual factors. It also speaks to the importance of balancing the abilities of individuals with the challenges and risks of their environments (Kirmayer et al., 2011; Masten & Wright, 2010). Throughout the text we return to the many ways abnormal child and adolescent psychology can be studied in a developmentally sensitive, systems-oriented manner.

These conceptual shifts are gradually changing the face of mental health and educational services for children and youths, with important implications for pediatrics, psychology, psychiatry, social work, nursing, education, and child development. How individuals think about health, how daily life is organized and experienced, how social policy is developed, how social resources are allocated, and how people are trained to implement these policies have reached their greatest potential in history for achieving major improvements in services to assist younger populations who cannot speak for themselves. Although this tremendous impact on the field of mental health, and on children and youths in particular, has not yet become reality, we are encouraged by how society has progressed in addressing the needs of children.

Study Resources

SECTION SUMMARIES

KEY TERMS

3

Research

If we knew what it was we were doing, it would not be called research, would it?

—Albert Einstein (1879–1955)

PRELIMINARY EDITION

IN THIS CHAPTER, WE look at the process of research and the many challenges faced by those who study children and adolescents with problems and their families. **Research** is generally viewed as a systematic way of finding answers to questions—a method of inquiry that follows certain rules.

A SCIENTIFIC APPROACH

The aim of science is not to open a door to infinite wisdom,
but to set a limit to infinite error.

—Brecht, *The Life of Galileo*

Scientific research strategies can be used to understand children with problems and how they can be helped. A scientific approach is an organized way of investigating claims that improves on using common sense and casual observations. However, science is more than just organized common sense. Science requires that a claim be based on theories backed up by data from well-designed studies that test alternative explanations and that observations be checked and repeated before conclusions are drawn (Rutter & Solantaus, 2014). A scientific approach is especially important in abnormal child psychology. Although relationships between variables of interest may seem obvious when observed casually—a child consumes too much sugar and becomes hyperactive—these relationships are often not as straightforward as they seem. What we initially may think is a simple cause-and-effect connection may be obscured by complex interactions and a combination of variables. Parents and professionals who work with children have a tendency to interpret and relate information according to their own belief systems and experiences. These relationships sometimes become firmly established, independent of whether they are supported by facts. Even when new information comes along, such as studies indicating a lack of correlation between sugar and hyperactivity, one's previous views or understanding can be difficult to change.

Folklore, home remedies, and fad treatments ranging from chicken soup to swimming with dolphins are unscientific aspects of abnormal child psychology. Simple explanations, such as "sugar causes hyperactivity," or simple solutions, such as "spare the rod and spoil the child," may appeal to parents or teachers because they promise an easy answer or quick remedy for a complex problem. Folklore and fad treatments, unintentionally or otherwise, play to the vulnerabilities of parents of children with problems, parents who desperately want the best for their children. More often than not, easy answers or quick remedies do not work, and sometimes they bring unfortunate consequences and costs for children with problems and their families.

People have always been skeptical about scientific research leading to new knowledge. Consider the following comments:

> After a few more flashes in the pan, we shall hear very little more of Edison and his electric lamp. Every claim he makes has been tested and proved impracticable. (*New York Times*, January 16, 1880)

> Louis Pasteur's theory of germs is ridiculous fiction. (Pachet, professor of physiology [Toulouse, 1872])

Fortunately, the light bulb, pasteurization, and many other ideas once viewed with skepticism have clearly caught on. Nevertheless, people are skeptical about research in abnormal child psychology for good reason. First, experts on childhood problems frequently disagree. Newspapers, magazines, websites, and TV talk shows provide a steady diet of conflicting opinions. The answers we get (e.g., violence on television makes children more aggressive, daycare has a harmful effect on children's emotional adjustment) often depend on which "expert" we ask.

Second, research studies that appear in mainstream media are frequently oversimplified, and the way in which findings are presented can make them more or less believable. For example, people are more likely to agree with the findings of a study when the findings are presented with a photo of a brain image, as compared with the same findings presented without a brain image or with a bar graph (McCabe & Castel, 2008). In the absence of information about the limitations of brain-imaging procedures, findings can be misrepresented or misunderstood.

Third, research findings in abnormal child psychology are often in conflict with one another. For example, most studies find that elementary-school-age girls are more prone to depression than boys, but some studies report higher rates of depression in boys, and other studies report no differences. How do we make sense out of inconsistent and sometimes contradictory findings? As we will discuss in this chapter, conflicting findings are often the result of how different studies are conducted—for example, the way depression is defined or how children for the study are selected (e.g., from clinics vs. from the general population).

A fourth reason for skepticism is that research has led to different recommendations regarding how children with problems should be helped. In some cases the same treatment (e.g., antidepressant medication) has been shown to be helpful, to have no effect, or to be harmful. As one practitioner put it after hearing about an effective new treatment method at a conference, "I'd better hurry home and use it quickly before a new study is published to show that it doesn't work!" Many conclusions from research with children are

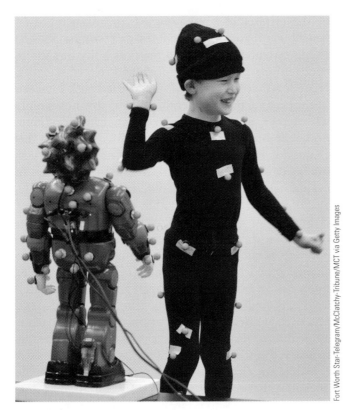

Abnormal child psychology can involve novel research methods, such as the possibility of using robots to help to understand, diagnose, and treat children with autism spectrum disorder.

qualified—rarely are there clear-cut answers. A moderate amount of discipline is good; too little or too much discipline is bad. Certain treatments may work for some children but not for others, for older but not for younger children, or for children with certain cultural backgrounds but not for others.

Finally, even when scientific evidence is relatively clear and produces a consensus, many parents and professionals may dismiss the findings because they have encountered an exception, usually one drawn from personal experience. For example, despite the large amount of research showing that the habitual use of harsh physical punishment by parents can have extremely negative effects on children, a parent may still say, "My father used his belt on me when I was a kid and it sure taught me how to behave properly!"

Because no single study is perfect, it is important to be an informed consumer and to keep in mind that it is the *accumulation* of findings—not one study—that advances the field. Research in abnormal child psychology using a scientific approach has led to exciting new advances in understanding children with problems and how they can best be helped. For example, in Chapter 6, we discuss studies that have identified brain abnormalities in children with autism that may tell us why these children have difficulty making social connections

with people. Other research—using home videotapes of 12-month-old infants who are later diagnosed with autism at 2 to 3 years of age—has identified early social markers for autism such as the infant "not responding to her name when called" or "rarely making eye contact." The discovery of possible biological and social markers helps identify children with autism at a younger age than ever before. This is critical, because the earlier a child with autism receives help, the better the outcome. In studies of autism and other disorders, findings from different studies do not always agree. Nevertheless, the accumulation of new findings from scientific research into the neurobiology, early social development, and intervention for children with autism has greatly advanced our understanding of this disorder and continues to suggest new ways to help these children.

When Science Is Ignored

The greatest enemy of knowledge is not ignorance, it is the illusion of knowledge.

—Stephen Hawking

The example of *facilitated communication* (FC) illustrates some of the lessons to be learned when scientific methods and evidence are ignored or dismissed. FC is a seemingly well-meant but highly controversial and misused procedure for teaching children with autism and other impairments to communicate. Using this method, a facilitator provides manual assistance by lightly holding a child's hand, wrist, or arm (see photo), while the child supposedly communicates by typing on a keyboard or by pointing to letters on an alphabet board. The alleged purpose of the manual assistance by the facilitator is to help the child press the keys that she or he wants to press—not to influence key selection. However, because the assistance is continued indefinitely, the possibility of direct influence by the facilitator exists.

Facilitated communication: Who's doing the communicating?

FC received widespread exposure in the media when it was reported that children who received it showed feats of literacy and intellectual competence far exceeding their presumed abilities (Biklen, 1990). The results were considered remarkable because the typical youngster using FC had a lifelong history of autism, profound intellectual disability, or both and had never talked (Jacobson, Mulick, & Schwartz, 1995). Proponents claim that, with this method, children with autism can generate phrases and sentences describing complex memories and feelings and demonstrate other advanced language skills (Biklen & Cardinal, 1997).

However, critics of FC view the method as quackery—no different from a Ouija board. Are the extraordinary outcomes attributed to FC fact, or are they fiction? Scientific research would indicate fiction. Controlled studies have consistently found that the child's supposed communication is being controlled by the facilitator (Mostert, 2001). In one revealing study, different questions were delivered through headphones to facilitators and individuals with autism ranging in age from 16 to 30 years (both were unaware that the questions were different). The resulting answers by the individuals with autism were found to match the questions given to the facilitator, not the client, indicating that it was the facilitator who was doing the communicating (Wheeler et al., 1993).

Unfortunately, FC continues to be used each day with thousands of youngsters with disabilities throughout the world (Grayson et al., 2012), which illustrates the potentially damaging effects of using practices not based on scientific evidence (Lilienfeld, 2007; Mostert, 2010). As reflected in the following comments by the father of a young boy with autism, parents who want the best for their children are particularly vulnerable to the false promise of questionable interventions:

> Professionals are very quick to dismiss the abilities of autistics. . . . So when facilitated communication proponents say they have found a way around the wall, parents are quick to believe. . . . But . . . the workshops can cost $250. The equipment $800 more. And what do we get for our money? Parents themselves "can't facilitate," they tell us. Our children will require facilitated communication for life, they say, and will never communicate on their own. . . . In short, the price we are asked to pay in an effort to communicate with our children is to allow strangers into our families to mediate our relationships with our own kids and to accept everything the stranger tells us on blind faith. (Mark S. Painter, Sr. [Dillon, 1993])

FC is of special interest to our discussion of a scientific approach to research because it meets many of the criteria of *pseudoscience*: demonstrations of benefit are based on anecdotes or testimonials, the child's baseline abilities and the possibility of spontaneous improvement are ignored, and related scientific procedures are disavowed. The differences between scientific and pseudoscientific claims are not simply whether or not they are based on evidence (Finn, Bothe, & Bramlett, 2005). As we discuss later in this chapter, it is the quality of the evidence, how it was obtained, and how it is presented that are crucial in evaluating whether claims are scientifically believable. Scientists are certainly capable of making incorrect claims. What distinguishes them from pseudoscientists is that they play by the rules of science, are prepared to admit when they are wrong, and are open to change based on new evidence (Lilienfeld, Lynn, & Lohr, 2003). Because a scientific approach to research is diverse and complex, many criteria, methods, and practices are necessary to depict how this approach is applied in abnormal child psychology. This will be our focus in the sections that follow, where we consider research in abnormal child psychology—from the questions that researchers who study childhood disorders typically seek to address, to the research process, to the methods and research designs used to study problems in children. In the last section, we discuss important ethical and pragmatic issues. The research that we present throughout this book emphasizes a scientific approach to abnormal child psychology. As we begin this journey, it is also important to keep in mind that science is a social enterprise undertaken by humans, and research is inevitably influenced by scientists' values (Sonuga-Barke, 2011).

Section Summary

A Scientific Approach

- A scientific approach to abnormal child psychology is a way of thinking about how best to understand and answer questions of interest, not just an accumulation of specific methods, practices, or procedures.

- Science requires that theories be backed up by evidence from controlled studies and that observations be checked and repeated before conclusions are drawn.

- Facilitated communication (FC) meets many of the criteria of pseudoscience because demonstrations of benefit are based on anecdotes or testimonials, the child's baseline abilities and the possibility of spontaneous improvement are ignored, and typical scientific procedures are disavowed.

- What distinguishes science from pseudoscience is that scientists play by the rules of science, are prepared to admit when they are wrong, and are open to change.

THE RESEARCH PROCESS

Science is not a collection of facts, any more than opera is a collection of notes. It's a process, a way of thinking, based on a single insight—that the degree to which an idea seems true has nothing to do with whether it is true, and that the way to distinguish factual ideas from false ones is to test them by experiment.

—Ferris (1998)

Research in abnormal child psychology is best characterized as a multistage process involving key decisions at various points. The process typically begins with the researcher(s) developing a hypothesis (research question) on the basis of observation, theory, and previous findings, and deciding on a general approach to research. The next stage involves identifying the sample to be studied, selecting measurement methods, and developing a research design and procedures. The research design and procedures must balance practical considerations with the adequacy of the research to address the hypotheses under investigation. The final stage consists of gathering and analyzing the data and interpreting the results in relation to theory and previous findings in an attempt to resolve the problem that initially led to the research. In this ongoing process, findings and interpretations from the study can then be used to generate future research questions and stimulate further research.

The main stages of the research process are summarized in ● Figure 3.1. Keep in mind that ethical considerations in conducting research with children and families must be considered at every stage of this process. We will discuss these ethical considerations in the final section of this chapter, "Ethical and Pragmatic Issues."

Since there is no one "correct" approach to research, most problems in abnormal child psychology are best studied by using multiple strategies and multiple methods (Rutter & Solantaus, 2014). Research is much like any decision-making process. This process requires an understanding of the conceptual, methodological, and practical considerations to make informed decisions about when certain research methods and strategies are appropriate and when they are not. To study abnormal child psychology, researchers must include research designs and methods of data analysis that can identify direct and indirect effects and different causal pathways for various disorders (Cicchetti & Hinshaw, 2003). We discuss common research questions and topics in abnormal child psychology in the sections that follow, addressing specific issues encountered at different stages of the research process.

Common Research Questions and Topics

Parents typically ask similar questions about their children, and the cases of Whitney (age 14) and Tito (age 7) provide examples.

WHITNEY

Always Sad

I don't understand why Whitney is so sad all the time. She's continually arguing with her brother, hates school, and has no friends. She's always been a moody child, but became much worse after my husband and I divorced. Is her sadness due to her moody personality, the divorce, or is something at home or at school making her feel this way? (Based on authors' case material)

● **FIGURE 3.1** | The research process in abnormal child psychology.

© Cengage Learning®

Constantly Fighting

Tito is constantly fighting with other kids at school. He never does what we ask him to do. When things don't go his way, he has a full-blown tantrum and throws and breaks things. My husband thinks Tito's just a tough kid, and that all he needs is firm discipline. He uses his belt a lot with Tito, but it doesn't seem to make a difference. I'm really worried. Will Tito outgrow his behavior? Is my husband being too strict? What can I do about it? (Based on authors' case material)

These case examples include typical questions that parents ask about their children's problem behavior and development. They are also questions that generate abnormal child behavior research: for example, research on the impact of divorce on children's mood and behavior, as in Whitney's case, or whether fighting and destructive behavior are likely to decrease with age, as in the case of Tito. As noted above, research typically begins with a hypothesis based on a theory, which predicts certain outcomes or behavior. Research hypotheses guide the researcher's choice of methods and the research designs most appropriate for answering certain questions. Research questions and topics are often based on theories of atypical development and behavior (discussed in Chapter 2). Some studies test predictions drawn from a single theory, whereas others test predictions based on different theories. When little or no theoretical knowledge is available, investigators may also develop a research question without an explicit prediction. For example, are there more depressed children today than there were a generation ago? Is child abuse more prevalent in our society than in other parts of the world?

Nature and Distribution of Childhood Disorders

Questions regarding the nature and distribution of childhood disorders include how disorders are defined, diagnosed, and expressed at different ages and in different settings. Related questions are directed at patterns of symptoms, base rates for various child problems and competencies, and natural progressions of problems and competencies over time. Such questions are frequently addressed through **epidemiological research,** which is the study of the incidence, prevalence, and co-occurrence of childhood disorders and competencies in clinic-referred and community samples (Costello, Egger, & Angold, 2005a). **Incidence rates**

reflect the extent to which new cases of a disorder appear over a specified period (e.g., the number of youths who develop a depressive disorder during the school year). **Prevalence rates** refer to all cases, whether new or previously existing, observed during a specified period of time (e.g., the number of teens with conduct disorder in the general population during 2012 and 2013). Estimates of incidence and prevalence can be obtained over a short period, such as 6 months, or over a much longer period. For example, *lifetime prevalence* indicates whether children in the sample have had the disorder at any time in their lives.

Knowledge about the risk for, and expression of, an individual disorder over the life course helps us understand the nature of the disorder and use this understanding as the basis for prevention and treatment (Costello & Angold, 2006). For example, studies of teens over time have found depression to be a recurrent disorder with poor long-term outcomes for many youngsters. This knowledge about the course of the disorder has resulted in promising new approaches to prevent and treat depression in young people, which we present in Chapter 10, "Depressive and Bipolar Disorders."

As we noted in Chapter 1, about 10% to 20% of children worldwide have a clinically diagnosable disorder, and many more exhibit specific symptoms or subclinical problems (Belfer, 2008). However, overall rates obscure the enormous variability in reported rates from study to study. It can be very confusing when one study reports a prevalence rate of 1% and another reports a rate of 20% for the same disorder at roughly the same point in time. Similarly, rates of reported problems in children have been found to vary from 6% to 20% when reported by teachers and from 10% to 40% when reported by parents (Costello & Angold, 2006). Some studies would lead you to conclude that almost every child you encounter has a problem; for others, the problem is so rare you wonder whether it even exists. Which conclusion is accurate?

To answer this question, we must know something about epidemiological research and how estimates of the number of cases (e.g., children with a problem or disorder) are made. Cases may be defined in terms of single symptoms, multiple symptoms, or patterns of symptoms with likely causes and associated characteristics. Estimates of prevalence vary widely depending on which definition we use, with estimates based on single symptoms being much higher than those based on patterns of symptoms. It is sobering to learn that lifetime prevalence estimates of mental disorders obtained prospectively (studying the same sample of children over time and assessing them at periodic intervals) are *double* those found in retrospective studies (asking people to remember what occurred at an earlier time), which are subject to recall failure (Moffitt et al., 2010). Case definition in abnormal child psychology is complex because children do not refer themselves for treatment. Therefore, equating illness with seeking treatment can be misleading. The factors that lead to referral sometimes have more to do with the child's parents, teachers, or doctor than with the child's behavior. Therefore, it is important that we study problems in children who are not referred to clinics for treatment as well as those who are. Throughout this book you will see many examples of striking differences in prevalence rates and other research findings, depending on whether children from clinics or children from community samples are the focus of study.

Prevalence rates also vary depending on whether cases are defined in terms of patterns of symptoms, impairment in functioning (e.g., difficulties at home or at school), or both. Fewer cases are identified when both symptoms and impairment in functioning are used than when definitions are based on either one or the other.

The rate and expression of childhood symptoms and disorders often vary in relation to demographic and situational factors, such as socioeconomic status (SES) (e.g., the social, economic, and physical environment in which the child lives as reflected in measures such as family income, education, or occupation); parents' marital status; and the child's age, gender, and cultural background, to name but a few. Consequently, these variables must be assessed and controlled for in most studies. For example, children from one ethnic group may display higher rates of learning problems than those from another ethnic group and may also have a lower SES. If we don't take SES into account we might conclude that differences in learning are related to ethnicity when they are instead a function of factors associated with lower SES such as poor nutrition and fewer learning opportunities. Similarly, although conduct problems are reported to be more frequent in African American than in Caucasian youngsters (McLaughlin, Hilt, & Nolen-Hoeksema, 2007), this finding is likely an artifact related to SES. That is, conduct problems are more prevalent in low-SES families and, since African American children are overrepresented in such families in North America, it is likely that the link between race and conduct problems is accounted for by stressful conditions associated with growing up in a poor family (Bird et al., 2001). In support of this, few differences in conduct problems in African American versus Caucasian youth are reported for primarily middle-class samples (Sameroff, Peck, & Eccles, 2004). The importance of cultural differences is highlighted in A Closer Look 3.1, which shows an

Children's socioeconomic status and cultural background play an important role in the rate and expression of childhood symptoms and disorders

example of epidemiological research into the types of child behavior problems reported by parents in seven cultures.

Correlates, Risks, and Causes

Whitney, in the case at the beginning of this section, displays persistent sadness that seems to be related to several variables: her history of being a moody child, her parents' divorce, her problems at school, and her lack of friends. Do any of these variables, alone or in combination, account for her sadness? If so, in what ways? Three variables of interest in abnormal child psychology are correlates, risk or protective factors, and causes of other variables. Most research in abnormal child psychology is designed to answer questions about the relation between the three general variables and childhood disorders. Because virtually all childhood disorders are the result of multiple variables interacting with one another over time, answers to these questions are rarely straightforward.

Correlates refer to variables that are associated at a particular point in time with no clear proof that one precedes the other. For example, Whitney's having no friends is associated with her sadness. Is she sad because she has no friends, or has her sadness prevented her from making friends? Since we don't know which variable came first, her lack of friends and her sadness are correlated variables.

A *risk factor* is a variable that precedes an outcome of interest and increases the chances of a negative outcome (see Chapter 1). For example, Whitney's depressed mood got worse following her parents' divorce. Do you think parental divorce is a risk factor for the development of depression or other problems in children? Remember that a risk factor increases the chances for

Cross-Cultural Epidemiological Research: Behavior Problems Reported by Parents of Children in Seven Cultures

Widespread movements of refugees and immigrants are placing millions of children into new and unfamiliar environments. Evaluating the mental health of these children can be difficult because of cultural variations in what constitutes abnormal behavior, how to identify such behavior, and what to do about it. Crijnen, Achenbach, and Verhulst (1997) examined the 6-month prevalence rates of child behavior problems as reported by parents or parent surrogates in studies carried out in seven cultures, using the same measurement instrument—the Child Behavior Checklist (CBCL) (Achenbach, 1991a). As shown in the figure, the total problem scores of children in Puerto Rico and China were well above the overall mean. In contrast, the total problem scores of children in Germany and Israel, were well below the overall mean. This epidemiological study indicates that parents in different cultures report different rates of problem behavior in their children. However, the findings do not indicate why these differences occur. Other kinds of studies are needed to answer that question—for example, research into cultural variations in child-rearing practices or expectations for child behavior (Achenbach & Rescorla, 2007).

Total problem scores for children in seven different cultures. Overall mean Child Behavior Checklist (CBCL) problem scores and mean CBCL problem scores for each culture at ages 6 through 11 and ages 12 through 17. Overall mean scores across cultures for each age grouping are indicated by solid horizontal lines. China did not provide enough 12- through 17-year-olds for analysis.

Based on Journal of the American Academy of Child & Adolescent Psychiatry, 36, A.A.M. Crijnen, T.M. Achenbach & F.C. Verhulst, Comparisons of Problems Reported by Parents of Children in 12 Cultures: Total Problems, Externalizing, and Internalizing, 1269–1277.

a certain outcome. It does not mean that it will occur; its occurrence will depend on other factors. Obviously, most children of parents who divorce do not become clinically depressed. Divorce is not necessarily a cause of a youngster's depression and low self-esteem, but it can be a risk factor (Hetherington, Bridges, & Insabella, 1998). A *protective factor* is a positive variable that precedes an outcome of interest and decreases the chances that a negative outcome will occur. The close relationship enjoyed by Whitney and her mother may serve as a protective factor against future episodes of depression.

Research into risk and protective factors often requires that large samples of children be studied and that multiple domains of child functioning—physical, cognitive, psychosocial—be assessed over long periods of time. This is necessary because: (1) only a small proportion of children at risk for a problem will actually develop the disorder; (2) the areas of child functioning

that will be affected, and how they will be affected, are not known in advance; and (3) the ages at which a disorder may occur or reoccur are also not known in advance. Sometimes the effects of exposure to a risk factor during infancy or early childhood may not be visible until adolescence or adulthood. The possibility that delayed, or *sleeper,* effects will occur complicates the study of risk and protective factors, since children must be studied for many years if delayed effects are to be detected.

Finally, other variables are *causes*. They influence, either directly or indirectly through other variables, the occurrence of a behavior or disorder of interest. Tito's father uses severe punishment when his son misbehaves. Is this punishment a cause of Tito's aggressive behavior? Is Tito learning aggressive behavior from his father? Questions about causes are complicated because what qualifies as a cause will vary according to the variables of interest and how far back in time a causal chain can be traced. Because childhood disorders are the result of multiple factors acting in concert, a challenge for researchers is to identify the relative contributions of each factor and—more importantly—to determine how they combine and interact over time to produce specific outcomes (Dodge & Pettit, 2003). When it comes to childhood disorders, "with very few exceptions, there is no such thing as a single basic necessary and sufficient cause" (Rutter, 2007b, p. 378). However, scientific research can help strengthen or weaken certain inferences about the causal role of some variables versus others.

Moderating and Mediating Variables

The key difference between moderating and mediating variables is that moderators have an independent effect on the existing relationship between two variables, whereas mediators account for some or all of the apparent relationship between two variables. **Moderator variables** influence the *direction* or *strength* of the relationship of variables of interest. The association between two variables depends on or differs as a function of moderating variables, such as the child's age, sex, SES, or cultural background. For example, as illustrated in ● Figure 3.2, in a study examining the relation between adolescents' self-reported history of physical abuse and their self-reports of internalizing problems such as anxiety and depression, McGee, Wolfe, and Wilson (1997) found that the correlation between the severity of physical abuse history and internalizing problems was greater for females than for males. The child's sex was a moderator variable; that is, the relationship between two of the variables (in this case, abuse and internalizing problems) differed, depending on the third (if the adolescent was a boy or a girl).

Mediator variables refer to the process, mechanism, or means through which a variable produces a particular outcome. Mediators describe what happens at the psychological or neurobiological level to explain how one variable results from another. In one study, Snyder (1991) found that on days when mothers of 4- to 5-year-old children experienced negative moods and frequent hassles, they were most likely to respond negatively to their children's misbehavior and to reinforce their children's coercive tactics during mother–child conflicts. In turn, the use of these types of maternal discipline was related to an increase in same-day child behavior problems. As shown in ● Figure 3.3, these findings indicate that the relationship between maternal distress and child conduct problems is partly mediated by the type of discipline mothers use on days when they feel distressed. Mothers' disciplinary strategies help explain the relationship between maternal distress and child conduct problems.

Outcomes

What are the long-term outcomes for children who experience problems? Many childhood problems decrease or go away as children mature, but we need to know at approximately what age such improvements may be expected. Similarly, will other problems emerge, such as the child developing a low opinion of himself or herself because of trouble with, say, wetting the bed or worrying too much about school? Returning to Tito's oppositional and aggressive behaviors, will we expect his problems to decrease or go away as he gets older, or do they forecast continued conflict with peers, future school problems, and later difficulties in social adjustment? The study of outcomes in abnormal

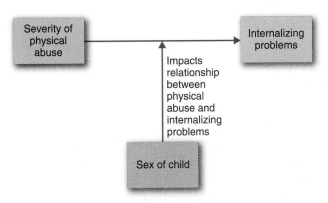

● **FIGURE 3.2** | Example of a moderator variable: Sex of the child moderates the relationship between abuse and internalizing problems.

© Cengage Learning®

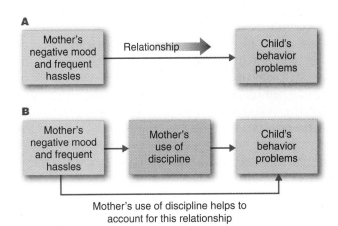

● **FIGURE 3.3** | Mediating variables: The type of discipline used by mothers on days they are feeling distressed mediates the relationship between maternal distress and child behavior problems.

© Cengage Learning®

child psychology is perhaps one of the most important research topics in the field today.

Interventions

How effective are our methods for treating or preventing childhood problems? Are some types of treatment more effective than others? Questions about treatment and prevention are concerned with evaluating the short- and long-term effects of psychological, environmental, and biological treatments; comparing the relative effectiveness of differing forms and combinations of treatment; and identifying the reasons that a particular treatment works. The questions also concern identifying factors that influence the referral and treatment process; understanding how processes such as the child–therapist relationship contribute to treatment outcomes; and assessing the acceptability of equivalent forms of treatment to children, parents, and teachers.

Many treatments for children and adolescents have not been evaluated, although this situation is steadily improving (Silverman & Hinshaw, 2008). These days, numerous studies evaluate treatment outcomes using **randomized controlled trials (RCTs)**, in which children with a particular problem are randomly assigned to different treatment and control conditions. We discuss the importance of random assignment later in this chapter. Findings from controlled research studies indicate that children who receive treatment are generally better off than children who do not.

However, an important distinction needs to be made between treatment efficacy and treatment effectiveness (Chorpita et al., 2011). **Treatment efficacy** refers to whether the treatment can produce changes under well-controlled conditions. In efficacy research, careful control is exercised over the selection of cases, therapists, and delivery and monitoring of treatment. In contrast, **treatment effectiveness** refers to whether the treatment can be shown to work in clinical practice, not just in well-controlled research settings. In research on effectiveness, treatment is evaluated in clinical settings, clients are usually referred rather than selected, and therapists provide services without many of the rigorous controls used in research. The benefits of treatment for children with problems have generally been found to be lower in clinical practice settings (effectiveness trials) than in controlled research settings (efficacy trials) (Weisz et al., 2013). As a result, a high priority for intervention research is on developing and testing interventions in settings where clinical services for youths are typically provided and finding ways to strengthen the bridge between research, public policy, and clinical practice (Chorpita & Daleiden, 2014; Weisz, 2014; Weisz, Ng, & Bearman, 2014). Relatedly, there is a growing interest in the design, development, and investigation of new technologies as a service delivery vehicle that could help to reduce the gap between intervention research and clinical practice (Jones, 2014).

Section Summary

The Research Process

- Research is a multistage process that involves generating hypotheses, devising an overall plan, selecting measures, developing a research design and procedures, gathering and analyzing the data, and interpreting the results.
- One's theory of abnormal child behavior determines the variables studied, the choice of research methods, and the interpretation of research findings.
- Questions about the nature and distribution of childhood problems are addressed through epidemiological research into the incidence and prevalence of childhood disorders and competencies in clinic-referred and community samples.
- Other common research topics in abnormal child psychology focus on correlates, risk and protective factors, causes, moderating and mediating variables, outcomes, and interventions for childhood disorders.

METHODS OF STUDYING BEHAVIOR

The study of children's behavioral and emotional problems requires that the methods we use to measure these problems generate scores that are reliable and valid. This is no easy task. Children's problems must be evaluated based on samples of their behavior in different situations (e.g., home or school) that often reflect differing perspectives of adults. These evaluations are likely to be affected by the child's age, sex, and cultural background and by the assessors' personal expectations and values. As a result, no single measurement can provide a complete picture of a child's problems, and multiple measures and sources of information are needed.

Standardization, Reliability, and Validity

The methods and measures that we use to study child and family behavior must undergo careful study to determine how well they measure constructs such as depression, anxiety, and intellectual disability. The use of well-standardized, reliable, and valid measures and procedures is essential to scientific research, as depicted in ● Figure 3.4.

Standardization is a process that specifies a set of standards or norms for a method of measurement that are to

Standardization	Application of certain standards or norms to a technique to ensure consistency in the way it is used by different assessors and across measurement occasions
Reliability	The degree to which a measurement obtained using the same technique is consistent, for example, over time or across assessors
Validity	The degree to which a technique measures what it is designed to measure

● **FIGURE 3.4** | Concepts that determine the value of our methods of measurement and assessment.

© Cengage Learning®

be used consistently across different assessments of the construct of interest. These standards and norms relate to the procedures that must be followed during administration, scoring, and evaluation of findings—for example, as specified in a manual for an intelligence test. Without standardization, it is nearly impossible to replicate the information obtained using a method of measurement. In addition, results are likely to be unique to the situation in which they are obtained and will not apply to other situations. In some cases, the measure may be applied to many children who vary in age, gender, race, SES, or diagnosis. The scores are then used for comparison purposes. However, the test scores of an 8-year-old boy from a low-SES background should be compared with the scores of other children like him, not with the scores of a 16-year-old girl from an upper-SES background.

Reliability refers to the consistency, or repeatability, of results obtained using a specific method of measurement. One type of reliability, *internal consistency,* refers to whether all parts of a method of measurement contribute in a meaningful way to the information obtained. To be reliable, information must also not depend on a single observer or clinician; various people must agree on what they see. This is known as *interrater reliability.* Imagine how you might react if you took your child to see three different psychologists and received three different diagnoses and three different treatment recommendations. How would you know which one was correct? In this case, the diagnoses would not be reliable because two or more of the psychologists did not agree. Similarly, tests or interviews repeated within a short time interval should yield similar results on the two occasions. In other words, the results need to be stable over time, which is referred to as *test–retest reliability.*

Reliability alone isn't enough to determine whether a method reflects the investigator's goals—validity must also be demonstrated. The **validity** of a method refers to the extent to which it actually measures the dimension or construct that the researcher sets out to measure. Validity is not all or none but rather a matter of degree, and it can be assessed in many ways. First, the measure can be examined for its *face validity,* or the extent to which it appears to assess the construct of interest. A questionnaire that asks whether you get nervous before taking an exam would be a face-valid measure of test anxiety, whereas one that asks if you think you are a parrot would not. *Construct validity* refers to whether scores on a measure behave as predicted by theory or past research. For example, a test of intelligence has construct validity if children who obtain high scores on the test also have better grades in school, understanding of concepts, verbal reasoning, recall, and parent ratings of intelligence than do children who obtain low scores on the test. Two components of construct validity are convergent validity and discriminant validity. *Convergent validity* reflects the correlation between measures that are expected to be related—for example, a teen's report of her depression in a screening interview and her scores on a depression questionnaire. It is an indication of the extent to which the two measures assess similar or related constructs—in this case, depression. This is in contrast to *discriminant validity,* which refers to the degree of correlation between measures that are not expected to be related to one another. For example, scores on a measure designed to assess depression and another designed to assess intelligence should not correlate.

Finally, *criterion-related validity* refers to how well a measure predicts behavior in settings where we would expect it to do so—at the same time (concurrent validity), or in the future (predictive validity). For example, a child's high scores on a measure of social anxiety should predict that the child would display anxiety or avoidance in current social situations and will perhaps have difficulties making friends in the future. Criterion-related validity tells whether scores on a measure can be used for their intended purpose.

Measurement Methods

A variety of measurement method options are available to assess important dimensions of children's behavioral, cognitive, emotional, and neurodevelopmental functioning. These methods are explicit plans to observe and assess children and their surroundings in ways that will reveal relatively clear relations among variables of interest.

Among the measurement options in abnormal child psychology are interviews, questionnaires,

TABLE 3.1 | Interview, Questionnaire, and Observation

	Interview	Questionnaire	Observation
Structure of situation	Semistructured or structured	Highly structured	Structured or unstructured
Structure of responses	Probe, expand, and clarify	Highly structured; no opportunity for probes or clarification	Vary from very inclusive observation of all behaviors to highly selective coding of very specific behaviors (e.g., number of "smiles")
Resource requirements	Considerable time needed for interviewing and coding responses and scoring.	Little investigator time needed for administration	Extensive time needed for observing and for coding and summarizing observations
Sources of bias	Relies on participants' perceptions and willingness to report; responses may be influenced by interviewer characteristics and mannerisms	Relies on participants' perceptions and willingness to report	Does not rely on participants' providing specific information, but what is observed may be influenced by the presence of the observer
Data reduction	Requires analysis or recoding of narrative responses	Little data reduction needed	Highly influenced by the complexity of the observation system

© Cengage Learning®

checklists and rating scales, psychophysiological recordings, brain imaging, performance measures, and direct observations of behavior (Mash & Barkley, 2007). A variety of intellectual, academic, and neuropsychological tests are also used (Sattler, 2008). In this chapter, we focus primarily on how these methods are used in research. We talk more about their use in clinical practice and about tests and testing in Chapter 4.

As presented in a comparison of three of the most commonly used methods of gathering data—interviews, questionnaires, and observations—shows how they differ on important dimensions. Because the information we obtain from children and families often varies as a function of the method used, researchers frequently rely on several methods to define and assess the constructs of interest.

Reporting

Reporting methods assess the perceptions, thoughts, behaviors, feelings, and past experiences of the child, parents, and teachers. These instruments include relatively unstructured clinical interviews, highly structured diagnostic interviews, and questionnaires. An important question regarding reporting methods relates to who is reporting on behavior. For example, with a *self-report measure,* a child or parent will provide information about his or her own behavior, feelings, and thoughts. Alternatively, using an *informant-report measure,* a person who is well acquainted with the child, usually a parent or a teacher, will provide information about a child's behaviors, feelings, or thoughts based on his or her observations of the child.

A concern with self- and informant-report methods is how accurately children, parents, or teachers report their own or others' thoughts, feelings, and behaviors. Inaccuracies may occur because of a failure to recall important events, selective recall or bias, and in some cases, intentional distortions. Some individuals may try to make themselves or others look better or worse than they actually are. Reporting methods also require a certain level of verbal ability and may not accurately assess individuals who have difficulty expressing themselves. Obviously, young children would fall into this category—children under the age of 7 or 8 are usually not reliable reporters of their own behavior. Individuals from a cultural background different from the one in which a reporting method was developed may have difficulty understanding and responding to certain questions. For this reason, it is essential that the reporting method used be sensitive to the language and cultural background of the person being evaluated.

Psychophysiological Methods

Psychophysiological methods assess the relationship between physiological processes and behavior to identify which nervous system structures and processes contribute to children's atypical development and behavior. Among the most common measures are autonomic nervous system activity, such as heart rate, blood pressure, breathing, pupil dilation, and electrical conductance of the skin. Changes in heart rate, for example, may be related to emotional responses. In addition, specific patterns of autonomic arousal may be associated with differences in children's temperament—their degree of shyness with people or responses to novel events (discussed in Chapter 11).

There are many limitations associated with psychophysiological measures, especially with young children. Sometimes, findings for these measures are inconsistent from one study to the next, and researchers may have to infer how the child may have processed a particular event or stimulus. Also, a child's physiological response can be influenced easily by other factors, such as the child's reaction to the recording equipment or to hunger, fatigue, or boredom. These extraneous influences must be minimized if conclusions are to be based on psychophysiological measures.

Many studies have used an *electrophysiological measure* of brain functioning, the **electroencephalogram (EEG)**, to link the brain's measurable electrical activity with ongoing thinking, emotion, or state of arousal (Rothenberger, 2009). The EEG records electrical brain activity using electrodes attached to the surface of the child's scalp. Because different EEG waves are related to different states of arousal, differential patterns of EEG activation may suggest sleep disturbances or various emotional states. For example, with respect to emotional states, a greater amount of electrical activity in the right frontal lobe of the brain as compared with the left frontal lobe is associated with anxiety and depression (McManis et al., 2002).

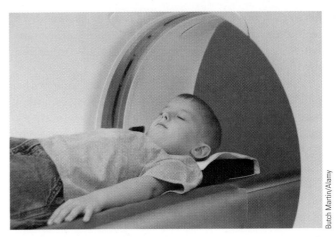

A child about to be evaluated using computed tomography (CT or CAT) scan

Neuroimaging Methods

Neuroimaging methods are used to examine the structure and/or function of the living brain (Wong, Grunder, & Brasic, 2007). These methods provide new ways of testing neurobiological and other theories for many childhood disorders—for example, by identifying abnormalities in the structure or functioning of specific brain regions or in how regions of the brain communicate with one another. These brain abnormalities, for instance, may cause the problems that children with autism have in recognizing people's facial expressions. *Structural* brain imaging procedures include *magnetic resonance imaging* (MRI) and *computed tomographic* (CT) scans. MRI uses radio signals generated in a strong magnetic field and passed through brain tissue to produce fine-grained analyses of brain structures. CT scans also reveal the various structures of the brain. As we will see in Chapter 8, findings from CT and MRI studies have led to the hypothesis of abnormal neural maturation in children with attention-deficit/hyperactivity disorder (ADHD).

Two types of functional imaging procedures are *functional magnetic resonance imaging (fMRI)* and *positron-emission tomography* (PET). fMRI is a form of MRI that registers neural activity in functioning areas of the brain. By doing so, it can show which brain areas are active during particular mental operations such as solving a specific type of problem or reacting to a fear-inducing stimulus. PET scans assess cerebral glucose metabolism. Glucose is the brain's main source of energy, so measuring how much is used is a good way to determine the brain's activity level.

Diffusion MRI (dMRI) is a magnetic imaging method that produces images showing *connections*

An electroencephalogram (EEG) is used to monitor electrical activity of the brain in a young girl

between brain regions. This method has become a key technology in the creation of the *human connectome*, which is the structure and organization of connections throughout the central nervous system.

Neuroimaging studies tell us that children with a particular disorder have structural differences, abnormal activity in certain areas of the brain, or abnormal brain connectivity, but they do not tell us why. Although remarkable advances have been made in the use of brain-imaging procedures with children during the past two decades, their promise for advancing our understanding or diagnosis of developmental disorders is just beginning (Insel, 2010; Peterson, 2003).

Observation Methods

You can observe a lot just by watching.

—Yogi Berra

Using systematic *observational methods,* a researcher can directly observe the behavior of the child and others under conditions that range from unstructured observations in the child's natural environment (referred to as **naturalistic observation**) to highly structured situations involving specific tasks or instructions usually carried out in the clinic or laboratory (referred to as **structured observation**). When using naturalistic observation, the researcher goes into the child's home, classroom, or day-care center to observe and record the behaviors of interest of the child and often of parents, teachers, siblings, and peers with whom the child interacts. Alternatively, the researcher may make a video recording of behavior in the natural environment, which can be analyzed at a later time.

A researcher who uses structured observations in the laboratory or clinic sets up a situation or provides instructions to elicit behaviors of particular interest (Roberts & Hope, 2001). For example, numerous studies of child–caregiver attachment have assessed young children's reactions to increasingly stressful episodes of separation from and reunion with their caregivers in the laboratory using the *Strange Situation* procedure (Ainsworth et al., 1978). By structuring the situation to elicit specific attachment behaviors (e.g., seeking to be close to the mother), the Strange Situation permits researchers to assess the security or insecurity of children's attachment by noting how effectively they can use their caregivers as a source of comfort during times of distress.

Structured laboratory- or clinic-based observations are cost-effective and offer the advantage of focusing observations on the phenomena of interest. The method is especially useful for studying child behaviors that occur infrequently in everyday life. Structured

A researcher might observe this young girl's behavior on the playground, as other children play around her, to help determine the cause of her emotional problems.

observations give the researcher greater control over the situation than do naturalistic observations, and they permit the use of other assessment procedures. For example, when a problem-solving discussion is recorded on video, replaying the interaction for family members can be used to ask them what they were thinking or feeling during the discussion (Sanders & Dadds, 1992). One negative aspect of using structured observations is that questions may arise as to whether observations in the laboratory or clinic provide a representative sample of the behaviors of interest (Mash & Foster, 2001). Knowing that they are being observed through a one-way mirror may make families feel as though they are in a fishbowl; children and parents may not behave in the laboratory as they do in real-life settings. Nevertheless, in general, samples of behavior obtained using observational methods—in the laboratory or in real-world settings—can be very informative. However, they should be regarded as "behavior in the presence of an observer," as the observer's presence is likely to influence the behavior of the children and parents who are being observed.

Section Summary

Methods of Studying Behavior

- The measures and methods used to study child and family behavior must be standardized, reliable, and valid.
- Self-report and informant-report methods include unstructured clinical interviews, structured diagnostic interviews, and questionnaires.
- Psychophysiological methods are used to assess the relationship between physiological processes and behavior; these methods include measures of heart rate, blood pressure, breathing, pupil dilation, and electrical conductance of the skin.

- Electrophysiological measurements, such as the EEG, link electrical brain activity with ongoing thinking, emotion, or state of arousal.
- Neuroimaging methods are used to examine the structure and/or function of the brain, and connections between parts of the brain.
- Observational methods are used to directly observe the behavior of the child and others in unstructured settings, such as the home, classroom, or playground, and in structured task situations in the laboratory or clinic.

RESEARCH STRATEGIES

The research strategies used to study children with problems ultimately contribute to the overall accuracy of research findings and conclusions. If a researcher is biased while selecting participants or chooses a research task that does not represent the problem of interest, then the validity of the results may be on shaky ground—the study may not be a fair test of the research question.

Research studies may be examined with respect to their internal and external validity. **Internal validity** reflects how much a particular variable, rather than extraneous influences, accounts for the results, changes, or group differences. Extraneous influences that could explain the results are called *threats to internal validity*. They include maturation, the effects of testing, subject-selection biases, and others. For example, suppose you found that providing relaxation training over several months to a group of 5-year-old children decreased their nighttime fears. It is possible that the observed decrease may be due to the extraneous influences of *maturation* or *the effects of testing*—the children's fears decrease because they are getting older or because they are being assessed repeatedly, rather than as a result of the relaxation training.

The reduction in fears could also be due to *subject-selection biases,* which are factors that operate in selecting subjects or in the selective loss or retention of subjects during the study. For example, if children with only mild fears are selected for our study, a high likelihood exists that their fears will decrease over time, even in the absence of treatment, as compared with children with more severe fears. Also, if children with more severe fears or children who do not benefit from relaxation training dropped out of the study prematurely, the observed decrease in fears may be the result of this selective loss of the most fearful subjects rather than a result of the treatment.

External validity refers to the degree to which findings can be generalized, or extended to people, settings, times, measures, and characteristics other than the ones in a particular study. Threats to external validity may include characteristics of the participants that apply to some people but not others, the reactivity of subjects to participating in the research, the setting in which the research is carried out, or the time when measurements are made. For example, many research studies in abnormal child psychology underrepresent cultural minorities and children from low-SES backgrounds, often because of difficulties in recruiting and retaining participants or because cultural minorities are less likely to receive mental health services for their problems (Cummings & Druss, 2011). Because of this, it is difficult to generalize the findings from these studies to these other groups of children. As another example, children or parents may not behave naturally in an unfamiliar laboratory setting. If findings from a study in the laboratory are quite different from what is found in real-life settings, this study too would have low external validity.

As much as possible, potential threats to internal and external validity need to be addressed when designing a research study. As we discuss in the sections that follow, careful attention to how the sample is identified, how variables of interest are defined and measured, how participants are assigned to conditions or groups, and the types of control groups used are just a few of the many research-design considerations needed to increase our confidence that our findings are best accounted for by the variable(s) of interest and are not due to extraneous influences.

Identifying the Sample

The validity of any research study in abnormal child psychology depends on the classification systems used to identify the samples of children who participate in the research. First, a careful definition of the sample is critical for comparability of findings across studies and for clear communication among researchers. Without such uniform standards, wide differences may result in estimated base rates for various childhood disorders and for many other findings.

In addition to our sample definition, a second issue is the need to consider possible comorbidities within our sample. **Comorbidity** is the simultaneous occurrence of two or more childhood disorders that is far more common than would be predicted from the general population base rates of the individual disorders. Comorbidity has direct implications for the selection of research participants and for the interpretation of results. Research samples drawn from clinical populations will have a disproportionately high rate of comorbidity because referral for treatment is most likely based on the combined symptoms of all disorders.

A failure to consider comorbidity may result in an interpretation of findings in relation to one disorder, when these findings are more validly attributed to a second disorder or to a combination of disorders. To deal with comorbidity in research samples, some researchers may select only participants with single, or pure, disorders. This strategy may yield small, atypical samples whose findings do not generalize to other populations. Although there is no single research strategy to address questions about comorbidity, studies that compare children showing single disorders with children showing comorbid disorders are needed to help disentangle the effects of comorbidity. It also needs to be recognized that much of the comorbidity among disorders may be artifactual, related more to the overlap in symptoms used to define and diagnose childhood disorders than to the co-occurrence of distinct conditions (Drabick & Kendall, 2010; Rutter, 2010).

A third issue is that we must be sensitive to the setting and source of referral of children for research.

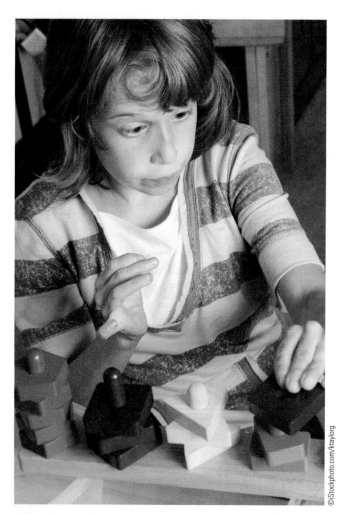

Comorbidity: A 10-year-old girl with multiple disabilities, including intellectual disability, autism, and epilepsy.

Random selection occurs when subjects are drawn from a population in a way that gives each individual in that population an equal chance of being selected for the study. This is rare in studies of child psychopathology. At the other end of the spectrum are studies that use *samples of convenience*, in which subjects are selected for a study merely because of their availability, regardless of whether they provide a suitable test of the questions or conditions of interest. Research samples in abnormal child psychology have been selected from numerous settings, including outpatient psychology and psychiatry clinics, schools, hospitals, day-care centers, and the community. Effects related to different settings are often confounded with effects related to different referral sources (e.g., physicians, teachers, and parents), since referral sources also differ across settings.

General Research Strategies

There are several different, yet complementary, approaches to research design that offer various advantages and disadvantages. The choice of approach frequently depends on the research questions being addressed, the nature of the childhood disorder under investigation, and the availability of resources (Hartmann, Pelzel, & Abbott, 2011).

Nonexperimental and Experimental Research

One goal of scientific research is to simplify and isolate variables in order to study them more closely. Varying or manipulating values of the variable(s) of interest while trying to control or hold constant other factors that could influence the results meets this goal. Doing this makes it possible to study the association between the particular variables of interest. The basic distinction between nonexperimental versus experimental research reflects the degree to which the investigator can manipulate the experimental variable or, alternatively, must rely on examining the natural covariation of several variables of interest. The *independent variable* is manipulated by the researcher. Based on a research hypothesis, the independent variable is anticipated to cause a change in another variable. The variable expected to be influenced by the independent variable is called the *dependent variable*. The greater the degree of control that the researcher has over the independent variable(s), the more the study approximates a true experiment.

In a **true experiment** the researcher has maximum control over the independent variable or conditions of interest and can use random assignment of subjects to groups, include needed control conditions, and control possible sources of bias. Conversely, the less control the

©iStockphoto.com/ktaylorg

researcher has in determining which participants will and will not be exposed to the independent variable(s), the more nonexperimental the research will be. Most variables of interest in child psychopathology cannot be manipulated directly, including the nature or severity of the child's disorder, parenting practices, or genetic influences. As a result, much of the research conducted on children with problems and their families relies on nonexperimental, correlational approaches.

In *correlational studies,* researchers often examine relationships among variables by using a **correlation coefficient,** a number that describes the degree of association between two variables. A correlation coefficient can range from –1.00 to +1.00. The size of the correlation indicates the strength of the association between two variables. A zero correlation indicates no relationship; the closer the value gets to –1.00 or +1.00, the stronger the relationship is. The sign of the correlation coefficient (plus or minus) indicates the direction of the relationship. A positive sign (+) indicates that as one variable increases in value, so does the other, whereas a negative sign (–) indicates that as one variable increases, the other decreases.

For example, a positive correlation of +0.70 between symptoms of anxiety and symptoms of depression indicates that children who show many symptoms of anxiety are also likely to display symptoms of depression. Alternatively, children who show few symptoms of anxiety are likely to display few symptoms of depression. However, a negative correlation of –0.70 between symptoms of depression and social skills, for example, indicates that children who show many symptoms of depression have fewer social skills.

The primary limitation of correlational studies is that interpretations of causality cannot be made. A correlation between two variables does not mean that one variable causes the other. If we find a relationship

Children's symptoms of anxiety and depression are often positively correlated.

between depression in children and depression in their parents, it could mean that being around a child who is depressed may lead to depression in parents, that parental depression may lead to depression in the child, or that depression in the child and parent may both be due to another, more fundamental variable, such as a shared genetic disposition to depression.

In experimental investigations, researchers must take steps to control for characteristics of participants that could decrease the accuracy of the findings. For example, if two groups of children differ with respect to education, intelligence, SES, or the presence of related disorders, it would be impossible to determine whether the independent variable or the other characteristics led to the results. **Random assignment** of participants to treatment conditions protects against this problem because the probability of a subject's appearing in any of the groups is the same. By assigning participants to groups on the basis of the flip of a coin, numbers drawn from a hat, or a table of random numbers, the chance is increased that characteristics other than the independent variable will be equally distributed across treatment groups.

As we have noted, many hypotheses in abnormal child psychology cannot be tested by randomly assigning participants to conditions or by manipulating conditions in the real world. A compromise involves the use of natural experiments, also called *quasi-experimental designs* or *known-group comparisons.* In **natural experiments,** comparisons are made between conditions or treatments that already exist. The experiments may involve children with different disorders, parents with different problems, or different family environments (e.g., children who have suffered from neglect vs. children who have not). These studies are essentially correlational, but the subjects are selected to ensure that their characteristics are as comparable as possible, with the exception of the independent variable. Despite the extreme care exercised by researchers to equate existing groups, natural experiments cannot achieve the same level of precision and rigor as true experimental research. Nevertheless, for many important questions in abnormal child psychology, natural experiments using known-group comparisons are the only option (Rutter, 2007b).

Prospective and Retrospective Research

Research designs that address questions about the causes and long-term outcomes of childhood disorders may differ with respect to the time the sample is identified and the time data are collected. In a **retrospective design,** a sample of people is identified at the current time and asked for information relating to an earlier time. Individuals are identified who already show the outcome of interest, and they are compared with controls who do not show the outcome. Assessments focus on characteristics in the past, and inferences are made about past characteristics and the current outcome. For example, a sample of young adults with a substance-use disorder might be asked to provide retrospective ratings and descriptions of their early family experiences.

Although data are immediately available in retrospective studies, they are also highly susceptible to bias and distortion in recall. Parents of teenagers diagnosed with schizophrenia may reinterpret their views of the teen's childhood, distorting their recollection of the teen's prior behavior or friendships. Moreover, retrospective designs fail to identify the individuals who were exposed to certain earlier experiences but did not develop the problem. Young adult females with an eating disorder may report more childhood experiences of sexual abuse. However, this finding could not serve as the basis for a conclusion that childhood sexual abuse is a specific precursor to eating disorders in young adulthood. The retrospective study fails to identify children who experienced childhood sexual abuse but did not develop an eating disorder as young adults.

In **real-time prospective designs**, the research sample is identified and then followed over time, with data collected at specified time intervals. The same youngsters are followed or assessed over time in order to understand the course of change or differences that may develop over time or during important developmental transitions such as middle-school entry or adolescence. For example, infants who are fearful in response to novel events may be followed over time to determine whether they later develop anxiety disorders or other problems to a greater extent than infants who are not fearful.

Prospective designs correct for several of the problems associated with retrospective research. By following a sample over time we can identify children who develop a disorder as well as those who do not. Since information is collected in real time, problems relating to bias and distortion in recall are minimized. Disadvantages of prospective designs include loss of participants over time and the extended length of time needed to collect data.

Analogue Research

Analogue research evaluates a specific variable of interest under conditions that only resemble or approximate the situation for which one wishes to generalize. Analogue studies focus on a circumscribed research question under well-controlled conditions. Often, the purpose of the research is to illuminate a specific process that would otherwise be difficult to study.

For example, Lang et al. (1989) were interested in whether the higher-than-normal rates of alcohol consumption observed in fathers of boys with attention-deficit/hyperactivity disorder (ADHD)/conduct disorder (CD) might be partly due to the distress associated with interacting with their difficult children (these researchers must have been parents, too!). Male and female single college students who were social drinkers were randomly assigned to interact with boys who were trained to perform behaviors characteristic of either typical children (friendly and cooperative) or children with ADHD/CD (overactive and disruptive). Participants also rated their own mood before and after interactions with the child. After the interaction, participants were given a 20-minute break while they anticipated another interaction with the same child. During the break, beer was freely available for their consumption. Both male and female participants reported comparable levels of elevated distressed mood after interacting with children enacting the ADHD/CD role. However, only the men who had interacted with these children drank enough to increase blood alcohol levels.

The findings suggest that interacting with a child with ADHD/CD may increase alcohol consumption in fathers. However, an analogue study only resembles the conditions of interest—the study participants were single college students, not parents of children with ADHD/CD; the children did not really have ADHD/CD; drinking was confined to an artificial laboratory setting; and only beer was available. Therefore, it is difficult to know whether similar effects would occur in real-life circumstances (despite anecdotal reports by some parents that their kids drive them to drink!). These conditions raise the question of external validity, or the generalizability of research findings.

Research Designs

Research designs are the strategies used to examine question(s) of interest. They refer to the ways in which a researcher arranges conditions to draw valid inferences about the variables of interest.

Case Study

The **case study**, which involves an intensive, usually anecdotal, observation and analysis of an individual child, has a long tradition in the study of abnormal development and behavior. Itard's description of Victor, the Wild Boy of Aveyron; Freud's treatment of a phobia in Little Hans; John Watson's conditioning of a phobic reaction in Albert B.; and many other similar case studies have played an influential role in shaping the way we think about children's problems. The case study, especially as used in the clinical context, brings together a wide range of information about an individual child from various sources, including interviews, observations, and test results. The goal is to get as complete a picture as possible of the child's psychological functioning, current environment, and developmental history. Sometimes the goal is to describe the effects of treatment on the child.

Case studies yield narratives that are rich in detail and provide valuable insights into factors associated with a child's disorder. Nevertheless, they also have drawbacks. They are typically viewed as unscientific and flawed because they are characterized by uncontrolled methods and selective biases, by inherent difficulties associated with integrating diverse observations and drawing valid inferences among the variables of interest, and by generalizations from the particular child of interest to other children. Hence, case studies have been viewed primarily as rich sources of descriptive information that provide a basis for subsequent testing of hypotheses in research using larger samples and more controlled methods. They may also provide a source for developing and trying out new treatment methods.

Despite their unscientific nature, there are compelling reasons why systematically conducted case studies are likely to continue to play a useful role in research on childhood disorders. First, some childhood disorders, such as childhood-onset schizophrenia, are rare, making it difficult to generate large samples of children for research. Second, the analyses of individual cases may contribute to the understanding of many striking symptoms of childhood disorders that either occur infrequently or are hidden and therefore difficult to observe directly. Third, significant childhood disturbances such as posttraumatic stress disorder (see Chapter 12) often develop as the result of a natural disaster, severe trauma, or abuse. These extreme events and circumstances are not easily studied using controlled methods.

Single-Case Experimental Designs

Single-case experimental designs have most frequently been used to evaluate the impact of a clinical treatment, such as reinforcement or stimulant medication, on a child's problem (Kazdin, 2011). The central features of single-case experimental designs that distinguish these from uncontrolled case studies include systematic repeated assessment of behavior over time, the replication of treatment effects within the same subject over time, and the participant's serving as his or her own control by experiencing all treatment conditions (Barlow, Nock, & Hersen, 2009). Many single-subject designs exist, the most common being the A-B-A-B (reversal) design and the multiple-baseline design carried out across behaviors, situations, or individuals.

In an **A-B-A-B reversal design**, a baseline of behavior is first taken (A), followed by an intervention phase (B), then a return-to-baseline phase during which the intervention is removed (A), and a final phase in which the intervention is reintroduced (B). When changes in behavior only occur during the intervention phases, this provides evidence that changes in behavior are due to the intervention. Findings from a study using a *reversal design* are presented in ● Figure 3.5. In this example, a behavioral intervention was used to reduce self-injurious behavior (SIB) in Ann, a 5-year-old girl with profound intellectual disability and multiple handicaps. Ann's SIB consisted of biting her hand and wrists during grooming activities, such as brushing her teeth. These behaviors were getting progressively worse and causing open wounds. During the initial baseline phase, the percentage of intervals during which Ann engaged in SIB during three brief sessions of toothbrushing ranged from 20% to 60%.

Intervention consisted of a negative reinforcement procedure in which Ann was permitted to briefly escape from the grooming activity when she performed an appropriate competing behavior (in this case, pushing a button that, when activated, played the message "Stop!"). She was also physically guided by a trainer to brush her teeth whenever she engaged in SIB. When these procedures were implemented during the intervention phase,

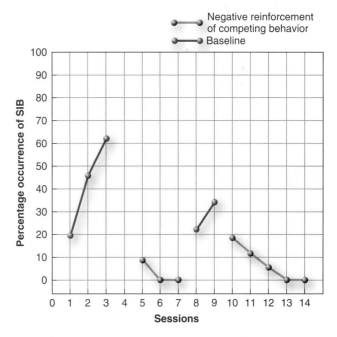

● **FIGURE 3.5** | A-B-A-B (reversal) design: treatment of Ann's self-injurious behavior (SIB).

Based on Use of Negative Reinforcement in the Treatment of Self-Injurious Behavior by M.W. Steege, D.P. Wacker, K.C. Cigrand, W.K. Berg, G.C. Novak, T.M. Reimers, G.M. Sasso & A. DeRaad, 1990, Journal of Applied Behavior Analysis, 23, 459–467.

an immediate reduction of SIB to 10% resulted, with no SIB occurring in the next two sessions. During the reversal, or return-to-baseline, phase, treatment was withdrawn and Ann's SIB increased to previous baseline levels. When treatment was reinstituted, SIB decreased again, and no biting was observed during the final two sessions. The finding that Ann's levels of SIB decreased only during the intervention phases, and not during the baseline or return-to-baseline phases, suggests that the reductions in Ann's SIB resulted from the intervention procedures.

Although the reversal design is applicable for use with a wide range of behaviors, there are limitations. One limitation is that if a treatment really works, the behavior may not reverse during the return-to-baseline phase. Do you see any other limitations of this design? Once Ann stopped engaging in SIB after intervention, do you think there was sufficient justification for reinstituting her harmful behavior for experimental purposes? We intentionally selected this example to illustrate a major limitation of the A-B-A-B design, which is the ethical concerns surrounding the return-to-baseline condition following effective treatment for undesirable or even dangerous behaviors. The

multiple-baseline design that we describe next gets around this concern, because no reversal is needed once intervention is introduced.

In a **multiple-baseline design** across behaviors, different responses of the same individual are identified and measured over time to provide a baseline against which changes may be evaluated. Each behavior is then modified in turn. If each behavior changes only when it is specifically treated, a cause-and-effect relationship between the treatment and the behavior change is inferred. Other common varieties of multiple-baseline designs involve successive introductions of treatment for the same behavior in the same individual across different situations or for the same behavior across several individuals in the same situation. The critical feature of the multiple-baseline approach is that change must occur only when treatment is instituted and only for the behavior, situation, or individual that is the target of treatment. Simultaneous changes must not occur for untreated behaviors, situations, or individuals until the time that each is, in turn, targeted for treatment.

Findings from a study using a multiple-baseline design across situations are presented in ● Figure 3.6.

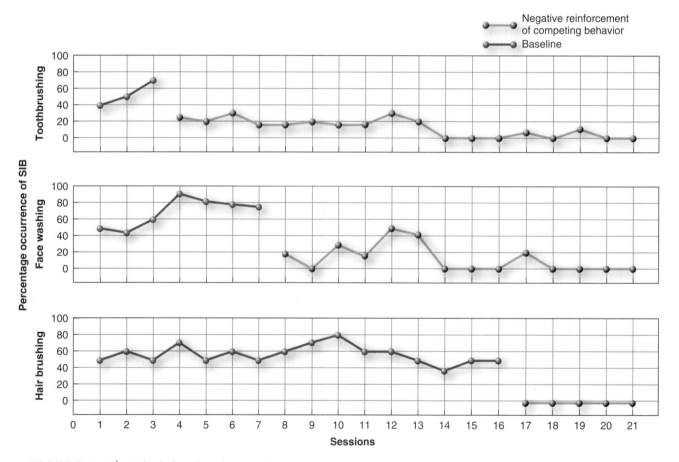

● **FIGURE 3.6** │ Multiple-baseline design across situations: treatment of Dennis's self-injurious behavior (SIB).

Based on Use of Negative Reinforcement in the Treatment of Self-Injurious Behavior, by M. W. Steege, D. P. Wacker, K. C. Cigrand, W. K. Berg, G. C. Novak, T. M. Reimers, G. M. Sasso & A. DeRaad, 1990, Journal of Applied Behavior Analysis, 23, 459–467.

In this example, the same intervention procedures used with Ann were used to reduce self-injurious behavior (SIB) in Dennis, a 6-year-old boy who also had profound intellectual disability and multiple handicaps. Dennis's SIB consisted of biting his hands, wrists, or arms during grooming activities such as toothbrushing, face washing, and hair brushing. His SIB was getting worse and causing open wounds. During the initial baseline phase, the percentage of intervals during which Dennis engaged in SIB averaged 50% or more during toothbrushing, face washing, and hair brushing. When an intervention was implemented during toothbrushing, an immediate decrease in Dennis's SIB resulted, with consistently low rates of SIB maintained throughout treatment. Moreover, no changes in Dennis's SIB were observed during face washing or hair brushing until the intervention was introduced during those situations.

Because changes in Dennis's SIB occurred only when an intervention was introduced during each of the specific situations, there is support for the hypothesis that intervention led to those changes. A multiple-baseline design avoids the problem associated with the reversal design of having to return to baseline when treating dangerous or unwanted behaviors.

Several advantages and limitations are associated with the use of single-case experimental designs. These designs preserve the personal quality of the case study and offer some degree of control for potential alternative explanations of the findings, such as the effects of maturation and reactivity to observation. Single-case designs also provide an objective evaluation of treatment for individual cases, permit the study of rare disorders, and facilitate the development and evaluation of alternative and combined forms of treatment. The negative aspects of the design are the possibilities that specific treatments will interact with unique characteristics of a particular child, the limited generalization of findings to other cases, and the subjectivity involved when visual inspection rather than statistical analysis is used to evaluate the data. The findings for Ann and Dennis were fairly clear-cut. Difficulties in interpretation arise when baseline data or observed changes are highly variable.

Between-Group Comparison Designs

Many research designs are based on comparisons between one group of children assigned to one or more conditions and other groups of children assigned to one or more different conditions. When participants are randomly assigned to groups, and groups are presumed to be equivalent in all other respects, one group typically serves as the *experimental group* and the other serves as the *control group*. Any differences observed between groups are then attributed to the experimental condition.

The choice of an appropriate control or comparison group often depends on what we know prior to the study and the questions we wish to answer. For example, if an established and effective treatment for adolescent depression exists, testing a new approach against a no-treatment control group will likely answer the wrong question, not to mention that it may raise ethical concerns about withholding a proven effective treatment. We do not want to know whether the new approach is better than nothing—we want to know whether it is better than the best available alternative treatment.

In many cases, assignment of participants to groups may not be possible, particularly when one wishes to make comparisons between known or intact groups, such as children who have been referred to clinics for depression versus those with depression who have not been referred. In these types of known-group comparisons there is no assignment; rather, the selection criteria for including or excluding participants from the groups must be carefully specified.

Cross-Sectional and Longitudinal Studies

Researchers interested in developmental psychopathology need information about the ways in which children and adolescents change over time. To obtain this information, researchers extend correlational and experimental approaches to include measurements taken at different ages. Both cross-sectional and longitudinal designs are research strategies in which a comparison of children of different ages serves as the basis for research.

In **cross-sectional research**, different youngsters at different ages or periods of development are studied at the same point in time, whereas in **longitudinal research**, the same children are studied at different ages or periods of development. In cross-sectional studies, researchers do not have to worry about the many problems associated with studying the same group of children over a long period. When participants are measured only once, researchers need not be concerned about selective loss of participants, practice effects, or general changes in the field that would make the findings obsolete by the time the study is complete. Although cross-sectional approaches are efficient, they are limited in the information they generate with regard to developmental changes. Evidence about individual change is not available. Rather, comparisons are limited to age-group averages.

Longitudinal designs are conducted prospectively. Data collection occurs at specified points in time from

Longitudinal Research: Does Child Maltreatment Lead to More Peer Rejection over Time?

Dodge, Pettit, and Bates (1994a) assessed a representative sample of 585 boys and girls for physical maltreatment in the first 5 years of life and then followed them for 5 consecutive years, from kindergarten through the fourth grade. Twelve percent of the sample was identified as having experienced maltreatment. The children's peers, teachers, and mothers independently rated the maltreated children as being more disliked, less popular, and more socially withdrawn than the nonmaltreated children in every year of evaluation—and the magnitude of the difference increased over time. As shown in the accompanying figure, by grade 4 more than twice as many maltreated as nonmaltreated children were rejected by their peer group. The results suggest that early maltreatment may disrupt relationships with adults, which in turn impairs a child's ability to form effective relationships with other children.

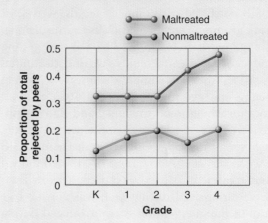

Proportions of maltreated and nonmaltreated children rejected by their peer group.

Based on Effects of Physical Maltreatment on the Development of Peer Relations by K.A. Dodge, G.S. Pettit & J.E. Bates, 1994, Development and Psychopathology, 6, 43–55.

the same individuals initially selected because of their membership in one or more populations of interest. In studies of child psychopathology, the populations of interest often consist of children at risk for developmental problems due to exposure to any one of a number of factors—for example, having a mother with depression or growing up in an abusive family situation.

The prospective longitudinal design allows the researcher to identify patterns that are common to all youngsters and to track differences in developmental paths that children follow. For example, a longitudinal study can tell that certain fears may decrease with age for all children but that some children may have an anxious disposition and show less of a reduction in specific fears with age. Because data are collected on the same individuals at time 1 and time 2, causal inferences between earlier events and later events and behavior based on temporal ordering can be made. Such inferences of causality cannot be made in cross-sectional designs, in which different individuals are assessed at the two time points. Longitudinal designs also allow for identification of individual developmental trends that would be masked by averaging data over individuals. The prepubertal growth spurt exemplifies this, where rapid accelerations in growth

occurring at different ages across the population are not reflected in growth measures averaged across adolescents. An example of a longitudinal study is presented in A Closer Look 3.2.

Despite their advantages, longitudinal designs have many practical and design difficulties (Hudziak & Novins, 2013). Practical concerns include obtaining and maintaining research funding and resources over many years and the long wait for meaningful data. Design difficulties relate to aging effects and cohort effects. *Aging effects* are general changes that occur because as participants age there are increases in physical prowess, impulse control, or social opportunity. *Cohort effects* are influences related to being a member of a specific **cohort**—a group of individuals who are followed during the same time and experience the same cultural or historical events. For example, the cohort of teens who lived in war-torn Yugoslavia in the early 1990s differ in many respects from North American teenagers living through the technological boom of the early 1990s.

The experience of being repeatedly studied, observed, interviewed, and tested may also threaten the validity of a longitudinal study. Children and adults may become more sensitized to the thoughts, feelings, and behaviors under investigation, thus thinking about them and revising them in ways that have nothing to do with age-related changes. Furthermore, with repeated testing, participants may improve as the result of practice effects, including greater familiarity with test items and better test-taking skills. Finally, changes within the field of abnormal child psychology may create problems for longitudinal studies conducted over an extended period. Theories and methods are constantly changing, and those that first led to the longitudinal study may become outdated.

Qualitative Research

Qualitative research focuses on narrative accounts, description, interpretation, context, and meaning (Denzin & Lincoln, 2011). The purpose of qualitative research is to describe, interpret, and understand the phenomenon of interest in the context in which it is experienced (Daly, 2007; Patton, 2002). This approach can be contrasted with a quantitative approach, which emphasizes operational definitions, careful control of the subject matter, the attempted isolation of variables of interest, quantification of dimensions of interest, and statistical analysis. Rather than beginning with already developed observational systems or assessment tools, qualitative researchers strive to understand the phenomenon from the participant's perspective. Qualitative data are typically collected through observations or open-ended interviewing and are recorded narratively as case study notes, for example. The observations and narrative accounts obtained are examined to build general categories and themes.

Proponents of qualitative research believe that it provides an intensive and intimate understanding of a situation that is rarely achieved in quantitative research (Denzin & Lincoln, 2011). Qualitative methods, such as the use of examples or stories, may be particularly engaging to children and enable the discussion of sensitive topics, while allowing the children a sense of control over the research situation (Barter & Renold, 2000). On the other hand, qualitative methods may also be biased by the researcher's values and preferences, and the findings cannot easily be generalized to individuals and situations other than the ones studied. Nonetheless, quantitative and qualitative research methods can be used in complementary ways (Lyons & Coyle, 2007). Qualitative methods can be used to identify important dimensions and theories that can then be tested quantitatively. Alternatively, qualitative case studies may be used to illuminate the meaning of quantitatively derived findings (Guerra et al., 2011). In addition, if qualitative data have been reduced to numbers through word counts or frequency counts of themes, the data can be analyzed using quantitative methods.

To give you a feel for qualitative research, consider a study by Petalas and colleagues (2009), who were interested in the experiences and views of siblings growing up in families that included a child with autism spectrum disorder (ASD). Eight typically developing children (9 to 12 years of age) with a brother with ASD were interviewed. Semi-structured interviews were analyzed using *interpretive phenomenological analysis* (IPA), a qualitative research approach that seeks to capture the richness and diversity of participants' accounts by uncovering central themes that emerge from their talk (Smith, Flowers, & Larkin, 2009). From this perspective, each sibling participant is seen as an expert on his or her personal experience. Each sibling interview lasted about 20 minutes on average and was audio-recorded and fully transcribed, resulting in 70 single-spaced pages of data. Analysis of these data involved reading and rereading of the transcripts until emergent themes were extracted. Briefly, one of the investigators listened to the recording and read the transcript to become familiar with the interview content. Transcripts were then read line by line, noting comments in the margins (e.g., summaries of meaning). Transcripts were then reread multiple times until themes emerging from the data were extracted by grouping sibling comments that clustered together. The themes were then checked and validated by the investigators to be sure that they were grounded in the data. This process, yielded five main themes, which are shown in A Closer Look 3.3, along with examples of a few of the sibling comments on which the themes were based.

The themes and examples highlight several features of the experiences of children growing up with a brother with ASD. You can see that siblings differ in their attitudes and interpretations of their experiences, and, to varying degrees, all mention positive aspects of having a brother with ASD. Siblings also describe different ways they were affected by having a brother with ASD, such as becoming socially isolated, changing their own behavior to cope with their brother's odd mannerisms and aggressive behavior, and having less family time for leisure and recreation. The exploratory findings from this qualitative study can be used to inform future larger-scale studies and quantitative research. They may also have implications for practice—for example, the need to develop enhanced support services for siblings of children with ASD (Petalas et al., 2009).

Qualitative Research: Siblings Talk about Their Brothers with Autism Spectrum Disorder (ASD)

Theme 1. Living with a Brother with ASD: Siblings' accounts of the impact on themselves and their families

- "I never feel like the youngest, even when I was small. ... I suppose I learned how to take care of people just like if I had a younger brother." [Lizzie]
- "Jake's loud and he won't stop running into my bedroom when we're talking; and then he just wants to play with us all the time. I get very irritated and I can't get him out. That's why I have a lock on my bedroom door now. [Maddie]
- "I feel quite angry, because he has spoiled a day, which we were all enjoying to that point. I feel quite sad because my Mom and Dad spend that money on us, and then he has to go and spoil it by having a tantrum." [Kevin]

Theme 2. Others' Reactions: Implications for siblings

- "It's quite annoying because they don't see Jack for who he really is; they just see a big person that's got Asperger's and [who] is really annoying. [Leah]
- "So if he starts swearing or starts kicking, you know, it's quite embarrassing because people might think, oh, you know, their mother or father taught him to do that, so it's quite embarrassing to me to think that people sort of disrespecting my family and me and my brother." [Kevin]
- "Just sometimes they sort of—well, when you make new friends they ask what's wrong with him and I have to explain it. And they get used to it when they get to know him. You tell them more about it, and you tell them stories and stuff. [Lizzy]

Theme 3. Acceptance and Wanting Change

- "Jack's just like an average person, that he's just got this Asperger's; but he's just like a normal. He's just got Asperger's. ... He's just like my normal brother; I never even think about it. I just recognize him as just another human. [Dylan]
- "... I like him the way he is. He's my brother. I'd never make him normal because I knew him like this. And I can't imagine a brother any other way. Well, not like Tyler any other way. I can't imagine him any other way, I wouldn't change anything." [Lizzy]

- "I'd like to tell him how much I appreciate him, because I don't really do that enough. He's often said to me, you're the worst brother in the world, you know, I don't like you, and I could show my appreciation more towards him than I do now." [Kevin]

Theme 4. Positive Views and Experiences

- "He's good at remembering things, like if he puts something up on his textbook, he'll remember it there, he'll remember it easier than anyone else. [Eddie]
- "I like that he always shows who he is. He always shows that he does have a personality and he is someone. And also just so he can't talk doesn't mean he doesn't have anything to say. He can sort of speak to you in a way." [Lizzy]
- "Last year, I'm not quite sure, he won a computer by doing horse riding. He didn't win, but he got it for doing so well, which I was really pleased by him for doing that. Not just for winning the computer, but because he'd done so well." [Kevin]

Theme 5. Support

- "He had someone called Lana who took him out on days out which was fun for him, and gave us as a family some time to go to places that maybe he wouldn't like to go. Like just as a family, without him, so that he would go where he liked to go, and us where we liked to go. Like just daytrips." [Lizzy]
- "I feel quite annoyed, because there's no one really to talk to about when I feel angry with Jack, and when he always gets his own way, and stuff about that. [Leah]
- "Mom went to a meeting for people who had children like Ryan and once she had to take me, and I met two other girls there, who had brothers who were autistic which is cool because you can still have a laugh with them and that, but they understand it better." [Kelsey]

From Petalas, M. A., Hastings, R. P., Nash, S., Dowey, A., & Reilly, D. (2009). "I like that he always shows who he is": The perceptions and experiences of siblings with a brother with autism spectrum disorder. *International Journal of Disability, Development and Education, 56*, 381–399.

Section Summary

Research Strategies

- Careful attention must be given to the way in which samples are identified for research in abnormal child psychology, including issues such as how the disorder of interest is defined, criteria for inclusion in the study, comorbidity, the setting from which subjects are drawn, and sample size.
- We can distinguish between nonexperimental and experimental research strategies on the basis of the degree to which the investigator can manipulate the experimental variable or, alternatively, must rely on examining the covariation of variables of interest.

- In prospective research, a sample is followed over time, with data collected at specified intervals. In retrospective research, a sample is identified at the current time and the sample members asked for information relating to an earlier time.

- Analogue research evaluates a specific variable under conditions that only resemble the situation for which the researcher wishes to generalize.

- The case study involves an intensive, usually anecdotal, observation and analysis of an individual child.

- Single-case designs involve repeated assessments of the same subject over time, the replication of treatment effects within the same subject, and the subject's serving as his or her own control. Two common examples are the A-B-A-B (reversal) design and multiple-baseline design across behaviors, situations, or individuals.

- Between-group designs compare the behavior of groups of individuals assigned to different conditions, such as an experimental group, or a comparison group and a control group.

- In cross-sectional research, different individuals at different ages or stages of development are studied at the same point in time. In longitudinal research, the same individuals are studied at different ages or stages of development.

- Qualitative research focuses on narrative accounts, description, interpretation, context, and meaning, and strives to understand the phenomenon from the participant's perspective and in the context in which it is experienced.

ETHICAL AND PRAGMATIC ISSUES

The image of overzealous scientists in white lab coats using children as guinea pigs for their experiments is a far cry from current research practices in abnormal child psychology. Researchers and policy makers have become increasingly sensitive to the possible ethical misuses of research procedures and are correspondingly more aware of the need for standards to regulate research practices (Fisher et al., 2013; Hoagwood & Cavaleri, 2010).

Research in abnormal child psychology must meet certain standards that protect children and families from stressful procedures. Any study must undergo careful ethical review before it can be conducted. Current ethical guidelines for research with children are provided through institutional review boards, federal funding agencies, and professional organizations such as the American Psychological Association and the Society for Research in Child Development.

Ethical standards for research with children attempt to strike a balance between supporting freedom of scientific inquiry and protecting the rights of privacy and the overall welfare of the research participants. Finding this balance is not always easy, especially with children. Although researchers are obligated to use nonharmful procedures, exposing the child to mildly stressful conditions such as a brief separation from their parent or exposure to an anxiety-producing stimulus may be necessary in some instances if benefits associated with the research are to be realized. Children are more vulnerable than adults to physical and psychological harm, and their immaturity may make it difficult or impossible for them to evaluate exactly what research participation means. In view of these realities, precautions must be taken to protect children's rights during the course of a study.

Informed Consent and Assent

The individual's fully informed consent to participate, obtained without coercion, serves as the single most protective regulation for research participants. **Informed consent** requires that all participants be fully informed of the nature of the research—as well as the risks, benefits, expected outcomes, and alternatives—before they agree to participate. Informed consent also includes informing participants of the option to withdraw from the study at any time, and of the fact that participation or nonparticipation in the research does not affect eligibility for other services.

Regarding research with children, protection is extended to obtaining both the informed consent of the parents or other legal guardian acting for the child and the assent of the child. **Assent** means that the child shows some form of agreement to participate without necessarily understanding the full significance of the research, which may be beyond younger children's cognitive capabilities. Guidelines for obtaining assent of the child call for doing so when the child is around the age of 7 or older. Researchers must provide school-age children with a complete explanation of the research activities in language they can understand. Factors that require particular attention when seeking children's assent include age, developmental maturity, psychological state, family factors, and the influence of the investigator seeking assent (Meaux & Bell, 2001). In addition to parents and children, consent must be obtained from other individuals who act on behalf of children, such as institutional officials when research is carried out in schools, day-care centers, or medical settings.

Voluntary Participation

Participation in research is to be voluntary, yet some individuals may be more susceptible to subtle pressure and coercion than others. Protection for vulnerable populations, including children, has received considerable attention. Families of high-risk infants and children are potentially more vulnerable, owing in part to the families' distress over their children's high-risk status. Although instructed otherwise, parents recruited from social service agencies or medical settings may still feel that their treatment or quality of care will be threatened if they do not participate in the research. Parents who mistreat their children may feel that their failure to participate in research could result in the loss of their child, a jail sentence, or failure to receive services.

The role of the researcher requires balancing successful recruiting with not placing pressure on potential participants. Volunteerism is itself a biasing factor in research. Individuals who agree to participate in research obviously differ from those who are approached but refuse. The question of whether volunteerism significantly biases findings on the variables of interest remains unanswered.

Confidentiality and Anonymity

Information revealed by individuals through participation in research is to be safeguarded. Most institutions require that individuals be informed that any information they disclose will be kept confidential and that they be advised regarding any exceptions to confidentiality. Adult informants must be told about the limits of confidentiality prior to their participation in research. In research with children, one of the most frequently encountered challenges to confidentiality occurs when the child or parent reveals past abuse or information that would suggest the possibility of future abuse of the child. Procedures for handling this situation vary across studies. They depend on the circumstances of the disclosure (e.g., by an adult within the context of therapy) and the reporting requirements of the state or province.

Nonharmful Procedures

No research procedures should be used that may harm the child either physically or psychologically. Whenever possible, the researcher is also obligated to use procedures that are the least stressful to the child and family. In some instances, psychological harm may be difficult to define, but when doubt is present, the researcher has the responsibility to seek consultation from others. If harm seems inevitable, alternative methods must be found or the research must be abandoned. In cases in which exposure of the child to stressful conditions may be necessary if therapeutic benefits associated with the research are to be realized, careful deliberation and analysis of the risks and benefits by an institutional review board are needed.

Other Ethical and Pragmatic Concerns

Sensitivity to ethical concerns is especially important when the research involves potentially invasive procedures, deception, the use of punishment, the use of participant payment or other incentives, or possible coercion. In longitudinal research, investigators must be particularly sensitive to the occurrence of unexpected crises, unforeseen consequences of research, and issues surrounding the continuation of the research when findings suggest that another course of action is required to ensure the child's well-being.

Many research problems typically addressed through standardized instructions and procedures are compounded by children's limited experience and understanding of novel research tasks and the particular characteristics of children with problems and their families. Researchers working with children with mental health problems and/or developmental disorders may face unique research challenges, such as motivating the children; keeping within time limitations; ensuring that instructions are well understood; and coping with possible boredom, distraction, and fatigue. Similarly, the families of children with problems often exhibit characteristics that may compromise their research participation and involvement. These characteristics include high levels of stress, marital discord, parental psychiatric disorders, substance-use disorders, restricted resources and/or time for research, and limited verbal abilities.

The final responsibility for the ethical integrity of any research project lies with the investigator. Researchers are advised or—in the case of research funded by government agencies—required to seek advice from colleagues. Special committees exist in hospitals, universities, school systems, and other institutions to evaluate research studies on the basis of risks and benefits. This evaluation involves weighing the costs of the research to participants in terms of inconvenience and possible psychological or physical harm against the value of the study for advancing knowledge and improving the child's life situation. If there are any risks to the safety and welfare of the child or family that the research does not warrant, priority is always given to the participants.

Section Summary

Ethical and Pragmatic Issues

- Research in abnormal child psychology must meet certain standards that protect children and families from stressful procedures, including informed consent and assent, voluntary participation, confidentiality and anonymity, and nonharmful procedures.

- To ensure that research meets ethical standards, researchers seek advice from colleagues and have their research evaluated by institutional ethics review committees. The final responsibility for the ethical integrity of any research project is with the investigator.

Study Resources

SECTION SUMMARIES

KEY TERMS

4

Assessment, Diagnosis, and Treatment

If there is anything that we wish to change in the child, we should first examine it and see whether it is not something that could better be changed in ourselves.

—C. G. Jung

PRELIMINARY EDITION

CHAPTER PREVIEW

OST CHILDREN AND ADOLESCENTS referred for assessment and treatment have multiple problems. More often than not, the accumulation of these problems over time results in a referral. We have emphasized that most childhood disorders involve breakdowns in normal development. Felicia (see below), for example, is having difficulty coping with the demands of adolescence—gaining autonomy from her parents, getting along with peers, performing well in school, establishing her self-identity, and regulating her emotions. Felicia also experienced the added stress of her mother's hospitalization for pneumonia.

The clinician who sees Felicia will need to evaluate how well Felicia can cope with life events; her appraisal of the events; her physical status, cognitive abilities, behavioral skills, and personality; and support from her parents, teachers, or peers. To sort out the importance of these complex and interacting forces, we must devise an effective plan of assessment that leads to diagnostic and treatment decisions. We will be revisiting Felicia's case throughout the chapter to see how we address these issues.

CLINICAL ISSUES

In this chapter, we emphasize the clinical strategies and methods used to assess children with psychological and behavioral problems, and the various approaches to the classification and diagnosis of childhood disorders. We also provide a brief introduction to treatment—a topic that we will discuss in detail for the individual disorders in the chapters that follow. We begin this important overview of clinical issues with a look at the decision-making process that surrounds assessment, diagnosis, and treatment.

The Decision-Making Process

How do we determine whether Felicia has a psychological disorder that requires professional attention or whether she will simply outgrow or overcome her problems on her own? Mental health clinicians have to systematically consider many important questions to understand a child's basic problem(s) and to make diagnoses and devise treatment plans. In many ways, this process is like good detective work. It requires sorting through the many factors that bring a child or adolescent to the attention of professionals, and checking out alternative hypotheses and plans. This ongoing decision-making process is aimed at finding answers to both immediate and long-term questions about the nature and course of the child's disorder and its optimal treatment (Mash, 2006).

The decision-making process typically begins with a clinical assessment. **Clinical assessments** use systematic problem-solving strategies to understand children with disturbances and their family and school

FELICIA

Multiple Problems

Felicia seemed unhappy and withdrawn at home and at school.

Felicia, age 13, was referred because of her depression, school refusal, social withdrawal at home and school, and sleep disturbance. Her parents first noticed her recent difficulties about a year ago, just after her mother was hospitalized for pneumonia. Felicia was in a regular eighth-grade class and began to refuse to attend school. She complained of frequent stomach pains before school as a reason not to attend. Her social behavior also got worse at this time. She wanted to be close to her mother at all times and frequently requested her mother's help with homework or chores. Felicia became extremely quiet, appeared sad and unhappy, and withdrew from social activities. Not long afterward, she began to complain of sleep problems and a loss of appetite. At about this time her grades in school dropped from mostly Bs to Cs and Ds. She reported that no one liked her, that she couldn't do anything well, and that her life was hopeless.

Based on Depression, by D. J. Kolko, 1987. In M. Hersen and V. B. Van Hasselt (Eds.), Behavior Therapy with Children and Adolescents: A Clinical Approach, p. 160.

Clinical assessment is like good detective work.

© Cengage Learning®

environments (Mash & Hunsley, 2007). Strategies typically include an assessment of the child's emotional, behavioral, and cognitive functioning, as well as the role of environmental factors (Sattler & Hoge, 2006). These strategies—which should be based on scientific evidence and clinical expertise—form the basis of a flexible and ongoing process of hypothesis testing regarding the nature of the problem, its causes, and the likely outcomes if the problem is treated as opposed to leaving it untreated (Haynes, Smith, & Hunsley, 2011).

Clinical assessment is much broader than interviewing or testing alone. The ultimate goal of assessment is to achieve effective solutions to the problems children and their families face, and to promote and enhance their well-being. *Clinical assessments are meaningful to the extent that they result in practical and effective interventions.* In other words, a close and continuing partnership between assessment and intervention is vital; they should not be viewed as separate processes (Mash & Hunsley, 2005; Youngstrom, 2013).

The focus of clinical assessment is to obtain a detailed understanding of the *individual* child or family as a unique entity (e.g., Felicia and her family), referred to as **idiographic case formulation**. This is in contrast to a **nomothetic formulation**, which emphasizes broad general inferences that apply to large *groups* of individuals (e.g., children with a depressive disorder). A clinician's nomothetic knowledge about general principles of psychological assessment, normal and abnormal child and family development, and specific childhood disorders is likely to result in better hypotheses to test at the idiographic level (Haynes, Mumma, & Pinson, 2009).

As you can imagine, the process of decision-making is similar to studying for several exams at the same time. You must be familiar with fundamental information in areas such as childhood depression or specific learning disorders and then be able to integrate this knowledge in new ways to make it applicable to help solve a particular problem. Like studying for exams, this process at first seems like you are trying to cram everything into a funnel to distill what is most important. Unlike studying for exams, however, working with children and families and applying your training and experience to new situations is often very enjoyable!

Clinicians begin their decision making with an assessment, which can range from a clinical interview with the child and parents to more structured behavioral assessments and psychological testing. Keep in mind that assessment is not something done *to* a child or family—it is instead a collaborative process in which the child, family, and teacher all play active roles. Because adults play a critical role in defining the child's problem and providing information, it is particularly important to establish a rapport with them, and active family and teacher involvement are important for both assessment and intervention (Dowell & Ogles, 2010).

Developmental Considerations

Diversity is the one true thing we all have in common. Celebrate it every day.

—Anonymous

In assessing children and families, one needs to be sensitive to the child's age, gender, and cultural background as well as to normative information about both typical and atypical child development. Such knowledge provides the clinician with a context for evaluating and understanding the behavior and circumstances of an individual child and family.

Age, Gender, and Culture

A crucial building block for assessment and treatment is recognizing diversity within children's developmental functions and capacities at various ages. How might Felicia's age, gender, or cultural background influence our approach to assessment, diagnosis, and treatment?

School refusal in a 13-year-old like Felicia is significant because it results in missed educational and social opportunities. In contrast, a 13-year-old's refusal to travel by airplane may be inconvenient or distressing, but in most cases would not have the same serious consequences as missing school. A child's age has implications not only for judgments about deviancy but also for selecting the most appropriate assessment and treatment methods. For example, at what age can a child provide reliable information in an interview? With respect to treatment, how might time-out for misbehavior for a 3-year-old differ from time-out for a school-age child?

Like age, the child's gender also has implications for assessment and treatment. Numerous studies have reported gender differences in the rates and expression of childhood disorders (Bell, Foster, & Mash, 2005). As shown in Table 4.1, some childhood disorders and conditions are more common in males than in females, others are more common in females than in males, and still others are equally common in the two sexes (Rutter, Caspi, & Moffitt, 2003). In general, boys are about three to four times more likely than girls to display early-onset disorders such as autism spectrum disorder (ASD) and attention-deficit/hyperactivity disorder (ADHD), whereas girls are more likely than boys to display disorders that have their peak onset in adolescence, such as depression and eating disorders (Martel, 2013).

As we have emphasized, most childhood disorders are identified and defined by adults, usually because adults find the child's symptoms particularly salient or troublesome. In general, overactivity and aggression are more common in boys than in girls; girls tend to express their problems in less observable ways such as sadness, fear, and shame (Chaplin & Aldao, 2013). In fact, among the symptoms that best distinguish boys who are referred for treatment are "showing off or clowning" (as reported by parents) and "disturbing other pupils" (as reported by teachers) (Achenbach & Rescorla, 2001). Thus, boys may receive an excess of referrals, and girls may be overlooked because of their less visible forms of suffering. Our assessments and interventions must be sensitive to possible referral biases related to gender and gender differences. The difficulty in distinguishing between true gender differences and differences in reporting is illustrated by the finding that the rate of ADHD diagnoses during the early to mid-1990s increased approximately threefold among girls, as compared with twofold for boys (Robison et al., 2002). Could the rate of ADHD in girls possibly increase threefold during one decade? It is more likely that increasing recognition of the disorder and its various forms of expression in girls contributed to the dramatic increase in these ADHD diagnoses (Hinshaw & Blachman, 2005). In considering gender differences, it is critical to keep in mind that there is great variability not just between boys and girls but also within each group. In addition, gender differences in emotional expression and behavior have been shown to vary depending on the age of the child, the interpersonal context in which the child is observed, and the personal relevance and demands of the situation (Chaplin & Aldao, 2013).

The study of gender differences has contributed enormously to our understanding and assessment of childhood disorders (Rose & Rudolph, 2006). However, it is also extremely important to study both girls and boys as distinct groups in their own right. An exclusive focus on sex differences could delay careful study of the expression of and underlying processes associated with specific disorders in one group or the other (Hinshaw, 2008). For example, studies into social aggression in girls have found that when angry, girls show aggression indirectly through verbal insults, gossip, ostracism, getting even, or third-party retaliation—referred to as *relational aggression* (Crick & Rose, 2000). As girls move into adolescence, the function of their aggressive behavior increasingly centers on group acceptance and affiliation. When adjustment problems are studied in relation to the issues most salient for girls (e.g., relationships, body image), it has been shown that girls experience significant problems during childhood. These problems include relational aggression and also behaviors that are self-serving, directed outward, and intended to physically harm others. This combination of relational and physical aggression is the strongest predictor of future psychological–social adjustment problems in girls (Crick, Ostrov, & Werner, 2006). Interestingly, children who engage in forms of social aggression that are not typical of their sex (overtly aggressive girls and relationally aggressive boys) are significantly more maladjusted than are children who engage in gender-normative forms of aggression (Crick, 1997).

Finally, cultural factors must be carefully considered during assessment and treatment (Achenbach & Rescorla, 2007; Nikapota, 2009). There is a rapidly changing demographic and cultural landscape in the United States as its population becomes increasingly

TABLE 4.1 | **Gender Patterns for Selected Problems of Childhood and Adolescence**

More Commonly Reported among Males

Attention-deficit/hyperactivity disorder	Autism spectrum disorder
	Language disorder
Childhood conduct disorder	Specific learning disorder
Intellectual disability	Enuresis

More Commonly Reported among Females

Anxiety disorders	Eating disorders
Adolescent depression	Sexual abuse

Equally Reported among Males and Females

Adolescent conduct disorder	Feeding disorder
Childhood depression	Physical abuse and neglect

Source: Adapted from "Gender differences in the diagnosis of mental disorders: Conclusions and controversies of DSM-IV," by C. M. Hartung and T. A. Widiger, 1998, *Psychological Bulletin*, 123, 260–278. Copyright © 1998 by the American Psychological Association. Reprinted with permission. APA is not responsible for the accuracy of this translation.

Biology and socialization interact to create different interests and behavior profiles of girls and boys.

multiracial and multicultural. By 2030, European-Americans in the United States will no longer constitute the majority among children under 18 years of age, and this is already true in children under 8 years of age (U.S. Census Bureau, 2013). Consequently, cultural sensitivity in the assessment, diagnosis, and treatment of children with emotional and behavioral problems and their families has become increasingly important (Pumariega et al., 2013). Consistent with this view is the expanded cultural emphasis in the most recent revision of the *Diagnostic and Statistical Manual of Mental Disorders* DSM (DSM-5; APA, 2013). The DSM-5 includes a framework for developing a cultural formulation of the child's disorder based on the child and family's cultural identity; their cultural concepts of distress; psychosocial stressors and cultural features of vulnerability and resilience; cultural aspects of the relationship between the child, family, and clinician; and an overall cultural assessment including a culturally appropriate plan for treatment. To assist, the DSM-5 also contains a "Cultural Formulation Interview," with a module for children and adolescents, to gather information about the impact of culture on the child's presenting problems and implications for treatment (APA, 2013; available at www.psychiatry.org/practice/dsm/dsm5/online-assessment-measures).

Cultural patterns reflect learned behaviors and values that are shared among members, are transmitted to group members over time, and distinguish the members of one group from those of another group. Culture can include ethnicity, language, religious or spiritual beliefs, race, gender, socioeconomic status (SES), age, sexual orientation, geographic origin, group history, education and upbringing, and life experiences.

Children who are ethnic minorities may have a greater risk of being misdiagnosed or underdiagnosed. For example, one study found that psychiatrically hospitalized African American adolescents were more often diagnosed with organic/psychotic disorders and less often diagnosed with mood/anxiety disorders than Caucasian teens (Kilgus, Pumariega, & Cuffe, 1995). In addition, African American and Hispanic children are less likely than white children to receive treatment (Zimmerman, 2005). Culturally competent assessment and treatment practices require that clinicians examine their own belief systems and the culturally based assumptions that guide their clinical practice.

A cultural formulation is necessary to establish a relationship with the child and family, motivate family members to change, obtain valid information, arrive at an accurate diagnosis, and develop meaningful recommendations for treatment. Ethnic identity and racial socialization are key factors to consider in the assessment of all children and families, including those from the dominant culture (Dishion & Stormshak, 2007b).

Cultural syndromes refer to a pattern of co-occurring, relatively invariant symptoms associated with a particular cultural group, community, or context (APA, 2013). For example, *mal de ojo* or the "evil eye" is a concept that is widespread throughout Mediterranean cultures and Latino communities throughout the world. A malady to which children are especially vulnerable and believed to be caused by a hateful look or glance from a malicious person, the evil eye can cause fitful sleep, crying without apparent cause, diarrhea, vomiting, and fever in children. Cultural syndromes rarely fit neatly into one Western diagnostic category (Alarcón, 2009). In addition, although the cross-cultural validity of Western diagnostic criteria varies widely depending on the disorder, data regarding their validity across cultures for many childhood disorders is lacking (Canino & Alegria, 2008). Therefore, it is important that clinicians assess the extent to which a child's cultural background and context affect the expression of both individual symptoms and clinical disorders. Although cultural syndromes may not be recognized as disorders in the culture in which they occur, distress and other illness features may still be recognized by an outside observer (APA, 2013).

What is considered abnormal child behavior may vary from one cultural group to the next (Serafica & Vargas, 2006). For example, a child's shyness and over-sensitivity are likely to lead to peer rejection and social maladjustment in Western cultures, but the same qualities may be associated with leadership, school competence, and educational achievement in Chinese children (Chen, Rubin, Li, & Li, 1999). In addition, it may be difficult to engage parents from some cultures if mental health issues are seen as particularly taboo, if intervention into personal family matters by strangers is viewed negatively, or if the causes of the illness in that culture are seen as physical or spiritual (Yasui & Dishion, 2007).

In negotiating assessment and treatment plans with children and families who may not share the clinician's concept of mental illness, a clinician must recognize the diversity that exists across and within racial and ethnic groups in lifestyle and patterns of acculturation (i.e., level of adaptation to dominant culture versus background culture). Generalizations about cultural practices frequently fail to capture these regional, generational, SES, and lifestyle differences. For example, SES level is a major confound in findings of differences in rates of psychopathology between various cultures because ethnic minority cultures are frequently overrepresented in low SES populations (Glover & Pumariega, 1998). An individual's acculturation level can also significantly

Recognizing diversity across and within ethnic groups is an important role of the clinician.

impact assessment and subsequent interventions. The lower the level of one's acculturation, the higher one scores on measures of psychopathology, particularly in conjunction with low SES and education level (Cuéllar, 2000). Having an awareness of the cultural customs and values that can affect behaviors, perceptions, and reactions to assessment and treatment, as well as recognizing the major confound of SES with these factors, puts the clinician in a better position to develop a meaningful assessment and intervention strategy.

Normative Information

Felicia's school refusal and sad mood started after her mother's hospitalization. Is Felicia's reaction normal for a stressful life event? How common are these symptoms in girls her age after a brief period of separation from a parent? Felicia also withdrew from social contact and experienced sleep disturbances. Adolescence is a time of biological and social upheaval for many youths. Therefore, we need to know whether Felicia is different from other girls her age with respect to these problems; if she is different, when should we become concerned and take action?

Knowledge, experience, and basic information about norms of child development and behavior problems are the crucial beginning to understanding how children's problems or needs come to the attention of professionals. As many parents discover, figuring out what to expect of their children at various ages can be challenging. Parents are faced with determining what difficulties are likely to be chronic versus those that are common and transient, deciding when to seek advice from others, and determining what treatment is best for their child. Immigrant parents can have even more difficulty with these tasks when trying to assess their second-generation child's behavior as the child attempts to navigate at least two different cultures (Falicov, 2003).

Isolated symptoms of behavioral and emotional problems generally show little correspondence with children's overall adjustment. Usually, the *age inappropriateness, severity,* and *pattern* of symptoms, rather than individual symptoms, define childhood disorders. Also, the extent to which symptoms result in impairment in the child's functioning is a key consideration. Nevertheless, certain symptoms do occur more frequently in children referred for assessment and treatment. Table 4.2 provides examples of parent- and teacher-rated symptoms that occur more frequently or in more extreme forms in children ages 6 to 18 who are referred for treatment and that best discriminate them from same-age children who are not referred for treatment. As you can see, these symptoms are relatively common behaviors that occur to some extent in all children—sadness, a lack of concentration, and demands for attention top the list.

Purposes of Assessment

Children and families are assessed for one or more purposes. These purposes guide the assessment process, including decisions regarding the use of particular assessment methods. As described below, three common purposes of assessment are description and diagnosis, prognosis, and treatment planning (McLeod, Jensen-Doss, & Ollendick, 2013).

Description and Diagnosis

"Diagnosis is not the end but the beginning of practice."

–Fischer (1879–1962)

The first step in understanding a child's problem is to provide a **clinical description,** which summarizes the unique behaviors, thoughts, and feelings that together make up the features of the child's psychological disorder. A clinical description attempts to establish basic information about the child's (and usually the parents') concerns at presentation, especially how the child's behavior or emotions are different from or similar to those of other children of the same age, sex, socioeconomic, and cultural background.

If you conducted an evaluation of Felicia, what information would be most important to include in your clinical description? You would start by describing how her behavior differs from normal behavior of girls her age. First, assessing and describing the *intensity, frequency,* and *severity* of her problem would communicate a sense of how excessive or deficient her behavior is, under what circumstances it may be a problem, how often it does or does not occur, and how severe the occurrences are. Second, you would need to describe the *age at onset* and *duration* of her difficulties. Some problems are transient and will spontaneously remit, while others persist over time. Like frequency and intensity, age at onset and duration of the problem behavior must be appraised with respect to what is considered normative for a given age. Finally, you would want to convey a full picture of her *different symptoms and their configuration.* Although Felicia needed help because of particular problems at school and with her peers, you need to know the full range, or profile, of her strengths and weaknesses to make informed choices about the likely course, outcome, and treatment of her disorder.

After establishing an initial picture of Felicia's presenting symptoms, you would next determine whether this description meets the criteria for diagnosis of one or more psychological disorders. **Diagnosis** means analyzing information and drawing conclusions about the nature or cause of the problem, or assigning a formal diagnostic label for a disorder. Does Felicia meet standard diagnostic criteria for a major depressive disorder and, if so, what might be the cause?

Diagnosis has acquired two separate meanings, which can be confusing. The first meaning is *taxonomic diagnosis,* which focuses on the formal assignment of cases to specific categories drawn from a system of classification such as the DSM-5 (APA, 2013) or from empirically derived traits or dimensions (discussed later in this chapter) (Achenbach & Rescorla, 2001). *Problem-solving analysis,* the second, much broader meaning of diagnosis, is similar to clinical assessment and views diagnosis as a process of gathering information that is used to understand the nature of an individual's problem, its possible causes, treatment options, and outcomes.

Thus, Felicia's assessment will involve a complete diagnostic (problem-solving) analysis to get the most comprehensive picture possible. In addition, Felicia may receive a formal diagnosis of *major depressive*

TABLE 4.2 | **Parent- and Teacher-Rated Problems That Best Discriminate between Referred and Nonreferred Children**

• Unhappy, sad, or depressed	• Poor schoolwork
• Can't concentrate	• Inattentive
• Demands attention	• Stubborn
• Disobedient at school	• Moody
• Doesn't get along with others	• Sulks
• Impulsive	• Temper
• Nervous	

Based on Achenbach, T. M. and Rescorla, L. A. (2001), Manual for the ASEBA School-Age Forms & Profiles, ISBN 978-0-938565-73-4. Burlington, VT: University of Vermont, Research Center for Children, Youth, and Families) p. 144.

"They're trying to figure out whether it's a chemical thing or I'm just a crybaby."

disorder (discussed in Chapter 10), which means that she possesses characteristics that link her to similar youths presumed to have the same disorder (taxonomic diagnosis). A secondary diagnosis of an anxiety disorder, such as separation anxiety disorder or school refusal, may be necessary for Felicia, since comorbidity of depression and anxiety is very common among girls her age. Comorbidity exists when certain disorders among children and adolescents are likely to co-occur within the same individual, especially disorders that share many common symptoms (see Chapter 3). Awareness of one disorder alerts us to the increased possibility for another disorder. Some of the more common comorbid disorders are conduct disorder and ADHD, ASD and intellectual disability, and childhood depression and anxiety (Drabick & Kendall, 2010).

Prognosis and Treatment Planning

Prediction is very difficult, especially if it's about the future.

—Attributed to Niels Bohr (1885–1962)

Prognosis is the formulation of predictions about future behavior under specified conditions. If Felicia does not receive help for her problem, what will likely happen to her in the future? Will her problems diminish as she gets older, or will they get worse?

Naturally, parents and others immediately want to know the possible short- and long-term outcomes for their child and what events might alter such projections. Remember that many childhood concerns, such as fears, worries, and bed-wetting, are common at certain ages, so any decision to treat a child's particular problem must be based on an informed prognosis. Clinicians must weigh the probability that circumstances will remain the same, improve, or deteriorate with or without treatment, as well as what course of treatment should be followed.

In addition, treatments for children and adolescents often focus on enhancing the child's development rather than merely on removing symptoms or restoring a previous level of functioning. In Felicia's case, for example, an assessment might reveal that she has poor social skills, so intervention plans might focus on efforts to teach her these skills in a concerted fashion to reduce the chances of continuing social relationship difficulties. A prognosis based on careful assessment can also serve to inform parents and others about the importance of doing something now that may reduce the likelihood of major problems later.

Treatment planning and evaluation means using assessment information to generate a plan to address the child's problem and to evaluate the effectiveness of the treatment. Felicia's mother keeps her daughter home from school when Felicia complains of stomach pains. She also does Felicia's homework. Does this information suggest a possible course of action? Felicia thinks she can't do anything well. Will helping her to change this and other irrational beliefs make a difference in her depression? When action is taken, how can we evaluate whether it is having the desired effect?

Treatment planning and evaluation may involve further specification and measurement of possible contributors to the problem, determination of resources and motivation for change, and recommendations for the treatments likely to be the most feasible, acceptable, and effective for the child and family. For example, are Felicia's parents unintentionally rewarding her physical complaints and school refusal by giving her extra attention when she doesn't go to school? Is Felicia willing to discuss with a therapist why she refuses to go to school? Are her parents willing to set limits on her behavior despite a history of struggle and failure with previous attempts?

Section Summary

Clinical Issues

- Clinical assessment is directed at differentiating, defining, and measuring the child's behaviors, cognitions, and emotions of concern, the environmental circumstances that may contribute to these problems, and the child's strengths and competencies.

- Assessments are meaningful to the extent that they result in effective interventions; a close and continuing partnership must exist between assessment and intervention.

- Age, gender, and culture influence how children's symptoms and behavior are expressed and recognized, and have implications for selecting the most appropriate methods of assessment and treatment.

(continues)

- The age inappropriateness, the severity, and the pattern of symptoms, rather than individual symptoms, usually define childhood disorders.

- Three purposes of assessment are: (1) description and diagnosis that determine the nature and possible causes of the child's problem, (2) prognosis that predicts future behavior under specified conditions, and (3) treatment planning and evaluation.

ASSESSING DISORDERS

If something exists, it exists in some amount. And if it exists in some amount, then it is capable of being measured.

–René Descartes

Not everything important can be measured, and not everything that can be measured is important.

–Albert Einstein

If you were planning to assess Felicia's problems, where would you begin and what might you include in your assessment? Should you interview Felicia, both parents, and her teacher? Do you need to observe Felicia at home? At school? Are there psychological tests or questionnaires to help you pinpoint Felicia's strengths and weaknesses, such as intelligence, emotion regulation, concentration, social skills, and learning ability?

You'll quickly recognize how massive the decision-making process can seem. In view of this complexity, many clinical settings use a multidisciplinary team approach to assessment. Psychological test administration and interpretation experts work with others to generate the most complete picture of a child's mental health needs. Multidisciplinary teams may include a psychologist, a physician, an educational specialist, a speech pathologist, and a social worker.

Some children may need to be referred for a medical exam as part of a comprehensive assessment to investigate whether a physical problem is related to their disorder. For example, a physiological problem may be causing a particular child's bed-wetting or sleep disorder. A thorough medical assessment by a physician could evaluate Felicia's stomach pains, sleep disturbances, and weight loss and be used to determine whether Felicia's depression was related to drug use or a general medical condition such as hypothyroidism (low levels of thyroid hormones).

Ideally, the clinical assessment of children experiencing difficulties relies on a **multimethod assessment approach,** which emphasizes the importance of obtaining information from different informants in a variety of settings and using a variety of methods that include interviews, observations, questionnaires, and tests. Deciding which assessment is best for a specific case is based on whether the assessment is for diagnosis, treatment planning, or treatment evaluation; on whether the problem is observable (like aggression) or internal (like anxiety); and on the child's and family's characteristics and abilities. In addition, the methods used need to be reliable, valid, cost-effective, and useful for treatment (Hunsley & Mash, 2008).

Clinical assessment consists of many strategies and procedures designed to help understand the child's thoughts, feelings, and behaviors as they occur in specific situations. Clinical interviews are usually conducted with the parents and child separately or in a family interview, and they help establish a good working relationship with the child and family. They are also extremely useful in obtaining basic information about existing concerns as viewed by the child and family members and in pinpointing directions for further inquiry. Behavioral assessments, checklists and rating scales, and psychological tests are then used in accordance with a decision-making approach. Information is also obtained from teachers and other significant individuals who interact with the child in various settings. The purpose is to obtain the most complete picture possible in order to develop and implement an appropriate treatment plan, within the limits of available resources.

A comprehensive assessment requires that some consideration be given to evaluating the child's strengths and weaknesses in areas ranging from basic language and self-care skills to coping and leadership abilities. If our detective work suggests that a particular area of functioning deserves closer scrutiny, then a more in-depth assessment of that area is warranted. However, if initial assessments indicate that certain areas of functioning are not a problem, then further assessments may not be necessary. For example, for a child who performs poorly in school, an assessment of intellectual functioning and academic performance is essential. On the other hand, for a child who experiences difficulties at home but is doing fine at school, assessment of intellectual and academic functioning may be unnecessary. Keep in mind that the most comprehensive assessment procedures will have little clinical impact if they are not practical to use in the settings in which youths with mental health problems are typically assessed. Thus, practitioners and policy makers more and more are seeking assessment protocols that are cost-effective and feasible to use in real-world service delivery settings (Ebesutani et al., 2012).

Clinical Interviews

Children and adolescents don't usually refer themselves for treatment. Typically, they are referred because of the impact of their behavior on others. Thus, they often do not understand why they are seeing a mental health profession, and in fact they may not even experience any distress or recognize any cause for concern. (To be fair, some adults are like this, too!) The initial clinical interview can be very important not only in obtaining information, but also in setting the stage for collaboration and cooperation among the child, family members, and other concerned parties.

The clinical interview is the assessment procedure usually used with parents and children. However, based on interviewers' theoretical orientations, styles, and purposes, interviews may vary considerably in terms of the kinds of information obtained and the meaning assigned to that information (Sattler & Mash, 1998). Interviews allow professionals to gather information in a flexible manner over many sessions. The findings can then be integrated with more time-consuming assessments, such as family observations or psychological testing.

Clinical interviews use a flexible, conversational style that helps the child or parent to present the most complete picture possible. Interviewees will be encouraged to tell their stories with minimal guidance, which permits the children and parents to convey their thoughts and feelings in ways that approximate how they think in everyday life. During the clinical interview, the interviewer may observe nonverbal communications by the child and parent, such as facial expressions, body posture, voice, mannerisms, and motor behavior. These informal observations can provide the clinician with additional insights

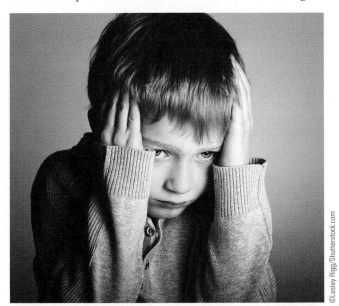

Children's initial reactions to seeing a mental health professional are often ones of fear and resistance.

©Lesley Rigg/Shutterstock.com

into the parent–child relationship that may be relevant in determining the presenting problem and the direction for treatment planning.

Clinical interviews can provide a large amount of information during a brief period. For example, during an hour-long interview with a parent, much detail about the child's developmental history, likes and dislikes, behavioral strengths and deficits, responses to discipline, relationships with others, and school performance can be obtained—far more than would be learned by observing the parent and child interacting for the same amount of time (Sattler, 1998).

Many clinicians develop their own style for engaging school-age children and adolescents in discussing their situation. We often use video games, crafts, and similar enticements to help the child feel more comfortable. When younger children are referred, it may be more appropriate to involve one parent in a joint game or activity. Younger children are more likely to "be themselves" with their parents than with a stranger. (For this age group, drawing, coloring, and similar fun activities are almost always successful in initiating a new relationship.) Also, because of their developmental level, younger children or children with intellectual disabilities may be capable of providing only general impressions of their internal states, behavior, and circumstances.

Depending on the child's age, you may want to adopt a child-friendly approach for the interview that fits with the child's developmental status, the nature of the problem, and the interview purpose. The interview typically will attempt to elicit information about the child's self-perceptions and perceptions of others, and to obtain samples of how the child responds in a social situation with an adult. Children's views of why they were brought to the clinic, their expectations for improvement, and their understanding of the assessment situation are all important to consider, along with the manner in which they interpret significant events such as divorce or family violence. Engaging unwilling children can be difficult. Since other people typically seek help on behalf of the child, some children and adolescents may feel that they do not have a problem and therefore they see no need to be interviewed.

What questions would you ask Felicia's parents? Perhaps you want to know how long Felicia's reluctance to separate from her parents has been a concern and whether help has been sought previously. You might also want to discuss the exact nature of the problems her parents are concerned about and to provide them with some indication of the next steps in the assessment and treatment process.

Developmental and Family History

Initial assessments often include a **developmental history** or **family history,** in which information is obtained from the parents regarding potentially significant developmental milestones and historical events that might impact the child's current difficulties. Often this information is gathered via a background questionnaire or interview that typically covers the following areas (Sattler, 1998):

▶ *The child's birth and related events,* such as pregnancy and birth complications or the mother's use of drugs, alcohol, or cigarettes during pregnancy

▶ *The child's developmental milestones,* such as age at which walking, use of language, bladder and bowel control, and self-help skills started

▶ *The child's medical history,* including injuries, accidents, operations, illnesses, and prescribed medications

▶ *Family characteristics and family history,* including the age, occupation, cultural background, and marital status of family members and the medical, educational, and mental health history of parents and siblings

▶ *The child's interpersonal skills,* including relations with adults and other children, and play and social activities

▶ *The child's educational history,* including schools attended, academic performance, attitudes toward school, relations with teachers and peers, and special services

▶ *The adolescent's work history and relationships,* including relationships with others of the same sex and the opposite sex

▶ *A description of the presenting problem,* including a detailed description of the problem and surrounding events, and how parents have attempted to deal with the problem in the past

▶ *The parents' expectations* for assessment and treatment of their child and themselves

Here is part of the developmental and family history given by Felicia's parents:

FELICIA

History

Her parents reported that Felicia was the result of an unplanned pregnancy following an initial miscarriage, the adoption of a son, and the birth of a sister. The pregnancy and Felicia's early life were described as uncomplicated and generally happy. Felicia reached developmental milestones late, required extra assistance with tasks, was quite reserved and uncommunicative, and experienced speech articulation problems. Her parents said they tended to "baby" Felicia, since she was seen as "slow." She was similarly described as developmentally immature by her teachers. As a result, she had repeated the first grade even though her attendance and academic performance were consistently good.

Felicia's adopted brother, age 23, attended a local college and lived at home. Her sister, age 16, also lived at home and attended high school. Felicia's mother had trained to become a registered nurse; her father held a Ph.D. in chemistry and managed the research department of a large company. No significant problems were reported for the other children, with the exception of some difficulty on the part of the brother in establishing independence.

Felicia's mother described experiencing a significant depression after each of her pregnancies and following her own father's death the previous year, a loss that was reported to have been very painful for Felicia also. Felicia's father reported no difficulties and was considered a stable and dependable person.

Based on Depression, by D. J. Kolko, 1987. In M. Hersen and V. B. Van Hasselt (Eds.), Behavior Therapy with Children and Adolescents: A Clinical Approach, pp. 163–164.

Many events presented in this developmental and family history may be relevant to the assessment of Felicia's current problems and must be explored as the assessment proceeds. For example, the babying described by Felicia's parents may reflect a more general pattern of overdependency on her parents that is contributing to her school refusal. The significant depression experienced by Felicia's mother following her pregnancies may suggest a family risk for depression. The death of Felicia's grandfather a year earlier may have been a triggering event, leading to a mood disturbance in both Felicia and her mother. During the early stages of assessment, these are hypotheses; as evidence accumulates with ongoing detective work, hypotheses can be supported or rejected as indicated by new data.

Semistructured Interviews

Most interviews with children and parents are unstructured. Clinicians use their preferred interview style and format, as well as their knowledge of the disorder, to pursue various questions in an informal and flexible manner. Unstructured clinical interviews provide a rich source of clinical hypotheses. However, their lack of standardization may result in low reliability and selective or biased gathering of information. To address this problem, clinicians sometimes use **semistructured interviews** that include specific questions designed to elicit information in a relatively consistent manner regardless of who is conducting the interview. The format of the interview usually ensures that the most important aspects of a particular disorder are covered. An appealing feature of semistructured interviews, especially for older children and youths, is that they can be administered by computer, something many children find entertaining and often less threatening at first than a face-to-face interview. The semistructured format also permits the clinician to follow up on issues of importance that may emerge during the interview. For younger children, a semistructured interactive interview using hand puppets may provide useful information about the child's emotional, behavioral, and peer problems (Ringoot et al., 2013).

The consistency and coverage of semistructured interviews may be offset by a loss of spontaneity between the child and the clinician, especially if the interview is conducted too rigidly. Under such circumstances, children and adolescents may be reluctant to volunteer important information not directly relevant to the interviewer's questions. With appropriate modifications that make the interview process easier to follow, however, semistructured interviews are reliable and very useful in assessing a wide range of children's symptoms (Edelbrock, Crnic, & Bohnert, 1999). Sample questions from a semistructured interview for young people like Felicia who are experiencing depression are presented in Table 4.3.

Behavioral Assessment

The clinical interviews described in this chapter are valuable in eliciting information from parents and school-age children. They provide an initial look at how the child and family think, feel, and behave and an initial hypothesis with regard to the factors that might be contributing to the child's problems. However, it is often necessary to obtain a firsthand look at the child's behavior in everyday life situations at home or at school or to ask someone who sees the child on a regular basis to observe the child's behavior.

Behavioral assessment is a strategy for evaluating the child's thoughts, feelings, and behaviors in specific settings, and then using this information to formulate hypotheses about the nature of the problem and what can be done about it (Haynes & Heiby, 2004). Behavioral assessment frequently involves observing the child's behavior directly, rather than inferring how children think, behave, or feel on the basis of their descriptions of inkblots or the pictures they draw.

Using behavioral assessment, the clinician or another person who sees the child regularly identifies **target behaviors,** which are the primary problems of concern, with the goal of then determining what specific factors may be influencing these behaviors. Sometimes this is a

TABLE 4.3	Semistructured Interview Questions for an Older Child or Adolescent with Depression

Depressed Mood/Irritability

- Do you feel sad?
- Do you get moody?

Loss of Interest

- Have you lost interest in doing things, like your hobbies?
- Is there anything you look forward to doing?

Self-Deprecatory Ideation

- Do you feel that you are worthless?
- Have you thought about committing suicide?

Sleep Disturbances

- Do you have trouble sleeping lately?
- Do you need more sleep than usual lately?

Change in School Performance

- Do you have trouble concentrating in school?
- Have you ever refused to go to school?

Decreased Socialization

- Have there been any changes in your relationships with friends?
- Do you feel a need to be alone?

Somatic Symptoms

- Do you get pains in your stomach?
- Do you get muscle pains and aches?

Loss of Usual Energy

- Do you feel you have less energy to do things?
- Do you often feel tired?

Change in Appetite and/or Weight

- Do you have to force yourself to eat?
- Has there been a change in your weight?

Based on Clinical and Forensic Interviewing of Children and Families: Guidelines for the Mental Health, Education, Pediatric, and Child Maltreatment Fields by J. M. Sattler, pp. 938-940.

straightforward task, as with a child who complains of illness every Monday morning and, as a result, is kept out of school for the day (sound familiar?). In other cases, the child displays multiple problems at home or school. Felicia's school refusal appears to be part of a larger pattern of difficulties that includes social withdrawal, depression, and possibly separation anxiety.

Even the seemingly simple task of identifying what is bothering a child can be a challenge. Remember that an adult usually decides that the child has a problem and that the child should be referred for an assessment. Adults often disagree about the nature of the child's problem, especially when they observe children in different settings (De Los Reyes & Kazdin, 2005). Ratings by various people may be influenced by differences between their cultures and that of the child. For example, when teachers rate youths from another cultural background, they are more likely to rate them higher on behavioral and emotional problems than are the teachers who have a similar background, the parents, or the children themselves (Skiba, Knesting, & Bush, 2002). Further, a child's presenting problem can often be very different from the one eventually identified as the target for intervention.

A commonly used and simple framework for organizing findings in behavioral assessment has been dubbed the "ABCs of assessment":

A = Antecedents, or the events that immediately precede a behavior

B = Behavior(s) of interest

C = Consequences, or the events that follow a behavior

In Felicia's case we might observe the following sequence: (A) Whenever Felicia's mother asks her to go to school (antecedent), (B) Felicia complains that she has stomach pains and refuses to go (behaviors), and (C) her mother lets Felicia stay home (consequence). This antecedent–behavior–consequence sequence might suggest that Felicia is being reinforced for her physical complaints and school refusal by not having to go to school. In addition, because there are no positive consequences for going to school and no negative ones for staying at home, Felicia might act this way on future school days. The ABCs of assessment can be used to organize information in specific contexts, as just described, or as an overall framework for assessment.

Behavior analysis or **functional analysis of behavior** is the more general approach to organizing and using assessment information in terms of antecedents, behaviors, and consequences (Hanley, Iwata, & McCord, 2003). As shown in ● Figure 4.1, functional analysis can be used to identify a wide range of antecedents and consequences that might be contributing to Felicia's school refusal and depression. The antecedents and consequences for Felicia's behavior include events in the immediate situation (a reduction in anxiety), more remote occurrences (being teased at school), events in the external environment, and Felicia's inner thoughts and feelings.

The goal of functional analysis is to identify as many factors as possible that could be contributing to a child's problem behaviors, thoughts, and feelings and to develop hypotheses for the factors that are most important and/or the most easily changed. In some cases, hypotheses can be confirmed or rejected by changing the antecedents and consequences to see whether the behavior changes. For example, we might teach Felicia to relax when thinking about going to school in order to reduce her anxiety (changing an antecedent) to see whether this decreases her school refusal. Or she could be instructed to substitute more positive self-statements ("I can succeed in school") for her negative ones ("I'm no good at anything") to see whether this decreases her depressive symptoms and raises her self-esteem. In these examples, you can see a close interplay between assessment and intervention when carrying out a functional analysis.

The process of gathering information about the child's behavior in specific settings takes many different forms. Often it involves either asking the parent, teacher, or child about what goes on in specific situations or observing the child. Clinicians develop their initial hypotheses based on information provided by the parents and the child during the interview; they pursue their hypotheses further using behavioral assessments, such as behavior checklists and rating scales and observations of behavior in real life or in role-play simulations. In general, behavioral assessment can be viewed as an approach to organizing assessment information for an individual child and developing hypotheses for treatment (Francis & Chorpita, 2004).

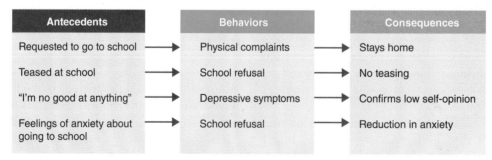

Antecedents	Behaviors	Consequences
Requested to go to school →	Physical complaints →	Stays home
Teased at school →	School refusal →	No teasing
"I'm no good at anything" →	Depressive symptoms →	Confirms low self-opinion
Feelings of anxiety about going to school →	School refusal →	Reduction in anxiety

● **FIGURE 4.1** | Functional analysis: antecedents, behaviors, consequences.

Checklists and Rating Scales

Reports concerning child behavior and adjustment can be obtained using global checklists and problem-focused rating scales. Global behavior checklists are used to ask parents, teachers, and sometimes the youths themselves to rate the presence or absence of a wide variety of child behaviors or to rate the frequency and intensity of these behaviors.

Unlike a clinical interview, the use of a well-developed checklist is strengthened by its known degree of standardization and by the opportunities to compare an individual child's score with a known reference group of children of a similar age and the same gender (Fernandez-Ballesteros, 2004). Checklists are economical to administer and score, and they provide a rich source of information about parents' or teachers' reports about children's behavior, including possible differences in the reports by parents in the same family and differences between parent and teacher reports. Keep in mind, however, that informants may differ in their views of the child's strengths and weaknesses because they interact with the child in different surroundings and circumstances. These discrepancies are not necessarily bad because they inform the clinician about the possible range of behavior in which the child engages, the possible circumstances that increase or decrease target behaviors, and the possibly unrealistic demands or expectations placed on the child.

Nevertheless, these discrepancies underscore the importance of obtaining information from multiple observers (Grigorenko, Geiser, Slobodskaya, & Francis, 2010).

The Child Behavior Checklist (CBCL) developed by Thomas Achenbach and his colleagues is a leading checklist for assessing behavioral problems in children and adolescents ages 6 to 18 (Achenbach & Rescorla, 2001). The CBCL is widely used in treatment settings and schools, and its reliability and validity has been documented in numerous studies. One form of the CBCL, which is completed by the parent, is often used in combination with teacher-completed and youth-completed checklists, classroom observations, and interviews designed to assess the same child behavior problems (Achenbach, 2009). A notable feature of the CBCL is that it has been used to assess children in 80 or more cultural groups throughout the world and as such provides a robust measure for evaluating immigrant, refugee, and minority children from diverse backgrounds (Achenbach et al., 2008).

The scales of the CBCL can be used to create a profile that gives the clinician an overall picture of the variety and degree of the child's behavioral problems. A CBCL profile derived from a checklist completed by Felicia's mother is shown in ● Figure 4.2. The profile shows that her major areas of concern about her daughter are with respect to symptoms of *anxious/depressed*

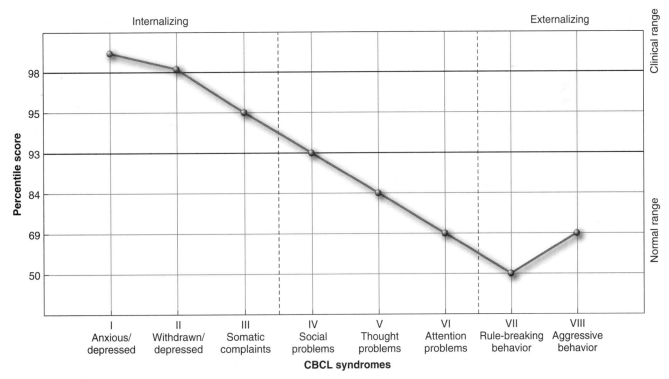

● **FIGURE 4.2** | Child Behavior Checklist (CBCL) profile for Felicia.

Based on Achenbach & Rescorla, 2001. Reference Crediting: Achenbach, T. M., & Rescorla, L. A. (2001). Manual for the ASEBA school-age forms & profiles. Burlington: University of Vermont, Research Center for Children, Youth, and Families.

(e.g., "fears school," "cries a lot"), *withdrawn/depressed* (e.g., "rather be alone," "enjoys little"), and *somatic complaints* (e.g., "feels dizzy," "aches"). Felicia's scores on these dimensions are extreme, and place her in the upper 5% or higher (clinical or near-clinical range) as compared with girls of a similar age.

Brief problem checklists based on scales such as the CBCL may also be administered to children and caregivers in a brief rating scale or interview format. These checklists provide a practical and cost-effective way to assess ongoing progress in treatment and to consider modifying treatment if our assessments indicate a lack of progress (Achenbach et al., 2011; Chorpita et al., 2010). Other checklists assess progress in relation to a small number of "top problems" identified by the child or parents as important (Weisz et al., 2011).

In addition to checklists such as the CBCL that span a wide range of behavior problems, other rating scales focus mainly on specific disorders—depression, anxiety, ADHD, ASD, or conduct problems—or on particular areas of functioning, such as social competence, adaptive behavior, or school performance (Mash & Barkley, 2007). Children are usually rated by parents and teachers. Self-report checklists, administered in an engaging, child-friendly manner to increase the child's interest in the material, is another option. We like to administer questionnaires to adolescents by computer, simply because they find this approach more interesting. With younger children, we like to hand them a card showing the range of responses they may have, using happy or sad faces and similar images that appeal to that age group. Rating scales provide the clinician with a look at specific problems that is more focused than that provided by a global behavior checklist. You will see many examples of rating scales used to assess specific problems in the chapters to follow.

Behavioral Observation and Recording

Since some children are not old enough or skilled enough to report on their own behavior, parents, teachers, or clinicians may keep careful records of specific target behaviors. Parents or other observers typically record *baseline* (prior to intervention) data on one or two problems that they wish to change—for example, how often their child complies with their requests or how often he or she throws a temper tantrum (Dishion & Granic, 2004). Portable electronic devices that cue the parent or older child to record and rate the intensity of specific symptoms or behaviors "in the moment" at various times during the day

can also provide valuable information (Whalen et al., 2011).

Recordings by parents have the advantage of providing ongoing information about behaviors of interest in life settings that might not otherwise be accessible to observation by the clinician. Parental monitoring may also provide secondary benefits that are not directly related to assessment—teaching parents better observation skills, assessing parental motivation, and providing parents with realistic estimates of their child's rate of responding and feedback with regard to the effects of treatment. However, many practical problems may arise in asking parents to keep accurate records; for example, children often know when they are being watched and may not act in their usual way. A Closer Look 4.1 illustrates why observing behavior can be a useful part of any clinical assessment.

The clinician may also set up a *role-play simulation* in the clinic to see how the child and family might behave in daily situations encountered at home or school or in a problem-solving situation, such as figuring out how to play a game together (Roberts & Hope, 2001). When observing families who have physically abused their preschool-age child, for example, we choose activities most likely to elicit both parent–child cooperation and conflict: We first ask parents to play with their child so that we can observe their teaching style; then we ask them to have the child put away her or his favorite toys, which often results in noncompliance and conflict.

In Felicia's case, role-play simulations were used to assess her social skills. The clinician first described the situation to Felicia as follows: "You're sitting in the school cafeteria eating lunch by yourself when Maria, a girl from your math class, comes over to your table and sits across from you." Next, the clinician takes the role of Maria and says, "Hi Felicia. How's your lunch?" Felicia then responds, and the interaction continues, giving the clinician a chance to directly observe Felicia's social skills in a situation that might come up in everyday life.

Remember, direct observation is not foolproof. Clinicians must take into account the informant, the child, the nature of the problem, and the family and cultural context because any of these issues can distort the findings. Despite its limitations, direct observation is a valid and beneficial step in the decision-making process for most families who voluntarily seek assistance and understand what may be required to conduct a thorough assessment and treatment plan. Direct observation can be quite helpful in assessing less motivated families as well.

Observing Behavior: Seeing the Whole Picture

Sometimes observations of a child with his or her parent can be extremely illuminating. Recently, the mother of Sammy, a 4-year-old child with severe behavior problems, came to one of our clinics for assistance. During the interview she told the clinician that her son was "impossible to get dressed," and "doesn't listen to a thing I say to him." She had been told by a family member that Sammy seemed "hyperactive," and her family doctor had requested a psychological assessment as a result of her insistence on this diagnosis.

A note from his preschool teacher painted a very different picture of this young boy. His teacher spoke frankly of Sammy's undeveloped skills at following directions or concentrating on a task for any length of time, but pointed out how he settled down much like the other children once he found something that he enjoyed to do. This boy seemed calm during our visit with him at the clinic, so we decided to get a clearer picture of the situation by visiting his home and school.

When we visited the home, the problem stood out within minutes. His home was littered with his toys and games, which his mother let him rummage through and toss around the room freely. Attempts to get her to provide some structure to his play and other activities resulted in an immediate confrontation between the two—he simply turned away and grabbed the toys he wanted, and she became upset and started to chase after him, yelling at him to put his toys away. "See," she said, turning to the observer, "he doesn't do a thing I ask him to do." The boy clutched his toys and quieted down at this point, turned on the TV, and plunked himself in front of it.

Similar attempts on Sammy's part to avoid doing what his teacher asked were observed during our school visit, although his teacher was more successful at getting him back to the activity at hand by using praise and other positive rewards.

Obviously, the description this mother gave us of her son's behavior lacked a few of the details that make an accurate diagnosis possible. Her description also failed to mention how upset she got when Sammy "didn't listen" and that the home

Observing behavior directly assists in obtaining an accurate picture of the child's behavior under certain circumstances

environment was rather chaotic and unstructured for a child his age. If we had not made this home observation visit, our assessment of the problem and recommendations for treatment might have been quite different; we may have attributed his misbehavior primarily to hyperactivity, as the mother initially led us to assume. Instead, we developed strategies to teach the mother how to structure her home in a child-friendly manner, how to spend time playing with her son, and how to encourage his compliance by starting with simple requests and using the positive rewards of praise, attention, and activities he enjoyed.

Source: Based on authors' case material.

Psychological Testing

A **test** is a task or set of tasks given under standard conditions with the purpose of assessing some aspect of the child's knowledge, skill, or personality. Most tests are standardized on a clearly defined reference group—for example, children of a certain age, sex, or SES, referred to as a *norm group*. An individual child's scores can then be compared with the scores of a comparable group of children to determine the extent to which that child's scores deviate from the norm. The prevalence and visibility of test use in our culture have led some people to adopt the mistaken view that testing and psychological assessment

are one and the same. Although tests play an important role in a child's assessment, they represent only one part of the overall decision-making process.

It is also important to keep in mind that many psychological tests, because they may have been "normed" on narrow and limited samples, may not be appropriate to use with individuals from racial, ethnic, or cultural groups other than those with whom the tests were normed. It has also been argued that many standardized tests, particularly intelligence and achievement tests, are culturally biased, unfairly penalizing children whose family, SES, and cultural background are different from those of Euro-American middle-class children.

These and other valid criticisms have led to improved tests. For example, test developers now select normative groups that are representative of the population, and test items that are as free of cultural bias as possible. In addition, several professional organizations have joined together to develop a Code of Fair Testing Practices, which presents guidelines for professionals for "fulfilling their obligation to provide and use tests that are fair to all test takers regardless of age, gender, disability, race, ethnicity, national origin, religion, sexual orientation, linguistic background, or other personal characteristics" (Joint Committee on Testing Practices, 2004, p. 2). As a result of these efforts, clinicians have become increasingly sensitive to the role of cultural factors in test administration and interpretation (Sattler, 2008).

Clinicians commonly use developmental scales, intelligence and educational tests, projective tests, personality tests, and neuropsychological tests to assess children's disorders of development, learning, and behavior (Sattler & Hoge, 2006). In fact, tests (particularly intelligence tests) are among the most frequently used assessment methods with children (Cashel, 2002). Remember, however, that test scores should always be interpreted in the context of other assessment information. Often, observations of a child's behavior during the test situation can tell us as much or more about the child as his or her test scores.

Developmental Testing

Developmental tests are used to assess infants and young children, and are generally carried out for the purposes of screening, diagnosis, and evaluation of early development. **Screening** refers to identifying children at risk, who are then referred for a more thorough evaluation. Infants and young children at risk for developing later mental health problems are now being assessed more frequently. This is the result of a growing recognition of the importance of early identification, intervention, and prevention, which in turn, have resulted in new laws and public policies requiring such screening (National Infant & Toddler Child Care Initiative, 2010; Wissow et al., 2013). As we discuss in Chapter 6, early screening of children for ASD in primary care settings is now seen as a key to early intervention. Because screening tests are brief, a more thorough assessment of a young child's development is also needed.

Intelligence Testing

Evaluating a child's intellectual and educational functioning is a key ingredient in clinical assessments for a wide range of childhood disorders (Sattler, 2008). For some children, impairments in thinking and learning may result from their behavioral or emotional problems. The drop in Felicia's grades from Bs to Cs and Ds was likely a function of the impact of her school refusal

and depression on her school performance. For other children, particularly those with intellectual disability or language and specific learning disorders, problems in thinking and learning may be part of the disorder itself.

In many other cases, the nature of the relationship between the child's disorder and disturbances in thinking and learning is less clear. For example, children with ADHD score lower on standard tests of intelligence and do more poorly in school than other children. Is this lowered performance related to their inattentiveness in the test situation or classroom, or to some other more basic deficit in how they process information? Intellectual and educational assessments can help answer some of these questions.

How would you define intelligence? In Western cultures, most people think intelligence involves problem-solving ability, verbal ability, and social intelligence. David Wechsler, whose test has come to be the one most frequently used to assess intelligence in children, defined intelligence as "the overall capacity of an individual to understand and cope with the world around him" (Wechsler, 1974, p. 5). This definition is consistent with the theories on which commonly used intelligence tests are based. Although debate remains about how to define *intelligence*, intelligence tests are primarily used in clinical settings to identify children who may have difficulty succeeding in a regular classroom and to plan interventions.

Numerous intelligence tests for children exist, each with its own strengths and weaknesses. The Wechsler Intelligence Scale for Children (WISC-IV), the most recent version of a test that was introduced over 60 years ago, is the most popular (Wechsler, 2003). The WISC-IV is made up of 10 mandatory and 5 supplementary subtests that span the age range of 6 to 16 years. According to Wechsler, these subtests assess the child's global capacity in different ways, but do not represent different types of intelligence. Relative to earlier versions, the WISC-IV places greater emphasis on fluid reasoning abilities, higher-order reasoning, and information-processing speed and less emphasis on possible externally or culturally influenced factors such as arithmetic knowledge (Prifitera, Saklofske, & Weiss, 2005). Tests to assess intelligence in younger children include the Wechsler Preschool and Primary Scale of Intelligence—III (WPPSI-R) (Wechsler, 2002), the Stanford–Binet intelligence scales, 5th edition (SB5) (Roid, 2003), and the Kaufman Assessment Battery for Children (K-ABC-II) (Kaufman & Kaufman, 2004).

Examples of questions and items included on each WISC-IV subtest are shown in A Closer Look 4.2. The WISC-IV is individually administered to the child by a highly trained examiner who follows prescribed procedures. The test produces a Full Scale IQ, derived from four indices: Verbal Comprehension Index,

Items Similar to Those Included in WISC-IV

I. Verbal Comprehension Index

Similarities (23 items)

> In what way are a pencil and a piece of chalk alike?
> In what way are tea and coffee alike?
> In what way are an inch and a mile alike?
> In what way are binoculars and a microscope alike?

Vocabulary (36 items)

> What is a ball?
> What does *running* mean?
> What is a poem?
> What does *obstreperous* mean?

Comprehension (21 items)

> Why do we wear shoes?
> What is the thing to do if you see someone dropping a package?
> In what two ways is a lamp better than a candle?
> In the United States, why are we tried by a jury of our peers?

Information (33 items)

> How many legs do you have?
> What must you do to make water freeze?
> Who developed the theory of relativity?
> What is the capital of France?

Word Reasoning (24 items)

The task is to identify the common concept being described with a series of clues.
Clue 1: This has a motor . . .
Clue 2: . . . and it is used to cut grass.

II. Perceptual Reasoning Index

Block Design (14 items)

The task is to reproduce stimulus designs using four or nine blocks (see below).

Picture Concepts (28 items)

The task is to choose one picture from each of two or three rows of pictures in such a way that all the pictures selected have a characteristic in common (see below).

Matrix Reasoning (35 items)

The task is to examine an incomplete matrix and select whichever of the five choices best completes the matrix (see below).

Picture Completion (38 items)

The task is to look at a picture—such as that of a car without a wheel, a scissors without a handle, or a telephone without numbers on the buttons—and identify the essential missing part (see below).

III. Working Memory Index

Digit Span (16 items; 8 in Digit Span Forward, 8 in Digit Span Backward)

In one part, the task is to repeat in a forward direction a string of from 2 to 9 digits presented by the examiner (example: 1–8). In the other part, it is to repeat in a backward direction a string of from 2 to 8 digits (example: 6–4–9).

Letter-Number Sequencing (10 items, each with 3 trials)

The task is to listen to a string of from 2 to 8 letters and digits (example: 1–b) and repeat it back with the numbers in ascending order followed by the letters in alphabetical order (example: e–6–d–9 would be repeated back as 6–9–d–e).

Arithmetic (34 items)

> If I have one piece of candy and get another one, how many pieces will I have?
> At 12 cents each, how much will 4 bars of soap cost?
> If suits sell for 1/2 of the regular price, what is the cost of a $120 suit?

(continues)

(continued)

IV. Processing Speed Index

Coding *(59 items in Coding A and 119 items in Coding B)*
The task is to copy symbols from a key (see below).

1	2	3	4	5	6
x	o	=	L	/	V

2	4	1	5	6	3	5	2	1	6	4	3

Symbol Search *(45 items in Part A and 60 items in Part B)*
The task is to decide whether a stimulus figure (a symbol) appears in an array (see below).

⌂ ◇	☼ □ ◇ ± △ = ¤	YES	NO
☼ ±	◇ △ ± □ = ¤ ⌂	YES	NO
= ¤	△ ⌂ ☼ □ ± x ◇	YES	NO

Cancellation *(2 items, one Random and one Sequenced)*
The task is to scan both a random arrangement and a sequenced arrangement of pictures and mark target pictures (animals) within a specified time limit (see below).

Note: All of the above items resemble those that appear on the WISC-IV but are not actually from the test.

Based on Sattler, J. M., Assessment of Children: WISC-IV and WPPSI-III Supplement, Exhibit 9–1 in Assessment of Children: Cognitive Foundations, Sixth Edition, 2008 (pp. 268–269).

Perceptual Reasoning Index, Working Memory Index, and Processing Speed Index. The profile of these four abilities represents key indicators of the cognitive strengths and weaknesses considered important to the assessment of learning disabilities, executive functions, attention disorders, traumatic brain injuries, intellectual disability, giftedness, and various other medical and neurological concerns (Prifitera et al., 2005). Nevertheless, the best evidence indicates that the overall general intelligence score should be favored over the individual indices when interpreting the WISC-IV (Watkins, 2010). True to tradition, IQ scores on the WISC-IV are good predictors of academic achievement.

Felicia obtained a Verbal Comprehension IQ score of 107, a Perceptual Reasoning Index score of 105, a Working Memory Index score of 104, a Processing Speed Index score of 105, and a Full Scale IQ score of 106 on the WISC-IV, which means that her intelligence is in the average range. With this information, the clinician next considers how her test scores relate to each other and whether there is a pattern to the results that might clarify her relative strengths and weaknesses. He or she must also consider any circumstances in the testing situation that might have affected Felicia's performance—anxiety, personality factors, motivation, or medication—and how her scores compare with those of other girls of comparable age, grade, ethnic group, or disability. Finally, and most important, the clinician must consider how the test scores will be used in treatment and educational planning. To assist with treatment planning modified versions of the core and supplemental WISC-IV subtests may be used to gather additional information about how

and why a child obtained a low score on one or more of the subtests (Benson, Hulac, & Bernstein, 2013).

Projective Testing

Projective tests present the child with ambiguous stimuli such as inkblots or pictures of people, and the child is asked to describe what she or he sees. The hypothesis is that the child will "project" his or her own personality—unconscious fears, needs, and inner conflicts—onto the ambiguous stimuli of other people and things. Without being aware, the child discloses his or her unconscious thoughts and feelings to the clinician, thus revealing information that would not be shared in response to direct questioning (Leichtman, 2004). Many "junior-sized" versions of projective tests have been developed for younger children, for whom the ambiguous stimuli have been made child-friendly by incorporating family scenes or pictures of animals (Levitt & French, 1992).

Projective testing has generated more controversy over the past century than any other clinical assessment method. Most clinicians have strong views about projective testing, either pro or con. You may very well have your own strong opinions about the Rorschach inkblot and similar methods. Some clinicians believe that projective tests provide a rich source of information about the child's coping styles, affect, self-concept, interpersonal functioning, and ways of processing information (Mihura et al., 2013). Other clinicians see them as inadequate with respect to meeting minimum standards for reliability and validity (Lilienfeld, Wood, & Garb, 2006; Wood et al., 2000).

100 **PART 1** Understanding Abnormal Child Psychology

Despite the controversy surrounding their use, projective tests continue to be one of the most frequently used clinical assessment methods (Cashel, 2002). Representative of the many projective techniques used with children and adolescents are human figure drawings, the Rorschach inkblot test, and thematic picture tests, in which children are asked to tell a story in response to pictures of children in everyday situations with their families, peers, or alone. Clinicians may also attempt to assess the child's inner life through play—for example, through the use of puppets, storytelling, or other material (Chethik, 2000). Although they are not formal projective tests, play and drawings are presumed by some clinicians to function in much the same way as projective tests—as a window into the child's unconscious processes.

Personality Testing

Personality is usually considered an enduring trait or pattern of traits that characterize the individual and determine how he or she interacts with the environment (Roberts & DelVecchio, 2000). For example, children who withdraw from social contact may be characterized by their parents as shy; others who are socially busy are characterized as outgoing. In a sense, a child's early temperament provides a foundation on which personality is built (discussed in Chapter 2). Several dimensions of personality have been identified, including whether a child or adolescent is timid or bold, agreeable or disagreeable, dependable or undependable, tense or relaxed, reflective or unreflective (Shiner, 2007). These central dimensions of personality have been dubbed the "Big 5" factors (Mervielde & Fruyt, 2002). Many of the methods already discussed, such as interviews, projective techniques, and behavioral measures, provide some information about the child's personality. However, many objective inventories focus specifically on personality, using either the child or a parent as the informant. Two personality inventories frequently used with children are the Minnesota Multiphasic Personality Inventory—Adolescent (MMPI-A) (Butcher et al., 1992/2006) and the Personality Inventory for Children, Second Edition (PIC-2) (Lachar, 1999). Examples of the type of content that may be included in personality inventories are shown in Table 4.4.

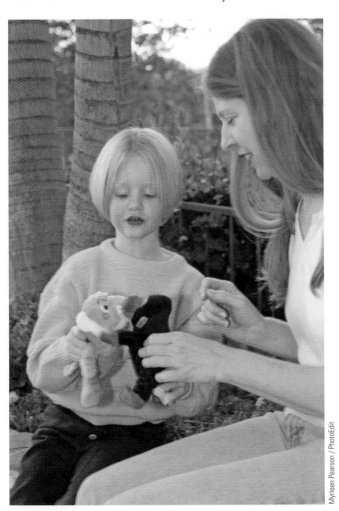

Some clinicians may use puppets or other play materials to engage young children in the assessment.

Myrleen Pearson / PhotoEdit

TABLE 4.4 | **Self-Report of Personality Scale Definitions**

Construct	Definition
Anxiety	Feelings of nervousness, worry, and fear; the tendency to be overwhelmed by problems
Attitude to school	Feelings of alienation, hostility, and dissatisfaction regarding school
Attitude to teachers	Feelings of resentment and dislike of teachers; the belief that teachers are unfair, uncaring, or overly demanding
Atypicality	The tendency toward bizarre thoughts, or other thoughts and behaviors considered odd
Depression	Feelings of unhappiness, sadness, and dejection; a belief that nothing goes right
Interpersonal relations	The perception of having good social relationships and friendships with peers
Locus of control	The belief that rewards and punishments are controlled by external events or people
Relations with parents	A positive regard toward parents and a feeling of being esteemed by them
Self-esteem	Feelings of self-esteem, self-respect, and self-acceptance

Based on Behavior Assessment System for Children, Second Edition (BASC-2).

Neuropsychological Assessment

Put simply, neuropsychology is the study of brain–behavior relations (Pennington, 2009). In the clinical context, **neuropsychological assessment** attempts to link brain functioning with objective measures of behavior known to depend on an intact central nervous system. For example, try closing your eyes and then touching the tip of your nose with your ring finger, first with your right hand and then with your left. How do you think you would do on this task if you were sleep-deprived? Even a simple task like this one depends on many psychological functions as well as on an intact nervous system. For children with certain brain injuries or dysfunctions, carrying out this or other tasks may prove difficult.

The premise underlying neuropsychological assessments is that behavioral measures can be used to make inferences about central nervous system dysfunction and, more important, the consequences of this dysfunction for the child. Neuropsychological assessments use this information clinically for determining a diagnosis, planning treatment, documenting the course of recovery, measuring subtle but significant improvements, and performing follow-up care with children who have neurological impairments or learning disorders (Reynolds & Fletcher-Janzen, 2009).

Neuropsychological assessments usually consist of comprehensive batteries that assess a full range of psychological functions: verbal and nonverbal *cognitive functions* such as language, abstract reasoning, and problem solving; *perceptual functions* including visual, auditory, and tactile-kinesthetic; *motor functions* relating to strength, speed of performance, coordination, and dexterity; and *emotional/executive control* functions such as attention, concentration, frustration tolerance, and emotional functioning.

Although neuropsychological assessments were originally used to identify an underlying brain injury or process, this is no longer their primary purpose. The routine use of neuroimaging procedures (Chapter 3), combined with mixed or inconsistent neuropsychological findings, has turned the focus away from diagnosis and toward obtaining information about strengths and deficits in functioning. This information can lead to effective intervention for children with a wide range of neurodevelopmental and learning problems (Riccio, Sullivan, & Cohen, 2010).

Section Summary

Assessing Disorders

- Clinical assessment relies on a multimethod assessment approach, which emphasizes obtaining information from different informants in a variety of settings, using a variety of methods.
- The clinical interview continues to be the most universally used assessment procedure with parents and children.
- In unstructured interviews, interviewers use their preferred style and format to pursue various questions in an informal and flexible manner. In contrast, semistructured interviews include specific questions designed to elicit information in a relatively consistent manner regardless of who is conducting the interview.
- Behavioral assessment evaluates the child's thoughts, feelings, and behaviors in specific settings and uses this information to formulate hypotheses about the nature of the problem and what can be done about it.
- Reports concerning child behavior and adjustment can be obtained using global checklists and problem-focused rating scales. An individual child's scores can be compared with a known reference group of children of a similar age and the same gender.
- Tests are tasks given under standard conditions with the purpose of assessing some aspect of the child's knowledge, skill, or personality.
- Evaluating a child's intellectual functioning is a key ingredient in clinical assessments for a wide range of childhood disorders.
- Projective tests present children with ambiguous stimuli to assess their inner thoughts and feelings that reflect aspects of their personality.
- Objective personality tests assess traits such as whether a child is timid or bold, agreeable or disagreeable, dependable or undependable, tense or relaxed, reflective or unreflective.
- Neuropsychological assessment attempts to link brain functioning with objective measures of behavior that are known to depend on central nervous system functioning.

CLASSIFICATION AND DIAGNOSIS

Over the past two decades, major changes have occurred in the classification of childhood disorders (Rutter & Uher, 2012). By **classification,** we mean a system for representing the major categories or dimensions of child psychopathology, and the boundaries and relations among them. As you may recall, one definition of *diagnosis* refers to the assignment of cases to categories of a classification system.

We begin our discussion of this important topic by considering some of the reasons for classification and diagnosis with children and adolescents, and we will go into some detail about current approaches. Because diagnosis is not without criticism, we also raise awareness of the impact of labeling children. Until now, we have looked at Felicia's problems on a very individual basis. We looked at her depression, school refusal, and social skills deficits, and we assessed her general intellectual functioning and behavior. This information tells us what is unique about Felicia and how she differs from others her age. Isn't this enough, you might ask? Why do we need to pigeonhole Felicia by tagging her with a diagnostic label such as "major depressive disorder"? Can't we just find a way to help her with her problems based on what we have learned about her unique characteristics?

Treating every child as unique has its drawbacks: research into the causes and treatments of childhood disorders would be impossible to conduct, and we would have little direction about how to proceed in treating an individual (Waldman & Lilienfeld, 1995). For this reason, we also need to consider what Felicia has in common with others who present with similar problems or symptoms and whether there are general principles that apply to many children. In effect, we do this throughout this text, as we learn about the core symptoms of child and adolescent disorders, their prevalence and course, their associated features, their prognosis, and their treatment. Without such information to use for comparison, making the best decisions concerning Felicia's problem and course of action would be difficult.

As you may recall from our earlier discussion, clinical assessment and diagnosis involve two related strategies for determining the best plan for a given individual. We use an *idiographic* strategy to highlight a child's unique circumstances, personality, cultural background, and other features that pertain to his or her particular situation. Each child who comes in for an assessment has unique strengths and challenges that make his or her problem a little different from the "textbook" case.

In addition, we use a *nomothetic* strategy as part of our assessment in order to benefit from all the information accumulated on a given problem or disorder and to determine the general category for the presenting problem. That is, we attempt to name or classify the problem using an existing system of diagnosis, such as the DSM-5 (APA, 2013) or the ICD-10 (International Classification of Diseases, 10th rev.) Classification of Mental and Behavioural Disorders (World Health Organization [WHO], 1992/2010). Classifying the problem leads to a foundation of knowledge from which we can draw in an attempt to understand the child and family; classification also helps us to communicate with others and to select an intervention, preferably one shown by research to be effective for children with similar difficulties.

Although most of us recognize the advantages of classification for medical and psychological problems,

developing a classification system that is simple and concise enough to be of practical benefit is not an easy task (Taylor, 2011). In fact, despite years of effort, there is no single, agreed-upon, reliable, and valid worldwide classification system for childhood disorders. The DSM has become the standard in North America, but—although it has been used with children across a wide age range—concerns continue to be raised about its limited coverage of childhood disorders, the overlap in symptoms across different childhood disorders, and its insensitivity to the developmental complexities that characterize these problems (e.g., changes in symptom expression with age), particularly for very young children (Pine et al., 2011; Regier et al., 2011). As we discuss below, the DSM-5 has attempted to address these and other concerns, but not without controversy.

Categories and Dimensions

The first approach to diagnosing child psychopathology involves the use of categorical classification systems. **Categorical classification** systems such as DSM-5 are based primarily on informed professional consensus, an approach that has dominated and continues to dominate the field of child (and adult) psychopathology. A *classical* (or pure) categorical approach assumes that every diagnosis has a clear underlying cause, such as an infection or a malfunction of the nervous system, and that each disorder is fundamentally different from other disorders. Therefore, individual cases can be placed into distinctive categories.

We might say, for example, that Felicia meets the criteria for a major depressive disorder but not for separation anxiety disorder. The disadvantage to this approach, of course, is that children's behavior seldom falls neatly into established categories, so a certain degree of confusion remains. Moreover, categories of behavior (as opposed to some medical diseases) do not typically share the same underlying causes; thus, the mental health field has had to modify the classical categorical approach to accommodate the current state of knowledge. Children given the same diagnosis don't necessarily share the same etiology, nor do they respond to the same treatment. It is therefore crucial to understand that current diagnostic categories represent only our current knowledge about how symptoms cluster together.

The second approach to describing abnormal child behavior involves empirically based dimensional classification. **Dimensional classification** approaches assume that many independent dimensions or traits of behavior exist, and that all children possess them to varying degrees. For example, rather than saying that Felicia's symptoms fit the category of major depressive disorder, we might say that she is significantly above average (often referred to as being within the *clinical range*) on the dimensions of depression and anxiety. These and other traits or dimensions are typically derived using statistical methods from samples drawn from both clinically referred and nonreferred child populations to establish ranges along each dimension (Achenbach & Rescorla, 2001).

Although they are more objective and potentially more reliable than clinically derived categorical systems, dimensional approaches based on statistical data also have limitations. First and foremost, the derived dimensions are dependent on sampling, method, and informant characteristics, as well as on the age and sex of the child (Mash & Hunsley, 2007). Consequently, integrating information obtained from different methods, from various informants, and over time or across situations can be challenging (De Los Reyes et al., 2013). Dimensional approaches may also be insensitive to contextual influences. For example, suppose you were a parent and were asked to describe whether your child "acts too young" using the scale "never, sometimes, a lot." You might want to clarify the circumstances or context under which she sometimes acts too young ("whenever I take her grocery shopping" or "when she is playing with other children"). Dimensions provide a useful estimate of the degree to which a child displays certain traits and not others, yet they often have to be tailored to the child's unique circumstances and developmental opportunities.

Many dimensions of child psychopathology have been identified through research. These include the *externalizing behavior* and *internalizing behavior* dimensions, which reflect aggressive/rule-breaking behaviors and anxious/withdrawn/depressed behaviors, respectively. Some of the most common dimensions identified in children and adolescents are presented in Table 4.5, along with examples of specific associated problem behaviors.

Although the debate about which approach is "best" has not been resolved, there is a growing consensus that each approach has value in classifying childhood disorders and that a combined approach may be needed (Pickles & Angold, 2003). In fact, to some extent, current approaches attempt to do this. For example, the DSM-5 includes dimensional ratings of severity for categorical diagnoses such as ADHD and ASD, and items drawn from empirically derived dimensions such as "anxious/depressed" have been used to develop rationally derived DSM-oriented scales identified by experts from different cultures as being consistent with DSM categories. However, it is not yet known whether combining the two approaches makes an appreciable difference in diagnosis as compared with using just one approach or the other (Ebesutani

| TABLE 4.5 | Commonly Identified Dimensions of Child Psychopathology and Examples of Items That Reflect Each Dimension |

Anxious/ Depressed	Withdrawn/ Depressed	Social Problems
Cries a lot	Would rather be alone	Too dependent
Worries	Refuses to talk	Doesn't get along
Feels worthless	Secretive	with peers
Nervous, tense	Shy, timid	Gets teased

Somatic Symptoms	Thought Problems	Aggressive Behavior
Feels dizzy	Hears things	Argues
Overtired	Sees things	Mean to others
Aches, pains	Strange behavior	Attacks people
Headaches	Strange ideas	Destroys others' things

Attention Problems	Rule-Breaking Behavior	
Inattentive	Lacks guilt	
Can't concentrate	Bad companions	
Can't sit still	Lies	
Confused	Runs away from home	

Based on Achenbach, T. M. & Rescorla, L. A. (2001). Manual for the ASEBA School-Age Forms and Profiles. (Burlington, VT: University of Vermont, Research Center for Children, Youth, and Families, 2001.

et al., 2010). Some severe forms of intellectual disability may be best conceptualized as qualitatively distinct conditions (categories), whereas most other childhood disorders, such as depression or anxiety, may be best described as extreme points on one or more continuous dimensions.

Also, depending on whether the purpose is clinical diagnosis or research, one approach may be more useful than the other. A dimensional approach to conceptualizing psychological factors such as behavior, affect, and cognitive abilities among children is compatible with research methods that determine the degree of association between two or more variables. Therefore, a dimensional approach is often preferred by those conducting psychological research. A categorical approach, on the other hand, is often more compatible with clinical purposes, for which the objective is to incorporate the whole pattern of the child's behavior into a meaningful diagnosis and treatment plan. In addition, categories are useful for communicating among clinicians, and categorical diagnoses are often required for clinical decisions—for example, to determine a child's eligibility for specialized services. In light of the different types of information provided by dimensions and categories, it is important to incorporate dimensions into current diagnostic practices while also finding feasible ways to reach categorical decisions (Rutter, 2011b).

The *Diagnostic and Statistical Manual of Mental Disorders* (DSM-5)

We begin our discussion of the DSM-5 with a brief synopsis of the evolution of current systems of diagnosis to show how far we have come in recognizing mental disorders in children and adolescents. The terminology and focus of prior systems reflected the major theoretical views of mental illness at the time; a shift to a more objective, informed approach occurred by the 1990s and continues today.

Historical Context

The slow process of formal recognition of the prevalence and significance of mental disorders began in 1948, when the *International Classification of Diseases* (ICD-6) added a section on mental disorders (WHO, 1948). Because many thought that the early ICD system was inadequate, in 1952 the American Psychiatric Association (APA, 1952) developed its own *Diagnostic and Statistical Manual of Mental Disorders* (DSM-I), which was revised in 1968 (DSM-II) (APA, 1968). These first efforts were not a huge success, but they did launch a sustained effort to improve the classification of mental disorders, an effort that continues today. Unfortunately, children and adolescents were neglected in the early versions of DSM; most childhood disorders were relegated to the adult categories, with the exception of mental retardation (intellectual disability), schizophrenia–childhood type, and transient disturbances in behavior or mood.

The DSM-III and DSM-III-R (APA, 1980, 1987) provided significant advances over the earlier versions. They discarded psychodynamic assumptions about etiology used in the earlier versions in favor of an atheoretical descriptive approach based on observable signs and symptoms. Clinical descriptions were replaced by explicit diagnostic criteria that helped to increase diagnostic reliability. In addition, they included more child categories and placed a greater emphasis on empirical data. With these changes came a shift in diagnostic systems and causal models. Less focus was put on the disorder existing within the child alone, and more emphasis was placed on the surrounding context in which the problem occurred. The DSM-III-R was developed to be a *prototypical* classification system by

which a child could be diagnosed with a certain subset of symptoms without having to meet all symptom criteria. This was an important change, especially in view of the heterogeneity of symptoms associated with most childhood disorders (Mash & Hunsley, 2007). On the other hand, it also means that individuals with the same diagnosis can and often do show very different patterns of symptoms. Consider that there were nearly 150 million different ways for an individual to meet the DSM-III-R criteria for an antisocial personality disorder (Widiger, 1993). The DSM-IV was published in 1994, followed by a revision in 2000 (DSM-IV-TR). Many changes were made to the classification system, the criteria sets for diagnosis, and the descriptive text in order to keep up with new research, correct factual errors, and provide new information.

DSM-5 Disorders

The DSM-5 was published in 2013, nearly two decades after the DSM-IV. The child and adolescent knowledge base has changed dramatically in the past 20 years. These changes necessitated conceptual, diagnostic, and procedural revisions, which are described in later chapters on disorders. We first introduce you to DSM-5 disorders that apply to children and adolescents. The first grouping, *Neurodevelopmental Disorders,* is shown in Table 4.6, and will be discussed in detail in the chapters to follow. Historically, these disorders were thought of as first occurring in childhood or as exclusive to childhood. However, it is now apparent that these early-occurring disorders continue into adolescence and adulthood for many of those affected. In addition to

TABLE 4.6 | Neurodevelopmental Disorders

DSM-5
Intellectual Disabilities (Intellectual Disability [Intellectual Developmental Disorder] [mild, moderate, severe, profound], Global Developmental Delay)
Autism Spectrum Disorder (with or without accompanying intellectual or language impairment)
Communication Disorders (Language Disorder, Speech Sound Disorder, Childhood-Onset Fluency Disorder [Stuttering], Social [Pragmatic] Communication Disorder)
Specific Learning Disorder (with impairment in reading, written expression, or mathematics)
Attention-Deficit/Hyperactivity Disorder (predominantly hyperactive/impulsive predominantly inattentive, or predominantly combined presentation)
Motor Disorders (Developmental Coordination Disorder, Stereotypic Movement Disorder, Tourette's Disorder, Persistent (Chronic) Motor or Vocal Tic Disorder)

Source: Diagnostic and Statistical Manual of Mental Disorders, Fifth Edition. American Psychiatric Association.

their early age at onset, the grouping of these disorders is also based on a suggested overlap of risks (e.g., genetic, developmental trajectories) that are not shared by disorders in other groups (Andrews et al., 2009). This grouping also recognizes that neurodevelopmental disorders frequently have overlapping symptoms and that they often co-occur in the same individual (e.g., a comorbid diagnosis of ASD and ADHD, or ADHD and Specific Learning Disorder) (Pettersson et al., 2013).

Table 4.7 presents other major disorders that apply to children and adolescents. Under the DSM-5 guidelines, diagnostic criteria for nearly all disorders (e.g., ADHD, ASD, mood, anxiety, eating, sleep) can apply to children as well as adults and both groups can be diagnosed using essentially the same criteria with some adjustment for developmental factors such as age and context (e.g., PTSD for Children Age 6 Years or Younger). A child can (and often does) receive more than one DSM-5 diagnosis, with the principal diagnosis listed first (e.g., ADHD; anxiety disorder). You should not try to memorize all of these terms right now, but simply get a feel for the organization and coverage to follow in later chapters.

DSM-5 Specifiers

After assessment using DSM-5 diagnostic criteria, **specifiers** are used to describe more homogeneous subgroupings of individuals with the disorder who share particular features and to communicate information that is relevant to treatment of the disorder. Specifiers may be used to rate subtypes of the disorder, co-occurring conditions, or the course or severity of the disorder, as appropriate. Common examples are: a subtype specifier such as "Predominantly inattentive presentation" for a child with ADHD; a co-occurring condition specifier such as "language impairment" or "intellectual impairment" for a child with ASD; a course specifier such as "onset prior to age 10 years" for a child with conduct disorder; or a severity specifier such as "mild," "moderate," "severe," or "profound" for a child with intellectual disability (ID) (APA, 2013).

Specifiers may also be used to note general medical conditions relevant to the understanding or management of the individual's mental disorder. Because DSM-5 assumes that mental disorders are closely related to physical and biological factors, the purpose of specifying general medical conditions is to encourage thoroughness in evaluation and to enhance communication among health care providers. General medical conditions can be related to mental disorders in a variety of ways. In some cases, the disorder may play a direct role in the development of physical problems, such as a disruption in sleep due to depression. In other cases, a child's clinical disorder, such as anxiety, may be a psychological reaction to a medical condition, such as being diagnosed with childhood cancer or diabetes. Clearly, it is important to document the co-occurrence and temporal order of problems to gain an overall understanding and to develop an appropriate treatment plan for an individual.

TABLE 4.7 | Other Selected Disorders of Childhood and Adolescence

Disruptive, Impulse Control, and Conduct Disorders (Oppositional Defiant Disorder, Conduct Disorder [childhood-onset or adolescent-onset type; with limited prosocial emotions], Antisocial Personality Disorder) **DSM-5**
Depressive Disorders (Disruptive Mood Dysregulation Disorder, Major Depressive Disorder, Persistent Depressive Disorder [Dysthymia])
Bipolar Disorders (Bipolar I Disorder, Bipolar II Disorder, Cyclothymic Disorder)
Anxiety Disorders (Separation Anxiety Disorder, Selective Mutism, Specific Phobia, Social Anxiety Disorder [Social Phobia], Panic Disorder, Agoraphobia, Generalized Anxiety Disorder)
Obsessive–Compulsive and Related Disorders (Obsessive-Compulsive Disorder, Body Dysmorphic Disorder, Hoarding Disorder, Trichotillomania [Hair-Pulling Disorder], Excoriation [Skin-Picking] Disorder)
Trauma- and Stressor-Related Disorders (Reactive Attachment Disorder, Disinhibited Social Engagement Disorder, Post-Traumatic Stress Disorder [PTSD] including PTSD for Children 6 Years and Younger, Acute Stress Disorder, Adjustment Disorders)
Feeding and Eating Disorders (Pica, Rumination Disorder, Avoidant/Restrictive Food Intake Disorder, Anorexia Nervosa, Bulimia Nervosa, Binge Eating Disorder)
Elimination Disorders (Enuresis, Encopresis)
Sleep-Wake Disorders (Insomnia Disorder, Hypersomnolence Disorder, Narcolepsy, Breathing-Related Sleep Disorders, Parasomnias)
Somatic Symptoms and Related Disorders (Somatic Symptom Disorder, Illness Anxiety Disorder, Conversion Disorder, Psychological Factors Affecting Other Medical Conditions, Factitious Disorder (including imposed on self and imposed on another)
Others: Substance-Related and Addictive Disorders, Personality Disorders

Source: Diagnostic and Statistical Manual of Mental Disorders, Fifth Edition. American Psychiatric Association.

Other Considerations

In making a diagnosis, it is also important to consider *psychosocial and environmental problems* that may affect the diagnosis, treatment, and prognosis of clinical disorders. Such problems include negative life events, environmental disruptions or deficiencies, family or other interpersonal stress, and lack of social support or personal resources. Typically, clinicians note only the problems that have been present over the past year, unless prior events—for example, an automobile accident—have likely contributed to the mental disorder. Contextual factors, such as child abuse or parental unemployment, are potentially important for understanding an individual's behavior and emotions. We remind you of this important consideration throughout our discussion of various disorders of childhood and adolescence because a child's presenting problem is often better understood if we can see the whole picture. Although DSM-5 did not develop its own classification of psychosocial and environmental problems, it refers clinicians to selected codes from the most current version of the ICD (ICD-10; WHO, 1992/2010).

Based on our clinical assessment Felicia was given the DSM-5 diagnosis of "Major Depressive Disorder, single episode," with "mild anxious distress," and a current severity rating of "Moderate" (based on the number and intensity of her symptoms and her impairment in social and school functioning). A diagnosis of Major Depressive Disorder (MDD), which we discuss in Chapter 10, was made because Felicia showed symptoms of depressed mood, loss of interest in almost all activities, significant weight loss, insomnia nearly every night, and feelings of worthlessness that persisted for more than 2 weeks and represented a change from her previous functioning. These symptoms were causing significant distress and impairment in Felicia's social and school functioning. We also noted that Felicia was experiencing mild anxious distress based on her reports of feeling tense and finding it difficult to concentrate on most days when she was depressed. Although the loss of her grandfather may have been a factor in Felicia's depression, it did not seem to be the major factor accounting for her symptoms.

Criticisms of DSM-5

Although DSM-5 includes numerous improvements over previous versions because of its greater emphasis on empirical research and more explicit diagnostic criteria sets, it is not faultless. Because DSM-5 focuses on descriptions of symptoms as the basis for generating categories, it has been criticized for failing to capture the complex adaptations, transactions, and setting influences that we have identified as crucial to understanding and treating psychopathology in children (Mash & Hunsley, 2007). DSM-5 also gives relatively less attention to disorders of infancy and childhood than to those of adulthood, and it fails to fully capture the interrelationships and overlap known to exist among many childhood disorders.

A further difficulty with DSM-5 diagnostic criteria for children is the relative lack of emphasis on the situational and contextual factors surrounding and contributing to various disorders in making a clinical diagnosis (Beauchaine, 2003). This reflects the fact that DSM-5 views a mental disorder as an individual psychopathology or risk for psychopathology, rather than in terms of problems in psychosocial adjustment or adaptation. However, DSM-5 explicitly gives much greater consideration than did its predecessors to factors such as culture, age, and gender that are associated with the expression of each disorder, and it has increased its recognition of the importance of family problems and extrafamilial relationship difficulties. In all likelihood, this awareness of the context for childhood disorders will encourage a greater sensitivity to developmental factors in diagnosing these disorders.

A different type of criticism deals with how DSM-5 is used rather than with the classification system itself. In some cases, DSM-5 categorical diagnoses can be an impediment to gaining proper services to address children's needs. For example, to qualify for a special education class, a child may be required to meet specific diagnostic criteria for a specific learning disorder. In the "typical" case, such requirements are usually met. However, some children may not have developed problems to the degree that they meet specific diagnostic criteria, or their problems may relate to more than one DSM category. These children may not qualify for services that otherwise could prove beneficial. It might be difficult to access programs to *prevent* future problems from developing in these at-risk children.

Finally, there are broader concerns about current classification systems such as DSM-5. One concern is that current systems contain excessively large numbers of diagnostic categories of limited validity, particularly in relation to improving treatment selection and outcomes (Uher & Rutter, 2012). A second is that they define disorders based on observable signs and symptoms that fail to map closely onto the underlying causes for these disorders. In response, the National Institute of Mental Health (NIMH) launched an initiative—the Research Domain Criteria (RDoC)—to classify mental disorders based on their biological origins

(Insel et al., 2010; Sanislow et al., 2010). The goal of RDoC is to develop future classification systems based on research findings for domains of functioning that map onto the underlying pathophysiology of the disorder rather than onto its observable symptoms. Preliminary work has defined various domains of functioning (e.g., cognitive systems, arousal/regulatory systems), broken down into specific constructs within domains (e.g., attention, circadian rhythms) that have units of analysis at the genetic, molecular, neural, and behavioral levels (Cuthbert & Kozak, 2013; Insel et al., 2010). We already know that many, if not all, of these levels of analysis will cut across disorders as they are currently defined, which suggests to some that an alternative approach based on underlying neurobiological systems is needed (Hayden & Mash, 2014).

RDoC proponents believe that this approach will eventually displace current classification systems and that laboratory-based approaches will supplant those classification systems in clinical assessment, leading to the identification of more precise and effective treatments (Insel, 2013; Insel et al., 2010). This is an ambitious goal in light of the currently limited ability of genetic and neuroimaging findings to predict treatment response or other important clinical outcomes; at present, most constructs that predict clinical outcomes (e.g., age at onset, negative life events) would be regarded as "psychological" or "behavioral" rather than biological (Hayden & Mash, 2014). The RDoC initiative is still in its infancy. It remains to be seen whether this approach will achieve its expressed objectives and also lead to a classification system that viable for use in clinical practice.

Pros and Cons of Diagnostic Labels

What's the use of their having names, the gnat said, "if they won't answer to them?" No use said Alice, "but it's useful to the people that name them, I suppose. If not, why do things have names at all?"

—Lewis Carroll, 1871

Despite every attempt to the contrary, the history of the classification of mental disorders has been fraught with disparaging and negative connotations that become attached to the labels used to describe these disorders (Hinshaw & Stier, 2008). The terms *moron*, *imbecile*, and *idiot*, for instance, were originally chosen in the

● **FIGURE 4.3** │ Classification of Child and Adolescent Disorders: 60 Years and Still Developing
Developments in child and adolescent diagnosis increased dramatically with the appearance of DSM-III in 1980. Current developments, such as the RDoC initiative, are focusing on the development of a classification system based on what we know about the genetic, brain, and other processes underlying child and adolescent disorders.

Source: Pine, D. (2013). A 60-Year Climb on the Mountain of Nosology. *Journal of the American Academy of Child & Adolescent Psychiatry, 55,* 1254.

early 1900s as neutral terms to describe lower levels of intellectual functioning, but they quickly became insults when they began to be used in common language. As a result, they gave way to terms such as *mental deficiency* and then *mental retardation,* which has now given way to the term *intellectual disability* for much the same reason. Stigma, it would seem, rapidly catches up with changes in terminology.

Much has been written about the positive and negative aspects of assigning diagnostic labels to children. On the positive side, labels help clinicians summarize and order observations, which can facilitate communication among professionals and sometimes aid parents by providing more recognition and understanding of their child's problem. Providing a label that communicates that the basis of the child's disorder is a condition (e.g., neurodevelopmental disorder) that is outside the control of the family or child and is not the result of something the parents did may also be welcomed. Moreover, descriptive labels are consistent with the natural tendency to think in terms of categories. That is, we tend to talk about ourselves, our friends, and our children as being happy, angry, depressed, or fearful, rather than use a number on a scale that signifies a range of emotion, even if a number might give a more accurate account. Finally, the use of descriptive terms or labels assists clinicians in locating a relevant body of detailed research and clinical data, and facilitates research on the causes, epidemiology, and treatment of specific disorders.

On the negative side are criticisms as to whether current diagnostic labels are effective in achieving any of the aforementioned purposes. There are also concerns about negative effects and stigmatization associated with assigning labels to children (Ben-Zeev, Young, & Corrigan, 2010; Hinshaw, 2007a). Public stigma and media messages allow negative attitudes to grow around children who are labeled. Once labeled, others may perceive and react to a child differently ("he's a hyperactive boy—you'll never get him to listen"). Classmates pick up on the use of labels, especially labels associated with visible treatments such as taking medication. A note sent by a classmate to a boy with ADHD reflects this: "Jack was ill, he took his pill, let's hope it makes him sit still." Standing out and being teased or bullied by other children may worsen the problem. Equally disturbing is that labels can negatively influence children's views of themselves and their behavior. In general, the reactions of others to persons who seem different or who have been diagnosed with a mental illness versus a physical illness reveal a tendency to generalize inappropriately from the labels (Corrigan, 2000; Martinez et al., 2011).

Section Summary

Classification and Diagnosis

- Classification refers to a system for representing the major categories of child psychopathology and the relations among them.
- Diagnosis refers to the assignment of cases to categories of the classification system.
- Childhood disorders have been classified using categories and dimensions.
- Categorical classification systems such as the DSM-5 have been based primarily on informed professional consensus and overt symptoms.
- Dimensional classification approaches assume that many independent dimensions or traits exist and that all children possess these to varying degrees.
- The terminology and focus of early classification systems reflected the major theoretical views of mental illness at the time; a shift to a more objective, informed approach occurred by the 1990s and continues today.
- The DSM-5 includes a number of neurodevelopmental disorders that have an onset in early childhood, as well as a broad range of other clinical disorders relevant to children.
- The DSM-5 incorporates the use of *specifiers* to define more homogeneous subgroupings of individuals with the disorder who share particular features and to communicate information that is relevant to treatment of the disorder.
- The DSM-5 has been criticized for failing to capture the complexity of child psychopathology, for giving less attention to disorders of infancy and childhood than to those of adulthood, for its relative lack of emphasis on situational and contextual factors, and for its emphasis on symptoms rather than on underlying etiology.
- Although diagnostic labels can facilitate communication among professionals, concerns have been raised about the negative effects and stigmatization associated with the assignment of labels to children.

TREATMENT AND PREVENTION

I have found the best way to give advice to your children is to find out what they want and then advise them to do it.

—Harry S Truman

Over the past two decades, effective treatment approaches for children and adolescents with behavioral and emotional problems and their families have grown tremendously in their sophistication and their breadth (Chorpita et al., 2011; Kaslow et al., 2012). Interventions today are planned by combining the most effective approaches to particular problems in an ongoing developmentally sensitive manner (Mash, 2006). Behavioral reward programs, for example, may be very useful for teaching parents of a young, difficult child ways to encourage desirable behavior. Once the child is a bit older, he or she may profit from cognitive–behavioral methods that address how the child thinks about social situations, such as making friends and avoiding conflicts.

A thorough clinical assessment and diagnosis constitute a critical first step in helping Felicia and other children who have psychological problems and their families. However, assessment and diagnosis are only the beginning of an ongoing helping process. We next must ask: "How can we help Felicia reduce her feelings of depression and hopelessness, eliminate her sleep disturbances and other somatic symptoms, increase her school attendance and performance, and improve her social skills and relationships with other children and her parents?" This is where intervention comes into play.

How do we determine the best type of intervention for children like Felicia and for those with other problems? We will consider this question in some detail for each disorder discussed in the chapters that follow; thus, our coverage of treatment and prevention in this section is intended to provide only a brief introduction. Our discussion of interventions in later chapters addressing specific problems follows from our general conviction that the most useful treatments are based on what we know about the nature, course, associated characteristics, and potential causes of a particular childhood disorder. However, this is not enough. We also need data to show that our interventions work (Silverman & Hinshaw, 2008). Interventions that zoom in on a specific problem with clear guidelines for treatment appear to be the most effective. Thus, our chapter-by-chapter coverage of treatments will be selective, focusing primarily on interventions that are tailored to what we know about each disorder and that have evidence for their effectiveness in treating youths with this disorder.

In this section, we provide an overview of what we mean by intervention, cultural considerations in treatment, treatment goals, ethical and legal considerations, main approaches to helping children with problems and their families, and what we know about the effectiveness of interventions for young people. The overall goal is to introduce you to important foundational issues associated with interventions for youths and their families.

Intervention

Better put a strong fence 'round the top of the cliff than an ambulance in the valley.

–Joseph Malins (1895)

Intervention is a broad concept that encompasses many different theories and practices directed at helping the child and family adapt more effectively to their current and future circumstances. There is no one best single approach to working with children and families— multiple problems require multiple solutions. Clinical assessment and diagnosis are usually followed by efforts to select and implement the most promising approach to intervention. Since psychological disorders typically represent failures in adaptation on the part of the child and/or his or her social environment, problem-solving strategies are part of a *spectrum* of activities for treatment, maintenance, and prevention.

● Figure 4.4 illustrates a spectrum of interventions and intervention settings for children and families. As shown, the strengths of youths, their families, communities, and cultures are nourished and maintained by effective interventions across a variety of life settings using a coordinated system of care (American Academy of Child and Adolescent Psychiatry [AACAP], 2007a). Interventions in the upper portion of the figure range from the most universal (directed at groups not having specific risks, problems, or disorders) on the left, to those that focus specifically on youths with lasting long-term conditions (e.g., autism) on the right (Weisz et al., 2005).

Note that interventions cover a wide range of actions, from prevention to maintenance. **Prevention** efforts are directed at decreasing the chances that undesired future outcomes will occur (Ialongo et al., 2006). They are based on the premise that it is inherently better to promote health and prevent problems before they occur, for example, by using school-based programs to prevent bullying and victimization (Farrington & Ttofi, 2009). **Treatment** refers to corrective actions that will permit successful adaptation by eliminating or reducing the impact of an undesired problem or outcome that has already occurred; **maintenance** refers to efforts to increase adherence to treatment over time to prevent relapse or recurrence of a problem. Prevention, treatment, and maintenance efforts complement one another by focusing on different stages of problem development with youths identified in different ways and in different settings, including those who may never seek help. By targeting both risks *and* existing problems and disorders, the combination of prevention and treatment has enormous potential to reach a diverse range of youths and families across a wide range of settings (Weisz, Donenberg et al., 1995).

Interventions are best depicted as part of the ongoing decision-making approach emphasized throughout this chapter. Our assessments should help us answer many questions that are essential for intervention. In Felicia's case, our answers to some of the following questions will guide us in determining which, if any, of the numerous available treatment options will be used:

▸ Should Felicia's difficulties be treated? If so, which ones? Depression? School refusal? Social skills deficits? Relations with family members? All of them?

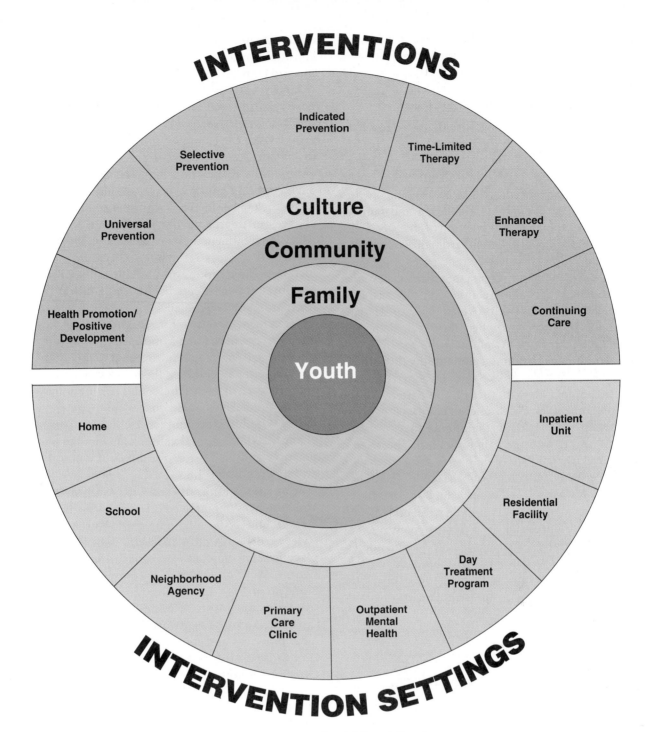

INTERVENTIONS

Indicated Prevention

Selective Prevention

Time-Limited Therapy

Universal Prevention

Enhanced Therapy

Culture

Community

Family

Youth

Continuing Care

Health Promotion/ Positive Development

Home

Inpatient Unit

School

Residential Facility

Neighborhood Agency

Day Treatment Program

Primary Care Clinic

Outpatient Mental Health

INTERVENTION SETTINGS

● **FIGURE 4.4** | The intervention spectrum and settings for childhood disorders.

Based on Weisz, J. R., Sandler, I. N., Durlak, J. A., and Anton, B. S. (2005). Promoting and protecting youth mental health through evidence-based prevention and treatment.

▶ What are the projected outcomes for Felicia in the absence of treatment?

▶ Based on the evidence, what treatments are likely to be most effective, efficient, and cost-effective for Felicia's depression, school refusal, and social skills deficits?

▶ What treatments are likely to be most acceptable to Felicia and to her family?

▶ When should treatment for Felicia begin? When should treatment be terminated?

▶ Is the intervention having the desired impact on Felicia's behavior? Are the changes meaningful for Felicia and her family? Do they make a real difference in their lives?

The ultimate goal of addressing these questions should be to achieve effective solutions to the problems faced by Felicia, her family, and other children like her, and then to promote and enhance long-term adjustments.

Cultural Considerations

Most interventions for youths with problems have failed to incorporate the unique experiences of ethnic minority children and their families (Yasui & Dishion, 2007). However, as evidence-based interventions have advanced, so has a growing awareness of the cultural context of children and families receiving psychological interventions (Huey & Polo, 2008; Scott et al., 2010). Parents from different ethnic groups and cultures have different parenting values and use different child-rearing practices. They also have different beliefs about childhood problems, how mental health services are provided, how to describe their children's problems when they seek help, and preferred interventions (Yasui & Dishion, 2007; Yeh et al., 2005). The **cultural compatibility hypothesis** states that treatment is likely to be more effective when it is compatible with the cultural patterns of the child and family. The importance of cultural sensitivity in treatment is reflected in the finding that for some problems and treatments, ethnic similarity between a child's caregiver and the therapist is associated with better treatment outcomes for the child (Halliday-Boykins, Schoenwald, & Letourneau, 2005).

Culturally competent children's mental health services may be provided in a number of ways. For example, in therapy for Hispanic children and adolescents, cultural competence may be achieved by matching children and families with clinicians of the same ethnicity; by customizing the treatment to Hispanic

cultural values, beliefs, and customs (e.g., familism, spiritualism, and *respeto*); or by incorporating ethnic and cultural narratives and role play into therapy (Malgady, 2010). In recent years, existing evidence-based treatments have been successfully adapted and implemented to meet the needs of specific cultural groups—as, for example, in the case of a cognitive–behavioral intervention for trauma in American Indian youths (Goodkind, LaNoue, & Milford, 2010). Such cultural adaptations of existing treatments may include changes in treatment surface structure (e.g., changes in treatment materials, mode of service delivery, or treatment setting), as well as deep structure changes that focus on factors unique to a particular racial or ethnic group, such as cultural beliefs regarding how trauma affects health and cultural practices for treating these problems.

Treatment services for children must not only attend to the presenting symptoms but must also consider the specific values, norms, and expectations present within many cultures; the various religious beliefs and practices of each family; and other circumstances that might make what is a successful treatment for one family a failure for another (Schwoeri, Sholevar, & Combs, 2003). Cultural values and common parenting practices and beliefs for five different cultural groups are shown in Table 4.8.

Can you think of how these cultural beliefs and practices might lead us to use different treatments? One issue might be the different parenting styles cross-culturally. African American families place greater emphasis on strict discipline, whereas Latino and Native American parents are generally more permissive. In helping families establish effective rules and forms of discipline for their children, the clinician must be aware of these important cultural practices and find methods that each parent is comfortable using. As we emphasized earlier, generalizations about cultural practices and beliefs may fail to capture the diversity that exists within and across cultural groups, so we must be extremely careful not to stereotype individuals of any cultural group.

Treatment Goals

What are the typical goals of treatment? Reducing symptoms (problems), producing more substantial changes that will enhance the child's long-term functioning, or both? Since both are important, treatment goals often focus on building children's adaptation skills to facilitate long-term adjustment, rather than on merely eliminating problem behaviors or briefly

"I like to think that each generation will need a little less therapy than the generation before."

TABLE 4.8 | Cultural Values and Parenting Practices and Beliefs

	African American	Latino American	Asian American	Native American	European American
Cultural Values	Communalism Individualism Kinship relations Unity Creativity Cooperation Authenticity Racial identity	Family loyalty Interpersonal connectedness Mutual respect Self-respect	Self-control Social courtesy Emotional maturity Respect for elders	Centrality of family Sharing Harmony Humility	Independence Autonomy Individualism Initiative Acquisition of skills Self-development Standing up for one's own rights
Parenting Practices and Beliefs	Authoritarian parenting No-nonsense parenting Unilateral parental decision-making Egalitarian family structure Strict discipline Communal parenting	Authoritarian parenting Patriarchal family structure High expression of parental warmth Communal parenting Freedom	Authoritarian parenting Structural and managerial parental involvement Patriarchal family structure Strict discipline Parental control Negotiation of conflict Parent as teacher	Permissive, lax parenting Shame as discipline Patriarchal and matriarchal family structures Communal parenting	Authoritative parenting Egalitarian family structure Parent as manager Demanding

Sources: Adapted from Forehand and Kotchik, 1996; and from Yasui and Dishion, 2007.

reducing subjective distress. Other treatment goals and outcomes are also of crucial importance to the child, family, and society (Jensen, Hoagwood, & Petti, 1996; Kazdin, 1997). These include:

▸ *Outcomes Related to Child Functioning:* Reduction or elimination of symptoms, reduced degree of impairment in functioning, enhanced social competence, improved academic performance

▸ *Outcomes Related to Family Functioning:* Reduction in family dysfunction, improved marital and sibling relationships, reduction in stress, improvement in quality of life, reduction in burden of care, enhanced family support

▸ *Outcomes of Societal Importance:* Improvement in the child's participation in school-related activities (increased attendance, reduced truancy, reduction in school dropout rates), decreased involvement in the juvenile justice system, reduced need for special services, reduction in accidental injuries or substance abuse, enhancement of physical and mental health

The interlocking network of physical, behavioral, social, and learning difficulties that characterizes most childhood disorders requires a multidisciplinary approach to attain these treatment and prevention goals.

In many instances, children require medication or medical intervention that must be coordinated with psychosocial interventions, such as in connection with ADHD, ASD, eating disorders, depression, and chronic medical conditions. Thus, the use of combined treatments is common. In addition, psychological interventions for children and adolescents often require integration with effective teaching strategies, as illustrated in later chapters addressing intellectual disability, communication disorders, and specific learning disorder. Finally, some children require integration of community and social services to aid in their protection and basic needs, which we discuss in Chapter 12 in the section on child abuse and neglect.

Ethical and Legal Considerations

Many children referred for assessment and treatment experience multiple disadvantages and arguably need special help and protection. Both ethically and legally, clinicians who work with children and families are required to think about the impact that their actions will have not only on the children themselves, but also on the responsibilities, rights, and relationships that connect the children and their parents (Dishion & Stormshak, 2007a; Prout & Prout, 2007).

Cultural background is an important consideration in understanding the child's uniqueness and expectation.

The ethical codes of professional organizations, such as the American Academy of Child and Adolescent Psychiatry (2009) and the American Psychological Association (2002, 2010), provide minimum ethical standards for practice, including: (a) selecting treatment goals and procedures that are in the best interests of the client; (b) making sure that client participation is active and voluntary; (c) keeping records that document the effectiveness of treatment in achieving its objectives; (d) protecting the confidentiality of the therapeutic relationship; and (e) ensuring the qualifications and competencies of the therapist. There is also an increasing emphasis on involving children, depending on their developmental level, as active partners in decision making with regard to their own psychological or medical treatment (McCabe, 1996, 2006).

In addition to these general ethical standards, there is a growing recognition of the unique challenges and ethical dilemmas associated with mental health interventions for children and their families (Belitz &

Bailey, 2009). Several core ethical issues for mental health interventions with children and families versus interventions with adults are highlighted in Table 4.9. Ethical issues with children are complex because of ongoing changes in the legal status of children and a trend toward recognition of minors' constitutional rights, including self-determination and privacy (Melton, 2000). However, a more basic issue is determining when a minor is competent to make his or her own decisions, rather than determining only whether he or she has the legal right to do so. Some of the challenging issues faced by clinicians working with children include deciding when a minor can provide informed consent or refuse treatment as well as balancing the child's rights to confidentiality against the rights of the parents and the integrity of the family.

In addition to these ethical and legal concerns, much larger ethical questions concern the provision of services for children and families. Many interventions currently used to treat children with complex problems are known to be limited in scope—for example, 1 hour per week of therapy—and cannot realistically be expected to have a meaningful or lasting impact on children who are experiencing severe problems. Furthermore, a number of currently used interventions are intrusive,

TABLE 4.9 | **Ethical Issues in Clinical Work with Children and Families**

1. Children are inherently more vulnerable than adults.
2. Children's abilities are more variable and change over time.
3. Children are more reliant upon others and upon their environment.
4. Ethical principles and practices in the treatment of adults must be modified in response to the child's current developmental abilities and legal status.
5. Boundary and role issues are often more prevalent and more complex when caring for children than for adults.
6. Adult practices, and the adult knowledge base, do not transfer reliably to the care of children.
7. Practitioners must develop skills to work with families, agencies, and systems.
8. It is key to monitor one's own actions and motivations.
9. Seeking consultation and advice is helpful in difficult situations.
10. It is essential to maintain an absolute commitment to the safety and well-being of the patient.

Source: Reprinted from *Psychiatric Clinics of North America, 32,* Belitz, J. & Bailey, R. A., Clinical ethics for the treatment of children and adolescents: A guide for general psychiatrists, 243–257, Copyright 2009, with permission from Elsevier.

expensive, and not supported by data (Kazdin, 2000). A more fundamental and thorny ethical question in some cases is whether we should provide any treatment when we know that the treatment may not make a difference or, even worse, may have harmful effects.

Clinicians who work with children and their parents need to be aware of federal, state, and local laws that affect both assessment and treatment of children with special needs. Many of these laws apply to children with mental and physical disabilities and handicaps and are based on the recognition that disability is a natural part of the human experience and that all citizens (children included) are entitled to equal treatment and education. Two laws that have had a profound influence on services for children with disabilities are the Education for All Handicapped Children Act (1975) and its amendment, the Individuals with Disabilities Education Improvement Act (2004). The following are two of the many purposes of these laws:

▸ To ensure that all children with disabilities have available to them a free, appropriate public education that emphasizes special education and related services designed to meet their unique needs and prepare them for employment and independent living.

▸ To ensure that the rights of children with disabilities and of the parents of such children are protected.

General Approaches to Treatment

The number and diversity of treatments for children have grown tremendously; currently, more than 550 treatments are currently in use to help children (Kazdin, 2000). While we will (thankfully) not attempt to cover them all, in the remainder of this chapter we provide a brief overview of several of the major approaches. More than 70% of practicing clinicians who work with children and families identify their approach as *eclectic*; this means that they use different approaches for children with different problems and circumstances and that they see most of these approaches as having value. In light of this practice, the large number of treatments specified above likely represents a vast underestimate of the full range of treatments used with children. Let's now turn to a brief overview of some of the general approaches to treatment and see how they might apply to Felicia.

Psychodynamic Treatments

Psychodynamic approaches view child psychopathology as determined by underlying unconscious and conscious conflicts (Lesser, 1972). Therefore, the focus is on helping the child develop an awareness of unconscious factors that may be contributing to his or her problems (AACAP, 2012; Galatzer-Levy et al., 2000). With younger children, this awareness can occur through play therapy (Chethik, 2000); with older children, it occurs through verbal interactions with the therapist. As underlying conflicts are revealed, the therapist helps the child resolve the conflicts and develop more adaptive ways of coping. Research has found some support for the effectiveness of both long- and short-term approaches to psychodynamic psychotherapy with children and adolescents (Abbass et al., 2013; Midgley & Kennedy, 2011), although further controlled studies are needed.

In Felicia's case, a therapist would help her gain insight into her problems through an intensive process of psychotherapy, perhaps lasting months or even years. The therapist might explore her earliest memories of her relationship with her parents by having her recall positive and negative memories and exploring how she constructs her childhood memories and relationships. The assumption is that once she resolves the underlying problems, such as an insecure attachment to her mother, Felicia's overt symptoms of depression, social withdrawal, school refusal, and physical symptoms will be alleviated (Muratori et al., 2003).

Behavioral Treatments

Behavioral approaches assume that many abnormal child behaviors are learned. Therefore, the focus of treatment is on re-educating the child, using procedures derived from theories of learning or from research. Such procedures include positive reinforcement, time-out, modeling, and systematic desensitization (Morris & Kratochwill, 2007). Behavioral treatments often focus on changing the child's environment by working with parents and teachers.

In Felicia's case, a therapist might try to decrease her school refusal by instructing her parents to not let her stay at home when she protests and by rewarding her for going to school with praise or a preferred activity. In addition, the therapist might use modeling, role-playing, and reinforced practice to help Felicia learn more effective social skills.

Cognitive Treatments

Cognitive approaches view abnormal child behavior as the result of deficits and/or distortions in the child's thinking, including perceptual biases, irrational beliefs, and faulty interpretations (Kendall, 2011b). For example, for an attractive girl who gets A grades but thinks she is ugly and is going to fail in school, treatment emphasis is on changing these faulty cognitions. As cognitions change, the child's behaviors and feelings are also expected to change.

In Felicia's case, she may believe that she can't do well in school, that if she goes to school then harm will befall her mother, or that children at school will think she's stupid. Changing these negative views by challenging them and by helping Felicia develop more rational and more adaptive forms of thinking, should lead to changes in her behavior.

Cognitive–Behavioral Treatments

Cognitive–behavioral approaches view psychological disturbances as the result of both faulty thought patterns, and faulty learning and environmental experiences. These approaches begin with the basic premise that the way children and parents think about their environment determines how they will react to it (Meichenbaum, 1977). Combining elements of both the behavioral model and the cognitive model, the cognitive–behavioral approach grew rapidly as behavior therapists began to focus on the important role of cognition in treatment for both the child and the family (Kendall, 2011a).

Faulty thought patterns that are the targets of change include distortions in both cognitive content (e.g., erroneous beliefs) and cognitive process (e.g., irrational thinking and faulty problem solving). As you will learn, cognitive distortions and biases have been identified in children with a variety of problems, including, for example, depression, conduct disorder, and anxiety disorders.

The major goals of cognitive–behavioral treatment are to identify maladaptive cognitions and replace them with more adaptive ones, to teach the child to use both cognitive and behavioral coping strategies in specific situations, and to help the child learn to regulate his or her own behavior. Treatment may also involve how others respond to the child's maladaptive behavior. Using a cognitive–behavioral approach, a therapist would help Felicia learn to think more positively and to use more effective social skills and coping strategies.

Client-Centered Treatments

Client-centered approaches view child psychopathology as the result of social or environmental circumstances that are imposed on the child and interfere with his or her basic capacity for personal growth and adaptive functioning. The interference causes the child to experience a loss or impairment in self-esteem and emotional well-being, resulting in even further problems. The therapist relates to the child in an empathic way, providing unconditional, nonjudgmental, and genuine acceptance of the child as an individual, often through the use of play activities with younger children and verbal interaction with older youths (Axline, 1947). The therapist respects the child's capacity to achieve his or her goals without the therapist's serving as a major adviser or coach—the therapist respects the child's self-directing abilities.

In Felicia's case, being babied by her parents, who view her as slow, may have led to interference with her adaptive functioning and to low self-esteem. In treatment, a therapist would comment on what Felicia is saying and feeling to help her understand her feelings and to increase the congruence between her feelings and her behavior. In therapy, Felicia would lead the way as the clinician follows.

Family Treatments

Family models challenge the view of psychopathology as residing only within the individual child and, instead, view child psychopathology as determined by variables operating in the larger family system. Like other approaches, the many varieties of family therapy differ widely in their underlying assumptions and approach to treatment. However, nearly all of the approaches view individual child disorders as manifestations of disturbances in family relations (Rivett, 2008).

Treatment involves a therapist (and sometimes a co-therapist) who interacts with the entire family or a select subset of family members, such as the parents and child or the husband and wife. Therapy typically focuses on the family issues underlying problem behaviors. Depending on the approach, the therapist may focus on family interaction, communication, dynamics, contingencies, boundaries, or alliances. It is also essential to adapt family interventions to the cultural context of the family (Kumpfer et al., 2002).

In Felicia's case, her overall helplessness and physical symptoms may be serving to maintain her role as the baby in the family, or may be serving as the parents' way of avoiding their own marital difficulties by focusing the problem on Felicia. A therapist would assist Felicia and her family in identifying and changing these and other dysfunctional ways in which family members relate to one another.

Neurobiological Treatments

Medical models view child psychopathology as resulting from neurobiological impairment or dysfunction and rely primarily on pharmacological and other biological approaches to treatment. Examples include the use of stimulant medications for the treatment of ADHD, antipsychotic medications for the treatment of schizophrenia or serious aggressive and destructive behavior, and selective serotonin reuptake inhibitors (SSRIs) such as fluoxetine (Prozac) for the treatment of depression and anxiety, along with practice guidelines for their use (AACAP, 2009a). Although still in a very early stage, there is also a growing interest in developing pharmacological interventions that target basic mechanisms such as gene expression, neurotransmission abnormalities, and other abnormal processes underlying the child's disorder (Vitiello & Grabb, 2013). Table 4.10 provides a summary of medications and their typical uses with children and adolescents, which you may find helpful when reviewing treatment for specific disorders discussed in other chapters.

Other, much more controversial forms of biological intervention include electroconvulsive therapy (ECT) for severe depression, the administration of large doses

TABLE 4.10 | Descriptions of Common Medications for Children and Youths[a]

Type of Medication	Treatment Uses	Examples
Stimulant and non-stimulant medications for ADHD	Attention-deficit hyperactivity disorder (ADHD)	*Stimulants*: Dextroamphetamine (*Dexedrine, Adderall*), Methylphenidate (*Ritalin, Metadate, Concerta, Focalin*) *Nonstimulant*: Atomoxetine (*Strattera*)
Antidepressant medications	Depression, school phobias, panic attacks, and other anxiety disorders, bed-wetting, eating disorders, obsessive–compulsive disorder, post-traumatic stress disorder, and ADHD	*Selective serotonin reuptake inhibitors (SSRIs):* Fluoxetine (*Prozac*), Sertraline (*Zoloft*), Paroxetine (*Paxil*), Fluvoxamine (*Luvox*), Venlafaxine (*Effexor*), Citalopram (*Celexa*), and Escitalopram (*Lexapro*). *Tricyclic antidepressants (TCAs):* Amitriptyline (*Elavil*), Clomipramine (*Anafranil*), Imipramine (*Tofranil*), and Nortriptyline (*Pamelor*). *Monoamine oxidase inhibitors (MAOIs):* Phenelzine (*Nardil*) and Tranylcypromine (*Parnate*).
Antipsychotic medications	Controlling psychotic symptoms (delusions, hallucinations), disorganized thinking, motor tics, and Tourette's syndrome. They are occasionally used to treat severe anxiety and may help in reducing very aggressive behavior.	*First-generation antipsychotics*: Chlorpromazine (*Thorazine*), Thioridazine (*Mellaril*), Fluphenazine (*Prolixin*), Trifluoperazine (*Stelazine*), Thiothixene (*Navane*), and Haloperidol (*Haldol*) *Second-generation antipsychotics (also known as atypical or novel):* Clozapine (*Clozaril*), Risperidone (*Risperdal*), Paliperidon (*Invega*), Quetiapine (*Seroquel*), Olanzapine (*Zyprexa*), Ziprasidone (*Geodon*), Aripiprazole (*Abilify*), Iloperidone (*Fanapt*), Lurasidon (*Latuda*), and Asenapine (*Saphris*).
Mood stabilizers and anticonvulsant medications	Bipolar disorder, severe mood symptoms and mood swings (manic and depressive), aggressive behavior and impulse control disorders.	Lithium (lithium carbonate, *Eskalith*), Valproic acid (*Depakote, Depakene*), Carbamazepine (*Tegretol*), Lamotrigine (*Lamictil*), and Oxcarbazepine (*Trileptal*)
Anti-anxiety medications	Selective serotonin reuptake inhibitors are used to treat anxiety in children and adolescents and are included above in the section on antidepressants. Other medications (presented here) used to treat anxiety in adults are rarely used with children and adolescents, but may be helpful for brief treatment of severe anxiety.	*Benzodiazepines:* Alprazolam (*Xanax*), Lorazepam (*Ativan*), Diazepam (*Valium*), and Clonazepam (*Klonopin*) *Antihistamines:* Diphenhydramine (Benadryl), and Hydroxyzine (Vistaril) *Atypical:* Buspirone (*BuSpar*) and Zolpidem (*Ambien*).

[a]These medications are often used in association with other forms of intervention such as psychotherapy, parent training, etc.

Source: Based on Psychiatric medication for children and adolescents Part. II: Types of medications, American Academy of Child & Adolescent Psychiatry, 2004, Updated May 2012.

of vitamins or minerals to children with autism, and the scrupulous elimination of food additives and preservatives from the diets of children with ADHD. In Felicia's case, a psychiatrist might consider using SSRIs to treat her depressive symptoms. As shown in ● Figure 4.5, the use of psychotropic medications for children's mental health problems increased significantly from the late 1980s to the mid-1990s, which can be attributed to increasing public acceptance of these medications as part of the treatment of mental health problems among children and youths during that time period (Olfson et al., 2002). Growth in the use of medications for children's mental health problems has slowed or leveled off over the past decade, although the percentage of children receiving more than one class of medication has increased (Comer, Olfson, & Mojtabai, 2010). Along with increased use, concerns have been expressed about the frequent use of medications with very young children (Chirdkiatgumchai et al., 2013; Gleason et al., 2007), and their frequent misuse and abuse by adolescents (Zosel et al., 2013). The use of prescription medication also varies in relation to racial/ethnic status. For example, more than 20% of non-Hispanic white adolescents report using prescription medication for depression versus 4% to 9% of Asian, black, and Hispanic youths (Cummings & Druss, 2011).

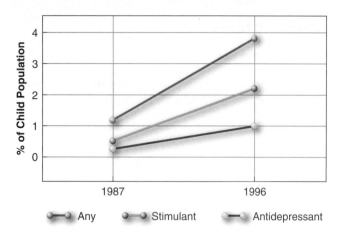

● **FIGURE 4.5** | Usage of psychiatric medication by children in the United States between 1987 and 1996.

Based on Olfson, M., Marcus, S. C., Weissman, M. M., & Jensen, P. S. (2005). National trends in the use of psychotropic medications by children. Journal of the American Academy of Child & Adolescent Psychiatry, 41, 514–521.

Combined Treatments

Combined treatments refer to the use of two or more interventions, each of which can stand on its own as a

treatment strategy (Kazdin, 1996a). In some instances, combinations of stand-alone interventions may consist of different conceptual approaches—using behavioral parent training and pharmacological treatments for children with ADHD, or using cognitive–behavioral treatment and family therapy in combination. In other instances, combined treatments may be derived from the same overall conceptual approach—using social skills training and cognitive restructuring in a group treatment program for adolescents with a social phobia, or using individual behavior management and family behavior therapy in the treatment of children with oppositional disorders.

More communities are now implementing comprehensive mental health programs for children, often delivered through schools to reach the most children and their families and to integrate mental health intervention and education (Walker & Gresham, 2013). In addition, youths who participate in school-based universal social and emotional learning programs have been found to show significantly improved social and emotional skills, attitudes, behavior, and academic performance (Durlak et al., 2011). A Closer Look 4.3 describes an innovative

A CLOSER LOOK 4.3

Model Comprehensive Mental Health Program: A Culturally Competent School-Based Mental Health Program

Program	Dallas School-Based Youth and Family Centers
Goal	To establish the first comprehensive, culturally competent, school-based program in mental health care in the 12th-largest school system in the nation. The program overcomes stigma and inadequate access to care for underserved minority populations.
Features	Annually serves the physical and mental health care needs of 3,000 low-income children and their families. The mental health component features partnerships with parents and families, treatment (typically six sessions), and follow-up with teachers. The well-qualified staff, who reflect the racial and ethnic composition of the population they serve (more than 70% Latino and African American), train school nurses, counselors, and principals to identify problems and create solutions tailored to meet each child's needs.
Outcomes	Improvements in attendance, discipline referrals, and teacher evaluation of child performance. Preliminary findings reveal improvement in children's standardized test scores in relation to national and local norms.
Biggest challenge	To sustain financial and organizational support of collaborative partners despite resistance to change or jurisdictional barriers. The school district contributes $3.5 million to the program, and an additional $1.5 million comes from Parkland Hospital.
How other organizations can adopt	Recognize the importance of mental health for the school success of all children, regardless of race or ethnicity. Rethink how school systems can more efficiently partner with and use state and federal funds to deliver culturally competent school-based mental health services.
Sites	Dallas and Fort Worth, Texas
Follow-up	This model program continues to provide school-based quality physical and mental health care to children and families. It promotes the wholeness of the family and engages families in their children's health and education, thereby reducing barriers to academic success. The 11th Youth and Family Center was opened in Dallas in 2012.

Sources: President's New Freedom Commission on Mental Health, 2003; www.dallasisd.org/Page/1427

school-based program that pays particular attention to the cultural diversity of families in their community.

In Felicia's case, we used a combined treatment approach that included cognitive–behavioral treatment for depression, behavioral treatment for school refusal, and social skills training.

Treatment Effectiveness

A growing emphasis on improving outcomes and reducing the costs of health care in general has led to the development of best practice guidelines for treating children and families with psychological problems.

FELICIA

Multiple Solutions

Our clinical assessment of Felicia suggested a combined treatment approach to treat three significant problems: school refusal, depression, and social difficulties.

To treat Felicia's school refusal, a behavioral program was implemented that required her to attend class daily. Felicia earned points for her attendance, class participation, and completion of class assignments, which could later be traded in for the opportunity to engage in preferred activities such as going to a movie or for money that could be used to purchase music apps and other things that Felicia had previously selected.

When Felicia refused to go to school, she lost points and was given a brief period of time-out from positive reinforcement. She had to sit in the kitchen by herself and was not permitted to read or watch TV. This behavioral program resulted in consistent school attendance and much-improved academic performance.

To treat Felicia's depressive symptoms, we used a cognitive–behavioral approach. Felicia learned that depression can occur for many reasons—the loss of her grandfather, thinking lots of negative thoughts, and not having any friends. We next taught Felicia how to relax to give her some immediate relief and provide her with a successful experience. Felicia then learned to monitor and rate her mood daily, and to identify thoughts and events that accompanied both her positive and negative moods. Felicia increased her positive thinking by learning to identify, challenge, and change her negative cognitions. After several weeks of treatment, Felicia began to feel less depressed, as reflected in her positive daily mood ratings and reports by her parents.

Both Felicia's teacher and her parents felt that her feelings of depression might be the result of her social interaction difficulties at home and school and that she might become less depressed if these problems could be decreased. Therefore, a social–cognitive skills training program was also implemented to simultaneously address her depressive symptoms and interpersonal difficulties. This program consisted of three parts. In the first part, Felicia was given behavioral social skills training that consisted of instruction, modeling of appropriate and inappropriate social behaviors, role playing and rehearsal, coaching, feedback, and a final role play. This training focused on those social skills, such as making eye contact and speaking clearly, that our initial assessment identified as lacking. Training was conducted in the situations that Felicia and her therapist identified as being problematic—for example, the role play we described earlier in which another teen sits at Felicia's table in the school cafeteria.

The second part of the treatment focused on cognitive skills, including general problem-solving skills, self-evaluation, and self-reinforcement. Felicia was taught to use certain cues that would prompt the correct use of her individual social skills in different situations—"What do I want to accomplish?" or "How do I do this now?" She also learned to evaluate the adequacy of her social behavior and whether she had improved on each social skill. To support Felicia's use of these strategies, a third behavioral component was included whereby Felicia could earn points for the accuracy of her judgments and the effectiveness of her social skills during the role plays. The results of the behavioral role-playing social skills intervention for Felicia are shown in ● Figure 4.6.

Following treatment, Felicia began to show increased emotional expressiveness and social responsiveness at home. She smiled more and argued less with her parents. She also began to assert herself more appropriately. Attempts by her teacher to have her speak up in class were met with considerable success. Gradually, she began to engage in more interactions with her peers and to participate in activities. Her mood also began to brighten as she made efforts to initiate conversations and engage in more reciprocal interactions with other children, her teacher, and her parents. At the end of the treatment program Felicia was more interactive and assertive and had learned to be more socially appropriate during interactions. She was less depressed and more animated.

One year following her treatment, Felicia reported no symptoms of depression and few feelings of hopelessness. She was attending school regularly, showed improved academic performance, and was participating in activities and interacting more with other children. In this example, a combined approach of cognitive–behavioral therapy, behavioral social skills training, and cognitive problem-solving training was successful in helping Felicia and her family.

Based on Depression, by D. J. Kolko, 1987. In M. Hersen and V. B. Van Hasselt (Eds.), Behavior Therapy with Children and Adolescents: A Clinical Approach, pp. 159–160.

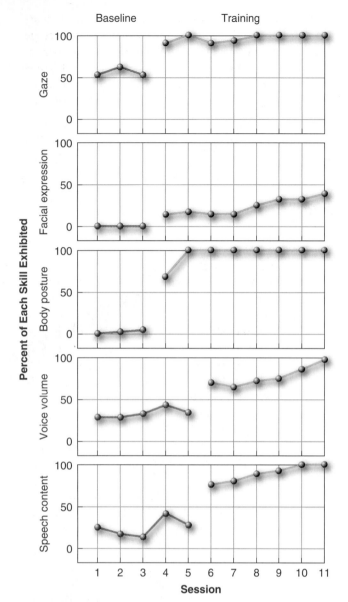

● **FIGURE 4.6** | Results of behavioral role-play intervention.

Based on Depression by D. J. Kolko, 1987. In M. Hersen and V. B. Van Hasselt (Eds.),"Behavior Therapy with Children and Adolescents: A Clinical Approach", pp. 163–164.

Best practice guidelines are systematically developed statements to assist practitioners and patients with decisions regarding appropriate treatment(s) for specific clinical conditions. These guidelines are intended to offer recommendations on the most effective and cost-effective treatments for children with particular problems and their families (March et al., 2007).

Two main approaches have been used to develop best practice guidelines. The *scientific approach* derives guidelines from a comprehensive review of current research findings. This approach emphasizes **evidence-based treatments (EBTs)**, which are clearly specified treatments shown to be effective in controlled research with specific populations (Weisz & Kazdin, 2010). Most EBTs have been evaluated in large-scale clinical trials involving large numbers of children and careful comparisons with other EBTs or other forms of treatment (e.g., medication). The *expert-consensus approach* uses the opinions of experts to fill in the gaps in the scientific literature—for example, when research is inconclusive or when there is a lack of information about multicultural issues. Thus, *evidence-based practice* is not the blind application of research findings, but rather it involves the use of the best available scientific evidence combined with good individual clinical expertise and provides for consumer choice, preference, and culture (Institute of Medicine, 2011; Sackett et al., 2000).

A number of professional organizations whose members provide mental health services to children and their families have developed excellent best practice guidelines, for example, the Society of Clinical Child and Adolescent Psychology (www.effectivechildtherapy.com) and the American Academy of Child and Adolescent Psychiatry (www.aacap.org). In the chapters that follow, we will discuss many of the best practice interventions that are recommended for youths with particular problems.

Consistent with the growing emphasis on improving outcomes, efforts to evaluate treatments for childhood disorders have intensified (Chorpita et al., 2011; Weisz & Kazdin, 2010). These efforts allow us to take a closer look at the overall effectiveness of commonly used treatment methods.

Let's begin with the good news:

▸ Changes achieved by children receiving psychotherapy are consistently greater than changes for children not receiving psychotherapy.

▸ The average child who is treated is better off at the end of therapy than at least 75% of children who did not receive treatment, particularly with respect to symptom reduction.

▸ Treatments have been shown to be effective for children with a wide range of problems, including both internalizing and externalizing disorders.

▸ Treatment effects tend to be lasting, with the effects at follow-up (usually around 6 months after treatment) similar to those found immediately after treatment.

▸ Effects are about twice as large for problems that are specifically targeted in treatment as they are for changes in nonspecific areas of functioning. This

PRELIMINARY EDITION

result suggests that treatments are producing focused changes in targeted areas such as anxiety rather than producing nonspecific or global effects such as changes in how the child feels (Weisz, 1998).

▶ The more outpatient therapy sessions children receive, the more improvement is seen in their symptoms (Angold et al., 2000).

So what's the bad news? Although research findings present a generally positive picture of psychotherapy with children and of behavioral and cognitive–behavioral approaches in particular, there are a number of important limitations.

First, although research generally shows that most treatments are effective in reducing symptoms such as anxiety, depression, and oppositional behavior, fewer than 20% of treatments demonstrate evidence that they reduce impairment in life functioning (Becker, Chorpita, & Daleiden, 2011). Thus, greater attention to the development and evaluation of interventions that also result in meaningful changes in the child's overall life functioning is needed. Second, we must be aware of the critical difference between research therapy that is carried out in laboratory-based outcome studies and therapy that is carried out in community-based clinics (Wagner, Swenson, & Henggeler, 2000). Most of the evidence-based treatment outcome studies for specific disorders fall into the category of research therapy. However, as compared with research therapy, clinical therapy is typically conducted with more severe cases, directed at a diverse set of problems and children, and carried out in clinic or hospital settings by professional career therapists with large caseloads (Weisz & Weiss, 1993). In general, clinical therapy is less structured and more flexible than research therapy, and it uses relatively more nonbehavioral methods, such as psychodynamic and eclectic approaches. In contrast to the findings for research therapy, similar analyses for studies of clinical therapy have resulted in minimal effects (Andrade, Lambert, & Bickman, 2000; Weisz et al., 2013). These findings suggest that conventional services for children as they are currently carried out may have limited effectiveness. However, few controlled studies exist of child therapy outcomes in settings where it is typically conducted, although this situation is changing. Thus, it is premature to draw any conclusions from the findings from clinic and community studies until more empirical data about therapy in clinical practice are available (Weisz, Jensen-Doss, & Hawley, 2006; Weisz et al., 2013).

In summary, although the efficacy of treatments for many child and adolescent mental health problems is substantial, testing of the effectiveness and cost-effectiveness of these treatments in real-world settings and dissemination of this information and its use in public settings are key issues that require further attention (Novins et al., 2013).

NEW DIRECTIONS

Knowing is not enough; we must apply

Willing is not enough; we must do

–Goethe

Despite the availability of many potentially effective assessment and treatment procedures, as many as 70% to 80% of children and families with significant mental health needs do not receive any specialized assessment or treatment services (Merikangas et al., 2011). Service rates are highest for children with ADHD and other behavior disorders, but fewer than one in five youths receive services for their anxiety, eating, or substance use disorders. This situation is even worse for youths from low-income families, ethnic minority youths, and those in the child welfare and juvenile justice systems. This raises the larger issue of whether current evidence-based practices are, by themselves, a viable way to help these large, unrecognized, and underserved groups of children and to reduce the gap between children's mental health needs and the availability and access to effective services (Kazak et al., 2010).

In response to this issue there has been a general "call to action" from many family, public, professional, and scientific organizations to address these challenges and actively promote the uptake of evidence-based assessment and treatment practices into public health, school, and mental health systems. This has led to an increasing number of opportunities for partnerships among the various stakeholders, along with financial incentives at the state and federal levels to support these efforts. The result has been several exciting new initiatives that focus on:

1. Increasing the recognition of children's mental health needs, not only on the part of laypersons, but also among education, welfare, juvenile justice, and health care professionals (Jensen et al., 2011).

2. Developing a much wider range of child mental health service delivery models based on: (a) the use of new technologies (e.g., Internet, smart phones, video-conferencing assessment and treatment services for rural youths [Duncan, Valasquez,

& Nelson, 2014; Trull & Ebner-Priemer, 2013]); (b) nontraditional service providers (e.g., parents, health counselors); (c) self-help interventions (e.g., self-help books, recordings, Internet); (d) the media (e.g., education entertainment); and (e) special settings where youths in need of mental health services are typically present (e.g., schools, primary care, community-based family wellness centers) (Kazdin & Blase, 2011; Rotheram-Borus, Swendeman, & Becker, 2013; Weist et al., 2014).

3. Broadening the framework and delivery systems for children's mental health assessment and intervention services to include multiple systems and disciplines and their coordination (Chorpita & Daleiden, 2014; Kazak et al., 2010).

The goal of these new initiatives is to translate evidence-based practices into real-world settings so as to significantly reduce the personal, social, and economic costs of children's mental health problems and related conditions, at both the individual and societal levels.

Section Summary

Treatment and Prevention

- Interventions for childhood disorders cover a wide range of strategies and settings related to prevention, treatment, and maintenance.

- Treatment goals now include outcomes related to child and family functioning as well as those of societal importance.

- Both ethically and legally, clinicians who work with children are required to think not only about the impact that their actions will have on the children they see, but also on the responsibilities, rights, and relationships that connect children to their parents.

- A tremendous number and diversity of treatments for children and families now exist, including psychodynamic, behavioral, cognitive, cognitive–behavioral, client-centered, family, biological, and combined approaches.

- Best practice guidelines are systematically developed statements derived from research findings and clinical consensus that assist clinicians and families with decisions regarding appropriate treatment(s) for specific childhood problems.

- Reviews of controlled treatment outcome studies have found that the changes achieved by children receiving therapy are consistently greater than changes for children not receiving therapy. However, these differences are not consistently found in studies of treatment outcomes based on clinic samples.

- The goal of new treatment initiatives is to better serve unrecognized and underserved populations of children with mental health problems and to translate evidence-based practices into real-world settings in ways that will significantly reduce the personal, social, and monetary costs associated with these problems.

Study Resources

SECTION SUMMARIES

KEY TERMS

5

Intellectual Disability (Intellectual Developmental Disorder)

Everybody is a genius. But if you judge a fish by its ability to climb a tree, it will live its whole life believing that it is stupid.

—Albert Einstein

PRELIMINARY EDITION

CHAPTER PREVIEW

INTELLIGENCE AND INTELLECTUAL DISABILITY

The Eugenics Scare

Defining and Measuring Children's Intelligence and Adaptive Behavior

The Controversial IQ

FEATURES OF INTELLECTUAL DISABILITIES

Clinical Description

Severity Levels

Prevalence

DEVELOPMENTAL COURSE AND ADULT OUTCOMES

Motivation

Changes in Abilities

Language and Social Behavior

Emotional and Behavioral Problems

Other Physical and Health Disabilities

CAUSES

Inheritance and the Role of the Environment

Genetic and Constitutional Factors

Neurobiological Influences

Social and Psychological Dimensions

PREVENTION, EDUCATION, AND TREATMENT

Prenatal Education and Screening

Psychosocial Treatments

124

UNTIL THE MID-NINETEENTH CENTURY, children and adults who today would be diagnosed as having an intellectual disability were labeled "idiots" and often were lumped together with persons suffering from mental disorders or medical conditions. They typically were ignored or feared, even by the medical profession, because their differences in appearance and ability were so little understood.

Although age-old fears, resentment, and scorn continue to overshadow many important discoveries about subnormal intelligence, the field of intellectual disability has experienced monumental gains over the past century in determining causes and providing services. Advances in understanding the development of children with intellectual disability, along with research in genetics, psychopathology, and other areas, have dramatically changed the face of this field.

The term *intellectual disability* has replaced the previous term *mental retardation* in the *Diagnostic and Statistical Manual of Mental Disorders,* 5th edition (DSM-5), based on consensus among professionals, advocacy groups, and the lay public. Intellectual disability is a neurodevelopmental disorder, a group of conditions with onset in the developmental period that produce impairments of social, personal, academic or occupational functioning (APA, 2013). Intellectual disability (ID) is characterized by significant limitations in mental abilities (such as reasoning, planning, and judgment) that result in impairments in adaptive functioning, such as conceptual, social, and practical skills needed to fulfill aspects of everyday life (Tassé et al., 2012). Although the name has changed, the three essential elements defining this condition have remained the same for the past 50 years: intellectual limitations, deficits in adaptive skills, and early onset.

Importantly, modern definitions of intellectual disability take into account a person's intellectual functioning within the context of what is typical for that individual's peers and culture. Cultural and linguistic diversity, as well as differences in communication, sensory, motor, and behavioral factors, must be carefully considered in determining a deficit or disability (American Association on Intellectual and Developmental Disabilities [AAIDD], 2010). Understanding improvements in knowledge about and treatment of intellectual disability, as well as understanding the prejudice and ignorance that had to be overcome, can be gained by looking at how the disorder has been viewed over the years.

INTELLIGENCE AND INTELLECTUAL DISABILITY

Throughout recorded history, persons with intellectual and other disabilities have suffered scorn and rejection from others, largely because of fear and ignorance.

The prevailing misunderstanding and mistreatment of children with intellectual disabilities changed very little until the end of the eighteenth century, fueled by the discovery of feral children such as Victor, the "wild boy of Aveyron" (discussed in Chapter 1), and by the expansion of humanitarian efforts to assist other oppressed or neglected groups, such as slaves, prisoners, the mentally ill, and persons with physical disabilities.

By the mid-nineteenth century, the concept of mental retardation had spread from France and Switzerland to much of Europe and North America. During the same period, Dr. Samuel G. Howe convinced his contemporaries that training and educating the "feeble-minded" was a public responsibility, and he opened the first humanitarian institution in North America for persons with intellectual disability—the Massachusetts School for Idiotic and Feeble-Minded Youth.

Parents of children with ID can be credited with advancing a perspective and response to the need for long-term care that was completely different from the prevailing public and professional opinions. By the 1940s, parents began to meet in groups and create local diagnostic and guidance centers to increase the availability of humane care. These groups organized in 1950 to form the National Association for Retarded Children (now known as The Arc), which quickly established a scientific board made up of representatives from every specialty possible to study, prevent, and care for persons with intellectual disability (Kanner, 1964). These efforts gained momentum when President John F. Kennedy, who had a sister with intellectual disability, formed the President's Panel on Mental Retardation in 1962 and called for a national program to combat intellectual disability. Soon thereafter, exposés in the media of the use of solitary confinement and restraints

Ignorance resulted in the segregation of children with intellectual disabilities, who were subjected to inhumane treatment. Today, most children with ID are integrated into regular classrooms.

for persons with ID increased public awareness of and outrage at the treatment of these individuals.

The Eugenics Scare

Three generations of imbeciles are enough.

— Justice Oliver Wendell Holmes Jr., commenting on the Supreme Court's 1927 decision to uphold eugenics sterilization laws

Evolutionary degeneracy theory, a pervasive nineteenth-century phenomenon, attributed the intellectual and social problems of children with intellectual disability to regression to an earlier period in human evolution (Bowler, 1989). In fact, mental deficiency experts in the nineteenth century believed they had found the "missing link" between humans and lower species (Gelb, 1995). J. Langdon H. Down, best known for the clinical description of the genetic syndrome that bears his name, interpreted the "strange anomalies" among his medical sample of persons with intellectual disability as an evolutionary throwback to the Mongol race (Down, 1866). Down believed that parents in one racial group might give birth to a child with intellectual disability who was a "retrogression" to another group. While grounded in speculation and misinformed conclusions, evolutionary degeneracy theory and its notion of inferiority received growing support by the late-nineteenth century as an explanation for insanity, mental deficiency, and social deviance. A Closer Look 5.1 depicts how this popular theory was conveniently used to explain undesirable human characteristics.

By 1910, the eugenics movement was gaining momentum. **Eugenics** was first defined by Sir Francis Galton (Charles Darwin's cousin) in 1883 as "the science which deals with all influences that improve the inborn qualities of a race" (cited in Kanner, 1964, p. 128). Public

and professional emphasis shifted away from the needs of persons with intellectual disability toward a consideration of the needs of society; society was to be protected from the presumable harm done by the presence of these persons in the community.

Consequently, persons with intellectual disability often were blamed for the social ills of the time, which is a powerful example of how labeling a problem can quickly become an explanation for it. A Closer Look 5.2, in fact, shows a 1912 *New York Times* article reflecting this public sentiment. The appearance, ability, and behavior of persons with intellectual disability were considered evidence of their lack of moral fiber, a belief that led to the diagnostic term *moral imbecile*, or *moron*, used to describe and explain their differences. This concept became a straightforward explanation for acts of deviance and justified wide-ranging attempts to identify and control such individuals. Morons, considered the least intellectually impaired (roughly comparable to mild intellectual disability today) were seen as a threat to society because, unlike the insane, they could easily pass for normal (Gelb, 1995). The intellectually impaired and other "undesirables" were seen as a public menace, to be feared and ostracized.

Defining and Measuring Children's Intelligence and Adaptive Behavior

Around 1900, the pioneering work of two French educators, Alfred Binet and Theophile Simon, led to some of the first major advancements in the field of children's intellectual functioning. Binet and Simon were asked to develop a way to identify schoolchildren who might need special help in school. They approached this monumental task by developing the first intelligence tests to measure judgment and reasoning, which they believed were basic

---

A CLOSER **LOOK** 5.1

The Infamous Kallikaks

Psychologist Henry Goddard, who began one of the largest training schools for intellectual disability in the early twentieth century, was also a proponent of the popular degeneracy theory and eugenics movement. In his book *The Kallikak Family: A Study in the Heredity of Feeble-Mindedness* (1912), Goddard traced two lines of descendants from a Revolutionary War soldier, Martin Kallikak, who fathered a child by a "feebleminded barmaid" during the war, which began the first line, and then fathered other children by a "respectable girl" he married after the war. The name "Kallikak" was invented by Goddard from a combination of two Greek words: *kalos,* meaning "attractive, pleasing," and *kakos,* meaning "bad, evil."

Goddard reported that many descendants of the first union were feebleminded, delinquent, poor, and alcoholic, whereas those of the second union were of good reputation. He claimed this outcome was evidence for the inheritance of intelligence, although he overlooked the two families' obvious environmental differences (Achenbach, 1982). A closer look at the disclaimer from the preface to the book is telling: "It is true that we have made rather dogmatic statements and have drawn conclusions that do not seem scientifically warranted by the data." (Based on authors' case material.)

Early-Twentieth-Century Perspectives on Mental Retardation

WEAK-MINDED FILL RANKS OF CRIMINALS
DR. HENRY GODDARD SAYS SOCIAL PROBLEMS
CAN BE SOLVED BY SEGREGATING THEM

WOULD NOT LET THEM MARRY
THIS POLICY WOULD IN TIME LARGELY
REDUCE CRIMES, DISEASE, AND DRUNKENNESS,
HE BELIEVES

From the army of 300,000 feeble-minded persons in the United States come the recruits that swell the ranks of the drunkards, criminals, paupers, and other social outcasts. Twenty-five per cent of the girls and boys in our reformatories are lacking in mental fibre and are unable to discern the difference between right and wrong or are too weak in character to do right whenever there is any inducement to do wrong. Sixty-five per cent of the children have a mother or a father, or both, who are feeble-minded. This country has so far taken no steps to segregate these irresponsible persons, so the number of them is constantly increasing....

This army furnishes the ranks of the criminals, paupers, drunkards, the ne'er-do-wells, and others who are social misfits. Their incapacity would be a priori cause of believing that they eventually will become public charges in one form or another, and investigation, in fact, proves that the groups of criminals, paupers, etc., actually do contain large percentages of people mentally irresponsible.

Source: The New York Times, March 10, 1912.

By convention, IQ scores (with a mean of 100 and a standard deviation of 15) are derived from a standardized table based on a person's age and test score. Because intelligence is defined along a normal distribution, approximately 95% of the population has scores within 2 standard deviations of the mean (i.e., between 70 and 130). Subaverage intellectual functioning is defined, accordingly, as an IQ of about 70 or below (approximately 2 standard deviations below the mean).

As we will discuss later in this chapter, the definition of intellectual disability includes not only subaverage intellectual functioning, but also a subaverage level of adaptive functioning. **Adaptive functioning** refers to how effectively individuals cope with ordinary life demands, and how capable they are of living independently and abiding by community standards (Hodapp et al., 2011). Note that some children and adolescents may learn to adapt quite well to their environment despite their lower intelligence as measured by an IQ test; therefore, they would not be considered to have an intellectual disability. Table 5.1 gives examples of the three major categories of adaptive behavior (conceptual, social, and practical adaptive skills). Similar to IQ, these skills are typically

TABLE 5.1 | **Specific Examples of Adaptive Behavior Skills**

Conceptual Skills
Receptive and expressive language
Reading and writing
Money concepts
Self-directions

Social Skills
Interpersonal
Responsibility
Self-esteem
Gullibility (likelihood of being tricked or manipulated)
Naiveté
Follows rules
Obeys laws
Avoids victimization

Practical Skills
Personal activities of daily living such as eating, dressing, mobility, and toileting
Instrumental activities of daily living such as preparing meals, taking medication, using the telephone, managing money, using transportation and doing housekeeping activities

Occupational Skills
Maintaining a safe environment

Source: From the American Association on Intellectual and Developmental Disabilities(AAIDD).

processes of higher thought. These early test questions asked children to manipulate unfamiliar objects such as blocks or figures and to solve puzzles and match familiar parts of objects. The test later became the Stanford–Binet scale, which remains one of the most widely used intelligence tests.

From these beginnings in intellectual testing, **general intellectual functioning** is now defined by an intelligence quotient (IQ or equivalent) that is based on assessment with one or more of the standardized, individually administered intelligence tests, such as the Wechsler Intelligence Scales for Children, 4th edition (WISC-IV), the Stanford–Binet, 5th edition (SB5), and the Kaufman Assessment Battery for Children, 2nd edition (KABC-II). These tests assess various verbal and visual–spatial skills (such as knowledge of the world, reasoning, and similarities and differences) and mathematical concepts, which together are presumed to constitute the general construct known as "intelligence."

assessed using standardized instruments such as the Adaptive Behavior Assessment System—Second Edition (ABAS-II; Harrison & Oakland, 2003) or the Vineland Adaptive Behavior Scales—Second Edition (VABS-II; Sparrow, Cicchetti, & Balla, 2005).

The Controversial IQ

If a person's intelligence is relatively stable over time, it would be tempting to conclude that it is largely innate and fixed. On the other hand, if intellectual and cognitive development is significantly shaped by environment, perhaps cognitive growth can be stimulated at an early age and the level of intellectual disability decreased.

Because intelligence is measured in relation to age-mates, IQ generally is stable from childhood through adulthood (Carr, 2005; Whitaker, 2008). One exception to this general rule is IQ that is measured during early infancy, when considerable fluctuation can still occur. For typically developing children, IQ measured prior to the first birthday has virtually no correlation with the IQ score achieved at age 12; however, by the time children are 4 years old, the correlation with IQ 12 years later is high ($r = 0.77$) (Neisser et al., 1996).

The picture is dramatically different, however, for infants and children with developmental delays or intellectual disability. At the lower IQ levels (say, below 50), even the youngest infants show IQ stability over time, with correlations between infant and childhood test scores ranging from 0.50 to 0.97 (Sattler, 2006). Researchers have discovered a similar pattern of IQ stability from middle childhood to young adulthood among children with mild to moderate intellectual delays (Mortensen et al., 2003; Toth & King, 2010).

Even though the IQ of cognitively delayed infants and young children is unlikely to change, proper environmental circumstances will help children reach their fullest potential. Since the early 1960s, researchers in child development and intellectual disability have been investigating ways to provide early stimulation programs that will help children with developmental delays to build on their existing strengths. Despite its strong genetic component, mental ability is always modified by experience. Not surprisingly, infancy through early childhood offer the most significant opportunity for influencing intellectual ability because of the young child's rapid brain development and response to environmental stimulation (Campbell & Ramey, 2010; Pungello et al., 2010).

The importance of genetic makeup not with standing, for some individuals IQ can and does change by 10 to 20 points between childhood and adolescence

(Simonoff, Bolton, & Rutter, 1996). Differences in outcome vary widely in relation to opportunities for each child to learn and develop. Children who live in healthy environments, where caregivers provide appropriate levels of stimulation and help them manage ambient levels of stress, are most likely to reach their full potential. Moreover, tests can sample only a limited spectrum of intellectual ability, and are incapable of accounting for each individual's unique learning history (Sattler, 2006).

Are We Really Getting Smarter?

Scores have risen sharply since the beginning of IQ testing, ranging from a 5- to a 25-point increase in a single generation (Kanaya, Scullin, & Ceci, 2003). When James Flynn brought this phenomenon of rising IQ scores to the attention of scientists in 1987, it became known as the "Flynn effect." The gain has averaged about 3 IQ points per decade, adding up to more than a full standard deviation since the 1940s. Once a test is re-normed (about every 15 to 20 years) the mean is reset to 100, resulting in a brief reversal of this gain in IQ scores.

In attempting to explain the Flynn effect, scientists have considered the rising standards of living, better schooling, better nutrition, medical advances, more stimulating environments, even the influence of computer games and complex toys (Flynn, 2007; 2012). IQ tests themselves have once again come under scrutiny, as have children's exposure to problems similar to those on the tests—like the mazes and puzzles they see on their cereal boxes and fast-food bags. Yet the consistent IQ gains are too large to be the result simply of increased familiarity with testing methods.

Although the exact cause of the effect remains unknown, experts on children's intelligence suspect that the gains reflect a meaningful aspect of intellectual growth and development. A relatively permissive and child-focused parenting style has emerged during recent decades, which may have given children greater facility with language and stronger overall cognitive capacity. Moreover, there are unprecedented cultural differences between successive generations—daily life and occupational experiences are far more complex today than in the past. There is a possible downside to the Flynn effect, however. Test scores drop an average of 5.6 points among persons with borderline and mild intellectual disability after a test is re-normed, which can have a significant impact on a child's eligibility for proper educational placement and other related services (Kanaya et al., 2003).

Are IQ Tests Biased or Unfair?

Many express concern over the relatively lower mean of the distribution of intelligence test scores of African Americans, typically about 1 standard deviation (about 15 IQ points) below that of whites (Jencks & Phillips, 1998). Although recent estimates suggest that African Americans have gained 4 to 7 IQ points on non-Hispanic whites since 1972 (Dickens & Flynn, 2006), considerable concern remains as to why differences in test results exist at all.

The controversy in IQ score differences is fueled by researchers who argue that IQ is 80% heritable and therefore largely genetically determined (Rushton & Jensen, 2006). Other researchers argue that economic and social inequality—not test bias or racial differences—are the simplest explanations for existing group differences in test performance between African Americans and whites (Brooks-Gunn, Klebanov et al., 2003; Nisbett et al., 2012). For example, when personal and family background characteristics are statistically controlled for, African American and white children achieve similar test scores. However, once these students enter school, the gap between white and African American children grows, which researchers believe may be due to lower-quality schools in the lower-income neighborhoods where some African-Americans live (Levitt & Fryer, 2004; Nisbett, 2009). A much higher proportion of African Americans and children from other ethnic minority groups in the United States as well as in other countries are poor and have fewer opportunities for advancement as compared with their white counterparts. Poverty and inequality are linked to poor nutrition, inadequate prenatal care, fewer intellectual resources, and similar realities that can have negative effects on children's developing intelligence (Christian et al., 2013; Sternberg, 2010).

Section Summary

Intelligence and Intellectual Disability

- The early history of intellectual disability was plagued by ignorance and blame.
- By the mid-twentieth century, progress toward understanding intellectual disability moved more rapidly, as parents, researchers, politicians, and the public sought better answers regarding its causes and better ways to assist both children and adults with ID.
- Intellectual disability refers to limitations in both intelligence and adaptive behavior. However, many persons with this disorder are capable of learning and of leading fulfilling lives.
- Despite its drawbacks, the IQ has become a principal standard for diagnosing intellectual disability, combined with other skills and abilities of the child.

FEATURES OF INTELLECTUAL DISABILITIES

MATTHEW

Gaining at His Own Pace

Matthew was almost 6 years old when he was referred for a psychological assessment. His brief school record described him as "developmentally delayed," and the school was concerned that his speech and social skills were very limited. He also had temper tantrums at home, and his new first-grade teacher had expressed concerns about his aggressive behavior toward other children in his class.

I first met with Matt in his home. "Show me some of your favorite toys or games," I suggested, unsure of how comfortable he was with a stranger at his home. He was a thin boy, with curly hair and a cautious, reserved expression. He looked me over for what must have been several minutes while I spoke with his mother and father. Although he said "OK," I wasn't sure he meant it—he stayed put and seemed uninterested in my request. Matt had turned 6 a few months ago, but I noticed that his clothes, games, and vocabulary were closer to those of my 3-year-old daughter. "I don't want to talk about school stuff!" he exclaimed, quite loudly, when I asked about his favorite subjects. "I only like recess and lunchtime—the stuff they won't let you do till the bell rings!" There was a certain degree of truth, and humor, to his statement, although I don't think he intended it as such.

Matt became a bit more interested when I brought out some testing materials. He completed with ease a puzzle designed for toddlers and was able to make the sounds of animals in the puzzle. But his emotional expression remained subdued, with little spontaneous laughter or joy. He seemed watchful and cautious. "Tell me about this story," I said to Matt, holding up a card showing some animals arguing over a ball. "What do you think is going on in this picture, and what are the characters, like the elephant and the zebra, thinking and feeling?" Matt started right in: "He's mad 'cuz the zebra grabbed the ball and ran away with it into the woods. That's all I see." My attempts to elicit more detail were met with only an inquisitive look.

After a few minutes of this, we took a break and brought out his toys. "Do you like *Harry Potter*?" he asked. We found some common ground among the characters in the book, and under these "ideal" conditions, Matt's communication became more at ease and spontaneous. He expressed a wide range of emotion throughout the interview, and settled in to his own comfortable level of relating. Gradually, his language production increased as we continued with the more relaxed play sessions.

(continues)

(continued)

In private, Matt's mother told me about his behavior problems around other children, such as hitting, biting, throwing objects, and demanding attention. I saw a brief episode of it myself when his 3-year-old sister came into the room: "Get out! This man is here to play with me!" Overall, Matt behaved like a much younger child—for example, by shouting or pushing when he couldn't get his way immediately. When we met for the second time, in my office, Matt's WISC-IV full-scale IQ was assessed at 64, and his adaptive abilities score was 68, based on his mother's report on the Vineland Adaptive Behavior Scales. Despite his mild intellectual disability, however, Matt has been gaining over the past year in school, and he is showing a healthy gain in his developmental milestones as well. (Based on authors' case material.)

You judge a person by how they look or how they talk or what the tests show, but you can never really tell what is inside the person.

—Ed, 27 years old, who was labeled mentally retarded and placed in a state institution at age 15 (Bogdan & Taylor, 1982)

Intellectual disabilities encompass perhaps the widest variation in cognitive and behavioral abilities of any childhood disorder. Some of these children function quite well in school and the community, whereas others with significant physical and cognitive impairments require daily supervision and assistance. The situations of Matthew, age 6, and Vanessa, age 8, illustrate some of the unique challenges children with intellectual disability face every day.

Matthew was diagnosed as having mild intellectual disability. Although his speech and language development were delayed, he was developing effective verbal skills and was capable of attending a regular classroom. Establishing friendships with children at school was sometimes problematic because he was often slow at understanding the rules of games and was teased by some children because of his slowness.

Vanessa was diagnosed as having moderate intellectual disability. She could feed and dress herself with minimum assistance, and she communicated in short sentences, although her speech was not always discernible to people outside her family. Vanessa required daily assistance to complete her routines, but she too was able to attend a local school during part of the day. As these cases show, the special needs of both children were sometimes overshadowed by economic and educational limitations, which required creativity and coordinated assistance on the part of parents, teachers, and other professionals.

VANESSA

Gaining at Home

Vanessa is an 8-year-old girl with moderate intellectual disability (IQ = 52) and limited communication skills. She was diagnosed prior to her fourth birthday, after medical and psychological examinations were undertaken to determine why she was not making many speech sounds or learning basic self-help skills. Vanessa's mother told us about how her daughter's special needs were poorly met while she was a resident in a special school for children with intellectual disabilities, and how this led to her parents' decision to raise Vanessa at home with the help of their community:

When our family moved here we were told that we would receive $75 per month to care for her at home, or she could live at the Children's Training Center. Vanessa had been diagnosed with moderate intellectual disability prior to her fourth birthday, and we knew that we could not care for her daily needs at home with the limited assistance being offered. So we made the difficult decision to place her at the training center. But, even though Vanessa came home every weekend, we felt there was something missing from her life; something beyond staff care and attention was needed to foster her growth.

About 2 years later, things changed dramatically. Vanessa was injured by another resident, and we decided that she should return home once and for all. We made every effort to find services she needed for her training and education in our own community. She now attends an integrated classroom at the same school as her older brother, and her teachers have noticed strong gains in her behavior and language. She participates in recreational programs, and has become an accomplished swimmer and basketball player. (Based on authors' case material.)

Clinical Description

When the psychiatrist interviewed me he had my records in front of him—so he already knew I was mentally retarded. It's the same with everyone. If you are considered mentally retarded there is no way you can win. There is no way they give you a favorable report.

—Ed, describing part of his intake interview at the state institution (Bogdan & Taylor, 1982)

Children with intellectual disability show a considerable range of abilities and interpersonal qualities. With proper assistance, children with mild intellectual impairments, such as Matthew, can carry out their daily routines much like other children. They can attend a regular classroom, adjust to the demands of physical and intellectual challenges, and develop meaningful and lasting relationships with peers and adults. Many show normal physical development and can learn the physical coordination required to ride a bike. Others, like Vanessa, who have more severe impairments, will require greater daily supervision and care throughout their childhood and sometimes into early adulthood, at which time they may have developed the necessary skills to live more independently.

Both Matthew and Vanessa, however, experience limitations that involve most areas of daily living. Their most obvious difficulties are learning to communicate effectively, due to their limited speech and language skills. Although Matthew eventually learned effective verbal communication, for several years Vanessa had to rely on sign language and nonverbal expressions or gestures to express her needs. Both children had problems developing friendships with other children because of their limited ability to comprehend what other children were expressing, especially during games and social activities that require stamina and formal rules. Many cognitive abilities, such as language and problem solving, are affected; therefore, most children with ID have difficulty with some aspect of learning. The degree of difficulty depends on the extent of cognitive impairment, which is the primary reason current definitions of intellectual disability emphasize this aspect.

Table 5.2 summarizes the DSM-5 diagnostic criteria for intellectual disability (also known as intellectual developmental disorder). These criteria consist of three core features that describe this disorder in both children and adults. First, such individuals must have deficits in the intellectual functions of reasoning, problem-solving, planning, abstract thinking, judgment, academic learning, and learning from experience. Such deficits are typically determined by clinical assessment and intelligence testing. But note that the DSM-5 does not provide specific IQ cutoff limits for meeting diagnostic criteria, as was the case in previous editions.

The second criterion for diagnosing intellectual disability requires deficits in adaptive functioning, which result in failure to meet developmental and sociocultural standards for personal independence and social responsibility. In effect, a subnormal IQ score is not sufficient to warrant a diagnosis of intellectual disability. A person also must show significant limitations in adaptive behavior, such as communication, self-care, social/interpersonal skills, or functional academic or work skills (Lancioni et al., 2009). This aspect of the definition is important because it specifically excludes persons who may function well in their own surroundings, yet for various reasons they may not perform well on standard IQ tests. Importantly,

| TABLE 5.2 | Diagnostic Criteria for Intellectual Disability (Intellectual Developmental Disorder) |

Intellectual disability (intellectual developmental disorder) is a disorder with onset during the developmental period that includes both intellectual and adaptive functioning deficits in conceptual, social, and practical domains. The following three criteria must be met:

(A) Deficits in intellectual functions, such as reasoning, problem-solving, planning, abstract thinking, judgment, academic learning and learning from experience, confirmed by both clinical assessment and individualized, standardized intelligence testing.

(B) Deficits in adaptive functioning that result in failure to meet developmental and sociocultural standards for personal independence and social responsibility. Without ongoing support, the adaptive deficits limit functioning in one or more activities of daily life, such as communication, social participation, and independent living, across multiple environments, such as home, school, work, and community.

(C) Onset of intellectual and adaptive deficits during the developmental period.

Note: The diagnostic term *intellectual disability* is the equivalent term for the ICD-11 diagnosis of *intellectual developmental disorders*.

Specify current severity (see Table 5.3): Mild, Moderate, Severe, or Profound

Source: Diagnostic and Statistical Manual of Mental Disorders, Fifth Edition, American Psychiatric Association.

whether a child or adolescent exhibits these various adaptive skills is related not only to ability, but also to experience and opportunity. Using public transportation, walking to a neighborhood store, and making simple purchases all can be affected by the individual's place of residence (urban versus rural, for example), or their concerns about neighborhood safety. Clinicians and educators must make educated guesses regarding a person's potential for performing a certain task if the person has not had experience with a particular skill on the test.

The third and final criterion for intellectual disability stipulates that the child's intellectual and adaptive deficits must have begun during the developmental period (generally considered to be before age 18). The purpose of establishing this upper limit for the age of onset is twofold. First, it acknowledges that intellectual disability is a developmental disorder that is evident during childhood and adolescence. Problems in learning and comprehension typically occur during this time of rapid brain development. Second, this age criterion rules out persons who may show mental deficiencies caused by adult-onset degenerative diseases, such as Alzheimer's disease, or by head trauma.

A diagnosis of intellectual disability specifies the level of impairment—mild, moderate, severe, or profound—similar to other disorders in the DSM-5. Although these four levels of impairment remain the same as in previous editions, they are specified in considerably more detail, as described below. Similarly, as mentioned above, the DSM-5 does not provide specific IQ cutoffs for meeting diagnostic criteria, to allow greater focus on adaptive functioning and levels of support that may be required. However, individuals with ID generally have an IQ score 2 standard deviations or more below the population mean (e.g., 70 points or below, allowing for a margin of error of 5 points).

Changes in DSM-5 criteria for ID have sought to focus more on the nature or qualities of the person rather than on the IQ score, based on years of controversy over IQ measurement and social influences (Toth & King, 2010). These criteria are not likely to result in a major shift in the numbers of people diagnosed with ID—as before, the majority of people diagnosed with intellectual disability fall into the mild range. However, because the ramifications of diagnosing someone with intellectual disability can be serious, every attempt is made to consider other factors that may limit one's mental abilities. As Ed described so well, a careful balance must be struck between identifying the special needs of persons with intellectual disabilities and labeling them as having a disability on the basis of somewhat arbitrary criteria (Schalock et al., 2007).

In addition, the definition and identification of intellectual disability depend somewhat on our social institutions. When children enter the school system, it is a significant point at which their abilities are compared and deficiencies are most likely to be detected. If children are placed in a poorly matched learning environment, their developmental progress can be disrupted. Following their school years, persons with mild intellectual disability often blend into the larger population, and their "diagnosis" no longer has as much meaning (Hodapp et al., 2011).

Severity Levels

The four levels of severity noted in Table 5.3 are defined on the basis of adaptive functioning in three primary domains: conceptual, social, and practical. These definitions reflect a major shift in focus away from IQ scores and more toward needed supports. This shift emphasizes the resources and strategies necessary to promote the overall adjustment and well-being of a person with intellectual disability. Specific needs of

TABLE 5.3 | Severity levels for Intellectual Disability (Intellectual Developmental Disorder)

Severity Level	Conceptual Domain	Social Domain	Practical Domains
Mild	• For preschool children: no obvious conceptual differences. • For school-aged children and adults: learning difficulties in academic skills involving reading, writing, arithmetic, time, or money, the support needed in one or more areas to meet age-related expectations. • In adults: impaired abstract thinking, executive function, short-term memory, and functional use of academic skills. There is a somewhat concrete approach to problems and solutions as compared with age-mates.	Children: • Show immaturity in social interactions. • Have difficulty in perceiving peers' social cues. • Show immature or more concrete communication, conversation, and language for age. • Show difficulty regulating age-inappropriate emotion and behavior; may be noticed by peers. • Have limited understanding of risk in social situations. • Display immature social judgment for age. • Are at risk of being manipulated by others (gullibility).	Children: • May function age-appropriately and maintain personal care. • May need some support with complex daily living tasks as compared with peers. Adults: • Typically need support with shopping, transportation, home and child care, organizing, cooking, and money management. • Participate in recreational skills similar to age-mates, but need support with well-being and organization. • May hold jobs that do not emphasize conceptual skills. • Need support with health care and legal decisions and with learning a vocation. • Often need support raising a family.

(continues)

Severity Level	Conceptual Domain	Social Domain	Practical Domains
Moderate	Conceptual skills lag markedly behind those of peers. • For preschoolers, language and pre-academic skills develop slowly. • For school-aged children, academic skill develops slowly and are limited as compared with those of peers. • For adults, academic skill development is typically at an elementary level, and support is required for all use of academic skills and work and personal life. • Adults need daily assistance with conceptual tasks of day-to-day life.	Individual: • Shows marked differences from peers in social and communicative behavior across development. • Uses less complex spoken language as primary tool for social communication. • Shows capacity for relationships in life-long ties to family and friends. • May inaccurately perceive or interpret social cues. • Shows limited social judgment and decision-making abilities. • Needs caretakers to assist with life decisions. • Has friendships with typically developing peers that are often affected by communication or social limitations. • Needs social and communicative support in work settings.	Adults: • Eat, dress, eliminate, and practice hygiene age-appropriately after extended teaching, time practicing, and reminders. • Participate in all typical household tasks after extended period of teaching and ongoing. • May achieve independent employment in jobs that require limited conceptual communication skills, but need considerable support from co-workers/supervisors. • Develop a variety of recreational skills, but will need additional, extended supports and learning opportunities. • Maladaptive behaviors present in a significant minority and cause social problems.
Severe	Individual: • Attains few conceptual skills. • Has little understanding of written language or of concepts involving numbers. • Needs caretakers to provide problem-solving support throughout life.	Individual: • Exhibits limited spoken language in terms of vocabulary and grammar. • Speaks using single words or phrases and may be supplemented through augmentative means. • Exhibits speech and communication focused on the present. • Uses language for social communication more than for explication. • Understands simple speech and gestural communication. • Has relationships with family members and familiar others for pleasure and help.	Individual: • Needs support for daily living (e.g., eating, dressing, bathing, elimination). • Needs supervision at all times. • Unable to make responsible decisions regarding well-being of self or others. • Needs long-term teaching and ongoing support in all domains to acquire skills. • Maladaptive behavior, including self-injury, is present in a significant minority.
Profound	Conceptual skills generally involve the physical world rather than symbolic processes. Individual: • May use objects in goal-directed fashion for self-care, work, and recreation. • Uses visuospatial skills, such as matching and sorting based on physical characteristics. However, co-occurring motor and sensory impairments may prevent functional use of objects.	Individual: • Has very limited understanding of symbolic communication in speech or gestures. • May understand some simple instructions or gestures. • Nonverbally, nonsymbolically expresses most desires and emotions. • Enjoys relationships with well-known family members, caretakers, and familiar others. • Initiates a response to social interactions through gestural and emotional cues. • May have co-occurring sensory and physical impairments, which may prevent many social activities.	Individual: • Is dependent on others for all aspects of daily physical care, health, and safety, but may participate in some of these activities. • Without severe physical impairments may assist with some daily work tasks at home. • May perform simple actions with objects, with extended support, related to vocational activities. • Enjoys recreational activities with the support of others. • May have physical and sensory impairments that prevent participation (beyond watching) in home, recreational, and vocational activities. • May exhibit maladaptive behaviors (only a significant minority.)

Source: Diagnostic and Statistical Manual of Mental Disorders, Fifth Edition, American Psychiatric Association.

the individual are evaluated and strategies and services are developed to optimize individual functioning. Concrete examples of support areas and support activities are shown in Table 5.4.

Children with intellectual disability vary widely in their degree of disability. Some show cognitive impairments from early infancy, such as limited vocalizations or poor self-regulation, whereas other impairments may go relatively unnoticed throughout the elementary school years. Because of the wide variation in cognitive functioning and impairment, classification systems for intellectual disability have always attempted to delineate various degrees of cognitive impairment. The DSM-5 has continued the tradition by specifying disability as mild, moderate, severe, or profound; however, these designations are based primarily on ability and needed supports rather than on IQ scores, as in the past.

Children and adolescents with **mild intellectual disability** constitute the largest group; it is estimated that as many as 85% of people with ID have the mild form of the disorder (King et al., 2009). Children with mild intellectual disability often show small delays in development during the preschool years, but typically are not identified until academic or behavior problems emerge during the early elementary years. This category also has an overrepresentation of minority group members, most likely due to the social and economic disparities noted previously.

As a group, children with mild intellectual disability typically develop social and communication skills during the preschool years (ages 0–5 years), perhaps with modest delays in expressive language. They usually have minimal or no sensorimotor impairment and engage with peers readily (although peers may see them as immature). Like Matthew, some children with mild ID may find school and peer relationships to be challenging. By their late teens, these children can acquire academic skills up to approximately the sixth-grade level. During their adult years, they usually achieve social and vocational skills adequate for minimum self-support, but may need supervision, guidance, and assistance, especially when under unusual social or economic stress. With appropriate supports, individuals with mild intellectual disability usually live successfully in the community, either independently or in supervised settings.

Persons with **moderate intellectual disability** constitute about 10% of individuals with ID. Children and adolescents at this level of impairment are more intellectually and adaptively impaired than someone with mild intellectual disability, and usually they are identified during the preschool years, when they show delays in reaching early developmental milestones. By

TABLE 5.4	Examples of Support Areas and Support Activities

Teaching and Education Activities:

- Interacting with trainers and teachers and fellow trainees and students
- Learning and using problem-solving strategies
- Using technology for learning
- Learning and using functional academics (reading signs, counting change, etc.)

Home Living Activities:

- Preparing and eating food
- Housekeeping and cleaning
- Dressing
- Bathing and taking care of personal hygiene and grooming needs

Community Living Activities:

- Using transportation
- Participating in recreation and leisure activities
- Visiting friends and family
- Shopping and purchasing goods

Employment Activities:

- Learning and using specific job skills
- Interacting with co-workers
- Completing work-related tasks with speed and quality
- Accessing and obtaining crisis intervention and assistance

Health and Safety Activities:

- Accessing and obtaining therapy services
- Avoiding health and safety hazards
- Accessing emergency services
- Maintaining mental health/emotional well-being

Behavioral Activities:

- Learning and making appropriate decisions
- Incorporating personal preferences into daily activities
- Maintaining socially appropriate behavior in public
- Controlling anger and aggression

Social Activities:

- Participating in recreation and leisure activities
- Making appropriate sexual decisions
- Making and keeping friends
- Engaging in loving and intimate relationships

Protection and Advocacy Activities:

- Managing money and personal finances
- Protecting self from exploitation
- Exercising legal rights and responsibilities
- Using banks and cashing checks

Source: Frequently Asked Questions on Intellectual Disability and the AAIDD Definition, by American Association on Intellectual and Developmental Disabilities (AAIDD), 2010.

the time they enter school, these children may communicate through a combination of single words and gestures, and show self-care and motor skills similar to an average 2- to 3-year-old. Many persons with Down syndrome function at the moderate level of impairment. Because their social judgment and decision-making abilities are limited, children and youth with moderate ID often require supportive services to function on a daily basis.

Like Vanessa, most individuals with this level of intellectual disability acquire limited communication skills during their early years, and by age 12 they may be using practical communication skills. They benefit from vocational training and, with moderate supervision, can attend to their personal care. They also can benefit from training in social and occupational skills, but they are unlikely to progress beyond the second-grade level in academic subjects. Adolescents with moderate intellectual disability often have difficulty recognizing social conventions, such as appropriate dress or humor, which interferes with peer relationships. By adulthood, persons with moderate intellectual disability typically adapt well to living in the community and can perform unskilled or semiskilled work under supervision in sheltered workshops (specialized manufacturing facilities that train and supervise persons with intellectual disability) or in the general workforce.

Those with **severe intellectual disability** constitute approximately 4% of persons with ID. Most of these individuals suffer one or more organic causes of impairment, such as genetic defects, and are identified at a very young age because they have substantial delays in development and visible physical features or anomalies. Milestones such as standing, walking, and toilet training may be markedly delayed, and basic self-care skills are usually acquired by about age 9. In addition to intellectual impairment, they may have problems with physical mobility or other health-related problems, such as respiratory, heart, or physical complications.

Most persons functioning at the severe level of intellectual disability require some special assistance throughout their lives. During early childhood they acquire little or no communicative speech; by age 12, they may use some two- to three-word phrases. Between 13 and 15 years of age, their academic and adaptive abilities are similar to those of an average 4- to 6-year-old. They profit to a limited extent from instruction in pre-academic subjects, such as familiarity with the alphabet and simple counting, and can master skills such as sight reading "survival" words such as "hot," "danger," and "stop." During their adult years, they may be able to perform simple tasks in closely supervised settings. Most adapt well to life in the community, in group homes or with their families, unless they have an associated disability that requires specialized nursing or other care (Toth & King, 2010).

Persons with **profound intellectual disability** constitute approximately 2% of those with ID. Such individuals typically are identified in infancy because of marked delays in development and biological anomalies such as asymmetrical facial features. During early childhood they show considerable impairments in sensorimotor functioning; by the age of 4 years, for example, their responsiveness is similar to that of a typical 1-year-old. They are able to learn only the rudiments of communication skills, and they require intensive training to learn basic eating, grooming, toileting, and dressing behaviors.

Persons with profound intellectual disability require lifelong care and assistance. Almost all of these individuals show organic causes for their ID, and many have severe co-occurring medical conditions, such as congenital heart defect or epilepsy, that sometimes lead to death during childhood or early adulthood. Most of these individuals live in supervised group homes or small, specialized facilities. Optimal development may occur in a highly structured environment with constant aid and supervision and an individualized relationship with a caregiver. Motor development, as well as self-care and communication skills, may improve if appropriate training is provided. For example, persons with profound intellectual disability usually can perform simple tasks, such as washing their hands and changing their clothes, provided they have close supervision.

The DSM-5 criteria for ID focuses on needed supports, which reflects the consensus that determining the level of functioning of an individual with intellectual disability should be based on the interaction between the person and the environment (AAIDD, 2010). The criteria also remove specific IQ cutoff scores or ranges, which acknowledges that IQ scores are approximations of a person's mental abilities that require additional knowledge of their actual abilities. With a DSM-5 diagnosis of intellectual disability (*moderate severity*), Vanessa would likely also receive the following descriptive diagnosis: "Vanessa is a child with intellectual disability who needs limited supports in home living, academic skills, and development of self-help skills." Matthew's diagnosis of intellectual disability (*mild severity*) might also clarify: "Matt is a child with intellectual disability who requires support on an as-needed basis, especially during stressful or demanding times—for example, during the transition to school, when making new friends, and when faced with new academic challenges."

Prevalence

Based on available evidence and estimates, the total number of children and adults with intellectual disability is approximately 1% of the general population (Maulik et al., 2011). However, each person applies his or her own cognitive abilities in unique ways that may be more or less adaptive in her or his own environment. Thus, prevalence estimates vary across time and across countries as a result of IQ measurement problems, different definitions of ID, and varying study designs (Witwer, Lawton, & Aman, in press).

Sex Ratio

Among children with mild intellectual disability (by far the most common diagnosis), males outnumber females at a ratio of 1.6:1. Males outnumber females among the other levels of severity as well, but these ratios are inconsistent across studies and tend to be small. Similar to racial differences in the diagnosis of intellectual disability, gender differences in ID may be an artifact of identification and referral patterns rather than true differences in prevalence (Einfeld et al., 2010). If a true male excess of intellectual disability does exist, researchers suspect this may be due to the occurrence of X-linked genetic disorders such as fragile-X syndrome (discussed later in the chapter), which affect males more often than females (Handen, 2007).

Socioeconomic and Cultural Influences

It is a well-established finding that intellectual disability is more prevalent among children of lower socioeconomic status (SES) and children from minority groups (Witwer et al., in press). This link is found primarily among children in the mild intellectual disability range; children with more severe levels are identified almost equally in different racial and economic groups. Whether or not signs of organic etiology are present, diagnoses of mild intellectual disability increase sharply from near zero among children from higher SES categories to about 2.5% in the lowest SES category (APA, 2000). These figures indicate that SES factors play a suspected role both in the cause of intellectual disability and in the identification and labeling of persons with intellectual disability (Maulik et al., 2011).

The overrepresentation of minority and low-SES children in the group with mild intellectual disability is a complicated and unresolved issue. As we noted, average IQ levels for the African American population are lower than IQ levels found in the white population, resulting in more African American children among samples of children with mild intellectual disability. What specific environmental circumstances might create such an imbalance in IQ findings? To answer this

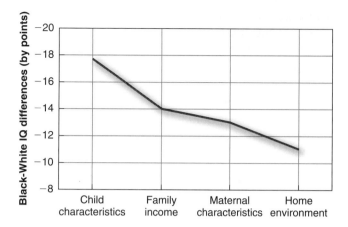

● **FIGURE 5.1** | Factors accounting for differences in IQ scores between white and African American children at 5 years of age.

Based on data from Brooks-Gunn, J., Klebanov, P. K., Smith, J., Duncan, G. J., & Lee, K. (2003). The Black-White test score gap in young children: Contributions of test and family characteristics. Applied Developmental Science, 7(4), pp. 239–252

question, Brooks-Gunn et al. (2003) tested the theory that the differences can be partially explained based on social and economic disadvantage. They accounted for initial IQ differences of over 17 points in African American versus white children by the independent effects of economic deprivation, home environment, and maternal characteristics. As shown in ● Figure 5.1, initial IQ differences were almost 18 points between a sample of African American and white children at 5 years of age, controlling for gender and birth weight. However, these differences were reduced by about 71% after adjusting for differences in poverty and home environment. Similar gains in IQ performance are found when children are adopted from working-class into middle-class homes, reinforcing the significant role of the environment in shaping one's intellectual and adaptive abilities (Nisbett et al., 2012). These data remind us that the likelihood of a diagnosis of intellectual disability is shaped and influenced by social and cultural forces such as racial discrimination, poverty, and cultural insensitivity (Emerson, 2012).

Section Summary

Features of Intellectual Disabilities

- The DSM-5 criteria for intellectual disability consist of deficits in intellectual functioning (confirmed by IQ testing and clinical assessment), deficits in adaptive functioning, and onset of intellectual and adaptive deficits during the developmental period.

- Children with intellectual disability vary widely in their degree of disability and level of functioning.

- IQ scores are no longer used to determine level of impairment. Rather, DSM-5 describes four levels of severity—mild, moderate, severe, or profound—based on adaptive functioning that determines a person's level of needed supports.
- Intellectual disability occurs in an estimated 1% of the population, more often among males than females.
- Intellectual disability occurs more often among children from lower socioeconomic and minority groups. Economic disadvantage and discrimination practices often account for these findings.

DEVELOPMENTAL COURSE AND ADULT OUTCOMES

To appreciate the manner in and extent to which children with intellectual disabilities achieve various developmental milestones, consider how typically developing children express themselves. An infant exploring his or her world relies on primitive sensorimotor functions—touching, tasting, and manipulating objects—to learn about the environment. At this stage of development everything is new, and the brain is establishing literally millions of new connections each day.

Then, between 18 and 24 months of age, the toddler begins to acquire language and to draw on memories of past experience to aid in understanding the present. For an intellectually normal child, it is during this stage that the child's environmental conditions and opportunities are known to play a crucial role in fostering enthusiasm for learning and in establishing the roots of intellectual sophistication. Although the majority of children with ID progress through each developmental milestone in roughly the same manner as other children, important differences in their developmental accomplishments are evident.

Much of the knowledge about other issues involved in the developmental course and adult outcomes for children with intellectual disability is derived from studies of children with Down syndrome. Chromosome abnormalities are the single most common cause of moderate to severe intellectual disability. **Down syndrome** is the most common disorder resulting from these abnormalities. children with Down syndrome, along with their parents, have frequently participated in studies comparing their development with that of their normally developing peers.

Dan, a 15-year-old with Down syndrome, describes how his early development was similar to, but much slower than, that of his younger brother.

Dan, with moderate intellectual disability, is describing how his younger brother Brian, with normal

DAN

With His Brother's Help

When I was almost 3 and my sister was 5, we had a baby brother. I helped feed him and take care of him until he was almost 3. I was 5 by then, and could do most of the things he could do, but about that time he caught up to me. I could still do some things he couldn't, but not many. He could do some things I had trouble with. We became good friends. Every time he learned a new skill, I would either learn it with him, or he would teach me later. I was really little for my age, so we were pretty close in size. We shared a bunk bed, toys, and clothes. We learned to do a lot of things together. When he learned to ride a bike, and I wasn't ready to learn yet, mom and dad got me a Powerwheel motorized bike so I could ride, too. When he learned to read, he taught me how, too. When he played baseball and football, he took me with him.

In those days, I still went to school in another district, so most of my friends were his friends. Now that we go to the same school it is sometimes hard for him to remember that I have my own friends, too. I have to tell him I am the big brother. He sometimes gets teased at school because he is my brother, but he is learning to explain instead of fight. Mostly, the kids are all nice to us. (Based on authors' case material.)

intelligence, caught up with him by the time Brian was 2 years old, and progressed through developmental milestones at a faster pace. Does Dan's development follow the same organized sequence as Brian's? Will his development show specific deficits in certain intellectual abilities such as language? Or will he eventually catch up? This case illustrates the developmental-versus-difference controversy (Weiss, Weisz, & Bromfield, 1986), an issue that has intrigued those in the field of child development and intellectual disability for some time. Simply stated, the **developmental-versus-difference controversy** is this: Do all children—regardless of intellectual impairments—progress through the same developmental milestones in a similar sequence, but at different rates? Or do children with intellectual disability develop in a different, less sequential, and less organized fashion?

The developmental position, which applies primarily to individuals not suffering from organic impairment, consists of two primary hypotheses: First, the *similar sequence hypothesis* argues that all children, with or without intellectual disability, pass through stages of cognitive development in an identical (invariant) order; they differ only in their rate and upper limit of development (Bennett-Gates & Zigler, 1998). Second, the *similar structure hypothesis* suggests that children with intellectual disability demonstrate the same behaviors and underlying processes as typically developing children at the same level of cognitive functioning (such as Dan and his younger brother were at ages 5 and 2). That is, if children with intellectual disability are matched to typically developing children by their mental age, then the children with intellectual disability will show equivalent performance on cognitive tasks, such as problem solving, spelling, and moral reasoning. The developmental position rejects the notion of a specific deficit or difference among children with intellectual disability and instead emphasizes how these children traverse the stages more slowly and attain a lower developmental ceiling than typically developing children (Bennett-Gates & Zigler, 1998).

In contrast, the **difference viewpoint** argues that cognitive development of children with intellectual disability differs from that of children without intellectual disability in more than developmental rate and upper limit. According to this position, even when his mental age is matched to his younger brother's, Dan will show qualitatively different reasoning and problem-solving strategies, and he may never be able to accomplish some tasks beyond a certain level.

Evidence supports the developmental hypothesis for children with familial, not organic, types of intellectual disability, but this issue has not yet been resolved. Children with familial intellectual disability generally follow developmental stages in an invariant order, the same as children with normal intellectual abilities, with the possible exception of some children with co-occurring brain abnormalities or autism (Bennett-Gates & Zigler, 1998). The similar structure hypothesis has also been supported for children with familial intellectual disability, with some exceptions. Children with familial intellectual disability show slight deficits in memory and information processing as compared with mental-age–matched children without intellectual disability (Schuchardt, Gebhardt, & Mäehler, 2010), which may be due to the children's difficulty in staying motivated to perform repetitive, boring tasks (Weisz, 1999).

The picture for children with organically based intellectual disability (such as Dan, who has Down syndrome) is more straightforward. They often have one or more specific deficit areas that cause them to perform more poorly than mental-age–matched children without intellectual disability. Thus, Dan is likely to show some differences in his performance in certain areas of development, including his expressive language. Nevertheless, he will likely pass through the same developmental sequences as his younger brother, but at a slower pace.

Motivation

Many children who fall within the range of mild intellectual disability are bright enough to learn and to attend regular schools and classrooms. However, they are more susceptible to a sense of helplessness and frustration, which places additional burdens on their social and cognitive development. As a consequence, they begin to expect failure, even for tasks they can master; in the absence of proper instruction, their motivation to tackle new demands decreases (Harris, 2006).

Ed, describing his memory of comments made by his teacher in elementary school, expresses this phenomenon well:

> Her negative picture of me stood out like a sore thumb. That's the problem with people like me—the schools and teachers find out we have problems, they notice them, and then we are abandoned. That one teacher was very annoyed that I was in her class. She had to put up with me. (Bogdan & Taylor, 1982)

Children with intellectual disability, consequently, expect little success, set lower goals for themselves, and settle for minimal success when they are able to do better, as compared with typically developing children of their same mental age (Weisz, 1999). This learned helplessness may be unwittingly condoned by adults. When they are told a child is "retarded," adults are less likely to urge that child to persist after failure than they are to urge a normal child at the same level of cognitive development. On the other hand, young children with mild intellectual disability improve in their ability to remain on task and they develop goal-directed behavior when

"Acknowledge our children's differences but respect their uniqueness." —Parent of a child with Down syndrome

provided with stimulating environments and caregiver support (Wilkins & Matson, 2009).

Changes in Abilities

Intellectual disability is not necessarily a lifelong disorder. Although it is a relatively stable condition from childhood into adulthood, the IQ score can fluctuate in relation to the level of impairment and type of intellectual disability. Children such as Matthew who have mild intellectual disability may, with appropriate training and opportunities, develop good adaptive skills in other domains and may exceed the level of impairment required for a diagnosis of intellectual disability.

The major cause of a child's intellectual disability certainly affects the degree to which his or her IQ and adaptive abilities may change. The IQ of children with Down syndrome, who are not representative of the course of intellectual disability in general, may plateau during the middle childhood years and then decrease over time. For example, from 1 to 6 years of age, children with Down syndrome often show significant age-related gains in adaptive functioning, but as they grow older, their pace of development levels off or even declines (Margallo-Lana et al., 2007). A similar deceleration is often seen in the rate of social development of these children as they grow older (Hazlett et al., 2011). This observation has been termed the *slowing and stability hypothesis* (Hodapp et al., 2011), and it affirms that children with Down syndrome may alternate between periods of gain in functioning and periods of little or no advance. Although these children continue to develop in intelligence, they do so at progressively slower rates throughout the childhood years.

Language and Social Behavior

Research on language development and social functioning among children and adolescents with Down syndrome suggests that their development follows a largely predictable and organized course (Filippi & Karmiloff-Smith, 2013). Because their cognitive development, play, self-knowledge, and knowledge of others are interrelated in organized and meaningful ways, the underlying symbolic abilities in children with Down syndrome are believed to be largely intact.

However, important differences in language development exist between children with Down syndrome and their typically developing age-mates. Perhaps the most striking difference for children with Down syndrome is the considerable delay in the expressive language development that is necessary to establish independent living skills. Their expressive language is often much weaker than their receptive language, especially as they attain communication abilities beyond the 24-month level (Filippi & Karmiloff-Smith, 2013).

Another major milestone of infancy and early childhood development is the ability to form secure attachments with caregivers. Although their attachments form more slowly than usual, many children with Down syndrome form secure attachment relationships with their caregivers by 12 to 24 months of developmental age (Dykens, Hodapp, & Evans, 2006). Still, a significant number of these children may have problems in developing a secure attachment because they express less emotion than other children. In one study, children with Down syndrome were not picked up and held by either the mother or the stranger in the strange situation to the same extent as non-delayed children. (See Table 2.2 for a description of the "strange situation" method of assessing child–caregiver attachment.) Even when these children made approaches with appropriate signals for contact, mothers and strangers rarely completed the contact, presumably because the children did not show the distress signals of crying, reaching, or holding on that typically tell the parent "I want to be picked up!" (Vaughn, Contreras, & Seifer, 1994). This finding has important implications for parents of young children with Down syndrome: Even though they may show few signals of distress or desire for contact, these infants and toddlers need to be held and nurtured just as others do.

Following the attachment period, the next important developmental milestones relate to the emergence of a sense of self, which establishes the early foundations of personality. Like other children, toddlers with Down syndrome begin to delight at recognizing themselves in mirrors and photos, although this milestone is often delayed. The experience of self-recognition in most infants is immediately met by smiles and laughter, and this experience is also found among toddlers with Down syndrome (Mans, Cicchetti, & Sroufe, 1978). This positive affect accompanying their visual self-recognition suggests that these children feel good about themselves. However, as toddlers and preschoolers, children with Down syndrome show delayed and aberrant functioning in their *internal state language,* the language that reflects the emergent sense of self and others (through the use of words such as "mad" and "happy"). Because internal state language is critical to regulating social interaction and providing a foundation for early self–other understanding, these children may be at increased risk for subsequent problems in the development of the self-system (Huck, Kemp, & Carter, 2010).

Children with intellectual disability, especially those with moderate to mild impairments, learn symbolic play—games, puppets, and sports—in much the same manner as do other children. Nevertheless, they often fail to gain their peers' acceptance in regular education settings, because they may have deficits in social skills and social–cognitive abilities (Cook & Oliver, 2011). Concerns about the social development of children with intellectual disability are increasing as a result of the movement to include children with different levels of ability in regular classrooms and schools, rather than only placing them in institutions or specialized facilities. Typically developing children seem to prefer playing with other typically developing children, and as a result, children with intellectual disability are more socially isolated from other children their age (Guralnick, Connor, & Johnson, 2011). These integrated classrooms allow children with intellectual disabilities, despite their limited social skills, to interact with typically developing peers, which in turn has a positive impact on their social status (Leffert, Siperstein, & Widaman, 2010; Siperstein, Glick, & Parker, 2009).

Emotional and Behavioral Problems

PATTIE

Disturbed or Disturbing?

Pattie was labeled mentally retarded and lived in over 20 homes and institutions before being committed to a state school at age 10. At the age of 20, she discussed some of her experiences and feelings: "I guess I was very disturbed. I call it disturbed, but it was when I was very upset. A lot of people at (the institution) ... told me I was disturbed—that I was disturbed and that I was retarded—so I figure that all through my life I was disturbed. Looking at the things I done, I must have been disturbed. ... Upset and disturbed are the same in my mind. Crazy to me is something else. It is somebody that is really gone. I mean really out. Just deliberately kill somebody just to do it. That is what I call crazy. I guess what I was was emotionally disturbed—yeah. Emotionally disturbed is a time when too many things are bothering me. They just build up till I get too nervous or upset. My mind just goes through all these changes and different things. So many things inside that were bothering me." (Based on Bogdan & Taylor, 1982.)

Pattie's description of her feelings while living in various institutions illuminates how "disturbing" her behavior could be. But are her feelings a function of her environment and personal limitations? Many children and adolescents with intellectual disability have to face many obstacles related to their intellectual, physical, and social impairments, and often they have little control over their own lives.

In the early 1970s, a major study was conducted to gain some understanding of the extent of psychiatric disorders among children and adults with and without intellectual disability (Rutter et al., 1976). Ratings by both parents and teachers revealed that about one-third of the children with mild intellectual disability and one-half of the children with more severe forms of intellectual disability showed major signs of emotional disturbance, suggesting that these problems are common. Since then, research has estimated that the risk of emotional and behavioral disturbances among children with intellectual disabilities is approximately three to five times greater than among typically developing children (Einfeld, Ellis, & Emerson, 2011). These problems are due largely to limited communication skills, additional stressors, and more neurological deficits faced by these children and youths (Adams & Oliver, 2011).

The nature and course of psychiatric disorders in children and adolescents with and without intellectual disabilities is likely very similar. Problem behaviors of youths with mild and moderate disabilities are similarly stable and persistent over the course of their development (de Ruiter et al., 2008; Einfeld et al., 2011). Impulse control disorders, anxiety disorders, and mood disorders are the most commonly diagnosed psychiatric diagnoses for children with intellectual disability. Although these problems are sometimes severe and often require intervention, they are considered to be part of the spectrum of problems that coexist with intellectual disability, and as not indicators of other psychiatric illnesses (Hodapp et al., 2006). By early adulthood, persons with intellectual disabilities continue to show a greater risk for psychopathology than the general population, although problems in attention and aggression show a significant decline from childhood rates (Buckles, Luckasson, & Keefe, 2013).

Adjustments usually are needed in how DSM-5 diagnostic criteria for other mental disorders are applied, however. The frequency of temper tantrums, hyperactivity, and mood disorders among these children requires consideration of what is normal or typical for other children with similar levels of intellectual disability. For example, the diagnosis of attention-deficit/hyperactivity disorder (ADHD) requires the presence of behavioral disturbance that is inappropriate for an individual's developmental level. Attention spans, distractibility, and on-task behaviors vary considerably among individuals with profound intellectual disability. An individual with profound intellectual disability must be compared with other children with profound intellectual disability for the purpose of diagnosing any other psychiatric disturbance (APA, 2013).

Internalizing Problems

Adolescence is a developmental period of increased risk for mood disorders and other internalizing symptoms, which is especially true for those with intellectual disability (Hodapp & Dykens, 2009). Like their normally developing peers, adolescents with Down syndrome and other forms of intellectual disability may show a decline in their previously sociable and cheerful behaviors, and in some cases they may suffer from significant symptoms of depression and social withdrawal.

ADHD-Related Symptoms

Teachers and parents of children and adolescents with intellectual disability commonly report ADHD-related symptoms that require adjustments in instruction and child-management strategies (Neece et al., 2013). When a teacher is present to prompt the appropriate behavior and participate in the activity, children with intellectual disability with and without ADHD generally will remain on task. However, when instructed to work without teacher assistance, differences between those with and without ADHD emerge (Handen et al., 1998). When children with intellectual disability and ADHD are placed on stimulant medication, they are able to remain on task for longer periods and their accuracy on cognitive tasks improves, similar to the responses of children with normal IQs (Simonoff et al., 2013).

Other Symptoms

Children and adults with intellectual disability may show additional symptoms that can be particularly troublesome. Pica (discussed in Chapter 14), which can result in the ingestion of caustic and dangerous substances, is seen in its more serious forms among children and adults with intellectual disability. **Self-injurious behavior (SIB)** is a serious and sometimes life-threatening problem that affects about one in five young children with ID (MacLean & Dornbush, 2012). Some common forms of SIB include head banging, eye gouging, severe scratching, rumination, some types of pica, and inserting objects under the skin. The long-term prognoses for pica and SIBs are not favorable. Emotional withdrawal, stereotypies (frequent repetition of the same posture, movement, or form of speech—e.g., head banging, hand or body movements), and avoidance of eye contact are often still evident more than 20 years later among persons with more severe forms of intellectual disability (Taylor, Oliver, & Murphy, 2011).

Thus, children with intellectual disability may show emotional and behavioral problems that require special recognition and learning strategies. In general, these problems do not constitute major psychiatric disorders, but they do reflect the greater challenges these children may have in learning to express their needs and in adapting to their surroundings. A 7-year-old girl with mild intellectual disability, for instance, may be at a developmental level comparable to that of a typically developing 4-year-old. In the classroom, therefore, she may have difficulty sitting in her seat and remaining on task. She may not always control her emotions or her behavior as well as other 7-year-olds in the class, leading to occasional outbursts of laughter or anger. It is important to keep these problems within a developmental perspective. We would not expect a 4-year-old to behave as well in the classroom as an older child, and expectations and teaching methods have to be adjusted accordingly. As expressed so well by Ed and Pattie, labeling a child with a diagnostic term that implies pathology or inability is often ill-conceived and counterproductive. Such terms must be used sparingly—only in circumstances, such as self-injurious behaviors, for which special attention is warranted.

Other Physical and Health Disabilities

Children with intellectual disabilities may also suffer other physical and developmental disabilities that can affect their health and development in pervasive ways. Such disabilities are usually related to the degree of intellectual impairment. Based on a meta-analysis of 31 studies, the prevalence of chronic health conditions in this population is much higher than in the general population (Oeseburg et al., 2011). ● Figure 5.2 shows some of the more common developmental disabilities found among children with intellectual disabilities.

Despite major co-occurring physical and intellectual disabilities, children and adults with Down syndrome now have a life expectancy approaching 60 years, largely as a result of better medical treatments for respiratory infections and congenital heart disorders (Dykens, 2013). However, most individuals with Down syndrome who live beyond the age of 40 demonstrate cognitive decline (much like Alzheimer's disease) due to gene damage on chromosome 21 (Torr et al., 2010).

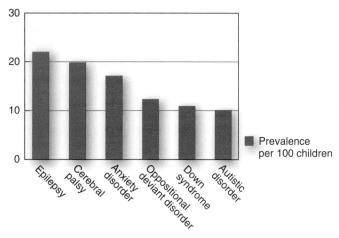

● **FIGURE 5.2** | Chronic health conditions among children with intellectual disabilities.

Based on Data from Oeseburg et al. (2011)

Section Summary

Developmental Course and Adult Outcomes

- Children with intellectual disability follow developmental stages in the same order as do typically developing children. However, their goals and motivation are reduced over time because of feelings of frustration, which often lead to expectations of failure.

- Adaptive skills and level of impairment may improve over time, especially for children with mild intellectual disability, if appropriate training and opportunities are provided.

- Developmental disabilities, such as speech and language problems and behavioral disturbances, are common. Emotional and behavioral problems are considered part of the spectrum of problems coexisting with intellectual disability, rather than indicators of mental disorder.

- Children with intellectual disability have a greater chance of having other physical and developmental disabilities, such as cerebral palsy, epilepsy, and emotional and behavioral disorders that can affect their health and development in pervasive ways.

CAUSES

It is astounding to consider that there are over 1,000 genetic disorders associated with intellectual disability, in addition to other organic causes (Hodapp & Dykens, 2009). Yet, despite the number of known causes, scientists are unsure of the causes of the majority of intellectual disability, especially mild ID. A genetic or environmental cause is known for almost two-thirds of individuals with moderate to profound intellectual disability, whereas the causes are known for only about

one-quarter of the individuals with mild intellectual disability (McDermott et al., 2007; van Bokhoven, 2011). Some causes happen before birth (prenatal), as is the case with all genetic disorders and accidents in the womb. Other causes are birth-related (perinatal) insults, such as prematurity or a lack of oxygen (anoxia) at birth. Still other causes are an inflammation of the brain lining (meningitis), head trauma, and other factors that occur after birth (postnatal).

Historically, causes of intellectual disabilities were divided into two fairly distinct groups—an organic group and the cultural–familial group (Hodapp & Dykens, 2003). The causes in the **organic group** have a clear biological basis and are usually associated with severe and profound intellectual disability, whereas causes in the **cultural–familial group** have no clear organic basis and are usually associated with mild intellectual disability (Hodapp et al., 2006).

Four major categories of risk factors contribute to intellectual disabilities: biomedical, social, behavioral, and educational. These four risk factors interact across time and even across generations from parent to child and provide a more comprehensive explanation of the interacting causes of problems associated with intellectual impairments (AAIDD, 2010; Chapman, Scott, & Stanton-Chapman, 2008). The definitions, characteristics, and causes of intellectual disability on the basis of these four risk factors are summed up in Table 5.5.

Although a distinction between organic and non-organic risk factors clarifies the underlying causes of intellectual disability, keep in mind that the distinctions are less clear in milder forms of intellectual disability than they are in more severe forms. For example, the large majority of persons at more severe levels of intellectual impairment (96%) show a clear etiology for the disorder, whereas a sizable percentage (32%) of those with mild impairments does not (Simonoff et al., 1996).

Considerable knowledge exists about organic intellectual disability because of the strong biological factors involved. Also, the increased ability to diagnose organic problems has led to increased estimates of this type of intellectual disability relative to cultural–familial causes—about one-third to one-half of all persons with intellectual disability show a clear organic cause (Hodapp et al., 2006). In stark contrast, the cultural–familial group remains somewhat of a mystery, although it comprises one-half to two-thirds of all persons with intellectual disability (Witwer et al., in press). As noted in Table 5.5, the prime suspects are environmental and situational factors such as poverty, inadequate child care, poor nutrition, and parental psychopathology, which mostly affect the psychological, and not the biological, development of the child. However, more

TABLE 5.5 | Risk Factors for Intellectual Disability

Timing	Biomedical	Social	Behavioral	Educational
Prenatal	1. Chromosomal disorders 2. Single-gene disorders 3. Syndromes 4. Metabolic disorders 5. Cerebral dysgenesis 6. Maternal illness 7. Parental age	1. Poverty 2. Maternal malnutrition 3. Domestic violence 4. Lack of access to prenatal care	1. Parental drug use 2. Parental alcohol use 3. Parental smoking 4. Parental immaturity	1. Parental cognitive disability without supports 2. Lack of preparation for parenthood
Perinatal	1. Prematurity 2. Birth injury 3. Neonatal disorders	1. Lack of access to prenatal care	1. Parental rejection of caretaking 2. Parental abandonment of child	1. Lack of medical referral for intervention services at discharge
Postnatal	1. Traumatic brain injury 2. Malnutrition 3. Meningoencephalitis 4. Seizure disorders 5. Degenerative disorders	1. Impaired child–caregiver interaction 2. Lack of adequate stimulation 3. Family poverty 4. Chronic illness in the family 5. Institutionalization	1. Child abuse and neglect 2. Domestic violence 3. Inadequate safety measures 4. Social deprivation 5. Difficult child behaviors	1. Impaired parenting 2. Delayed diagnosis 3. Inadequate early intervention services 4. Inadequate special education services 5. Inadequate family support

specific cause-and-effect relationships have not been determined. Accordingly, both genetic and environmental factors are implicated in milder forms of intellectual disability, but in a manner as yet to be determined (Toth & King, 2010).

The relative importance of the environment also stands out in the two-group distinction. The socioeconomic background of the organic group is about the same as that for the general population, which fits with the notion that severe forms of intellectual disability can affect anyone, regardless of SES. The familial group is overrepresented by those of lower SES and social disadvantage and is significantly related to a family history of intellectual disability. This fits with the assertion that an impoverished social environment can influence intellectual growth and ability in subtle, yet crucial, ways.

In most cases, the risk factors for intellectual disabilities have been supported empirically, with some adjustments as noted earlier in terms of nonorganic risk factors. First, the percentage of individuals with a clear organic cause has increased over the past few decades because of the greater knowledge of genetic and organic causes. Also, the original assumption that mild intellectual disability is not due to biomedical (organic) causes had to be tempered by findings that epilepsy, cerebral palsy, and other organic disorders are found more often among persons with mild intellectual disability than among those without intellectual disabilities (Hodapp et al., 2011).

Inheritance and the Role of the Environment

The study of human intelligence has received the lion's share of attention in terms of the underlying processes involved in genetic makeup and the environmental factors that influence genetic expression. Still, the long-standing debate concerning the relative contributions of genes and environment is far from being fully resolved (McDermott et al., 2007). Conceivably, genetic influences on development are potentially modifiable by environmental input, although the practicality of the modifications is another matter. Similarly, environmental influences on development involve the genes or structures to which the genes have contributed (Neisser et al., 1996). Simply stated, children do not inherit an IQ—they inherit a **genotype**, which is a collection of genes that pertain to intelligence. The expression of the genotype in the environment—the gene–environment interaction—is referred to as the **phenotype**. The **heritability** of a trait describes the proportion of the variation of a trait attributable to genetic influences in the population (Neisser et al., 1996). Heritability of any given trait, therefore, can range from none (0%) to 100% genetically determined.

Is it possible to estimate the heritability of intelligence and, by implication, the heritability of intellectual disability? This intriguing question can now be answered with some degree of confidence, but little fanfare. The overwhelming evidence points to a heritability of intelligence of approximately 50%; that is, both genetic and nongenetic factors play powerful roles in the makeup and expression of intelligence (Davis, Arden, & Plomin, 2008).

There are so many specific genetic causes of intellectual disability that some skepticism about the importance of environmental effects still remains. The difficulty of identifying, pinpointing, and measuring specific, nongenetic variables certainly adds to this dilemma. However, considerable evidence has demonstrated that major environmental variations do affect cognitive performance and social adjustment in children from disadvantaged backgrounds (Ramey, Ramey, & Lanzi, 2007). For example, children born to socially disadvantaged parents and then adopted into more privileged homes have higher IQ scores, stronger self-esteem, and fewer acts of delinquency than siblings reared by their disadvantaged, biological parents (Juffer & van IJzendoorn, 2007; van der Voort et al., 2013).

The prenatal environment may influence IQ to a greater extent than was previously appreciated. A review of studies of twins and nontwin siblings revealed that a shared prenatal environment (i.e., all children shared the same mother) accounted for 20% of IQ similarity in twins but only 5% in nontwin siblings (Devlin, Daniels, & Roeder, 1997). These findings imply that prenatal influences such as nutrition, hormone levels, and toxic substances may be misidentified as genetic when in fact they are environmental (Rutter, 2011). The practical benefits of this research are important to consider. If early environmental (prenatal) influences have a significant impact on intellectual functioning, then expanding public health initiatives aimed at improving maternal nutrition and reducing prenatal exposure to toxins may not only improve maternal prenatal care, but may also improve children's intellectual and cognitive functioning.

Genetic and Constitutional Factors

Despite the rapid expansion of knowledge regarding the genetic mechanisms underlying conditions associated with intellectual disability, the actual biological mechanisms that cause impaired intellect are poorly understood (Hodapp & Burack, 2006). Identification of abnormal genes, or genes involving an increased risk for particular disorders, is invaluable for genetic screening and counseling, but the identification does not specify a more effective treatment mode for intellectual disability.

Because so many conditions cause intellectual disability, the focus in this section will be on several different disorders or classes of disorder, including Down syndrome, fragile-X syndrome, Prader–Willi and Angelman syndromes, and single-gene conditions. Each disorder illustrates different aspects of genetic mechanisms. The various ways in which genes may interact with environmental influences also are highlighted.

Chromosome Abnormalities

The most common disorder that results from a chromosome abnormality is Down syndrome. These abnormalities also can occur in the number of sex chromosomes, resulting in intellectual disability syndromes such as Klinefelter's (XXY, a disorder in which males have an extra X chromosome) and Turner's (XO, a disorder in which women are missing a second X chromosome). These latter disorders are somewhat common—about 1 in 400 live births—but they are generally less devastating than genetic irregularities in their effects on intellectual functioning (Simonoff et al., 1996).

The number of children with Down syndrome has gradually decreased from 1 in 700 births to 1 in 1,000 births over the past two decades, due to increased prenatal screening and termination of pregnancies diagnosed with Down syndrome (Hazlett et al., 2011; Roizen & Patterson, 2003). The syndrome produces several distinguishing physical features, including a small skull; a large tongue protruding from a small mouth; almond-shaped eyes with sloping eyebrows; a flat nasal bridge; a short, crooked fifth finger; and broad, square hands with a simian (monkeylike) crease across the palm. These physical features are sometimes inconspicuous, and they can appear in varying degrees.

In most cases of Down syndrome, the extra chromosome results from **nondisjunction**, which is the failure of the 21st pair of the mother's chromosomes to separate during meiosis. When the mother's two chromosomes join with the single 21st chromosome from the father, the result is three number 21 chromosomes instead of the normal two (known as trisomy 21). Because nondisjunction is strongly related to maternal age, the incidence of Down syndrome increases from about 1 per 1,000 live births for mothers less than 35 years old to about 20 per 1,000 when the mother is 45 years of age or older (Wu & Morris, 2013).

Although the chromosomal basis of Down syndrome is well understood, the specific cause of intellectual disability in these children is not known. Gene mapping of chromosome 21 has resulted in the belief that some genes may have localized effects on brain development (Roizen, 2007). Testing this theory from a functional perspective, researchers pinpointed differences in hippocampal function among young children with and without Down syndrome based on neuropsychological testing (Pennington et al., 2003). Because the hippocampus plays an important role in long-term memory, these findings help to explain some of the underlying processes that affect the ability of children with Down syndrome to acquire normal language skills (a fundamental aspect of IQ).

Fragile-X syndrome is the most common cause of inherited intellectual disability (Down syndrome occurs more frequently but is rarely inherited). This disorder affects about 1 in 4,000 males and 1 in 8,000 females (Hagerman, 2011). Physical features of fragile-X syndrome are more subtle than those of Down syndrome and may include a large forehead, a prominent jaw, and low, protruding ears. Intellectual disability is generally in the mild to moderate range, although some children are profoundly handicapped and others have normal intelligence (Cornish et al., 2013). Males suffer more detrimental effects of fragile-X syndrome; intellectual disability occurs in most males who have fragile-X syndrome, as compared with only about half of females (Reiss & Hall, 2007).

Children and adolescents with fragile-X syndrome, which affects twice as many boys as girls.

Although the gene for fragile-X syndrome, known as the FMR-1 gene, is located on the X chromosome, this syndrome does not follow a traditional X-linked inheritance pattern. About one-third to one-half of the females who carry and transmit the disorder are themselves affected with a variant of the syndrome and show a slight degree of cognitive or emotional impairment. Further, about 20% of males with the FMR-1 gene transmit the disorder but are not affected themselves (Fatemi & Folsom, 2011).

The behavioral characteristics of fragile-X syndrome are often subtle but distinctive. The majority of affected males have unusual social and communication patterns marked by shyness and poor eye contact, as well as significant delays in cognitive and communication development (Einfeld, 2005). Social anxiety and avoidance are also common in girls with this disorder, even if unaccompanied by intellectual disability (Gerenser & Forman, 2007). Notably, most males and about one-third of females with fragile-X syndrome show some autism-like behaviors, such as flapping hands, biting themselves, repetitive actions, and walking on toes, and close to half of children with fragile-X syndrome meet the criteria for a diagnosis of autism (McCary & Roberts, 2013).

Prader–Willi syndrome is a complex genetic disorder that includes short stature, intellectual disability or learning disabilities, incomplete sexual development, low muscle tone, and an involuntary urge to eat constantly. The syndrome is rare and estimated to affect only about 5 to 10 per 100,000 births (Dykens, Cassidy, & DeVries, 2011). Between ages 2 and 6, children with this syndrome develop extreme overeating, foraging, and hoarding. They need fewer calories than normal to maintain an appropriate

This micrograph shows the "pinched chromosome" found in fragile-X syndrome.

Chico Sanchez/Alamy

The Washington Times/ZUMAPRESS/Newscom

This 8-year-old boy has Prader–Willi syndrome (left). Nineteen-year-old Danna has Angelman syndrome and is part of the inclusion program at her school, allowing her to be with students from the general population (right)

weight because they are small, and they invariably become obese (Hinton, Isles, Williams, & Parkinson, 2010; Theodora, Talebizadeh, & Butler, 2006).

Angelman syndrome is associated with intellectual disability that is usually moderate to severe. The behavior of children with this disorder is characterized by ataxia (awkward gait), jerky movements, hand flapping, seizures, and the absence of speech. Distinctive facial features include a large jaw and an open-mouthed expression (Didden et al., 2009).

Both Prader–Willi and Angelman syndromes are associated with an abnormality of chromosome 15, but they are not considered inherited conditions. Rather, these syndromes are believed to be spontaneous genetic birth defects that occur at or near the time of conception. For reasons that are still not well understood, genes in the affected region on the mother's chromosome 15 are not expressed (functional). This lack of a gene or genes that are very close to each other appears to be the cause of the related syndromes. The origin— whether maternal or paternal—of the absent genetic material is the likely cause of the marked phenotypic differences.

Much is being discovered about the genetic influences on intelligence and adaptive abilities. Because these influences are by no means uniform or exact, a challenge remains in accounting for the mechanisms that cause these effects on intelligence and the variations in phenotypic expression. Even with Down syndrome, for example, the range in IQ extends into mild intellectual disability and some individuals have an IQ within the normal range. Molecular genetic and biological techniques are beginning to make it possible to understand why such variation occurs, although knowledge to date is extremely limited (Handen, 2007).

Single-Gene Conditions

Other syndromes affecting intelligence and cognitive functioning can result from genetically based metabolic defects, known as inborn errors of metabolism. Such defects cause excesses or shortages of certain chemicals that are necessary during particular stages of development. Inborn errors of metabolism account for 3% to 7% of cases of severe intellectual disability (Antshel & Arnold, 2007; Wolfe & Krasnewich, 2013).

One of the best understood examples of a single-gene condition is *phenylketonuria* (PKU), a rare disorder occurring in approximately 1 in 15,000 individuals (Waisbren, 2011). Unlike chromosomal abnormalities that cause Down syndrome, the cause of PKU is a recessive gene transmitted by typical mendelian mechanisms. Children receive the gene from both parents (neither of whom necessarily has PKU), which results in a lack of liver enzymes necessary for converting the amino acid phenylalanine into tyrosine, another essential amino acid. Tyrosine is normally converted into other chemicals needed for physical development. Because the individual is unable to metabolize phenylalanine, which is found in many foods, it accumulates in the body and is converted to phenylpyruvic acid, another abnormal metabolite. This metabolite, in turn, causes brain damage, intellectual disability, musty body odor, hyperactivity, seizures, and dry, bleached skin and hair.

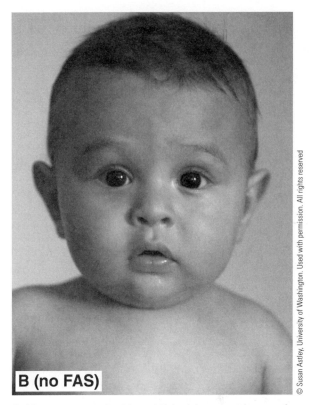

A (FAS)　　　**B (no FAS)**

Characteristics of children with fetal alcohol spectrum disorders (left) as compared with a child without evidence of the disorder (right). Children with FASD show features such as skin folds at the corners of the eyes, low nasal bridge, short nose, smooth area between nose and upper lip, small head circumference, small eye opening, small midface, and thin upper lip. These facial features are consistent in children with fetal alcohol spectrum disorders across geographic locations and from different ethnic backgrounds

PKU is a good example of a genetic disorder that can be treated successfully by environmental changes. Most countries now screen all infants for the presence of this defect at birth, and affected infants are immediately placed on a restricted diet. However, now that affected individuals have received early treatment, young women with PKU have begun to reproduce, resulting in high rates of birth defects and subsequent intellectual disability in their offspring. Severe dietary restriction, begun prior to conception, is currently the best precaution for these problems (Waisbren, 2011).

Neurobiological Influences

Fetal and infant development also can be affected by adverse biological conditions such as malnutrition, exposure to toxic substances, and various prenatal and perinatal stressors. These conditions directly or indirectly cause lowered intelligence and intellectual disability in some, but by no means all, cases. The effects often depend on the degree of insult to the fetus and the time of fetal development (the first trimester being the period of greatest susceptibility).

Pregnancy and delivery are times of greatest susceptibility to trauma, infections, or other complications and account for about 10% of intellectual disability overall. Other general medical conditions acquired during infancy or childhood, such as infections, traumas, and accidental poisonings, account for about 5% of suspected or known causes of intellectual disability (Hodapp et al., 2011).

Prenatal exposure to alcohol through maternal alcohol consumption during pregnancy is the most widely recognized preventable cause of intellectual disability. *fetal alcohol spectrum disorder* (FASD) is an umbrella term that covers the range of outcomes associated with all levels of prenatal alcohol exposure (Riley, Infante, & Warren, 2011). Even small amounts of alcohol may have negative effects on the growth and intellectual abilities of a fetus. For example, significant deficits in physical development were found among children and adolescents with prenatal alcohol exposure when mothers had, on average, less than one drink per day; exposure during the second half of the first trimester was especially harmful (Day et al., 2002; Feldman et al., 2012).

Lip-Philtrum (space between the nose and upper lip) Guide

This series of photos provides a more detailed look at degrees of philtrum groove smoothness. In Photo 1, you see a normal lip-philtrum groove. As your eye moves to the right, you see philtrums that are progressively smoother. In Photo 5, you see the smoothness characteristic of FAS

The most extreme form of FASD, **fetal alcohol syndrome,** is considered to be a leading known cause of intellectual disability because of its clear link to intellectual impairment. Fetal alcohol syndrome is estimated to occur in 0.5 to 2.0 per 1,000 live births (Centers for Disease Control and Prevention, 2011c), although it is considered to be grossly underdiagnosed and may be considerably more common. Alarmingly, the incidence of this disorder is about 4 times higher among African Americans and 16 times higher among Native Americans as compared with majority populations (MMWR, 2002). Despite over two decades of public health warnings about abstaining from alcohol immediately before and during pregnancy, fetal alcohol spectrum disorders have not declined (Watson et al., 2011).

Fetal alcohol syndrome is characterized by central nervous system (CNS) dysfunction, abnormalities in facial features, and growth retardation, with affected children falling below the 10th percentile. The mechanism that causes the abnormalities is not clear but is believed to involve the *teratogenic* (damage to fetal development) effects of alcohol on the development of the central nervous system and the related damage from metabolic and nutritional problems associated with alcoholism (Niccols, 2007). On average, the IQ of children and youths with this disorder is in the mild range of intellectual disability (Streissguth, 2007). In addition to intellectual deficits, these children often have long-term difficulties that resemble ADHD, including attention deficit, poor impulse control, and serious behavior problems, which often persist into adulthood and carry high treatment costs (Amendah, Grosse, & Bertrand, 2011; Vaurio, Crocker, & Mattson, 2013).

Several teratogens other than alcohol are known to increase the risk of intellectual disability because of their effect on CNS development. Viral infections, such as rubella (German measles), contracted by the mother during the first 3 months of pregnancy can cause severe defects in the fetus. However, immunization has virtually eliminated this cause of intellectual disability in most developed countries. Syphilis, scarlet fever, tuberculosis of the nervous system, degenerative diseases of the nerves, and sometimes measles and mumps can lead to intellectual disability. ID also can be caused by x-rays, certain drugs taken by the mother during pregnancy, mechanical pressure on the child's head during birth, lack of oxygen due to delays in breathing at birth, poisons such as lead and carbon monoxide, and tumors and cysts in the head (Hodapp & Dykens, 2003). In essence, any biochemical or infectious substance that cannot be destroyed or regulated by the mother's immune system or regulatory system can pose a risk to fetal development and, in turn, intellectual ability.

Social and Psychological Dimensions

The final group of factors that cause intellectual disability, or occur in association with it, is perhaps the least understood and most diverse. Broadly defined, these factors include many environmental influences, such as deprived physical and emotional care and stimulation of the infant, and other mental disorders that are often accompanied by intellectual disability, such as autism spectrum disorder. Together these factors account for about 15% to 20% of intellectual disability. Although quite broad in scope, these influences are largely indirect and unproven because they often are embedded in different layers and degrees of individual and family circumstances. Parental deviance, such as abuse or neglect, and how it can affect intellectual and behavioral development is discussed in greater detail in Chapter 12.

Parents not only provide their children with their genes, but also provide the child-rearing environment and atmosphere that serve to direct and shape the child's psychological development right from the beginning. Consider the comments by the father of a young child with Down syndrome, who had to learn how to ask for proper assistance and to connect with other families of children with Down syndrome:

I will never forget when the nurse told us how much these children can achieve. Her advice to contact a local association for children with Down syndrome was an important beginning. Other parents at the association helped me understand that Down syndrome was a chromosomal aberration and not a disease, and [gave advice on] how to look for help. My son was hardly a month old when he began physiotherapy to help him learn and interact with others. Jake is 3 years old now and he is full of life. He walks, repeats several words, and understands directions. (Adapted from Martin, 1995)

How do families who have a child with intellectual disability contribute to the child's healthy development or, alternatively, to his or her decline? In recent years, the field of intellectual disabilities has shown a major change in how this question is addressed. Rather than focusing only on the family's negative influence, researchers are interested in learning how some families successfully cope with the additional stress and demands of raising a child with intellectual disability. As is the case when dealing with other stressors, individual members and the family unit can be affected negatively as well as positively, such as when a couple or siblings are brought closer together by caring for a child with special needs (Hodapp & Dykens, 2012; Lobato et al., 2011; Neece, Blacher, & Baker, 2010).

One way in which parents adapt successfully to having a child with special needs is to use social supports and community resources, although individual preferences regarding the type of support used may vary, and supports that help mothers may not help fathers. Mothers often are concerned about how raising a child with intellectual disability may affect their personal relationships with their husbands and about the restrictions the child's care may place on their role in the family, whereas fathers worry about not feeling close to the child. Thus, mothers and fathers differ in how they understand and relate to the child with intellectual disability, the aspects of raising the child they see as stressful, and the factors that best alleviate stress (Gerstein, Crnic, Blacher, & Baker, 2009).

Understanding how young people with Down syndrome function socially and independently has helped identify the factors that affect their adjustment to community living. Not surprisingly, early cognitive development is a strong predictor of developmental progress and self-sufficiency among such children, as shown in areas such as language (Filippi & Karmiloff-Smith, 2013). However, family factors are also important, particularly mothers' strategies for coping with their children's problems and their families' levels of social support (Gray et al., 2011).

Section Summary

Causes

- The two-group approach emphasizes the important etiological differences between organic and cultural–familial causes of intellectual disability.
- Organic causes include genetic and constitutional factors, such as chromosome abnormalities, single-gene conditions, and neurobiological influences.
- Suspected cultural–familial, or nonorganic, causes of intellectual disability include diverse social, behavioral, and educational risk factors.
- Some of the established risk factors for intellectual disability include alcohol, lead, and other toxins or injuries that affect prenatal and postnatal development. Other risk factors affect the quality of physical and emotional care and stimulation of the infant and small child, such as poverty and inadequate family supports.

PREVENTION, EDUCATION, AND TREATMENT

We plead for those who cannot plead for themselves.

—Motto of Highgate, the first public institution for persons with intellectual disability, established in London, England, October 1847

As we turn our discussion toward treatment methods for children with intellectual disability, consider for a moment how you would apply your knowledge of psychological and educational treatments to best assist a child such as Vanessa or Matthew. Would you first try to get Matthew's behavior problems under control and then teach him other skills? Would Vanessa likely benefit from individualized treatment that emphasizes gradual speech training and self-help skills?

As is true for several other disorders we have discussed, such as ADHD and some types of conduct disorders, the primary presenting problems—in this case, intellectual deficiency and limited adaptive abilities—are chronic conditions that pose limitations across many important areas of development. Consequently, programs often must be designed to fit the educational and developmental levels of each individual child even more so than, say, treatment programs for children with behavior or anxiety problems. It is useful to begin this task with an overview of major environmental and individual characteristics that may increase the risk of adjustment problems, or serve to protect the child from such problems.

A child's overall adjustment is a function of parental participation, family resources, and social supports (on the environmental side), combined with his or her level of intellectual functioning, basic temperament, and other specific deficits (on the individual side). Treatment can be designed to build on the child's existing resources and strengths in an effort to bolster particular skill areas or learning abilities. In other words, it is not necessary to focus attention primarily on what the child lacks, but rather on how best to match teaching and therapeutic methods to the child's own levels and abilities to accomplish realistic, practical goals. Thus, treatment and education for children with ID involves a multicomponent, integrated strategy that considers children's needs within the context of their individual development, their family or institutional setting, and their community (Wilkins & Matson, 2009).

The severity of intellectual disability can be prevented or reduced in some instances by taking proper precautions. Therefore, we begin this section by discussing current health care practices involving parental education and prenatal screening. These procedures, implemented in many communities, are designed to inform parents about proper prenatal care and risks and to detect abnormal fetal development. We then turn to psychosocial treatments for children with intellectual disability and their families, which have become a common part of many treatment and education plans. In short, treatment focuses on teaching the child necessary skills and abilities, such as language, personal care and hygiene, and social skills, as well as on teaching skills and providing supports to parents and other caregivers.

Psychopharmacological interventions for children and adults with intellectual disabilities have been hindered by both professional and public perceptions that psychotropic drugs are used to control behavior—a view based on unfortunate and inappropriate use in the past and on the drugs' major side effects. Although many newer classes of compounds that reduce unpleasant side effects have become available over the past decade, these compounds have not been systematically studied in treating people with intellectual disability. Nevertheless, drug treatment is beneficial in some cases. As with other childhood disorders, drug treatment can be targeted at desirable changes in specific behaviors or dimensions, such as compulsions, aggression, or self-injury, rather than at treating the underlying disorder itself (Golombek & King, 2010; Ghuman et al., 2009).

Prenatal Education and Screening

One of the best opportunities to promote healthy outcomes occurs during prenatal development (Hodapp & Burack, 2006). Although not all forms of intellectual disability can be prevented prenatally, many debilitating forms related to fetal alcohol syndrome, lead poisoning, or rubella can easily be prevented if proper

precautions are taken. A much larger number of children are positively affected by prenatal education and health care if one includes not only the prevention of specific risks, but also the promotion of proper child care, especially during the child's first 2 years.

Not too long ago, a pregnant woman would have seen her doctor for several visits prior to childbirth, and may have gained additional knowledge through reading and from family members. At that time, the focus was largely on the medical needs of the pregnancy, with little opportunity to consider what it means to raise a child and to prepare for the added stress and complexity that child care involves.

Today, almost all communities have prenatal programs for parents, and fathers have taken on a much larger role. Parents are provided with information about the different periods of fetal development and are cautioned about the use of alcohol, tobacco, nonprescribed drugs, and caffeine during pregnancy. These programs, often run by public health nurses, community colleges, churches, and other community organizations, have filled much of the gap in services between basic medical care and basic child care that parents need prior to the birth of a baby. The stresses of childbirth and postnatal adjustment are described, with opportunities for parents to consider the additional supports they may need and the changes they may need to make to ensure the child's health and safety. Many programs also include discussion of children with special needs, so that parents are not left feeling confused and alone (Ramey et al., 2007).

In providing these important prenatal services, there is an increasing multicultural focus that sensitively and appropriately considers the cultural background of the recipients (Pumariega et al., 2013). We now recognize that family members make choices based on cultural influences. To be of most help, prenatal and postnatal services must be culturally diverse and culturally sensitive. Meeting this goal involves working with informal support and assistance networks, such as churches, community and spiritual leaders, and community organizations, in ways that extend self-determination. Prenatal programs are increasingly breaking away from a set curriculum and are being modified to establish a better fit with each cultural group or community—for example, by providing information on ways to access health care and family services for persons with limited transportation, limited income, and so forth.

Prenatal screening constitutes a particular form of genetic screening that is used to determine whether a fetus has a genetic abnormality, such as Down syndrome, which would lead to a seriously handicapping condition. Ultrasound scanning can detect many conditions associated with physical defects, and testing of amniotic fluid during fetal development assists the prenatal diagnosis of chromosomal abnormalities and genetic diseases identifiable at the DNA level (Roizen & Patterson, 2003). Substantial advances in genetic screening allow for much greater precision in genetic counseling. For example, noninvasive molecular genetic techniques are replacing invasive techniques, such as amniocentesis, for women whose pregnancies are considered to be at an increased risk for certain chromosome abnormalities, which allows for quicker diagnosis of a broad range of genetic disorders (Devers et al., 2013). Ethical and practical guidelines are still under review, however, because there is a fundamental difference between using genetic information to prevent an illness or disease and altering genetic material to promote desired (or get rid of undesired) personal characteristics.

Psychosocial Treatments

The first psychosocial treatment we consider involves intensive, broad-ranging, early-intervention services for families with young children that are designed to reduce risk factors and promote healthy child development. Although expensive to deliver, these services are proving to be of considerable benefit to children and families over the long term, and they accomplish a great deal more than merely reducing intellectual deficits. We then take a close look at the existing educational and therapeutic methods that have successfully benefited children with various levels of intellectual disability. We discuss the application of behavioral, cognitive–behavioral, and family-oriented interventions, with an emphasis on the task of integrating known treatments that best match the different needs of these children.

As a prelude to the discussion of psychosocial treatments, we acknowledge the importance of community-based activities that offer people with disabilities a choice of ways to develop their interpersonal and practical skills and self-confidence. Studies find that athletes who participate in Special Olympics score higher on measures of social competence and have more positive self-perceptions than do their nonathlete counterparts (Special Olympics, 2007).

Early Intervention

For over 50 years, involving caregivers and other adults in early, intensive, child-focused activities has been one of the most promising methods for enhancing the intellectual and social skills of young children with developmental disabilities, including children with intellectual disability, learning disabilities, and lack of environmental stimulation (Wilkins & Matson, 2009). Many of these children would be described as disadvantaged or high-risk, synonymous terms referring to family circumstances such as low income, insufficient

health care, and poor housing; child characteristics such as low IQ, poor adaptive abilities, and physical or health disabilities; or a combination of the two. Early educational intervention consists of systematic efforts to provide high-risk children with supplemental educational experiences before they enter school, and this intervention frequently includes other family and child services.

One of the more successful examples of an early educational intervention is the Carolina Abecedarian Project (Campbell & Ramey, 2010). The intervention was offered to children of poor families (98% of whom were African American), who were provided with enriched environments from early infancy through the preschool years. In follow-up studies of over 100 children, results showed that by age 2, the test scores of children in the enrichment group were already higher than the test scores of children in control groups, and at age 15, they remained some 5 points higher, 10 years after the end of the program. At age 15, members of the treated group were less likely to score in the intellectual disability or low-normal range of intellectual functioning. The enrichment group also outperformed the control groups in academic achievement through 10 years in school for both reading and mathematics, and there were fewer instances of grade retention or special education classes (Ramey et al., 1999, 2000). By age 30, those who received the intervention had better educational attainment, with some evidence of economic benefit as well (Campbell et al., 2002; Campbell et al., 2012; Pungello et al., 2010).

Based on these and related findings, the optimal timing for intervention appears to be during the preschool years (Hodapp & Burack, 2006). Early education programs such as the Abecedarian project are highly relevant to the issue of environmental effects in intellectual disability because they involve children from socially disadvantaged backgrounds, who have a much higher risk of intellectual disability. Although the programs show effectiveness, the lasting benefits depend on the stability and continuation of environmental changes that foster healthy child development. A Closer Look 5.3 offers a set of practical recommendations for enhancing children's lives through early intervention.

Dan's mother added some additional ideas, based on her own experiences:

Be creative. He learns by repetition, so the more closely you follow the "house" system and coordinate all the topics of all the classes, the easier he and the other students can learn. He can learn spelling words of items he touches in science lab. He can learn history related to his library book of the week. Combine the lesson plans to touch all phases of the subject.

Practical Recommendations for Enhancing Children's Lives through Early Intervention

- *Encouragement of exploration.* Children are encouraged by adults to explore and gather information about their environments.
- *Mentoring in basic skills.* A trusted, familiar adult teaches children basic cognitive skills such as labeling, sorting, sequencing, and comparing.
- *Celebration of developmental advances.* Family and others who know the child celebrate and reinforce each of the child's accomplishments.
- *Guided rehearsal and extension of new skills.* Responsible others assist the child in rehearsing and extending newly acquired skills.
- *Protection from harmful displays of disapproval, teasing, or punishment.* Constructive criticism and negative consequences for unacceptable behaviors are used.
- *A rich and responsive language environment.* Adults provide a predictable and understandable environment for communication. Spoken and written language are used to convey information, provide social awards, and encourage the learning of new material and skills.

Source: C. T. Ramey and S. L. Ramey, 1992.

Behavioral Treatments

As noted earlier, for many years the way to deal with problems faced by persons with ID was to isolate them from society by placing them in institutions or separate schools, a practice that curtailed their ability to interact with typically developing peers. Behavioral interventions first emerged in the context of these restricted settings and were initially seen primarily as a means to control or redirect negative behaviors, such as aggression or self-injury.

Through the efforts of concerned behavioral therapists, important principles were established concerning the implementation of behavioral methods with children and other persons who are unable to provide fully informed consent. The Association for Behavior Analysis (ABA) Task Force stipulated that each individual has the right to the least-restrictive effective treatment, as well as a right to treatment that results in safe and meaningful behavior change (Van Houten et al., 1988). These efforts, coupled with continued input from parents and educators, led to a greater emphasis on positive methods for teaching basic academic and social skills in both schools and communities to help children and adolescents with intellectual disability adapt in the most normal fashion.

Vanessa's treatment plan typifies how several important behavioral methods are successfully applied. Language training often is considered a fundamental starting point for teaching more advanced skills to children with intellectual disability, and behavioral methods are well suited for this purpose (Matson, Matson, & Rivet, 2007; van der Schuit et al., 2011). The plan developed for Vanessa offers a useful example of how these methods are applied. Vanessa participated in one-to-one therapy sessions during which she was reinforced (by edibles and praise) for emitting sounds that imitated the therapist's sounds. The speech therapist used a *shaping* procedure that began by forming a list of responses (such as "ge," "ga," "oh") that were progressively more similar to the target response (in this case, the word go). After Vanessa mastered the first sound, she was reinforced only for attempts at the next sound on the list, and so on, until the desired sound or word was gradually shaped.

To encourage her speech sounds and simple words to become functional speech and language, the therapist taught Vanessa to imitate the names of pictures shown to her. If she said the name of the picture, such as "dog," within a few seconds, she received social rewards and, if necessary, tangible rewards such as candy. As Vanessa became more adept at naming the pictures, the therapist began to use some of the trained words in response to questions he would pose, such as "What is this?" Gradually, Vanessa's mother and father were brought into the sessions with the therapist to begin asking her similar questions and promoting her use of functional speech. As her speech grew, new words and short sentences were introduced—ones that would be of most use to Vanessa on a daily basis at home, at the cafeteria, and when asking to use the bathroom.

Vanessa's behavior during mealtimes also presented considerable problems for her parents. She had difficulty getting food onto her fork or spoon, so her parents were taught to use simple methods of *modeling* and *graduated guidance* to assist. After demonstrating how to hold a spoon, they would show her how to pick up her food and bring it to her mouth. They carefully demonstrated each step involved, from dipping the spoon to placing it in the mouth, each time praising her for her attempts. As required, they would guide her hand to show her how each step was done.

Unfortunately, without much warning, Vanessa would sometimes throw or spit her food, so her parents were also taught how to respond to such outbursts. Their first attempt to stop this problem was to remove her food for half a minute or so. If this tactic did not settle the behavior, or if she became more aggressive, they used time-out from reinforcement. They provided a short reprimand ("Don't throw food!")

Social and sports events are an important way of fostering independence, social competence, and self-esteem in persons with intellectual disability.

and told her why she was in time-out. Without ceremony, they turned her chair into the corner for about a minute. At the first sign of settling her behavior, they turned Vanessa around in her chair to face them and returned to a positive, guided method of helping her to learn to feed herself.

In addition to their training in basic skills to promote language and readiness to learn, many older children and adolescents with ID benefit from training in specific social skills to promote their integration into regular classrooms and other activities. As mentioned previously, individuals with intellectual disability have various degrees of difficulty in communication, self-control, anger management, correct recognition and labeling of affect in others, social problem solving, and a host of other interpersonal limitations that often lead to victimization by peers (Fisher, Moskowitz, & Hodapp, 2013).

Tailored to each student's individual needs, social skills training uses positive reinforcement strategies to teach and reward important interpersonal skills such as smiling, sharing, asking for help, attending, taking turns, following directions, and solving problems (Kemp et al., 2013). Peers without disabilities also can be taught effective ways to interact socially with children with intellectual disability, a method known as social inclusion. This method is successful in increasing the quantity and quality of interactions between children with disabilities and their peers without disabilities, and it promotes the development of friendships (Harada et al., 2011; Siperstein et al., 2009).

Cognitive–Behavioral Therapy

The same theories that led to the development of cognitive therapy techniques for children with other types of learning and behavior problems generally apply to children with intellectual disability as well. These methods are most effective for children with some receptive and expressive language skills—like the skills Vanessa acquired after careful and prolonged training through the use of visual and physical prompts. Once children are able to follow adult verbal directives and to verbally describe their own actions, they are in a position to benefit from verbal self-regulation and behavioral-inhibition training programs (Cobb et al., 2006; Bexkens et al., 2014). Self-instructional training is most beneficial for children who have developed some language proficiency but still have difficulty understanding and following directions. **Self-instructional training** teaches children to use verbal cues, initially taught by the therapist or teacher, to process information, to keep themselves on task ("I'm not gonna look. I'm gonna keep working."), and to remind themselves of how to approach a new task ("What do I have to do here? First, I have to. …").

Education of children with intellectual disability has been plagued by the fact that specific cognitive skills can be taught, yet children often lack the higher-order (metacognitive) capabilities to apply these skills in new situations. Children with intellectual disabilities use fewer, simpler, and more passive cognitive strategies in memory and learning task situations than do children without such disabilities (Hodapp et al., 2011). Therefore, instructional methods developed to assist the average or above-average learner are often ineffective. Coupled with this concern is the continued reliance on verbal instruction to teach behavioral and cognitive skills to normal and exceptional children.

Language problems may require verbal instructional techniques to be replaced by methods that capitalize on a particular child's strongest learning channels. These methods often rely less on verbal, symbolic representation and more on perceptual, visually oriented techniques such as modeling and picture cuing.

Specific learning techniques also can be used to improve memory and learning. For example, in addition to being taught various basic math skills, students learn to identify the type of math problem they confront and then to choose the appropriate strategy for solving the problem. The first goal of this training is to teach the child to be *strategical*—to use cognitive strategies—and then to be *metastrategical*—to make discriminations regarding how to apply different strategies in different situations. This method has been successful in teaching children with learning difficulties a range of adaptive skills, such as math and language (Hay et al., 2007).

Family-Oriented Strategies

The presence in the family of a child with intellectual disability is a challenge, but it is not an insurmountable problem. Families are central to the development of any child, but care of a child with intellectual disability involves an expanded commitment of time, energy, and skills. The needs of the child often dictate that family members participate in various community services and educational systems with which they may be quite unfamiliar. In the end, the majority of parents of children with intellectual disability come to see their child as a positive contributor to their family and quality of life, although the family experiences a higher-than-average level of stress and parental depressive symptoms (Gerstein et al., 2009; Hodapp & Dykens, 2012). This view of the child as a positive contributor is reassuring, given the finding that individual services provided for the child are usually more effective when family members are active participants (AAIDD, 2010).

What exactly do the parents of a child with intellectual disability need to be most effective? Family members need support and guidance, access to necessary services, opportunities for a short caregiving break, such as a weekend off, and the availability of goal-oriented counseling to cope with the practical difficulties of demanding caregiving tasks, such as sleep disruption, marital discord, and restricted leisure and social opportunities. Short-term, problem-focused behavioral therapy for the parents is one of the most successful approaches (Bagner & Eyberg, 2007). Each family's treatment goals are developed individually; then parents are provided with solutions matched to their needs. For example, parents may be taught assertiveness skills or behavior-management techniques (discussed in the next paragraph). In some instances, the solutions involve obtaining new resources from teachers or day-care staff or from neighbors and extended family.

Parent training has been widely used to assist parents of children with intellectual disability. As opposed to the focus of many other applications of parent training, when the child has intellectual disability the primary focus on behavior change is skill acquisition rather than reduction of behavior problems (Bagner & Eyberg, 2007). The parents' roles as primary teachers often continue well past the normal childhood years, so parent training often entails a relevant focus on development to prepare the family to tackle each new challenge.

There are three critical, but not exclusive, periods during the family life cycle in which parent training and family counseling are most beneficial. The first occurs during the child's infancy and toddlerhood, when parents are coming to terms with the child's disability and may need assistance in learning ways to provide adequate stimulation of early language formation and similar developmental skills. A second critical time is during the preschool and school years, when parents often want to know more about the best way to teach their child basic academic and social skills. Intensive programs, which demand a considerable amount of the parents' time, are usually best suited for the preschool years, when the family is most focused on child developmental issues (Brown et al., 2008). Finally, parental concerns resurface during the child's emergence into young adulthood. At this age, the child is no longer eligible for funded schooling, and new issues of housing, employment, relationships, and financial planning associated with independent living become concerns.

Many children with intellectual disabilities attend regular schools. The **inclusion movement** (and the Individuals with Disabilities Education Improvement Act) gives children with disabilities the option of being educated in regular classroom settings, regardless of the severity of the disability. The school curriculum must be adaptable to meet the individual needs and abilities of children with intellectual disability. For example, because children with Down syndrome often have strong visual short-term memories, a visually based approach to teach them how to read has been determined to be more effective than traditional phonetic approaches (Hazlett et al., 2011). Furthermore, this movement has raised anew the issue of how persons with disabilities are perceived and treated by professionals and peers.

Some children and adolescents with intellectual disability benefit from **residential care,** or out-of-home placement, which also carries with it unique responsibilities of family members. Residential care services are seldom a full replacement for the love and attention of the family, yet they may be necessary and beneficial under some circumstances, such as aggressive behavior of the child or the need for specialized language or social skills training that cannot be provided adequately in the home or regular school setting. Residential care (also known as "respite care") ranges from part-time care, when the child returns home each evening or weekend, to full-time care, when home visits are less frequent. Some residential programs may serve only a few children at a time, much like a group home; others may be large, multidisciplinary tertiary care facilities serving persons of all ages with various disabilities.

Regardless of the structure of the residential program or respite services, research has determined that family involvement plays a critical role in children's adaptation to and benefit from such settings. Facilities that offer ways to promote family involvement, such as weekend visits and participation in classroom activities, strengthen the important attachment between children with intellectual disability and their families (Grant, Ramcharan, & Flynn, 2007). Because one goal of residential care is often to enable the child to live at home or in a family-like community setting, efforts to maintain family involvement are invaluable (Chan et al., 2012).

Section Summary

Prevention, Education, and Treatment

- Intervention efforts are most successful when offered at the earliest point in time, especially through the preschool years.
- Interventions for children with intellectual disability are matched to the child's individual needs and abilities, and are integrated with the family, school, and community.
- Successful interventions often include behaviorally based training and educational components that teach specific skills and reduce undesired behavior.

Study Resources

SECTION SUMMARIES

KEY TERMS

6

Autism Spectrum Disorder and Childhood-Onset Schizophrenia

It wasn't just that she didn't understand language. She didn't seem to be aware of her surroundings. She wasn't figuring out how her world worked, learning about keys that fit into doors, lamps that turned off because you pressed a switch, milk that lived in the refrigerator … If she was focusing on anything, it was on minute particles of dust or hair that she now picked up from the rug, to study with intense concentration. Worse, she didn't seem to be picking up anyone's feelings.

Catherine Maurice, mother of a child with autism (1993a)

CHAPTER PREVIEW

AUTISM SPECTRUM DISORDER (ASD)

THE COMPELLING DESCRIPTION THAT begins this chapter, from a mother talking about her 2-year-old daughter offers a first glimpse into the mystery of autism, perhaps the most captivating and telling of all childhood disorders. **Autism,** or **autism spectrum disorder (ASD),** is a complex neurodevelopmental disorder characterized by abnormalities in social communication and unusual behaviors and interests. ASD touches every aspect of the child's interaction with his or her world, involves many parts of the brain, and undermines the traits that make us human—our social responsiveness, ability to communicate, and feelings for other people.

Description and History

Imagine yourself the parent of an infant or toddler who won't cuddle, look into your eyes, or respond to your affection or touching. Unlike other children, who are social beings from the start, your child doesn't seem to form a loving relationship with you as you interact with him. In fact, he seems incapable of forming a normal relationship or communicating with anyone. As he grows older, he rarely speaks. When he does speak, he talks in unusual ways, for example, by parroting what you say to him or blurting out seemingly meaningless phrases, such as "Dinosaurs don't cry." Your child doesn't use facial expressions or gestures to communicate his needs or to tell you how he feels—no smiles, no nods, no head shakes, no holding up toys for you to look at. Nor does he seem to understand the smiling faces that you and others make as you try to engage him socially. Your child shows little interest in sharing pride or pleasure with you or anyone else. Over the first few years of life, he becomes more and more isolated. He becomes caught up in his own little world of rituals and interests, and if these are interrupted, he becomes extremely upset. Something is seriously wrong. Naturally, you are concerned and have many questions.

In this chapter, we address a number of critical questions asked by families of children with ASD (Interagency Autism Coordinating Committee [IACC], 2011). These include: When should I be concerned? How can I understand what is happening? What caused this to happen? Which treatments will help? Where can I turn for services? What does the future hold for my child as a teenager and adult? As you read this chapter, you might want to keep these questions in mind and consider how you would respond to them as you learn more about ASD.

ASD is a DSM-5 disorder characterized by significant and persistent deficits in social interaction and communication skills and by restricted, and repetitive patterns of interests and behaviors (APA, 2013). As we shall see, ASD

Children with ASD behave in unusual and frequently puzzling ways, like exhibiting odd interests in the sensory aspects of the environment, atypical facial expressions, and a lack of interest in others.

is not one particular thing. Although all children with ASD display its core features, children vary widely in the form, pervasiveness, and severity of their symptoms, abilities, associated conditions, and needed supports.

Although *childhood-onset schizophrenia* (COS) is not on the autism spectrum in DSM-5, we conclude the chapter with a separate section about this disorder. Historically, autism and COS were thought of as a single condition. Subsequently, they came to be viewed as distinct disorders, with different family histories, outcomes, and associated features (Fitzgerald, 2014). However, findings from recent studies using newer research methods suggest that there may be more overlap between autism and COS than previously thought, and the possibility that the two are linked may need to be reexamined (de Lacy & King, 2013; Sullivan et al., 2013).

Most people have seen or heard the frequent media messages about ASD. Although interest in ASD is at an all-time high, ancient stories suggest that children with this disorder have been around for centuries. For example, stories of elfin children, left in the place of real human babies who were stolen away by the "little people," describe these "changelings" as strange and remote, much like a child with ASD (Wing & Potter, 2002). The factual history of autism begins in 1943, when psychiatrist Dr. Leo Kanner described 11 children who, in the first few years of life, displayed more attention to objects than to people, avoided eye contact, lacked social awareness, had limited or no language, and displayed stereotyped motor activities. They also exhibited **preservation of sameness,** which is an anxious and obsessive insistence on the maintenance of sameness in daily routines and activities, which no one but the child may disrupt. Their parents described them as "acting as if people weren't there" and "oblivious to everything around him" (Kanner, 1943, p. 242). Around the same time, Dr. Hans Asperger, an Austrian doctor, described a milder form of this disorder that became known as *Asperger's disorder* (Asperger, 1944). Because of the intense interests of the children he studied and their lengthy descriptions of these interests, he compared them to "absent-minded professors." Interestingly, Dr. Asperger's own preoccupations, interests, and social aloofness suggest that he himself may have had symptoms of the disorder (Lyons & Fitzgerald, 2007).

Kanner (1943, 1944) used the term *early infantile autism* (*autism* literally means "within oneself") to describe these children. There is, said Kanner, "an extreme autistic aloneness that, whenever possible, disregards, ignores, shuts out anything that comes to the child from outside" (1943, p. 242). He described the parents of the children he observed as highly intelligent and obsessive people who were cold, mechanical, and detached in their relationships—called the "refrigerator parent" (who, according to Kanner, just happened to "defrost enough to produce a child"). Although he clearly saw autism as an inborn deficit, he also planted the seeds for the psychoanalytic view that "the precipitating factor in infantile autism is the parent's wish that his child should not exist" (Bettelheim, 1967, p. 125). This early view that autism resulted from a child's defensive withdrawal from an intellectual, coldhearted, and hostile parent is unsupported. Children with autism have not withdrawn from reality because of a mental disorder—rather, they have failed to enter reality because of widespread and serious disturbances in their development. Autism is now recognized as a strongly biologically based lifelong neurodevelopmental disorder that is present in the first few years of life (Rutter, 2013).

Children with ASD behave in unusual and frequently puzzling ways. They may squeal with excitement at the sight or sound of a wheel spinning on a toy car, yet ignore or have a full-blown tantrum if someone attempts to play with them. At times they may look through you as if you are a pane of glass, but other times stare directly into your face or tug on your arm to lead you to something they want. When you speak to a child with ASD, she may act as if she is deaf, but then quickly turn in the direction of the faint crinkling sound of a candy wrapper in another room.

Some children with ASD display extreme fear or avoidance of noisy or moving objects such as running water, swings, elevators, battery-operated toys, or even the wind. One child was so afraid of a vacuum cleaner that he would not go anywhere near the closet where it was kept. When someone used it in the house, he ran to the garage and covered his ears. Yet the same child was oblivious to the sounds of traffic roaring by him on a dangerous freeway. Although children with ASD fear many things, they are also attracted to and preoccupied with other objects and activities—for example, a rotating fan or a flickering light. These children often develop unusual attachments or reactions to odd objects, such as a rubber band, a piece of sandpaper, or a string.

Other children with ASD may have extraordinary perceptual abilities—for example, identifying the brand of a vacuum cleaner by its sound alone. These perceptual abilities may result in distress in response to minor changes in the environment—shown, for instance, by screaming, kicking, and lashing out at others if a chair is moved from its usual location. They may spend hour after hour playing in a corner of their room, engaged in stereotyped or repetitive motor activities, such as rocking, lining up objects, or repeatedly flapping their hands and fingers as they flip through pages of a magazine. Rather than seeing the big picture, children with ASD are much more likely to fixate on a minuscule object or event in their world, such as a tiny spot on their shirt. Whereas most of us see the hugeness of trees in the forest, a child with autism is more likely to fixate on one pine needle.

Section Summary

Autism Spectrum Disorder

- ASD is a DSM-5 disorder characterized by significant and persistent deficits in social communication and interaction skills and restricted, repetitive patterns of behaviors, interests, or activities.

- Historically, autism and childhood-onset schizophrenia (COS) were lumped together as a single condition; now recognized as separate disorders, recent research suggests that there may be more overlap of the two disorders than was previously thought.

- ASD has increasingly come to be recognized as a biologically based lifelong neurodevelopmental disorder that is present in the first few years of life.

- Children with ASD behave in unusual and frequently puzzling ways.

- They may spend hours engaging in stereotyped or repetitive motor activities or focus on minuscule details of their world rather than their entire environment.

DSM-5: DEFINING FEATURES OF ASD

DSM-5 criteria for ASD are presented in Table 6.1. As shown, the core features of ASD are represented by two symptom domains: (1) social communication and social interaction and (2) restricted, repetitive patterns of behavior, interests, or activities. These domains are well supported by research (Guthrie et al., 2013). In order to receive a diagnosis of ASD the child must display symptoms in *both domains*. The symptoms must also be persistent, occur in multiple settings, and be present early in development. Those who display only deficits in social communication and interaction but not restricted and repetitive behaviors would receive a diagnosis of Social (Pragmatic) Communication Disorder, a newly designated type of language disorder (see Chapter 7).

Social Communication and Interaction. DSM-5 lists three symptom types in this category, with all three required for an ASD diagnosis: (1) deficits in social–emotional reciprocity; (2) deficits in nonverbal communication behaviors used for social interaction; and (3) deficits in developing maintaining, and understanding relationships. Table 6.1 includes specific examples of symptoms for each type.

Restrictive and Repetitive Behaviors. Four types of symptoms are specified in this category, with *at least two* types required for an ASD diagnosis: (1) stereotyped or repetitive motor movements, use of objects, or speech; (2) insistence on sameness, inflexible adherence to routines, or ritualized patterns of verbal or nonverbal

TABLE 6.1 | Diagnostic Criteria for Autism Spectrum Disorder

DSM-5

(A) Persistent deficits in social communication and social interaction across multiple contexts, as manifested by the following, currently or by history (examples are illustrative not exhaustive):

    (1) Deficits in social-emotional reciprocity, ranging, for example, from abnormal social approach and failure of normal back-and-forth conversation; to reduced sharing of interests, emotions, or affect; to failure to initiate or respond to social interactions.

    (2) Deficits in nonverbal communicative behaviors used for social interaction, ranging, for example, from poorly integrated verbal and nonverbal communication; to abnormalities in eye contact and body language or deficits in understanding and use of gestures; to a total lack of facial expressions and nonverbal communication.

    (3) Deficits in developing, maintaining and understanding relationships, ranging, for example, from difficulties adjusting behavior to suit various social contexts; to difficulties in sharing imaginative play or in making friends; to absence of interest in peers.

    Specify current severity based on social communication impairments and restricted, repetitive patterns of behavior.

(B) Restricted, repetitive patterns of behavior, interests, or activities, as manifested by at least two of the following, currently or by history (examples are illustrative, not exhaustive):

    (1) Stereotyped or repetitive motor movements, use of objects, or speech (e.g., simple motor stereotypies, lining up toys or flipping objects, echolalia, idiosyncratic phrases).

    (2) Insistence on sameness, inflexible adherence to routines, or ritualized patterns of verbal or nonverbal behavior (e.g., extreme distress at small changes, difficulties with transitions, rigid thinking patterns, greeting rituals, need to take same route or eat same food every day).

    (3) Highly restricted, fixated interests that are abnormal in intensity or focus (e.g., strong attachment to or preoccupation with unusual objects, excessively circumscribed or perseverative interests).

    (4) Hyper- or hyporeactivity to sensory input or unusual interest in sensory aspects of environment (e.g., apparent indifference to pain/temperature, adverse response to specific sounds or textures, excessive smelling or touching of objects, visual fascination with lights or movement).

    Specify current severity based on social communication impairments and restricted, repetitive patterns of behavior.

(C) Symptoms must be present in early developmental period (but may not become fully manifest until social demands exceed limited capacities, or may be masked by learned strategies in later life).

(D) Symptoms cause clinically significant impairment in social, occupational, or other important areas of current functioning.

(E) These disturbances are not better explained by intellectual disability (intellectual developmental disorder) or global developmental delay. Intellectual disability and autism spectrum disorder frequently co-occur; to make comorbid diagnoses of autism spectrum disorder and intellectual disability, social communication should be below that expected for general developmental level.

Note: Individuals with a well-established DSM-IV diagnosis of autistic disorder, Asperger's disorder, or Pervasive Developmental Disorder, Not Otherwise Specified, should be given the diagnosis of autism spectrum disorder. Individuals who have marked deficits in social communication, but whose symptoms do not otherwise meet criteria for autism spectrum disorder, should be evaluated for social (pragmatic) communication disorder.

Specify if:
With or without accompanying intellectual impairment
With or without accompanying language impairment
Associated with a known medical or genetic condition or environmental factor
Associated with another neurodevelopmental, mental, or behavioral disorder
With catatonia

Source: Diagnostic and Statistical Manual of Mental Disorders, Fifth Edition. American Psychiatric Association.

behavior; (3) highly restricted, fixated interests that are abnormal in intensity or focus; and (4) hyperreactivity or hyporeactivity to sensory input or unusual interest in sensory aspects of the environment. Table 6.1 includes examples of specific symptoms for each type.

DSM-5 also specifies that a *severity* rating of current symptoms be made for each domain. Severity ratings reflect the extent to which the symptoms interfere with the child's functioning. More severe deficits are rated as requiring greater levels of support, as follows: requiring support (level 1); requiring substantial support (level 2); and requiring very substantial support (level 3). Severity level ratings should help in guiding the types of programs and services needed to help the child and family, but since symptom severity may fluctuate across situations and over time, these ratings are not intended to be used in determining the child's eligibility for services.

DSM-5 criteria for ASD provide a relatively new way of looking at autism. In light of this, we highlight several key changes in ASD criteria from DSM-IV to DSM-5 and why they were made. First, the DSM-5 organization of symptoms into two domains represents a change from DSM-IV, in which deficits in social interaction and those in communication were viewed as separate domains along with the third domain of restricted and repetitive behavior. However, research does not support viewing social interaction and communication as distinct domains (Frazier et al., 2012), and clinicians have difficulty separating the symptoms of each. For example, is difficulty engaging in two-way conversation a deficit in social reciprocity or in communication skills? (Klinger et al., 2014)

Second, DSM-5 eliminated all previous subtypes of ASD (e.g., Autistic Disorder, Asperger's Disorder, Pervasive Developmental Disorder, Not Otherwise Specified [PDD-NOS]) and substituted a single overarching category—ASD. One reason for doing this was to increase the consistency of diagnosing ASD. In DSM-IV, the criteria for autism subtypes were not well conceptualized or defined. Although clinicians could readily distinguish ASD from other neurodevelopmental disorders (e.g., intellectual disability, specific learning disorder), distinctions between subtypes were unreliable and inconsistent and were related more to where the diagnosis was made, the child's level of intellectual ability, and co-occurring conditions, than to the child's ASD symptoms (Lord et al., 2012). A second reason for using a single ASD category rather than subtypes was a recognition that changes in developmental level can lead to changes in symptom presentation. Although an ASD diagnosis is stable after 2 years of age, children often changed diagnosis from one subtype to another because of age-related changes in their social and cognitive skills (van Daalen et al., 2009). Thus, rather than representing true change, these

age- and skill-related fluctuations in diagnosis are best viewed as variability within a single disorder.

The elimination of subtypes in DSM-5 does not mean that these distinctions are unimportant. As we have noted, ASD is not one thing, and there is a great deal of heterogeneity within the disorder. What is important is having a classification system that can address this variability (Rutter, 2013). To do this, DSM-5 includes the use of *specifiers* to indicate when other important conditions, such as intellectual and/or language impairment, are present and whether the child's ASD is associated with a known medical or genetic condition or with another neurodevelopmental, mental, or behavioral disorder. This provides a more detailed description of the full range and severity of the child's problems, which is critical to developing an appropriate treatment plan.

There is support for the conceptual validity of using a single ASD category. However, many individuals with ASD, their families, advocacy groups, and clinicians suggest that fewer individuals will be diagnosed, especially those with milder symptoms and normal intellectual abilities who were previously diagnosed with Asperger's disorder. Therefore, the use of DSM-5 could result in reduced eligibility for services for these children. Although research to date suggests that most children diagnosed with Asperger's disorder will receive a diagnosis of ASD using DSM-5 criteria (Huerta et al., 2012), it is not yet known whether this will be the case in clinical practice. The possibility that some individuals could be disadvantaged by changes in DSM-5 criteria will require further monitoring and evaluation (Kent et al., 2013).

ASD across the Spectrum

When we hear the term *autism*, or *ASD*, we may think of Raymond, the main character in the movie *Rain Man*, or Temple Grandin (who was the subject of an HBO film), a high-functioning and insightful woman with ASD who is a Professor of Animal Sciences, one of the top scientists and consultants in the humane livestock handling industry, and a leading advocate for persons with ASD (Grandin & Panek, 2013). Although some individuals with ASD display the abilities and special talents that are often portrayed in the movies, most do not.

ASD is defined as a **spectrum disorder** because its symptoms, abilities, and characteristics are expressed in many different combinations and in any degree of severity (Lai et al., 2013). Thus, ASD is not an "all or nothing" phenomenon. At one end of the spectrum we may find a child who is mute, crouched in a corner of his room, spinning a paper clip over and over again for hours; at the other end of the spectrum is a researcher who is also able to hold a corporate job—as long as

Dr. Temple Grandin (left) with award-winning actress Clare Danes, who portrayed her in the highly acclaimed film, *Temple Grandin*.

it doesn't require interacting with customers. Although children with ASD vary widely in intellectual ability, language, age, socioeconomic (SES), gender, and race, the majority of them display most of the core features of the disorder (Mayes & Calhoun, 2011). Nevertheless, despite the similarities in their core profile, they show enormous variability in the expression and severity of their symptoms. This variability among children with ASD applies widely across both their social communication and behavioral impairments (Jones & Klin, 2009).

Children with ASD not only differ widely in their core symptoms, but they may also, in varying degrees, display features not specific to ASD—most commonly, intellectual disability and epilepsy. Thus, children with the same diagnosis of ASD can be vastly different from one another in their intellectual ability, severity of language problem, and degree of progress. To illustrate this key point, let's compare and contrast two children, Lucy and John, both diagnosed with autism.

LUCY

ASD with Intellectual Disability

Lucy's parents watched her development right from the start because there had been so many difficulties during pregnancy and delivery. Labor began 3 weeks early and lasted 23 hours, so that forceps were needed to assist the delivery. Lucy had to have oxygen to revive her, spent 4 days in the special-care unit, and received treatment for jaundice.

Indeed, it seemed that everything in Lucy's development was troubling. For example, she was always too distressed to feed or she fed so ravenously and quickly

that she vomited. Nights were no better—she took hours to settle and always woke early. By her first birthday she had only just started to sit up, and was still not crawling. The family physician said that Lucy was indeed delayed in her development. At 14 months, she began to crawl (6 months is typical), and at 19 months she pulled herself up on the furniture (most children do this at around 12 months); she made little progress in other areas.

At 2 years of age, Lucy still did not use any words, and was unresponsive to her parents' attempts to engage her in simple games like peek-a-boo. At 30 months, she started to walk (most children walk by 14 months). However, her main sounds were a strange clicking noise made with the back of her tongue and a variety of screams. She still seemed oblivious to people around her (including her parents) unless they had something she wanted. A pediatrician thought the delay in her development might be due to the difficulties with her delivery and suggested that Lucy be checked every 12 months.

She loved to play with a particular blue and red rattle that she would shake or spin for hours. Once she had the rattle she did not look at anyone, and if someone tried to take it from her she screamed and banged her head on the floor. Understandably, this devastated her parents. Lucy took great interest in odors, sniffing food, toys, clothes, and (to her parents' embarrassment) people. She also liked to feel things, and often tried to stroke stockings on women's legs, even those of complete strangers. If they tried to stop her, she had a tantrum.

When Lucy was 4 years old, her pediatrician suspected she had ASD, and referred her to a psychologist for a detailed assessment. The diagnosis was confirmed, and her parents were told that Lucy was generally delayed in her development. They were heartbroken, but they felt that finally Lucy would get the help she desperately needed. (Autism: The Facts, by Baron-Cohen and Bolton, (1993) pp. 1–8.)

JOHN

ASD with Average Intellectual Ability

John was born after a normal pregnancy and delivery. As an infant, he was easy to feed and slept well. He seemed happy and content to lie in his crib for hours. He sat unsupported at 6 months (which is in the normal range), and soon after, he crawled. His parents saw him as independent and willful. However, his grandmother thought John lacked interest in people.

John walked on his first birthday (in sharp contrast to Lucy, who did not walk until 30 months of age); yet during his second year he did not progress as well as

(continues)

(continued)

expected. Although he made sounds, he did not use words. Indeed, his ability to communicate was so limited that even when he was 3 years old, his mother still found herself trying to guess what he wanted (as if he were a much younger child). Occasionally he would grab hold of her wrist and drag her over to the sink, yet he never said anything like "drink."

At this time his parents also became concerned about John's extreme independence. Even when he fell down and hurt himself, he would not come to his parents for help. He never became upset when his mother had to go out and leave him with a neighbor or relative. In fact, he seemed to be more interested in his toy bricks than in people. He spent hours lining the bricks up in exactly the same way and in precisely the same sequence of colors.

After his third birthday his parents became increasingly concerned, despite reassurances from their doctor. John used no words and showed no interest in other children. He did not wave bye-bye or show any real joy when they tried to play peek-a-boo. John always wriggled away from his mother's cuddles and only seemed to like rough-and-tumble play with his father. His mother worried that she had done something wrong, and she felt depressed, rejected, and guilty.

When John was 3.5 years old, he was referred to a child psychiatrist, who told his parents that John had ASD, but added that his abilities in spatial tasks (such as jigsaw puzzles) suggested normal intelligence in these areas. Although it was still too early to tell how John would progress, there were indications he would do better than most children with ASD. John received speech therapy, and a psychologist helped his parents plan ways of encouraging communication and reducing temper tantrums.

At age 4, John suddenly began to speak in complete sentences. However, his speech was quite unusual. For example, he often repeated back word for word whatever his parents had said. If they asked him "Do you want a drink?" he would say "you want a drink" in reply. At other times, John made rather surprising remarks. For instance, he would say "You really tickle me" in a tone of voice exactly similar to that of a family friend who had first used the expression some days before. However, his use of this phrase, and most of his speech, was usually inappropriate to the setting, and lacked any clear meaning. Autism: The Facts, by Baron-Cohen and Bolton, (1993) pp. 1–8.

her as "living in a glass bubble." Extreme social unresponsiveness is typical of many children with ASD. John is more socially outgoing and talkative when he approaches others; however, his efforts at social contact are repetitive and unnatural. His abnormalities in communication are less obvious than his social deficits, and consist of speaking in one-sided and stereotyped phrases. In contrast, Lucy is seriously lacking in her ability to communicate and is silent most of the time (Baron-Cohen & Bolton, 1993).

In addition to their abnormalities in social and language development, John and Lucy both display ritualistic behavior. Lucy checks the location of little pieces of thread that she has tied on all the chairs in her house, and John insists on taking exactly the same route to school each day. John and Lucy also have repetitive interests: John likes nothing better than counting lampposts, while Lucy, if allowed to do so, watches the same video over and over again. Both children can spend hours absorbed in nothing but these narrow interests, and these obsessions may lead to other problems. For example, John or Lucy may scream intensely if even a minor change occurs in one of their daily routines (Baron-Cohen & Bolton, 1993).

Despite the many similarities shown by John and Lucy, their stories also show how children with ASD can be quite different from one another. Three critical factors contribute to these differences:

▸ *Level of intellectual ability:* Intellectual ability ranges from profound disability to above-average intelligence. John is of average intelligence, whereas Lucy has a severe intellectual disability. Because of her intellectual disability, Lucy was slow to develop in all areas. As a result of Lucy's limited overall level of functioning, she shows a much narrower range of interests and activities than John shows.

▸ *Severity of their language problems:* John speaks quite a lot, whereas Lucy is mute. Children with ASD can fall anywhere between these two extremes.

▸ *Behavior changes with age:* Some children make little progress, whereas others develop speech or become more outgoing. When significant gains are made, they are usually made by children like John, who have average or above-average intelligence and acquire speech at a young age.

Section Summary

DSM-5: Defining Features of ASD

• In DSM-5, autism or ASD is a severe neurodevelopmental disorder with an onset in early development, which is

Lucy and John both display the defining features of ASD. They failed to develop normal two-way social relationships and communication in the first few years of life, and displayed repetitive interests and preoccupations. When Lucy was young, her parents described characterized by significant and persistent deficits in social interaction and communication skills and by stereotyped patterns of behaviors, interests, and activities.

- ASD is a spectrum disorder, which means that its symptoms and characteristics are expressed in many different combinations and in any degree of severity.

CORE DEFICITS OF ASD

Despite 70 years of research, considerable debate continues today about the core deficits of ASD. Most likely, ASD consists of several deficits, not one primary deficit, that affect the child's social–emotional, language, and cognitive development (Dawson & Toth, 2006). As we discuss each core deficit of ASD, keep in mind that these aspects of development are interconnected—they do not develop in isolation. For example, children with ASD may display a decreased ability to regulate levels of alertness, which in turn is related to increased deficits in social communication (Keehn et al., 2010).

Social Interaction and Communication Deficits

Social Interaction Deficits

Children with ASD experience profound difficulties in relating to other people, even when they have average or above-average intelligence (Pelphrey et al., 2011). From a young age, they show deficits in many skills that are crucial for early social development. Such deficits include the following:

- a lack of monitoring of the social activities of others;
- a lack of social and emotional reciprocity;
- unusual nonverbal behaviors such as using atypical facial expressions, eye-to-eye gaze, body postures, and gestures to regulate social interaction;
- lack of interest and/or difficulty relating to others, especially other children; and
- a failure to share enjoyment and interests with others (e.g., Landa et al., 2011; Shic et al., 2011).

They may also display difficulties in imitating others' social behavior, sharing a focus of attention with others, and engaging in make-believe play (Klinger et al., 2014).

Children with ASD have limited social expressiveness and sensitivity to social cues, impaired recognition of complex emotions and mental states in everyday life, and experience little sharing of experiences or emotions with other people. These children have great difficulty integrating the social, communicative, and emotional behaviors that are required when greeting a familiar person. Their lack of understanding of

people as social partners may lead to their treating people as objects, or to directing their actions at the body parts of other people, as when the child attacks a restraining hand rather than the person (Phillips et al., & Riviere, 1995).

Children with ASD display atypical processing of faces and facial expressions (Dawson, Webb, & McPartland, 2005). In processing information about the human face, they may overemphasize one part of the face, such as the mouth, rather than attending to its overall shape or focusing on the eyes as most children do (Joseph & Tanaka, 2003). The child's focus on the mouth rather than the eyes may reflect a tendency to attend to stimuli in which sound and motion co-occur (Klin et al., 2009). They also display deficits in recognizing facial expressions of emotion, particularly in detecting fear. This may be because the identification of fear relies more heavily on the eye region than does other emotions, and individuals with ASD do not look at the eyes as often as others when viewing faces (Boraston et al., 2008). Atypical face processing in individuals with ASD may be related to a less generalized or narrower face detection system, which may also contribute to their reduced social interest (Churches, Baron-Cohen, & Ring, 2012).

Children with ASD display impairments in **joint attention,** which is the ability to coordinate attention to a social partner and an object or event of mutual interest (Mundy & Newell, 2007). Joint attention, which typically emerges between 9 and 14 months of age, involves making a social connection with another person by directing that person's attention to objects or people by pointing, showing, and looking, and by communicating shared interest. Although children with ASD may bring an object to a person or point to an object when they want something done for them, they show little desire to share interest and attention with another person for the sheer pleasure of interaction. Poor quality of eye contact and smiling during parent–infant interactions in the first year of life may be related to deficits in joint attention in the second year of life in children later diagnosed with ASD (Clifford & Dissanayake, 2008). In turn, deficits in joint attention have been found to impede language development in infants with ASD at 20 months and to predict greater problems in language, communication, and social behavior at age 42 months (Charman, 2003; Luyster et al., 2008).

Although it was once thought that children with ASD failed to form a social bond with their parents or that they could not tell the difference between their parents and other adults, research has proved this wrong (Rutgers et al., 2004). Most children with ASD are more responsive to their caregivers than to unfamiliar adults, directing more social behavior and seeking to be closer to them than to strangers after a brief separation (Dissanayake & Sigman, 2000). In addition, once the children's disoriented and disorganized repetitive motor behaviors are taken into account, children with ASD display slightly lower—but comparable—rates of secure attachment to their mothers than normal controls. When lower rates of secure attachment are found, it is usually in children with lower intellectual ability and greater ASD severity (Naber et al., 2008). Most show a preference for their mother over a stranger, use their mother as a secure base for exploration, and are comforted by their mother when distressed. Importantly, the quality of infant–mother attachment in young children with ASD contributes substantially to the development of the child's play behavior, which is important for the development of social skills (Naber et al., 2007).

Children with ASD do not have a global deficit in their ability to form attachments. Rather, the deficit seems to be in their ability to understand and respond to social information (Rogers, Ozonoff, & Maslin-Cole, 1993). As shown in A Closer Look 6.1, a child with ASD will likely notice when his mother leaves the room and will look for her, both signs of attachment. However, unlike a normal child, he may have little understanding of the event or how to respond in order to change the situation, making it seem as if he has no attachment. Thus, although children with ASD are attached to their parents, the way they express attachment is unusual and difficult to "read." As a result, parents may feel that their child is not attached at all, and may feel disheartened by the child's lack of the cuddling, reaching, and responsiveness that typically accompany attachment behavior.

It is important to note that the Strange Situation, a traditional assessment of attachment, conceptualizes deficits in social functioning in relation to the concept of security/insecurity, which may not be relevant to understanding the deficits in social functioning that characterize most children with ASD. As a result, questions have been raised regarding whether the Strange Situation is a useful way to evaluate the unusual qualities of social relationships associated with ASD (Rutter, Kreppner, & Sonuga-Barke, 2009).

In addition to their social difficulties, children with ASD have difficulty processing emotional information contained in body language, gestures, facial expressions, or the voice. Preschool-age children with ASD do not look for or attend to the emotional cues provided by other people. In contrast to other children of the same mental age, they may sort pictures of people according

---

A CLOSER LOOK 6.1

Attachment in Children with ASD

This young boy with ASD notices that his mother has left the room. He wanders around the room looking for her, but there's essentially no change in his expression. He doesn't seem to know what to do to change the event.

© 1991 Alvin Perlmutter

A child his age without ASD is likely to react like this:

© 1991 Alvin Perlmutter

This child's facial expression changes in 10 seconds from "Oh no, she's not really leaving me" to "You gotta be kidding" to "Oh my god, she's gone." He's crying, but as soon as his mother returns, he's comforted and he's fine.

Source: Behavior Disorders of Childhood, produced by Alvin H. Perlmutter, Inc. in association with Toby Levine Communications.

to the type of hat a person is wearing rather than by emotional expressions (Weeks & Hobson, 1987).

Children with ASD also have difficulties in understanding emotional information, and their own bodily expressions of emotion—often characterized by limited spontaneous use of expressive gestures and bizarre, rigid, or mechanical facial expressions—are very different from those of typical children (Loveland et al., 1994; Trevarthen & Delafield-Butt, 2013). They also have difficulties in recognizing emotions from the body movements of others (Atkinson, 2009). Thus, children with ASD both process and express emotional information in unusual ways.

Social Communication Deficits

For two years the mother of a young man with autism would correct her son by saying, "Don't do that. It doesn't look normal." The son would stop the inappropriate behavior. Then she would add, "You want to look normal, don't you?" The son would say, "Yes." Then one day it occurred to the mother to ask her son, "Do you know what normal means?" "Yes," he said, and the mother was impressed. She pushed for his definition. He said, "It's the second button from the left on the washing machine."

—From Our Old Ways Just Aren't Working: Donnellan by Karin Melberg Schwier, p. 8, Saskatchewan Association for Community Living, Dialect, February 1988

Most children have passed predictable milestones on the path to learning language by age 3; one of the earliest is babbling. By the first birthday, a typical toddler says words, turns when he hears his name, points when he wants a toy, and when offered something he does not like, makes it clear that the answer is "no." In contrast, children with ASD display serious abnormalities in communication and language that appear early in their development and persist (Mitchell et al., 2006). Atypical early vocalizations are a sensitive indicator of a heightened risk for later ASD symptoms in infants with a family history of ASD (Paul et al., 2011). Even before children learn to talk, they have at their disposal a rich array of facial expressions, vocalizations, and gestures to communicate their needs, interests, and feelings. One of the first signs of language impairment is the inconsistent use of these early preverbal communications. For example, a typical child with ASD may point to a stuffed animal she wants that is out of reach. By doing this, she is demonstrating the ability to use **protoimperative gestures**—gestures or vocalizations that are used to express needs. However, this child will fail to use **protodeclarative gestures**—gestures or vocalizations that direct the visual attention of other people to objects of shared interest.

The primary purpose of protodeclarative gestures is to engage other people in interaction; for example, a toddler excitedly points to a dog to direct her mother's attention to this fascinating creature that she sees. The use of protodeclarative gestures requires shared social attention and an implicit understanding of what other people are thinking—abilities that are lacking in children with ASD. They are also missing other declarative gestures, for example, the *showing gesture*, which young children without ASD use to show someone else something of interest, such as a newly discovered object (or a handful of shaving cream; see A Closer Look 6.2).

As many as half of all children with ASD do not develop useful language; this includes some children who begin to speak and then regress in their speech development, usually between 12 and 30 months of age. Children with ASD with no speech or only limited speech rely on primitive forms of communication, such as pulling their mother's hand in a desired direction or bringing her a box to be opened. Children with ASD may use *instrumental gestures* to get someone else to do something for them immediately, but they fail to use *expressive gestures* to convey feelings (Frith, 2003). These two types of gestures are illustrated in ● Figure 6.1.

Instrumental Gestures

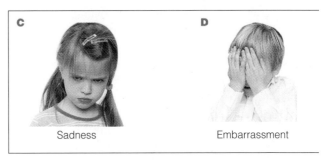

Expressive Gestures

● **FIGURE 6.1** | Instrumental and expressive gestures. Children with ASD may use gestures to get others to do things for them but not to convey feelings.

Photo Credits: (a) Karin Dreyer/Stockbyte/Getty Images (b) Image Source/Photodisc/Getty Images (c) Michaela Begsteiger/Getty Images (d) Digital Vision/Photodisc/Getty Images

Early Communication in ASD

When a dab of shaving cream is put in the hand of this child with ASD, he pays attention to the shaving cream, and that's all he pays attention to. He is oblivious to the fact that his father is a foot away and his mother is close by. He shows no signs of wanting to share his experience with others.

This normally developing child is delighted with the shaving cream, and immediately incorporates everyone into his experience by showing his mother what he has in his hand. He has something to communicate and wants to let everyone in on it.

Source: Behavior Disorders of Childhood, produced by Alvin H. Perlmutter, Inc.

Children with ASD who develop language usually do so before age 5. Although almost all children with ASD show delays in their language development, it is their lack of spontaneity and their use of qualitatively unusual forms of communication that is most striking (Chiang & Carter, 2008). The rhythm and intonation of their speech is often unusual (Peppe et al., 2007), but most noticeable is their lack of social chatter—their failure to use language for social communication. Parents and teachers of children with ASD describe their communications as nonsensical, silly, incoherent, and irrelevant, having little meaningful connection with the situation in which they occur. This is illustrated in the following interview with Jerry, a 5-year-old boy with ASD who has a great deal of expressive language (Bemporad, 1979, pp. 183–184):

INTERVIEWER: "Would you draw a man or a woman?"

JERRY: "A man was business to a lady."

INTERVIEWER: "What does that mean?"

JERRY: "No, a man is present to a lady, yes, yes, yes. A radio. Lady gives the pedal. Great big handkerchief and napkin, all tucked in. So see, there it is. We'll paint the picture and put it in a frame."

Language impairments in children with ASD occur at many levels (Stefanatos & Baron, 2011). For example, a common language impairment in children with ASD is **pronoun reversal**, which occurs when the child repeats personal pronouns exactly as heard, without changing them to suit the situation. For example, a child named Tim when asked, "What's your name?" answered, "Your name is Tim," rather than "My name is Tim." However, their primary problem is not so much with the computational (sounds, words, and grammar) or the semantic (meaning) use of language. Rather, these children display profound impairments in **pragmatics,** which is the appropriate use of language in social and communicative contexts. An example of pragmatics (or, in this case the lack of it) is shown in ● Figure 6.2. The point of the

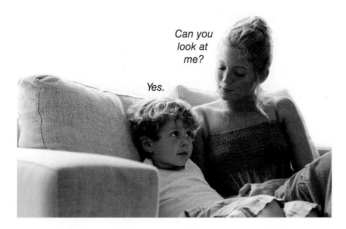

Can you look at me?

Yes.

● **FIGURE 6.2** | Children with ASD have difficulty with the pragmatic use of language.

PhotoAlto/Eric Audras/Getty images

question "Can you look at me?" is to request that an action be taken, not to request information about the child's ability to look at his mother. To understand this, a child must know more than what words mean—a child must "read" the context in which words are used. Lacking in pragmatic competence, children with ASD often have difficulty understanding nonliteral statements or adjusting their language to fit the situation (Dawson, 1996; Tager-Flusberg, 1993).

High-functioning children with ASD who have mastered word order and have large vocabularies may continue to display impairments in pragmatics. In addition, they continue to show both nonverbal and verbal deficits that reflect a basic failure to recognize the thoughts, feelings, and intentions of other people. At a nonverbal level, their monotonic voice and lack of gestures suggest difficulty in communicating emotions. At a verbal level, they display problems with narrative discourse, including stories lacking in detail and difficulty providing sufficient information to others. As they get older, children with ASD make little use of language for social convention, for example, to greet others or to be polite. It has been suggested that the common element underlying all the communication deficits in ASD is a general failure to understand that language can be used to inform and influence other people (Tager-Flusberg, Paul, & Lord, 2005).

Restricted and Repetitive Behaviors and Interests

Children with ASD display a wide variety of restricted and repetitive behaviors and narrow patterns of interests and activities, such as a fascination with arithmetic, lining up toys, or insistence on driving the same route to the school (Leekam, Prior, & Uljarevic, 2011). **Restricted and repetitive behaviors** are characterized by their high frequency, repetition in a fixed manner, and desire for sameness in the environment. Some children may perform stereotyped body movements, such as rocking or flapping their hands and arms, with such intensity that they begin to perspire; others may react explosively to a minor change in their routine; others may show a preoccupation with unusual objects, such as an electrical cord. They may show stereotyped and repetitive behaviors at times when they are not explicitly directed to engage in another activity, suggesting a possible deficit in their ability to initiate activities on their own. Other stereotyped behaviors occur in unpredictable or demanding situations and may provide the child with a sense of control over the environment and a way to cope with changes that are not understood (Klinger et al., 2014).

The category of restricted and repetitive behaviors was expanded in DSM-5 to include repetitive speech and idiosyncratic phrases that were previously identified in DSM-IV as deficits in communication. A common type of repetitive speech in children with ASD is **echolalia,** which is the child's parrot-like repetition of words or word combinations that she or he has heard, either immediately after hearing them, or at a later time. A child who is asked the question "Do you want a cookie?" responds by repeating, "Do you want a cookie?" Although echolalia was once thought to be pathological, it may actually be a critical first step in language acquisition for many children with ASD. Echolalia and other verbal behaviors, such as *perseverative speech*—incessant talking about one topic and incessant questioning—may also serve a variety of communicative and developmental functions for children with ASD. These behaviors may reflect the child's desire to communicate, although in a very primitive way (Prizant, 1996; Prizant & Wetherby, 1989).

Research has identified two dimensions of restricted repetitive behaviors in children with ASD: (1) "repetitive sensory and motor behaviors" (e.g., hand and body mannerisms, repetitive object use, and unusual sensory interests) and (2) "insistence on sameness behaviors" (e.g., compulsions and rituals, resistance to change). The frequency of the former remains relatively high over time, whereas the latter starts low and increases or worsens over time (Richler et al., 2010).

Self-stimulatory behaviors are stereotyped as well as repetitive body movements or movements of objects. Hand flapping or pencil spinning are examples. Although self-stimulatory and repetitive behaviors also occur in typically developing children and children with other forms of neurodevelopmental disorders, they are more frequent and persistent in those with ASD (Leekam et al., 2011; Watt et al., 2008). A particular self-stimulatory behavior, such as moving

Pamela engaging in self-stimulation as a 7-year-old child and 20 years later as an adult

the fingers in front of the eyes, may persist from childhood through adulthood. In the accompanying photos of Pamela, taken 20 years apart, her self-stimulatory behavior looks amazingly similar. Self-stimulation may involve one or more of the senses, for example, staring at lights, rocking, or smelling objects.

The exact reasons why children with ASD engage in self-stimulatory and other repetitive behaviors are not known, although many theories have been advanced (Turner, 1999). One theory is that these children crave stimulation, and self-stimulation serves to excite their nervous system. Another theory is that their environment may be too stimulating and that they engage in repetitive self-stimulation as a way of blocking out and controlling unwanted stimulation. Other theories maintain that self-stimulation is maintained by the sensory reinforcement it provides, or that repetitive behaviors provide a calming influence, a way of regulating extreme levels of emotion (Joosten, Bundy, & Einfeld, 2009). Finally, restricted and repetitive behaviors may be linked to genetic disorders, such as fragile-X syndrome, that may co-occur with ASD (Moss et al., 2009). In the case of an individual child, any one of these reasons may apply (Leekam et al., 2011).

Atypical reactions to sensory input or unusual interests in sensory aspects of the environment are now included in the DSM-5 in the restrictive and repetitive behaviors category (Mandy, Charman, & Skuse, 2012). Many sights, sounds, smells, or textures that most children find normal can be confusing or even painful to children with ASD. A child with ASD may perceive and react to a specific person's voice as to a loud shriek, to a gentle stroke on the arm as to a sharp pain. Temple Grandin said that it wasn't that she didn't want contact with her mother but "the sensory overload of a hug shorted out my nervous system" (Grandin & Panek, 2013, p. 8). Such *sensory overresponsivity* involves a negative response to or avoidance of sensory stimuli and is accompanied by

overreactive brain responses in the primary sensory areas of the brain and areas related to affective processing and regulation, including touch (Green et al., 2013; Voos, Pelphrey, & Kaiser, 2013). A variety of sensory abnormalities are both common and persistent in children with ASD, with 90% or more having problems in two or three sensory domains that continue well into adulthood (Klintwall et al., 2011; Leekam et al., 2007). These include oversensitivities or undersensitivities to certain stimuli (e.g., unusual reactions to auditory stimulation), overselective and impaired shifting of attention to sensory input, and impairments in mixing across sensory modalities—for example, an inability to simultaneously see the movement and hear the sound of a person's clapping (Reynolds & Lane, 2008; Rogers & Ozonoff, 2005).

Children with ASD may display deficits such as sensory dominance and stimulus overselectivity. *Sensory dominance* is the tendency to focus on certain types of sensory input over others—for example, a preference for sights over sounds. *Stimulus overselectivity* is the tendency to focus on one feature of an object or event in the environment while ignoring other equally important features. A selective focus on one narrow part of the environment while ignoring other important features gives children with ASD the appearance of having tunnel vision or tunnel hearing, making it very difficult for them to learn about their world (Robertson et al., 2013).

Section Summary

Core Deficits of ASD

- Children with ASD experience profound difficulties in relating to other people, including deficits in orienting to social stimuli, imitating others, sharing a focus of attention with others, and noticing and understanding other people's feelings. They also display deficits in social communication, including the use of preverbal vocalizations and gestures, language oddities such as pronoun reversal, and difficulties with the appropriate use of language in social contexts.

- Children with ASD exhibit restricted and repetitive patterns of behaviors, interests, and activities. These generally fall into two categories: (1) *repetitive sensory and motor behaviors*, which include unusual sensory interests, oversensitivities or undersensitivities to certain stimuli, stereotyped hand and body movements, and repetitive speech or object use, and (2) *insistence on sameness behaviors*, which include compulsions and rituals, and resistance to change.

ASSOCIATED CHARACTERISTICS OF ASD

In addition to their core deficits, children with ASD display a number of associated characteristics. These include intellectual deficits and strengths, cognitive and motivational deficits, and medical conditions and physical characteristics.

Intellectual Deficits and Strengths

Intellectual disability (ID) is common in children with ASD and is a strong predictor of later functioning (Matson & Shoemaker, 2009). The intellectual ability of children with ASD varies widely, from profound disability to superior ability. Those with superior abilities often capture media attention, yet, in reality, 70% of children with ASD have been estimated to have co-occurring ID. Approximately 40% have severe to profound ID, and 30% have mild to moderate ID. The remaining 30% have average intellectual ability or above (Fombonne, 2003, 2005). However, recent reports indicate that ID in children with ASD is lower, closer to 40% to 50% (Centers for Disease Control and Prevention [CDC], 2014; Charman et al., 2011). The more recent lower estimates most likely reflect the increase in ASD diagnoses in higher-functioning individuals as well as more children receiving early intervention (Matson & Shoemaker, 2009).

Assessing intellectual ability in children with ASD can be challenging, since intellectual tests often require skills such as language and imitation that may be limited in these children (Klinger, O'Kelley & Mussey, 2009). Intelligence in children with ASD has typically been assessed using the Wechsler Intelligence Scale for Children (WISC-IV; Mayes & Calhoun, 2008). Most children with ID without ASD show a general delay across all areas of intellectual functioning on this test. In contrast, the performance of children with ASD tends to be uneven across different WISC subtests. One common pattern is a relatively low score on verbal subtests such as comprehension, and relatively high scores on nonverbal subtests involving short-term memory for strings of numbers or arranging blocks to form a specific pattern. However, there is limited evidence that individuals with ASD show one distinctive IQ test profile (Charman et al., 2011). Studies have also found that children with ASD score higher on other tests of intellectual functioning than they do on the commonly used WISC-IV, also suggesting that intelligence in this population may be higher than previously estimated (Dawson et al., 2007).

Despite their intellectual deficits, a small but significant number of individuals with ASD develop *splinter skills* or *islets of ability*. Their special talents may be in spelling, reading, mathematics, music, or drawing. As many as 25% of children with ASD display a special cognitive skill that is above average for the general population and well above their own general level of intellect (Howlin et al., 2004). These special abilities are more strongly related to the restricted and repetitive characteristics of children with ASD than to their deficits in social interaction and communication (Vital et al., 2009).

In addition, about 5% of children with ASD develop an isolated and often remarkable talent that far exceeds normally developing children of the same age. These children, referred to as *autistic savants*, display supernormal abilities in calculation, memory, jigsaw puzzles, music, or drawing (Treffert, 2010). One boy with ASD had an IQ of 60 but could recite the daily lottery numbers for the past 5 years. Another boy learned to play the piano by reproducing any tune he heard on the radio, from Brahms to Bacharach. Psychologists who studied this boy estimated that he had more than 2,000 tunes in his head (Gzowski, 1993, p. 91). Nadia, a girl with ASD, was obsessed with horses; she drew hundreds of pictures of them with incredible vividness and accuracy when she was only 3 years old. One of Nadia's drawings at age 5 is reproduced in ● Figure 6.3. After seeing a picture of a horse in a story, Nadia could generate endless images of what this horse would look like in any pose (Baron-Cohen & Bolton, 1993). Interestingly, Nadia did not retain her savant skills as she got older, suggesting that, for some, later developing higher-order cognitive skills may interfere with the types of processing that support their special abilities (Selfe, 2011).

It is not clear whether the special abilities of a few children with ASD reflect intact abilities or indicate a cognitive deficit. However, superior performance by children with ASD has typically been viewed as a side effect of abnormal brain functioning, rather than as a reflection of genuine intelligence. One idea is that autistic savants tend to segment information into parts rather than looking at the whole, which leads to exceptional performance in certain domains (Pring, Hermelin, & Heavey, 1995). Another explanation is that children with ASD think in images rather than in abstract ideas, which allows them to remember material in the manner

(Age 5)

● **FIGURE 6.3** | Drawing of a horse by Nadia at age 5.

Nadia: A Case of Extraordinary Drawing Ability, L. Selfe, 1977. Copyright Elsevier 1977.

of a camera or a recorder (Hurlbert, Happé, & Frith, 1994). Unfortunately, despite the fascination and appeal of the skills of autistic savants or the more common splinter skills, in most cases the skills are not used constructively to enhance everyday living.

Cognitive and Motivational Deficits

Two types of cognitive limitations proposed to underlie ASD are: (1) specific cognitive deficits in processing social–emotional information, and (2) more general cognitive deficits in information processing, planning, and attention.

Deficits in Processing Social–Emotional Information

The social and communication deficits of children with ASD have generated much interest in how they process social–emotional information, such as emotional expressions, voice and facial cues, and internal mental states. As we have discussed, their unusual social behavior suggests a significant impairment in their social sensitivities. Social interaction is not entirely absent or impaired, but rather they have great difficulty in situations that require social understanding.

At around 12 months, most normally developing infants can tell when they and another person are attending to the same thing. They begin to recognize that people's actions are driven by desires and directed at goals. This ability contributes to the emergence of pretend, or "as if," play. Young children with ASD, however, don't understand pretense, nor do they engage in pretend play (Stanley & Konstantareas, 2007). For example, a normally developing child may give a doll a drink of water from an empty cup while making the appropriate slurping sounds, whereas a child with ASD may simply spin the cup repetitively. The deficits in spontaneous pretend play in young children with ASD led to the hypothesis that these children would also display impairments in their understanding of beliefs and desires or other mental states in themselves or others that cannot be seen directly. The development of such an awareness of mental states in themselves and others is referred to as **mentalization** or **theory of mind (ToM)** (Baron-Cohen, Tager-Flusberg, & Cohen, 2000). By age 4, most children can comprehend what others might know, think, and believe; this is something that even older individuals with ASD have great difficulty doing. The ToM hypothesis of ASD begins with the premise that the ability to read the intentions, beliefs, feelings, and desires of others from their external behavior has adaptive significance in human evolution. ToM proposes that all humans are, by nature, mind readers. We spend our waking lives reading subtle cues that enable us to fill in the blanks about other people's beliefs and intentions. We do this automatically and with little conscious effort.

Suppose, for example, that a student walked into your class about 10 minutes after it began, looked around the room, and then left. How would you explain the student's behavior? As a mind reader, you may have thought: "Maybe she was *trying* to find a book she lost, and she *thought* she left it in this classroom," or "Maybe she *wanted* to find a friend who was taking this class, but *realized* that her friend was not in class today." No doubt you can come up with many explanations for this student's behavior, and most will be based on her mental states (the words in italics). You may not be 100% certain of the reason, but chances are you can easily generate many possibilities.

It has been proposed that many of the primary problems of individuals with ASD stem from a deficit in their ToM mechanism. In other words, children with ASD suffer in varying degrees from "mindblindness"; that is, "they fail to develop the capacity to mindread in the normal way" (Baron-Cohen, 1995, p. 5). Interestingly, when asked what brains do, most 5-year-olds say that brains are for thinking, dreaming, keeping secrets, and so on. But when children with ASD are asked this question, they may say that the brain is what makes people move—expressing nothing about mental activity (Baron-Cohen, 1995). A child with ToM deficits may be able to learn, remember, and know things about the social world but has little understanding of their meaning.

The original test used to determine children's ability to detect mental states of others was called the Sally–Anne Test. A similar test is described in A Closer Look 6.3. This test, which is extremely simple, illustrates what it means to have an everyday ToM.

The Sally–Anne Test: What It Means to Have a Theory of Mind

Two dolls, Sally and Anne, are used as props. Sally has a basket; Anne has a box. Sally puts a marble in her basket and covers it, then leaves the room. Anne takes the marble from the basket and hides it in her own box. Next, Sally comes back from her walk and wants to play with her marble. The critical question is: Where will Sally look for her marble?

Most 4-year-olds can answer this question reliably. Sally will look for her marble in her basket where she put it. Even children with intellectual disabilities realize that Sally will think that the marble is where she had left it. They also indicate that Sally did not know what Anne did because she was out of the room when Anne moved the marble.

This understanding demonstrates that young children have attributed a mental state to another person. They grasp that someone can have a false belief about a situation. The false belief is a mental state, not a physical state, and it can very helpfully explain and predict behavior—for instance, that Sally will look for her marble in her basket. Understanding false belief naturally implies an understanding of true belief, of knowledge and ignorance, and of intentions and feelings. This is a theory of mind (ToM).

Most children with ASD, even of a mental age far in excess of 4 years, find the simple Sally–Anne test a great puzzle and tend to get it wrong. They say that Sally will look for the marble in Anne's box (where it really is)—even though they remember correctly that Sally had put the marble into her basket and was not present when Anne transferred it to her box. Despite remembering the simple sequence of events, they cannot make sense of them by inferring that Sally has a false belief—so they do not take into account what Sally thinks; they miss the important change (her previously correct belief is now false). Thus, they cannot predict Sally's behavior. Their lack of understanding of false belief reflects a lack of understanding of others' mental states; hence the claim that individuals with ASD do not have a theory of mind (ToM).

Source: Adapted from *Autism* By Uta Frith, From *Scientific American*, June 1993.

A small but significant number of children with ASD (estimates range widely, from 15% to 60%) demonstrate some knowledge of ToM—they pass the Sally–Anne Test or tests like it (Happé, 1995a). In contrast to the children with ASD who do not pass false-belief tests, children with ASD who pass the tests display insightful and interactive behavior and have better verbal and communication abilities (Frith & Happé, 1994). They also display far more verbal ability than other children of the same chronological age, suggesting that they may work out ToM tasks in a conscious and logical way (Happé, 1995a, 1995b). All children who succeed at ToM tasks, including children with ASD, usually understand metaphors, irony, and a range of speaker emotions, such as the intention to lie or tell a joke. However, youngsters with ASD who understand a false belief give laborious explanations for their insights, suggesting the use of conscious and deliberate strategies to discern mental states. In contrast, understanding a false belief may be so natural, automatic, and unconscious for most children that they may have difficulty explaining how they come up with their answer (Happé, 1995a).

Brain scan studies suggest that the ability to mentalize is associated with a specific region of the brain that is connected to a widespread network of brain regions involved in social cognition (van Veluw & Chance, 2013). Regarding the difficulties displayed by children with ASD, these findings may have implications for understanding the neural basis of ASD, which we will return to in a later section. Although specific social-emotional cognitive deficits, as in ToM, are very common in children with ASD, the fact that they do not occur in all of these children suggests that mechanisms other than ToM are needed to explain the cognitive deficits in autism.

General Deficits

Children with ASD display a general deficit in higher-order planning and regulatory behaviors (Russell, 1997). These processes, called *executive functions,* permit us to maintain effective problem solving by inhibiting inappropriate behaviors, engaging in thoughtful actions, sustaining task performance and self-monitoring, using feedback, and flexibly shifting from one task to another. This presence of a general deficit in executive functioning in children with ASD is suggested by their difficulties in cognitive functions such as planning and organizing, changing to a new cognitive set, disengaging from salient stimuli, processing information in novel and unpredictable environments, and generalizing previously learned information to new situations (O'Hearn et al., 2008).

There are many types of executive functions, so it will be important to identify which deficits in executive function are specific to individuals with ASD (Russo et al., 2007). For example, children with ASD display executive functioning deficits that are more generalized and profound than those seen in ADHD; children with ASD share some deficits with children who have ADHD (e.g., vigilance, inhibitory) and have other deficits that are different (e.g., cognitive flexibility/switching) (Corbett et al., 2009).

Another general cognitive deficit hypothesized to underlie ASD is a weak drive for **central coherence,** which refers to the strong tendency of humans to interpret stimuli in a relatively global way that takes the broader context into account (Frith, 1993). By doing this, we can extract meaning from complex sets of information and remember the main points rather than the precise details. It has been proposed that individuals with ASD have a weak tendency for central coherence and tend to process information in bits and pieces rather than looking at the big picture (Frith & Happé, 1994). Understanding other peoples' words, gestures, or feelings can be extremely difficult for someone who lacks central coherence, as reflected in this statement by Donna Williams, an adult with ASD who has written extensively about what it is like to have this disorder:

> It is hard to care or be interested in what a person feels when you perceive a body and then a hand and an eye and a nose and other bits all moving but not perceived in any connected way, with no perception of the context. (Nemeth, 1994, p. 49)

Consistent with a general deficit in central coherence, individuals with ASD perform surprisingly well on tasks in which a focus on parts of a stimulus, rather than the overall pattern, serves to facilitate performance. One such task, the Embedded Figures Test (Jolliffe & Baron-Cohen, 1997) is shown in ● Figure 6.4. The advantage for individuals with ASD on this task may be caused by their spontaneous mental segmentation of the figures into unconnected and meaningless units (Brosnan, Gwilliam, & Walker, 2012). This happens to facilitate the identification of the figure embedded in the whole pattern, resulting in higher scores on this task.

A deficit in ToM and weak central coherence in a child with ASD may also affect the generalized knowledge of what happens at everyday real-life events such as going on a field trip (Loth, Gomez, & Happé, 2008). These types of mental scripts are important tools in structuring the child's social experiences while accounting for the variability that surrounds real-life events, and may be impaired in children with ASD.

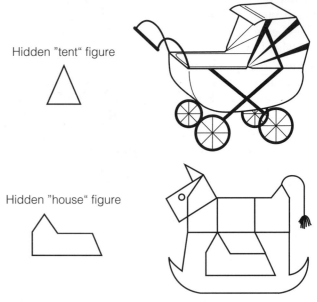

Embedded Figures

● **FIGURE 6.4** | Embedded Figures Test: Children with ASD perform relatively well on tasks that require attention to details of a figure rather than the overall pattern.

From *A Manual for the Embedded Figures Test* by H. A. Witkin, P. K. Oltman, E. Raskin, and S. A. Karp, pp. 21–26. Consulting Psychologists Press, Inc. Copyright © 1971 by Stephen Karp. Reprinted by permission of S. A. Karp.

Are These Cognitive Deficits Specific to ASD?

Of the cognitive deficits that we have described, lack of ToM seems to be the one most specific to children with ASD as compared with children with ID or specific language deficits. However, studies of ToM across a variety of other disorders, including schizophrenia, ADHD, and conduct disorder, suggest that these children also have difficulties in accurately interpreting other people's intentions (Sprung, 2010). Deficits in processing social–emotional information appear to be less specific to ASD than are ToM deficits; the former occur in many other conditions, including schizophrenia and ID. There is even less diagnostic specificity for executive functioning deficits, which occur in many other clinical groups of children, including those with ADHD and conduct disorder (Griffith et al., 1999). Further work is needed to determine whether the kinds of deficits in executive functioning in children with ASD differ from those in children with other problems (Hill, 2004).

Are These Cognitive Deficits Found in All Individuals with ASD?

As we have noted, some individuals with ASD pass ToM tests. However, it is not yet clear whether individuals with ASD who have normal IQs have actually developed a ToM. Studies of high-functioning school-aged children and adolescents with ASD suggest that they understand the theoretical principles of advanced mental state reasoning but do not apply them in everyday life situations (Scheeren et al., 2013).

It seems unlikely that a single cognitive abnormality can explain all the deficits present in children with ASD (Tager-Flusberg, 2007). The presence of multiple cognitive deficits, some specific and some general, may help us explain why ASD exists in so many forms and levels of severity. Finally, although we have discussed the general and specific deficits in cognitive functioning in ASD individually, note that they are related to one another. For example, there is likely a link between the development of certain executive functions and the emergence of children's ToM.

In addition to the cognitive deficits previously discussed, another view is that children with ASD have an underlying impairment in *social motivation*—that is, they fail to find social stimuli intrinsically rewarding (Dawson et al., 2002). For example, most infants find the mutual exchange of positive emotions during social interactions involving eye-to-eye contact rewarding, and it motivates them to notice and attend to social and emotional cues. In contrast, infants who are later diagnosed with ASD initially show as much eye contact as infants who do not go on to develop ASD, but then show a decline in eye contact from 2 to 6 months of age, a pattern not seen in infants who do not develop ASD (Jones & Klin, 2013). Children with ASD may fail to find eye-to-eye contact rewarding and thus are less motivated and less likely to attend to social cues, extract meaning from others' emotional expressions, and participate in social exchanges. As a result, they have fewer opportunities to engage in behaviors essential for the development of social communication and language (Garcia-Perez, Hobson, & Lee, 2008; Hobson, 2002/2004). As one adolescent with ASD put it, "I still have to remind myself that there are people." Motivational theories remind us that the poor perspective-taking skills of children with ASD are not only manifestations of a cognitive deficit in their perspective-taking abilities, but may also reflect their disinclination to shift their perspective.

Medical Conditions and Physical Characteristics

About 10% of children with ASD have a coexisting medical condition that may play a causal role in their disorder (Challman et al., 2003; Fombonne, 2003). These include motor and sensory impairments, seizures, immunological and metabolic abnormalities, sleep problems, and gastrointestinal symptoms (IACC, 2011). About 25% of individuals with ASD experience seizures (Mouridsen, Rich, & Isager, 2011). Seizure onset usually occurs either in early childhood or more often in late adolescence or early adulthood (Bolton et al., 2011; Parmeggiani et al., 2010), with early-onset seizures typically associated with greater ID and poorer outcomes (Saemundsen, Ludvigsson, & Rafnsson, 2008). Sleep disturbances are also common, occurring in about 65% of children with ASD, and are typically related to the sleep–wake rhythm and problems with sleep onset and maintenance (Dawson, 2010; Hollway & Aman, 2011). Sleep disorders in children with ASD are associated with a wide variety of behavior problems, making it essential to assess and treat these disorders when working with these children (Rossignol & Frye, 2011; Schwichtenberg et al., 2013). Also common are gastrointestinal symptoms such as abdominal pain, constipation, bloating, diarrhea, and nausea, occurring in about 50% of children with ASD (Chaidez, Hansen, & Hertz-Picciotto, 2013). These may be related to food selectivity and unusual eating habits and obsessions ranging from minor problems in eating, to disruptive mealtime behaviors, to clinically significant feeding problems, and to anxiety (Mazurek et al., 2013; Seiverling, Williams, & Sturmey, 2010).

Children with ASD are usually described as having a normal or attractive physical appearance, and they do not display the visible physical deviations that often accompany severe ID that is not associated with ASD. They may have subtle but distinctive minor physical anomalies such as facial asymmetries, which suggest the influence of genetic or other prenatal factors (Ozgen et al., 2010).

As many as 90% of individuals with ASD have a head size that is above average. About 20% have a significantly larger-than-normal head size that places them in the upper 3% of the general population (Redcay & Courchesne, 2005). This characteristic is more common in higher-functioning individuals and distinguishes them from individuals with ID, language disorder, and ADHD (Gillberg & de Souza, 2002). Interestingly, infants with ASD tend to have a smaller-than-average head size at birth, but then show an excessive increase in growth from 6 to 12 months, leading to the larger-than-normal head size observed at a later age, which is then followed by a deceleration in head growth (Courchesne, Carper, & Akshoomoff, 2003; Dawson et al., 2007). The cause of this rapid growth during the first year of life is not known, but one implication is that the overproduction of brain connections too quickly makes it difficult for developing children with ASD to adapt to and make sense out of their experiences (Lewis & Elman, 2008). However, a recent reevaluation of head-circumference data in ASD studies raises the important concern that previous findings could be an artifact of using outdated norms and that when current norms for early brain growth are used there are few observed differences between changes in early brain growth in infants with ASD and other children (Raznahan et al., 2013). Thus, it remains to be established whether the "accelerated" growth in head size is specific to children with ASD when contemporary norms are used or whether it also occurs in samples of healthy children and those with other psychiatric disorders (Rommelse et al., 2011).

Accompanying Disorders and Symptoms

The disorders that most often accompany ASD are ID and epilepsy (Bolton et al., 2011). Additional behavioral and psychiatric symptoms may include ADHD (Hanson et al., 2013), conduct problems (Guttmann-Steinmetz, Gadow, & DeVincent, 2009), anxieties and fears (Hallett et al., 2013), and mood problems (Magnuson & Constantino, 2011). Some children with ASD also engage in extreme, and sometimes potentially life-threatening, *self-injurious behavior* (SIB)—any self-inflicted behavior that can cause tissue damage to the child's own body (see Chapter 5). The most common forms of SIB are head banging, hand or arm biting, and excessive scratching and rubbing. Head banging, if not prevented, can be severe enough to produce bleeding or even brain injury. SIB may occur for a variety of reasons—self-stimulation, to gain attention, or to eliminate unwanted demands—or, it may occur for no apparent reason (Furniss & Biswas, 2012). Whatever the reasons, rates of emergency/hospital treatment for self-inflicted injuries in children with ASD are seven times greater than for typically developing children (McDermott, Zhou, & Mann, 2008). However, SIB may not occur more frequently in young children with ASD than in those with other forms of developmental delay. For children with ASD, ID, atypical sensory processing, need for sameness, repetitive behaviors, and impulsivity are among the strongest risk factors for SIB (Duerden et al., 2012; Richman et al., 2013).

Section Summary

Associated Characteristics of ASD

- Previous estimates were that about 70% of children with ASD also have ID. However, recent reports suggest that ID in individuals with ASD is closer to 40% to 50%, a decrease that is most likely related to increased diagnoses of ASD in higher-functioning individuals and to the effects of early intervention.

- Children with ASD display a deficit in theory of mind (ToM)—the ability to understand other people's and one's own mental states, including beliefs, intentions, feelings, and desires.
- Children with ASD display a general deficit in higher-order planning and regulatory behaviors (e.g., executive functions).
- They may display co-occurring medical conditions and physical features such as seizures, sleep problems, gastrointestinal symptoms, or increased head size.
- Children with ASD may display co-occurring symptoms of ADHD, conduct problems, anxieties and fears, and mood problems.

PREVALENCE AND COURSE OF ASD

For decades, ASD was thought to be a rare disorder, affecting about 1 per 2,500 children (Tanguay, 2000). However, recent findings worldwide indicate a much higher prevalence rate—as many as 1 per 68 children or between 1% and 2% (CDC, 2014; Elsabbagh et al., 2012). ASD affects over 2 million individuals in the U.S. and tens of millions more worldwide (Autism Speaks, 2013). In terms of economic burden, the total estimated annual societal costs of caring for children with ASD in the United States are $11.5 billion or more (Ganz, 2007; Levelle et al., 2014). Health care costs for children with ASD are at least six times higher than for those without ASD and even higher for those with ASD and a co-occurring condition such as ID, ADHD, or epilepsy (Peacock et al., 2013). Given the increasing prevalence and growing emphasis on early identification and intervention for children with ASD, it is likely that these costs will continue to rise.

Many causes for the apparent dramatic increase in ASD have been proposed—vaccines, mercury, diet, acetaminophen, caffeine, antibiotics, allergies, environmental pollutants, and electromagnetic radiation—but to date none has been scientifically substantiated. It seems likely that most, if not all, of the rise in prevalence is caused by a greater awareness among parents and professionals; a broadening of the concept and its definition over the years; greater recognition and diagnosis of milder forms of ASD; changes in diagnostic criteria and categories; diagnostic substitution (i.e., the number of children receiving special education under other diagnostic categories, primarily ID, speech impairment, and learning disabilities, has decreased as those diagnosed with ASD have increased); and better case-finding methods (King & Bearman, 2009; Wazana, Besnahan, & Kline, 2007). However, whether there is also a real increase in prevalence due to an unidentified cause remains an open question. Interestingly, in contrast to scientific opinion that the increase in ASD prevalence is mainly due to changes in awareness and diagnostic practices, many laypeople continue to believe that the increase is due to increased exposure to new environmental, medical, and technological hazards (e.g., vaccinations, cell phone towers) (Russell, Kelly, & Golding, 2009).

ASD is found in all social classes and has been identified worldwide. It is about four to five times more common in boys than in girls, a ratio that has remained fairly constant over the years, even with increasing prevalence estimates (CDC, 2014). The sex difference is most apparent among children with IQs in the average to above-average range, perhaps being as high as 10:1 in higher-functioning individuals. However, among children with ASD and profound ID, the numbers of boys and girls are similar. Thus, although girls are less often affected by ASD than are boys, when they are affected, they tend to have more severe intellectual impairments (Dworzynski et al., 2012). Girls with ASD who do not have an intellectual impairment are more likely to be formally diagnosed at a later age than boys (Giarelli et al., 2010). Girls with comparable high levels of ASD symptom severity as boys are also less likely to be diagnosed, suggesting that there is a bias in diagnosis or that in the absence of co-occurring intellectual or behavioral deficits girls may be better able to cope with the same level of ASD symptoms (Constantino & Charman, 2012). In general, the clinical manifestations of ASD are quite similar for boys and girls, although there may be some differences in their cognitive profiles (Carter et al., 2007). For example, it has been found that girls with ASD engage in more pretend play than do boys, suggesting that impairment in pretense may be less of a problem for girls (Knickmeyer, Wheelwright, & Baron-Cohen, 2008). Findings also suggest brain differences underlying ASD in males and females (Lai et al., 2013).

In considering the high ratio of males to females with ASD, Simon Baron-Cohen (2002, 2009) proposed the *extreme male brain theory of ASD*. Those with ASD are presumed to fall at the extreme high end of a continuum of cognitive abilities associated with systemizing (understanding the inanimate world), and at the extreme low end of abilities associated with empathizing (understanding our social world). Both abilities are present in all males and females, but males are presumed to show more systemizing and females more empathizing. Frequent interests and behaviors that occur among individuals with ASD (e.g., attention to detail, collecting, an interest in mathematics, mechanical knowledge, and scientific and technical information) are presumed to reflect an extreme on the systemizing dimension of the male brain, and a relative absence of empathizing (e.g., mindreading, empathy, eye contact, and communication) (Baron-Cohen et al., 2003). Interestingly, one brain study found that females with ASD displayed masculinization at the neural level (Lai et al., 2013). The extreme male brain theory is intriguing but somewhat controversial. Further research into the neurocognitive aspects of these dimensions in individuals with ASD will be needed before we can infer that they are "from Mars and not Venus."

Rates of ASD are comparable across different racial and ethnic groups. Where differences are found, prevalence is higher among non-Hispanic white children than among members of other groups, most likely because of underidentification in non-Hispanic black and Hispanic children (CDC, 2012a). Different racial and ethnic groups do not differ in core symptoms of or risk factors for ASD (CDC, 2012a; Cuccaro et al., 2007). However, African American children are nearly three times more likely than white children to receive another diagnosis such as ADHD or adjustment disorder before being diagnosed with ASD, and they are nearly three times more likely to experience delays in receiving intervention (Mandell et al., 2007). Societies differ in how they integrate ASD into their cultural frameworks. For example, in contrast to viewing ASD as a disorder, some cultures view children with ASD as having special skills or as being more in touch with the spirit world. Cultural views range from those of the Navajo, who embrace their children with ASD as being blessed (Kapp, 2011), to the South Koreans, who may hide their children with ASD to protect siblings from being considered tainted and unmarriageable (Grinker, 2007).

Age at Onset

The *diagnosis* of ASD is usually made in the preschool period or later. However, most parents of children with ASD become seriously concerned a year or more before a diagnosis is made, typically during the months preceding their child's second birthday (McConkey, Truesdale-Kennedy, & Cassidy, 2009) At this time, their child's lack of progress in language, imaginative play, and social relations stands in sharp contrast to rapid developments in these areas by other children of the same age. Although deficits of ASD become increasingly noticeable around age 2, elements are probably present and noticed earlier, as reflected in Anne-Marie's solemn reaction to her first birthday party (Yirmiya & Charman, 2010).

ANNE-MARIE

First Birthday

We were celebrating Anne-Marie's first birthday and had just paraded in, bearing the cake with much fanfare. Daniel, her big brother, almost two and a half years old, and greatly excited, joined us in singing. Anne-Marie, in her high-chair, gazed solemnly at the cake, her baby body still, her mouth unsmiling. ... I couldn't help once again making a silent comparison to her brother, who at his first birthday party had squealed with delight. ... Who knows, really, what the first sign was, at what point Anne-Marie began to slip away from us? Was it around that first celebration, or after or before? (Based on Maurice, 1993b)

At present, the period from 12 to 18 months seems to be the earliest point in development at which ASD can be reliably detected. For example, an interesting study found that children with ASD generally did not show signs of the disorder at 6 months of age, but between 6 and 12 months they failed to gain new social skills or showed a loss of previously acquired ones (Ozonoff et al., 2010). Most children with ASD showed a subtle and gradual loss of specific social skills between 6 and 18 months that went unnoticed by parents. These findings suggest that traditional views that symptoms of ASD are present at birth or that the child shows dramatic regression at a later age may not accurately depict how ASD develops. Instead, the onset of symptoms may be more accurately represented as being on a continuum based on the amount and timing of loss of previously acquired skills (Ozonoff et al., 2009). Consistent with this view are recent findings that an early decline in eye contact over the first 6 months may precede the gradual loss of specific social skills that occurs from 6 to 12 months of age. Children who later developed ASD and typically developing children did not differ in eye contact in the first month of life, but for those who later developed ASD, eye contact gradually decreased over the first 6 months of life (Jones & Klin, 2013).

Currently, diagnoses of ASD that are made around age 2 to 3 years are stable for most children (Bryson, Rogers, & Fombonne, 2003; Kleinman et al., 2008). However, with increasing research into key early indicators, systematic screening and direct observation of infants at risk for ASD (e.g., those with older siblings with the disorder), and universal screening of young infants, it is likely that ASD can and will be reliably detected at earlier ages, particularly for those with low

IQ (Bryson et al., 2008; Oosterling et al., 2010; Pierce et al., 2011). Features of atypical development, that are very similar to those found in ASD but are less severe, have recently been detected in infant siblings of children with ASD by the infants' first birthday (Ozonoff et al., 2014). Possible early indicators of ASD may include: "uses few gestures to express social interest," "doesn't respond when name is called," "rarely makes eye contact when interacting," "limited babbling, particularly in a social context," and "displays odd or repetitive ways of moving hands and/or fingers" (Zwaigenbaum et al., 2009). Children with ASD have been found to differ from typically developing children on most of these indicators between the ages of 12 and 24 months. However, in one study, only early communicative gestures were found to distinguish children with ASD from those with developmental delay or language impairment (Vaness et al., 2012). As part of its campaign to raise awareness about the importance of early identification for intervention, the American Academy of Pediatrics (AAP) recommended that all children be screened for ASD at 18 months and 24 months (Hampton, 2007). The organization Autism Speaks has a video glossary on its website (www.autismspeaks.org) where you can view fascinating video clips that show some of the early red flags for ASD as well as examples of commonly used treatments. To date, efforts to implement screening approaches in community settings have had positive results. However, the extent to which these results have brought about reduced time to diagnosis and enrollment in services has not yet been tested (Daniels et al., 2013).

Course and Outcome

Children with ASD develop along different pathways. Some show abnormal behavior soon after birth; some, 25% or more, show seemingly normal development for the first year or longer followed by *regression* (the loss of previously acquired language and social skills, with an onset of ASD) (Parr et al., 2011); while others appear to improve significantly over time (Fein et al., 2013). The symptoms of children with ASD change over time. Most symptoms gradually improve with age, even though children continue to experience many problems. During adolescence, some symptoms, such as hyperactivity, self-injury, and compulsivity, may worsen (Spector & Volkmar, 2006). During later adolescence and adulthood, abnormalities such as stereotyped motor movements, anxiety, and socially inappropriate behaviors are common, even in high-functioning individuals; these individuals also often experience loneliness, social disadvantage and exclusion, and work difficulties (Howlin, 2013). Complex obsessive–compulsive rituals may develop, and talking may be characterized by idiosyncratic and perseverative speech, monotonous tone, and self-talk (Newsom & Hovanitz, 2006).

Findings from early studies of children with ASD who received limited help indicated that an overwhelming majority (70% or more) showed poor outcomes with limited progress and continuing handicaps that did not permit them to lead an independent existence (Lotter, 1978). More recent follow-up studies report slightly better, but quite similar, outcomes (Eaves & Ho, 2008; Howlin et al., 2004; Howlin et al., 2013). Very few adults with ASD achieve high levels of independence. Most remain quite dependent on their family and other support services, with few friends and no permanent job (Roux et al., 2013). These adults continue to display problems in communication, stereotyped behaviors and interests, and poor reading and spelling abilities. Overall, children with better language skills, higher intellectual ability, and higher scores on measures of reciprocal social interaction at the time of diagnosis show better long-term outcomes, but outcomes can be variable even for high-functioning individuals (Bennett et al., 2008). It is possible that better long-term outcomes will be achieved by more recent generations of children with ASD who were diagnosed at a younger age, are higher-functioning, and received intensive early intervention. However, future longitudinal research will be needed before we know. Whatever the outcome, the reality is that children with ASD grow up, and most will continue to require age-appropriate supports and services. To date, far greater attention has been given to research, programs, and services for children with ASD than to adolescents and adults with ASD. Further efforts to address the needs of older individuals with ASD are sorely needed (Bailey, 2012; Wilczynski, 2013).

Section Summary

Prevalence and Course of ASD

- ASD is a disorder that affects as many as 1 in 68 children, or between one and two percent. It is four to five times more common in boys than in girls. ASD is found across all social classes and has been identified in every country in which it has been studied.
- ASD is most often identified around age 2 years or older, although elements are present at a much earlier age.
- Children with ASD may develop along different pathways. Some show abnormal behavior soon after birth; others

show seemingly normal development for the first year or longer followed by regression; while others appear to improve significantly over time.

- Most children with ASD show gradual improvement of their symptoms with age, although they continue to display social impairments that make them different from other people throughout their lives.
- The two strongest predictors of adult outcomes in children with ASD are intellectual ability and language development.

CAUSES OF ASD

No single abnormality can account for all the impairments associated with ASD, or for the many forms of the disorder, ranging from mild to severe. Although the precise causes of ASD are still not known, our understanding of possible mechanisms has increased dramatically (Klinger et al., 2014). These advances are evident when we consider that, not long ago, autism was being attributed to cold and unloving parents. It is now generally accepted that ASD is a biologically based neurodevelopmental disorder with multiple causes involving genetic and environmental risk factors (Faja & Dawson, 2013). To understand ASD, we must consider problems in early development, genetic influences, and neuropsychological and neurobiological findings.

Problems in Early Development

Children with ASD experience more health problems prenatally, at birth, or immediately following birth than do other children. Although not proven as independent risk factors, prenatal and neonatal complications such as preterm birth, bleeding during pregnancy, toxemia (blood poisoning), viral infection or exposure, a lack of vigor after birth, and others have been identified in a small percentage of children with ASD (Gardener, Spiegelman, & Buka, 2009, 2011). One study found that very preterm birth (gestational age of <26 weeks) was associated with a much higher rate of ASD, with a prevalence of 8% diagnosed by age 11 (Johnson et al., 2010). Other risk factors that affect the prenatal environment may place the fetus at increased risk for ASD. These include increased maternal age, in vitro fertilization, maternal use of prescription and nonprescription drugs, toxic chemicals in the environment during pregnancy, maternal fever or maternal illnesses such as diabetes or infections during pregnancy, chronic hypertension, and prepregnancy obesity (Szatmari, 2011). For example, with regard to parental age, a study of over 7 million children in California found that older mothers and fathers were more likely to have a child with ASD than were younger parents (Grether et al., 2009). It was found that an increase of 10 years in maternal age was associated with a 38% greater risk of ASD and that the same increase in paternal age was associated with a 22% greater risk. The relationship between increasing parental age and ASD suggests that age could be a contributing factor in the increase in ASD, and also raises questions about possible mechanisms including age-related gene variants or epigenetic dysfunction (Sandin et al., 2012). Exposure to antidepressant medication (SSRIs) during the first trimester of pregnancy has also been found to increase the risk of ASD (Croen et al., 2011). Although problems during pregnancy and birth may not be the primary cause of ASD, they do suggest that fetal or neonatal development has been compromised (Szatmari, 2011).

A controversial and widely publicized proposal was that some cases of ASD in children who speak only a few words and have other social–communicative behaviors that disappear in the second year of life might be linked to vaccinations. Two hypotheses attracted the most attention. The first incriminated the measles components of combination vaccines for measles–mumps–rubella (MMR) (Wakefield et al., 1998; *retracted* February, 2010). The second lay blame on exposure to ethyl mercury (thimerosal), a preservative used in other vaccines (Ball, Ball, & Pratt, 2001). Both hypotheses claimed that the apparent ASD "epidemic" coincided with the introduction of MMR vaccines and/or increased exposure to thimerosal as a result of the increased number of recommended childhood vaccinations in the first 3 years of life. However, current scientific evidence does not support an association between MMR vaccines or thimerosal and ASD (Fombonne, 2008; Institute of Medicine, 2004; see also The Editors of The Lancet, 2010). Nevertheless, a large number of parents of children with ASD still believe that their child's disorder was caused by vaccinations (Harrington et al., 2006).

Genetic Influences

Studies of specific chromosomal anomalies and gene disorders, findings from family and twin studies, and specific gene studies indicate a substantial role for genetic factors in ASD (Rutter, 2005). However, despite strong evidence for a genetic contribution and some noteworthy findings emerging from tests of hundreds of genes, the rate of progress in gene discovery has been slow, and the genetic architecture of ASD remains largely unknown (El-Fishawy & State, 2010).

Chromosomal and Gene Disorders

The discovery of the fragile-X anomaly (see Chapter 5) in about 2% to 3% of children with ASD led to increased attention to this and other chromosomal defects that might be related to ASD (Turk & Graham, 1997). In general, individuals with ASD have an elevated risk, about 5%, for chromosomal anomalies (Barton & Volkmar, 1998; Dykens & Volkmar, 1997). However, these anomalies alone do not indicate the specific gene sites underlying the disorder, because ASD has been associated with anomalies involving several chromosomes (Freitag et al., 2010).

ASD is also associated with *tuberous sclerosis,* a rare single-gene disorder. The manifestations of this disorder can vary widely from mild to severe; they may include neural deficits, seizures, and learning disabilities. Most cases are derived from de novo mutations, cases in which no family history of the disorder existed (Bailey, Phillips, & Rutter, 1996). About 25% or more of children with tuberous sclerosis also have ASD. This makes the association between ASD and tuberous sclerosis greater than that for any other genetically based condition.

Family and Twin Studies

Some studies have found that as many as 15% to 20% of siblings of individuals with ASD also have the disorder, a number nearly twice that seen in earlier reports (Ozonoff et al., 2011). Also, at 3 years of age, high-risk siblings who do not receive a diagnosis of ASD show greater severity of symptoms of ASD and lower levels of developmental functioning than do low-risk children (Messinger et al., 2013). In addition, family members of children with ASD display higher-than-normal rates of social and language deficits and unusual personality features that are very similar to those found in ASD but are less severe (Gerdts et al., 2013; Ozonoff et al., 2014). Referred to as the *broader autism phenotype,* these deficits include social oddities such as aloofness, lack of tact, and rigidity; pragmatic language problems such as over-communicativeness or undercommunicativeness; and poor verbal comprehension. Family members with the broader phenotype do not, however, display the atypical language (e.g., pronoun reversal), extreme stereotyped repetitive behavior, or the ID and epilepsy that are often associated with a formal diagnosis of ASD (Rutter, 2000). These findings are consistent with a general family risk for ASD that is genetically mediated. In addition, a growing number of studies have reported similar neurophysiological correlates (e.g., atypical brain activation, reduced white matter) for children with ASD *and* their "unaffected siblings," suggesting a family susceptibility to ASD involving a wide array of brain regions and networks (Barnea-Goraly, Lotspeich, & Reiss, 2010; Belmonte, Gomot, Baron-Cohen, 2010).

Twin studies have reported concordance rates for ASD in identical twins ranging from 70% to 90%, in contrast to near-zero rates for fraternal twins (Rutter, 2005). These findings indicate that the heritability of an underlying liability for ASD may be as high as 90% and suggest that almost all the variance in the expression and stability of ASD over time can be attributed to inherited genetic influences (Freitag et al., 2010; Holmboe et al., 2013; Lichtenstein et al., 2010). One exception is a finding that a large proportion of the variance in susceptibility to ASD could be explained by *shared environmental experiences* (58%), with heritability accounting for a smaller amount (38%) (Hallmayer et al., 2011). If replicated, this finding suggests that susceptibility to ASD may have a moderate genetic heritability component and a substantial shared twin environmental component. To date, the major focus of research on ASD has been on genetic influences, with minimal attention paid to environmental factors. The finding that shared environmental experiences have a significant influence on ASD susceptibility suggests that environmental risk factors occurring prior to or by the end of the first year of life could play an important role. Thus, further research into problems in early development of the type discussed previously, such as low birth weight, multiple births, maternal infections during pregnancy, and parental age, may help to advance our understanding of ASD (Hertz-Picciotto, 2011).

Molecular Genetics

New research using molecular genetics has pointed to particular areas on many different chromosomes as possible locations for *susceptibility genes* for ASD (Klinger et al., 2014). Susceptibility genes are causally implicated in the susceptibility to ASD but do not cause it directly on their own. Although several searches for major ASD genes have been undertaken, they have not yielded consistent results (Freitag et al., 2010). No single gene has been found to be relevant for most cases of ASD. Inconsistent findings in gene studies may be due to the considerable etiologic heterogeneity within ASD and the diverse ways in which it appears. Rather than a single gene, ASD is associated with rare mutations that have a strong effect for a very small proportion of individuals with ASD who have such genes, and a few common variants of small effect in several genes that seem to be a factor for many cases of ASD (Anney et al., 2012). Thus, ASD is likely to be a complex genetic disorder resulting from both rare mutations and simultaneous genetic variations (e.g., submicroscopic deletions or insertions of segments of DNA) in multiple genes (El-Fishawy & State, 2010). Moreover, the expression of ASD gene(s) may be influenced by environmental factors (e.g., exposure to drugs, maternal illness)—a "a second hit" that occurs primarily during fetal brain development. The possible role of such gene–environment interactions (GxE) and also gene–environment correlations (rGEs) in ASD requires further study (Corrales & Herbert, 2011; Meek et al., 2013).

Finally, there are a number of situations in which epigenetic dysregulation (changes in gene expression caused by mechanisms other than changes in the underlying DNA sequence) may be associated with the development of ASD, For example, co-morbid genetic conditions such as fragile-X syndrome or genes or genomic regions exhibiting abnormal epigenetic regulation (Grafodatskaya et al., 2010) may be associated with ASD. Thus, in searching for genetic alterations responsible for ASD, it may also be necessary to look beyond mutations and variations in specific genes into epigenetic regulation of gene function (Rangasamy, D'Mello, & Narayanan, 2013).

Brain Abnormalities

Although there is no known biological marker for ASD, impressive advances have been made in documenting the neurobiological basis of the disorder (Neuhaus, Beauchaine, & Bernier, 2010; Pelphrey et al,, 2011). Current research suggests that the behavioral features of ASD may result from abnormalities in brain structure and functioning that are consistent with early disturbances in neural development, possibly tracing back to prenatal development (Minshew, Johnson, & Luna, 2000; Stoner et al., 2014; Xiao et al., 2014). Importantly, although many brain regions are implicated, the disorder does not seems to lie in an abnormality localized in one part of the brain. Rather, it results from a lack of normal connectivity across brain networks that underlie the core features of ASD (Rudie et al., 2012; Stigler et al., 2011; Waterhouse & Gillberg, 2014).

Neuropsychological impairments in ASD occur in many domains, including verbal intelligence, orienting and selective attention, memory, pragmatic language, and executive functions (Dawson et al., 2002). The widespread nature of these deficits suggests that multiple regions of the brain are involved at both the cortical and subcortical levels (Happé & Frith, 1996). The types of neuropsychological deficits also vary as a function of the severity of the child's disorder. For example, low-functioning children with ASD may show impairments in basic memory functions, such as visual recognition memory, which are mediated by the brain's medial temporal lobe (Barth, Fein, & Waterhouse, 1995). In contrast, high-functioning children may have more subtle deficits in working memory or in encoding complex verbal material, suggesting the involvement of higher cortical functions (Dawson, 1996).

Biological Findings

Brain imaging studies have looked for structural and functional abnormalities in brain development or consistently localized brain lesions associated with the symptoms of ASD (Williams & Minshew, 2007). In terms of abnormal brain development, one longitudinal study examined brain growth at multiple points in time from ages 1.5 to 5 years in normal toddlers and toddlers who received a confirmed diagnosis of ASD at around 4 years of age (Schumann et al., 2010). The toddlers with ASD showed evidence of overgrowth of cerebral gray and white matter in all regions by age 2.5 years, around the time that their clinical symptoms began to appear. Almost all brain regions were found to develop at an abnormal rate; this finding was more pronounced in girls.

In terms of localized brain abnormalities, studies have consistently identified structural abnormalities in the cerebellum and in the medial temporal lobe and related limbic system structures (Bauman & Kemper, 2005; Courchesne et al., 2007). The *cerebellum*, a relatively large part of the brain located near the brain stem, is most frequently associated with motor movement. However, it is also partially involved in modulating emotion, language, executive function, learning, thought, and attention (Hodge et al., 2010). Specific areas of the cerebellum are found to be significantly smaller than normal in youngsters with ASD, particularly in those with a higher level of functioning (Scott et al., 2009). It has been proposed that cerebellar abnormalities may underlie the problem that children with ASD have in rapidly shifting their attention from one stimulus to another (Courchesne et al., 2007).

A second localized brain abnormality is in the medial temporal lobe and connected limbic system structures such as the amygdala and hippocampus (Groen et al., 2010; Johnson et al., 2013; Schumann & Amaral, 2009). These areas of the brain are associated with functions that are often disturbed in children with ASD—for example, learning, memory, and emotion regulation (Mazefsky et al., 2013). The amygdala plays an especially important role in recognizing the emotional significance of stimuli, in orienting toward social stimuli, in the perception of eye gaze direction, and, along with the hippocampus, in long-term memory (Schulkin, 2007). Findings from brain scan studies suggest that there are both structural and functional abnormalities in the amygdala of those with ASD (although not in all cases) (Monk, 2008). For example, enlargement of the amygdala in toddlers with ASD is correlated with the severity of their social and communication impairments (Schumann et al., 2009).

Studies of brain metabolism in individuals with ASD suggest decreased blood flow in the frontal and temporal lobes. Studies have also found a decrease in the functional connections between cortical and subcortical regions and a delay in the maturation of the frontal cortex, as indicated by reduced cerebral blood flow in the frontal brain regions of preschool-age children with autism (Zilbovicius et al., 1995).

In relation to connections among specific brain regions and tracts (parts of the brain that carry signals from one brain region to another and allow communication between the two hemispheres), abnormalities in the corpus callosum, frontal lobe cortex, and other brain tracts have been found in youngsters with ASD (Kumar et al., 2010; Shukla, Keehn, & Muller, 2011) and in their unaffected siblings (e.g., Barnea-Goraly et al., 2010). Reductions in the area of the corpus callosum (the main fiber tract connecting the hemispheres) have been found in children with ASD, supporting the role of abnormalities in connectivity in the disorder (Frazier & Hardan, 2009). Another study found significantly reduced interhemispheric connectivity specific to brain regions with functional relevance to ASD (Anderson et al., 2011). Postmortem studies of single axons in prefrontal regions of the brain have revealed a disconnection of long-distance brain pathways, excessive connections between adjacent areas, and inefficiency in pathways for emotion, which may account for why individuals with ASD have difficulty in shifting attention, engage in repetitive behavior, and avoid social interactions (Zikopoulos & Barbas, 2010).

Atypical patterns of connectivity in the *default mode network* (DMN) have also been found in children with ASD (von dem Hagen et al., 2013). The DMN is a network of brain regions that are active when the individual is not focused on the external world and the brain is at wakeful rest—focusing on internal tasks such as daydreaming, thinking about the future, retrieving autobiographical memories, and assessing others' perspectives. These findings are important, since the DMN includes brain regions (e.g., medial prefrontal cortex, medial temporal lobe) hypothesized to be involved in the higher-order social–cognitive processes that are impaired in children with ASD—for example, memory, theory of mind, and integration of information (Stigler et al., 2011).

ASD as a Disorder of Risk and Adaptation

Based on the causal factors we have discussed, a model of risk and adaptation is needed to understand how

ASD develops. Genetic and environmental factors lead to abnormalities in brain development, which in turn lead to generalized disturbances in how the child processes information and interacts with his or her environment (Faja & Dawson, 2013). These disturbances are likely to disrupt critical input affecting brain development during early periods of sensitivity (Dawson et al., 2002). Therefore, the relationship between the child's early risk for ASD and later outcomes will be mediated by alterations in how the child interacts with and adapts to his or her environment. For example, Wan et al. (2013) found that the quality of interaction between infants at risk for ASD and their caregivers at 12 to 15 months correlated with an autism diagnosis at age 3 years. Depending on the interaction between early risk factors and the environment in which the child develops, different children will follow different developmental pathways. Although pathways may change at any point in development, the longer the child is on a maladaptive pathway, the more difficult it is for change to occur. Thus, as we discuss in the next section on treatment, the earlier the risk for ASD can be identified and the sooner intervention begins, the greater the likelihood that the child will have a better outcome (Sigman, Spence, & Wang, 2006).

Section Summary

Causes of ASD

- ASD is a biologically based neurodevelopmental disorder that may result from multiple causes.
- Some children with ASD experience prenatal and neonatal complications such low birth weight, bleeding during pregnancy, toxemia (blood poisoning), viral infection or exposure, and a lack of vigor after birth.
- ASD is a genetic disorder, although specific genes with large effects have not been identified. More likely, ASD is a complex genetic disorder resulting from rare mutations and simultaneous genetic variations in multiple genes. Shared environmental experiences and epigenetic factors may also be involved.
- Nonautistic relatives of individuals with ASD display higher-than-normal rates of social, language, and cognitive deficits that are similar in quality to those found in ASD, but are less severe and are not associated with intellectual deficits or epilepsy.
- Neuropsychological impairments occur in many areas of functioning, including intelligence, attention, memory, language, and executive functions.
- Structural abnormalities in the cerebellum and the medial temporal lobe, prefrontal cortex, and related limbic system structures have been found.

- ASD is not represented by a localized abnormality in one part of the brain but rather by a lack of normal connectivity and communication among brain networks that underlie the core features of ASD.
- The relationship between the child's early risk for ASD and later outcomes will be mediated by how the child interacts with and adapts to his or her environment.

TREATMENT OF ASD

I have not counted the trials of medication, the diets, ... the behavioral programs. If they total five hundred, there are five hundred fewer to try. ... I'm a believer. ... I believe my son can get well.

—From Swackhamer (1993)

Autistic people suffer from a biological defect. Although they cannot be cured, much can be done to improve their lives.

—U. Frith (1997)

These two sentiments—the first by the mother of a child with ASD, the second by an ASD expert—underscore the promise, pain, and uncertainty that surround efforts to help children with ASD and their families. Parents of children with ASD report having tried, on average, seven to nine different therapies for their child, and are currently using four to six (Goin-Kochel, Myers, & Mackintosh, 2007). It has been estimated that about *400 different treatments* are being used by individuals with ASD (Interactive Autism Network, 2011). The fact that no one treatment has been successful in eliminating the symptoms of ASD makes many parents vulnerable to new claims of dramatic improvements. This is especially true for a dizzying array of widely publicized treatments such as vitamins, nutritional supplements, special diets (e.g., gluten- and casein-free diets), medications (e.g., antipsychotics, stimulants, antidepressants), hyperbaric oxygen therapy (sealing the child in a pressurized oxygen chamber), chelation therapy (removal of heavy metals from the body), weighted vests (to provide "calming" stimulation), secretin (a hormone that controls digestion), immunotherapy (use of substances that target a variety of hypothesized but as yet unproven immune system abnormalities), auditory training, music therapy, dance/movement therapy, repetitive transcranial magnetic stimulation (stimulating key motor cortical sites to improve motor activity), sensory integration, facilitated communication, horseback riding, use of trained service dogs, and even swimming with dolphins (Schreck, Russell, & Vargas, 2013). Unfortunately, most of these treatments have not lived up to their claims under close scientific scrutiny, and some may have harmful effects (Research Autism, 2013; Umbarger, 2007).

Although behavioral, educational, and medical treatments may improve learning and behavior, and may permit a few children to achieve near-normal functioning, there is no known cure for ASD. The goals for most treatments are to minimize the core problems of ASD, maximize the child's independence and quality of life, and help the child and family cope more effectively with the disorder (Myers, Johnson, and the Council on Children with Disabilities, 2007). These goals can be facilitated by treatments designed to enhance development and learning, to reduce associated maladaptive behaviors, and to educate and support parents in meeting these goals. Understanding parents' beliefs about the causes of their child's ASD may also be important for treatment (Dardennes et al., 2011).

Promising new programs of early intervention, community-based education, and community living options are all reasons for optimism about improving outcomes for children with ASD (Rogers & Wallace, 2011; Volkmar et al., 2014). The most benefit is likely to come from developmentally oriented, early behavioral interventions that involve parents and that are used along with special educational methods (Rutter, 2006b). Most children treated using these newer evidence-based methods show significant gains in language, communication, and measured IQ and a modest reduction in the severity of the core symptoms of autism (Virués-Ortega, 2010; Young et al., 2010). However, questions remain concerning how intensive the interventions need to be (e.g., 20 vs. 40 hours per week), how much change can be achieved, and the extent to which changes can be directly attributed to the intervention. Additional controlled studies are needed before long-term outcomes can be fully assessed (Charman, 2011; Vismara & Rogers, 2010).

Overview

EMILIE

A Full-Time Job

When Emilie was 2 she was diagnosed with autism, Emilie's mother recalled, her eyes brimming with tears. "We've been relying on ourselves ever since." Emilie's mother and father have read about children with autism who became accomplished scientists and musicians—but progress for Emilie, now age 4, has been slow. Two months ago they hired a specialist to teach them a new one-on-one approach for

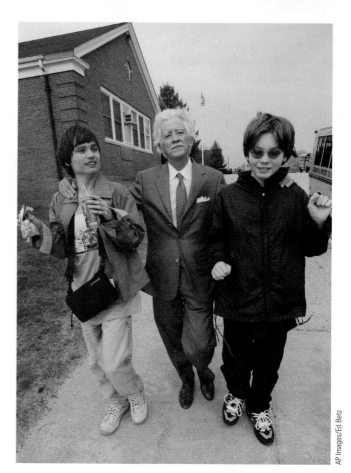

The demands of parenting a child with ASD are considerable.

getting through to Emilie with a reward system. Pictures of food are taped to hallway walls. On the fridge is a cutout of a glass of milk. After years of shrieking and kicking for what she wants, Emilie is learning to express her needs. When she points to what she wants, she gets a reward—a potato chip or an activity she likes. Every afternoon mother and daughter spend 2 hours on the floor, face to face, their legs interlocked. "Listen to maman, Emilie. Look at me. Look at me. Say 'yes.' Say 'yes.' Do you like chips, Emilie? You can have one if you just say the word, 'yes.'"

Emilie's mother coaxes patiently, firmly, holding out a bowl of chips. But Emilie runs to the radiator and climbs it, teetering there. When her mother pulls her down Emilie shrieks, kicks, and falls to the floor crying. In a minute the episode is over, and the lesson begins again. This time Emilie looks at her mother, says "yes," and holds out her hand for a chip. "Bravo, sweetheart. You did it. I knew you could," her mother beams. Emilie's mother has used the reward system to build Emilie's vocabulary to 22 words. That, to her parents, has been a monumental breakthrough.

"We have to motivate her," says her mother, whose only respite is an evening out once or twice a month with

AP Images/Ed Betz

her husband. "If we let her be, she'd just climb or hide under the cover all day long. That's my nightmare, that she'll end up in a psychiatric hospital, withdrawn from the world. I can see that we are slowly beginning to get through to her," Emilie's mother says with a deep sigh. "She didn't pay any attention to us at all before. She never showed any affection or made eye contact. But now she looks at me and says 'maman.' Sometimes she hugs me. It doesn't happen every day. But it grabs my heart when it does."

From Susan Semenak, *The Gazette*, November 21, 1996, pp. A1 and A15. Reprinted by permission.

Emilie's case captures the demands, frustrations, aspirations, and hopes of a family trying to do the best possible for their child with ASD. A number of treatments are available for helping children with ASD, such as Emilie, and their families. These treatments focus on the specific social, communication, behavioral, and cognitive deficits of ASD that we have discussed throughout this chapter. They include strategies for engaging children in treatment; decreasing disruptive behaviors; teaching appropriate social behavior, including joint attention, imitation, and reciprocal interaction; increasing functional, spontaneous communication; promoting cognitive skills such as symbolic play and perspective taking; and teaching adaptive skills that prepare the child for increased responsibility and independence. Family interventions enable parents to participate fully in their child's treatment and to cope with the substantial demands and parenting-related stress associated with raising a child with ASD (Estes et al., 2014; Rivard et al., 2014). In addition, educational interventions and speech and language therapy are commonly used. Also, for some children, antipsychotic medications (e.g., risperidone, aripiprazole) may help to decrease interfering and challenging behaviors and symptoms such as irritability, severe tantrum behavior, physical aggression, and repetitive behaviors (Volkmar et al., 2014), particularly when they are combined with intensive behavioral intervention (Arnold et al., 2012; Frazier et al., 2010). However, the effectiveness of these medications must be balanced against their known adverse effects, such as weight gain or liability to cause metabolic disorders (McPheeters et al., 2011).

Because children with ASD have great difficulty making changes and generalizing previously learned skills to new environments, these areas must be directly addressed in treatment. It is also critical that treatment be tailored to meet the needs of the individual child and the family, thus making it possible for each child to meet his or her full potential. In the following paragraphs we highlight how several of the treatment components mentioned previously are implemented.

Initial Stages

Initially, treatment focuses on building rapport and teaching the child learning-readiness skills. Various procedures help the child feel comfortable being physically close to the therapist and to identify rewards to strengthen the child's social behavior, affection, and play. Imitating the child's use of toys may increase eye contact, touching, and vocalizations directed toward the therapist. Prompting the child to engage in play with a preferred toy may decrease social avoidance.

Children with ASD must learn to sit in a chair, come when called, and attend to their teacher if they are to progress. These readiness skills are taught using two approaches. The first is a step-by-step approach to presenting a stimulus and requiring a specific response, referred to as **discrete trial training**. The second attempts to strengthen behavior by capitalizing on naturally occurring opportunities, referred to as **incidental training**. Most interventions use a combination of these approaches (Ghezzi, 2007).

Reducing Disruptive Behavior

Young children with ASD display many disruptive and interfering behaviors, such as tantrums or throwing objects, as well as self-stimulation, aggression, and self-injury. These behaviors are common reactions to demands on the child that are made early in treatment, and they must be eliminated if the child is to learn more adaptive forms of social interaction and communication. Many procedures are effective in eliminating disruptive behavior, including rewarding competing behaviors, ignoring the behavior, and mild forms of punishment.

Teaching Appropriate Social Behavior

Teaching appropriate social behavior is a high treatment priority (White, Keonig, & Scahill, 2007). The salience of social cues may be increased by pairing people with whom the child has contact with actions, activities, and events that the child finds pleasant or useful. Younger children are also taught ways to express affection through smiling, hugging, tickling, or kissing—behaviors that enable them to return the affection they receive from others. Other ways to enhance social interaction include teaching social toy play, social pretend play, and specific social skills such as initiating and maintaining interactions, taking turns and sharing, and including others in activities. Developmental and relationship approaches foster parental use of child-centered responsive interactions that embed numerous opportunities for teaching social and emotional behaviors into play. Parent-assisted Children's Friendship Training programs for school-age children with ASD target conversational skills, peer group entry skills, developing friendship networks, good sportsmanship, good host behavior during play dates, and handling teasing (Laugeson et al., 2012). Group social skills interventions have also been shown to improve social behaviors in high functioning children with ASD (Derosier et al., 2010).

One strategy for teaching appropriate social behavior to children with ASD involves teaching normal or mildly handicapped peers to interact with them. Peers are taught to initiate age-appropriate social behaviors such as playing with toys, commenting about activities, or acknowledging their partner's responses. Teachers may signal and reward the peers' social initiations with the child with ASD. Other strategies use prompts and rewards for teaching the child with ASD to initiate interactions, and in some cases to involve siblings as trainers (Kohler, Strain, & Goldstein, 2005).

Teaching Appropriate Communication Skills

Several strategies are used to help children with ASD communicate more appropriately. **Operant speech training** is a step-by-step approach that first increases the child's vocalizations and then teaches imitation of sounds and words, the meanings of words, labeling objects, making verbal requests, and expressing desires. The emphasis is on teaching the child to use language more spontaneously and more functionally in everyday life situations to influence others and to communicate better (Newsom & Hovanitz, 2006).

Executive Function Intervention

Recent interventions have also focused on the executive functioning deficits displayed by children with ASD. One such school-based program, Unstuck and On Target [UOT], uses cognitive–behavioral strategies

The mother of Max, a 4-year-old boy with ASD, spends hours each day teaching communication skills to her son.

to reduce insistence on sameness and to teach flexibility, goal-setting, and planning (Kenworthy et al., 2013). A controlled study compared third- and fifth-graders with ASD and average or above-average intellectual ability who received the UOT intervention with a comparable group of children with ASD who received social skills training. After intervention, children in both groups improved, but those receiving UOT showed significantly greater improvement in their problem-solving, flexibility, and planning/organizing skills. When observed in their classroom, children who had received UOT were better able to follow rules, make transitions, and be more flexible (Kenworthy et al., 2013). Both groups made equivalent gains in social skills. These findings are promising in showing that children with ASD with average or above-average intellectual ability can learn higher-level cognitive skills and apply them in a mainstream classroom.

Early Intervention

As methods to identify ASD at a very young age are developed, possibilities for effective early intervention with infants and toddlers increase dramatically (Wallace & Rogers, 2010). The promise of early intervention derives, in part, from the plasticity of neural systems early in development (Mundy & Neal, 2001) and the fascinating hypothesis that providing very young children with ASD with intensive and highly structured experiences may alter their developing brains in ways that permit outcomes that are not otherwise possible (Dawson, 2008). In an important investigation, Dawson et al. (2012) found that 18-to-30–month-old children with ASD who received early intervention showed significantly greater improvement than comparison children after intervention in their ASD symptoms, IQ, language, and adaptive and social behaviors. In support of the hypothesis of altering the developing brain through early intervention, at 48 to 77 months of age, children who had received the early intervention also displayed more normal patterns of brain activation when viewing faces versus objects than did comparison children, and these brain changes were associated with improved social behavior. Nowadays, whenever possible, intensive interventions for children with ASD begin before the age of 3—the earlier the intervention, the better the outcome is likely to be (Rogers et al., 2012).

Comprehensive early-intervention programs include many of the specific treatments for ASD that we have described (Harris, Handleman, & Jennett, 2005). A variety of early-intervention programs are available, some based on a learning/behavioral model (e.g., Applied Behavior Analysis; Lovaas & Smith, 2003; Smith, 2011), others based on a structured teaching model (e.g., TEACCH; Mesibov, Shea, & Schopler, 2005), and others based on developmental (e.g., Early Start Denver Model; Dawson et al., 2010) and/or relationship-focused (DIR or Floor Time; Greenspan & Wieder, 2006) approaches. Although these and other programs may differ in philosophy and emphasis, they share many common goals and features, which is why different models may result in similar outcomes when applied in standard-practice preschool or school settings (Kasari & Smith, 2013). There is a growing consensus that the most effective interventions for children with ASD include the following features (Myers et al., 2007):

▶ *Early:* Begin intervention as soon as an ASD diagnosis is seriously considered.

▶ *Intensive:* Active engagement of the child at least 25 hours a week, 12 months a year, in systematically planned, developmentally appropriate educational activities with specific objectives.

▶ *Low Student–Teacher Ratio:* Allow sufficient one-on-one time and small-group instruction to meet specific individualized goals.

▶ *High Structure:* Use predictable routines, visual activity schedules, and clear physical boundaries to minimize distractions.

▶ *Family Inclusion:* Include a family component, with parent training as indicated.

▶ *Peer Interactions:* Promote opportunities for interactions with typically developing peers.

▶ *Generalization:* Teach child to apply learned skills in new settings and situations and to maintain the use of these skills.

▶ *Ongoing Assessment:* Monitor child's progress and make adjustments in treatment as needed.

The average age of children with ASD entering early-intervention programs has been 3 to 4 years or younger. These children have an average IQ in the mid-50s, although many are not testable at the time of their intake for treatment. Early intervention provides direct one-to-one work with the child for 15 to 40 hours per week and active involvement of the family. In effect, these programs become a way of life for the family—24 hours a day, 7 days a week. Programs are carried out at home and in the preschool, and efforts are made to include the child in interactions with normal peers, especially later in treatment.

Comprehensive reviews of outcomes for children with ASD completing early-intervention programs find that many of them are able to function in regular educational placements, although the type of setting and amount of support services needed varied considerably. Most children also show developmental gains, as reflected in improvements in their social behavior and communication, IQ scores, and scores on developmental tests and as found on classroom observations (Dawson et al., 2010; Eikeseth et al., 2007; Howard et al., 2005).

The UCLA Young Autism Project

The UCLA Young Autism Project began about 50 years ago under the direction of Dr. Ivar Lovaas (1927–2010). Now referred to as the Applied Behavior Analysis (ABA) or Early Intensive Behavioral Intervention (EIBI) approach, it is the most detailed and labor-intensive of the early intervention programs and begins the earliest. It is one of the few programs that currently qualifies as an evidence-based treatment for ASD based on outcomes evaluated against control groups of similar-age children receiving less-intensive intervention (Lord & Jones, 2013; Rogers & Vismara, 2008). For these reasons, we focus on this approach, although we recognize that other potentially useful approaches have yet to be evaluated and that a few others that have been evaluated are also available.

The program includes many of the key elements of early intervention and is based on principles of applied behavior analysis, including the use of rewards and punishment and shaping by successive approximation (Lovaas, 2003; Smith, 2011). Parents are taught to act as the primary therapists for their children, with direction and help from therapists who work with them in the home. The average age of children entering the program is 32 months.

In a landmark research investigation, children with ASD were assigned to one of three groups. Although this assignment was not carried out randomly, the groups were found to be comparable with respect to age, language, intellectual functioning, and other measures prior to intervention. The experimental group of 19 children received 40 hours per week of intensive intervention. Control group 1 consisted of 19 children

Early intervention is essential for children with ASD.

who attended special education classes and received 10 hours per week of one-to-one instruction. Control group 2 consisted of 21 children from a larger study who also attended special education classes but did not receive one-to-one instruction.

For children in the experimental group, the first year of the program emphasized reducing disruptive behaviors and teaching appropriate behaviors such as compliance, imitation, and appropriate toy play. The second year emphasized expressive and abstract language and interactive play. Children were also taught how to function in a preschool group and, if possible, were enrolled in regular education preschool. The third year of the program emphasized the appropriate expression of emotions, pre-academic tasks, assertiveness, and observational learning.

The first outcome data were obtained when the children were 7 years old. Remarkably, 47% of the children in the experimental group were found to be functioning educationally and intellectually at a normal level. They successfully completed a regular first-grade class without support, were recommended for promotion by their teachers to a regular second-grade class, and scored at or above average on standardized IQ tests. On average, the IQ scores of these children increased by 37 points, from 70 to 107; overall, the experimental-group children showed an increase in mean IQ from 53 to 83. Children in the two control conditions did not fare nearly as well, resulting in only 1 of 40 children placed in a regular first-grade class; overall, these children showed only minimal increases in IQ scores. The experimental-group children were assessed again when their average age was 13 years, with similar results. The nine children who were placed in regular classrooms were virtually indistinguishable from same-age normal peers.

Nearly all children with ASD benefit from early intervention, but uncertainty remains as to: (1) how much the rate of progress depends on the severity of the child's ASD, the child's IQ and language ability, and the area of functioning being targeted (i.e., cognitive performance, language skills, adaptive behavior), and (2) what the long-term outcomes will be (Institute of Education Sciences, 2010; Reichow & Wolery, 2009; Warren et al., 2011). Additional studies have supported the effectiveness of the ABA approach in comparisons with other treatments and when used in community settings (Rogers & Vismara, 2008; Magiati, Charman, & Howlin, 2007). Claims have been made that some children with ASD can achieve normal functioning if given intensive intervention before age 3. However, earlier reports of "recovery" have not been replicated, and the question of whether they can achieve full recovery is a matter of some debate (Gresham & MacMillan, 1997; Smith & Lovaas, 1997).

Medications

Many children with ASD receive psychotropic medication, most commonly antidepressants, stimulants, and tranquilizers/antipsychotics (Mandell et al., 2008). As with many of the other childhood disorders we have discussed, medication use for children with ASD has also increased, and many of these children receive multiple medications (Oswald & Sonenklar, 2007; Spencer et al., 2013). Although certain medications may help in the alleviation of specific behavioral symptoms, their benefits are limited, variable from child to child, and do not alter the core deficits of children with ASD (McCracken, 2011). Given the limited evidence of the effectiveness of medications, particularly for very young children, it is crucial that their risks, benefits, and costs be carefully evaluated (McPheeters et al., 2011).

Section Summary

Treatment of ASD

- Treatments for ASD are directed at maximizing the child's potential and helping the child and family cope more effectively with the disorder.

- Treatments for ASD focus on the specific social, communication, cognitive, and behavioral deficits displayed by children with this disorder.

- The most effective treatments use highly structured skill-oriented strategies that are tailored to the individual child and provide education and supportive counseling for the family.

- Nearly all children with ASD benefit from early intervention; however, controlled studies are needed to evaluate long-term outcomes.

- Medications may help in alleviating some symptoms. However, their benefits are limited, variable from child to child, and do not change the core deficits of children with ASD.

A teenage boy with ASD and his parents: Active family involvement is a key ingredient for successful treatment outcomes.

CHILDHOOD-ONSET SCHIZOPHRENIA (COS)

I have a special power in my nose and I can control what's on TV and what people say or do.

—From "Schizophrenia: Hidden Torment," by M. Nichols, *Maclean's*, January 30, 1995

This statement by a young girl with schizophrenia highlights the seriousness of this disorder. **Schizophrenia** is a neurodevelopmental disorder of the brain that is expressed in abnormal mental functions and disturbed behavior (White & Hilgetag, 2011). It is characterized by severe psychotic symptoms, including: bizarre delusions (false beliefs), hallucinations (false perceptions), thought disturbances, grossly disorganized behavior or catatonic behavior (motor dysfunctions ranging from wild agitation to immobility), extremely inappropriate or flat affect, and significant deterioration or impairment in functioning (APA, 2013).

Early-onset or **childhood-onset schizophrenia (COS)** is a progressive neurodevelopmental disorder that causes significant distress and disability (Rapoport & Gogtay, 2011). Rather than being a distinct form of schizophrenia, COS is a rare and possibly more severe form of schizophrenia that has an onset prior to age 18 and worse long-term outcomes (Kyriakopoulos & Frangou, 2007; Remschmidt et al., 2007). Although there is some overlap in symptoms, susceptibility genes, and social–cognitive patterns in children with ASD and those with COS, the two are distinct disorders. Clinically, those with COS have a later age at onset of their problem, less intellectual impairment, less severe social and language deficits, less ritualistic and repetitive behavior, hallucinations and delusions as the child gets older, and periods of remission and relapse (J. R. Asarnow & Asarnow, 2003).

Initially, a category for schizophrenia in childhood, distinct from the category of schizophrenia in adults, was used to diagnose the disorder. However, current thinking is that the criteria used to diagnose schizophrenia in adults can also be used to diagnose this disorder in young people (Asarnow, Tompson, & McGrath, 2004). Nevertheless, there are differences in presentation. For example, COS most often presents with hallucinations, thought disorder, and flattened affect; systematic delusions are observed less frequently (McClellan, Stock, & American Academy of Child and Adolescent Psychiatry [AACAP] Committee on Quality Issues [CQI], 2013).

In the initial stages of COS, the afflicted youngster may have difficulty concentrating, sleeping, or doing schoolwork, and may start to avoid friends. As the illness progresses, she or he may begin to speak incoherently and see or hear things that no one else does. Periods of improvement may be followed by terrifying relapses that are characterized by disordered thinking in which the youngster leaps illogically from one idea to another. The youngster may experience hallucinations, paranoia, and delusions. During their psychotic phases, youngsters with schizophrenia may be convinced that they have godlike powers or that people are spying on them. When in the grip of a psychosis, they may behave unpredictably and may become violent and suicidal.

Several of the clinical features of COS are illustrated in the case of Mary, a girl who first began to display symptoms of the disorder when she was about 10 years old.

MARY

Depressed, Disorderly, Doomed

Mary had always been a very shy child. At times she would become mute, she had severe difficulty making friends, was frequently oppositional, and occasionally wet the bed. By age 10, Mary had problems in school in addition to her continuing social isolation. She became depressed, felt that the devil was trying to make her do bad things, believed that her teacher was trying to hurt her, and became preoccupied with germs. Her behavior became increasingly disorganized; she talked of killing herself, appeared disheveled, and ran in front of a moving car in an apparent suicide attempt.

This episode precipitated an inpatient psychiatric evaluation, during which Mary continued to show bizarre behavior. She lapsed into periods of intense anxiety and had one episode of uncontrolled screaming. At times she would stare blankly into space and was frequently mute. Although Mary's functioning improved during hospitalization and she returned to her family, throughout her childhood and adolescence she was tormented by fears, hallucinations, the belief that others were out to get her, and occasional bouts of depression, often accompanied by suicide attempts. She continued to be socially isolated and withdrawn and to perform poorly at school. At age 17, after several brief inpatient hospitalizations, Mary was admitted to a state hospital, where she remained until the age of 19. During this period her affect was increasingly flat, and her psychotic symptoms persisted. One week after discharge from the hospital, Mary went into her room, locked the door, and overdosed on her medications. She was found dead the next morning.

Based on J. R. Asarnow & Asarnow, 2003.

Mary's tragic story illustrates several key features of COS.

- Although most cases have their onset during late adolescence or early adulthood, schizophrenia does occur during childhood (Nicolson & Rapoport, 1999).

- COS has a gradual rather than a sudden onset in childhood, with the child displaying a wide range of impairments that precede his or her psychotic symptoms (Nicolson et al., 2000).

- When the disorder is present in childhood, the symptoms likely will persist into adolescence and adulthood.

- COS has a profound negative impact on the child's developing social and academic competence.

Mary's futile 10-year struggle with schizophrenia underscores the tremendous pain and personal suffering experienced by youngsters with this illness.

DSM-5: DEFINING FEATURES OF SCHIZOPHRENIA

DSM-5 criteria for schizophrenia are presented in Table 6.2. In addition to the presence of hallmark symptoms such as delusions, hallucinations, grossly disorganized speech and behavior, and negative symptoms such as flat affect, continuous signs of disturbance must persist for at least 6 months. In addition, the individual must show a significant decrement in one or more areas of functioning or, in the case of children and adolescents, a failure to achieve expected levels of interpersonal, academic, or occupational achievement. Although minor modifications in the symptom criteria for schizophrenia were made in DSM-5, research has found minimal effects of these changes on diagnosis, with over 98% of patients previously diagnosed with the disorder using DSM-IV

TABLE 6.2 | Diagnostic Criteria for Schizophrenia

DSM-5

(A) *Severe disturbance in sensory functioning and/or behavior*: Two (or more) of the following, each present for a significant portion of the time during a 1-month period (or less if successfully treated). At least one of these must be (1), (2), or (3):

(1) Delusions.

(2) Hallucinations.

(3) Disorganized speech (e.g., frequent derailment or incoherence).

(4) Grossly disorganized or catatonic behavior.

(5) Negative symptoms (i.e., diminished emotional expression or avolition)

(B) *Social/occupational dysfunction*: For a significant portion of the time since the onset of the disturbance, level of functioning in one or more major areas such as work, interpersonal relations, or self-care is markedly below the level achieved prior to the onset (or when the onset is in childhood or adolescence, there is failure to achieve expected level of interpersonal, academic, or occupational functioning).

(C) *Duration*: Continuous signs of the disturbance persist for at least 6 months. This 6-month period must include at least 1 month of symptoms (or less if successfully treated) that meet Criterion A (i.e., active-phase symptoms) and may include periods of prodromal or residual symptoms. During these prodromal or residual periods, the signs of the disturbance may be manifested by only negative symptoms or by two or more symptoms listed in Criterion A present in an attenuated form (e.g., odd beliefs, unusual perceptual experiences).

(D) *Schizoaffective and Mood Disorder exclusion*: Schizoaffective disorder and depressive or bipolar disorder with psychotic features have been ruled out because either 1) no major depressive or manic episodes have occurred concurrently with the active-phase symptoms, or 2) if mood episodes have occurred during active-phase symptoms, they have been present for a minority of the total duration of the active and residual periods of the illness.

(E) *Substance/medical condition exclusion*: The disturbance is not attributable to the physiological effects of a substance (e.g., a drug of abuse, a medication) or another medical condition.

(F) *Relationship to autism spectrum or communication disorder*: If there is a history of autism spectrum disorder or a communication disorder of childhood-onset, the additional diagnosis of schizophrenia is made only if prominent delusions or hallucinations, in addition to the other requirements of schizophrenia, are also present for at least 1 month (or less if successfully treated).

Specify if: **With catatonia**

Specify current severity:

Severity is rated by a quantitative assessment of the primary symptoms of psychosis including delusions, hallucinations, disorganized speech, abnormal psychomotor behavior and negative symptoms. Each of these symptoms may be rated for its current severity (more severe in the last 7 days) on a 5-point scale ranging from 0 (not present) to 4 (present and severe).

Note: Diagnosis of schizophrenia can be made without using this severity specifier.

Source: Diagnostic and Statistical Manual of Mental Disorders, Fifth Edition. American Psychiatric Association.

criteria also receiving a DSM-5 diagnosis (Tandon, Bruijnzeel, & Rankupalli, 2013). The traditional subtypes of schizophrenia (e.g., paranoid, disorganized) were eliminated in DSM-5, and catatonia is included as a specifier, not a subtype.

The use of the same diagnostic criteria for children and adults facilitates comparisons between cases of childhood-onset and adult-onset schizophrenia and the identification of important continuities in the disorder during the course of development. However, schizophrenia may be expressed differently at different ages. For example, hallucinations, delusions, and formal thought disturbances are extremely rare and difficult to diagnose before the age of 7; when they do occur, they may be less complex and reflect childhood themes (Caplan, 1994). A failure to adjust diagnostic criteria for developmental changes, such as social withdrawal or peer problems, may overlook children who show early signs of schizophrenia but may not develop the full-blown adult type until a later age (McClellan et al., 2003).

Other developmental considerations may also come into play in making a diagnosis. For example, it is sometimes difficult to distinguish between pathological symptoms, such as delusions, and the rich imaginative fantasies typical of many young children. Also, because cognitive and language processes are developing during childhood, it is extremely difficult to diagnose the symptom of disorganized speech (e.g., switching topics midsentence, incoherent or tangential speech). One difference between children with schizophrenia and adults with schizophrenia is that young children may not see their psychotic symptoms as distressing or disorganizing. Thus, when psychotic symptoms appear early in development, children may have difficulty distinguishing them from normal experience (Russell, 1994).

Symptoms of schizophrenia fall into two categories. The first, positive symptoms (also called psychotic or active symptoms), involve excesses or disturbances in normal functioning, such as delusions or hallucinations. The second, negative symptoms, involve a loss in normal functioning, for example, disturbances in sleep patterns.

Positive Symptoms

Youngsters with COS may display psychotic symptoms such as delusions and hallucinations (Polanczyk et al., 2010). **Delusions** are disturbances in thinking involving disordered thought content and strong false beliefs that are misrepresentations of reality in the context of one's life experience and culture. **Hallucinations** are disturbances in perception in which things are seen, heard, or otherwise sensed even though they are not real or present. They can present

in any sensory modality, including smell or touch. The most common presenting symptom for children with schizophrenia is auditory hallucinations (e.g., hearing voices that other people cannot hear and are experienced as separate from the individual's thoughts); they occur in about 80% of patients who have an onset prior to age 11. About 40% to 60% of children with schizophrenia also experience visual hallucinations, delusions (David et al., 2011), and thought disorders characterized by loose associations, illogical thinking, and impaired discourse skills (Caplan et al., 2000). Examples of psychotic symptoms reported by children with schizophrenia are presented in A Closer Look 6.4.

Negative Symptoms

Negative symptoms of schizophrenia may include slowed thinking, speech, and movement; emotional apathy; lack of drive; indifference to social contact; and

---

A CLOSER LOOK 6.4

Psychotic Symptoms in Children with Schizophrenia

Hallucinations

An 8-year-old boy stated: "I once heard a noise coming from the south and the east; one told me to jump off the roof and one told me to smash my mom."

A 12-year-old boy saw a ghost (man) with a red, burned, scarred, and cut face on multiple occasions and in different locations. He had been seeing this since age 5.

Delusions

A 9-year-old boy was convinced he was a dog (his parents were German Shepherds) and was growing fur; on one occasion, he refused to leave a veterinarian's office unless he received a shot.

An 11-year-old boy described "waste" produced when the good and bad voices fought with each other; the "waste" came out of his feet when he swam in chlorinated pools.

Thought Disorder

"I used to have a Mexican dream. I was watching TV in the family room. I disappeared outside of this world and then I was in a closet. Sounds like a vacuum dream. It's a Mexican dream. When I was close to that dream earth, I was turning upside down. I don't like to turn upside down. Sometimes I have Mexican dreams and vacuum dreams. It's real hard to scream in dreams."

Source: From A. T. Russell, The Clinical Presentation of Childhood-Onset-Schizophrenia, Schizophrenia Bulletin, 1994, volume 20, 631–646.

self-neglect. These symptoms generally reflect a loss of motivation and can range from minor to severe. Although these symptoms are much less dramatic than the positive symptoms, they can be very persistent and difficult to treat. They also may be difficult to recognize in young people, because some of these changes are behaviors that might be expected to occur to some degree during adolescence.

Section Summary

DSM-5: Defining Features of Schizophrenia

- Schizophrenia is a neurodevelopmental disorder of the brain that is expressed in abnormal mental functions and disturbed behavior.

- Unlike children with ASD, children with COS have a later age at onset, show less intellectual impairment, display less severe social and language deficits, develop hallucinations and delusions as they get older, and experience periods of remission and relapse.

- COS is a more severe form of adult-onset schizophrenia rather than a different disorder.

- Youngsters with COS may display psychotic symptoms, such as delusions and hallucinations, and negative symptoms, such as a slowing of thinking, speech, and movement, and indifference to social contact.

PRECURSORS AND COMORBIDITIES

For a majority of children with COS, the onset of their disorder is gradual rather than sudden, with nearly 95% showing a clear history of behavioral, social, and psychiatric disturbances before the onset of psychosis (Paya et al., 2013). For example, Mary was oppositional and had difficulty making friends well before she began to display her psychotic symptoms.

Developmental precursors for the onset of schizophrenia include speech and language problems, learning problems, static cognitive impairments and maturational delays, problems in motor development, movement abnormalities (e.g., facial tics, grimaces), higher levels of social impairment (e.g., social withdrawal, social oddities), unusual thought content, suspicion/paranoia, substance abuse, and a genetic risk for schizophrenia with a recent deterioration in functioning (Cannon et al., 2008; **Dickson et al., 2012;** Paya et al., 2013).

About 10% to 20% of children and adolescents with COS have IQs in the borderline range of intellectual functioning or lower. They also display impairments in attention, memory, and executive functions,

as well as global intellectual deficits (Frangou, 2013). Children with COS often present with other symptoms and disorders, such as anxiety and depression, ADHD, conduct problems, movement abnormalities, and suicidal tendencies (Frazier et al., 2007). About 70% of children meet criteria for another diagnosis, most commonly mood disorder or oppositional/conduct disorder (Russell, Bott, & Sammons, 1989). Returning to the question of whether ASD and COS are related, one study found that COS is preceded by ASD in 30% to 50% of cases (Rapoport et al., 2009). In addition, epidemiological and family studies have found associations between the two disorders, and both display deficits in theory of mind and mirror neuron impairments (mirror neurons fire both when an individual acts and when they see the same action performed by another) impairments. Both disorders also show signs of accelerated brain development at ages near the onset of the disorder, and brain imaging studies also find similar abnormalities in neural connectivity (de Lacy & King, 2013). A small but significant genetic correlation and similar risk genes and rare small chromosomal variants have also been found (Cross-Disorder Group of the Psychiatric Genetics Consortium, 2013; King & Lord, 2011). Taken together, these findings suggest several potentially important links between COS and ASD.

Prevalence

Schizophrenia is extremely rare in children under 12 years of age. It begins to increase dramatically in frequency in adolescence and early adulthood, with a modal onset at around 22 years of age (Abel, Drake, & Goldstein, 2010; McClellan et al., 2013)

▸ Estimates of COS indicate a prevalence of less than 1 child per 10,000, with an increased rate in more recent years (J. R. Asarnow & Asarnow, 2003; Okkels et al., 2013).

▸ These estimates suggest that schizophrenia occurs at least 100 times more often in adults than in children (Bromet & Fennig, 1999).

▸ COS has an earlier (by 2 to 4 years) age at onset in boys as in girls (Häfner et al., 1998), and an onset prior to 12 years of age is about twice as common in boys as in girls. However, this sex difference disappears in adolescence (Frazier et al., 2007).

The reasons that more males have COS are not known; a greater general biological vulnerability of males for neurodevelopmental disorders and different causes have both been suggested as possibilities. For adults, the rates of schizophrenia are higher in lower socioeconomic groups. However, there is little information regarding the relationship between social class and COS. In a related vein, the incidence rates and pattern of symptoms in adults with schizophrenia are similar across cultures, countries, and racial groups (Myers, 2011), but little information regarding cross-cultural patterns is available for COS (J. R. Asarnow & Asarnow, 1994).

Section Summary

Precursors and Comorbidities

- For a majority of children with COS, the onset of the disorder is gradual rather than sudden, with nearly 95% of children showing a clear history of behavioral, social, and psychiatric disturbances before the onset of psychosis.
- Developmental precursors for the onset of schizophrenia include speech and language problems, cognitive impairments and delays, problems in motor development, social impairment, unusual thought content, substance abuse, and a genetic risk for schizophrenia with a recent deterioration in functioning.
- Children with COS often display other symptoms and disorders, such as anxiety and depression, ADHD, conduct problems, movement abnormalities, and suicidal tendencies.
- Recent findings suggest several links between COS and ASD.

Prevalence

- Schizophrenia is extremely rare in children under 12 years of age, occurring much less often than in adolescents and adults.
- COS has an earlier age at onset in boys, and an onset prior to 12 years of age is about twice as common in boys as in girls. This sex difference disappears in adolescence.

CAUSES AND TREATMENT OF COS

We are just beginning to understand the possible causes of COS and ways of helping these children and their families. In the following sections, we discuss research into biological and family factors that have been implicated thus far, as well as recent treatments for this disorder.

Causes

A key issue in understanding schizophrenia is why a genetically based, neurobiological disorder is not expressed clinically until 15 to 20 years after birth, at which time it progressively disables its victims. In understanding this issue, investigators have proposed a **neurodevelopmental model of schizophrenia** in which a genetic vulnerability and early neurodevelopmental insults result in impaired connections between many brain regions, including the cerebral cortex, white matter, hippocampus, cerebellum, and parts of the limbic system (Rapoport, Addington, & Frangou, 2005; Rapoport, Giedd, & Gogtay, 2012). This model is supported by findings suggesting that gene mutations leading to schizophrenia may produce disruptions in the development of fetal prefrontal cortical circuitry (Gulsuner et al., 2013). This defective neural circuitry creates a vulnerability to dysfunction that is revealed by developmental processes and events during puberty (e.g., synaptic and hormonal changes), and by exposure to stress (Lewis & Lieberman, 2000). The neurodevelopmental model provides a useful framework for understanding how a condition like schizophrenia, which first presents as a disorder in adolescence or early adulthood, can be partly understood as a function of events occurring much earlier in development (Owen et al., 2011). A model of early-occurring neural pathology in schizophrenia is consistent with the findings that infants and children who later develop COS often display developmental impairments well before the onset of their psychotic symptoms, including deficits in motor, language, and cognitive and social functioning (Marenco & Weinberger, 2000).

Biological Factors

Evidence suggests a strong genetic contribution to schizophrenia in childhood, with heritability estimates around 80% (R. F. Asarnow et al., 2001; Gejman, Sanders, & Duan, 2010). For example, the rate of schizophrenia among relatives of children with COS is about double the rate for family members of adults with schizophrenia. One landmark twin study found concordance rates of 88% and 23%, respectively, for identical versus fraternal twins with schizophrenia with an onset prior to 15 years of age (Kallman & Roth, 1956). Molecular genetic studies have identified a number of potential susceptibility genes for COS, many of which have been previously linked with schizophrenia in adults (Kyriakopoulos & Frangou, 2007). Several common gene variants with small effects have been implicated, along with some extremely rare gene variants with potentially large effects (Pogue-Geile & Yokley, 2010). However, specific gene findings account for a very small amount of the variance, and most of the genetic influences on susceptibility to schizophrenia have yet to be identified. Given the large number of weak genetic (and environmental) risk factors, it is likely that COS is best represented by a continuum of risk involving many GxE interactions (Rapoport & Gogtay, 2011). For example, one study found a ninefold increased risk of schizophrenia in cases in which the presence of a parent with psychosis was combined with maternal depression during pregnancy (Maki et al., 2010). In light of the enormous number of genes, gene regulatory mechanisms associated with brain development, and mutational mechanisms that can disrupt these processes, it is possible that most affected individuals with COS have a unique genetic cause (Kuniyoshi & McClellan, 2014).

The occurrence of central nervous system dysfunction among individuals with schizophrenia, and the dramatic improvements associated with the administration of medications, suggest that schizophrenia is a disorder of the brain (Lewis & Lieberman, 2000). Brain scan studies of youngsters with COS have found enlarged ventricles and a shrinkage in brain gray matter that spreads across the brain during adolescence, beginning in the rear brain structures involved in attention and perception and spreading to the frontal parts of the brain involved in executive functions such as planning and organization (Vidal et al., 2006). The progressive loss of gray matter was accompanied by delayed/disrupted white matter growth, hippocampal volume loss, and a progressive decline in cerebellar volume. Interestingly, most of these changes were also found in the nonpsychotic siblings of the children with COS. However, siblings showed later normalization of the earlier gray matter abnormalities, suggesting a role for restorative/protective factors. In contrast, the hippocampal volume loss across age in children with COS was not shared by their siblings; thus it appears to be specific to schizophrenia (Rapoport & Gogtay, 2011). Another study found that atypical neural activity in a network of language-associated brain regions during discourse processing was associated with subsequent thought disorder severity and social outcome in youth at risk for psychosis (Sabb et al., 2010). Findings like this are important in identifying potential biomarkers for COS that may suggest strategies for intervention and prevention.

No single brain lesion has been identified in all cases of COS, and the lesions that have been found in some cases are not specific to schizophrenia (Kyriakopoulos & Frangou, 2007). In addition, atypical developmental patterns of brain development over time are often more prominent than are anatomic brain differences at any one time point (Rapoport & Gogtay, 2011). In general, brain research on COS points to a widespread developmental disruption of neural connectivity. These disrupted neural connections likely involve susceptibility genes that impact developmental processes involved in establishing connectivity within and between brain regions (Karlsgodt et al., 2008; Rapoport et al., 2012).

Environmental Factors

COS is a familial disorder, but the less than 100% concordance rates for identical twins suggest that nongenetic influences contribute to the likelihood of a child developing schizophrenia. Nongenetic factors, including exposure to infectious, toxic, or traumatic insults and stress during prenatal or postnatal development, may interact with a genetic susceptibility for schizophrenia (Arseneault et al., 2011; Lahti et al., 2009; Rapoport et al., 2005). Several nongenetic factors occurring during pregnancy and birth are associated with an increased risk for later schizophrenia, including: maternal diabetes, low birth weight, older paternal age, winter birth, and prenatal maternal stress (King, St-Hilaire, & Heidkamp, 2010). Each of these factors alone is associated with a slight increase in risk, which multiplies when they are combined with each other and/or with other risk factors. In considering other nongenetic influences, the elevated likelihood of psychiatric illness in parents of children with schizophrenia will likely have a negative effect on the ability of the affected parent to function in a parental role.

By themselves, psychosocial factors do not cause COS. However, they may interact with biological risk factors to affect the onset, course, and severity of the disorder. Parents of children with schizophrenia score higher than parents of children with depression on **communication deviance,** which is a measure of interpersonal signs of attentional and thought disturbance. Children from families with high communication deviance display the most severe impairment and the poorest attentional functioning. These findings suggest that communication deviance may be associated with a severe form of schizophrenia or that family interaction may worsen the severity of dysfunction (J. R. Asarnow, Goldstein, & Ben-Meir, 1988). Parents of children with schizophrenia are more likely to use harsh criticism of their children than are parents of depressed children or normal controls, which could be a reaction to their child's severe difficulties.

Support for the role of the family environment comes from studies showing that exposure to a poor family environment and certain patterns of communication may interact with a genetic risk for schizophrenia to further increase a child's risk for developing a schizophrenia-spectrum disorder. For example, in a longitudinal study of children of biological mothers with schizophrenia-spectrum disorders who were adopted at an early age, poor child-rearing environments and communication deviance of the adoptive parents predicted which adoptees developed a schizophrenia-spectrum disorder (Wahlberg et al., 2004; Wynne et al., 2006). Children with a dysfunctional child-rearing environment and adoptive parents who displayed high rates of communication deviance were significantly more likely to develop schizophrenia-spectrum disorder than those raised in more positive family environments. For children with a low genetic risk for schizophrenia, a poor family environment and deviant parent communication patterns did not increase the risk for the later development of a schizophrenia-spectrum disorder.

Family findings highlight the stress, distress, and personal tragedy often experienced by families of children with schizophrenia (J. R. Asarnow & Asarnow, 2003). In the words of June Beeby, the mother of 17-year-old Matthew, who was diagnosed with schizophrenia and believed that God wanted his mother and his sister to die:

> "It's quite horrendous. First of all, you've got somebody that you love, a child that you've raised. And then suddenly, the child becomes a crazy person" (M. Nichols, 1995, p. 70). On a dark and cold winter day, June Beeby arrived home to find her son dead in a pool of blood. "He had taken two ordinary dinner knives ... and plunged them into his eyes until they pierced his brain" (p. 70). In a diary entry that he had made 2 years before he took his life, Matthew had described an encounter with God: "He used his power and he controlled my brain for nine months. ... God wanted me to feel that I would die, in order for individuals to live forever in heaven" (p. 74).

Treatment

As a parent you feel you have a tremendous responsibility to keep a son or daughter safe. ... But when your child is schizophrenic you can't do that, because the person doesn't want help.

—From "Schizophrenia: Hidden Torment," by M. Nichols, *Maclean's*, January 30, 1995

COS is a chronic disorder with a poor long-term outcome for most sufferers, although some youngsters may display more positive outcomes (McClellan et al., 2013; Röpcke & Eggers, 2005). In either case, outcomes for most afflicted individuals are vastly improved over what they once were. Current treatments emphasize the use of antipsychotic medications (e.g., clozapine, risperidone) combined with psychotherapeutic and social and educational support programs (McClellan et al., 2013; National Institute of Health and Clinical Excellence [NICE], 2013b). Although we know far less about the use of antipsychotic

medications with children than with adults, they are widely used to treat young people with schizophrenia, and a majority of youngsters with schizophrenia will spend much of their life on some medication (Findling et al., 2014). Medications help control psychotic symptoms in children with schizophrenia by blocking dopamine transmission at the D2 dopamine receptor. However, adverse effects with antipsychotic treatment are prevalent and are associated with reduced adherence to treatment. Depending on the type of medication, these side effects can be serious and may include increased levels of prolactin, motor dysfunction (e.g., tremor), weight gain, sedation, or dysregulation of glucose. Thus, it is extremely important that these side effects be carefully monitored and managed with changes in dose or type of medication as needed (Tiffin, 2007). There is also a need for psychosocial treatments, such as family intervention, social skills training, and cognitive–behavioral therapy (Addington, Piskulic, & Marshall, 2010). The need for educational support that provides factual information about the illness and its treatment within a recovery-focused discussion with the patient and family is also widely recognized in clinical practice (McDonnell & Dyck, 2004; Tiffin, 2007). Although findings from psychosocial treatments with older individuals with schizophrenia are promising, more controlled studies with children and adolescents are needed (Tiffin & Welsh, 2013).

Using a prevention framework, recent efforts have focused on a variety of pharmacological, biological, psychosocial, and family interventions for high-risk younger individuals well before the onset of psychotic symptoms. Findings to date have suggested that these interventions can be effective in reducing the risk of transition to full-blown psychosis over the short term but over the longer term may only delay transition to psychosis (Preti & Cella, 2010). Further research into the prediction and prevention of psychosis in youths at high clinical risk for psychosis is needed, particularly in relation to possible long-term benefits (Addington & Heinssen, 2012).

Section Summary

Causes and Treatment of COS

- Current views regarding the causes of COS are based on a neurodevelopmental model in which a genetic vulnerability and early neurodevelopmental insults result in impaired connections between many brain regions. This impaired neural circuitry may increase the child's vulnerability to stress.

(continues)

Section Summary (continued)

- COS is a disorder that involves multiple genes and is associated with environmental and developmental vulnerability factors.
- Brain studies in COS suggest a shrinkage in brain gray matter that spreads across the brain during adolescence; it begins in the rear brain structures involved in attention and perception and spreads to the frontal parts of the brain involved in executive functions such as planning and organization.
- Although medications may help control psychotic symptoms in children with schizophrenia, psychosocial treatments such as social skills training, family intervention, cognitive–behavioral therapy, and educational support are also needed.

Study Resources

SECTION SUMMARIES

KEY TERMS

PRELIMINARY EDITION

7

Communication and Learning Disorders

If you can read this, thank a teacher.

—Anonymous

EVERYONE HAS IMPORTANT NEEDS and ideas. Imagine not being able to get them across. Sights and sounds surround you, but you cannot focus your attention long enough to make sense of them. When you are shown how to read or add, you find that the letters and numbers look and sound too much alike. Children and adolescents with communication and learning disorders experience these difficulties daily. Everyday tasks can be confusing and frustrating, and sometimes result in a cycle of academic failure and lowered self-esteem.

JAMES

Smart but Can't Read

James, age 9, was a growing concern for his teacher: "James is obviously a very bright boy, and he wants to do well. I've noticed that he likes art, and is always wanting to draw. But he gets really upset when I ask him to do some work in class.

He looks like he dreads coming to school. And he complains that some words he tries to read don't make sense to him. I'm worried that his increasing frustration is going to cause other problems in school or with friends. Sometimes he gets mad at something and he has trouble calming down. If he is trying to create something that doesn't turn out the way he envisioned it, he explodes and slams his fist against the wall."

What James's mother heard was all too familiar. She knew that her son would get involved in something only if he could do it his own way. Her mind wandered briefly to when he was a toddler and sometimes got so anxious and worried about something that he had trouble sleeping or felt sick. She shared with his teacher her frustration at trying to find out what the problem was: "Getting him to read at home is like pulling teeth. He won't read at all on his own because he knows he can't read many of the words." (Based on authors' case material.)

FRANCINE

Shunned and Falling Behind

Francine, age 7, was entering a new school for the second time in 2 years. The first school was too challenging, and the other kids teased her because she "doesn't know what 2 plus 2 is." She is content to play for hours by herself and is not interested in the things that other kids her age are doing. "Most of the time," her mother explained, "Francine seems sad and in a bit of a fog." Although school performance was a major concern, her mother was also quite worried about Francine's lack of friends and the way other children treated her.

Her mother and father proudly shared their daughter's early childhood history and developmental milestones with me during our first interview. "Francine walked before she was a year old, and was a very talkative baby and toddler, who picked up new words quite quickly. She was a healthy and normal baby—we can't figure out why she seems so uninterested in school and other kids." They went on to explain: "When she entered preschool and kindergarten, she seemed uninterested in making friends. The other kids basically ignored her, even though she didn't do anything to bother them. My husband and I didn't think much of it at first. In fact, we bragged about how she took an early interest in reading and would spend a lot of her time alone with a book or magazine, even when she was 4 or 5, although she didn't usually understand what she read. But we grew more concerned around age 5 because she paid little attention to popular movies, toys, and things other kids her age played with. When she was a preschooler, we also noticed that she had trouble with numbers and understanding concepts like "more," "less," or "bigger." She knows what these words mean now, but she is still confused when we ask her to count something.

Yesterday I gave her her allowance and just for the heck of it, I used pennies, nickels, and dimes to see if she could add them up. No matter how hard we tried, she became confused, switching from one coin to the other, and she thought she had a bigger allowance if I stacked the pennies up! And if you ask her to arrange something, like setting the table for dinner, you never know what you'll end up with!" (Based on authors' case material.)

Children with communication or learning disorders can learn, and they are as intelligent as anyone else. Their disorders usually affect only certain limited aspects of learning, and rarely are they severe enough to impair the pursuit of a normal life—but they can be very stressful. Consider the experiences of James and Francine: James and Francine have different learning problems. James's are with language and reading. His ability to distinguish between different language sounds (phonemes) is underdeveloped, which is the primary reason for his poor word recognition and writing ability. Francine's problems are mostly with nonverbal learning, such as math. She can read quite well, but she has difficulty understanding some of the subtleties of others' facial expressions and gestures. She also confuses terms and instructions that describe numerical or spatial relationships, such as "larger than" or "sit beside the couch."

The field of learning and communication disorders, broadly referred to as "learning disabilities," has changed dramatically during the past 50 years. For many years, learning problems were attributed to poor motivation or poor instruction. Fortunately, breakthroughs in neuroimaging techniques has led to increased recognition of the differences in the neurological makeup and development of children with problems in language and related cognitive tasks. With recent advances in detection and intervention aimed at early language development, signs of communication problems are detected at an early age and children are taught using alternative methods that build on their developmental strengths.

In this chapter, we emphasize the relationship between language development and the subsequent appearance of a learning problem once the child enters school. We put these problems in a developmental context by showing how communication disorders (diagnosed primarily in early childhood) and learning disorders (identified most often during early school years) have interconnected features and underlying causes. As a case in point, preschoolers with communication disorders are more likely to develop a learning disability by middle childhood or early adolescence (Beitchman & Brownlie, 2014).

DEFINITIONS AND HISTORY

Learning disability (LD) is still commonly used as a general term for learning problems that occur in the absence of other obvious conditions, such as intellectual disability or brain damage. In the *Diagnostic and Statistical Manual of Mental Disorder*, 5th edition (DSM-5) two more specific terms are used, *communication disorders* and *learning disorders*, but the common use of the term *learning disability* requires that it be clarified and defined.

A learning disability affects how individuals with normal or above-average intelligence take in, retain, or express information. Incoming or outgoing information can be scrambled as it passes between the senses and the brain. Unlike most physical disabilities, a learning disability is hidden and is often undetected in young children (Lovett & Lewandowski, in 2014). Thus, children with learning disabilities often must cope not only with their limitations in reading, writing, or math but also with the frustration of convincing others that their problems are as legitimate as visible disabilities.

Learning difficulties often show up in schoolwork and can impede a child's ability to learn to read, write, or do math, but they also can affect many other parts of life, including work, daily routines, family life, and friendships. Some learning problems are specific and

Slowly but surely, most children learn the letters of the alphabet and how to use them to read and write words. For children with certain learning disabilities, however, the shapes and sounds of different letters continue to be confusing.

affect a narrow range of ability, whereas others may affect many different tasks and social situations. Each type of learning disability, whether it is related to reading, writing, math, or language, is characterized by distinct definitions and diagnoses. Knowledge of communication and learning disorders is growing rapidly as a result of increased scientific interest and research support. We now recognize that a learning disability, though challenging, does not have to be a handicap. Many well-known people with learning difficulties used their talents in exceptional ways, including Albert Einstein, Winston Churchill, and Thomas Edison.

The main characteristic all children with learning difficulties share is failing to perform at their expected level in school. Otherwise, symptoms vary tremendously (Beitchman & Brownlie, 2014). Many children and adults who are unable to acquire academic skills at a normal rate have been helped by recognizing and attending to specific learning problems.

Children with learning disabilities constitute a third of all children in the United States and Canada who receive special education services (National Center for Educational Statistics, 2012). Yet, experts still struggle to adequately define learning disabilities because of their many forms and overlapping symptoms, which you will note in the following lengthy definition:

Learning disability is a lay term (not a diagnostic term) that refers to significant problems in mastering one or more of the following skills: listening, speaking, reading, writing, reasoning, and mathematics. Learning disabilities do not include visual, hearing, or physical impairments; intellectual disability; emotional disturbance; or environmental disadvantage. Emotional and social disturbances and other adaptive deficiencies may occur with learning problems, but they do not by themselves constitute a learning disability (Individuals with Disabilities Education Improvement Act [IDEA], 2004).

In Chapter 5 we described intellectual disability as involving deficits in basic cognitive abilities that include problem solving, verbal skills, and mental reasoning. But the broader concept of intelligence also includes logical, mathematical, and language abilities that reflect a pattern of relative strengths and weaknesses possessed by everyone. For example, we are all stronger in some areas of learning and performance than in others (e.g., we enjoy writing and reading, but don't ask us to fix your car). Similarly, children with specific learning disorders who have normal intelligence show a pattern of relative strengths and weaknesses that can make some learning tasks much more difficult. This pattern is noteworthy mostly because it is so extreme and unexpected for a child who otherwise shows normal cognitive and physical development.

Communication disorder is a diagnostic term that refers to deficits in language, speech, and communication (APA, 2013). Communication disorders include the following diagnostic categories:

Few realize that Albert Einstein had early speech and language difficulties, given his monumental contributions to society.

Bettmann/Corbis

▶ language disorder (problems using language to communicate, such as spoken words or sign language, or understanding what other people say)

▶ speech sound disorder (deficits in productive speech sounds)

▶ childhood-onset fluency disorder (problems in speech fluency, such as stuttering)

▶ social (pragmatic) communication disorder

These communication disorders are developmentally connected to the later onset of learning disorders.

Specific learning disorder is a diagnostic term that refers to specific problems in learning and using academic skills. The DSM-5 integrates the frequently co-occurring problems in reading, mathematics, and written expression into this one category, and uses specifiers to designate impairments in one or more of these areas. Specific learning disorder is determined by achievement test results that are substantially below what is expected for the child's age, schooling, and intellectual ability.

An unexpected pattern of strengths and weaknesses in learning was first noted and studied during the late nineteenth century by physicians who were treating patients with medical injuries (Hammill, 1993). Franz Joseph Gall, a pioneer of language disorders, was struck by what he observed among some of his brain-injured patients: They had lost the capacity to express their feelings and ideas clearly through speech, yet they did not seem to suffer any intellectual impairment. One of his patients could not speak, but had no problem writing his thoughts on paper. Because he knew that this patient had normal speech before the head injury, Gall reasoned that the problem must have resulted from brain damage that had disrupted the neurological processes related to speech. For the first time, scientists began to pinpoint areas in the brain that control the ability to express and receive language processes.

These early observations, based on known medical injuries, raised the possibility that people with learning disabilities differ from people with intellectual disability in terms of relative strengths and deficits. People with learning disabilities have normal intellectual processes in most areas but are relatively weaker in others, which is known as having an **unexpected discrepancy** between measured ability and actual performance. This premise remained the foundation of most definitions of learning disability for many years. However, researchers and practitioners eventually agreed that subaverage performance on achievement tests, rather than a discrepancy between potential and actual performance, was a better way to capture these learning difficulties (Maehler & Schuchardt, 2011).

The links between intellectual disability, organic brain damage, and learning problems fascinated scientists, who had a firmer understanding of brain–behavior relationships by the 1940s. During that time, the question still remained as to why some children who did not fit the definition of intellectual disability based on IQ had significant problems in learning. Could intellectual disability be restricted to only certain intellectual abilities? Were academic problems the same as those assessed by measures of general intelligence?

Strauss and Werner (1943) shed light on this issue by pointing out that children learn in individual ways, challenging the concept that learning is a relatively uniform, predictable process in children without intellectual disabilities. Three important concepts from this period continue to influence the field to this day (Hallahan, Pullen, & Ward, 2013):

1. Children approach learning in different ways, so each child's individual learning style and uniqueness should be recognized and used to full advantage.

2. Educational methods should be tailored to an individual child's pattern of strengths and weaknesses; one method should not be imposed on everyone.

3. Children with learning problems might be helped by teaching methods that strengthen existing abilities rather than emphasize weak areas.

By the early 1960s, the modern learning disabilities movement had begun. Parents and educators were dissatisfied that children often had to be diagnosed with an intellectual disability in order to receive special education services. A category was needed to describe learning problems that could not be explained on the basis of intellectual disability, lack of learning opportunities, psychopathology, or sensory deficits (Lyon, Fletcher, & Barnes, 2003).

Thus, the emerging concept of learning disabilities made intuitive sense to many who were familiar with the varied needs of children, and it was welcomed as states and provinces began to support special education programs and services. The domination of physicians and psychologists in the field gave way to greater input from educators, parents, and clinicians. Teacher training expanded to include new ways to teach youngsters who could not respond to typical classroom methods. Professionals trained in speech and language pathology became an important part of school-based services.

As the focus of the learning disabilities movement shifted from the clinic to the classroom, parents and educators assumed a major role in programming and placement. They were encouraged by the fact that the term *learning disabled* did not stigmatize children, but rather brought them needed services (Hammill, 1993).

The fact that these children had normal intelligence gave parents and teachers hope that difficulties in reading, writing, and math could be overcome if only the right set of instructional conditions and settings could be identified (Lyon et al., 2003). These developments led to the recent Response-to-Intervention (RTI) movement, which views LD in terms of what academic help children need rather than what disability they might have (Lovett & Lewandowski, in press). Thus, with the collaborative leadership of parents, educators, and specially trained professionals, the field of learning disabilities grew from its beginning in the 1960s to the major component of educational services it is today.

Section Summary

Definitions and History

- *Learning disability* is a general lay term for communication and learning problems that occur in the absence of other obvious conditions such as intellectual disability or brain damage.
- Children and adults with learning disabilities show specific deficits in using spoken or written language, often referred to as relative strengths and weaknesses.
- Parents and educators assumed a major role in bringing recognition and services to children with learning disabilities.

LANGUAGE DEVELOPMENT

From birth, infants selectively attend to parental speech sounds and soon learn to communicate with basic gestures and sounds of their own. Usually, by their first birthday they can recognize several words and use a few of their own to express their needs and emotions. Over the next 2 years, their language development proceeds at an exponential pace, and their ability to formulate complex ideas and express new concepts is a constant source of amazement and amusement for parents. Adults play an important role in encouraging language development by providing clear examples of language and enjoying the child's expressions.

Language consists of **phonemes**, which are the basic sounds (such as sharp *ba*'s and *da*'s and drawn-out *ee*'s and *ss*'s) that make up language. When a child hears a phoneme over and over, receptors in the ear stimulate the formation of dedicated connections to the brain's auditory cortex. A perceptual map forms that represents similarities among sounds and helps the infant learn to discriminate among different phonemes. These

From an early age, children love to express themselves.

maps form quickly; 6-month-old children of English-speaking parents already have auditory maps different from infants in non-English-speaking homes, as measured by neuron activity in response to different sounds (Kuhl et al., 2006). By their first birthday, the maps are complete, and infants are less able to discriminate sounds that are not important in their own language.

Rapid development of a perceptual map is why learning a second language after—rather than with—the first language is difficult; brain connections are already wired for English, and the remaining neurons are less able to form basic new connections for, say, Swedish. Once the basic circuitry is established, infants can turn sounds into words, and the more words they hear, the faster they learn language. The sounds of words serve to strengthen and expand neural connections that can then process more words. Similar cortical maps are formed for other highly refined skills, such as musical ability (Huss et al., 2011). A young child who learns to play a musical instrument may strengthen the neural circuits that underlie not only music, but verbal memory as well (Ho, Cheung, & Chan, 2003).

Phonological Awareness

Not all children progress normally through the milestones of language development. Some are noticeably delayed, continuing to use gestures or sounds rather than speech. Others progress normally in some areas, such as following spoken directions and attending to commands, but have trouble finding the words to express themselves clearly.

Although the development of language is one of the best predictors of school performance and overall intelligence (Sattler, 2008), delays or differences in development are not a definitive sign of intellectual disability or cognitive disorder. Rather, such deviations from normal may be just that—deviations—and may be accompanied by superior abilities in other areas of cognitive functioning. Albert Einstein, who is considered an intellectual genius, began speaking late and infrequently, causing his parents to worry that he was "subnormal." According to family members, when his father asked his son's headmaster what profession his son should adopt, the answer was simply, "It doesn't matter, he'll never make a success of anything" (R. W. Clark, 1971, p. 10).

Since language development is an indicator of general mental development, children in whom language fails to develop or who show severe delays in acquiring language are considered at risk of having a language-based learning disability. Albert Einstein notwithstanding, early language problems are considered highly predictive of subsequent communication and learning disorders (Heim & Benasich, 2006; Williams, 2010).

Phonology is the ability to learn and store phonemes as well as the rules for combining the sounds into meaningful units or words. Deficits in phonology are a chief reason that most children and adults with communication and learning disorders have problems in language-based activities such as learning to read and spell (Larkin & Snowling, 2008; Nation, Snowling, & Clarke, 2007).

A young child is required to recognize that speech is segmented into phonemes (the English language contains about 42, such as *ba*, *ga*, *at*, and *tr*). This task is difficult for many children because speech does not consist of separate phonemes produced one after another. Instead, sounds are *co-articulated* (overlapped with one another) to permit rapid communication, rather than pronounced sound-by-sound (Liberman & Shankweiler, 1991). About 80% of children can segment words and syllables into their proper phonemes by the time they are 7 years old. The other 20% cannot, and it is these children who struggle hardest to read (S. E. Shaywitz & Shaywitz, 2013; Vellutino et al., 2004).

Generally, early language problems surface as learning problems when children enter school, because in school children are taught to connect spoken and written language. Those who do not easily learn to read and write often have difficulty learning the alphabetic system—the relationship of sounds to letters. They also cannot manipulate sounds within syllables in words, which is called a lack of phonological awareness and is a precursor to reading problems (Rvachew, 2007).

Phonological awareness is a broad construct that includes recognizing the relationship between sounds and letters, detecting rhyme and alliteration, and being aware that sounds can be manipulated within syllables in words. Primary-grade teachers detect phonological awareness as they ask children to rhyme words and manipulate sounds. For example, the teacher can say "hat" and ask the child to say the word without the *h* sound, or say "trip" and have the child say the word without the *p*. To assess the child's ability to blend sounds, teachers can say the three sounds *t*, *i*, and *n*, for example, and see whether the child can pull the sounds together to say "tin."

In addition to serving as a prerequisite for basic reading skills, phonological awareness and processing also appear highly related to expressive language development (Boada & Pennington, 2006). Readers with core deficits in phonological processing have difficulty segmenting and categorizing phonemes, retrieving the names of common objects and letters, storing phonological codes in short-term memory, and producing some speech sounds. Reading and comprehension depend on the rapid and automatic ability to decode single words. Children who are slow and inaccurate at decoding have the most difficulties in reading comprehension (Melby-Lervåg, Lyster, & Hulme, 2012).

Section Summary

Language Development

- Language development is based on innate ability and environmental opportunities to learn, store, and express important sounds in the language. It proceeds very rapidly during infancy.

- Deficits in phonological awareness—the ability to distinguish the sounds of language—have been identified as a major cause of communication and learning disorders.

COMMUNICATION DISORDERS

Children with communication disorders have difficulty producing speech sounds, using spoken language to communicate, or understanding what other people say. In DSM-5, communication disorders include the diagnostic subcategories of *language disorder, speech sound disorder, childhood-onset fluency disorder (stuttering),* and *social (pragmatic) communication disorder.* These subcategories are distinguished by the exact nature of the child's impairment.

Recall that during development phonological problems appear before problems in language reception or expression, yet they have strong similarities. The following discussion focuses on language disorder in an effort to highlight early childhood problems that represent the fundamental features of communication

disorders. (Stuttering has a unique clinical feature and developmental course, so it is discussed separately.)

Consider Jackie's communication problems at age 3 years:

JACKIE

Screaming, Not Talking

Jackie's mother explained with no hesitation why she asked for help: "My 3-year-old daughter is a growing concern. Since she was a baby, she has been plagued by ear infections and sleep problems. Some nights she screams for hours on end, usually because of the ear infections. She has violent temper outbursts and refuses to do simple things that I ask her to do, like get dressed or put on her coat."

The child, waiting in the playroom, could be heard screaming over her mother's voice. Jackie was asking my assistant for something, but she could not make out what Jackie was saying. It was pretty obvious how frustrated both the child and her mother must feel on occasion. Her mother explained how she and Jackie's father had divorced when Jackie was less than 2 years old, and that after weekend exchanges it sometimes took a few days for Jackie's routine to return to some degree of normalcy.

I opened the letter she had brought from Jackie's preschool teacher, someone who I knew had a great deal of experience with children of this age. "Jackie is a bright and energetic child," the letter began, "but she is having a great deal of difficulty expressing herself with words. When she gets frustrated, she starts to give up or becomes angry—she won't eat her meals or she fights with staff at nap time, even if she is hungry or tired. If a new teacher at day care is introduced, it takes Jackie a long time to get used to the new person. Jackie seems to understand what she is being asked, but can't find the words to express herself, which understandably leads to an emotional reaction on her part." (Based on authors' case material.)

Language Disorder

Jackie's problems met the criteria for a **language disorder,** which is a communication disorder characterized by difficulties in the comprehension or production of spoken or written language. As a result of these deficits, Jackie showed her frustration loudly and inappropriately.

Children's language development follows specific steps, although each child may proceed through the steps at a different pace. Normal variations can make it difficult to predict that a given child's early communication problems will later become major problems in learning. A common example is the child who points to different objects and makes grunting or squealing noises that the parent quickly recognizes as "more milk" or "no peas." Prior to age 3 or so, many children communicate this way unless parents actively encourage using words and discourage nonverbal communications. Nevertheless, despite plenty of verbal examples and proper language stimulation, some children do not develop in some areas of speech and language, and they later have problems in school. This developmental connection makes the study of communication disorders highly pertinent to understanding and treating subsequent learning problems.

Table 7.1 shows the major features of the DSM-5 diagnostic criteria for language disorder. Children with a language disorder, such as Jackie, do not suffer from intellectual disability or from autism spectrum disorder, which affect speech and language. Rather, they show persistent difficulties in acquiring and using language to communicate (Criterion A). A child's ability to use language depends on both receptive skills (i.e., receiving and comprehending language) and expressive skills (i.e., production of vocal, gestural, or verbal signals). Thus, children with this disorder often show reduced vocabulary, limited sentence structure, or impairments in their ability to carry on a conversation. A child's expressive and receptive abilities may differ such that his or her language comprehension, for example, is stronger than his or her language expression. For example, when asked by her parents to go upstairs, find her socks, and put them on, Jackie was quite capable of complying. When asked by her mother to describe what she has just done, however, she might respond simply, "find socks."

The linguistic abilities of children with language disorders vary significantly, based on the severity of the disorder and the age of the child. Most often, these children begin speaking late and progress slowly in their speech development. Their vocabulary often is limited and is marked by short sentences and simple grammatical structure, as in Jackie's response. To fit the diagnostic criteria, these problems must be substantially below the abilities of other children of the same age, resulting in functional limitations in communication, social participation, or academic achievement (Criterion B). In addition, the symptoms must begin in the early developmental period (Criterion C) and not be attributable to other sensory impairments or medical conditions (Criterion D).

Although their hearing is normal, children with language disorder may have difficulty understanding particular types of words or statements, such as complex if–then sentences. In severe cases, the child's ability to understand basic vocabulary or simple sentences may be impaired, and there may be deficits in auditory processing of sounds and symbols and in their storage, recall, and sequencing. Understandably, these problems make the child seem inattentive or noncompliant, and the disorder can be easily misdiagnosed. Imagine how it would feel to be in Greece visiting an English-speaking host and her Greek husband. Unless your host is present, trying to engage in friendly conversation can be frustrating and uncomfortable. Even if both you and the husband can each understand a few words the other is saying, you probably cannot actually converse. If you have ever faced a similar communication barrier, you probably have an appreciation of the frustration and discomfort that accompany a language disorder.

When the developmental language problem involves articulation or sound production rather than word knowledge, a **speech sound disorder** may be an appropriate diagnosis. Children with this disorder have trouble controlling their rate of speech, or lag behind playmates in learning to articulate certain sounds. Typically, children learn phonemes and use intelligible speech by the age of 3 years or so, with the exception of some of the more difficult sounds such as *l, r, s, z, th,* and *ch,* which may take a few years longer to articulate (APA, 2013).

TABLE 7.1 | Diagnostic Criteria for Language Disorder

DSM-5

(A) Persistent difficulties in the acquisition and use of language across modalities (i.e., spoken, written, sign language, or other) due to deficits in comprehension or production that include the following:

  (1) Reduced vocabulary (word knowledge and use).

  (2) Limited sentence structure (ability to put words and word endings together to form sentences based on the rules of grammar and morphology).

  (3) Impairments in discourse (ability to use vocabulary and connect sentences to explain or describe a topic or series of events or have a conversation).

(B) Language abilities are substantially and quantifiably below those expected for age, resulting in functional limitations in effective communication, social participation, academic achievement, or occupational performance, individually or in any combination.

(C) Onset of symptoms is in the early developmental period.

(D) The difficulties are not attributable to hearing or other sensory impairment, motor dysfunction, or another medical or neurological condition and are not better explained by intellectual disability (intellectual developmental disorder) or global developmental delay.

Source: Diagnostic and Statistical Manual of Mental Disorders, 5th edition. American Psychiatric Association.

Depending on the severity of the disorder, the speech quality of these children may be unusual, and even unintelligible. For example, at age 6, James still said "wabbit" instead of "rabbit" and "we-wind" for "rewind." Preschoolers, of course, often mispronounce words or confuse the sounds they hear, which is a normal part of learning to speak. When these problems persist beyond the normal developmental range (age 4) or interfere with academic and social activities by age 7, they deserve separate attention.

Prevalence and Course

Children usually reveal problems in speech articulation and expression as they attempt to tackle new sounds and express their own concepts. Even though prevalence estimates account for normal variations in language development and are based on individuals who meet specific diagnostic criteria, the degree of severity can vary considerably. For example, in early childhood, milder forms of speech sound disorder are relatively common, affecting close to 10% of preschoolers. Many of these children outgrow their earlier difficulties, so only 2% to 3% of preschoolers meet the criteria for speech sound disorder. However, language disorder is a bit more common, affecting about 7% of younger school-age children across studies (Beitchman & Brownlie, 2014; Heim & Benasich, 2006).

Communication disorders are identified almost twice as often in boys as in girls (Pinborough-Zimmerman et al., 2007); boys' language difficulties are more often accompanied by behavior problems, and consequently, they are referred and diagnosed with communication learning disorders more often than girls (Vellutino et al., 2004). By 4 years of age a child's individual differences in language stabilize, so problems that remain past this age are highly predictive of later outcomes. About 50% fully outgrow their problems, whereas the other 50% may show improvement but still have some degree of impairment into adulthood. Children with receptive language impairments, in particular, have a poor prognosis as compared with those with primarily expressive impairments. Receptive language problems are more resistant to treatment and are often associated with reading difficulties throughout their education (APA, 2013).

Even though language problems usually diminish with time, children with communication disorders often have higher-than-normal rates of negative behaviors that began at an early age (van Daal, Verhoeven, & van Balkom, 2007). Associated behavior problems, such as attention-deficit/hyperactivity disorder (ADHD) and social skill limitations, can add to communication problems and further alter the course of development in terms of how these children relate to peers or keep up with educational demands (Durkin & Conti-Ramsden, 2010). To give children with special needs the opportunity to interact with typically developing children, school systems have begun to include these children in regular, rather than segregated, classrooms. **Inclusion** education strategies are based on the premise that the abilities of children with special needs will improve from associating with normally developing peers and that by doing so these children will be spared the effects of labeling and special placements.

Causes

Notable findings that support the role of genetics, brain function, and environmental risk factors associated with a higher incidence of learning disorders are discussed in the following sections.

Genetics

Language processes appear to be heritable to a significant degree, although the specific genetic underpinnings are difficult to pinpoint. About 50% to 75% of all children with a language disorder show a positive family history of some type of learning disability (American Speech–Language–Hearing Association [ASHA], 2008; Heim & Benasich, 2006). Twin studies and adoption studies also suggest a genetic connection (McGrath et al., 2007; Plomin, Haworth, & Davis, 2010; Whitehouse et al., 2011).

Scientists are zeroing in on specific deficits in brain functioning that lead to communication disorders and may be heritable. Studies comparing language-impaired children with and without an affected parent suggest that *temporal processing deficits* occur significantly more often in children with a positive family history for a language-based learning disability (Caylak, 2011; Flax et al., 2003). That is, affected children have more difficulty deciphering certain speech sounds because of subtle but important differences in the way neurons fire in response to various sounds. In a twin study, Bishop et al. (1999) found that the variation in temporal processing was due to environmental factors and not to genetics because twin–twin correlations were similar for monozygotic (MZ) and dizygotic (DZ) twins. However, what does appear to be genetic is a deficit in phonological short-term memory.

The Brain

Language functions develop rapidly and are housed primarily in the left temporal lobe of the brain

Neurons form a vast, miniaturized informational network that transmits information in the form of electrical signals. When electrical signals move through a neuron, the cell ejects chemicals called neurotransmitters into the synapses (spaces between neurons). The neurotransmitters then cross the synapses and act like switches to turn adjacent cells on or off.

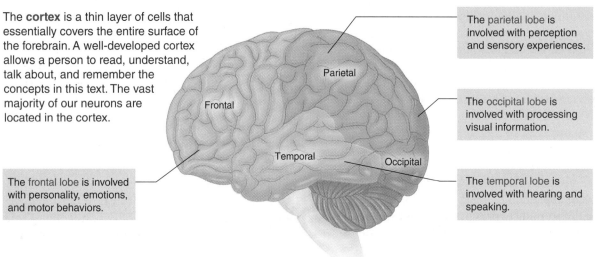

The cortex is a thin layer of cells that essentially covers the entire surface of the forebrain. A well-developed cortex allows a person to read, understand, talk about, and remember the concepts in this text. The vast majority of our neurons are located in the cortex.

The parietal lobe is involved with perception and sensory experiences.

The occipital lobe is involved with processing visual information.

The frontal lobe is involved with personality, emotions, and motor behaviors.

The temporal lobe is involved with hearing and speaking.

● **FIGURE 7.1** | Areas of the brain involved in language functions.

From Plotnik/Kouyoumdjian. Introduction to Psychology, 9th ed. 2011 Wadsworth, a part of Cengage Learning, Inc

(see ● Figure 7.1). A circular feedback loop helps strengthen the developmental process of language reception and expression. The better children comprehend spoken language, the better they will be able to express themselves. Feedback from their own vocalizations, in turn, helps shape their subsequent expressions. Lack of comprehension and absence of feedback reduces verbal output, and thus interferes with the development of articulation skills (Vellutino et al., 2007).

Anatomical and neuroimaging studies show that deficits in phonological awareness and segmentation are related to problems in the functional connections between brain areas, not to a specific dysfunction of any single area of the brain (Lyon et al., 2006; Richlan, Kronbichler, & Wimmer, 2011). Some brain imaging studies have indicated that poor performance on tasks demanding phonological awareness is associated with less brain activity in the left temporal region, suggesting that phonological problems may stem from neurological deficits or deviations in posterior left-hemisphere systems that control the ability to process phonemes (Richlan et al., 2011; S. E. Shaywitz et al., 2009). We return to these findings on brain function later, in our discussion of reading disorders.

Recurrent otitis media (middle ear infection) in early childhood was long thought to contribute to language difficulties, because hearing loss accompanies frequent or long bouts of infections. Although otitis media that occurs often during early childhood may lead to speech and language delays, these delays improve relatively quickly and largely disappear by age 7 (Zumach et al., 2010).

In summary, although biological findings point to abnormal brain functioning, how this abnormality originates is still unclear. The best guess is that communication disorders result from an interaction of genetic influences, slowness or abnormalities of brain maturation, and possibly, minor brain lesions that escape clinical detection (S. E. Shaywitz, Morris, & Shaywitz, 2008).

Home Environment

How much does the home environment contribute to communication disorders? Do some parents fail to provide adequate examples to stimulate their children's language? Because of the important role parents play in children's development, psychologists have studied this issue carefully.

We noticed when we first visited Jackie at home that her stepfather was a very quiet man who often communicated nonverbally—a gesture, a frown, a short phrase. Her mother used very simple speech when talking to Jackie but not when talking to Jackie's 6-year-old sister. These observations match those of researchers (St. James-Roberts & Alston, 2006; Whitehurst & Lonigan, 1998) who compared verbal interactions of families with and without a child who had a language disorder. They found that parents changed the way they spoke to their children, depending on their children's abilities. When the child spoke in simple, two- or three-word sentences, the parents adjusted their speech accordingly. Note that, except in extreme cases of child neglect or abuse, it is unlikely that communication disorders are caused by parents. Parental speech and language stimulation may affect the pace and range of language development, but not the specific impairments that characterize the disorders (Glascoe & Leew, 2010; McGrath et al., 2007).

Treatment

Although communication disorders in some children may self-correct by age 6 or so, those with more severe communication and language difficulties will continue to lag behind their peers and are at risk of havingbehavioral or social problems if the difficulties are left untreated. Thus, parents should seek help in understanding their child's speech delays and to ensure that they are doing everything possible to stimulate language development. In general, treatment for children with communication disorders is based on three principles (Beitchman & Brownlie, 2014): (1) treatment to promote the child's language competencies; (2) treatment to adjust the environment in ways that accommodate the child's needs; and (3) therapy with the child (or youth) to equip him or her with knowledge and skills to reduce behavioral and emotional symptoms.

Specialized preschools, for example, have had good results using a combination of computer- and teacher-assisted instruction to teach early language skills to young children, which helps to pace the child's practice of new skills (Hatcher et al., 2006; Loo et al., 2010; Smith-Lock et al., 2013).

For Jackie, we designed ways that her parents and day-care teachers could build on her existing strengths. Her day-care teacher had an excellent idea: Because Jackie loved to draw and to talk about her artwork, why not use her interest in drawing to increase her enthusiasm for speaking? When I visited her class, Jackie ran up to show me her drawing, exclaiming, "I draw picture of mom, dad, kitty, and lake." We agreed that her behavior problems could be managed by simple forms of ignoring and distracting and the occasional time-out. Jackie became attached to computer graphics and images, and she soon was able to identify letters and small words and to move shapes around the screen. All the while, her expressive language improved, and by age 5 she could pronounce all the letters of the alphabet and was eager to start kindergarten.

Childhood-Onset Fluency Disorder (Stuttering)

Childhood-Onset Fluency Disorder (Stuttering) is the repeated and prolonged pronunciation of certain syllables that interferes with communication. It is quite normal for children who are still learning to speak to go through a period of nonfluency, or unclear speech, as part of their development. It takes practice and patience for a child to develop the coordination for the tongue, lips, and brain to work in unison to produce unfamiliar or difficult combinations of sounds. For most children, this period of speech development passes without notice, and for most parents it is full of wonder and amusement as their children wrestle with new words. Some children, however, progress slowly through this stage, repeating (*wa-wa-wa*) or prolonging (*n-ah-ah-ah-o*) sounds; they struggle to continue or develop ways to avoid or compensate for certain sounds or words. Four-year-old Sayad has speech problems that typify the pattern of stuttering:

SAYAD

Family Legacy

Sayad's parents had received a lot of informal advice from friends and relatives about their son's speech problems, but most of what they said was worrisome. "He'll struggle with this for most of his life," his grandmother had warned. "If something isn't done right away, he'll become a stutterer, and be so self-conscious that he won't be able to keep up in school or with his friends."

(continues)

(continued)

Sayad started repeating and prolonging some of his words when he was about 2, but now his problem had grown more noticeable. As he spoke, he pursed his lips, closed his eyes, and shortened his breathing, seeming to tense up his face. Yet his interactions with me were friendly and at ease. "M-m-m-m-y words get stuck in m-m-m-m-y m-m-mouth," he explained, "and I-I-I-I talk t-t-t-t-too fast. Wh-wh-wh-why can't I talk right?" I soon discovered why his grandmother was so concerned: The child's great-grandfather and great-uncle both stuttered, and Sayad's father had been a stutterer until he was a teenager.

Sayad's mother had been trying to ignore the problem and not draw attention to it, but she was growing more aware that Sayad's peers teased and imitated him. She explained why she came for an assessment: "We were on the way to the store when Sayad kept saying 'where' over and over. After I stopped the car and unfastened his seatbelt, he finished his question—'is daddy?' After that, I gave up on my 'leave it alone' notion and began trying ways to slow Sayad down a bit." (Based on authors' case material.)

DSM-5 diagnostic criteria for Childhood-Onset Fluency Disorder (Stuttering) are shown in Table 7.2. This disorder involves disturbance in the normal fluency and time patterning of speech that is atypical for the child's age and that occurs often and persists over time. Stuttering is characterized by sound and syllable repetitions, sound prolongations, pauses within a word, word substitutions to avoid problematic words, and similar pronunciation and speech difficulties. These difficulties lead to anxiety about speaking or participating in activities that require effective communication or social participation. Over time the child may develop a fearful anticipation of speaking in front of others and attempt to avoid speech situations such as talking by telephone or in class. The disorder may be accompanied by motor movements such as eye blinks, tics, tremors of the lips or face, etc. (APA, 2013).

Prevalence and Course

Stuttering is relatively common as young children learn to articulate sounds clearly and appropriately. Population-based surveys indicate that 11% of children stutter by age 4, with girls affected as much as boys (Reilly et al., 2013; Yairi & Ambrose, 2013). However, few children receive a diagnosis of childhood-onset fluency disorder because about 80% recover from stuttering as they attend school for a year or so (Packman, Code, & Onslow, 2007). The prevalence of stuttering across

TABLE 7.2 | Diagnostic Criteria for Childhood-Onset Fluency Disorder (Stuttering)

DSM-5

(A) Disturbances in the normal fluency and time of patterning of speech that are inappropriate for the individual's age and language skills, persist over time, and are characterized by frequent and marked occurrences of one (or more) or the following:

(1) Sound and syllable repetitions.

(2) Sound prolongations of consonants as well as words.

(3) Broken words (e.g., pauses within a word).

(4) Audible or silent blocking (filled or unfilled pauses in speech).

(5) Circumlocutions (word substitutions to avoid problematic words).

(6) Words produced with an excess of physical tension.

(7) Monosyllabic whole-word repetitions (e.g., "I-I-I-I" see him).

(B) The disturbance causes anxiety about speaking or limitations in effective communication, social participation, or academic or occupational performance, individually or in any combination.

(C) The onset of symptoms is in the early developmental period (*Note:* Later-onset cases are diagnosed as adult-onset fluency disorder).

(D) The disturbance is not attributable to a speech-motor or sensory deficit, dysfluency associated with neurological insult (e.g., stroke, tumor, trauma), or another medical concern and is not better explained by another mental disorder.

Source: Diagnostic and Statistical Manual of Mental Disorders, 5th ed. American Psychiatric Association.

the lifespan (i.e., the number of individuals of all ages who meet the diagnostic criteria at any point in time) is below 1% (Yairi & Ambrose, 2013). Higher rates of parent-reported stuttering have been noted among African American and Hispanic children in the United States, although how racial and cultural factors may affect stuttering remains unclear (Boyle et al., 2011).

Causes and Treatment

Many myths and falsehoods surround stuttering. The widely held view that stuttering is caused by an unresolved emotional problem or by anxiety is not supported by any evidence (Packman et al., 2007). Because the problem runs in families, researchers have focused on family characteristics as the major causes. However, it is not likely this behavior is acquired primarily as a function of the child's linguistic environment. Sayad's grandmother and mother would be relieved to know that the communicative behavior of mothers does not significantly contribute to the development of stuttering (Howell & Davis, 2011).

Genetic factors play a strong role in the etiology of stuttering, accounting for approximately 70% of the variance in the causes of stuttering (Dworzynski et al., 2007). Environmental factors, such as premature birth or parental mental illness, account for the remaining causal influences (Ajdacic-Gross et al., 2010). Genetic factors most likely influence speech by causing an abnormal development in the location of the most prominent speech centers in the brain, which are usually in the left hemisphere. This biological source for stuttering explains many of its clinical features, including the loss of spontaneity and occasional problems in self-esteem (Howell, 2011; Kell et al., 2009).

Since most children outgrow stuttering, one of the most frustrating problems for parents and therapists is to decide whether therapy would be intervention or interference. Therapy is usually recommended if sound and syllable repetitions are frequent, if the parent or child is concerned about the problem, or if the child shows, like Sayad, facial or vocal tension. A common psychological treatment for children who stutter is to teach parents how to speak to their children slowly and use short and simple sentences, consequently removing the pressure the child may feel about speaking (Howell, 2011; Rousseau, Packman, Onslow, Harrison, & Jones, 2007). Other beneficial treatments for stuttering include contingency management, which uses positive consequences for fluency and negative consequences for stuttering (Bothe et al., 2006; Murphy, Yaruss, & Quesal, 2007), and habit reversal procedures, such as learning to regulate breathing (Bate et al., 2011).

Social (Pragmatic) Communication Disorder

Social (Pragmatic) Communication Disorder (SCD) is a new disorder in DSM-5. It involves persistent difficulties with pragmatics—the social use of language and communication (APA, 2013). Pragmatics are culturally specific practices and skills related to social uses of language, conversational norms, and the use of nonverbal communication, such as eye contact and gestures (Beitchman & Brownlie, 2014). Pragmatic difficulties involve both expressive and receptive skills—being able to adapt one's communication to the social context and being able to understand the nuances and social meanings expressed by others.

The first requirement for a diagnosis of social (pragmatic) communication disorder involves persistent difficulties across four areas (Table 7.3):

▸ Deficits in using communication for social purposes. A child may show difficulty greeting others or sharing information appropriately.

TABLE 7.3 **Diagnostic Criteria for** Social (Pragmatic) Communication Disorder

DSM-5

(A) Persistent difficulties in the social use of verbal and nonverbal communication as manifested by all of the following:

  (1) Deficits in using communication for social purposes, such as greeting and sharing information, in a manner that is appropriate for the social context.

  (2) Impairment of the ability to change communication to match context or the needs of the listener, such as speaking differently in a classroom than on a playground, talking differently to a child than to an adult, and avoiding use of overly formal language.

  (3) Difficulties following rules for language and storytelling, such as taking turns in conversation, rephrasing when misunderstood, and knowing how to use verbal and nonverbal signals to regulate interaction.

  (4) Difficulties understanding what is not explicitly stated (e.g., making inferences) and nonliteral or ambiguous meanings of language (e.g., idioms, humor, metaphors, multiple meanings that depend on the context for interpretation).

(B) The deficits result in functional limitations in effective communication, social participation, social relationships, academic achievement, or occupational performance, individually or in combination.

(C) The onset of the symptoms is early in the developmental period (but deficits may not become fully manifest until social communication demands exceed limited capacities).

(D) The symptoms are not attributable to another medical or neurological condition or to low abilities in the domains of word structure and grammar, and are not better explained by autism spectrum disorder, intellectual disability (intellectual developmental disorder), global developmental delay, or another mental disorder.

Source: Diagnostic and Statistical Manual of Mental Disorders, 5th ed. American Psychiatric Association.

▸ Difficulties changing their communication to match the situation or the listener, such as the classroom versus the playground.

▸ Problems following the rules of language, such as taking turns in a conversation,

▸ Difficulties understanding what someone is not explicitly saying, such as being able to make inferences based on the context of the situation.

A diagnosis of SCD is not typically made until the child is 4 or 5 years old, to determine whether he or she has shown adequate developmental progress in speech and language. Signs of language impairment, such as a history of delay in reaching language milestones, are common, but it is the specific deficits in social communication that determine this disorder. As with other communication disorders, onset must be early in development and result in functional limitations in communication, social participation, social relationships or academic functioning.

Social (pragmatic) communication disorder was added to the DSM because of the number of children who did not meet conventional criteria for an autism spectrum disorder (ASD) yet who had persistent difficulties with social aspects of communication and peer relations. SCD is differentiated from ASD largely on the basis of fewer restricted/repetitive patterns of behaviors and interests (Gibson et al., 2013). The symptoms of SCD also overlap with ADHD, social anxiety disorder, and intellectual disability in that they share problems in social, pragmatic communication. Although this diagnostic category is new, studies based on similar samples of children suggest that some children show improvement over time while others continue to show social communication deficits into adulthood. Regardless of improvements in social communication, children with SCD may suffer lasting impairments in peer relations due to their early difficulties. Thus, peer-assisted interventions are recognized as effective ways to build pragmatic communication and social skills for these children (Murphy, Faulkner, & Farley, 2014).

Section Summary

Communication Disorders

- Speech and language problems that emerge during early childhood include difficulty producing speech sounds, demonstrating speech fluency, using spoken language to communicate, or understanding what other people say.

- Even though most children with communication disorders acquire normal language by mid-to-late adolescence, early communication disorders are developmentally connected to the later onset of learning disorders.

- Language disorder is a communication disorder involving difficulties in comprehension or production of spoken or written language.

- Childhood-Onset Fluency Disorder (Stuttering) is relatively common among younger children, and declines significantly once the child enters school.

- Social (Pragmatic) Communication Disorder is new to DSM-5. Its primary characteristics involve difficulties in the social use of verbal and nonverbal communication.

- Causes of communication disorders include genetic influences and slow or abnormal brain maturation.

- Many communication disorders resolve themselves after children begin attending school. Treatment is recommended for children who show significant language delays or difficulties; it involves accommodating the child's needs to strengthen speech and language skills.

SPECIFIC LEARNING DISORDER

People do not understand what it costs in time and suffering to learn how to read. I have been working at it for eighty years, and I still can't say that I've succeeded.

—Goethe (1749–1832)

Whether we are studying Roman history or calculus, applying ourselves to the task of learning requires exertion and concentration. Like physical activities, some learning activities are more difficult than others, especially for younger children who have not developed a foundation of good study habits and successful learning experiences. Parents and teachers may notice that a child is struggling unusually hard to master a particular skill, such as reading, and wonder why. The problem may be formally assessed by an IQ test and various standardized tests that assess abilities in specific academic areas.

When achievement in reading, math, or writing is well below average for the child's age and intellectual ability, he or she may be diagnosed with a specific learning disorder (SLD). In other words, a child with a specific learning disorder is intellectually capable of learning key academic concepts of reading, writing, and math, but seems unable to do so. The phrase "unexpected academic underachievement" captures this notion that the child's learning problems are indeed *specific* and not due to intellectual disability or global developmental delay (APA, 2013).

JAMES

Strong Points Shine

The look on the 9-year-old's face said it all—he did not want to be here. "I'm tired of talking to people" was his terse greeting. I wondered for a moment whether he would talk to me at all, but as soon as he saw my computer, he brightened a bit. To allow time for him to feel more comfortable, I invited James to play a quick game or two. His skill at the action games told me a lot about his basic energy and problem-solving ability—he was a whiz at figuring out the rules of each game and getting a high score. We spoke casually during the warm-up, but it was clear to me that he preferred to concentrate on the game.

A half hour passed, with little more than a few sentences exchanged. A quick trip to the snack bar gave us the common ground we needed to open up and talk a bit. "Why does my teacher want me to come here?" he reasonably asked. As he listened and replied to my explanation, his language problems stood out. His sentences were short, simple, and rapid. Here is an example:

"James, tell me something about your favorite story or a recent movie you've seen."

"I like the movie. Lots of dogs."

"What movie is that, James?"

"Dog movie."

During testing, James often tried to start before I had finished telling him what to do. He was eager to do what I asked, but he stopped abruptly as soon as he had trouble. James could focus on only one sound at a time, so if he missed early cues or initial instructions, he would become disoriented, frustrated, and uncooperative. James wanted to do well, but I could see he was struggling. He completed the WISC-IV (Wechsler Intelligence Scale for Children, 4th ed.) in less than an hour, hurrying almost as if to escape his own mistakes. His measured general intelligence was within the normal range, but his performance abilities (performance IQ, 109) were much stronger than his verbal abilities (verbal IQ, 78). It was obvious as well that the test underestimated his true ability, as a result of his eagerness to finish and his difficulty with understanding some of the instructions.

To my surprise, James was ready to continue on to the next test after only a short computer game break. He explained why this was so: "I put things together, like puzzles. I make cars and planes at my house." As long as I gave him small breaks on the computer, he was willing to tackle the material on the tests. Some of his spelling errors stood out immediately, such as *skr* for *square*, and *srke* for *circle*. When asked to write the sentence "he shouted a warning," he wrote "he shtd a woin." He read "see the black dog" as "see the black pond," and "she wants a ride to the store" as "she was rid of the store." He seemed to use a "best guess" strategy in tackling reading, based on the sounds that he knew: When asked to write the word bigger, he wrote just her. But I noticed that James's enthusiasm picked up a bit as he began telling stories from pictures he was shown, and he marveled at his own ability to rotate shapes on the computer to complete a picture. He left my office more animated and talkative than when he arrived, which showed how nice it must have felt for him to experience success. (Based on authors' case material.)

James, at age 9, had problems primarily in reading and spelling. Contrast his reading difficulties with those of Tim, who struggles with spatial orientation and mathematical reasoning.

TIM

Warming with Interest

When I first saw Tim, he seemed aloof and disinterested. His eyes stayed focused on the floor, and his body remained expressionless, as if to say, "Leave me alone, and let me outta here." As I searched for something to say, I asked Tim to tell me a little about his family: "Do you have any brothers or sisters? Does your family like to do anything special together?" His tired response, "I have two brothers, my father works all day, mom plays piano. We want a boat," sent me a clear message as to his mood and interest in this activity. My usual ploy of turning on the computer games fell flat—"I hate computers" was Tim's preemptive response. I wondered, "Is he depressed, angry, hurt, frustrated? Just what is going on here?"

Having looked at his school record, I knew he was struggling, especially in math and physical sciences, but his speech and affect expressed more than only academic problems. His school records flashed the news that Tim had a specific learning disorder, as evidenced by his WISC-IV performance score of 79 that fell in the borderline-to-low-average range, and his verbal score of 108 that fell in the average range. The test administrator had politely described Tim's test-taking approach as "reluctant." Notes by teachers indicated that he commonly had problems on tasks involving drawing, particularly if they required memory, and his math and social skills were far below those of others in his class.

I pulled out my *Where's Waldo?* book and we began looking at it together. In addition to being fun, looking for Waldo and his friends (small figures amidst millions of figures and colors) required Tim to be patient. At first he balked, but I noticed that he improved if he used his own verbally mediated strategy to solve the problem. Tim talked to himself as he thought aloud: "Look around the edges first, then start to look closer and closer to the middle of the page. Look for Waldo's red and white shirt—look closely at each section!" The more interested he was, the more he would talk. Once he warmed up, his smile appeared, along with his admission that "this sure beats math lesson." (Based on authors' case material.)

James's pattern of strengths and weaknesses shows that although he has reading problems, other strengths compensate for this disability. He has strong talents for figuring out how things work and for drawing ideas on paper. Tim has several strengths, too, especially in linguistic skills such as word recognition, sentence structure, and reading. In contrast to James, Tim has problems primarily in the visual, spatial, and organizational spheres, which show up as difficulties with tactile (touch) perception, psychomotor activity (e.g., throwing and catching), and nonverbal problem solving (e.g., figuring out math problems and assembling things).

Both boys fit the diagnostic criteria for SLD. Note how Tim's academic problems, in particular, were almost masked by his frustration and low self-esteem.

For children with specific learning disorders, following simple instructions can be confusing and frustrating.

Emotional problems are often seen in children who are bright enough to recognize that their performance is below that of others and are frustrated with their poor performance at school. The limitations of both James and Tim can affect every aspect of their formal education as well as their interpersonal abilities; therefore, these disorders require comprehensive and ongoing treatment plans.

To understand the nature of specific learning disorders, picture yourself asking for directions to a famous monument at an information booth in an unfamiliar town. The attendant hands you a map with written directions: "Go out the driveway and turn right. Go till you reach the second light, turn left, and look for the sign to Amityville. It's about 3 miles down the road. You'll pass a cemetery and a red schoolhouse, and go under a railroad trestle before you get to Highway 18. When you see the sign, turn right." Most of us would have trouble recalling these verbal directions, so having them written in the map makes them easier to follow. However, children or adults with an SLD in reading experience confusion in these common situations that involve understanding the meaning of what is read. Specific learning problems can be difficult to recognize because, for most of us, the material in question is straightforward and simple. The child may be blamed for not listening, not paying attention, or for being "slow," which further disguises the true nature of the learning problems.

The main diagnostic feature of SLD is that the child has difficulties learning keystone academic skills of reading, writing, spelling, or math (see Table 7.4). These difficulties may appear in one or more of these

TABLE 7.4 | Diagnostic Criteria for Specific Learning Disorder

DSM-5

(A) Difficulties learning and using academic skills, as indicated by the presence of at least one of the following symptoms that have persisted for at least six months, despite the provision of interventions that target those difficulties:

(1) Inaccurate or slow and effortful word reading (e.g., reads single words aloud incorrectly or slowly and hesitantly, frequently guesses words, has difficulty sounding out words).

(2) Difficulty understanding the meaning of what is read (e.g., may read text accurately but not understand sequence, relationships, inferences, or deeper meanings of what is read).

(3) Difficulties with spelling (e.g., may add, omit, or substitute vowels or consonants).

(4) Difficulties with written expression (e.g., makes multiple grammatical or punctuation errors within sentences; employs poor paragraph organization; written expression of ideas lacks clarity).

(5) Difficulties mastering number sense, number facts, or calculation (e.g., has poor understanding of numbers, their magnitude, and relationships; counts on fingers to add single-digit numbers instead of recalling the math fact as peers do; gets lost in the midst of arithmetic computation and may switch procedures).

(6) Difficulties with mathematical reasoning (e.g., has severe difficulty applying mathematical concepts, facts, or procedures to solve quantitative problems).

(B) The affected academic skills are substantially and quantifiably below those expected for the individual's chronological age, and cause significant interference with academic or occupational performance, or with activities of daily living, as confirmed by individually administered standardized achievement measures and comprehensive clinical assessment. For individuals aged 17 years and older, a documented history of impairing learning difficulties may be substituted for the standardized assessment.

(C) The learning difficulties begin during school-age years but may not become fully manifest until the demands of those affected academic skills exceed the individuals limited capacities (e.g., as in timed tests, reading or writing lengthy complex reports for a tight deadline, excessively heavy academic loads).

(D) The learning difficulties are not better accounted for by intellectual disabilities, uncorrected visual or auditory acuity, other mental or neurological disorders, psychosocial adversity, lack of proficiency in the language of academic instruction, or inadequate educational instruction.

Note: The four diagnostic criteria are to be met based on a clinical synthesis of the individual's history (developmental, medical, family, educational), school reports, and psychoeducational assessment.

(continues)

TABLE 7.4 | Diagnostic Criteria for Specific Learning Disorder (*continued*)

Specify if:

With impairment in reading:

Word reading accuracy

Reading rate or fluency

Reading comprehension

With impairment in written expression:

Spelling accuracy

Grammar and punctuation accuracy

Clarity or organization of written expression

With impairment in mathematics:

Number sense

Memorization of arithmetic facts

Accurate or fluent calculation

Accurate math reasoning

Specify current severity:

Mild: Some difficulties learning skills in one or two academic domains, but of mild enough severity that the individual may be able to compensate or function well when provided with appropriate accommodations or support services, especially during the school years.

Moderate: Marked difficulties learning skills in one or more academic domains, so that the individual is unlikely to become proficient without some intervals of intensive and specialized teaching during the school years. Some accommodations or supportive services at least part of the day at school, in the workplace, or at home may be needed to complete activities accurately and efficiently.

Severe: Severe difficulties learning skills, affecting several academic domains, so that the individual is unlikely to learn these skills without ongoing intensive individualized and specialized teaching for most of the school years. Even with an array of appropriate accommodations or services at home, at school, or in the workplace, the individual may not be able to complete all activities efficiently.

Source: Diagnostic and Statistical Manual of Mental Disorders, 5th ed. American Psychiatric Association.

skills, including inaccurate or slow reading, difficulty understanding the meaning of what is read, difficulties with spelling and/or written expression, or difficulties mastering number sense, calculation, or mathematical reasoning. The affected academic skills would need to be substantially below what it should be for the child's age and intellectual ability. In practice, this often means that the child's achievement test scores in academic subjects are at least 1.5 standard deviations below average for their age and sex (which translates to a standard score of 78, or below the seventh percentile).

To be classified as a disorder, the performance problems must significantly interfere with academic achievement or daily living, and to persist for more than 6 months despite efforts to improve them. (Some children and adults have found ways to compensate for their learning problems and therefore do not display a disability, despite their test findings or poor achievement.) Finally, the learning difficulties appear during the school-age years, and cannot be better accounted for by a sensory problem (such as impaired hearing or sight), intellectual disability, psychosocial adversity, or inadequate educational instruction.

Because many aspects of speaking, listening, reading, writing, and arithmetic overlap and build on the same functions of the brain, it is not surprising that a child or adult can have more than one form of SLD (Scanlon, 2013). Recall that phonological awareness facilitates the ability to speak and, later on, to read and write. A single gap in the brain's functioning can disrupt many types of cognitive activity. These disruptions, in turn, can interfere with the development of important fundamental skills and compound the learning difficulties in a short time. Moreover, as we saw with both James and Tim, numerous secondary problems can emerge, such as temper outbursts and withdrawal from social situations, as a result of frustration and lack of success.

As noted earlier in this chapter, DSM-5 integrates the frequently co-occurring problems in reading, mathematics, and written expression into one category, and uses specifiers to designate all academic domains and subskills that are impaired. Table 7.4 also describes the degrees of severity (mild, moderate, or severe) associated with each impairment. Degrees of severity reflect both the extent of the child or adolescent's learning difficulties as well as the appropriate accommodations or supports he or she requires to learn the academic skill(s) and complete activities at school, work or home as efficiently as possible. Below we take a closer look at the three core academic skill impairments specified in SLD.

SLD with Impairment in Reading

He has only half learned the art of reading who has not added to it the more refined art of skipping and skimming.

—Arthur James Balfour

Children are naturally attracted to reading, and its importance in our society is unequaled by any other academic accomplishment. We are surrounded by written signs and messages and, by about age 5 or so, most children want to know what they mean. (Capitalizing on this natural curiosity, advertisers have become expert in pairing recognizable symbols with the names of their product or establishment so that children can "read" more quickly.) By the first grade, natural interest and developmental readiness are channeled into formally learning how to read. For many children, this process is difficult and tedious; for a sizable minority, however, it can be confusing and upsetting. The role of parents in this process is critical, because children need positive feedback and need to feel satisfied with their performance, regardless of their speed and accuracy.

When you consider everything involved in learning the basics of reading, such as associating shapes of letters (graphemes) with sounds (phonemes), it is not surprising that some children have difficulty and can quickly fall behind. Read the following sentence: "I believe that abnormal child psychology is one of the most fascinating and valuable courses I have taken." As you read the sentence, did you notice that you had to simultaneously:

▶ Focus attention on the printed marks and control your eye movements across the page?

▶ Recognize the sounds associated with letters?

▶ Understand words and grammar?

▶ Build ideas and images?

▶ Compare new ideas with what you already know?

▶ Store ideas in memory?

Most of us have forgotten all the effort that goes into reading, especially in the beginning. Not surprisingly, children's initial attempts are laborious and monotonous as they wrestle with the sounds and complexities of combined letters. Such mental processing requires a complex intact network of nerve cells that connect our vision, language, and memory centers (Grigorenko, 2007). A small problem in any area can cause reading difficulties. The most common underlying feature of a reading disorder, however, is an inability to distinguish or to separate the sounds in spoken words. Phonological skills are fundamental to learning to read, and therefore this deficit is critical.

To assess a child's need for additional practice in mastering phonemes and words, it is important to understand that there are two systems that operate when one reads words, which are essential in the development of reading. The first system operates on individual units (phonemes) and is relatively slow; the second system operates on whole words more quickly. In normal readers, whole words are learned through the development of phonologically based word analysis. However, persistently poor readers seem to rely on rote memory for recognizing words (S. E. Shaywitz & Shaywitz, 2013).

Many clinical signs of reading disorders are first evident only to a trained eye. Some testing methods developed by teachers and school psychologists show how children with reading disorders function in the classroom. They often have trouble learning basic sight words, especially those that are phonetically irregular and must be memorized, such as *the, who, what, where, was, laugh, said,* and so forth. These children have developed their own unique and peculiar reading patterns, which signal the need for different teaching methods. Typical errors include *reversals (b/d; p/q), transpositions* (sequential errors such as *was/saw, scared/sacred*), *inversions (m/w; u/n)*, and *omissions* (reading *place* for *palace* or *section* for *selection*). However, these errors are common in many younger children who are just learning to read and write and do not necessarily imply a reading disorder.

To assess a child's need for additional practice in certain areas, teachers may log the types of errors the child makes while reading out loud. In addition to decoding words, reading comprehension is assessed by having the student retell a story or suggest the next episode. Average readers rely heavily on auditory and visual modalities for gathering new information, but children with reading disorders may prefer a mode of touch or manipulation to assist them in learning. These various patterns of strengths and weaknesses, if adequately assessed, can then be used to the child's advantage in planning additional teaching methods such as computer-based learning (S. E. Shaywitz et al., 2008).

A child with a SLD with impairment in reading lacks the critical language skills required for basic reading: word reading accuracy, reading comprehension, and reading rate or fluency. **Dyslexia** is an alternative term sometimes used to describe this pattern of reading difficulties. These core deficits stem from problems in **decoding**—breaking a word into parts rapidly enough to read the whole word—coupled with difficulty reading single small words (Vellutino et al., 2007). When a child cannot detect the phonological structure of language and automatically recognize simple words, reading development will very likely be impaired (Peterson & Pennington, 2010). The slow and labored decoding of single words requires substantial effort and detracts from the child's ability to retain the meaning of a sentence, much less a paragraph or page.

SLD with Impairment in Written Expression

CARLOS

Slowly Taking Shape

Carlos, age 7, was about to finish second grade when his teacher and parents met to discuss his handwriting problems. The year had gone well in general, but his parents were bracing for bad news. Smiling and pulling out some workbooks, Carlos's teacher lined up examples of how he had gradually become able to print some letters over the course of the year. But what his parents saw was self-explanatory: His shapes were very poor and looked more like those of his 3-year-old sister. Sensing both parents' apprehension, his teacher clarified: "Carlos is having a few problems in his fine motor coordination, in activities such as artwork, putting puzzles together, and similar tasks. He goes too fast when trying to do these tasks, and he forgets to be careful or to follow the pattern. He makes a half-hearted attempt on his writing assignments and then starts talking to his classmates. I'd like him to be seen by a psychologist for testing, and hopefully next fall his new teacher can strengthen his writing and fine motor skills with some additional exercises."

During the initial interview, Carlos took an immediate interest in my computer games, exclaiming how easy it was to use the mouse to draw figures. When asked to use a pencil and paper, however, Carlos balked. I asked him to copy by hand some of the figures he drew on the computer, after first printing them for him on paper. In doing so, he switched to his preferred hand in the middle of the task. He also showed several letter reversals (b/d; p/q), and pushed down very hard on the pencil in an attempt to trace or draw the figures. Throughout these tasks he talked freely and asked a lot of questions, making me wonder at times who was assessing whom.

Carlos showed evidence on neuropsychological testing of finger *agnosia* (he could not tell which finger I touched when his hand was behind his back), especially with his left hand. He also had considerable difficulty copying a triangle, a circle, and a square based on examples shown to him (see ● Figure 7.2). On the WISC-IV he obtained a performance score of 91, in the low-average range, and a verbal IQ score of 117, in the high-average range. On performance subtests he had particular problems with block design and puzzles, such as object assembly. He had more difficulty with verbal IQ subtests that involved concentration and attention, such as math and digit-span tasks. Throughout the testing, I found Carlos to be impulsive and sometimes quite defiant: If he didn't want to do something, he simply would not do it. These observations were consistent with his parents' frustration at his immature behavior and defiance at home.

● **FIGURE 7.2** | *Top*: Drawings produced by Carlos when asked to copy a triangle, a circle, and a square. *Bottom*: Examples of a triangle, circle, and square from a typically developing 7-year-old boy.

(Based on authors' case material.)

Carlos has a specific learning disorder related to written expression. He has strong language and reasoning abilities, as well as normal problem-solving skills for his age, yet he is considerably weaker in his visual–motor abilities, as shown by his writing, figure copying, and figure rotation. Like reading and math, writing derives from several interconnected brain areas that produce vocabulary, grammar, hand movement, and memory.

SLD with impairment in written expression may manifest as problems in spelling accuracy, grammar and punctuation accuracy, and/or clarity or organization of written expression. This particular SLD is often found in combination with SLD in reading or mathematics, which also have underlying core deficits in language and neuropsychological development.

Children with impairment in written expression often have problems with tasks that require eye–hand coordination, despite their normal gross motor development. Teachers notice that, as compared with children who have normal writing skills, children with impairments in writing produce shorter, less interesting, and poorly organized essays and are less likely to review spelling, punctuation, and grammar to increase clarity (Hooper et al., 2011, 2013). However, spelling errors or poor handwriting that do not significantly interfere with daily activities or academic pursuits do not qualify a child for this diagnosis. In addition, problems in written expression signal the possibility of other learning problems because of shared metacognitive processes: planning, self-monitoring, self-evaluation, and self-modification (Heim & Benasich, 2006).

SLD with Impairment in Mathematics

During their preschool years, children are not as naturally drawn to mathematical concepts as they are to reading. This changes rapidly as they discover that they need to count and add to know how much money it takes to buy something or how many days remain until vacation. As in reading, the need to know propels children to learn new and difficult concepts, and little by little their new skills help them understand the world better.

For some children, like Francine and Tim, this curiosity about numbers is compromised by their inability to grasp the abstract concepts inherent in many forms of numerical and cognitive problem solving. Francine's difficulty with numbers and concepts began to show up well before she attended school, which is typically the case. When she encountered math concepts in second grade that required some abstract reasoning, she fell further and further behind.

The DSM-5 criteria for SLD with impairment in mathematics include difficulties in number sense, memorization of arithmetic facts, accurate or fluent calculation, and/or accurate math reasoning. *Dyscalculia* is an

● **FIGURE 7.3** | Errors in math computation by a 10-year-old girl with a mathematics disorder.

From "Learning Disabilities" by H.G. Taylor, 1988, p. 422. In E.J. Mash and L.G. Terdal (Eds.) "Behavioral Assessment of Childhood Disorders", 2nd ed.

alternative term sometimes used to describe this pattern of math difficulties. Many skills are involved in arithmetic: recognizing numbers and symbols, memorizing facts (the multiplication table), aligning numbers, and understanding abstract concepts such as place value and fractions. Any or all may be difficult for children with a mathematics disorder (Vukovic & Siegel, 2010). Children and adults with this disorder may have difficulty not only in math, but also in comprehending abstract concepts or in visual–spatial ability. Examples of calculation errors typical of children with a mathematics disorder are shown in ● Figure 7.3, an example that points out errors that suggest spatial difficulties and directional confusion.

Children with an SLD with impairment in mathematics typically have core deficits in arithmetic calculation and/or mathematics reasoning abilities, which include naming amounts or numbers; enumerating, comparing, and manipulating objects; reading and writing mathematical symbols; understanding concepts and performing calculations mentally; and performing computational operations (Andersson, 2010; Lyon et al., 2006). These deficits imply that the neuropsychological processes underlying mathematical reasoning and calculation are underdeveloped or impaired.

Prevalence and Course

Estimates of the prevalence of SLD across all three domains (reading, writing, and math) range from 5% to 15% among school-aged children (APA, 2013). Reasons for this large range focus on the notion that SLD in reading—the most common form—may be part of a continuum of reading abilities rather than a discrete, all-or-none phenomenon. Children with reading disorders are essentially those who fall at the lower end of the reading continuum (Snowling, 2008). This consideration of the range of ability is useful and important because, clearly, there are strong readers and weak readers, and no definitive cutoff point easily distinguishes the two. Estimates of the prevalence of SLD with impairment in mathematics or written expression are unclear due to the overlap among all three subtypes, although consensus is that they occur at a much lower rate than do reading difficulties (Landerl & Moll, 2010).

SLD impairments are considered lifelong, although the course varies based on severity and available supports. Recognition of SLD typically emerges during elementary school years, when a student falls significantly behind classmates in one or more of these subjects, though parents often note problems in language delays or counting in early childhood. Parents and teachers may notice specific delays in early skill development, or notice behavioral signs of the child's struggles, such as his or her unwillingness to learn to read, write, or work with numbers. In elementary school, the child shows marked difficulty in learning letter–sound correspondence and may commit reading errors by connecting sounds and letters (e.g., "big" for "got") and have difficulty sequencing numbers and letters (APA, 2013).

By the middle grades children with SLD may show poor reading comprehension and poor spelling and written work. They may be able to read and pronounce the first part of a word correctly but then guess the rest of the word. As they struggle with these difficulties throughout elementary school, being fearful of or refusing to read aloud is common. By adolescence through to adulthood, these patterns often shift from basic coding difficulties to marked problems in reading comprehension and written expression, including poor spelling and poor mathematical problem solving. Over time, teens and adults learn to manage these difficulties to the best of their ability, but may avoid situations that require reading, writing, or numerical ability. Thus, over the life span SLD is associated with many functional consequences, such as lower academic achievement, higher school dropout rates, poor overall mental health and well-being, and lower employment and income (APA, 2013).

Cultural, Class, and Gender Variations

Social and cultural factors are less relevant to SLD than other types of cognitive and behavioral problems; in fact, the diagnostic criteria state that they cannot be attributed to these factors. Nevertheless, some cultural and ethnic factors may affect how children with SLD are identified and treated (Johansson, 2006).

Many childhood disorders reflect an interaction between the child's inherent abilities and resources and the opportunities that exist in the child's local environment, as emphasized throughout this text. In the case of learning to read, some teaching approaches do not explicitly emphasize specific sound–symbol relationships that are inherent in the dialect of children from diverse ethnic backgrounds. For example, an interesting study by Wood et al. (1991) illustrated the point that deficits in phonological awareness occur more frequently among populations that use nonstandard English. They followed a random sample of 485 Caucasian (55%) and African American (45%) children from first grade through third grade, and they found that although African American youngsters read at the same grade level as Caucasian children at the beginning of the first grade, they show marked declines in reading by the third grade and severe declines by the fifth grade. These findings suggest that greater attention to differences in dialect can lead to better learning opportunities.

Whereas attention to cultural and ethnic issues pertaining to SLD is a recent addition to research, sex differences have a long and contentious history. Boys are more often referred for learning difficulties than girls, perhaps because boys are more likely to show associated behavior problems such as aggression or inattention. Girls with learning problems often are quiet and withdrawn rather than loud and attention seeking, and they may be overlooked unless educators and parents are well informed. Nonetheless, when male–female ratios of SLD are derived from epidemiological estimates rather than from referrals, the ratio of boys to girls falls between 2:1 and 3:1 (APA, 2013).

Psychological and Social Adjustment

For many years, a diagnosis of learning disability or disorder required a discrepancy between IQ and performance, which hampered early identification because the assessment often was not done until the child had attempted and failed at reading, usually by the third grade. By that time, the child's achievement would be low enough to warrant a diagnosis, but the child had failed in reading for 2 to 3 years and may have developed other behavioral and emotional problems as a result.

Today's recognition of SLD as an early neurodevelopmental disorder is improving detection of children with difficulties, but they still face significant obstacles in their peer adjustment and academic progress. Children with SLD often do not know how or why they are different, but they do know how it feels to be unable to keep up with others in the classroom. Hearing themselves described as "slow," "different," or "behind," they may identify more with their disabilities rather than with their strengths. These daily experiences may cause some children to act out by either withdrawing or becoming angry and noncompliant. Like James, they may stop trying to learn. Like Francine, they may become isolated and limit their participation in activities that their peers enjoy.

Students with SLD with reading impairment feel less supported by their parents, teachers, and peers than do normal readers, and they are more likely to express poor academic or scholastic self-concepts (Heim & Benasich, 2006). Perhaps as a result of the interaction of their disorder and their environment, children and adolescents with SLD are more likely than their peers to show internalizing problems such as anxiety (Nelson & Harwood, 2011) and mood disorders (Maughan et al., 2003), as well as externalizing behaviors such as ADHD (Goldston et al., 2007). The range and types of problems are generally similar for both younger and older age groups. Accordingly, issues pertaining to both younger and older children and adolescents with SLD are considered jointly unless particular developmental differences warrant attention. Many of these issues are common to all domains of SLD unless otherwise noted.

The connection between SLD and behavioral or emotional disorders has generated considerable interest but only cautious conclusions. Common sense suggests that children with SLD encounter considerable challenges that are likely to take a toll on self-esteem and, in time, their social relationships. However, children's self-concepts in sports and appearance are usually less affected (Lyon et al., 2006).

Parents and teachers describe children with SLD as being more difficult to manage than typical children, beginning at an early age. Although overall reports of behavior problems increase considerably for all children between early and middle childhood, behavior problems among children with SLD are about three times higher than typically developing children by 8 years of age (i.e., 32% vs. 9%; Benasich, Curtiss, & Tallal, 1993) (see ● Figure 7.4). Most of these problems are not specific to SLD but cover a broad range

of problems that overlap with features of conduct disorder (CD), oppositional defiant disorder (ODD), and attention-deficit/hyperactivity disorder (ADHD) across all ages (APA, 2013).

These co-occurring problems are often interpreted as individual reactions and coping styles in response to failure, frustration, and, in some instances, punishment and negative attention. However, in terms of development, it is hard to say which comes first: Behavior problems may precede, follow, or co-occur with learning problems (Hinshaw, 1992). Whereas many of these behavioral and emotional problems gradually decrease from childhood to adolescence, adolescents with SLD continue to face challenges in their social relationships (St Clair et al., 2011).

Based on a review of over 150 studies, Kavale and Forness (1996) found that about three of every four students with SLD have significant deficits in social skills. As a group, they are more isolated and less popular among peers than other children, and they tend to make negative impressions on others (Durkin & Conti-Ramsden, 2010). Like Francine, who was described by her mother as "humorless and in a bit of a fog," most children with SLD have difficulty grasping the nuances of social interaction and may not know how to greet others, make friends, or join in playground games. Subtle cues of social interaction may be missed or ignored. These children may not always interpret correctly or respond appropriately to the frequent nonverbal—but very expressive—communication of other children, such as rolling the eyes to show dislike or disinterest. When children with SLD misunderstand the situation and act inappropriately, other children turn away.

A child with SLD also can be an emotional burden for family members. Parents may experience a wide range of emotions, including denial, guilt, blame, frustration, anger, and despair. Brothers and sisters often feel annoyed, embarrassed, or jealous of the attention their sibling receives. Because behavioral problems are usually so disruptive, a child's distress and emotional needs may easily be overlooked.

Adult Outcomes

Unfortunately, the social and emotional difficulties connected to communication and learning disorders may continue into adulthood, largely because of inadequate recognition and services (Johnson et al., 2010). Adults may find ways to disguise their problems, such as watching television news rather than reading newspapers. On the other hand, many excel in nonacademic subjects such as art, music, dance, or athletics. Still others may become outstanding architects and engineers,

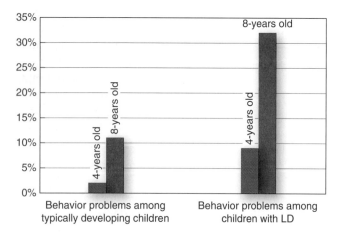

● **FIGURE 7.4** | Percentage of clinically significant behavior problems among children with and without learning disorders, at 4 years and 8 years of age.

Data from Benasich et al., 1993

or they may have extraordinary interpersonal skills (Lyon et al., 2006). Each child and adolescent has many strengths that can be developed to compensate for his or her known deficits. Thus, despite their earlier risk for academic failure and psychosocial problems, many adults with SLD lead successful and productive lives (Lovett & Lewandowski, in press).

Men with SLD with impairments in reading do not differ from their peers regarding feelings of global self-worth; symptoms of depression; feelings of competency and satisfaction with jobs, marriages, and other relationships; or frequency of antisocial behavior (Boetsch, Green, & Pennington, 1996). However, men still perceive lower levels of social support from parents and relatives—the only people still in their lives who knew of their problems as children—which confirms the indelible impressions left by early experiences.

One adult describes his own way of compensating for learning problems:

> I faked my way through school because I was very bright. I resent most that no one picked up my weaknesses. Essentially I judge myself on my failures. . . . [I] have always had low self-esteem. . . . A blow to my self-esteem when I was in school was that I could not write a poem or a story. . . . I could not write with a pen or pencil. The computer has changed my life. I do everything on my computer. It acts as my memory. I use it to structure my life and for all of my writing since my handwriting and written expression has always been so poor. (Polloway, Schewel, & Patton, 1992, p. 521)

Whereas the long-term outlook for men with SLD is generally positive, the troublesome issue of sexism arises when considering how adult women with SLD fare over time. As a group, women with SLD have more adjustment problems than men as they leave school and face the demands of adult life. Similar to other adults with disabilities, they also face greater risk of sexual assault and related forms of abuse (Brownlie et al., 2007). Problems and breakdowns in relationships are common, which may reflect the lack of opportunity available to these women to achieve in areas that capitalize on their strengths.

Reading problems often cause poorly qualified graduates to take relatively undemanding and unrewarding jobs. Women who lack competitive skills and strong career options because of school failure tend to get involved at an early age in intimate relationships that are generally unsupportive (Fairchild, 2002). Young men, in contrast, have more wide-ranging options once they leave school, which facilitates more positive social functioning in adulthood. Thus, if they are able to select their own environments in adulthood

Factors That Increase Resilience and Adaptation

Several personal characteristics and circumstances aid those with learning disorders in their successful adaptation from childhood, through adolescence, to young adulthood. As part of a longitudinal study of all children born in 1955 on the island of Kauai, Hawaii, E. E. Werner (1993) followed 22 children with learning disabilities and 22 matched controls. She found that most children with learning disabilities adapted successfully to adult life. Those who showed the greatest resilience and flexibility over time had: (1) a basic temperament that elicited positive responses from others; (2) a well-developed sense of efficacy, preparedness, and self-esteem that guided their lives; (3) competent caregivers and supportive adults; and (4) opportunities for a second chance if they made mistakes or got into trouble with the law. Although some of these characteristics are present from birth (e.g., temperament), many of the other supportive factors can be increased through the efforts of family members, schools, and communities. (Based on authors' case material.)

(and women have more obstacles in this regard than men), both men and women with SLD can build on their existing strengths, skills, and talents (Hatch, Harvey, & Maughan, 2010).

It is safe to say that even though aspects of SLD may remain, people who are given proper educational experiences have a remarkable ability to learn throughout their life spans (Gregg, 2011). A Closer Look 7.1 describes some of these important opportunities that increase resilience. Adults can learn to read, although it is difficult because brain development slows down after puberty. Current gains in knowledge of the causes and early signs of SLD are likely to have a positive impact on early recognition and proper instruction. Nonintrusive electrophysiological measurements of brain reactivity may permit an early diagnosis based on underlying deficits in phonological processing rather than on performance alone. Thus, early identification and intervention may be the key to preventing the long-term consequences of these disorders (S. E. Shaywitz & Shaywitz, 2013).

Causes

Most learning disorders do not stem from problems in a single area of the brain, but from difficulties in bringing information from various brain regions together so that information can be integrated and understood

(Damasio et al., 2004; Meyer & Damasio, 2009). Minute disturbances may underlie phonological processing deficits. Emerging evidence suggests that in many cases these subtle disturbances begin very early during development, perhaps prenatally (McGrath et al., 2007; Raschle, Chang, & Gaab, 2011).

Recent findings suggest two distinguishable types of children with reading disorders—children who are persistently poor readers and those who are accuracy-improved (i.e., they learn ways to compensate for their reading difficulties and improve over time) (S. E. Shaywitz, Mody, & Shaywitz, 2006). Persistently poor readers and accuracy-improved readers have comparable reading skills and socioeconomic status when they begin school, but by the time they are young adults, the accuracy-improved readers show better cognitive ability. The presence of compensatory factors, such as stronger cognitive ability, may allow the accuracy-improved individuals to minimize the consequences of their phonological defect over time (Ferrer et al., 2010). These compensatory factors may be genetically based, and thus the child's ability improves with maturity, whereas the persistently poor readers may face greater environmental challenges, often associated with poverty and inequality, that reduce reading opportunities.

Genetic and Constitutional Factors

Children who lack some of the skills needed for reading, such as hearing the separate sounds of words, are more likely to have a parent with a related problem. Around the turn of the twentieth century this problem was studied largely by physicians, who considered reading disorders to be an inherited condition called *congenital word blindness* (W. P. Morgan, 1896). Today, estimates based on behavioral genetic studies indicate that heritability accounts for over 60% of the variance in reading disorders (V. M. Bishop, 2006; Plomin et al., 2010), although the exact mode of transmission remains undetermined.

Most attention paid to heritability is aimed at genetic transmission of critical brain processes underlying phonetic processing (Scerri & Schulte-Körne, 2010; Vellutino et al., 2004). Because a parent's learning disorder may take a slightly different form in the child—the father may have a writing disorder and his child an expressive language disorder—it seems unlikely that subtypes of specific learning disorders are inherited directly. More likely, what is inherited is a subtle brain dysfunction that, in turn, can lead to a learning disorder (Newbury et al., 2011; Richlan et al., 2011; Scerri & Schulte-Körne, 2010). For example, on chromosome 6 an area has been identified that predisposes children to reading disorders (Grigorenko, 2007). Genetic transmission provides a plausible explanation for the relative risk of SLD in reading or mathematics being 4 to 8 times and 5 to 10 times higher, respectively, in first-degree relatives of persons with SLD as compared to those without it (APA, 2013; Shalev, 2007). Keep in mind that environmental factors also play a role in moderating genetic influences on SLD outcomes (i.e., gene–environment interaction; Petrill, 2013).

Neurobiological Factors

Our understanding of learning disorders, particularly reading-based and language-based problems, took an important new direction in the mid-1980s with the discovery that the brains of people with these problems were characterized by cellular abnormalities in the left hemisphere, which contains important language centers (Galaburda et al., 1985). The fact that these cellular abnormalities could occur only during the fifth to seventh months of fetal development strengthened the view that learning disorders evolve from subtle brain deficits present at birth (Lyon et al., 2003). Initial autopsy findings were confirmed by sophisticated brain imaging technology that reveals the brain directly at work and makes it possible to detect subtle malfunctions that never could be seen before.

The suspected deficits, which likely are genetically based, involve specific discrimination tasks, such as detecting visual and auditory stimuli, as well as more pervasive visual–organizational deficits associated with reasoning and mathematical ability (Benassi et al., 2010; Pennington, 2006). A probable location of these deficits is a structure called the "planum temporale," a language-related area in both sides of the brain. In a normal brain, the left side of the planum temporale is usually larger than the right side; however, in the brain of an individual with a reading disorder, the two sides are equal (Tallal, 2003).

B. A. Shaywitz et al. (2002) found lower activation in numerous sites—primarily the left hemisphere of the brains of dyslexic children as compared with non-impaired children—including the inferior frontal, parietotemporal, and occipitotemporal gyri. These three areas of the brain are responsible for understanding phonemes, analyzing words, and automatically detecting words, respectively. Once a word is learned, this three-part center recognizes it automatically, without first having to decipher it phonetically (S. E. Shaywitz & Shaywitz, 2013).

From a cognitive standpoint, these neurological findings suggest that children with learning disorders are distinctively disadvantaged as compared with average readers in terms of the processing underlying their short-term and working memory. Impairments in short-term memory affect the recall of phonemes

Primary auditory cortex

Auditory association area

Temporal lobe

How the brain processes speech

1 The primary auditory cortex (shown in red), which is located on the top edge of each temporal lobe, receives electrical signals from receptors in the ears and transforms these signals into meaningless sound sensations, such as vowels and the consonants in *ba* and *ga*.

2 The meaningless sound sensations are sent from the primary auditory cortex to another area in the temporal lobe, called the auditory association area.

3 The auditory association area (shown in blue), which is located directly below the primary auditory cortex, transforms basic sensory information, such as noises or sounds, into recognizable auditory information, such as words or music. Here, sounds are matched with existing patterns that have been previously formed and stored.

● **FIGURE 7.5** | How the brain processes speech.

From Plotnik/Kouyoumdjian. *Introduction to Psychology*, 9E. © 2011 Wadsworth, a part of Cengage Learning, Inc. Reproduced by permission. www.cengage.com/permissions.

and numbers; similarly, impairments in working memory affect how such information is processed and stored so that it can be rapidly accessed. Considerable support now exists concerning how memory deficits explain the performance difficulties of children with a learning disorder (Carretti et al., 2009; Maehler & Schuchardt, 2011; Swanson, Zheng, & Jerman, 2009).

We have stressed that most children with reading and writing disorders have difficulty distinguishing phonemes that occur rapidly in speech. But why is this so? Consider what is involved, as shown in ● Figure 7.5. The sound must be processed by various brain areas as it is carried by nerve impulses from the ear to the thalamus to the nerve cells within the auditory cortex, where it is matched to existing patterns, or phonic bins, that have been previously formed and stored.

Compare this process to listening to music. When you first hear a new song, do you recognize aspects that resemble other recordings by that group or another group? Can you distinguish the music of one group from another? As we listen, we tend to cluster sounds into various categories, acquiring our taste for music as we store more collections and melodies into memory. Each time we hear new music, we match it to what we already know and appreciate. Young people are particularly adept at assimilating new sounds, thereby broadening their tastes. In contrast, people who have already formed specific musical tastes tend to stick to what they know, rejecting unrecognizable sounds. This gap in music appreciation is analogous to the gap researchers describe in the phonic abilities of children with learning disorders—they lack certain auditory sites that allow certain sounds to be recognized, so their appreciation of certain words is compromised.

Each neuron in the language-processing areas of the brain has immense specificity. Some neurons fire when you silently name an object but not when you read the object's name out loud, and vice versa. Certain neurons are activated when bilingual people speak one language, but not when they speak the other (Ojemann, 1991). Someone can have an expressive language problem despite full comprehension, because the same neurons that are active when a person hears a word are not active when that person speaks it.

In the visual system, different aspects of what you see, such as form, color, and motion, are routed to different regions of the visual cortex. When something moves in your visual field, the region of the cortex that responds to visual motion is activated. Eden et al. (1996) first discovered that adults with reading disorders show no activation in visual motion when asked to view randomly moving dots. A specific defect in the perception of visual motion may interfere with many different brain functions, and it has been noted among children with autism as well as those with learning disorders (Benassi et al., 2010; Skottun & Skoyles, 2008). To detect differences between consonant sounds—such as *b* and *t*—we must be able to distinguish between very rapid changes in sound frequency. A subtle neurological deficit in sensitivity could prohibit this distinction, which would then show up clinically as problems in reading and phonological processing (Raschle et al., 2011).

Thus, two major findings implicate specific biological underpinnings of reading disorders: (1) language difficulties for people with reading disorders are specifically associated with the neurological processing of phonology and storage of such information into memory; and (2) behavioral and physiological abnormalities are found in the processing of visual information. It is not surprising, therefore, that phonological and visual processing problems often coexist among people with reading disorders (Skottun & Skoyles, 2008).

Studies of the causes of SLD mostly involve children with reading disorders, but the findings apply to disorders in written expression and mathematics as well. Many—but not all—disabled writers show deficits in reading (Lyon et al., 2003), and some mathematical concepts require reading and writing as well as mathematics skills. Similar to how deficits in phonological awareness underlie SLD with reading impairment, certain cognitive deficits involving concepts of numbers appear to underlie SLD with impairment in mathematics (Geary, 2013). For instance, if you show small sets of dots, usually up to four dots per set, to typically developing children they can tell you instantly (i.e., without counting the items) how many items are in each set, a process known as *subitizing*. But children with SLD with impairments in mathematics appear to have trouble subitizing even three items, suggesting a deficit in their rapid visual processing of enumeration concepts (Ashkenazi, Mark-Zigdon, & Henik, 2013). Similarly, most children can

quickly say which of two numbers is larger (e.g., "13" vs. "31"), but students with mathematics disorder are slower and less accurate than their peers at doing so (Rousselle & Noël, 2007).

Recall that Francine had well-developed word recognition and spelling abilities, but significantly worse mechanical–arithmetic skills. SLD with impairment in mathematics, and perhaps SLD with impairment in written expression as well, are associated with brain deficits that differ from those described for language-based learning disorders. These deficits are largely found in areas not related to verbal ability, which has led to the term nonverbal learning disability. **Nonverbal learning disability** (NLD) is associated with deficits related to right-hemisphere brain functioning, which are characteristic of children who perform considerably worse at math than reading. These deficits involve social/emotional skills, spatial orientation, problem solving, and the recognition of nonverbal cues such as body language (Hulme & Snowling, 2009). In addition to math deficiencies, NLD may be accompanied by neuropsychological problems such as poor coordination, poor judgment, and difficulties adapting to novel and complex situations (Lyon et al., 2003; Semrud-Clikeman et al., 2010). To date, the unique aspects of NLD remain unconfirmed. Critics argue that it may simply be a form of SLD with impairment in mathematics (Fine et al., 2013; Spreen, 2011).

Social and Psychological Factors

Emotional and behavioral disturbances and other signs of poor adaptive ability often accompany SLD. This is no surprise, because children with one neurodevelopmental disorder (i.e., communication disorder, SLD, ADHD, or intellectual disability) are about 40% more likely to have another neurodevelopmental disorder, most likely because of shared etiological factors (Gooch et al., 2013). The overlap between SLD with impairment in reading and ADHD, for example, ranges from 30% to 70% depending on how ADHD is defined (Del'Homme et al., 2007; Fletcher, Shaywitz, & Shaywitz, 1999). Although this degree of overlap suggests that behavioral and learning problems have certain common aspects, they are still distinct and separate disorders (Lyon et al., 2006). SLD is commonly associated with deficits in phonological awareness, whereas ADHD has more variable effects on cognitive functioning, especially in areas of rote verbal learning and memory (Jakobson & Kikas, 2007). ADHD, moreover, is relatively unrelated to phonological awareness tasks. However, some children with SLD show symptoms similar to those of ADHD, including inattention, restlessness, and hyperactivity (Del'Homme et al., 2007).

Prevention and Treatment

What can be expected of Francine, James, Tim, and Carlos during their school years and beyond? Proper planning and goal setting are the cornerstones of the helping strategies for home and for school. Specific learning disorders are not usually outgrown, but there is reason for optimism if educational planning and accommodations are ongoing (Beitchman & Brownlie, 2014).

Although SLD has strong biological underpinnings, intervention methods rely primarily on educational and psychosocial methods. Psychosocial treatments for James, Francine, Carlos, and Tim must be comprehensive and ongoing, with each new task broken down into manageable steps, including examples, practice, and ample feedback. Combined with proper teaching strategies, children and their families may benefit from counseling aimed at helping the children develop greater self-control and a more positive attitude toward their own abilities. Support groups for parents also can fill an important gap between the school and the home by providing information, practical suggestions, and mutual understanding.

Someday, breakthroughs in brain research may lead to new medical interventions, but at present no biological treatments exist for speech, language, and academic disabilities. In cases in which significant problems coexist in concentration and attention, some children respond favorably to stimulant medications that may temporarily improve attention, concentration, and the ability to control their impulsivity, albeit with little or no improvement in learning. Typically, the medication schedule ensures that the drug is active during peak school hours, when reading and math are taught.

Francine's problems in making friends were a major concern to everyone, and we believed that they were directly linked to her learning disability. A cognitive–behavioral intervention plan was developed in conjunction with her educational program. Because of Francine's strong verbal skills, we taught her to problem solve through role playing, and encouraged her mother to invite one child at a time for her to play with so that she could practice her skills. Francine had drifted into being a loner and seemed disinterested in looking after herself, so we also discussed ways to develop better self-care at home by giving her an allowance for completing household chores. We spent considerable time explaining the nature of her problems to her parents, and this guidance led to relief and understanding.

We saw the family once again one year later; although some of Francine's problems still existed, her social abilities had improved. She still had difficulties in developing friendships and tended to prefer being alone, but the problem had clearly lessened from the previous year. (Based on authors' case material.)

Consider the coordinated planning and effort that went into the treatment programs for Francine: Francine was able to get help because her problems were detected; recall, however, that by the time she was referred, she had already begun to fail at formal schooling. The first step in solving any problem is to realize that it exists. The nature of learning disorders makes this difficult for many children and parents. Although numerous signs of language-based learning disorders are present from early childhood, sophisticated means of assessing problems are not yet available before children are old enough to be formally tested.

FRANCINE

Slowly but Surely Improving

To reduce Francine's difficulties with math and, especially, with peer relationships, we considered several factors. First, we decided that teaching should be primarily verbal, with an understanding that she would have the most difficulty in math and science. Her teachers favored allowing Francine to use a calculator and a computer to assist her in learning new concepts. An emphasis on physical education was also planned, to help her with her visual–motor coordination. Her math teacher agreed that using graph paper might help her visualize numerical relationships, which led to noticeable improvements in her schoolwork.

Phanie/Science Source

Treatment of specific learning disabilities usually begins with a careful assessment of a child's abilities.

Issues of identification are important because a brief window of opportunity may exist for successful treatment. If a problem is detected in early childhood—say, by kindergarten—then language-based deficits can often be remediated successfully. If the problem is not detected until age 8 or so, the rates of response to treatment are much lower (Hatcher et al., 2006). This is why prevention of reading difficulties is a hot topic: Training children in phonological awareness activities at an early age may prevent subsequent reading problems among children at risk (Duff & Clarke, 2011; Snowling & Hulme, 2012). These activities involve games of listening, rhyming, identifying sentences and words, and analyzing syllables and phonemes. For example, the child might analyze *sand* as *s-and* and then synthesize it into *sand,* or colored alphabet blocks might be used to break the word into separate phonetic sounds (*s-a-n-d*).

Knowledge of communication and learning disorders has played leapfrog with the philosophy and practice of classroom instruction during the past decade. Discoveries in neurosciences, as noted above, challenged some prevailing educational practices, leading to more systematic ways of assisting children with learning disorders, as explored in the following sections.

The Inclusion Movement

Integrating children with special needs into the regular classroom began as the *inclusion movement* during the 1950s, based on studies showing that segregated classes for students with disabilities were ineffective and possibly harmful (Baldwin, 1958). Resource rooms and specially trained teachers replaced the special classes that had been in vogue, a change that had the further advantage of removing the need to label and categorize children. The Education for All Handicapped Children Act of 1975 in the United States (currently known as Individuals with Disabilities Education Improvement Act [IDEA], 2004) and the provincial Education Acts in Canada mandate that children with special needs must be afforded access to all educational services, regardless of their handicaps. Today, children with special educational needs in the United States, Canada, and many other countries are placed in regular classrooms whenever possible.

In 2002, the No Child Left Behind Act was signed into law in the United States. This act allowed for more intensified efforts by each state to improve the academic achievement of public school students considered at risk for school failure. Today, almost 14% (about 6.6 million) of school-age children in the United States from all walks of life receive some level of support through special education, and students with specific learning disabilities account for close to half of these students (National Center for Educational Statistics (2012).

Response to Intervention Models

IDEA provides for the use of response to intervention (RTI) models to identify and assess children. RTI consists of tiered instruction, in which children who have difficulty learning to read using typical methods of instruction are provided with small-group, intensive instruction. Those who need additional intervention may receive one-on-one special education. This approach seeks to provide each child with the appropriate level of instruction required for his or her individual needs (National Institutes of Health, 2007).

Initiatives to allow children with special needs to receive services without being diagnosed or labeled as intellectually disabled, learning disabled, and so forth have become widely available and hold considerable promise. However, implementation and teacher training, as well as the question of whether such initiatives succeed in meeting the special needs of students, continue to be unresolved (Lovett & Lewandowski, in 2014).

Instructional Methods

Although controversy remains over the practical aspects of including all children in regular classrooms, most educators today favor direct instruction for children with learning disorders. **Direct instruction** is a straightforward approach to teaching based on the premise that to improve a skill, the instructional activities must approximate those of the skill being taught (see example in A Closer Look 7.2) (Hammill et al., 2002). Direct instruction in word structure is necessary because of the child's phonological deficits. Direct instruction in reading emphasizes the specific learning of word structure and word reading until the skill is learned, without concern for the full context of the sentence or story. This method is based on the premise that a child's ability to decode and recognize

---

A CLOSER **LOOK** 7.2

Steps in Direct Behavioral Instruction

1. Review the child's existing abilities.
2. Develop a short statement of goals at the beginning of each lesson.
3. Present new concepts and material in small steps, each followed by student practice.
4. Provide clear and detailed instructions and explanations.
5. Provide considerable practice for all students.

6. Check student understanding of concepts continually, in response to teacher questions.
7. Provide explicit guidance for each student during initial practice.
8. Provide systematic feedback and corrections.
9. Provide explicit instruction and practice for exercises completed by students at their desks.

Source: From Treatment of Learning Disabilities by G. R. Lyons and L. Cutting, 1998. In E. J. Mash and L. C. Terdal (Eds.), Treatment of Childhood Disorders.

The following example illustrates how the steps in direct behavioral instruction are applied.

Example: Direct Instruction Lesson

A typical DI lesson includes explicit and carefully sequenced instruction provided by the teacher (model) along with frequent opportunities for students to practice their skills (independent practice) over time (review). For example, if the sound /m/ appeared for the first time, the teacher might say, "You're going to learn a new sound. My turn to say it. When I move under the letter, I'll say the sound. I'll keep on saying it as long as I touch under it. Get ready. mmm" (model). "My turn again. Get ready. mmm" (model). "Your turn. When I move under the letter, you say the sound. Keep on saying it as long as I touch under it. Get ready." (independent practice). "Again. Get ready." (independent practice). If an error occurs during instruction, the teacher would model the sound ("My turn. mmm"), use guided practice ("Say it with me. Get ready. mmm"), and have students practice independently ("Your turn. Get ready"). A "starting over" would be conducted based on this error; this might include starting over at the top of a column or row of sounds so that students get increased practice on the /m/ sound. The /m/ would appear throughout the lesson and in subsequent lessons to ensure skill mastery (firm responding) over time.

Source: Marchand-Martella, Martella, & Ausdemore (2005). An Overview of Direct Instruction.

words accurately and rapidly must be acquired before reading comprehension can occur (Hammill et al., 2002; Haager, Klinger, & Vaughn, 2007).

To prevent dyslexia, it is important to provide early interventions that teach both phonological and verbal abilities. Children must be able to learn the sounds of words to decode them, but they must also understand the meaning of a word to understand the message of the text (S. E. Shaywitz & Shaywitz, 2013). The techniques that have been demonstrated to work are practicing manipulating phonemes, building vocabulary, increasing comprehension, and improving fluency, which helps strengthen the brain's ability to link letters to sounds (Nation et al., 2007).

In brief, the components of effective reading instruction are the same whether the focus is prevention or intervention—phonemic awareness and phonemic decoding skills, fluency in word recognition, construction

of meaning, vocabulary, spelling, and writing (Snowling & Hulme, 2012). Evidence-based evaluations show dramatic reductions in the incidence of reading failure when direct and explicit instruction in these components is provided by the classroom teacher (Duff & Clarke, 2011; Haager et al., 2007; Schuele & Boudreau, 2008). Empirical support for teaching phonics from an early age also is emerging from brain imaging studies. For example, instruction in phonemic awareness, phonics, and other reading skills produces more activation in the automatic recognition process, noted previously (see section on "Causes," above). After undergoing such training, brain scans of people who were once poor readers begin to resemble those of good readers (National Institutes of Health, 2007).

We now turn to some practical examples of how reading, writing, and math can be taught by applying well-established principles of learning. Behavioral and cognitive–behavioral strategies have been highly beneficial in remediating the problems of children and adolescents with communication and learning disorders (Lyon et al., 2006). In addition, new methods based on the use of technology offer some children additional ways to acquire basic and advanced academic skills.

Behavioral Strategies

Many problems that children with communication and learning disorders have stem from the fact that the material is simply presented too fast for them (Tallal & Benasich, 2002). Thus, a strategy to provide children with a set of verbal rules that can be written out and reapplied may be more beneficial than one that relies on memory or on grasping the concept all at once. Tried-and-true behavioral principles of learning are well suited to this task of teaching systematically.

In addition to academic concepts, some of the associated problems with peers can be addressed in the same fashion, as we saw with Francine. A simple, gradual approach is more beneficial than an approach that tries to solve the problem all at once. Children also need help learning to generalize new information to different situations. An individualized, skills-based approach does not have to be boring or routine; in fact, speech and language therapists are skilled at providing a stimulating but structured environment for hearing and practicing language patterns. During an engaging activity with a younger child, the therapist may talk about toys and then encourage the child to use the same sounds or words. The child may watch the therapist make the sound, feel the vibration in the therapist's throat, and then practice making the sounds himself or herself in front of a mirror.

Behavioral methods often are used in conjunction with a complete program of direct instruction, which typically proceeds in a cumulative, highly structured manner (Wright & Jacobs, 2003), as shown in A Closer Look 7.2. Because this method places a strong emphasis on the behavior of the teacher in terms of explicit correction, reinforcement, and practice opportunities, it is sometimes referred to as "faultless instruction": Each concept should be so clearly presented that only one interpretation is possible. Each lesson is structured according to field-tested scripts. Teachers work with one small group of students at a time, and shoot questions at them at a rate as high as 10 to 12 per minute.

This highly structured, repetitive method is clearly effective. Students who receive direct behavioral instruction typically outperform students who receive standard classroom instruction by almost 1 standard deviation on various learning measures (Lyon et al., 2003).

Cognitive–Behavioral Interventions

Cognitive–behavioral interventions are also highly suited for children with communication and learning disorders. Like behavioral methods, these procedures actively involve students in learning, particularly in monitoring their own thought processes. Considerable emphasis is placed on self-control by using strategies such as self-monitoring, self-assessment, self-recording, self-management of reinforcement, and so on (Alwell & Cobb, 2009; Cobb et al., 2006). Essentially, children are taught to ask themselves several questions as they progress, to make themselves more aware of the material. Try it yourself: "Why am I reading this? What's the main idea the authors are trying to get across? Where can I find the answer to this question? How does this follow from what I learned a minute ago?"

Carlos's treatment program shows how some of these procedures were applied to his particular writing problems:

CARLOS

Plans

In third grade, Carlos's treatment plan was to integrate a cognitive–behavioral approach into regular teaching methods. Rather than using one-to-one instruction, I discussed with his teacher ways of blending some behavioral methods into the classroom. For example, his strengths are in the areas of thinking and speaking, so I discussed using computers and tape recorders to help him learn the materials. He seemed to like these

methods, and they helped him bypass some aspects of his writing disability. I discussed practice strategies for visual–motor integration, such as drawing and tracing and gradually made the task more complex. Because cursive writing is often easier for children than printing, I suggested that Carlos bypass learning to print. A continuous pattern of output is easier for Carlos to plan and produce than a discrete form of output, such as printing.

To help Carlos write a paper, I adopted a basic planning strategy from Graham, MacArthur, Schwatz, and Voth (1992), which helped him structure the tasks into related subproblems. The acronym PLANS helps him to remember to:

Pick goals (related to length, structure, and purpose of the paper)
List ways to meet goals
And
make Notes
Sequence notes

This mnemonic was used in a three-step writing strategy to assist Carlos to: (1) do PLANS, (2) write and say more, and (3) evaluate whether he is successful in achieving his goals. (Based on authors' case material.)

Computer-Assisted Learning

Studies have shown that a similar level of efficacy in phonetic ability can be achieved by teachers as by clinicians (Duff & Clarke, 2011), which has led to a growing number of computer and Internet training programs. One problem in reading instruction is maintaining a balance between the basic, but dull, word decoding and the complex, but engaging, text comprehension. Not all the issues have been resolved, but computer-assisted methods for spelling, reading, and math provide more academic engagement and achievement than traditional pencil-and-paper methods.

Computers have been used as simple instructional tools to deliver questions and answers since the 1970s. Since discovering phonological awareness and timing problems in the brain, researchers are now testing whether computers can remedy some basic auditory problems. Some children with communication and learning disorders are unable to process information that flashes by too quickly, such as the consonant sounds *ba* and *da*, and this deficit interferes with vital speech processes. Computer programs are able to slow down these grammatical sounds, allowing young children to process them more slowly and carefully (Loo et al., 2010; Gaab et al., 2007; Palmer, Enderby, & Hawley, 2007).

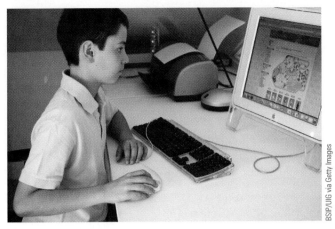

New research raises cautious hope that computer games and exercises can help children with learning disabilities develop key mental skills.

to ensure competency. As they progress, they should practice more and more reading that is contextualized. Reading materials should have controlled vocabularies that contain mostly words the children can decode. As children develop a core sight vocabulary, introduce only those irregular words that can be read with high accuracy. Guessing is counterproductive.

5. *Teach for automaticity.* Once basic decoding is mastered, children must be exposed to words often enough that they become automatically accessible. This usually requires a great deal of practice, which should be as pleasant and rewarding as possible.

Source: From Rebecca H. Felton, Effects of Instruction on the Decoding Skills of Children with Phonological-Processing Problems, Journal of Learning Disabilities, 26, 583–589

Whether taught by computers, teachers, or both, studies of interventions for learning disorders indicate that successful approaches typically include explicit instruction in phonemic awareness and phonemic decoding. These interventions also provide students with practice reading text and comprehending what they read, with ample assistance and almost daily sessions (Torgesen et al., 2010).

In summary, treatment methods for communication and learning disorders are varied and beneficial. A Closer Look 7.3 reviews some of the basic elements of a successful beginning reading program, elements that apply to other disabilities as well. For children with reading disorders to learn how to read, they must receive a balanced intervention program composed of direct and explicit instruction in phonemic awareness, a systematic way to generalize this learning to the learning of sound–symbol relationships (phonics), and many opportunities to practice these coding skills by reading meaningful, interesting, and controlled texts. The sooner this intervention occurs in schools, the better (Haager et al., 2007).

A CLOSER **LOOK** 7.3

Critical Elements for a Successful Beginning Reading Program

1. *Provide direct instruction in language analysis.* Identify at-risk children early in their school careers—preferably in kindergarten—and teach phonological awareness skills directly.

2. *Provide direct teaching of the alphabetic code.* Code instruction should be structured and systematic, in a sequence that goes from simple to more complex. Teach the regularities of the English language before introducing the irregularities. Nothing should be left to guesswork—be as explicit as possible. Teach a child who is overly reliant on letter-by-letter decoding to process larger and larger chunks of words.

3. *Teach reading and spelling in coordination.* Children should learn to spell the words they are reading correctly.

4. *Provide intensive reading instruction.* Children may need 3 or more years of direct instruction in basic reading skills

Section Summary

Specific Learning Disorder

- Specific learning disorder (SLD) includes problems in reading, mathematics, or writing ability, with reading disorders being the most common. Mathematics and writing disorders overlap considerably with reading disorders.

- Although SLD overlaps with behavioral disorders, they are distinct problems. Opportunities to develop and use particular strengths lead to more successful adult outcomes.

- SLD in reading may be caused by phonological problems that arise from physiological abnormalities in the processing of visual information in the brain. These deficits are believed to be largely inherited.

- Treatments for children with communication and learning disorders involve educational strategies that capitalize on existing strengths, and behavioral strategies involving direct instruction.

- Cognitive–behavioral techniques and computer-assisted instruction are also used successfully.

Study Resources

SECTION SUMMARIES

KEY TERMS

PRELIMINARY EDITION

8

Attention-Deficit/Hyperactivity Disorder (ADHD)

ADHD is not a problem with knowing what to do; it is a problem with doing what you know.

—Russell A. Barkley (2006a)

DESCRIPTION AND HISTORY

WE BEGIN OUR DISCUSSION of attention-deficit/hyperactivity disorder (ADHD) with a description of the primary symptoms and behaviors of children with this disorder. We then consider the different views of ADHD that have been presented since it was first described as a disorder more than 200 years ago.

JOHN

Inattentive, Hyperactive, Impulsive

John is a 7-year-old whose mother is desperate for help. "He walked at 10 months and has kept me running ever since. As a child he was always bouncing around the house and crashing into things. He's in constant motion, impulsive, and never listens. When I ask him to put his shirt in the hamper, I find him playing, his shirt still on the floor. John has no routines and seldom sleeps. Discipline doesn't work, nor do the techniques that work for my other boys. He's oblivious to his behavior. He never finishes anything, and except for sitting down to play a video game, rarely watches TV except on the run."

John's teacher says his main problems in school are staying on task and keeping track of what's happening. "He blurts things out in class and is constantly fidgeting or out of his chair," she says. Although John can complete his assignments, he forgets to bring home the book he needs to do his homework. When he does complete his homework, he forgets to put it in his backpack or to hand it in. John has great difficulty waiting his turn or following rules with other children. Other kids think he's weird and don't want to play with him. John's parents are demoralized and don't know what to do.

From *The Hyperactive Child Book*, by Patricia Kennedy, Leif Terdal, and Lydia Fusetti, pp. 8–9. New York: St. Martin's Press.

Description

Attention-deficit/hyperactivity disorder (ADHD) describes children who, like John, display persistent age-inappropriate symptoms of inattention, hyperactivity, and impulsivity that are sufficient to cause impairment in major life activities (APA, 2013).

The term *ADHD* may be new, but children who display overactive and unrestrained behaviors have been around for some time. In 1845, Heinrich Hoffmann, a German neurologist, wrote in a child's storybook one of the first known accounts of hyperactivity. His humorous poem described the mealtime antics of a child aptly named "Fidgety Phil," who "won't sit still; / He wriggles, / And jiggles," and "swings backwards and

Fidgety Phil, 1845, and Dusty N., 1994: Mealtimes are an especially trying time for children with ADHD and their parents

forwards, / And tilts up his chair." When his chair falls, Philip screams and grabs the tablecloth, and "Down upon the ground they fall, / Glasses, plates, knives, forks, and all" (Hoffmann, 1845).

More recently, a compelling article about ADHD titled "Life in Overdrive" described the behavior of 7-year old Dusty N.:

Dusty awoke at 5:00 one recent morning in his Chicago home. Every muscle in his 50-pound body flew in furious motion as he headed downstairs for breakfast. After pulling a box of cereal from the cupboard, Dusty started grabbing cereal with his hands and kicking the box, scattering the cereal across the room. Next he began peeling the decorative paper covering off the TV table. Then he started stomping the spilled cereal to bits. After dismantling the plastic dustpan he had gotten to clean up the cereal, he moved on to his next project: grabbing three rolls of toilet paper from the bathroom and unraveling them around the house. (Adapted from *Time*, July 18, 1994, p. 43)

Although the accounts of Phil and Dusty N. are separated by almost 150 years, the mealtime behaviors of both boys typify the primary symptoms of ADHD. The boys are **inattentive**, not focusing on mealtime demands and behaving carelessly; **hyperactive**, constantly in motion; and **impulsive**, acting without thinking.

ADHD has no distinct physical symptoms that can be seen in an x-ray or a lab test. It can only be identified by characteristic behaviors that vary considerably from child to child. As we shall discuss, ADHD has become a blanket term used to describe several different patterns of behavior that likely have different causes.

The behavior of children with ADHD is puzzling and full of contradictions. Rash and disorganized behaviors are a constant source of stress for the child and for parents, siblings, teachers, and classmates. Why can't he sit still? Why can't she ever get anything done? Why does he make so many careless mistakes? Nothing seems physically wrong with the child, and at certain times or in some situations the child with ADHD seems fine. Such inconsistencies may cause others to think the child could do better if only she tried harder or if her parents or teachers would set firmer limits. However, increased effort and stricter rules usually don't help, because most children with ADHD are already trying hard. They want to do well but are constantly thwarted by their limited self-control. As a result, they experience the hurt, confusion, and sadness of being blamed for not paying attention or being called names like "space cadet." They may be scolded, put down, or even spanked for failing to complete homework or chores. Unfortunately, they may not know why things went wrong or how they might have done things differently.

Feelings of frustration, being different, not fitting in, and hopelessness may overwhelm a child with ADHD (Young et al., 2008). For example, David says: "I got no friends cause I don't play good and when they call me Dope Freak and David Dopey I cry, I just can't help it" (Ross & Ross, 1982). Such comments leave little doubt that ADHD can severely disrupt an individual's life, consume vast amounts of energy, produce emotional pain, damage self-esteem, and seriously disrupt relationships. In addition to the individual's personal suffering and exposure to stigmatizing attitudes by others (Lebowitz, 2013), the societal costs of ADHD in youth are also high, with an estimated cost of $38 billion to $72 billion a year in the United States, the highest costs related to health care and education. Estimated costs for adults with ADHD, which take productivity and income losses into account, are nearly two to three times higher than for young people. These estimates, along with the additional billions in spillover costs borne by family members of individuals with ADHD, indicate that the economic impact of ADHD across the lifespan for individuals with ADHD in the United States is considerable (Doshi et al., 2012).

History

The symptoms of ADHD were first described in a 1775 medical textbook by the German physician, Melchior Adam Weikard (Barkley & Peters, 2012). Since then there have been numerous explanations for the troublesome behaviors of ADHD (Barkley, 2014e). In 1798, a Scottish-born physician, Sir Alexander Crichton described a syndrome similar to ADHD that included early onset, restlessness, inattention, and poor school performance. These individuals described themselves as having "the fidgets," and displayed a severe problem attending no matter how hard they tried (Palmer & Finger, 2001). Symptoms of overactivity and inattention were described as a disorder in 1902 by the English physician George Still (what a coincidence!), who believed that the symptoms arose out of poor "inhibitory volition" and "defective moral control" (see ● Figure 8.1). In the early 1900s, the onset of widespread compulsory education demanded self-controlled behavior in a group setting, which further focused attention on children with the symptoms of ADHD.

Another view of ADHD arose from the worldwide influenza epidemic from 1917 to 1926. A number of children who had developed encephalitis (brain inflammation) and survived experienced multiple behavior problems, including irritability, impaired attention, and hyperactivity. These children and others who had suffered birth trauma, head injury, or exposure to toxins displayed behavior problems that were labeled *brain-injured child syndrome*, which was associated with intellectual disability. In the 1940s and 1950s, this label was then erroneously applied to children displaying similar behaviors, but with no evidence of brain damage or intellectual disability, and led to the terms *minimal brain damage* and *minimal brain dysfunction (MBD)* (Strauss & Lehtinen, 1947). These terms provided a convenient way to attribute behavior problems to a physical cause. Although certain head injuries can explain some cases of ADHD, the brain damage theory was eventually rejected because it did not explain the majority of cases (Rie, 1980).

In the late 1950s, ADHD was referred to as *hyperkinesis*, which was attributed to poor filtering of stimuli

The Goulstonian Lectures

ON

SOME ABNORMAL PSYCHICAL CONDITIONS
IN CHILDREN.

*Delivered before the Royal College of Physicians of
London on March 4th, 6th, and 11th, 1902,*

BY GEORGE F. STILL, M.A., M.D. CANTAB.,
F.R.C.P. LOND.,

ASSISTANT PHYSICIAN FOR DISEASES OF CHILDREN, KING'S
COLLEGE HOSPITAL; ASSISTANT PHYSICIAN TO THE
HOSPITAL FOR SICK CHILDREN, GREAT
ORMOND-STREET.

———

LECTURE II.

Delivered on March 6th.

———

MR. PRESIDENT AND GENTLEMEN,——In my first lecture I drew your attention to some points in the psychology and development of moral control in the normal child and then considered the occurrence of defective moral control in association with general impairment of intellect; before going further it may be well to review briefly the points which have been raised. Moral control, we saw, is dependent upon three psychical factors, a cognitive relation to environment, moral consciousness, and volition, which in this connexion might be regarded as inhibitory volition. Moral control, therefore, is not present at birth, but under normal psychical conditions is gradually developed as the child grows older. The variation in the degree of moral control which is shown by different children at the same age and under apparently similar conditions of training and environment suggested that the innate capacity for the development of such control might also vary in different individuals.

Courtesy of The Lancet, April 19, 1902.

● **FIGURE 8.1** | English physician George Still was one of the first to describe the symptoms of ADHD.

entering the brain (Laufer, Denhoff, & Solomons, 1957). This view led to the definition of the *hyperactive child syndrome,* in which motor overactivity was considered the main feature of ADHD (Chess, 1960). However, it was soon realized that hyperactivity was not the only problem; there was also the child's failure to regulate motor activity in relation to situational demands.

In the 1970s, it was argued that in addition to hyperactivity, deficits in attention and impulse control were also primary symptoms of ADHD (Douglas, 1972). This view was widely accepted and has had a lasting impact on the criteria of the *Diagnostic and Statistical Manual of Mental Disorders* (DSM) for defining ADHD. In the 1980s, interest in children with ADHD increased dramatically, and the sharp rise in the use of stimulants generated controversy

that continues to this day (Mayes & Rafalovich, 2007).

More recently, in addition to inattention and hyperactivity–impulsivity, the problems of poor self-regulation, difficulty in inhibiting behavior, and reward and motivational deficits have been emphasized as central impairments of the disorder (Nigg, Hinshaw, & Huang-Pollack, 2006). Increasingly, "multipathway models" have emerged that include both attention-related and motivation-related theories. These models propose different pathways to ADHD with different neural substrates, meaning that different children with ADHD may have different reasons for their behavior (Nigg & Barkley, 2014). Although there is growing agreement about the nature of ADHD, views continue to evolve as a result of new findings and discoveries. As you will learn, despite the label for this disorder, the main difficulties in ADHD are far more complex than simply a deficit in attention (Nigg & Barkley, 2014).

Section Summary

Description and History

- Attention-deficit/hyperactivity disorder (ADHD) is manifested in children who display persistent age-inappropriate symptoms of inattention, hyperactivity, and impulsivity that cause impairment in major life activities.

- ADHD can only be identified by characteristic patterns of behavior, which vary quite a bit from child to child.

- The behavior of children with ADHD is a constant source of stress and frustration for the child and for parents, siblings, teachers, and classmates; it also has high costs to society.

- The disorder that we now call ADHD has had many different names, primary symptoms, and presumed causes, and views of the disorder are still evolving.

CORE CHARACTERISTICS

ADHD is included in DSM-5 as a *neurodevelopmental disorder* because it has an early onset and persistent course, is associated with lasting alterations in neural development, and is often accompanied by subtle delays and problems in language, motor, and social development that overlap with other neurodevelopmental disorders such as autism spectrum disorder (ASD) and specific learning disorder (APA, 2013). Experts developed the DSM-5 criteria for ADHD after reviewing research, re-analyzing data, conducting field trials with children throughout North America, and receiving several rounds of public feedback (APA, 2013). Table 8.1

(A) A persistent pattern of inattention and/or hyperactivity-impulsivity that interferes with functioning or development, as characterized by (1) and/or (2): `DSM-5`

  (1) Inattention: Six (or more) of the following symptoms have persisted for at least 6 months to a degree that is inconsistent with developmental level and that negatively impacts directly on social and academic/occupational activities:

  Note: The symptoms are not solely the manifestation of oppositional behavior, defiance, hostility, or failure to understand tasks or instructions. For older adolescents and adults (age 17 and older), at least five symptoms are required.

   (a) Often fails to give close attention to details or makes careless mistakes in schoolwork, at work, or during other activities (e.g., overlooks of misses details, work is inaccurate).

   (b) Often has difficulty sustaining attention in tasks or play activities (e.g., has difficulty remaining focused during lectures, conversations, or lengthy reading).

   (c) Often does not seem to listen when spoken to directly (e.g., mind seems elsewhere, even in the absence of any obvious distraction).

   (d) Often does not follow through on instructions and fails to finish schoolwork, chores, or duties in the workplace (e.g., starts tasks but quickly loses focus and is easily sidetracked).

   (e) Often has difficulty organizing tasks and activities (e.g., difficulty managing sequential tasks: difficulty keeping materials and belongings in order; messy, disorganized work; has poor time management; fails to meet deadlines).

   (f) Often avoids, dislikes, or is reluctant to engage in tasks that require sustained mental effort (e.g., schoolwork or homework; for older adolescents and adults, preparing reports, completing forms, reviewing lengthy papers).

   (g) Often loses things necessary for tasks or activities (e.g., school materials, pencils, books, tools, wallets, keys, paperwork, eyeglasses, mobile telephones).

   (h) Is often easily distracted by extraneous stimuli (for older adolescents and adults, may include unrelated thoughts).

   (i) Is often forgetful in daily activities (e.g., doing chores, running errands; for older adolescents and adults, returning calls, paying bills, keeping appointments).

  (2) Hyperactivity and Impulsivity: Six (or more) of the following symptoms have persisted for at least 6 months to a degree that is inconsistent with developmental level and that negatively impacts directly on social and academic/occupational activities:

  Note: The symptoms are not solely a manifestation of oppositional behavior, defiance, hostility, or a failure to understand tasks or instructions. For older adolescents and adults (age 17 or older), at least five symptoms are required.

   (a) Often fidgets with or taps hands or feet or squirms in seat.

   (b) Often leaves seat in situations when remaining seated is expected (e.g., leaves his or her place in the classroom, in the office or other workplace, or in other situations that require remaining in place).

   (c) Often runs about or climbs in situations where it is inappropriate

  Note: In adolescents or adults, may be limited to feeling restless.

   (d) Often unable to play or engage in leisure activities quietly.

   (e) Is often "on the go," acting as if "driven by a motor" (e.g., is unable to be or is uncomfortable being still for extended time, as in restaurants, meetings; may be seen by others as being restless or difficult to keep up with).

   (f) Often talks excessively.

   (g) Often blurts out answers before a question has been completed (e.g., completes people's sentences; cannot wait for a turn in conversation).

   (h) Often has difficulty waiting his or her turn (e.g., while waiting in line).

   (i) Often interrupts or intrudes on others (e.g., butts into conversations, games or activities; may start using other people's things without asking or receiving permission; for adolescents and adults, may intrude into or take over what others are doing).

(B) Several inattentive or hyperactive–impulsive symptoms were present before age 12 years.

(C) Several inattentive or hyperactive-impulse symptoms are present in two or more settings (e.g., at home, school, or work; with friends or relatives; in other activities).

(D) There must be clear evidence that the symptoms interfere with, or reduce the quality of, social academic, or occupational functioning.

(E) The symptoms do not occur exclusively during the course of schizophrenia or another psychotic disorder and are not better explained by another mental disorder (e.g., mood disorder, anxiety disorder, dissociative disorder, personality disorder, substance intoxication or withdrawal).

(continues)

Specify whether:

Combined presentation: If both Criterion A1 (inattention) and Criterion A2 (hyperactivity–impulsivity) are met for the past 6 months.

Predominantly inattentive presentation: If Criterion A1 (inattention) is met but Criterion A2 (hyperactivity–impulsivity) is not met for the past 6 months.

Predominantly hyperactive–impulsive presentation: if Criterion A2 (hyperactivity–impulsivity) is met but Criterion A1 (inattention) is not met for the past 6 months.

Specify if:

In partial remission: When full criteria were previously met, fewer than the full criteria have been met for the past 6 months, and the symptoms still result in impairment in social, academic, or occupational functioning.

Specify current severity:

Mild: Few, if any, symptoms in excess of those required to make the diagnosis are present, and symptoms result in no more than minor impairments in social or occupational functioning.

Moderate: Symptoms or functional impairment between "mild" and "severe" are present.

Severe: Many symptoms in excess of those required to make the diagnosis, or several symptoms that are particularly severe, are present, or the symptoms result in marked impairment in social or occupational functioning.

Source: Diagnostic and Statistical Manual of Mental Disorders, Fifth Edition. American Psychiatric Association.

shows the two lists of key symptoms that were identified for defining ADHD and distinguishing it from related problems. The first list includes symptoms of *inattention*; the second list includes symptoms of *hyperactivity–impulsivity*.

Quantitative studies support a model of ADHD consisting of a unitary ADHD component with two separable specific dimensions of inattention and hyperactivity–impulsivity (Burns et al., 2013). These two dimensions are well documented in research with thousands of individuals across various age, ethnic, and cultural groups throughout the world (Toplak et al., 2012). The two dimensions are highly correlated but they do predict different behavioral and cognitive impairments and likely have different neural correlates (Kuntsi et al., 2013; Willcutt et al., 2012). For example, symptoms of inattention tend to predict academic problems and peer neglect, whereas those of hyperactivity–impulsivity tend to predict aggressive behavior and peer rejection, among other problems.

To define the two core dimensions of ADHD as inattention and hyperactivity–impulsivity oversimplifies the disorder. First, each dimension includes many distinct processes that have been defined and measured in various ways. Second, although we discuss attention and impulse control separately, the two are closely connected developmentally—attention helps the child regulate behavior, emotions, and impulses (Nigg et al., 2006).

Inattention

LISA

Just Can't Focus

At age 17, Lisa struggles to pay attention and act appropriately. But this has always been hard for her. She still gets embarrassed thinking about the time that her parents took her to a restaurant to celebrate her 10th birthday. She was so distracted by the waitress's bright red hair that her father had to call her name three times before she remembered to order. Then, before she could stop herself, she blurted, "Your hair dye looks awful!"

In school, Lisa was quiet and cooperative but often seemed to be daydreaming. She was smart, yet couldn't improve her grades no matter how hard she tried.

Several times she failed exams. She knew the answers, but couldn't keep her mind on the test. Her parents responded to her low grades by taking away privileges and scolding her, "You're just lazy, Lisa. You could get better grades if you only tried."

Lisa found it agonizing to do homework. Often, she forgot to plan ahead by writing down the assignment or bringing home the right books. And when trying to work, every few minutes she found her mind drifting to something else. As a result, she rarely finished and her work was full of errors. One day, after Lisa had failed yet another exam, her teacher found her sobbing, "What's wrong with me?"

Adapted from National Institute of Mental Health [NIMH], 1994a.

Inattention refers to an inability to sustain attention or stick to tasks or play activities, to remember and follow through on instructions or rules, and to resist distractions. It also involves difficulties in planning and organization and in timeliness and problems in staying alert (Nigg & Barkley, 2014). Children who are inattentive find it difficult, during work or play, to focus on one task. While playing soccer, as the rest of the team heads downfield with the ball, the child with ADHD may get sidetracked by playing in a mud puddle. The child may attend automatically to enjoyable things, but have great difficulty focusing on less enjoyable tasks. Common complaints about inattention are that the child doesn't or won't listen, follow instructions, or finish chores or assignments. Since inattention can result from a failure in one or more cognitive processes that control attention (Petersen & Posner, 2012), it is not sufficient to say that a child has an attention deficit. The child could have a deficit in only one type or in more than one type.

Attentional capacity is the amount of information we can remember and attend to for a short time. When someone gives you directions or a phone number, how much information can you attend to and remember briefly? Children with ADHD do not have a deficit in their attentional capacity. They can remember the same amount of information for a short time as do other children (Taylor, 1995).

Selective attention is the ability to concentrate on relevant stimuli and ignore task-irrelevant stimuli in the environment. When you're studying for a test (relevant stimuli), how easily are you distracted by voices in another room?

Distractibility is a term commonly used to indicate a deficit in selective attention. Distractions can be disruptive to all children, including those with ADHD. However, children with ADHD are much more likely than others to be distracted by stimuli that are *highly salient and appealing* (Milich & Lorch, 1994).

Sustained attention, or *vigilance*, is the ability to maintain a persistent focus over time on unchallenging, uninteresting tasks or activities or when fatigued (Langner & Eickhoff, 2013). When you're tired and have to study for a test, can you still pay attention until you've reviewed all the required material? A primary attention deficit in ADHD seems to be sustained attention. When children with ADHD are assigned an uninteresting or repetitive task, their performance is poor as compared with that of other children. Although no one

likes to work on uninteresting tasks, most of us will when we have to. Children with ADHD may not be able to persist at such tasks even when they want to. They work best on self-paced tasks that they themselves have chosen—playing a computer game or building a model airplane—and on tasks they find especially interesting that do not require sustained attention. Most tasks, though, require sustained attention for successful performance, and many tasks are not particularly interesting.

Deficits in sustained attention are one of the core features of ADHD. However, children with ADHD may show performance deficits from the very beginning of a task or response, not just a decline over time. This suggests that their attentional problems may also be in alerting and preparing for the task from the outset, and not only in sustaining attention during the task. **Alerting** refers to an initial reaction to a stimulus; it involves the ability to prepare for what is about to happen. It helps the child achieve and maintain an optimally alert attentional state. A child with an alerting deficit (such as the lack of alertness you may experience when you are very tired) may respond too quickly in situations requiring a slow and careful approach and too slowly in situations requiring a quick response. This pattern of responding is often seen in children with ADHD. Thus, one view is that the deficit in sustaining attention may be partly related to the difficulty in alerting (Mullane et al., 2011).

"I need you to line up by attention span."

Hyperactivity–Impulsivity

MARK

Junior Wild Man

Mark, age 14, has more energy than most boys his age. But then, he's always been overactive. At age 3 he was a human tornado, dashing around and disrupting everything in his path. At home, he darted from one activity to the next, leaving a trail of toys behind him. At meals, he upset dishes and talked non-stop. He was reckless and impulsive, running into the street despite oncoming cars, no matter how often his mother explained the danger or scolded him. At the playground, his tendency to overreact—like socking playmates simply for bumping into him—had already gotten him into trouble several times. His parents didn't know what to do. Mark's doting grandparents reassured them, "Boys will be boys. Don't worry, he'll grow out of it." But he didn't.

Adapted from NIMH, 1994a.

Hyperactivity–impulsivity involves the undercontrol of motor behavior, poor sustained inhibition of behavior, the inability to delay a response or defer gratification, or an inability to inhibit dominant responses in relation to ongoing situational demands (Nigg & Barkley, 2014). Although the symptoms of hyperactivity and impulsivity are conceptually distinct, when children display one symptom they usually display the other as well. These symptoms are best viewed as a single dimension of behavior called *hyperactivity–impulsivity* (Willcutt et al., 2012). The strong link between hyperactivity and impulsivity suggests a deficit in regulating behavior. There are different reasons for hyperactivity–impulsivity. For example, a child may be constantly out of his seat in the classroom because he wants to look outdoors, because he is anxious about completing an assigned task, or because he can't control his motor behavior.

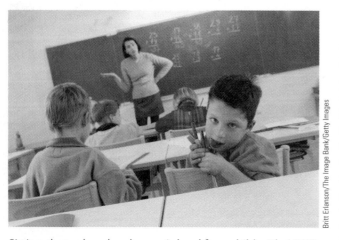

Sitting through a class lesson is hard for a child with ADHD

Britt Erlanson/The Image Bank/Getty Images

Hyperactivity

The image of a motor-driven ball of speed is the stereotype of a child with ADHD. Sitting still through a class lesson can be impossible for children with ADHD. They may fidget, squirm, climb, run about the room aimlessly, touch everything in sight, or noisily tap a pencil. Parents and teachers describe them as "always on the go" and "talking incessantly." Their activity is excessively energetic, intense, inappropriate, and not goal-directed. The children are extremely active, but unlike other children with a high energy level, they accomplish very little. Recordings of body movements indicate that even when they sleep, children with ADHD display more motor activity than other children (Teicher et al., 1996). However, the largest differences are found in situations requiring the child to inhibit motor activity—to slow down or sit still in response to the structured task demands of the classroom.

Impulsivity

Children who are impulsive seem unable to bridle their immediate reactions or think before they act. They may take apart an expensive clock with little thought about how to put it back together. It's very hard for them to stop an ongoing behavior or to regulate their behavior in accordance with the demands of the situation or the wishes of others. As a result, they may blurt out inappropriate comments or give quick, incorrect answers to questions that have not yet been completed. Because it is difficult to wait or take turns, they interrupt conversations, intrude on others' activities, and lash out in frustration when upset. They also experience difficulty resisting immediate temptations and delaying gratification (Sonuga-Barke et al., 2008). Minor mishaps are common, such as spilling drinks or knocking things over, but more serious accidents and injuries can result from reckless behavior, such as running into the street without looking (Brehaut et al., 2003).

Impulsivity may take different but related forms and is expressed across many life domains, including school and interpersonal relationships (Sharma, Markon, & Clark, 2013; Tsukayama, Duckworth, & Kim, 2013). *Cognitive impulsivity* is reflected in disorganization, hurried thinking, and the need for supervision. (Remember John not handing in his homework even though it was done?) It may also involve impulsive decision making, for example, in the child's valuing of immediate rewards. *Behavioral impulsivity* includes impulsively calling out in class or acting without considering the consequences. Children who are behaviorally impulsive have difficulty inhibiting their response when the situation requires it. A child may touch a stove to see if it is hot even when she is old enough to know better. Cognitive and behavioral impulsivity (and inattention) predict problems with academic achievement, particularly in reading (Rabiner, Coie, & the Conduct Problems Prevention Research Group, 2000). Only behavioral impulsivity, however, predicts rule-breaking behavior and thus may be a specific sign of increased risk for conduct problems (Willoughby et al., 2000). *Emotional impulsivity* is demonstrated by impatience, low frustration tolerance, hot temper, quickness to anger, and irritability. The term generally refers to how quickly and how likely an individual will react with negative emotions in response to negative events as compared with others of the same age or developmental level (Barkley, 2014c). Although less studied than other types of impulsivity, some findings suggest that emotional impulsivity may be an important component of ADHD that contributes to poor educational, occupational, and other adult outcomes beyond those associated with inattention and hyperactivity–impulsivity (Barkley, 2014c).

In summary, the core features of ADHD—inattention and hyperactivity–impulsivity are made up of many processes. Children with ADHD display a unique constellation and severity of symptoms but may not differ from comparison children on all types and measures of inattention and hyperactivity–impulsivity. The primary attention deficit in ADHD is an inability to engage and sustain attention and to follow through on directions or rules while resisting salient distractions. The primary impairment in hyperactivity–impulsivity involves undercontrol of motor behavior, poor sustained inhibition of behavior, the inability to delay a response or defer gratification, and an inability to voluntarily inhibit dominant responses in relation to situational demands.

Presentation Type

Investigators have become increasingly interested in identifying the different ADHD presentations (Milich, Balentine, & Lynam, 2001). **Presentation type** refers to a group of individuals with something in common—symptoms, etiology, problem severity, or likely outcome—that makes them distinct from other groupings. DSM specifies three presentation types of ADHD based on the individual's primary symptoms:

▸ **Predominantly inattentive presentation (ADHD-PI)** describes children who meet symptom criteria for inattention but not hyperactivity–impulsivity.

▸ **Predominantly hyperactive–impulsive presentation (ADHD-HI)** describes children who meet symptom criteria for hyperactivity-impulsivity but not inattention.

▸ **Combined presentation (ADHD-C)** describes children who meet symptom criteria for both inattention and hyperactivity–impulsivity.

Children with ADHD-PI are described as inattentive to details, easily distracted, careless, not listening, unfocused, disorganized, unable to sustain effort, and forgetful (Interestingly, the same 1845 storybook that described the hyperactive–impulsive behavior of "Fidgety Phil" also described a very inattentive, distractible young boy named "Hans Look-in-the-Air"). They may have a learning disability, find it hard to remember things, and display low academic achievement (Massetti et al., 2008). They are often described as anxious and apprehensive and socially withdrawn and may display mood disorders (Maedgen & Carlson, 2000). Children with ADHD-PI represent the most common presentation in the general population, but they are less often referred to clinics than are those with ADHD-C (Willcutt, 2012).

One concern about the ADHD-PI presentation is that it may contain at least three diagnostic subgroups (Diamond, 2005; Milich, Balentine, & Lynam, 2001). One group includes children who display both clinically significant symptoms of inattention and subclinical (below the DSM cutoff), but still substantial, levels of hyperactivity–impulsivity. Thus, it is not clear whether this group is qualitatively different from those with ADHD-C or just different in their degree of impairment. Another group with the ADHD-PI presentation consists of children whose inattentive symptoms are linked to problems with arousal and **sluggish cognitive tempo (SCT)**, a cluster that includes symptoms such as daydreaming, trouble staying awake/alert, mentally foggy/easily confused, slow processing of information, stares a lot, spacey, loses train of thought, forgets what was going to say, and appearing lethargic, hypoactive, or even sleepy (Barkley, 2013b; McBurnett et al., 2013). Symptoms of SCT have been viewed both as a core component of some forms of ADHD or as an entirely separate disorder from ADHD that coexists with it in up to 50% of all cases (Barkley, 2014f). Qualitative differences exist between individuals with the SCT subset of ADHD-PI and those with "subthreshold" ADHD-C, suggesting that these groups may have different disorders (Barkley, 2013b). A third subgroup of individuals who meet criteria for ADHD-PI consists of those who originally met criteria for the ADHD-C presentation but experience an age-related reduction in symptoms of hyperactivity–impulsivity and, as a result, no longer meet criteria for the ADHD-C presentation. These individuals with ADHD-PI likely have a different disorder from those whose symptoms have always been consistent with the ADHD-PI presentation.

Children with the ADHD-HI and ADHD-C presentations are more likely to display problems in inhibiting behavior and in behavioral persistence (Solanto et al., 2007). They are also more likely to be aggressive, defiant, rejected by peers, and suspended from school or placed in special education classes (Short et al., 2007). Children with ADHD-C are the ones most often referred for treatment (Willcutt, 2012). ADHD-HI is the rarest presentation and includes primarily preschoolers. Many of those diagnosed with ADHD-HI as preschoolers do not meet diagnostic criteria for ADHD at a later age, suggesting that the preschool diagnosis reflects a typical developmental phase or possibly a time-limited behavior disorder (Roberts, Milich, & Barkley, 2014).

Although children with different ADHD presentation types are diverse, research findings do not fully support the three subgroup distinctions (Nigg, Tannock, & Rohde, 2010). Presentations may also be unstable over time—a child described as ADHD-PI at one time may be categorized as ADHD-HI or ADHD-C at another point in time, and vice versa (Lahey & Willcutt, 2010). Valo and Tannock (2010) found that 50% of ADHD cases were reclassified from one presentation to another depending on the number of people reporting on the child's symptoms, the methods used to assess symptoms, and how information across reporters and methods was combined.

The heterogeneity of ADHD symptoms is widely acknowledged, but many issues remain regarding the reliability and validity of the presentations specified in DSM-5 and their symptom criteria (Nikolas & Nigg, 2013). Our knowledge of ADHD presentations is clearly still "under construction." It is important to keep this in mind since inconsistencies in the literature may reflect findings that mix together samples of children with different presentations.

Additional DSM Criteria

Not every child who displays inattention and/or hyperactive–impulsive behavior has ADHD. Most children blurt out things they didn't mean to say, jump from one activity to another, make careless mistakes, or become forgetful and disorganized at times. This doesn't mean they will have a lifelong disorder. ADHD also differs in *severity*—the number of symptoms in excess of those required to make the diagnosis and the degree of impairment in functioning. Symptoms and degree of impairment are used to rate the child's "current severity" of ADHD, ranging from mild to moderate to severe. To diagnose ADHD using DSM-5, the symptoms must also:

▶ appear before age 12 [*Note:* This represents a change from DSM-IV, which required that symptoms appear before age 7. The age criteria was raised because there was little difference between children with an onset before or after age 7; about half of children with ADHD-PI are not identified until well after age 7; and extending the requirement from age 7 to age 12 does not significantly change the overall prevalence of ADHD (Kieling et al., 2008; Polanczyk et al., 2010)]

▶ persist for more than 6 months;

▶ occur more often and with greater severity than in other children of the same age and sex;

▶ occur across two or more settings (e.g., home, school, other activities)

▶ interfere with, or reduce the quality of, social, academic, or occupational functioning; and

▶ not be better explained by another mental disorder (e.g., mood disorder, anxiety disorder).

Illnesses, accidents, middle ear infections, mild seizures, chronic abuse, or stressful life events such as a major move can result in behaviors that mimic the symptoms of ADHD. A normally agreeable 9-year-old boy who becomes inattentive or argumentative immediately after his parents separate is likely having an adjustment reaction, not experiencing ADHD. The disruptive behaviors of youngsters with mild intellectual disabilities, learning disorders, or conduct problems may be mistaken for ADHD, as can the inattentive or restless behaviors of those with anxiety disorders. In fact, most people have trouble concentrating if they are overloaded with too many things to do or a lot of pressure to hurry—sound familiar? Therefore, it is essential to investigate other possible reasons for the individual's symptoms (Smith, Barkley, & Shapiro, 2007).

Depending too heavily on individual symptoms or rating scales to diagnose ADHD can be unreliable and misleading (Solanto & Alvir, 2009). Before a diagnosis of ADHD is made, it is essential to carry out a thorough assessment that includes a developmental history, parent and teacher reports, normed assessment instruments, and behavioral observations (Johnston & Mah, 2008). Importantly, since there is only a modest relationship between ADHD symptoms and impairment in childhood, a child can display ADHD symptoms without necessarily displaying significant impairment. Conversely, a child may display remitted or subclinical levels of ADHD symptoms but still suffer significant maladjustment (Mick et al., 2011). Thus, in evaluating ADHD, it is important to assess both the child's symptoms and impairment in functioning (Gathje, Lewandowski, & Gordon, 2008).

What DSM Criteria Don't Tell Us

The DSM-5 criteria for ADHD have a number of limitations (Roberts et al., 2014):

▶ *Developmentally insensitive.* Although DSM states that clinical judgment may be used to assess whether symptoms are "inconsistent with developmental level," it applies the same symptoms to individuals of all ages, even though some symptoms, particularly for hyperactive–impulsive behaviors (running and climbing), apply more to young children (Pine et al., 2011). Similarly, the number of symptoms needed to make a diagnosis is not adjusted for age or level of maturity in younger children, even though hyperactive–impulsive symptoms show a general decline with age. One age adjustment that is included in DSM-5 is a reduced number of ADHD symptoms (from six to five) needed to make the diagnosis in older adolescents and adults (age 17 and older) (APA, 2013). The DSM-5 also includes clarifying examples of how these symptoms might be expressed in teens and adults. The validity of these changes in symptom number and expression in diagnosing and predicting impairment in teens and adults with ADHD has yet to be tested.

▶ *Categorical view of ADHD.* According to DSM, ADHD is a disorder that a child either has or doesn't have. However, because the number and severity of symptoms are also calculated on a scale, children who fall just below the cutoff for ADHD are not necessarily different from children just above the cutoff. In fact, over time, some children may move in and out of the DSM category as a result of fluctuations in their behavior. Both statistical and neurobiological research support the idea that ADHD is a dimensional rather than a categorical disorder, representing an extreme or a delay in normal traits that all children possess to a degree (Shaw et al., 2011; Sonuga-Barke, 2013). However, it may still be useful to talk about categories even when a disorder is of a continuous or changing nature. For example, there is no magic cutoff for defining high blood pressure, but most of us would agree that people with high blood pressure are at greater risk for certain negative outcomes.

These limitations highlight the fact that DSM criteria are designed to classify and diagnose. They help shape our understanding of ADHD but are also shaped by—and in some instances lag behind—new research findings.

Section Summary

Core Characteristics

- DSM-5 uses two lists of symptoms to define ADHD. The first list includes symptoms of inattention, poor concentration, and disorganization. The second list includes symptoms of hyperactivity–impulsivity.
- Children who are inattentive find it difficult to sustain mental effort during work or play and find it difficult to resist salient distractions while doing so.
- Children with ADHD are extremely active, but unlike other children with a high energy level, they accomplish very little.
- Children with ADHD are impulsive, which means they seem unable to bridle their immediate reactions or they may fail to think before they act.
- DSM specifies three presentation types of ADHD based on primary symptoms: predominantly inattentive, predominantly hyperactive–impulsive, or both.
- A diagnosis of ADHD requires the appearance of symptoms before age 12, a greater frequency and severity of symptoms than in other children of the same age and gender, persistence of symptoms, occurrence of symptoms in several settings, and impairments in functioning.
- Although useful, the DSM criteria have several limitations; an important one is developmental insensitivity.

ASSOCIATED CHARACTERISTICS

In addition to their primary difficulties, children with ADHD often display other problems. For example, Lisa was failing in school and Mark was getting into fights. In the sections that follow, we consider the characteristics and problems commonly associated with ADHD, including cognitive deficits, speech and language impairments, medical and physical concerns, and social problems.

Cognitive Deficits

Children and adolescents with ADHD display a variety of cognitive deficits, including deficits in executive functions, intellectual deficits, impairments in academic functioning, learning disorders, and distorted self-perceptions. These are discussed in the sections that follow.

Executive Functions

Executive functions (EFs) are cognitive processes in the brain that activate, integrate, and manage other brain functions (Pennington & Ozonoff, 1996). They underlie the child's capacity for self-regulation functions such as self-awareness, planning, self-monitoring, and self-evaluation. Having EFs in the brain is like having an air traffic control system at a busy airport to manage the arrivals and departures of dozens of planes on multiple runways. They help us focus on multiple streams of information at the same time, filter distractions, and revise plans as necessary (Center on the Developing Child at Harvard, 2011). EFs are varied and include (Barkley, 2012):

▶ *Cognitive processes*, such as working memory (holding facts in mind while manipulating information), mental computation, planning and anticipation, flexibility of thinking, and the use of organizational strategies.

▶ *Language processes*, such as verbal fluency and the use of self-directed speech.

▶ *Motor processes*, such as allocation of effort, following prohibitive instructions, response inhibition, and motor coordination and sequencing.

▶ *Emotional processes*, such as self-regulation of arousal level and tolerating frustration.

For most children, these different processes work in concert, enabling them to exercise deliberate control of their attention and impulses and to maintain problem-solving behaviors in order to attain a future goal. Many EFs reflect abilities that emerge and develop rapidly in preschool children, continue to mature in older children and adolescents, and peak in young adults (Best & Miller, 2010). However, most (not all) children with ADHD show deficits in one or more EFs, especially response inhibition, vigilance, working memory, and planning (Holmes et al., 2010). In fact, as shown in Table 8.2, many symptoms of inattention and hyperactivity–impulsivity reflect impairments in EFs. The number of children with ADHD who display EF deficits may vary depending on how these deficits are measured, with EF rating scales generally finding more deficits than psychometric tests (Weyandt & Gudmundsdottir, 2014). It is also important to keep in mind that children with ADHD may differ in the type of EF deficits they display; for example, some may show poor inhibitory control, others may show poor set shifting, and others may not display any EF deficits (Roberts, Martel, & Nigg, 2013). Children with ADHD with different EF deficit profiles may also differ in other characteristics; for example, their intellectual ability, academic achievement, and co-occurring symptoms or disorders (Roberts et al., 2013).

In light of their close connection with symptoms of ADHD, impairments in EF are viewed as a key deficit in ADHD. However, EF deficits are not *uniquely* associated with ADHD. They also occur in children with other disorders, such as ASD and conduct disorder (Banaschewski et al., 2005; Salcedo-Marin et al., 2013). In addition, EF deficits occur in only about half of

TABLE 8.2 | **Impaired Executive Functions in ADHD and Examples of Resulting Impairments**

Impaired Executive Function	Resulting Impairment
1. Organize, prioritize, and activate	Trouble getting started Difficulty organizing work Misunderstand directions
2. Focus, shift, and sustain attention	Lose focus when trying to listen Forget what has been read and need to reread Easily distracted
3. Regulate alertness, effort, and processing speed	Excessive daytime drowsiness Difficulty completing a task on time Slow processing speed
4. Manage frustration and modulate emotion	Very easily irritated Feelings hurt easily Overly sensitive to criticism
5. Working memory and accessing recall	Forget to do a planned task Difficulty following sequential directions Quickly lose thoughts that were put on hold
6. Monitor and regulate action	Find it hard to sit still or be quiet Rush things, slapdash Often interrupt, blurt things out

Source: Based on Brown, 2000.

children with ADHD (Lambek et al., 2011), suggesting that they are one important component of ADHD but that other deficits also need to be examined. One study of children with ADHD with and without EF deficits found that the two groups were comparable in ADHD symptoms and school functioning. However, those with EF deficits had lower IQ scores and displayed greater response variability. In contrast, those with ADHD without EF deficits showed more aversion to delay of reward. If confirmed, these and other findings suggest multiple pathways for ADHD (Lambek et al., 2010), a point we return to in a later section on causes.

Intellectual Deficits

Most children with ADHD are of at least average overall intelligence, and some are quite bright (Antshel et al., 2008). Their difficulty lies not in a lack of intelligence, but rather in applying their intelligence to everyday life situations (Barkley, 2006a). As a result, the children never quite live up to their potential. They do score about

5 to 9 points lower on IQ tests than both control children and their own siblings (McConaughey et al., 2009). Since IQ tests such as the Wechsler Intelligence Scale for Children, Fourth Edition (WISC-IV) include subtests related to specific deficits of children with ADHD (e.g., working memory), their lower test scores are not surprising (Frazier, Demaree, & Youngstrom, 2004). In addition, lower IQ scores can be the direct result of the effects of ADHD symptoms on test-taking behavior. For example, a child who scores lower on an IQ test because he or she is not paying attention to instructions or is engaging in off-task behaviors is not necessarily less intelligent. On average, inattention has been estimated to account for about a 2- to 5-point lowering of overall IQ-test scores in children with ADHD (Jepsen, Fagerlund, & Mortensen, 2009). Other factors that may contribute to a lower overall IQ score include possible family influences, co-occurring learning disabilities, and deficits in executive functioning.

Impaired Academic Functioning

Most children with ADHD experience severe difficulties in school; this is especially true for those with co-occurring disorders (DuPaul & Langberg, 2014). They frequently have lower productivity, grades, and scores on achievement tests. They may also fail to advance in grade or may be placed more frequently in special education classes. Finally, they may be expelled and fail to finish high school or obtain post-secondary education (Loe & Feldman, 2007). Particularly disturbing are findings that the academic skills of children with ADHD are impaired before they enter the first grade (Barkley, Shelton et al., 2002).

Specific Learning Disorder

As many as 45% of children with ADHD have a specific learning disorder (DuPaul, Gormley, & Laracy, 2013); that is, they have trouble with certain academic skills, such as reading, spelling, and math (Weyandt & Gudmundsdottir, 2014). When learning disorder is broadly defined as performance below expected grade level, nearly 80% of children with ADHD qualify for a learning disorder by late childhood. However, when defined more narrowly as a significant delay in reading, arithmetic, or spelling that is relative to the child's general intellectual functioning, or defined as extremely low achievement in a specific academic subject(s), the number drops to around 25% (Barkley, 2006a). Children with ADHD and those with learning problems show distinct patterns of cognitive deficits, which may be present in combination in those with both disorders (Gooch, Snowling, & Hulme, 2011).

Different pathways may underlie the association between ADHD and learning disorders (Taylor, 2011). For example, the child's cognitive and intellectual deficits

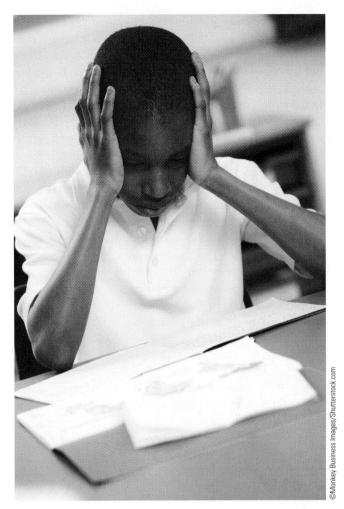

The structured demands of a classroom can be painful for a child with ADHD

may directly lead to learning problems. The impact of childhood ADHD symptoms on long-term academic achievement may also be indirect—they influence later school grades as a result of their effects on homework management and classroom performance (Langberg et al., 2011). ADHD may also predispose the child to conduct problems (to be discussed in Chapter 9) in school that may in turn result in poor academic performance. The association could also be due to common neuropsychological deficits (McGrath et al., 2011; Rajendran et al., 2013) or a common genetic link, although findings suggest that the two disorders are transmitted independently within families (Del'Homme et al., 2007).

Distorted Self-Perceptions

The many failures experienced by children with ADHD have led to the common belief that these children must suffer from low self-esteem—and there is some support for this (Treuting & Hinshaw, 2001). However, many children with ADHD report a higher self-esteem than warranted by their behavior (Owens et al., 2007). For example, they may perceive their relationships with their parents, teachers, or peers no differently than do control children, even though their parents, teachers, or peers see things in a more negative light (Gerdes, Hoza, & Pelham, 2003; Normand et al., 2013). This exaggeration of one's competence is referred to as a **positive bias**. Positive bias can occur in relation to social competence, where it may be particularly problematic, or in other areas such as academic performance or behavioral conduct (Hoza et al., 2012). Some findings suggest that self-esteem in children with ADHD may vary with the type of ADHD presentation, the accompanying disorders, and the area of performance being assessed (e.g., conduct, scholastic achievement). Children with ADHD who display inattentive and depressive/anxious symptoms tend to report lower self-esteem, whereas those with symptoms of hyperactivity–impulsivity and conduct problems appear to exaggerate their self-worth (Owens et al., 2007). The bias in the latter group is most dramatic in the areas of performance in which the child is most severely impaired. Increases in positively biased self-perceptions of behavior in children with ADHD have also been found to predict greater aggression over time (Hoza et al., 2010). In general, research has found that children with ADHD and a positive social or behavioral bias are more likely to display persistent social impairments and more negative behaviors than those with ADHD without this bias (McQuade & Hoza, 2014).

Several explanations for the positive bias in children with hyperactivity–impulsivity have been proposed—it serves a self-protective function that allows the child to cope every day despite frequent failures; it reflects a diminished self-awareness as a result of impairments in executive functions (McQuade et al., 2011); or it is a result of not knowing what constitutes successful or unsuccessful performance (Ohan & Johnston, 2002). To date, there is some support for the self-protective function of positive bias (Hoza et al., 2010), although other explanations may also apply.

Children with ADHD also display distortions in their perceptions of **quality of life**, which refers to a person's subjective perception of their position in life as evidenced by their physical, psychological, and social functioning. According to parents, the impact of their child's ADHD on the child's quality of life is substantial, particularly when the child has co-existing emotional and conduct problems (Schei et al., 2013). However, despite experiencing many life difficulties, children with ADHD rate their own quality of life more positively than others rate it (Danckaerts et al., 2010).

Speech and Language Impairments

About 30% to 60% of children with ADHD also have impairments in their speech and language (Helland

et al., 2012). Interestingly, the type of speech and language impairment may be related to the child's specific ADHD symptoms. For example, one study with preschoolers found that symptoms of hyperactivity–impulsivity were related to poor language skills, whereas those of inattention were more highly correlated with weaker receptive and expressive vocabulary skills (Gremillion & Martel, 2013). In addition to showing a higher prevalence of formal speech and language disorders (see Chapter 7), children with ADHD may have difficulty in understanding others' speech and in using appropriate language in everyday situations (McInnes et al., 2003; Wassenberg et al., 2010). The pragmatic aspects of speech, along with impaired verbal working memory and discourse analysis, are primary difficulties (Bellani et al., 2011). Impairment in pragmatic language skills has been related to these children's social difficulties, and may, in part account for these difficulties (Staikova et al., 2013). Excessive and loud talking, frequent shifts and interruptions in conversation, inability to listen, and inappropriate conversation are a few common examples of impairments.

Children with ADHD not only ramble on, but also their conversation is characterized by speech production errors, fewer pronouns and conjunctions, tangential and unrelated comments, abandoned utterances, and unclear links (Mathers, 2006; McGrath et al., 2008). Can you understand the following statement by a boy with ADHD?

> And all of a sudden the soldiers—and all of a sudden he gets faint and you know when he says "Good doctors, I want to talk with you" and all of a sudden he goes in the door and inside they come off it from the thing. So he puts—I think this something on the doorknob. (Tannock et al., 1995)

When speech is unclear, as in this example, it is difficult for the listener to understand who and what the child is talking about. Unfortunately, miscommunication is all too common in children with ADHD.

Medical and Physical Concerns

In addition to the difficulties we have discussed, children and adolescents with ADHD also experience a number of medical and physical concerns, including having health-related problems, being accident-prone, and demonstrating risk-taking behaviors (Barkley, 2014d; Nigg, 2013).

Health-Related Problems

In terms of specific problems, some studies have reported higher rates of enuresis and encopresis (Shreeram et al., 2009) and asthma (Fasmer et al., 2011). One prospective study found that asthma in early life increased the risk of developing ADHD during the school years (Chen et al., 2013). Other health concerns for which individuals with ADHD are at elevated risk include dental health problems, poor fitness, obesity, and eating problems and disorders (in females) (Barkley, 2014d). Sleep disturbances are also common in children with ADHD (Cortese et al., 2009, 2013; Owens et al., 2013). Resistance to going to bed, difficulty in falling asleep, fewer total hours asleep, and involuntary sleep movements such as teeth grinding or restless sleep may be the most significant disturbances (Spruyt & Gozal, 2011). Some of the sleep problems in children with ADHD may be related to their use of stimulant medications, and/or co-occurring conduct or anxiety disorders, rather than to only their ADHD (Mick, Biederman et al., 2000).

Accident-Proneness and Risk Taking

Given their problems with impulsivity, motor inhibition, and lack of planning and forethought, it is not surprising that over 50% of parents of children with ADHD describe their child as accident-prone. These children are about three times more likely to experience serious accidental injuries, such as broken bones, lacerations, severe bruises, burns, poisonings, or head injuries (Barkley, 2014d). Young adult drivers with ADHD are at higher risk than others for traffic accidents, and deviant peer associations may play an important role (Cardoos, Loya, & Hinshaw, 2013; Cox, Madaan, & Cox, 2011).

ADHD is a significant risk factor for the early initiation of cigarette smoking, substance-use disorders, Internet- and videogame-use problems and addictions, and risky sexual behaviors such as multiple partners and unprotected sex (Barkley, 2014d; Lee et al., 2011). Substance-use disorders among young people with ADHD are also more frequent, severe, and persistent than substance-use disorders in those without ADHD (Charach et al., 2011). There are a number of possible reasons that ADHD may lead to substance-use problems, a notable one being co-occurring or later conduct problems (Wilens, 2011). Overall, these findings suggest a progression of hyperactive–impulsive behaviors during childhood to a pattern of irresponsible and risky adolescent and adult behavior.

In support of this, a prospective 33-year follow-up study of 8-year-old boys with ADHD but without conduct disorder found that as adults they had relatively more risky driving behaviors, sexually transmitted diseases, head injuries, and emergency department admissions than a comparison group and that lifetime risk-taking was related to negative health outcomes and more deaths not related to specific medical conditions. Importantly, the relationship between ADHD and risk taking was accounted for by the later development of Conduct Disorder (CD)/Antisocial Personality Disorder (APD). Over their lifetime, individuals with ADHD who did not develop CD/APD did not differ from the comparison group in risk-taking behaviors (Ramos Olazagasti et al., 2013).

Impulsive behavior is the most significant childhood characteristic that predicts reduced life expectancy (an average of 8 years less), according to a longitudinal study spanning over a half century (Friedman et al., 1995). A reduced life expectancy for individuals with ADHD may also be predicted by a pattern of accident-proneness, auto accidents, and risk taking, combined with a reduced concern for health-promoting behaviors, such as exercise, proper diet, safe sex, and moderate use of tobacco, alcohol, and caffeine, especially for those with co-occurring CD/APD symptoms (Barkley, 2014d).

The need for further research into health-related problems in children and adolescents with ADHD is accentuated by findings that show they have significantly higher rates of inpatient and outpatient hospitalizations and emergency department visits. Average medical costs for children with ADHD are more than double the costs for those without ADHD (Le et al., 2013; Leibson et al., 2001) and at least comparable to the costs for children with asthma (Chan, Zhan, & Homer, 2002). The multitude of health and related problems and costs indicate that "ADHD is more than just a serious mental health problem—it is a serious *public health* problem" (Barkley, 2014d).

Social Problems

DENNIS

Nothing Sticks

With my other children, I could tell them one time, "Don't do that," and they would stop. But Dennis, my child with ADHD, I could tell him a hundred times, "Dennis, don't carve soap with my potato peeler," "Don't paint the house with used motor oil," or "Don't walk on Grandma's white sofa in your muddy shoes," but he still does it. It's like every day is a brand new day and yesterday's rules are long forgotten. ... I just cannot stay one step ahead of him. He does things my other kids never thought of.

From *The Hyperactive Child Book*, by Patricia Kennedy, Leif Terdal, and Lydia Fusetti, pp. 8–9. New York: St. Martin's Press.

Social problems in family life and at school are common in children with ADHD (Johnston & Chronis-Tuscano, 2014; McQuade & Hoza, 2014). Those who experience the most severe social disability are at greatest risk for poor adolescent outcomes and other disorders, such as depression and conduct disorder (Greene et al., 1996). Children with ADHD don't listen and are often hostile, argumentative, unpredictable, and explosive. As a result, they are frequently in conflict with adults and other children. It is common for children with ADHD to be removed from swimming lessons because of disruptive behavior or to be kicked out of gymnastics. For one child with ADHD taking dance lessons, the teachers offered to buy back her shoes if only her parents would take her out!

To get along with others, you must follow social rules and respect conventions. Children with ADHD do not play by the same rules as others and don't seem to learn from past mistakes, despite their awareness of expected social behaviors and a desire to conform to them. Many social blunders by children with ADHD appear more thoughtless than intentional. Even with good intentions, their behaviors have an annoying quality that is a source of great distress for their parents, siblings, teachers, and classmates. In the words of one mother: "Our grade one parent interview was highly traumatic; her teacher cried!"

Family Problems

Families of children with ADHD experience many difficulties, including interactions characterized by negativity, noncompliance by the child, excessive parental control, and sibling conflict (Johnston & Chronis-Tuscano, 2014). Parents may experience high levels of distress and related problems—most commonly, depression in mothers and antisocial behavior, such as substance abuse, in fathers. Further stress on family life stems from the fact that parents of children with ADHD may themselves have ADHD and other associated conditions (Johnston et al., 2012). This can also be a barrier to effective treatment for the child (Sonuga-Barke, Daley, & Thompson, 2002).

Families of children with ADHD also report less parenting competence, fewer contacts with extended family members, greater caregiver strain, less instrumental support, and slightly higher rates of marital conflict, separation, and divorce (Bussing et al., 2003; Johnston & Mash, 2001). They report generally higher levels of parenting stress, which may fluctuate over the course of the day in relation to the child's ADHD-related behaviors (Theule et al., 2013; Whalen et al., 2011). Parents of these children also show increased alcohol consumption that, in some instances, could be a direct result of stressful interactions with their children (Pelham & Lang, 1999). Many also report stigmatizing experiences, including concerns about how society would label their child, social isolation and rejection, and perceptions that health care and school personnel are dismissive of their concerns (dosReis et al., 2010; Moldavsky & Sayal, 2013). Finally, when interviewed, siblings of children with ADHD report that they feel victimized by their ADHD sibling and that this experience is often minimized or overlooked (Kendall, 1999).

It is important to note that the links between ADHD and high levels of family conflict, parental psychopathology, and marital discord are, in many cases, due to the child's co-occurring conduct problems rather than to ADHD symptoms alone (Johnston & Mash, 2001).

Things I've learned from my ADHD child (honest and no kidding):

> If you hook a dog leash over a ceiling fan, the motor is not strong enough to rotate a 42-pound boy wearing batman underwear and a superman cape. It is strong enough, however, if tied to a paint can, to spread paint on all four walls of a 20 × 20 foot room. (An anonymous mother in Austin, Texas)

Peer Problems

Peer problems in both boys and girls with ADHD are apparent at an early age and are quickly evident when the child enters a new social situation. These children display little of the give-and-take that characterizes other children (McQuade & Hoza, 2014). Children with ADHD can be bothersome, stubborn, socially awkward, and socially insensitive. Others describe them as socially conspicuous, loud, intense, and quick to react. They are socially active but usually "off the mark" with respect to the style, content, or timing of their behavior, which often has an annoying quality that brings out the worst in other children (Whalen & Henker, 1992). Children with ADHD seem to get into trouble even when trying to be helpful, and although their behavior seems thoughtless, it is often unintentional. They often see their own behavior more favorably than it is perceived by others, and they may be puzzled by others' negative reactions (Nijmeijer et al., 2008).

In light of their social difficulties, it is not surprising that children with ADHD are disliked and uniformly rejected by peers, have few friends, and report receiving low social support from peers (Gardner & Gerdes, 2013; McQuade & Hoza, 2014). Their lack of skill in correctly recognizing emotions in others and in regulating their own emotions and behavior (Kats-Gold, Besser, & Priel, 2007) and the aggressiveness that frequently accompanies ADHD often lead to social conflict and a negative reputation (Erhardt & Hinshaw, 1994). For girls with ADHD-PI, internalizing symptoms may play a particularly salient role in their being disliked or rejected by peers (Becker et al., 2013). The social problems of these children may increase the later risk of having disorders other than ADHD and may spill over into other areas of development (Murray-Close et al., 2010). Once they are labeled "ADHD" by their peers, a negative process begins whereby the child suffers more negative treatment and rejection by peers, leading to a cascading of negative effects over time.

Children with ADHD are not deficient in social reasoning or understanding (Whalen & Henker, 1992). They simply do not use what they know during social exchanges, and they may continue to be dominant or assertive even when the situation changes and requires accommodation, negotiation, or submission (Landau & Milich, 1988). Their social agenda may also differ from the agenda of their peers, especially when ADHD is accompanied by aggression. They may actually value and prefer troublemaking, sensation seeking, and having fun at the expense of following rules and getting along with others (Melnick & Hinshaw, 1996).

Despite their many social problems with peers, some adolescents with ADHD may meet their social needs by maintaining one or two positive close friendships (Glass, Flory, & Hankin, 2012). The social premise for such relationships may differ from those of other teens, possibly with a mutual focus on "having fun" rather than on seeking emotional support. Positive friendships may buffer the negative outcomes of peer rejection commonly seen in children with ADHD. Since most research on ADHD has examined peer relationships in general, further research into close friendships is needed to determine their nature and function during adolescence.

Section Summary

Associated Characteristics

- Besides their primary difficulties, children with ADHD display other problems, such as cognitive and learning deficits, speech and language impairments, motor incoordination, medical and physical concerns, and social problems.
- Children with ADHD display deficits in executive functions (EFs), the higher-order mental processes that underlie the child's capacity for planning and self-regulation.
- Children with ADHD score slightly lower on IQ tests, but most are of normal intelligence. Their difficulty is in applying their intelligence to everyday life situations.
- Children with ADHD experience school performance difficulties, including lower grades, a failure to advance in grade, and more frequent placements in special education classes.
- Many children with ADHD have a specific learning disorder, typically in reading, spelling, or math.
- Some children with ADHD report a higher self-esteem than is warranted by their behavior, referred to as a " positive bias."
- They often have speech and language impairments and have difficulty using language in everyday situations.
- They may experience many health-related problems, including enuresis and encopresis, asthma, obesity, eating

problems, and sleep disturbances and tend to be accident-prone. The costs of and medical service use in those with ADHD are high.

- They experience numerous social problems with family members, teachers, and peers.

ACCOMPANYING PSYCHOLOGICAL DISORDERS AND SYMPTOMS

Children with ADHD typically present a mixed bag of symptoms and impairments, with ADHD being only one, albeit a significant one. Nearly two-thirds of parents report behaviors other than the core symptoms of ADHD as being the most worrisome, typically aggression and defiance (Findling et al., 2009). Co-occurring psychological disorders are also common, usually with an onset after that of the ADHD (Yoshimasu et al., 2012). In community samples, up to 44% of children with ADHD have at least one other disorder, and 43% have at least two or more other disorders (Willcutt et al., 2012). One reason that ADHD is so challenging is that as many as 80% of clinic-referred children with ADHD have a co-occurring psychological disorder, and up to 50% have two or more disorders (Pliszka, 2014). Common co-occurring disorders include oppositional and conduct disorders, anxiety disorders, mood disorders, and motor coordination and tic disorders. As we noted previously, learning disorders are also quite common, as are substance-use disorders in adolescence (see Chapter 13). Some children with ADHD display symptoms of ASD (see Chapter 6), possibly originating from similar familial/genetic factors (Rommelse et al., 2011). Children with ADHD and ASD traits display higher rates of psychopathology, neuropsychological deficits, social difficulties with peers, and restricted and repetitive behaviors than do those with ADHD without ASD traits (Kotte et al., 2013; Martin et al., 2014).

Oppositional Defiant Disorder and Conduct Disorder

SHAWN

Bad Boy

Shawn, now an energetic and talkative young adult, recalls his childhood with ADHD as a total disaster: "I did really bad in school. My parents and teachers were always on my back. They bugged me about being too loud, too defiant, too explosive, and too aggressive. Then I began to use drugs: marijuana, and later, cocaine. I barely managed to squeeze through high school. I

(continues)

(continued)

couldn't concentrate at all. I'd study for hours and then forget everything I'd read. I had to cheat my way through high school." (Based on authors' case material.)

About half or more of all children and adolescents with ADHD—mostly boys, like Shawn—meet criteria for oppositional defiant disorder (ODD) by age 7 or later (Pliszka, 2014). Children with ODD overreact by lashing out at adults and other kids. They are stubborn, short-tempered, argumentative, and defiant. The symptoms of ODD generally fall into two types—irritability (e.g., tantrums, crankiness) and defiance (e.g., talking back, argumentativeness) (Kuny et al., 2013). About 30% to 50% of children with ADHD eventually develop conduct disorder (CD) (Beauchaine, Hinshaw, & Pang, 2010), which is more severe than ODD. Children with CD violate societal rules and are at high risk for getting into serious trouble at school or with the police. They may fight, cheat, steal, set fires, or destroy property. CD is also associated with the use of illegal drugs, which may explain why children with ADHD may have a higher risk for developing substance-use problems in adolescence (Szobot & Bukstein, 2008). ADHD that occurs early, particularly when it is accompanied by severe symptoms of hyperactivity–impulsivity, increases the odds of ODD/CD by about 10-fold, making it one of the most reliable predictors of these disorders (Angold, Costello, & Erkanli, 1999). Longitudinal studies have found that ADHD leads to ODD and CD rather than vice versa (Thapar et al., 2006). Interestingly, persistent and severe ODD and CD outcomes among children with ADHD are related to variations in

a specific gene (*COMT*) known to be associated with the regulation of neurotransmitters in the areas of the brain implicated in ADHD. These findings suggest the existence of a subgroup of children with ADHD who are at biological risk for later developing conduct problems (Caspi et al., 2008). Finally, ADHD is also a risk factor for the later development of antisocial personality disorder (APD) (Storebø & Simonsen, 2013), a pervasive pattern of disregard for, and violation of, the rights of others, as well as involvement in multiple illegal behaviors.

ADHD, ODD, and CD run together in families, which suggests a common predisposing cause. In support of this, there is a substantial common genetic contribution for the three disorders, especially between ADHD and ODD (Coolidge, Thede, & Young, 2000; Hamshere et al., 2013). There is also evidence for a contribution from a shared environment, perhaps related to family adversity and deficits in parenting (Burt et al., 2001). We discuss ODD, CD, and APD in greater detail in Chapter 9.

Anxiety Disorders

T.J.

Overactive and Anxious

T. J. was first referred for help at age 6. He had been very active and impulsive since he was a toddler. His parents reported that he had trouble sleeping and would wake up several times each night. They also said that he showed great anxiety during even brief separations from them and seemed to be worrying about something the whole time. T. J. confirmed that he had "terrible bad dreams" and felt that no one liked him.

Based on Tannock, 2000.

"Sam, neither your father nor I consider your response appropriate."

Edward Koren / The New Yorker Collection / www.cartoonbank.com

About 25% or more of children with ADHD experience excessive anxiety (Manassis, 2007). These children worry about being separated from their parents, trying something new, taking tests, making social contacts, or visiting the doctor. They may feel tense or uneasy and constantly seek reassurance that they are safe and protected. Because these anxieties are unrealistic, more frequent, and more intense than normal, they have a negative impact on the child's thinking and behavior. Findings regarding whether or not co-occurring anxiety worsens the symptoms or severity of ADHD are inconsistent (Hammerness et al., 2010). However, children with co-occurring ADHD and anxiety display social and academic difficulties and experience greater long-term impairment and mental health problems than those with either condition alone (Manassis et al., 2007).

Mood Disorders

As many as 20% to 30% of young people with ADHD experience depression (Daviss, 2008; Spencer et al., 2000), and even more will develop depression or another mood disorder by early adulthood (Fischer et al., 2002). Being diagnosed with ADHD between 4 and 6 years of age is a risk factor for future depression and suicidal behavior in adolescence, particularly for girls (Chronis-Tuscano, Molina, et al., 2010). These youths feel so sad, hopeless, and overwhelmed that they are unable to cope with everyday life. Depression lowers self-esteem; reduces interest or pleasure in favorite activities; increases irritability; and disrupts sleep, appetite, and the ability to think (Mick, Santangelo et al., 2000). Youths with ADHD have higher rates of suicidal ideation and deliberate self-harm than controls, although the highest risk for suicide is among those with ADHD with co-occurring depression and conduct problems (Pliszka, 2014).

The association between ADHD and depression may be a function of the fact that family risk for one disorder increases the risk for the other. This suggests that depression in a child with ADHD is not due solely to the child's demoralization as a result of their ADHD symptoms (Biederman, Mick, & Faraone, 1998).

Controversy abounds regarding the association between ADHD and pediatric bipolar mood disorder (BP) (to be discussed in Chapter 10). In part, this is due to the difficulty in distinguishing between symptoms of ADHD and the unregulated high energy level, poor judgment, and over-talkativeness of children with BP, as well as to possible shared underlying mechanisms (Youngstrom & Algorta, 2014; Youngstrom, Arnold, & Fraser, 2010). The relationship between the two disorders seems to go mainly in one direction—a diagnosis of childhood BP sharply increases the child's risk for previous or co-occurring ADHD, but a diagnosis of ADHD does not appear to increase the child's risk for BP (Pataki & Carlson, 2013; Skirrow et al., 2012).

Developmental Coordination and Tic Disorders

As many as 30% to 50% of children with ADHD display motor coordination difficulties—such as clumsiness, poor performance in sports, or poor handwriting—especially when they attempt to execute complex motor sequences (Fliers et al., 2010). Impairments often appear in the motor skills domains of strength, visual motor coordination, adjusting speed, and dexterity. As many as 50% of children with ADHD may have a

developmental coordination disorder (DCD), a condition characterized by marked motor incoordination and delays in achieving motor milestones (Brossard-Racine et al., 2012; Fliers et al., 2012). About 20% of children with ADHD also have tic disorders—sudden, repetitive, nonrhythmic motor movements or sounds such as eye blinking, facial grimacing, throat clearing, and grunting (Murphy et al., 2013; Simpson, Jung, & Murphy, 2011). These children experience more behavioral, social, and academic difficulties than do those with ADHD alone. When present, tic disorders decline to low rates by adolescence and do not appear to significantly affect later psychosocial functioning (Peterson et al., 2001).

Section Summary

Accompanying Psychological Disorders and Symptoms

- A factor that makes ADHD so challenging is that children with the disorder have much higher than expected rates of other psychiatric disorders, particularly conduct problems, anxiety, and mood disorders.
- As many as 50% of children with ADHD also meet criteria for oppositional defiant disorder or conduct disorder.
- About 25% or more of children with ADHD experience excessive anxiety. The presence of co-occurring anxiety is associated with more social and academic difficulties, and greater long-term impairment and mental health problems.
- As many as 20% to 30% children with ADHD experience depression or another mood disorder. Although depression may be partly related to demoralization as a result of their symptoms, it also can result from an elevated risk for depression in families of children with ADHD.
- The relation between ADHD and bipolar disorder is controversial. A diagnosis of childhood bipolar disorder appears to sharply increase the child's risk for previous or co-occurring ADHD, but a diagnosis of ADHD does not appear to elevate the child's risk for bipolar disorder.
- Children with ADHD may display motor coordination difficulties and tic disorders.

PREVALENCE AND COURSE

When we began our studies in the 1960's no one believed such children existed; while now people find them under every rock.

—Dr. Leon Eisenberg, child psychiatrist and ADHD pioneer (1922–2009)

The striking increase in ADHD alluded to in the above quote likely reflects an increase in diagnostic practices rather than an epidemic of ADHD. This increase is based partly on growing knowledge about ADHD, pressures from parents seeking treatment for children, and adults identifying their own ADHD (Taylor, 2009). The growing recognition of ADHD has established that it affects millions of children throughout the world and across all socioeconomic levels (Erskine, 2013). Although rates can vary widely with sampling methods (Rowland et al., 2013), the best estimate is that about 5% to 9% of all children and adolescents 4 to 17 years old in North America are currently diagnosed with ADHD; worldwide, just over 5% have ADHD (APA, 2013; Polanczyk et al., 2007; Visser et al., 2013). These estimates suggest that about 3 million to 5 million school-age children and adolescents in the United States are affected. As many as half of all children referred to clinics display ADHD symptoms either alone or in combination with other disorders, making ADHD one of the most common referral problems (Barkley, 2006a).

Reports from parents, teachers, and doctors are all used to identify children with ADHD. However, these people do not always agree, because the child's behavior may differ from setting to setting. Also, different adults may emphasize different symptoms when making a judgment. Teachers, for example, are most likely to rate a child as inattentive when the child also displays oppositional symptoms (Abikoff et al., 1993). Prevalence rates and patterns of comorbidity also differ when teacher's reports are compared with parent's reports (Gadow & Nolan, 2002). Since adults may disagree, prevalence estimates of ADHD are much higher when based on one person's opinion rather than on a consensus.

Gender

ADHD occurs more frequently in boys than in girls, with estimates ranging from 2% to 4% for girls and 6% to 9% for boys 6 to 12 years of age (Owens, Cardoos, & Hinshaw, 2014; Polanczyk & Jensen, 2008). In adolescence, overall rates of ADHD decrease slightly for both sexes, but boys still outnumber girls by the same ratio of about 2.5:1, a ratio that declines by adulthood to about 1.6:1 or lower (Kessler et al., 2005; Merikangas et al., 2010), possibly because of an underidentification of girls in childhood. This ratio is even higher in clinic samples, in which boys outnumber girls by 6:1 or more—most likely because boys are referred more frequently because of their overt defiance and aggression or because parents and teachers may think that learning assistance is less effective for girls than for boys with ADHD (Ohan & Visser, 2009).

ADHD in girls may go unrecognized and unreported because teachers fail to recognize and report inattentive behavior unless it is accompanied by the disruptive symptoms normally demonstrated by boys. In addition, the symptoms used to diagnose ADHD

may also contribute to the sex difference in prevalence. DSM criteria were developed and tested mostly with boys with ADHD, and many of the symptoms—excessive running around, climbing, and blurting out answers in class— are generally more common in boys than girls. Thus, the specified cutoffs and symptoms may be more appropriate to boys than to girls, because girls with ADHD may have to display not only extreme behavior but also behavior that is uncharacteristic as compared with their same-sex peers before they will be referred (Hinshaw & Blachman, 2005). Interestingly, when girls with ADHD also display defiance and aggression, they are referred at a younger age than boys, a finding that implies lower tolerance by adults or a greater concern for these behaviors when they occur in girls (Silverthorn et al., 1996). Girls with ADHD may be more likely than boys to display inattentive/disorganized symptoms characteristic of a sluggish cognitive tempo, including forgetfulness, lethargic behavior, mental confusion, drowsiness, tendency to daydream (McBurnett, Pfiffner, & Frick, 2001), anxiety, depression (Rucklidge & Tannock, 2001), and hyperverbal rather than hyperactive motor behavior (Nadeau, Littman, & Quinn, 1999). Thus, current DSM criteria may be insensitive to the problems that are especially relevant to girls (Ohan & Johnston, 2005). Although it may be premature to expand the current symptom lists for ADHD to include additional items appropriate to girls, it is clear that sampling, referral, and definition biases may all contribute to reports of ADHD being more prevalent in boys than in girls.

In the past, girls with ADHD were a highly understudied group (Hinshaw & Blachman, 2005). Although girls with ADHD tend to display inattentive/disorganized symptoms, some research shows more similarity between girls and boys with ADHD than was previously thought to exist. Some studies have found that among clinic-referred school-age children with ADHD, boys and girls are quite similar with respect to their expression and severity of symptoms, brain abnormalities, deficits in response inhibition and executive functions, level of impairment, family correlates, response to treatment, and outcomes (Biederman et al., 2006; Owens et al., 2014). Follow-up studies of girls with ADHD indicate clear evidence of major problems through adolescence and young adulthood, including anxiety; depression; romantic relationship difficulties; conflict with mothers; significant peer rejection and conduct problems; large deficits in academic achievement; continuing deficits in attention, executive functions, and language; impaired decision making; and high rates of service utilization (Babinski et al., 2010; Biederman et al., 2010; Mick et al., 2011; Miller et al., 2013; Owens et al., 2014).

It is noteworthy that girls with ADHD who display hyperactive–impulsive behaviors are more likely to develop symptoms of eating disorders (bingeing–purging

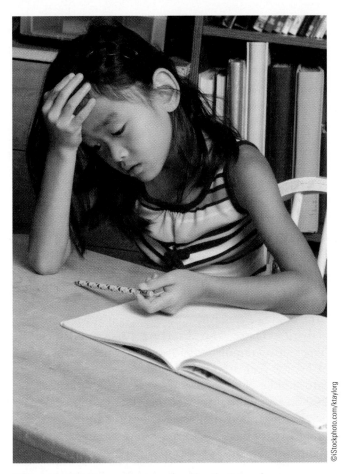

Girls with ADHD may be described by their teachers as "spacey" or "in a fog." Without hyperactivity and disruptive behavior, ADHD in girls may go unrecognized or be ignored.

behaviors, body dissatisfaction) and to engage in self-injury and suicide attempts than are girls with ADHD who display only symptoms of inattention or girls who do not have ADHD (Hinshaw et al., 2012; Mikami et al., 2008; Swanson, Owens, & Hinshaw, 2013). These findings support the need to consider behaviors and outcomes for girls with ADHD that reflect female-relevant domains of impairment.

Socioeconomic Status and Culture

ADHD affects children from all social classes, although there are slightly more children with ADHD in lower socioeconomic status (SES) groups (Akinbami et al., 2011). Low family income in childhood is also associated with an increased likelihood of ADHD (Larsson et al., 2013). The relationship between ADHD and SES may be related to co-occurring conduct problems in children with ADHD, since conduct problems are related to conditions that accompany low SES, such as family adversity and stress (Szatmari, Offord, & Boyle, 1989). Consistent with this view, family conflict and attachment links ADHD with SES (Russell et al., 2014).

Research on the relationships among ADHD, race, and ethnicity have been inconsistent, and it remains unclear whether current tools for assessing ADHD adequately capture the expression of ADHD in minority groups. By kindergarten entry, children in the United States who are black are 70% less likely to be diagnosed with ADHD than otherwise similar white children—even though they are equally likely to display ADHD-related behaviors in the classroom (Morgan et al., 2014). However, for older children, teacher-rated ADHD and observed rates of ADHD behavior are higher for black than for white children, which are not explained by rater bias or SES (Miller, Nigg, & Miller, 2009). Slightly lower rates of ADHD have been reported for Hispanic, Asian, American Indian, and Pacific Islander children (Cuffe, Moore, & McKeown, 2005). Knowledge about ADHD and access to treatment seem to be greater among Caucasian, non-Hispanic, and more highly educated families (McLeod et al., 2007; Miller et al., 2009). However, some research suggests that when families from different ethnic groups do receive treatment, they do not differ in the benefits derived (Jones et al., 2010).

ADHD has been identified in every country where it has been studied. Estimates vary across countries and cultures, with the highest rates found in South America and Africa (8% to 12%) and the lowest rates in Japan and China (2% to 5%). European and North American rates are in between (4% to 9%). These variations are mainly the result of differences in source of information (e.g., parents, teachers) and the way ADHD is diagnosed across studies done in different parts of the world. When a uniform diagnostic method is used, the rates of ADHD are highly similar worldwide (Buitelaar et al., 2006).

Varying cultural norms and tolerance for the symptoms of ADHD may explain the different diagnosis rates across cultures (Weisz, Weiss et al., 2006). In cultures that value reserved and inhibited patterns of child behavior, such as Thailand, symptoms of ADHD are less common than in the United States. Moreover, when ADHD symptoms do occur, teachers in Thailand view them as more problematic—likely because of their culture-linked values and expectations (Weisz, Chayaisit et al., 1995). Thus, a child being identified as having ADHD is partly a function of the discrepancy between a child's behavior and cultural expectations about how children ought to behave (Moffitt & Melchior, 2007).

Course and Outcome

In the sections that follow, we describe how symptoms of ADHD change with development. These changes over the life span are illustrated with the experiences of Alan, now age 35, who was diagnosed with ADHD in grade 1.

Infancy

ALAN

Off and Running

Our baby-sitter swears I was sitting up watching TV by 4 months. Then from a crawling position I ran, and we were off. … I was all over the house, into everything, and Mom soon realized I could not be left alone. Darting here, there, and anywhere, I didn't like playing with my toys, preferring to explore on my own.

From R. A. Barkley and L. J. Pfiffner, "Off to School on the Right Foot: Managing Your Child's Education. In: Barkley, R. A. Taking Charge of ADHD: The Complete, Authorized Guide for Parents, 1995, p. 208.

It is likely that signs of ADHD are present at birth (one mother reported her child was so overactive in the womb that the kicking nearly knocked her over!). Home-based activity-level assessments in the home—using motion detectors—are related to mothers' ratings of ADHD symptoms in children as young as 2 years of age (Ilott et al., 2010). Similarly, when parents of an older child with ADHD describe what their child was like as a baby, they often say their baby had a difficult temperament—extremely active, unpredictable, oversensitive or undersensitive to stimulation, and irritable with erratic sleep patterns or feeding difficulties. Early markers of ADHD symptoms may be present in infancy and toddlerhood, but reliable identification of ADHD is difficult prior to age 3 (Arnett, MacDonald, & Pennington, 2013). In addition, there are issues with these reports that suggest the early presence of ADHD. First, parents' recollections may be colored by their child's later difficulties. Second, most infants with a difficult temperament do not develop ADHD. Although a difficult temperament in infancy may indicate something amiss in development—and in some cases may be a risk factor for later ADHD—it cannot by itself be taken as an early sign of ADHD. For example, one study reported an association between persistent crying during infancy and a 10-fold higher risk for hyperactivity at 8 to 10 years of age (Wolke, Rizzo, & Woods, 2002). However, most infants who cry persistently do not go on to develop ADHD.

Preschool

ALAN

Preschool Outcast

I often wondered why I wasn't in group-time in preschool. The teacher sent me in the corner to play with a toy by

myself. Because of being singled out I didn't have many friends. I was different, but I didn't know why or what it was.

From R. A. Barkley and L. J. Pfiffner, "Off to School on the Right Foot: Managing Your Child's Education. In: Barkley, R. A. Taking Charge of ADHD: The Complete, Authorized Guide for Parents, 1995, p. 208.

With the growing number of hyperactive–impulsive symptoms at 3 to 4 years of age, ADHD becomes an increasingly visible and significant problem (Greenhill et al., 2008). Preschoolers with ADHD act suddenly and without thinking, dashing from activity to activity, grabbing at immediate rewards; they are easily bored and react strongly and negatively to routine activities (Campbell, 2006). Parents find it very difficult to manage the hyperactivity and noncompliance of their child, who may also be defiant and aggressive. Preschoolers with ADHD often roam about the classroom or daycare, talking excessively and disrupting other children's activities. Those who display a persistent pattern of hyperactive–impulsive and oppositional behavior for at least 1 year are likely to continue on to difficulties into middle childhood and adolescence (Olson et al., 2000). Difficulties in resisting temptation, delaying gratification, and inhibiting behavior during the preschool years have also been found to predict ADHD symptoms in third grade (Campbell & von Stauffenberg, 2009). At this age, the combination of severe ADHD-related symptoms and disruptions in the parent–child relationship is especially predictive of continuing ADHD behavior patterns (Campbell, Shaw, & Gilliom, 2000).

Elementary School

ALAN

I Couldn't Do Anything Right

Toward the middle half of first grade, the teacher called my Mom in for a conference. She was telling my Mom, "I'm always having to call on Alan. 'Alan, be still. Please. Yes, you can sharpen your pencil for the third time. You have to go to the bathroom again?'" By the time I got to third grade things were getting off track. I felt like nothing I did was right. I would try to do good work. My teacher would write on my papers, "Needs to concentrate more on answers," "Needs to turn in all work," "Needs to follow directions." I really didn't think my teacher liked me. She was very stern, never seemed to smile, and was always watching me.

From R. A. Barkley and L. J. Pfiffner, "Off to School on the Right Foot: Managing Your Child's Education. In: Barkley, R. A. Taking Charge of ADHD: The Complete, Authorized Guide for Parents, 1995, p. 208.

Symptoms of inattention become especially evident when the child starts school. Classroom demands for sustained attention and goal-directed persistence are formidable challenges for these children (Kofler, Rapport, & Alderson, 2008). Not surprisingly, this is when children are usually identified as having ADHD and referred for special assistance. Symptoms of inattention continue through grade school, resulting in low academic productivity, distractibility, poor organization, trouble meeting deadlines, and an inability to follow through on social promises or commitments to peers. The hyperactive–impulsive behaviors that were present in preschool continue, with some decline, from 6 to 12 years of age (Barkley, 2006a).

During elementary school, oppositional defiant behaviors may increase or develop. By 8 to 12 years of age, defiance and hostility may take the form of serious problems, such as lying or aggression. During the school years, ADHD increasingly takes its toll, as children experience problems with self-care, personal responsibility, chores, trustworthiness, independence, social relationships, and academic performance (Stein et al., 1995).

Adolescence

ALAN

A Parent's Viewpoint

It wasn't until Alan was 13 that I understood that ADHD was a lifelong condition. His inability to block out the high level of activity in junior high caused him to become a frequent visitor to the principal's office. And he began to do poorly in math, the subject he had always done well at, because he couldn't concentrate on all the steps involved. I had him thoroughly evaluated for ADHD again and discovered he wasn't outgrowing it. In fact, it was causing him more trouble, not less. It was then that I realized how ADHD shapes personality, torments the victims, and fragments relationships.

From R. A. Barkley and L. J. Pfiffner, "Off to School on the Right Foot: Managing Your Child's Education. In: Barkley, R. A. Taking Charge of ADHD: The Complete, Authorized Guide for Parents, 1995, p. 208.

Many children with ADHD do not outgrow their problems when they reach adolescence, and sometimes their problems can get much worse. Although hyperactive–impulsive behaviors decline significantly by adolescence, they still occur at a higher level than in 95% of same-age peers who do not have ADHD. The disorder continues into adolescence for at least 50% or more of clinic-referred elementary school children (Spencer, Biederman, & Mick, 2007). In addition, most teens continue to display significant impairments in their emotional, behavioral, and social

functioning (Barkley, 2006b; Lee et al., 2008). Childhood symptoms of hyperactivity–impulsivity (more so thansymptoms of inattention) are generally related to poor adolescent outcomes (Barkley, 2006b).

Adulthood

ALAN

Adult Challenges

Alan is now 35 years old. He frequently feels restless, cannot sit at a desk for more than a few minutes, cannot get organized, does not follow through on plans because he forgets them, loses his keys and wallet, and fails to achieve up to his potential at work. During conversations, his mind wanders and he interrupts others, blurting out whatever comes to mind without considering the consequences. He often gets into arguments. His mood swings and periodic outbursts make life difficult for those around him. Now his marriage is in trouble. He feels helpless and frustrated. (Based on authors' case material)

Although difficult to confirm, many well-known and highly successful adults, including inventor Thomas Edison, recording star and actor Justin Timberlake, celebrity Paris Hilton, and 18-time Olympic gold medal winner in swimming Michael Phelps may have had ADHD as children. Some children with ADHD either outgrow their disorder or learn to cope with it, particularly those with mild ADHD and without conduct or oppositional problems. Better outcomes are more likely for children whose symptoms are less severe and who receive good care, supervision, and support from their parents and teachers and who have access to economic and community resources, including educational, health, and mental health services (Kessler et al., 2005).

Unfortunately, like Alan, most children with ADHD will continue to experience problems, leading to a lifelong pattern of suffering and disappointment (Barkley, 2014a, b). Once thought of primarily as a disorder of childhood, ADHD is now well established as an adult disorder. Adults with ADHD are restless, easily bored, and constantly seeking novelty and excitement; they may experience work difficulties, impaired social relations, and suffer from depression, low self-concept, substance abuse, and personality disorder (Barkley, 2014a, b). Although the situation is changing, many adults with ADHD have never been diagnosed, particularly those without accompanying behavior problems. As a result, they may feel that something is wrong with them, but they don't know what it is. Since many adults with ADHD are bright and creative individuals, they often feel frustrated about not living up to their potential. Alan has had to contend with a number of significant problems as he continues to adapt to adult responsibilities of marriage, finances, and work. The help he has received for his ADHD helps him cope, but it is an ongoing challenge.

A few words of caution are in order regarding the developmental course and outcomes for ADHD. First, age at onset, course, and outcomes may differ depending on the samples, measures used, accompanying disorders, and the presentation type of ADHD (Faraone, Biederman, & Mick, 2006; Owens et al., 2014). For example, negative outcomes are much greater in clinic samples as compared with community samples and for children with accompanying conduct problems. Little information is currently available regarding long-term outcomes for youngsters with ADHD-PI. Interestingly, ADHD symptoms and impairments in adulthood are more severe when reported by other adults than by the person with ADHD (Barkley et al., 2002). Thus, the developmental course and outcomes we have presented describe an overall pattern, but additional follow-up studies are needed to fill in important details.

Section Summary

Prevalence and Course

- The best estimate is that ADHD affects about 5% to 9% of all school-age children.
- The diagnosis of ADHD is about two to three times more common in boys than in girls.
- Girls with ADHD have a significant disorder; clinic-referred girls with ADHD display many of the same features and outcomes as boys with ADHD.
- ADHD occurs across all socioeconomic levels and has been identified in every country where it has been studied.
- Symptoms of ADHD change with development. A difficult temperament as an infant may be followed by hyperactive–impulsive symptoms at 3 to 4 years of age, which are followed, in turn, by the increasing visibility of symptoms of inattention around the time that the child begins school.
- Although some symptoms of ADHD may decline in prevalence and intensity as children grow older, for many individuals ADHD is a lifelong and painful disorder.

THEORIES AND CAUSES

The word cause is an altar to an unknown god.

—William James (1842–1910)

Many explanations for ADHD have been advanced, and some are highly controversial. For example, it has been argued (without much support) that ADHD is a trait left over from our evolutionary past as hunters (Hartmann, 1993). Others contend that ADHD is a myth, a disorder that has been fabricated because as a society we need it (Baughman, 2006; Breggin, 2001).

Clear answers about the nature and causes of ADHD have been elusive because diagnostic practices are not standardized and research is challenging. Nevertheless, research into the basic nature of ADHD leads to fascinating theories about possible mechanisms and causes (Martel, 2009; Nigg & Barkley, 2014). As summarized in A Closer Look 8.1, theories

A CLOSER LOOK 8.1

Interrelated Theories of ADHD

Cognitive Functioning Deficits

Children with ADHD display specific cognitive deficits in sustained attention, response inhibition (i.e., inability to delay initial reactions to events or to stop behavior once it gets going), working memory, and executive functions. These in turn may lead to other cognitive, language, and motor difficulties. Cognitive deficits are important for understanding ADHD. However, since more than 50% of children with ADHD do not show major impairment on any specific cognitive task, the evidence does not support a *single* cognitive deficit as the cause of ADHD (Nigg, 2005).

Reward/Motivation Deficits

Children with ADHD display an abnormal sensitivity to rewards (i.e., higher reward threshold) and usually a heightened sensitivity or an aversion to delay (Sonuga-Barke et al., 2008). As a result, they have difficulty motivating themselves and performing well when rewards are unavailable or delayed (Aase & Sagvolden, 2006). In support of this theory, some research has connected ADHD with disruptions in the dopamine reward pathways of the brain (Volkow et al., 2009).

Arousal Level Deficits

Children with ADHD have an abnormal level of arousal—either too high or, more commonly, too low. Hyperactivity–impulsivity reflects an underaroused child's effort to maintain an optimal level of arousal by excessive self-stimulation (Zentall, 1985). Although this theory has received some support (Antrop et al., 2000), it has not yet been presented as a comprehensive model to account for the full range of problems found in children with ADHD.

Self-Regulation Deficits

Children with ADHD have a higher-order deficit in their ability to self-regulate—to use thought and language to direct their behavior. Deficiencies in self-regulation and effortful control lead to impulsivity, poor maintenance of effort, poor modulation of arousal level, emotion dysregulation, and attraction to immediate rewards. Self-regulatory theories examine the interplay among cognitive, arousal, and reward/motivational processes to understand how individuals with ADHD regulate their behavior in specific contexts (Douglas, 1999; Martel, 2009).

emphasize deficits in cognitive functioning, reward and motivation, arousal level, and self-regulation. No single theory can explain the many difficulties associated with ADHD. For example, despite having similar levels of ADHD symptoms, children with ADHD may show differences in the kinds of problems they experience related to response inhibition, arousal, and response variability (Fair et al., 2012). However, identifying the influences of the processes emphasized by each theory helps increase our understanding of ADHD and develop more integrative models (Shiels & Hawk, 2010).

Numerous causes for ADHD have been proposed. However, many have not been adequately tested or have fallen by the wayside in the face of weak, inconsistent, or nonexistent support. Among these are that ADHD is caused by too much sugar intake, yeast, fluorescent lighting, motion sickness, bad parenting, poor school environment, urban living, or too much TV.

While many factors may lead to ADHD, current research strongly suggests that ADHD is a neurodevelopmental disorder for which genetic and neurobiological factors play a central role (Faraone, 2014; Kieling, Gonclaves, Tannock, & Castellanos, 2008; Scasselatti et al., 2012). However, biological and environmental risk factors together shape the development of behavioral and emotional regulation and the expression of ADHD symptoms over time, following several different pathways (Froehlich et al., 2011; Nigg et al., 2006; Sonuga-Barke et al., 2005). Since ADHD is a complex and chronic disorder involving genetic, neural, cognitive, and behavioral mechanisms, any explanation that focuses on just one cause is likely to be inadequate (Banerjee, Middleton, & Faraone, 2007; Coghill et al., 2005). Although data do not yet permit a comprehensive causal model, ● Figure 8.2 shows a possible developmental pathway for ADHD that highlights several known causal influences and outcomes. We discuss each of these causal influences in the sections that follow.

Genetic Influences

Several lines of evidence point to genetic influences as key causal factors in ADHD (Faraone & Mick, 2010).

▶ *ADHD runs in families.* About one-third of the biological relatives of children with ADHD also have the disorder (Smalley et al., 2000). Remarkably, if a parent has ADHD, the risk to their child is nearly 60% (Biederman et al., 1995).

▶ *Adoption studies.* Rates of ADHD are nearly three times higher in biological parents of children with

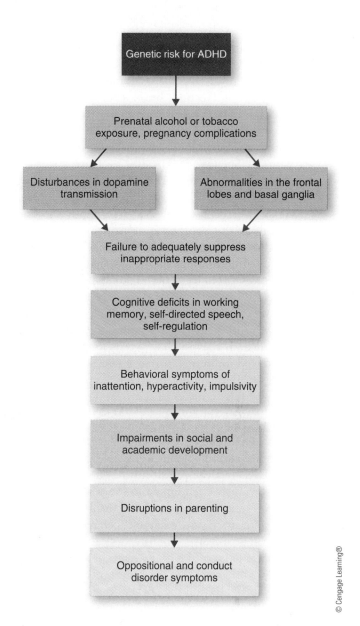

● **FIGURE 8.2** | A possible developmental pathway for ADHD.

ADHD, as compared with adoptive parents of children with ADHD (Sprich et al., 2000).

▶ *Twin studies.* Twin studies report extraordinarily high heritability estimates for ADHD, averaging about 75% for hyperactive–impulsive and inattentive behaviors, making ADHD among the most heritable of the childhood disorders (Nikolas & Burt, 2010). Further, ADHD concordance rates for identical twins average 65%, about twice that for fraternal twins (Levy & Hay, 2001).

▶ *Specific gene studies.* Molecular genetic analysis suggests that specific genes may contribute to the expression of ADHD (Banaschewski et al., 2010).

The focus has been on genes involved in dopamine regulation, for three primary reasons. First, dopamine is a neurotransmitter used by the brain and has a central role in psychomotor activity and reward seeking. Second, brain structures implicated in ADHD (see below) are rich with dopamine innervation, and neuroimaging studies have found evidence for dopamine dysregulation in these brain structures (Spencer et al., 2007). Third, primary medications that reduce ADHD symptoms act primarily by blocking the dopamine transporter (DAT1), a receptor on the presynaptic neuron involved in the re-uptake of dopamine, thereby increasing the availability of dopamine in the synapse. Research findings on the association between variants in DAT1 and ADHD have been mixed (Li et al., 2006). However, this may be related to a gene–environment interaction. For example, children with this genetic risk who are also exposed to environmental risks such as psychosocial adversity or maternal smoking during pregnancy may develop a greater number of ADHD symptoms than those who are not exposed to the environmental risk (Laucht et al., 2007).

Studies consistently show an association between ADHD and a variant of one of the dopamine receptor genes, DRD4 (seven-repeat form). Interestingly, this gene has previously been linked to the personality trait of sensation seeking (high levels of thrill seeking, impulsive, exploratory, and excitable behavior) (Ebstein et al., 1996); it affects responsiveness to medication; and it impacts parts of the brain associated with executive functions and attention. In addition to the association between ADHD and the DRD4 dopamine receptor gene, several other genes related to the regulation of dopamine, as well as noradrenaline, have recently been identified (Faraone & Mick, 2010; Nikolas et al., 2010).

Findings that implicate specific genes within the dopamine system in ADHD are intriguing, and they are consistent with a model suggesting that reduced dopaminergic activity may be related to the behavioral symptoms of ADHD. For example, preliminary findings indicate that brain activity related to inhibitory control of behavior in children with ADHD may differ as a function of variations in specific genes within the dopamine system (Bédard et al., 2010). Keep in mind, however, that the effects of individual gene variants are very small and—in the vast majority of cases—the heritable components of ADHD are likely to be the result of multiple genes interacting on several different chromosomes (Neale et al., 2010). For example, associations have also been found between ADHD and genes within the serotonin system (Guimarães et al., 2009),

and gene mutations that impair maternal serotonin production during pregnancy may increase the risk of ADHD-related symptoms in offspring (Halmøy et al., 2010). Some work has also implicated genes associated with serotonin function in aversion to reward delay, suggesting that different genes may regulate different ADHD behaviors (Sonuga-Barke et al., 2011b). Thus, it is extremely unlikely that ADHD is caused by only one gene. As Kates (2007) noted, "Finding a gene mutation that transmits risk for ADHD is like looking for a needle in a haystack of the 3 billion base pairs of DNA that constitute the human genome" (p. 547). Nevertheless, taken together, the findings from family, adoption, twin, and specific gene studies strongly indicate that the risk for ADHD is inherited, although the precise mechanisms are not yet known (Mick et al., 2010). Findings from genomewide association studies are just beginning to reveal the specific neurodevelopmental networks that may be involved in ADHD (Poelmans et al., 2011). To date, these findings indicate that many common DNA variants combine to create a genetic predisposition to ADHD that accounts for about 20% to 30% of the disorder's heritability (Smoller et al., 2003; Yang et al., 2013). These findings from genomewide studies do not specify the particular DNA or variants that make up the predisposition to ADHD but do suggest that such variants will likely be found as more data are collected (Faraone, 2014). Importantly, the more we discover about the genetics of ADHD, the more evident it becomes that environmental factors play a powerful role in shaping neurodevelopmental processes and pathways. Therefore, the role of environment will need to be incorporated into any explanation of ADHD based on genetic influences (Sonuga-Barke, 2010).

Pregnancy, Birth, and Early Development

Many factors that can compromise the development of the nervous system before and after birth may be related to ADHD symptoms, including pregnancy and birth complications, maternal exposure to environmental toxins or severe stress during pregnancy, low birth weight, malnutrition, early neurological insult or trauma, and diseases of infancy (Lindström, Lindblad, & Hjern, 2011; Linnet et al., 2003; Martel et al., 2007). Although these early factors predict later symptoms of ADHD, they may not be specific to ADHD; that is, they may elevate the risk of developing many later problems in addition to ADHD.

A mother's use of cigarettes, alcohol, or other drugs during pregnancy can have damaging effects on her unborn child. One study found that mothers of children with ADHD reported higher rates of heavy smoking

(10 cigarettes per day) and more psychosocial stress during pregnancy as compared with mothers of unaffected control children (Motlagh et al., 2010). Consistent support has been found for an association between maternal cigarette smoking during pregnancy and ADHD, particularly for female offspring, and for children who carry a specific genetic risk for ADHD (Braun et al., 2006; Neuman et al., 2007). Whether this association is causal or due to other unmeasured environmental or genetic factors is unclear (Obel et al., 2011; Thapar et al., 2009). Evidence suggests that most (but not necessarily all) of the association between maternal cigarette smoking during pregnancy and ADHD is due to genetic mediation, not to the direct effects of nicotine exposure in the womb (Rutter & Solantaus, 2014). Exposure to alcohol before birth may also lead to symptoms of inattention, hyperactivity, impulsivity, and associated impairments in learning and behavior (Mick et al., 2002).

Evidence suggests that mothers of children with ADHD use more alcohol, tobacco, and drugs than do control parents, even when they are not pregnant (Mick et al., 2002). Since parental substance use is often associated with a chaotic home environment both before and after birth, it is difficult to disentangle the influence of substance abuse and other factors that occur prior to birth from the cumulative impact of a negative family environment that occurs during later development. Other substances used during pregnancy, such as cocaine, can adversely affect the normal development of the brain and lead to higher-than-normal rates of ADHD and other psychiatric disorders (Weissman et al., 1999). To summarize, although pregnancy and birth complications and substance use during pregnancy are not the cause of most cases of ADHD, they may be important contributing factors for some children.

Neurobiological Factors

ADHD is far from well understood, but there is substantial support for neurobiological causal factors (Krain & Castellanos, 2006). Evidence comes from research showing differences between children with and without ADHD on measures of brain function (Barkley, 2006a; Kieling et al., 2008), including:

▸ Differences on psychophysiological measures (e.g., electroencephalography, galvanic skin response, and heart-rate deceleration), suggesting diminished arousal or arousability (Beauchaine et al., 2001; Loo & Makieg, 2012).

▸ Differences on measures of brain activity during vigilance tests, suggesting underresponsiveness to stimuli and deficits in response inhibition (Pliszka, Liotti, & Woldorff, 2000).

▸ Differences in blood flow to the prefrontal regions of the brain and the pathways connecting these regions to the limbic system and cerebellum, suggesting decreased blood flow to these regions (Hendren, De Backer, & Pandina, 2000).

Brain Abnormalities

Brain-imaging studies make it possible to test hypotheses about the location of brain dysfunction in ADHD and to provide assessments of brain structure and function (Cortese et al., 2012). Findings from these studies suggest abnormalities primarily in the **frontostriatal circuitry of the brain** (Bush, 2008). This region consists of the prefrontal cortex and interconnected areas of gray matter located deep below the cerebral cortex, collectively known as the *basal ganglia* (basement structures) (Hart et al., 2013). These areas of the brain are associated with attention, executive functions, delayed responding, and response organization. Lesions in this region result in symptoms similar to those of ADHD. Children with ADHD have a smaller right prefrontal cortex than children without ADHD (Filipek et al., 1997) and have structural abnormalities in several regions of the basal ganglia (Sobel et al., 2010). Interestingly, in identical twins discordant for ADHD, it is only the twin with ADHD who displays abnormalities in these brain structures (Castellanos et al., 2003).

Brain differences may not be restricted exclusively to the prefrontal cortex and parts of the basal ganglia. Some findings indicate that children with ADHD have smaller total and right cerebral volumes (by 3% to 4%) and a smaller cerebellum. These data provide support for the growing notion that some deficits associated with ADHD, such as learning temporal associations and events and their consequences, may involve a cerebellar–prefrontal–striatal network (Mackie et al., 2007; Valera et al., 2007). Some work also suggests that specific regions of the thalamus may also be involved in the brain circuitry of ADHD, with different thalamic subcircuits associated with differing ADHD symptoms linked with the regulation of motor and emotional responses (Li et al., 2012). The default mode network (discussed in Chapter 6) also operates abnormally in ADHD. This network tends to be active at rest but tends to shut off during task engagement—but not as effectively in those with ADHD (Cortese et al., 2012).

In addition to identifying brain abnormalities, brain-scan studies now focus on how brain connections and networks are wired during development. Newer studies suggest that circuits may develop differently or later in ADHD (Fair et al., 2010; Shaw et al., 2007). For example, one study (see A Closer Look 8.2) identified a delay in brain maturation in children with ADHD, particularly in the prefrontal regions (Shaw et al., 2007). Another study found differences in brain development between individuals with ADHD whose symptoms persisted into adulthood and those whose symptoms did not persist. Those whose symptoms persisted showed an increase in cortical thinning in areas of the prefrontal cortex. In contrast, only individuals whose ADHD remitted showed a trajectory of cortical thickening or minimal thinning (Shaw et al., 2013). These findings help to advance our understanding of developmental pathways to adult ADHD.

In summary, brain-scan studies indicate the importance of the frontostriatal region of the brain in ADHD and the pathways connecting this region with the limbic system (via the striatum) and the cerebellum and thalamus. However, further research is required to reliably identify more localized abnormalities. Furthermore, although neuroimaging studies can tell us that children with ADHD have a structural difference or less activity in certain regions of the brain, they don't tell us why.

A few additional words of caution are needed when evaluating the neurobiological evidence for ADHD. First, samples have been defined differently across studies and sample sizes are generally small. This gives rise to inconsistent findings and presents problems

---

A CLOSER **LOOK** 8.2

Does the Brain Develop Abnormally in Children with ADHD, or Is It Just Delayed?

Findings from brain-imaging studies suggest the latter. Dr. Philip Shaw and his colleagues at the National Institute of Mental Health studied a large group of children with ADHD and a comparison group of typically developing children at different ages (Shaw et al., 2007). Using magnetic resonance imaging (MRI), the researchers tracked changes in the cortical thickness of the children's brains. Typically, the cortex reaches a peak thickness at around 7 or 8 years of age. However, as shown in the accompanying photograph, in children with ADHD, there was about a 2- to 3-year delay in reaching this peak thickness as compared with typically developing controls. The greatest delay (about 5 years) was in the prefrontal cortex, which regulates self-control.

The overall pattern of brain development was the same for both groups, suggesting a developmental delay and not abnormal development in children with ADHD. The brains of children with ADHD did reach one developmental milestone earlier than did the brains of typically developing children—maturation of the motor cortex, which plans and controls movements. The researchers proposed that the delay in the development of areas of the cortex related to self-control, combined with the earlier development of the motor cortex, may account for the fidgety, restless, and uncontrolled hyperactive behavior of children with ADHD.

Interestingly, other brain-imaging studies have found that delayed cortical maturation in the prefrontal cortex is associated with a greater number of symptoms of hyperactivity–impulsivity, even in typically developing children who have not been diagnosed with ADHD (Shaw et al., 2011).

Although these brain-scan findings are captivating, they raise other important issues. First, the cause of the maturational delay in children with ADHD is not known at this time, although some work suggests that delayed or decreased myelination

Greater than 2 years' delay

0 to 2 years delay

Regions where the ADHD group had delayed cortical maturation, as indicated by an older age of attaining peak cortical thickness

From Proceedings of the National Academy of Sciences, "Attention-deficit/hyperactivity disorder is characterized by a delay in cortical maturation," edited by Leslie G. Ungerleider, National Institutes of Health, Bethesda, MD, and approved October 5, 2007, © 2007 by The National Academy of Sciences of the USA.

may be a factor (Nagel et al., 2011). Second, if ADHD is just a delay in development, why do so many children continue to display ADHD as adults? Delay alone may not fully characterize all children with ADHD. In addition, even when brain maturation "catches up," the expression of behavior may still be different, since the timing of brain maturation may be as important as its end point (Fair et al., 2010). Answers to these questions await further research. The hope is that brain-imaging studies will increase our understanding of how ADHD develops and in doing so may one day help to tailor treatments for children with ADHD. (Based on authors' case material.)

"Young man, go to your room and stay there until your cerebral cortex matures."

with interpretation and generalization. Second, ADHD includes a complex set of symptoms, making the search for a single neurobiological cause too simplistic. Third, the differences in brain structure and activity seen in ADHD (and other disorders) are usually meaningful only when comparing group statistics. The amount of variation in brain structure or function from one brain to the next is simply too great to be diagnostic or predictive for an individual, given what we currently know (Insel, 2010). Thus, although research using brain imaging has greatly increased our understanding of ADHD, much research remains to be done before neuroimaging procedures can be integrated into clinical practice (Bush, 2008).

Neurophysiological and Neurochemical Findings

Precise neurophysiological and neurochemical abnormalities underlying ADHD have been extremely difficult to document (Scassellati et al., 2012). No consistent differences have been found between the biochemistry of urine, plasma, blood, and cerebrospinal fluid of children with and without ADHD. At a neurochemical level, the known action of effective medications for ADHD suggests that the neurotransmitters dopamine, norepinephrine, epinephrine, and serotonin may be involved, with most evidence suggesting a selective deficiency in the availability of both dopamine and norepinephrine (Barkley, 2006a). However, we must be cautious in drawing conclusions from the effects of medications alone. Using medication for effective treatment of ADHD symptoms does not prove that deficits in the chemical or its action are the cause of the symptoms, any more than the elimination of a headache by aspirin implies that the headache was caused by aspirin deficiency. Medications may operate at levels of neuroanatomy

and neurochemistry that are far removed from the primary causal influences.

Diet, Allergy, and Lead

The connection between sugar and hyperactivity achieved epic significance when "What is sugar?" was the correct question for the answer "The major cause of hyperactivity in North America" on the popular TV show *Jeopardy* (Barkley, 1995). However, study after study has conclusively shown that sugar is not the cause of hyperactivity (Milich, Wolraich, & Lindgren, 1986). So why do nearly half of the parents and teachers who are asked think that children are sugar-sensitive? It may be the power of suggestion.

In one study, mothers who believed their children were sugar-sensitive were told that their children would be given a drink of Kool-Aid™ containing either sugar or, as a placebo, the sugar substitute aspartame. After the children drank their Kool-Aid, they and their mothers spent time playing and working together. In fact, none of the children was given sugar—they all received Kool-Aid with aspartame. But the mothers who thought their children had received sugar rated them as more hyperactive than the mothers who believed their children had received aspartame. Perhaps even more telling was that during play and task interactions, mothers who thought their children had received sugar were more critical of them, hovered more, and talked to them more frequently (Hoover & Milich, 1994). These findings suggest that what parents believe about the causes of their children's ADHD can affect their views of their children and how they treat them (Johnston & Leung, 2001). Such beliefs may be fueled by media portrayals—for example, when Bobby Hill, the son on the TV show *King of the Hill*, is diagnosed with ADHD after eating at least four bowls of "Cookie Crunch" cereal (the last with extra sugar!). His mother, Peggy, "a hotshot substitute teacher," wonders if she should stay at home more often so she can give Bobby more attention, a notion reinforced by Bobby's father, Hank, who comments, "Well, it is called attention *deficit* disorder" (Kennedy, 2008).

There has been a long-time controversy about the possibility that allergic reactions and diet cause ADHD. A popular view in the 1970s and 1980s was that food additives caused children to be hyperactive and inattentive, and parents were encouraged to withhold foods containing artificial flavorings, colorings, preservatives, and sugars. By the 1990s, food additives appeared to have been discarded as an explanation for ADHD (McGee, Stanton, & Sears, 1993). However, some studies have revived this idea, focusing on the moderating role of genetic factors to explain why food additives may affect the behavior of some children more than that of others (McCann et al., 2007; Stevenson, 2010; Stevenson et al., 2010). In a close vote (8 to 6), a Food and Drug Administration Advisory Panel (March 31, 2011) concluded that foods that contain artificial dyes do not need warning labels, but this issue continues to be debated. Dietary research on ADHD is now focusing on micronutrients, with much interest currently in essential fatty acids—which are commonly lacking in the diet of North American children—as well as in other nutrients such as zinc and iron, which may be metabolized abnormally in some children (Arnold & DiSilvestro, 2005; Howard et al., 2011; Stevens et al., 2003).

Exposure to low levels of lead found in dust, water, soil, and flaking paint in areas where leaded gasoline and paint were once used may be associated with ADHD symptoms in the classroom (Fergusson, Horwood, & Lynskey, 1993). Although most children with ADHD do not have significantly elevated lead levels in their teeth or blood (Kahn, Kelly, & Walker, 1995), some work persistently links ADHD to slight, subclinical elevations in lead exposure (Goodlad, Marcus, & Fulton, 2013). All children have a little lead in their blood, and those with ADHD have a little more. In addition, lead exposure in combination with other risk factors, such as exposure to nicotine during pregnancy, may further increase a child's risk for ADHD (Froehlich et al., 2009). These findings suggest a possible role of lead exposure that requires further follow-up using causally informative prospective studies (Nigg et al., 2010).

Family Influences

Twin studies find that psychosocial factors in the family account for only a small amount of the variance in ADHD symptoms (Nikolas & Burt, 2010), and explanations for ADHD based exclusively on negative family influences have received little support (Barkley, 2006a). Nevertheless, family influences are important in understanding ADHD for several reasons (Johnston & Chronis-Tuscano, 2014; Mash & Johnston, 2005).

▶ *Family influences may lead to ADHD symptoms or to a greater severity of symptoms.* In some cases, ADHD symptoms may be the result of interfering and insensitive early caregiving practices (Carlson, Jacobvitz, & Sroufe, 1995), especially in children with a specific genetic risk for ADHD (Martel et al., 2011). Thus, parenting practices may interact with the child's genetic makeup to moderate risk for ADHD. In addition, for children at risk for ADHD, family conflict may raise the severity of their hyperactive–impulsive symptoms to a clinical level (Barkley, 2003). Especially important

is the **goodness of fit**, or the match between the child's early temperament and the parent's style of interaction (Chess & Thomas, 1984). An overactive child with an overstimulating parent is a seemingly poor fit. As we have seen, many parents of children with ADHD also have the disorder, which means that the parents' ADHD symptoms may disrupt early parent–child interactions (Johnston et al., 2012). For example, mothers with higher levels of ADHD symptoms have been found to show less involvement, less positive parenting, and more inconsistent discipline with their children than mothers with lower levels of ADHD symptoms (Chronis-Tuscano et al., 2008). Finally, one study found that mothers with variants in DAT1 were more like to display negative and controlling behaviors when interacting with their children, particularly when their children were highly disruptive (Lee et al., 2010). Although preliminary, these findings are fascinating, in that they suggest the possible importance of a parent-gene × child-gene interaction in families of children with ADHD, with the effects mediated by the child-rearing environment.

▶ *Family problems may result from interacting with a child who is impulsive and difficult to manage* (Mash & Johnston, 1990). The clearest support for this child-to-parent direction of effect comes from double-blind placebo-controlled drug studies in which children with ADHD who received stimulant medications showed a decrease in their symptoms. The decreases in children's ADHD symptoms produced a corresponding reduction in the negative and controlling behaviors that parents had previously displayed when their children were not medicated (Barkley, 1988).

▶ *Family conflict is likely related to the presence, persistence, or later emergence of associated oppositional and conduct disorder symptoms.* In children with an inherited biological risk for ADHD, family conflict may heighten the emergence of early ODD and later comorbid ADHD and CD (Beauchaine et al., 2010). For example, children with ADHD report observing more interparental conflict than do children without ADHD, which may worsen ADHD and related ODD and CD symptoms in those who have a genotype that makes them particularly vulnerable to the effects of the emotional stress and self-blame associated with interparental conflict (Nikolas et al., 2010). Many ADHD interventions aim to change patterns of family interaction to prevent an escalating cycle of oppositional behavior and conflict. Family influences may play a major role in determining the outcome of ADHD and its associated problems, even if the influences are not the primary cause of ADHD (Johnston, Hommersen, & Seipp, 2009; Kaiser, McBurnett, & Pfiffner, 2011).

In summary, ADHD has a strong biological basis and is an inherited condition for many children. It is likely that ADHD is a heterogeneous disorder, particularly at the level of neurobiology. Although evidence is converging on specific brain areas and circuits, findings are correlational, and we do not yet know the specific causes of the disorder. We are just beginning to understand the complex ways in which biological risk factors, brain development, early environmental experiences and events, family relationships, and broader system influences interact to shape the development and outcome of ADHD (Nigg & Barkley, 2014).

Section Summary

Theories and Causes

- Theories about possible mechanisms and causes for ADHD have emphasized deficits in cognitive functioning, reward/motivation, arousal level, and self-regulation.

- There is strong evidence that ADHD is a neurodevelopmental disorder; however, biological and environmental risk factors together shape its expression.

- Findings from family, adoption, twin, and specific gene studies suggest that ADHD is inherited, although the precise mechanisms are not yet known.

- Many factors that compromise the development of the nervous system before and after birth may be related to ADHD symptoms, such as pregnancy and birth complications, maternal smoking during pregnancy, low birth weight, malnutrition, maternal alcohol or drug use, early neurological insult or trauma, and diseases of infancy.

- ADHD appears to be related to abnormalities and developmental delays in the frontostriatal circuitry of the brain and the pathways connecting this region with the limbic system, the cerebellum, and the thalamus.

- Neuroimaging studies tell us that in children with ADHD there is a structural difference or less activity in certain regions of the brain, but they don't tell us why.

- The known action of effective medications for ADHD suggests that several neurotransmitters are involved, with most evidence suggesting a selective deficiency in the availability of both dopamine and norepinephrine.

- Psychosocial factors in the family do not typically cause ADHD, although they are important in understanding the disorder. Family problems may lead to a greater severity of symptoms and relate to the emergence of co-occurring conduct problems.

- ADHD is likely the result of a complex pattern of interacting influences, perhaps giving rise to the disorder through several nervous system pathways.

TREATMENT

MARK

Medication and Behavior Therapy

In third grade, Mark's teacher threw up her hands and said, "Enough!" In one morning, Mark had jumped out of his seat six times to sharpen his pencil, each time accidentally charging into other children's desks and toppling books and papers. He was finally sent to the principal's office when he began kicking a desk he had overturned. In sheer frustration, his teacher called a meeting with his parents and the school psychologist.

But even after they developed a plan for managing his behavior in class, Mark showed little improvement. Finally, after an extensive assessment, they found that he had ADHD with symptoms of both inattention and hyperactivity–impulsivity. He was put on Ritalin, a stimulant medication, to control the hyperactivity during school hours. With a psychologist's help, his parents learned to reward desirable behaviors and to have Mark take time out when he became too disruptive. Soon Mark was able to sit still and focus on learning.

Adapted from NIMH, 1994a.

LISA

Behavior Therapy and Counseling

Because Lisa wasn't disruptive in class, it took a long time for teachers to notice her problem. Lisa was first referred to the school evaluation team when her teacher realized that she was a bright girl with failing grades. The team ruled out a learning disability but determined that she had the inattentive subtype of ADHD. The school psychologist recognized that Lisa was also dealing with depression.

Lisa's teachers and the school psychologist developed a treatment plan that included a program to increase her attention and develop her social skills. They also recommended that Lisa receive counseling and cognitive behavior therapy to help her recognize her strengths and overcome her depression.

Adapted from NIMH, 1994.

In recent years, the number of children with ADHD receiving help has more than doubled. However, it is still the case that less than half, particularly those in greatest clinical need, actually receive specialty services for ADHD (Visser et al., 2013; Zima et al., 2010). Of those who do receive services, many do not continue their treatment for any length of time (Hechtman, 2006). Although there is no known cure for ADHD, a variety of treatments can be used to help children like Mark and Lisa cope with their symptoms and any secondary problems that may arise (Antshel & Barkley, 2008; Pelham & Fabiano, 2008). An overview of these treatments is presented in Table 8.3.

The primary treatment approach, as recommended by *Consumer Reports* and the U.S. Surgeon General, combines stimulant medication, parent management training, and educational intervention (AACAP, 2007c; Kaiser & Pfiffner, 2011; NICE, 2013a). Interventions

TABLE 8.3 | Treatments for Children with ADHD

Primary Treatments	Focus of Treatment
Stimulant medication	Managing ADHD symptoms at school and home
Parent management training	Managing disruptive child behavior at home, reducing parent–child conflict, and promoting prosocial and self-regulating behaviors
Educational intervention	Managing disruptive classroom behavior, improving academic performance, teaching prosocial and self-regulating behaviors
Intensive Treatment	**Focus of Treatment**
Summer treatment programs	Enhancing present adjustment at home and future success at school by combining many of the primary and additional treatments in an intensive summer treatment program
Additional Treatments	**Focus of Treatment**
Family counseling	Coping with individual and family stresses associated with ADHD, including mood disturbance and marital strain
Support groups	Connecting adults with other parents of children with ADHD, sharing information and experiences about common concerns, and providing emotional support
Individual counseling	Providing a supportive relationship in which the youth can discuss personal concerns and feelings

© Cengage Learning®

that use elements of all these approaches have also been provided in intensive summer treatment programs and controlled clinical trials (Smith & Shapiro, 2014). Additional treatments, for which there is far less evidence, include family counseling and support groups and child-focused treatments, such as individual counseling and traditional forms of social skills training (Mikami, 2014; Smith, Barkley, & Shapiro, 2006). Other treatments, such as brain-wave neurofeedback/biofeedback (Lofthouse et al., 2011) and complementary and alternative biomedical treatments, such as special diets (e.g., restricted elimination diets, artificial food color elimination) and vitamin/mineral supplements (e.g., supplementation with free fatty acids) (Hurt & Arnold, 2014; Millichap & Lee, 2012) are used despite limited or inconsistent supporting evidence to date (Sonuga-Barke et al., 2013; Vollebregt et al., 2013). However, given that some studies have reported modest beneficial effects for both neurofeedback and dietary treatments for a small proportion of children with ADHD, further evaluation of these approaches seems warranted (Gevensleben et al., 2014; Nigg et al., 2012; Stevenson et al., 2014).

A rationale and procedures for early detection and early intervention for ADHD are now beginning to emerge (Sonuga-Barke et al., 2011a). However, one 6-year follow-up study of 207 children 3 to 5 years old who had ADHD who were treated with stimulant medication found little improvement, suggesting that further study of moderating variables (e.g., co-occurring behavior problems, family adversity) and other interventions for this age group may be needed (Riddle et al., 2013). Focused interventions for specific ADHD core deficits—for example, working memory (Beck et al., 2010; Rapport et al., 2014), inattention (Rabiner et al., 2010), self-control (Diamond, 2012), and organization, time-management, and planning (Abikoff et al., 2013) are also receiving attention (Evans, Owens, & Bunford, 2013). Further work is needed to determine whether these approaches produce changes that are long-lasting and generalize to other tasks and situations beyond the training context (Dunning, Holmes, & Gathercole, 2013).

Although similar treatments are used for children and adolescents with ADHD, research with teens has been extremely limited (Barkley, 2006b). Similarly, only a few studies have looked at treatment efficacy for specific ADHD presentation types, such as children with predominantly inattentive symptoms (e.g., Pfiffner et al., 2007). Therefore, although recognizing that children with different ADHD symptoms may have different treatment needs (Solanto et al., 2009), most of our discussion centers on treatments for school-age children with ADHD who show symptoms of both inattention and hyperactivity–impulsivity.

Medication

When I'm not medicated … my muscles just don't want to relax. They don't want to settle down. I just feel very "go-go-go." I can't be still. My body tries to keep up with my mind but it can't just do it fast enough.

—Angelique (Waite & Ramsey, 2010, p. 429)

The use of stimulants and other medications to treat the symptoms of ADHD in children has been the subject of considerable and heated debate. Most of you likely have opinions about stimulants for ADHD—perhaps that they are overprescribed, used as a quick fix, do not let kids be kids, lead to overdiagnosis, or lead to later substance use. Let's look at the role of stimulant medications and the controversy that surrounds them.

Stimulants

Stimulant medications have been used to treat the symptoms of ADHD since the chance discovery of their effectiveness in the 1930s (see A Closer Look 8.3).

A CLOSER **LOOK** 8.3

The "Accidental" Discovery of Math Pills

The use of stimulant medication for children with learning and behavior problems was first reported in 1937 by Charles Bradley, the medical director of a small hospital for children with major difficulties in learning or behavior. Dr. Bradley described dramatic improvements in some of the children he treated with Benzedrine. Why did Dr. Bradley decide to use stimulants to treat these problems in the first place?

Dr. Bradley was a very conscientious physician, and all patients were given careful workups. These workups included a spinal tap, which naturally led to headaches afterward that frequently were lasting, severe, or both, and were presumed to be due to the loss of spinal fluid. Dr. Bradley speculated that if he could stimulate the choroid plexus to secrete spinal fluid at a faster rate, the headaches would be relieved more quickly. He decided to proceed along these lines and chose the most potent stimulant available at the time, Benzedrine. (*Note:* This type of powerful stimulant is no longer used.) The effect on the headaches was negligible, but to his astonishment, the teachers reported major improvements in learning and behavior in many children that lasted until the Benzedrine regimen was withdrawn. The children themselves noted the greater ease of learning and called the medication "math pills," presumably because mathematics was the hardest subject for them, and their improved ability to learn was most noticeable in that subject.

Source: Based on Gross, 1995.

Several other types of medications have also been used, including noradrenergic drugs, antidepressants, and antihypertensives (Daughton & Kratochvil, 2009). We focus our discussion on stimulants because they are the most studied, most effective, and most commonly used treatment for the management of symptoms of ADHD and its associated impairments. Nevertheless, it is important to keep in mind that many other potentially effective medication options are available for children with ADHD, including nonstimulant drugs such as atomoxetine (Strattera) and a patch that releases stimulant medication directly through the skin into the bloodstream, eliminating the need to take medication orally (Pelham et al., 2011). Other medications may be used for children who do not respond well to stimulants, cannot tolerate the side effects of stimulants, or have other conditions along with ADHD (Connor, 2014).

Stimulants come in several types, including both short- and long-acting forms. Among the most effective stimulants in treating individuals with ADHD are dextroamphetamine (Dexedrine or Dextrostat), amphetamine-dextroamphetamine (Adderall), and **methylphenidate** (Ritalin), the most commonly used drug by far (Faraone & Buitelaar, 2010). These medications alter activity in the frontostriatal region of the brain by affecting neurotransmitters (dopamine) important to this region. Interestingly, preliminary findings from brain-scan studies of individuals with ADHD suggest that stimulants may also help to normalize structural abnormalities and functional connections within this region (Sheridan, Hinshaw, & D'Esposito, 2010; Sobel et al., 2010).

For about 80% of children with ADHD, stimulants produce dramatic increases in sustained attention, impulse control, and persistence of work effort and decreases in task-irrelevant activity and noisy and disruptive behaviors. Stimulants may also improve the child's academic productivity; cooperation and social interactions with parents, teachers, and peers; and, occasionally, physical coordination such as handwriting or sports ability (Barkley, 2006a; Prasad et al., 2013). Stimulant medications used appropriately and with proper supervision are usually quite safe (Connor, 2014). Some children may experience side effects such as reduced appetite, weight loss, slowing of expected gains in height and weight, increase in heart rate and blood pressure, or problems falling asleep. However, most potential side effects are typically benign and can be carefully monitored and often eliminated by reducing the dose of the medication (Graham et al., 2011). Although stimulants can be addictive if misused or abused (one recreational name for Ritalin is Vitamin R!), they are not addictive for most children who take them, nor do they lead to an increased risk for later

Stimulant medications are commonly used to treat children with ADHD

substance abuse (Chang et al., 2013; Humphreys, Eng, & Lee, 2013; Molina et al., 2013). Stimulants seldom make children "high," nervous, or jumpy, or turn them into nonfeeling zombies. Qualitative findings suggest that young people taking medication are generally positive about taking it and report that it reduces their disruptive behavior, improves their relationships with peers, and increases their ability to meet normative expectations (Singh, 2013; Singh et al., 2010).

The short-term benefits of medication are well documented (Spencer, Biederman, & Wilens, 2000). Unfortunately, follow-up studies raise questions about their long-term benefits (Jensen et al., 2007). The effects of stimulants are temporary and occur only while the individual is taking the medication. In this sense, the use of stimulants is similar to other important treatments for chronic conditions, such as insulin used for diabetes; however, they are not a cure. Many young people receiving stimulants for severe behavior problems remain impaired, despite many years of medication treatment. The limited long-term benefits of stimulants raise important issues about their clinical use that have yet to be resolved, particularly their use in preschool children (Riddle et al., 2013).

Controversy: The Ritalin Wars

There is no pharmacologic free lunch. The key question is always this: Is the gain to public health from proper use of an agent ... greater than the danger of wide-scale misuse or the social cost of the regulatory machinery itself?

—Leon Eisenberg (2007)

Public awareness of and controversy about the potential misuse of medication is evidenced by efforts(ultimately unsuccessful) to introduce legislation in the U.S. Congress with the express purpose

"to protect children and their parents from being coerced into administering a controlled substance in order to attend school, and for other purposes" (Child Medication Safety Act of 2007). Why the concern? Community and physician surveys, increased production of Ritalin, and pharmacy audits all indicate that stimulant consumption has more than tripled since 1990 in North America (Scheffler et al., 2007). The co-prescription of stimulants with other medications, most commonly antidepressants, has also increased during this period (Comer, Olfson, & Mojtabai, 2010). Over 3.5 million children and adolescents in the United States (6% of 4- to 17-year-olds) are currently taking stimulants for ADHD, a 28% increase from 2007–2008 to 2011–2012 (Visser et al., 2013). Moreover, the use of Ritalin is at least five times higher in North America than in the rest of the world, although its use worldwide is also increasing. This increase may stem from a widening of the diagnostic criteria for ADHD, greater use of stimulants among girls and older individuals, widespread third-party medication coverage, and direct-marketing efforts by drug companies. Also, as changes in public policy and laws increase eligibility for special education and other services for individuals with ADHD, more individuals may receive this diagnosis and subsequently be prescribed medication (DuPaul & Stoner, 2003). Some findings indicate that although stimulant use in children ages 15 and younger in the United States has leveled off over the past decade, it continues to increase in older adolescents and young adults (McCabe & West, 2013). This increase is related to the growing recognition of ADHD in adults, and has also raised concerns about a possible diversion of stimulants from medical to nonmedical use in older individuals (Rabiner, 2013). In fact, among high school seniors in the United States, the self-reported lifetime prevalence of medical and nonmedical use of stimulants is the same (9.5%) (McCabe & West, 2013).

Given the astronomic increase in the use of stimulants to treat ADHD in North America, despite the similarities of prevalence across different parts of the world, we need to ask whether ADHD is overdiagnosed and whether stimulants are overprescribed (Eisenberg, 2007). Because of the wide variability in diagnostic practices, treatment decisions, and rates of stimulant use in various schools, communities, geographic regions, and populations, it is not surprising that research findings concerning diagnosis and medication use are inconsistent (Angold et al., 2000; Jensen et al., 1999). Perhaps the best overall conclusion to be drawn from the research is that in many cases stimulants are currently being used inappropriately: underprescribed in some cases and overprescribed in others. We need a better understanding of the factors leading to the diagnosis of ADHD and stimulant use so that further steps can be taken to increase appropriate use—for example, improved screening and diagnosis and better education of service providers (Jensen, 2000; Kovshoff et al., 2013). Consider the following comments by the parents of a child with ADHD:

> When all is said and done, we stand in the middle on the issue of medication—not dramatically opposed, but not wildly enthusiastic either. Ideally, stimulants should be prescribed, monitored carefully, and there should be ongoing communication with parents and school personnel. However, the world being what it is, a lot of people seem to be falling short of the ideal a lot of the time. (McCluskey & McCluskey, 2000, p. 11)

Despite their limitations, stimulants—when properly used—remain among the most effective treatments for managing symptoms of ADHD. Nevertheless, since stimulants do not address many of the associated individual, family, academic, and peer problems of children with ADHD, additional primary interventions such as parent management training and educational interventions are needed.

Parent Management Training (PMT)

Being the parent of a child who is overactive, disorganized, irritable, and does not listen or follow directions is difficult and exhausting. Usual discipline tactics such as reasoning, warning, or scolding often don't work. Thus, parents may feel powerless and at a loss as to what to do. Out of frustration, they may spank, ridicule, or yell at their child, even though they know it is not effective. These reactions leave everyone in the family feeling more upset than ever. **Parent management training (PMT)** focuses on teaching both effective parenting practices and strategies for coping with the challenges of parenting a child with ADHD (Chacko et al., 2014). It provides parents with a variety of skills to help them:

▸ manage their child's oppositional and noncompliant behaviors;

▸ cope with the emotional demands of raising a child with ADHD;

▸ contain the problem so that it does not worsen; and

▸ keep the problem from adversely affecting other family members.

Parents are first taught about ADHD so that they understand the biological basis of the disorder. This helps to remove the burden of guilt from parents who may think they have caused the problem. Parents are also given a set of guiding principles for raising a child with ADHD, such as using more immediate, frequent, and powerful consequences; striving for consistency; planning ahead; not personalizing the child's problems; and practicing forgiveness (Barkley, 2013c).

Parents are next taught behavior management principles and techniques, such as identifying behaviors they wish to encourage or discourage, using rewards and sanctions to achieve specified goals, establishing a home token program, noticing what their child does well, and praising their child's strengths and accomplishments. For disruptive behavior, parents also learn to use penalties such as loss of privileges or time-out as well as how to manage noncompliance in public places. Parents may also learn to use a school–home-based reward program, in which teachers evaluate the child on a daily report card (Owens et al., 2012). This card serves as a means for rewards or punishments (usually tokens) that will be administered at home for classroom conduct. Parents also learn how to manage future misconduct and are given follow-up sessions (Smith et al., 2006).

Parents are encouraged to spend time each day sharing an enjoyable activity with their child. They learn to structure situations in ways that will maximize the child's success and minimize failures. For example, if the child has difficulty completing tasks, it may be necessary to break the task into smaller steps and then praise the completion of each step. In PMT, parents also learn to reduce their own levels of arousal through relaxation, meditation, or exercise. Reduced arousal or anger allows parents to respond more calmly to their child's behavior.

Numerous studies support the effectiveness of PMT and other psychosocial interventions in treating children with ADHD (Chacko et al., 2014; Evans et al., 2013; Fabiano et al., 2009; Mulqueen, Bartley, & Block, 2013); however, the relative advantages and long-term benefits of PMT when used on its own to treat ADHD continue to be debated (Chronis-Tuscano, Chacko, & Barkley, 2013; Sonuga-Barke et al., 2013). As we will discuss, the effects of stimulants appear to be as strong as or stronger than the effects of PMT in treating the primary symptoms of ADHD. PMT may produce additional therapeutic benefits by treating the associated problems, improving family functioning, and increasing consumer satisfaction (Chronis et al., 2004a). To date, PMT has focused mainly on teaching parents to manage the overt disruptive behaviors that accompany their child's ADHD rather than on changing the deficits underlying the child's ADHD. New approaches that combine PMT with therapy that is directed at the parent–child processes that mediate the development of attention and self-regulatory skills may provide incremental benefits for children with ADHD (Sonuga-Barke et al., 2006).

Educational Intervention

Boxed in at School

My teacher wanted to make me concentrate better, so one day she put my desk in the far corner, separated from the rest of the class. A few days had passed. I still wasn't finishing my work on time, but I was trying. My teacher didn't care; it wasn't finished. She then put a refrigerator box around my desk so I couldn't see anyone. I could hear as other kids in class would make fun of me. It really hurt; I was ashamed of myself and mad at my teacher. I couldn't tell my Mom because I might get into trouble. I hated school, didn't like my teacher, and started not liking myself. ... It was hard to face the next day. A week had passed, and I poked holes in the cardboard so I could see who was making fun of me. I started peeping through the holes, making the other kids laugh. The teacher would get so annoyed. So I became the class clown. I was expelled for two days. When my Mom found out what was going on, boy, did she get angry; she was mad that the teacher would do this and mad that the principal allowed it and no one could see what this was doing to me.

From R. A. Barkley and L. J. Pfiffner, "Off to School on the Right Foot: Managing Your Child's Education. In: Barkley, R. A. Taking Charge of ADHD: The Complete, Authorized Guide for Parents, 1995, p. 208.

Classroom requirements to sit still, pay attention, listen to instructions, wait your turn, complete assignments, and get along with classmates are not easily met by children with ADHD. Their inattention and hyperactivity–impulsivity make learning very difficult, at times even painful. Although some children with ADHD are placed in a special education class for all or part of the day, most remain in the regular classroom. Whenever possible, it is preferable to keep children with ADHD in classes with their peers.

Educational interventions focus on managing inattentive and hyperactive–impulsive behaviors that interfere with learning and on providing a classroom environment that capitalizes on the child's strengths (DuPaul & Stoner, 2003). Techniques for managing classroom behavior are similar to those recommended to parents. The teacher and child set realistic goals and objectives, set up a mutually agreed-upon reward system, carefully monitor performance, and reward the child for meeting goals. Disruptive or off-task classroom behaviors may be punished with **response-cost procedures** that involve the loss of privileges, activities, points, or tokens following inappropriate behavior or with brief periods of time-out. These procedures have proved to be effective in reducing disruptive classroom behavior and enhancing academic productivity (Pfiffner & DuPaul, 2014).

Many strategies for instructing children with ADHD are simply good teaching methods. Letting children know what is expected of them, using visual aids, providing cues for expected behavior, and giving written as well as oral instructions all help children focus their attention and remember important points. In addition, children with ADHD may require other accommodations to help them learn. For example, the teacher may seat the child near the teacher's desk, provide a designated area in which the child can move about, establish a clearly posted system of rules, and give the child frequent cues for expected behaviors. A card or a picture on the child's desk can provide a visual reminder for acceptable behavior such as raising a hand instead of shouting out. Repeating instructions, providing extra time, writing assignments on the board, and listing all of the books and materials needed for a task may increase the likelihood that children with ADHD will complete their work (Pfiffner & DuPaul, 2014).

School-based interventions for ADHD have received considerable support. A meta-analysis of 60 studies spanning 15 years found that school-based programs, including academic, contingency management, and self-regulation interventions, were related to moderate to large improvements in academic and behavioral functioning of students with ADHD (DuPaul, Eckert, & Vilardo, 2012). Some efforts have focused on a variety of school-based interventions for ADHD, including those for individual students in regular and special education classes, combined home and school interventions, and schoolwide interventions that incorporate both universal and targeted treatments (Pfiffner & Dupaul, 2014; Waschbusch, Pelham, & Massetti, 2005).

Intensive Interventions

There are no quick cures for ADHD. More intensive (and ongoing) treatments than previously used may be required to produce meaningful changes in long-term outcomes. As described below, the Summer Treatment Program and the Multimodal Treatment Study for Children with ADHD are two examples of programs that have provided intensive treatment to children with ADHD and their families.

Summer Treatment Program

Over the past 30 years, Dr. William Pelham and his colleagues have developed and disseminated an exemplary intensive summer treatment program (Pelham et al., 2010). In this program, treatment is provided to children with ADHD ages 5 to 15 in a camplike setting where they engage in classroom and recreational activities with other children. Summer treatment has two major advantages over other interventions: It maximizes opportunities to build effective peer relations in normal settings, and it provides continuity to academic work to ensure that gains made during the school year are not lost. These programs are coordinated with stimulant medication trials, parent management training, social skills training, and educational interventions in an all-out treatment effort.

The Summer Treatment Program packs 360 hours of day-treatment into a period of 8 weeks, the equivalent of 7 years of weekly therapy. Ratings by parents and counselors suggest that children who participate show overall improvements in behavior, decreases in problem severity, and improvements in social skills and academic performance. Children also rate themselves as doing better, and parents report higher levels of self-efficacy. Dropout rates are low and consumer satisfaction is high. The program is also cost-effective as compared with more traditional treatments. Preliminary findings from controlled studies of outcomes are promising (Chronis et al., 2004b; O'Connor et al., 2012; Pelham et al., 2000; Sibley et al., 2013); however, although growing in use, these programs are not yet widely available and it is still too early to tell whether this kind of intensive program will make a long-term difference for these children.

The MTA Study

The Multimodal Treatment Study of Children with ADHD (MTA Study) is a landmark multisite study sponsored by the U.S. National Institute of Mental Health (NIMH) and the U.S. Department of Education. It represents the first large, randomized clinical trial for children with ADHD. The study sought to answer three questions: How do long-term medication and behavioral treatments compare with one another? Are there additional benefits when they are used together? What is the effectiveness of systematic carefully delivered treatments versus routine community care? (MTA Cooperative Group, 1999a).

Children with ADHD participating in a Summer Treatment Program

Carefully diagnosed children 7 to 9 years of age with ADHD were randomly assigned to one of four treatment groups, followed by major assessments at periodic intervals during and after treatment.

▸ *Medication Management:* This group received stimulant medication 7 days a week;

▸ *Behavioral treatment:* This group received 35 sessions of parent management training, up to 10 teacher and school visits per year, and participation in an intensive 8-week summer treatment program, which taught academic and social skills and had a classroom aide who continued to reinforce strategies learned in the summer treatment program in the child's actual classroom for half a day, 5 days per week, for 12 weeks;

▸ *Combined behavioral treatment and medication:* This group received both medication and behavioral treatment; or

▸ *Routine community treatment:* This group received treatment as it was routinely delivered in community care. In fact, 66% of children in this group received stimulant medication.

The major finding from the MTA Study after 14 months of active treatment was that all groups showed reductions in ADHD symptoms over time, but there were significant variations in the amount of change. First, stimulant medication was superior to behavioral treatment and to routine community care in treating the symptoms of ADHD. Second, combining behavioral treatments with medication resulted in no additional benefits for the core symptoms of ADHD over medication alone, but it did provide modest benefits for non-ADHD symptoms and other outcomes related to positive functioning (MTA

Cooperative Group, 1999a). Composite outcome measures showed that combined treatment was best, followed by medication, then behavior therapy, and finally, community treatment (Conners et al., 2001; Swanson et al., 2001).

The benefits of combined treatment were also found at 24 months of follow-up (MTA Cooperative Group, 2004a, b). However, by 36 months there were no significant treatment group differences, with all groups showing equal benefits for ADHD symptoms (Jensen et al., 2007). Consistent with this result, findings from the MTA Study at 6 and 8 years after enrollment in the program indicate that the effects of both medication and behavioral treatments either decline or cease entirely when the treatment stops (Molina et al., 2009). Thus, the efficacy of treatment for children with ADHD will require that these treatments continue to be provided in a comprehensive, carefully monitored, and ongoing fashion. The interventions in the MTA Study were more intensive and monitored more closely than is typically the case in real-world clinical practice. Further research will be needed to determine the intensity of intervention and frequency of monitoring needed to maintain treatment gains and optimal functioning over time and across contexts in light of available treatment resources (Abikoff, 2009).

Other questions from the MTA Study that continue to be addressed concern which treatments work best for which children, for which outcomes, and why? (Hinshaw, 2007b). For example, children with ADHD and comorbid anxiety and children from families on social assistance may benefit more from behavioral treatments than those without these difficulties (MTA Cooperative Group, 1999b), and behavioral treatments may be associated with less substance use at a later age (Molina et al., 2007). In general, the long-term findings from the MTA study indicate that the initial clinical presentation in childhood (e.g., severity, co-occurring conduct problems, social disadvantage) and the strength of ADHD symptom response to *any* treatment are better predictors of adolescent outcomes than the type of treatment received in childhood (Molina et al., 2009).

The MTA Study findings can be interpreted in different ways and are likely to be debated for some time to come. It seems that for children who have uncomplicated ADHD with no co-occurring disorders, adequate social functioning, and good academic performance, medication management may be the best treatment option. However, for those who have ADHD complicated by oppositional symptoms, poor social functioning, and ineffective parenting, combining medication and behavioral treatment may be the best option. In both cases, ongoing interventions will likely be needed. Whatever the final verdict, findings from the MTA study continue to raise numerous questions of clinical importance for children with ADHD and their families.

Additional Interventions

Other interventions have been used to provide support to children with ADHD and their families. Among these interventions are family counseling and support groups and individual counseling for the child. (A brief overview of these interventions can be found in Table 8.3.)

Family Counseling and Support Groups

Many families of children with ADHD experience frustration, blame, and anger for some time. As we have discussed, siblings may feel neglected or resent the time their parents spend with the child with ADHD. Family members may require special assistance not only in managing behavior but also in dealing with their own thoughts and feelings. Counseling the family helps everyone develop new skills, attitudes, and an ability to relate more effectively.

Support groups for people who are coping with ADHD in various ways can be very helpful to members. There are many local and national support groups for parents of children with ADHD. Members share information, emotional support, personal frustrations and successes, referrals to qualified professionals, discoveries about what works, and their aspirations for their children and themselves. There are also online bulletin boards and discussion groups. Sharing experiences with others that have similar concerns helps parents feel that they are not alone.

Individual Counseling

Life can be very hard for children with ADHD. They have few successes on which to build their sense of self-competence. Perhaps as a result, even when they succeed, they may attribute their success to uncontrollable factors such as task ease or luck (Hoza et al., 2000). Being punished or told they are stupid or bad is often their main form of attention. They have few friends and are constantly in trouble. The cumulative impact can leave them feeling isolated and believing that they are abnormal, stupid, or doomed to failure. Individual counseling attempts to address these concerns, although evidence for its effectiveness in treating children with ADHD is limited. Children usually come into counseling with many questions about ADHD and treatment that are addressed at the outset and in later sessions (see A Closer Look 8.4. How would you answer these questions?).

Questions Asked by Children and Adolescents with ADHD

Children (Ages 4 to 10)

I just found out I have ADHD. How can I keep this secret from my brother?

I heard ADHD means you're weird. Is that right?

Is it true that if you have ADHD you can think faster than other people?

Will the medicine make me smarter?

Adolescents (Ages 11 to 17)

How do you know the medicine isn't dangerous?

Any advice on how to deal with the fact that I feel like a reject because I have ADHD?

How long am I going to have ADHD?

How can I convince [my teacher] that ADHD exists and that it affects my performance?

Source: Based on Hallowell and Ratey, 1994.

need. I'm not dumb. You can't always measure smartness by tests. I feel I'm doing better now. It helps to talk to people who understand. What I'm trying to say is: no matter what comes my way, I can survive. I have those who really care, and from that I draw my strength.

From R. A. Barkley and L. J. Pfiffner, "Off to School on the Right Foot: Managing Your Child's Education. In: Barkley, R. A. Taking Charge of ADHD: The Complete, Authorized Guide for Parents, 1995, p. 208.

A Comment on Controversial Treatments

Understandably, parents want to explore all possible ways to help their children with ADHD. Over the years, many treatments that sound plausible have been proposed. Some are enthusiastically endorsed by professionals, and individual patient reports claim dramatic success; others are pure charlatanism. Treatments proposed for children with ADHD that have not been scientifically substantiated include allergy treatments, homeopathic treatments, medication to correct inner ear problems, vestibular stimulation, running, walks in the park, treatment for yeast infection, megavitamins, sensory integration training, chiropractic adjustment, eye training, special colored glasses, metronome therapy, and applied kinesiology (realigning bones in the skull). Untested or fad treatments may prove to be expensive, provide false hope for a quick cure, delay the use of evidence-based treatments that are known to be of some benefit, and in some cases may even be harmful (AACAP, 2013; Waschbusch & Hill, 2003).

Keeping Things in Perspective

MARK

Good Support System

Through my years so far, I've been through a lot. My Mom says I have a good heart; I care about those in

Young people with ADHD have problems that should not be minimized, especially if doing so prevents children and adolescents with ADHD and their families from receiving help. However, as Mark's comments illustrate, in helping those with ADHD and their families, it is important not to lose sight of the fact that each child is unique and has assets and resources that need to be recognized and supported. These assets can serve as a buffer in reducing the child's behavior problems and referral concerns (Short et al., 2007).

In closing, many of our current treatments for ADHD developed prior to advances in our theory and knowledge about the possible causes of ADHD. Efforts are now underway to design more effective treatments that are sensitive to the different types of ADHD and to specific cognitive and behavioral deficits of individual children (Casey, Nigg, & Durston, 2007).

Section Summary

Treatment

- There is no cure for ADHD, but a variety of treatments can be used to help children cope with their symptoms and any secondary problems that may arise over the years.

- The primary approach to treatment combines stimulant medication, parent management training, and educational intervention.

- Stimulants are the most effective treatment for managing symptoms of ADHD; however, their limited long-term benefit raises important issues about their clinical use that are yet to be resolved.

- Parent management training (PMT) provides parents with a variety of skills to help them manage their child's oppositional and defiant behaviors and cope with the difficulties of raising a child with ADHD.

- Educational interventions focus on managing inattentive and hyperactive–impulsive behaviors that interfere with learning and on providing a classroom environment that capitalizes on the child's strengths.

- Findings from the MTA Study, a landmark controlled comparison of intensive treatments for ADHD, suggest that for children with uncomplicated ADHD, medication may be the best treatment option; however, for those with ADHD and oppositional symptoms, poor social functioning and ineffective parenting, combining medication and behavioral treatment may be the best option.
- Additional interventions for ADHD include family counseling and support groups, and individual counseling for the child.

Study Resources

SECTION SUMMARIES

KEY TERMS

9

Conduct Problems

Our youth now love luxury. They have bad manners, contempt for authority and disrespect for their elders. Children nowadays are tyrants.

—Socrates, 470–399 B.C.E.

CHILDREN'S CONDUCT PROBLEMS HAVE long been a societal concern and been considered to be forerunners of juvenile delinquency and adult criminality. However, despite enormous public, scientific, and professional attention, substantial numbers of youths continue to display antisocial, destructive, and violent behaviors, many of which are hidden from public view. Many types of adolescent conduct problems have increased substantially over the past 25 years, a change that has affected males and females, all social classes, and all family types (Collishaw et al., 2004). Since 1994, the most lethal forms of youth violence in the United States steadily decreased and then leveled off in the 2000s, and the number of youths arrested for violent crimes in 2010 was at its lowest in at least 30 years (Puzzanchera, 2013). However, the prevalence of other forms of antisocial behavior (e.g., aggravated assault) remains alarmingly high, and the proportion of females involved in violent crimes has increased (Zahn et al., 2008). A nationally representative survey of U.S. high school students in 2011 found that about 33% had been in a physical fight at least once in the past year, 25% reported being bullied on school property, 17% reported carrying a weapon in the past month, and 8% reported being threatened or injured with a weapon on school property (CDC, 2012b; Robers, Kemp, & Truman, 2013). Tragically, there are many victims of youth violence. Guns killed more children in the United States in 2008–2009 than the number of U.S. military deaths in both the Iraq and Afghanistan wars to date (Children's Defense Fund, 2012).

The high prevalence of youths with conduct problems and the harm inflicted on their victims create an urgent need for understanding and assistance. Tragic school shootings by youths, such as the mass murder–suicide at Sandy Hook Elementary School in Newtown, Connecticut, in 2012 that resulted in the deaths of 20 children and 6 adult staff members, provide stark reminders of the societal impact of youth violence. These youths often have a background that suggests a history of social isolation and rejection, unusual social behavior, and a fascination with violent themes. As such, these incidents raise important questions about factors that contribute to violence and other antisocial behavior by young people in our society (McNamara & Findling, 2008).

Unfortunately, school shootings and media portrayals of extreme antisocial acts may also fuel popular beliefs that aggression is inherent in humans, that some children are born bad, or that youth violence is symptomatic of a decaying society. In fact, although it is an ongoing and extremely serious problem, much progress has been made in understanding, reducing, and preventing youth violence as well as less harmful but still serious forms of antisocial conduct (Moffitt et al., 2008).

DESCRIPTION OF CONDUCT PROBLEMS

"[T]hose who violate social and criminal codes do so for very many reasons. …[B]efore studying our cases we must do our best to group them into different sorts. …"

—John Bowlby (1907–1990)

ANDY

Young Rage

"Andy threw his booster seat in my face and hit my jaw. He thought it was funny. He was acting up, and I think he had already had one time-out for yelling and screaming and interrupting us at the table. And I said, "Fine, you are not having dessert." He flew into a rage. He picked up a metal fork and threw it at me with all his force, and hit me—barely missed my eye. There was blood on my forehead. I was hysterical. I was terrified to see that type of rage in a 4-year-old."

Based on Troubled Families—Problem Children: Working with Parents: A Collaborative Process by C. Webster-Stratton and M. Herbert, 1994, pp. 44–45

Early conduct problems may be forerunners of delinquency and adult criminal behavior

Masterfile

MARVELLE

Defiant

"She just drives me up the wall. She's irritable all the time and never does anything I ask her to do. When she doesn't get her way she throws a full-blown tantrum. Her behavior is also a problem at school. Her teacher can't get her to do schoolwork—she simply refuses. She's also defiant, won't stay in her seat, and talks constantly. She's disrupting the entire class. I'm worried that she's headed for serious problems if she doesn't shape up soon." (Based on authors' case material)

NICK

Not Like Other Kids

Outwardly, Nick is a normal 10-year-old. He loves sports, especially football. He has a talent for drawing and an aptitude for math ... but Nick isn't like other kids. At age 2, he put a can of cat food on the stove, and lit the burner—it exploded. In one 5-day period last March, he threw a rock at a girl at the YMCA, hitting her in the head and drawing blood; set fire to his room; pushed his sister down the stairs; whipped the family dog with a chain; and stole $20 from his mother's wallet.

Adapted from Colapinto, 1993, p. 122.

STEVE

Not without Cause

Twelve-year-old Steve was referred because he stabbed his father in the leg and stole a car. He had a history of lying, fighting at school, and theft and was constantly in trouble with school personnel and police. He readily admitted stabbing his father in the leg, but his story included some interesting details that hadn't come up previously. He and his two brothers were in their parents' bedroom while the father was raping the mother. She was screaming for help and panicked. Steve went and got a knife from the kitchen; his brothers tried to restrain him but could do so only partially. He stabbed his father in the calf, deeply and with a long cut. After the stabbing, Steve felt he was going to get beaten, because his father had a long history of physically abusing the boys. He fled to his grandfather's house, took the car keys without permission, drove off, and crashed the car in a field. The police brought Steve to us. By all accounts, he had stabbed his father. And indeed he stole a car.

Based on Kazdin, A. E. (1995). Conduct disorders in childhood and adolescence (2nd ed.). Thousand Oaks, CA: Sage.

---

in many cases, aggressive behaviors are an adaptation to home and neighborhood violence and neglect. These circumstances do not excuse the behaviors, but they do provide an important backdrop for understanding and preventing these problems. Consider the case of Steve.

Conduct problem(s) and antisocial behavior(s) are terms used to describe a wide range of age-inappropriate actions and attitudes of a child that violate family expectations, societal norms, and the personal or property rights of others (Kimonis, Frick, & McMahon, 2014). These children experience problems in controlling their emotions and behavior. Like the children in our examples, youths with conduct problems display a variety of disruptive and rule-violating behaviors, ranging from annoying but relatively minor behaviors such as whining, swearing, and temper tantrums to more serious forms of antisocial behavior such as vandalism, theft, and assault. Given such diversity, we need to consider many types, pathways, causes, and outcomes of conduct problems.

Although we may be shocked by their actions, children with severe conduct problems frequently (not always) grow up in extremely unfortunate family and neighborhood circumstances, where they experience physical abuse, neglect, poverty, or exposure to criminal activity (Lahey, Miller et al., 1999). Thus,

Steve's tragic family situation may evoke sympathy and concern. Youths with severe conduct problems are often seriously disturbed and need help. At the same time, the callousness of their deeds often evokes outrage, concern for innocent victims, and a desire to severely punish or confine them. This creates an inconsistency between society's concern for children who experience early adversity or abuse and the tendency to criminalize and demonize youths who display violent behaviors. As they grow older, these youths walk a fine line between pleas from the mental health and juvenile justice systems for understanding and rehabilitation and demands from the general public and the criminal justice system to punish the offenders and protect the victims (Steinberg, 2009). Most people have opinions about the nature of youth violence and what can be done about it. To examine some of your own views, consider the statements in A Closer Look 9.1.

Section Summary

Description of Conduct Problems

- Conduct problems or antisocial behavior(s) are age-inappropriate actions and attitudes of a child that violate family expectations, societal norms, and the personal or property rights of others. These children display problems in the self-control of emotions and behaviors.

- The nature, causes, and outcomes of conduct problems in children are wide-ranging, requiring that we consider several different types and pathways.

- Many children with severe conduct problems grow up in extremely unfortunate family and neighborhood circumstances.

CONTEXT, COSTS, AND PERSPECTIVES

"[T]he extent to which any of us conform with the social and criminal codes is a matter of degree. ..."

—John Bowlby (1950)

To understand antisocial behavior in young people and its impact on society, we next consider its expression in the context of normal development, its societal costs, and the different ways in which such behavior has been viewed by the juvenile justice, mental health, and public health systems.

Context

Most young people break the rules from time to time. Did you ever defy authority, lie, spread rumors, fight, skip school, run away, break curfew, destroy property, steal, text while driving, or drive under the influence of alcohol? If so, welcome to the club—many young people admit to these antisocial acts. In 2011, about 71% of high school students in the United States had consumed alcohol, 45% smoked cigarettes, 40% used marijuana, 33% texted or e-mailed while driving, and 8% had driven after drinking alcohol (CDC, 2012b). In fact, very few adolescents (about 6%) refrain from antisocial behavior entirely, and those who do describe themselves as excessively conventional, anxious, and socially inhibited—not well adjusted at all during adolescence (Moffitt et al., 2002).

Antisocial behaviors appear and then decline during normal development (Tremblay, 2003). Most toddlers hit, kick, intentionally break things, tell lies, and resist adult authority, but most also learn to control these behaviors by the time they enter school. About 50% of parents report that their preschoolers steal, lie, disobey, or destroy property, in contrast to 10% of parents who report the same about young adolescents (Achenbach, 1991a). This decline partially reflects the parents' lack of awareness of the trouble their teens may be getting into. However, teens also report that their antisocial behaviors decrease with age (Achenbach, 1991b). Frequencies of three common antisocial behaviors for clinic-referred and non-referred boys and girls of different ages, as reported by their parents, are shown in ● Figure 9.1.

The graphs in Figure 9.1 illustrate several important features of antisocial behaviors in the context of normal development:

▶ Antisocial behaviors vary in severity, from minor disobedience to fighting.

Policies and practices that place youths with conduct problems together can increase their antisocial and delinquent behavior.

- Some antisocial behaviors decrease with age (e.g., disobeying at home), whereas others increase with age and opportunity (e.g., hanging around with kids who get into trouble).
- Antisocial behaviors are more common in boys than in girls during childhood, but this difference narrows in adolescence.

Even though many antisocial behaviors decrease with age, children who are the most physically aggressive in early childhood maintain their relative standing over time (Broidy et al., 2003). Longitudinal studies find aggressive acts such as persistent physical fighting to be highly stable, with an average correlation of about 0.70 for measures of these behaviors taken at different times (Loeber, Green et al., 2000). This makes aggressive behavior about as stable as IQ scores!

Social and Economic Costs

The staggering costs borne by the educational, health, criminal justice, social service, and mental health systems that deal with youths with conduct problems make it the most costly mental health problem in North America (Welsh et al., 2008). Although antisocial acts are universal in young people, an early, persistent, and extreme pattern of antisocial behavior occurs in only about 5% of children (Hinshaw & Lee, 2003). These children cause considerable and disproportionate amounts of harm, accounting for over 50% of all crime in the United States, and about 30% to 50% of clinic referrals (Loeber, Burke et al., 2000).

More teenagers in the United States die from firearm injuries than from all diseases combined, and they are more than twice as likely as adults to be victims of violence, most often committed by other teens (Snyder & Sickmund, 2006). The costs of antisocial behavior can be understood in terms not only of lives but also of dollars. As much as 20% of all mental health expenditures in the United States are attributable to crime (National Institute of Justice, 1996). The additional public costs per child with conduct problems across the health care, juvenile justice, and educational systems are enormous—at least $10,000 or more a year (Foster, Jones, & The Conduct Problems Prevention Research Group, 2005). The lifetime costs to society for one youth to leave high school for a life of crime and substance abuse have been estimated to be about $3.2 million to $5.5 million (Cohen & Piquero, 2009).

Perspectives

Conduct problems have been viewed from several perspectives, each using different terms and definitions to

● **FIGURE 9.1** | Parent-reported frequencies for common antisocial behaviors in clinic and nonreferred boys and girls ages 4 to 18.

From *Manual for the Child Behavior Checklist/4-18 and 1991 Profile* by T. M. Achenbach, 1991, pp. 131, 134, 138, 145. University of Vermont. Copyright by T. M. Achenbach. Reproduced by permission.

describe similar patterns of behavior. These include the legal, psychological, psychiatric, and public health perspectives (Loeber, Burke, & Pardini, 2009).

Legal

Legally, conduct problems are defined as delinquent or criminal acts. The broad term **juvenile delinquency** describes children who have broken a law, ranging from sneaking into a movie without paying to homicide. Delinquent acts include property crimes (e.g., vandalism, theft, breaking and entering) and violent crimes (e.g., robbery, aggravated assault, homicide). Legal definitions depend on laws that change over time or differ across locations. Delinquency, the legal definition, involves apprehension and court contact and excludes the antisocial behaviors of very young children that usually occur at home or school. It is also important to distinguish official records of delinquency from self-reported delinquency. Youths who display antisocial behavior and are apprehended by police may differ from youths who display the same patterns but are not apprehended because of their intelligence or resourcefulness. Debate is ongoing about the age at which children should be held responsible for their delinquent behavior. The minimum age of criminal responsibility ranges from 7 to 14 years in most states and provinces, but this has fluctuated over the years in relation to society's tolerance or intolerance of antisocial behavior in youth.

Given the large numbers of youths involved in criminal activities, we must ask whether these behaviors are understandable (albeit objectionable) adaptations to a hostile environment—the most common reason that youths give for carrying a weapon is self-defense (Simon, Dent, & Sussman, 1997). Unfortunately, no clear boundaries exist between delinquent acts that are a reaction to environmental conditions, such as a high-crime neighborhood, and those that result from factors within the child, such as impulsivity. Some criminal behaviors, such as arson and truancy, are arbitrarily included in current mental health definitions, whereas selling drugs, receiving stolen property, and prostitution are not. Similarly, some symptoms of mental health problems do not necessarily violate laws (e.g., bullying, staying out late without permission). A legal definition of delinquency may result from one or two isolated acts, whereas a mental health definition usually requires the child to display a variety and persistent pattern of antisocial behaviors. Thus, only a subgroup of youths who meet a legal definition of delinquency will also meet the definition for a mental disorder (Waldman & Lahey, 2013).

Psychological

From a psychological perspective, conduct problems fall along a continuous dimension of **externalizing behavior** (Burns et al., 1997). Children at the upper extreme of this dimension, usually one or more standard deviations above the mean, are considered to have conduct problems. The externalizing dimension itself consists of two related but independent subdimensions, labeled "rule-breaking behavior" and "aggressive behavior" (Achenbach & Rescorla, 2001). Rule-breaking behaviors include running away, setting fires, stealing, skipping school, using alcohol and drugs, and committing acts of vandalism. Aggressive behaviors include fighting, destructiveness, disobedience, showing off, being defiant, threatening others, and being disruptive at school.

Two additional independent dimensions of antisocial behavior have been identified: overt–covert and destructive–nondestructive (Frick et al., 1993). The **overt–covert dimension** ranges from overt visible acts such as fighting to covert hidden acts such as lying or stealing. Children who display overt antisocial behavior tend to be negative, irritable, and

Two sides of the externalizing dimension: overt (left) and covert (right)

resentful in their reactions to hostile situations and to experience higher levels of family conflict (Kazdin, 1992). In contrast, those displaying covert antisocial behavior are less social, more anxious, and more suspicious of others and come from homes that provide little family support. Most children with conduct problems display both overt and covert behaviors. These children are in frequent conflict with authority, show the most severe family dysfunction, and have the poorest long-term outcomes (Loeber, Lahey, & Thomas, 1991). The **destructive–nondestructive dimension** ranges from acts such as cruelty to animals or physical assault to nondestructive behaviors such as arguing or irritability.

As shown in ● Figure 9.2, crossing the overt–covert with the destructive–nondestructive dimension results in four categories of conduct problems: (A) covert–destructive, or property violations; (B) overt–destructive, or aggression; (C) covert–nondestructive, or status violations; and (D) overt–nondestructive, or oppositional behavior. Children who display overt–destructive behaviors, particularly persistent physical fighting, are at especially high risk for later psychiatric problems and impairment in functioning (Broidy et al., 2003).

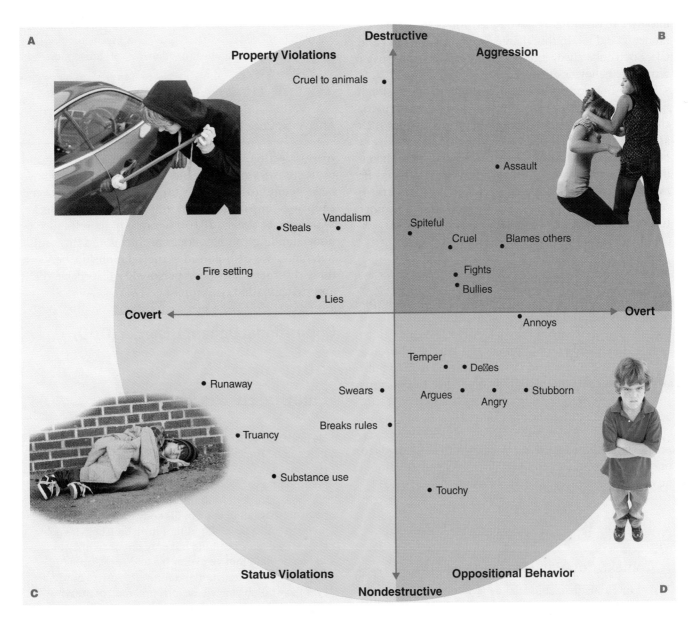

● **FIGURE 9.2** | Four categories of conduct problems.

Based on "Oppositional Defiant Disorder and Conduct Disorder: A Meata-Analytic Review of Factor Analyses and Cross-Validation in a Clinic Sample," by P. J. Frick, Y. Van Horn, B. B. Lahey, M.3A. G. Christ, R. Loeber, E. A. Hart, L. Tannenbaum & K. Hanson, Clinical Psychology Review, 13, 319–340.

Photo Credits: (a) Paul Bradbury/OJO Images/Getty Images; (b) Weston Colton/Getty Images; (c) ©iStockphoto.com/plherrera; (d) © Monkey Business Images/Dreamstime.com

Psychiatric

From a psychiatric perspective, conduct problems are defined as distinct mental disorders based on DSM-5 symptoms (APA, 2013). DSM-5 contains the general category of disruptive, impulse-control, and conduct disorders. All disorders in this category involve problems in the self-control of emotions and behaviors, including two that refer to persistent patterns of antisocial behavior in youth—oppositional defiant disorder (ODD) and conduct disorder (CD). This general category also includes *intermittent explosive disorder* (i.e., impulsive aggressive outbursts in response to minor provocations), *pyromania* (i.e., multiple episodes of deliberate and purposeful fire setting), and *kleptomania* (i.e., recurrent failure to resist impulses to steal items not needed for personal use or monetary value). In this chapter, we focus on ODD and CD, often collectively referred to as conduct problems or **disruptive behavior disorders**.

Note: Both categorical (psychiatric) and dimensional (psychological) perspectives have proven validity for classifying conduct problems in youth. Categories such as CD or ODD are associated with different patterns of behaviors and outcomes. On the other hand, dimensional measures of externalizing behavior in adolescence may be better predictors of adult outcomes than categorical measures (Fergusson, Boden, & Horwood, 2010). In other words, each perspective provides useful information.

Public Health

This perspective blends the legal, psychological, and psychiatric perspectives with public health concepts of prevention and intervention (U.S. Department of Health and Human Services, 2001). The goal is to reduce the number of injuries and deaths, personal suffering, and economic costs associated with youth violence, in the same way that other health concerns such as automobile accidents or tobacco use are addressed. The public health approach cuts across disciplines and brings together policy makers, scientists, professionals, communities, families, and individuals to understand conduct problems in youths and determine how they can be treated and prevented (Dodge, 2011).

Section Summary

Context, Costs, and Perspectives

- For most children, antisocial behaviors appear and then decline during normal development, although children who are most aggressive maintain their relative standing over time.
- Costs to the educational, health, social service, criminal justice, and mental health systems that deal with youth

make conduct problems one of the most costly mental health problems in North America.

- From a legal perspective, conduct problems are defined as criminal acts that result in apprehension and court contact and are referred to as "delinquency."
- From a psychological perspective, conduct problems fall along a continuous dimension of externalizing behavior, which includes a mix of impulsive, overactive, aggressive, and rule-breaking acts.
- From a psychiatric perspective, conduct problems are viewed as distinct categories of mental disorder based on DSM symptoms. These are called disruptive, impulse control, and conduct disorders, and include oppositional defiant disorder (ODD) and conduct disorder (CD).
- A public health perspective cuts across disciplines and blends the legal, psychological, and psychiatric perspectives with public health concepts of prevention and intervention.

DSM-5: DEFINING FEATURES

In this section, we discuss the defining features and characteristics of ODD and CD. Both disorders have been found to predict future psychopathology and enduring impairment in life functioning (Burke, Waldman, & Lahey, 2010). Because of its relevance to understanding youth conduct problems and their adult outcomes, we also consider the relationship between these disorders, antisocial personality disorder (APD), and psychopathic symptoms.

Oppositional Defiant Disorder (ODD)

GORDON

Enjoying His Power

He just digs his heels in, "That's it, I am not wearing these socks! Forget it, I'm not going!" And he is right. He's gone to school in his pajamas, without lunch, in the pouring rain without a coat. ... He will explain to me, "Mom, we are done with this discussion." ... He doesn't have an easy-going bone in his body. He is not ever going to say, "Okay, I'll put that turtleneck on." It's going to be, "I will do something but only on my terms. ... I will do nothing that you want me to do and furthermore I'll throw such a tantrum and throw this cereal bowl all over the wall, so you will be late, and mad at me when you clean it up." ... He enjoys that power.

Adapted from *Troubled Families—Problem Children: Working with Parents: A Collaborative Process* by C. Webster-Stratton and M. Herbert, 1994, p. 47.

Gordon's frequent arguing and active defiance of his mother are consistent with a diagnosis of **oppositional defiant disorder (ODD)**. These children display an age-inappropriate recurrent pattern of stubborn, hostile, disobedient, and defiant behaviors (see Table 9.1 for DSM-5 diagnostic criteria for ODD). ODD usually appears by age 8, and it was included in the DSM to capture early displays of antisocial and aggressive behavior by preschool and school-age children (Keenan, 2011). Many of these behaviors, such as temper tantrums or arguing, are extremely common in young children. However, severe and age-inappropriate ODD behaviors can have extremely negative effects on parent–child interactions (Greene & Doyle, 1999). Children with ODD also are at considerable risk for developing later impulse-control, substance-use, and mood and anxiety disorders, even after controlling for common co-occurring childhood disorders such as ADHD and CD (Frick & Nigg, 2012; Nock et al., 2007). Child and adolescent ODD symptoms also predict a variety of social and interpersonal difficulties in early adulthood, including poor functioning with peers and poor romantic relationships (Burke, Rowe, & Boylan, 2014).

Some findings indicate that symptoms of ODD can be grouped into three dimensions that reflect *negative affect* (angry/irritable mood), *defiance* (defiant/headstrong behavior), and *hurtful behavior* (vindictiveness), which differentially predict later emotional and behavioral disorders in early adulthood (Burke, 2012; Burke, Hipwell, & Loeber, 2010; Stringaris, Maughan, & Goodman, 2010). For example, in one study, all three dimensions of ODD were related to CD, whereas only negative affect predicted later depression, defiance predicted later behavior disorders, and vindictiveness was related to callous and unemotional behavior (Stringaris & Goodman, 2009). All three dimensions of ODD are highly correlated. However, symptoms of the hurtful behavior dimension do not seem to occur as consistently with symptoms of the other two dimensions, suggesting that they might be more related to the severe conduct problems of CD than to ODD (Burke et al., 2010; Rowe et al., 2010).

DSM-5 organizes ODD symptoms into three symptom clusters, which is consistent with research: *angry/irritable mood* (i.e., loses temper, touchy or easily annoyed, angry and resentful); *argumentative/defiant behavior* (i.e., argues with or defies authority figures, annoys or blames others); and *vindictiveness* (i.e., spiteful and vindictive) (see Table 9.1).

DSM-5 uses severity ratings for ODD of "mild," "moderate," or "severe," depending on whether symptoms are present in one, two, or three or more settings. Settings are home, school, and with peers.

TABLE 9.1 | **Diagnostic Criteria for** Oppositional Defiant Disorder

DSM-5

(A) A pattern of angry/irritable mood, argumentative/defiant behavior, or vindictiveness lasting at least 6 months as evidenced by at least four symptoms from any of the following categories, and exhibited during interaction with a least one individual who is not a sibling.

Angry/Irritable Mood

(1) Often loses temper.

(2) Is often touchy or easily annoyed.

(3) Is often angry or resentful.

Argumentative/Defiant Behavior

(4) Often argues with authority figures or, for children and adolescents, with adults.

(5) Often actively defies or refuses to comply with requests from authority figures or with rules.

(6) Often deliberately annoys others.

(7) Often blames others for his or her mistakes or misbehavior.

Vindictiveness

(8) Has been spiteful or vindictive at least twice within the past 6 months.

Note: The persistence and frequency of these behaviors should be used to distinguish a behavior that is within normal limits from behavior that is symptomatic. For children younger than 5 years, the behavior should occur on most days for a period of at least 6 months unless otherwise noted (Criterion A8). For individuals 5 years or older the behavior should occur at least once per week for 6 months, unless otherwise noted (Criterion A8). While these frequency criteria provide guidance on a minimal level of frequency to define symptoms, other factors should also be considered, such as whether the frequency and intensity of the behaviors are outside a range that is normative for the individual's developmental level, gender, and culture.

(B) The disturbance in behavior is associated with distress in the individual or others in his or her immediate social context (e.g., family peer group, work colleagues), or it impacts negatively on social, educational, occupational, or other important areas of functioning.

(C) The behaviors do not occur exclusively during the course of a psychotic, substance-use, depressive, or bipolar disorder. Also, the criteria are not met for disruptive mood disorder.

Specify current severity:

Mild: Symptoms are confined to only one setting (e.g., at home, at school, at work, with peers).

Moderate: Some symptoms are present in at least two settings.

Severe: Some symptoms are present in three or more settings.

Source: Diagnostic and Statistical Manual of Mental Disorders, Fifth Edition. American Psychiatric Association.

Most clinic-referred children with ODD (about 90%) display symptoms in two or more settings, but even those who show impairments only at home still display significant adjustment problems, albeit not as severe as those of children who display impairments across multiple settings (Kimonis et al., 2014).

Conduct Disorder (CD)

GREG

Dangerous Distress

Greg, age 10, was referred because of his excessive fighting, hyperactivity, temper tantrums, and disruptive behavior at home and at school. At home, Greg argued with his mother, started fights with his siblings, stole from his parents, and constantly threatened to set fires when disciplined. On three separate occasions, he actually had set fires to rugs, bedspreads, and trash in his home. One fire led to several thousand dollars in damages. Greg also lied frequently; at school, his lying got others into trouble, precipitating frequent fights with peers and denials of any wrongdoing.

Greg was brought to the clinic because his parents felt that he was becoming totally unmanageable. A few incidents were mentioned as unusually dangerous—for example, Greg's attempt to suffocate his 2-year-old brother by holding a pillow over his face. Also, Greg had recently wandered the streets at night and had broken windows of parked cars.

Greg's parents occasionally resorted to severe punishment, using paddles and belts, or locking him in his room for 2 to 3 days. His father has been employed only sporadically for the past 2 years, and spent much of his time at home sleeping or watching TV. The loss of income led to increased stress. Greg said that he could not stand to be with his dad because his dad got mad all the time over little things. Greg's mother worked full time and was not at home very much. She had a history of depression, with two suicide attempts in the past 3 years. She was hospitalized on each occasion for approximately 2 months. Greg's behavior became even worse during these periods.

Although Greg's intelligence was within the normal range, his academic performance was behind grade level, and he was in a special class because of his overactive and disruptive behavior. His parents were told that unless they got help, Greg could not return to the school the next year. His parents did not know where to turn. They talked about giving Greg up or putting him in a special boarding school, where more discipline might make him "shape up."

Based on Conduct Disorders in Childhood and Adolescence by A. E. Kazdin, pp. 2–3.

Greg's chronic and unmanageable behavior qualifies for a diagnosis of **conduct disorder (CD)**. Children with conduct disorder display a repetitive and persistent pattern of severely aggressive and antisocial acts that involve inflicting pain on others or interfering with the rights of others through physical and verbal aggression, stealing, or vandalism. The DSM-5 groups symptoms of CD into four dimensions: aggression to people and animals (e.g., bullying, physical cruelty), destruction of property (e.g., fire setting, vandalism), deceitfulness or theft (e.g., conning, shoplifting), and serious violations of rules (e.g., truancy, running away from home). (see Table 9.2 for DSM-5 diagnostic criteria for CD).

Greg's case illustrates several key features of CD (Kazdin, 1995):

▸ Children with CD engage in severe antisocial behaviors. Greg set fires and tried to suffocate his 2-year-old brother. He also displayed less severe problems, such as noncompliance and temper tantrums, but these weren't the main reasons for referral. DSM-5 includes severity ratings for CD of "mild," "moderate," and "severe" based on the number of symptoms in excess of the three required to make the diagnosis or the amount of harm caused to others.

▸ They often have co-occurring problems such as ADHD, academic deficiencies, and poor relations with peers.

▸ Their families often use child-rearing practices, such as harsh punishment, that contribute to the problem and often have their own problems and stresses, such as marital discord, psychiatric problems, and unemployment. Greg's mother had a history of depression and his father was frequently unemployed.

▸ Their parents feel these children are out of control, and they feel helpless to do anything about it. Greg's parents want to give him up or put him in a boarding school.

CD and Age at Onset

Is the age at which symptoms of CD first occur important? DSM makes the distinction between youths with an early or late onset of CD. Those with **childhood-onset conduct disorder** display at least one symptom of the disorder before age 10, whereas those with **adolescent-onset conduct disorder** do not. Increasing evidence points to the importance of age at onset in diagnosing and treating children with CD (Odgers et al., 2008). Children diagnosed with childhood-onset CD are more likely to be boys, show more aggressive symptoms, account for a disproportionate amount of

TABLE 9.2 | **Diagnostic Criteria for** Conduct Disorder

(A) A repetitive and persistent pattern of behavior in which the basic rights of others or major age-appropriate societal norms or rules are violated, as manifested by the presence of at least three of the following 15 criteria in the past 12 months from any of the categories below, with at least one criterion present in the past 6 months:

DSM-5

Aggression to People and Animals

(1) Often bullies, threatens, or intimidates others.

(2) Often initiates physical fights.

(3) Has used a weapon that can cause serious physical harm to others (e.g., a bat, brick, broken bottle, knife, gun).

(4) Has been physically cruel to people.

(5) Has been physically cruel to animals.

(6) Has stolen while confronting a victim (e.g., mugging, purse snatching, extortion, armed robbery).

(7) Has forced someone into sexual activity.

Destruction of Property

(8) Has deliberately engaged in fire setting, with the intention of causing serious damage.

(9) Has deliberately destroyed others' property (other than by fire setting).

Deceitfulness or Theft

(10) Has broken into someone else's house, building, or car.

(11) Often lies to obtain goods or favors or to avoid obligations (i.e., "cons" others)

(12) Has stolen items of nontrivial value without confronting a victim (e.g., shoplifting, but without breaking and entering; forgery).

Serious Violations of Rules

(13) Often stays out at night despite parental prohibitions, beginning before age 13 years.

(14) Has run away from home overnight at least twice while living in parental or parental surrogate home, or once without returning for a lengthy period.

(15) Is often truant from school, beginning before age 13 years

(B) The disturbance in behavior causes clinically significant impairment in social, academic, or occupational functioning.

(C) If the individual is 18 years or older, criteria are not met for Antisocial Personality Disorder.

Specify whether:

Childhood-onset type: Individuals show at least one symptom characteristic of conduct disorder prior to age 10 years.

Adolescent-onset type: Individuals show no symptom characteristic of conduct disorder prior to age 10 years.

Unspecified onset: Criteria for a diagnosis of conduct disorder are met, but there is not enough information available to determine whether the onset of the first symptom was before or after age 10 years.

Specify if:

With limited prosocial emotions: To qualify for this specifier, an individual must have displayed at least two of the following characteristics persistently over at least 12 months and in multiple relationships and settings. These characteristics reflect the individual's typical pattern of interpersonal and emotional functioning over this period and not just occasional occurrences in some situations. Thus, to assess the criteria for the specifier, multiple information sources are necessary. In addition to the individual's self-report, it is necessary to consider reports by others who have known the individual for extended periods of time (e.g., parents, teachers, co-workers, extended family members, peers).

Lack of remorse or guilt: Does not feel bad or guilty when he or she does something wrong (excludes remorse when expressed only when caught and/or facing punishment). The individual shows a general lack of concern about the negative consequences of his or her actions. For example, the individual is not remorseful after hurting someone or does not care about the consequences of breaking rules.

Callous–lack of empathy: Disregards and is unconcerned about the feelings of others. The individual is described as cold and uncaring. The person appears more concerned about the effects of his or her actions on himself or herself, rather than their effects on others, even when they result in substantial harm to others.

Unconcerned about performance: Does not show concern about poor/problematic performance at school, at work, or in other important activities. The individual does not put forth the effort necessary to perform well, even when expectations are clear, and typically blames others for his or her poor performance.

Shallow or deficient affect: Does not express feelings or show emotions to others, except in ways that seem shallow, insincere, or superficial (e.g., actions contradict the emotion displayed; can turn emotions "on" or "off" quickly) or when emotional expressions are used for gain (e.g., emotions displayed to manipulate or intimidate others).

(continues)

TABLE 9.2 | **Diagnostic Criteria for** Conduct Disorder (*continued*)

Specify severity:

Mild: Few if any conduct problems in excess of those required to make the diagnosis are present, and conduct problems cause relatively minor harm to others (e.g., lying, truancy, staying out after dark without permission, other rule breaking).

Moderate: The number of conduct problems and the effect on others are intermediate between those specified in "mild" and those in "severe" (e.g., stealing without confronting a victim, vandalism).

Severe: Many conduct problems in excess of those required to make the diagnosis are present, or conduct problems cause considerable harm to others (e.g., forced sex, physical cruelty, use of a weapon, stealing while confronting a victim, breaking and entering).

Source: Diagnostic and Statistical Manual of Mental Disorders, 5th ed. American Psychiatric Association.

illegal activity, and persist in their antisocial behavior over time (Lahey, Goodman, et al., 1999). In contrast, youths diagnosed with adolescent-onset CD are as likely to be girls as boys and do not display the severity or psychopathology that characterizes the childhood-onset group. They are also less likely to commit violent offenses or to persist in their antisocial behavior as they get older. Age at onset does make a difference.

The ODD and CD Connection

There is much overlap between the symptoms of ODD and CD. This raises the question of whether ODD is a separate disorder from CD; a milder, earlier version; or a reflection of the same underlying temperament and deficits (Waldman & Lahey, 2013). Symptoms of ODD typically emerge 2 to 3 years before CD symptoms, at about 6 years of age for ODD versus 9 years for CD (Nock et al., 2007). Since ODD symptoms emerge first, it is possible that they are precursors of CD for some children. However, nearly half of all children with CD have no prior ODD diagnosis (Rowe et al., 2010), and most children who display ODD do not progress to more severe CD—at least 50% maintain their ODD diagnosis without progressing, and another 25% cease to display ODD problems entirely (Burke et al., 2010). Thus, for most children, ODD is an extreme developmental variation and a strong risk factor for later ODD and other problems, but not one that necessarily signals an escalation to more serious conduct problems (Keenan et al., 2011). Thus, ODD and CD appear to be distinguishable yet highly correlated aspects of child psychopathology.

Antisocial Personality Disorder (APD) and Psychopathic Features

Persistent aggressive behavior and CD in childhood may be a precursor of adult **antisocial personality disorder (APD)**, a pervasive pattern of disregard for, and violation of, the rights of others, including repeated illegal behaviors, deceitfulness, failure to plan ahead, repeated physical fights or assaults, reckless disregard for the safety of self or others, repeated failure to sustain work behavior or honor financial obligations, and a lack of remorse (APA, 2013). Research has found that as many as 40% of children with CD develop APD as young adults (Lahey et al., 2005). In addition to their early CD, adolescents with APD may also display **psychopathic features**, which are defined as a pattern of callous, manipulative, deceitful, and remorseless behavior—the more menacing side of human nature (Blair et al., 2006). Consider these chilling comments by Jason.

JASON

No Conscience

Jason, age 13, had been involved in serious crime—including breaking and entering, thefts, and assaults on younger children—by age 6. Listening to Jason talk was frightening. Asked why he committed crimes, this product of a stable, professional family replied, "I like it. My f___ parents really freak out when I get in trouble, but I don't give a sh ___ as long as I'm having a good time. Yeah, I've always been wild." About other people, including his victims, Jason had this to say: "You want the truth? They'd screw me if they could, only I get my shots in first." He liked to rob homeless people, especially "f_gots," "bag ladies," and street kids, because, "They're used to it. They don't whine to the police. ... One guy I got into a fight with pulled a knife and I took it and rammed it in his eye. He ran around screaming like a baby. What a jerk!"

Adapted from Hare, 1993, p. 162.

Like Jason, youths who display psychopathic features appear to be aware that their aggressive behavior will cause others to suffer—but they don't care. Rather, their goals in conflict situations involve revenge, dominance, and forced respect (Pardini, 2011). Although less is known about psychopathic features in children than in adults this situation is changing. Signs of a lack of conscience occur in some children as young as 3 to 5 years (Kochanska et al., 1994). Other children, like Jason, began committing brutal acts of violence at age 6 with little remorse. A subgroup of preschoolers with behavior problems show a worrisome increase in their lack of concern for others as they begin to enter middle childhood (Hastings et al., 2000). Finally, adolescents with CD are less likely than peers to show affective empathy or embarrassment, which suggests a failure to inhibit emotions and actions in accordance with social conventions (Lovett & Sheffield, 2007).

These and many other findings point to a subgroup of children with CD whose lack of concern for others may place them at especially high risk for extreme antisocial and aggressive acts and for poor long-term outcomes. They display a **callous and unemotional (CU) interpersonal style** characterized by an absence of guilt, lack of empathy, uncaring attitudes, shallow or deficient emotional responses, and related traits of narcissism and impulsivity (Frick et al., 2014; Kahn et al., 2012). Children with CU traits display a greater number and variety of conduct problems, and they have more frequent contact with police and a stronger parental history of APD than other children with conduct problems (Frick & White, 2008). Research with children and adolescents has found that CU interpersonal and affective traits predict persistent delinquency, future recidivism, and symptoms of APD in early adulthood (Byrd, Loeber, and Pardini, 2012; McMahon et al., 2010; Pardini & Loeber, 2008). CU symptoms in childhood are about as stable as ODD and CD symptoms over time, but developmental changes have also been noted, suggesting that these are not unchanging characteristics of the child. For example, some children display stable high levels of CU traits, others show increasing or decreasing levels, and others show stable low levels (Fontaine et al., 2011). CU traits in childhood and early adolescence are likely precursors of adult forms of psychopathy, although further research is needed to confirm this (Lynam et al., 2007).

Given the evidence in support of CU traits in identifying an important characteristic of children with conduct problems, DSM-5 uses the specifier **"with limited prosocial emotions"** to describe youth with CD who display a persistent and typical pattern of interpersonal and emotional functioning involving at least two of the following three characteristics: lack of remorse or guilt; callous–lack of empathy; and unconcerned about performance. The term "limited prosocial emotions" was used, in part, in DSM-5 to avoid the possible negative connotations associated with the term "callous-unemotional" (Frick & Nigg, 2012).

At this point you might want to consider A Closer Look 9.2 to sharpen your knowledge of DSM-5 criteria for ODD and CD by considering whether or not TV cartoon personality Bart Simpson qualifies for a diagnosis of one, both, or neither of these disorders.

Section Summary

DSM-5: Defining Features

- Children with oppositional defiant disorder (ODD) display an age-inappropriate pattern of stubborn, hostile, and defiant behaviors that reflect symptoms of emotionality

A CLOSER **LOOK** 9.2

Bart Simpson: What's the Diagnosis?

Sharpen your knowledge of DSM-5 criteria for ODD and CD by considering whether TV cartoon personality Bart Simpson qualifies for a diagnosis of one, both, or neither of these disorders. Here is a list of antisocial acts displayed by Bart:

- Flushes a cherry bomb down the toilet
- Rearranges party snacks to say "Boy our party sucks"
- Loosens the top on Milhouse's salt shaker
- Lights Homer's tie on fire
- Tricks Flanders kids into giving cookies away
- Pretends to be Timmy (trapped in a well)
- Blames Lisa for making long distance calls
- Pulls carpet up, writes "Bart" on carpet
- Plays with and later breaks grandpa Abe's false teeth
- Flushes Homer's wallet and keys down toilet
- Cuts all of baby Maggie's hair off
- Paints extra lines on parking lot
- Leaves box factory tour
- Pops heads off Mr. Burns's statues/floods his car
- Smashes Mr. Burns's windows
- Recounts throwing mail in sewer with Milhouse
- Phones 911 to get babysitter into trouble

Comment: Based on Bart's symptoms of aggression, destruction of property, deceitfulness, and serious violation of rules, he easily qualifies for a DSM diagnosis of CD. Like most children with CD, Bart also displays symptoms of ODD (e.g., not complying with rules, deliberately annoying others, blaming others for his misbehavior, engaging in spiteful behavior) and qualifies for this diagnosis as well. (Based on authors' case material.)

and temperamental activity. ODD symptoms can be grouped into three dimensions: negative affect, defiance, and vindictiveness.

- Conduct disorder (CD) describes children who display severe aggressive and antisocial acts involving inflicting pain upon others or interfering with the rights of others through physical and verbal aggression, stealing, or committing acts of vandalism.

- Children who display childhood-onset CD (before age 10) are more likely to be boys, show more aggressive symptoms, account for a disproportionate amount of illegal activity, and persist in their antisocial behavior over time.

- Children with adolescent-onset CD are as likely to be girls as boys and do not display the severity or psychopathology that characterizes the childhood-onset group.

- There is much overlap between CD and ODD. However, most children who display ODD do not progress to more severe CD.

- Persistent aggressive behavior and conduct problems in childhood may be a precursor of adult antisocial personality disorder (APD), a pervasive pattern of disregard for, and violation of, the rights of others.

- A subgroup of children with conduct problems display psychopathic features, including callous–unemotional (CU) traits such as lacking in guilt, not showing empathy, and not displaying feelings or emotions. These children also display a preference for novel and perilous activities and a diminished sensitivity to cues for danger and punishment when seeking rewards.

- DSM-5 uses the specifier "with limited prosocial emotions" to describe youth with CD who display a pattern of interpersonal and emotional functioning involving a lack of remorse or guilt, empathy, or concern about performance.

ASSOCIATED CHARACTERISTICS

Many child, family, peer, school, and community factors are associated with conduct problems in youths. Some factors co-occur with conduct problems, others increase their likelihood, and still others are the result of these problems. To fully understand conduct problems, we must examine these various factors and how they interact over time.

Cognitive and Verbal Deficits

Although most children with conduct problems have normal intelligence, they score nearly 8 points lower than their peers on IQ tests (Pajer et al., 2008). This IQ deficit may be greater (more than 15 points) for children with childhood-onset CD, and cannot be accounted for solely by socioeconomic disadvantage, race, or detection by the police (Lynam, Moffitt, &

Stouthamer-Loeber, 1993). Lower IQ scores in children with CD may be related to the co-occurrence of ADHD (Waschbusch, 2002). When ADHD is also present, the association between a lower IQ and an increased risk for CD is clear. It is less clear how a lower IQ mediates this risk (Rutter, 2003b).

Verbal IQ is consistently lower than performance IQ in children with CD, suggesting a specific and pervasive deficit in language (Zadeh, Im-Bolter, & Cohen, 2007). This deficit may affect the child's receptive listening, reading, problem solving, pragmatic language, expressive speech and writing, and memory for verbal material (Brennan et al., 2003; Gremillion & Martel, 2013; Jaffee & D'Zurilla, 2003). Some suggest that verbal and language deficits may contribute to conduct problems by interfering with the development of self-control, emotion regulation, or the labeling of emotions in others, which may lead to a lack of empathy (Hastings et al., 2000). One study found that poor language ability predicted the development of later conduct problems, suggesting that targeting language deficits may be useful in preventing or treating conduct problems (Peterson et al., 2013).

Verbal deficits are present early in a child's development, long before the emergence of conduct problems. However, their presence alone does not predict future aggression—family factors are also important. Children with both verbal deficits and family adversity display four times as much aggressive behavior as children with only one factor (Moffitt, 1990). Thus, verbal deficits may increase the child's vulnerability to the effects of a hostile family environment. How this occurs is not known, but one possibility is that a child's verbal deficits may make it more difficult for parents to understand their child's needs, which leads to parents' frustration, fewer positive interactions, more punishment, and greater difficulties in teaching social skills (Patterson, 1996). Verbal deficits, such as poor receptive language skills, may also lead to rejection by mainstream peers, adding to the development of conduct problems (Menting, van Lier, & Koot, 2011).

It is important to keep in mind that the relationship between different cognitive/verbal deficits and antisocial behavior may vary for specific types of antisocial behaviors. For example, one study found that verbal abilities were negatively related to physical aggression but positively associated with theft, and that inductive reasoning was negatively associated with increases in theft across adolescence (Barker et al., 2011). These findings highlight the importance of studying specific types of conduct problem behaviors in order to better understand their possible underlying mechanisms.

Children with conduct problems rarely consider the future consequences of their behavior or its impact

"How am I supposed to think about consequences before they happen?"

on others. They fail to inhibit their impulsive behavior, keep social values or future rewards in mind, or adapt their actions to changing circumstances. This pattern suggests deficits in executive functions similar to those of children with ADHD (Raine et al., 2005). Because ODD/CD and ADHD frequently co-occur, the observed deficits in executive functions in these children could be due to the presence of co-occurring ADHD (Pennington & Ozonoff, 1996).

It is also possible that the types of executive functioning deficits experienced by children with ODD and CD may differ from those experienced by children with ADHD (Nigg et al., 2006). For example, Rubia (2010) has made the distinction between *cool* (as in temperature, not as in Lady Gaga) cognitive executive functions, such as attention, working memory, planning, and inhibition, and *hot* executive functions that involve incentives and motivation. Both cool and hot executive functions are associated with distinct but interconnected brain networks. Cool executive function deficits are thought to be more characteristic of children with ADHD, whereas hot executive function deficits are more characteristic of children with conduct problems. Children with both ADHD and conduct problems, which is common, likely display a combination of the two types of executive function deficits.

School and Learning Problems

Every time you stop a school, you will have to build a jail.

—Mark Twain (November 23, 1900)

Children with conduct problems display many school difficulties, including academic underachievement, grade retention, special education placement, dropout,

suspension, and expulsion (Roeser & Eccles, 2000). Although the frustration and demoralization associated with school failure can lead to antisocial behavior in some children (Maughan, Gray, & Rutter, 1985), there is little evidence that academic failure is the primary cause of conduct problems, particularly in early childhood. Since many young children display patterns of disruptive behavior long before they enter school, it is more likely that a common factor, such as a neuropsychological or language deficit, lack of self-control, or socioeconomic disadvantage, underlies both conduct problems and school difficulties (Lahey & Waldman, 2003).

Over time, underachievement and conduct problems influence each other. Subtle early language deficits may lead to reading and communication difficulties, which in turn may heighten conduct problems in elementary school. Children with poor academic skills are increasingly likely to lose interest in school and to associate with delinquent peers. By adolescence, the relationship between conduct problems and underachievement is firmly established, which, in one pathway, may lead to anxiety or depression in young adulthood (Masten et al., 2005).

Family Problems

He is so violent with his sister. He split her lip a couple of times. And he almost knocked her out once when he hit her over the head with a 5-pound brass pitcher. He's put plastic bags over her head.

—Webster-Stratton and Herbert (1994)

Family problems are among the strongest and most consistent correlates of conduct problems (Dishion & Patterson, 2006). Two types of family disturbances are related to these problems in children. *General family disturbances* include parental mental health problems, a family history of antisocial behavior, marital discord, family instability, limited resources, and antisocial family values. *Specific disturbances in parenting practices and family functioning* include excessive use of harsh discipline, lack of supervision, lack of emotional support and involvement, and parental disagreement about discipline.

The two types are interrelated, since general family disturbances such as maternal depression often lead to poor parenting practices that can lead to antisocial behavior and feelings of parental incompetence that may lead to increased maternal depression, which completes the circle.

High levels of conflict are common in families of children with conduct problems. So, too, are poor parenting practices such as ineffective discipline, negative control, inappropriate use of punishment and rewards, failure to follow through on commands, and a lack of involvement in child rearing (Larsson et al., 2008; Trentacosta & Shaw, 2008). Parents may also exhibit social–cognitive deficits similar to those of their children, which suggests that the tendency of antisocial children to infer hostile intent of others may mirror the social perceptions of their parents (Healy et al., 2013). Finally, there is often a lack of family cohesion, which is reflected in emotional detachment, poor communication and problem solving, low support, and family disorganization (Henggeler, Melton, & Smith, 1992). Household chaos—characterized by high noise levels, crowding, people coming and going all the time—and a lack of predictability and family routines is also associated with child conduct problems (Deater-Deckard et al., 2009).

From Cain and Abel to TV's Bart and Lisa Simpson, conflict between siblings has generated much attention (Johnston & Freeman, 1998). Conflict is especially high between children with conduct problems and their siblings. Nonreferred siblings sometimes display as much negative behavior as their referred siblings, even when the sibling with conduct problems is not present

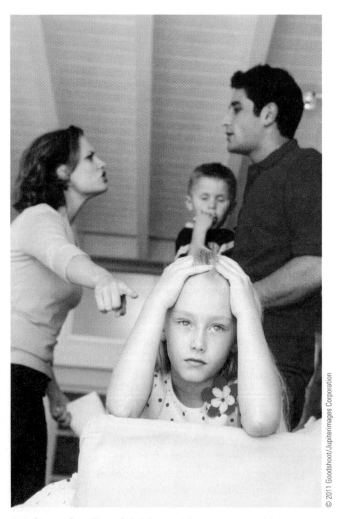

Conflict in families of children with conduct problems is common.

(Dishion & Patterson, 2006). This suggests that their difficulties are not simply immediate reactions to the annoying behaviors of their antisocial brother or sister. There are many possible reasons for the similarities in the problem behaviors of siblings, including poor parenting practices, the effects of modeling, direct influence of the other sibling, marital discord, parent mental health problems, and shared hereditary influences. Whatever the reasons, the collaboration of siblings in one another's deviant behavior can be as powerful as deviant peer relationships in heightening the risk for later conduct problems, and may also contribute to later aggression toward peers (Ensor et al., 2010).

In this section, we have described many common problems in families of children with conduct problems. Later in this chapter, we consider how these family problems might combine with other factors to cause additional difficulties.

Peer Problems

He is so aggressive around other children. We can't really trust him not to walk up and wallop the smaller ones. He pokes them in the eyes or pushes them down. ... It's almost like he seeks out other children to hurt them.

—Webster-Stratton and Herbert (1994)

Young children with conduct problems display verbal and physical aggression toward other children as well as poor social skills (Miller & Olson, 2000). Preschoolers who show poor self-regulation have difficulty understanding the perspectives of others, experience corporal punishment from their parents, and display higher levels of peer aggressiveness during the transition to grade school (Olson et al., 2011). As they grow older, most children with conduct problems are rejected by their peers, although some may remain quite popular (Rodkin et al., 2000). Peer rejection in elementary school is a strong risk factor for adolescent conduct problems. For example, children rejected for 2 or 3 years by grade 2 are about 5 times more likely than others to display conduct problems later in adolescence (Laird et al., 2001). As they enter school, some of these children become bullies, a particularly offensive pattern associated with continuing conduct problems into adolescence and adulthood (see A Closer Look 9.3).

Children with conduct problems are able to make friends. Unfortunately, their friendships are often with like-minded antisocial individuals (Button et al., 2007). Notably, the combination of early antisocial behavior and associating with deviant peers is a powerful predictor of conduct problems during adolescence (Laird et al., 2005). Involvement with antisocial peers becomes increasingly stable during childhood and

Bullies and Their Victims

For 2 years, Johnny, a quiet 13-year-old, was a human plaything for some of his classmates. The teenagers badgered Johnny for money, forced him to swallow weeds and drink milk mixed with detergent, beat him up in the restroom, and tied a string around his neck, leading him around as a "pet" (Olweus, 1995, p. 196).

Bullying among school children is a very old, familiar, and particularly offensive form of antisocial behavior. **Bullying** occurs when one or more children intentionally and repeatedly expose another child, who cannot readily defend himself or herself, to negative actions (Olweus, 2013). Such actions may take the form of physical contact, offensive words, making faces or dirty gestures, and intentional exclusion from a group. Bullying usually involves an imbalance of power, so that the victim has difficulty defending herself or himself (Guerra, Williams, & Sadek, 2011). The scope of this problem is large. In 2007, about 32% of students 12 to 18 years of age reported having been bullied at school, most commonly by being made fun of; being the subject of rumors; or being pushed shoved, tripped, or spit on (Robers et al., 2013). Boys are much more likely than girls to bully other children and are also somewhat more likely to be the victims of bullying. Victims are typically perceived as vulnerable, weak, or different. The following comments by high school students capture the diverse factors related to victimization and being seen as different (Guerra et al., 2011):

Radius Images/Masterfile

> You can get bullied because you are weak or annoying or because you are different. Kids with big ears get bullied. Dorks get bullied. You can also get bullied because you think too much of yourself and try to show off. Teacher's pet gets bullied. If you say the right answer too many times in class you can get bullied. … If you do not want to get bullied you have to stay under the radar, but then you might feel sad because no one pays attention to you. (p. 306)

No youth who is seen as different is exempt. For example, at a 2011 White House Conference on the Prevention of Bullying, President Barack Obama admitted that as a youth he was a victim of bullying: "I have to say, with big ears and the name that I have, I wasn't immune. I didn't emerge unscathed" (Brown, 2011). Although victimization by a bully is strongly associated with emotional problems, some children are resilient. Interestingly, in one study, youths with a particular genotype (involving the serotonin transporter 5-HTT gene) were found to be less likely to suffer adverse effects following bullying victimization—another example of gene-environment interaction (Sugden et al., 2010).

Unfortunately, widespread access to the Internet and smart phones has led to new forms of bullying by youths who use electronics to taunt, insult, threaten, harass, or intimidate a peer. Electronic/Internet or cyberbullies may use instant text messaging, e-mails, tweets, defaming websites, and online "slam books" to aggress against peers by circulating rumors,

secrets, insults, and threats to harass, manipulate, and harm their victims (Kowalski et al., 2014). Most cyberbullying occurs outside of school hours, although it is likely that many, if not most, episodes originate in school settings. Media accounts and some studies have reported that cyberbullying is a rapidly growing problem, maybe even be more common than face-to-face bullying. However, some findings suggest that rates of cyberbullying have remained relatively constant in recent years, and are approximately 65% to 75% lower than traditional forms of bullying (Olweus, 2013). There is also a huge overlap between traditional and cyberbullying. About 90% of traditional bullies are also cyberbullies, and about 90% of victims of traditional bullies are also victims of cyberbullies (Olweus, 2013; Raskauskas & Stoltz, 2007). This suggests that the new electronic media have actually created relatively few new victims and bullies. These findings should not downplay or trivialize the significance of cyberbullying but rather serve to provide perspective on its prevalence and nature relative to traditional forms of bullying.

A child's status as a victim or a bully is likely to be stable over time, and victims and bullies display certain typical characteristics. Typical victims are characterized by anxious and submissive patterns of behavior, low self-esteem, and, in the case of boys, by physical weakness. These children send a signal to others that if they are attacked or insulted, they won't retaliate. Typical bullies are distinguished by their aggressiveness toward both peers and adults. They are often impulsive, need to dominate other people, are stronger than other boys, show little empathy for their victims, and derive satisfaction and, often, material gain from inflicting injury and suffering on their victims. One study found that nearly 40% of boys who were bullies in school were later convicted of three or more criminal offenses by the

(continues)

(continued)

time they were 24 years old (Olweus, 1995). Thus, bullying in school appears to be part of a more general pattern of antisocial behavior.

The high prevalence of bullying and its impact on victims (sadly, some may commit suicide) make it a significant social problem. Studies of long-term outcomes for former bullies and victims provide strong evidence that bullying is not simply a harmless and passing school problem, but one that has serious adjustment and public health consequences with large costs to society (Copeland et al., 2013; Olweus, 2013). To combat this problem, websites (e.g., http://stopbullyingnow.hrsa.gov) and schoolwide interventions and policies that increase awareness of the problem, develop clear rules against bullying, and provide support and protection for victims have been developed and successfully used in countries throughout the world (Karna et al., 2011).

supports the transition to adolescent criminal acts such as stealing, truancy, and substance abuse (Patterson, 1996). In fact, about two-thirds of all recorded youth offenses are committed in the company of two to three peers (Snyder & Sickmund, 2006). Involvement with deviant peers is also one of the strongest predictors of accelerated autonomy and early sexual activity in adolescence (French & Dishion, 2003).

TOM AND MATTHEW

Murderous Meeting of Minds

On February 16, 1995, in the small Minnesota town of Delano, 14-year-old Tom and his best friend Matthew ambushed and killed Tom's mother. ... These boys spent much time together. They admitted to planning the ambush (one saying they had planned it for weeks, the other, for a few hours). They were armed and waiting when Tom's mother came home from work. One conclusion seems relatively certain: This murder was an unlikely event until these antisocial friends reached consensus about doing it.

Adapted from Hartup, 1996, p. 1.

Friendships between antisocial boys are abrasive, unstable, of short duration, and not very productive (Dishion & Patterson, 2006). Positive exchanges, when they do occur, are compromised by the bossy and coercive behaviors that accompany them. Antisocial friends may engage in "deviant talk," selectively rewarding one another for discussions of rule breaking, but having little to say about prosocial behavior. As a result of this differential reinforcement, they may become more alike in their antisocial tendencies over time, leading to a further escalation in the frequency and variety of their antisocial activities (Piehler & Dishion, 2007).

The fact that deviant peer involvement is an especially strong predictor of substance use, delinquent behavior, and violence makes intervention in this area a high priority. Unfortunately, many well-intentioned programs such as group therapy, unstructured after-school programs, summer programs, or boot camps tend to create groups for youths with conduct problems—the very situation that may produce the most damage (Dishion, Bullock, & Granic, 2002; Gottfredson, 2010).

Aggressive children also show distortions in how they think about social situations. They underestimate their own aggressiveness and its negative impact, and they overestimate the amount of aggression directed at them. Subgroups of aggressive children may think about social situations in different ways. For example, *reactive–aggressive* children (those showing an angry, defensive response to frustration or provocation) display a **hostile attributional bias**, which means they are more likely to attribute hostile and mean-spirited intent to other children, especially when the intentions of others are unclear (e.g., when another child accidentally bumps into him, a reactive–aggressive child is likely to think the other child did it on purpose). In contrast, *proactive–aggressive* children (those who use aggressive behavior deliberately to obtain a desired goal) are more likely to view their aggressive actions as positive and to value social goals of dominance and revenge rather than affiliation (Crick & Dodge, 1996). Proactive-aggressive children display a lack of concern for others, and their solutions to social problems are few in number, mostly aggressive, and inappropriate (Hastings et al., 2000; Dodge & Pettit, 2003). Proactive–aggressive youths are also likely to display reactive–aggression, whereas reactive–aggressive youths display only reactive aggression and are less aggressive overall (Crapanzano, Frick, & Terranova, 2010).

The hostile attributions of children with conduct problems are directly related to similar attributions by their parents. For example, one longitudinal study found that maternal hostile attributions were related to psychosocial adversity, poor parenting behavior, hostile attributions of the child, and child aggression at 5 years of age (Healy et al., 2013). It is important to keep in mind that many children with conduct problems live in highly aggressive and threatening circumstances. In some cases, their bias toward seeing threat and aggression in others may be an accurate reflection of the realities of living in a hostile social world, and their aggressive style of responding may be an adaptive reaction to that world.

Self-Esteem Deficits

Although many children with conduct problems have low self-esteem, there is little support for the view that low self-esteem is the primary cause of conduct problems. Rather, these problems seem to be related to an inflated, unstable, and/or tentative view of self (Baumeister, Bushman, & Campbell, 2000). For example, aggressive children may overestimate their social competence and acceptance by other children (David & Kistner, 2000). Any perceived threat to their biased view of self (e.g., rejection) may lead to aggressive behavior, which provides a way to avoid a lowering of self-concept (Orobio de Castro et al., 2007). Consistent with this view, self-esteem among youth gang members seems to conform to a pattern in which any increment in self-esteem—from increased status, respect, or prestige—for one group member takes away from what is available for others (Anderson, 1994). Thus, youths with conduct problems may experience high self-esteem that over time permits them to rationalize their antisocial conduct (Menon et al., 2007).

Health-Related Problems

Young people with persistent conduct problems engage in many behaviors that place them at high risk for personal injuries, illnesses, drug overdoses, sexually transmitted diseases, substance abuse, and physical problems as adults (Odgers et al., 2007a). Rates of premature death (before age 30) due to various causes (e.g., homicide, suicide, accidental poisoning, traffic accident, or drug overdose) are three to four times higher in boys with conduct problems than in boys without these problems (Kratzer & Hodgins, 1997). Antisocial behavior in childhood predicts an early onset and persistence of sexual activity and sexual risk-taking by age 21 (Ramrakha et al., 2007; Wymbs et al., 2013). This exposes young people to more years at risk for contracting sexually transmitted diseases and unwanted pregnancies through contact with multiple partners and a failure to use contraceptives.

Substance-use disorders and adolescent antisocial behavior are strongly associated with each other (Conner & Lochman, 2010). For example, youths who have used or sold drugs are more likely than nonusers to carry a handgun, belong to a gang, use alcohol, or engage in a host of other antisocial behaviors (Snyder & Sickmund, 2006). Adolescent substance abuse is related to the imminent dangers of accidents, violence, school dropout, family difficulties, and risky sexual behavior (Gilvarry, 2000). Early conduct problems are a known risk factor for adolescent substance use (Fergusson, Horwood, & Ridder, 2007). The prevalence of delinquent behavior varies with the severity of substance abuse, with about

10% of adolescents who use multiple drugs committing more than 50% of all felony assaults, felony thefts, and various other reported crimes (Johnston et al., 2012). Thus, the evidence indicates that conduct problems during childhood are a risk factor for adolescent and adult substance abuse, and this relationship is mediated by drug use and delinquency during early and late adolescence (Fergusson et al., 2007; Hopfer et al., 2013). We talk more about substance use problems in Chapter 13, when we discuss health-related disorders.

Section Summary

Associated Characteristics

- Many children with conduct problems show cognitive, verbal, and language deficits, despite their normal intelligence.
- These children experience a variety of school difficulties, including academic underachievement in language and reading, which may result from co-occurring ADHD.
- General family disturbances, and disturbances in parenting practices and family functioning, are among the strongest and most consistent correlates of conduct problems.
- Children with conduct problems have interpersonal difficulties with peers, including rejection and bullying. Their friendships are often with other antisocial children.
- Antisocial behavior may be related to an inflated, unstable, and/or tentative view of self.
- Youths with conduct problems engage in many behaviors that place them at high risk for health-related problems, including personal injuries, illnesses, sexually transmitted diseases, and substance abuse.

ACCOMPANYING DISORDERS AND SYMPTOMS

Most children with conduct problems suffer from one or more additional disorders, most commonly ADHD, depression, and anxiety (Waldman & Lahey, 2013).

Attention-Deficit/Hyperactivity Disorder (ADHD)

More than 50% of children with CD also have ADHD. There are several possible reasons for this overlap (Beauchaine, Hinshaw, & Pang, 2010; Rhee et al., 2008), among them:

▶ A shared predisposing vulnerability such as impulsivity, poor self-regulation, or temperament may lead to both ADHD and CD.

- ADHD may be a catalyst for CD by contributing to its persistence and escalation to more severe forms, particularly when shaped by ineffective parenting emotional reactions and behaviors.
- ADHD may lead to childhood onset of CD, which is a strong predictor of continuing problems.

Despite the large overlap, two lines of research suggest that CD and ADHD are distinct disorders. First, a model that includes both CD and ADHD consistently provides a better fit to the data than a model based on only a single disorder (Waschbusch, 2002). Second, CD is less likely than ADHD to be associated with cognitive impairments, neurodevelopmental abnormalities, inattentiveness in the classroom, and higher rates of accidental injuries (Hinshaw & Lee, 2003).

Depression and Anxiety

About 50% of youths with conduct problems also receive a diagnosis of depression or anxiety (Wolff & Ollendick, 2006). Some evidence suggests that it is ODD and not CD that best accounts for the connection between conduct problems and depression and that this relationship is driven by the negative mood symptoms of ODD (e.g., anger/irritability) rather than by its behavioral symptoms of defiance (Burke & Loeber, 2010). Boys with combined conduct and internalizing problems have poor outcomes in early adulthood, including having the highest risk of later psychiatric disorders and criminal offenses (Sourander et al., 2007). Most girls with CD develop a depressive or anxiety disorder by early adulthood, and for both sexes, increasing severity of antisocial behavior is associated with increasing severity of depression and anxiety (Zoccolillo et al., 1992). Adolescent CD is also a risk factor for completed suicide in young people with a family history of depression (Renaud et al., 1999).

Findings regarding the relation between anxiety disorders and antisocial outcomes for children with conduct problems are puzzling but quite interesting (Drabick, Ollendick, & Bubier, 2010). In some studies, co-occurring anxiety has been identified as a protective factor that inhibits aggressive behavior (Pine et al., 2000). However, other studies have found that anxiety increases the risk for later antisocial behavior (Rutter, Giller, & Hagell, 1998). Boys with CD and anxiety disorder show a higher level of salivary cortisol associated with a greater degree of behavioral inhibition, which supports the theory of anxiety as a protective factor (McBurnett et al., 1991). In boys with CD only, lower levels of salivary cortisol are directly associated with more aggressive and disruptive behaviors (McBurnett et al., 2000). It has been hypothesized that the

relation between anxiety and antisocial outcomes may depend on the type of anxiety. In this formulation, anxiety related to shyness, inhibition, and fear may protect against conduct problems, whereas anxiety associated with negative emotionality and social avoidance/withdrawal based on a lack of caring about others may increase the child's risk for conduct problems (Lahey & Waldman, 2003). Consistent with this view, children with callous–unemotional traits show less anxiety than other children with conduct problems (Frick et al., 1999). It has been proposed that different pathways underlie the relationship between conduct problems and anxiety, such that anxiety may serve as a buffer or facilitator of conduct problems, depending on the underlying conditions (Drabick et al., 2010).

Section Summary

Accompanying Disorders and Symptoms

- About 50% of children with CD also have ADHD. Despite the overlap, CD and ADHD appear to be distinct disorders.
- About 50% of children with conduct problems are diagnosed with depression or a co-occurring anxiety disorder. Symptoms of negative mood associated with ODD best account for the relationship between conduct problems and depression.
- Anxiety related to shyness, inhibition, and fear may protect against conduct problems, whereas anxiety associated with negative emotionality and social avoidance/withdrawal based on a lack of caring about others may increase the child's risk for conduct problems.

PREVALENCE, GENDER, AND COURSE

In the sections that follow we consider the prevalence of conduct problems, the important role that gender plays in the expression of antisocial behavior, and the different ways that conduct problems emerge over the course of development.

Prevalence

ODD is more prevalent than CD during childhood, but by adolescence they occur equally often. *Lifetime prevalence estimates* are 12% for ODD (13% for males, and 11% for females), and 8% for CD (9% for males and 6% for females) (Merikangas et al., 2010). The reason overall lifetime prevalence rates are comparable is that ODD either declines or stays constant from early childhood to adolescence, whereas CD increases over the same time period. Prevalence estimates for CD and ODD are similar across cultures, although most comparisons to date have been made between Western countries rather than between Western and non-Western countries (Canino et al., 2010; Erskine et al., 2013).

Gender

In all of the recorded history of the more than ten million animal species, including four thousand mammals which populate the planet, only two species have been documented to engage in warfare... male chimpanzees and male humans.

—From Eme (2007)

ANN

Runaway

Until recently, Ann, age 13, lived with her mother, stepfather, and younger brother. For the past 6 months, she has been living in a youth shelter under the custody of the courts, because she repeatedly ran away from home. Ann was described by her parents as defiant and argumentative, and she frequently lied and stole. She often stole clothes and jewelry from the homes of relatives and friends, as well as from her parents. ... Over the past 3 years, Ann had run away from home on four occasions. Each time, the police had to be called. Running away was precipitated by being grounded for stealing or smoking cigarettes. ... One time, Ann was gone for 3 nights. The police found her wandering the streets late at night on the other side of town (about 10 miles from her home). Ann would not tell them who she was or where she lived.

Based on Conduct Disorders in Childhood and Adolescence by A. E. Kazdin, p. 17.

Clear gender differences in the frequency and severity of antisocial behavior are evident by 2 to 3 years of age (Dodge, Coie, & Lynam, 2006). During childhood, rates of conduct problems are about 2 to 4 times higher for boys than for girls, with boys showing an earlier age at onset and greater persistence (Eme, 2007; Lahey et al., 2006). Boys also display more conduct problems and report using more physical aggression than girls across countries throughout the world (Erskine et al., 2013; Lansford et al., 2012). This gender difference does not imply that girls do not display severe conduct problems, including physically aggressive behavior, they just do so much less often than boys.

The gender disparity in conduct problems increases through middle childhood, narrows greatly in early adolescence—due mainly to a rise in covert nonaggressive antisocial behavior in girls (McDermott, 1996)—and then increases again in late adolescence when boys are at the peak of their delinquent behavior (Lahey et al., 2006). Ann steals, lies, and runs away from home, but she is not physically aggressive. In contrast to boys, whose early symptoms of CD are aggression and theft, early symptoms for girls are usually sexual misbehaviors (Offord, Alder, & Boyle, 1986). Antisocial girls are more likely than others to develop relationships with antisocial boys, then become pregnant at an earlier age and display a wide spectrum of later problems, including anxiety, depression, and poor parenting (Foster, 2005).

Although gender differences in the overall amount of antisocial behavior decrease in early adolescence, boys remain more violence-prone than girls throughout their life span, and are more likely to engage in repeated acts of physical violence (Odgers & Moretti, 2002). For conduct problems that are chronic from early childhood to adulthood, the male-to-female ratio is marked, about 10:1. In contrast, more transient forms of antisocial behavior in adolescence show a male-to-female ratio of about 2:1 (Moffitt et al., 2001).

In addition, physical aggression by girls during childhood, when it does occur, does not seem to forecast continued physical violence and other forms of delinquency in adolescence, as it does for boys (Broidy et al., 2003). This does not mean that girls are nonviolent—about 25% of teenage girls commit at least one violent act such as getting into a serious fight at school or work, taking part in a group-against-group fight, or attacking others with the intent to seriously harm them (compared with about 50% of teenage boys) (Substance Abuse and Mental Health Services Administration [SAMHSA], 2009). Interestingly, the sex difference in antisocial behavior has decreased by more than 50% over the past 60 years, suggesting that females may be more susceptible to or more affected by contemporary risk factors, such as family discord or media influences and/or that there is a growing recognition of these problems in girls (Rutter et al., 1998). Unfortunately, antisocial behavior is increasingly becoming an equal

Girls will be girls.

opportunity affliction—conduct problems are one of the most common mental disorders in adolescent girls.

Explaining Gender Differences

The precise reasons for gender differences in antisocial behavior are not known, although genetic, neurobiological, and environmental risk factors have all been implicated (Eme, 2007; Messer et al., 2006). Genetic and environmental risk factors for antisocial behavior in childhood may also be qualitatively different for males and females (Meier et al., 2011). Gender differences may be partly related to definitions of conduct problems that place a strong emphasis on physical aggression and minimal emphasis on the less physically aggressive forms of antisocial behaviors shown by girls (Crick, Bigbee, & Howes, 1996). When girls are angry they are more likely to use indirect forms of **relational aggression** (see A Closer Look 9.4), such as verbal insults, gossip, tattling, ostracism, threatening to withdraw one's friendship, getting even, or third-party retaliation rather than physical forms of aggression (Cote et al., 2007; Crapanzano et al., 2010). In addition, girls are more likely than boys to become emotionally upset by aggressive social exchanges (Crick, 1995). As girls move into adolescence, the function of their aggressive behavior increasingly revolves around group acceptance and affiliation, whereas for boys, aggression remains confrontational (Crick & Rose, 2000).

Fewer differences in antisocial behaviors exist between boys and girls referred for treatment than for children in community samples. Although boys and girls with conduct problems who are referred to clinics display comparable amounts of externalizing behavior (Dishion & Andrews, 1995), referred girls are more deviant than boys in relation to their same-age, same-sex peers (Webster-Stratton, 1996; Zoccolillo, 1993). Girls' behavior is considered more covert because boys typically engage in more rough and tumble play, bullying, fighting, and noncompliance than girls. With overt antisocial behavior more common in boys, their symptoms are more noticeable at a younger age, which could account for the reported earlier age at onset of conduct problems in boys. Longitudinal research has found that age at onset is prior to age 10 in nearly 90% of girls with CD (Keenan et al., 2010). Although research does not support the development of gender-specific criteria for CD at this time (Frick & Nigg, 2012), it does suggest that further study of relational aggression and callous–unemotional features in girls may prove useful in detecting girls with CD at a younger age (Keenan et al., 2010; Kroneman et al., 2011).

Some girls have an early menarche, which may indirectly heighten their conduct problems by increasing their

---

A CLOSER LOOK 9.4

Social Aggression in Girls: "I Hurt Her through the Grapevine"[1]

Over the course of a school day, Rachel Simmons (2002) met with eight groups of 9th-grade girls and began each meeting with the same question:

Girls are more likely than boys to use indirect forms of social aggression, such as gossiping and spreading rumors.

"What are some of the differences between the ways guys and gals are mean?"

From periods one through eight she heard the same responses: "Girls can turn on you for anything." "Girls whisper." "They glare at you." "They destroy you from the inside." "Girls are manipulative." "There's an aspect of evil in girls that there isn't in boys." "Girls target you when they know you're weakest." "Girls do a lot behind each other's backs." "Girls plan and premeditate."

"In bold, matter-of-fact voices, girls described themselves … as disloyal, untrustworthy, and sneaky. They claimed girls use intimacy to manipulate and overpower others. They said girls are fake, using each other to move up the social hierarchy. They described girls as unforgiving and crafty, lying in wait for a moment of revenge that will catch the unwitting victim off guard, and with an almost savage eye-for-an-eye mentality."

[1]Crick et al. (2001, p. 15)

Adapted from Simmons, 2002, pp. 15–16.

involvement with deviant peers (Burt et al., 2006). Interestingly, an early onset of menarche predicts increased delinquency primarily for girls who attend mixed-gender schools rather than all-girl schools. In mixed-gender schools, exposure to boys who model antisocial behavior and pressure girls for early sexual relations may interact with the early physical maturation of girls. Such exposure may lead to antisocial behavior in these girls, who are more likely to find rewards and opportunities for antisocial activities in the company of boys than girls (Moffitt et al., 1992). In contrast to earlier findings, one study found that girls reaching menarche at an early age had a greater risk of early pregnancy and sexually transmitted infection by age 18, but it found little evidence to indicate that age at menarche was related to later antisocial or criminal behavior (Boden, Fergusson, & Horwood, 2011). Although the reason for these discrepant findings is not known, they do suggest that early age at menarche plays a role in determining sexual behavior outcomes but not necessarily in determining longer-term outcomes in other areas of adjustment, such as antisocial behavior.

Another study found that *both* early maturing girls and early maturing boys were at risk for being exposed to peers who may draw them into delinquent behavior (Negriff, Ji, & Trickett, 2011). However, for early-maturing children who had been maltreated, exposure to abuse had a greater effect on the development of delinquency than did exposure to delinquent peers. These findings suggest that different mechanisms may underlie the relationship between early maturation and delinquency for different groups of children. Most likely, both early-maturing girls and early-maturing boys are vulnerable to an interaction between genetic and environmental risks for delinquent behavior (Harden & Mendle, 2012).

Developmental Course and Pathways

Longitudinal studies have greatly advanced our understanding of antisocial patterns by revealing both a general developmental progression and important variations on this theme (Frick & Viding, 2009).

General Progression

An approximate ordering of the different forms of disruptive behavior and antisocial behavior from early childhood through adolescence is shown in ● Figure 9.3.

Although there are isolated reports, such as that of a 9-month-old infant being expelled from day care for punching other children, early signs of conduct problems are usually not so obvious (Kazdin, 1995, p. 27). The earliest indications of conduct problems may be a *difficult temperament* in the first few years of life, expressed as fussiness, irritability, irregular sleeping and eating patterns, or fearfulness in response to novel events. Interestingly, fussiness in the first year of life was a stronger predictor of later conduct problems in boys, whereas fearfulness was a stronger predictor of later conduct problems in girls (Lahey et al., 2008). As is the case for ADHD, although difficult temperament often precedes later conduct problems, it may not be specific to these problems. The evidence regarding early temperament and later conduct problems suggests a general link, but has not yet identified specific aspects of temperament that predict distinct types of maladjustment (Loeber et al., 2009).

During the preschool and early school years, a child with a difficult temperament displays an increase in hyperactivity and impulsivity with growing mobility, weak emotion-regulation skills, and a heightened risk for

Preschool   Elementary School   Adolescence

| Difficult temperament | Hyperactivity | Overt conduct problems aggressiveness/ oppositionality | Withdrawal | Poor peer relationships | Academic problems | Covert or concealing conduct problems | Association with deviant peers | Delinquency (Arrest) |

● **FIGURE 9.3** | Approximate ordering of the different forms of disruptive and antisocial behavior from childhood through adolescence.

Based on Development and Risk Factors of Juvenile Antisocial Behavior and Delinquency by R. Loeber, 1990, 'Clinical Psychology Review', 10, 1–41. *Photo Credits (left to right):* © Andrewblue/Dreamstime.com; © iStockphoto.com/ Christopher Futcher; Elena Rostunova/Shutterstock.com simple forms of oppositional and aggressive behaviors that peak during the preschool years (Tremblay, 2000). Preschoolers with ODD display stubbornness, temper tantrums, irritability, and spitefulness—problems that remain stable from 2 to 5 years of age. Discipline problems and poor self-control and emotion regulation during early childhood, especially when accompanied by harsh parenting and high levels of stress, are strong indicators that the child will continue to experience behavior problems and negative outcomes across nearly every area of life functioning in adolescence and adulthood (Campbell et al., 2010; Fergusson, Boden, & Horwood, 2013; Moffitt et al., 2011).

Most children with conduct problems show *diversification*—they add new forms of antisocial behavior over time rather than simply replacing old behaviors. Poor social skills and social–cognitive deficits often accompany early oppositional and aggressive behaviors, predisposing the child to poor peer relationships, rejection by peers, and social isolation and withdrawal. When the child enters school, impulsivity and attention problems may result in reading difficulties and academic failure. Covert conduct problems, such as truancy or substance use, also begin to appear during the elementary school years and increase into early adolescence. From ages 8 to 12, behaviors such as fighting, bullying, fire setting, vandalism, cruelty to animals and people, and stealing begin to emerge.

In this progression, we see a snowballing negative cycle over time, where one deficit or problem behavior produces direct and indirect changes in others. For example, peer rejection leads to social–cognitive deficits and aggression; social–cognitive deficits lead to peer rejection and aggression; aggression leads to peer rejection (Lansford et al., 2010). Conversely, better social–cognitive skills may increase peer acceptance and lower aggressiveness. These cascading effects highlight the importance of looking at the progression of antisocial behavior over time as a dynamic developmental process involving relationships among neurobiological dispositions, social environments, cognitions, and behavior (Lansford et al., 2010).

Across cultures, major conduct problems become more frequent during adolescence. Delinquent behavior shows a dramatic rise in middle adolescence and peaks around the age of 17, followed by an equally dramatic drop in late adolescence and young adulthood (Hirschi & Gottfredson, 1983). Adolescence is characterized by a growing association with deviant peers and by increasing rates of arrest, re-arrest, and conviction as the minimum age of criminal responsibility is met. From ages 12 to 14, property destruction, running away from home, truancy, mugging, breaking and entering, use of a weapon, and forced sex occur with increasing frequency (Lahey & Waldman, 2003). By age 18, many young people with conduct problems display antisocial personality development and behaviors that forecast an antisocial future, including substance dependence, unsafe sex, dangerous driving habits, delinquent friends, and unemployment (Moffitt et al., 1996).

Does this developmental progression mean that every young child with conduct problems goes on to become a delinquent adolescent? Definitely not. The sequence in Figure 9.3 shows a maximum progression that begins early in life and persists through adolescence. Although some children display this maximum progression, others will desist their antisocial behavior at a young age. About 50% of children with early conduct problems do improve. Those who do so are those who tend to display less extreme levels of early conduct problems, have higher intelligence and socioeconomic status (SES), fewer delinquent friends, mothers who were not teenagers when they gave birth, and parents with more social skills and fewer mental health problems (Lahey et al., 2002; Nagin & Tremblay, 2001). It is important to note, however, that even among children who display antisocial behavior and then desist at a young age, other problems may emerge in young adulthood, suggesting that their recovery is far from complete (Moffitt et al., 2002). Some children may not display problems until adolescence, and not all children display the full range of difficulties described. Still others may display a chronic low level of persistent antisocial behavior from childhood or adolescence through adulthood (Fergusson & Horwood, 2002). These differences lead us to consider important variations in the general progression.

Pathways

There are likely as many unique pathways to the development of antisocial behavior as there are children who display these problems. Although a number of different pathways have been identified (Hoeve et al., 2008), evidence across cultures and countries supports two common pathways—the life-course–persistent (LCP) path and the adolescent-limited (AL) path (Moffitt, 2006). As shown in ● Figure 9.4, a small number of individuals with conduct problems (less than 10%) show a persistent pattern of antisocial behavior throughout their lives, whereas the majority display antisocial behavior that occurs mainly during adolescence. Keep in mind that, although the designation of two pathways is a useful way to think about how conduct problems develop in different ways, it is likely that children display a range of levels of severity and continuity over time and that many do not fit neatly on one pathway or the other (Waldman & Lahey, 2013). For example, other pathways that have been identified include the low-level chronic offense path and the adult-onset antisocial behavior path (Loeber et al., 2009).

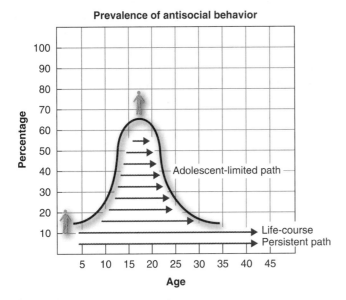

Prevalence of antisocial behavior

● **FIGURE 9.4** | The changing prevalence of participation in antisocial behavior across the life span.

Based on Adolescence-Limited and Life-Course-Persistent Antisocial Behavior: A Developmental Taxonomy by T. E. Moffitt, 1993, 'Psychological Review', 100, 674–701.

The **life-course–persistent (LCP) path** describes children who engage in aggression and antisocial behavior at an early age and continue to do so into adulthood (Moffitt et al., 1996). They may display "biting and hitting at age 4, shoplifting and truancy at age 10, selling drugs and stealing cars at age 16, robbery and rape at age 22, and fraud and child abuse at age 30" (Moffitt, 1993, p. 679). Their underlying disposition remains, but the way it is expressed changes with new "opportunities" at different points in development. For these children, antisocial behavior begins early because of subtle neuropsychological deficits that may interfere with their development of language, memory, and self-control, resulting in cognitive deficits and a difficult temperament by age 3 or younger. These deficits heighten the child's vulnerability to antisocial elements in the social environment, such as abuse or poor parenting, which in turn lead to oppositional and conduct problems (Lansford et al., 2011; Moffitt, 1993). These children experience greater social adversity (e.g., maternal insensitivity, single parenting, low income) than their peers from infancy through mid-adolescence (Roisman et al., 2010).

About half of the children who display high levels of childhood-onset antisocial behavior continue on the LCP path by engaging in less serious nonaggressive antisocial behaviors (e.g., stealing and truancy) during middle childhood, followed by affiliation with delinquent peers and more serious delinquent activities during adolescence (Brame, Nagin, & Tremblay, 2001; Dandreaux & Frick, 2009). This subgroup of teens is most likely to commit violent crimes and to drop out of school. LCP youths display consistency in their behavior across situations—for example, by lying at home, stealing from stores, and cheating at school. As young adults, they have difficulty forming lasting relationships and may display a hostile mistrust of others, aggressive dominance, impulsivity, and psychopathic features. Complete spontaneous recovery is rare after adolescence. The LCP path is associated with a family history of externalizing disorders and is often perpetuated by the progressive accumulation of its own consequences (Odgers et al., 2007b). For example, poor self-control and diminished verbal intellect may lead to irreversible decisions, such as dropping out of school or abusing drugs, which further limit opportunities for recovery.

The **adolescent-limited (AL) path** describes youths whose antisocial behavior begins around puberty and continues into adolescence, but who later cease these behaviors during young adulthood. This path includes most juvenile offenders whose antisocial behavior is limited primarily to their teen years (Hamalainen & Pulkkinen, 1996). Teens on the AL path display less extreme antisocial behavior than those on the LCP path, are less likely to drop out of school, and have stronger family ties. Their delinquent activity is often related to temporary situational factors, especially peer influences. The behavior of AL youths is not consistent across situations; they may use drugs or shoplift with their friends while continuing to follow rules and to do well in school. Although these children do not display antisocial behavior in childhood, they do experience, like youngsters on the LCP path, greater social adversity and personal risk during childhood relative to other youths, suggesting that the AL pathway is not simply part of normal adolescent development (Roisman et al., 2010).

MARCUS

Call of the Wild

"I grew up in a real poor family. My mom was on welfare all my life—we never had much. As soon as I got to the age of 11, I was interested in other kids who were breaking the rules. I used to see what they used to do—and what they had."

Marcus joined a gang when he turned 13. Two years later, after a number of arrests and four detentions in a juvenile facility, he became disillusioned with gang life and managed to turn his life around. He is now 17 and works as a youth minister for a church dedicated to helping other young people like himself.

Adapted from Goldentyer, 1994.

The attraction of still-forbidden adult privileges, such as drinking alcohol, driving a car, and having sex, may motivate some youths with few previous risk signs to engage in antisocial behavior as they enter adolescence. These youths may observe their LCP peers obtaining desired adult privileges via illicit means and may mimic their delinquent activities. Eventually, when access to adult privileges becomes available, AL youths cease breaking laws and rely instead on the more adaptive and prosocial behaviors and values they learned prior to adolescence (Moffitt, Lynam, & Silva, 1994).

Contrary to expectations, some youths on the adolescent-limited path continue to display antisocial behavior well into their 20s before they eventually stop. Others do not desist in their 20s at all but continue to display higher-than-normal levels of impulsivity, substance abuse and dependence, property crimes, and mental health problems (Moffitt et al., 2002). Persistence in early adulthood is often the result of *snares*, or outcomes of antisocial behavior that close the door to getting a good job, pursuing higher education, or attracting a supportive partner. Common snares include unplanned parenthood, dropping out of school, addiction to drugs or alcohol, disabling injuries, unemployment or erratic work history, severed family connections, imprisonment, bad reputation, and a delinquent self-image (Moffitt et al., 1994). Thus, despite their potential, some individuals with no history of childhood antisocial behavior who initiate delinquent activity in adolescence continue to experience problems well into adulthood (Moffitt et al., 2002). Therefore, referring to these individuals as "adolescent-limited" is somewhat misleading.

The identification of the LCP and AL pathways (and their variations) helps us understand why adult antisocial behavior is almost always preceded by antisocial behavior during childhood and adolescence (Brame et al., 2001). Nevertheless, most antisocial adolescents do not go on to become antisocial adults. At the crossroads of early adulthood, LCP and most AL teens go different ways. Antisocial behavior is stable for youths on the LCP path, who continue on the same road, but unstable for those on the AL path.

Adult Outcomes

The number of active offenders decreases by about 50% in the early 20s, and almost 85% of former delinquents desist from offending by their late 20s. This general relationship between age and crime applies to males and females, for most types of crimes, and in numerous Western nations (Caspi & Moffitt, 1995). Most children with conduct problems do not grow up to be antisocial adults (Maughan & Rutter, 2001). However,

adult outcomes depend not only on the type and variety of conduct problems developed during childhood and adolescence, but also on the number and combination of risk and promotive factors in the child, family and community (Kokko & Pulkkinen, 2000). Also, even when antisocial behavior decreases in adulthood, coercive interpersonal styles may sometimes persist, along with family, health, and work difficulties.

A significant number of children with conduct problems, particularly those on the LCP path, do go on as adults to display criminal behavior, psychiatric problems, social maladjustment, health problems, lost productivity, and poor parenting of their own children (Fergusson, Horwood, & Ridder, 2005). As adults, they are more likely to be downwardly socially mobile and to display an erratic work history, perhaps because of lower skill attainment and difficulties in getting along with co-workers and supervisors. They also have more violent marriages and cohabitations and higher rates of divorce and are more likely than others to select partners with similar antisocial characteristics, providing the next generation with a double dose of both genetic and environmental risk (Moffitt et al., 2002). One follow-up study of adult women who were arrested for severe conduct problems in adolescence found that most continued to display these problems. A majority had depressive and anxiety disorders, 6% died a violent death, many had dropped out of school, one-third were pregnant before the age of 17 years, half were re-arrested, and many had suffered traumatic physical injuries (Zoccolillo & Rogers, 1991, 1992). Thus, males and females experience different but poor adult outcomes. Males are at higher risk for criminal behavior, work problems, and substance abuse, whereas females are more likely to experience depression, suicidal behavior, and health problems (Moffitt et al., 2001).

Section Summary

Prevalence, Gender, and Course

- ODD is more prevalent than CD during childhood, but by adolescence the two occur about equally. The lifetime prevalence rates for ODD and CD are about 12% and 8%, respectively.
- During childhood, conduct problems are about 2 to 4 times more common in boys than in girls. This difference narrows greatly in early adolescence, due mainly to a rise in covert nonaggressive antisocial behavior in girls, and then increases again in late adolescence and beyond.
- Girls are more likely than boys to use indirect forms of relational aggression—for example, verbal insults, gossip, or third-party retaliation.

- There is a general progression of antisocial behavior from difficult early temperament and hyperactivity, to oppositional and aggressive behavior, to social difficulties, to school problems, to delinquent behavior in adolescence, to antisocial personality development, to criminal behavior in adulthood.
- The life-course–persistent (LCP) path describes children who display antisocial behavior at an early age and who continue to do so into adulthood.
- The adolescent-limited (AL) path describes teens whose antisocial behavior begins around puberty and continues into adolescence and who later cease these behaviors in young adulthood.
- A significant number of children with conduct problems continue to experience difficulties as adults, including criminal behavior, psychiatric problems, social maladjustment, health and employment problems, and poor parenting of their own children.

CAUSES

When it comes to conduct problems, there are no simple or single causes. Consider two brothers—one, John Edgar Wideman, is an award-winning author (*Brothers and Keepers*), while his younger brother Robby is in prison for murder. How do we account for such striking differences between brothers raised in the same family? Are they due to differences in genetic make-up, neurobiological functioning, birth complications,

"We won't know till they're older which one is the evil twin."

Sidney Harris/Cartoon Bank.com

temperament, intelligence, family experiences, peer influences, difficulties in school, or some combination of these factors?

Historically, conduct problems were viewed as either the result of an inborn characteristic or learned through poor socialization practices. Early theories focused mainly on the child's aggression and invoked one primary cause, such as an aggressive drive, frustration, poor role models, or reinforcement. However, most of these "smoking gun" explanations can be challenged on one point or another. For example, not all children behave aggressively, as would be predicted by the aggressive-drive theory, and frustration sometimes leads to cooperation rather than aggression. Although each single-cause theory highlights a potentially important determinant, no single theory can explain all forms of antisocial behavior.

We next consider a wide number and diversity of risk factors for youth conduct problems. Although we examine them separately, conduct problems are best accounted for by the interplay among predisposing child, family, community, and cultural factors that operate in a transactional fashion over time (Granic & Patterson, 2006). It is also important to recognize that subgroups of youths with conduct problems (e.g., child versus adolescent onset, those with CU traits) may have distinct risk factors underlying their antisocial and aggressive behaviors (Kimonis et al., 2014). These risk factors are summarized in Table 9.3.

Genetic Influences

Heredity is something a man believes in until his own son begins behaving like a delinquent.

—Author unknown

The universality of aggressive behavior and antisocial behavior in humans and the fact that such behaviors run in families within and across generations highlight the importance of genetic influences. Adoption and twin studies indicate that 50% or more of the variance in antisocial behavior is attributable to heredity for both males and females. This influence is somewhat higher for aggressive versus nonaggressive conduct problems and in childhood versus adolescence. Research indicates that parents pass on a general liability for externalizing disorders to their children that may be expressed in different ways, including oppositional and conduct problems, inattention, and hyperactivity–impulsivity (Bornovalova et al., 2010). The heritability of conduct problems also varies by age at onset and other factors (Burt & Neiderhiser, 2009). For example, the strength of the genetic contribution is higher for children who display the LCP versus the AL pattern and for those with callous–unemotional traits (Viding et al., 2008). However, all externalizing disorders appear to share substantial genetic influences, suggesting at least some common causal factors among them(Lahey et al., 2011). Overall, adoption and twin studies suggest that both genetic and environmental factors contribute to antisocial behavior across

TABLE 9.3 | **Summary of Risk Factors for Antisocial Behaviors**

Child
Genetic risk, prenatal and birth complications, exposure to lead and other toxins, low arousal and reactivity, anterior and posterior cingulate cortex development, functional and structural deficits in prefrontal cortex, reduced amygdala activity, blunted emotional and cortisol reactivity (CU -type), insensitivity to stress (CU-type), fearlessness/low anxiety (CU-type), difficult temperament, emotion dysregulation, attention-deficit/hyperactivity disorder (ADHD), insecure/disorganized attachments, childhood onset of aggression, social avoidance and withdrawal, social–cognitive deficits (hostile attributional bias), lowered verbal intelligence and verbal deficits, executive functioning deficits

Family
Antisocial family values, parental antisocial or criminal behavior, paternal antisocial personality disorder, maternal depression, parental substance abuse, marital discord, teen motherhood, single parenthood, family stress/conflict/instability, chaotic household, large family, low socioeconomic status, low education of mother, family carelessness in permitting access to weapons

Ineffective Parenting
Poor supervision and monitoring, inconsistent discipline, avoidance of discipline due to concerns about the child's reaction, harsh discipline and maltreatment, discordant parent–child interactions, poor communication and problem solving, low parental involvement, parental neglect, low parental warmth, parental hostile attributional bias

Peers
Early peer aggression, rejection by peers, association with deviant siblings, association with deviant peers, bullying

School
Poor academic performance, weak bonding to school, low educational aspirations, low school motivation, poorly organized and functioning schools

Neighborhood and Community
Neighborhood disadvantage and poverty, disorganized neighborhoods, gang membership, availability of weapons

Sociocultural
Media portrayal of violence, cultural attitudes encouraging use of aggression, socialization of children for aggression

Adapted from Loeber and Farrington, 2000, p. 749.

development. The studies do not, however, specify the mechanisms by which the factors operate.

It is likely that genetic risks for antisocial behavior operate via several pathways (Rutter, 2003b). First, genetic factors may be related to a difficult temperament, lack of response to distress in others, impulsivity, a tendency to seek rewards, or an insensitivity to punishment that combine to create an antisocial "propensity" or "personality" (Waldman et al., 2011). Second, genetic factors may increase the likelihood that a child will be exposed to environmental risk factors, such as prenatal stress, parental maltreatment, divorce, or other negative life events that are associated with an increased risk of antisocial behavior. Third, children's genotype and neurobiology may moderate their susceptibility to these environmental insults in determining whether they later develop antisocial behavior (Ellis & Boyce, 2011; Zohsel et al., 2014). These and other pathways will need to be addressed if the causes of antisocial behavior are to be understood (Rutter, 2006a).

Exciting new studies into gene variants have identified possible gene–environment (G×E) interactions in the development of conduct problems (Dodge, 2009). A variant of the gene that encodes the neurotransmitter-metabolizing enzyme monoamine oxidase A (MAOA) has been of particular interest because this gene is related to neural systems involved in aggression. When threatened or provoked, humans naturally feel rage and an impulse to react aggressively. Activation of the MAOA enzyme helps us inhibit that response; thus, it plays a key role in regulating behavior following threatening events. Research has found that maltreated children with a low-active MAOA genotype are much more likely to develop antisocial behavior than maltreated children who do not have this genotype (Kim-Cohen et al., 2006). An interaction between the low-active MAOA genotype and physical discipline before age 5 has also been found to be related to adolescent delinquent behavior (Edwards et al., 2010). Brain imaging studies have also found that individuals with the low-active MAOA genotype show patterns of arousal in areas of the brain that are associated with aggression in response to emotion-provoking stimuli (Buckholtz & Meyer-Lindenberg, 2008).

In addition to MAOA, other genes and G×E interactions have been implicated in the association between negative parenting and childhood conduct problems (Albaugh et al., 2010; Lahey et al., 2011). Findings to date suggest that some of these genes may not be specific to any one type of externalizing disorder but will predispose individuals to a broad spectrum of conduct problems (Dick, 2007). G×E interaction effects in conduct disorders are fascinating. However, research into these effects is just beginning, and replication studies are needed (Hebebrand et al., 2010). Similarly, research into how G×E interaction effects develop over time is still in its infancy (Dodge, 2009).

Prenatal Factors and Birth Complications

A number of pregnancy and birth factors (e.g., low birth weight) are related to the development of serious conduct problems (Brennan, Grekin, & Mednick, 2003). Malnutrition during pregnancy is associated with later antisocial behavior, which may be mediated by protein deficiency (Raine, 2002). Exposure to lead before and after birth and the mother's use of nicotine, marijuana, and other substances during pregnancy may also be associated with later conduct problems (Carpenter & Nevin, 2010; Gaysina et al., 2013; Murray et al., 2010; Nigg & Breslau, 2007). There is also support for maternal alcohol use during pregnancy playing a role in conduct problems— the greater the amount of alcohol consumed, the greater the risk of child conduct problems (D'Onofrio et al., 2007; Larkby et al., 2011). Although pregnancy and birth factors are correlated with conduct problems, strong evidence of direct biological causation is lacking (Hodgins, Kratzer, & McNeil, 2001). For example, it is likely that the relation between mothers' smoking during pregnancy and adolescent conduct problems and criminality is best accounted for by the transmission of an underlying antisocial tendency from mother to child and other family background variables, rather than by exposure to cigarette by-products during pregnancy (D'Onofrio et al., 2008, 2010b; Gatzke-Kopp & Beauchaine, 2007).

Neurobiological Factors

Gray (1987) proposed that people's behavioral patterns are related to two subsystems of the brain, each having distinct neuroanatomical regions and neurotransmitter pathways. The **behavioral activation system (BAS)** stimulates behavior in response to signals of reward or nonpunishment. In contrast, the **behavioral inhibition system (BIS)** produces anxiety and inhibits ongoing behavior in the presence of novel events, innate fear stimuli, and signals of nonreward or punishment. Other behavioral patterns may result from the relative balance or imbalance of activity in these two neural systems. Think of the BAS as similar to the gas pedal and the BIS as similar to the brake pedal—some individuals ride one more heavily than the other.

It has been proposed that antisocial patterns of behavior result from an overactive BAS *and* an underactive BIS—a pattern determined primarily by genetic predisposition. Consistent with an overactive BAS,

children with conduct problems show a heightened sensitivity to rewards (Frick et al., 2003). In addition, they fail to respond to punishment and continue to respond under conditions of no reward—patterns that are consistent with an underactive BIS (Fowles, 2001). Strikingly, a lack of fear conditioning at age 3 has been found to predict criminal offending 20 years later (Gao et al., 2010).

Individual differences in antisocial behavior have been related to variations in stress-regulating mechanisms, including the hypothalamic–pituitary–adrenal (HPA) axis and the autonomic nervous system (ANS), serotonergic functioning, and structural and functional deficits in the prefrontal cortex of the brain (van Goozen et al., 2007). Children with CD who show an early onset of aggressive symptoms display low psychophysiological/cortical arousal and low reactivity of the autonomic nervous system (e.g., a lower resting heart rate) (Lorber, 2004; Raine, 2002). Low arousal and autonomic reactivity may lead to diminished avoidance learning in response to warnings or reprimands, a poor response to punishment, and a fearless, stimulus-seeking temperament. In turn, this may lead to antisocial behavior, a failure to develop the anticipatory fear needed to avoid such behavior, and a lack of conscience. Most children respond to discipline and punishment by reducing their antisocial behavior. Often, the opposite occurs with children with conduct problems—when disciplined or punished they may increase their antisocial behavior and become even more defiant (Briggs-Gowan et al., 2014).

Neuroimaging studies have identified structural and functional brain abnormalities in several brain regions in youths with conduct disorders, including in those with high levels of psychopathic features (Pardini et al., 2013). These brain regions include the amygdala, prefrontal cortex, posterior and anterior cingulate, and insula, as well as interconnected regions. Imaging studies also show reduced activation in some of these areas (e.g., the amygdala) when viewing emotional stimuli such as angry or sad faces, or during tasks that require learning not to respond to punishing stimuli (Finger et al., 2011; Huebner et al., 2008; Passamonti et al., 2010). These brain regions are involved in processing social and emotional information. Therefore, abnormalities in these regions likely underlie the social–cognitive and emotional deficits that characterize youths with conduct problems. Interestingly, as described in A Closer Look 9.5, similar brain abnormalities may be present both in youths with early-onset and those with adolescent-onset conduct disorders (Fairchild et al., 2011).

Although much additional work is needed, early findings from neuroimaging and other studies suggest three neural systems underlying cognitive, social, and emotional differences across different types of conduct problems. The first includes subcortical neural systems that lead to

Do the Brains of Children with Early-Onset Conduct Disorders Differ from Those of Children with Adolescent-Onset Conduct Disorders?

Despite the many differences between children with early-onset and those with adolescent-onset CD, brain-imaging findings suggest that the two groups may display similar brain abnormalities as compared with children without CD. Using magnetic resonance imaging (MRI), neuroscientists in England measured the size of specific brain regions of 65 teenage boys with CD and 27 teenage boys without CD (Fairchild et al., 2011). They found that the amygdala, a region of the brain involved in reading others' emotions, empathy, and recognizing when others are distressed, was markedly smaller in teens with CD than in the healthy comparison group. However, no differences were found between teens with early-onset and those with adolescent-onset conduct disorders. The image to the right, shows the amygdala (for each side of the brain), the region of the brain for which the reduction in volume was largest for teens with CD versus healthy comparison children.

These preliminary findings are important, since it has been argued that early-onset CD is a neurodevelopmental condition, whereas adolescent-onset CD is mostly the result of teens associating with and mimicking other teens who are getting into trouble. However, this study shows that abnormalities in

Courtesy of Dr. Giuseppe Iaria

brain structures underlying social-information processing may contribute to the emergence of both adolescent-onset as well as early-onset CD (Fairchild et al., 2011).

---

aggressive behavior. In this context, dysfunction in the integrated functioning of brain circuits involving the amygdala has been implicated (Blair, 2011). The second neural circuit includes prefrontal cortex decision-making circuits and socioemotional information-processing circuits that assess social cues and evaluate the consequences of aggressing or not aggressing; the third neural circuit includes frontoparietal regions involved in regulating emotions and impulsive motivational urges (Coccaro et al., 2011). In the future, further research into these neural circuits may help to reveal mechanisms through which inborn dispositions may place a child at risk for later conduct problems (Viding & Jones, 2008).

Social–Cognitive Factors

Social–cognitive abilities refer to the skills involved in attending to, interpreting, and responding to social cues. There is a strong relationship between social–cognitive deficits and antisocial behavior across all types of conduct-problem trajectories (e.g., childhood limited, adolescent-onset, early-onset persistent), especially for children showing early-onset persistent conduct problems. As many as 40% of boys and 25% of girls with persistent conduct problems display significant social–cognitive impairments (Oliver et al., 2011).

The connection between children's thinking in social situations and their aggressive behavior has been looked at in several ways. Some approaches focus on immature forms of thinking, such as egocentrism, a lack of social perspective taking, theory of mind deficits, or deficits in moral reasoning (Blair, 2010; Olson et al., 2011). Others emphasize cognitive deficiencies, such as a child's failure to use verbal mediators to regulate his or her behavior (Meichenbaum, 1977), or cognitive distortions, such as interpreting a neutral event as an intentionally hostile act (Crick & Dodge, 1994). Other approaches focus more broadly on the social–cognitive processes involved in antisocial decision making (Fontaine et al., 2010). Some research has also found deficits in facial expression recognition and eye contact in children with conduct problems, which may further contribute to their antisocial behavior and social difficulties (Dadds et al., 2011; Fairchild et al., 2009).

Dodge and Pettit (2003) have presented a comprehensive social–cognitive framework to account for aggressive behavior and antisocial behavior in children. In their model, cognitive and emotional processes play a central mediating role. Children are presumed to develop social knowledge about their world based on a unique set of predispositions, life experiences, and sociocultural contexts. In specific social situations, children

TABLE 9.4 | Steps in the Thinking and Behavior of Aggressive Children in Social Situations

Step 1: Encoding. Socially aggressive children use fewer cues before making a decision. When defining and resolving an interpersonal situation, they seek less information about the event before acting.

Step 2: Interpretation. Socially aggressive children attribute hostile intentions to ambiguous events.

Step 3: Response Search. Socially aggressive children generate fewer and more aggressive responses and have less knowledge about social problem solving.

Step 4: Response Decision. Socially aggressive children are more likely to choose aggressive solutions.

Step 5: Enactment. Socially aggressive children use poor verbal communication and strike out physically.

Source: From A Review and Reformulation of Social information Processing Mechanism in Children's Social Adjustment by N. R. Crick and K. A. Dodge, 1994, *Psychological Bulletin,* 115, 74–101.

then use this social knowledge to guide their processing of social information in ways that lead directly to certain behaviors. For example, when teased in the schoolyard by peers, does the child laugh with the crowd, walk away, or strike back aggressively? A set of emotional and thought processes are presumed to occur between the social stimulus of being teased and the child's reaction. The thinking and behavior of antisocial/aggressive children in social situations are often characterized by deficits in one or more of these steps, as outlined in Table 9.4.

Family Factors

I am convinced that increasing rates of delinquency are due to parents who are either too careless or too busy with their own pleasure to give sufficient time, companionship, and interest to their children.

—Former FBI director J. Edgar Hoover, *The New York Times,* December 6, 1947

Many family factors have been implicated as possible causes of children's antisocial behavior—early maternal age at childbearing, poor disciplinary practices, harsh discipline, a lack of parental supervision, a lack of affection, marital conflict, family isolation, and violence in the home (D'Onofrio et al., 2009; Hoeve et al., 2008; Lansford et al., 2011). For children who are at genetic risk for antisocial behavior, positive parenting practices may reduce the influence of the child's genotype on later antisocial behavior, whereas negative parenting practices can have the opposite effect (Feinberg et al., 2007). Although the association between family

factors and conduct problems is well established, the nature of this association and the possible causal role of family factors continue to be debated.

Family difficulties are related to the development of both ODD and CD, with a stronger association for children on the LCP as compared with those on the AL path (Lahey et al., 1992). A combination of individual child risk factors (e.g., difficult temperament) and extreme deficits in family management skills most likely accounts for the more persistent and severe forms of antisocial behavior (Caspi & Moffitt, 1995).

Family factors are related to children's antisocial behavior in complex ways. For example, physical abuse is a strong risk factor for later aggressive behavior. One reason for this link between factors appears to be deficits in the child's social information processing that result from the physical abuse (Dodge & Pettit, 2003). As we have seen, the child's genotype can also moderate the link between maltreatment and later antisocial behavior, a possible reason that not all children who have been abused grow up to victimize others (Caspi et al., 2002).

Several factors may affect the consequences of marital conflict on children's aggressive behavior; these include the parents' unavailability, the use of

Physical abuse is a strong risk factor for later aggressive behavior.

Bob Kalman / The Image Works

inconsistent or harsh discipline, lax monitoring, and how the child interprets conflict between parents (Cummings & Davies, 2002). Other conditions associated with marital conflict or divorce such as stress, depression, loss of contact with one parent, financial hardship, and greater responsibility at home may also contribute to antisocial behavior (Emery, 1999). Interestingly, contact with an absent father after the breakup of the parents' marriage can be either a risk or a protective factor for antisocial behavior, depending on whether or not the father is antisocial (Jaffee et al., 2003).

Nick's mother says:

Nick hit a neighborhood kid on the head with a two-by-four; the injured child required 16 stitches. Then he killed another kitten by jumping on it from his bunk bed. I lost control. I told him I hated him, I grabbed him by the cheek, I pinched it a little too hard. I didn't know what to do. (Colapinto, 1993, p. 150)

Cruel and aggressive child behaviors can evoke strong reactions, like the anger and overly harsh response by Nick's mother. An important concept for understanding family influences on antisocial behavior is **reciprocal influence**, which means that the child's behavior is both influenced by and influences the behavior of others. Negative parenting practices and parent–child conflict may lead to antisocial behavior, but they may also be a reaction to the oppositional and aggressive behaviors of their children (Klahr et al., 2011).

For example, in an interesting study of reciprocal influence, mothers of boys with and without CD were asked to interact with three boys—their own son, a boy with CD, and a boy without CD (Anderson, Lytton, & Romney, 1986). All mothers were more demanding and negative when interacting with a child with CD, which supports a child-to-parent effect. However, mothers of boys with CD responded most negatively to their own sons, suggesting that previous negative interactions with their child also had an effect. Reciprocal influence is a useful way to think of the interplay between family influences and antisocial behavior over the course of development. However, it is also possible that some aspects of the family environment are related to antisocial behavior as a result of a shared genetic predisposition that leads parent and child to display similar behavior patterns.

Some studies generally support the view that child behaviors exert greater influence on parenting behaviors than the reverse, perhaps more so for mothers than fathers (Narusyte et al., 2011). This suggests that the inborn level of emotional dysregulation that children bring to their interactions with parents may have a greater influence on outcomes than ineffective parenting behaviors (Loeber et al., 2009). Nevertheless, as we will

A child's oppositional behavior may also lead to negative parenting behavior.

discuss, interventions directed at changing ineffective parenting behaviors are among the most effective methods for reducing children's conduct problems.

Coercion Theory

Gerald Patterson's **coercion theory** contends that parent–child interactions provide a training ground for the development of antisocial behavior (Patterson, Reid, & Dishion, 1992). This occurs through a four-step, escape-conditioning sequence in which the child learns to use increasingly intense forms of noxious behavior to escape and avoid unwanted parental demands. The *coercive parent–child interaction* described in A Closer Look 9.6 begins when a mother finds her son Paul, who is failing in school, watching TV rather than doing his homework. Coercive parent–child interactions are made up of well-practiced actions and reactions, which may occur with little awareness. This process is called a "reinforcement trap" because, over time, all family members become trapped by the consequences of their own behaviors. For example, mothers of antisocial children are eight times *less* likely to enforce demands than are mothers of nonproblem children (Patterson et al., 1992).

The relationship between parenting and conduct problems also appears to be affected by a child's callous–unemotional traits. In one report, ineffective parenting was related to conduct problems, but only in children who were rated low on CU traits (Wootton et al., 1997). Children with CU traits displayed significant conduct problems regardless of the quality of parenting they received. The relationship between parental discipline and conduct problems may also be affected by the amount of discipline—too much or too little can both have adverse effects. The relationship between parental discipline and antisocial behavior may also vary with the family's cultural background, the emotional climate in which discipline is used, and the gender of the parent–child pair. For example, discipline may be most effective in same-gender parent–child pairs: discipline of daughters by mothers and sons by fathers (Deater-Deckard & Dodge, 1997).

Attachment Theories

Attachment theories emphasize that the quality of children's attachment to parents will determine their eventual identification with parental values, beliefs, and standards. Secure bonds with parents promote a sense of closeness, shared values, and identification with the social world. Attachment theories contend that children refrain from antisocial behavior because they have a stake in conformity.

Children with conduct problems often show little internalization of parent and societal standards. Even when they comply with parental requests, they may do so because of perceived threats to their freedom or physical safety (Shaw & Bell, 1993). When these threats are not present, such as when the child is unsupervised, antisocial behavior is likely to occur. Weak bonds with parents may lead the child to associate with deviant peers, which in turn may lead to delinquency and substance abuse (Elliott, Huizinga, & Menard, 1989).

Research findings support a relationship between insecure attachments, particularly for children with disorganized attachments, and the development of antisocial behavior during childhood and adolescence (Pasco Fearon et al., 2010). However, it is unclear whether attachment quality by itself can predict current or future variation in the severity of conduct problems. It is likely that the relationship between attachment and antisocial behavior is affected by many factors, including the child's gender, clinical status, temperament, and family management practices (Pasco Fearon et al., 2010).

Other Family Problems

In addition to the negative parenting practices and attachment problems that we have discussed, other family factors such as family instability and stress, and parental criminality and psychopathology may also contribute to children's conduct problems.

JAKE AND REGGIE

All Odds Against Them

Linda M., single mother of 2-year-old Jake and 4-year-old Reggie, sought treatment because Reggie was engaging in severe and uncontrollable aggressive behaviors, including hitting, kicking, and biting Jake. She was depressed and at risk for suicide. Her boyfriend Hank is the father of the two children. He lives nearby and demands that she come over so he can see the children. During these visits, he engages her in what she refers to as "forced sex" (i.e., rape), and he demands that Jake and Reggie remain with them and watch. In principle, Linda could have refused the visits. However, Hank threatened that if she did not comply, he would stop paying child support, take Jake and Reggie away in a custody battle, kill himself, or come over to the house and kill her and the two boys. These threats of violence were to be taken seriously because Hank had a prior arrest record for assault and brandished a gun.

Based on Conduct Disorders in Childhood and Adolescence by A. E. Kazdin, p. 17.

Family Instability and Stress

Families of children with conduct problems are often characterized by an unstable family structure, with frequent transitions, including changes in parents and changes in residence (Dishion & Patterson, 2006). Family instability is related to a child's heightened risk for antisocial behavior, academic problems, anxiety and depression, association with deviant peers, and criminal conviction (Kasen et al., 1996). In most cases, the impact of divorce on a child's antisocial behavior is related to the family disruption and conflict that accompany it (Emery, 1999). In some cases, a child's antisocial behavior may contribute to family instability by increasing the chances of divorce (Block, Block, & Gjerde, 1986).

High family stress is associated with negative child behavior in the home, and may be both a cause and an outcome of antisocial behavior. Unemployment, low SES, and multiple family transitions are all related to childhood conduct problems. Among family stressors, poverty is one of the strongest predictors of children having CD and high rates of criminal activities (Pagani et al., 1999). But what constitutes the "active ingredient" in the link between poverty and antisocial behavior? In this regard, instability, residential mobility, and disruptions in parenting practices have all been found to be important (Dodge, Pettit, & Bates, 1994b). The **amplifier hypothesis** states that stress amplifies the maladaptive predispositions of parents (e.g., poor mental health), thereby disrupting family management practices and compromising parents' ability to be supportive of their children (Conger et al., 1994).

Parental Criminality and Psychopathology

Aggressive and antisocial tendencies run in families, within and across generations (Blazei, Iacono, & Krueger, 2006; D'Onofrio et al., 2007). In fact, children's aggression is correlated with their parents' childhood aggression at the same age (Huesmann et al., 1984). Parents of antisocial children have higher rates of arrests, motor vehicle violations, license suspensions, and substance abuse (Dishion & Patterson, 2006). Antisocial individuals are likely to be ineffective parents, especially during disciplinary confrontations during which they display an irritable, explosive style of interaction. Certain types of parental psychopathology, such as APD, are strongly and specifically related to CD in their children (Herndon & Iacono, 2005). This relationship is particularly clear for fathers, as is the link between paternal criminal behavior and substance abuse and child antisocial patterns (Waldman & Lahey, 2013). The strong association between paternal APD and a child's antisocial behavior is independent of whether the father lives in the home and of the degree of contact between father and child (Tapscott, Frick,

Wootton, & Kruh, 1996). For mothers, antisociality, histrionic personality (excessive emotionality and attention seeking), and depression are related to children's antisocial behavior (Dishion & Patterson, 2006).

Societal Factors

Causes of antisocial behavior at the level of the individual and family tell only part of the story, since they interact with the larger societal and cultural context in determining conduct problems (Sampson, 1992). There is little doubt that poverty, neighborhood crime, family disruption, and residential mobility are related to crime and delinquency in young people (Cooley-Strickland et al., 2009; Schonberg & Shaw, 2007). However, the specific mechanisms by which these conditions lead to crime and delinquency are not known.

Theories of social disorganization propose that community structures impact family processes that then affect the child's adjustment (Sampson & Laub, 1994). Adverse contextual factors (e.g., low SES) are associated with poor parenting, particularly coercive and inconsistent discipline and poor parental monitoring (Lahey, Van Hulle et al., 2008). In turn, these factors are associated with an early onset of antisocial behavior, arrests at an early age, and chronic offending during adolescence (Capaldi & Patterson, 1994). A vicious cycle of adaptational failure and added stress places downward pressure on both the parent and the child. An antisocial individual is more vulnerable and at greater risk of entering a class of divorced, unemployed, and disadvantaged people (Dishion & Patterson, 2006). For example, social disadvantage, increased mobility, divorce, early sexual activity, and working-mother status may lead to an increase in mothers who are at greater risk for antisocial parenting practices. Also, less skilled antisocial mothers may drift into areas of large cities that isolate them from family and neighbors and lead them to function in an atmosphere of mistrust and minimal communication. When these women become pregnant again, they may have reduced access to public health services. Poor diet and drugs may result in a higher incidence of low birth weight, prematurity, and birth defects in their offspring, which in turn make their infants and toddlers more difficult to parent. The combination of a difficult infant and an unskilled parent increases the likelihood of antisocial behavior and the subsequent likelihood of behaviors that result in arrest. In this way, the generation of conduct problems cycles again and again.

Neighborhood and School

Antisocial behavior in youths is disproportionately concentrated in poor neighborhoods characterized by a criminal subculture that supports drug dealing and prostitution, peer group violence, delinquent gang membership, frequent transitions and mobility, and low social support from neighbors or religious groups (Leventhal & Brooks-Gunn, 2000). In addition, antisocial people tend to select neighborhoods populated by other people who are like them (Harden et al., 2009). The **social selection hypothesis** states that people who move into different neighborhoods differ from one another before they arrive, and those who remain differ from those who leave. For individuals with antisocial traits, this creates a community organization that minimizes productive social relations and effective social norms, leading to the antisocial behavior becoming the rule (Sampson, Raudenbush, & Earls, 1997). The effects of community characteristics on crime and delinquency are likely to be reinforced by neighborhood social disorganization characterized by few local friendship and acquaintance networks, low participation in local community organizations, and an inability to supervise and control teenage peer groups (Sampson & Groves, 1989). In fact, the main influence of effective parents in high-risk neighborhoods seems to be in countering gang membership (Tolan, Gorman-Smith, & Henry, 2003).

In high-risk neighborhoods, enrollment in a poor-quality school is associated with antisocial and delinquent behavior, whereas a positive school experience can be a protective factor for the development of these behaviors (Rutter, 1989). A good school environment characterized by clear requirements for homework completion, high academic expectations, clear and consistent discipline policies, and incentives for appropriate school behavior and achievement may partially compensate for poor family circumstances. Systematic interventions to promote these school characteristics have resulted in schoolwide reductions in children's conduct problems (Gottfredson, Gottfredson, & Hybel, 1993).

Weapons signs, such as this one in the area of Austin, Texas, are routinely posted outside schools.

Media

I believe that this kind of vicarious adventure, escape, excitement, even blood and thunder is necessary and important to most children as outlets for their own emotions, particularly their feelings of aggression.

—Josette Frank, Media Consultant

Programs interestingly depicting antisocial conduct, crime, and murder, influence children to antisocial attitudes and lead to aggression.

—Judge Jacob Panken, New York City Children's Court

These contrasting expert opinions were presented about 70 years ago (*The New York Times*, April 14, 1946), in reference to the influence of radio on children. The controversy regarding media influences on aggression in young people continues today. Parents, teachers, policymakers, and the press have expressed concerns about the possible adverse impact of violence in movies, TV, video games, text messages, and the Internet on children's social development and aggressive behavior. In considering media influences on children's antisocial behavior, we discuss the relation between TV violence and children's aggressive behavior because most of the research has been conducted in this area. Research into the new media is increasing at a rapid pace (Varnhagen, 2006). The findings from studies of TV violence and children's aggressive behavior should help us in answering questions about young people's use of the Internet, their exposure to unwanted or undesirable information, and how they are affected by this exposure.

At one extreme, some researchers claim that TV violence verges on child maltreatment and that we can reduce murders by unplugging the TV; others argue that there is little evidence for a causal relation between TV violence and aggressive behavior. By the time a child in the United States reaches grade 6, he or she has witnessed 8,000 or more murders on TV and well over 100,000 other acts of violence (Leland, 1995). The concern is that this steady diet of violence leads children to think violence is normal, to become desensitized to the suffering of real people, or to become aroused by images they see and want to mimic those violent acts. For example, one 5-year-old boy, after watching his favorite cartoon characters pull one of their famous arson stunts, set his house ablaze; his younger sister was killed in the fire. Thus, exposure to media violence can be both: (1) a short-term *precipitating* factor for aggressive and violent behavior that results from priming, excitation, or imitation of specific behaviors, and (2) a long-term *predisposing* factor for aggressive behavior acquired via desensitization to violence and observational learning of an aggression-supporting belief system (i.e., "the world is a hostile place," "aggression is acceptable," "aggression can be used to solve social problems") (Huesmann et al., 2003).

Exposure to media violence may reinforce pre-existing antisocial tendencies in some children. For example, in a series of studies spanning more than a decade, children with conduct problems were found to view relatively large amounts of violent material, prefer aggressive characters, and believe fictional content to be true (Gadow & Sprafkin, 1993). However, it is not only children with preexisting violent tendencies who are likely to be affected. Long-term studies have found that childhood exposure to media violence between ages 6 and 9, identification with aggressive TV characters, and perceived realism of TV violence predict serious aggressive and criminal behavior 15 years later (Huesmann et al., 2003).

The correlation between TV violence and aggression is indisputable—but does TV violence cause aggression, and if so, how? Although research suggests a causal relation (Anderson & Bushman, 2002; Johnson et al., 2002), answers to these questions remain elusive despite decades of research and a pressing urge to act on research findings through social policies to filter violent content and inform users. It is unlikely that media influences (TV or other forms) alone can account for the substantial amount of antisocial behavior in young people (Rutter & Smith, 1995). Like other risk factors, media influences interact with child, family, community, and cultural factors in contributing to conduct problems. But clearly they are an important and unique contributing factor. Exposure to media violence will not turn an otherwise well-adjusted child into a violent criminal. However, "just as every cigarette one smokes increases a little bit the likelihood of a lung tumor some day ... every violent TV show increases a little bit the likelihood of a child growing up to behave more aggressively in some situation" (Huesmann et al., 2003, p. 218).

Cultural Factors

Cultural differences in the expression of aggressive behavior are dramatic. Across cultures, socialization of children for aggression has been found to be one of the strongest predictors of aggressive acts such as homicide and assault. As the following examples of contrasting socialization practices illustrate, aggression may be an inadvertent consequence of a culture's emphasis on training "warriors":

The Kapauku of Western New Guinea:

At about 7 years of age, a Kapauku boy begins to be under the father's control, gradually sleeping and eating only with the men and away from his mother. ... His training [to be a brave warrior] begins when the father engages his son in mock stick fights. Gradually the fights become more serious and possibly lethal when the father and son shoot real war arrows at each other. Groups of boys play at target shooting; they also play at hitting each other over the head with sticks. (Ember & Ember, 1994, p. 639–640)

The homicide rate among the Kapauku from 1953 to 1954 was estimated at 200 per 100,000, approximately 40 times the current murder rate in the United States.

The Lepcha of the Indian Himalayas:

The Lepcha are very clear about what they expect from their children. "Good children help out with the work, tell the truth, listen to teaching from elders, help old people, and are peaceable. Bad children quarrel with and insult people, tell lies, draw their

Calvin and Hobbes   by Bill Watterson

knives in anger when reprimanded, and do not do their share of the work." (Ember & Ember, 1994, p. 641)

Interviews with the Lepcha people revealed that the only authenticated murder in their culture had occurred about 200 years ago (Ember & Ember, 1994).

Rates of antisocial behavior vary widely across and within cultures, and not necessarily in relation to technological gains, material wealth, or population density. For example, some third world countries that value interdependence are characterized by high rates of prosocial behavior, and some places with high population density have very low rates of violence. The United States is by far the most violent of all industrialized nations, with homicide rates about 5 times higher than those in Europe and 10 times higher than those in Japan (OECD, 2013).

Minority status is related to antisocial behavior in the United States, with elevated rates of antisocial behavior in African American, Hispanic American, and Native American youths (Elliott, Huizinga, & Ageton, 1985). However, studies of national samples have reported either no or very small differences in antisocial behavior related to race or ethnicity when SES, gender, age, and referral status are controlled for (Lahey et al., 1995). Thus, although externalizing problems are reported to be more frequent among minority-status youths, this finding is likely related to disparities that include economic hardship, limited employment opportunities, residence in high-risk urban neighborhoods, and membership in antisocial gangs (Children's Defense Fund, 2007; Egley & Howell, 2013). Importantly, both Mexican American and African American children who live in dangerous or disadvantaged neighborhoods and who have high levels of family support show fewer antisocial behaviors than children who have low or no family support (Schofield et al., 2012). For immigrant groups in the United States, the risk for CD also seems to vary according to migration status and amount of exposure to American culture. For example, one study found that the risk for CD was highest among Mexican American children of U.S.-born parents as compared with children of Mexican-born immigrants raised in the United States or the general population of Mexico (Breslau et al., 2012).

Section Summary

Causes

- Conduct problems in children are best accounted for by multiple causes or risk and protective factors that operate in a transactional fashion over time.
- Adoption and twin studies indicate that genetic influences account for about 50% of the variance in antisocial behavior.

- Genetic contributions to overt forms of antisocial behavior, such as aggression, are stronger than for covert acts, such as stealing or lying.
- Antisocial behavior may result from an overactive behavioral activation system (BAS) and an underactive behavioral inhibition system (BIS). Low levels of cortical arousal and autonomic reactivity and deficits in the amygdala, prefrontal cortex, and other brain regions play an important role, particularly for childhood-onset/persistent CD.
- Many family factors have been implicated as possible causes of children's antisocial behavior, including marital conflict, family isolation, violence in the home, poor disciplinary practices, a lack of parental supervision, and insecure attachments.
- Family instability and stress, parental criminality and antisocial personality, and antisocial family values are risk factors for conduct problems.
- The structural characteristics of the community provide a backdrop for the emergence of conduct problems by giving rise to community conditions that interfere with the adoption of social norms and the development of productive social relations.
- School, neighborhood, and media influences are all potential risk factors for antisocial behavior, as are cultural factors, such as minority group status and ethnicity.

TREATMENT AND PREVENTION

SCOTT

Salvageable?

Scott, age 10, was referred after setting a fire in the schoolyard. While his therapist saw Scott as "potentially salvageable," his parents were not willing to pursue therapy. As a result, Scott was placed in a boarding school for "troubled boys." ... After 3 weeks at this school, he was expelled for burning down the dorm. ... Charges were pressed and he was sent to a group home for delinquent boys. He remained there for 3 months before he and two older boys ran away. They were caught a few days later when they attacked a homeless man, stealing his money ($4.85) and beating him. As a result of this crime, Scott was sent to a detention facility until he turned 18. His therapist heard nothing further.

Based on Morgan, 1999.

Many forms of treatment will be tried throughout the life of a child with severe conduct problems. Treatment may begin during the preschool years or, more typically, as was the case with Scott, when severe antisocial behavior at school leads to referral. Ongoing contacts with the educational, mental health, and judicial systems may result in referral for one or more of a wide range of treatments. The most promising treatments use a combination of approaches that are applied across individual, family, school, and community settings (Kazdin, 2007; Lochman et al., 2011; Sanders, 2012). In addition, treatment frequently requires that related family problems, such as maternal depression, marital discord, abuse, and other stressors be addressed if gains are to be generalized and maintained (McMahon, Wells, & Kotler, 2006).

Most people understand that family dysfunction, abuse, school expulsion, association with drug-using peers, residence in a high-crime area, and minimal parental supervision contribute to serious conduct problems (Henggeler, 1996). However, despite this recognition, typical and often court-mandated treatments such as psychotherapy, group therapy, tutoring, punishment, wilderness programs, and boot camps fail to meaningfully address these determinants, and thus are among the least effective approaches (Lipsey, 1995). Despite their lack of effectiveness in treating serious antisocial behavior, office-based individual counseling and family therapy are often provided because they can be relatively inexpensive (Tate, Reppucci, & Mulvey, 1995). Group treatments that bring together antisocial youth may only make the problem worse, since associating with like-minded individuals often encourages antisocial behavior (Dishion & Dodge, 2005).

As we saw for Scott, restrictive approaches such as residential treatment, inpatient psychiatric hospitalization, and incarceration also show little effectiveness and have the additional disadvantage of being extremely expensive (Henggeler & Santos, 1997). Unfortunately, a significant proportion of mental health dollars for youths continues to be spent on restrictive out-of-home placements that may cause more harm than good (Sondheimer, Schoenwald, & Rowland, 1994). Incarceration may not even serve a community protection function, since youths who are incarcerated and then released often commit more crimes than youths kept at home and given treatment (Henggeler, 1996).

Since youth conduct problems are known to show a developmental progression, diversification, and escalation over time, treatments must be sensitive to where a youth is in this trajectory. Treatment methods and goals will differ for preschoolers, school-age children, and adolescents and will differ according to the type and severity of the child's conduct problems. In general, the more progressed the antisocial behavior, the greater is the need for intensive interventions and, unfortunately, for children like Scott, the poorer is the prognosis. In fact, if early-onset antisocial behavior is not changed by the end of grade 3, it might best be treated as a chronic condition, much like diabetes, which cannot be cured but can be managed or contained through ongoing interventions and supports (Kazdin, 1995). This troubling situation of high treatment effort and cost with less return for older children has led to a reevaluation of priorities and a growing emphasis on early intervention and prevention (Powell, Lochman, & Boxmeyer, 2007). A comprehensive, two-pronged approach to the treatment of conduct problems is needed that includes (Frick, 2000):

▶ *Early intervention/prevention* programs for young children at risk for or just starting to display problem behaviors

▶ *Ongoing interventions* to help older youths and their families cope with the many associated social, emotional, and academic problems

To illustrate the many treatments for children and adolescents with conduct problems, we next highlight three representative treatment approaches that have had some proven success (Eyberg, Nelson, & Boggs, 2008)—parent management training (PMT), problem-solving skills training (PSST), and multisystemic therapy (MST) (see Table 9.5). We also discuss promising new

TABLE 9.5 | **Effective Treatments for Children with Conduct Problems**

Treatment	Overview
Parent Management Training (PMT)	Teaches parents to change their child's behavior in the home and in other settings using contingency management techniques. The focus is on improving parent–child interactions and enhancing other parenting skills (e.g., parent–child communication, monitoring, and supervision).
Problem-Solving Skills Training (PSST)	Identifies the child's cognitive deficiencies and distortions in social situations and provides instruction, practice, and feedback to teach new ways of handling social situations. The child learns to appraise the situation, change his or her attributions about other children's motivations, be more sensitive to how other children feel, and generate alternative and more appropriate solutions.
Multisystemic Therapy (MST)	An intensive approach that draws on other techniques such as PMT, PSST, and marital therapy, as well as specialized interventions such as special education, and referral to substance abuse treatment programs or legal services.

© Cengage Learning

preventive interventions for young children. Almost all forms of treatment provide corrective interpersonal experiences with parents, siblings, and peers because most antisocial acts, including violence, occur between the child and family members or peers. In addition, given the pervasiveness of conduct problems across settings, nearly all treatments include components designed to change the child's behavior at home, in the community, and at school (Liber et al., 2013).

Parent Management Training (PMT)

Parent management training (PMT) teaches parents to change their child's behavior at home and in other settings (Brinkmeyer & Eyberg, 2003; McMahon & Forehand, 2003). Its underlying assumption is that maladaptive parent–child interactions are at least partly responsible for producing and sustaining the child's antisocial behavior. Changing the way parents interact with their child will lead to improvements in the child's behavior. Although both child and parent behavior jointly contribute to negative parent–child interactions, the easiest and most desirable point of entry in modifying these interactions is changing parent behavior. The goal of PMT is for the parent to learn specific new skills (Forgatch & Patterson, 2010). To achieve this goal, many of the same procedures that we have discussed for working with children with ADHD and their families are used (see Chapter 8). These include teaching parents to monitor their children's behavior, to present clear commands and rules, and to systematically provide rewards and minor forms of punishment such as time out from positive reinforcement. Many variations of PMT can be individual versus group training, training in the clinic versus in the home, or the use of live versus videotaped training materials.

PMT has a number of strengths and some limitations (McMahon et al., 2006). Many excellent treatment manuals and training materials have been developed that facilitate its widespread use (e.g., Barkley, 2013a; McMahon & Forehand, 2003). In addition, PMT has been evaluated more than any other treatment for conduct problems (Eyberg et al., 2008). These evaluations have repeatedly demonstrated short-term effectiveness in producing changes in parent and child behavior. The average child whose parents participate in PMT shows better adjustment after treatment than 80% of referred children whose parents do not participate (Serketich & Dumas, 1996). In addition to changes in the referred child, PMT has also been associated with reductions in the problem behaviors of siblings and reduced stress and depression in the parents.

PMT has been most effective with parents of children younger than 12 years of age and less so with adolescents (Dishion & Patterson, 1992). In light of this, promising adaptations of these interventions have also been developed for working with older adolescents and their families (Dishion & Kavanagh, 2003). Although PMT can produce short-term gains, its long-term effectiveness is less clear (McMahon et al., 2006). In addition, PMT makes numerous demands on parents to master and implement procedures in the home, attend meetings, and maintain phone contact with the therapist. For families under stress and with few resources, these demands may be too great to allow the family to continue in treatment (Lundahl, Risser, & Lovejoy, 2006). In order to increase engagement of low-income families, smart phone–enhanced versions of PMT have been developed to include series of skills videos, brief daily surveys, text message reminders, video recording of home practice, and midweek video calls (Jones et al., 2014). There is also growing recognition of the importance of identifying barriers to, and facilitators of, access/engagement of parents in PMT programs (Koerting et al., 2013).

The application of PMT is rarely straightforward. The need to change their own parenting practices may not be recognized by parents who believe that difficulties occur because their child is stubborn, their marriage is bad, work is interfering with the time they spend together, or school personnel are unfair. In fact, parents of children with conduct problems frequently believe they use good parenting practices but their child fails to respond. It is important to address these parental beliefs and concerns if treatment is to be successful (Morrisey-Kane & Prinz, 1999). In addition, PMT practitioners have increasingly come to recognize the importance of marital and social support, therapy style and engagement, and ethnic and cultural factors in treatment (Scott et al., 2010; Yasui & Dishion, 2007).

Problem-Solving Skills Training (PSST)

Problem-solving skills training (PSST) is a form of cognitive behavioral therapy that focuses on the cognitive deficiencies and distortions displayed by children and adolescents with conduct problems in interpersonal situations (Kazdin, 2010). PSST is used both alone and in combination with PMT, as required by the family's circumstances. The underlying assumption of PSST is that the child's perceptions and appraisals of environmental events will trigger aggressive and antisocial responses, and that correcting faulty thinking will lead to changes in behavior. As described in A Closer Look 9.7, the child is taught to use five problem-solving steps to identify thoughts, feelings, and behaviors in problem social situations.

During PSST, the therapist uses instruction, practice, and feedback to help the child discover different

Cognitive Problem-Solving Steps

Problem Situation

Jason, one of the kids in your class, has taken your Nintendo game. You want to get it back. What do you do?

Step 1: What Am I Supposed to Do?

I want to get my Nintendo game back from Jason.

Step 2: I Have to Look at All My Possibilities

I can beat him up and take it back, ask him to give it back, or tell my teacher.

Step 3: I Had Better Concentrate and Focus

If I beat him up, I would get into trouble. If I asked him, he might give it back.

Step 4: I Need to Make a Choice

I'll try asking him, and if that doesn't work, I will tell my teacher.

Step 5: I Did a Good Job or I Made a Mistake

I made a good choice. I won't get into trouble. Jason and I can still be friends if he returns my Nintendo game. If not, I did my best to get it back before asking my teacher for help. I did a good job!

Based on Kazdin, A. E. (1996). "Problem solving and parent management training in treating aggressive and antisocial behavior." In E. D. Hibbs & P. S. Jensen (Eds.), Psychosocial Treatments for Child and Adolescent Disorders (pp. 377–408). Washington, DC: American Psychological Association.

ways to handle social situations. To accomplish this, children learn to appraise the situation, identify self-statements and reactions, and alter their attributions about other children's motivations. They also learn to be more sensitive to how other children feel, to anticipate others' reactions, and to generate appropriate solutions to social problems.

PSST is effective with children and youths who are clinically referred for conduct problems, with benefits extending to parent and family functioning (Kazdin, 2010). Research supports the emphasis on the relationship between maladaptive cognitions and aggressive behavior on which PSST is based, and PSST procedures are carefully specified in treatment manuals. Until relatively recently it was not clear whether changes in maladaptive cognitions were responsible for behavioral improvements. Indeed, the alteration of social–cognitive processes may not necessarily lead to changes in behavior. However, in one major study using a multifaceted intervention (Fast Track) it was found that 27% of the intervention's impact on antisocial behavior was mediated by its effect on three social–cognitive processes: reducing hostile-attribution biases, increasing competent response generation to social problems, and devaluing aggression (Dodge, Godwin, & The Conduct Problems Prevention Research Group, 2013). Finally, although most children improve as a result of PSST, some may continue to display more problems than their nondeviant peers. Thus, more enduring PSST and other interventions are being developed to meet the needs of families of children with conduct problems whose problems are particularly severe.

Multisystemic Therapy (MST)

Multisystemic therapy (MST) is an intensive empirically supported family and community-based treatment for adolescents with severe conduct problems that make out-of-home placement highly likely (Henggeler & Schaeffer, 2010). MST views the adolescent with conduct problems as functioning within interconnected social systems, including the family, school, neighborhood, and court and juvenile services (Henggeler et al., 2009). Antisocial behavior results from, or can be maintained by, transactions within or between any of these systems. MST seeks to empower caregivers to improve youth and family functioning (Cunningham et al., 1999). Thus, treatment is carried out with all family members, school personnel, peers, juvenile justice staff, and other individuals in the child's life. MST is an intensive approach that also draws on PMT, PSST, and marital therapy, as well as specialized interventions such as special education and referral to substance-abuse treatment programs or legal services. In effect, MST attempts to address the many determinants of severe antisocial behavior (Wells et al., 2010). The guiding principles of MST are outlined in Table 9.6.

Outcome studies of MST with extremely antisocial and violent youths have found this approach to be superior to usual services, individual counseling, community services, and psychiatric hospitalization. In addition, studies have found decreases in delinquency and aggression with peers, improved family relations, and reductions in out-of-home placements (Weiss et al., 2013). Importantly, MST has been found to reduce long-term rates of criminal behavior for as long as 5 years after treatment. MST is also cost-effective; its costs are 10 times less than conventional interventions and its estimated savings over the years are about $10 to $20 for each dollar spent on MST (Klietz, Borduin, & Schaeffer, 2010).

Since studies of MST have not yet differentiated between adolescents who show life-course–persistent and those with adolescence-limited patterns of antisocial behavior, it is difficult to know whether successful outcomes reported for this approach apply

TABLE 9.6 | The Nine Principles of Multisystemic Therapy (MST)

1. **Finding the fit** The primary purpose of assessment is to understand the "fit" between the identified problems and their broader systemic context.

2. **Positive and strength-focused** Therapeutic contacts emphasize the positive and use systemic strengths as levers for change.

3. **Increasing responsibility** Interventions are designed to promote responsible behavior and decrease irresponsible behavior among family members.

4. **Present-focused, action-oriented, and well defined** Interventions are present-focused and action-oriented, targeting specific and well-defined problems.

5. **Targeting sequences** Interventions target sequences of behavior within and between multiple systems that maintain identified problems.

6. **Developmentally appropriate** Interventions are developmentally appropriate and fit the developmental needs of the youth.

7. **Continuous effort** Interventions are designed to require daily or weekly effort by family members.

8. **Evaluation and accountability** Intervention efficacy is evaluated continuously from multiple perspectives, with providers assuming accountability for overcoming barriers to successful outcomes.

9. **Generalization** Interventions are designed to promote treatment generalization and long-term maintenance of therapeutic change by empowering caregivers to address family members' needs across multiple systemic contexts.

Based on Table 2.1 in Multisystemic Therapy for Antisocial Behavior in Children and Adolescents (2nd ed.), by S. W. Henggeler, S. K. Schoenwald, C. M. Borduin, M. D. Rowland, & P. B. Cunningham. New York: Guilford Press.

equally to both groups. It is possible that part of the success of MST may be in helping youths on the adolescent-limited path decrease their association with deviant peers and, by doing so, lowering the age at which they cease delinquent behavior.

Preventive Interventions

Until recently, treatments for older children with conduct problems were given far greater attention than programs for early intervention and prevention. Fortunately, this situation is changing, with a growing recognition of the need for intensive home and school-based interventions that can compete with the child's negative developmental history, poor family and community environment, and deviant peer associations (Prinz & Sanders, 2007; Wilson & Lipsey, 2007). Annual family checkups that provide tailored PMT to preschool-age children within the context of early childhood social, health, and educational services have also been developed to prevent early-onset pathways of antisocial behavior (Dishion et al., 2013). The main assumptions of preventive interventions are (Webster-Stratton, 1996):

▶ Conduct problems can be treated more easily and more effectively in younger than in older children.

▶ By counteracting risk factors and strengthening promotive factors at a young age, it is possible to limit or prevent the escalating developmental trajectory of increased aggression, peer rejection, self-esteem deficits, conduct disorder, and academic failure that is commonly observed in children with childhood-onset conduct problems.

▶ In the long run, preventive interventions will reduce the substantial costs to the educational, criminal justice, health, and mental health systems that are associated with conduct problems.

Carolyn Webster-Stratton has developed an intensive and multifaceted early-intervention program for parents and teachers of 2- to 10-year-old children with or at risk for conduct problems (Incredible Years; Webster-Stratton & Reid, 2010). This program uses interactive videotapes as a foundation for training, which permits widespread use at a relatively low cost. In addition to teaching child management skills, the program also addresses the associated individual, family, and school difficulties that accompany conduct problems. Parents are taught personal self-control strategies for managing anger, depression, and blame. As a result, they learn effective communication skills, strategies for coping with conflict at home and at work, and ways to strengthen social supports. Teachers are taught ways to strengthen positive relationships with students, effective classroom discipline, strategies for teaching social skills, anger management, problem-solving skills, and how to increase collaboration with parents (Webster-Stratton & Herman, 2010). In addition to the parent and teacher training programs, there is also an Incredible Years Child Training program for 3- to 8-year-olds, who meet with a therapist in groups of six for 2 hours a week. Children view videotapes of conflict situations at school and home that illustrate problem-solving and social skills. Following this, children discuss feelings, generate ideas for more effective responses, and role-play alternative behaviors.

A number of studies have provided support for the effectiveness of these early interventions in reducing later conduct problems and maintaining positive outcomes in adolescence for two-thirds or more of children whose parents are involved (Webster-Stratton, Reid, & Hammond, 2004; Webster-Stratton, Rinaldi, & Reid, 2010). This early intervention/prevention program is now more frequently based in schools, with a growing emphasis on matching the type, timing, and amount of intervention to the level of risk and specific needs of the child and family (Webster-Stratton & Reid, 2010).

An innovative program designed to prevent the development of serious chronic antisocial behavior in high-risk children is Fast Track (Conduct Problems Prevention Research Group, 2007, 2010)—a multisite, collaborative research project that exemplifies the comprehensive effort needed to treat children at risk for serious conduct problems. The program was directed at high-risk kindergarten children who were identified in terms of their disruptive behavior and poor peer relations. The intervention began in grade 1 and continued through grade 10. It was divided into an elementary school phase and a transition to middle and high school phase, with each phase including goals and interventions relevant to successful adjustment during each of these developmental periods.

The goals were to reduce disruptive and aggressive behaviors at home and school and to improve the quality of the child's relationships with parents, teachers, and peers. Children were taught the social–cognitive skills needed for effective interpersonal problem solving and emotion regulation. Other important goals were to strengthen academic skills, especially reading, and to improve the quality of the relationship between family members and school personnel. During the transition to adolescence, issues related to peer affiliation and peer influence, academic achievement and orientation, social cognition and identity development, and parent and family relations were addressed.

Five integrated treatment components were used to achieve these goals: (1) parent management training; (2) home visiting/case management; (3) social–cognitive skills training; (4) academic tutoring; and (5) teacher-based classroom intervention. Fast Track interventions were implemented with close collaboration among parents, teachers, and project staff. The strengths of the program were that they targeted the deficits and determinants that research has shown to be important in youths with conduct problems and that they used treatment procedures for which there is already some empirical support (Eyberg et al., 2008).

The findings from the Fast Track intervention are complex, since multiple behaviors and attitudes were assessed over a wide age range and outcomes for various behaviors and areas of functioning differed over time. In general, the overall results indicate that the intervention had a significant impact, particularly with respect to reducing conduct problems and enhancing the child's social competence and family relations. However, interventions were less successful in reducing disruptive behavior in the classroom or improving academic performance. Importantly, by grade 9, for children who initially had the highest risk for conduct problems (top 3%), the intervention prevented 75% of CD cases. In contrast, the intervention had little impact on children who were initially at only moderate levels of risk (Slough, McMahon, & The Conduct Problems Prevention Research Group, 2008). Taken together, the findings support the efficacy of the Fast Track intervention for children at highest initial risk for conduct problems. For these children, Fast Track was effective in preventing diagnoses of CD, ODD, and ADHD, highlighting the importance of interventions that target children with the highest risk at a young age (Conduct Problems Prevention Research Group, 2011). Only time will tell whether this all-out effort will result in changes in public policy and will achieve its intended long-term goal of preventing serious chronic antisocial behavior and to enhance psychosocial outcomes into late adolescence and young adulthood (Dodge & McCourt, 2010).

Although tremendous advances have been made in the treatment and prevention of conduct problems, much work remains to be done. The main conclusion to be drawn from intervention and prevention efforts over the past 100 years is that *the degree of success or failure in treating antisocial behavior depends on the type and severity of the child's conduct problem and related risk and protective factors* (Kazdin & Wassell, 1999). Children who come from mostly middle-class healthy families and who have mild conduct problems are likely to benefit from individual, parent, family, and school-based interventions; those who come from highly dysfunctional homes and poor neighborhoods and who display severe and persistent problems are likely to benefit very little, if at all, unless early, much more intensive, and long-term interventions are used. If interventions are to succeed, it will also be necessary to find cost-effective interventions and ways to help families persevere with interventions that could prove to have real benefits (Rutter, 2003b). Although significant short-term gains for children with severe conduct problems have been achieved using intensive interventions, the degree of normalization and long-term impact of these approaches is yet to be determined.

Section Summary

Treatment and Prevention

- Considerable efforts to help children and adolescents with conduct problems have led to several approaches with some proven success.

- The focus of parent management training (PMT) is on teaching parents to change their child's behavior in the home.
- The underlying assumption of problem-solving skills training (PSST) is that faulty perceptions and appraisals of interpersonal events trigger antisocial responses. The focus is on changing behavior by changing the way the child thinks in social situations.
- Multisystemic therapy (MST) is an intensive approach that is carried out with all family members, school personnel, peers, juvenile justice staff, and other individuals in the adolescent's life.
- Recent efforts have focused on trying to prevent conduct problems through intensive programs of early intervention/prevention.
- The degree of success or failure in treating antisocial behavior depends on the type and severity of the child's conduct problem and related risk and protective factors.

Study Resources

SECTION SUMMARIES

KEY TERMS

10

Depressive and Bipolar Disorders

This is my depressed stance. When you're depressed, it makes a lot of difference how you stand. The worst thing you can do is straighten up and hold your head high because then you'll start to feel better. If you're going to get any joy out of being depressed, you've got to stand like this.

—Charlie Brown (Charles M. Schulz, 1922–2000)

CHAPTER PREVIEW

DONNA

Desperate Despair

Donna, age 12, says, "Sometimes I feel like jumping off the roof or finding some other way to hurt myself." Over the past 3 months, Donna has become more and more withdrawn, and her feelings of sadness, worthlessness, and self-hatred scare her. Her teacher describes Donna as "a loner who seems very troubled and unhappy." She's always been a good student, but she is now having difficulty concentrating, is failing tests, and feels totally unmotivated. At home, Donna is having trouble sleeping, has no appetite, and frequently complains of headaches. Most days she stays in her room and does nothing. When her mother asks her to do something, Donna becomes extremely upset. Her mother says Donna is "moody and irritable most of the time." (Based on authors' case material)

MICK

Up and Down

Mick, age 16, is moody all of the time. Sometimes he is sad, sullen, and apathetic. At other times he is full of life and energy, or intensely angry. When full of energy, he can go with little or no sleep for days without feeling tired. He moves constantly, talks incessantly, and cannot be interrupted. These extreme changes in mood make Mick feel out of control, and sometimes he thinks about hurting himself. He is frightened by his thoughts and drinks or uses drugs when they are available to reduce the pain. (Based on authors' case material)

PERHAPS YOU KNOW A child or teen who seems constantly unhappy, shows little enthusiasm for anything, is moody, or—at worst—thinks life just isn't worth living. This child may have a **mood disorder** (also called an *affective disorder*), in which a disturbance in mood is the central feature. Mood is broadly defined as a feeling or emotion—for example, sadness, happiness, anger, elation, or crankiness. Children with mood disorders suffer from extreme, persistent, or poorly regulated emotional states, such as excessive unhappiness, ongoing irritability or anger, or swings in mood from deep sadness to high elation. Mood disorders are one of the most common, chronic, and disabling illnesses in young people (Kessler et al., 2012a, b).

OVERVIEW OF MOOD DISORDERS

Mood disorders come in several types. At one end of the spectrum is severe depression. Like Donna, children who have severe depression suffer from **dysphoria**, a state of prolonged bouts of sadness (Kovacs & Yaroslavsky, 2014). They feel little joy in anything they do and lose interest in nearly all activities, a state known as **anhedonia**. In the words of one depressed teen:

> Depression makes you lose interest in all the stuff you used to think was fun. You might quit playing guitar or drop out of yearbook, and claim that you just don't have the energy or desire to pursue extracurricular activities—or curricular activities, for that matter. From Solin, 1995.

Many young people with depression express these combined feelings of sadness and loss of interest or pleasure. However, some may never report feeling sad. Rather, they express their depression through their irritable mood. **Irritability** refers to easy annoyance and touchiness, characterized by an angry mood and temper outbursts (Stringaris, 2011). Others may describe these children as cranky, grouchy, moody, short-fused, or easily upset. Being around them is difficult because any little thing can set them off. Irritability is one of the most common co-occurring symptoms of depression, present in as many as 80% of clinic-referred and 36% of community samples of youngsters with depression (Stringaris et al., 2013).

At the other end of the mood spectrum are a smaller number of youths, those like Mick, who also experience episodes of **mania**, an abnormally elevated or expansive mood, increased goal-directed activity and energy, and feelings of **euphoria**, which is an exaggerated sense of well-being. They suffer from an ongoing combination of extreme highs and extreme lows, a condition known as **bipolar disorder** (BP) or *manic–depressive illness*. Their highs may alternate with lows, or they may feel both extremes at about the same time.

The two major types of mood disorders in the *Diagnostic and Statistical Manual of Mental Disorders*, 5th edition (DSM-5) are depressive disorders and bipolar disorders. We discuss each of these in the sections that follow.

Section Summary

Overview of Mood Disorders

- Children with mood disorders suffer from extreme, persistent, or poorly regulated emotional states—for example, excessive unhappiness, irritability, or swings in mood from deep sadness to high elation.

(continues)

- Mood disorders are common and are among the most persistent and disabling illnesses in young people.
- There are two major types of mood disorders: depressive disorders and bipolar disorders.

DEPRESSIVE DISORDERS

"And how are you?" said Winnie-the-Pooh.

Eeyore shook his head from side to side.

"Not very how," he said. "I don't seem to have felt at all how for a long time."

—A. A. Milne, *Winnie-the-Pooh* (1926)

Depression refers to a pervasive unhappy mood, the kind of gloomy feeling displayed by Eeyore, the sad and indecisive old gray donkey in *Winnie-the-Pooh*. The symptoms of depression are so universal that depression is sometimes called "the common cold of psychopathology." Everyone feels sad, blue, out of sorts, or "down in the dumps" at times. (Even reading or writing about depression can be a real downer—can anyone think of a way to put a positive spin on feelings of dejection, hopelessness, irritability, loneliness, or self-blame?) Sometimes our sadness is a normal reaction to an unfortunate event in our lives like losing a friend or a job. At other times, we may feel depressed without really knowing why. These feelings soon pass, however, and we resume our normal activities. Clinical depression, in contrast, is more severe than the occasional blues or mood swings that everyone gets from time to time.

Childhood is usually thought of as a happy and carefree time, a period unfettered by the worries, burdens, and responsibilities of adulthood. We tend to think of young people as positive and upbeat, not depressed. In fact, a common reaction to hearing that a child is depressed is "What does she have to be depressed about?" Even when children experience disappointment, disapproval, or other inevitable negative events in their lives, their sadness, frustration, and anger are expected to be short-lived. When children become sad, irritable, or upset, parents often attribute the negative moods to temporary factors—such as a lack of sleep or not feeling well—and expect the moods to pass. Thus, for a long time it was thought that children did not get depressed, and when they did, the depression would be short-lived. We now know this is not true. Current estimates indicate that more than 3 million children and adolescents in the United States suffer from significant depression each year (Kessler et al., 2012a).

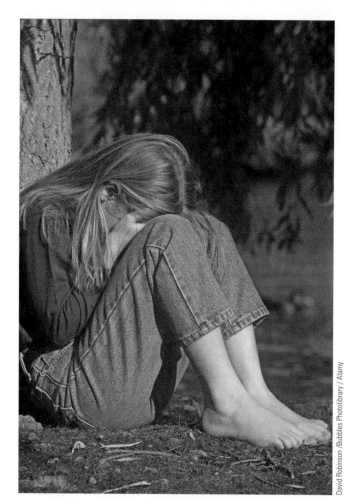

Depression in children goes well beyond normal mood swings.

Unlike most children, who bounce back quickly when they are sad, children who are depressed cannot seem to shake their sadness, and it begins to interfere with their daily routines, social relationships, school performance, and overall functioning. Depressed youths often have accompanying problems such as anxiety or oppositional/conduct disorders. Although clinical depression may resemble the normal emotional dips of childhood, for many young people it is pervasive, disabling, long-lasting, and life-threatening (Abela & Hankin, 2008b; Hammen, Rudolph, & Abaied, 2014). Unfortunately, depression often goes unrecognized and untreated because parents and, in some cases, teachers may not recognize the child's underlying subjective negative mood.

History

Not long ago, people doubted the existence of depression in children. This mistaken belief was rooted in traditional psychoanalytic theories, which viewed depression as hostility or anger turned inward. Because children lacked sufficient superego development to permit aggression to be directed against the self, it was believed that they were incapable of experiencing depression (Rochlin, 1959). In another mistaken view, symptoms of depression were considered normal and passing expressions of certain stages of development, a belief that also has proved false. Depression in young people is a recurrent problem, as it is for adults.

As depression in children was acknowledged, a popular view emerged that children express depression in a much different way than adults, ways that are often indirect and hidden. This idea came to be known as *masked depression*. It was thought that any known clinical symptom in children, including hyperactivity, learning problems, aggression, bed-wetting, separation anxiety, sleep problems, and running away, could be a sign of an underlying but masked depression (Cytryn & McKnew, 1974). Because this concept is too encompassing to be useful, the once popular notion of masked depression has been rejected. Depression in children is not masked, but it may simply be overlooked because it frequently co-occurs with more visible disorders, such as conduct problems.

Depression in Young People

Almost all young people experience some symptoms of depression, and many experience significant depression at some time (Avenevoli et al., 2008). These youngsters display lasting depressed mood while facing real or perceived distress and experience disturbances in their thinking, physical functioning, and social behavior. Suicidal behavior among teens, which is frequently associated with depression, is also a very serious concern (Cha & Nock, 2014).

As many as 90% of youngsters with depression show significant impairment in their daily functions, and, even when they recover from their depression, they are likely to experience recurrent bouts of depression and continued impairments (Simonoff et al., 1997). The long-lasting emotional suffering, problems in everyday living, and heightened risk of these youths for suicide, substance use, other mental health problems, poorer health outcomes, and higher health care costs make depression in young people a significant concern (Fombonne et al., 2001a; Keenan-Miller, Hammen, & Brennan, 2007).

Depression and Development

Children express and experience depression differently at different ages (Weiss & Garber, 2003). An infant may show sadness by being passive and unresponsive; a preschooler may appear withdrawn and inhibited; a school-age child may be argumentative and combative or complain of feeling sick; a teenager may express feelings of guilt and hopelessness, sulk, or feel misunderstood. These examples are not various types of depressions, but likely represent different stages in the developmental course of the same process.

No one pattern fits all children within a particular age group or developmental period, and depression is not clearly recognizable as a clinical disorder using DSM criteria until children are older. Depression in children under the age of 7 is diffuse and less easily identified. However, some studies have found that age-adjusted diagnostic criteria can be used to identify and treat depression in children as young as 3 to 5 years (Luby, 2013). It is important to recognize depressive symptoms in preschool children, since their symptoms can persist or reoccur and develop into depressive disorders during late childhood or early adolescence (Luby, Si et al., 2009).

We know the least about depression in infants (Guedeney, 2007). In the 1940s, American psychoanalyst René Spitz described a condition he called *anaclitic depression*, in which infants raised in a clean but emotionally cold institutional environment displayed reactions that resembled depression (Spitz & Wolf, 1946). These infants displayed weeping, withdrawal, apathy, weight loss, and sleep disturbance. They also showed an overall decline in development, and in some cases, death. Although Spitz attributed this depression to an absence of mothering and the lack of opportunity to form an attachment, other factors, such as physical illness and sensory deprivation, may also have played a role. Nevertheless, even young children exposed to institutional neglect and later adopted may display emotional and behavioral disturbances that place them at heightened risk for depression and other internalizing disorders (Stellern et al., 2014).

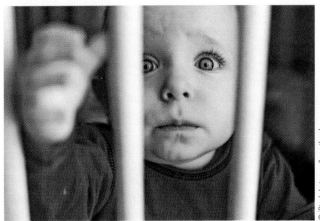

Depression in institutionalized infants: When observed over time, these infants display a physical appearance that in an adult might be described as depression.

It also became clear that similar symptoms could occur even in noninstitutionalized infants raised in severely disturbed families in which the mother was depressed, psychologically unavailable, or physically abusive. These infants may experience sleep disturbances, loss of appetite, increased clinging, apprehension, social withdrawal, crying, and sadness (Goodman & Brand, 2009).

Preschool children who are depressed may appear extremely somber and tearful. They generally lack the exuberance, bounce, and enthusiasm in their play that characterize most preschoolers. They may display excessive clinging and whiny behavior around their mothers, as well as fears of separation or abandonment. In addition to getting upset when things do not go their way, many are irritable for no apparent reason. Negative and self-destructive verbalizations may occur, and physical complaints such as stomachaches are common (Luby et al., 2003).

School-age children with depression display many of the symptoms of preschoolers in addition to increased irritability, disruptive behavior, temper tantrums, and combativeness. A parent may say, "Nothing ever pleases my child—she hates herself and everything around her." School-age children may look sad, but are often unwilling to talk about their sad feelings. Physical symptoms may include weight loss, headaches, and sleep disturbances. Academic difficulties and peer problems are also common, and may include frequent fighting and complaints of not having friends or being picked on. Suicide threats may also begin to occur at this age.

Preteens and teens with depression display many of the symptoms of younger children, in addition to increasing self-blame and expressions of low self-esteem, persistent sadness, and social inhibition. A child may say, "I'm stupid" or "Nobody likes me." Feelings of isolation from family are also common. The preteen may also experience an inability to sleep or may sleep excessively. Disturbances in eating are also common. Teens show increased irritability, loss of feelings of pleasure or interest, and worsening school performance. Angry discussions with parents regarding normal parent–teen issues, such as choice of friends or curfew, are also more common. Other symptoms at this age include a negative body image and self-consciousness, physical symptoms such as excessive fatigue and energy loss, feelings of loneliness, guilt, and worthlessness, and suicidal thoughts, plans, and attempts.

Many of these symptoms and behaviors may also occur in children and teens who are developing normally or in those with other disorders or conditions. Therefore, the presence of sad mood, diminished interest or pleasure, or irritability is essential for diagnosing depression. In addition, regardless of the child's age, the symptoms must reflect a change in behavior, persist over time, and cause significant impairment in functioning (Rudolph & Lambert, 2007).

Anatomy of Depression

The term *depression* has been used in various ways. It is important to distinguish between depression as a symptom, depression as a syndrome, and depression as a disorder.

As a *symptom*, depression refers to feeling sad or miserable. Depressive symptoms often occur without the existence of a serious problem, and they are relatively common at all ages. For most children, symptoms of depression are temporary, related to events in the environment, and not part of any disorder.

As a *syndrome*, depression is more than a sad mood. A syndrome refers to a group of symptoms that occur together more often than by chance. Along with sadness, the child may display a reduced interest or pleasure in activities, cognitive and motivational changes, and somatic and psychomotor changes. As a syndrome, depression represents an extreme on a dimension reflecting the number or severity of co-occurring symptoms that the child displays. The occurrence of depression as a syndrome is far less common than isolated depressive symptoms, and it often includes mixed symptoms of anxiety and depression, which tend to cluster on a single dimension of *negative affect* (Ollendick et al., 2003).

As a *disorder*, depression comes in several forms. We will consider three types. The first, **major depressive disorder (MDD)**, has a minimum duration of 2 weeks and is associated with depressed or irritable mood, loss of interest or pleasure, other symptoms (e.g., sleep disturbances, difficulty concentrating, feelings of worthlessness), and significant distress or impairment in functioning. The second, **persistent depressive disorder [P-DD]**, or **dysthymia**, is associated with depressed or irritable mood, generally fewer, less severe, but longer-lasting symptoms (a year or more in children) than MDD, and significant impairment in functioning. The third, **disruptive mood dysregulation disorder (DMDD)**, is a recently introduced depressive disorder characterized by: (1) frequent and *severe temper outbursts* that are extreme overreactions to the situation or provocation; and (2) chronic, persistently *irritable or angry mood* that is present between the severe temper outbursts.

The common characteristic of all depressive disorders is the presence of sad, empty, or irritable mood, along with somatic and cognitive symptoms that interfere with the individual's functioning. The differences among depressive disorders are related to their duration, timing, associated features, or presumed causes. As we discuss next, these disorders are defined using DSM-5 criteria.

- Depression in young people involves numerous and persistent symptoms, including impairments in mood, behavior, attitudes, thinking, and physical functioning.

- For a long time it was mistakenly believed that depression did not exist in children in a form comparable to depression in adults.

- It is now known that depression in young people is prevalent, disabling, and often under-referred.

- The way in which children express and experience depression changes with age.

- It is important to distinguish between depression as a symptom, a syndrome, and a disorder.

- Three types of DSM-5 depressive disorders are major depressive disorder (MDD), persistent depressive disorder [P-DD], or dysthymia, and disruptive mood dysregulation disorder (DMDD).

MAJOR DEPRESSIVE DISORDER (MDD)

JOEY

Feeling Worthless and Hopeless

Ten-year-old Joey's mother and teacher are concerned about his irritability and temper tantrums at home and at school. With little provocation, he bursts into tears, yells, and throws objects. In class he seems to have difficulty concentrating and seems easily distracted. Increasingly shunned by his peers, he plays by himself at recess, and at home spends most of his time in his room watching TV. His mother notes that he has been sleeping poorly and has gained 10 pounds over the past couple of months from constant snacking. The school psychologist has ruled out learning disabilities or ADHD; instead, she says Joey is a deeply unhappy child who expresses feelings of worthlessness and hopelessness, and even a wish that he would die. These feelings began about 6 months ago when Joey's father, divorced from his mother for several years, remarried and moved to another town, and now spends far less time with Joey.

Adapted from Hammen & Rudolph, 2003.

ALISON

"I Couldn't Take It Any More"

Alison, age 17, gets high grades, is a talented musician, and is attractive. However, for the past 3 years, she has been fighting to stay alive. "There are times when I was in school and I would start to cry—I had no idea why. My friends would say, 'What have you got to be depressed about, Alison? You're smart, talented, and can have any boy you want.' When my closest friend moved away 3 years ago, I was really lonely," says Alison. "I'd write notes about suicide and talk about killing myself. I couldn't eat and was tired most of the time. Even the smallest decision was overwhelming. Some days I'd never get out of bed I was so depressed. I couldn't stand school and hated everyone." Alison's feelings of hopelessness lasted for days, then weeks, then months. Finally, "I couldn't take it anymore," says Alison. "I wanted to die—so I tried to kill myself." (Based on authors' case material)

Although Joey and Alison differ in age and symptoms, both display the key features of MDD: sadness, loss of interest or pleasure in nearly all activities, irritability, plus a number of additional specific symptoms that are present during the same 2-week period. These symptoms must also represent a change from previous functioning. DSM-5 criteria for MDD are presented in Table 10.1.

A diagnosis of MDD depends on the presence of a major depressive episode plus the exclusion of other conditions, such as the prior occurrence of a manic episode (in this case, a diagnosis of bipolar disorder would be made). It also requires ruling out physical factors such as the physiological effects of a substance, another medical condition that may have caused or prolonged the depression, depression that is part of normal bereavement, and underlying thought disorders. Finally, the symptoms must cause clinically significant distress or impairment in important areas of life functioning (e.g., social, academic).

If full criteria are currently met for MDD, DSM-5 also provides for severity ratings of "mild," "moderate," or "severe" based on the number of symptoms in excess of those required to make the diagnosis, the amount of symptom distress and its manageability, and the extent of impairment in life functioning caused by the symptoms. In addition to severity, other specifiers are used to designate whether this is a single or recurrent depressive episode; whether a previous episode is in partial or full remission; whether the episode includes psychotic features (presence of delusions and/or hallucinations); or, whether the episode is accompanied by other features, for example, anxious distress (e.g., feeling tense, restless, or that something awful may happen).

The cases of Joey and Alison highlight three important points about the diagnosis of MDD in children and adolescents (Hammen et al., 2014):

TABLE 10.1 | Diagnostic Criteria for Major Depressive Disorder

(A) Five (or more) of the following symptoms have been present during the same 2-week period and represent a change from previous functioning; at least one of the symptoms is either (1) depressed mood or (2) loss of interest or pleasure.

Note: Do not include symptoms that are clearly attributable to another medical condition.

(1) Depressed mood most of the day, nearly every day, as indicated by either subjective report (e.g., feels sad, empty, hopeless) or observation made by others (e.g., appears tearful). (**Note:** In children and adolescents, can be irritable mood.)

(2) Markedly diminished interest or pleasure in all, or almost all, activities most of the day, nearly every day (as indicated by subjective account or observation).

(3) Significant weight loss when not dieting or weight gain (e.g., a change of more than 5% of body weight in a month), or decrease or increase in appetite nearly every day. (**Note:** In children, consider failure to make expected weight gains).

(4) Insomnia or hypersomnia nearly every day.

(5) Psychomotor agitation or retardation nearly every day (observable by others, not merely subjective feelings of restlessness or being slowed down).

(6) Fatigue or loss of energy nearly every day.

(7) Feelings of worthlessness or excessive or inappropriate guilt (which may be delusional) nearly every day (not merely self-reproach or guilt about being sick).

(8) Diminished ability to think or concentrate, or indecisiveness, nearly every day (either by subjective account or as observed by others)

(9) Recurrent thoughts of death (not just fear of dying), recurrent suicidal ideation without a specific plan, or a suicide attempt or a specific plan for committing suicide.

(B) The symptoms cause clinically significant distress or impairment in social, occupational, or other important areas of functioning.

(C) The episode is not attributable to the physiological effects of a substance or to another medical condition.

Note: Criteria A-C represent a major depressive episode.

Note: Responses to a significant loss (e.g., bereavement, financial ruin, losses from a natural disaster, a serious medical illness or disability) may include the feelings of intense sadness, rumination about the loss, insomnia, poor appetite, and weight loss noted in Criterion A, which may resemble a depressive episode. Although such symptoms may be understandable or considered appropriate to the loss, the presence of a major depressive episode in addition to the normal response to a significant loss should also be carefully considered. This decision inevitably requires the exercise of clinical judgment based on the individual's history and the cultural norms for the expression of distress in the context of loss.

(D) The occurrence of the major depressive episode is not better explained by schizoaffective disorder, schizophrenia, schizophreniform disorder, delusional disorder, or other specified and unspecified schizophrenia spectrum and other psychotic disorders.

(E) There has never been a manic episode or hypomanic episode.

Note: This exclusion does not apply if all of the manic-like or hypomanic-like episodes are substance-induced or are attributable to the physiological effects of another medical condition.

Source: Diagnostic and Statistical Manual of Mental Disorders, Fifth Edition, American Psychiatric Association.

- The same DSM-5 criteria for diagnosing adults can be used to diagnose school-age children and adolescents.

- Because children's disruptive behaviors attract more attention, or are more easily observed as compared with internal, subjective suffering, depression in children can be easily overlooked.

- Some features of depression are likely more common in children and adolescents than in adults—notably, irritable mood. In light of this, DSM-5 specifies that irritable mood can substitute for depressed mood in diagnosing depression in children. However, most children with depression display either depressed mood alone (58%) or depressed and irritable mood (36%)—irritable mood alone is rare (6%) (Stringaris et al., 2013).

Young people with MDD frequently display similar symptoms and have comparable rates of comorbidity and recurrence as adults (Birmaher et al., 2004). However, as compared with adults, clinic-referred youths with MDD have almost exclusively first-episode depressions, will recover somewhat faster from their depressive episodes, and are at greater risk for developing bipolar disorder. Children who develop MDD suffer from their disorder for many years longer than adults, making early-onset of this disorder a particularly severe form of affective illness (Kovacs, 1996).

Prevalence

Between 2% and 8% of all youths aged 4 to 18 experience MDD each year (Costello, Erkanli, & Angold, 2006; Kessler et al., 2012a). Depression is relatively rare among preschool and school-age children (about 1% to 3%; Bufferd et al., 2012; Egger & Angold, 2006), but increases twofold to threefold by adolescence (NIMH, 2003). Since depression comes and goes, prevalence estimates vary with the time frame during which symptoms are assessed. Lifetime prevalence estimates—whether a young person has ever been depressed—range from about 10% to 20% or higher (Merikangas et al., 2010; Rohde, Lewinsohn et al., 2013).

Even though these rates are so high, they may underestimate the problem. First, the estimates using a DSM-5 diagnosis of MDD might be lower than the self-reported symptoms of depression. Second, many children who just barely fail to meet diagnostic criteria for MDD still show significant impairments in their social competence, cognitive attributions, coping skills, family relations, and experience of stress. They are also at greater risk than other youths for developing future depression and other disorders, such as substance abuse (Gotlib, Lewinsohn, & Seeley, 1995).

The modest increase in depression from preschool to elementary school is likely not biologically based, but rather is a reflection of the school-age child's growing self-awareness and cognitive capacity, verbal ability to report symptoms, and increased performance and social pressures. In contrast, the sharp increase in depression in adolescence appears to be the result of biological maturation at puberty interacting with important developmental changes that occur during this tumultuous period. This hypothesis is supported by the emergence of large sex differences in depression after puberty, the emergence of bipolar disorder, and the relative stability in rates of depression through adolescence (Birmaher et al., 1996).

Comorbidity

RAYMOND

Depressed and Enraged

Raymond, age 16, lives alone with his single mother. For the past few months he has been persistently sad and unhappy, overcome with feelings of worthlessness. He is socially withdrawn, and he spends most of his time alone at home or avoiding contact with peers on the days when he manages to attend school. He is constantly tired but still finds it difficult to sleep, lying awake at night for hours and then struggling to drag himself from bed in the morning. Both he and his mother are concerned about his weight, which has increased substantially due to his inability to control his appetite for chips, candy, and soda. Even if he makes it to school, he finds he is unable to concentrate on his work.

Raymond's listlessness and withdrawal are countered, however, by his defiance and repeated outbursts of anger and aggression. He frequently lashes out in rage at his mother, and he recently punched his fist through a wall and a door at home. He also has been in several fights with other students at school as a result of being teased by his peers. He rarely complies with rules and limits at home or at school, leading to frequent conflicts with his mother and with school authorities. The event that precipitated Raymond's current referral was his arrest for shoplifting at a local store.

(Adapted from Compas & Hammen, 1994)

Like Raymond, who has MDD and a co-occurring conduct disorder, as many as 90% of young people with depression have one or more other disorders, and 50% have two or more (Simonoff et al., 1997). The most frequent co-occurring disorders in youngsters with MDD are anxiety disorders, particularly generalized anxiety disorders, specific phobias, and separation anxiety disorders. Depression and anxiety become more visible as separate but co-occurring disorders as the severity of the child's problem increases and as the child gets older (Gurley et al., 1996). Persistent depressive disorder, conduct problems, attention-deficit/hyperactivity disorder (ADHD), and substance-use disorder are also common in youngsters with MDD (Birmaher et al., 1996; McKowen et al., 2014). In the case of conduct problems, the extent to which young people with MDD experience oppositional defiant disorder (ODD) or conduct disorder (CD) seems to be directly related to the presence of irritable mood (Stringaris et al., 2013). Further, about 60% of adolescents with MDD have a comorbid personality disorder, which is most commonly borderline personality disorder—characterized by instability of interpersonal relationships, self-image, and affects and marked impulsivity (Muehlenkamp et al., 2011).

Many co-occurring disorders are present before MDD manifests, and they are likely to persist after the child is no longer depressed. For example, an early-onset anxiety disorder is a strong predictor of later depression and precedes depression in 85% of young people with both disorders (Kessler et al., 2012c; Rohde, 2009). A multiple-pathways model for understanding the strong relationship between anxiety and depression has been proposed by Cummings, Caporino, and Kendall (2013). In one common pathway, the child may have a general propensity (temperamental, biological, environmental) to anxiety.

If left untreated, this may lead to anxiety-related impairments (e.g., cognitive biases, negative affectivity) that become risk factors for the development of depression.

The presence of a co-occurring disorder is significant because it can increase the risk for recurrent depression, increase the duration and severity of depressive episodes, and increase the risk for suicide attempts. The presence of another disorder also decreases a depressed youth's response to treatment and is related to less effective treatment outcomes (Birmaher et al., 1996).

Onset, Course, and Outcome

The onset of depression in adolescence may be gradual or sudden. Either way, a youth typically has a history of milder episodes of depression that do not meet DSM-5 diagnostic criteria. Most adults with depression recall having their first depressive episode between the ages of 15 and 19 (Kessler, Merikangas, & Wang, 2007). However, prospective studies of children and adolescents usually find earlier ages at onset, most commonly between the ages of 13 and 15 (Merikangas et al., 2010).

The average episode of MDD in clinically referred children and adolescents lasts about 8 months, with longer episodes if a parent has a history of depression (Kaminski & Garber, 2002). Initial episodes are of shorter duration in community samples, with the average ranging from 4 months in childhood to 2 months in adolescence (Rohde, Lewinsohn et al., 2013). Although almost all young people eventually recover from their initial depressive episode, their disorder itself, unfortunately, does not go away (Birmaher, Arbelaez, & Brent, 2002). MDD has a chance of recurrence of about 25% within 1 year, 40% within 2 years, and 70% within 5 years. Thus, a significant number of youngsters develop a chronic, relapsing disorder that persists into young adulthood (Fombonne et al., 2001a).

Those with an onset of depression prior to age 15 and a recurrent episode prior to age 20 display more severe, chronic, suicidal depressions; greater co-occurring anxiety and worse social functioning at age 15; and poorer psychosocial outcomes at age 20 (Hammen et al., 2008). For youths who are hospitalized for depression, nearly half will be rehospitalized within 2 years after remission. In addition, about one-third of adolescents with MDD will develop a bipolar disorder within 5 years after the onset of their depression, known as a *bipolar switch* (DelBello et al., 2003). Thus, depression is a condition that endures over the course of development, creating a long-term social, emotional, and economic burden for the youth and the family.

Why do depressive episodes re-occur, and why does the length of time between episodes get progressively shorter? One possible explanation is that the first episode may sensitize the child to future episodes (Rudolph & Flynn, 2007). According to this idea, the first episode may be linked to a specific stressor and is accompanied by lasting changes in biological processes that heighten future reactivity to stress (Post et al., 1996). The initial externally produced changes in the brain can be conditioned so that following the first depressive episode, individuals are increasingly vulnerable to stress, and even nonsevere stress or minor events that resemble loss or stress experiences may result in depression (Stroud et al., 2011). This process is known as *stress sensitization* (Post & Weiss, 1998).

In addition to their recurring bouts of depression, the immediate and long-term prospects for children with MDD may include many other negative outcomes (Fergusson, Boden, & Horwood, 2007). For example, a history of depression during the school years also increases the risk for later delinquency, tobacco use, substance-use disorder, suicidal behavior, impairment, school dropout, poor work record, marital problems, and health-service use (Gotlib et al., 1998; Rice et al., 2007).

The overall outcome for young people with depression is not optimistic. Although almost all youths will recover from their depression, they continue to be at high risk for later episodes of mood and other disorders and for impaired social and academic functioning. One mother of a depressed teen paints a realistic picture of the long-term outcome for a child who suffers from depression:

> Depression in kids, when it hits them in their teens, leaves a hole in their lives. When they're young and just starting out in life, they're supposed to become independent. But that doesn't happen with depressed kids. They're out of synch and get left behind. And they never really catch up. That leaves a permanent scar. (Adapted from Owen, 1993, p. C1)

As they become adults, youngsters with a history of MDD continue to experience many negative long-term outcomes that include a high rate of suicidal behavior, adult depression and other psychiatric disturbances, high rates of psychiatric and medical hospitalizations, alcohol abuse/dependence, psychosocial impairments, lower educational achievement, and employment problems (Fombonne et al., 2001b; Jaycox et al., 2009). In general, these outcomes underscore the need for effective prevention and early intervention programs for young people with depression, which we discuss in a later section.

Gender

In what has been called depression's double standard, females are twice as likely as males to suffer from depression, are more susceptible to milder mood disorders, and are more likely to experience recurrent episodes (Zahn-Waxler, Race, & Duggal, 2005). This sex difference is not present among children ages 6 to 11, at which ages depression is reported to be equally common in boys and girls (Kessler et al., 2012a; Merikangas et al., 2010). However, sex differences in emotional reactivity are present in children who are depressed or at risk for depression as early as the preschool period, with boys displaying more anger and girls more sadness (Luby, Essex et al., 2009). In addition, sex differences in specific symptoms that forecast later depression (e.g., fearfulness, feelings of inadequacy, negative self-evaluation, and negative affect) may in fact be present prior to 10 years of age, with girls reporting significantly more of these symptoms than boys (Rudolph, Hammen, & Daley, 2006).

Sex differences in diagnosable depression begin between ages 13 and 15, when the rate rises for girls (Wade, Cairney, & Pevalin, 2002). As shown in ● Figure 10.1, rates of depression as well as sex differences in rates increase dramatically between ages 15 and 18 (Hankin, Wetter, & Cheely, 2008). The ratio of girls to boys is about 2:1 to 3:1 after puberty, a pattern that continues throughout adolescence and adulthood.

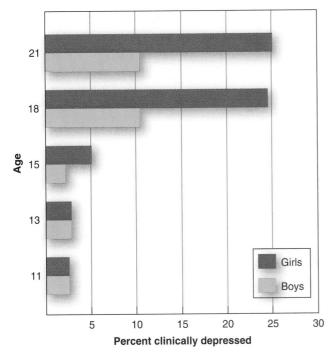

● **FIGURE 10.1** | The overall rate of depression and the proportion of females with depression increase dramatically during adolescence.

Based on "Development of Depression from Preadolescence to Young Adulthood: Emerging Gender Differences in a 10-year-Longitudinal Study" by B. L. Hankin L. Y. Abramson, T. E. Moffitt, P. A. Silva, R. McGee & K. E. Andell, 1998, 'Journal of Abnormal Psychology', 107, 128–140.

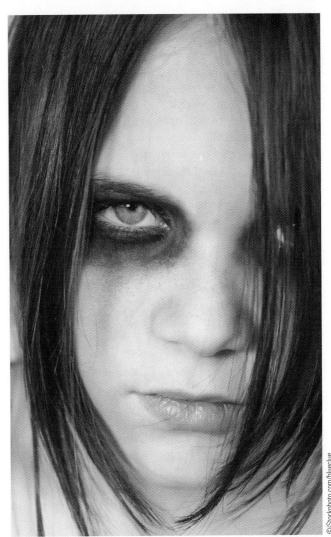

Teenage girls are particularly vulnerable to depression and related problems.

Although depression occurs more frequently in girls than in boys, symptom presentation is generally quite similar for the two sexes. (Slightly more girls than boys report symptoms related to weight and appetite disturbances and feelings of worthlessness and guilt [Lewinsohn, Pettit et al., 2003].) However, the correlates of depression may differ for the sexes. For example, depression is more highly related to school-related stress in boys than in girls (Sund, Larsson, & Wichstrom, 2003).

The increase in depression during adolescence and the emergence of sex differences in depression at this time have led to a special interest in this developmental period (Rudolph et al., 2006). Many physical, psychological, and social changes during adolescence may heighten the risk for depression in girls. Hormonal changes in estrogen and testosterone may affect brain function, increasing sexual maturity may affect social roles, interpersonal changes and expectations may result in heightened exposure to stressful life events, and nonnormative changes such as early maturation may lead to isolation from one's peer group (Hankin et al., 2008).

These changes may diminish self-worth, lead to depressed mood, and evoke self-focused attention. It is also thought that girls may be at higher risk than boys because they have a greater orientation toward cooperation and sociality. They also use ruminative coping styles to deal with stress (focusing on the symptoms of distress and its causes rather than on solutions)—especially stress involving interpersonal loss and disruptions. These two characteristics may put girls at a disadvantage during adolescence, when they face somewhat greater biological and stressful role-related challenges than boys (Zahn-Waxler et al., 2005). Interpersonal stress and a lack of social support are particularly salient aspects of depression for adolescent girls (Rudolph & Flynn, 2007).

Low birth weight has been found to predict depression in adolescent girls but not in adolescent boys, and girls born at a low birth weight are especially vulnerable to adversity after puberty (Costello et al., 2007; Van Lieshout & Boylan, 2010). This suggests that low birth weight may be a marker for poor intrauterine conditions that lead to adjustments in fetal development, which in turn have long-term consequences for girls' response to stress in adolescence. Research also suggests that increased levels of testosterone and estrogen at puberty, particularly when they occur in combination with social stress, increase the risk for depression in girls (Angold, Worthman, & Costello, 2003). Hormones and sleep cycles, which can alter mood, differ dramatically between boys and girls. One study of blood flow in regions of the brain during periods of sadness in men and in women found that although men and women considered themselves to be equally sad, their brain activity differed. When asked to feel sad on cue, both sexes activated regions of the prefrontal cortex, but women showed a much wider activation of the limbic system (George et al., 1996). These and other findings suggest that sex differences in depression may be partly rooted in biological differences in the brain processes that regulate emotions (Martel, 2013).

Ethnicity and Culture

The incidence of depression has been found to vary across regions worldwide (Culbertson, 1997); however, few studies have examined ethnic, racial, or cultural differences in clinically depressed youths, and findings have been inconsistent (Anderson & Mayes, 2009). One study compared the prevalence of MDD across nine ethnic groups in a large community sample of children in grades 6 to 8 (Roberts, Roberts, & Chen, 1997). Of these groups, African American and Hispanic youths both had significantly higher rates of depression. However, only Hispanic youths with depression showed an elevated risk for impaired functioning. In another study, pubertal status was found to be a better predictor of depressive symptoms than chronological age in Caucasian girls, but not in African American or Hispanic girls (Hayward et al., 1999). Similarly, obesity in the sixth grade was found to be associated with a greater likelihood of depressed mood in the eighth grade for Caucasian girls but not for African American or Hispanic girls (Anderson et al., 2011).

A large community study of high school students found that nonwhite (African American, Hispanic, and Asian) adolescents reported more symptoms of depression than white adolescents (Rushton, Forcier, & Schectman, 2002). However, these differences likely reflect differences in socioeconomic status (SES), since depression and lower SES are related. Race and ethnicity are known sources of varying levels of exposure to stress and availability of resources. As a result, low SES may increase vulnerability to stress, and by doing so it may increase the likelihood of depression. In a longitudinal study of four race–ethnic groups (whites, African Americans, Hispanics, and Asians) during the transition from adolescence to young adulthood, it was found that race and ethnicity were important in understanding depressive symptoms during this period (Brown, Meadows, & Elder, 2007). In females, initial rates of depressive symptoms were highest for Hispanic and Asian teens and lowest for whites, with African American youths falling in between. As expected, males displayed lower levels of symptoms, but the findings for race–ethnic group differences were similar to those for females. Within gender, all groups showed decreases in symptoms over time; however, whites continued to display fewer depressive symptoms than the other three groups, particularly as compared with African Americans. This lasting race–ethnic inequality in depressive symptoms creates a risk for emotional and physical health in later life, as stress may accumulate in the context of a lack of resources.

Section Summary

Major Depressive Disorder (MDD)

- The key features of MDD are sadness, loss of interest or pleasure in nearly all activities, and irritability, plus many specific symptoms that are present for at least 2 weeks.

- The overall prevalence of MDD annually for youths 4 to 18 years of age is between 2% and 8%, with rates that are low during childhood but increase dramatically during adolescence. The likelihood that a youth has ever had MDD is higher, from 10% to 20% or more.

- The most frequent accompanying disorders in young people with MDD are anxiety disorders, persistent depressive disorder, conduct problems, ADHD, and substance-use disorder.
- Almost all young people recover from their initial depressive episode, but about 70% have another episode within 5 years and many develop bipolar disorder.
- Depression in preadolescent children is equally common in boys and girls, but the ratio of girls to boys is about 2:1 to 3:1 after puberty.
- The relationship between depression and race/ethnicity during childhood and adolescence is an understudied area.

In the next section, we discuss persistent depressive disorder, a milder but more chronic form of depression, about which we know relatively little as compared with MDD. Many children with persistent depressive disorder eventually develop MDD; therefore, the two disorders are related.

PERSISTENT DEPRESSIVE DISORDER [P-DD] (DYSTHYMIA)

DEBORAH

A Childhood without Laughter

A few months ago, my mother unearthed some pictures of me as a baby that I had never seen before. One showed me at about 9 months old, crawling on the grass of Golden Gate Park. I was looking directly at the camera, my tongue sticking out of the corner of my mouth, and I was laughing happily. My face was lit from within and looked more than a little mischievous. I was absolutely transfixed by that photo for days. I would continually take it out of my wallet and stare at it, torn between laughter and tears. For a while I couldn't figure out what it was about the picture that drew me. Finally it hit me; this was the only picture of myself as a child that I had seen that showed me laughing. All the photos I had ever seen depicted a child staring solemnly or smiling diffidently, but never laughing. I looked at the Golden Gate Park picture and wished that I had remained that happy and that depression had not taken away my childhood. When I first was diagnosed with depression at age 24, I discussed my childhood with my doctor. Although it is hard to diagnose a child from 20 years in the past, it seemed clear to both of us that I had suffered from dysthymia (mild, long-term depression) probably from the time I was a small child.

Based on A Childhood Without Laughter by D. M. Deren.

Like Deborah, young people who suffer from **persistent depressive disorder (P-DD)** experience symptoms of depressed mood that occur for most of the day, on most days, and persist for at least 1 year. They are unhappy or irritable most of the time. (The sad and gloomy life of Eeyore the donkey in the 100 Acre Wood likely qualifies for a diagnosis of P-DD.) Combined with their chronic depressed (or irritable) mood, these children also display at least two somatic (e.g., eating problems, sleep disturbances, low energy) or cognitive symptoms (e.g., lack of concentration, low self-esteem, feelings of hopelessness) that are present while they are depressed. Although the symptoms of P-DD are chronic, they are less severe than those for children with MDD.

P-DD is a "new" category in DSM-5; it combines the previous DSM-IV categories of Dysthymic Disorder and MDD—Chronic. This was done because of the lack of differences between youths with a dysthymic disorder and those with a chronic type of major depression. In comparison to nonchronic MDD, chronic forms of depression, whether referred to as dysthymic disorder, chronic major depression, or P-DD are associated with a poorer response to treatment, greater long-term morbidity at follow-up, and greater familial loading for affective disorders (McCullough et al., 2003).

Children with P-DD are characterized by poor emotion regulation, which includes constant feelings of sadness, feelings of being unloved and forlorn, self-deprecation, low self-esteem, anxiety, anger, and temper tantrums (Masi et al., 2003). Some may experience **double depression**, in which MDD is superimposed on the child's previous P-DD, causing the child to present with both disorders (Klein, Shankman, & Rose, 2008).

The chronic nature of P-DD raises the issue of whether it is a mood disorder or a general personality style (Daley et al., 1999). For example, we all know people we would describe as "sad sacks"—nothing ever seems to make them happy. However, P-DD seems to follow a chronic course that is typical of mood disorders, and the similarities between P-DD and MDD in young people suggest that it is a mood disorder, not a personality style (Renouf & Kovacs, 1995). One study found that children with either MDD or P-DD alone did not differ in their clinical features, demographics, or associated characteristics, leading to unanswered questions about the validity of this distinction. However, those with both disorders were more severely impaired than children with just one of them (Goodman et al., 2000).

Prevalence and Comorbidity

Rates of P-DD are lower than those of MDD, with approximately 1% of children and 5% of adolescents displaying the disorder (Birmaher et al., 1996). The most prevalent co-occurring diagnosis with P-DD is MDD. During the course of their P-DD, as many as 70% of children may have an episode of major depression (Renouf & Kovacs, 1995). About half of the children with P-DD also have one or more co-occurring non-affective disorders that preceded the P-DD, including anxiety disorders, CD, and ADHD (Kovacs et al., 1994).

Onset, Course, and Outcome

P-DD develops about 3 years earlier than MDD, most commonly around 11 to 12 years of age (Kovacs et al., 1997). Since P-DD frequently precedes MDD, it could be a precursor to its development (Lewinsohn, Hops et al., 1993). Childhood-onset P-DD has a prolonged duration, with an average episode length of 2 to 5 years.

Almost all children eventually recover from P-DD. On the other hand, they also have an extremely high risk of developing other disorders, especially MDD, anxiety disorders (separation anxiety disorder and generalized anxiety disorder are the most common), and conduct disorder (Klein et al., 2008; Masi et al., 2003). They are also at increased risk for the subsequent development of bipolar and substance-use disorders (Kovacs et al., 1994).

Adolescents with a history of P-DD report receiving less social support from friends. This finding appears to be unique to children with P-DD as compared with children with MDD (Klein, Lewinsohn, & Seeley, 1997). Those who recover from their P-DD have the same family relationships, cognitive styles, and school functioning as other children. The only area that continues to be affected is psychosocial functioning (Klein et al., 1997). However, it is not known whether deficits in psychosocial functioning precede or follow P-DD. They may be a predisposing factor for the development of P-DD, or a lasting scar of the illness (Renouf & Kovacs, 1995).

The early onset and extended duration of P-DD make it a serious problem. Children who develop the disorder at age 9 then recover 4 years later will have spent more than 30% of their entire lives and over 50% of their school-age years being depressed. Since depression is associated with many other academic, cognitive, family, and social problems, these long-lasting episodes of P-DD can have extremely harmful effects on development (Renouf & Kovacs, 1995). Since early-onset P-DD is almost always followed by MDD and sometimes by bipolar disorder, its early diagnosis may help to identify children at risk for later mood disorders and has important implications for prevention.

Section Summary

Persistent Depressive Disorder [P-DD] (Dysthymia)

- Children with P-DD display a depressive or irritable mood for most of the day, on most days for at least 1 year. While depressed, they also experience a number of somatic and cognitive symptoms.
- About 5% of children and adolescents have an episode of P-DD by the end of adolescence.
- The most common disorders accompanying P-DD are superimposed MDD, anxiety disorders, CD, and ADHD.
- The most common age at onset for P-DD is between 11 and 12 years, with an average episode length of between 2 and 5 years.
- Almost all young people eventually recover from their P-DD, but many will develop MDD.
- Children who recover from their P-DD differ from other children mainly on measures of psychosocial functioning.
- P-DD is a revised category in DSM-5 that combines the previous DSM-IV categories of Dysthymic Disorder and MDD—Chronic. This was done because of the lack of differences between youths with a dysthymic disorder and those with a chronic type of major depression.

DISRUPTIVE MOOD DYSREGULATION DISORDER (DMDD)

The central feature of **disruptive mood dysregulation disorder** (DMDD) is chronic, severe persistent irritability. This severe irritability has two main clinical features. The first is frequent verbal or physical *temper outbursts* that usually occur in response to frustration and are totally out of proportion to the provocation or situation. These outbursts must occur frequently (three or four times a week) over 1 year in at least two of three settings (i.e., at home, at school, with peers), and must be age-inappropriate. The second feature of severe irritability is a chronic, persistently *irritable or angry mood* that is present most of the day, nearly every day, between the severe temper outbursts. This mood must have an onset prior to age 10 years; be characteristic of the child; be present most of the day, nearly every day; and be noticeable to others. A diagnosis of DMDD cannot coexist with ODD (in this case. a diagnosis of DMDD only would be made) or bipolar disorder (in this case. a diagnosis of BP would be made), but can co-occur with MDD, ADHD, CD, or substance-use disorder (APA, 2013).

DMDD is a new depressive disorder in DSM-5, and it is the one that we know the least about. In addition, its inclusion in DSM-5 as a depressive disorder has generated some controversy. In light of this, we briefly consider the context in which DMDD was established as a diagnostic category and some of the issues that surrounded its development. DMDD was formulated in two contexts. The first included findings on severe irritability as a salient characteristic of mood, not just as a manifestation of MDD (Stringaris, 2011). For example, studies have found that irritability at age 3 predicts depression, ODD, and functional impairment in early childhood (Dougherty et al., 2013) and that irritability in adolescence predicts self-reports of depressive and anxiety disorders up to 20 years later (Stringaris et al., 2009). The second context was research on bipolar disorder (to be discussed later in this chapter) that identified children with severe mood dysregulation problems whose symptoms did not fit neatly into traditional definitions of bipolar disorder (Towbin et al., 2013). Importantly, the development of the diagnosis of DMDD was a direct response to concerns about increasing rates of bipolar disorder diagnoses in young children and the growing use of medications to treat these children. Thus, much of the initiative in creating the category of DMDD was to provide an alternative to diagnosing BP in young children too frequently (Youngstrom & Algorta, 2014).

As described by Youngstrom and Algorta (2014), the definition of DMDD changed several times during its development in DSM-5, first described as "severe mood dysregulation disorder," then as "temper dysregulation disorder," and lastly as a "disruptive mood regulation disorder." Significantly, it was also moved from the Disruptive, Impulse-Control, and Conduct Disorders section of DSM-5 to the Depressive Disorders section—not to the Bipolar Disorders section. Significant concerns have been expressed about using DMDD clinically as a new diagnosis, given the absence of data about its prevalence, course, and response to treatment. A central concern is the extent to which the criteria developed for DMDD can be used to reliably differentiate it from other mood and behavior disorders, particularly ODD, which as you may recall, also includes irritability, anger, and defiance as key features (Axelson et al., 2011). This concern appears to be justified, as field trials report overall reliabilities of the DSM-5 criteria for DMDD in clinical practice to be quite low (kappa = 0.25), and to vary widely across settings (Regier et al., 2013). Thus, it may prove difficult for clinicians to reliably distinguish DMDD from other mood and behavioral problems (Youngstrom & Algorta, 2014).

According to DSM-5, DMDD is common in clinic samples, occurs predominantly in males and in school-age children, has high comorbidity with anxiety, mood, and disruptive behavior disorders, and markedly disrupts the youth's family and peer relationships and school performance. Currently, we know there are a number of youngsters with severe irritability and mood

dysregulation problems who do not meet criteria for bipolar disorder. What we do not know is whether DMDD as currently defined is distinct from other mood and conduct problems, its prevalence, characteristic course and outcomes, or how it can be best treated (Axelson et al., 2011; Towbin et al., 2013). Further research and clinical data are sorely needed to determine if the DMDD diagnosis will prove to be reliable, valid, and useful in clinical practice.

Section Summary

Disruptive Mood Dysregulation Disorder (DMDD)

- Disruptive mood dysregulation disorder (DMDD) is characterized by frequent and severe temper outbursts and chronic, persistently irritable or angry mood.
- DMDD is a new disorder in DSM-5, and it is the one we know the least about.
- The development of the DMDD category was a response to increasing rates of bipolar disorder (BP) diagnoses in young children; it was intended to provide an alternative to diagnosing BP in young children too frequently.
- Further research and clinical data are needed to determine whether the DMDD diagnosis will prove to be reliable, valid, and useful in clinical practice.

Now that you have some familiarity with MDD, P-DD, and DMDD, we next consider their associated characteristics and possible causes.

ASSOCIATED CHARACTERISTICS OF DEPRESSIVE DISORDERS

Young people with depressive disorders experience deficits in intellectual performance and academic achievement and disturbances in self-perceptions, self-esteem, social problem solving, interpersonal behavior, and life stressors (Garber & Kaminsky, 2000). Since depression often occurs with anxiety and other disorders, we do not always know whether these associated deficits and disturbances are specific to depression or related to the presence of psychopathology in general. In addition, it is often difficult to know whether cognitive and psychosocial deficits are an outcome or a cause of depression.

Intellectual and Academic Functioning

Certain depressive symptoms—difficulty concentrating, loss of interest, and slowness of thought and movement—are likely to have a harmful effect on a child's intellectual and academic functioning. However, the overall intellectual potential of youths who are depressed is comparable to the potential of those who are not depressed. The association between severity of depression and children's overall intelligence is weak, suggesting that the effects of depression on cognitive functions may be selective. For example, depression may be associated with impairments while performing nonverbal tasks that require attention, coordination, speed, or recall of emotionally coded information, such as facial expressions (Guyer et al., 2011), but not necessarily on tasks that require verbal skills or overall intelligence (Wilkinson & Goodyer, 2006). Depression may also be associated with broad impairments in executive functions, for example, maintaining task goals in working memory (Snyder, 2013).

Youngsters with depression perform more poorly than others in school. They score lower on standard achievement tests, are rated by their teachers as achieving less academically, and have lower levels of grade attainment (Cole, 1990). Poor concentration and thinking ability, slowed movement or agitation, fatigue, insomnia, and somatic symptoms may lead to repeating a grade, being late or skipping school, failure to complete homework, and dissatisfaction with or refusal of school. Jenn, a 15-year-old girl with MDD, and her mother had this to say about school:

> "School is a big waste of time," says Jenn. "I don't want to be there. I don't have the energy or motivation for school. I just say I'm sick so I can stay at home in bed and sleep all day." Jenn's mother says, "We used to fight about school so much that eventually I'd let her stay home—just to avoid having another fight."

It is difficult to determine whether depression is a cause or an outcome of learning difficulties. Most likely it can be both. For example, learning difficulties in adolescents, particularly girls, has been found to lead to feelings of inadequacy as a student, which predict depressive symptoms (Kiuru et al., 2011). It is unclear whether depression has an enduring effect on school performance. Some studies find that school difficulties do not follow the child's recovery from depression, while others report that academic problems continue even after recovery (Kovacs & Goldston, 1991). In general, the association between depression and school difficulties is not as strong as the association between depression and social dysfunction (Lewinsohn, Gotlib, & Seeley, 1997).

Cognitive Biases and Distortions

"Good morning, Pooh Bear," said Eeyore gloomily. "If it is a good morning," he said. "Which I doubt."

—A. A. Milne, *Winnie-the-Pooh* (1926)

ELLIE

Life's Hardly Worth It

"... like everything's worthless, like it's just not worth it to even be. ... It's—it seems like it's a silly thing to even go through life and exist. And from one day to the next you're always wondering if you're going to make it to the next day if it's—if you can stand it, if it's worth trying to get to tomorrow. ... It's just—just, I feel like—I feel mostly like I'm worthless, like there's something wrong with me. It's really not a pleasant feeling to know that you're a total failure, a complete nothing, and I get the feeling that I never do nothing right or worthwhile or anything."

Adapted from McKnew, Cytryn, & Yahraes, 1983.

Many children with depression experience biases, deficits, and distortions in their thinking (Lakdawalla, Hankin, & Mermelstein, 2007). These children commonly notice depression-relevant cues such as sad facial expressions more often than positive cues such as happy facial expressions (Ehrmantrout et al., 2011; Hankin et al., 2010). Given the importance of accurately reading emotional cues for successful social relationships, these selective attentional biases can contribute to adverse relationships with family members and peers.

Some cognitive disturbances, such as Ellie's painful feelings of worthlessness, are part of the diagnosis of depression. Negative beliefs ("I never do nothing right.") and attributions of failure ("I'm a total failure.") are not part of the diagnosis but typically accompany the disorder. Negative thoughts that are self-critical and automatic, such as "I'm a real loser," "I'm ugly," or "I'm gonna fail," are common. Unfortunately, these thoughts can't simply be swept aside by suggesting to a depressed youth that she or he "look at the bright side."

Depressed children often devalue their own performance by not acknowledging their accomplishments. They dismiss praise when it is given and frequently make inaccurate interpretations of their experiences (Fichman, Koestner, & Zuroff, 1996). To focus narrowly and passively on negative events for long periods is referred to as a **depressive ruminative style** (Nolen-Hoeksema, Girgus, & Seligman, 1992). These youngsters view themselves as ineffective in most areas of their lives, and they make self-directed disparaging comments when faced with further failure or rejection (e.g., "It must be my fault."). They misread situations, feel slighted by harmless remarks, and are easily frustrated—small setbacks are seen as major catastrophes. Negative thinking and faulty conclusions are generalized across situations, so the depressed youth sees no hope of gaining any pleasure or satisfaction.

Depression in young people is associated with negative thoughts and feelings of worthlessness.

Negative Self-Esteem

Eeyore, the old grey Donkey, stood by the side of the stream and looked at himself in the water. "Pathetic," he said. "That's what it is. Pathetic."

—A. A. Milne, *Winnie-the-Pooh* (1926)

FARAH

Never Good Enough

Fifteen-year-old Farah's mother says that Farah is a "model daughter," who is near the top of her class, active in school activities, and extremely popular. Her mother is concerned about "how hard Farah is on herself, thinking that she has to be perfect." If Farah doesn't get the highest grade on a test, she won't allow herself to see her friends for a week, and spends most of the time in her room studying. Farah acknowledges that she sets very high standards for herself and if she fails to meet these standards becomes extremely self-critical and self-punitive. She has even slapped herself in the face after what she saw as academic "failure" (getting an A minus rather than an A). Farah's accomplishments bring her little satisfaction, and any perceived failure leads to immediate self-condemnation. Farah's overall self-worth is low and her sense of self, which is based on competency in academic achievement, is highly vulnerable. (Based on authors' case material)

It is not unusual for young people with depression to think that no one can help them out of their misery. Many report hopelessness or negative expectations about the future that are related to diminished self-esteem and to suicidal ideations and attempts (Marciano & Kazdin, 1994). Since feelings of hopelessness dominate their lives, they experience a vicious downward cycle in which self-defeating negative thoughts become pervasive and impair performance at school and home. As performance deteriorates they perceive more failure, and receive—and even seek—further negative feedback. These outcomes maintain their low opinions of themselves and their view of an inability to change, and these lead to further impairments in functioning.

The pessimistic outlook of young people with depression also places them at greater risk for depressive symptoms, especially in response to stressful life events. Since their pessimism may continue after remission of depressive symptoms, they remain at risk for future depressive episodes. We will return to the role of cognitive disturbances in depression later, in the section on cognitive theories.

Almost all young people with depression experience negative self-esteem. In fact, low self-esteem is the symptom that seems most specifically related to depression in adolescents (Lewinsohn et al., 1997). Self-esteem in children with depression is also highly reactive to daily life events, and such daily fluctuations in self-esteem appear to be related to depression following exposure to major life stresses (Roberts & Gotlib, 1997). Thus, both low self-esteem and unstable self-esteem seem to play an important role in depression.

Since physical appearance and approval from peers are especially important as sources of self-esteem for most adolescents, perceived incompetence in these areas may heighten the risk for depression. The fact that self-esteem problems in adolescent girls are often related to a negative body image may partly contribute to their higher risk for depression (Hankin & Abramson, 2001).

An interesting developmental model of self-esteem and depression hypothesizes that young people seek and receive feedback from others about their competence or incompetence in several domains: academics, social relations, sports, conduct, and physical appearance

(Jordan & Cole, 1996). Self-views are constructed from this feedback, and the outcome may be a varied and positive self-view leading to optimism, energy, and enthusiasm. Or it may be a narrow and negative self-view leading to pessimism, a sense of helplessness, and possibly, depression (Seroczynski, Cole, & Maxwell, 1997). Children whose self-views are negative and narrowly focused in one domain—for example, in academics—may show instability in their self-esteem because they lack alternative compensatory areas of functioning, such as sports or social relations. This may make them vulnerable to developing depression when faced with stress in their primary domain.

Social and Peer Problems

Young people who are depressed experience significant disruptions in their relationships. They have few friends or close relationships, feel lonely and isolated, feel that others do not like them (which, unfortunately, often becomes a reality), and display extensive impairments in their social skills (Rudolph, Flynn, & Abaied, 2008). The low social status of youngsters with depression has been found to emerge via two pathways (Agoston & Rudolph, 2013). In the first pathway, depressive symptoms promote socially helpless behavior and subsequent neglect by peers. In the second pathway, depressive symptoms promote aggressive behavior and subsequent rejection by peers. Chronic peer-related loneliness during childhood has also been found to predict depressive symptoms in early adolescence (Qualter et al., 2010). In addition, children with depression who report poor friendships at the time of referral have a reduced likelihood of recovery from depression (Goodyer et al., 1997). Even when children recover from their depression, they continue to experience some social impairment.

Social withdrawal is common in youngsters with depression. They often spend significant amounts of time alone, show little interest in seeing friends, and engage in few activities. Their social withdrawal may reflect an inability to maintain social interactions—possibly related to negative, irritable, and aggressive behavior toward others—and deficits in initiating conversations or making friends (Rockhill et al., 2007). These factors can seriously interfere with social development, depriving youngsters with depression of the social exchanges that lead to healthy interpersonal relationships.

Youngsters who are depressed use ineffective styles of coping in social situations. For example, they use less active and problem-focused coping and more passive, avoidant, ruminative, or emotion-focused coping (Hammen et al., 2014). A strong risk factor for the onset of depression in adolescent females is **co-rumination**, a

negative form of self-disclosure and discussion between peers focused narrowly on problems or emotions to the exclusion of other activities or dialogue (Stone et al., 2011). Co-rumination seems to be one mechanism underlying adolescent females' heightened risk for depression. Ironically, co-rumination between peers is associated with higher ratings of friendship quality and closeness, which in turn, have been found to predict increases in co-rumination. Thus, what appear to be socially rewarding and supportive relationships with peers not only fail to protect female teens from distress, but also may increase their risk for depression when based on maladaptive styles of interaction (Stone et al., 2011).

Depressed teens may also make poor choices in dealing with social problems, such as turning to alcohol or drugs in response to a break-up with a boyfriend or girlfriend. In the words of Page, age 17:

> I was so unhappy that I didn't care about myself—even about being safe. I was out drinking a lot, doing a lot of pot. Sometimes I would just black out and not know what was happening. One night I think a bunch of guys had sex with me when I passed out, I don't know. I never remembered anything, it was all hearsay the next day. I made some really bad boyfriend choices. I would date guys who reinforced my view of myself as ugly, stupid, and uncool. I dropped my preppy boyfriend and started dating a 20-year-old guy who was living in his own apartment and playing in a band. He had tattoos on his arms and stomach. I would date guys just so I could get a ride, even though I didn't like them. I would pick boyfriends who were depressed or ones that my parents really didn't like. (From "I Did Not Want to Live," by Sabrina Solin Weill, 1995. *Seventeen*, April 1, 1995, pp. 154–156, 176.)

Interestingly, the basic understanding required for appropriate social relations appears to be relatively intact in youngsters with depression. They are generally capable of providing cognitive solutions to interpersonal problems (Kovacs & Goldston, 1991). However, as with Page, their deficits in social problem solving and behavior in real-life situations, particularly when they are under stress, are in sharp contrast to their social understanding (Calhoun et al., 2012). Adolescents with depression and poor social problem-solving skills are likely to show increases in the severity of their depression over time (Becker-Weidman et al., 2010).

Family Problems

Youngsters with depression experience less supportive and more conflictual relationships with their mothers, fathers, and siblings than do children who do not have depression. They report feeling socially isolated from

"It's my youth, and I don't have to enjoy it if I don't want to."

their families and prefer to be alone rather than with them. In family situations, the child's social isolation may not be a social skill deficit, but rather a reflection of the child's desire to avoid conflict. Family relationship difficulties have been found to persist even when children are no longer clinically depressed (Sheeber et al., 2007).

During interactions, these youngsters may be quite negative toward their parents, and their parents in turn may respond in a negative, dismissing, or harsh manner. When repeated over time, these interactions may adversely affect family relationships. Children with depression who are irritable, unresponsive, and unaffectionate provide little positive reinforcement for their parents, and they frustrate their parents' desire for satisfaction in the parenting role (Kovacs, 1997).

Depression and Suicide

CARLA

"It Became Too Much"

Carla, age 12, was admitted to the intensive care unit unconscious and unstable after ingesting eight of her mother's 50-mg Elavil tablets, an unknown quantity of antidepressants, and approximately 20 tablets of Tylenol 3. This suicide attempt, her first, came after arguing with her father over chores and restrictions imposed because her grades were so bad. Carla said she went to the medicine cabinet and ingested everything she could find because "it became too much" and she "did not want to live." For the previous month, she had displayed a noticeable change of mood, behaving with more instability and depression, feeling worthless and hopeless. During this period she had lost her appetite and had dropped two dress sizes. She had increasingly isolated herself, staying alone in her room. Her school performance, for which her father had restricted her, had declined from B's the previous term to D's.

From Adolescent Suicide: Assessment and Intervention by A. L. Berman and D. A. Jobes, 1991, p. 144.

Carla's case illustrates the profound feelings of hopelessness, helplessness, and despair that often lead a youngster with depression to attempt suicide. Most youngsters with depression report suicidal thinking, and as many as one-third who think about killing themselves actually attempt it (Goldston, Daniel, & Arnold, 2006). Drug overdose and wrist cutting are among the most common methods for adolescents who attempt suicide. In one long-term follow-up study, adolescents with MDD had a fivefold increased risk of a first suicide attempt as compared with controls without MDD, and nearly 8% of them committed suicide within 15 years of their first episode of MDD (Weissman et al., 1999b). For adolescents who complete suicide, the most common methods are firearms (45%), suffocation (40%), and poisoning (8%) (CDC, 2013).

The link between depression, suicidal behavior, and completed suicide is undeniable, strong, and sobering (Dervic, Brent, & Oquendo, 2008). Suicidal ideation (e.g., thinking about killing oneself) is common across many different types of psychological disorders, but actual suicide attempts are much more common during depression (Nock et al., 2013) (see A Closer Look 10.1). In one 7-to 9-year follow-up of youngsters with psychiatric disorders, 84% of all suicide attempts were found to occur because of depressive disorders (Shaffer et al., 1996).

About 60% of youngsters who are clinically depressed report having thoughts about suicide, and 30% attempt suicide by 17 years of age, with most attempts coming within the first year after the onset of suicidal thoughts. Unfortunately, about half of them eventually make further attempts (AACAP, 2001). The suicide attempts of youngsters with depression almost never occur during times when they are symptom-free—90% or more have depressive features at the time of their suicidal episode. Finally, among youngsters who kill themselves, the odds of having major depression are 27 times higher than among controls (Brent et al., 1993; Shaffer et al., 1996).

Although rates of suicidal behavior vary across countries, the two strongest risk factors for suicidal behavior are consistent worldwide—having a mood disorder and

Depressive Disorder Is Associated with Suicide Thoughts and Suicide Attempts

What's the Use?

I look ~~srott~~ around here and all I see,
Is a school and a world
that could do without me.
I've gotten here but only by fate.
My death, I'm sure, will not come late.
I try each day to see the use of being here.
There is none.
I try to find a meaning,
But the wars have been fought,
my battle is yet to come.
When I close my eyes the pain goes.
When I open them again the pain. snows.
I try to not cry aloud,
Wouldn't matter anyway I'm lost in this crowd.
You can pretend I don't live,
But I'll keep living 'till my life gives.

Teri's note

Teri: What's the Use?

Teri, age 15, had been depressed since her father died when she was 11. According to her mother, over the past 14 months her behavior had gone from moody to sullen. She had disobeyed restrictions imposed as punishments and had run away from home on several occasions. She labeled herself as "stupid," spoke and wrote often of death and suicide (see accompanying note). On three occasions she had cut her wrists, albeit only superficially. Her school performance had declined and she spoke now of hating school. Her peer associations were almost exclusively with other alienated teens, described by her as "punks and other anarchists."

Source: Adolescent Suicide: Assessment and Intervention by A. L. Berman and D. A. Jobes, 1991, p. 144.

being a young female (Cha & Nock, 2014; Nock et al., 2008). In general, young females with depression show more suicidal ideation and attempt suicide more often than young males (Nock et al., 2013). The risk factors for nonfatal suicide attempts are similar for males and females (Thompson & Light, 2010). However, since girls typically do not use guns, they are usually less successful in completing suicide than boys (Goldston et al., 2006). Ages 13 and 14 are peak periods for a first suicide attempt by youngsters with depression. Suicide prior to puberty is rare, most likely because depression and substance abuse before puberty are also rare. In adolescents with depression, suicide attempts double during the teen years but show an abrupt decline after age 17 or 18. It is possible that as young people mature, they are better able to tolerate their negative mood states and acquire more resources for coping, thus making it less likely that they will attempt suicide during periods of sadness (Borowsky, Ireland, & Resnick, 2001).

In light of the strong connection between symptoms of depression and suicidal ideation and behavior, a primary strategy for reducing suicide in young people is to increase the availability of effective treatments for depression (Brown et al., 2007). We discuss these treatments later in this chapter. Prevention and treatment programs for suicidal behavior generally focus on family involvement and support, and they emphasize intervening early after the suicidal crisis (Brent et al., 2013; Pineda & Dadds, 2013). Since racial and ethnic groups are known to differ in rates of suicidal behaviors and the circumstances under which they occur (e.g., precipitants, risk and protective factors, and patterns of seeking help), it is also important that suicide prevention and treatment programs are sensitive to these cultural differences (Goldston et al., 2008).

Our discussion of suicidal behavior in this chapter has focused primarily on its relationship with depressive disorders. However, it is important to recognize that self-injurious thoughts and behaviors in young people is a significant topic in its own right, and one that is just beginning to receive the attention it deserves (Cha & Nock, 2014). Self-injurious thoughts and behaviors range from nonsuicidal self-injury such as self-cutting, to suicidal ideation, suicide attempts, and completed suicide. Suicide is especially worrisome, as it is the second leading cause of death among adolescents and young adults in the United States, resulting in about 4,600 deaths per year (CDC, 2013). DSM-5 includes two newly proposed disorders in its section on conditions for further study: Suicidal Behavior Disorder describes individuals who have made a suicide attempt within the past 24 months, and Nonsuicidal Self Injury describes individuals who engage in intentional self-inflicted damage to the surface of the body (e.g., cutting, burning, stabbing, excessive rubbing) without suicidal intent. These proposed diagnoses and other efforts will hopefully bring further attention and understanding to self-injurious behaviors in young people so we can learn how to best predict and prevent these behaviors (Cha & Nock, 2014).

Section Summary

Associated Characteristics of Depressive Disorders

- Youngsters with depression have normal intelligence, although certain symptoms such as difficulty concentrating, loss of interest, and slowness of thought may negatively affect intellectual functioning.

- They perform more poorly than others in school, score lower on standard achievement tests, and have lower levels of grade attainment.

- They often experience deficits and distortions in their thinking, including negative beliefs, attributions of failure, and self-critical automatic negative thoughts.

- Almost all youngsters with depression experience low or unstable self-esteem.

- Youngsters with depression have few friends and close relationships, feel lonely and isolated, and feel that others do not like them.

- They experience poor relationships and conflict with their parents and siblings, who in turn may respond in a negative, dismissing, or harsh manner.

- Most youngsters with depression report suicidal thinking, and about 30% who think about killing themselves actually attempt it.

THEORIES OF DEPRESSION

Many theories have been proposed to explain the onset and course of depression. Until recently, however, most were developed to explain depression in adults, then directly applied to children with minimal regard for developmental differences (Garber & Horowitz, 2002). In the sections that follow, we consider several of these theories. Keep in mind, however, that depression is likely a final, common pathway for interacting influences that predispose a child to develop the disorder (Hammen et al., 2014). No one theory can explain all forms of depressive disorder and differences in symptoms and severity within the same disorder. An overview of the primary theories of depression is presented in Table 10.2.

Psychodynamic

Early psychodynamic theories viewed depression as the conversion of aggressive instinct into depressive

TABLE 10.2 | Overview of Theories of Depression

Psychodynamic	Actual or symbolic loss of love object (e.g., caregiver) that is loved ambivalently; anger toward love object turned inward; excessive severity of the superego; loss of self-esteem
Attachment	Insecure early attachments; distorted internal working models of self and others
Behavioral	Lack or loss of reinforcement or quality of reinforcement; deficits in skills needed to obtain reinforcement
Cognitive	Depressive mindset; distorted or maladaptive cognitive structures, processes, and products; negative view of self, world, and future; poor problem-solving ability; hopelessness
Self-Control	Problems in organizing behavior toward long-term goals; deficits in self-monitoring, self-evaluation, and self-reinforcement
Interpersonal	Impaired interpersonal functioning related to grief over loss; role dispute and conflict; role transition; interpersonal deficit; single parenting; social withdrawal; interaction between mood and interpersonal events
Socio-environmental	Stressful life circumstances and daily hassles as vulnerability factors; social support, coping, and appraisal as protective factors
Neurobiological	Neurochemical and receptor abnormalities; neurophysiological abnormalities; neuroendocrine abnormalities; genetic variants; abnormalities in brain structure and function; effects of early experience on the developing brain

Based on A Developmental Cognitive Model of Unipolar Major Depression, by D. J. A. Dozois, unpublished manuscript.

affect. Depression is presumed to result from the loss of a love object (e.g., mother). This loss can be actual, as in the case of the death of a parent, or symbolic, as a result of emotional deprivation, rejection, or inadequate parenting. The individual's subsequent rage toward the love object is then turned against the self. Since children and adolescents were believed to have inadequate development of the superego or conscience, the hostility directed against internalized love objects that have disappointed or abandoned them does not produce guilt, so they do not become depressed (Bemporad, 1994; Poznanski, 1979). However, more recent studies have found that high levels of maladaptive guilt and shame are related to the onset of depression in children as young as 3 to 5 years of age (Luby, Belden et al., 2009). Furthermore, the fact that depression does occur in many youngsters who do not experience loss or rejection—and doesn't occur in many children who do—casts doubt on the psychodynamic model. Contrary to this theory, many children do experience clinical depression.

Attachment

Attachment theory focuses on parental separation and disruption of an attachment bond as predisposing factors for depression. John Bowlby hypothesized that a child confronted with unresponsive and emotionally unavailable caregiving goes through a typical sequence involving protest, despair, and detachment (Bowlby, 1961). A parent's consistent failure to meet the child's needs is associated with the development of an insecure attachment, a view of the self as unworthy and unloved, and a view of others as threatening or undependable. These factors may place the child at risk for later depression, particularly in the context of stressful interpersonal relationships (Rudolph, Hammen, & Burge, 1997). Attachment relationships also serve to regulate biological and behavioral systems related to emotion. For example, a secure attachment may help to reduce distress, whereas an insecure attachment may lead to difficulties in regulating emotion, which in turn may become a risk factor for later depression. In support of this theory, children with insecure attachments are more likely than children with secure attachments to display symptoms of depression (e.g., Toth & Cicchetti, 1996). In addition, children and adolescents with depression are more likely to experience disturbances in attachment than are children without depression (Stein et al., 2000). In one study, only 8% of adolescents with depression were securely attached (vs. 52% of controls), and 40% of them had an insecure attachment that was unresolved with regard to loss or abuse (Ivarsson et al., 2010).

Behavioral

Behavioral views emphasize the importance of learning, environmental consequences, and skills and deficits during the onset and maintenance of depression.

Depression is related to *a lack of response-contingent positive reinforcement* (Lewinsohn, 1974). This lack of positive reinforcement may occur for three reasons. First, a youngster may be unable to experience available reinforcement, often because of interfering anxiety. Second, changes in the environment, such as the loss of a significant person in the child's life, may result in a lack of availability of rewards. Finally, a youngster may lack the skills needed to have rewarding and satisfying social relationships.

Children may also receive sympathy for their sadness, which produces the desired attention and concern. However, this sympathy is usually short-lived because even people who care about the youngster begin to avoid him or her. This reduction in attention may then lead to withdrawal, impairment in functioning, and heightened feelings of depression. Few studies have tested specific behavioral hypotheses with children, and this model seems incomplete in the light of what is known about other factors that may lead to a vulnerability to depression. Nevertheless, the behavioral model highlights the importance of learning processes in the emergence, expression, and outcome of depression in young people.

Cognitive

Cognitive theories focus on the relation between negative thinking and mood (Abela & Hankin, 2008a). The underlying assumptions are that how young people view themselves and their world will influence their mood and behavior and that cognitive vulnerabilities interact with negative events to increase depressive symptoms. A variety of negative cognitions, attributions, misperceptions, and deficiencies in cognitive problem-solving skills are related to depression in young people (Lakdawalla et al., 2007). Cognitive theories emphasize **depressogenic cognitions**, which are the negative perceptual and attributional styles and beliefs associated with depressive symptoms.

For example, **hopelessness theory** proposes that depression-prone individuals tend to make internal, stable, and global attributions to explain the causes of negative events. In other words, when something bad happens, they think that they are responsible (internal attribution), that the reason they are to blame will not change over time (stable attribution), and that the reason that something bad happened applies to most things they do and in most situations (global attribution) (Abramson, Seligman, & Teasdale, 1978). In contrast, they attribute positive events to something outside themselves (external), which is not likely to happen again (unstable), and is seen as unique to this event (specific). A *negative* *attributional style* results in the individual's taking personal blame for negative events in his or her life and leads to helplessness and avoidance of these events in the future. Helplessness may in turn lead to hopelessness about the future, which promotes further depression (Abramson, Metalsky, & Alloy, 1989).

The cognitive model developed by Aaron Beck (1967) proposes that depressed individuals make negative interpretations about life events because they use biased and negative beliefs as interpretive filters for understanding these events. Depressed individuals show cognitive problems in three areas.

First, they display *information-processing biases*, or errors in their thinking in specific situations, called *negative automatic thoughts*. These often include thoughts of physical and social threat, personal failure, and hostility (Schniering & Rapee, 2004). They may selectively attend to negative information, assume blame for negative events, maximize and exaggerate negative events, and minimize positive events. They also assign negative labels to events and then react emotionally to the label rather than to the event. For example:

▸ EVENT: Child didn't receive an invitation to Ashley's party.

▸ LABEL: "I didn't receive an invitation because Ashley doesn't like me. *Nobody likes me.*"

▸ EMOTIONAL REACTION: Unhappiness and depression.

Second, depression is believed to be associated with a negative outlook in the following three areas, referred to as the **negative cognitive triad** (see ● Figure 10.2):

▸ Negative views about *oneself* (e.g., "I'm no good," "I'm boring")

▸ Negative views about the *world* (day-to-day experiences) (e.g., "They're no good," "It's too hard")

▸ Negative views about the *future* (e.g., "It's always going to be this bad," "I'll never graduate")

These negative views become increasingly more stable with age, maintain feelings of helplessness, undermine the youngster's mood and energy level, and are related to the child's severity of depression (LaGrange et al., 2008).

Third, depressed youngsters have **negative cognitive schemata**, which are stable structures in memory that guide information processing, including self-critical beliefs and attitudes. These schemata are rigid and resistant to change even in the face of contradictory evidence and may heighten the youngster's sensitivity to depression, especially when activated by stress.

Applying cognitive theories to depression in young people raises questions about the cognitive capacities

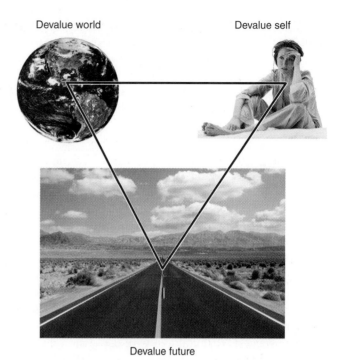

Devalue world   Devalue self

Devalue future

● **FIGURE 10.2** | The Negative Cognitive Triad: Depression is related to a devaluation of self, the world, and the future.

Photo credits: Tom Merton/OJO Images/Getty Images; ©worker/Shutterstock.com; ©kavram/Shutterstock.com

of children at various stages of development and the development and stability of cognitive structures that may be involved in their depressive thinking (Abela & Hankin, 2008a). A well-developed sense of self and a time perspective for the future are needed to experience depression; these cognitive processes are still developing in children. In addition, many of the cognitive errors and distortions discussed so far, such as illogical thinking or faulty attributions, are normal ways of thinking in young children!

Although higher rates of negative thinking are found in youngsters with depression, there are still many unanswered questions about the relation between cognition and depression (Lakdawalla et al., 2007). More information is needed about how negative cognitions develop. Are the negative cognitions that accompany depression the result of parental rejection and negative parenting practices? Is there a relation between maternal and child cognitions, as suggested by the relationship between mothers' and children's negative thinking (Stark, Schmidt, & Joiner, 1996)? One study found an association between a maternal depressogenic cognitive style during pregnancy and offspring cognitive style 18 years later (Pearson et al., 2013). How and when does a cognitive vulnerability for depression interact with stress to result in depression (Cole et al.,

2008)? At this time, there is support for a cognitive vulnerability–stress interaction in adolescents, and possibly for children as young as 7 years of age (Hayden et al., 2013; Lakdawalla et al., 2007). Longitudinal studies are needed to answer these and other questions concerning the role of cognition in the development of depression in young people.

Other Theories

Self-control theories view youngsters with depression as having difficulty organizing their behavior in relation to long-term goals and as displaying deficits in self-monitoring, self-evaluation, and self-reinforcement. As a result, they selectively attend to negative events and to the immediate consequences of their behavior. These youngsters set excessively high standards for performance, make negative causal attributions, administer insufficient self-rewards, and use excessive self-punishment. Research suggests that children with depression display a number of these deficits (Rehm & Sharp, 1996).

Interpersonal models view disruptions in interpersonal relationships, especially with family and peers, as the basis for the onset and maintenance of depression (Hammen, 1999). Depressive symptoms in adolescence are associated with increases in the negative quality and decreases in the positive quality of relationships over time (Oppenheimer & Hankin, 2011). The behaviors of a depressed youngster are unpleasant to others, leading family members and others to become annoyed and frustrated. As the youngster becomes more aware of how others are reacting, he or she feels even more needy, and then unthinkingly and annoyingly seeks excessive reassurance, which in turn leads to further interpersonal rejection (Joiner, 1999). Interpersonal models also propose that the child's depression may serve a function in the family—for example, to reduce conflict between parents.

Socioenvironmental models emphasize the relationship between stressful life events and depression. Adolescents with depression experience significantly more psychosocial adversity than controls or adolescents with other psychiatric disorders (Ivarsson et al., 2010). Some life situations related to the onset of depression are being social disadvantaged, having an unemployed parent, having a single parent, being part of a large family, experiencing a personal loss, being abused, and having poor social support. Stressful life events may be linked to depression in several ways. First, depression can be a direct reaction to the occurrence of stressful life events, such as the loss of a parent. Second, the impact of stress may be moderated by individual risk factors, such as genetic risk. This is referred to as the **diathesis–stress model of depression** because the

occurrence of depression depends on the interaction between the youngster's personal vulnerability (diathesis) and life stress. Third, negative environmental events may be internalized as negative cognitive styles (e.g., rumination), which then predispose the child to depression (Abela & Hankin, 2011). Finally, depression may result in behaviors and impairments in functioning that generate stressful life circumstances that in turn lead to depressive reactions (Hammen, Brennan, & Le Brocque, 2011). The generation of stress following depression may also be heightened by early developmental risk factors such as child abuse and neglect (Harkness, Lumley, & Truss, 2008).

Neurobiological models of depression in young people focus on genetic vulnerabilities and neurobiological processes, including the effects of early experiences such as stress, child maltreatment, or maternal depression on the developing brain. Several neurobiological abnormalities have been identified, although findings are less consistent for children than for adults (NIMH, 2003). We consider possible biological and other factors in the next section, on causes.

Section Summary

Theories of Depression

- Psychodynamic theories presume that depression results from the actual or symbolic loss of a love object and view depression as the conversion of aggressive instinct into depressive affect.

- Attachment theories focus on insecure attachment, a view of the self as unworthy and unloved, and a view of others as threatening or undependable as risk factors for later depression, particularly in the context of stressful interpersonal relationships.

- Behavioral views emphasize the importance of learning, environmental consequences (particularly a lack of response-contingent reinforcement), and skills deficits during the onset and maintenance of depression.

- Cognitive theories of depression focus on the relation between negative thinking and mood, with the underlying assumption that how young people view themselves and their world will influence their mood and behavior.

- Other theories of depression have emphasized the role of deficits in self-control, interpersonal disturbances, stressful life events, and genetic and neurobiological processes.

CAUSES OF DEPRESSION

In light of the many vulnerability, risk, and protective factors that have been implicated, an integrative framework is necessary to account for depression in young

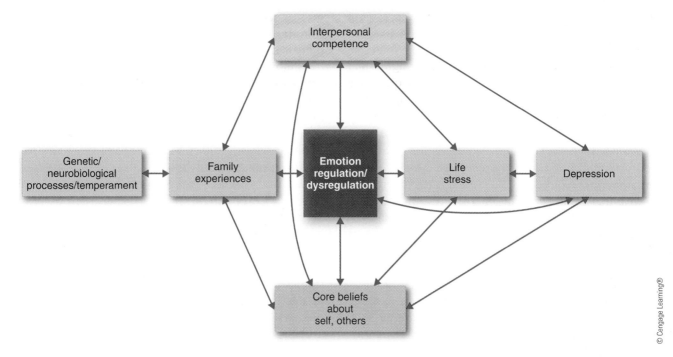

● FIGURE 10.3 | A developmental framework for depression in young people.

people and for its nonoccurrence in the presence of risk (Hammen et al., 2014; Miller, 2007). The framework presented in ● Figure 10.3 highlights possible causes of depression in young people and the interplay among genetic, neurobiological, family, cognitive, emotional, interpersonal, and environmental factors. Given these many interacting influences, multiple pathways to depression are likely (Eaves, Silberg, & Erkanli, 2003).

Within this framework, genetic risk influences neurobiological processes and is reflected in an early temperament characterized by oversensitivity to negative stimuli, high negative emotionality, and a disposition to feeling negative affect. These early dispositions increase exposure to and are shaped by negative experiences within the family and continue to exert influence throughout development. Core beliefs about self and others develop as a result of experiences within the family. Parenting that is insensitive, disengaged, or rejecting may lead to an insecure attachment and a view of the self as incompetent, other people as threatening or unresponsive, and relationships as negative and unpredictable. Negative family experiences may also create an inconsistent emotional and social environment, which makes it difficult for the child to effectively regulate emotions and interpersonal behavior and to cope with stress (Compas et al., 2001).

Cognitive, emotional, and interpersonal problems may lead directly to depression, or they may elicit conflict, rejection by others, and social isolation, which will eventually lead to depression. In other instances, negative beliefs, poor social relationships, and difficulty in

regulating emotions may create a *vulnerability* to develop depression when confronted with life stresses. In any of these scenarios, the child's depression may then interfere with future development by further disrupting interpersonal relationships, damaging existing competencies, producing further difficulties in regulating emotions, creating additional stress, and confirming the child's already negative views about self and others (Hammen et al., 2014).

In the sections that follow, we examine several of these possible interacting causal influences for depression.

Genetic and Family Risk

Twin and other genetic studies suggest a moderate genetic influence on depression in children and adolescents, with heritability estimates ranging from 30% to 45% across studies for males and females (Franic et al., 2010; Lemery & Doelger, 2005). There is consistent evidence that MDD in young people runs in families across generations (Oquendo et al., 2013). In fact, the single best predictor of a child's risk for MDD is a high family incidence for this disorder (Weissman et al., 2005). Children with a parent who suffered from depression as a child are 14 times more likely than controls to become depressed themselves *before the age of 13* (Weissman et al., 1988).

Children of parents with depression have about 3 times the risk of having depression as compared with children of parents with no psychiatric disorders

(Weissman et al., 2006). The child's risk for depression is even higher when both parents have a mood disorder. Children of depressed parents also have an earlier age at onset for their depression (by about 3 years of age) and are more likely to show an onset before puberty than children of nondepressed parents (Weissman et al., 1997). This is a significant factor because a family history of depression is most likely associated with recurrence of depression and a continuation of depression into adulthood for children with an onset of depression before puberty (Wickramaratne, Greenwald, & Weissman, 2000). In addition to depression and other mood disorders, children of depressed parents also display a variety of other emotional and behavioral disturbances, including anxiety, conduct problems, and substance-use disorders (Batten et al., 2012; Oquendo et al., 2013).

The lifetime prevalence of depression in mothers of children with depression is also high, about 50% to 75% (Kovacs, 1997). A family history of depression is also greater in first-degree relatives of children with depression than in children without depression (Wickramaratne et al., 2000). Although depression in young people is a family disorder, the extent to which transmission in families is genetic, psychosocial, or, most likely, both is not yet known. Causal influences may also differ with development, with support for a greater role for environmental influences for depression during childhood in contrast to a greater genetic influence during adolescence (Scourfield et al., 2003).

Studies into possible genetic markers for early-onset depressive disorders have implicated regions on several chromosomes. However, findings generally suggest that no specific region makes a large contribution to the risk of MDD and that multiple regions are involved (Holmans et al., 2007). Studies of specific genes have focused primarily on those involved in the synthesis, release, and reuptake of the neurotransmitter serotonin and to a lesser extent on other genes, such as brain-derived neurotrophic factor (BDNF), that have been implicated in brain plasticity and response to stress (Chen, Li, & McGue, 2013; Levinson, 2006).

In general, family and twin studies and specific gene studies suggest that a vulnerability to negative affect may be inherited and that certain environmental stressors may be required for these vulnerabilities to result in depression (Eley & Stevenson, 2000; Rice, Harold, & Thapar, 2003). Support for gene–environment (G×E) interactions comes from several studies. One 3-year longitudinal study found that the effects of family conflict on depressive symptoms were greater for children and adolescents at genetic risk for depression (Rice et al., 2006). A second study found that individuals with variants in the serotonin transporter gene displayed more depressive symptoms, diagnosable depression, and suicidality in relation to stressful life events than those who did not (Caspi et al., 2003). Research has also found that youths with variants in the serotonin transporter gene who experienced more stressors as compared with the typical level displayed increases in depressive but not anxious symptoms over time, suggesting a G×E interaction specific to depression (Hankin et al., 2011). Another study found a higher risk for depression in children who were maltreated, but only in children with variants in both the BDNF and serotonin transporter genes. Importantly, social support was also found to ameliorate the child's genetic risk for depression (Kaufman et al., 2006). Finally, other genes (such as COMT) have been found to reduce the risk for depressive symptoms in children exposed to severe psychosocial deprivation as a result of being raised in an institution from a young age (Drury et al., 2010).

The findings that specific genes may increase or decrease sensitivity to stress through their impact on the brain's emotional and arousal systems and, by doing

"Son, it's important to remember that it's O.K. to be depressed."

<Caption and credit info to come>

so, heighten or reduce the child's risk for depression are fascinating (Bradley et al., 2008; Gatt et al., 2010). However, it is important to note that there have been few studies with children and that results have been inconsistent (e.g., Karg et al., 2011; Risch et al., 2009). Thus, findings in this area, particularly those for the serotonin transporter gene (Culverhouse et al., 2013), must be viewed cautiously until they can be confirmed in studies that consider how multiple genes interact with multiple sources of environmental adversity in youngsters with and without depression (Fergusson et al., 2011). Findings from some studies in animals have also suggested that epigenetic processes known to cause stable and lasting changes in gene function may be involved in depression, although further studies will be needed to extend these findings to human depression (Mahgoub & Monteggia, 2013).

Neurobiological Influences

Although we cannot point to one part of the brain that causes a young person to become depressed, abnormalities in the structure and function of several brain regions have been implicated. Most studies of young people with depression have focused on neural systems that regulate emotional functions such as neuroendocrine stress responses, autonomic activity, and reward sensitivity. Brain scan studies have identified multiple abnormalities in the structure and function of the amygdala, cingulate and prefrontal cortex, and related limbic and striatal brain areas (Miller, 2007). For example, the amygdala, hippocampus, and thalamus have been found to have smaller volumes in adolescents and adults with depressive disorders. Interestingly, maternal depression during pregnancy is related to the microstructure of the right amygdala of newborn infants (Rifkin-Graboi et al., 2013). Smaller volumes of several of the aforementioned brain structures in infants as young 6 weeks of age have been associated with higher levels of internalizing behaviors at 18 and 36 months of age (Herba et al., 2010). These findings suggest a possible biological vulnerability for the development of internalizing problems that may be present early in life. Studies have also identified cortical thinning in the right hemispheres of children and adults with or at risk for depression based on family history (Fallucca et al., 2011; Peterson et al., 2009). Cortical thinning in the right hemisphere might produce disturbances in arousal, attention, and memory for social stimuli that predispose the individual to developing a depressive disorder.

In general, brain activity has been found to be less active than normal in regions of the brain associated with attention, executive functions, and sensory processes, but more active than normal in regions

involved in recognizing and regulating emotions, mediating stress responses, and learning and recalling emotion-arousing memories (Ho et al., 2013; Sylvester et al., 2013; Yurgelun-Todd, Sava, & Dahlgren, 2007). For example, the amygdala may overstimulate brain structures involved in forming certain types of memories, perhaps accounting for the tendency of depressed youngsters to ruminate on past negative life events. Overactivity of the amygdala may also affect the recognition and consolidation of social stimuli (e.g., faces, tone of voice) from a very early age so that ordinary interpersonal events are seen or recalled as aversive or emotionally arousing (Gaffrey et al., 2011; Lau et al., 2009; Monk et al., 2008). Consistent with this hypothesis, one study found elevated amygdala activity during face processing in 4- to 6-year-old children with depression, which was also related to parent-reported child emotion dysregulation and negative affect (Gaffrey et al., 2013) (see ● Figure 10.4). Neuroimaging studies of youngsters with MDD have also identified disruptions in neural activity in areas of the brain associated with decision making about future rewards and responses to rewarding outcomes (Forbes et al., 2006).

The hippocampus, one of the brain's memory centers, has also been implicated in depression. Parts of the hippocampus are involved in recognizing the environmental contexts for reward or danger, including sensitivity to stress. Brain-scan studies have found that individual variations in hippocampal volume interact with family stress to prospectively predict differences in depressive symptoms in adolescent girls over a period of 2.5 years (Whittle et al., 2011). Because of

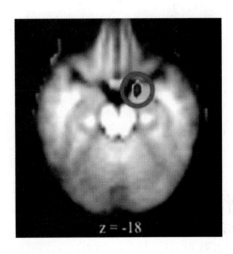

● **FIGURE 10.4** | Brain scans of preschoolers with depression revealed elevated activity in the amygdala (the small area in the red circle) during face processing when compared with scans of young children exhibiting no signs of depression.

Washington University School of Medicine

variants in the hippocampus, individuals with depression may experience a constant state of anxiety and have difficulty recognizing situations that are safe (Davidson, Pizzagalli, & Nitschke, 2002). Studies of other brain regions have found that healthy adolescents who respond to peer rejection with greater activation of the anterior cingulate cortex are more likely to show an increase in depressive symptoms over the following year (Masten et al., 2011). These findings suggest that activity in brain regions involved in affective processing of socioemotional stimuli may provide a possible neurobiological marker for predicting healthy youngsters' future risk for depression.

Other studies into the neurobiological correlates of depression in young people have focused on hypothalamic–pituitary–adrenal (HPA)-axis dysregulation; sleep abnormalities suggestive of reduced neuroplasticity; variants in BDNF, which is involved in nerve growth and development; and the brain neurotransmitters serotonin, dopamine, and norepinephrine, which are widely spread throughout brain circuits thought to underlie mood disorders (Miller, 2007). Although findings related to these neurobiological correlates are suggestive, keep in mind that studies of children are few in number, and the findings are far less consistent than those for adults (Kaufman et al., 2001).

HPA-axis dysregulation is evidenced by abnormal cortisol responses in children and adolescents with depression, including higher baseline levels and atypical or overactive responses to stressors (Lopez-Duran, Kovacs, & George, 2009). HPA-axis and other neurobiological findings have led to a strong interest in the impact of early exposure to stress on later negative moods. Mounting evidence suggests that early adversity (e.g., prenatal stress, harsh or neglectful parenting) may produce HPA-axis abnormalities (e.g., alterations in corticotropin-releasing hormone [CRH] circuits), which sensitize the child to later stress, thus increasing the risk for developing depression (Heim & Nemeroff, 2001; Huizink, Mulder, & Buitelaar, 2004).

Infants of depressed mothers show higher levels of salivary cortisol (the stress hormone) and less relative left frontal lobe electrical activity than infants of mothers without depression (Dawson et al., 1997). Like higher levels of cortisol, decreased relative left frontal lobe activity may be a vulnerability factor for negative emotional states and later onset of depression (Nusslock et al., 2011; Forbes et al., 2008), although not all studies support this finding (e.g., Shankman et al., 2011). Nevertheless, research suggests that interactions between depressed mothers and their infants may produce biochemical and neurological changes that form and perpetuate a lasting basis for depressive disorder (Cytryn & McKnew, 1996; Post et al., 1996).

In summary, findings from studies of neurobiological correlates suggest that youngsters with depression may have a heightened sensitivity to stress. Repeated neuroendocrine activation related to stress might increase youngsters' susceptibility to chronic depressive symptoms, which in turn may lead to further extreme biological activation and psychosocial stress. Neurobiological findings over a wide age range of children are suggestive of widespread abnormalities in executive, affective, and motor networks of the brain, and in brain areas supporting emotional regulation (Ho et al., 2013). However, further research will be needed to clarify the specific neural circuits underlying depression in young people. The characteristics, severity, course, and outcome of a depressive episode may depend on the extent to which different neural circuits and processes are involved in response to environment demands and on when during development these networks are formed (Gabbay et al., 2013; Goodyer, 2008).

Family Influences

"I was always able to explain away my daughter's symptoms," says the mother of a 12-year-old. *"When she was 10 and fought with me about everything, I just wrote it off as preadolescent hissy fits. When she dropped out of gymnastics—which had been her raison d'être—and started losing weight, I told myself she was just searching for a new identity. But when her best friend came to me and told me that my daughter was talking about suicide, I was forced to face the truth. I keep blaming myself. What did I do to cause this depression? What could I have done to prevent it?"*

—From "Childhood Depression," by K. Levine, pp. 42–45, *Parents,* October 1995.

Family influences play an important role in the development, onset, maintenance, and course of depression in young people (Schwartz et al., 2013; Restifo & Bögels, 2009). One approach to examining these influences looks at families of children and adolescents with depression; the second approach considers families in which parents, particularly mothers, are depressed.

When Children Are Depressed

Families of children with depression display more critical and punitive behavior toward their depressed child than toward other children in the family. As compared with families of youngsters without depression, these families display more anger and conflict, greater use of control, poorer communication, more overinvolvement, and less warmth and support (Sheeber et al., 2007; Stein et al., 2000). They often experience high levels of stress, disorganization, marital discord, and a lack of social support (Messer & Gross, 1995; Slavin & Rainer, 1990). Youngsters with depression describe their families as less cohesive and more disengaged than do youngsters without depression (Kashani et al., 1995).

Research points strongly to the link between childhood depression and family dysfunction. One longitudinal study found that less support and more conflict in the family were associated with more depressive symptoms in adolescents both concurrently and prospectively over a 1-year period. In contrast, more depressive symptoms did not predict a worsening of family relationships over the same time period. Thus, family problems precede and may be directly related to the development of depressive symptoms (Sheeber et al., 1997).

When Parents Are Depressed

To mother appropriately requires the action of systems that regulate sensation, perception, affect, reward, executive function, motor output and learning. When a mother is at risk to engage in less than optimal mothering, such as when she is depressed … the function of many or all of maternal and related systems may be affected.

—Barrett & Fleming, 2011, p. 368

MRS. D.

Not Up to Mothering

Mrs. D. is depressed and has been helpless and needy for most of her 5-year-old daughter Maria's life. She moves ever so slowly to prepare breakfast for Maria and herself. Wringing her hands, she pays little attention to events around her. Maria has been tugging at her mother for some time, apparently wanting food. Mrs. D. mumbles something, sobs continuously, and wipes tears from her cheek as she moves between the cupboard and kitchen table. Maria persists in trying to gain her mother's attention, and finally Mrs. D. hugs her and strokes her hair. At first Maria pulls back; then she snuggles against her mother's legs. Finally, Mrs. D. fills a bowl with cereal, and she and Maria sit down to eat in total silence, during which Mrs. D. looks sadly at her daughter. Deep bouts of depression periodically incapacitate Mrs. D., and any problem that Maria has sends her to bed. Mostly, Maria is left on her own to handle problems.

Adapted from Radke-Yarrow & Zahn-Waxler, 1990.

Depression interferes with a parent's ability to meet the basic physical and emotional needs of a child, including feeding, bedtime routines, medical care, and safety practices. Mothers who suffer from depression, like Mrs. D.,

also create a child-rearing environment teeming with negative mood, irritability, helplessness, less emotional flexibility, and unpredictable displays of affection. When their children display negative emotions and distress, mothers with a history of depression are less likely to respond supportively with comfort, empathy, or assistance and are more likely to disapprove, dismiss, punish, or ignore their child's negative emotions (Silk et al., 2011). Depressed mothers also display less energy in stimulating play, less consistent discipline, less involvement, poor communication, lack of affection, and more criticism and resentment of their children than mothers without depression (Goodman, 2007). High levels of marital conflict, family discord, and stress may also be present in the home when a parent is depressed (Hammen, 2002). Critically, this type of negative family environment in combination with a child's genetic predispositions can adversely affect the development of stress regulatory systems and predispose the child to a lifetime of depressive illness and other negative health outcomes (Taylor, Way, & Seeman, 2011).

Maternal depressions during and shortly after pregnancy have been found to be independent risk factors for major depression in the offspring at age 18 years (O'Connor, Monk, & Fitelson, 2014; Pearson et al., 2013). The first year of a child's life seems to be a particularly sensitive period for the effects of maternal depression on the child's later behavior and other adverse outcomes (Bagner et al., 2011). Depressed mothers may differ from one another in their styles of interaction; some are more intrusive and others are more withdrawn. These differences are important because they may be associated with different child outcomes. For example, children of depressed mothers with an intrusive maternal style display avoidance and "tuning out," whereas children of depressed mothers with a withdrawn maternal style display heightened

Chris Rout / Alamy

Maternal depression interferes with the mother's ability to meet the needs of her children sociability toward strangers (Hart, Jones, & Field, 2003). Thus, the offspring of mothers with depression attempt to cope with the unpredictability of their environment in different ways, which are often maladaptive and show reactions ranging from aggressive behavior to withdrawal, failure to thrive, school refusal, depression, and even suicidal behavior (Goodman & Tully, 2008). Like Maria, they must take care of themselves and learn how to handle their own problems.

It is not surprising that children of depressed mothers show cognitive deficits, emotional delays, separation difficulties, insecure attachments, and less positive affect during their development (Olino et al., 2011). These children also display early signs of a cognitive vulnerability to depression. They tend to be self-critical, display a negative attributional style, and have a lower self-concept. They also have difficulties regulating their emotions and experience decreased social acceptance as young as age 5 (Dagne & Snyder, 2011; Maughan et al., 2007). As a result of these disturbances in emotion regulation, the children are ill equipped to cope effectively with stressful events, which subsequently places them at risk for higher levels of depression, lower functioning across multiple domains, and lower perceived competence (Garber & Cole, 2010; Goodman et al., 2011). Given the emotion-regulation disturbances seen in both depressed mothers and their children, it is not surprising that by adolescence or earlier, maternal depression is associated with greater *mutual* engagement in negative affect during parent–child interactions, rather than solely reflecting the mothers' own negativity (Connell et al., 2011).

Follow-up studies of these children confirm the risks associated with growing up in a family with a depressed parent. Over a 10-year period, children of depressed parents had not only increased rates of depression, particularly before puberty, but also higher rates of phobias, panic disorder, and alcohol dependence (Weissman et al., 1997). As compared with controls, offspring of depressed parents received more outpatient treatment over 10 years and had poorer overall functioning in work, family, and marital relationships. In terms of health-care use, children of depressed parents have a higher rate of medically attended physical injuries in the home, emergency and sick visits, and inpatient and specialty-service use and a lower rate of well-child care visits (Phelan et al., 2008; Sills et al., 2007). The findings from follow-up studies are sobering in documenting the serious long-term negative outcomes and impairments in children whose parents suffer from depression (Weissman et al., 2006).

Several issues regarding the relationship between maternal depression, child depression, and family factors need to be considered. First, the kinds of family difficulties we have described are related to many other child disorders, and they may not be specific to depression. Second, it is difficult to know whether family problems are the result of one or more co-occurring conditions, such as child conduct problems, or maternal anxiety disorder or antisocial behavior, rather than depression. It is generally found that, although statistically significant, severity of maternal depression by itself accounts for only a small amount of the variance in child outcomes, indicating that other risk factors will also need to be considered (Goodman, 2014). Third, most studies are correlational, making it impossible to determine the direction of influence. An adverse family environment can lead to child depression, but child depression may also evoke negative and critical reactions from family members and produce distress in others. Fourth, another factor, such as genetic risk, may account for both depression and family disturbances. Fifth, protective factors in the mother or child may reduce the risk of negative child outcomes. For example, one study reported that the presence of a specific maternal genotype markedly reduced the impact of maternal depression on child psychopathology (Apter-Levy et al., 2013). Some support exists for all these mechanisms of family influence on child depression.

Finally, a shortcoming of existing research has been the relative lack of attention to fathers with depression. A steadily growing number of studies indicate that paternal depression has significant but small effects on parenting, with depressed fathers showing less positive and more negative parenting behaviors than those who are not depressed (Wilson & Durbin, 2010). However, few studies have examined paternal behavior in relation to child outcomes. Although internalizing and externalizing problems in children are more strongly associated with depression in mothers as compared with depression in fathers, depression in fathers still may play an important moderating role—for example, through its impact on the marital relationship (Connell & Goodman, 2002; Kane & Garber, 2004).

The high frequency of maternal depression combined with the numerous associated developmental, health, and behavioral problems in children of depressed mothers creates a pressing need for effective treatments for depressed mothers and their children (Wachs, Black, & Engle, 2009). Importantly, some studies have found that reductions in parents' depressive symptoms with treatment can lead to both immediate and longer-term decreases in their children's problem behaviors and symptoms and to favorable changes in their child's global functioning (Wickramaratne et al., 2011). Regulated early child-care services may also help to buffer the negative effects of maternal depression on children's internalizing problems (Herba et al., 2013).

Stressful Life Events

Depression is associated with both severe and nonsevere stressful life events (Rudolph et al., 2006). Severely stressful events may include a move to a new neighborhood, a change of schools, a serious accident or family illness, an extreme lack of family resources, a violent family environment, or parental conflict or divorce (Gilman et al., 2003; Goodyer et al., 1997). At times, nonsevere stressful events, or "daily hassles," such as a poor grade on a test, an argument with a parent, criticism from a teacher, a fight with a boyfriend, or a broken date, may also result in depression. Relative to nondepressed youngsters, those who become depressed experience significantly more severe and nonsevere stressful life events in the year preceding their depression—especially events related to romantic relationships, education, relationships with friends or parents, work, and health (Birmaher et al., 1996).

Triggers for depression often involve interpersonal stress or actual or perceived personal losses, such as the death of a loved one, abandonment, rejection, or a threat to one's self-esteem (Eley & Stevenson, 2000; Goodyer, 1999). For example, a recent relationship break-up seems to be an especially significant predictor for first versus later episodes of major depression during adolescence (Monroe, Rohde, Seeley, & Lewinsohn, 1999). Sadness and depression following loss are common. In children 6 to 17 years of age who had recently suffered the most horrible loss possible—the loss of a parent—all experienced sadness, grief, and other symptoms (Cerel et al., 2006). Thirty percent of adolescents who had lost a friend or peer through suicide developed a depressive disorder within 6 months after the loss (Brent et al., 1992). Yet depressive disorder is not an inevitable outcome to personal losses—most children who experience the loss of a parent or friend show far fewer depressive symptoms than children who are clinically depressed, and they do not develop major depression (Cerel et al., 2006).

Emotion Regulation

Emotion regulation refers to the processes by which emotional arousal is redirected, controlled, or modified to facilitate adaptive functioning and the balance maintained among positive, negative, and neutral mood states (Cole & Hall, 2008). Youngsters demonstrate wide differences in regulating their emotions and managing their negative mood states (Keenan, 2000). For example, if a favorite playmate cannot be found, one child may cry and cannot be comforted; another may cry for a short time and then find someone else to play with; and another child may look to an adult for comfort. Children's strategies for self-regulation play a crucial role in overcoming, maintaining, or preventing negative emotional states. As we have discussed, young children who experience prolonged periods of emotional distress and sadness, or who are exposed to maternal negative moods, may have problems regulating negative emotional states and may be prone to the development of depression (Dagne & Snyder, 2011; Durbin & Shafir, 2008).

A variety of skills are necessary to manage one's own emotions. These include recognizing changes in emotion, accurately interpreting the conditions that led to mood change, setting goals to change one's mood, and implementing effective coping responses. Youngsters with depression may show deficits in one or more of these regulatory skills and, as a result, have difficulty overcoming their negative moods (Sheeber et al., 2000; Yap et al., 2011). They may use avoidance or negative behavior to regulate their distress, rather than more problem-focused and adaptive coping strategies. Since emotion regulation encompasses neurobiological regulatory processes, acquired behavioral and cognitive strategies, and external resources for coping, depression may result from difficulties in any one or more of these areas (Cole & Hall, 2008).

Section Summary

Causes of Depression

- Depression is likely a final common pathway for interacting influences that predispose a child to develop the disorder.

- Family and twin studies and specific gene studies suggest that what may be inherited is a vulnerability to depression and anxiety and that certain environmental stressors may be required to express these disorders.

- Youngsters with depression may experience heightened reactions to stress that increase their vulnerability to depression. Studies of neurobiological correlates have focused on limbic and prefrontal neural circuits; the HPA axis; sleep abnormalities; growth hormone; variants in

(continues)

Section Summary (continued)

BDNF, which is involved in nerve growth and development; and the brain neurotransmitters serotonin, dopamine, and norepinephrine.

- Families of children with depression display anger and conflict, greater use of control, less effective communication, more overinvolvement, and less warmth and support than families of children who are not depressed.

- Children of depressed parents experience increased rates of depression before puberty; higher rates of phobias, panic disorder, and alcohol dependence as adolescents and adults; and other negative health outcomes.

- Depression is associated with both severe stressful life events, such as a move to a new neighborhood, and less severe stressful events or daily hassles, such as criticism from a teacher or an argument with a boyfriend.

- Young children who experience prolonged periods of emotional distress and sadness may have problems in regulating their negative emotional states and may be prone to the development of depression.

TREATMENT OF DEPRESSION

LEETA

Feeling Better

Leeta, age 16, sat slumped in her chair. Disheveled and distracted, she answered questions in a vague and unfocused manner. She was admitted to the hospital after she slit her wrists with a knife; she had become despondent, irritable, and out of control at home. Leeta's thoughts and reasoning were distorted. She expressed a pervasive sense of hopelessness and was certain that she would remain in hospitals for the rest of her life.

Fortunately, this was not the case. She became involved in cognitive–behavioral therapy that focused on accurate reasoning, a more positive self-image, and ways to lessen family turmoil and was also treated with antidepressant medication. One year later, Leeta entered our office for a follow-up interview with energy and excitement. "I never thought that I would feel like hanging out with friends and doing things again. It's not that I don't get sad once in a while, but it doesn't take over my whole life."

Adapted from Oster & Montgomery, 1995.

Many potentially effective psychosocial and psychopharmacological treatments are available to treat youngsters with depression (Brent, Poling, & Goldstein, 2011; David-Ferdon & Kaslow, 2008; Maalouf & Brent, 2012). Despite this availability, less than half of children with depression receive help for their problem (Olfson et al., 2003). Rates of treatment vary by racial/ethnic background, being highest for non-Hispanic white youths (40%) and lowest for Asian youths (19%). About one-third of African American and Hispanic youths receive treatment for their depression (Cummings & Druss, 2011). In one study of adolescents who killed themselves, most of whom had a depressive disorder, only 7% had been in treatment prior to their suicide (Brent et al., 1988). The high comorbidity, associated deficits, and recurrence of depression in young people require a combination of treatments, with an emphasis on eliminating depressive symptoms, maintaining positive outcomes, and preventing relapse (AACAP, 2007d; Cheung et al., 2007).

Cognitive–behavioral therapy (CBT), the treatment used with Leeta, has shown the most success in treating children and adolescents with depression (Watanabe et al., 2007). In addition, Interpersonal Psychotherapy for Adolescent Depression (IPT-A), which focuses on improving interpersonal functioning by enhancing communication skills in significant relationships, has also proven to be an effective treatment (Mufson et al., 2004). CBT and IPT-A are also more efficacious for treating depression than other forms of therapy (e.g., family therapy or nondirective supportive therapy) (David-Ferdon & Kaslow, 2008).

With regard to psychopharmacological treatment, tricyclic antidepressants have not proven to be nearly as effective for depressed young people as for depressed adults (Papanikolaou et al., 2006). In contrast, new-generation antidepressants, especially the selective serotonin reuptake inhibitors (SSRIs), have demonstrated moderate efficacy in controlled studies with young people (Fombonne & Zinck, 2008). However, concerns have been raised about their effectiveness, overuse, and possible side effects, which we discuss later in this section. In addition to CBT, IPT-A, and medications, many variations in these treatments (e.g., individual versus group format, increasing amounts of parental involvement, combined treatments, computer-based treatments, and online treatments) are available. Other treatments that emphasize self-control, social support, family relationships, and increasing social and academic functioning, have also been used with varying degrees of success (David-Ferdon & Kaslow, 2008). Screening for and treating maternal depression may also benefit the child's response to his or her own treatment and help the mother to be a more effective participant in her child's treatment (Kovacs & Yaroslavsky, 2014). To date, studies have reported some benefits for older depressed children whose mothers were treated for depression, but short-term or no benefits for infants and toddlers whose mothers received treatment. These findings suggest that direct treatment of very young children with depression may be needed to sustain developmental changes (Luby, 2013).

An early onset of depression places youngsters at greater risk for experiencing multiple episodes of major depression throughout their lives. Therefore, it is critical that treatment begin as soon as possible; very early and aggressive intervention is warranted to reduce the length of a depressive episode, reduce the likelihood of future episodes, minimize associated impairments in functioning, and reduce the risk of suicide. An overview of the main treatments for youngsters with depression is presented in Table 10.3.

Psychosocial Interventions

Most psychosocial interventions for depression in young people use an integrated approach derived from two traditions—behavior therapy and cognitive therapy. These two approaches for depression were originally developed with adults, but have since been adapted and extensively applied with children and adolescents.

Behavior therapy maintains that depression results from and is sustained by a lack of reinforcement due to a restricted range of potential reinforcers, few available reinforcers, or inadequate skills for obtaining rewards (Lewinsohn, 1974). Consequently, the treatment focuses on increasing pleasurable activities and events and providing the youngster with the skills needed to obtain more reinforcement. Interventions such as social skills training teach children assertiveness, communication, how to accept and give feedback, social problem solving, and conflict resolution skills in order to increase positive social interactions. Strategies such as daily monitoring, structuring activities, and scheduling activities are used to help youngsters with depression become more active, engage in rewarding experiences, and solve problems (McCauley et al., 2011).

Cognitive therapy teaches youngsters with depression to identify, challenge, and modify negative thought processes such as misattributions, negative self-monitoring, short-term focus, excessively high performance standards, and a failure to self-reinforce. They are taught to identify and eliminate negative thoughts, such as "It's my fault," or "What's the point?" and taught to replace them with positive thoughts, such as "She really likes me," or "I'm an interesting person." A child who has been rejected by a friend might be encouraged to think, "She was in a bad mood," rather than "She hates me." When youngsters are presented with specific situations and examples of irrational negative thinking, they are taught to substitute alternative logical explanations that are more positive. For example:

▸ SITUATION: Two girls, Diana and Colleen, both ask friends to get together with them after school. Both girls' friends say they can't because they have too much homework to do.

▸ IRRATIONAL THINKING: Diana feels rejected and thinks, "Because my friend won't get together with me, she doesn't like me, and she'll never want to do anything with me again."

▸ RATIONAL THINKING: In contrast, Colleen thinks, "Well, my friend is busy today, but we can get together some other time. She's still my best friend."

TABLE 10.3 | **Treatments for Youngsters with Depression**

Behavior Therapy	Aims to increase behaviors that elicit positive reinforcement and to reduce punishment from the environment. May involve teaching social and other coping skills, and using anxiety management and relaxation training.
Cognitive Therapy	Focuses on helping the youngster with depression become more aware of pessimistic and negative thoughts, depressogenic beliefs and biases, and causal attributions of self-blame for failure. Once these self-defeating thought patterns are recognized, the child is taught to change from a negative, pessimistic view to a more positive, optimistic one.
Cognitive–Behavioral Therapy (CBT)	The most common form of psychosocial intervention. Combines elements of behavioral and cognitive therapies in an integrated approach. Attribution retraining may also be used to challenge the youngster's pessimistic beliefs.
Interpersonal Psychotherapy for Adolescent Depression (ITP-A)	Explores family and interpersonal interactions that maintain depression. Family sessions are supplemented with individual sessions in which youngsters with depression are encouraged to understand their own negative cognitive style and the effects of their depression on others and to increase pleasant activities with family members and peers (Mufson, et al., 2004).
Medication	Treats mood disturbances and other symptoms of depression using antidepressants, especially selective serotonin reuptake inhibitors (SSRIs).

In practice, behavior therapy and cognitive therapy are integrated into a unified cognitive behavior therapy (CBT) approach, in which more adaptive cognitions are hypothesized to lead to more adaptive behavior and vice versa. Examples of these integrated CBT approaches for children and adolescents follow.

Primary and Secondary Control Enhancement Training (PASCET)

John Weisz and his colleagues (2003) have developed a 15-session, individualized CBT-based program for youngsters 8 to 15 years of age who have depression. In treatment sessions and in take-home assignments, youngsters learn and practice two types of coping skills:

▸ *Primary control skills* (ACT skills) for changing objective events in their lives (e.g., changing the activities they engage in, learning to relax) to conform with their wishes.

▸ *Secondary control skills* (THINK skills) for altering the subjective impact of stressful life events (e.g., altering their negative thoughts and feelings).

The focus of the PASCET program is to help the child change conditions that are changeable and to change the subjective impact of those that are not. Parents are also involved in the program and are encouraged to support their children in using these coping skills. PASCET is an excellent example of a program that has evolved since its initial use in the schools to reduce depressive symptoms. It is now being implemented and evaluated in community mental health clinics with youngsters who have been referred for depression (Bearman & Weisz, 2009). A current and ongoing priority for PASCET and similar CBT programs is on identifying the treatment components needed to effectively deploy them in intervention settings where youngsters with depression are typically referred for help and treated by clinical practitioners (Bearman et al., 2010; Weisz et al., 2013).

The ACTION Program

Kevin Stark and his colleagues (2012) have developed a comprehensive CBT approach for children with depression. The primary components of this treatment are appropriate for children and adolescents and for boys as well as girls. However, the current format is designed to be gender-sensitive, with treatment activities, skills emphasized, and a focus on interpersonal relationships specific to girls in the 9- to 13-year age range (Stark et al., 2008). Like the PASCET program, ACTION uses a holistic approach that involves both child and parents. The ACTION acronym is used to nourish the idea that youngsters can have an impact on their moods, and it is presented to them as follows (Stark & Kendall, 1996, p. 14):

A = Always find something to do to feel better.
C = Catch the positive.
T = Think about it as a problem to be solved.
I = Inspect the situation.
O = Open yourself to the positive.
N = Never get stuck in the negative muck.

Multiple treatment procedures are used to reduce the child's mood disturbances, behavioral deficits, and cognitive symptoms:

▸ *Dysphoria, anger, anhedonia,* and *excessive anxiety* are treated by educating the child about the relation between mood, thinking, and behavior, and by using anger management procedures, scheduling pleasant activities, and relaxation training.

▸ *Interpersonal deficits* are treated using social skills training.

▸ *Cognitive distortions* and *negative and self-critical thinking* are addressed by using cognitive-restructuring procedures and training in effective problem-solving and self-control procedures.

Interventions can be carried out in both individual and group formats, and they make use of a workbook that includes a variety of exercises such as this one:

▸ SITUATION: You accidentally drop your books … a group of classmates are talking and laughing at the other side of the room.

▸ NEGATIVE THINKING: Now look at what I've done. They must think I'm a complete idiot.

▸ COPING RESPONSE: No, they're probably laughing at something else. Besides, I know them. They're not like that. It's not like I'm the first person ever to drop her books. It's really no big deal.

Interventions with parents are used to facilitate the child's use of effective coping strategies outside of treatment and to change events that may contribute to and prolong the child's problems. Since negative parent–child interactions may result in negative thinking, changing maladaptive patterns within the family is an important feature of the ACTION program. Several methods are used to change parental and family cognitions and behavior, including teaching parents effective forms of discipline, ways to manage anger, and ways to change negative thinking. Interventions with the entire family teach negotiation and conflict-resolution skills, recreational planning, and effective problem solving and family communication (Stark et al., 2012). ACTION is a promising intervention built on a sound theoretical and research base. The program continues to be evaluated as a comprehensive treatment package for depression (Stark et al., 2010).

Adolescent Coping with Depression Program (CWD-A)

One of the most well-established and comprehensive CBT programs for the treatment of depression in adolescents is the Adolescent Coping with Depression Program (CWD-A) (Clarke, Lewinsohn, & Hops, 2001). CWD-A is a nonstigmatizing psychoeducational approach that emphasizes skills training to promote adolescents' control over their moods and enhancement of their ability to cope with problematic situations. Treatment is provided in 16 two-hour sessions over an 8-week period for groups of up to 10 adolescents ages 13 to 18. Adolescents use a workbook that includes brief readings, short quizzes, structured learning tasks, and forms for homework assignments for each session. The core treatment sessions with adolescents involve group activities and role playing. In addition, complementary therapy with the youngsters' parents is carried out to accelerate and support the learning of new skills, and to assist in applying the skills learned in the group to everyday life situations. Periodic "booster sessions" help to maintain the skills taught during treatment (Clarke & DeBar, 2010).

Initially, adolescents learn that depression can have many causes, including inherited tendencies, stress, and excessive negative thinking. Relaxation training is then used to quickly provide a successful experience and some immediate relief. Subsequent sessions include the following components (Clarke & DeBar, 2010):

▸ Self-change skills, such as self-monitoring of mood and behavior, and ways to establish realistic goals, are taught.

▸ Pleasurable activities and opportunities for reinforcement are increased.

▸ Positive thinking is increased by identifying, challenging, and changing negative cognitions.

▸ Training in social, communication, and problem-solving skills is integrated throughout the program.

▸ Specific skills are taught, such as conversational skills, ways to plan social activities, and ways to make friends.

▸ Goal setting is used to identify short- and long-term life goals and potential barriers to these goals.

▸ Final sessions emphasize integrating the skills learned and making plans for the future.

The CWD-A program and modified versions (e.g., group format, brief treatment protocol) have demonstrated beneficial, albeit moderate and in some cases not long-lasting, treatment and prevention effects in many controlled studies by its developers and others (Cuijpers et al., 2010; Rohde, Stice et al., 2010, 2013). However, as with the other treatments we have discussed, there is a need for further evaluation by independent investigators, extending its use to a wider variety of depressed youngsters, longer-term follow-up studies, and comparisons with other treatments for depression, particularly medication (Clarke & DeBar, 2010).

Interpersonal Psychotherapy for Adolescent Depression (IPT-A)

IPT-A is based on the idea that adolescent depression affects relationships, which in turn affect mood. Thus, treatment focuses on the adolescent's depressive symptoms and the social context in which these symptoms occur (Young & Mufson, 2008). The emphasis in IPT-A is on increasing adolescents' independence and negotiating their interdependence on others by addressing relevant developmental issues such as romantic relationships, separation from parents, and peer relationships. The adolescent takes an active role in identifying a specific problem area (e.g., loss and grief, interpersonal disputes, role transitions, interpersonal deficits), discussing communication and problem-solving techniques for that area, practicing these skills in session, and applying them outside sessions in the context of significant relationships. The treatment is structured around addressing the identified problem areas, and both the therapist and adolescent are expected to play an active role (Mufson, et al., 2004).

IPT-A is designed as a once-weekly, 12-session outpatient program. Treatment is divided into three phases. The *initial phase* (4 sessions) addresses the diagnosis of depression, educates the adolescent and family about depression, introduces the principles of IPT-A and the structure of treatment, identifies an interpersonal problem area, and makes a treatment contract. The *middle phase* (5 sessions) further clarifies the problem, identifies strategies for effectively targeting the problem, and implements interventions to resolve the problem. A number of techniques are used. For example, if an adolescent reports a fight with her boyfriend, she would be asked how this made her feel and whether or not this affected her depressive symptoms. This helps to educate the adolescent about the link between interpersonal events and mood, and makes her feel more comfortable and skilled at identifying and communicating feelings. Other techniques in this phase focus on helping the adolescent to recognize the impact of her communication on others, the feelings generated, and how modifying the communication may impact the outcome of the interaction and the adolescent's associated feelings. Additional techniques involve problem solving in interpersonal situations, role playing both communication and problem-solving skills, and the use of homework to practice these skills between sessions (Young & Mufson, 2008).

The *termination phase* (3 sessions) reviews progress in the identified problem area, links changes in interpersonal functioning and relationships to improved mood and decreased depressive symptoms, and identifies strategies that have been most helpful. It also addresses the importance of continuing to use the learned strategies following treatment, highlights areas that still need improvement, and considers what to do if symptoms of depression return.

IPT-A has been shown to be an effective treatment for adolescent depression in a number of controlled studies in clinic, school, and community settings, using both individual and group formats (Mufson, 2010; Mufson et al., 2012). In an effort to reach more youngsters, IPT-A is also being developed as a preventive intervention ("Teen Talk") for adolescents in grades 7 to 10 who display elevated levels of depressive symptoms. Preliminary findings suggest that IPT-A and Teen Talk may useful approaches to preventing more severe forms of depression and reducing symptoms of anxiety (Young et al., 2012; Young, Mufson, & Davies, 2006).

In concluding our discussion of psychosocial treatments, the good news is that a wide variety of treatments for young people with depression have been shown to be effective for most youths who receive them (March & Vitiello, 2009; TADS Team, 2009). However, nearly half of those who recover, especially girls, have a relapse of their depression (Curry et al., 2011), and effect sizes have been moderate and smaller than those reported for adults (Weisz, McCarty, & Valeri, 2006). Hence, there is a need to explore more effective treatments that build on our growing understanding of childhood depression; reduce the rate of depression relapse or deterioration; personalize treatment to meet the child's cognitive, emotional, and developmental profile; and are likely to be used in clinical practice settings (Brent & Maalouf, 2009; Weisz et al., 2013). There is also a need to study treatments of longer duration and the use of booster sessions following treatment and to evaluate outcomes over longer follow-up periods.

Medications

"I kept hearing about Prozac in the news," says one father, *"and when we finally brought my 9-year-old to a psychiatrist, I thought he could just give her this pill and change our lives. After a year, I can say that things are a bit better. But it took lots of trials with lots of different pills."*

—From "Childhood Depression," by K. Levine, pp. 42–45, *Parents*, October 1995. Reprinted by permission of the author/

Antidepressant medications are commonly used to treat youngsters with depression. An estimated 1.4 million youngsters in the United States received antidepressant medication in 2002 (Vitiello, Zuvekas, & Norquist, 2006), with over 60% of those treated in outpatient settings filling prescriptions for these drugs (Olfson et al., 2014). For many youngsters, antidepressant medications can shorten a depressive episode and return them to the important developmental tasks of childhood and adolescence. As we have noted, although tricyclic antidepressants are effective with adults, they have consistently failed to demonstrate any advantage over placebo in treating depression in young people, and may have some potentially serious cardiovascular side effects (Fombonne & Zinck, 2008). As a result they are no longer regarded as primary drugs for the management of depressive symptoms in young people.

SSRIs have clearly become the first line of antidepressant medication treatment for youngsters with depression, with one national survey reporting that over 90% of prescriptions written for these youngsters were for SSRIs (Olfson et al., 2003). Among the most commonly used SSRIs are fluoxetine (Prozac), sertraline (Zoloft), and citalopram (Celexa). SSRIs achieve their antidepressant effects by blocking the reuptake of serotonin, thereby increasing its availability in the synapse and stimulating the postsynaptic neuron. At present, the only SSRI that is approved by the Food and Drug Administration (FDA) for use with children and adolescents with MDD is fluoxetine.

A number of controlled investigations have demonstrated that some SSRIs are moderately effective in reducing symptoms of depression in children and adolescents. One meta-analysis found that 40% to 60% of children responded to Prozac versus 20% to 35% of those on placebo (Hetrick, McKenzie, & Merry, 2010). Support for the effectiveness of other SSRIs was limited. There was also little evidence that children and adolescents who took SSRIs showed improvement in their school performance, interpersonal relations, or social functioning on a day-to-day basis (Hetrick et al., 2010). Others have argued that research supports the use of SSRIs, that combined treatments using medication and CBT in combination are likely to be the most effective, and that greater treatment effects are obtained for children with more severe depressions (March, 2010).

After they were first marketed in the late 1980s, the use of Prozac and other SSRIs increased dramatically. For example, nearly three-quarters of a million prescriptions for SSRIs for children ages 6 to 18 were written in 1996—an 80% increase in only 2 years (*APA Monitor*, December 1997). However, despite some support for their efficacy, both professional and public concerns have been voiced about their use with children and adolescents. The main concerns are possible serious side effects such as suicidal thoughts and self-harm and a lack of information about the long-term effects of these medications on the developing brain. Related to these concerns and warnings by the FDA, the use of SSRIs with young people has decreased by about 20% in more recent years (Gibbons et al., 2007; Libby et al., 2007). In 2004, the FDA asked all manufacturers of antidepressant medications to include in their labeling a boxed warning (black box) and Patient Education Guide to alert consumers about the increased risk of suicidal thinking and behavior in youngsters treated with these medications. A summary of the main points included in these black box warnings is presented in A Closer Look 10.2.

The FDA warnings were based on a pooling of findings from 24 short-term, placebo-controlled studies of antidepressant trials with more than 4,400 youngsters with MDD and other disorders. The overall findings indicated an increased risk of suicidal thinking or behavior in youngsters with depression (4% on active medication vs. 2% on placebo) (Hammad, Laughren, & Racoosin, 2006). The risk for untreated youths with depression, the long-term effects of medication, and the combination of medication and psychosocial interventions were not evaluated, and there were no completed suicides in any of the studies. In addition, findings regarding increases in suicidality from other studies have been inconsistent (Gibbons et al., 2012). Also inconsistent are findings regarding the use of medications either alone or in combination with psychosocial interventions. Some studies have found a benefit of combined treatment versus medication alone, with an enhancement of the safety of medications when used in combination with CBT (e.g., Treatment of Adolescents with Depression Study [TADS] Team, 2004, 2007), whereas others have not (e.g., Goodyer et al., 2007).

Thus, despite much research, the risks, long-term safety, and benefits associated with the use of antidepressant medications with young people remain uncertain (Moreno et al., 2007a). In light of the potential effectiveness of the psychosocial treatments for depression in youths that we have discussed, careful consideration must be given to determining which youngsters are most or least likely to benefit from antidepressant medication (AACAP, 2007d).

Notwithstanding these concerns, untreated depression has profound long-term consequences, including a high risk for suicide, and there is some evidence that a higher use of antidepressant medications across counties in the United States is associated with lower rates of suicide in young people (Gibbons et al., 2006). Thus, there may be possible risks that go along with not using medications relative to the risks from suicidal ideation and suicide attempts, especially when numerous research and clinical studies indicate that many young people benefit from drug treatment (Bridge et al., 2007).

In the absence of better data regarding drug effects, side effects, and long-term safety of medication use with depressed children, there are currently no easy answers to this dilemma. Some say it is unethical to treat depressed children using medications in light of the potential dangers. Others say that the risks associated with drug treatment are no greater than risks for other treatments and that it is unethical to withhold treatment in light of the known benefits. Given the many social, political, and economic implications surrounding the use of medications to treat depression in young people, we may hear a lot more about this issue for some time to come (e.g., Riddle, 2004).

In concluding our discussion of the treatment of depression, we note that controlled studies of psychological treatments and medication have found that up to 60% of youngsters with depression respond to placebo (Bridge et al., 2007) and about 15% to 30% respond to brief treatment (Goodyer et al., 2007). Thus, in youngsters with mild or brief depression, an absence of suicidality, and minor impairment in functioning, the use of education, support, and case management related to school and family stressors may be effective. However, for those who are more severely depressed, display suicidal ideation and behavior, and show significant impairment in functioning, the specific types of

A CLOSER LOOK 10.2

Summary of Food and Drug Administration (FDA) Black Box Warnings for the Use of Antidepressants with Children and Adolescents

- Youths with MDD are at an increased risk for suicidal thinking or behavior.
- When considering an antidepressant for a child or adolescent, it is important to weigh the increased risk of suicidality with the possible benefits of the medication.
- When starting young people on antidepressants, they must be very closely monitored for worsening of symptoms, suicidality, or unusual changes in behavior.
- Family members must closely observe the youngster for increases in symptoms or worsening of functioning, and immediately communicate any such observations to their provider.
- A statement needs to be included regarding whether the medication is approved for use with children and adolescents.

© Cengage Learning®

off the mark
by Mark Parisi

THAT'S THE WAY, UH, HUH UH, HUH...
I LIKE IT! UH, HUH UH, HUH...

EEYORE WHEN HE REMEMBERS HIS PROZAC

www.offthemark.com

ATLANTIC FEATURE © 1996 MARK PARISI

Atlantic Feature © 1996 Mark Parisi

psychological and pharmacological treatments that we have discussed will likely be needed (AACAP, 2007d; Cheung, Kozloff, & Sacks, 2013).

Prevention

In view of the recurring nature of depression, successful efforts during childhood and adolescence to prevent the onset of depression may reduce a lifelong risk of illness and reduce the use and costs of health care resources (Horowitz & Garber, 2006; Stice et al., 2009).

Early studies of prevention with grade school and high school students with subclinical symptoms of depression found CBT/problem-solving approaches to be effective in reducing depressive symptoms and lowering the risk for developing depression up to 2 years after treatment (Gillham & Reivich, 1999; Shochet et al., 2001). However, not all programs have reported benefits. For example, in a later controlled study, a comprehensive school-based program for adolescents attempted to develop individual resiliency skills and enhance protective factors in the environment. The program failed to produce significant changes in levels of depressive symptoms or risk or protective factors in participating adolescents over the 3 years of the study (Sawyer et al., 2010). These negative results, despite extensive efforts to use evidence-based interventions, highlight some of the challenges in implementing school-based, universal prevention programs. Among

these challenges are the need for effective teacher training over a large and diverse geographical area so that programs are implemented as prescribed, the difficulty in engaging young adolescents in prevention programs, and the amount of time required to implement policy and practice changes at "whole school" levels (Sawyer et al., 2010).

Other large-scale prevention efforts (e.g., *Columbia Teen Screen*) have been directed at the early detection of high school students at risk for depression and suicide to ensure that these students receive help (Shaffer et al., 2004). The importance of school-based screening is highlighted by the finding that although 90% of parents report that they are confident in their ability to tell if their child is thinking about suicide, the parents of only about one-third of teens with mental health problems know that their child has these problems. School-based screening for suicide has had moderate success in identifying students who are at high risk for suicide and other mental health problems, but concerns have been raised regarding the number of youngsters who are falsely identified as being at risk (Scott, Wilcox, et al., 2010).

In recent years, prevention efforts have also focused on providing cognitive–behavioral prevention to adolescents at risk for depression by virtue of having a parent with a history of a depressive disorder. In a randomized controlled study, a cognitive–behavioral prevention program demonstrated sustained effects as compared with a usual-care group in preventing the onset of depressive episodes in at-risk youths over a 3-year period (Beardslee et al., 2013). However, group differences were not found when parents were actively depressed at baseline. Other similar prevention programs have used family cognitive–behavioral interventions with 9- to 15-year-old children of parents with a history of MDD (Compas et al., 2011). Depressed parents and their children are taught a wide array of problem-solving and coping skills, including teaching children ways of coping with their parent's depression. The goals of the program are to educate families about depression, to increase awareness of the impact of stress and depression on functioning, to help families recognize and monitor stress, to facilitate the use of effective ways of coping with stress, and to improve parenting skills. In a randomized controlled study, children who participated in the preventive intervention were compared with those in a comparison group who received written information. Those who received the intervention showed significantly lower rates of MDD over a 2-year period, significantly lower rates of internalizing and externalizing symptoms at 18 months, and significantly lower rates of externalizing symptoms at 24 months. Marginal effects were found for reductions in parents' symptoms of depression at 18 and 24 months but not for episodes of MDD (Compas et al., 2011). Preventive programs like these have the potential to protect unaffected children of depressed parents from developing the disorder and to improve outcomes for children with depression who are currently receiving treatment.

A high priority must be given to the development and continued refinement of identification, early intervention, and prevention efforts for youngsters at risk for depressive disorders (Barrera, Torres, & Munoz, 2007; Farrell & Barrett, 2007). The development of programs for preschool children with depression (Lenze, Pautsch, & Luby, 2011) and online and computer-based interactive programs for use in primary care, school, and other settings are examples of promising new prevention approaches (Gladstone et al., 2014; Spence et al., 2011).

Section Summary

Treatment of Depression

- Cognitive–behavioral therapy and interpersonal psychotherapy have had the most success in treating depression in young people.
- SSRIs have been recommended as the first line of drug treatment for children with depression, but concerns have been raised about their use.
- A high priority needs to be given to programs aimed at preventing depression in young people.

BIPOLAR DISORDER (BP)

In a sense, depression is a view of the world through a dark glass, and mania is that seen through a kaleidoscope—often brilliant but fractured.

—K. R. Jamison (1997)

BEN

Extreme Mood Swings

Ben, age 14, was living in a residential treatment center. He had a history of moodiness, hyped-up activity, sleeplessness, and a sexual preoccupation with the girls in his class—he had even approached his teacher with offers of sexual intimacy. Ben's thoughts raced, his speech was rapid and fragmented, and he had wide mood swings. At the high extreme, Ben rarely slept, and he yelled, sang, and disturbed everyone—charging about the residence day and night with a seemingly endless supply of energy. He felt "absolutely terrific" at these times and thought he could fly. The low extreme found Ben curled up in a ball beneath a stack of blankets, a withdrawn and hopeless young man who expressed feelings of worthlessness and thoughts of suicide. (Based on authors' case material)

Ben displays the essential features of **bipolar disorder (BP)**: a striking period of unusually and persistently elevated, expansive, or irritable mood, accompanied by increased goal-directed activity or energy, and alternating with or accompanied by one or more major depressive episodes. The two mood states associated with the manic phase of BP are elation and a profound sense of well-being (euphoria). However, these feelings can quickly change to anger and hostility if something interferes with the youngster's behavior. Since many youngsters with BP have simultaneous feelings of depression, they are easily reduced to tears. It is at once remarkable and almost inconceivable how a young person with this disorder such as Ben can be so manic, elated, energetic, and wild at one moment; so depressed and immobile the next; and at other times seemingly so normal (Geller & Luby, 1997).

Symptoms of BP in young people were recognized as early as 150 c.e., when the physician Aretaeus of Cappadocia described manic behavior in young men in puberty (Kotsopoulos, 1986). In modern times, BP was generally considered an adult illness, receiving very little attention in children and adolescents (Geller & DelBello, 2003). More recently, there has been upsurge of professional and public interest in children and adolescents with BP as reflected in increasing rates of research, diagnosis, treatment, and media coverage (Fristad & Algorta, 2013; Youngstrom & Algorta, 2014). For example, since 1994, the estimated number of youth outpatient office visits for BP has increased at least 40-fold, with about 90% of the youngsters receiving prescriptions for psychotropic medication during these visits (Moreno et al., 2007b). As we will discuss, along with the increased interest has come considerable controversy—BP in young people is difficult to identify because it occurs infrequently, shows extreme variability of clinical presentation within and across episodes, and overlaps in symptoms with more common childhood disorders such as ADHD and conduct problems (Youngstrom & Algorta, 2014).

Debate continues as to the appropriate criteria for diagnosing BP in children and adolescents (Carlson, 2011). At the center of the controversy is whether BP can be diagnosed in prepubertal children. Some clinicians avoid the use of this label entirely, and instead label young children who display unstable moods with the less stigmatizing categories of ADHD or depression. Others use the label of BP liberally in young children, often based solely on the presence of mood swings, irritability, and aggression, leading to concerns about overdiagnosis. Thus, clinicians presented with identical diagnostic information vary widely in their assessment of BP in children, from 0% risk to 100% risk (Jenkins et al., 2010). A focal point of this debate is whether BP looks the same in young children as in adults. If it does, then mania in children should be diagnosed narrowly, with distinct episodes that are a clear departure from the youngster's usual behavior and functioning, and should have the same symptoms as those for adults (e.g., euphoria, grandiosity). If not, then a broader definition that includes early childhood onset of chronic emotion dysregulation with symptoms of ADHD, ODD, and other comorbidities, as well as severe irritability, extended outbursts of rage, and modified symptoms of mania would be sufficient to make the diagnosis (Carlson & Klein, 2014). How the BP label is used with young children has important implications for treatment, given the few available medications for stabilizing mood in children and the greater risks of using these medications for children than for adults (Ghaemi & Martin, 2007).

Young people who meet DSM-5 diagnostic criteria for BP display significant impairment in functioning, including previous hospitalization, MDD, treatment with medications, and co-occurring disruptive behavior and anxiety disorders. A history of psychotic symptoms and suicidal ideation and suicide attempts are also common (Axelson et al., 2006). They show severe and cyclical mood changes and outbursts. Thus, in its fully developed state, this condition is clearly different from a child's usual behavior (Carlson, 2002). During a manic episode, youths with BP may display intense symptoms, such as irritability and rage. Or they may show silly, giddy, overexcited, overtalkative behavior coupled with expansive, grandiose beliefs (e.g., a teen who feels she has a special connection to God). It is normal for children to pretend to have special powers or abilities, but a youngster with BP, during a manic episode, will actually believe he is the X-Man Wolverine and that he is indestructible and all-powerful. He might believe he can walk on water, control traffic, or jump off buildings without hurting himself—but he does not believe he might kill himself in the process.

Restlessness, agitation, and sleeplessness are also typical of youngsters with BP. Sexual disinhibition (like Ben's propositioning his teacher) may also occur when the youth becomes uncharacteristically preoccupied with sexual themes, sexually touching others, or "talking dirty." Youths with BP may experience unrealistic elevations in self-esteem (believing they are "the chosen one") and vast surges of energy; they may go with little or no sleep for days without feeling tired. They may be able to concentrate for hours on one activity that interests them, such as drawing or becoming engrossed in a mentally demanding fantasy game. At the same time, however, they may be highly distractible, constantly jumping from one thing to another (Geller & Luby, 1997).

The elated mood of youths with mania may (erroneously) give them the appearance of being happy and cheerful. Like Ben, they may say, "I feel absolutely terrific." It is difficult to recognize that a laughing, happy youngster also has a history of misery and distress. For this reason, evaluating a youth's current mood in relation to his or her developmental history is essential, particularly when there is an inconsistency between the child's elated mood and his or her history of trouble at home or school (Youngstrom, 2007).

Current research suggests that BP with an onset prior to age 18 is essentially the same disorder that occurs in adults, although possible differences in long-term outcomes and associated characteristics are not known (Carlson et al., 2004). Although not without problems, the diagnosis of BP can be made in children and adolescents using the same DSM-5 criteria used for adults. There are four primary types of BP: bipolar I disorder; bipolar II disorder; cyclothymic disorder; and other specified bipolar disorder. These different types are related to whether the youngster displays a manic or hypomanic episode. A *manic episode,* which is the hallmark feature of BP, involves a discrete period of a week or more during which the youngster displays an ongoing, pervasive, and unusually elevated or irritable mood and persistently increased goal-directed activity or energy. This episode is accompanied by the types of symptoms we have been describing such as an exaggerated self-esteem, a reduced need for sleep, racing thoughts, rapid and frenzied speech, attention to irrelevant details, increased activity, or overinvolvement in pleasurable but often reckless and risky behaviors. In addition, the youngster does not meet criteria for a depressive episode during the period of mood disturbance and increased energy and activity; the mood disturbance is not due to substance use or abuse or to a medical condition; and the disturbance causes significant impairment in usual activities or requires hospitalization in order to prevent the child or others from harm. A *hypomanic episode* has features that resemble a manic episode in quality but are less intense—the mood disturbance and increased activity or energy are less severe, of shorter duration, and produce less impairment in functioning than a manic episode.

A diagnosis of *bipolar I disorder* requires evidence for a manic episode and one or more major depressive episodes; a *bipolar II disorder* requires a hypomanic episode in combination with one or more major depressive episodes; a *cyclothymic disorder* describes children or adolescents who display numerous and persistent hypomanic and depressive symptoms for a year or more that cause considerable distress and impairment in functioning, but do not meet criteria for a manic episode or for a major depressive disorder

(Van Meter et al., 2013); and an *other specified bipolar disorder* describes individuals who display characteristic symptoms of BP that cause significant functional impairment but do not meet criteria for any of the other types of bipolar disorder. DSM-5 also includes a specifier of "*with mixed features,*" which can be used when a current manic or hypomanic episode includes subthreshold symptoms of depression or dysthymia or when an episode of MDD includes subthreshold symptoms of mania or hypomania.

Atypical symptom presentation makes it difficult to use DSM-5 criteria for BP to diagnose youngsters with mania (Youngstrom, 2007). Changes in mood, psychomotor agitation, and mental excitation are often volatile and erratic rather than persistent. Irritability, belligerence, and mixed manic–depressive features occur more frequently than euphoria. Unlike for adults, developmental limitations and the social environment place constraints on children's reckless behaviors, which typically involve school failure, fighting, dangerous play, and inappropriate sexual conduct. Thus, classic manic symptoms of grandiosity, psychomotor agitation, and reckless behavior must be differentiated from manic symptoms of common childhood disorders, such as ADHD and conduct problems, and from typical childhood behaviors, such as bragging, imaginary play, overactivity, and youthful blunders (American Academy of Child and Adolescent Psychiatry [AACAP], 2007c).

How are some of the more notable symptoms of mania expressed in youngsters with BP? When in a manic state, youngsters show great conviction about the correctness or importance of their ideas. Adolescents with BP may show grand delusions—illogical and strong beliefs that lead to poor judgment and impulsive behavior (Jamison, 1997). For example, they may badger their teachers about how to teach. This badgering may become so intense that teachers contact the parents, pleading with them to ask their children to cease. Youngsters with BP may intentionally fail subjects, acting on their illogical belief that children can choose what to pass or fail because they believe they are not being taught correctly. They may steal expensive items and be unresponsive to efforts by police or parents to explain that their actions are wrong and illegal. Although these youngsters know that stealing is illegal for others, they believe they are above the law. They may believe that they will achieve great fame, for example, as a brain surgeon, even though they are failing all of their classes at school. Similarly, a youngster with BP who is short, clumsy, and lacks any athletic ability may practice basketball with great fervor and strongly believe that he will become the next LeBron James. Another child may feel she has the ability to change the weather at will.

In contrast to youngsters with depression, who cannot fall asleep and may lie in bed for hours fretting and brooding, those with mania show high levels of activity at bedtime, spend very little time in bed, and require very little sleep. A child with mania might spend several hours at bedtime rearranging clothes in a dresser or closet, or an adolescent may wait until his or her parents are asleep and then sneak out of the house to go a party.

For children with mania, their words, thoughts, and actions occur in fast motion. Increased verbal production with puns, word plays, and incessant speech are common. At all ages, children with mania show *pressured speech*—they talk too much and too fast, change topics too quickly, and cannot be interrupted. They also have *racing thoughts* that they may describe in concrete terms—for example, by saying they can't do their schoolwork because their thoughts keep interrupting. In the words of one teen, "I wish I had a switch on my forehead so I could turn off my racing thoughts" (Geller & Luby, 1997). Like an adult with BP, a child with the disorder also shows a *flight of ideas*, which is an illogical jump from one idea to another. For example, in reply to the question, "Do you live in Los Angeles?" the child may reply, "Some people like to swim in the ocean. Do you have a dog?"

For children with mania of all ages, even slight changes in their surroundings can lead to significant distractibility. Heightened psychomotor agitation and goal-directed actions resemble normal activities carried out in excess, with a seemingly endless supply of energy. During a brief period of time, a manic youngster might draw several pictures, read a book, work on the computer, prepare a snack, make multiple phone calls, write a letter, and vacuum the house.

Accepting dares is common for youngsters with BP. In older adolescents, this may appear as a pattern of reckless driving that results in multiple tickets for speeding or driving under the influence. In preadolescents, it may be expressed as grandiose delusions of being able to jump out the window because they believe they can fly. They also may push the limits on usual childhood climbing on things, based on the strong belief that they are above the possibility of danger (Geller & Luby, 1997). In extreme cases, they may experience violent agitation with delusional thinking as well as visual and auditory hallucinations.

Prevalence

Lifetime prevalence estimates of BP in community samples of youths 7 to 21 years of age range from about 0.5% to 2.5% worldwide (Merikangas et al., 2012; Van Meter, Moreira, & Youngstrom, 2011). In light of the complicated presentation of symptoms and the difficulties in making an accurate diagnosis, it is possible that BP in young people is more common and occurs at a younger age than previously thought (Luby & Belden, 2006; Youngstrom, 2007).

The duration of manic symptoms in young people often does not meet the DSM-5's distinct 1-week duration requirement to be a manic episode. In an epidemiological study of 8- to 19-year-olds, it was found that recurrent episodes of mania or hypomania that met the DSM-5 criteria for episode duration were extremely rare (<0.3%), and restricted to 16- to 19-year-olds (Stringaris et al., 2010). Children with BP are also likely to present with rapid cycling episodes (at least four episodes of a mood disturbance over a 1-year period), with about 80% of children showing this course (Geller et al., 1995).

In light of these findings, the most common diagnoses are the milder bipolar II disorder, cyclothymic disorder, and other specified BP rather than bipolar I disorder (Lewinsohn, Klein, & Seeley, 1995). Children with a diagnosis of cyclothymic disorder or other specified BP are quite similar in terms of their current symptom severity and functional impairment to those with bipolar I disorder, suggesting that these disorders are on the same bipolar spectrum (Hafeman et al., 2013). It is of interest to note that studies of community samples have reported a stable rate of BP in young people over the past two decades, which is in contrast to the large increase in BP diagnoses in clinical samples over this period (Youngstrom & Algorta, 2014). This suggests a growing awareness and recognition of BP symptoms rather than an actual increase in rates, similar to what we described in Chapter 6 for increasing rates of ASD diagnoses.

Despite accounts of the onset of mania in children as young as 5 or 6 years old, the incidence of BP prior to puberty is extremely rare, but it increases during adolescence and is nearly as high as it is for adults (Lewinsohn, Klein, & Seeley, 2000). In sharp contrast to the effects of depression, BP affects boys and girls equally. However, symptoms may be expressed differently, with boys showing more manic moods and girls more depressed moods (Duax et al., 2007). In studies of youngsters with early-onset BP, boys seem to be affected more often than girls, especially when the age of onset is younger than 13 years. Rates of BP have not been found to differ by ethnicity or culture, but few studies have investigated this issue in children and adolescents (AACAP, 2007c). Given the many different definitions and methods that have been use to assess the prevalence of BP in young people, the most consistent results that emerge are that prevalence rates are higher in: clinic versus community samples; older versus younger participants; and

samples that define BP more broadly and include participants with cyclothymic disorder and other specified BP (Youngstrom & Algorta, 2014).

Comorbidity

Co-occurring disorders are extremely common in youngsters with BP. They include anxiety disorders, ADHD, ODD, CD, substance-use problems, and suicidal ideation and suicide attempts (Goldstein et al., 2012; Hauser, Galling, & Correll, 2013; Sala et al., 2010). These disorders share many overlapping symptoms with BP, possibly related to shared underlying processes for what are currently assumed to be distinct disorders (Youngstrom & Algorta, 2014). In addition to these disorders, sleep disturbances, disrupted relationships with family and peers, risk-taking behaviors, and medical problems such as overweight status or obesity, cardiovascular and metabolic disorders, epilepsy, and migraine headaches are also common in youngsters with BP, which further complicates how it is managed (Goldstein et al., 2013; Sheffer & Linden, 2007; Youngstrom & Algorta, 2014).

More than 60% of youngsters with BP display one or more comorbid anxiety disorders, and as many as 50% have two or more anxiety disorders. In addition to their frequency, comorbid anxiety disorders have been found to adversely affect the course of BP in young people, suggesting the need for early recognition and treatment (Sala et al. 2014). Many youngsters with BP display co-occurring symptoms of ADHD, such as poor judgment, distractibility, inattention, irritability, hyperactivity, anger, poor impulse control, demanding behaviors, and the tendency to jump from one topic or activity to another. For youngsters first seen because of symptoms of BP, about 60% to 90% of prepubertal children and 30% of adolescents also have ADHD (Geller & Luby, 1997).

ODD and CD occur in as many as 80% of children and adolescents with BP (Leibenluft & Rich, 2008). Symptoms of grandiosity, mania, and poor judgment in BP may be confused with symptoms of conduct problems. For example, one 11-year-old boy with BP, who believed he would be a famous rock star, stole several hundred dollars' worth of music and was totally unaffected when questioned by the police. CD overlaps with BP on symptoms such as running away, driving under the influence, substance abuse, sexual promiscuity, and stealing. Similarly, the flight of ideas and/or pressured speech associated with mania may be mistaken for a language disorder (Carlson, 2002; Geller & Luby, 1997).

In trying to differentiate the symptoms of BP from those of comorbid conditions, if symptoms occur or worsen only during a mood episode, they may indicate mania. However, if they are chronic, occur between episodes, and represent the child's typical level of behavior, the presentation would be more consistent with ODD, ADHD, or anxiety disorder (Leibenluft & Rich, 2008).

Onset, Course, and Outcome

About 60% of patients with BP experience their first episode prior to the age of 19 years, with a peak age of onset between 15 and 19 years (Merikangas et al., 2007; Post et al., 2008). Although BP in preschool children may be identified using age-adjusted mania symptoms (Luby, Tandon, & Belden, 2009), onset prior to age 10 is extremely rare. Younger children in clinical samples display higher overall levels of manic symptoms, whereas adolescents display higher rates of depressive symptoms. However, the core symptoms of depression and mania appear to be consistent across age groups (Youngstrom & Algorta, 2014). Youngsters with BP may first present with either depressive or manic episodes, although most report that their first mood episode was major depression. This is consistent with the reported high rates of switching from depression to mania (Geller & Luby, 1997).

Risk factors for eventual mania include a major depressive episode (characterized by rapid onset, psychomotor retardation, disrupted sleep patterns, and psychotic features) and a family history of mood disorders, especially BP (AACAP, 2007c). When a young person presents with a first episode of obvious mania, further manic episodes will very likely follow. Bipolar episodes are generally shorter than major depressive episodes, lasting from 4 to 6 months if left untreated. About 70% of adolescents recover from their initial episode within 6 months, but 50% will have at least one recurrent episode (Birmaher et al., 2006).

Adolescents with mania often have complex presentations that include psychotic symptoms such as hallucinations, paranoia, and thought disorder. They also have unstable moods with mixed manic and depressive features, and severe deterioration in behavior. These diverse forms of presentation may result in an underdiagnosis of BP in teens and may be misdiagnosed as schizophrenia.

Because it is difficult to recognize symptoms of BP in young people, the symptoms are commonly noticed well before a youngster is treated or hospitalized, but they are not labeled as BP (Youngstrom et al., 2005). A look back at the histories of adults with BP symptoms often shows that mood swings began around puberty; however, there is frequently a 5- to 10-year lag between the onset of symptoms and display of the disorder serious enough to be recognized and treated (Carlson, 1994).

The early onset and the course of BP make it chronic and resistant to treatment, with a poor long-term prognosis similar to that in adults (AACAP, 2007c). In a 5-year prospective follow-up study of adolescents with BP, nearly 50% had a relapsing course or never achieved complete remission (Strober et al., 1995). As compared with adults, adolescents with BP may have a more prolonged early course and a poorer response to treatment. However, long-term prognosis appears to be similar to that for adults, with most patients continuing to experience significant symptoms and functional impairment (DelBello et al., 2007).

Causes

JESSI

Runs in the Family

"Jessi's father had been an alcoholic and a manic depressive," says her mother, "probably since he was an adolescent. He died of dehydration that occurred during a manic episode. His illness had been a mystery to us. Growing up, Jessi knew her father was ill, and when she was older, she began to worry about what his sickness might mean for her. I worried too," says Jessi's mother. "By the time Jessi was in her early twenties, something was clearly wrong. At first, I noticed only that she had become less reliable—forgetting things, arriving late, and occasionally missing appointments with me. Frequently, she complained of fatigue, a cold, flu, or a stomachache. Increasingly, her responses were brief, perfunctory. Though we didn't know it then, Jessi was experiencing a huge mood shift that was taking months to complete itself. Jessi had MDD, without the manic swings of the bipolar disorder her father had suffered from."

Adapted from Dowling, 1992.

Relatively few studies have examined the causes of BP in young people, although research with adults, and more recently with children, indicates that BP is one of the most heritable forms of mental disorder (McInnes et al., 2003). Findings from family and gene studies indicate that BP is the result of a genetic vulnerability combined with environmental factors, such as life stress or a negative family climate. When an identical twin has BP, there is only a 65% chance that the other twin will have it too, suggesting that in addition to genes, other factors are important. Although BP can affect anyone, it has definitely been shown to run in families (Oquendo et al., 2013). Offspring of mothers with BP are more likely to exhibit greater physiological dysregulation in response to stress than controls at as young as 6 months of age; this is a possible early vulnerability factor for later mood disorders (Johnson et al., 2014). If one or both parents have BP, the chances are about 5 times greater that their children will also develop BP or often, like Jessi, another recurrent mood disorder (Hodgins et al., 2002; Mesman et al., 2013).

Besides mood disorder, children at risk for BP by virtue of having parents with the disorder also display a wide range of psychopathology, particularly conduct problems and ADHD, as well as social and academic difficulties (Singh et al., 2007). Relatives of youngsters with BP also have a higher incidence of the disorder. Family incidence and risk for a broad range of psychiatric problems are highest in cases of early-onset BP, with lifetime prevalence rates of about 15% in first-degree relatives (AACAP, 2007c; Rende et al., 2007). This rate is 15 times greater than the prevalence of the disorder in the general population.

Increasing evidence suggests that BP arises from multiple genes, and some studies have identified several chromosomal regions and susceptibility genes (Alsabban, Rivera, & McGuffin, 2011; McInnis et al., 2003). As we have found for other disorders, specific genes that have been identified contribute only a small amount to the risk for BP. In addition, several of these genes have also been identified for youths with depression, anxiety, ADHD, or psychosis. There is likely a complex mode of inheritance rather than a single dominant gene. Individuals with a genetic predisposition do not necessarily develop BP, since environmental factors also play an important role in determining how genes are expressed (Geller & Luby, 1997).

A number of nonspecific risk factors that raise the risk for BP include poor maternal health or nutrition during pregnancy, substance use during pregnancy, a stressful early environment, exposure to traumatic events, and parental mood disorders (Youngstrom & Algorta, 2014). The ways in which environmental factors play a role are not well understood. However, one study suggests that parental BP may create a negative family climate, including problem-solving and communication deficits, which predict family conflict, which in turn predicts childhood BP (Du Rocher et al., 2008).

Brain scans of children identified as being at risk for BP that were taken before and after the onset of a manic episode have shown changes in the brain that reflect a pattern of emotion dysregulation in general, rather than one that is specific to BP onset (Gogtay et al., 2007). Generally, mood fluctuations in BP have been related to abnormalities in the structure and function of the amygdala, prefrontal and anterior cingulate cortex, hippocampus, thalamus, and basal ganglia, but findings have not always been consistent with respect to the types of abnormalities (Garrett & Chang,

2008; Gogtay et al., 2007). Such inconsistencies may be related to ongoing brain changes that are occurring in young people and the point in development at which brain structure and function are assessed.

Some studies have found that BP in adolescents is related to reduced volumes of the amygdala and hippocampus (Beardon et al., 2007; Blumberg et al., 2003). As you may recall, we discussed the importance of the amygdala for recognizing and regulating emotions in relation to depression. Research has found that youngsters with BP misread neutral facial expressions as hostile and in doing so show heightened activation of the amygdala and its connectivity to other parts of the brain involved in processing facial information (Perlman et al., 2013; Rich et al., 2008). These and other findings suggest that youths at risk for and those with BP may display unique neural correlates and deficits in facial emotion processing and dysregulation in brain regions associated with emotion regulation (Brotman et al., 2010; Garrett et al., 2012). Such deficits may be related to the poor social skills, aggression, and irritability that characterize youngsters with BP. In addition, adolescents with BP also show abnormal activation of prefrontal and subcortical areas of the brain during the anticipation of and response to monetary gains and loss, which suggest problems in reward processing, motivation, and goal pursuit (Singh et al., 2012).

Treatment

Treatment of BP in children and adolescents is receiving increasing attention. Although there is currently no cure for BP, in most cases treatment can stabilize mood and allow for management and control of symptoms. Treatment of BP generally requires a multimodal plan that includes close monitoring of symptoms, educating the patient and the family about the illness, matching treatments to individuals, administering medications such as lithium or atypical antipsychotics to stabilize mood, and performing psychotherapeutic interventions to address the youngster's symptoms and related psychosocial impairments (AACAP, 2007c; Kowatch et al., 2005). The general goals of treatment are to decrease the child's symptoms and to prevent relapse, while also reducing long-term illness and enhancing the youngster's normal health and development (Geller & Delbello, 2008).

Medications

Multiple medications have been used to treat youngsters with BP (Goldstein, Sassi, & Diler, 2012). The FDA has approved lithium for use in children as young as 12 years of age. However, there are currently no drugs that are FDA-approved for the treatment of BP in children younger than this (AACAP, 2007c). Medications are typically used to address manic or mixed symptoms and depressive symptoms or to prevent relapse. Clinical trials of medication have had some success, and controlled studies of medication treatment for adolescents with BP are rapidly increasing in number, although few studies have evaluated effects in children younger than age 10 years of age (Goldstein et al., 2012; Liu et al., 2011). Until very recently, recommended treatments were based on findings with adults; however, as we saw with tricyclic antidepressants, such an extrapolation may not be warranted (Geller et al., 1998). Hence, mood-stabilizing medications need to be used with caution and conservatively with young people with BP, particularly in those who do not fit the classic presentation of symptoms seen in adults with bipolar I disorder; these youngsters may constitute as many as 75% of cases of BP (Horst, 2009; Merikangas & Pato, 2009).

Based on its use with adults with BP, lithium has been the agent of first choice in the treatment of youths with BP, and its efficacy has been demonstrated in a number of controlled studies (Goldstein et al., 2012). Lithium is a common salt that is widely present in the natural environment—for example, in drinking water—usually in amounts too small to have any effects. However, the side effects of therapeutic doses of lithium can be serious, especially when used in combination with other medications; side effects may include toxicity (poisoning), renal and thyroid problems, and substantial weight gain (Gracious et al., 2004). It can be given to young people when used with the same safety precautions and similar careful monitoring used for adults. However, lithium cannot be given to children in chaotic families or to children who are unable to keep the multiple appointments needed for monitoring potentially dangerous side effects (Carlson, 1994; Geller & Luby, 1997). In addition, one study found that only 35% of adolescents with BP reported full adherence with the medication regimen (DelBello et al., 2007). Some studies have found atypical antipsychotic agents to be more efficacious than lithium in treating acute manic and mixed episodes in young people with BP, suggesting that these medications may be a preferred option for many youths with BP (Goldstein et al., 2012). However, they too have many metabolic side effects. In addition, adjunctive medications to treat secondary symptoms such as ADHD, depression, and anxiety have also been used (AACAP, 2007c; Sanchez & Soares, 2011).

Psychosocial Treatments

A focus on biological causes and pharmacological interventions for BP has resulted in a relative lack of attention to psychosocial treatments, although this situation is changing (Fristad & MacPherson, 2014). There is also a pressing need for studies on prevention, targeted interventions to delay or prevent progression to full manic or depressive episodes, and approaches that focus on possible environmental moderators of risk (Youngstrom & Algorta, 2014).

Medications may decrease symptoms of BP, but they do not help with the associated functional impairments or preexisting or co-occurring substance-use disorders, learning and behavior problems, and family- and peer-related issues. Nonadherence to medication regimens has been shown to be a major contributor to relapse. Thus, the family must be educated about the negative effects of nonadherence and to recognize possible symptoms of relapse. Psychosocial interventions focus on providing information to the child and family about the disorder, symptoms and course, possible impact on family functioning, and heritability of the disorder. Youths and parents are also taught ways of coping with symptoms and preventing relapse by using problem-solving, communication, emotion regulation, and cognitive—behavioral skills (Fristad, Goldberg Arnold, & Leffler, 2011; Fristad & MacPherson, 2014). Controlled research on psychosocial treatments for youngsters with BP is beginning to appear (Fristad et al., 2009; Goldstein et al., 2007; Miklowitz et al., 2011). This has resulted in several promising new early interventions for high-risk youths using family-focused therapy, CBT, and combined treatments to reduce symptoms of BP (Fristad & MacPherson, 2014; Miklowitz et al., 2013). Further efforts to identify young children at risk for developing BP are needed to enhance opportunities for both psychosocial and pharmacological preventive interventions (Howes & Falkenberg, 2011; Luby & Navsaria, 2010).

Section Summary

Bipolar Disorder

- A recent surge in interest in the diagnosis of bipolar disorder (BP) in children and adolescents has generated considerable controversy surrounding difficulties in identifying the disorder in young people.
- Youngsters with BP show periods of abnormally and persistently elevated, expansive, and/or irritable mood.
- They may display symptoms such as an inflated self-esteem, decreased need for sleep, pressured speech, flight of ideas, distractibility, and reckless behavior.
- BP is far less common than MDD in young people, with lifetime prevalence estimates of 0.5% to 2.5% worldwide.
- BP has a peak age at onset in late adolescence and, unlike depression, affects males and females about equally.

(continues)

Section Summary (continued)

- The most common accompanying disorders are ADHD, anxiety disorders, conduct problems, and substance abuse.
- Very few studies have examined the causes of BP in children and adolescents. Family and gene studies with adults indicate that BP is the result of a genetic vulnerability in combination with environmental factors, such as life stress or disturbances in the family.
- Brain-imaging studies of youngsters with BP point to abnormalities in regions of the brain involved in emotion regulation, including the amygdala and anterior cingulate cortex.
- BP in young people requires a multimodal treatment plan with education of the patient and the family about the illness, medication, and psychosocial interventions to address the youngster's symptoms and related psychosocial impairments.

Study Resources

SECTION SUMMARIES

KEY TERMS

11

Anxiety and Obsessive—Compulsive Disorders

It is hard to be brave, when you're only a very small animal.

—Piglet (Pooh's Little Instruction Book, 1995)

Separation Anxiety: Brad is terrified of being separated from his mother. He follows her around the house constantly, always needing to know where she is.

Social Anxiety: Li-Ming is very preoccupied with what others think of her. She doesn't interact with anyone at school, and feels completely isolated.

Panic Disorder: Claudia describes her sudden attack of overwhelming anxiety. "My heart started pumping so fast I thought it would explode. I thought I was going to die."

Generalized Anxiety: Jared "worries about everything"—how he is doing in school, events in the news, and family finances.

Obsessive–Compulsive Disorder: Georgina can't stop thinking about not being able to sleep. Every night before bedtime she goes through the same routine of counting and grouping all the clothes and shoes in her bedroom closet and opening and closing the closet door.

ALL CHILDREN EXPERIENCE FEAR, worry, or anxiety as a normal part of growing up, but each child in our examples suffers from an anxiety or related disorder that is excessive and debilitating. An anxiety disorder is one of the most common mental health problems in young people, with lifetime prevalence estimates between 8% and 30% (Kessler et al., 2012a; Merikangas et al., 2010). Estimates vary widely with the child's age, type of anxiety disorder, and whether impaired functioning is part of the diagnosis. Conservatively, at least one child in every elementary school classroom is likely to have an anxiety disorder (Cartwright-Hatton, McNicol, & Doubleday, 2006). Despite their early onset, high frequency, persistence, and associated problems, anxiety disorders in children often go unnoticed and untreated (Gregory et al., 2007). Fewer than 20% of youngsters with anxiety disorders receive services for their problem, as compared with about 45% to 60% of those with conduct or attention disorders (Merikangas et al., 2011). This may be due to the frequent occurrence of fears and anxiety during normal development, the invisible nature of many symptoms (e.g., a knot in the stomach), and the fact that anxiety is not nearly as damaging to other people or property as are conduct problems (Higa-McMillan, Francis, & Chorpita, 2014).

For a long time, anxiety in children was thought to be a mild and transitory disturbance that would fade over time with normal life experiences. However, we now know that many children who experience anxiety display impairments in their school, social, and family/home functioning and will continue to display anxiety and other problems into adolescence and adulthood (Bittner et al., 2007; Langley et al., 2014). Having an anxiety disorder in childhood or adolescence is also one of the strongest predictors of most other later mental disorders (Kessler et al., 2012c). Although isolated symptoms of fear and anxiety are usually short-lived, anxiety disorders have a more chronic and stable course (Carballo et al., 2010). In fact, nearly half of those affected have an illness duration of 8 years or longer (Keller et al., 1992), and parents' reports of their child's anxiety symptoms predict anxiety disorders 24 years later (Reef et al., 2010). The societal costs for clinically anxious youths are also substantial, with estimated costs (e.g., health care, child care, missed work or school days) about 20 times higher for families with an anxious child versus those from the general population (Bodden, Dirksen, & Bögels, 2008). Thus, anxiety disorders in children are common, distressing, long-lasting, and costly (Rapee, Schneiring, & Hudson, 2009).

We begin our discussion with anxiety disorders, the primary focus of this chapter. We also discuss obsessive–compulsive disorder (OCD), a closely related disorder that was considered to be one of the anxiety disorders in previous versions of the *Diagnostic and Statistical Manual of Mental Disorders* (DSM). OCD is now included in a separate chapter of DSM-5, with related disorders such as hoarding, hair-pulling, skin-picking, and body dysmorphic disorder (i.e., perceived defects or flaws in physical appearance). As we shall discuss, there is a close relationship between the anxiety disorders and some of these disorders (especially OCD), with respect to their behavioral and cognitive symptoms and other features.

DESCRIPTION OF ANXIETY DISORDERS

Anxiety is a mood state characterized by strong negative emotion and bodily symptoms of tension in which the child apprehensively anticipates future danger or misfortune (Barlow, 2002). This definition captures two key features of anxiety—strong negative emotion and an element of fear. Children who experience excessive and debilitating anxieties are said to have **anxiety disorders.** These disorders occur in many forms. Some children, like Brad, feel anxious whenever they are separated from their mother or are away from home. Others feel anxious only in certain situations, such as when they have to travel by airplane or, like Li-Ming, when they have to give a talk in class. Some youngsters, like Claudia, have unpredictable bouts of such sudden and intense anxiety that they become terrified and immobilized. Others, like Jared, worry about almost everything and feel anxious most of the time for no apparent reason. Some children, like Georgina, experience repeated, intrusive, and unwanted thoughts that produce anxiety, and they spend hours in ritualized behavior in an effort to alleviate that anxiety.

Many youngsters with anxiety disorders suffer from more than one type, either simultaneously or at separate times during their development (Costello, Egger, & Angold, 2005b). In view of the substantial overlap among these disorders, we begin this chapter by discussing the general features and mechanisms of anxiety that apply across all types. The common occurrence of fears and anxieties in childhood and adolescence requires that we also consider the role of these emotions in normal development. We then examine each anxiety disorder and what makes it unique.

Experiencing Anxiety

> When Isabella saw a dog running loose in front of her house, she became pale, sweaty, cold, and trembly. Her thoughts raced so fast that she couldn't think. She froze. Her heart pounded, she felt tense, and she found it difficult to breathe.

Isabella is experiencing anxiety in response to an event she sees as potentially threatening or dangerous. As humans, we are programmed to detect and react to signs of anxiety in ourselves and in others. In fact, anxiety is both expected and normal at certain ages and in certain situations. One-year-old infants become distressed when separated from their mothers, and almost all young children have short-lived specific fears—of the dark, for example. The child's world can be a strange and menacing place, full of unknown dangers—some real, others imagined. Although no one likes to feel anxious, not feeling anxious when the situation calls for it is far worse.

Anxiety often hits us when we do something important, and in moderate doses it helps us think and act more effectively. You will probably be better prepared for your next exam if you're just a little bit nervous about taking it. Similarly, some anxiety may help a child prepare harder for an upcoming oral report or athletic event. In this sense, anxiety is an adaptive emotion that readies children both physically and psychologically for coping with people, objects, or events that could be dangerous to their safety or well-being.

Although some anxiety is good, too much is not. Excessive, uncontrollable anxiety can be debilitating. A child may fail a test because she spends too much time thinking about how awful it would be to fail, making it nearly impossible to think about anything else (e.g., how to solve a math problem). In children with anxiety disorders, this normally useful emotion works against them.

When children experience fears beyond a certain age, in situations that pose no real threat or danger, and to an extent that seriously interferes with daily activities, anxiety is a serious problem. Even if the child knows there is little to be afraid of, he or she is still terrified and does everything possible to escape or avoid the situation. This pattern of self-defeating behavior, known as the **neurotic paradox** (Mowrer, 1950), can become self-perpetuating—much like Sisyphus repeatedly pushing the rock up the hill, only to have it roll back down each time.

First and foremost, anxiety involves an immediate reaction to *perceived* danger or threat—a reaction known as the **fight/flight response**. All of its effects are aimed at escaping potential harm, either by confronting the source of danger (fight) or by evading it (flight). If you look up to see a grand piano about to fall in your direction and experience no anxiety whatsoever, you will pay serious consequences. To avoid such a fate, your fight/flight response would kick into overdrive and you would jump out of harm's way.

Think of a recent situation that made you anxious. What was it about the situation that made you anxious? What physical symptoms did you notice? What were you thinking? What did you do? Describing what it's like to be anxious is not easy, because anxiety is a complex reaction with many symptoms, as shown in Table 11.1.

Youngsters with anxiety experience strong negative emotion and physical tension, and anticipate future danger.

TABLE 11.1 | The Many Symptoms of Anxiety

Physical		
Increased heart rate	Dizziness	Blushing
Fatigue	Blurred vision	Vomiting
Increased respiration	Dry mouth	Numbness
Nausea	Muscle tension	Sweating
Stomach upset	Heart palpitation	

Cognitive		
Thoughts of being scared or hurt	Thoughts of incompetence or inadequacy	Thoughts of bodily injury
Thoughts or images of monsters or wild animals	Difficulty concentrating	Images of harm to loved ones
Self-deprecatory or self-critical thoughts	Blanking out or forgetfulness	Thoughts of going crazy
	Thoughts of appearing foolish	Thoughts of contamination

Behavioral		
Avoidance	Trembling lip	Avoidance of eye contact
Crying or screaming	Swallowing	Physical proximity
Nail biting	Immobility	Clenched jaw
Trembling voice	Twitching	Fidgeting
Stuttering	Thumb sucking	

Based on Fears and Anxieties, by B. A. Barrios and D. P. Hartmann, 1997, p. 235. In E. J. Mash and L. G. Terdal (Eds.), Assessment of Childhood Disorders, 3rd ed.

How many of these symptoms did you experience? What do these many symptoms have in common?

The symptoms of anxiety are expressed through three interrelated response systems: the *physical system,* the *cognitive system,* and the *behavioral system.* It is essential to know how the three sets of symptoms work, since more than one may be evident in different children with the same anxiety disorder. Also, as we will discuss, different response systems are more dominant in certain anxiety disorders. Let's take a closer look at how each response system works.

Physical System

When a person perceives or anticipates danger, the brain sends messages to the sympathetic nervous system, which produces the fight/flight response. The activation of this system produces many important chemical and physical effects that mobilize the body for action:

▸ *Chemical effects.* Adrenaline and noradrenaline are released from the adrenal glands.

▸ *Cardiovascular effects.* Heart rate and strength of the heart beat increase, readying the body for action by speeding up blood flow and improving delivery of oxygen to the tissues.

▸ *Respiratory effects.* Speed and depth of breathing increase, which brings oxygen to the tissues and removes waste. This may produce feelings of breathlessness, choking or smothering, or chest pains.

▸ *Sweat gland effects.* Sweating increases, which cools the body and makes the skin slippery.

▸ *Other physical effects.* The pupils widen to let in more light, which may lead to blurred vision or spots in front of the eyes. Salivation decreases, resulting in a dry mouth. Decreased activity in the digestive system may lead to nausea and a heavy feeling in the stomach. Muscles tense in readiness for fight or flight, leading to subjective feelings of tension, aches and pains, and trembling.

These physical symptoms are familiar signs of anxiety. Overall, the fight/flight response produces general activation of the entire metabolism. As a result, the individual may feel hot and flushed and, because this activation takes a lot of energy, he or she feels tired and drained afterward.

Cognitive System

Since the main purpose of the fight/flight system is to signal possible danger, its activation produces an immediate search for a potential threat. For children with anxiety disorders, it is difficult to focus on everyday tasks because their attention is consumed by a constant search for threat or danger. When these children can't find proof of danger, they may turn their search inward: "If nothing is out there to make me feel anxious, then something must be wrong with me." Or they may distort the situation: "Even though I can't find it, I know there's something to be afraid of." Or they may do both. Children with anxiety disorders will invent explanations for their anxiety: "I must be a real jerk." "Everyone will think I'm a dummy if I say something." "Even though I can't see them, there are germs all over the place." Activation of the cognitive system often leads to subjective feelings of apprehension, nervousness, difficulty concentrating, and panic.

Behavioral System

The overwhelming urges that accompany the fight/ flight response are aggression and a desire to escape the threatening situation, but social constraints may prevent fulfilling either impulse. For example, just before a final exam you may feel like attacking your professor or not showing up at all, but fortunately for your professor and your need to pass the course, you are likely to inhibit these urges! However, they may show up as foot tapping, fidgeting, or irritability (consider the number of teeth marks in pencils) or as escape or avoidance by getting a doctor's note, requesting a deferral, or even faking illness. Unfortunately, avoidance perpetuates anxiety, despite the temporary feeling of relief. Avoidance behaviors are negatively reinforced; that is, they are strengthened when they are followed by a rapid reduction in anxiety. As a result, each time a child is confronted with an anxiety-producing situation, the faster she or he gets out of it, the faster the anxiety drops off—so the more the child avoids such situations. As children with anxiety disorders engage in more and more avoidance, carrying out everyday activities becomes exceedingly difficult.

CHANTELLE

The Terror of Being Home Alone

When Chantelle, age 14, realized she was at home alone, she was terrified. Her thoughts raced so fast it was impossible to think clearly. She forgot all the right things to do. Her heart pounded and she tensed up. She felt like she couldn't breathe, and she began to sob. She wanted to run but felt completely immobilized. (Based on authors' case material.)

Chantelle's reactions show how the three response systems of anxiety interact and feed off one another. Physically, Chantelle's heart pounded, she tensed, and she had difficulty breathing. Cognitively, she could not think clearly. Behaviorally, she was completely immobilized.

Anxiety versus Fear and Panic

It is important to distinguish anxiety from two closely related emotions—fear and panic. **Fear** is an immediate alarm reaction to current danger or life-threatening emergencies. Although fear and anxiety have much in common, the fear reaction differs both psychologically and biologically from the emotion of anxiety. Fear is a *present-oriented* emotional reaction to current danger marked by a strong escape tendency and an all-out surge in the sympathetic nervous system.

The overriding message is alarm: "If I don't do something right now, I might not make it at all." In contrast, anxiety is a *future-oriented* emotion characterized by feelings of apprehension and lack of control over upcoming events that might be threatening. Fear and anxiety both warn of danger or distress. However, only anxiety is frequently felt when no danger is actually present (Barlow, 2002).

Panic is a group of physical symptoms of the fight/flight response that unexpectedly occur in the absence of any obvious threat or danger. With no explanation for physical symptoms such as a pounding heart, the child may invent one: "I'm dying." The sensations themselves can feel threatening and may trigger further fear, apprehension, anxiety, and panic (Barlow, 2002).

Normal Fears, Anxieties, Worries, and Rituals

Since fear and anxiety in moderate doses are adaptive, it is not surprising that emotions and rituals that increase feelings of control are common during childhood and adolescence. It is only when the emotions and rituals become excessive, occur in a developmentally inappropriate context, or lead to impairment in functioning such as an inability to go to school, make friends, complete academic tasks, or meet other developmental goals that they are of concern.

Normal Fears

Since young people and their environments constantly change, fears that are normal at one age can be debilitating a few years later. For example, fear of strangers may serve a protective function for infants and young children, but when it persists beyond a certain age it can seriously interfere with the development of peer relations (Brooker et al., 2013). Whether or not a specific fear is normal also depends on its effect on the child and how long it lasts. If a fear has little impact on the child's daily life or lasts only a few weeks, it is likely a part of normal development.

The number and types of common childhood fears change over time, with a general age-related decline in number (Gullone, 1999). Even so, specific fears are common in older children, and many teens report that their fears cause them considerable distress and significantly interfere with daily activities (Ollendick & King, 1994). Girls tend to have more fears than boys at almost every age; they also rate themselves as more fearful and report fears that are more intense and disabling than do boys. Although fears show a general decline with age, some, such as school-related fears, remain stable; others, such as social fears, may increase (Muris, 2007). Common fears and anxieties of infants, children, and adolescents are shown in Table 11.2. Also shown are possible relevant symptoms and corresponding DSM-5 anxiety disorders that may develop in relation to these symptoms.

TABLE 11.2 | Common Fears and Anxieties of Infancy, Childhood, and Adolescence; Possible Symptoms; and Corresponding DSM-5 Diagnoses

Developmental Period	Age	Common Fears and Anxieties	Possible Symptoms	Corresponding DSM-5 Anxiety Disorder
Early Infancy	Within first weeks	Loss of physical support, loss of physical contact with caregiver	—	—
	0–6 months	Intense sensory stimuli (loud noises)	—	—
Late Infancy	6–8 months	Shyness/anxiety with stranger, sudden, unexpected, or looming objects	—	Separation anxiety disorder
Toddlerhood	12–18 months	Separation from parent, injury, toileting, strangers	Sleep disturbances, nocturnal panic attacks, oppositional defiant behavior	Separation anxiety disorder, panic attacks
	2–3 years	Fears of thunder and lightning, fire, water, darkness, nightmares	Crying, clinging, withdrawal, freezing, avoidance of salient stimuli (e.g., turning the light on), night terrors, enuresis	Specific phobias (natural environment), panic attacks
		Fears of animals	—	Specific phobias (animal)
Early Childhood	4–5 years	Separation from parents, fear of death or dead people	Excessive need for reassurance	Separation anxiety disorder, generalized anxiety disorder, panic attacks
Primary/Elementary School Age	5–7 years	Fear of specific objects (animals, monsters, ghosts)	—	Specific phobias
		Fear of germs or of getting a serious illness	—	Obsessive–compulsive disorder (OCD)
		Fear of natural disasters, fear of traumatic events (e.g., getting burned, being hit by a car or truck)	—	Specific phobias (natural environment), acute stress disorder, post-traumatic stress disorder, generalized anxiety disorder
	5–11 years	School anxiety, performance anxiety, physical appearance, social concerns	Withdrawal, timidity, extreme shyness with unfamiliar adults and peers, feelings of shame	Social anxiety disorder (social phobia)
Adolescence	12–18 years	Personal relations, rejection from peers, personal appearance, future, natural disasters, safety	Fear of negative evaluation	Social anxiety disorder (social phobia)

Based on Beesdo, Knappe, & Pine, 2009.

All children experience some fear, anxiety, and worry as a normal part of growing up.

Jacqueline Veissid/Photodisc/Getty Images

Normal Anxieties

Like fears, anxieties are very common during childhood and adolescence. Various types of anxiety are evident by age 4 (Eley, Lichenstein, & Moffitt, 2003), and about 25% of parents report that their child is too nervous, fearful, or anxious (Achenbach, 1991a). The most frequent symptoms in samples of children with normal anxieties are separation anxiety, test anxiety, overconcern about competence, excessive need for reassurance, and anxiety about harm to a parent (Barrios & Hartmann, 1997).

Younger children generally experience more anxiety symptoms than do older children, primarily about separation from parents. Girls display more anxiety than boys, but they generally experience similar types of symptoms. Although some specific anxieties decrease with age, such as separation anxiety and anxiety about school, nervous and anxious symptoms may not show the age-related decline observed for many specific fears (Hale et al., 2008). Anxious symptoms may reflect a stable trait that predisposes children to develop excessive fears related to their stage of development. Thus, the disposition to be anxious may remain stable over time, even though the objects of children's fears change.

Normal Worries

If worrying about the future is so unproductive, why do we do so much of it? Part of the reason seems to be that the process of worry—thinking about all possible negative outcomes—serves an extremely useful function in normal development. In moderate doses, worry can help children prepare for the future—for example, by checking their homework before they hand it in or by rehearsing for an upcoming class play. Worry is a central feature of anxiety, and anxiety is related to the number of children's worries and to their intensity (Silverman, La Greca, & Wasserstein, 1995). Children of all ages worry, but the forms and expressions change. Older children report a greater variety and complexity of worries and are better able to describe them than are younger children (Chorpita et al., 1997).

Normal Rituals and Repetitive Behavior

Ritualistic, repetitive activity is extremely common in young children (Peleg-Popko & Dar, 2003). A familiar example is the bedtime ritual of saying good night—addressing people in a certain order or giving a certain number of hugs and kisses. Normal ritualistic behaviors in young children include preferences for sameness in the environment (e.g., watching the same DVD over and over again), rigid likes and dislikes, preferences for symmetry (e.g., carrying a toy in each hand), awareness of minute details or imperfections in toys or clothes (e.g., being bothered by a minuscule thread on a jacket sleeve), and arranging things so they are "just right" (e.g., insisting that different foods not touch each other on the plate). Rituals help young children gain control and mastery over their social and physical environments and make their world more predictable and safer (Evans et al., 1997). Any parent who has violated these rituals and paid the price can appreciate how important they are to the young child.

Many common routines of young children fall into two distinct categories: repetitive behaviors and doing things "just right." These categories are strikingly similar to those found for older individuals with OCD and related disorders, which we discuss later in the chapter. It is not known whether OCD is an extreme point on a continuum of normal developmental rituals or an entirely different problem (Evans, Gray, & Leckman, 1999). However, research suggests that the neuropsychological mechanisms underlying compulsive, ritualistic behavior in normal development and those in OCD may be similar (Pietrefesa & Evans, 2007).

Anxiety Disorders According to DSM-5

Anxiety disorders in DSM-5 are divided into seven categories that closely define the focus of the child's anxiety and the types of reaction and avoidance. To give you an overall picture, these disorders are described briefly in A Closer Look 11.1. The number of youths with multiple anxiety disorders increases with age. Keep in mind that significant associations exist between nearly all anxiety disorders. These associations are best explained by a model that

Main Features of Seven DSM-5 Anxiety Disorders

Separation Anxiety Disorder (SAD)

Characterized by excessive worry regarding separation from home or parents. Youths may show signs of distress and physical symptoms on separation, experience unrealistic worries about harm to self or others when separated, and display an unwillingness to be alone.

Specific Phobia

Characterized by severe and unreasonable fears and avoidance of a specific object or situation, for example, dogs, spiders, darkness, or riding on a bus.

Social Anxiety Disorder (SOC) (Social Phobia)

Characterized by a severe and unreasonable fear of being embarrassed or humiliated when doing something in front of peers or adults.

Selective Mutism

Characterized by a consistent failure to speak in specific social situations in which there is an expectation for speaking (e.g., school), even though the child may speak loudly and frequently at home or in other settings.

Panic Disorder (PD)

Characterized by recurrent, unexpected and severe panic attacks. These attacks may consist of an accelerated heart rate, shortness of breath, sweating, upset stomach, dizziness, fear of dying, and others. The individual also experiences a persistent concern or worry about additional panic attacks or their consequences, or displays a significant maladaptive change in behavior to avoid having panic attacks (e.g., avoidance of exercise or new situations).

Agoraphobia

Characterized by fear or anxiety about two or more situations such as using public transportation, being in open spaces (e.g., parking lots, marketplaces), being in enclosed spaces (e.g., theaters), being in a crowd, or being outside of the home alone. The fear or anxiety about these situations occurs because the individual thinks that escape might be difficult or help not available if they were to develop panic-like or other incapacitating symptoms.

Generalized Anxiety Disorder (GAD)

Characterized by ongoing and excessive worry about many events and activities. Youths may worry about their grades in school, their relations with peers, and their own or others' safety. They may constantly seek comfort or approval from others to help reduce their worry.

---

specifies multiple distinct anxiety syndromes that are related to a higher-order factor (e.g., negative affect) that is common to most if not all anxiety disorders, as well as depression (Higa-McMillan et al., 2014).

Section Summary

Description of Anxiety Disorders

- Anxiety disorders are among the most common mental health problems in children and adolescents, but they often go unnoticed and untreated.

- Anxiety is an adaptive emotion that prepares youngsters to cope with potentially threatening people, objects, or events. Strong negative emotions, physical tension, and apprehensive anticipation of future danger or misfortune characterize it.

- The symptoms of anxiety are expressed through three interrelated response systems: physical, cognitive, and behavioral.

- Fear is a present-oriented emotional reaction to current danger. In contrast, anxiety is a future-oriented emotion characterized by feelings of apprehension and a lack of control over upcoming events that might be threatening.

- Fears, anxieties, worries, and rituals in children are common, change with age, and follow a predictable developmental pattern with respect to type.

- DSM-5 specifies several types of anxiety and related disorders based on types of reaction and avoidance.

SEPARATION ANXIETY DISORDER

BRAD

"Don't Leave Me!"

Brad, age 9, is unable to enter any situation that requires separation from his parents—playing in the backyard, going to other children's homes, or staying with a babysitter. When forcibly separated from his parents, Brad cries or throws a full-blown tantrum. When his mother plans to leave the house, he runs through all the horrible things that might happen to her, in an endless series of what-if questions. When she becomes frustrated and angry, Brad becomes even more anxious. The more anxious he gets, the more he argues with his mother, and the angrier she gets. Brad has also threatened to hurt himself if forced to go to school.

Brad's separation problems began about a year ago, when his father was drinking too much and was frequently absent for long periods. Brad's problem gradually worsened over the course of the year, until he completely refused to go to school. Help was sought, but Brad continued to get worse. He developed significant depressive symptoms, including sadness, guilt about his problems, and occasional wishes to die.

Adapted from Last, 1988.

Separation anxiety is important for the young child's survival and is normal at certain ages. From about age 7 months through the preschool years, almost all children fuss when they are separated from their parents or others to whom they are close. In fact, a lack of separation anxiety at this age may suggest insecure attachment or other problems. Unfortunately, like Brad, some children continue to display such anxiety long after the age at which it is typical or expected. When anxiety persists for at least 4 weeks and is severe enough to interfere with normal daily routines such as going to school or participating in recreational activities, the child may have a separation anxiety disorder. The DSM-5 criteria are presented in Table 11.3.

Children with **separation anxiety disorder (SAD)** display age-inappropriate, excessive, and disabling distress related to separation from their parents or other major attachment figures and fear of being alone (Cooper-Vince et al., 2014). Young children with SAD may have vague feelings of anxiety or repeated nightmares about being kidnapped or killed or about the death of a parent. They frequently display excessive demands for parental attention by clinging to their parents and shadowing their every move. Often, they are reluctant to sleep separated from their parents, and they try to climb into their parents' bed at night or sleep on the floor just outside their parents' bedroom door (Allen et al., 2010). Older children with SAD may have difficulty being alone in a room during the day, sleeping alone even at home, running errands, going to school, or going to camp. They may also have specific fantasies of illness, accidents, kidnapping, or physical harm.

Children with SAD fear new situations and may display physical symptoms. To avoid separation, they may fuss, cry, scream, or threaten suicide if the parent leaves (although serious suicide attempts are rare);

TABLE 11.3 | **Diagnostic Criteria for Separation Anxiety Disorder (SAD)**

DSM-5

(A) Developmentally inappropriate and excessive fear or anxiety concerning separation from those to whom the individual is attached, as evidenced by at least three of the following:

(1) Recurrent excessive distress when anticipating or experiencing separation from home or from major attachment figures.

(2) Persistent or excessive worry about losing major attachment figures or about possible harm to them, such as illness, injury, disasters, or death.

(3) Persistent and excessive worry about experiencing an untoward event (e.g., getting lost, being kidnapped, having an accident, becoming ill) that causes separation from a major attachment figure.

(4) Persistent reluctance or refusal to go out, away from home, to school, to work, or elsewhere because of fear of separation.

(5) Persistent and excessive fear of or reluctance about being alone or without major attachment figures at home or in other settings.

(6) Persistent reluctance or refusal to sleep away from home or to go to sleep without being near a major attachment figure.

(7) Repeated nightmares involving the theme of separation.

(8) Repeated complaints of physical symptoms (e.g., headaches, stomachaches, nausea, vomiting) when separation from major attachment figures occurs or is anticipated.

(B) The fear, anxiety, or avoidance is persistent, lasting at least 4 weeks in children and adolescents and typically 6 months or more in adults.

(C) The disturbance causes clinically significant distress or impairment in social, academic, occupational, or other important areas of functioning.

(D) The disturbance is not better explained by another mental disorder, such as refusing to leave home because of excessive resistance to change in autism spectrum disorder; delusions or hallucinations concerning separation in psychotic disorders; refusal to go outside without a trusted companion in agoraphobia; worries about ill health or other harm befalling significant others in generalized anxiety disorder; or concerns about having an illness in illness anxiety disorder.

(E) criteria and Specify if should be deleted in their entirety. No substitutions for either.

Source: Diagnostic and Statistical Manual of Mental Disorders, Fifth Edition, American Psychiatric Association.

physical symptoms may include rapid heartbeat, dizziness, headaches, stomachaches, and nausea. Not surprisingly, parents, especially mothers, become highly distressed. Over time, as we saw with Brad, children with SAD may become increasingly withdrawn, apathetic, and depressed, and are at risk for developing a variety of other anxiety disorders during adolescence (Lewinsohn et al., 2008).

Prevalence and Comorbidity

SAD is one of the two most common anxiety disorders to occur during childhood (the other is specific phobia), and it is found in about 4% to 10% of all children (Merikangas et al., 2010). It is common in both boys and girls, although it is more prevalent in girls. About two-thirds of children with SAD have another anxiety disorder, and about half develop a depressive disorder following the onset of SAD. They may also display specific fears of getting lost or of the dark. School reluctance or refusal is also quite common in older children with SAD (Albano, Chorpita, & Barlow, 2003).

Onset, Course, and Outcome

Of children referred for anxiety disorders, SAD has the earliest reported age at onset (7 to 8 years) and the youngest age at referral (Shear et al., 2006). SAD generally progresses from mild to severe. It may begin with harmless requests or with symptoms such as restless sleep or nightmares, which progress to the child sleeping nightly in his or her parents' bed. Similarly, school mornings may evoke physical symptoms and an occasional absence from school, which escalates into daily tantrums about leaving for school and outright refusal. The child may become increasingly concerned about the parents' daily routine and whereabouts (Albano et al., 2003).

Often, SAD occurs after a child has experienced major stress, such as moving to a new neighborhood, entering a new school, death or illness in the family, or an extended vacation. Brad's SAD emerged after his father developed a problem with alcohol and subsequently left home. The symptoms of SAD may also fluctuate over the years as a function of stress and transitions in the child's life. Although they may lose friends as a result of their repeated refusal to participate in activities away from home, children with SAD are reasonably skilled socially and get along with others. However, their school performance may suffer as a result of frequent school absences. The child may require special assignments just to keep up; in extreme cases, they may have to repeat the school year (Albano et al., 2003).

SAD persists into adulthood for more than one-third of children and adolescents. As adults, these individuals are more likely than others to experience relationship difficulties (e.g., never marry or become separated or divorced), other anxiety disorders and mental health problems (particularly panic disorder and depression),

and functional impairment in their social and personal lives (Milrod et al., 2014; Shear et al., 2006).

School reluctance and refusal are quite common in youngsters with SAD.

ERIC

Won't Go to School

Eric, age 12, was referred by a school psychologist and his parents for his intense school refusal behavior. On entering seventh grade and a new school, he began to experience a variety of negative symptoms, such as hyperventilation, anxiety, sad mood, and somatic symptoms. Although attendance was not a problem at first, by mid-September Eric began to report severe headaches on school mornings. School attendance then became intermittent. By late September, his aversion to school had worsened and he was staying at home on most days.

Adapted from Kearney, 1995.

School Reluctance and Refusal

Although starting school is exciting and enjoyable for most children, many are reluctant to go to school and—for a few—school may create so much fear and anxiety that they will not go. These children can become literally sick with worry, let minor physical symptoms keep them at home, or pretend to be ill. **School refusal behavior** is defined as the refusal to attend classes or difficulty remaining in school for an entire day. It includes youngsters who resist going to school in the morning but eventually attend, those who go to school but leave at some point during the day, those who attend with great dread that leads to future pleas for nonattendance, and those who miss the entire day (Kearney, 2007).

School refusal is equally common in boys and girls, and it occurs most often between the ages of 5 and 11 years. Excessive and unreasonable fears of school usually first occur during preschool, kindergarten, or first grade and peak during the second grade. However, school refusal can occur at any time and may have a sudden onset at a later age, as happened with Eric. Children who refuse school may complain of a headache, upset stomach, or sore throat just before it's time to leave for school, then begin to "feel better" when permitted to stay at home, only to feel "sick" again the next morning. As the time for school draws near, the child may plead, cry, and refuse to leave the house and may even have a full-blown panic reaction. School refusal often follows a period at home during which the child has spent more time than usual with a parent (e.g., brief illness, holiday break, or summer vacation). At other times, school refusal may follow a stressful event such as a change of schools (as happened with Eric), an accident, or the death of a relative or family pet.

For many children, fear of school is really a fear of leaving their parents—separation anxiety. However, school reluctance and refusal can occur for many reasons (Kearney & Albano, 2004). Most children who refuse to go to school have average or above-average intelligence, suggesting that it is not a difficulty with academics that leads to this problem. A fear of school may be associated with submitting for the first time to authority and rules outside the home, being compared with unfamiliar children, and experiencing the threat of failure. Some children fear school because they are afraid of being ridiculed, teased, or bullied by other children or being criticized or disciplined by their teachers. In other cases, the child's fear may result from an excessive or irrational fear of being socially evaluated or embarrassed when having to recite in class or undress in front of unfamiliar people in a gym class. Eric was extremely anxious about meeting new people, being late for class,

School reluctance and refusal are common problems related to anxiety.

moving from class to class, taking classes involving public speaking, and participating in gym class. He refused to attend school mainly to escape being socially evaluated and, to a lesser extent, to gain attention from his parents (Kearney & Silverman, 1996).

The possible long-term consequences are serious for a child who displays a persistent pattern of school refusal behavior and does not receive help. Academic or social problems may develop as a result of missed instruction and peer interaction. Treatment usually emphasizes an immediate return to school and other routines and must take into account the specific functions being served by school refusal behaviors (Kearney & Albano, 2007).

Section Summary

Separation Anxiety Disorder

- Children with SAD display age-inappropriate, excessive, and disabling distress related to separation from and fear of being alone without their parents or other major attachment figures.

- SAD is one of the most common anxiety disorders of childhood, with the earliest reported age at onset and the youngest age at referral.

- School refusal behavior is defined as the refusal to attend classes or difficulty remaining in school for an entire day.

SPECIFIC PHOBIA

CHARLOTTE

Arachnophobia

For 2 years, Charlotte, age 8, has complained of an intense fear of spiders. "Spiders are disgusting," she says. "I'm scared to death that one will crawl on me, especially when I'm sleeping. When I see a spider, even a little one, my heart pounds, my hands feel cold and sweaty, and I start to shake." Charlotte's mother says that her daughter goes completely pale when she sees a spider, even at a distance, and tries to avoid any situation where she thinks there might be one. Charlotte's fear is beginning to interfere with her daily activities. For example, she won't play in the backyard and refuses to go on class or family outings where she might encounter a spider. She is afraid to go to sleep at night because she thinks a spider might crawl on her. (Based on authors' case material.)

Many children have specific fears that are mildly troubling, come and go rapidly until about age 10, and rarely require special attention. However, if the child's fear occurs at an inappropriate age, persists, is irrational or exaggerated, leads to avoidance of the object or event, and causes impairment in normal routines, it is called a **specific phobia.** Like Charlotte, children with a specific phobia display a marked fear or anxiety about specific objects or situations (e.g., animals, heights) for at least 6 months. The DSM-5 criteria for specific phobia are shown in Table 11.4.

Children with a specific phobia show an extreme and disabling fear about objects or situations that in reality pose little or no danger or threat; these children go to great lengths to avoid these objects or situations. They experience extreme fear or dread, physiological arousal to the feared stimulus, and fearful anticipation and avoidance when confronted with the object of their fear. Their fear or anxiety may be expressed by crying, tantrums, freezing, or clinging. Their thinking usually focuses on threats to their personal safety, such as being stung by a bee or struck by lightning. Anticipatory anxiety is also common. For example, a child with a phobia of dogs may think: "What if a big dog is running loose on my way to school and I get attacked and bitten in the face?" These worries cause distress severe enough to disrupt everyday activities. The children are constantly on the lookout for the feared stimulus and, as we saw with Charlotte, go to great lengths to avoid contact.

Children's beliefs regarding the danger of the feared stimulus are likely to persist despite evidence that no danger exists or despite efforts to reason with them. Unlike most adults with a specific phobia, children often do not recognize that their fears are extreme and unreasonable. If the feared object is rarely encountered, the phobia may not lead to serious impairment. However, if it is encountered regularly or if the fear causes significant distress or seriously interferes with important life events, the child's phobia can become a serious problem (Albano et al., 2003).

The phobias that can develop in children and adolescents seem limitless; they include fears of telephones, water, menstruation, newspapers, mathematics, haircuts, and bowel movements, to name just a few. Although it is possible to develop a phobia about almost any object, situation, or event—ranging from A (apiphobia, a fear of bees) to Z (zemmiphobia, a fear of the great mole rat)—children are much more likely to develop certain fears than others (Depla et al., 2008).

TABLE 11.4 | **Diagnostic Criteria for Specific Phobia**

(A) Marked fear or anxiety about a specific object or situation (e.g., flying, heights, animals, receiving an injection, seeing blood). | **DSM-5**

Note: In children, the fear or anxiety may be expressed by crying, tantrums, freezing, or clinging.

(B) The phobic object or situation almost always provokes immediate fear or anxiety.

(C) The phobic object or situation is actively avoided or endured with intense fear or anxiety.

(D) The fear or anxiety is out of proportion to the actual danger posed by the specific object or situation and to the sociocultural context.

(E) The fear, anxiety, or avoidance is persistent, typically lasting 6 months or more.

(F) The fear, anxiety or avoidance causes clinically significant distress or impairment in social, occupational, or other important areas of functioning.

(G) The disturbance is not better accounted for by another mental disorder, including fear, anxiety, and avoidance of situations associated with panic-like symptoms or other incapacitating symptoms (as in agoraphobia); objects or situations related to obsessions (as in obsessive–compulsive disorder); reminders of traumatic events (as in post-traumatic stress disorder); separation from home or attachment figures (as in separation anxiety disorder); or social situations (as in social anxiety disorder).

Specify if (code based on the phobic stimulus):

Animal (e.g., spiders, insects, dogs)

Natural environment (e.g., heights, storms, water)

Blood, injection, injury (e.g., needles, invasive medical procedures)

Situational (e.g., airplanes, elevators, enclosed places)

Other (e.g., situations that may lead to choking or vomiting; in children, loud sounds or costumed characters)

Source: Diagnostic and Statistical Manual of Mental Disorders, Fifth Edition, American Psychiatric Association.

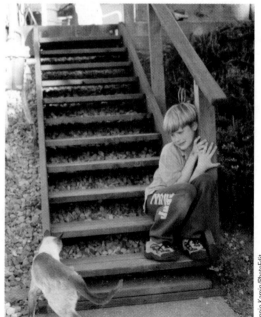

Fear of animals is one of the most common and heritable specific phobias.

According to evolutionary theory, human infants are biologically predisposed as a result of natural selection to learn certain fears (Seligman, 1971). The sources of most children's phobias can be traced to the natural dangers encountered during human evolution—snakes, the dark, predators, heights, blood, loud noises, and unfamiliar places. For example, when listening to evolutionary fear-relevant sounds (e.g., snake hissing), infants as young as 9 months of age display heart rate slowing, an increased eye-blink startle response, and more visual orienting, as compared to when they listen to modern fear-relevant sounds (e.g., siren wailing) or pleasant sounds (e.g., crowd cheering) (Erlich, Lipp, & Slaughter, 2013). These fears are adaptive in an evolutionary sense because they alert the individual to possible sources of danger, thereby increasing the likelihood of survival. It is not only by chance that the most common and most heritable specific phobias in children are a fear of events in the natural environment (e.g., heights, thunder) and a fear of animals, particularly dogs, snakes, insects, and mice (Essau, Conradt, & Petermann, 2000). Although evolutionary theory explains a readiness to acquire specific types of fears, it does not explain why children differ in their fearfulness or why some children develop extreme and disabling anxiety.

As specified in DSM-5, common types of specific phobias in young people include fears of animals or insects (e.g., dogs or spiders); fears of natural events (e.g., heights or thunderstorms); fears of blood, injuries, or medical procedures (e.g., seeing blood or receiving an injection); and fears of specific situations (e.g., flying in airplanes, riding on a bus). Both similarities (e.g., age at onset, gender, treatment response) and differences (e.g., focus of fear, physiological reaction, neural response patterns, impairment, comorbidity) have been found across these types, with natural environment and animal phobias having the most in common with other types, and blood, injury, and injection phobias the least (LeBeau et al., 2010; Lueken et al., 2011).

Prevalence and Comorbidity

About 20% of all youngsters experience specific phobias at some time in their lives, and those with this disorder tend to have multiple phobias (Kessler et al., 2012a; Merikangas et al., 2010). However, very few of these children are referred for treatment, suggesting that most parents do not view specific phobias as significantly harmful. There does seem to be a family vulnerability for particular types of phobias—children are at increased risk for the phobic disorder exhibited by their parent (LeBeau et al., 2010). Family risk can be attributed to both genetic and environmental factors. Specific phobias, particularly blood phobia, are more common in girls than boys

(Essau et al., 2000). The most common co-occurring disorders for youngsters with a specific phobia are another anxiety disorder and depressive disorders (Leyfer et al., 2013). Although comorbidity is frequent for children with specific phobias, it tends to be lower than for other anxiety disorders (LeBeau et al., 2010).

Onset, Course, and Outcome

Phobias involving animals, darkness, insects, blood, and injury typically have their onset at 7 to 9 years of age, which is similar to normal development. However, even though fears and phobias decline with age, clinical phobias are more likely to persist over time than are normal fears. Specific phobias can occur at any age but seem to peak between 10 and 13 years of age (LeBeau et al., 2010).

Section Summary

Specific Phobia

- Children with a specific phobia exhibit an extreme and disabling fear of particular objects or situations that in reality pose little or no danger.
- Evolutionary theory contends that human infants are biologically predisposed to learn certain fears that alert them to possible sources of danger. This may explain why the most common specific phobia in children is a fear of animals, such as dogs, snakes, and insects.
- DSM-5 categorizes specific phobias into five subtypes based on the focus of the phobic reaction and avoidance: animal; natural environment; blood, injection, injury; situational; and other.
- About 4% to 10% of children experience specific phobias, but only a very few are referred for treatment. Specific phobias can occur at any age, but seem to peak between 10 and 13 years of age.

SOCIAL ANXIETY DISORDER (SOCIAL PHOBIA)

To understand the world one must not be worrying about one's self.

—Albert Einstein (1879–1955)

▶ Kaylie is terrified to use the phone because, she says, she doesn't know how to have a conversation and would be embarrassed by the long periods of silence.

▶ Eugene is too embarrassed to use a public restroom.

▶ Li-Ming is terrified of speaking in front of her class—she's afraid of being humiliated.

Each of these youngsters has a **social anxiety disorder** (SOC [for "social"]) or **social phobia**—a marked and persistent fear of social or performance requirements that expose them to scrutiny and possible embarrassment (Knappe, Beesdo-Baum, & Wittchen, 2010). They go to great lengths to avoid these situations, or they may face the challenge with great effort, wearing a mask of fearlessness. Long after the age at which a fear of strangers is considered normal, children with SOC continue to shrink from people they do not know. When in the presence of other children or adults, they may blush, fall silent, cling to their parents, or try to hide. To be classified as SOC, their anxiety must occur in peer settings, not just when interacting with adults. The DSM criteria for SOC are shown in Table 11.5.

In addition to their extreme anxiety in social situations that make many people anxious, youngsters with SOC may feel anxious about the most mundane activities—handing out papers in class, buttoning their coat in front of others, or ordering a Big Mac and fries at McDonalds. Their most common fear is doing something in front of other people. They fear that if they speak in public, they may stumble over their words; if they ask a question, they may sound stupid; if they enter a room, they may trip and look awkward. One teenage girl was so fearful of being the focus of attention during meals that she spent every lunch period during her first year in high school sitting in a bathroom stall (Albano et al., 2003, p. 287).

Youngsters with SOC are more likely than other children to be highly emotional, socially fearful, and inhibited, sad, and lonely. They frequently experience socially distressing events with which they are unable to cope effectively, in part related to a lack of social skills (Beidel, Turner, & Morris, 1999). These children want to be liked by other people. However, their fear of acting in a way that may invite humiliation is so intense and pervasive that it often leads to loneliness and suffering because they cannot form the relationships they desire (La Greca & Lopez, 1998). If other people attempt to push them into social situations they may cry, have a tantrum, freeze, or withdraw even further. They fear most social situations, are afraid to meet or talk with new people, avoid contact with anyone outside their family, and find it extremely difficult to attend school, participate in recreational activities, or socialize (Beidel et al., 2007; Bernstein et al., 2008). Current evidence supports the view of SOC as existing on a continuum of severity from lesser to greater as a function of the number of social situations that are feared and/or avoided (Bögels et al., 2010).

The anxiety associated with SOC can be so severe that it produces stammering, sweating, upset stomach, rapid heartbeat, or a full-scale panic attack. Adolescents with SOC frequently believe that their visible physical reactions will expose their hidden feelings of

TABLE 11.5 | **Diagnostic Criteria for** Social Anxiety Disorder (Social Phobia)

DSM-5

(A) Marked fear or anxiety about one or more social situations in which the individual is exposed to possible scrutiny by others. Examples include social interactions (e.g., having a conversation, meeting unfamiliar people), being observed (e.g., eating or drinking), or performing in front of others (e.g., giving a speech).

Note: In children, the anxiety must occur in peer settings and not just during interactions with adults.

(B) The individual fears that he or she will act in a way or show anxiety symptoms that will be negatively evaluated (i.e., will be humiliating or embarrassing; will lead to rejection or offend others).

(C) The social situations almost always provoke fear or anxiety.

Note: In children, the fear or anxiety may be expressed by crying, tantrums, freezing, clinging, shrinking away, or failing to speak in social situations.

(D) The social situations are avoided or endured with intense fear or anxiety.

(E) The fear or anxiety is out of proportion to the actual danger posed by the social situation and to the sociocultural context.

(F) The fear, anxiety, or avoidance is persistent, typically lasting for 6 months or more.

(G) The fear, anxiety, and avoidance causes clinically significant distress or impairment in social, occupational, or other important areas of functioning.

(H) The fear, anxiety, and avoidance is not attributable to the direct physiological effects of a substance (e.g., a drug of abuse, a medication) or another medical condition.

(I) The fear, anxiety, or avoidance is not better explained by the symptoms of another mental disorder, such as panic disorder, body dysmorphic disorder, or autism spectrum disorder.

(J) If another medical condition (e.g., Parkinson's disease, obesity, disfigurement from burns or injury) is present, the fear, anxiety, or avoidance is clearly unrelated or is excessive.

Specify if:

Performance only: If the fear is restricted to speaking or performing in public.

Source: Diagnostic and Statistical Manual of Mental Disorders, Fifth Edition, American Psychiatric Association.

inadequacy, which makes them even more anxious. In a repeating cycle, children with SOC anticipate their awkwardness and poor performance, which triggers further anxiety as they approach the feared situation, and further increases their nervousness and physical symptoms. As a result, they avoid social activities such as calling a classmate for missed homework, asking the teacher to explain something, answering the telephone, going to parties, and dating (Albano, 1995).

SOC encompasses a variety of social fears, including fear of performance situations, such as speaking in front of others, and fear of interaction situations, such as talking to others at a party. Some research has suggested that performance- and interaction-related social fears may differ from one another in their risk factors and clinical characteristics and that identifying children with SOC who differ in their types of social fears may help to further our understanding of this disorder (Knappe et al., 2011). To this end, DSM-5 provides a "performance only" specifier to identify youngsters with SOC whose anxiety is restricted to performance situations such as speaking in front of others or performing in public (e.g., at a sporting event or musical recital).

Prevalence, Comorbidity, and Course

SOC is common; it has a lifetime prevalence of 6% to 12% and affects nearly twice as many girls as boys (Knappe et al., 2010). Girls may experience greater social anxiety because they are more concerned with social competence than are boys and attach greater importance to interpersonal relationships and evaluation by peers (Inderbitzen-Nolan & Walters, 2000). Some support for this hypothesis comes from a brain functional magnetic resonance imaging study into the

neural correlates of anticipated evaluation by peers in 9- to 17-year-old male and female adolescents (Guyer et al., 2009). Females who thought that a peer they wished to interact with was evaluating them showed age-related increases in activation of brain regions (e.g., hippocampus) associated with processing emotional information. These increases did not occur in males. Representative findings from this study are shown in ● Figure 11.1 and suggest that, relative to males, adolescent females may have an increasing biological sensitivity to being evaluated by peers, which may, over time, increase their vulnerability to developing SOC.

Among children and adolescents referred for treatment for anxiety disorders, about one-third have SOC as their primary diagnosis. It is also the most common secondary diagnosis for children referred for other anxiety disorders (Leyfer et al., 2013). Even so, many cases of SOC are overlooked because shyness is common and because these children are not likely to call attention to their problem even when they are severely distressed (Essau, Conradt, & Petermann, 1999).

Two-thirds of children and adolescents with SOC have another anxiety disorder—most commonly, generalized anxiety disorder (Bernstein et al., 2008; Leyfer et al., 2013). Other common comorbid anxiety disorders are SAD and specific phobias (Beidel et al., 2007). About 20% of adolescents with SOC also suffer from major depression. They may also use alcohol and other drugs as a

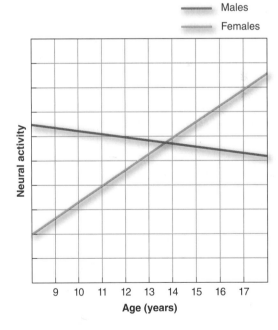

● **FIGURE 11.1** | (a) Increased neural activity as detected in the hippocampus while participants appraised how they thought preferred peers would evaluate them. (b) As age increased, neural activity in the hippocampus increased in females but did not change in males.

(a) © 2009, Amanda E. Guyer, Erin B. McClure-Tone, Nina D. Shiffrin, Daniel S. Pine, Eric E. Nelson; "Probing the Neural Correlates of Anticipated Peer Evaluation in Adolescence" *Child Development*, © 2009, Society for Research in Child Development, Inc. (b) From Probing the neural correlates of anticipated peer evaluation in adolescence by Guyer et al. *Child Development, 80*, 1000–1015. Journal Compilation © 2009, Society for Research in Child Development, Inc. John Wiley and Sons.

form of self-medication to reduce their anxiety in social situations and are at risk for later substance-use problems (Albano et al., 2003; Buckner et al., 2008).

SOC is extremely rare in children under the age of 10, and it generally develops after puberty, with the most common age at onset in early- to mid-adolescence (Wittchen, Stein, & Kessler, 1999). However, given the nature of the disorder, individuals with SOC are often the most reluctant to seek treatment following the onset of their problem. The prevalence of SOC appears to increase with age, with considerable persistence and fluctuations in symptom severity over time (Beesdo-Baum et al., 2012). As adults, individuals with SOC may experience significant impairment in role functioning, including relationship problems, educational difficulties, and poorer overall quality of life. The average duration of symptoms of social anxiety is about 20 to 25 years—thus, it is not a short-lived condition of adolescence and young adulthood. In the absence of effective treatment, the likelihood of a complete and long-lasting remission for SOC is the lowest for all anxiety disorders (Knappe et al., 2010).

Section Summary

Social Anxiety Disorder (SOC) (Social Phobia)

- Children with SOC fear being the focus of attention or scrutiny or of doing something in public that will be intensely humiliating.
- SOC is common, with a lifetime prevalence of 6% to 12%, and affecting nearly twice as many girls as boys.
- SOC generally develops after puberty, at a time when most teens experience heightened self-consciousness and worries about what others think of them.

SELECTIVE MUTISM

KEISHA

Mum's the Word

Keisha, age 6, doesn't speak at kindergarten to teachers or peers and did not do so during her 2 years in preschool. Two years ago she had difficulties being left at preschool and it took about 2 months before she could be left without crying. Although she doesn't talk to other children, she interacts with them and participates in school activities. Keisha speaks openly to all family members at home but does not speak to them in public if others might hear her. She says that she does not know why she doesn't talk, but has told her mother that she feels scared. Her mother says Keisha is shy and is a worrier.

Adapted from Leonard & Dow, 1995.

Children with **selective mutism** fail to speak in specific social situations in which there is an expectation to speak (e.g., at school), even though they may speak loudly and frequently at home or in other settings (Viana, Beidel, & Rabian, 2009). The DSM-5 criteria also require that the child's disturbance interferes with educational or work achievement or with social communication, that it is present for at least 1 month, that it is not limited to a lack of knowledge or discomfort with the spoken language required in the social situation, that it is not better explained by a communication disorder, and that it does not occur only during the course of autism spectrum disorder, schizophrenia, or another psychotic disorder (APA, 2013).

Prevalence, Comorbidity, and Course

Selective mutism is rare, estimated to occur in about 0.7% of all children in community samples (Bergman, Piacentini, & McKracken, 2002). Prevalence does not seem to vary by sex or race/ethnicity. The most common co-occurring disorders are other anxiety disorders, particularly SOC and specific phobia. Oppositional behaviors may also occur, but these may be limited to situations in which the child is required to speak (Cunningham, McHolm, & Boyle, 2006). The average age at onset is about 3 to 4 years; however, there is often a considerable lag between onset and referral, possibly because the child's mutism may not occur at home. With school entry and the associated increase in social interaction and tasks (e.g., reading aloud), the child is more likely to be identified and referred. The persistence of selective mutism is variable, although many children seem to "outgrow" the disorder. However, research in this area is limited, and the long-term course of the disorder is not known (APA, 2013).

Although it was not previously included as a diagnosable disorder in DSM-IV, selective mutism has many features in common with the anxiety disorders (Leonard & Dow, 1995), which resulted in its inclusion as an anxiety disorder in DSM-5. For example, about 45% to 75% of children with selective mutism meet diagnostic criteria for SOC in ways other than their reluctance to speak (Viana et al., 2009), and nearly 40% of their parents have also been diagnosed with SOC during their lifetime (Chavira et al., 2007). Other common comorbidities include communication, elimination, and oppositional disorders (Cohan et al., 2008).

Based on the similarities between selective mutism and SOC, it has been suggested that selective mutism may be a developmentally specific variant of SOC in young children or an early precursor to SOC, rather than a unique disorder (Bergman et al., 2002; Dummit et al., 1997). However, there are also differences between the two disorders—for example, nonverbal social engagement and oppositional features occur in selective mutism, but less so in SOC (Yaganeh, Beidel, & Turner, 2006). Relatedly, one study identified three subgroups of children with selective mutism: anxious—mildly oppositional; (2) anxious—communication delayed; and (3) exclusively anxious (Cohan & Chavira, 2008). Anecdotal accounts from adults who suffered from selective mutism as children also suggest that in some cases trauma played a role and not talking was a self-protective response (Omdal, 2007). For example, Dr. Maya Angelou, a celebrated African-American poet and writer who captivated audiences with her words, was mute for nearly 5 years after suffering the trauma of being raped at 8 years old.

Section Summary

Selective Mutism

- Children with selective mutism fail to talk in specific social situations where there is an expectation to do so, even though they may speak in other settings.

- Selective mutism is a rare disorder occurring in about 0.7% of all children. Its prevalence does not seem to vary by sex or race/ethnicity.

- The most common co-occurring disorders are other anxiety disorders, particularly SOC and specific phobia.

- The average age at onset is about 3 to 4 years, but there is often a considerable lag between onset and referral.

- Selective mutism and SOC are currently viewed as distinct but strongly related disorders.

PANIC DISORDER AND AGORAPHOBIA

CLAUDIA

An Attack Out of Nowhere

Claudia, age 16, was watching TV after a noneventful day at school. She suddenly felt overwhelmed by an intense feeling of light-headedness and a smothering sensation, as if she couldn't get any air to breathe. Her heart started to pound rapidly, as if it would explode. The attack came on so fast and was so intense that Claudia panicked and thought she was having a heart attack that would kill her. She began to sweat and tremble, and she felt the room was spinning. These feelings reached a peak within 2 minutes ... but this was the seventh attack that Claudia had experienced this month. She frantically ran to her mother and pleaded to be taken to the hospital emergency room—again. (Based on authors' case material.)

Prior to DSM-5, panic disorder and agoraphobia were connected because diagnosing panic disorder included the designation "with" or "without" agoraphobia (i.e., a marked fear or avoidance of certain situations in which the individual thinks that escape may be difficult, or help not available, if they were to experience panic-like or other incapacitating symptoms). However, in DSM-5, panic disorder and agoraphobia are now separate disorders with different diagnostic criteria. This change was based on research suggesting that a number of adolescents and adults experience agoraphobia without panic symptoms. However, to date, most studies of young people have considered the two conditions together (Higa-McMillan et al., 2014). Therefore, we discuss both disorders in this section.

Adolescents like Claudia with a **panic disorder (PD)** display recurrent unexpected panic attacks followed by at least 1 month of persistent concern or worry about having another attack and its consequences or a significant change in their behavior related to the attacks in order to avoid having them. The DSM-5 diagnostic criteria for Panic Disorder are presented in Table 11.6.

A **panic attack** is a sudden and overwhelming period of intense fear or discomfort that is accompanied by four or more physical and cognitive symptoms characteristic of the fight/flight response (see Table 11.6). Usually, a panic attack is short, with symptoms reaching maximal intensity in 10 minutes or less and then diminishing slowly over the next 30 minutes or the next few hours. Panic attacks are accompanied by an overwhelming sense of imminent danger or impending doom, and

Panic

Chris Collins/Cusp/Corbis

TABLE 11.6 | Diagnostic Criteria for Panic Disorder

DSM-5

(A) Recurrent unexpected panic attacks. A panic attack is an abrupt surge of intense fear or intense discomfort that reaches a peak within minutes and during which time four (or more) of the following symptoms occur:

Note: The abrupt surge can occur from a calm state or an anxious state.

(1) Palpitations, pounding heart, or accelerated heart rate.
(2) Sweating.
(3) Trembling or shaking.
(4) Sensations or shortness of break or smothering.
(5) Feelings of choking.
(6) Chest pain or discomfort.
(7) Nausea or abdominal distress.
(8) Feeling dizzy, unsteady, light-headed, or faint.
(9) Chills or heat sensations.
(10) Paresthesias (numbness or tingling sensations).
(11) Derealization (feelings of unreality) or depersonalization (being detached from oneself).
(12) Fear of losing control or "going crazy."
(13) Fear of dying.

Note: Culture-specific symptoms (e.g., tinnitus, neck soreness, headache, uncontrollable screaming or crying) may be seen. Such symptoms should not count as one of the four required symptoms.

(B) At least one of the attacks has been followed by 1 month (or more) of one or both of the following:

(1) Persistent concern or worry about additional panic attacks or their consequences (e.g., losing control, having a heart attack, "going crazy")

(2) Significant maladaptive change in behavior related to the attacks (e.g., behaviors designed to avoid having panic attacks, such as avoidance of exercise or unfamiliar situations).

(C) The disturbance is not attributable to the physiological effects of a substance (e.g., a drug of abuse, a medication) or another medical condition (e.g., hyperthyroidism, cardiopulmonary disorders).

(D) The disturbance is not better accounted for by another mental disorder.

Source: Diagnostic and Statistical Manual of Mental Disorders, Fifth Edition, American Psychiatric Association.

by an urge to escape. Although they are brief, they can occur several times a week or month. It is important to remember that although the symptoms are dramatic, they are not physically harmful or dangerous.

Panic attacks are easily identified in adults, but some controversy exists over how often they occur in children and adolescents. Although panic attacks are extremely rare in young children, they are common in adolescents (Mattis & Ollendick, 2002). One explanation is that young children lack the cognitive ability to make the catastrophic misinterpretations (e.g., "my heart is beating rapidly and I'm sitting here watching TV like I always do—I must be going crazy") that usually accompany panic attacks (Nelles & Barlow, 1988). However, research suggests that young children may in fact be capable of such misinterpretations (Mattis & Ollendick, 1997).

If limited cognitive capacity is not the primary reason that panic attacks are so rare in young children, what is? In a revealing study, the relationship between the occurrence of panic attacks and pubertal stage was assessed in 754 girls in the sixth and seventh grades. Importantly, increasing rates of panic were related to pubertal development, not to increasing age (Hayward et al., 1992). The significance of pubertal development and anxiety disorders in females has received general support (Reardon, Leen-Feldner, & Hayward, 2009). For example, in one study, sixth- to eighth-grade females who developed internalizing symptoms were on average 5 months earlier in their pubertal development than females who did not develop symptoms (Hayward et al., 1997). Given that spontaneous panic attacks are rare before puberty and are related to pubertal stage, and that adolescence is the peak time for the onset of the disorder, the physical changes that take place around puberty seem critical to the occurrence of panic.

Why do the physical symptoms of the fight/flight response occur if an adolescent is not initially frightened? One possibility is that things other than fear can produce these symptoms. A youngster may be distressed for a particular reason and that stress may increase production of adrenaline and other chemicals that produce physical symptoms of panic. Increased adrenaline may be chemically maintained in the body even after the stress is no longer present. Another possibility is that the youngster may breathe a little too fast (subtle hyperventilation), which also can produce symptoms. Because the over-breathing is very slight, the child gets used to it and does not realize that he or she is hyperventilating. A third possibility is that some youngsters are experiencing normal bodily changes but, because they are constantly monitoring their bodies (as adolescents are prone to do), they notice these sensations far more readily (Barlow, 2002).

Adolescents with PD may avoid locations where they've had a previous panic attack or situations or activities in which they fear an attack might occur. An adolescent with PD might think: "It would be bad enough to have an attack at all, but it would be really dangerous if I had one while riding my bike to school. I'd be totally preoccupied with the attack and would have an accident. I'd probably destroy my bike and wind up seriously hurting myself or someone else in the process!" The youth's avoidance of riding a bike to school could be misinterpreted as a fear of bike riding, when it is actually a fear of having a panic attack while riding the bike.

If not recognized and treated, PD and its complications can seriously interfere with relationships at home and at school and with school performance. Some adolescents with PD may be reluctant to go to school or be separated from their parents. In severe cases, the tendency to avoid everyday life circumstances may increase and generalize, to the point at which the older adolescent with PD becomes terrified to leave the house at all.

Agoraphobia is characterized by marked fear or anxiety in certain places or situations (i.e., being in a crowd, being outside the home alone; see Table 11.7). The individual fears or avoids these situations because of thoughts that escape might be difficult, or help might not be available, if they were to experience panic-like or other incapacitating symptoms (e.g., fear of falling in an elderly person) (Craske et al., 2010; Wittchen et al., 2010). An older adolescent with agoraphobia who dares to venture into a feared situation does so only with great distress or when accompanied by a family member or a friend.

Agoraphobia is a distinct disorder that can be conceptualized independently from both panic attacks and panic disorder. Support for this comes from a 10-year longitudinal follow-up study of a normative sample of 3,000 individuals 14 to 24 years of age at the outset of the study (Wittchen et al., 2008). Sex and age differences in incidence and age at onset were observed between those with agoraphobia and those with panic attacks and panic disorder. The course and stability of agoraphobia also differed from that of panic disorder, and panic attacks did not reliably predict the onset of agoraphobia. Thus, rather than being an outcome of panic disorder, consistent with DSM-5, agoraphobia appears to be an anxiety disorder in its own right (Higa-McMillan et al., 2014).

Prevalence and Comorbidity

Panic attacks are common among nonreferred adolescents, affecting about 16% of teens (Mattis & Ollendick, 2002). PD and agoraphobia are much less common, with an estimated lifetime prevalence for both of about 2.5% for youths 13 to 17 years of age (Merikangas et al., 2010). Adolescent females are about twice as likely as adolescent males to experience panic attacks, and a fairly consistent association has been found between panic attacks and stressful life

TABLE 11.7 | **Diagnostic Criteria for Agoraphobia**

DSM-5

(A) Marked fear or anxiety about two (or more) of the following five situations:

  (1) Using public transportation (e.g., automobiles, buses, trains, ships, planes).

  (2) Being in open spaces (e.g., parking lots, marketplaces, bridges).

  (3) Being in enclosed spaces (e.g., shops, theatres, cinemas).

  (4) Standing in line or being in a crowd.

  (5) Being outside of the home alone.

(B) The individual fears or avoids these situations because of thoughts that escape might be difficult or help might not be available in the event of developing panic-like symptoms or other incapacitating or embarrassing symptoms (e.g., fear of falling in the elderly; fear of incontinence).

(C) The agoraphobic situations almost always provoke fear or anxiety.

(D) The agoraphobic situations are actively avoided, require the presence of a companion, or are endured with intense fear or anxiety.

(E) The fear or anxiety is out of proportion to the actual danger posed by the agoraphobic situations and to the sociocultural context.

(F) The fear, anxiety, or avoidance is persistent, typically lasting for 6 months or more.

(G) The fear, anxiety, or avoidance causes clinically significant distress or impairment in social, occupational, or other important areas of functioning.

(H) If another medical condition (e.g., inflammatory bowel disease, Parkinson's disease) is present, the fear, anxiety, or avoidance is clearly excessive.

(I) The fear, anxiety, or avoidance is not better explained by the symptoms of another mental disorder.

Note: Agoraphobia is diagnosed irrespective of the presence of panic disorder. If an individual's presentation meets criteria for panic disorder and agoraphobia, both diagnoses should be assigned.

Source: Diagnostic and Statistical Manual of Mental Disorders, Fifth Edition. American Psychiatric Association.

events (King, Ollendick, & Mattis, 1994). Most referred adolescents with PD have one or more other disorders, most commonly an additional anxiety disorder (particularly generalized anxiety disorder or SAD) and major depressive disorder. Other comorbid conditions include mania and hypomania, attention-deficit/hyperactivity disorder (ADHD), and oppositional defiant disorder (ODD) (Doerfler et al., 2007). The most common comorbidities for agoraphobia are other anxiety disorders (e.g., PD, specific phobias, and SOC), major depressive disorder, post-traumatic stress disorder, and alcohol-use disorder (APA, 2013).

Did Darwin Have a Panic Disorder?

Charles Darwin (1809–1882) was a gregarious and daring traveler and outdoorsman in his college days. However, in his late 20s—just a year after returning to England after a 5-year voyage to South America and the Pacific aboard the HMS *Beagle*—he started to have an "uncomfortable palpitation of the heart." The symptoms arose shortly after he began keeping a secret notebook that, 22 years later, would become his book-length elaboration of the theory of evolution, *On the Origin of Species*. Over the years, his affliction was described as a case of bad nerves, a tropical disease, intellectual exhaustion, arsenic poisoning, suppressed gout, and a host of other symptoms. However, in his journal Darwin described his malady as a "sensation of fear … accompanied by troubled beating of the heart, sweat, trembling of muscles."

From Desmond & Moore, 1991.

The relation between SAD and PD has received considerable attention, to see whether separation experiences during childhood contribute to the development of later PD or whether SAD is a childhood form of adult panic disorder (Craske et al., 2010). Findings generally support SAD as a strong predictor of PD. However, since SAD also predicts other anxiety disorders (but not depressive or substance-use disorders), it may be an early marker for anxiety disorders in general, rather than a specific risk factor for PD (Kossowsky et al., 2013).

After months or years of unrelenting panic attacks and the restricted lifestyle that results from avoidance behavior, adolescents and young adults with PD and agoraphobia may develop severe depression and may be at risk for suicidal behavior. Others may begin to use alcohol or drugs as a way of alleviating their anxiety (Higa-McMillan et al., 2014).

Onset, Course, and Outcome

Although PD has been found to occur in young children, few cases have been reported (Higa-McMillan et al., 2014). The average age at onset for a first panic attack in adolescents with PD is 15 to 19 years, and 95% of adolescents with the disorder are postpubertal (Bernstein, Borchardt, & Perwien, 1996). PD occurs in otherwise emotionally healthy youngsters about half the time. The most frequent prior disturbance, if one exists, is a depressive disorder (Last & Strauss, 1989). Unfortunately, PD and agoraphobia are stable over time and have one of the lowest complete remission rates for any of the anxiety disorders (Wittchen et al., 2000). Individuals with PD and those with PD and agoraphobia with an

early onset are more likely to experience comorbid disorders and a recurrence of symptoms following a period of remission than those with a later onset, indicating that early onset PD and agoraphobia are particularly serious disorders (Ramsawh et al., 2011). In the absence of treatment, these disorders are likely to have a persistent and chronic course.

Section Summary

Panic Disorder and Agoraphobia

- A panic attack is a sudden and overwhelming period of intense fear or discomfort accompanied by physical and cognitive symptoms.
- Adolescents with PD display recurrent unexpected panic attacks followed by persistent concern about having another attack, constant worry about the consequences, or a significant maladaptive change in their behavior related to the attacks, designed to avoid having additional attacks.
- Agoraphobia is characterized by marked fear or anxiety in certain situations. The individual fears or avoids these situations because of thoughts that escape might be difficult or help might not be available if they were to experience panic-like or other incapacitating symptoms.
- Many postpubertal adolescents experience panic attacks, but PD and agoraphobia are much less common, affecting about 2.5% of teens, and females about twice as often as males. Average age at onset for a first panic attack in adolescents with PD is 15 to 19 years.
- PD and agoraphobia are associated with many other disorders, most commonly other anxiety disorders.

- PD and agoraphobia are stable and over time and have one of the lowest rates of complete remission for any of the anxiety disorders.

GENERALIZED ANXIETY DISORDER

JARED

Perpetual Worrywart

Jared, age 13, was referred because of his excessive anxiety, worry, and somatic symptoms—his mother describes him as overly concerned about everything. Jared says he worries about most things, but especially about not being good enough for his parents, being teased by other kids, not doing well at school, making mistakes, and being in an accident in which he or his parents are injured. Jared ruminates for days about things that have already occurred, such as what he said in class the previous day or how he did on last week's test. Once he begins to worry, he says, "I just can't stop, no matter how hard I try." Jared reports that when he is worrying about the past or anticipating an upcoming event he has headaches, stomachaches, and a rapid heartbeat. His mother (who also worries a lot, but not nearly as much as Jared) says that Jared is extremely self-critical and needs constant reassurance. (Based on authors' case material.)

Some worrying is a part of normal development. However, children like Jared with a **generalized anxiety disorder (GAD)** experience excessive and uncontrollable anxiety and worry about many events or activities on most days. They worry when there is nothing obvious to provoke the worry. For children with GAD, worrying can be episodic or almost continuous. The worrier is unable to relax and may experience physical symptoms such as muscle tension, headaches, or nausea. Common symptoms of GAD include irritability, difficulty concentrating, and a lack of energy, difficulty falling asleep, and restless sleep (Comer et al., 2012; Layne et al., 2009). The DSM-5 criteria for GAD are presented in Table 11.8.

In other anxiety disorders, anxiety converges on specific situations or objects, such as separation, social performance, animals or insects, or bodily sensations. In contrast, the anxiety experienced by individuals with GAD is widespread and focuses on a variety of everyday life events (Andrews et al., 2010). It was once thought that children who were generally anxious did not focus their anxiety on one specific thing, which is referred to as "free-floating anxiety." However, these youngsters do, in fact, focus their anxiety, but they focus it on many different things. Hence, the term *generalized anxiety* is more accurate.

TABLE 11.8 | **Diagnostic Criteria for Generalized Anxiety Disorder (GAD)**

(A) Excessive anxiety and worry (apprehensive expectation) occurring more days than not for at least 6 months, about a number of events or activities (such as work or school performance). **DSM-5**

(B) The individual finds it difficult to control the worry.

(C) The anxiety and worry are associated with three (or more) of the following six symptoms (with at least some symptoms present for more days than not for the past 6 months).

Note: Only one item is required for children.

(1) Restlessness or feeling keyed up or on edge.

(2) Being easily fatigued.

(3) Difficulty concentrating or mind going blank.

(4) Irritability.

(5) Muscle tension.

(6) Sleep disturbance (difficulty falling or staying asleep, or restless unsatisfying sleep).

(D) The anxiety, worry, or physical symptoms cause clinically significant distress or impairment in social, occupational, or other important areas of functioning.

(E) The disturbance is not due to the general physiological effects of a substance (e.g., a drug of abuse, a medication) or a another medical condition (e.g., hyperthyroidism).

(F) The disturbance is not better explained by another mental disorder.

Source: Diagnostic and Statistical Manual of Mental Disorders, Fifth Edition, American Psychiatric Association.

Children with GAD are likely to pick up on every frightening event in a movie, on the Internet, or on TV and relate it to themselves. If they see a news report on TV about a car accident, they may begin to worry about being in a car accident themselves. They always expect the worst possible outcome and underestimate their ability to cope with situations or events that are less than ideal. They do not seem to realize that the events they worry about have an extremely low likelihood of actually happening. Thus, their thinking often consists of what-if statements: "What if the school bus breaks down?" "What if I get hit by lightning?" Children with GAD do not restrict their worries to frightening or catastrophic events; they also worry excessively about minor everyday occurrences, such as what to wear or what to watch on TV. This generalized worry about minor events distinguishes children with GAD from those with other anxiety disorders (Albano et al., 2003).

Like Jared, children with GAD are often self-conscious, self-doubting, and worried about meeting others' expectations. Their worry may lead to significant interpersonal problems, especially those involving a tendency to be overly nurturing to others. Children with GAD seek constant approval and reassurance from adults and fear people whom they perceive as unpleasant, critical, or unfair. They tend to set extremely high standards for their own performance and are highly self-critical when they fall short. Moreover, they continue to worry even when evidence contradicts their concern. For example, a child with GAD who received a grade of A on every previous class assignment may worry about failing on the next assignment (Silverman & Ginsburg, 1995). Children with GAD also show an intolerance of uncertainty, which may be a cognitive disposition for GAD that may result in impaired decision making under conditions of uncertainty, as well as other cognitive processes that serve to maintain worry (Fialko, Bolton, & Perrin, 2012; Krain et al., 2006).

Children with GAD cannot seem to stop worrying even when they recognize how unhappy they are making themselves and others. This characteristic is what makes their anxiety abnormal. A normal child who is

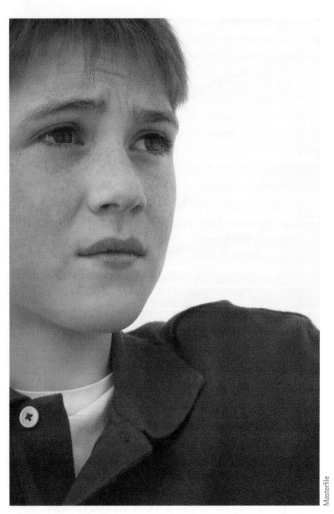

Youngsters with a generalized anxiety disorder worry about almost everything.

worried about an upcoming sports competition can still concentrate on other tasks and will stop worrying once the competition is over. However, for children with GAD one "crisis" is followed by another in a never-ending cycle. The intensity of the child's worries is one of the best predictors of impairment in children with GAD (Layne et al., 2009). It may also lead to a sense that the worry is uncontrollable, which is an important clinical feature of GAD (Kertz & Woodruff-Borden, 2011). The cognitive beliefs that children with GAD hold about worry may also play a role. *Meta-worry*, or worrying about worry, involves the development of beliefs such as worrying is uncontrollable or that it can lead to negative consequences for the worrier. For children with GAD, these negative beliefs about worry may lead to even higher levels of anxiety and more widespread anxiety (Ellis & Hudson, 2010; Esbjørn et al., 2014).

Prevalence and Comorbidity

GAD was the least common anxiety disorder reported in a large national survey of more than 10,000 teens (13 to 18 years of age) in the United States, with a lifetime prevalence rate of 2.2% (Merikangas et al., 2010). In contrast, a more recent study found that it was the most common anxiety disorder diagnosis (37%) among children referred to an anxiety specialty clinic (Leyfer et al., 2013). In general, the disorder is equally common in boys and girls, with a slightly higher prevalence in older adolescent females. Children with GAD have a high rate of other anxiety disorders. For younger children, co-occurring SAD and conduct problems are most common; older children with GAD tend to have specific phobias, SOC, panic disorder, and MDD, as well as impaired social adjustment, low self-esteem, and an increased risk for suicide (Keller et al., 1992; Leyfer et al., 2013; Masi et al., 2004). Rates of co-occurring MDD for GAD are especially high, in some cases, even higher than for other anxiety disorders (Higa-McMillan et al., 2014).

Onset, Course, and Outcome

The average age at onset for GAD is in early adolescence (Beesdo et al., 2010). Older children present with a higher total number of symptoms and report higher levels of anxiety and depression than younger children, but these symptoms may diminish with age (Strauss et al., 1988). In a community sample of adolescents with GAD, the likelihood of their having GAD at follow-up was higher if symptoms at the time of initial assessment were severe (Cohen, Cohen, & Brook, 1993). Nearly half of severe cases were rediagnosed after 2 years, suggesting that severe GAD symptoms persist over time, even in youngsters who have not been referred for treatment.

Generalized Anxiety Disorder

- Youngsters with a GAD experience chronic or exaggerated worry and tension, often accompanied by physical symptoms.
- GAD occurs in about 2% of children in community samples, but it is one of the most common anxiety disorders in children who are referred to specialty clinics for treatment of anxiety.

OBSESSIVE—COMPULSIVE AND RELATED DISORDERS

Insanity: doing the same thing over and over again and expecting different results.

—Attributed to Albert Einstein

OCD was previously included as an anxiety disorder in the DSM. While recognizing its close relationship with the anxiety disorders, the DSM-5 includes OCD in a separate chapter with a number of related disorders that are distinct from OCD but contain overlapping diagnostic features such as preoccupations and repetitive behaviors or mental acts in response to the preoccupations (Piacentini, Chang, et al., 2014). This grouping was based on similarities that have been found between OCD and these related conditions in terms of their features, comorbidity, familial and genetic factors, brain circuitry, and response to treatment (Bienvenu et al., 2012). To give you a brief overview of the OCD-related disorders, the main features of each are described in A Closer Look 11.3. We will focus our discussion on OCD since it is the disorder that is most closely connected to the anxiety disorders and the one we know the most about.

Obsessive–Compulsive Disorder

ETHAN

Counting and Cleaning

Ethan, age 15, is continually distracted by powerful and peculiar thoughts, such as counting how many times he blinks and how many steps it takes to get to the kitchen. He avoids stepping on any floor tiles with dirt on them because he doesn't want to get germs on his feet. He is obsessed with germs on door handles and feels compelled to avoid touching them unless he first uses a cloth (which he always has with him) to clean the handle off. On those rare occasions that he misplaces or forgets to bring a clean cloth with him, he gets extremely anxious, freezes, and feels sick to his stomach. (Based on authors' case material.)

A CLOSER **LOOK** 11.3

Main Features of DSM-5 OCD-Related Disorders

Body Dysmorphic Disorder
Body dysmorphic disorder is characterized by a preoccupation with defects or flaws in physical appearance that are not observable or appear slight to others. During the course of the disorder, the individual engages in repetitive behaviors (e.g., mirror checking, excessive grooming, seeking reassurance) or mental acts (comparing her or his appearance to others) in response to appearance concerns. This preoccupation causes significant distress or impairment in important areas of life functioning (e.g., social, occupational).

Hoarding Disorder
Hoarding disorder is characterized by persistent difficulty discarding or parting with possessions, regardless of their actual value. This difficulty is due to a perceived need to save the items and to distress associated with discarding them. The difficulty discarding possessions results in an accumulation of possessions that congest and clutter active living areas and substantially compromises their intended use. The hoarding causes significant distress or impairment in important areas of life functioning (e.g., social, occupational, maintaining a safe environment).

Trichotillomania (Hair-Pulling Disorder)
Trichotillomania is characterized by recurrent pulling out of one's hair, resulting in hair loss (not attributable to another medical condition), repeated attempts to decrease or stop hair pulling, and significant distress or impairment in important areas of life functioning.

Excoriation Disorder (Skin-Picking Disorder)
Excoriation disorder (skin-picking disorder) is characterized by recurrent skin picking resulting in skin lesions, repeated attempts to stop skin picking, and significant distress or impairment in important areas of life functioning.

Source: Diagnostic and Statistical Manual of Mental Disorders, Fifth Edition, American Psychiatric Association.

Ethan has an **obsessive–compulsive disorder (OCD)**, which is an unusual disorder of ritual and doubt. Youngsters with OCD experience recurrent, time-consuming (taking more than 1 hour a day), and disturbing obsessions and compulsions (Evans & Leckman, 2006). **Obsessions** are persistent and intrusive thoughts, urges, or images that are experienced as intrusive and unwanted, and generally cause significant anxiety or distress. Most children describe their obsessions as very similar to worries. However, obsessions are much more than heightened worries about everyday problems, such as homework or popularity. They are excessive and irrational and are focused on improbable or unrealistic events or on greatly exaggerated real-life events. Children with OCD may complain about being unable to stop "hearing" recurring rhymes or songs or may experience fears of having a serious disease such as cancer or of being attacked by an intruder. In children with OCD, the most common obsessions focus on contamination, fears of harm to self or others, or concerns with symmetry and exactness, whereas in adolescents, sexual, somatic, and religious preoccupations also become more common (Geller et al., 1998). Since these and other obsessions create considerable anxiety and distress, children with OCD go to great lengths to try to neutralize them with another action, known as a compulsion.

Compulsions are repetitive, purposeful, and intentional behaviors (e.g., hand washing) or mental acts (e.g., repeating words silently) that are performed in response to obsessions in an attempt to suppress or neutralize them. For example, as a result of an obsession with germs, a child with OCD may feel compelled to clean door handles, check for dirt, or engage in some other ritual as a way of decreasing anxiety. One 7-year-old boy was so obsessed with germs that he felt compelled to wash his homework! Multiple compulsions are the norm, the most common being excessive washing and bathing (occurring in about 85% of cases), repeating, checking, touching, counting, hoarding, and ordering or arranging (Geller et al., 1998). The DSM-5 criteria for OCD are presented in Table 11.9.

Most children with OCD have multiple obsessions and compulsions, and certain compulsions are commonly associated with specific obsessions. For example, washing and cleaning rituals are likely to be associated with contamination obsessions, such as a concern with dirt or germs, a concern or disgust with body wastes or secretions (e.g., urine, feces, saliva), or an excessive concern about chemical or environmental contamination. Compulsions involving counting over and over to a certain number are frequently related to a concern about harm—that something terrible might happen, such as the death of a parent or a

fire. Obsessions with symmetry, exactness, or order are often associated with compulsions for arranging and ordering, such as repeatedly packing and unpacking a

TABLE 11.9 | **Diagnostic Criteria for Obsessive–Compulsive Disorder (OCD)**

DSM-5

(A) Presence of obsessions, compulsions, or both:

Obsessions are defined by (1) and (2):

(1) Recurrent and persistent thoughts, urges, or images that are experienced, at sometime during the disturbance, as intrusive and unwanted, and that in most individuals cause marked anxiety or distress.

(2) The individual attempts to ignore or suppress such thoughts, urges, or images, or to neutralize them with some other thought or action (i.e., by performing a compulsion).

Compulsions are defined by (1) and (2):

(1) Repetitive behaviors (e.g., hand washing, ordering, checking) or mental acts (e.g., praying, counting, repeating words silently) that the individual feels driven to perform in response to an obsession or according to rules that must be applied rigidly.

(2) The behaviors or mental acts are aimed at preventing or reducing anxiety or distress, or preventing some dreaded event or situation; however, these behaviors or mental acts are not connected in a realistic way with what they are designed to neutralize or prevent, or are clearly excessive.

Note: Young children may not be able to articulate the aims of these behaviors or mental acts.

(B) The obsessions or compulsions are time-consuming (e.g., take more than 1 hour per day) or cause clinically significant distress or impairment in social, occupational, or other important areas of functioning.

(C) The obsessive–compulsive symptoms are not attributable to the physiological effects of a substance (e.g., a drug of abuse, a medication) or another medical condition.

(D) The disturbance is not better explained by the symptoms of another mental disorder.

Specify if:

With good or fair insight: The individual recognizes that obsessive–compulsive disorder beliefs are definitely or probably not true or that they may or may not be true.

With poor insight: The individual thinks obsessive–compulsive disorder beliefs are probably true.

With absent insight/delusional beliefs: The individual is completely convinced that obsessive–compulsive disorder beliefs are true.

Specify if:

Tic-related: The individual has a current or past history of a tic disorder.

Source: Diagnostic and Statistical Manual of Mental Disorders, Fifth Edition. American Psychiatric Association.

suitcase or rearranging drawers (Piacentini, 1997). Interestingly, in adults, each symptom dimension of OCD (e.g., contamination-related, symmetry-related) may be mediated by a distinct but partially overlapping neural system; however, this may not be the case for children. This suggests important developmental differences in the neural mechanisms of OCD symptoms in children versus adults (Gilbert et al., 2009).

How can children with OCD be so reasonable about some things yet so disturbed with respect to their obsessions and compulsions? Most children over age 8 persist in their obsessions or compulsions even though they recognize them as excessive and unreasonable (children ordinarily use the words *dumb* or *stupid*). However, OCD is extremely resistant to reason, even when the child recognizes the "silliness" of the routines. For example, one of 10-year-old Emilio's obsessive thoughts is that a long, flexible, pipe-like structure protrudes from his chest. He knows this is not so, but he must behave as if the pipe is there and move in such a way that no person or object comes too close in front of him (Despert, 1955).

Children with OCD often involve family members in their rituals; for example, demanding that their clothes be washed two or three times a day, not allowing others to eat certain foods for fear of illness or contamination, or having a parent get up at 5 a.m. to assist them in dressing rituals that may take hours to complete (Piacentini, 1997; Waters & Barrett, 2000). Some children with OCD insist that certain phrases be repeated or that questions be answered in a certain way. Consider this exchange between Heather, age 11, and her mother:

> HEATHER: You said before that we were having dessert. Now you say we're having ice cream. Which one is it?
>
> MOTHER: Ice cream is dessert.
>
> HEATHER: But which one is right?
>
> MOTHER: Both.
>
> HEATHER: But are we having ice cream or dessert?
>
> MOTHER: We're having ice cream.
>
> HEATHER: So why did you say we were having dessert?

Heather became so argumentative, insistent, and persistent that her mother thought she had a severe behavior problem. However, with further assessment, it became clear that Heather's oppositional behavior was an expression of OCD. When interviewed about her problem, Heather said: "I can't help it. When I'm with my mother, I have to make her say things 'just right' or I feel terrible."

Compulsions are intended to neutralize or reduce the anxiety and tension of the obsessions or to prevent some dreaded event or situation from happening. Although rituals may provide temporary relief from anxiety, in the long run they fail to achieve their intended purpose. As a result, children with OCD increasingly become trapped in a time-consuming and never-ending cycle of obsessions and compulsions. Many hours each day are dominated by disabling, alarming, and sometimes ridiculous thoughts and by repeated compulsive behaviors. The child's preoccupation with obsessions and rituals makes it extremely difficult, if not impossible, to focus on anything else. As we saw with Ethan, even a simple activity like opening a door may become an insurmountable problem.

As a result of such excessive preoccupations, normal activities of children with OCD are reduced, and health, social and family relations, and school functioning can be severely disrupted (Storch et al., 2010). Cleaning or washing rituals may lead to health problems, such as skin irritation of the hands and forearms as a result of prolonged washing or gum lesions as a result of prolonged toothbrushing. Dressing or washing rituals may result in chronic lateness. Counting and checking rituals and intrusive thoughts may prevent concentration at school and interfere with schoolwork. These rituals may require the child to check and recheck every answer on a test so often that he or she is unable to finish the test. Homework may become a daily struggle, as the child spends hours repeatedly checking and correcting the work. Bedtime rituals may preclude inviting friends to sleep over and cause repeated refusals to accept similar invitations from friends. Contamination fears may interfere with school attendance and social activities such as going to the movies or participating in sports (Piacentini, 1997).

Because of the odd and senseless nature of OCD symptoms, many children try to mask or hide their rituals, especially in social situations or at school (Rapoport et al., 2000). In less severe cases, teachers, friends, and family members may be unaware of the child's OCD for months or even years. However, as the rituals become more elaborate and time consuming, they become increasingly difficult to conceal. With considerable effort, children with OCD may muster the energy to suppress their symptoms for brief periods. However, suppression commonly has a rebound effect, with increased symptoms once the child is in a safe place. As the child becomes too overwhelmed by anxiety to cope, or when websites, magazine articles, or TV shows about OCD bring the problem into focus, others become more and more aware of its seriousness (Piacentini, 1997).

Prevalence and Comorbidity

The lifetime prevalence of OCD in children and adolescents is about 1% to 2.5%, suggesting that it occurs about as often in young people as in adults (Zohar, 1999). Clinic-based studies of younger children suggest that OCD is about twice as common in boys as in girls. However, this gender difference has not been observed in community samples of adolescents, which may be a function of age differences, referral bias, or both (Albano et al., 2003). Comorbid disorders are common, occurring in about 50% of children in community samples, and the rates are much higher in children in clinic samples (Geller et al., 2012). The most common comorbidities are anxiety disorders, ADHD, ODD, and vocal and motor tics, which usually improve or remit in the second decade of life. As the child gets older, depressive disorders, substance-use disorders, learning disorders, and eating disorders are also overrepresented in children with OCD (Piacentini et al., 2012, 2014).

Onset, Course, and Outcome

The mean age at onset of OCD is 9 to 12 years with two peaks, one in early childhood and another in late adolescence/early adulthood (S. Taylor, 2011). Children with an early age at onset of OCD (6 to 10 years) are more likely to be boys and more likely to have a family history of OCD than children with a later onset, suggesting a greater role of genetic influences in such cases (Walitza et al., 2010). These children have a high rate of co-occurring chronic tic disorders (Piacentini et al., 2014), **trichotillomania** (hair loss from compulsive pulling or twisting of hair) (Panza, Pittinger, & Bloch, 2013), and ADHD (Leckman et al., 2010). They may also have prominent motor patterns, engaging in compulsions without obsessions and displaying odd behaviors, such as finger licking or compulsively walking in geometric designs.

The developmental course of OCD in young children indicates that they typically have obsessions that are more vague than those of older children and are less likely to feel that their obsessions are abnormal. Young children with OCD often ask their parents endless questions related to their obsessions and make no effort to hide their discomfort. Most children over 8 years of age are aware that their obsessions are abnormal, and they are usually uncomfortable talking about them. They may try to hide or minimize them or deny they have them, which frustrates parents who know that something is wrong and want to help.

One half to two-thirds of children with OCD continue to meet the criteria for the disorder 2 to 14 years later. Although most children, including those treated

Haunted by their habits: washing, checking, and exactness

with medication, show some improvement in symptoms, fewer than 10% show complete remission, and many experience interpersonal problems, work difficulties, and lower quality of life as adults (Palermo et al., 2011). Predictors of a poorer outcome include a younger age at onset of OCD, a poor initial response to treatment, hoarding symptoms in childhood, a lifetime history of tic disorder, and parental psychopathology at the time of referral. Thus, OCD remains a serious and chronic disorder for a significant number of children (Evans & Leckman, 2006).

Section Summary

Obsessive–Compulsive and Related Disorders

- While recognizing the relatedness of OCD and anxiety disorders, DSM-5 groups OCD in a separate chapter with a number of related disorders that are distinct from OCD, but contain overlapping diagnostic features such as preoccupations and repetitive behaviors or mental acts in response to the preoccupations.

- OCD and related disorders include OCD, body dysmorphic disorder, hoarding disorder, trichotillomania (hair-pulling disorder), and excoriation (skin-picking) disorder.

- Youngsters with OCD experience repeated, intrusive, and unwanted thoughts or obsessions that cause anxiety, often accompanied by ritualized behaviors or compulsions to relieve the anxiety.

- Among the most common obsessions in children are contamination and fears of harm to self and others. Among the most common compulsions are washing and bathing, and repeating, checking, and arranging.

- OCD has a mean age of onset of 9 to 12 years and affects about 1% to 2.5% of all children. Children with an early onset are more likely to be boys and are more likely to have a family history of the disorder than are those with a later onset.

- OCD is a serious and chronic disorder, with as many as two-thirds of children continuing to have the disorder 2 to 14 years after being diagnosed.

ASSOCIATED CHARACTERISTICS

Youngsters with anxiety disorders and OCD display a number of associated characteristics, including cognitive disturbances, physical symptoms, social and emotional deficits, and depression.

Cognitive Disturbances

For most children, the development of cognitive maturity is associated with a reduction in fears. However, children with anxiety disorders continue to evaluate nonthreatening events as threatening, which suggests a disturbance in how they perceive and process information (Field, Hadwin, & Lester, 2011).

Intelligence and Academic Achievement

Young people with anxiety disorders typically have normal intelligence, and there is little evidence of a strong relationship between anxiety and IQ. However, excessive anxiety may be related to deficits in specific areas of cognitive functioning, such as attention, memory, and speech or language. High levels of anxiety can interfere with academic performance. One study found that anxiety in the first grade predicted anxiety in the fifth grade and significantly influenced fifth-grade achievement (Ialongo et al., 1995). The specific mechanisms involved could include anything from frequent absences to direct interference on cognitive tasks such as taking a test or solving a math problem. Youngsters with anxiety disorders, particularly SOC, may also fail to reach their academic potential because they drop out of school prematurely (Van Ameringen, Mancini, & Farvolden, 2003).

Threat-Related Attentional Biases

Children at risk for anxiety and those with anxiety disorders selectively attend to information that may be potentially threatening or dangerous (e.g., an angry-looking face)—a tendency referred to as anxious vigilance or hypervigilance (Bar-Haim et al., 2007; LoBue & Pérez-Edgar, 2014). The more severe the children's anxiety, the stronger is their attention to potentially threatening stimuli (Waters et al., 2010). Anxious vigilance permits the child to avoid potentially threatening events by early detection, with minimal anxiety and effort. Although this may benefit the child in the short term, it has the unfortunate long-term effect of maintaining and heightening anxiety by interfering with the information-processing and coping responses needed to learn that many potentially threatening events are not so dangerous after all (Lonigan et al., 2004).

Cognitive Errors and Biases

When faced with a clear threat, both nonanxious and anxious children use rules to confirm information about danger (e.g., seeing a large dog approaching who is growling with bared teeth) and minimize information about safety (e.g., that the dog is on a leash). However, highly anxious children often do this in the face of less obvious threats, suggesting that their perceptions of threats activate danger-confirming thoughts (Muris et al., 2003). Children with conduct problems also put a negative spin on ambiguous events. The main difference is that children with conduct problems select aggressive solutions in response to a perceived threat, whereas anxious children choose avoidant solutions that emphasize personal safety (Chorpita, Albano, & Barlow, 1996). Children with anxiety disorders employ more maladaptive and less adaptive cognitive coping strategies in response to stressful life events than nonanxious children. Their cognitive coping strategies rely more on catastrophizing (e.g., thinking that something is far worse than it actually is) and rumination and less on positive reappraisal and planning (Legerstee et al., 2010).

Although threat-related attentional biases and cognitive errors and biases are associated with anxiety in children, the precise nature of these errors and their role in causing anxiety has not yet been established (Alfano, Beidel, & Turner, 2002). One possibility is that the child's temperament may heighten attentional biases to threat and behavioral avoidance and by doing so promote the acquisition of fears (Field, 2006). In general, children with anxiety disorders see themselves as having less control over anxiety-related events than do other children. However, different types and degrees of cognitive errors may occur in children with different anxiety and related disorders—for example, inflated responsibility and overestimation of threat in those with OCD (Taylor & Jang, 2011) and more negative and less positive cognitive processing following a distressing social event in those with SOC (Schmitz et al., 2010).

Physical Symptoms

Many children with anxiety disorders have somatic symptoms, such as stomachaches or headaches. These symptoms are more common in youngsters with GAD, PD, and SAD than in youngsters with a specific phobia. Somatic symptoms are also more frequent in adolescents than in younger children and in children who display school refusal. One study found that 90% of youngsters with anxiety disorders experience at least one sleep-related problem, most commonly insomnia, nightmares, and reluctance/refusal to sleep alone (Alfano, Ginsburg, & Kingery, 2007). Some may experience *nocturnal panic*, an abrupt waking in a state of extreme anxiety that is similar to a daytime panic attack. Nocturnal panic attacks usually occur in adolescents who suffer from PD. They prevent a return to sleep and are vividly recalled the next day (Craske & Rowe, 1997).

Higher levels of anxiety in adolescence are associated with reduced accidents and accidental death in early adulthood but with higher rates of nonaccidental death in later life. High levels of anxiety in adolescence may reduce risky behaviors and by doing so lead to short-term survival benefits, but anxiety takes its toll over time by increasing the long-term risk of serious health problems (Lee, Wadsworth, & Hotopf, 2006).

Social and Emotional Deficits

Since many anxious children expect danger in social situations, it is not surprising that they experience interaction difficulties with other children, including siblings (Fox, Barrett, & Shortt, 2002; La Greca & Landoll, 2011). In fact, they display low social performance and high social anxiety, and their parents, teachers, and peers are likely to view them as anxious and socially maladjusted (Chansky & Kendall, 1997; Krain & Kendall, 2000). These children, particularly those with SOC, may also be less popular with their peers (Verduin & Kendall, 2008). Compared to their peers, children with anxiety disorders are more likely to see themselves as shy and socially withdrawn and to report low self-esteem, loneliness, and difficulties in starting and maintaining friendships.

Some difficulties with peers and siblings may be related to specific deficits in understanding emotion, particularly in hiding and changing emotions (Southam-Gerow & Kendall, 2000) and in differentiating between thoughts and feelings (Alfano et al., 2002). Findings regarding how other children view children with anxiety disorders are mixed (Kendall et al., 1997). Childhood anxiety disorders are most likely associated with diminished peer popularity when they coexist with depression.

Anxiety and Depression

We have already discussed co-occurring disorders in relation to each anxiety disorder, and it is important to keep in mind that a child's risk for accompanying disorders will vary with the type of anxiety disorder (Cummings et al., 2013). GAD, SAD, and SOC are more commonly associated with depression than is specific phobia (Watson, 2009). Depression is also diagnosed more often in children with multiple anxiety disorders and in children who show severe impairments in their everyday functioning (Woodward & Fergusson, 2001).

The strong and undeniable relationship between anxiety and depression in children and adolescents merits further discussion (Garber & Weersing, 2010). Does anxiety lead to depression? Are anxiety and depression the same disorder with different clinical features? Are they on a continuum of severity? Are they distinct disorders with different causes but some overlapping features?

Children with anxiety and depression have an older age at presentation than children with only anxiety, and in most cases symptoms of anxiety both precede and predict symptoms of depression (Avenevoli et al., 2008). Symptoms of anxiety and depression may form a single indistinguishable dimension in younger children, but they are increasingly distinct in older children and children with at least one diagnosable disorder (De Bolle & De Fruyt, 2010; Price et al., 2013).

The concept of negative affectivity is useful in understanding the nature of the link between anxiety and depression (Anderson & Hope, 2008). **Negative affectivity** is a persistent negative mood, as reflected in nervousness, sadness, anger, and guilt. In contrast, **positive affectivity** refers to a persistent positive mood that includes states such as joy, enthusiasm, and energy. Negative affectivity is related to both anxiety and depression, whereas positive affectivity is negatively correlated with depression but is independent of anxiety symptoms and diagnoses (Lonigan, Phillips, & Hooe, 2003). In general, children with anxiety do not differ from children with depression in their negative affect, which suggests that a general underlying dimension of negative affectivity is common between anxiety and depression (Chorpita, 2002). Rather, the difference between children who are anxious and children who are depressed may be the lower positive affectivity in those who are depressed. It has also been proposed that a third construct, *physiological hyperarousal* (e.g., somatic tension, shortness of breath, dizziness) may be unique to children who are anxious. Although this hypothesis has received some support, particularly with respect to panic disorder, fewer studies have investigated this construct and findings have been inconsistent (Anderson & Hope, 2008).

Consistent with the idea of anxiety and depression as distinct dimensions with different developmental pathways are findings that some of the predictors and environmental influences associated with anxiety are different from those of depression. In terms of predictors, social and externalizing problems predict later anxiety disorders, whereas internalizing symptoms are generally better predictors of mood disorders (Roza et al., 2003). In terms of environmental influences, threatening life events such as physical jeopardy or the risk of losing a parent are related to symptoms of anxiety but not of depression. In contrast, life events involving actual loss and stress, such as the death of a family member or family stress, are associated with depression but not anxiety (Eley & Stevenson, 2000).

Section Summary

Associated Characteristics

- Children with anxiety disorders display deficits in specific areas of cognitive functioning, such as attention, memory, and speech and language.
- They selectively attend to information that may be potentially threatening, a tendency referred to as "anxious vigilance."

- These children often have somatic symptoms, such as stomachaches or headaches, and may experience sleep disturbances.
- Children with anxiety disorders report being socially withdrawn and lonely, and may be viewed by others as socially maladjusted.
- There is a strong and undeniable relationship between anxiety and depression in children and adolescents. The difference between children who are anxious and those who are depressed may be the greater positive affectivity in those who are anxious.

GENDER, ETHNICITY, AND CULTURE

Studies across ethnicities and cultures have found a preponderance of anxiety disorders in girls during childhood and adolescence (Anderson & Mayes, 2010; McLean & Anderson, 2009). By age 6, twice as many girls as boys have experienced symptoms of anxiety, and this discrepancy persists through childhood, adolescence, and young adulthood (Roza et al., 2003; see ● Figure 11.2). The fact that boys are less likely than girls to report anxiety may contribute to this variation, although how much it contributes is not known (Wren et al., 2007). For adolescents with anxiety, the differences between genders cannot be accounted for solely by psychosocial factors such as stress, self-perceived social competence, or emotional reliance. This suggests

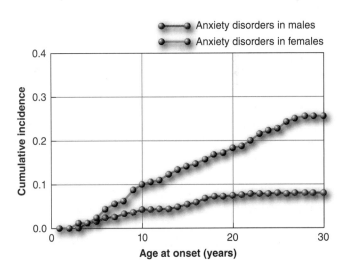

● **FIGURE 11.2** | Cumulative incidence of anxiety disorders in females and males.

Figure 1 from "Stable Prediction of Mood and Anxiety Disorders Based on Behavioral and Emotional Problems in Childhood: A 14-Year Follow-Up During Childhood, Adolescence, and Young Adulthood," by Sabine J. Roza, M.Sc.; Marijke B. Hofstra, M.D.; Jan van der Ende, M.S.; Frank C. Verhulst, M.D. *Am J Psychiatry* 2003;160:2116–2121. Adapted with permission from the *American Journal of Psychiatry* (Copyright © 2003). American Psychiatric Association.

© Cengage Learning, 2013

that female vulnerability to anxiety may also be related to genetic influences and related neurobiological differences, as well as to varying social roles and experiences (Lewinsohn et al., 1998).

One study of gender-role orientation in boys and girls with anxiety disorders found that self-reported masculinity was related to lower overall levels of fearfulness and fewer specific fears of failure and criticism, medical fears, and fears of the unknown (Ginsburg & Silverman, 2000). In contrast, no relation was found between self-reported femininity and fearfulness. This suggests that gender-role orientation, especially masculinity, may play a role in the development and persistence of fearfulness in children.

There is general support for a higher prevalence of anxiety in ethnic minority groups in the United States. However, symptom expression, biological factors, and family processes may differ somewhat by ethnic group (Anderson & Mayes, 2010). Studies comparing the number and nature of fears in African American and white youngsters have found the two groups to be quite similar (Ginsburg & Silverman, 1996). However, African American children generally report more symptoms of anxiety than do white children (Cole et al., 1998), although white children report more symptoms of SOC and fewer symptoms of SAD than do African American children (Compton, Nelson, & March, 2000). Among children who are referred for anxiety or related disorders, whites are more likely to present with school refusal and with higher severity ratings than African Americans. It has been found that symptoms of anxiety are higher in children of parents with fewer years of formal education, suggesting that variations in child anxiety across racial/ethnic groups may also be accounted for by group differences in parental education (Wren et al., 2007).

Patterns of referral, help-seeking behaviors, diagnoses, and treatment processes are also likely to differ across racial/ethnic groups. For example, African American parents who need help with their child's OCD symptoms may be more likely to turn to members of their informal social network, such as clergy or medical personnel, than to mental health professionals (Hatch, Friedman, & Paradis, 1996). Their family members are also less likely to be drawn into the child's OCD symptoms. Although ethnicity is not related to outcomes in the treatment of anxiety disorders, it may be related to premature termination of treatment (Kendall & Flannery-Schroeder, 1998).

Research comparing anxiety disorders in Hispanic and white children has found marked similarities in age at presentation, gender, primary diagnosis, proportion with school refusal, and proportion with more than one diagnosis. Hispanic children are more likely

to have a primary diagnosis of SAD. Hispanic parents also rate their children as more fearful than do white parents (Ginsburg & Silverman, 1996). Few studies have examined anxiety disorders in Native American children. Prevalence estimates from one study of Native American youths in Appalachia (mostly Cherokee) indicate rates of anxiety disorders similar to those for white youths, with the most common disorder for both groups being SAD. Rates of SAD were slightly higher for Native American youths, especially girls (Costello et al., 1997). Native Hawaiian adolescents display rates of OCD that are twice as high as those of other ethnic groups (Guerrero et al., 2003). When attempting to explain such differences, it is important to keep in mind that genetic and/or environmental risk factors may play a role.

The experience of anxiety is pervasive across cultures. Although cross-cultural research into anxiety disorders in children is limited (Lewis-Fernández et al., 2010), specific fears in children have been studied and documented in virtually every culture. Developmental fears (e.g., a fear of loud noises or of separation from the primary caregiver) occur in children of all cultures at about the same age. The details may vary from culture to culture, but the number of fears in children tends to be highly similar across cultures, as does the presence of gender differences in pattern and content.

Nevertheless, the expression, developmental course, and interpretation of symptoms of anxiety are affected by culture (Higa-McMillan et al., 2014; Ingman, Ollendick, & Akande, 1999). For example, in relation to panic-like symptoms, higher rates are found for paresthesias (feelings of tingling or numbing of the skin) among African Americans, trembling among Caribbean Latinos, dizziness among several East Asian Groups, and fear of dying among Arabs and African Americans (Craske et al., 2010).

Cultural differences in traditions, beliefs, and practices about children can affect the occurrence of anxiety and related symptoms and how they are perceived by others and experienced by the child (Wang & Ollendick, 2001). For example, James, a 16-year-old Chinese American boy, had been to multiple doctors throughout his life for treatment for stomach cramps, nausea, and hot flushes in the morning before going to school and also in anticipation of social interactions. James had a social anxiety disorder but both he and his family felt his problem was physical and wanted to focus only on his physical symptoms in therapy and not his subjective feelings of anxiety.

Increased levels of fear in children are found in cultures that favor inhibition, compliance, and obedience (Ollendick et al., 1996). Chinese cultural values such as human malleability and self-cultivation may heighten levels of general distress and specific fears (e.g., social evaluative) (Dong, Yang, & Ollendick, 1994). In addition, Chinese adolescents report higher levels of social anxiety than do American youths, including anxiety about humiliation and rejection and public performance fears (Yao et al., 2007). This is likely related to their collectivistic versus individualistic value orientation. Children in Thailand display more symptoms of anxiety, such as shyness and somatic symptoms, than children in the United States (Weisz et al., 2003). Perhaps the most accurate way to analyze cultural differences in anxiety is using Weisz and colleagues' (2003, p. 384) **behavior lens principle**, which states that child psychopathology reflects a mix of actual child behavior and the lens through which it is viewed by others in a child's culture.

Section Summary

Gender, Ethnicity, and Culture

- About twice as many girls as boys experience symptoms of anxiety, and this difference is present in children as young as 6 years of age.
- Children's ethnicity and culture may affect the expression and developmental course of fear and anxiety, how anxiety is perceived by others, and expectations for treatment.

THEORIES AND CAUSES

Over the years, numerous theories and causes have been proposed to explain the origins of fear and anxiety in children, including brain disease, mental strain, parenting practices, conditioning, and instinct (Treffers & Silverman, 2011). The study of fear and anxiety in children dates back to Freud's (1909/1953) classic account of the case of Little Hans; Watson and Rayner's (1920) conditioning of a fear in Little Albert; and Bowlby's (1973) monumental works on early attachment and loss. Although each early theory has been debated since it was introduced, all have had a lasting impact on how we think about anxiety in children.

Early Theories

Classical psychoanalytic theory views anxieties and phobias as defenses against unconscious conflicts rooted in the child's early upbringing. Certain drives, memories, and feelings are so painful that they must be repressed and displaced onto an external object or symbolically associated with the real source of anxiety. Thus, anxiety and phobias will protect the child against unconscious wishes and drives. Freud's most famous case of a phobia was Little Hans, a 5-year-old who feared horses. According to Freud, Little Hans unconsciously felt that he was in competition with his father for his mother's love and feared his father's revenge (the Oedipus complex). Hans's fear was repressed and displaced onto horses, a symbol of his castrating father. Having something specific to fear was less stressful for Hans than suffering from anxiety without apparent cause.

Behavioral and learning theories held that fears and anxieties were learned through classical conditioning. In the case of Little Albert, Watson and Rayner (1920) created what looked very much like a rat phobia (see A Closer Look 1.3), and claimed that fears were learned by association. Operant conditioning has been cited in explaining why fears persist once they are established. The principle is that behavior will continue if it is reinforced or rewarded. Once something has become frightening, there is the automatic reward of instant relief whenever the child avoids the feared object or situation. Thus, through negative reinforcement, avoidance of a feared stimulus becomes a learned response, which serves to maintain the child's fear even when not exposed to it. The combination of classical and operant conditioning in the learning and maintenance of fears is called the **two-factor theory** (Mowrer, 1947). Social learning theories also showed that children could learn fears through observation of others, without experiencing the feared stimulus directly (Bandura & Walters, 1963).

Bowlby's *theory of attachment* (1973) presents a very different explanation for children's fears. According to attachment theory, fearfulness in children is biologically rooted in the emotional attachment needed for survival. Infants must be close to their caregivers if their physical and emotional needs are to be met. Attachment behaviors, such as crying, fear of strangers, and distress, represent active efforts by the infant to maintain or restore proximity to the caregiver. Separation gradually becomes more tolerable as the child gets older. However, children who are separated from their mothers too early, who are treated harshly, or who fail to have their needs met consistently show atypical reactions to separation and reunion. Early insecure attachments become internalized and determine how children see the world and other people. Children who view the environment as undependable, unavailable, hostile, or threatening may later develop anxiety and avoidance behavior.

No single theory is sufficient to explain the various anxiety disorders in children, the differences among children in the expression of these disorders, or the variations in outcomes over time. It is important to recognize that different anxiety disorders may require different causal models. In contrast to early theories, current models of anxiety use a developmental psychopathology perspective that emphasizes the importance of interacting biological and environmental influences (Gregory & Eley, 2007; McClure & Pine, 2006). This approach takes into account brain development and psychopathology and integrates this knowledge with research on genetic variation and environmental effects (Monk, 2008). Genetic vulnerability reflects a disposition toward broad anxiety-related traits, whereas early environmental risk may influence developing neural circuitry as well as the specific types of anxieties that emerge. In the sections that follow, we consider the role of temperament, genetic and family risk, neurobiological factors, and family influences.

Temperament

Once I visited with a group of preschool children from the campus day care center when I noticed a little Caucasian boy slowly sneaking up behind a little Chinese girl who was walking in front of him. The boy came to within 2 feet of the girl, his presence still undetected, stopped, and then screamed at the top of his lungs, "BOO!!" Even though I saw it coming, the intensity of the boy's scream startled me a bit. However, much to my surprise, the intended victim showed hardly any reaction. Instead, this pint-sized version of Wonder Woman paused for a moment, slowly turned, looked at the boy (who appeared dumbfounded by this unexpected display of fearlessness), and with a relaxed smile on her face, calmly said, "I'm used to that sort of thing." She then turned and continued on her way, with the little boy trailing behind like a puppy dog (I think he was in love).

The lesson of this story is that children (like adults) differ markedly in their psychological and physical reactions to novel or unexpected events, perhaps because of their wiring, gender, cultural background, prior experience (in this example, perhaps with a pesky little brother?), or a combination of factors. How would you react if someone snuck up behind you and yelled "BOO!!"? Readiness to react to unfamiliar or discrepant events is one distinguishing feature of all mammals. Orienting, attending, vigilance, wariness, and motor readiness in response to the unfamiliar are important mechanisms for survival. From an evolutionary perspective, abnormal fears and anxieties reflect variation among infants in their initial behavioral reactions to novelty (Kagan, 2013).

This variation is partly the result of inherited differences in the neurochemistry of brain structures thought to play an important role in detecting discrepant events. These brain structures include the amygdala, which has a primary function of reacting to unfamiliar or unexpected events (Fitzgerald et al., 2006), and its projections to the motor system, the anterior cingulate and frontal cortex, the hypothalamus, and the sympathetic nervous system. Children with a high threshold for novelty, such as the little girl in the story, are presumed to be at low risk for developing anxiety disorders. Other children (about 15% to 20%) are born with a low threshold for becoming overexcited and to withdrawing in response to novel stimulation as infants, a tendency to be fearful and anxious as toddlers, and a tendency to be unusually shy or withdrawn in novel or unfamiliar situations as young children. This type of temperament is called **behavioral inhibition (BI)**, an enduring trait for some and a predisposing factor for the development of later anxiety disorders, particularly SOC (Chronis-Tuscano et al., 2009; Kagan, 2013). In one study, adolescents who were behaviorally inhibited as toddlers and young children showed social withdrawal in adolescence, and this relationship was moderated by a heightened attention bias to threat (Pérez-Edgar et al., 2010). One meta-analysis also found that childhood BI was associated with a greater than sevenfold increase in risk for developing SOC (Clauss & Blackford, 2012).

However, the road from BI during infancy and childhood to a later anxiety disorder is neither direct nor straightforward. Different risk factors and pathways to adolescent SOC have been identified—one, for example, based on gender and early BI, and another based on exposure to early maternal stress (Essex et al., 2010). Although BI may contribute to later anxiety disorders, this is not an inevitable outcome. Such an outcome may depend on whether the inhibited child grows up in an environment that fosters this tendency (Degnan, Almas, & Fox, 2010). For example, a parent's use of firm limits that teach children how to cope with stress may reduce their risk for anxiety. In contrast, it is possible that well-meaning but overinvolved or overcontrolling parents who shield their sensitive child from stressful events may inadvertently cause timidity to persist by preventing the child from confronting fears. By not confronting these fears, the child cannot eliminate them. Such tendencies in the parents of inhibited children may be common. Thus, inhibited children may be at high risk not only because of their inborn temperament, but also because of their elevated risk of exposure to an anxious, overinvolved, or overcontrolling parent (Hudson & Dodd, 2012; Lewis-Morrarty et al., 2012).

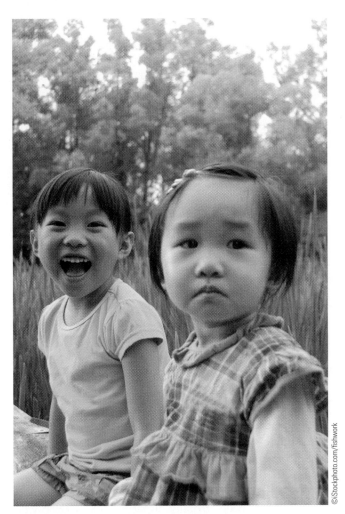

Early differences in temperament may predispose some children to develop anxiety disorders.

Family and Genetic Risk

I was always considered shy. … Now I see my daughter is just like I was. Did I do something to cause this?

—From Beidel and Turner (1998)

Family and twin studies suggest that children inherit general tendencies to be inhibited, tense, or fearful (Gregory & Eley, 2007). In addition, both shared and nonshared environmental influences have been shown to play a substantial role. Two lines of evidence suggest that anxiety disorders run in families. First, parents of children with anxiety disorders have increased rates of current and past anxiety disorders (Cooper et al., 2006). Second, children of parents with anxiety disorders have an increased risk for having anxiety disorders themselves (Merikangas et al., 1999). In general, family studies consistently show a relationship between an anxiety disorder in the child and anxiety disorders in first-degree relatives. Children of parents with anxiety disorders are about 5 times more likely to have anxiety disorders than are children of parents without anxiety disorders (Beidel & Turner, 1997). However, these children do not necessarily have the same disorders as their parents (Mancini et al., 1996). Nearly 70% of children whose parents have agoraphobia meet diagnostic criteria for disorders such as anxiety and depression and report more fear and anxiety and less control over various risks than do children of comparison parents without agoraphobia. However, the fears of parents with agoraphobia and the fears of their children are no more closely aligned than those of nonanxious parents and their children, once again supporting the view that for most anxiety disorders a general predisposition for anxiety is perpetuated in families (Capps et al., 1996).

Twin studies suggest that about one-third or more of the variance in childhood anxiety symptoms is accounted for by genetic influences (Gregory & Eley, 2011; Lamb et al., 2010). However, identical twin pairs do not typically have the same types of anxiety disorders. This is consistent with the view that a disposition to become anxious is inherited but the form of the disorder is shaped by environmental influences. The amount of genetic influence is highest for obsessive–compulsive behaviors and shyness/inhibition (Mataix-Cols et al., 2013; Taylor, Jang, & Asmundson, 2010). Although moderate genetic influence has also been reported for specific fears and separation anxiety in young children (Bolton et al., 2006), environmental factors such as maternal psychiatric problems, ineffective parenting, and poverty seem to play a relatively stronger role (Muris & Merckelbach, 2001). In general, genetic influences for anxiety tend to decrease with age, while shared environmental influences increase (Bartels et al., 2007).

Specific gene studies have focused on variants in genes related to the serotonin system (Lau et al., 2009). These variants have been associated with BI, particularly among those who are also exposed to environmental risk (Lau & Pine, 2008). They are of interest because the serotonin system has been implicated in anxiety and is the site of action for widely used antianxiety and antidepressant medications (Lesch et al., 1996). In addition to serotonin markers, other candidate genes that have received attention are those involved in the dopamine system and in mediating the response to stress through brain systems implicated in anxious and avoidant behavior (Rubin et al., 2013; Smoller et al., 2003). The most consistent findings thus far have linked genes to broad anxiety-related traits such as BI. Little research currently exists to support a strong direct link between specific genetic markers and *specific* types of anxiety disorders (Murray, Cresswell, & Cooper, 2009). Rather, it appears that small contributions from multiple genes seem related to anxiety when certain psychological and social factors are also present. Further studies into G×E interactions for anxiety are needed (Gregory & Eley, 2007). For example, one study found a significant G×E interaction in which stressful life events presented a greater risk for anxiety/depressive symptoms when a specific serotonin-related genotype was present (Petersen et al., 2012). Future research examining the ways in which multiple genetic factors interact with multiple sources of environmental adversity, may help to overcome the unreliability of findings in studies that attempt to identify interactions between a single gene and a single measure of environmental adversity (Fergusson et al., 2011).

Neurobiological Factors

No single structure or neurotransmitter controls the entire anxiety response system. Rather, several interrelated systems operate together in complex ways to produce anxiety. The parts of the brain most often connected with anxiety involve neural circuits related to potential threat and fear conditioning—the hypothalamic–pituitary–adrenal (HPA) axis; the limbic system (amygdala, hippocampus), which acts as a mediator between the brain stem and the cortex; the ventrolateral and dorsolateral prefrontal cortex; and other cortical and subcortical structures (Fitzgerald et al., 2013; Monk, 2008; Pine, 2011). Potential danger signals are monitored and sensed by the more primitive brain stem, which then relays the signals to the higher cortical centers through the limbic system. As noted in Chapter 9, this brain system is referred to as the *behavioral inhibition system,* and it is believed to be overactive in children with anxiety disorders. As we have discussed, anxious individuals display threat biases at multiple levels of information processing (e.g., attention to threat, fear learning). It has been proposed that abnormalities in learning safety cues in childhood may establish threat-related appraisal biases early in development, which may then lead to chronic anxiety disorders in adulthood (Britton et al., 2011). Consistent with this, healthy teens have greater difficulty distinguishing between threat and safety cues than adults, relying more on areas of the brain involved in basic fear responses (hippocampus, right amygdala) than on areas involved in more reasoned judgment about what is safe or not (prefrontal cortex) (Lau et al., 2011). This may be one reason why teens (and youths with anxiety disorders) generally report more pervasive worries and are more vulnerable to stress-related problems.

Particularly noteworthy are findings that the regulation of the brain circuits underlying threat and fear conditioning can be shaped by early life stress, thus providing a possible biological basis for an increased vulnerability to later stress and the development of fearfulness and anxiety disorders (Heim et al., 2010).

As we discussed in A Closer Look 2.2, activation of the HPA axis is closely related to the regulation of stress and fear and involves the release of cortisol needed to meet a challenging situation. Pathological anxiety has been related to elevations of cortisol secretion, reflected in an exaggeration of normal HPA reactions or a failure of the HPA axis response to habituate to repeated exposure to the same stressor (van der Vegt et al., 2010). Prolonged exposure to elevated levels of cortisol as a result of early stress or trauma may have neurotoxic effects on the developing brain—for example, reduced cerebral volume or changes in the volume of the hippocampus (Weems & Silverman, 2013). Early life stress may also produce lasting hyperreactivity of corticotropin-releasing factor (CRF) systems, which are closely related to the HPA axis, as well as alterations in other neurotransmitter systems that create a heightened response to stress (Pine, 2003).

Brain scans of children with GAD suggest abnormalities (larger volume) in brain regions and circuits associated with social–emotional information processing and fear conditioning (amygdala and superior temporal gyrus) (De Bellis, Keshavan, Frustaci, et al., 2002; De Bellis, Keshavan, Shifflett et al., 2002; Roy et al., 2013). These studies also report more pronounced right–left hemisphere brain asymmetries in children with GAD, which have also been reported in children who are behaviorally inhibited or anxious/depressed (Kagan & Snidman, 1999). As we have discussed, an overexcitable amygdala has been strongly implicated in children who are behaviorally inhibited and in youngsters with anxiety disorders (McClure et al., 2007b; Schwartz et al., 2003). The amygdala detects and organizes reactions to natural dangers by quickly scanning incoming stimuli that are novel and/or potentially threatening. Interestingly, children with anxiety disorders who have higher levels of pretreatment amygdala activation in response to emotional information show a better response to both cognitive–behavioral therapy and drug treatment (McClure et al., 2007a). In addition to the brain regions we have discussed, neuroimaging studies have also suggested the importance of other brain regions for specific anxiety-related disorders such as OCD (Friedlander & Desrocher, 2006; Hajcak et al., 2008).

The neurotransmitter system that has been implicated most often in anxiety disorders is the γ-aminobutyric acid–ergic (GABA-ergic) system. Neuropeptides are generally viewed as anticipatory stress modulators whose abnormal regulation may play a role in anxiety disorders (Sallee & Greenawald, 1995). A group of neurons known as the locus ceruleus ("deep blue place") is a major brain source for norepinephrine, an inhibitory neurotransmitter. Overactivation of this region is presumed to lead to a fear response, and underactivity to inattention, impulsivity, and risk-taking. Abnormalities of these systems may be related to anxiety states in children (Sallee & Greenawald, 1995).

New findings using brain scans have increased our understanding of the neurobiological mechanisms in anxiety disorders. The brain regions we have described have been consistently implicated in fear and anxiety. While acknowledging that pathways are likely to be complex, the plasticity of these neural systems during early development makes research into possible mechanisms a priority for both understanding and preventing future anxiety disorders in children.

Family Factors

As we have discussed, anxiety runs in families, and the relationship between family factors and childhood anxiety disorders has generated considerable attention (Knappe et al., 2010). Among the many family factors of interest are specific parenting practices, including the parent's use of discipline and modeling of anxious behaviors; broader family dimensions such as family functioning as a whole, parenting stress, and the marital relationship; the parent–child attachment relationship; and the beliefs that parents hold about their child's anxious behavior (Bögels & Brechman-Toussaint, 2006; Creswell et al., 2011; Manassis, 2011).

Parenting practices such as rejection, overcontrol, overprotection, and modeling of anxious behaviors have all been identified as contributors to childhood anxiety symptoms and disorders (Edwards, Rapee, & Kennedy, 2010; McLeod, Wood, & Weisz, 2007). Although most research has focused on mothers, fathers also play a role, and both parents may contribute to their child's anxiety in ways that are specific to their different parenting roles (Bögels & Phares, 2008). Parents of anxious children are often described as overinvolved, intrusive, or limiting of their child's independence.

Observations of interactions between 9- to 12-year-old children with anxiety disorders and their parents found that parents of children with anxiety disorders were found to grant less autonomy to their children than other parents; the children found their mothers and fathers to be less accepting than other parents (Siqueland, Kendall, & Steinberg, 1996). Other studies have found that mothers of children previously identified as behaviorally inhibited or anxious are more likely to be critical and to be less positive when interacting with their children (Whaley, Pinto, & Sigman, 1999). Emotional overinvolvement by parents is also associated with an increased occurrence of SAD in their children (Hirshfeld, Biederman, & Rosenbaum, 1997). These findings generally support the association between excessive parental control and anxiety disorders in children, although the

strength of this association appears to be small and the causal mechanisms and directionality of effect are not yet known (McLeod et al., 2007). One study found a relationship between mothers' use of extreme control and higher levels of child anxiety. However, the overlap between high child anxiety and maternal control was mainly due to shared genetic factors. This suggests that mothers not only influence their children's anxiety, but also that children with high levels of anxiety may elicit extreme maternal control (Eley et al., 2010).

Another study looked at the broader relationship between family functioning and child anxiety (Pagani et al., 2008). The dimensions of family functioning that were of interest included problem solving, communication, family roles, affective involvement, and emotional responsiveness. It was found that prolonged exposure to high levels of family dysfunction was associated with the most extreme trajectories of anxious behavior during middle childhood. This association was found to exist over and above the influence of other aspects of family dysfunction, such as marital transitions, socioeconomic status (SES), family size, and a parent's depressive symptoms. In general, findings in support of an association between family functioning and anxiety disorders are suggestive, but it is unclear whether family dysfunction relates specifically to anxiety disorders (Bögels & Brechman-Toussaint, 2006).

Not only are parents of children with anxiety disorders more controlling than other parents, they also have different expectations. For example, when they thought the child was being asked to give a videotaped speech, mothers of children with anxiety disorders expected their children to become upset and had low expectations for their children's coping (Kortlander, Kendall, & Panichelli-Mindel, 1997). It is likely that parental attitudes shape—and are shaped by—interactions with the child, during which parent and child revise their expectations and behavior as a result of feedback from each other (Barrett, Rapee, et al., 1996). This process may not only impact on the child's behavior, but may also play a role in the development of information-processing biases in the child (Hadwin, Garner, & Perez-Olivas, 2006).

Parental anxiety disorder alone may not lead to an elevated risk of anxiety disorders in children of high- or middle-SES parents, but it may increase risk in children of low-SES parents (Beidel & Turner, 1997). These findings are consistent with the idea that some children have a genetic vulnerability to anxiety, which may be actualized in the context of specific life circumstances, such as the stressful conditions that are often present in low-SES families. Children with an initial disposition to develop high levels of fear may be especially vulnerable to the type of power-assertive parenting often used by low-SES parents. These children may be particularly sensitive to punishment and, when exposed to physical discipline, may become hypervigilant to hostile cues and develop a tendency to react defensively or aggressively (Colder, Lochman, & Wells, 1997).

Insecure attachments may be a risk factor for the development of later anxiety disorders (Brumariu & Kerns, 2010; Kerns & Brumariu, 2014) and are associated with anxiety disorder symptoms in early adolescence (Muris & Meesters, 2002). Mothers with anxiety disorders have been found to have insecure attachments, and 80% of their children are also insecurely attached (Manassis et al., 1994). This relationship may be mediated by the impact of the mother's anxiety on her sensitivity to her child (Stevenson-Hinde et al., 2014).

Infants who are ambivalently attached have more anxiety diagnoses during childhood and adolescence than infants who are securely attached (Bernstein et al., 1996), although a clear link between specific types of insecure attachments and specific anxiety disorders has not been established. It may be a risk factor, but insecure attachment may be a nonspecific factor because many infants with insecure attachments develop disorders other than anxiety (e.g., depression, disruptive behavior disorder), and many do not develop disorders.

Clearly articulated causal models for anxiety disorders in children are just beginning to emerge (Muris, 2007). In the absence of an integrative model, we present the possible developmental pathway shown in ● Figure 11.3. Children with an inborn predisposition

● **FIGURE 11.3** │ A possible developmental pathway for anxiety disorders.

to be anxious or fearful who sense that the world is not a safe place may develop a psychological vulnerability to anxiety. Once anxiety occurs, it feeds on itself. The anxiety and avoidance continue long after the stressors that provoked them are gone. Keep in mind that many children with anxiety disorders do not continue to experience problems as adults. Therefore, it will be important to identify risk and protective factors that would explain these differences in outcomes (Pine & Grun, 1999). In addition, it is also important to keep in mind that different developmental pathways may occur for children with different anxiety disorders, or even for those with the same disorder.

Section Summary

Theories and Causes

- No single theory can explain the many different forms of anxiety disorder in children.
- Early theories viewed anxiety as a defense against unconscious conflicts, a learned response, or an adaptive mechanism needed for survival.
- Some children are born with a tendency to become overexcited and to withdraw in response to novel stimulation (behavioral inhibition)—an enduring trait for some, and a possible risk factor for later anxiety disorders.
- Family and twin studies suggest a moderate biological vulnerability to anxiety disorders.
- Anxiety is associated with specific neurobiological processes. The potential underlying vulnerability of children at risk for anxiety is most likely localized to brain circuits involving the brain stem, the limbic system, the HPA axis, and the frontal cortex.
- Anxiety is associated with a number of family factors, including specific parenting practices, family functioning, the parent–child attachment, and parents' beliefs about their children's anxious behavior.
- Children with anxiety disorders will likely display features that are shared across the various disorders, as well as other features that are unique to their particular disorder.

TREATMENT AND PREVENTION

CANDY

Afraid to Swallow

Candy, age 11, was hospitalized for dehydration. Her voice trembled and her eyes widened with fear as she described being rushed to the emergency room in an ambulance after she fainted. She was embarrassed that something as simple as eating was so hard for her, but it terrified her to even think about trying. Candy detested being thin, and desperately wanted to be "just like other kids." After talking with Candy, it was clear that she dreaded eating because she was afraid of vomiting in public. Her fear began when she couldn't eat in front of other kids in the school cafeteria, but advanced quickly to her not being able to eat at all. Candy doesn't have an eating disorder—she has a severe social anxiety disorder. (Based on authors' case material.)

Since many fears and anxieties are not associated with serious disturbances, deciding whether a child's anxiety is serious enough to warrant treatment is seldom easy. Although anxiety disorders are extremely disabling for the child and family, they are rarely life threatening. Children with anxiety disorders can be exceedingly quiet, shy, compliant, eager to please, or secretive, and their distress may go unnoticed. Sometimes a severe disruption to a normal routine may be needed before a parent seeks help. If a child is so afraid of spiders or dogs that she is terror-stricken when going outside regardless of whether a spider or dog is nearby, then treatment may be needed. Treatment may also be required when parents repeatedly make important decisions that interfere with family life to accommodate a child's fears, such as not going camping or not driving on holidays. Unlike children who provoke or offend others, children with anxiety disorders typically do not cause trouble, and as a result they receive far less professional attention than children with conduct problems. This situation is unfortunate, because many of these children can be helped with treatment (AACAP, 2007b; Shin-ichi et al., 2007).

In 1924, Mary Cover Jones worked with 3-year-old Peter, who was afraid of a rabbit. She eliminated Peter's fear by gradually exposing him to the rabbit when he was relaxed, by having him watch other children play with a rabbit, and by rewarding him for approaching the rabbit. These treatment techniques are still used today. Teaching children to use behavioral and cognitive coping skills to reduce anxious avoidance also increases the child's options and opportunities. In this regard, in addition to reducing or preventing symptoms of anxiety, early intervention may prevent future problems, such as loss of friends, failure to reach social and academic potential, low self-esteem, and depression (Rapee, 2002).

Overview

Timidity will always diminish if the occasions that produce it be skillfully repeated, until they cease to cause surprize, for the timid apprehend the unexpected.

—Yoritomo-Tashi (1916)

Decades of research from almost every perspective imaginable corroborate the popular adage that the best way to defeat your fears is to face them. Although specific procedures may vary, exposing children and adolescents to the situations, objects, and occasions that produce anxiety is the main line of attack in any treatment for anxiety disorders (Chorpita & Southam-Gerow, 2006). As described in A Closer Look 11.4, when former three-time world heavyweight boxing champion Evander Holyfield was only 17 years old, he faced his fears—and was never afraid again.

Treatments for anxiety are directed at modifying four primary problems (Barlow, 2002):

▸ Distorted information processing
▸ Physiological reactions to perceived threat
▸ Sense of a lack of control
▸ Excessive escape and avoidance behaviors

These central problems are addressed using a variety of treatment strategies that are matched to the types of anxiety symptoms the child is experiencing (Muris, 2007). In the following sections, we describe the most commonly used treatments for anxiety disorders, including behavior therapy, cognitive–behavioral therapy (CBT), family interventions, and medications. These treatments have been shown to be highly effective in treating anxiety disorders in young people (Piacentini, Bennett et al., 2014). Typically, combined forms of treatment that involve multiple components and target multiple symptoms and problems are used (Chorpita, 2007; Hannesdottir & Ollendick, 2007). It is also important that treatments for children with anxiety disorders are sensitive to the ethnic and cultural factors that we discussed earlier in the chapter (Harmon, Langley, & Ginsburg, 2006). We conclude by highlighting recent efforts directed at the prevention of anxiety.

Behavior Therapy

The main technique of behavior therapy for phobias and anxiety and related disorders is **exposure**, having children face what frightens them, while providing ways of coping other than escape and avoidance. Exposure procedures have been used successfully with boys and girls of all ages from a variety of ethnic backgrounds. About 75% of children with anxiety disorders

---

A CLOSER **LOOK** 11.4

Evander Holyfield: The Best Way to Defeat Fear Is to Face It

Evander Holyfield, a former three-time world heavyweight boxing champion, has the reputation of having no fear of failure or injury. In fact, Holyfield is amazed by his courage, since he used to be paralyzed by fear. From age 8, when he began boxing, until he was 17, he knew nothing but the constant anxiety of being bullied. "I was scared at everything I did, but especially boxing," he says. "I don't know how I ever got started, but I was scared. I don't know why I stayed. But I won a lot of fights, never got hurt, and as much torment as I was living in, I just assumed I would quit before I got to, say, 18. From watching the older kids box, I knew there came a time when you could get hurt, your nose would be bloody, your eye cut. I'd quit before that happened to me."

However, at 17, he suddenly found himself looking at a left hook from nowhere. Holyfield, then a slim 147 pounds of quivering nerves, was knocked unconscious, more or less, but he rose from the deck and charged his opponent. It was quite a little amateur fight.

The fight came back to him in a dream that night, after his head had cleared. He had been knocked down, yes, but he had

gotten up and fought, after a fashion. Amazingly, he remembered nothing from the experience except numbness; it hadn't hurt at all. "I was never afraid again" he says.

Adapted from "Lovestruck" by Richard Hoffer, *Sports Illustrated*, June 30, 1997.

are helped by this treatment (Chorpita & Southam-Gerow, 2006).

Usually the process is gradual and is referred to as **graded exposure**. The child and therapist make a list of feared situations, from least to most anxiety-producing, and the child is asked to rate the distress caused by each situation on a scale from 1 to 10; this is called a Subjective Units of Distress Scale (SUDS) or fear thermometer. The child is then exposed to each situation, beginning with the least distressing and moving up the hierarchy as the level of anxiety permits.

For Wayman, an 8-year-old-boy with OCD, leaving his bedroom closet door open was an anxiety-provoking situation with a SUDS rating of 8. Exposure was achieved by asking him to imagine being in this bedtime situation:

> THERAPIST: It is nighttime. Your parents have tucked you in and have gone to bed themselves. You reach over to shut off the light on the nightstand, and you notice that your bedroom closet door is open just a bit, just enough for something to crawl out and into your room. It's dark in that corner and you think you see something. You shut off the light and lie down. You hear a strange, scratching noise coming from the closet. It sounds like something is moving. What's your SUDS rating?
>
> WAYMAN: (Points to fear thermometer.) It's a seven.
>
> THERAPIST: Stay with it. Tell me about what happens next.
>
> WAYMAN: The closet door creaks open a bit more, and now I know that something is there. It can come get me. It's a monster.
>
> THERAPIST: You begin to sweat. You want so badly to go and shut that door, but you stay in bed. You close your eyes, but the sound doesn't stop. It seems to be getting closer. You look over and see a horrible face, with red eyes staring at you. You want to scream, but you know you can't. What's your SUDS rating now?
>
> WAYMAN: Eight. This is the worst part.
>
> THERAPIST: Okay, good, stay with the image. Stay with it. What's your SUDS rating now?
>
> WAYMAN: Five.

With repeated exposure to the fear, Wayman's SUDS ratings continued to decrease, and he was able to leave his bedroom closet door open without feeling anxious. (Adapted from Albano, Knox, & Barlow, 1995)

A second behavior therapy technique for treating children's fears and anxiety is **systematic desensitization**, which consists of three steps: (1) teaching the child to relax; (2) constructing an anxiety hierarchy; and (3) presenting the anxiety-provoking stimuli sequentially while the child remains relaxed. With repeated presentation, the child feels relaxed in the presence of stimuli that previously provoked anxiety.

In a third technique, known as **flooding**, exposure is carried out in prolonged and repeated doses (massed exposure). Throughout the process, the child remains in the anxiety-provoking situation and provides anxiety ratings until the levels diminish. Flooding is typically used in combination with **response prevention**, which prevents the child from engaging in escape or avoidance behaviors. More than other approaches, flooding may create distress, especially during the early stages of treatment. This procedure must be used carefully, especially with young children who may not understand the rationale. More recently, modified flooding procedures have been used in controlled settings to effectively treat a variety of specific phobias. For example, *one-session treatment* (OST) begins with pre-session meeting(s) with the child and family to build rapport and provide information about anxiety and therapy. This is followed by a 2.5- to 3-hour long, single-session of massed exposure therapy that, in addition to exposure, uses a variety of CBT techniques, such as reinforcement, participant modeling (see below), psychoeducation, skills training, and cognitive challenges (Ollendick & Davis, 2013). This approach has shown promising results but requires further evaluation with children in clinical practice settings.

In exposure-based therapies, the feared object can be confronted in many ways, including real-life, role playing, and imagining or observing others in contact with the feared object or situation (modeling). There is also evidence that exposure through virtual environments can be effective (Krijn et al., 2004; Sarver, Beidel, & Spitalnick, 2014).

One of the most effective procedures for treating specific phobias involves *participant modeling and reinforced practice*. Using this procedure, the therapist models the desired behavior (e.g., approaching the feared object), encourages and guides the child in practicing this behavior, and reinforces the child's efforts. Although all exposure procedures are effective, real-life, or in vivo exposure, works best—but it is not always easy to implement. Once the child faces her fear in a real-life situation with no adverse consequences, she is more confident about doing it again.

Other useful behavior therapies are directed at reducing the physical symptoms of anxiety. These include muscle relaxation and special breathing exercises. Children who are anxious often take rapid shallow breaths (hyperventilation) that can produce increased heartbeat, dizziness, and other symptoms. Relaxation procedures are often used with gradual exposure.

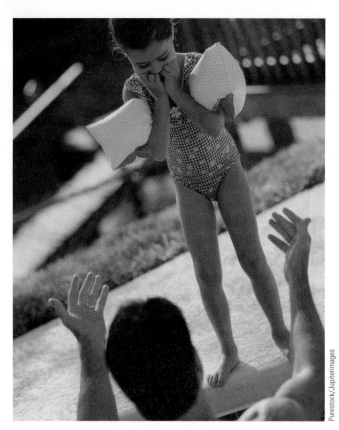

A 5-year-old girl with a fear of water is being encouraged and guided to enter a swimming pool.

Cognitive–Behavioral Therapy (CBT)

The most effective procedure for treating most anxiety disorders in young people is CBT (Chorpita et al., 2011; Silverman, Pina, & Viswesvaran, 2008). In addition to using behavior therapy procedures, CBT teaches children to understand how thinking contributes to anxiety and how to modify their maladaptive thoughts to decrease their symptoms (Kendall & Suveg, 2006). For example, as part of comprehensive CBT for panic disorder, a teen who becomes light-headed during a panic attack and fears she is going to die may be helped by a clinical strategy in which the therapist asks her to spin in a circle until she becomes dizzy. When she becomes alarmed and thinks, "I'm gonna die," she learns to replace this thought with one that is more appropriate; for example, "It's just a little dizziness—I can handle it" (Hoffman & Mattis, 2000). Making the youngster aware of thought patterns and ways to change them complements exposure and other behavioral therapy procedures, such as positive reinforcement and relaxation. CBT and exposure-based treatments are almost always used in combination. An example of a combined approach for treating adolescents with social anxiety disorder

is presented in A Closer Look 11.5 (Albano & DiBartolo, 2007). Similar programs for treating teens with social anxiety in the school setting have also proven effective (Warner et al., 2007).

The CBT treatment program *Coping Cat*, developed by Philip Kendall and his colleagues, is one of the most carefully evaluated treatments for youngsters 7 to 13 years old who have GAD, SAD, and SOC (Kendall, Furr, & Podell, 2010). A teen version is available, as is an Australian adaptation (*Coping Koala*). This approach emphasizes learning processes and the influence of contingencies and models, as well as the pivotal role of information processing. Treatment is directed at decreasing negative thinking, increasing active problem solving, and providing the child with a functional coping outlook. The intervention creates behavioral experiences with emotional involvement, while simultaneously addressing thought processes (Kendall et al., 2010).

Skills training and exposure are used to combat the problematic thinking that contributes to anxious distress and the behavioral avoidance that serves to maintain it. A variety of effective techniques are used, including modeling, role play, exposure, and relaxation training. Therapists use social reinforcement to encourage and reward the children, who are also taught to reward themselves for successful coping. Children first learn to use the following four steps of a "FEAR" plan:

F = Feeling frightened? (recognizing physical symptoms of anxiety)

E = Expecting bad things to happen? (recognizing anxious cognitions)

A = Attitudes and actions that will help (coping self-talk and behavior to use when anxious)

R = Results and rewards (evaluating performance and administering self-reward for effort)

After children learn the FEAR plan, the second part of the program is devoted to exposure and practice. Children attend 16 to 20 sessions over a period of 8 weeks. To enhance the skills learned in therapy, they must practice using them in anxiety-producing situations at home and school. Controlled evaluations of this approach have found it to be extremely effective. Most children show reductions in anxiety, with 71% of children freed of their primary diagnosis at the end of treatment and 54% not meeting the criteria for any anxiety disorder. For many children, these gains have been maintained for 7 to 19 years after treatment (Benjamin et al., 2013; Kendall et al., 2004). Compared to children who were responsive to the initial treatment, those who were not responsive had higher rates of panic disorder, alcohol dependence and drug abuse as adults

Cognitive–Behavioral Therapy for Adolescent Social Anxiety Disorder

Ann Marie Albano and her colleagues have developed a comprehensive group CBT treatment program for adolescents with a social anxiety disorder (Albano, 2003). Treatment is carried out in small groups of four to six teens and involves sixteen 90-minute sessions. The treatment includes a number of important elements (Albano, Detweiler, & Logsdon-Conradsen, 1999).

Psychoeducational

In this phase, teens are informed about the nature of anxiety. A model emphasizing the cognitive, physiological, and behavioral symptoms increases their awareness and understanding of what provokes and maintains their symptoms. They are taught self-monitoring to help them identify anxiety triggers and reactions. To help the teens identify their symptoms, they are placed in anxiety-provoking situations, such as entering a classroom late, and asked to describe their physical, cognitive, and behavioral reactions:

THERAPIST: What would you be feeling? (physical)

TEEN: Butterflies, dizziness, shortness of breath.

THERAPIST: What would you be thinking? (cognitive)

TEEN: Everyone will be looking at me. What if the teacher yells at me? My face will be all red; they'll see it.

THERAPIST: What would you do? (behavioral)

TEEN: Skip the class. Not look up at anyone. Go to the nurse's office instead.

(Adapted from Marten et al., 1991)

Skill Building

In this phase, teens learn cognitive restructuring, social skills, and problem-solving skills. Adolescents are taught to identify cognitive distortions—errors in thinking that perpetuate anxiety. Systematic rational responses are developed to replace these cognitions. Modeling, role-playing, and systematic-exposure exercises are used.

Specific social skills for interpersonal interactions, maintenance of relationships, and assertiveness are identified and taught. Adolescents first identify behaviors that negatively influence social interactions, such as not smiling, making nervous gestures, not showing interest, speaking too softly, or criticizing or ignoring others. They then practice better forms of social interaction (Marten et al., 1991).

Problem Solving

In this phase, a model for identifying problems and developing realistic goals is presented and rehearsed. The teen is taught how to cope by using a proactive approach rather than avoidance. Two therapists role-play a situation that produces social anxiety. They verbalize their automatic thoughts and rational coping responses to model stages of cognitive restructuring. One therapist (T1) verbalizes the automatic thoughts, and the other therapist (T2) acts as the "rational responder," as illustrated in the following example:

Scene: You Have Been Called on to Give a Brief Talk in Front of Your Class

T1: "Oh no, I can't do this!"

T2: "Okay, calm down, stay cool. Don't think so negatively."

T1: "Everyone will be looking at me. I'll mess up."

T2: "They have to do this too. We're all a little nervous."

T1: "What will I say? I can't think!"

T2: "Okay, I can say things clearly, I know this stuff."

T1: "My heart is beating so fast, I'm gonna be sick."

T2: "I feel nervous, but it will pass. I'll be fine."

T1: "Boy, I'm glad that's over, I'll never do this again."

T2: "Alright! I did it! That was okay. I made it!" (Adapted from Marten et al., 1991.)

Therapists then discuss the role play with the group, drawing on the members' experiences in similar situations.

Exposure

In this phase, teens develop a fear and avoidance hierarchy of social situations, which serves as the focus of in-session exposures. Group members and therapists simulate the situations. Exposures target the behavioral avoidance and cognitive component of anxiety, showing that anxiety will dissipate with habituation.

Generalization and Maintenance

To enhance generalization and maintenance of treatment effects, the prosocial and coping behaviors that the teen learns in the group are modeled and practiced during snack-time sessions. In addition, to increase generalization to the home setting, the program also includes a component for active parent participation (Marten et al., 1991).

When asked how she had changed following treatment for her social anxiety disorder, here's what one girl said:

"Well, my friends told me that when they used to ask my opinion about something, I would always say, 'I don't care' or 'I don't know.' Now when they ask me, I give them my opinion. They said they like me much better now because I say what I think." (Beidel & Turner, 1998, p. 223)

Used by permission of Ann Marie Albano.

(Benjamin et al., 2013). Replication studies using CBT have found gains to be maintained for 8 to 13 years after treatment (Saavedra et al., 2010). In general, children who are younger and have fewer internalizing symptoms, and whose mothers do not display depressive symptoms, generally show more favorable outcomes (Southam-Gerow, Kendall, & Weersing, 2001).

Computer-based, computer-assisted, and online CBT have also been shown to be effective in treating anxiety disorders and OCD in children and adolescents (Comer et al., 2014; Khanna & Kendall, 2010; Spence et al., 2011). These approaches have the added benefit of using less therapist time and/or providing greater access for families who have difficulty accessing clinic-based treatment, making it a viable and cost-effective option for many youngsters with anxiety disorders. Although CBT is effective in a variety of formats in treating childhood anxiety disorders, studies have not tested whether its effectiveness is through changes in the hypothesized key components—the child's cognitions and coping skills. Thus, CBT in a variety of formats works, but we do not yet know why. In addition, the treatment response to CBT may not be consistent across anxiety disorders. Evidence suggests that children with SAD and GAD may show more favorable outcomes than those with SOC (Rapp et al., 2013). One study found that youngsters with anxiety disorders who had more severe and impairing anxiety, greater caregiver strain, and a main diagnosis of SOC had less favorable treatment outcomes (Compton et al., 2014).

Family Interventions

Anxiety disorders often occur in a context of parental anxiety and problematic family relationships, which may influence the effectiveness of any of the treatment approaches. In some cases, child-focused treatment may have spillover effects into the family. For example, as children come to view themselves as more competent and less avoidant, parents' perceptions about what their child can and cannot do change as well. As a result, parents may begin to respond differently to their child, and their own feelings and functioning improve (Kendall & Flannery-Schroeder, 1998). Greater parental involvement in modeling and reinforcing coping techniques, inclusion of parental anxiety-management strategies, and inclusion of parent skills training may be especially important in treating younger children with anxiety. Some studies have found these types of modified CBT approaches for younger children and their families to be effective in reducing anxiety and improving coping skills in children in the 4-to-9-year age range,

with outcomes comparable to those for treatments for CBT with older children (Cartwright-Hatton et al., 2011; Hirshfeld-Becker et al., 2010). Several age-adapted forms of CBT have also been developed for preschool-age children with anxiety disorders. These adaptations mainly involve including the child's primary caregivers in treatment and the use of age-appropriate materials such as cartoons, drawings, and narratives (Luby, 2013).

Addressing children's anxiety disorders in a family context may result in more dramatic and lasting effects than focusing only on the child, particularly for children of anxious parents (Creswell & Cartwright-Hatton, 2007; Suveg et al., 2006). In one study, it was found that nearly 70% of the children with anxiety disorders who completed individual or family treatment did not meet criteria for any anxiety disorder at posttreatment. The addition of a family component that focused on interactions, managing emotion, communication, and problem solving significantly enhanced short-term outcomes and long-term maintenance (Barrett, Dadds, & Rapee, 1996).

Given the important role of the family in childhood OCD, treatments for OCD have increasingly emphasized family involvement (Waters & Barrett, 2000). The primary treatment for children with OCD involves CBT that helps them learn to confront their worst fears gradually (graded exposure) while being prevented from engaging in their rituals (response prevention) (Freeman et al., 2008; March & Mulle, 1998; Piacentini et al., 2012). Family treatment for OCD provides education about the disorder and helps families cope with their feelings, such as helplessness in not being able to relieve the child's pain, frustration that the child cannot "just stop," jealousy from siblings, and disappointment that the child is not "normal" (Piacentini, Jacobs, & Maidment, 1997). Both individual child CBT and family-based interventions have proven to be effective in treating children with OCD (Barrett et al., 2008; Freeman et al., 2014; Geller et al., 2012). A number of excellent CBT manuals and self-help books are also available for treating OCD and related disorders (see www.ocfoundation.org). Generally, CBT has been found to be most effective for less severe cases of OCD, in which children display less severe symptoms, less impairment, greater insight, and fewer externalizing symptoms (Garcia et al., 2010).

Medications

A variety of medications have been used to treat the symptoms of anxiety in children and adolescents; the most common and effective ones are selective serotonin reuptake inhibitors (SSRIs) (Reinblatt & Riddle, 2007; Rynn et al., 2011). Although used to treat all types of anxiety and related disorders, the strongest evidence of their effectiveness is in treatment of OCD (Garcia et al., 2010). Findings regarding the effectiveness of medications for treating anxiety and related disorders other than OCD have been less consistent (Huemer, Erhart, & Steiner, 2010). Nevertheless, a number of controlled studies have found SSRIs to be effective in managing the symptoms of anxiety for youngsters with SOC, SAD, and GAD, with effects comparable to those in CBT in some studies (Reinblatt & Riddle, 2007; Piacentini, Bennett et al., 2014).

Given the lack of controlled studies and possible adverse side effects associated with the use of SSRIs for children with anxiety disorders, CBT is generally considered the first line of treatment; medication is used for children with severe symptoms or comorbid disorders or when CBT is not available or proves unsuccessful (AACAP, 2007b). Some children who are severely anxious may require medication before they are able to participate in CBT. To date, there have been relatively few studies of the effectiveness of medications for the treatment of anxiety disorders in children, particularly for specific phobias; however, clinical trials and a growing number of controlled studies provide some knowledge about the use of these compounds (Geller et al., 2012; Reinblatt & Riddle, 2007).

Prevention

Given their frequency, early onset, and chronicity and the personal suffering and public health costs associated with anxiety disorders, early identification and prevention efforts need to be a priority. In an innovative prevention study, researchers first identified very young children (mean age, <4 years) who were at risk for later anxiety disorders (Rapee et al., 2010). As described in the case of Jack (see A Closer Look 11.6), children were selected based on both a

---

A CLOSER LOOK 11.6

Early Intervention and Prevention of Anxiety Disorders

Jack: "Participating with Confidence"
Background
"Jack," 3 years 11 months of age, was referred by his parents, who were concerned about his difficulty interacting with people outside the immediate family and participating in new activities. Despite attending the same preschool for 6 months, Jack was unable to initiate or reciprocate play with other children and spoke only to his main teacher. He tended to watch rather than participate in group activities. Jack's parents had withdrawn him from group swimming classes because he cried if he thought anyone was looking at him. His parents also avoided most social engagements because Jack constantly clung to them and demanded to go home. Both parents described themselves as having been very shy as children and were keen for Jack to avoid this experience.

Behavioral Inhibition Assessment
When Jack arrived at the laboratory for the behavioral inhibition assessment, he hid behind his mother when greeted and sat on his mother's lap rather than at the table with the assessor. He did not respond verbally to the assessor for over 30 minutes, and when he did, his speech was soft and monosyllabic and he avoided eye contact. He reacted fearfully in the cloaked stranger interaction and returned to his mother's lap. Jack did not approach the novel toy or interact with the other child in the peer interaction component. Jack's assessment showed that he met all criteria for behavioral inhibition, and he also met DSM-5 criteria for social anxiety disorder.

Intervention
Jack's parents were randomly allocated to the 6-week parent education program. In the program, Jack's parents were encouraged to reduce their overprotective parenting style by not allowing Jack to avoid situations that made him anxious, such as attending parties and new activities. They were also encouraged to give Jack the opportunity to speak for himself rather than answering for him. Jack's parents were assisted in developing a graded-exposure hierarchy to previously feared situations. They began with reinforcing Jack's efforts to reply when familiar people greeted him and gradually worked up to helping him to join in small group activities.

Outcome
At his final follow-up assessment, at 6 years 10 months of age, Jack no longer met the criteria for social anxiety disorder and was no longer as strongly inhibited. Jack's mother reported that he was still reserved when he first met unfamiliar people and that she would still describe him as "shy." However, he was participating with confidence in most school and extracurricular activities, and he had a small group of close friends.

Excerpt from Altering the Trajectory of Anxiety in At-Risk Young Children. Ronald M. Rapee, Ph.D.; Susan J. Kennedy, Ph.D.; Michelle Ingram, M.Clin.Psych.; Susan L. Edwards, Ph.D.; Lynne Sweeney, Ph.D. From the Centre for Emotional Health, Department of Psychology, Macquarie University. Am J Psychiatry 2010;167: 1518–1525. Adapted with permission from the American Journal of Psychiatry (Copyright © 2010). American Psychiatric Association.

high *withdrawal* score on a temperament questionnaire and high scores on a laboratory test of *behavioral inhibition*. A relatively brief intervention consisting of six 90-minute group sessions with parents was then carried out. The sessions provided an overview of the developmental aspects of anxiety, principles of parenting techniques (particularly the role that parental overprotection plays as a risk factor for anxiety), cognitive restructuring for parental worries about their child, and—for the children as they matured—the use of exposure hierarchies for the child, and the importance of ongoing use of these techniques, especially during high risk periods such as school entry. A no treatment control group was simply monitored in the clinic at 12-month intervals, on the same schedule as the parents who received intervention.

As shown in ● Figure 11.4, the overall number and the severity of diagnosed anxiety disorders decreased for both groups following the start of the study. Importantly, like Jack, children in the intervention group showed significantly fewer anxiety disorders and lower symptom severity at the last two follow-up visits

relative to controls. Mothers also reported that their children showed lower levels of anxiety 3 years after treatment, with a similar trend for children's reports of their own anxiety at the 3-year follow-up. Particularly interesting was that the intervention effects were modest at 1 year but stronger at 2 and 3 years. Also, the severity differences between treated and untreated children seem to be mainly due to an increase in symptoms for the control group, suggesting that untreated children may be on a worsening developmental trajectory (Cuthbert, 2010). Follow-up studies are needed to explore possible reasons for these outcomes. Universal programs of primary prevention have also proven to be a promising approach to preventing anxiety in older children (Barrett et al., 2006). With further research, these and other innovative programs of early intervention and prevention offer hope for the many children and families who suffer from anxiety disorders.

Section Summary

Treatment and Prevention

- Exposing youngsters to the situations, objects, and occasions that produce their anxiety is the main line of attack in treating fears and anxieties.

- The most effective procedures for treating specific phobias involve participant modeling and reinforced practice.

- Cognitive–behavioral therapy (CBT) teaches children to understand how their thinking contributes to anxiety, how to change maladaptive thoughts to decrease their symptoms, and how to cope with their fears and anxieties other than by escape and avoidance.

- Medications such as SSRIs are effective in treating children with anxiety disorders. CBT is generally considered the first line of treatment, with medication reserved for those with severe symptoms or comorbid disorders or when CBT is not available or proves unsuccessful.

- Family interventions for anxiety disorders may result in more dramatic and lasting effects than focusing only on the child.

- Prevention programs have had some success in decreasing symptoms of anxiety, although further research is needed to evaluate their long-term benefits.

● **FIGURE 11.4** | Number and severity of diagnosed anxiety disorders over 3 years in children whose parents received an intervention or who received only monitoring.

Reprinted with permission from the *American Journal of Psychiatry* (Copyright © 2010). American Psychiatric Association.

Study Resources

SECTION SUMMARIES

KEY TERMS

12

Trauma- and Stressor-Related Disorders

I think the thumbprint on the throat of many people is childhood trauma that goes unprocessed and unrecognized.

—Tom Hooper (British film and television director)

ALTHOUGH STRESS AND TRAUMA in childhood or adolescence have always existed, only recently have these events been receiving the attention they duly deserve. Considerable evidence supports the significant link between childhood trauma and immediate and long-term mental health consequences, leading some to call childhood trauma "the hidden epidemic" (Lanius, Vermetten, & Pain, 2010). Childhood trauma has the potential to undermine healthy child development and cause many of the forms of abnormal child development described in this text, such as anxiety, depression, eating disorders, and many others (Chapman, Dube, & Anda, 2007).

It is now known that trauma occurring during childhood or adolescence is common, with about one in four youths reporting some form of major trauma before age 16 (Costello et al., 2002). **Traumatic events** are defined as exposure to actual or threatened harm or fear of death or injury and are considered uncommon or extreme stressors. Such terrifying or life-threatening events are wide-ranging. They include careless or intentional acts such as physical and sexual abuse, neglect, and exposure to domestic and community violence, as well as unintended medical traumas, accidents, natural disasters, war, terrorism, refugee trauma, and traumatic loss (Gerson & Rappaport, 2013). **Stressful events** are typically more common and less extreme than traumatic events. Stressors may be a single event, such as parental separation or romantic breakups, or may involve multiple or ongoing stressful situations or events. Some stressful events are developmentally connected—for example, going to school or leaving home for the first time. Even childhood bullying, once considered a common rite of passage, is now recognized as a major stressor that contributes to adult mental health problems for some individuals (Copeland et al., 2013). Although many traumatic and stressful events do not lead to a mental health disorder, they can affect ongoing developmental processes in insidious and disruptive ways.

Trauma- and stressor-related disorders is a new category in the *Diagnostic and Statistical Manual of Mental Disorders*, 5th edition (DSM-5); it includes Acute Stress Disorder, Adjustment Disorder, and Posttraumatic Stress Disorder (PTSD), which were classified as anxiety disorders in previous editions of the DSM. This category also includes two other stressor-related disorders previously listed as "Disorders usually first diagnosed in infancy, childhood, or adolescence": Reactive Attachment Disorder and Disinhibited Social Engagement Disorder. These changes were made to create the more specific category of trauma- and stressor-related disorders. These disorders have in common direct or indirect exposure to acute or chronic stressors or catastrophic events, which may consist of multiple events over time, such as child maltreatment.

Considerable research concerning child maltreatment has been done, so we refer to this literature throughout this chapter to illustrate the nature and scope of childhood trauma- and stressor-related disorders. **Child maltreatment** is a generic term that refers to four primary acts: physical abuse, neglect, sexual abuse, and **psychological abuse**. Maltreatment can take many forms, including acts experienced by many children, such as harsh corporal punishment, sibling violence, and peer assault, as well as acts experienced by a significant minority, such as beatings or abandonment (Centers for Disease Control [CDC], 2011d). Child maltreatment cuts across all lines of gender, national origin, language, religion, age, ethnicity, disability, and sexual orientation.

MARY ELLEN

Her Legacy

She is a bright little girl, with features indicating unusual mental capacity, but with a careworn, stunted, and prematurely old look. Her apparent condition of health, as well as her scanty wardrobe, indicated that no change of custody or condition could be much for the worse.

. . . On her examination [in court] the child made a statement as follows: "I don't know how old I am. . . . I have never had but one pair of shoes, but I cannot recollect when that was. I have had no shoes or stockings on this winter. . . . I am never allowed to play with any children, or to have any company whatever. Mamma has been in the habit of whipping and beating me almost every day. She used to whip me with a twisted whip—a raw hide. The whip always left a black and blue mark on my body. I have now the black and blue marks on my head which were made by mamma, and also a cut on the left side of my forehead which was made by a pair of scissors. She struck me with the scissors and cut me; I have no recollection of ever having been kissed by any one. . . . I have never been taken on my mamma's lap and caressed or petted. . . . I do not know for what I was whipped—mamma never said anything to me when she whipped me."

New York Times, April 10, 1874.

This heartbreaking and tragic report of Mary Ellen's abuse led to the formation in the winter of 1874 of the New York Society for the Prevention of Cruelty to Children, as citizens discovered that animals were protected from mistreatment but children were not. It took another 100 years to pass legislation that clearly defined and mandated the reporting of child abuse and neglect, finally launching new efforts to identify and assist abused and neglected children in North America. Despite these efforts, child abuse and neglect remain one of the most common causes of trauma- and stressor-related disorders across the lifespan (Wekerle & Wolfe, 2014).

In North America, before they reach adulthood, 1 in 10 children experiences some form of sexual victimization by an adult or peer (Finkelhor et al., 2009). Each year, about 1 in 10 children receives physical punishment by a parent or other caregiver harsh enough to put the child at risk of injury or harm (Straus & Stewart, 1999). Sadly, each day in the United States more than five children—most of whom are under 4 years old—die at the hands of their parents or caregivers (U.S. Department of Health and Human Services, Administration on Children, Youth, and Families [USDHHS], 2010). Countless other children suffer the effects of psychological abuse and neglect or are exposed to catastrophic events or accidents. Most show profound changes in mood, arousal, or behavior immediately after these events. Although many recover or manage to cope effectively, about one-third go on to develop symptoms of post-traumatic stress disorder (PTSD) or other mental disorders that affect their daily lives (Gerson & Rappaport, 2013).

For many generations, violence against children and other family members was viewed as a private matter, and its significant negative effects continue to be poorly acknowledged. Until very recently, violence between family members was considered, in the eyes of the law, to be less consequential, less damaging, and less worthy of society's serious attention than violence between strangers. Today we know better: violence against children occurs in numerous forms, from mild acts of frightening or yelling at children, to severe acts of assaulting them with fists and weapons. Moreover, violence and abuse wax and wane in a cyclical manner that creates tension, uncertainty, and fear in children, forcing them to cope with harsh realities and fearful demands (Wekerle et al., 2006).

Many forms of childhood trauma, especially child abuse and neglect, have considerable psychological importance because they often occur within ongoing relationships that are expected to be protective, supportive, and nurturing. Children from abusive and neglectful families grow up in environments that fail to provide

consistent and appropriate opportunities to guide their development; instead, these children are placed in jeopardy of physical and emotional harm (Jaffe, Wolfe, & Campbell, 2011). Yet, their ties to their families—even to the abuser—are very important, so child victims may feel torn between a sense of belonging and a sense of fear and apprehension. Because children are dependent on the people who harm or neglect them, they face other paradoxical dilemmas as well (American Psychological Association, 1996/2007):

- *The victim not only wants to stop the violence but also longs to belong to a family.* Loyalty and strong emotional ties to the abuser are powerful opponents to the victim's desire to be safe and protected.

- *Affection and attention may coexist with violence and abuse.* A recurring cycle may begin, whereby mounting tension, characterized by fear and anticipation, ultimately gives way to more abusive behavior. A period of reconciliation may follow, with increased affection and attention. Children are always hopeful that the abuse will not recur.

- *The intensity of the violence tends to increase over time, although in some cases physical violence may decrease or even stop altogether.* Abusive behavior may vary throughout the relationship, taking verbal, sexual, emotional, or physical forms, but the adult's abuse of power and control remains the central issue.

We begin our discussion of child trauma and stress with some significant historical issues, followed by consideration of the family's role in children's healthy socialization and safety.

HISTORY AND FAMILY CONTEXT

Because the most severe and long-lasting forms of childhood trauma occur at the hands of caregivers, we begin this discussion with a look at how society's view of child-rearing and intolerance of child abuse and neglect have evolved over a relatively short period. Intentional and unintentional forms of trauma have always existed, and most likely were even more common place in previous generations (Radbill, 1987), but these events were seldom identified as problematic. For generations, children were viewed as the exclusive property and responsibility of their fathers, who had full discretion as to how punishment could be administered. This right was unchallenged by any countermovement to seek more humane treatment for children up until the recognition of the abuse Mary Ellen experienced, just 140 years ago.

Ironically, the same legal system that was designed to support and assist the family has tolerated, and in some respects condoned, the abuse of family members, including children, women, and the elderly (Jaffe et al., 1996). Two major cultural traditions have influenced this position until recently: absolute authority over the family by the husband and the right to family privacy. The Roman Law of Chastisement (753 B.C.), for example, made women the possessions of men, who they were required to obey. English common law similarly allowed parents and others to punish their children using "moderate and reasonable" chastisement. For centuries since, it has been up to the courts in various countries to determine what is moderate and reasonable. Sadly, many developed and developing societies still adhere to this view of children as personal property to be managed however the parent wishes (Wolfe & Nayak, 2003).

Fortunately, over the past century and a half, particularly the past 30 years, the legal system's response has shifted to condemn such behavior throughout much of the Western world (albeit with considerable resistance). The UN Convention on the Rights of the Child (1989) spurred efforts to value the rights and needs of children, and to recognize their exploitation and abuse in many developed countries. Today, 42 countries have established an official government policy regarding child abuse and neglect, and about one-third of the world's population is included in the various countries that conduct an annual count of child abuse and neglect cases (International Society for Prevention of Child Abuse and Neglect, 2010). These efforts provide the critical first steps to identifying the scope of the problem, and justify the implementation of important societal, community, and cultural changes to combat child abuse and related forms of stress and trauma.

Healthy Families

You know the only people who are always sure about the proper way to raise children? Those who've never had any.

—Bill Cosby

It is difficult to talk about childhood trauma and maltreatment without talking about the importance of healthy families. Family relations are the earliest and most enduring social relationships that significantly affect a child's competence, resilience, and sense of well-being. For most of us, family influences are positive and beneficial, offering a primary source of support and nurturance that sets the stage for lifetime patterns of secure relationships and well-being. For others, however, family events and experiences are profoundly negative and harmful, providing the context for some of the most severe violence in society (Straus, Gelles, & Steinmetz, 2003).

As parents, we recognize that children require considerable direction and control and that they sometimes behave in ways that challenge our decisions and interfere with our plans. If you have not experienced this yourself, ask a parent you know if you can take their young child grocery shopping! Individuals who are ill-prepared for the vital and challenging role of being parents may rely heavily on child-rearing methods from their own childhood, without questioning or modifying those methods. Although this approach to parenting is natural and often appropriate, in some cases it can perpetuate undesirable child-rearing methods, such as physical coercion, verbal threats, and neglect of the child's needs (Gershoff, 2013; Wolfe, 1999).

Understanding the dire effects of trauma and abuse on the mental health of children and adults must begin with a discussion of what children should expect from a healthy family environment. For healthy development, children need a caregiving environment that balances their need for control and direction, or "demandingness," with their need for stimulation and sensitivity, or "responsiveness" (Maccoby & Martin, 1983). Determinants of healthy parent–child relationships and family roles derived from these two primary developmental needs include:

▶ Adequate knowledge of child development and expectations, including knowledge of children's normal sexual development and experimentation;

▶ Adequate skill in coping with the stress related to caring for small children, and knowledge of ways to enhance child development through proper stimulation and attention;

▶ Opportunities to develop normal parent–child attachment and early patterns of communication;

▶ Adequate parental knowledge of home management, including basic financial planning, proper shelter, and meal planning;

▶ Opportunities and willingness to share the duties of child care between two parents, when applicable;

▶ Provision of necessary social and health services.

These healthy patterns depend not only on parental competence and developmental sensitivity, but also on family circumstances and the availability of community resources, such as education and child-rearing information, as well as social networks and supports. The family situation itself, including the parents' marital relationship and the child's characteristics, such as temperament, health, and developmental limitations, provides the basic context for child-rearing.

Although we would expect a considerable range in ability and resources among North American families, certain features of a child's environment should be fundamental and expectable. For young children, an **expectable environment** requires protective and nurturing adults, as well as opportunities for socialization within a culture. For older children, an expectable environment includes a supportive family, contact with peers, and ample opportunities to explore and master their environment (Cicchetti & Valentino, 2006). Moreover, responsible parenting involves a gradual shifting of control from the parent to the child and the community. Seldom is this process a smooth one, but healthy families learn to move gradually from nearly complete parental control, through shared control, to the child's growing self-control and eventual independence as an adult.

Continuum of Care

Most of us agree that children who lack the basic necessities of life—food, affection, medical care, education, and intellectual and social stimulation—are placed in jeopardy, but different cultural values, community standards, and personal experiences make one person's abuse another person's discipline or education (Spilsbury & Korbin, 2013).

● Figure 12.1 depicts a hypothetical range of child care, from healthy to abusive and neglectful, that

Most Positive Parenting Style ⟵   ⟶ **Most Negative Parenting Style**

Positive/Healthy	Poor/Dysfunctional	Emotionally Abusive/Neglectful
Stimulation and Emotional Expressions	*Stimulation and Emotional Expressions*	*Stimulation and Emotional Expressions*
Provides a variety of sensory stimulation and positive emotional expressions	Shows rigid emotional expression and inflexibility in responding to child	Expresses conditional love and ambivalent feelings toward child
Expresses joy at child's efforts and accomplishments	Seems unconcerned with child's developmental/psychological needs	Shows little or no sensitivity to child's needs
Interactions	*Interactions*	*Interactions*
Engages in competent, child-centered interactions to encourage development	Often insensitive to child's needs; unfriendly	Emotionally or physically rejects child's attention
Friendly, positive interactions that encourage independent exploration	Poor balance between child independence and dependence on parent	Takes advantage of child's dependency status through coercion, threats, or bribes
Consistency and Predictability	*Consistency and Predictability*	*Consistency and Predictability*
Demonstrates consistency and predictability to promote their relationship	Often responds unpredictably, sometimes with emotional discharge	Responds unpredictably, accompanied by emotional discharge
Rules and Limits	*Rules and Limits*	*Rules and Limits*
Makes rules for safety and health	Unclear or inconsistent rules for safety and health	Sporadic, capricious
Appropriate safeguards for child's age		Exploits or corrupts for parent's benefit
Disciplinary Practices	*Disciplinary Practices*	*Disciplinary Practices*
Occasionally scolds, criticizes, interrupts child activity	Frequently uses coercive methods and minimizes child's competence	Uses cruel and harsh control methods that frighten child
Teaches child through behavioral rather than psychological control methods	Uses psychologically controlling methods that confuse, upset child	Violates minimal community standards on occasion
Emotional Delivery and Tone	*Emotional Delivery and Tone*	*Emotional Delivery and Tone*
Uses emotional delivery and tone that are firm but not frightening	Uses verbal and nonverbal pressure, often to achieve unrealistic expectations	Frightening, threatening, denigrating, insulting

● **FIGURE 12.1** | Continuum of Parental Emotional Sensitivity and Expression.

© Cengage Learning®

provides some guidelines and boundaries for acceptable behavior between parents and children (Wolfe & McIsaac, 2011). At the positive end of this continuum we see appropriate and healthy forms of child-rearing actions that promote child development. Competent parents encourage their child's development in a variety of ways and match their demands and expectations to the child's needs and abilities. Of course, parents are human, and many on occasion will scold, criticize, or even show insensitivity to the child's state of need; in fact, discipline often requires such firm control, with accompanying verbal statements and affect.

Poor/dysfunctional actions, shown in the middle of the diagram, represent greater degrees of irresponsible and harmful child care. Parents who show any discernible degree of these actions toward their child often need instruction and assistance in effective child care methods. Finally, the far right of the diagram depicts parents who violate their child's basic needs and dependency status in a physically, sexually, or emotionally intrusive or abusive manner. Similarly, their failure to respond to a child's needs is the cornerstone of neglect.

Section Summary

History and Family Context

- Traumatic events involve exposure to actual or threatened harm or fear of death or injury, and include a wide range of intentional acts and unintentional circumstances.

- Stressful events are typically more common and less extreme than traumatic events but can still play a significant role in adjustment and well-being.

- Child maltreatment is considered among the worst and most intrusive forms of trauma and stress. It refers to four primary acts: physical abuse, neglect, sexual abuse, and psychological abuse.

- Child care can be described along a hypothetical continuum ranging from healthy to abusive and neglectful.

- Boundaries between appropriate and inappropriate behavior toward children are not always clear or well established, but an awareness of what is right and what is wrong can go a long way in preventing maltreatment.

TRAUMA, STRESS, AND MALTREATMENT: DEFINING FEATURES

I think my biggest focus for myself is learning how to continue to get through the trauma that my father has caused in my life.

—Lindsay Lohan

Incidents of trauma, stress, and maltreatment that affect children's health and well-being usually involve actions by adults or circumstances beyond the child's control. Thus,

they are important risk factors for abnormal child behavior or compromised development, as well as for specific disorders to be discussed later on in this chapter. Because of their significance, DSM-5 considers some forms of child stress and maltreatment under the category "Other conditions that may be a focus of clinical attention." For example, if a child who was abused is also suffering from a clinical disorder such as depression, the maltreatment would be noted as part of the diagnosis in order to ensure proper treatment. Additional conditions that may be a focus of clinical attention (and child stress) include problems related to family upbringing, family dynamics, or divorce.

Trauma and Stress

Trauma and stressful experiences in childhood or adolescence may involve actual or threatened death or injury, or a threat to one's physical integrity. Children exposed to chronic or severe stressors, such as major accidents, natural disasters, kidnapping, brutal physical assaults, war and violence, or sexual abuse, have an elevated risk of PTSD, as discussed in the next section. Examples of well-known traumatic events associated with the onset of PTSD in children are the Oklahoma City bombing, the school shootings in Littleton, Colorado, the terrorist attacks on the United States on September 11, 2001, the ravaging impact of Hurricane Katrina on New Orleans and the U.S. Gulf Coast, and the 2004 great Indian Ocean earthquake and tsunamis (Comer & Kendall, 2007; Dean et al., 2008).

As a result of exposure to war in recent decades more than 2 million children worldwide have been killed, approximately 6 million have been injured or permanently disabled, 1 million have been orphaned, and 20 million have been displaced (Barenbaum, Ruchkin, & Schwab-Stone, 2004). Many others have been injured by land mines or targeted for ethnic cleansing and genocide. Millions of other children have

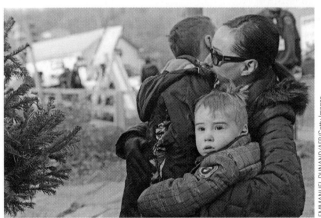

Parental support can mitigate the psychological harm from traumatic events in childhood.

Young Jason never goes unarmed. Grabbing his plastic gun and rubber knife, he tells his mother, "If daddy comes, I'll be able to stop him."

been exposed to bombing, shelling, sniper fire, and terrorist attacks resulting in untold loss of family, friends, and community support (Bellamy, 2002). The tragedy of these events underscores the need to understand how they affect children's mental health, and, more importantly, to find effective ways of helping the child victims of such atrocities (Ehntholt & Yule, 2006).

Estimates based on a nationally representative sample of dual-parent U.S. households indicate that over 15 million American children live in families in which partner violence occurred at least once in the previous year (McDonald et al., 2006). Child witnesses of abuse and violence in the home or in their community are exposed to traumatic events that pose a high risk to development (Jaffe et al., 2011; Wolfe et al., 2003). Younger children exposed to violence are fearful and often show regressive and somatic signs of distress, such as sleep problems, bed-wetting, headaches, stomachaches, diarrhea, ulcers, and enuresis. Older boys tend to be more aggressive with peers and dating partners; girls tend to be more passive and withdrawn and to have low self-esteem (Crooks & Wolfe, 2007). All of these symptoms can be directly or indirectly linked to a stressful family environment, as well as threats to the child's safety and the safety of one or more caregivers.

Less extreme, non-life-threatening forms of stressful experiences in childhood or adolescence are common, and most do not lead to enduring harm or disorders. Changing schools, parental separation, medical problems, and peer conflict are just a few of the myriad forms of stress that are a part of life, which some adults reflect back on as building character while others fear to discuss. However, teens today are reporting levels of stress that rival those of adults, which poses risks to their physical and emotional health (Bethune, 2014) (see A Closer Look 12.1).

How Stress Affects Children

To cope with everyday forms of stress, children and youths need a basic expectable environment to adapt successfully or their development may be compromised. All children must cope with various degrees of stress, and these experiences can be strengthening if they do not exceed the child's coping ability—that is, the nature and amount of stress is *manageable* (Masten & Wright, 2010). Stressful experiences that are mild, predictable, and brief are usually manageable and can actually enhance a child's biological and psychological competence (Thompson, 2014). However, a child's method of adapting to or coping with immediate environmental demands (such as avoiding an

"If you think you're stressed out, imagine being a teenager in today's society. American teens say they experience stress in patterns similar to those for adults, and during the school year they report stress levels even higher than those reported by adults. These were the prime conclusions of APA's poll *Stress in America™: Are Teens Adopting Adults' Stress Habits?*

Teens reported that their stress levels during the school year far exceeded what they believe to be healthy (5.8 vs. 3.9 on a 10-point scale) and topped adults' average reported stress levels (5.8 for teens vs. 5.1 for adults). Even during the summer, teens reported their stress during the prior month at levels higher than what they believe is healthy (4.6 vs. 3.9 on a 10-point scale).

Many teens also reported feeling overwhelmed (31%) and depressed or sad (30%) as a result of stress. More than one-third of teens reported feeling tired (36%) and nearly one-quarter of teens (23%) reported skipping a meal due to stress."

Source: Bethune (2014).

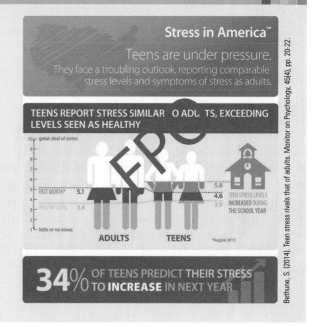

abusive caregiver) may later compromise his or her ability to form relationships with others. A child's successful methods of adapting to outbursts of anger and aggression between family members are constantly challenged. Signs of stress appear, such as increased illness, symptoms of fear and anxiety, and problems with peers or school (El-Sheikh et al., 2013; Kim & Cicchetti, 2010).

Stressful events in the child's family or immediate environment affect each child in different and unique ways. However, certain situations trigger more intense or more chronic stress reactions and carry more severe consequences than others. (Consider, for example, the difference between the stress of moving to a new school and the stress of being bullied by an older child.) Early, chronic stress challenges the child's developing biological and social development, influencing multiple neurobiological changes in an effort to adapt (described later in this chapter). However, such adaptation to threat and chronic stress carries trade-offs in children's abilities to perform at school, to interact with peers, and to control their impulses. Stress provokes strong biological responses (e.g., elevated blood pressure, activation of immunological and hormonal systems) that are designed for short-term reactions, such as fight or flight. Children who are chronically aroused by a stressful environment mobilize these biological responses repeatedly, often to the point of overload. Over time, some of these children may show signs of being *hyperresponsive* to stress: excessive threat vigilance, mistrust, poor social relationships, impaired self-regulation, and unhealthy lifestyle choices

(Miller, Chen, & Parker, 2011). Paradoxically, some children may become *hyporesponsive* to stressful events— underreacting to signs of danger or threat—indicating that their stress system is overtaxed and may be shutting down. **Allostatic load** is a concept used to describe this progressive "wear and tear" on biological systems due to the effects of chronic stress (Thompson, 2014).

Child maltreatment, exposure to domestic violence, and chronic child poverty are among the worst and most intrusive forms of childhood stress and trauma (Graham-Bermann et al., 2012; Yoshikawa, Aber, & Beardslee, 2012). These circumstances impinge directly on the child's daily life, may be ongoing and unpredictable, and are often the result of actions or inactions of people the child is supposed to trust and depend on. However, keep in mind that even events such as abuse, neglect, family violence, and poverty do not affect each child in a predictable, characteristic fashion. Rather, their impact depends on the child's makeup and available supports (El-Sheikh & Erath, 2011).

A prime factor in how children respond to various forms of stress is the degree of parental support and assistance they receive to help them cope and adapt. Parents provide a model that teaches the child how to exert some control even in the midst of confusion and upheaval. Understandably, a warm relationship with an adult who provides a predictable routine and consistent, moderate discipline, and who buffers the child from unnecessary sources of stress, is a valuable asset. Maltreated children may have the hardest time adapting appropriately to any form of stress when they are deprived of positive adult relationships, effective models of problem solving, and a sense of personal control or predictability (Luthar, 2006; Wekerle & Wolfe, 2014).

Maltreatment

Peace in society depends upon peace in the family.

—Augustine

Have you ever babysat a young child or been in charge of a group of children at a camp or school? If you saw bruises on a child, what would you do? First, you would consider that bruises on a child can be caused by any number of factors, so you would need to obtain more information, if possible, to see whether the bruises were accidental. You should be aware that all states and provinces in North America have civil laws, or statutes, that obligate persons who come in contact with children as part of their job or volunteer work (bus drivers, day-care workers, teachers, babysitters, and so forth) to report known or suspected cases of abuse to the police or child welfare authorities. These statutes also provide criteria for removing children from their homes if it is suspected that they are being maltreated. Criminal statutes further specify the forms of maltreatment that are criminally punishable. We all have a role to play in keeping children safe from harm, and it begins with being attentive to signs of possible abuse; professional or police involvement should be sought if you are concerned or uncertain.

Child maltreatment is broadly defined as "Any recent act or failure to act on the part of a parent or caretaker, which results in death, serious physical or emotional harm, sexual abuse, or exploitation, or an act or failure to act which presents an imminent risk of serious harm" (Child Welfare Information Gateway, 2011). Each year, over a million children in the United States experience maltreatment that results in some degree of harm, resulting in a rate of 17 per 1,000 children in the population (Sedlak et al, 2010). Incidence rates of maltreatment resulting in harm in Canada and the United Kingdom are similar, about 14 per 1,000 children (Public Health Agency of Canada, 2010; National Society for the Prevention of Cruelty to Children, 2011).

● Figure 12.2 shows the percentages of each subtype of abuse and neglect, based on U.S. data. As shown, child neglect (including medical neglect) continues to be a worrisome problem, accounting for four out of five documented cases of maltreatment in the United States. Physical abuse (10.9%), sexual abuse (7.6%), psychological maltreatment (7.6%), and other forms of maltreatment (e.g., abandonment or threats of harm, 9.6%) make up the remaining substantiated

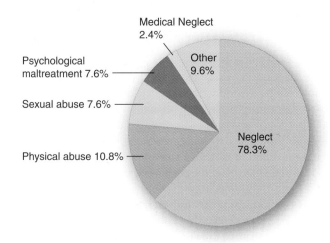

● **FIGURE 12.2** | Types of child maltreatment by percentage. "Other" forms of maltreatment include abandonment, threats of harm to the child, and congenital drug addiction. (Note that the percentages total more than 100% because children may have suffered from more than one type of maltreatment.)

Data from USDHHS (2010).

cases. In addition, about one in four of these children suffered more than one form of maltreatment.

Neglect

JANE AND MATT

Used to Neglect

Although Janet had worked for child protective services for over 10 years, she still cringed when she described the conditions of the home from which she had just removed two young siblings. "Neighbors and relatives have complained about the parents' never being around much, and how they often hear children crying," Janet explained during our interview. "I've been to the home before, and usually it stays clean for a few days after my visit. But this time the children were left with a teenaged babysitter, who went off to play in an arcade. They walked out of the home and had to be returned by the police. What I saw this time was worse than before. Little Matt, who's almost 3 years old, was running around in soiled diapers, crawling across broken dishes and spilled food, putting things in his mouth. His sister Jane, who turns 6 next month, was dressed in dirty clothes and looked like she hadn't eaten in a week. The odor from the house forced me to step outside for air. The children seemed used to it—they just moved things out of their way and didn't seem to care."

I met with both children once they were settled into a foster home, and offered ways for the foster parents to manage Jane's strong-willed behavior and Matt's delay in speech and toileting. The foster mother noted how both children seemed to need "constant attention and control" and how neither had knowledge of typical routines such as sitting down together for dinner, cleaning up, bed times, basic hygiene, and the need to wear clean clothing. (Based on authors' case material.)

These two children suffered the effects of physical and emotional neglect, characterized by a failure to provide for their basic physical, educational, and emotional needs. **Physical neglect** includes refusal or delay in seeking health care, expulsion from the home or refusal to allow a runaway to return home, abandonment, and inadequate supervision. **Educational neglect** involves actions such as allowing chronic truancy, failing to enroll in school a child who is of mandatory school age, and failing to attend to a child's special educational needs. **Emotional neglect**, one of the most difficult categories to define, includes actions such as marked inattention to the child's needs for affection, refusal or failure to provide needed psychological care, spousal abuse in the child's presence, and permission for drug or alcohol use by the child.

The determination of child neglect requires consideration of cultural values and standards of care, as well as recognition that the failure to provide the necessities of life may be related to poverty. The examples shown in Table 12.1 are actual cases of the three forms of neglect (Sedlak & Broadhurst, 1996).

Neglected children may suffer physical health problems, limited growth, and increased complications in other health conditions, such as diabetes, allergies, and failure to thrive (Lyons-Ruth et al., 2014; van Tilburg et al., 2010). They also may show behavior patterns that vacillate between undisciplined activity and extreme passivity as a result of the ways they adapt to an unresponsive caregiver (Hildyard & Wolfe, 2002). As toddlers, they show little persistence and enthusiasm; as preschoolers, neglected children show poor impulse control and are highly dependent on teachers for support and nurturance (Erickson & Egeland, 2002).

Child neglect, the most common form of maltreatment, is tied to poverty, substance abuse, and parental indifference.

TABLE 12.1 | The Three Forms of Child Neglect

Physical Neglect	Educational Neglect	Emotional Neglect
• A 2-year-old who was found wandering in the street late at night, naked and alone	• An 11-year-old and a 13-year-old who were chronically truant	• Siblings who were subjected to repeated incidents of family violence between their mother and father
• An infant who had to be hospitalized for near-drowning after being left alone in a bathtub	• A 12-year-old whose parents permitted him to decide whether to go to school, how long to stay there, and in which activities to participate	• A 12-year-old whose parents permitted him to drink and use drugs
• Children who were living in a home contaminated with animal feces and rotting food	• A special education student whose mother refused to believe he needed help in school	• A child whose mother helped him shoot out the windows of a neighbor's house

© Cengage Learning®

Abuse

Abused and Abusive

Four-year-old Milton's rambunctious nature and his mother's hair-trigger temper were an explosive mix. He was constantly in trouble at home and often was spanked, yelled at, and locked in his room. One evening his babysitter took him to the emergency department because she thought he had a bad cold. During the examination, the doctor discovered that Milton had a fracture to his left forearm that was a couple of weeks old. There was a goose egg on Milton's forehead and multiple bruises on his face at various stages of healing, as well as bruises on his back. Several people had noticed Milton's aggressive behavior—pushing other children or hitting them with something at preschool—but no one had realized that he was being abused. His preschool teacher told investigators, "I'm never sure from one minute to the next how Milton will react to the other children. He could be playing and suddenly become angry at something and start to destroy things or hit someone. I've also seen him become frightened—at what I don't know—and withdraw into a corner. I've tried several times to discuss these things with his mother, but she says he's just trying to get his way all the time." (Based on authors' case material.)

Milton has been physically abused. His behavior indicates growing up in an environment with punitive disciplinary methods that are the norm and are detrimental to child-centered stimulation and appropriate limit setting. **Physical abuse** is multiple acts of aggression that include punching, beating, kicking, biting, burning, shaking, or otherwise physically harming a child. In most cases, the injuries from physical abuse are not intentional, but they occur as a result of overdiscipline or severe physical punishment. The severity and nature of the injuries vary considerably, as shown by these sobering examples of physical abuse (Sedlak & Broadhurst, 1996):

▶ A 1-year-old child died of a cerebral hemorrhage after being shaken by her father.

▶ A teen's mother punched her and pulled out her hair.

▶ A child sustained second- and third-degree "stocking" burns to the feet after being held in hot water.

As a result of their harsh and insensitive treatment, physically abused children like Milton often are described as more disruptive and aggressive than their age-mates, with disturbances that reach across a broad spectrum of emotional and cognitive functioning (Teisl

& Cicchetti, 2008). Physical injuries may range from minor (bruises, lacerations), to moderate (scars, abrasions), to severe (burns, sprains, broken bones). These physical signs represent only the visible injuries; we will see later in this chapter that the psychological development of physically abused children often is impaired in less visible—but very serious—ways as well. We ask you to keep Milton's case in mind, since we refer to him several times throughout the chapter.

Some forms of abuse are psychological rather than physical, but carry a similar blow to a child's health and well-being. Harsh, emotionally abusive threats and put-downs from one's parents or caregivers can be as harmful to a child's development as physical abuse or neglect. **Psychological abuse** (also known as emotional abuse) includes repeated acts or omissions by the parents or caregivers that have caused, or could cause, serious behavioral, cognitive, emotional, or mental disorders. For example, parents or caregivers may use extreme or bizarre forms of punishment, such as confinement of a child in a dark closet. Psychological abuse also includes verbal threats and put-downs, habitual scapegoating, belittling, and name-calling. Psychological abuse exists, to some degree, in all forms of maltreatment, so the specific consequences of this form of maltreatment are less well understood than those of other forms of maltreatment (Glaser, 2011; Wolfe & McIsaac, 2011).

Sexual Abuse and Exploitation

No Haven at Home

Rosita was not quite 4 years old when her family doctor suspected that something was going on that troubled her. He expressed his concerns to child welfare, and Rosita reenacted several sexual acts for them, using dolls depicting her father and herself. "Daddy said I can play a game, and it's OK 'cause grownups do it," she hesitantly explained. Rosita made the dolls kiss, then the male doll rubbed the female doll's vagina. "But he hurt me, and it made me scared. I didn't want to get in trouble." To make matters worse, her mother became furious with Rosita and the agency when she heard the accusations, and was unwilling to ensure her daughter's protection and safety at home. "Rosita just wants a lot of attention—she's said this stuff before and I don't believe her one minute," was her mother's only comment. (Based on authors' case material.)

Rosita was sexually abused by her father and disbelieved by her mother; as a result, she faces many ongoing psychological complications. Because Rosita was seen several times throughout the course of her childhood and adolescent development, her case is discussed further in a later section of this chapter on the course of development of children and adolescents who have been sexually abused.

Sexual abuse includes fondling a child's genitals, intercourse with the child, incest, rape, sodomy, exhibitionism, and commercial exploitation through prostitution or the production of pornographic materials. The actual number of sexual abuse cases may be underreported because of the secrecy or "conspiracy of silence" that so often characterizes these cases, making determination of abuse difficult (Mitchell, Wolak, & Finkelhor, 2007). The following are actual reported cases of sexual abuse (Sedlak & Broadhurst, 1996):

▸ A 10-year-old girl who was raped by her father;

▸ Two sisters and a brother who were sexually molested by their mother's live-in boyfriend;

▸ A 4-year-old who was fondled by his father during weekend visitations.

The behavior and development of sexually abused children may be affected significantly, especially in relation to the duration or frequency of abuse, the use of force, the use of penetration, and a close relationship to the perpetrator (Berliner & Elliott, 2002). The physical health of these children may be compromised by urinary tract problems, gynecological problems, sexually transmitted diseases (including AIDS), and pregnancy (Maniglio, 2009).

About one-third of sexually abused children neither report nor exhibit visible symptoms, and about two-thirds of those who do show symptoms recover significantly during the first 12 to 18 months after the abuse (Kendall-Tackett, Williams, & Finkelhor, 2001). Nonetheless, the possibility of delayed emergence of symptoms, especially PTSD, is becoming more widely recognized (Fergusson, McLeod, & Horwood, 2013; Trickett, Noll, & Putnam, 2011). Children's reports of sexual abuse and their reactions and recovery vary depending on the nature of the sexual assault and the response of their important others, especially the mother (London et al., 2008). Many acute symptoms of sexual abuse resemble children's common reactions to stress, such as fears, increased anger, anxiety, fatigue, depression, passivity, difficulties focusing and sustaining attention, and withdrawal from usual activities.

In reaction to an abusive incident, it is common for younger children to regress temporarily, such as by becoming enuretic or easily upset or by having problems sleeping. In later childhood and early adolescence, these signs of distress may take the form of acting-out behaviors (such as delinquency, drug use, and promiscuity) or unhealthy relationships and self-destructive behavior (Trickett et al., 2011). Some sexually abused children may exhibit sexualized behaviors with other children or toys that may include excessive masturbation, age-inappropriate knowledge of sexual activity, and/or pronounced seductive or promiscuous behavior. Any of these symptoms of distress may be associated with a decline or sudden change in school performance, behavior, and peer relations.

Unlike physical abuse and neglect, sexual abuse rarely has any connection to child-rearing, discipline, or inattention to developmental needs. Rather, it constitutes a breach of trust, deception, intrusion, and exploitation of a child's innocence and status. Whereas all types of maltreatment share a common ground in relation to the abuse of power by an adult over a child, sexual abuse stands out from physical abuse and neglect in terms of these specific dynamics.

Children may also suffer trauma from commercial or sexual exploitation, such as child labor and child prostitution. Globally, as many as 10 million children may be victims of child prostitution, the sex industry, sex tourism, and pornography, although accurate statistics are not available (United Nations, 2006). Sadly, many exploited children began as victims of abuse and rape in their homes and are forced into commercial sexual activity at a young age (Cooper et al., 2005). Rates of child prostitution tend to be higher in Asia and Latin America, but an alarming growth has been recorded in Africa, North America, and Europe (Wolfe & Nayak, 2003). Poverty is the greatest factor in the child prostitution explosion, as migration of families from rural areas into cities creates unemployment, the breakdown of family structures, homelessness, and inevitably, an increase in child prostitution.

Characteristics of Children Who Suffer Maltreatment

Improvements in data-collection methods over the past decade indicate that trauma and maltreatment affect vulnerable or disadvantaged children disproportionately, as indicated by age, sex, and racial differences. For example, there is correspondence between certain types of maltreatment and children's ages. Younger children, who have the greatest need for care and supervision, are the most common victims of abuse and neglect, which corresponds to the emergence of their greater independence and to parental conflict during this developmental period. Sexual abuse, in contrast, is more common among the older age groups (>12 years). Other than for sexual abuse, the rate of victimization is inversely related to the age of the child (USDHHS, 2010).

Child maltreatment affects boys and girls almost equally except for sexual abuse, for which girls account for about 80% of the reported victims (USDHHS,

2010). Moreover, the dynamics of sexual abuse differ considerably for boys and girls. Although boys as well as girls are more likely to be abused by someone they know and trust than by a stranger, boys are more likely to be abused by male nonfamily members—camp staff, teachers, scout leaders—whereas girls are more likely to be sexually abused by male family members. Children with disabilities are also three times more likely than nondisabled children to be the victims of any sort of physical or sexual abuse (Jones et al., 2013).

In terms of racial characteristics, victims of maltreatment are predominately white (44%), African American (22%), or Hispanic (21%), and most suffer from neglect. African American children, American Indian or Alaska Native children, and children of multiple races have the highest rates of victimization in proportion to the same race or ethnicity in the general population. White children and Hispanic children both had rates of approximately 8 per 1,000 children of the same race or ethnicity, whereas Asian American children had the lowest rate (2.0 per 1,000 children of the same race or ethnicity; USDHHS, 2010). These racial differences have been consistent over many years and are believed to be a function of the disproportionate impact of poverty, stress, and disadvantage on minority children and their families (Jones, Finkelhor, & Halter, 2006). These demographic patterns suggest different vulnerabilities for children based on gender, disability, and social disadvantage; these differences have implications for safety and prevention (Wolfe et al., 2003).

Cross-culturally, child maltreatment is at epidemic proportions in many societies worldwide. International organizations estimate that by 14 years of age, 40 million children are victims of child abuse and neglect annually around the world (United Nations, 2006; World Health Organization, 2004a), confirming suspicions that child abuse is found in all societies and is almost always a highly guarded secret. Studies in which children or young adults were interviewed about their childhood experiences further confirm that rates of child sexual abuse in other Western societies are comparable to those in North America, which cluster around 20% for females, and 8% for males (Finkelhor, 2008; Pereda et al., 2009; Stoltenborgh et al., 2011).

Family Context

My father was frightened of his mother. I was frightened of my father and I am damn well going to see to it that my children are frightened of me.

—George V, King of England (1865–1936)

Why do some family relationships give rise to pain and conflict instead of support and harmony? There is no simple answer to this question, so we must rely on a combination of theory, clinical observations, and empirical findings. For physical abuse and neglect, an important consideration is that they are **relational disorders**. These forms of maltreatment occur most often during periods of stressful role transitions for parents, such as the postnatal attachment period, the early childhood and early adolescence "oppositional" periods of testing limits, and the times of family instability and disruption (Wolfe, 1999). The caregivers' failure to provide nurturant, sensitive, available, and supportive care, especially during critical periods, is a fundamental feature of maltreatment.

Notwithstanding the critical role of the adult offender, abuse and neglect are rarely caused by a single risk factor. In addition, even though the risk signs and indicators are present, it is still very difficult to predict who will become abusive and who will not. Remember that child maltreatment and other forms of trauma and stress are events, not a uniform disorder; therefore, it is necessary to consider multiple causes that interact unpredictably. Like a tornado that arises from just the right conditions of heavy wind, atmospheric pressure, and open terrain, child maltreatment may emerge in any given family if the "right" conditions exist. These causal conditions stem largely from the interaction of child, familial, and cultural influences, but it is not possible to predict specifically where and when they will detonate (Cicchetti & Valentino, 2006).

Stress is one of those forces of nature and humankind that can convert static, stable conditions into dynamic, chaotic patterns. For example, physical abuse and neglect occur most often in the context of social and economic family deprivation, which can transform any predisposed, high-risk parents into abusive or neglectful ones. A greater degree of stress experienced by the abusive parent in the social environment will increase the probability that violence will surface as an attempt to gain control or cope with irritating, stressful events. In the case of neglect, stress may be so severe that parents withdraw from their child-care responsibilities.

Sexual abuse also is influenced by cultural and familial practices, as well as the dynamic forces of stress. However, unlike physical abuse and neglect, sexual abuse is primarily a premeditated act, during which the adult offender plays a purposeful and intentional role. The abuser plans ways to circumvent the child's natural resistance and self-protection and controls the situation to avoid detection. Maltreatment seldom is caused by severe forms of adult psychopathology (Wolfe, 1999). Fewer than 10% of maltreating parents have a primary psychiatric illness that might cause them to harm a child. However, these parents with primary psychiatric illnesses are likely to have a history of learning and intellectual deficits and personality disorders that impede their day-to-day abilities to cope successfully with child-related and other stressors (Haskett, Scott, & Ward, 2004). Similarly, perpetrators of child sexual abuse often show various personality disorders related to immaturity and interpersonal adjustment, but these disorders do not fit a homogeneous pattern (Fagan et al., 2002).

Family characteristics remind us of the cultural and social forces that shape child-rearing methods and contribute potentially to stress and trauma. Most significant is the well-established finding that maltreatment is more common among the poor and disadvantaged (although it also occurs among higher-income families). This connection is not likely to be due to a reporting bias, because it has remained constant for the past 35 years, despite increased awareness and reporting (Wekerle & Wolfe, 2014). What it does imply, however, is that the economically based context—restricted child-care opportunities, crowded and unsafe housing, and lack of health care, to name a few conditions—is a powerful backdrop to the high incidence rates of child maltreatment and stressor-related disorders.

Family structure also is connected to the probability of child maltreatment. Children living with a single parent with a live-in partner are at significantly greater risk of all types of maltreatment. Maltreatment—especially physical and educational neglect—is more common in larger families, where additional children in the household mean additional tasks, responsibilities, and demands.

Who commits these acts? It should not surprise you that 80% of the victims suffer all forms of maltreatment by one or both parents. However, there are important exceptions, as well as key sex differences in the nature of abuse or neglect. Nearly 50% of sexually abused children are abused by persons other than parents or parent figures, as compared with only a small fraction in other categories. Child neglect is committed predominantly by mothers (about 90% of the time), which fits with the fact that mothers and mother substitutes tend to be the primary caregivers. In contrast, sexual abuse is committed more often by males (also about 90% of the time); about 50% of these abusers are the child's father or father figure. While males are the dominant perpetrators of sexual abuse, for child maltreatment in general the most common perpetrator pattern overall is a female parent acting alone, who typically is younger than 30 years of age (USDHHS, 2010).

Causes of Maltreatment

Because child maltreatment is perhaps the single most common type of trauma and stress to children and adolescents, we take a closer look at some of the causes and contributors to major forms of maltreatment.

To many parents like Brenda, child-rearing is a difficult and aversive event that can escalate unpredictably into a sudden abusive incident, or it may more gradually turn into avoidance and neglect. Lacking experience and guidance in child-rearing and facing overwhelming stress, these parents cannot think of ways to best handle the situation. Instead, they succumb to the irritation of the moment—the child—and respond emotionally, without thinking.

Brenda's history and situation are very typical: How would she know how to raise her child, given her own childhood experiences? Many abusive and neglectful parents had little past or present exposure to positive parental models and supports. Their own childhoods often were full of difficult, sometimes very traumatic, episodes of family violence, alcoholism, and harsh family circumstances related to frequent moves, unemployment, and poverty (Wolfe, 1999). As adults, they find daily living stressful and irritating, and they prefer to avoid potential sources of support because it takes additional energy to maintain social relationships. Chronic physical ailments and a pervasive mood of discontent are common problems, which are understandable in light of the circumstances and limited coping resources.

Adult Offenders

Physical abuse and neglect are not accidental events, although they are seldom planned or intentional. One parent described it this way:

I felt I was spinning out of control. Everywhere I went, things just built up and tension mounted. When

I tried to quiet my kids down, I would start shouting. When I tried to run away, everything followed me like a trail of debris. I just wanted the craziness to stop.

Like a chain reaction, a tragic combination of events can cause some predisposed individuals to maltreat a child in their care. Most of these events have one factor in common: They pose added stress for an individual who has already reached his or her limit.

Because child maltreatment usually occurs in relation to child-rearing demands, it is not surprising that maltreating parents interact with their children less often than other parents during everyday activities involving their children. In general, neglectful parents actively avoid interacting with their children, even when the child appropriately seeks attention, most likely because social interaction is unfamiliar and even unpleasant. Physically abusive parents, in contrast, tend to deliver a lot of threats or angry commands that exceed the demands of the situation when interacting with their children, rather than offer their children positive forms of guidance and praise (Azar & Wolfe, 2006; Wolfe, 1985).

Let's return to Brenda's situation and consider how her learning history, combined with her situational events, became a recipe for disaster. When her son misbehaved, she responded with a harsh combination of emotional and physical threats—the methods most familiar to her. At first, the physical punishment would stop Milton's misbehavior, but over time it led to a standoff, forcing her to increase the severity of her punishment, and the child to escalate his aversiveness to the punishment.

Brenda's cognitive perceptions and distortion of events also played a significant role in this coercive process. **Information-processing disturbances** cause maltreating parents to misperceive or mislabel typical child behavior in ways that lead to inappropriate responses and increased aggression (Berlin et al., 2011; Francis & Wolfe, 2008). They are unfamiliar with their roles as parents and with what is developmentally appropriate behavior for a child at a given age. Brenda believed not only that her son was able to understand—at age 4—what she was thinking and feeling, but also that he was able to put her needs ahead of his own.

Over time, Brenda thought Milton was misbehaving intentionally, presumably because, in her mind, he should have known better. ("I can never get him to listen—he's a troublemaker, and he knows how to push my buttons.") Some parents apply the same faulty reasoning to their own behavior as well, which results in lowered self-efficacy. ("I'm not a good mother; other mothers can get their children to do these things.") These unrealistic expectations and attributions of negative intent can lead to greater punishment for child misbehavior and less reliance on explanation and positive teaching methods (Azar & Wolfe, 2006).

Children are seen as deserving harsh punishment, and its use is rationalized as a way to maintain control. By now you can see where this process might end up.

Like a tropical storm with an unpredictable course, a conflict between the parent and child suddenly can increase in intensity and turn into a damaging hurricane, or it simply can blow over. Negative arousal and emotions are highly "conditionable," so that salient events later can trigger the same feelings. This conditioning may occur gradually and build into uncontrollable outbursts, or it may occur suddenly during highly stressful, provocative episodes of conflict (Averill, 2001).

To illustrate, imagine yourself trying to get your child ready for school each day, and going through the same frustrating chain of events: You're late for work and under pressure to get to a meeting, when your preschooler starts to fuss about wearing boots or combing hair. For all but a hearty few, this combination of stress and all-too-familiar child demands spells anger and frustration. While most of us manage to control our emotions to deal with the situation in the best possible way, parents who have deficits in child-rearing and information-processing skills may see the child as intentionally causing them to be late. Anger and arousal are powerful emotions, so rational problem solving quickly can give way to emotional and reflexive reactions.

Anger and rage are highly dependent on situational cues that usually stem from prior emotionally arousing events. In Brenda's case, certain "looks" that her son gave led her to believe that he wasn't going to comply. We discovered this interaction by videotaping the two of them playing together and then having Brenda ask Milton to straighten up the room. We played the tape back and asked Brenda to tell us whenever she felt that Milton was doing something that bothered her. She stopped the tape at several different points, telling us, "He's giving me that look," or "I know what he's thinking—why should I have to do what she says?" At this point, Brenda's tone of voice would become more tense and frustrated and her instructions to Milton more forceful and abrupt.

Although Brenda could acknowledge she was getting very angry, at first she was not able to interrupt this process and calm herself down. This demonstrates how parental arousal can be triggered by events, including past memories and current emotional tension, that may be highly specific to a particular parent–child relationship. This may lead to an overgeneralized—more angry, more aggressive—parental response, because the parent is responding impulsively to cues that in the past were associated with frustration and anger.

Neglectful parents have received far less research attention than physically abusive ones, perhaps because omissions of proper caretaking behaviors are more difficult to describe and detect than commissions

(Dubowitz & Bennett, 2007). As groups, the personality characteristics and lifestyle choices of abusive and neglectful parents overlap considerably. However, neglectful parents have more striking personality disorders and inadequate knowledge of children's needs, and they suffer more chronic patterns of social isolation than both abusive parents and parents who do not maltreat their children. Furthermore, neglectful caregivers typically disengage when they are under stress, whereas abusive parents become emotionally and behaviorally reactive. Neglectful parents try to cope with the stress of child-rearing and related family matters through escape and avoidance, which can lead to severe consequences for the child and to higher risk of substance abuse and similar coping failures for the parents (Hildyard & Wolfe, 2007).

Those seeking explanations for child sexual abuse have looked for evidence of deviant sexual histories in the adult offender, as well as environmental and cultural risk factors that play a role in the sexual exploitation of children. Yet, similar to physical abusers of children, sexual abusers are a very mixed group who defy most personality labels or psychiatric descriptors. Some are described as timid and unassertive, whereas others show a pattern of poor impulse control and domineering interpersonal style. Their common ground is a preference for sexual exploitation of children and adolescents who, because of their age and innocence, cannot consent to the activities or readily disclose the abuse to someone.

Sexual abusers of children come from many walks of life, and they are seldom discernible based on personality traits, occupation, or age (other than the conclusion that the vast majority of offenders are male). As a group, these offenders are more likely to have significant social and relationship deficits, including social isolation; difficulty forming emotionally close, trusting relationships; and low self-esteem (Marshall et al., 2008). Comorbid psychiatric disorders and substance abuse also emerge as proximate risk factors for sexual abuse of children (Fagan et al., 2002).

Persons who engage in sexual acts with minor children or youths (pedophiles) may limit their activities to incest that involves their own children, stepchildren, or other relatives, or they may victimize children outside their families (APA, 2013; Marshall et al., 2008). Significantly, over 50% of pedophiles report an awareness of their pedophilic interests before they turn 17 years old (63% of those who target male children and 50% of those who target female children), which they begin to act out, on average, by their late teens or early 20s (Abel, Osborn, & Twigg, 1993; Seto, 2008). Emerging evidence shows deficiencies in cerebral white matter in cortical regions of the brain that respond to sexual cues, suggesting that pedophilia may result from early neurodevelopmental problems that cause a partial disconnection within that network (Cantor & Blanchard, 2012; Kruger & Schiffer, 2011).

Those who victimize children develop complicated techniques to gain access to and compliance from the child, which emphasizes the sexually opportunistic and predatory nature of this behavior. Pedophiles may win the trust of the child's mother or have a relationship with a woman with a child. They may use methods to lower a child's resistance, such as initiating a friendship, playing games or giving presents, having hobbies or interests that appeal to the child, and using peer pressure (Wekerle et al., 2006; Wolak et al., 2008). They seldom resort to violence or force to gain the child's compliance; rather, they are attentive to the child's needs in order to gain the child's affection, interest, and loyalty as well as to reduce the chances that the child will report the sexual activity. Typically, sexual behavior takes place only after a period of "grooming," with a gradual indoctrination into sexual activity, underscoring how sex offenders of children are "sophisticated, calculating, and patient" (Singer, Hussey, & Strom, 1992, p. 884). As one offender asserted, "You can spot the child who is unsure of himself and target him with compliments and positive attention" (Elliott, Browne, & Kilcoyne, 1995, p. 584).

A perpetrator's efforts to establish a relationship with the child or youth, such as spending time alone with the child or singling the child out as favored or special, also may reduce the child's internal inhibition by distorting the roles of the relationship and blurring interpersonal boundaries. Special status as a teacher, religious figure, or scout leader may cover the abuser's intentions with a sense of entitlement or privilege with a child, distorting the role into one that is a central part of the child's life (Wolfe, Jaffe, et al., 2003). Sadly, children made more than 11,000 allegations of sexual abuse by over 4,000 priests between 1950 and 2002, which represents about 4% of the 110,000 priests who served during the 52 years covered by the study (U.S. Conference of Catholic Bishops, 2004).

Two meta-analyses comparing thousands of sexual offenders who targeted children and nonoffenders confirmed a link between offenders and a history of having been sexually abused during their own childhood (Jespersen, Lalumière, & Seto, 2009; Seto & Lalumière, 2010). One possibility is that negative childhood experiences—sexual abuse, as well as other forms of stress or maltreatment—set in motion a cautious, distrustful approach to intimate relationships. A history of child sexual abuse or exposure to other stressors may lead to atypical sexual interests in early adolescence for some male victims. In turn, deviant sexual fantasies provide a way of temporarily avoiding, interrupting, or reducing painful abuse-related mental states and psychiatric symptoms (Maniglio, 2011).

For example, an adolescent male with a history of unhealthy or exploitative relationships may justify using coercive and abusive actions toward others who are smaller or weaker because his other attempts at closeness have failed (Ward & Beech, 2008). His sexual interests and arousal become fused with his need for emotional closeness, which can lead to sexual preoccupation, promiscuity, and the possibility of increasing sexual deviancy as his attempts to gain intimacy escalate through sexual contact (Seto, 2008).

Certain situational factors increase children's vulnerability to sexual abuse, a fact that offenders exploit to their advantage. Offenders see children as more vulnerable if they have family problems, spend a lot of time alone, and seem unsure of themselves; they also admit to preferring victims who are attractive, trusting, and young (Elliott et al., 1995). To gain access to the child, offenders look for circumstances that create lax supervision or opportunities for them to become involved, such as parental unavailability, illness, stress, spousal abuse, or lack of emotional closeness to the child.

Child and Family Influences

Do certain child characteristics or behaviors increase the likelihood of trauma or maltreatment? Children have an uncanny ability to figure out what their parents are going to do before they actually do it, and they become amazingly accomplished at weighing the odds for desired outcomes. However, even though children might do things that are annoying, adults are fully responsible for abuse and neglect. No child—no matter how difficult to manage or how challenging to teach—ever deserves to be mistreated. Children's behavior or developmental limitations may increase the potential for abuse, but only if they are accompanied by the other critical factors noted previously. With the important exception of girls being sexually abused more often than boys, no child characteristic, such as conduct problems, has been associated with the risk of maltreatment, once environmental and adult factors are controlled (USDHHS, 2010). Unintentionally, however, the child may still play a role in the continuation or escalation of harsh or stressful relationships.

The kind of coercive family interactions that we discussed in Chapter 9 with regard to aggressive children, frequently occur in abusive families (Stith et al., 2009; Wolfe, 1999). Physically abused or neglected children, for example, may learn from an early age that misbehaving often elicits a predictable parental reaction—even though it's negative—which gives the child some

"I hate you! Never come back to my house," screamed an 8-year-old at his father as police arrested the man for attacking his wife.

sense of control. If crying and clinging are the only ways to get a parent's attention, these behaviors may escalate in intensity over time, especially if the parent fails to provide appropriate child stimulation and control.

This type of coercive interaction explains why abusive incidents occur most often during difficult—but not uncommon—episodes of child behavior such as disobedience, fighting and arguing, accidents, and dangerous behavior, which may produce anger and tension in some adults. In contrast, circumstances surrounding incidents of neglect relate more to chronic adult inadequacy that spills over into daily family functioning (Stith et al., 2009). Neglected children's early feeding problems or irritability may place an increased strain on the parents' limited child-care abilities, again setting in motion an escalation in the child's dependency needs and demands, accompanied by further parental withdrawal (Drotar, 1999).

Family circumstances, most notably conflict and marital violence, also have a causal connection to child maltreatment. In about half of the families in which adult partners are violent toward one another, one or both parents also have been violent toward a child at some point during the previous year (Edleson, 1999). Domestic conflicts and violence against women most often arise during disagreements over child-rearing, discipline, and each partner's responsibilities in child care (Gewirtz & Edleson, 2007). Children may be caught in the cross fire between angry adults, or in some cases they may instigate a marital conflict by misbehaving or demanding attention. In either case, an escalating cycle of family turmoil and violence begins, whereby children's behavioral and emotional reactions to the violence create additional stress on the marital relationship, further aggravating an already volatile situation.

The physical and psychological consequences of violence, moreover, cause abused women to be less capable of responding to their children's needs, which again increases pressure on the family system. Tragically, not only do marital violence and family turmoil frighten and disturb children in a direct manner, but the resulting fallout from these events—ranging from changes in financial status and living quarters to loss of family unity and safety—prolongs the stress and thus the harmful impact on children's development (Jaffe et al., 2011).

In a dynamic process, parental and situational factors interact over time to either increase or decrease the risk of physical abuse or neglect (MacKenzie, Kotch, & Lee, 2011). ● Figure 12.3 depicts this dynamic process in relation to three hypothetical transitional stages. These stages suggest that maladaptive interaction patterns, like adaptive ones, do not develop simply because of the predilections of the parent or child. On the contrary, these patterns are the result of complex interactions between child characteristics, parental personality and style, the history

Stage 1: Reduced tolerance for stress and disinhibition of aggression

Destabilizing factors	Compensatory factors
• Poor child-rearing preparation • Low sense of control and predictability • Stressful life events	• Supportive spouse • Socioeconomic stability • Success at work and school • Social supports and healthy models

Stage 2: Poor management of acute crises and provocation

Destabilizing factors	Compensatory factors
• Conditioned emotional arousal to child behavior • Multiple sources of anger and aggression • Belief that child's behavior is threatening or harmful to parent	• Improvement in child behavior • Community programs for parents • Coping resources

Stage 3: Habitual patterns of arousal and aggression with family members

Destabilizing factors	Compensatory factors
• Child habituates to physical punishment • Parent is reinforced for using strict control techniques • Child increases problem behavior	• Parental dissatisfaction with physical punishment • Child responds favorably to noncoercive methods • Community restraints/services

● **FIGURE 12.3** | An integrated model of physical child abuse.

Reprinted from Wolfe, 1999.

of the parent–child relationship, and the supportive or nonsupportive nature of the broader social context within which the family is embedded (Wolfe, 1999). This process, moreover, includes both destabilizing and compensatory factors that can influence the likelihood of abuse or neglect in a negative or positive fashion, respectively.

Social and Cultural Dimensions

What role does our culture play in childhood trauma, stress, and maltreatment? Again, considerable knowledge in this area stems from research on violence against children and youths. Intuitively, a primary focus on individual factors as singular causes of trauma to children and youth is very limiting, since we live in a society that not only condones violence but also glorifies it directly and indirectly.

Consider how the entertainment industry, including many aspects of the media and professional sports, earns billions of dollars in profits from exploiting our interests in violence in all of its forms. Equally disturbing is the portrayal of sex roles by society's envoys in the media and the entertainment industry: Females are stereotypically presented as relatively powerless and passive and men as vested with power; women are encouraged to defer to the benevolence of powerful men, and men are encouraged to challenge the autonomy of powerful and assertive women (Hedley, 2002). These cultural phenomena are ingrained through years of repeated imagery, and they are presumed to be the basis for the motivation of some men to maintain control and power in a relationship (Williams, 2003).

At the family level, we have noted that child maltreatment and other forms of trauma and stress usually occur in the context of homes and neighborhoods with multiple problems, where poverty, social isolation, and wide acceptance of corporal punishment significantly influence child development. These factors stem from racism and inequality, which are arguably the major sociocultural factors contributing to stress—not only for children, but also for many adults and especially for members of minority groups. The extent to which a society deems any particular group to be less worthy of recognition and economic or political support represents the level of vulnerability for that group to violence and a host of other indignities.

Perhaps as a result of cultural and social factors, maltreating families often lack significant social connections to others within their extended families, neighborhoods, and communities; they also tend to lack connections to social assistance agencies (Spilsbury & Korbin, 2013). Unfortunately, maintaining family privacy and isolation may result in restricted access to healthier child-rearing models and social supports. Neglectful families especially are prone to isolation and insularity, which may be related directly to the parents' significant interpersonal problems (Gaudin et al., 1996). Their coping abilities are impaired by their

circumstances and further constrained by their lack of resources and poor child-rearing models from their own upbringing. Thus, child maltreatment occurs to some extent because of limited cultural opportunities to learn appropriate child-rearing methods and receive necessary education and supports, as well as because of long-held social customs that endorse the use of physical force to resolve conflicts with children (Gershoff, 2013).

Cultural norms and practices influence the prevalence of sexual abuse as well. The erotic portrayal of children—not only in pornography but also in mainstream advertising—raises many concerns about personal boundaries and appropriate messages. There is also grave concern stemming from the quantity of child pornography circulating on the Internet, where sexual abusers of children share information, exchange pornography, and make contact with potential child victims. Children exposed to pornography, directly or through the Internet, may be desensitized and socialized into believing that the activity is normal (Wolak et al., 2008). Children used in the production of pornography show psychological symptoms such as emotional withdrawal, antisocial behavior, mood swings, depression, fear and anxiety, and disorders such as PTSD (Cooper et al., 2005).

Section Summary

Trauma, Stress, and Maltreatment: Defining Features

- Childhood trauma may involve actual or threatened death or injury, or a threat to one's physical integrity.
- Forms of childhood stress that may lead to poor adaptation include bullying, parental separation, peer conflict, and many others.
- Chronic stress challenges the child's developing biological and social development.
- Many forms of child trauma, stress, and maltreatment are connected to poverty and inequality, social isolation, and unhealthy cultural norms concerning child-rearing practices and family privacy.

TRAUMA AND STRESSOR-RELATED DISORDERS

In this section, we examine specific disorders most commonly linked to trauma, stress, and abuse. The first two, Reactive Attachment Disorder (RAD) and Disinihibited Social Engagement Disorder (DSED), are related to social neglect. These disorders may occur among children who experience an absence of proper care and nurturance and as a result show significant developmental delays or impairments in relating to adults. We then turn our attention to post-traumatic stress disorder (PTSD), a serious problem among children or youths who are exposed to stressful, fearful, or intrusive events that threaten their safety or self-esteem.

Reactive Attachment Disorder

Reactive attachment disorder (RAD) is characterized by a pattern of disturbed and developmentally inappropriate attachment behaviors (APA, 2013; see Table 12.2). When faced with any form of stress, such as a new situation or adult, children with RAD show no consistent effort to seek comfort or nurturance from their caregiver, and they fail to respond to their caregiver's efforts to comfort them (Criterion A). Children with RAD seldom express positive emotion when interacting with their caregivers, and their emotion regulation is compromised, leading to outbursts of fear, sadness, or irritability that fall outside the norm for their age (Criterion B). It is believed that they have the capacity to form appropriate attachments to caregivers but fail to do so, most likely because of a lack of proper opportunities in early childhood. Thus, RAD is linked to problems in the early caregiver–child relationship, which could be due to multiple caregivers, social neglect or deprivation, or being reared in an institution with very limited opportunities to develop secure attachments (Criteria C and D).

Disinhibited Social Engagement Disorder

Disinihibited social engagement disorder (DSED) is another possible outcome of social neglect. Rather than fear and avoidance, as with RAD, the child with DSED shows a pattern of overly familiar and culturally inappropriate behavior with relative strangers (Criterion A; Table 12.3).

TABLE 12.2 | **Diagnostic Criteria for** Reactive Attachment Disorder

(A) A consistent pattern of inhibited, emotionally withdrawn behavior toward adult caregivers, manifested by both of the following: **DSM-5**
(1) The child rarely or minimally seeks comfort when distressed.
(2) The child rarely or minimally responds to comfort when distressed.
(B) A persistent social and emotional disturbance characterized by at least two of the following:
(1) Minimal social and emotional responsiveness to others.
(2) Limited positive affect.
(3) Episodes of unexplained irritability, sadness or fearfulness that are evident even during nonthreatening interactions with adult caregivers.
(C) The child has experienced a pattern of extremes of insufficient care as evidenced by at least one of the following:
(1) Social neglect or deprivation in the form of persistent lack of having basic emotional needs for comfort, stimulation, and affection met by caregiving adults.
(2) Repeated changes of primary caregivers that limit opportunities to form stable attachments (e.g., frequent changes in foster care).
(3) Rearing in unusual settings that severely limit opportunities to form selective attachments (e.g., institutions with high child-to-caregiver ratios).
(D) The care in Criterion C is presumed to be responsible for the disturbed behavior in Criterion A (e.g., the disturbances in Criterion A began following the lack of adequate care in Criterion C).
(E) The criteria are not met for autism spectrum disorder.
(F) The disturbance is evident before 5 years of age.
(G) The child has a developmental age of at least 9 months.
Specify if: Persistent: The disorder has been present for more than 12 months.
Specify if: Severe: When a child exhibits all symptoms of the disorder, with each symptom manifesting at relatively high levels.

Source: Diagnostic and Statistical Manual of Mental Disorders, 5th ed. American Psychiatric Association.

TABLE 12.3 | **Diagnostic Criteria for** Disinhibited Social Engagement Disorder

(A) A pattern of behavior in which a child actively approaches and interacts with unfamiliar adults and exhibits at least two of the following: **DSM-5**
(1) Reduced or absent reticence in approaching and interacting with unfamiliar adults.
(2) Overly familiar verbal or physical behavior (that is not consistent with culturally sanctioned and with age-appropriate social boundaries).
(3) Diminished or absent checking back with adult caregiver after venturing away, even in unfamiliar settings.
(4) Willingness to go off with an unfamiliar adult with minimal or no hesitation.
(B) The behaviors in Criterion A are not limited to impulsivity (as in attention-deficit/hyperactivity disorder) but include socially disinhibited behavior.
(C) The child has experienced a pattern of extremes of insufficient care as evidenced by at least one of the following:
(1) Social neglect or deprivation in the form of persistent lack of having basic emotional needs for comfort, stimulation, and affection met by caregiving adults.
(2) Repeated changes of primary caregivers that limit opportunities to form stable attachments (e.g., frequent changes in foster care).
(3) Rearing in unusual settings that severely limit opportunities to form selective attachments (e.g., institutions with high child-to-caregiver ratios).
(continues)

(4) The care in Criterion C is presumed to be responsible for the disturbed behavior in Criterion A (e.g., the disturbances in Criterion A began following the lack of adequate care in Criterion C).

(5) The child has a developmental age of at least 9 months.

Specify if: Persistent: The disorder has been present for more than 12 months.

Specify if: Severe: When a child exhibits all symptoms of the disorder, with each symptom manifesting at relatively high levels.

Source: Diagnostic and Statistical Manual of Mental Disorders, 5th ed. American Psychiatric Association.

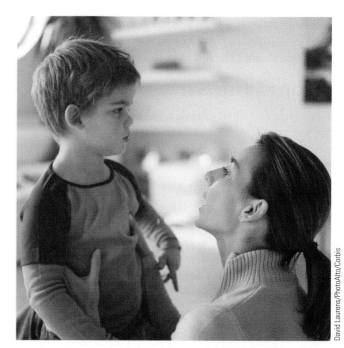

Young children with Reactive Attachment Disorder (RAD) seldom seek adult comfort or express positive emotion.

Instead of typical social reticence with unfamiliar adults or situations, toddlers and preschoolers with DSED fail to check with caregivers and may venture away. School-aged children may exhibit intrusive and overly familiar behavior with strangers, including asking overly personal questions, violating personal space, or initiating physical contact without hesitation. Obviously, such behavior can be dangerous, especially since the child may be willing to walk away with a stranger. Such actions are not limited to impulsivity, such as attention-deficit/hyperactivity disorder (ADHD), but must include socially disinhibited behavior as described above (Criterion B). Similar to RAD, children with DSED have experienced extremes of insufficient care that are presumed to be responsible for their disinhibited pattern with unfamiliar adults (Criteria C and D).

Prevalence and Development

RAD and DSED are diagnoses that apply only to children between the ages of 9 months and 5 years who display these symptoms. The prevalence is currently unknown for either disorder, although they are believed to be uncommon even among populations of severely neglected children (APA, 2013). Typically, children with either one of these disorders of social neglect show delays in cognitive and socioemotional development, which may persist for several years without intervention.

Despite very common etiologies (i.e., poor nurturance and/or deprivation), the courses of RAD and DSED differ substantially, with DSED being the more persistent of the two. For example, symptoms of RAD often disappear among children raised in an institution once they are adopted into a family, whereas signs of DSED often persist (Smyke et al., 2010). Young children with DSED fail to show reticence in situations with strangers, and as preschoolers they may show verbal and social intrusiveness and attention-seeking. It is not unusual

for these patterns to continue through middle childhood in adolescence, with the child or teen with DSED showing inauthentic expressions of emotion, superficial relationships, and more peer conflicts (APA, 2013). Not surprisingly, RAD in early childhood has been linked to subsequent internalizing disorders such as depression, whereas DSED has been linked to disruptive behavior disorders such as ADHD (Gleason et al., 2011).

Causes and Treatment

Both RAD and DSED stem from very inadequate care, as noted above, but they are considered to be distinct disorders rather than subtypes of a single disorder. Other than biological vulnerabilities, it is unknown what factors might cause one neglected child to become reticent and unresponsive to adults, while another becomes disinhibited and indiscriminate in seeking adult attention. What is known is that children with RAD typically recover from this disorder once they are placed in a secure, stable environment; those with DSED usually improve but may show more lasting difficulties, as noted above. Until more is known about the long-term consequences of the two disorders, interventions that focus on improving caregiving quality (e.g., stability, positive affection, and safety) are warranted (Lyons-Ruth et al., 2014).

Post-traumatic Stress Disorder

Most children show symptoms of anxiety or behavioral problems within the first year of being exposed to trauma; these symptoms gradually fade. However, a sizeable minority go on to suffer symptoms of PTSD and other clinical disorders for years to come (Nader & Fletcher, 2014). **Acute stress disorder** is characterized by the development during or within 1 month after exposure to an extreme traumatic stressor of at least nine symptoms associated with intrusion, negative mood, dissociation, avoidance, and arousal (these are largely the same symptoms as PTSD, described below, but last for 1 month or less). Similar to PTSD, the traumatic event is relived over and over, leading to attempts to avoid any reminders that arouse memories of it. Acute stress disorder emphasizes the more immediate, but short-term, dissociative reactions to trauma, whereas PTSD reflects the longer-lasting, ongoing pattern. Acute stress disorder occurs following trauma in about 10% to 20% of children and youths and, although short-lived, can be very disruptive and distressing, especially for those subjected to sexual assaults or witnessing mass shootings (Meiser-Stedman et al., 2007).

Children or adults who react to more common (and less severe) forms of stress in an unusual or disproportionate manner may qualify for a diagnosis of **adjustment disorder**. For example, a student who did poorly on an exam or a teen who broke up with his girlfriend may become angry, withdrawn, or refuse to attend school. Although such reactions to single or repeated stressors are not uncommon, if they result in clinically significant impairment in functioning or disproportionate distress, a diagnosis of adjustment disorder is given. An adjustment disorder is considered to be a short-term diagnosis (i.e., symptoms last no longer than 6 months after the stressor) in most cases; however, the criteria may still apply if the stress or its consequences are prolonged, such as chronic housing or family-related problems.

Children and youth with **post-traumatic stress disorder** (PTSD) display persistent anxiety following an overwhelming traumatic event that occurs outside the range of usual human experience. Such events include exposure to actual or threatened violence, harm to themselves or others, or even learning about traumatic events that occur to close family members or friends (Criterion A). When the diagnosis of PTSD was first introduced, the reference points were catastrophic events, such as war, torture, rape, natural disasters (e.g., earthquakes and hurricanes), and disasters of human origin (e.g., arson and automobile accidents). However, a broader definition is now used to include other highly aversive events, such as witnessing or hearing about harm to loved ones or being repeatedly exposed to aversive details of a traumatic event. Although traumatic experiences are typically considered extreme or unusual events, children who display PTSD-related symptoms may have experienced lower-magnitude—but still highly stressful—events such as parental conflict, maltreatment, or community violence that overwhelm their coping abilities (Copeland et al., 2010).

MARCIE

Not the Only Victim

While accompanying her mother to a neighbor's house, a large German shepherd viciously mauled the face of Marcie, age 6. Her brother Jeff, age 7, and her two younger sisters observed the incident. Although the mother warned the children to keep away from the dog, Marcie and Jeff let it approach and Jeff was able to pet the dog. Marcie then bent toward the dog to pet it, and the dog attacked. The mother immediately applied pressure to the bleeding wound, as the two youngest children clung to their mother's legs. The dog's owner (who had followed the dog down the driveway) panicked and ran to the children's home to get their father, leaving the dog unleashed and barking at the frightened family for about 20 minutes. The father took the family home, cleaned Marcie's wound, and then took her for emergency medical treatment. Marcie received stitches in her face while she was strapped down and in extreme distress.

Following the incident, all the children displayed some fear and reverted to behaviors displayed at a younger age, such as bed-wetting and finger sucking. They also displayed irritability and developed varying degrees of sleep disturbances and nightmares. Moreover, Marcie developed an intense fear of medical procedures or any situation that reminded her of a medical procedure. Thus, intense fear and panic reactions accompanied follow-up visits to the plastic surgeon. Excessive distress was shown in everyday first-aid situations such as caring for a minor scratch or scrape.

Adapted from *Behavioral Assessment and Treatment of PTSD in Prepubertal Children: Attention to Developmental Factors and Innovative Strategies in the Case Study of a Family* by A. M. Albano, P. P. Miller, R. Zarate, G. Cote, D. H. Barlow, 1997, pp. 245–262, 'Cognitive and Behavioral Practice', Vol. 2.

As shown in Table 12.4, a DSM-5 diagnosis of PTSD for children (over age 6) as well as adults involves four core features that persist longer than 1 month (APA, 2013):

▶ Symptoms of intrusion, such as distressing memories, dreams, or flashbacks that is often described as a feeling of reliving the traumatic event(s).

TABLE 12.4 | Diagnostic Criteria for Post-traumatic Stress Disorder

DSM-5

(A) Exposure to actual or threatened death, serious injury, or sexual violence in one (or more) of the following ways:

   (1) Directly experiencing the traumatic event(s).

   (2) Witnessing, in person, the event(s) as it happened to others.

   (3) Learning that the event(s) happened to a close relative or close friend. In cases of actual or threatened death of a family member or friend, the event(s) must have been violent or accidental.

   (4) Experiencing repeated or extreme exposure to aversive details of the traumatic event(s) (e.g., first responders collecting human remains; police officers repeatedly exposed to details of child abuse).

Note: Criterion A4 does not apply to exposure through electronic media, television, movies, or pictures, unless this exposure is work-related.

(B) Presence of one (or more) of the following intrusion symptoms associated with the traumatic event(s), beginning after the traumatic event(s) occurred:

   (1) Recurrent, involuntary and intrusive distressing memories of the traumatic event(s). **Note:** In young children, repetitive play may occur in which themes or aspects of the traumatic event(s) are expressed.

   (2) Recurrent distressing dreams in which the content and/or affect of the dream are related to the traumatic event(s). **Note:** In children, there may be frightening dreams without recognizable content.

   (3) Dissociative reactions (e.g., flashbacks) in which the individual feels or acts as if the traumatic event(s) were recurring. (Such reactions occur on a continuum, with the most extreme expression being a complete loss of awareness of present surroundings). **Note:** In young children, trauma-specific reenactment may occur in play.

   (4) Intense or prolonged psychological distress at exposure to internal or external cues that symbolize or resemble an aspect of the traumatic event(s).

   (5) Marked physiological reactions to internal or external cues that symbolize or resemble an aspect of the traumatic event(s).

(C) Persistent avoidance of stimuli associated with the traumatic event(s), beginning after the traumatic event(s) occurred, as evidenced by one or both of the following:

   (1) Avoidance of or efforts to avoid distressing memories, thoughts, or feelings about or closely associated with the traumatic event(s).

   (2) Avoidance of or efforts to avoid external reminders (people, places, conversations, activities, objects, situations) that arouse distressing memories, thoughts, or feelings about or closely associated with the traumatic event(s).

(D) Negative alterations in cognitions and mood associated with the traumatic event(s), beginning or worsening after the traumatic event(s) occurred, as evidenced by two (or more) of the following:

   (1) Inability to remember an important aspect of the traumatic event(s) (typically due to dissociative amnesia and not to other factors such as head injury, alcohol, or drugs).

   (2) Persistent and exaggerated negative beliefs or expectations about oneself, others, or the world (e.g., "I am bad," "No one can be trusted," "The world is completely dangerous," "My whole nervous system is permanently ruined").

   (3) Persistent distorted cognitions about the cause or consequences of the traumatic event(s) that lead the individual to blame himself/herself or others.

   (4) Persistent negative emotional state (e.g., fear, horror, anger, guilt, or shame).

   (5) Markedly diminished interest or participation in significant activities.

   (6) Feelings of detachment or estrangement from others.

   (7) Persistent inability to experience positive emotions (e.g., inability to experience happiness, satisfaction, or loving feelings).

(E) Marked alterations in arousal and reactivity associated with the traumatic event(s), beginning or worsening after the traumatic event(s) occurred, as evidenced by two (or more) of the following:

   (1) Irritable behavior and angry outbursts (with little or no provocation) typically expressed as verbal or physical aggression toward people or objects.

   (2) Reckless or self-destructive behavior.

   (3) Hypervigilance.

   (4) Exaggerated startle response.

   (5) Problems with concentration.

   (6) Sleep disturbance (e.g., difficulty falling or staying asleep or restless sleep).

(F) Duration of the disturbance (Criteria B, C, D and E) is more than 1 month.

(G) The disturbance causes clinically significant distress or impairment in social, occupational, or other important areas of functioning.

(H) The disturbance is not attributable to the physiological effects of a substance (e.g., medication, alcohol) or another medical condition.

(continues)

Specify if:

With Dissociative Symptoms: The individual's symptoms meet the criteria for post-traumatic stress disorder, and in addition, in response to the stressor, the individual experiences persistent or recurrent symptoms of either of the following:

(1) **Depersonalization:** Persistent or recurrent experiences of feeling detached from, and as if one were an outside observer of, one's mental processes of body (e.g., feeling as though one were in a dream; feeling a sense of unreality of self or body or of time moving slowly).

(2) **Derealization:** Persistent or recurrent experiences of unreality of surroundings (e.g., the world around the individual is experienced as unreal, dreamlike, distant or distorted).

Note: To use this subtype, the dissociative symptoms must not be attributable to the physiological effects of a substance (e.g., blackouts, behavior during alcohol intoxication) or another medical condition (e.g., complex partial seizures).

Specify if:

With Delayed Expression: If the diagnostic threshold is not exceeded until at least 6 months after the event (although it is understood that onset and expression of some symptoms may be immediate).

Source: Diagnostic and Statistical Manual of Mental Disorders, Fifth Edition. American Psychiatric Association.

▸ Avoidance of distressing memories, thoughts, or feelings, as well as avoidance of any reminders that arouse such thoughts or feelings.

▸ Distortions in thoughts or feelings (i.e., alterations in cognitions and mood) associated with the traumatic event(s), such as elevated fear, inability to feel positive emotions, self-blame and guilt.

▸ Symptoms of extreme arousal and reactivity, such as angry outbursts, self-destructive behavior, sleep problems, or hypervigilance (i.e., watchfulness).

PTSD symptoms usually begin within the first three months following the trauma, although a delay of many months or even years is not uncommon, especially in cases of physical and sexual abuse (Lyons-Ruth et al., 2014). Symptoms of PTSD are both conspicuous and complex. They may include intense fear, helplessness, and horror, which children may express as agitated behavior and disorganization. Some children with PTSD or partial-PTSD show many of the same symptoms as combat soldiers exposed to the horrors of war. They may experience physiological symptoms, nightmares, fears, and panic attacks either in the short term or for many years (Kirsch, Wilhelm, & Goldbeck, 2011). They may regress developmentally and display age-inappropriate behaviors, such as a fear of strangers. Children with PTSD avoid situations that could remind them of the traumatic event, or they may reenact the event in play. They may feel sadness or shame, become socially withdrawn, and/or have problems concentrating in school (Anthony, Lonigan, & Hecht, 1999).

Some key symptoms of PTSD are expressed differently in children than in adults. For example, instead of flashbacks and waking recall of the traumatic event, young children are likely to re-experience trauma in nightmares. Initially, the nightmares reflect the traumatic event, but over time they may become less specific and vague. Similarly, daytime recall may be expressed in play or through reenactment of the event or related themes. Trauma reactions of preschool children may include repetitive drawing and play focused on trauma-related themes, regressive behavior, antisocial or aggressive behavior, and destructive behavior (Perrin, Smith, & Yule, 2000).

Given these differences in how young children express their thoughts and emotions, DSM-5 criteria include different age-related manifestations for children age 6 and under (shown in Table 12.5). This category was added in DSM-5 to reflect findings that modified (simplified) criteria can more accurately diagnose PTSD among younger children. A principle difference between criteria for younger children and those for older children reflects younger children's use of play reenactment, rather than words, to display their feelings and memories (see Criterion B). Also, criteria for younger children combine symptoms of avoidance and symptoms of negative alterations in cognition into one category, using more age-appropriate examples.

Prevalence and Course

About 14% of children 2 to 17 years of age in the United States report lifetime exposure to natural disaster and about two-thirds experience one or more potentially traumatic events by age 16 (Becker-Blease,

(A) In children 6 years and younger, exposure to actual or threatened death, serious injury, or sexual violence in one (or more of the following ways):

DSM-5

    (1) Directly experiencing the traumatic event(s).

    (2) Witnessing, in person, the event(s) as it occurred to other, especially primary caregivers. **Note**: Witnessing does not include events that are witnessed only in electronic media, television, movies, or pictures.

    (3) Learning that the traumatic event(s) occurred to a parent or caregiving figure.

(B) Presence of one (or more) of the following intrusion symptoms associated with the traumatic event(s), beginning after the traumatic event(s) occurred:

    (1) Recurrent, involuntary, and intrusive distressing memories of the traumatic event(s). **Note:** Spontaneous and intrusive memories may not necessarily appear distressing and may be experienced as play reenactment.

    (2) Recurrent distressing dreams in which the content and/or affect of the dream are related to the traumatic event(s). **Note:** It may not be possible to ascertain that the frightening content is related to the traumatic event(s).

    (3) Dissociative reactions (e.g., flashbacks) in which the child feels or acts as if the traumatic event(s) were recurring. (Such reactions may occur on a continuum, with the most extreme expression being a complete loss of awareness of present surroundings). Such trauma-specific reenactment may occur in play.

    (4) Intense or prolonged psychological distress at exposure to internal or external cues that symbolize or resemble an aspect of the traumatic event(s).

    (5) Marked physiological reactions to reminders of the traumatic event(s).

(C) One (or more) of the following symptoms, representing either persistent avoidance of stimuli associated with the traumatic event(s) or negative alterations in cognitions and mood associated with the traumatic event(s), must be present, beginning after the event(s) or worsening after the event(s):

Persistent Avoidance of Stimuli

    (1) Avoidance of or efforts to avoid activities, places, or physical reminders that arouse recollections of the traumatic event(s).

    (2) Avoidance of or efforts to avoid people, conversations, or interpersonal situations that arouse recollections of the traumatic event(s)..

Negative Alterations in Cognitions

    (3) Substantially increased frequency of negative emotional states (e.g., fear, guilt, sadness, shame, confusion).

    (4) Markedly diminished interest or participation in significant activities, including constriction of play.

    (5) Socially withdrawn behavior.

    (6) Persistent reduction in expression of positive emotions.

(D) Alterations in arousal and reactivity associated with the traumatic event(s), beginning or worsening after the traumatic event(s) occurred, as evidenced by two (or more) of the following:

    (1) Irritable behavior and angry outbursts (with little or no provocation) typically expressed as verbal or physical aggression toward people or objects (including extreme temper tantrums.

    (2) Hypervigilance.

    (3) Exaggerated startle response.

    (4) Problems with concentration.

    (5) Sleep disturbance (e.g., difficulty falling or staying asleep or restless sleep).

(E) The duration of the disturbance is more than a month.

(F) The disturbance causes clinically significant distress or impairment in relationships with parents, siblings, peers, or with school behavior.

(G) The disturbance is not attributable to the physiological effects of a substance (e.g., medication or alcohol) or another medical condition.

Specify if:

With dissociative symptoms: The individual's symptoms meet the criteria for post-traumatic stress disorder, and the individual experiences persistent or recurrent symptoms of either of the following:

    (1) **Depersonalization:** Persistent or recurrent experiences of feeling detached from, and as if one were an outside observer of, one's mental processes or body (e.g., feeling as though one were in a dream; feeling a sense of unreality of self or body or of time moving slowly).

(continues)

(2) **Derealization:** Persistent or recurrent experiences of unreality of surroundings (e.g., the world around the individual is experienced as unreal, dreamlike, distant, or distorted). **Note:** To use this subtype, the dissociative symptoms must not be attributable to the physiological effects of a substance (e.g., blackouts) or another medical condition (e.g., complex partial seizures).

Specify if:

With delayed expression: If the full diagnostic criteria are not met until at least 6 months after the event (although the onset and expression of some symptoms may be immediate).

Source: Diagnostic and Statistical Manual of Mental Disorders, 5th ed. American Psychiatric Association.

Turner, & Finkelhor, 2010; Copeland et al., 2007). Most do not develop PTSD, except after several traumas or a history of anxiety. Nevertheless, a significant number of children and adolescents who are exposed to trauma develop PTSD, and many others experience some PTSD symptoms as well as other emotional disturbances (Briggs-Gowan et al., 2010; McLaughlin et al., 2010). In a large national sample of over 4,000 adolescents 12 to 17 years of age in the United States, the 6-month prevalence of PTSD was 3.7% for boys and 6.3% for girls. In addition, nearly 75% of youngsters with PTSD displayed a comorbid diagnosis of depression and/or substance abuse (Kilpatrick et al., 2003). Thus, PTSD is a significant problem, especially among children and youths who experience multiple or cumulative forms of trauma such as child maltreatment, exposure to domestic violence, bullying, assaults, and other forms of victimization (Cloitre et al., 2009).

The prevalence of PTSD symptoms is appreciably greater in children who are exposed to life-threatening events or prolonged interpersonal trauma (such as abuse) than children who are exposed to less severe trauma (Furr et al., 2010). For example, nearly 40% of children exposed to the Buffalo Creek Dam collapse in 1972 showed probable PTSD symptoms 2 years after the disaster (Fletcher, 2003). PTSD in children is also strongly correlated with degree of exposure. In children exposed to a schoolyard sniper attack, proximity to the attack was directly related to the risk of developing PTSD symptoms (Pynoos et al., 1987). In effect, traumatic events that have a personal or direct impact on a child are more likely to lead to strong reactions and more persistent symptoms of PTSD (Nader & Fletcher, 2014).

As many as half of victims of maltreatment involving sexual abuse or combined sexual and physical abuse meet criteria for PTSD during childhood or adolescence (Martin et al., 2013; Nooner et al., 2012; Scott, Wolfe, & Wekerle, 2003). The prevalence of PTSD among adults is equally disturbing: About one-third of the childhood victims of sexual abuse, physical abuse, or neglect meet criteria for lifetime PTSD (Koenen &

Widom, 2009; Widom, 1999). Among adults, women are twice as likely to develop PTSD as men, and women's symptoms last up to 4 times longer; but gender differences are less apparent among children and youths (Nader & Fletcher, 2014).

> The child trapped in an abusive environment is faced with formidable tasks of adaptation. She must find a way to preserve a sense of trust in people who are untrustworthy, safety in a situation that is unsafe, control in a situation that is terrifyingly unpredictable, power in a situation of helplessness.
>
> —From Herman (1992)

This statement by prominent clinician and researcher Judith Herman captures the essence of the world of children and youths who have suffered maltreatment or fear. Trauma and maltreatment are more than physical pain and transitory fear; to a child or adolescent, these events often represent threats to their emerging sense of self, their world, and their feelings of safety and well-being. We return to Rosita's case to illustrate this dramatic impact:

ROSITA

Feeling Trapped

At age 6, Rosita was brought to the hospital following two suicidal/self-harm gestures. While camping, she wrapped a rope that hung from a tree around her neck and her foster mother grabbed it and untangled it. She did not appear to be hurt, but she sat and cried for a long time while her foster mother cuddled her.

"Rosita is preoccupied with themes of death and self-harm, in her drawings, stories at school, and even with her classmates," her teacher explained. "She has problems making friends, because she acts silly when she tries to join their games. More than once she's asked other children to touch her vagina, and she has tried to put her finger in one girl's vagina. Needless to say, this

(*continues*)

(continued)

has alarmed other parents and teachers. But she's such a needy child—she'll go from a temper tantrum to becoming clingy in a matter of seconds."

Rosita's life became more settled, and by age 9 her school performance had improved noticeably. However, at age 15, her psychological condition rapidly grew worse. She made suicide attempts and began cutting her arm with glass and other sharp objects. When I saw her after her release from the hospital, she was very distraught, and felt unloved and abandoned. Her feelings of depression and anxiety were evident: "I'll jump or get really scared, for no reason. I just want to go somewhere and hide, and get away from people," she explained. "I can't trust anybody except for my friend Mary—but even she thinks I'm weird when I get like this. It's like I'm trapped or caught, and can't get away." My interview went on to reveal Rosita's sleeping problems and her constant crying and sadness.

Rosita had never forgotten the abuse she experienced as a child, and sometimes had intrusive reminders of what happened. "I feel tied in a knot, and I feel like I'm going crazy or something. That's when I might start cutting on my arm or something, just to feel like I'm not dreaming, that I'm real." Sometimes she even blamed herself for losing her family years ago, explaining that "no matter how bad it was I wish no one had ever found out, because it wasn't worth all the pain I'm going through." (Based on authors' case material.)

Rosita lacks a sense of self-esteem and a sense of the future. She is very vulnerable to recurring victimization because she lacks self-awareness and has limited self-protection skills. She feels a terrible loss and ambivalence over her family, sometimes blaming herself for the abuse or wishing it had never been discovered. Although she is a verbal and insightful young woman, she often is overcome with worries, anxiety, fear, and emotional distress related to her current circumstances.

What happens to the development of children who suffered trauma or maltreatment during their important formative years? Normal development follows a predictable, organized course (see Chapter 1), beginning with the child's mastery of physiological regulation (eating, sleeping) and continuing throughout the development of higher skills, such as problem solving and peer relationships. However, under abnormal and highly stressful circumstances, such as abuse and neglect, predictability and organization are disrupted and thrown off course, which often results in developmental impairments and limited adaptation.

Children with histories of trauma or maltreatment not only must face acute and unpredictable parental outbursts or betrayal, but also must adapt to environmental circumstances that pose developmental challenges. These influences include the more dramatic events, such as marital violence and separation of family members, as well as the mundane but important everyday activities that may be disturbing or upsetting, such as unfriendly interactions, few learning opportunities, and a chaotic lifestyle. Children who are sexually abused undergo pronounced interruptions in their developing view of themselves and the world that result in significant emotional and behavioral changes, indicative of their attempts to cope with such events. Because the source of stress and fear is centralized in their family, children who are maltreated are challenged regularly to find ways to adapt that pose the least risk and offer maximum protection and opportunity for growth (Collishaw et al., 2007).

The course of PTSD may begin during childhood with abuse-specific fears, such as fear of being alone and fear of men, as well as idiosyncratic fears related to specific events of abuse, such as fear of sleeping (van der Kolk, 2007). PTSD-related symptoms also are more likely to occur if the abuse was chronic and the perpetrator relied on a method of coercion or trickery to force compliance (Williams, 2003). But child trauma, like other forms of adversity during childhood, does not affect each child in a predictable or consistent fashion. On the contrary, the impact of trauma depends not only on the severity and chronicity of the specific events, but also on how the events interact with the child's individual and family characteristics. Without proper support and assistance, young children who initially may have achieved normal developmental milestones can show a dramatic downturn in their developmental progress as a result of chronic or acute trauma or similar types of stress (Crooks & Wolfe, 2007). Consequently, their core developmental processes are impaired, which results in emotional and behavioral problems ranging from speech and language delays to criminal behavior.

Associated Problems and Adult Outcomes

Longitudinal findings suggest that PTSD can become a chronic psychiatric disorder for some children and youths, persisting for decades and in some cases for a lifetime (Nader & Fletcher, 2014). Children and youths with chronic PTSD may display a developmental course marked by remissions and relapses. In a less common delayed variant, children exposed to a traumatic event may not exhibit symptoms until months or years later, when a situation similar to the original trauma triggers the onset of PTSD (Andrews et al., 2007). For example, attempts to develop sexual intimacy during adulthood may trigger PTSD in a survivor of childhood sexual abuse.

The developmental disruptions and impairments that accompany many forms of trauma and stress set in motion a series of events that increase the likelihood of adaptational failure. As stated earlier, not all children who face these developmental challenges will have psychopathology—let alone the same form of psychopathology—but they are at a much greater risk for significant emotional and adjustment problems.

There are often patterns linking the nature of child or adolescent trauma and subsequent adult expressions of either PTSD or its many associated features relating to fear, emotion regulation, avoidance, and physiological arousal. For example, adolescents and adults with histories of physical abuse and exposure to violence between parents are at increased risk of developing interpersonal problems marked by their own acts of aggression and violence or of violent victimization by others (Berlin, Appleyard, & Dodge, 2011; El-Sheikh & Erath, 2011). This relationship between being abused as a child and becoming abusive toward others as an adult is known as the **cycle-of-violence hypothesis.** Although victims of violence have a greater chance of becoming perpetrators of violence, this relationship is not inevitable and it can be attenuated through early intervention (Berlin et al., 2011).

Persons with histories of sexual abuse, on the other hand, are more likely than nonvictims to develop chronic impairments in self-esteem, to have physical health problems, and to lack emotional and behavioral self-regulation (Hillberg, Hamilton-Giachritsis, & Dixon, 2011; Irish, Kobayashi, & Delahanty, 2010). As adulthood approaches, developmental impairments that stem from child sexual abuse can lead to more pervasive and chronic psychiatric disorders and health problems, including anxiety and panic disorders, depression, eating disorders, sexual problems, and personality disturbances (Chapman et al., 2007; Maniglio, 2009; Paras et al., 2009). As we see below, some of the more significant impairments from which many sexual abuse victims suffer stem from PTSD and associated chronic regulatory problems with mood and affect (Campbell et al., 2008).

Traumatized children frequently exhibit symptoms of disorders other than PTSD, and children with other disorders may have PTSD as a comorbid diagnosis (Famularo et al., 1996). For example, PTSD that occurs in children traumatized by fires, hurricanes, or chronic maltreatment may worsen or lead to disruptive behavior disorders (Amaya-Jackson & March, 1995). In the following sections, we examine four prominent outcomes associated with trauma and PTSD—mood and affect disturbances, emotional and behavioral problems, sexual adjustment, and unhealthy relationships. We discuss these outcomes based on the extant literature on

child maltreatment, as they are more generally representative of child victims of trauma and stress.

Mood and Affect Disturbances

Some say that traumatic events, such as maltreatment, affect children to their very soul, since they disrupt and impair so many significant childhood memories and experiences. Perhaps this is why symptoms of depression, emotional distress, and suicidal ideation are common among children with histories of physical, emotional, and sexual abuse and why they often lead to PTSD (Crooks & Wolfe, 2007). As noted, the causes of these longer-term symptoms and problems sometimes can be avoided if children are provided with support by nonoffending family members and are given opportunities to develop healthy coping strategies and social supports. If symptoms of depression and mood disturbance go unrecognized, however, they are likely to increase during late adolescence and adulthood and can lead to suicide attempts and self-mutilating behavior, especially among those who have been sexually or physically abused since childhood (Fitzgerald et al., 2008; Mironova et al., 2011).

Similarly, teens with histories of maltreatment have a much greater risk of substance abuse that, in turn, increases the risk of other adjustment problems (Clark et al., 2010; Jones et al., 2013). Perhaps as a result of their chronic emotional pain, some teens and adults attempt to cope with unpleasant memories and current stressors by abusing alcohol and drugs in a futile effort to reduce or avoid their distress. Substance abuse may also temporarily bolster self-esteem and reduce feelings of isolation. Childhood sexual abuse also can lead to eating disorders, such as anorexia nervosa and bulimia nervosa (Murray, Macdonald, & Fox, 2008).

Many women, as well as men, with histories of childhood sexual abuse face lifelong struggles in establishing close and trusting relationships.

Walled Away

"What I would end up doing was separating from the physical feeling and couldn't comprehend the physical pain and emotional sensation. The only word I can use now—I didn't have the word when I was five—the word I use now is rape, and the only way I could deal with that was I would separate into the wallpaper and the wallpaper was all different ballerinas and different poses and what I could see from them was that they didn't move. They were always smiling or they always had this look on their face and they couldn't be touched. They just stood still. So I would become this ballerina and I couldn't be touched and whatever he did to me I couldn't feel it because I was in the wall."

"The body mends soon enough. The broken spirit, however, takes the longest to heal," by an adult survivor of sexual abuse. Transcribed from *The Nature of Things with David Suzuki*, executive producer, Michael Adler, for the Canadian Broadcasting Corporation, originally aired on October 6, 1994.

PTSD affects a significant number of men and women who have been subjected to severe physical or sexual abuse during childhood, but its expression may vary. Like Rosita, some adults may be haunted by intrusive thoughts or feelings of being trapped or, like Celia, they may dissociate or become emotionally numb, as they did originally to escape from the pain and fear.

In reaction to emotional and physical pain from abusive experiences, children or adults voluntarily or involuntarily may induce an altered state of consciousness known as **dissociation**, which can be adaptive when neither resistance nor escape are possible (Valentino et al., 2008). The process allows the victim to feel detached from the body or self, as if what is happening is not happening to him or her. Almost all people dissociate in minor ways, such as daydreaming, but abuse victims may rely on this form of psychological escape to the extent that profound disruptions to self and memory can occur (Macfie, Cicchetti, & Toth, 2001). Over time, this fragmentation of experience and affect can progress into borderline disorder, dissociative identity disorder, or chronic pain (Briere, Hodges, & Godbout, 2010; Raphael & Widom, 2011; Widom, Czaja, & Paris, 2009).

Emotional and Behavioral Problems

Girls and boys tend to differ in the ways they process and express their turmoil and symptoms of PTSD. Girls tend to show more internalizing signs of distress, such as shame and self-blame; boys, on the other hand, tend

to show heightened levels of physical and verbal aggression (Wekerle et al., 2008).

It comes as no surprise that the relationships children have with their peers and teachers typically mirror the models of relationships they know best. Instead of a healthy sense of autonomy and self-respect, models of relationships among children who experience violence or maltreatment have elements of victim and victimizer—those who rule and those who submit—and during interactions with peers, such children may alternate between being the aggressor and being the victim (Dodge, Pettit, & Bates, 1994a). Their strategies for adaptation, such as hypervigilance and fear, evolve to become highly responsive to threatening or dangerous situations. These strategies conflict, however, with the new challenges of school and peer groups. As a result, some children with histories of maltreatment may be more distracted by aggressive stimuli, and they may misread the intentions of their peers and teachers as being more hostile than they actually are (Dodge et al., 1994a).

The development of empathy and social sensitivity for others during the preschool years are prerequisites for the development of positive, reciprocal peer relationships. Physically abused and neglected children, however, show less skill at recognizing or responding to distress in others, since they have no experience with this (Smetana et al., 1999). Observational studies of the behavior of maltreated children and their nonmaltreated peers reveal that physically abused children engage in more stealing behavior, and neglected children engage in more cheating behavior and less rule-compatible behavior (Cicchetti & Valentino, 2006; Koenig, Cicchetti, & Rogosch, 2004).

Children with histories of physical abuse or neglect stand out as having the most severe and wide-ranging problems in school and interpersonal adjustment. Their performance on standardized tests of reading, language, and math is worse than that of other children (Mills et al., 2011). Teachers who are unaware of their backgrounds describe them as lacking maturity and academic readiness—pointing out their problems with completing schoolwork, lack of initiative, overreliance on teachers for help, and behavior that is both aggressive toward and withdrawn from their peers (Egeland et al., 2002). This pattern of poor adjustment often persists, contributing to higher rates of physical and mental health problems in later adolescence and adulthood (Clark, Thatcher, & Martin, 2010; Trickett, Negriff et al., 2011).

Longitudinal studies of girls who were sexually abused in childhood or early adolescence reveal deleterious effects across a host of biopsychosocial domains (the impact on men has received less attention, but similar patterns have been reported; Wolfe, Francis, &

Straatman, 2006). The most illustrative of these studies followed a sample of sexually abused girls for 23 years, documenting problems and concerns at home and school and with peers. The pattern and extent of harm to these girls was substantial: compared to a comparison group of girls who were not abused, those with histories of sexual abuse had significant neurodevelopmental differences in their responses to stress; earlier onsets of puberty; greater cognitive deficits; more mental health problems (especially depression and PTSD); higher rates of obesity; and more major illnesses and health-care utilization. They also had higher rates of dropping out of high school, self-mutilation, physical and sexual revictimization, teen motherhood, drug and alcohol abuse, and domestic violence in adulthood (Trickett, Noll et al., 2011).

Sexual Adjustment

Sexual abuse, in particular, can also lead to **traumatic sexualization**, in which a child's sexual knowledge and behavior are shaped in developmentally inappropriate ways. About 35% of preschoolers who have been sexually abused show age-inappropriate sexual behaviors, such as French-kissing, open masturbation, and genital exposure (Friedrich & Trane, 2002).

For some children, the offenders' means of enticement—gifts, privileges, affection, and special attention—teaches them that their own sexual behavior is a means to an end. Thus, the abused child may attempt to sexualize interpersonal relationships by indiscriminately hugging and kissing strange adults and children (i.e., signs of disinhibited social engagement disorder, discussed above), acts that are relatively uncommon among children who were not sexually abused (Cosentino et al., 1995). For others, however, sexual behavior is associated with strong emotions, such as fear, disgust, shame, and confusion. These feelings may translate into distorted views about the body and sexuality, in some cases leading to weight problems, eating disorders, poor physical health care, and physically self-destructive behaviors (Trickett, Noll et al., 2011).

Although sexualized behaviors are more common among younger abused children, they sometimes re-emerge during adolescence or young adulthood in the guise of promiscuity, prostitution, sexual aggression, and victimization of others (Tricket, Noll et al., 2011; Wilson & Widom, 2011). In fact, a history of any type of maltreatment among males is a significant risk factor for inappropriate sexual behaviors, alienation, and social incompetence during adolescence (Salter et al., 2003; Tewksbury, 2007). Women with childhood histories of sexual abuse, in particular, are more likely to report difficulties during adulthood related to sexual adjustment; these difficulties range from low sexual arousal to intrusive flashbacks, disturbing sensations, and feelings of guilt, anxiety, and low self-esteem concerning their sexuality (Merrill et al., 2003).

Because their normal development of self-awareness and self-protection was severely compromised, adult survivors of child sexual abuse may become less capable of identifying risky situations or persons or knowing how to respond to unwanted sexual or physical attention. Consequently, both men and women who were sexually abused as children are more likely to fall victim to further trauma and violence, such as rape or domestic violence, during adulthood (McIntyre & Spatz Widom, 2011; Widom, Czaja, & Dutton, 2008; Wolfe et al., 2006).

Unhealthy Relationships

Does violence beget violence, as predicted by the cycle-of-violence hypothesis discussed above? Although many persons convicted of heinous crimes and violence against others report histories of child abuse and neglect, most children who experience abuse or other traumas do not go on to commit crimes. How do we reconcile this obvious, but complicated, connection between victim and victimizer roles?

Consider the developmental importance of adolescence. This developmental stage may represent a critical transition between being a victim of child maltreatment and the future likelihood of becoming abusive or being abused as an adult (Scott et al., 2003). Social dating, a favorite—and significant—adolescent pastime, can be a testing ground wherein one's knowledge and expectations about relationships are played out. Youths who have learned to adapt to violence and intimidation as a way of life, and who lack suitable alternative role models or experiences, are more likely to enter the social dating arena with inappropriate expectations about relationships.

Indeed, youths (girls as well as boys) who grew up in violent homes report more violence—especially verbal abuse and threats—toward their dating partners and toward themselves (Wolfe et al., 2004). Dating violence that occurs during adolescence, when combined with a history of violence in their own family, is a strong pre-relationship predictor of intimate violence during early adulthood and marriage (White & Widom, 2003). Thus, adolescence may be the middle stage, or initiation period, in the formation of a violent dynamic in intimate partnerships.

As we said, most children with histories of maltreatment or trauma do not become violent offenders or child abusers as young adults. Nonetheless, there is a significant connection between these events and subsequent arrests as a juvenile or an adult, even among girls, or engaging in sexual and physical violence as a young adult, especially for males (Campbell et al., 2008; Lansford et al., 2007). A history of maltreatment is associated with an earlier mean age at first offense and a higher frequency of offenses, as well as a higher proportion of chronic offenses (Widom, 1989). Also, for about one in five mothers, a history of child physical abuse (but not neglect) was associated with physical abuse of their offspring (Berlin et al., 2011).

Growing up with power-based, authoritarian methods—even if they do not result in physical injuries or identified maltreatment—can be toxic to relationships and social patterns. Many investigators believe that the prolonged and significant harm created by acts

of child maltreatment by caregivers stems from the emotional and psychological damages implicit in such acts. In other words, child maltreatment involves more than physical harm to a child. Such acts by caregivers undermine the child's basic sense of trust and safety, leading to lifelong struggles in their interpersonal relationships and sense of well-being (Wekerle & Wolfe, 2014; Wolfe & McIsaac, 2011). Even the amount of routine violence—frequently being hit with objects or physically punished—that one experiences as a child is significantly associated with violent delinquent behavior later in life (Straus, 2001). A study that links childhood violence and adult criminal behavior is described in A Closer Look 12.2.

What Are the Long-Term Criminal Consequences of Child Maltreatment?

This important question has plagued the general public and the field of child maltreatment, from therapists and educators to policy makers and criminal justice officials. Cathy Widom (1996) addressed this question by examining the criminal records of over 900 individuals subjected as children to physical or sexual abuse or neglect prior to age 12, along with a matched cohort of children who were not maltreated. Both groups were followed into adolescence and early adulthood to determine whether they engaged in criminal or delinquent behavior as adolescents or adults.

The results are telling: Of the people who experienced any type of child maltreatment (physical abuse, sexual abuse, or neglect), 27% were arrested as juveniles, as compared with 17% of their nonabused counterparts. The same pattern continued into adulthood: 42% of the abused/neglected group, as compared with 33% of the controls, had arrest records as adults. Consistent with the cycle-of-violence hypothesis, those with histories of physical abuse (21%), neglect (20%), or both (16%) were particularly likely to be arrested for committing a violent crime (Maxfield & Widom, 1996).

One disturbing result is that women with histories of physical abuse and neglect were significantly more likely than women who were not maltreated to be arrested for a violent act (7% vs. 4%), whereas this relationship was barely significant for men (26% vs. 22%). Notably, persons with histories of sexual abuse were no different from the other maltreated children in their rates of criminal offenses.

But what about sex crimes? Are persons who were sexually abused during childhood more likely to commit sexual offenses, as suggested by the backgrounds of the known sexual offenders? If all types of abuse and neglect are combined, the odds of being arrested for a sex crime were 2 times greater for victims of maltreatment than for nonvictims. However, if maltreatment backgrounds were broken down by type, only

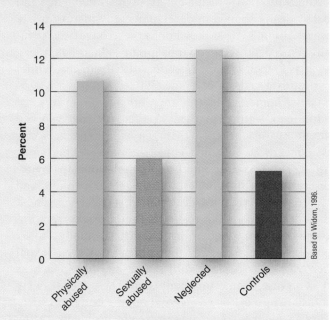

Based on Widom, 1996.

Sex crimes and maltreatment backgrounds

those with physical abuse and neglect backgrounds had increased arrests for sex crimes; those with sexual abuse backgrounds did not (this finding remained when only male subjects were compared). Children who were sexually abused were about as likely as the controls to be arrested later for any sex crime, and less likely than victims of physical abuse and neglect (see the accompanying figure).

Thus, although any type of maltreatment puts victims at higher risk for criminal behavior, persons who were sexually abused in childhood are less likely than victims of physical abuse or neglect to commit a sex crime, and no more likely than demographically similar individuals.

Causes

By definition, PTSD originates from severe trauma and/or threat that overwhelms a person's emotional, social, and biological capabilities. In this section, we examine the ways in which trauma affects critical homeostatic functions that, in turn, cause PTSD. Full- or partial-symptom PTSD can strike at any time throughout the life span. Its course depends on the age of the child or adolescent when trauma event(s) occurred and the nature of those events.

Because traumatic experience is filtered cognitively and emotionally before it can be appraised as an extreme threat, how trauma is experienced depends on a number of factors, including the child's developmental level and pre-disaster characteristics, such as level of anxiety and stress; cognitive appraisal of the threat and coping style; and characteristics of the disaster or traumatic experience, among other factors (Furr et al., 2010; Weems et al., 2007). In one study of children 6 years of age or younger who had PTSD, it was found that symptoms continued for 2 years after the event even with treatment (Scheeringa et al., 2005). This finding raises the troubling possibility that very young children who are vulnerable to developing PTSD after experiencing trauma may have an increased vulnerability to a more chronic course of the disorder, perhaps related to the impact of trauma on the developing brain (Bremner, 2007; Lyons-Ruth et al., 2014). Despite these differences related to age and timing, exposure to horrific or frightening events is traumatic to nearly all children.

Understanding the major factors that influence the development of PTSD requires consideration of the basic psychological and developmental processes that are impaired or delayed because of trauma, stress, or maltreatment. We examine the primary factors that contribute to adjustment after trauma, beginning with early attachment and affect regulation—the building blocks of the development of important self-regulatory and interpersonal competencies that can be compromised by trauma, stress, maltreatment, or related events. Whereas the diagnosis of PTSD may apply to only a minority of maltreated or traumatized children, PTSD *symptoms* in childhood, rather than a PTSD *diagnosis,* may serve to interfere with important psychological and neurobiological mechanisms. Over time, these symptoms may develop into delays and impairments that increase the likelihood of PTSD, as discussed below. Again, we reference the adjustment of maltreated children to illustrate these processes.

A common postulate of psychological causes of PTSD centers on the child's efforts to integrate a traumatic event into his or her existing cognitive view of the world, especially in cases in which the trauma stems from someone who cares for them and is in a position of trust. In simple learning terms, a traumatic experience can result in an individual's long-term response that continues well beyond the original stressor (Baum, O'Keefe, & Davidson, 1990). The process of conditioning—that is, the manner by which traumatic episodes become associated with particular eliciting stimuli such as odors, locations, or situations—can lead to overreactions that interfere with normal daily activities. In addition to the original event(s), major and minor stressful life events often occur as a result of the original traumatic event. For example, disclosure of sexual abuse gives rise to both immediate events (e.g., change in living arrangements, arrest of the perpetrator) and long-term events (e.g., loss of contact with the perpetrator) that can also reduce an individual's coping resources. These additional stressors can create a chronic, stress-filled lifestyle that disguises the original source of trauma or maltreatment.

Poor Emotion Regulation

Trauma, stress, and maltreatment can disrupt the important process of parent–child attachment and can interfere with children's ability to seek comfort and to regulate their own physiological and emotional processes. Parent–child attachment and the home climate play a critical role in emotion regulation, another early developmental milestone. As noted in Chapter 2, **emotion regulation** refers to the ability to modulate or control the intensity and expression of feelings and impulses, especially intense ones, in an adaptive manner (Kim & Cicchetti, 2010). For example, without consistent stimulation, comfort, and routine to aid in the formation of a secure attachment, maltreated infants and toddlers have considerable difficulty establishing a reciprocal, consistent pattern of interaction with their caregivers. Instead, they show a pattern described as *insecure–disorganized attachment,* characterized by a mixture of approach and avoidance, helplessness, apprehension, and a general disorientation (Cyr et al., 2010). The lack of a secure, consistent basis for relationships places maltreated children at greater risk of falling behind in their cognitive and social development and can result in problems regulating their emotions and behavior with others. Emotions serve as important internal monitoring and guidance systems; they are designed to appraise events as beneficial or dangerous and to provide motivation for action. Poor emotion regulation, in contrast, is at the heart of PTSD.

Because emotions provide important signals about our internal and external worlds, children must learn to interpret and respond to them appropriately. Most children learn this naturally through the emotional expressions and explanations given by their caregivers. Maltreated children, on the other hand, live in a world of emotional turmoil and extremes, making it difficult for them to understand, label, and regulate their internal states (Shipman et al., 2007). Expressions of affect, such as crying or signals of distress, may trigger disapproval, avoidance, or abuse, so maltreated youngsters tend to inhibit their emotional expression and regulation and remain more fearful and on alert. Similarly, they show increased attention to anger- and threat-related signals such as facial expressions, and less attention to other emotional expressions (Masten et al., 2008; Shackman, Shackman, & Pollak, 2007). When a new situation that involves a stranger or peer triggers emotional reactions, these children do not have the benefit of a caring smile or words from a familiar adult to assure them that things are okay (El-Sheikh & Erath, 2011).

Difficulties modulating emotions can be expressed as depressive reactions as well as intense angry outbursts. Accordingly, as maltreated children grow older and face new situations involving peers and other adults, poor emotional regulation becomes more and more problematic, resulting in unusual and self-harmful behaviors, such as Rosita's attempts to cut herself (Mironova et al., 2011). Over time, this inability to regulate emotions is associated with PTSD as well as other internalizing disorders, such as depression and fearfulness, and externalizing disorders, such as hostility, aggression, and various forms of acting out (Brensilver et al., 2011; Teisl & Cicchetti, 2008).

Emerging View of Self and Others

As normal development progresses, regulation of affect and behavior becomes less dependent on the caregiver and more and more autonomous (parents often use the vernacular expression, "terrible twos"). Toddlers' developing self-regulation is now applied to new situations, which further strengthens their emerging view of themselves and others. Importantly, children form complex mental representations of people, relationships, and the world during this developmental period. Their emerging view of themselves and their surroundings is fostered by healthy parental guidance and control that invoke concern for the welfare of others. To the degree that these opportunities are available to children with PTSD or with histories of maltreatment, emotional and behavioral problems are more likely to appear as a result of their maladaptive view of themselves and others.

Representational models of oneself and others are significant because they contain experience, knowledge, and expectations that carry forward to new situations (Cicchetti & Lynch, 1995). For example, consider how a child's internalized belief that "My mother is usually there for me when I need her" or that "I am loved and worthy of love" shapes his basic beliefs about himself and others, and how these ideas reflect a sense of well-being and connection. Maltreated children, in contrast, often lack these core positive beliefs about themselves and their world. Instead, they may develop negative representational models of themselves and others based on a sense of inner "badness," self-blame, shame, or rage, all of which further impair their ability to regulate their affective responses (Simon, Feiring, & McElroy, 2010; Valentino et al., 2008).

Feelings of powerlessness and betrayal often are described by children and adults who have been victims of maltreatment—feelings that become salient components of their self-identity (van der Kolk, 2007; Wolfe et al., 2003). In a situation of powerlessness, the child's will, desire, and sense of self-efficacy are thwarted and rebuked; these circumstances are often linked to fears, worries, and depression. In the words of one survivor, "It's as if the world was evil, it's coming to get you, and you could do almost nothing to defend from it" (Lisak, 1994, p. 533). Betrayal involves the degree to which the child feels the perpetrator gained his confidence through manipulation and coercion, as well as the position of trust or authority held by the perpetrator. As a consequence, the child's emotional needs may be compromised by intense and contradictory feelings of the need for closeness and the fear of it.

One's sense of personal power or self-efficacy can be undermined by significant trauma, stress, or maltreatment, as such events may devalue the child as a person. Feelings of betrayal can also challenge an individual's sense of self, because the person the individual depended on violated that trust and confidence. Such feelings may not be identified until years later, once the individual reaches an age at which he or she can recognize this betrayal dynamic as the source of feelings of self-blame, guilt, and powerlessness (Freyd, DePrince, & Gleaves, 2007; Williams, 2003). Thus, they are a significant aspect of the criteria for a diagnosis of PTSD.

Emotional reactions elicited by harsh punishment or sexual exploitation require the child to search for an answer to a fundamental question concerning responsibility and blame: "Why did this happen to me?" The previous quotes about self-esteem illustrate how some sexually abused children feel responsible for failing to recognize the abuse, for participating in the abuse, for causing their families' reactions to disclosure, for failing to avoid or control the abuse, and for failing to protect themselves. Rather than acknowledge or believe that one's own parents or a trusted adult could be the person at fault, some maltreated children may ascribe nonmalevolent intentions to the offender that can then be used to explain and justify to others their family problems and disruption. Shifting the blame to themselves or to situational factors that are less important than one's own parents provides a more acceptable explanation (McGee, Wolfe, & Olson, 2001). One male survivor describes this attribution of blame: "I had to make sense out of what was going on. And the sense I made out of this was that I'm not really a good person. There's something different about me and something wrong" (Lisak, 1994, p. 541).

Neurobiological Changes

Stressful childhood life experiences can influence brain development and lead to both anatomical and functional brain changes that underlie symptoms of PTSD. Neuroscientists have connected the behavioral signs of poor emotion regulation among children with PTSD to alterations in the developing brain, resulting in abnormalities in their ability to manage stress (Danese et al., 2011). For example, the concept of "limbic irritability" has been coined to account for symptoms of internalizing psychopathology after maltreatment because of its impact on the limbic system. Symptoms of limbic irritability include somatic, sensory, and behavioral phenomena believed to be due to increased excitatory neurotransmission after maltreatment in early childhood (Dackis et al., 2012).

The brain undergoes its most rapid growth and organization early in development, especially from birth to 2 years of age. The changes that occur during this sensitive period of rapid growth may become permanent and thus influence further development. In the case of PTSD, this means that exposure to trauma or maltreatment early in life could influence further development even when that adversity is no longer present, leading to enduring effects. For example, long-term alterations in the hypothalamic–pituitary–adrenal (HPA) axis and norepinephrine systems are found among maltreated children and adults with a history of childhood abuse, which have a pronounced effect on their responsiveness to stress (McCrory, De Brito, & Viding, 2010). The brain areas implicated in the stress response that can lead to long-term mental health problems include the hippocampus (learning and memory), the prefrontal cortex (planning and decision-making), and the amygdala (emotion regulation) (Cicchetti et al., 2010; Nunes et al., 2010; Roth & Sweatt, 2011).

In effect, acute and chronic forms of stress associated with maltreatment may cause changes in brain development and structure from an early age (Danese et al., 2011). The neuroendocrine system is designed to handle sudden stressful events by releasing cortisol to produce a fight-or-flight response (see Chapter 2). Elevated levels of stress hormones can act on structures in the brain such as the hippocampus and the amygdala to disrupt learning and memory and can lead to adverse brain development through accelerated neuronal loss, myelination delays, inhibition of neurogenesis, and decreased brain growth factors (McCrory et al., 2010). However, after prolonged and unpredictable stressful episodes associated with most forms of chronic childhood trauma and maltreatment, cortisol levels become depleted and the feedback systems that control hormone levels in the brain may not function correctly. Stress floods the brain with cortisol; the brain, in turn, resets the threshold at which cortisol is produced so that ultimately it circulates at a dramatically low level. As a result, the neuroendocrine system becomes highly sensitive to stress (Davies et al., 2009; Nunes et al., 2010).

Late childhood and adolescence are considered to be critical periods for the brain's prefrontal cortical development. These regions are responsible for the maturation of executive functioning, including attention and cognitive flexibility, and are among the last areas of the brain to develop (Anderson et al., 2001). Therefore, because executive skills develop later in life, difficulties in executive functioning would not become apparent until children are older. The neurobiological changes that occur in response to untoward early-life stress may partially account for PTSD and related disorders that emerge throughout the lives of children and youths exposed to maltreatment or trauma.

Section Summary

Trauma and Stressor-Related Disorders

- Children with reactive attachment disorder show little effort to seek comfort from a caregiver or adult,
- Children with disinhibited social engagement disorder show a pattern of overly familiar and culturally inappropriate behavior with relative strangers,
- Children with either disorder of social neglect show developmental delays that may persist for several years.
- Youngsters with post-traumatic stress disorder (PTSD) display persistent frightening thoughts after experiencing overwhelming traumatic events such as threatened death or injury, natural disasters, or maltreatment.
- Children with PTSD reexperience the traumatic event, avoid associated stimuli, and display symptoms of extreme arousal.
- Stress and trauma can result in significant PTSD-related symptoms at any time from childhood to adulthood, including mood disturbances, emotional and behavioral problems, difficulties in sexual adjustment, and unhealthy relationships.
- Causes of PTSD in children focus on psychological factors (such as emotion regulation and their view of self and others), as well as neurobiological factors that affect various brain areas and reactivity to stress.

TREATMENT AND PREVENTION

Violence against children is never justifiable. Nor is it inevitable. If its underlying causes are identified and addressed, violence against children is entirely preventable.

—Kofi Annan

Children who are maltreated or who experience violence at home, children who witness serious harm to others, or those who face other severe forms of stress and trauma will need some degree of help to restore their trust of others and feelings of safety and to cope with their fear and anxiety. Fortunately, there are well-supported intervention methods available to restore their healthy development (e.g., after being abused or neglected) and reduce immediate- and long-term problems that may arise from early stress or trauma (Thompson, 2014).

By providing proper knowledge and support, families and communities often play the most critical role in assisting children and youths who directly or indirectly experience traumatic or stressful events. Children may be protected, in part, from the effects of trauma or severe stress by a positive, supportive relationship with at least one important and consistent person in their lives who provides support and protection, such as other family members or peers (Haskett et al., 2006; Skopp et al., 2007). Paradoxically, this person could be a maltreating parent, a notion that at first may be hard to comprehend. Many maltreated children do not think of their parents as abusive; rather, they adapt to their own experiences as best as possible. Loyalty to one's parents is a powerful emotional tie—so from the child's point of view, a parent who at times yells, hits, and castigates, may at other times be a source of connection, knowledge, or love (Wekerle & Wolfe, 2003). In addition to the importance of supportive relationships, personality characteristics such as positive self-esteem and sense of self also are related to fewer negative outcomes among maltreated children (Afifi & MacMillan, 2011).

Exposure-Based Therapy

We begin our discussion of intervention by considering single-episode events, such as school shootings or other loss of life. Such events are a reality for some and a concern for everyone, so most school boards and communities have developed well-structured plans to be put into action in the event of tragedy or loss. Notably, a school's response can be instrumental in the immediate aftermath of traumatic events involving children or youths. Children can be affected by dire news or by witnessing tragic events, so schools play a crucial role in maintaining a reasonable routine, allowing for appropriate expression of grief or loss, identifying students who might be at risk, and helping students who need it to access available resources for assistance (Steele & Malchiodi, 2012).

Adults play a critical role in assisting children's recovery from traumatic events.

Effective intervention and prevention for children who have been exposed to trauma or maltreatment generally takes the form of structured therapy involving the child directly and/or programs for parents to assist them in supporting the child or changing their child-rearing methods (as in the case of maltreatment). Efforts to help children cope with their feelings and reactions after a disaster focus on helping the child acknowledge the experience and their reactions, and addressing pre- and post-disaster factors that are known to affect the child's adjustment, such as their developmental level, anxiety, coping style, and available social support (Gerson & Rappaport, 2013). Cognitive–behavioral treatment involving imagined or real-life exposure to feared stimuli, discussed below, has been shown to be effective treatment in helping children with PTSD and related symptoms after trauma or loss (AACAP, 2010; Silverman, Ortiz, et al., 2008).

Following acute stress or trauma, such as motor vehicle accidents, shootings, bombings, and hurricanes, the use of an early exposure intervention has reduced acute stress symptoms. Many of these interventions are brief, ranging from 1 to 10 sessions, and are often delivered in groups to reach as many children as possible. Psychological First Aid (PFA), for example, is based on the theory that children need information and support to reintegrate back into their school routine. PFA strives to provide safety and practical assistance, stability, and connection with needed supports for everyone affected by the event(s). This form of brief therapy is intended for secondary victims—children who have learned of harm to others such as classmates or community members—and to address the post-disaster reactions among victims, such as feeling displaced or at a loss (Forbes et al., 2011).

In-depth psychological interventions are available for children who are severely affected by a traumatic event. The child or youth typically begins by describing a particular traumatic incident (such as a classmate's suicide) and their feelings, thoughts, or attitudes about it. With the aid of the therapist, the child examines the incident, including aspects such as the time and duration, awareness of and connectedness to each incident, and a verbal report of the incident. In Grief and Trauma Intervention for Children (GTI), sessions address topics that are common to children who are experiencing grief and trauma, such as dreams (nightmares), questioning, anger, and guilt. The techniques are based on cognitive–behavioral therapy (CBT) and narrative therapy and include narrative exposure to the trauma through drawing, discussing, and writing. A child is encouraged to develop an in-depth, coherent narrative of what happened while expressing their thoughts and feelings, developing positive coping strategies, and making meaning of losses (Salloum & Overstreet, 2012). Through such graded exposure to memories and feelings stemming from the event, the child becomes more able to talk about the traumatic incident with a sense of emotional control without the intrusion of negative emotions and other reactions elicited by the incident. However, researchers are finding that children or adults who show signs of dissociation at the time at which treatment starts do not respond as well to such early intervention, most likely because of their degree of shock and disconnection (Price et al., 2014).

Trauma-focused cognitive–behavioral therapy (TF-CBT) is the most widely studied and supported form of exposure therapy for childhood trauma or stress. TF-CBT is a components-based psychosocial treatment model that incorporates elements of cognitive-behavioral, attachment, humanistic, empowerment, and family therapy models. This method has helped children and adults cope with the emotions and intrusive thoughts related to sexual abuse, domestic violence, traumatic loss, acts of violence and terrorism, and many other traumatic or stressful events (Barrera et al., 2013; Gerson & Rappaport, 2013).

TF-CBT involves a combination of exposure therapy and skill building to allow the individual to practice more effective ways of coping with intrusive memories and emotions (Cohen et al., 2010). Exposure strategies essentially involve having children or youths talk about the traumatic event and their feelings about it at a speed that is not too distressing for them. Children or youths are encouraged to create a coherent "narrative," or story of what happened, at their own pace, which enables them to master painful feelings about the event and to resolve the impact the event has on their life. During this process they are able to correct any untrue or distorted ideas about what happened, such as feeling they are to blame or could have done something to prevent it. Throughout each session, they are taught stress management and relaxation skills to help them cope with unpleasant feelings or intrusive memories about the trauma (see A Closer Look 12.3).

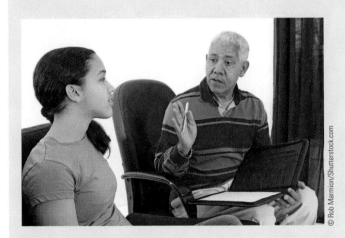

Some children have reactions to trauma that consist of more complex patterns extending beyond typical PTSD-related symptoms. **Complex trauma** often manifests as problems with attachment to others, emotion regulation, dissociation, behavior problems, and distorted self-concept. For example, we saw how children who have been sexually abused report engaging in health-compromising behaviors such as substance abuse, unsafe sex, and conduct problems (Fergusson et al., 2013; Homma et al., 2012). To meet these needs, TF-CBT has additional time allotted to teaching coping skills that incorporate safety and appropriate gradual exposure. Such modifications also allow for an adequate treatment-closure phase that includes traumatic grief components and ensures ongoing safety and trust (Cohen et al., 2012).

Special Needs of Maltreated Children

It should come as no surprise that child maltreatment exacts an enormous toll on society, in terms of both human suffering and economic loss. The total lifetime economic costs of medical, legal, educational, and child welfare services related to maltreatment are estimated to be a staggering $124 billion a year in the United States (Fang et al., 2012). Accordingly, there is a sense of urgency in addressing this issue at all levels of prevention and intervention (Wekerle, 2011a).

Consider these obstacles to intervention and prevention services for maltreating families: (1) Those most in need are least likely to seek help on their own; (2) these children are brought to the attention of professionals as a result of someone else's concern, usually after they have violated expected norms or laws; and (3) parents do not want to admit to problems because they fear losing their children or being charged with a crime (fears that are, of course, realistic).

Many children and adults who seek treatment related to child abuse and neglect are under some form of legal constraint. Similar to other psychological interventions, child-abuse treatments are based on the principle of beneficial assistance—but who wants assistance for something they will not admit is a problem? Therefore, treatments for child abuse and neglect have languished because of this basic dilemma: Access to treatment and prevention depends on admitting to or recognizing one's own culpability (Azar & Wolfe, 2006).

Despite these obstacles, through treatment, children and youths who have grown up with violence can make major shifts in how they relate to others, especially if treatment is begun early. Seeing their strengths and abilities, rather than their deficits, is a plausible approach to preventing physical abuse, neglect, and related social problems. Fifteen years after receiving pre- and postnatal home-visitation services to establish resource linkages and learn about their child's developmental needs, first-time parents—who were initially at risk of maltreating their child based on either low socioeconomic status, young age (under 19 years), or unmarried status—gained controls on important dimensions such as better family planning with regard to the number and spacing of children, less need for welfare, less child maltreatment, and fewer arrests of their children during adolescence (Eckenrode et al., 2010; Kitzman et al., 2010; Olds et al., 1997). As a result of intensive research, home-visitation programs to prevent child abuse and neglect have become widespread in many parts of North America (MacMillan et al., 2009).

Clearly, efforts to enhance positive experiences at an early stage in the development of the parent–child relationship hold considerable promise for prevention of child maltreatment and the reduction of its consequences. As shown in ● Figure 12.4, child-abuse

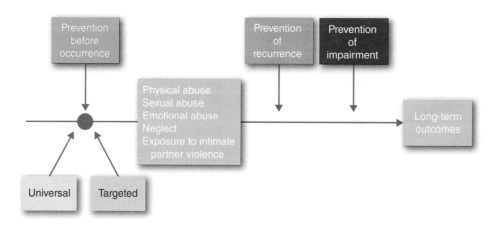

● **FIGURE 12.4** | A continuum depicting opportunities for preventing child abuse or its long-term outcomes.

Based on MacMillan et al., 2009

interventions include efforts to prevent such acts altogether (i.e., universal and targeted prevention), as well as efforts to prevent recurrence or significant impairments.

Similarly, programs that instruct children and their parents on how to avoid and report sexual abuse will improve children's responses to victimization, especially programs that encourage children to participate actively in prevention activities (Finkelhor, 2009). Formal treatment efforts also increase the chances of overcoming the harmful effects of abuse and neglect. We discuss treatments for physical abuse and neglect in the same section because of their close connection to child-rearing disturbances. Treatment of child sexual abuse is presented separately because of its unique nature and course.

Physical Abuse and Neglect

The results of any traumatic experience, such as abuse, can only be resolved by experiencing, articulating, and judging every facet of the original experience within a process of careful therapeutic disclosure.

—Alice Miller

Treatment of child abuse and neglect can be delivered in many ways: to individual parents, to children, to parents and children together, or to the entire family. Although most interventions emphasize desired changes in parental behavior, such changes can have a pronounced effect on their children's development as well.

Interventions for physical abuse usually involve ways to change how parents teach, discipline, and attend to their children, most often by training parents in basic child-rearing skills, accompanied by cognitive–behavioral methods that target specific anger patterns or distorted beliefs. Treatment for child neglect also focuses on parenting skills and expectations, coupled with teaching parents how to improve their skills in organizing important family needs—such as home safety, finances, and medical needs, among others—as well as drug and alcohol counseling (Azar & Wolfe, 2006). Similarly, children who have witnessed violence in the home benefit from interventions that address their needs in the context of their family circumstances. For example, their nonoffending mothers may attend treatment with them, so that mothers learn ways to deal with problematic child behavior while also providing appropriate maternal support (Graham-Bermann et al., 2007; Jaffe et al., 2011).

Because maltreating parents place too much emphasis on control and discipline, or ways to avoid contact and responsibilities, they seldom know how to enjoy their child's company. Therefore, treatment often begins with efforts designed to increase positive parent–child interactions and pleasant experiences. Parents are shown—through modeling, role playing, and feedback—how to engage with their children in daily activities that serve to strengthen the child's areas of deficiency and to promote adaptive functioning (Wolfe, 1991). Activities are selected to maximize the child's attention and provide ample opportunity for pleasant interchanges. Milton's treatment plan illustrates this important initial step:

MILTON'S TREATMENT

Session 1

It didn't take long to see what Brenda faced at home. Partway through our first session, Milton (age 4) wanted his mother's attention and became quite angry when she was asked to leave the room for a few minutes. During this outburst, he pushed an easy chair over and tried to hit Brenda with a rolled-up poster. She happily left for the observation room, leaving him and me together for the first time. I found a game and some puppets that he liked, and began the process of establishing a relationship. As soon as Milton started to lose interest, I switched to a new activity. I modeled for Brenda some ways simply to observe Milton's behavior and express my interest:

"Milton likes to explore everything! Look! I have a talking doll! Can you make him say something? Excellent—he spoke to you!" (Milton starts to go for the toy chest). "Look, Milton! I have a puppet. Would you like to hold him? Good, you're coming back to play with me. After we play with the puppet, mommy will come in and play too! When we're all done, we'll go get a drink. Can you stack these blocks? Oops, you knocked them down; that looked like fun. Let's try again; only this time, you put one on here for me." I closely guided Milton to new activities to reduce his distractibility, all the time talking aloud so that his mother could hear in the adjoining room where she was observing the interaction. (Based on authors' case material.)

Once parents learn a more flexible, adaptive teaching style that suits their child's development, efforts are begun to strengthen the child's compliance and self-control. Parents observe while the therapist models positive ways to encourage the child's attention and appropriate behavior, followed by practice and feedback. Therapists model for the parent how to express positive affect—with smiles, hugs, physical affection, and praise—and how to show dismay or concern when necessary with appropriate facial expression, firmer voice tone, and similar cues that express disapproval.

Parent training seldom goes smoothly, especially with families who have multiple problems. What do you do when a child just "acts himself" and doesn't follow your directions, while his parent watches? These situations often are valuable for helping a parent apply the new skills under naturalistic, this-is-what-it's-really-like conditions. Serendipitously, the value of modeling how to handle such a challenge was discovered a few sessions later:

MILTON'S TREATMENT

Session 4

Milton was tired of following my directions. Unaware that his mother was watching, he seized the opportunity to have some fun. He picked up toys and tossed them, and turned the light switch off and on. I thought I could simply get Milton to settle down by taking him down from his chair (which he was using to reach the light switch) and bringing him back to the couch. I was wrong. He started throwing a tantrum and screaming violently. With no other choice (child psychologists know when they're licked), I decided to talk above the noise so that his mother could hear how I was feeling and what I thought I might do: "I'm not sure just what to do yet. Milton seems to be uninterested in listening at the moment. Rather than getting angry, I think I'll wait a minute or two and try again. I've seen my 3-year-old do this, and I know you can't always expect kids to listen."

Brenda, familiar with this behavior at home, thought the situation was priceless—"Now you know what I have to deal with!" In lighthearted defense, I explained how there may not be an easy solution for these situations, which is why it is so important to maintain your composure and not expect or demand cooperation from Milton immediately. Tongue-in-cheek, I reminded her of Murphy's law of child behavior—"Anything that can go wrong, will"—and its corollary, "Just because it worked last time doesn't mean it will work every time!" (Based on authors' case material.)

From this and similar misadventures, we discovered how familiar problems that emerge during treatment delivery will add authenticity for parents (and conveniently happen whether or not we plan them!). These situations, as well as less stressful ones, also are used to teach parents how to manage themselves calmly, yet firmly. Therapists model how parents can express frustration and annoyance without becoming abusive and harsh, and parents then are encouraged to discuss and rehearse how they can handle the situation.

Gradually, they learn to replace physical punishment or apathy with more positive approaches. This process takes time, and parental frustration and impatience are to be anticipated. Cognitive–behavioral methods have been successful at teaching coping and problem-solving skills to abusive and neglectful parents as well as to parents at risk for maltreating their children (Mikton & Butchart, 2009; Thomas & Zimmer-Gembeck, 2011).

In addition to learning new ways to stimulate child development and structure child activities, neglectful parents often require very basic education and assistance in managing everyday demands, such as financial planning and home cleanliness (Allin, Wathen, & MacMillan, 2005). Programs like Project SafeCare provide multicomponent interventions, such as marital counseling, financial planning, and lessons on cleanliness and similar concerns, that address the various needs of neglectful and multiproblem families (Gershater-Molko, Lutzker, & Wesch, 2003). Treatment services for abused or neglected children are less common than parent-oriented interventions, largely because parental behavior is often the primary concern. We have seen, however, that maltreated children often lag in important developmental competencies, which is a strong rationale for focusing additional attention on these areas.

The wave of the future in preventing child abuse and neglect is likely to involve public health approaches that offer comprehensive assistance to parents and families based on their level of need and proper timing of assistance. For example, the well-supported Triple P program offers five tiers of assistance to best meet the needs of all parents in a community, from brief sessions to intense training and one-on-one assistance (Prinz et al., 2009). Similarly, information and guidance for parents of younger children can be readily provided by pediatric primary care providers as part of regular health visits (Dubowitz, Feigelman, Lane, & Kim, 2009).

Sexual Abuse

What allowed this to happen was that so many people were silent about it.

—Adult sexually abused as a child

Sexually abused children have experienced a world of secrecy, silence, and isolation. After they break that silence by disclosing the abuse, or the abuse is discovered by accident, the path toward healing can be difficult. They must access not only unpleasant memories, but also buried feelings of guilt, confusion, fear, and low self-worth. Sexual abuse, like many other problems of childhood, occurs in the context of other individual, family, and community problems that affect its impact and treatment. Elements of family functioning, especially maternal support and help-seeking in response to the crisis, are known to affect children's levels of distress and aid in their recovery, so treatment often must address these situational issues as well.

Treatment programs for children who have been sexually abused usually provide several crucial elements to restore the child's sense of trust, safety, and guiltlessness (Cohen, Mannarino, & Murray, 2011; Johnson, 2008). One major element of treatment involves education and support to help these children understand why this happened to them and how they can learn to feel safe once again. Information and education about the nature of sexual abuse helps clarify false beliefs that might lead to self-blame, and children's feelings of stigma and isolation often are addressed through reassurance or group therapy that involves other child victims. Animated films and videos offer ways for child victims to acknowledge and validate their feelings and to help them talk about their feelings, allowing these children to move toward the future with a sense of hope and empowerment. Children also are taught ways to prevent sexual abuse and restore their sense of personal power and safety. Through the use of animated films and behavioral rehearsal, children learn how to distinguish appropriate from inappropriate touches.

Cognitive–behavioral methods are particularly valuable in achieving these goals (Cohen et al., 2010, 2012). Preferably, education and support are provided not only to the child victim, but to (nonoffending) parents as well. The secretive betrayal that underlies the nature of sexual abuse causes some parents to feel ambivalent about whether to believe their child or how they feel about the alleged perpetrator, whom they may have trusted. Parents may need advice on ways to understand and manage their child's behavior, which because of the abuse may involve regressive or sexual behaviors. Parents often experience their own fears and worries as a result of the disclosure, and discussion with other parents and therapists can provide valuable support.

In conjunction with education and support, sexually abused children must express their feelings about the abuse and its aftermath—anger, ambivalence, fear—within a safe and supportive context. Younger children, for example, often cannot report their psychological reactions to the trauma unless they are asked specifically about the aspects of the trauma (Wolfe, Sas, & Wekerle, 1994). Sexual abuse elicits attempts by children to cope with powerful and confusing feelings, and it is understandable that some will use every method possible to avoid these feelings.

However, attempts to escape or avoid internal states of fear and anxiety, paradoxically, can make them worse.

For these reasons, TF-CBT has been adapted for child sexual abuse victims and others with complex trauma symptoms. The child is asked to recall gradually her memories of events, often to the point of feeling distressed, to allow the powerful emotions to be extinguished with repeated exposure. In addition, she learns to cope with negative thoughts and feelings about the abuse by using positive statements and imagery. Overall, gradual exposure, modeling, education, coping, and prevention-skills training have shown positive effects in the treatment of PTSD and other common outcomes of sexual abuse (Harvey & Taylor, 2010; Trask, Walsh, & DiLillo, 2011).

There is strong agreement that successful interventions for sexually abused children should result in several important outcomes (Berliner & Elliott, 2002). Treatment services should help children understand that what happened to them was abuse, that it was wrong, and that it may have caused them some temporary problems. Emotional and behavioral problems that may have arisen from the abuse should subside, and children should have the personal resources to handle future problems. Importantly, they should have supportive relationships in place, especially with parents and other caregivers who have received adequate knowledge and assistance to understand the possible impact the abuse may have on their children's behavior and adjustment. Finally, successful treatment results in children's regaining their normal rate of development.

A generation ago, psychology textbooks rarely discussed child sexual abuse. We had little knowledge of the devastating developmental, mental health, and societal consequences of abuse and neglect, and very few treatments were available. Since that time, considerable progress has been made in understanding and helping children who have been abused and neglected and their families. Most importantly, broader efforts at prevention and family support may help reduce or eliminate the likelihood of such unnecessary and harmful mistreatment of children and youths.

Section Summary

Treatment and Prevention

- Several factors appear to be important in children's course of recovery from PTSD, including the nature of the traumatic event, preexisting child characteristics, and family/social support.

(*continues*)

Section Summary (continued)

- Trauma-focused cognitive–behavioral therapy involves a combination of exposure therapy and skill building to allow the individual to practice more effective ways of coping with intrusive memories and emotions.
- Prevention of maltreatment holds considerable promise, especially if attempts are begun early in the formation of the parent–child relationship.
- Treatment of physical abuse involves training parents in more positive child-rearing skills, accompanied by cognitive–behavioral methods to target specific anger patterns or distorted beliefs.

- Treatment for child neglect focuses on parenting skills and expectations, coupled with training in social competence and household management.
- Interventions for children who have been sexually abused emphasize the children's needs for safety, understanding, and expression of emotional consequences.
- Cognitive–behavioral methods have shown value in working with sexually abused children, especially when accompanied by education and support for nonoffending, supportive caregivers.

Study Resources

SECTION SUMMARIES

KEY TERMS

13

Health-Related and Substance-Use Disorders

It is health that is real wealth and not pieces of gold and silver.

—Mahatma Gandhi

CHAPTER PREVIEW

JEREMIAH

Breath Is Life

Jeremiah Jager, age 4, loves blue. He drinks blue soda pop, picks the blue marshmallows out of his Magic Stars cereal, and grabs the blue crayon. But when he got croupy and turned his favorite color this past winter—lips, cheeks, nose—his mother panicked. It was Jeremiah's eighth visit to the ER. And the scariest. "When he turned blue, I said 'I want some answers,'" says Cathy, who figured that—like relatives on both sides of his family—Jeremiah was developing asthma. She called the 800 number for Lung Line at the National Jewish Medical and Research Center in Denver. "This is going to cost twice as much as our car," says Cathy. "But why give birth to them if you're not going to do all you can for them?" Within a week, the Jagers left Alliance, Nebraska, for the long drive to Denver. They had to find out what was wrong with their child.

From "An Epidemic of Sneezing and Wheezing," by C. G. Dowling and A. Hollister, *Life Magazine*, May 1997, p. 79. Copyright 1997. The Picture Collection Inc. Used with permission. All rights reserved.

FREDDIE

Too Worried to Sleep

Freddie, age 12, had considerable difficulty falling asleep. Each night it would take him an hour or two to fall asleep, which made it very difficult for him to get up for school at 6:00 A.M. the next morning. His typical nighttime routine was to watch television downstairs until 9:00 p.m. and then get ready for bed. Once in bed, he read for a while before turning out the lights. He explains: "I start to get sleepy when I'm reading, but as soon as I turn off the lights I'm wide awake. I can't stop from thinking about things, especially stuff that bothers me at school, like homework and making friends. My dad told me I would get sick because I don't sleep enough, and now I'm afraid I'll catch 'mono' like a friend of mine has at school. No matter what I do, I can't seem to just fall asleep like I used to."

Adapted from Bootzin & Chambers, 1990.

WHAT DO JEREMIAH AND Freddie have in common? To varying degrees, these children must face situations that affect their health and well-being; as a result, they and their family members are continually distressed and worried. Jeremiah's parents want answers for his breathing problems, which seem to occur without warning. Because doctors are unable to explain his episodes, Jeremiah's parents secretly wonder whether his breathing problems may be due to psychological causes.

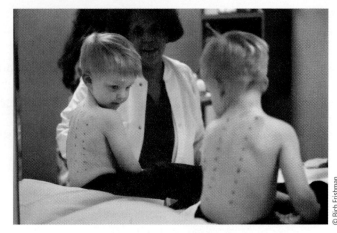

Jeremiah was thoroughly tested for allergies. The test results were all negative.

Similarly, Freddie's sleep problems are intermingled with worries brought on by his father's comments about him failing to get enough sleep. What role, if any, do psychological factors play in Jeremiah's and Freddie's development and adaptation to their health-related problems?

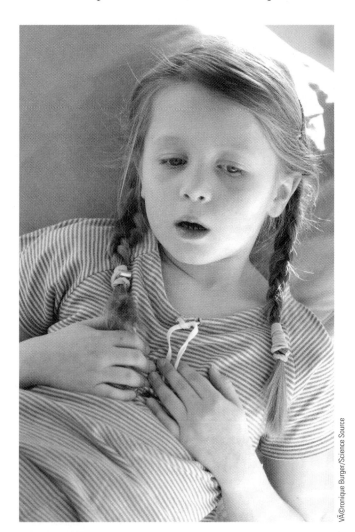

<Caption TBD>

Children, parents, and other family members are all deeply affected by children's health-related problems, which is why they have considerable psychological importance. The problems discussed in this chapter are not typically viewed as mental health disorders, rather they are viewed as health-related problems and medical stressors. Some stressors are mild, such as Freddie's problems falling asleep and sleeping through the night, but problems such as Jeremiah's asthma can be life-threatening and highly disruptive, and they may involve complicated and intrusive medical interventions.

Pediatric health-related disorders are a distinct area of specialization, but cover a wide range of concerns, from relatively minor, such as enuresis (bed-wetting) and encopresis (soiling), to chronic illnesses such as cancer and diabetes (Jackson, Alberts, & Roberts, 2010; Prinstein & Roberts, 2006). Health-related disorders are different from other mental disorders largely because children's adjustment problems are more directly connected to the impact of the physical illness. Moreover, the field of pediatric psychology stresses the interaction between physical and mental health because the various disorders and developmental problems all share medical, psychological, and psychosocial components (Peterson, Reach, & Grube, 2003). The involvement of psychologists and other mental health professionals in children's health-related problems has led to many highly successful ways to assist children and family members in coping with and adapting to their circumstances.

HISTORY

Psychological approaches to aiding children with health-related problems have gained considerable momentum over the past two decades, but a long history preceded these developments. Ever since Greek philosophers first suggested that pain and disease were caused by an imbalance in the body's basic elements of fire, air, water, and earth, various cultures have been both fascinated and perplexed by the interrelationship between the mind and the body. During the medieval period, these early philosophies were overshadowed by the belief that mental and physical illnesses were caused by demonic possession and required a quick and gruesome dispatch of the afflicted person.

Most new theories and research related to emotional and physical well-being remained dormant until the late 19th century. Charcot and Freud introduced their theories on the nature of hysteria and conversion disorders. However, debates about the importance of the mind–body connection dichotomy caused a clash between psychodynamic theory and modern medicine in the early 20th century (Siegel, Smith, & Wood, 1991).

Partially as a result of these controversies, an early distinction emerged between disorders caused by physical factors and those caused by emotional or psychological factors (Peterson et al., 2003). Physical disorders caused or affected by psychological and social factors were referred to as *psychosomatic*. Later, the term *psychosomatic* was replaced by the term *psychophysiological*, meaning that psychological factors affected somatic (physical) function. These terms are no longer used, however, because they wrongly implied that a person's physical symptoms were caused solely by mental problems.

Until 50 years ago, attention was rightfully placed on the acute, infectious diseases—such as smallpox, tuberculosis, diphtheria, and typhus—that claimed the lives of one in four children before their ninth birthday (Pollock, 1987). This statistic—simple, unemotional, impartial—belies the emotional toll this high infant and child mortality rate must have had on our ancestors. In fact, some historians argue that prior to the mid-19th century, children's highly unpredictable life spans contributed to a diminished emotional investment in children among parents and society (Garrison & McQuiston, 1989). In Western society today, it is difficult to conceive of these circumstances, even though high child mortality rates still exist in other countries around the world.

Sleep–wake disorders, elimination disorders, chronic illness, and substance-use disorders—all health-related problems addressed in this chapter—are good examples of how poorly understood physical symptoms can be misattributed to psychological causes. Moreover, diverse childhood experiences underscore how reliance on fashionable cures and untested folk wisdom, rather than on scientific findings, can be viewed by subsequent generations as unwise and sometimes harmful.

Consider children's sleep and elimination disorders. For centuries, these relatively common afflictions were unfairly attributed to children's inherent stubbornness and laziness. Societal attitudes toward addressing bed-wetting ranged from severe to lenient. By the turn of the 20th century, according to professional and public opinion, enuresis, like childhood masturbation, was a potential sign of emotional and behavioral disturbance. Early psychodynamic theory was gaining in popularity and proposed that toileting difficulties reflected unconscious conflicts that, if unresolved, could turn into troublesome personality styles. The sources of the underlying conflict were numerous: lack of parental love, the guilt value of feces, separation anxiety, pregnancy wishes, response to family problems, and traumatic separation from mother between the oral and anal stages of psychosexual development (Fielding & Doleys, 1988).

By the 1920s, the *Infant Care Bulletin,* the official publication of the U.S. Children's Bureau, reflected the harsh stance of society toward children's developmental problems. It advised parents to force their children to have bowel movements on a strict, regular schedule and to complete toilet training by 8 months of age at the latest! If the baby did not go along with this plan, elimination was induced by inserting a stick of soap into the rectum (Achenbach, 1982).

Fortunately, by the 1940s this advice mellowed toward more natural, developmentally sensitive approaches that allowed children's maturity to dictate when parents could shift from diapers to toileting, which occurred between 12 and 30 months of age. Toilet-training issues once again emerged during the rebellious 1960s, when renowned pediatrician Benjamin Spock was blamed for many social problems in North America because his advice on toileting and early childhood discipline from the 1940s was considered too lenient. Spock (1945) made it clear, though, that "the child supplies the power but the parents have to do the steering."

The Society of Pediatric Psychology was organized in 1968 to connect psychology and pediatrics, and it established the *Journal of Pediatric Psychology* in 1976. These two landmark events broadened the research and theory on physical outcomes of child health disorders to encompass the psychosocial effects of illness and the interplay between the two (Roberts & Steele, 2009).

How children adapt to the many situational, developmental, and chronic stressors affecting their health and well-being is a primary interest of pediatric health psychology. We begin by discussing sleep–wake disorders, pausing to consider how important sleep is to our psychological and physical development and its regulation from birth onward. Then we discuss elimination disorders and chronic illness in children and adolescents, areas in which monumental gains have been made in recent years in helping children overcome or adapt to these challenges. Finally, we describe substance-use disorders and related health-compromising behaviors that emerge in adolescence. How health-related problems interact with children's and adolescents' psychological well-being, and how they and their families adapt in response, are central themes throughout this chapter.

Section Summary

History

- For centuries, poorly understood physical symptoms have been misattributed to psychological causes.
- Today, pediatric health psychologists study how children's health-related problems interact with their psychological well-being and how they and their families adapt in response.

SLEEP–WAKE DISORDERS

People who say they sleep like a baby usually don't have one.

—Leo J. Burke

We all have problems sleeping at one time or another. Usually, the problems are not serious and do not interfere with the next day's activities, but sometimes sleep problems can seriously affect our physical and psychological health and well-being. As any parent, sibling, or roommate can attest, these problems can have a major impact on them as well. In fact, problems such as resistance at bedtime, difficulty settling at bedtime, night waking, difficulty waking up, and fatigue are among the most common concerns expressed by parents of young children (Meltzer & Mindell, 2007).

Arguably, sleep is the *primary* activity of the brain during the early years of development. Consider this: By 2 years of age the average child has spent almost 10,000 hours (nearly 14 months) asleep, and approximately 7,500 hours (about 10 months) in waking activities (Anders, Goodlin-Jones, & Sadeh, 2000). During those 2 years, the brain has reached 90% of its adult size and the child has attained remarkable complexity in cognitive skills, language, concept of self, socioemotional development, and physical skills (Dahl, 2007; Dahl & El-Sheikh, 2007). And most of these maturational advances occurred while the child was asleep.

By age 5 or so, a more even balance gradually emerges between sleep and wakefulness. Still, by the time they begin school, children have spent more time asleep than in social interactions, exploration of the environment, eating, or any other single waking activity. Why has evolution favored sleep over these important activities? Wouldn't it be to our advantage to have more waking time to learn language, acquire knowledge, and develop similar adaptive skills? Apparently, sleep serves a fundamental role in brain development and regulation (Dahl, 2007). This role explains why sleep disturbances can affect overall physical and mental health and well-being and why sleep disorders are important to abnormal child psychology.

Perhaps you have noticed how sleep problems co-occur with many different disorders, including attention-deficit/hyperactivity disorder (ADHD), depression, anxiety, conduct problems, and developmental disorders (Chorney et al., 2008; Kelly & El-Sheikh, 2013). This connection raises an important consideration: Do sleep problems cause other disorders, or do they result from them? The answer to this question requires an understanding of how sleep problems interact with a person's psychological well-being. Since sleep problems commonly arise from particular stressors—an upcoming exam or a relationship problem—we tend to think that sleep difficulties are secondary symptoms of a more primary problem. However, the relationship between sleep problems and psychological adjustment is bidirectional.

Sleep problems may cause emotional and behavioral problems among children and adolescents, and they may be caused by a psychological disorder. An underlying factor common to both sleep problems and other disorders may cause sleep issues in some cases. Problems in the brain's arousal and regulatory systems can cause increased anxiety and can affect sleep (see Chapter 11). Stress-related events, especially those that affect the child's safety—such as war, disaster, and family conflict—both increase arousal and interfere with normal sleep patterns (El-Sheikh, Bub, et al., 2013; Kelly & El-Sheikh, 2013). Simply stated, sleep–wake disorders can cause other psychological problems or they can result from other disorders or conditions. Sleep–wake disorders have considerable importance to abnormal child psychology because they mimic or worsen many of the symptoms of major disorders.

The Regulatory Functions of Sleep

We tend to think that sleep is a time when not much is happening—the "lights are on but nobody's home." This lack of activity and nearly complete loss of awareness during sleep suggests that sleep regulation has little to do with psychological processes such as attention, arousal, emotions, and behavior. So why does the brain—particularly, the developing brain—require long periods of relative inactivity?

Sleep, arousal, affect, and attention are all closely intertwined in a dynamic regulatory system (Dahl, 1996). This at odds with the popular image of sleep as simply rest. When the central nervous system (CNS) must increase arousal in response to possible danger,

Children's sleep patterns help regulate their mood and behavior.

the system must recover soon thereafter and restore the balance between sleep and arousal. It is fascinating how the system changes with development: During infancy, the balance is skewed in favor of more sleep, because safety and other needs are provided for by the child's caregivers. As children mature, they start looking after their own needs, becoming more alert and attentive to danger. Gradually, the cycle between sleep and arousal becomes skewed more in favor of arousal, which by then is adaptive and necessary, and the dynamic patterns of sleep help restore the balance.

Most college students suffer sleep loss or disruption as a result of all-night study sessions or late-night partying. So you are probably familiar with sleep's important role in regulating states of emotional arousal and restoration. The giddiness, silliness, and impulsive behaviors children and adults show if sleep-deprived signify impairment in the prefrontal cortex functions. The prefrontal cortex is an important *executive control* center in the brain—it is in charge of processing emotional signals and making critical decisions for response—so impairment results in signs of decreased concentration and diminished ability to inhibit, or control, basic drives, impulses, and emotions (Talbot et al., 2010).

The prefrontal cortex is uniquely situated in the brain where it can integrate thoughts (higher cortical functions) with emotions (basic CNS functions). If a person is sleep-deprived or otherwise impaired, the first functions affected are the more complex, demanding tasks that require integrating cognitive, emotional, and social input rapidly and accurately (Dahl, 1996). Ask any parent or teacher and they can tell you: Children with disrupted or inadequate sleep show less executive control the next day; they are more cranky, impulsive, distractible, and emotionally labile (meaning they switch abruptly from, say, laughing to crying). These symptoms are easily confused with those of ADHD, although sleep-related problems usually self-correct within a day or two (Cortese et al., 2013).

The physiology of sleep also has a fascinating connection to developmental problems that occur during childhood, and it further underscores the crucial role of sleep in restoring balance (Gregory et al., 2008). Specific stages of sleep are believed to produce an active *uncoupling,* or disconnection, of neurobehavioral systems (Dahl, 1996). In effect, separate aspects of the CNS take a break from their constant duty. Think about how your nervous system must use electrical signals to continuously maintain an active, close connection while you are awake. These signals require that our neurobehavioral systems maintain precise timing and frequency. (See our discussion of communication and learning disorders in Chapter 7.)

© Zits Partnership. Reprinted with special permission of King Features Syndicate

Sleep researcher R. E. Dahl describes the uncoupling process by comparing sleep's role to that of tuning instruments in a large orchestra: Tuning cannot be accomplished while the instrument is continuously playing, or "coupling," with the other instruments in the orchestra. Likewise, retuning or recalibration of the components of the CNS may require temporary uncoupling, or disconnection from other systems. Further, the uncoupling may be particularly critical for children. As children mature, regions of the brain rapidly differentiate and establish specific functions and patterns of interconnection within the CNS (Dahl, 1996, 2007), which requires considerable recalibration or retuning. In Dahl's music analogy, a new instrument must be retuned more often than one that has been broken in.

Maturational Changes

Our sleep patterns and needs change dramatically during the first few years of life, then gradually settle into a stable pattern as we reach adulthood. Newborns sleep about 16 to 17 hours each day, and 1-year-olds sleep about 13 hours a day, including daytime naps that range from 1 to over 2 hours (Acebo et al., 2005; Anders & Eiben, 1997). These maturational changes partially explain why the sleep problems of infants and children are different from those of older children, adolescents, and adults. Infants and toddlers have more night-waking problems, preschoolers have more falling-asleep problems, and younger school-age children have more going-to-bed problems. In contrast, sleep problems among adolescents and adults typically involve difficulty going to or staying asleep (insomnia) or not having enough time to sleep (Roberts, Roberts, & Xing, 2011).

Paradoxically, adolescents have an increased physiological need for sleep, but many get significantly less sleep than they did during early childhood. This results in many teens being chronically sleep-deprived, with daytime symptoms of fatigue, irritability, emotional lability, difficulty concentrating, and falling asleep in class (Roberts et al., 2011). The bottom line? Let sleeping teens lie—they need to catch up on their sleep!

Features of Sleep–Wake Disorders

Primary sleep–wake disorders are likely a result of abnormalities in the body's ability to regulate sleep–wake mechanisms and the timing of sleep, as opposed to sleep problems related to a medical disorder, a mental disorder, or the use of medications. There are 10 sleep–wake disorders in the *Diagnostic and Statistical of Mental Disorders*, 5th ed. (DSM-5), reflecting the increasing research and clinical overlap between sleep problems and mental health disorders (Reynolds & O'Hara, 2013). Only the major sleep–wake disorders most relevant to children and youths are discussed herein; for simplicity, these are divided into two categories: dyssomnias and parasomnias (Voderholzer & Guilleminault, 2012). **Dyssomnias** are disorders of initiating or maintaining sleep, characterized by difficulty getting enough sleep, not sleeping when you want to, not feeling refreshed after sleeping, and so forth. **Parasomnias**, in contrast, are sleep disorders in which behavioral or physiological events intrude on ongoing sleep. Whereas dyssomnias involve disruptions in the sleep process, parasomnias involve physiological or cognitive arousal at inappropriate times during the sleep–wake cycle, which can result in sleepwalking or in nightmares that jolt someone from sleep. Persons suffering from parasomnia sleep disorders often report unusual behaviors while asleep, rather than sleepiness or insomnia.

Dyssomnias

Dyssomnias, many of which are common during certain stages of development, are disturbances in the amount, timing, or quality of sleep. Freddie, for example, suffered from a common form of childhood insomnia in which he had difficulty getting to sleep. Fortunately, many sleep problems resolve themselves as the child matures, especially if parents are given basic information and guidance, such as to refrain from yelling at the child to go to sleep and instead to adhere to a bedtime routine (U.S. Department of Health and Human Services, 2011).

Table 13.1 provides a descriptive overview of childhood dyssomnias. For the most part, dyssomnias are common childhood afflictions, with the exception of narcolepsy, which is uncommon but may be underdiagnosed in children (Nevsimalova, 2009). Breathing-related sleep disorders can affect children of various ages as a result of allergies, asthma, or swollen tonsils and adenoids. Although relatively common, dyssomnias can sometimes have a significant impact on

TABLE 13.1 | Dyssomnias

Sleep Disorder	Description	Prevalence and Age	Treatment
Insomnia Disorder	Difficulty initiating or maintaining sleep, or sleep that is not restorative; in infants, repetitive night waking and inability to fall asleep	25% to 50% of 1-to 3-year-olds	Behavioral treatment, family guidance
Hypersomnolence Disorder	Excessive sleepiness that is displayed as either prolonged sleep episodes or daytime sleep episodes	Common among young children	Behavioral treatment, family guidance
Narcolepsy	Irresistible attacks of refreshing sleep occurring daily, accompanied by brief episodes of loss of muscle tone (cataplexy)	<1% of children and adolescents	Structure, support, psychostimulants, antidepressants
Breathing-Related Sleep Disorder	Sleep disruption leading to excessive sleepiness or insomnia that is caused by sleep-related breathing difficulties	1% to 2% of children; preschool, elementary ages	Removal of tonsils and adenoids
Circadian Rhythm Sleep Disorder	Persistent or recurrent sleep disruption leading to excessive sleepiness or insomnia due to a mismatch between the sleep–wake schedule required by a person's environment and his or her internal sleep cycle (circadian rhythm); late sleep onset (after midnight), difficulty awakening in morning, sleeping in on weekends, resistance to change	Unknown; possibly 7% of adolescents	Behavioral treatment, chronotherapy

children's behavior and emotional state, much like they impact adult behavior (Reid, Huntley, & Lewin, 2009).

Parasomnias

Parasomnias are somewhat common afflictions during early to mid-childhood and, we might add, are a bit easier to understand because of their more familiar terms and our own experiences. They include **nightmares** (repeated awakenings, with frightening dreams that you usually remember), **sleep terrors** (abrupt awakening, accompanied by autonomic arousal but no recall), and **sleepwalking** (getting out of bed and walking around, but with no recall the next day). Nightmares occur during rapid-eye-movement (REM) (dream) sleep, usually during the second half of the sleep period, whereas sleep terrors and sleep walking occur during non-REM (NREM) sleep (for this reason, DSM-5 combines sleep terrors and sleepwalking into one category: NREM sleep arousal disorders). Sleep terrors and sleepwalking occur during deep sleep in the first third of the sleep cycle, when the person is so soundly asleep that he or she is difficult to arouse and has no recall of the episode the next morning (Reid et al., 2009). Although girls and boys report similar rates of nightmares in childhood, by adolescence, girls report more nightmares

than boys, a pattern that continues into adulthood (Schredl & Reinhard, 2011). Fortunately, as with the dyssomnias, children typically grow out of parasomnias or recover from sleep disruption or sleep loss and do not develop a chronic condition that interferes with daily activities. Characteristics of parasomnia sleep disorders are shown in Table 13.2.

DSM-5 criteria for sleep disorders typically are not met in full by younger children because of the transitory nature of their sleep problems (Goodlin-Jones et al., 2009). Refer to Tables 13.1 and 13.2, in lieu of the specific criteria for children, to aid in understanding the major features and differences of the various sleep disorders. Also, note two considerations concerning diagnostic criteria: In addition to the symptoms pertaining to each sleep disorder, as listed in Tables 13.1 and 13.2, DSM-5 diagnostic criteria for all sleep-related disorders emphasize: (1) the presence of clinically significant distress or impairment in social, occupational, or other important areas of functioning; and (2) the requirement that the sleep disturbance cannot be better accounted for by another mental disorder, the direct physiological effects of a substance, or a general medical condition (other than a breathing-related disorder) (APA, 2013). These considerations apply to all the disorders discussed in this chapter.

TABLE 13.2 | Parasomnias

Sleep Disorder	Description	Prevalence and Age	Treatment
Nightmare Disorder	Repeated awakenings with detailed recall of extended and extremely frightening dreams, usually involving threats to survival, security, or self-esteem; generally occurs during the second half of the sleep period	Common between ages 3 and 8	Provide comfort, reduce stress
NREM Sleep Arousal Disorders			
Sleep Terrors	Recurrent episodes of abrupt awakening from sleep, usually occurring during the first third of the major sleep episode and beginning with a panicky scream; accompanied by autonomic discharge, racing heart, sweating, vocalized distress, glassy-eyed staring; difficult to arouse, inconsolable, disoriented; no memory of episodes in morning	3% of children; ages 18 months to 6 years	Reduce stress and fatigue; add late afternoon nap
Sleepwalking	Repeated episodes of arising from bed during sleep and walking about, usually during the first third of the major sleep episode; poorly coordinated, difficult to arouse, disoriented; no memory of episode in morning	15% of children have one attack; 1% to 6% have one to four attacks per week; age 4 to 12 years, rare in adolescence	Take safety precautions, reduce stress and fatigue, add late afternoon nap

Treatment

Sleeping difficulties in infants and toddlers often subside on their own, but any parent who has been awakened night after night by a screaming child can attest that "waiting for them to grow out of it" seems like forever. If going to sleep or staying asleep becomes difficult, the goal of behavioral interventions is to teach parents to attend to the child's need for comfort and reassurance, but to gradually withdraw more quickly from the child's room after saying goodnight. (This is an example of *extinction,* since parental attention is being removed.)

Parents also can be taught to establish good sleep hygiene appropriate to their child's developmental stage and the family's cultural values. Once established, positive reinforcement methods, such as praise or star charts, can be used to reward the child for efforts to follow the bedtime routine. Sleep hygiene may involve identifying suspected causes of disrupted sleep and involving other family members in maintaining a chosen routine. For example, individualized bedtime rituals, such as reading, singing, or playing a quiet game, establish a positive transition to bedtime, and regular bedtimes and waking times establish a consistent routine (Reid et al., 2009).

Treatment of circadian rhythm sleep disorders requires a highly motivated adolescent and a supportive family, because there are no shortcuts or medications that can easily restore a disrupted sleep–wake cycle. The goal of behavioral intervention is twofold: to eliminate the sleep deprivation and to restore a more normal sleep–wake routine. The adolescent is asked to keep a sleep–wake and daily activity log, with regular bedtimes and rise times. If begun early in the disorder, such supportive behavioral methods are often effective (Hasler et al., 2012). In addition to behavioral methods, melatonin (a natural hormone) supplements have shown to be effective with children and adolescents in advancing the sleep–wake rhythm and restoring the sleep cycle (van Geijlswijk, Korzilius, & Smits, 2010).

In contrast to treatment for some dyssomnias, prolonged treatment of child and adolescent parasomnias is usually not necessary, particularly if the episodes of sleep intrusion occur infrequently (Moturi & Avis, 2010; Sullivan, 2012). Treatment of nightmares consists of providing comfort at the time of occurrence and attempting to reduce daytime stressors. If nightmares or sleep terrors are intense and persistent, daytime stresses at school, family conflicts, or emotional disturbance may be implicated (El-Sheikh, Kelly, & Rauer, 2013; Keller et al., 2014). If sleepwalking is suspected, parents usually are asked to record episodes at home on video. If sleepwalking is confirmed, parents must take precautions to reduce the chance of injury to a child who may fall or bump into objects. Because of the possibility of fire or other emergencies, children should never be locked in their rooms. Excessive fatigue or unusual stresses during the daytime often precipitate sleepwalking. Therefore, brief afternoon naps can be beneficial.

Section Summary

Sleep–Wake Disorders

- Sleep disorders are important to abnormal child psychology because they mimic or worsen many symptoms of the major disorders.
- Sleep disorders can cause psychological problems, result from other disorders, or be a symptom of trauma or stress in the child's life.
- Dyssomnias are disorders of initiating or maintaining sleep, and include hypersomnia, narcolepsy, breathing-related sleep disorders, and circadian rhythm disorder.
- Parasomnias are sleep disorders in which behavioral or physiological events intrude on ongoing sleep, arousing the sleeper. They include nightmares, sleep terrors, and sleepwalking.
- Although most dyssomnias and parasomnias of childhood are common and often disappear with maturity, they still may have a negative impact on the child's daily activity and adjustment. Effective psychological treatments for most childhood sleep disorders involve the establishment and regulation of bedtime routines.

ELIMINATION DISORDERS

"Step 1: Before you begin, remove all stubbornness from the child." These instructions were provided by a popular toilet training manual years ago, apparently without a hint of irony. For generations, parents have half-jokingly referred to the bathroom, and toilet training in particular, as the "combat zone," where parental right meets child's might. Teaching toddlers how to use the toilet is one of the more significant challenges of parenting, but it is unlikely that it deserved the disproportionate amount of attention it received in the early abnormal child psychology literature.

Thanks to a better understanding of the biological and psychological underpinnings of elimination disorders, attention has been directed away from the child's personality or emotional trauma. However, for a significant minority of children, the problems associated with toileting continue well past the age when most children have achieved freedom and independence. Elimination problems can turn into distressing and chronic difficulties, and can affect participation in educational and social

activities, camps, sleepovers, and so forth. In extreme cases, toileting accidents can precipitate physical child abuse (Herrenkohl, Herrenkohl, & Egolf, 1983).

Two elimination problems that occur during childhood and adolescence are **enuresis** the involuntary discharge of urine during the day or night, and **encopresis**, the passage of feces in inappropriate places, such as in clothing or on the floor. Child psychologists have studied and treated these elimination problems among children because they can have strong implications on the development of self-competence and self-esteem. Even though most children eventually outgrow problems of enuresis or encopresis by age 10 or so, they may have suffered years of embarrassment and peer rejection that remain troublesome. Fortunately, in most instances the problems can be alleviated through education and retraining efforts involving both parents and children. These disorders are one of the few areas of abnormal child psychology in which early referral and treatment can virtually eliminate long-term consequences.

Enuresis

As many as 7 million children in the United States and Canada go through the same routine each night: turn off the lights, go to sleep, wet the bed. Most of the time the child cannot control the discharge, but on occasion it may be intentional. Although the problem is relatively common, it is stressful for parents and children.

Concerns about correcting children's bed-wetting have perplexed professionals and parents for generations. Here is how Thomas Phaer, "the father of English pediatrics," explained the early cure to physicians under the heading "Of Pyssying in the Bedde" in his *Boke of Children* (1544):

> Many times for debility of vertus retentive of the reines or blader, as wel olde men as children are often-times annoyed, whan their urine issueth out either in theyre slepe or waking against theyr wylles, having no power to reteine it whan it cometh, therfore yf they will be holpen, fyrst they must avoid al fat meates, til ye vertue be restored againe, and to use this pouder in their meates and drynkes. (Cited in Glicklich, 1951, p. 862)

The "pouder" was derived from the trachea of a cock or the "stones of a hedge-hogge." This remedy seems tame in view of more "enlightened" mechanical and surgical approaches to enuresis that emerged by the 18th century—yokes made of iron (mercifully covered with velvet) that prevented urination and steel spikes placed on the child's back to prevent lying on the back, because that position was believed to stimulate bladder function during sleep. If you did not want your child to be outfitted for one of these devices, other forms of treatment were available. Medicinals such as strychnine, belladonna, sacral plasters, and chloral hydrate were used presumably to stimulate the bladder (regardless of poisonous side effects), or the orifice of the urethra was cauterized (partially closed) with silver nitrate to make it more tender and responsive to the passage of urine (Glicklich, 1951). Throughout history, the treatment of childhood bed-wetting reflects society's generally poor understanding of and sensitivity to children's needs and problems at the time.

Most children have bed-wetting accidents until age 5 or so, therefore DSM-5 has narrowed the criteria to reflect the developmental nature of this disorder (see Table 13.3). The criteria stipulate that the problem must be frequent (at least twice a week for 3 consecutive months) or accompanied by significant distress or impairment in social, academic, or other important areas of functioning. A chronological age of 5 years, or the equivalent developmental level, was arbitrarily chosen as a developmental benchmark for the point at which most children achieve urinary continence. Finally, the voiding of urine into bed or clothes must not be due exclusively to a general medical condition or the result of a diuretic, which is a drug that reduces water retention.

DSM-5 distinguishes between three subtypes of enuresis (APA, 2013). *Nocturnal only* is the most common subtype, in which wetting occurs only during

sleep at night, typically during the first third of the night. Nocturnal enuresis is significantly more common among boys than girls (Su et al., 2011). Sometimes the child is dreaming of urinating, which indicates that the voiding took place during REM sleep. *Diurnal only* is defined as the passage of urine during waking hours, most often during the early afternoon on school days (APA, 2013). Diurnal enuresis is more common in females than males and is uncommon after age 9. Because of these features, suspected causes of diurnal enuresis often indicate a child's reluctance to use the toilet because of social anxiety or a preoccupation with a school event. Finally, *nocturnal* and *diurnal* can exist in combination.

Prevalence and Course

Because it is common for young children to wet the bed occasionally, it is not seen as a clinical problem unless it occurs more than once a month (Brown et al., 2008). Using one or more episodes a month as a cutoff, the incidence of nocturnal enuresis varies from about 4% to 13% for children 10 years of age or younger (Su et al., 2011). The prevalence of enuresis declines rapidly as children mature: By age 10, only 3% of males and 2% of females are affected, and this evens out to 1% of males and less than 1% of females by late adolescence (Mellon & Houts, 2006). Diurnal enuresis is much less common; it is estimated to affect 3% of 6-year-olds (Peterson et al., 2003). However, prevalence of both forms of enuresis is higher among those who are less educated, members of lower socioeconomic groups, and institutionalized children, perhaps due to less structure in their daily routines and added environmental stressors (APA, 2000).

Approximately 85% of children with enuresis have *primary enuresis,* because they have never attained at least 6 months of continuous nighttime control. By definition, primary enuresis starts at age 5. In contrast, *secondary enuresis* is less common and refers to children who have previously established urinary continence but then relapse, usually between the ages of 5 and 8 years (APA, 2013). Children with secondary enuresis often take a longer time establishing initial nighttime continence or have a higher number of stressful life events (Mellon & Houts, 2006). Most children do eventually stop wetting the bed, but for those who do not attain this on their own, treatment is particularly beneficial in preventing a lengthy and disruptive problem.

You can imagine how younger children are treated when peers discover that they have wet themselves in class or while sleeping over a friend's house. Teasing, name calling, and social stigmatization are common peer reactions to this unfortunate problem. Although

TABLE 13.3 | **Diagnostic Criteria for Enuresis**

(A) Repeated voiding of urine into bed or clothes, whether involuntary or intentional **DSM-5**

(B) The behavior is clinically significant as manifested by either a frequency of at least twice a week for at least 3 consecutive months or the presence of clinically significant distress or impairment in social, academic (occupational), or other important areas of functioning.

(C) Chronological age is at least 5 years (or equivalent developmental level)

(D) The behavior is not attributable to the physiological effects of a substance (e.g., a diuretic, an antipsychotic medication) or another medical condition (e.g., diabetes, spina bifida, a seizure disorder)

Specify if:

Nocturnal only: Passage of urine only during nighttime sleep

Diurnal only: Passage of urine during waking hours

Nocturnal and diurnal: A combination of the two subtypes above

Source: *Diagnostic and Statistical Manual of Mental Disorders,* 5th ed. (Copyright © 2013). American Psychiatric Association.

enuresis is a physical condition, it is often accompanied by some degree of psychological distress (Joinson et al., 2007; Van Hoecke et al., 2006). The impact of this distress often depends on three features related to the nature of the enuresis: (1) limitations imposed on social activities, such as sleeping away from home; (2) effects on self-esteem, including the degree of social ostracism imposed by peers; and (3) parental reactions, such as anger, punishment, and rejection (Christophersen & VanScoyoc, 2013; Houts, 2010). Parents are often poorly informed about the nature of enuresis and may respond by punishing or humiliating the child who suffers from it. Fortunately, these consequences are not inevitable or long-lasting. Many children with enuresis are able to establish their self-esteem and peer relationships despite their occasional embarrassment or anxiety. For others, treatment for bed-wetting usually has a positive impact on their self-concept and peer relations (Brown, Pope, & Brown, 2011).

sodapix/Getty images

Waking up to a wet bed is upsetting, and it can affect a young child's self-confidence if poorly managed.

Causes and Treatment

For most children with enuresis, one specific etiology cannot be identified (Fritz, Rockney, & the Work Group on Quality Issues, 2004). Children with nocturnal enuresis need to urinate at night, but they do not wake up when they need to urinate. By age 5 or so, most children have made the transition from urinating around the clock, as they did in infancy, to urinating only during waking hours.

Children who continue to need to urinate at night may have a deficiency during sleep of an important hormone known as *antidiuretic hormone (ADH)*. ADH helps concentrate urine during sleep hours, meaning that the urine contains less water and has therefore decreased volume. For normal children, this decreased volume usually means that their bladders do not overfill while they are asleep, unless they drank excessive fluids before bed. Children with enuresis, however, do not show the usual increase in ADH during sleep (Norgaard, Pederson, & Djurhuus, 1985). They continue to produce more urine during the hours of sleep than their bladders can hold, and if they fail to wake up, bed-wetting results.

The reason children with enuresis fail to wake up when they need to urinate can also be explained by developmental and biological factors. Older children and adolescents are able to sense a full bladder at night, which activates a nerve impulse from the bladder to the brain. This signal may initiate dreams about water or going to the toilet, which usually wakes them up. This signaling mechanism matures during early childhood, so infants understandably have very little ability to detect the need to urinate. Some children with primary enuresis, however, lack normal development of this signal processing in the brain (Ornitz et al., 1999).

Primary enuresis, the most common type, is decidedly not due to stress or child obstinacy. On the contrary, this trait appears to be inherited. If both parents were enuretic, 77% of their children are too; if only one parent was enuretic, then 44% of their offspring are also. If neither parent had this problem, only about 15% of their children develop enuresis. Concordance rates of enuresis for monozygotic (68%) and dizygotic (36%) twins also verify this connection (Bakwin, 1973; Sethi, Bhargava, & Phil, 2005).

Treatments for children with nocturnal enuresis have perhaps the most comprehensive track record of evaluation for any psychological intervention for childhood problems (Mellon & Houts, 2006). Dozens of promising behavioral methods have been investigated by hundreds of studies over several decades; they are joined by many other studies of pharmacological agents. Fortunately, these efforts have led to some strong conclusions as to what works best. (This example provides a good lesson in how long it often takes to verify successful treatment methods for psychological disorders.)

The standard behavioral intervention, based on classical conditioning principles, is using an alarm that sounds at the first detection of urine. Bed-wetting alarms have been around since Mowrer and Mowrer (1938) first invented the "bell and pad" (a battery-operated device that produced a loud sound as soon as a drop of urine closed the electrical circuit), and they are among the safest and most effective treatments. Modern alarms have a simple moisture sensor that snaps into a child's pajamas, with a small speaker attached to the shoulder to awaken the child. A single drop of urine completes the electronic circuit, setting off a piercing alarm that causes the child to tense and reflexively stop urinating. The one drawback to this method is the alarm's unpopularity with other household members. For the alarm to be effective, an adult must wake the child up, which usually is not easy; walk him to the bathroom; get him to finish urinating in the toilet; and then reset the alarm. If this ritual is carefully followed, the alarm will begin to wake the child directly within 4 to 6 weeks, and by 12 weeks he will likely master nighttime bladder control and no longer need the alarm. The modern urine alarm, when used in conjunction with other behavioral activities (e.g., monitoring and intermittent reinforcement), has been recommended by the American Academy of Child and Adolescent Psychiatry as a minimal standard in the treatment of enuresis (i.e., should apply in at least 95% of enuresis cases) (Fritz et al., 2004).

Another behavioral method, based on operant conditioning principles, involves variations of *dry-bed training*. Children, like adults, wake up more easily when the day holds promise and excitement. Reward systems, such as star charts or other tokens, capitalize on this anticipation. Dry-bed training was originally developed as a brief but intensive intervention in response to parents' frustration over the more intrusive and drawn-out urine alarm. During a single office visit, parents are instructed in bladder retention control training by having their child drink more and more fluids during the day, and then delay urination for longer periods (in an effort to strengthen bladder control); hourly wakings for trips to the toilet; a cleanup routine for accidents (overcorrection, or having the child clean more than just the sheets); and positive reinforcement for dry nights. This routine is practiced nightly for 1 or 2 weeks.

Dry-bed training methods combined with an alarm (referred to today as *full-spectrum home training*) are still commonly used, resulting in a success rate of about three in four children and a relapse rate of 10% after 1 year (Brown et al., 2011; Friman, 2008). In less severe or prolonged cases of primary enuresis, a simple incentive such as earning stars or similar tokens for dry nights is often enough to make children responsive to nighttime bladder fullness. Other children, however, may require the alarm treatment to get the message firmly implanted, coupled with close professional monitoring to help parents adhere to the training methods.

In the mid-1980s, desmopressin, a synthetic ADH administered by nasal spray before bedtime, became available as a treatment for enuresis. About 70% of children using desmopressin can avoid bed-wetting within a few days, and another 10% or so show significant improvement in the number of dry nights (Brown et al., 2011). Although desmopressin works very well while

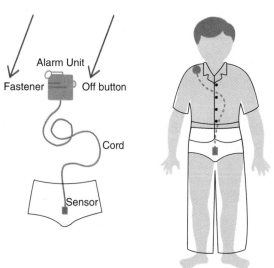

Alarm unit fastens onto outside of pajama top at shoulder

Cord runs under pajama top from alarm unit to sensor

Sensor clips to underpants

● **FIGURE 13.1** | CAPTION tbd

children are taking the medicine, the difficulty comes in keeping them dry when they stop taking it: the relapse rate can be as high as 80% (Fritz et al., 2004). Unlike alarm systems, which have most children cured of bed-wetting within 12 weeks, treatment with medication often requires some additional behavioral treatment before children are able to stop taking the medicine.

Psychological treatments for enuresis, especially the urine alarm, have been more effective overall than pharmacological treatments (Campbell, Cox, & Borowitz, 2009; Houts, 2010). In particular, treatment using the urine alarm was found to be superior to any other type of intervention. At the end of treatment, which generally lasts 12 weeks, children who used a urine alarm were equally as likely to have ceased bed-wetting as those who took desmopressin; however, at their 3-month follow-up visit, children using a urine alarm are almost twice as likely to have ceased bed-wetting as children who received other treatments, including desmopressin. On average, almost half of all children who used alarms remain dry at follow-up, compared with about one-third treated with other behavior therapies and one-quarter treated with tricyclic medications (an antidepressant that sometimes prevents bed-wetting) (Mellon & Houts, 2006). Enuresis is one of the few disorders for which treatments using psychological interventions are clearly superior to those using drugs; therefore, psychological interventions should be used instead of waiting for the child to grow out of the problem because of the distress it causes the child and family.

Encopresis

Encopresis refers to the passage of feces in inappropriate places, such as in clothing or on the floor. Like enuresis, this act is usually involuntary, but may occasionally be done intentionally. The diagnostic criteria stipulate that this event must occur at least once per month for at least 3 months, and that the child must be 4 years old or older (if the child is developmentally delayed, a mental age of at least 4 years is used). Fecal incontinence must not be due to an organic or general medical condition (see Table 13.4).

Two subtypes of encopresis are described in DSM-5: with or without constipation and overflow incontinence. Essentially, encopresis results from constipation that produces fecal impaction. Liquid stool above the impaction gradually develops sufficient pressure to leak around the impaction, thereby producing overflow incontinence in most cases (Christophersen & VanScoyoc, 2013).

Prevalence and Course

An estimated 1% of 5-year-old children have encopresis (APA, 2013). Similar to enuresis, encopresis is

| TABLE 13.4 | Diagnostic Criteria for Encopresis |

(A) Repeated passage of feces in inappropriate places (e.g., in clothing, on floor), whether involuntary or intentional.

(B) At least one such event occurs each month for at least 3 months.

(C) Chronological age is at least 4 years (or equivalent developmental level).

(D) The behavior is not attributable to the physiological effects of a substance (e.g., laxatives) or another medical condition, except through a mechanism involving constipation

Specify if:

With constipation and overflow incontinence: There is evidence of constipation on physical examination or by history.

Without constipation and overflow incontinence: There is no evidence of constipation or physical examination or by history.

Source: *Diagnostic and Statistical Manual of Mental Disorders,* 5th ed. (Copyright © 2013). American Psychiatric Association.

more common in boys than in girls, decreases rapidly with age, and involves primary and secondary types. Children with primary encopresis have reached age 4 without establishing fecal continence, whereas children with secondary encopresis had established a period of continence before the current episode of encopresis began.

As many as one in five children with encopresis show significant psychological problems, but these problems more likely result from, rather than initially cause, the encopresis (Mikkelsen, 2010; Peterson et al., 2003). Understandably, they may feel ashamed and try to avoid situations, such as camp or school, that might lead to embarrassment. As with enuresis, the degree of children's impairment and associated psychological distress is partially a function of social ostracism by peers, as well as anger, punishment, and rejection on the part of caregivers.

Causes and Treatment

Overly aggressive or early toilet training, family disturbance and stress, and child psychopathology have all been thought, at one time or another, to cause encopresis (Burket et al., 2006; Peterson et al., 2003). However, like enuresis, encopresis is a physical disorder that can lead to psychological factors, but it seldom results from these factors alone. The sooner it is diagnosed and treated, the less likely it is that the child will suffer any lasting emotional scars or disruptions in social relationships. Exceptions, of course, are children with oppositional defiant and conduct disorders (discussed in Chapter 9), in which encopresis and enuresis may occur as secondary symptoms of broader behavior patterns.

Understanding the etiology of encopresis leads to a discussion of toilet training, during which children first learn to control bowel movements. Children must learn how to recognize signals from the muscles and nerves that tell them when it is time for a bowel movement. Sometimes they try to avoid or suppress these signals, especially if something more enjoyable is going on. Some children attempt to suppress passing feces to avoid having an accident; this allows feces to build up in the colon over time, causing *megacolon*. If uncleared, the feces that stay in the bowel become large, hard, and dry, which causes later bowel movements to be painful. Over time, the stretched muscles and nerves give fewer and fewer signals to the child about the need to have a bowel movement. This decrease in signals results in stool accidents, and the colon and rectum often do not empty as they should.

About half of all children who develop this pattern of avoidance also have abnormal *defecation dynamics*; that is, they contract rather than relax the external sphincter when they attempt to defecate (Campbell et al., 2009). Combined with avoidance tactics, an increased risk of chronic constipation and encopresis develops. In case you're wondering how such dynamics develop, consider how some children (and adults) avoid using a bathroom if they are in a strange place or if they have been told that public toilets should be avoided because they are germ-infested. Anxiety about defecating in a particular place, or stressful and harsh toileting experiences, can cause chronic constipation. Without reversing this pattern of retention, the child becomes less able to perform the many skills required for successful toileting, including recognizing body cues, undressing, going into the bathroom, sitting on the toilet chair, and relaxing the appropriate muscles (Peterson et al., 2003).

Optimal treatment of encopresis involves both medical and behavioral interventions to help the child learn to empty the colon to allow it to return to normal size and function (Christophersen & VanScoyoc, 2013). To get the process moving, fiber, enemas, laxatives, or lubricants may be given to disimpact the fecal mass (Kuhl et al., 2010). Then, to establish a better routine and healthy pattern of elimination, behavioral methods are used in combination with laxatives or similar agents. Laxatives alone do not address the underlying behavioral mechanisms. Children who have large and impacted stools will find defecation frightening and painful, which further encourages them to ignore early rectal distention cues (the urge to defecate) and avoid going to the toilet.

Behavioral methods involve teaching a toilet-training procedure that encourages detection of and response to rectal distention cues, parental efforts to praise the child's clean pants and toilet use, and regularly scheduled toilet times after meals. During these times, children practice tensing and relaxing their external anal sphincter for several minutes; the practice time often is followed by fun time of reading or playing games to desensitize children to sitting on the toilet. Then they are taught to strain and attempt to have a bowel movement. With a combination of laxatives and behavioral treatment, most children improve significantly within the first 2 weeks of treatment, and over 75% maintain these improvements (Campbell et al., 2009; Houts, 2010). Internet-based behavioral treatments for encopresis have also shown success and have the advantage of wider access for families (Ritterband et al., 2013).

Section Summary

Elimination Disorders

- Enuresis is the involuntary discharge of urine during the day or night.
- Encopresis is the passage of feces in inappropriate places, such as in clothing or on the floor.
- Primary enuresis has a strong genetic component, whereas encopresis results from children's efforts to avoid defecation, resulting in chronic constipation.
- Combined pharmacological and psychological treatments of elimination problems are often very successful.

CHRONIC ILLNESS

Who has not feared that the very worst could somehow single out a family member? Who does not worry as a toddler wanders toward the curb, as a preschooler climbs a playground ladder, or as a teenager suddenly begins having severe headaches and dizziness? Chronic illnesses and medical conditions affect over 12 million children and adolescents in North America, so it is likely that we frequently will hear about these sad events. Here is one mother's reflection:

When does the pain go away? I don't think ever. It is a lifetime mourning for what could have been. It has nothing to do with lack of acceptance or understanding and everything to do with things we hold close in our hearts; the celebrations never realized. Sharing in the joy of watching others trying out for sports, having a first date, graduate, get accepted at university, or watch a beloved daughter walk down the aisle to be married, will never be experienced. Different experiences are ours. Instead of reflecting on what could have been, look for what's right with your child, not what's wrong. Be proud of all accomplishments. Different joys are ours. Celebrate each achievement, each milestone. They are great motivators for yourself, your child, and others. (Reprinted with permission from Greey, 1995.)

A **chronic illness** is one that persists longer than 3 months in a given year or that requires a period of continuous hospitalization of more than 1 month. Chronic medical conditions—the wide range of complications relating to physical growth, function, and development, such as a visual or hearing impairment—are part of this picture as well. About 10% to 20% of youths under the age of 18 years will experience one or more chronic health conditions, with approximately 5% of these children suffering from a disease so severe that it regularly interferes with their daily activities, such as forming friendships, attending school, and simply pursuing a normal quality of life (Brown, Daly, & Rickel, 2007).

Children and adolescents whose health and functional ability are compromised by a chronic medical condition face numerous challenges to their development and adjustment. Each day, children with insulin-dependent diabetes must monitor their blood-glucose level and diet and inject insulin. Children with asthma cautiously navigate new situations, on the alert for an attack that can literally leave them breathless, and children with cancer must cope with the stares or comments from peers who have little understanding or compassion for why another child looks different or seems frail. Like other developmental disorders, these conditions impact not only the child but also peers and family members. This impact, in turn, affects the child's ability to adapt to the condition (Havermans et al., 2011; Sharpe & Rossiter, 2002).

The DSM-5 addresses the mental health issues pertaining to health-related disorders in children and adults indiscriminately. However, there has been considerable effort to redirect the focus of health-related symptoms and disorders away from the absence of a medical cause and more toward the presence of distressing physical symptoms. **Somatic symptom and related disorders** (previously called "somatoform disorders") are a group of related problems involving distressing somatic symptoms, such as pain and dizziness, that interfere with daily activities. These somatic or health concerns are accompanied by excessive thoughts, feelings, and behaviors, such as anxiety or worry about the seriousness of the symptoms (APA, 2013).

For somatic symptom and related disorders, the emphasis is on the way a child or youth presents with and interprets their symptoms, rather than on the symptoms per se. For example, younger children may frequently complain of aches and pain, which is common; however, worrying day and night that something is not right about one's health might be indicative of a somatic symptom disorder if this pattern continues for more than 6 months. These symptoms are not intentionally produced or feigned, and they are real enough to cause the child significant distress or impairment. Because the etiology of these symptoms is unknown, there is no longer a presumption that they are caused by psychological factors. Rather, the DSM-5 has revised their take on somatic symptom and related disorders by recognizing the potential influence of genetic and biological vulnerability (such as increased sensitivity to pain), early traumatic experiences (such as those discussed in Chapter 12), and cultural norms that may stigmatize psychological suffering as compared with physical suffering (APA, 2013).

Somatic symptom disorders have been studied largely in adults, especially because they imply a chronic, established pattern that is often not detected until young adulthood (Abramowitz & Braddock, 2011). Thus, their diagnostic applicability in reference to children and adolescents is questionable and seldom used (Eminson, 2007; Schulte & Petermann, 2011). Nonetheless, we raise this topic primarily because the multiple somatic symptoms in children, especially recurrent abdominal pain, may be developmental precursors to adult somatic symptom disorders (Essau, 2007).

Somatic symptom and related disorders include a new category known as **psychological factors affecting other medical conditions**. This category may be relevant to children and youths with existing medical symptoms or conditions because psychological factors, such as distress or poor coping, may influence their physical condition or its treatment. For example, a child with diabetes who is depressed and refuses to monitor and regulate her glucose level can affect her

Chronic illness and medical conditions affect over 12 million children and adolescents in North America.

health condition significantly. However, this diagnostic category does not apply to most children with chronic health conditions because it is the medical condition and its limitations that affect their psychological adjustment, not the other way around. In other words, psychological symptoms may develop in response to the stress of having or being diagnosed with a general medical condition. Rather than depression affecting the course of diabetes, as in the previous example, it is more likely that diabetes causes adjustment difficulties, which sometimes (but by no means always) include clinical disorders, such as depression. Thus, some children and adolescents with chronic illness accompanied by significant adjustment or behavioral problems may receive a diagnosis of *adjustment disorder,* which better accounts for the nature of the stressor (APA, 2013).

Progress in the development of effective medical treatments and cures for children with chronic illness has been spectacular over the past three decades, greatly prolonging the lives of many who previously would have died during infancy or childhood. Remarkably, the survival rate for certain types of cancer, such as acute lymphoblastic leukemia, has increased from about one in five children in the 1950s to four in five children today (Brown et al., 2007). At the same time, however, these advances and improved survival rates have led to greater child and adult morbidity. **Morbidity** refers to the various forms of physical and functional consequences and limitations that result from an illness. Increased morbidity implies that more children and adolescents are adapting to the challenges of a chronic illness. For these children, illness has become a chronic life situation and stressor, and it can have repercussions well into adulthood.

As children's survival has improved and life-threatening illnesses are better controlled, attention has moved away from the acute, infectious diseases to a broader emphasis on promoting children's health and development and assisting in the care of children with chronic illness or handicapping conditions (Canter & Roberts, 2012). Pediatric health psychologists are particularly active in helping children with chronic health disorders to successfully adapt and to attain an optimal quality of life.

To increase our awareness of the ways children with chronic disease learn to cope and adapt to physical and social challenges, we take a look at how children normally think of and express health concerns. This helps distinguish between adaptive and maladaptive coping reactions among children with chronic illness.

Normal Variations in Children's Health

We now recognize that children can communicate about their pain and discomfort about as well as adults do, but this was not always true. It was once thought that infants did not experience pain at all and that children were far less sensitive to pain than adults. Because children seemed less able to communicate about their pain, it was wrongly concluded that they had higher pain thresholds than adults. However, children do have a good concept of what pain is and how to express that they are feeling it (McAlpine & McGrath, 1999). Their concepts of pain and its causes, their descriptions of pain, and their specific pain experiences seem remarkably well formed by an early age, both for boys and girls. Consider this comment:

> It [stomachache] was like bees in your stomach—stinging your stomach, yellow jackets going ping, pong, bop inside—like something just chopped down your stomach. [6-year-old boy].

> It [earache] felt like something is inside your ear like a sticker from a rose bush poking deep inside your ear, like way harder than just pricking. [9-year-old boy] (Ross & Ross, 1984, p. 184)

It is unlikely that children simply pick up pain descriptions from their parents or others. Consider the child-like imagery used by a 7-year-old boy in describing a headache:

> Like there's this big monster in there, see, and he's growing like crazy and there's no room and he's pulling the two sides of my head apart he's getting so big. (Ross & Ross, 1984, p. 189).

Now picture this common scene: Since age 6, Jackie has informed her parents from time to time that she was "too sick" to go to school. She then would carefully provide them with a list of her symptoms: "My tummy hurts; I feel hot, my throat hurts; I can't feel my toes." Careful questioning would usually result in a further list of symptoms—in fact, most were suggested by one of her parents: "Does your leg hurt too?" [yes]; "How does your head feel?" [achy]; "What does your skin feel like?" [stingy]. The astute reader might note that these symptoms emerged at about the time Jackie was entering the first grade. Would you consider this situation to be typical of how children learn about physical symptoms and their connection to life's responsibilities?

Are somatic symptoms in children (such as those expressed by Jackie) normal and commonplace? To no one's surprise, about a third of typical school-aged children report using pain for secondary gains, such as increased parental and peer attention, and avoidance of school and athletic activities. Undeniably, one of the most common ways children express their fears, dislikes, and avoidance is to complain of aches and pains, often of uncertain or dubious origin.

Girls and boys show interesting differences in this respect. When they are asked, girls report more symptoms of pain and anxiety than boys do (Kröner-Herwig et al., 2011). Under stressful circumstances, girls are more likely to cry, cling, and seek emotional support, and boys are more likely to be uncooperative, avoidant, and stoic. Similarly, excessive somatic symptoms are associated with emotional disorders in girls and disruptive behavior disorders in boys (Egger et al., 1999; Jellesma et al., 2011; Rose & Rudolph, 2006). Does this imply that girls are somehow more sensitive to pain or less able to manage their fear and anxiety than boys? Yes and no. These gender differences stem from socialization expectations as well as biological differences. We are all familiar with the ways boys are encouraged to adopt stoic attitudes about pain, whereas girls are reinforced for passive, affective expression. Both boys and girls react to distress, but they express it according to how they have been taught and what they wish to receive. Therefore, these complaints are within the normal developmental range and do not merit a psychiatric label.

Some children may be more likely than others to experience recurrent pain and physical symptoms because of their family influences. For example, children with functional abdominal pain and similar forms of recurrent unexplained pain are more likely to identify someone in their family who often expresses pain than are children whose pain is due to known organic causes (Marshall et al., 2007). In addition, children of mothers with a somatic disorder are 4 times more likely to express physical symptoms when emotionally upset (Craig, Cox, & Klein, 2002; Guite et al., 2007). These unexplained, recurrent pain symptoms among children, therefore, seem to originate primarily from family *pain models* (Peterson et al., 2003). Children also learn healthy adaptational patterns at home and elsewhere. Children with well-developed social and academic competence, for instance, are less likely to respond to negative life events, such as divorce or hospitalizations, with amplified stress and pain reactions (Walker et al., 2007).

Let's turn our attention now to children who have chronic health problems or conditions. Each chronic illness has unique challenges. Children with diabetes face daily medical routines, but they have a relatively predictable prognosis; children with cancer experience unpleasant side effects of treatment and must also cope with the uncertain prognosis of their illness.

The one important thing that all chronic illnesses and medical conditions have in common is that they constitute a major stressor that challenges and absorbs both the child's and the family's available coping resources. Viewing chronic illness in this way—as a form of major stress requiring adaptation—has allowed researchers to identify factors that promote successful adaptation to chronic illness. This view also has advanced new ways to assist children in coping with these challenges, as we will see.

It is estimated that in North America, 10% to 20% of the child population suffers from some form of chronic health-related disorder or condition (including obesity, diabetes, asthma, and others), and the rate has been rising dramatically in recent years (Brown et al., 2007; Van Cleave, Gortmaker, & Perrin, 2010). Of these children, about two-thirds have mild conditions; the remainder have conditions that result in moderate to severe activity restrictions and bothersome treatment regimens (Peterson et al., 2003). Asthma is the most common chronic illness in childhood, followed by neurological and developmental disabilities and behavioral disorders. Fortunately, severe forms of chronic illnesses—those that pose major physical and intellectual limitations that interfere with children's daily lives—are relatively rare, but their combined rates are sizable.

Table 13.5 shows the incidence rates (i.e., number of new cases occurring in a specified population during a year) of selected chronic childhood diseases and medical conditions. Survival rates for many of these illnesses have greatly improved in recent years (Jemal et al., 2009); therefore, these rates reflect a large proportion of children who have survived these childhood illnesses until 20 years of age or older. The impact of living with HIV and AIDS, currently the sixth leading cause of death among 15- to 24-year-olds in the United States, likely will be a major health issue in the years to come (Garvie et al., 2009; Howland et al., 2007).

TABLE 13.5	Incidence Rates of Selected Chronic Illnesses in U.S. Children and Adolescents, Ages 0 to 19
Illness	**Incidence (per population annually)**
Asthma	19.6% of child population[a]
Cancers and tumors	16/100,000 children diagnosed each year[b]
Diabetes mellitus	24/100,000 children diagnosed each year[c]
Sickle-cell anemia	1/500 African American newborns[d]

[a]Prevalence of the total child/youth population (Akinbami, Moorman, & Liu, 2011).
[b]Bloom, Cohen, and Freeman (2011).
[c]Centers for Disease Control and Prevention (CDC) (2011a).
[d]Amendah et al. (2010).

Most chronic childhood illnesses do not discriminate in terms of social class and ethnicity—they can affect children from all walks of life. However, there are certain exceptions to how illnesses affect children, such as the specific conditions genetically determined by racial or ethnic descent. For example, cystic fibrosis affects primarily whites, and sickle-cell disease affects primarily persons of African descent (Thompson & Gustafson, 1996). African American children are about 3 times more likely to be hospitalized for asthma than are their white peers; this difference may be due to the conditions associated with low income and disadvantage (Brown et al., 2007).

Also, a troubling connection exists between socioeconomic status (SES), ethnicity, and survival rates among children and adults with cancer in particular (Wich et al., 2011). Despite attempts to achieve more equitable health care delivery, residents of poorer communities still may receive inferior quality of care, even in universal health care systems like those in Canada (Booth, et al., 2010), Korea (Son et al., 2011), and the United Kingdom (Stringhini et al., 2010). In addition, the poor may have other ailments that make cancer survival more difficult, or parents may be less inclined to seek medical attention if they have other major life stressors or if they are not aware of critical symptoms. In general, children in poor families are 5 times as likely to be in fair or poor health as children in families that are not poor (Bloom et al., 2011). People with adequate means generally have more options and control over their lives, which translates into greater opportunities for proper medical care for their children. Later in this chapter, we consider some ways to empower families and achieve a greater balance in their roles and available resources.

We now take a closer look at two specific illnesses—diabetes mellitus and childhood cancer—that are representative of the course and patterns of adaptation faced by children with chronic illness.

Diabetes Mellitus

AMANDA

Daily Struggle with Diabetes

Amanda, age 14, was diagnosed with insulin-dependent diabetes mellitus about a year ago. Like most teenagers, she leads an active life, and eating the proper foods is difficult enough without the added burden of daily glucose monitoring and insulin injections. She shared with us some of the ways this disease has affected her life, and how she copes with its demands and limitations:

Becoming diabetic has completely changed my life. My best friend is the insulin I take and the machine.

I use the machine to test my blood sugar four times a day by poking my finger and putting blood on a test strip.

From the reading I am able to adjust my insulin and what I must eat. I am forced to eat a healthy balanced meal regularly about six times every day. I try not to have a negative attitude because I now realize just how lucky I am. I do not know what I would do if I did not have my machine or all of the sugar-free foods that are now available. Not only did diabetes change my physical life, but it altered my mental life as well. It helped me look at my life and realize what was important to me. My close friend, Germaine, helped me get through the first year at school, when some of the other kids wondered why I had to use needles and couldn't eat the same things they do. My parents have been great, and even my younger brother lays off me when he knows I'm having a particularly bad day. In a way, I'm more aware of how important health is to us than most kids at school, and I don't take things for granted the way I used to. (Based on authors' case material.)

Amanda suffers from **insulin-dependent diabetes mellitus,** a lifelong metabolic disorder in which the body is unable to metabolize carbohydrates because the pancreas releases inadequate amounts of insulin. This lack of insulin has a domino effect on the body's ability to regulate appetite, metabolize carbohydrates into necessary energy, and maintain a balance of blood chemistry. The lack of insulin prohibits glucose from entering the cells, which forces glucose to accumulate in the bloodstream and cause *hyperglycemia*. Glucose also tells the regulatory cells of the hypothalamus when a person is hungry or full, so without this information, the person tends to eat constantly but does not gain weight (Thompson & Gustafson, 1996). A treatment regimen consisting of insulin injections, diet, and exercise is necessary to approximate a normal metabolic state. Although current treatment regimens have greatly improved the health status of people with diabetes, the condition is still associated with significant morbidity and mortality.

Diabetes affects boys and girls equally, and its incidence is increasing: a child born in North America in 2000 stands a one in three chance of being diagnosed with diabetes in his or her lifetime (Canadian Diabetes Association, 2014). Initial symptoms often include fatigue, thirst, hunger, frequent urination, and weight loss despite excessive eating. It is a progressive disease; the more chronic complications that occur during young adulthood or beyond, including circulatory problems, can lead to blindness, kidney failure, and accelerated cardiovascular disease (Siegel, 2008). Individuals with

Adolescents with chronic illness, such as diabetes, must adhere carefully to a daily treatment regimen.

diabetes have an increased risk of illness and death, including a risk of cardiovascular disease double that for the population without diabetes (Franco et al., 2007). Given the seriousness of the illness and the long-standing, intrusive treatment requirements, it is understandable that children with diabetes and their families have an increased risk for conflict and adjustment problems (Ellis et al., 2007).

Children with diabetes face daily treatment tasks to maintain their metabolic control, such as blood-glucose monitoring, dietary restraints, insulin injections, and learning how to balance energy demands and insulin needs (Peterson et al., 2003). **Metabolic control** is the degree to which the patient's glucose levels are maintained within the normal range. Children and adolescents must carefully monitor their insulin levels—too little insulin can result in a diabetic coma, too much insulin can result in an insulin reaction called *hypoglycemia*. Hypoglycemic episodes are extremely unpleasant and can include irritability, headaches, and shakiness. Adding to the complexity is the fact that illness and

stress can upset the relationship between glucose and required insulin levels (Schwartz et al., 2011).

Children and teens must carefully follow the instructions given to them by their physicians; that is, they must practice careful *regimen adherence*. Good regimen adherence and metabolic control are linked to the individuals' correct knowledge about their disease and its treatment, their belief that adherence is important, and adequate problem-solving skills (Drotar, 2013; Rasmussen et al., 2011). As we saw with Amanda, adolescence is a particularly difficult period because of the impact that the illness can have on self-esteem and social and educational experiences—adolescence is difficult enough without the added burden of these daily treatment tasks. Therefore, psychologists have become active in developing ways to promote regimen adherence and metabolic control by helping family members adapt to the demands of the condition (Schwartz et al., 2011). Behavioral strategies have been quite successful in this regard, especially with methods that reinforce symptom reduction or medication use and self-control methods that teach patients to regulate dosage and monitor their symptoms, blood glucose, and medications (Drotar, 2006; Elkin & Stoppelbein, 2008; Jaser & White, 2011).

Childhood Cancer

CHEN

A Determined Boy Fighting Leukemia

Chen, age 9, explains his feelings about childhood leukemia and its impact on his family and peer relations:

I've had cancer now for 3 years. They're still trying to fight it with the right medicine but nothing has worked yet. My friends come visit me—they're pretty OK with everything. But sometimes if you try and tell other kids about it they don't understand because they don't have it. To them we're normal. They don't have any kind of problems that hold them back from doing things. They don't have to worry about being in the hospital, checkups and things, to see how you're doing. You can tell your friends why you have to stop and rest awhile, but they don't really understand—they don't really want to—they want to keep on going. I've got lots of family who care about me and I worry for them. I guess I'm used to all the doctors and medicines I take. Not that I like them but I know it's the only thing that might help. But I liked having the ability to do anything with my friends (or even my parents). I want to be able to get up and go. I'd tell someone else going through this to stay strong and keep the faith. And speak up when you need something!

(continues)

(continued)

Chen's mother explains the ordeal he and his family have undergone since his diagnosis:

Chen received a bone marrow transplant from his brother over a year ago and, thankfully, his leukemia went into remission. But when we went back 1 year later for a checkup, we were told Chen had suffered a relapse—the cancer had overtaken the bone marrow, and his prognosis is poor. Now our family focuses on enjoying our time together and doing things with Chen. We are fortunate—my employer has gone out of his way to help me stay at home with Chen. Their support over the past year has been incredible. In fact, our whole community has shown tremendous support to our family. But his turn for the worse has made it difficult for us to do the things we have done over the past few months. We are angry, hopeful, depressed, joyous, saddened all the time. It is the worst roller coaster that we have ever ridden. Yet, Chen's medical condition has made us more determined to do more than we had ever hoped for, and the kindness shown toward our family has been overwhelming. (Based on authors' case material.)

It is difficult for most of us to imagine what Chen and his family have experienced. Their words acknowledge the importance of their strength and determination and their human kindness when faced with a serious childhood illness, which in this case was terminal. Cancer can strike children very suddenly, more so than with adults, and children are often at a more advanced stage of cancer when they are first diagnosed (Brown et al., 2007). White children suffer the highest rates of cancer as compared to other ethnic groups, but reasons for this disparity are not known. Incidence rates for Hispanic and Asian/Pacific Islander children fall between those for African Americans and whites, while rates for American Indians are much lower than for any other group (Bloom et al., 2011).

<Caption TBD>

Ap images/Lea Suzuki,Pool

The most common form of childhood cancer is acute lymphoblastic leukemia (ALL), which accounts for close to half of all forms of childhood cancer (U.S. Cancer Statistics Working Group, 2013). ALL is actually a group of heterogeneous diseases in which there is a malignancy of the bone marrow, which produces blood cells. In ALL, the bone marrow produces malignant cells called "lymphoblasts" that progressively replace normal bone marrow with fewer red blood cells and more white blood cells, causing anemia, infection, and easy bruising or excessive bleeding (Friedman, Latham, & Dahlquist, 1998). Childhood cancer used to be fatal, but advances in medical treatment have resulted in dramatic improvements in survival rates. Still, long-term complications such as recurrent malignancy, growth retardation, neuropsychological deficits, cataracts, and infertility pose a risk to survival and quality of life.

Like those with diabetes, children with cancer undergo complicated medical treatment regimens, especially during the first 2 to 3 years after diagnosis. In addition, they face school absences, significant treatment side effects, and an uncertain prognosis. Chemotherapy and radiation therapy can cause hair loss and weight changes, as well as nausea, vomiting, increased fatigue, endocrine and growth retardation, and a depressed immune system (Friedman et al., 1998). Children with cancer also must cope with painful medical procedures, such as venipuncture, bone marrow aspiration, and lumbar puncture. Treatment requires children to be away from friends and some family members, which hinders their psychosocial development. Therefore, the psychosocial aspects of pediatric cancer have focused on managing the distress related to the multiple diagnostic and treatment procedures these children face.

Although approximately 80% of pediatric cancer patients survive, about half of the survivors will have a serious physical or mental illness as adults (Krull et al., 2010; Kwak et al., 2013; Zebrack et al., 2002). The most common illnesses include infertility, chronic anxiety, and recurrent cancers (Cantrell, 2011; Stuber et al., 2011). Many patients require long-term care into adulthood because they never learned the life-skills necessary for self-care.

Development and Course

Children with chronic illnesses are more likely than their healthy peers to suffer emotional and behavioral adjustment problems stemming from the burden of their disease and its treatment, especially children with chronic illness accompanied by disability (Hysing et al., 2009). Understandably, children whose normal functional abilities are limited face the greatest challenges in everyday activities; these challenges, in turn, increase behavioral, social, and school-adjustment difficulties. These problems are most often expressed as internalizing symptoms, such as anxiety, depression, or post-traumatic stress disorder, or a combination of both internalizing and externalizing problems (Pao & Bosk, 2011; Pinquart & Shen, 2011; Wechsler & Sánchez-Iglesias, 2013).

To keep these symptoms in perspective, one must recognize that the adjustment of children with chronic illness typically is better than that of children referred to mental health clinics for non-health-related problems (Wechsler & Sánchez-Iglesias, 2013). For the most part, children with chronic illness are exhibiting stress-related symptoms; the incidence of DSM-5-type disorders among these children is actually low. For example, a meta-analysis of 340 studies revealed that symptoms of depression among children with various chronic health conditions are only slightly higher than those of their healthy peers, an encouraging indication of successful adaptation among the vast majority of these children (Pinquart & Shen, 2011). Moreover, children with diabetes and children with cancer on average report symptoms of anxiety, depression, and low self-esteem within the normal range for their age and gender (Brown et al., 2007; Wechsler & Sánchez-Iglesias, 2013).

Although populations of chronically ill children are at risk for initial adjustment difficulties, it is difficult to say what causes particular symptoms or why some children adapt more successfully than others. When one considers how these children must cope with unpredictable events and challenges almost every day, it is understandable that they would have increased stress-related symptoms. It is especially encouraging to know that most can adapt successfully to the course and consequences of their illness. Symptoms of anxiety, depression, and anger can be thought of as normal responses to stressful experiences associated with the long-term illness and treatment regimens, rather than as psychiatric disorders (Wechsler & Sánchez-Iglesias, 2013). This is similar to the adjustment problems faced by children with intellectual disabilities and children who have been abused or neglected. Most children with chronic illness show considerable resilience in the face of stressful experiences associated with their condition, and we should exercise caution in applying psychiatric labels or descriptors that fail to capture the context and nature of their circumstances.

Effect on Family Members

The field of pediatric health psychology has clearly adopted a focus on the important role of family functioning in the adjustment of children with chronic illness.

The child's circumstances may result in family cohesion and support, as we saw in Amanda's and Chen's families, or it may result in family disruption and crisis. As parents try to understand and cope with the news of their child's diagnosis, they must at the same time start to accept that their child might always be different from other children. How they react and accept these realities determines, to a large extent, how their child and other siblings will react and adapt. Parents who fail to resolve this crisis are more likely to have problems with attachment and child-rearing, which further complicates the stressful nature of the child's illness (Mullins et al., 2007).

Learning that a child has a life-threatening disease causes trauma and stress to all family members and, in fact, qualifies as a traumatic event that can precipitate post-traumatic stress disorder (PTSD) (Kwak et al., 2013). A mother of an infant born with a chronic disability describes her initial reaction:

> I felt like I was bouncing around on a raft in the middle of a terrible storm. I didn't know where I was, where I was going, or what wave was going to break over my head next. Most of the time, I just hung on. Hanging on, I discovered, is the key to survival. (Medvescek, 1997, p. 67)

Many parents of children with chronic illness report that their fears resurface and memories return whenever their child has only a common illness, like a cold or flu (Pai et al., 2007). About 10% of mothers and fathers suffer symptoms of PTSD, a rate that is comparable to that for other types of traumatic stress exposure (Barakat, Hocking, & Kazak, 2013). Fortunately, the children themselves do not typically suffer PTSD-related symptoms upon learning of their disorder, probably because they are very young at the time of diagnosis. However, children's memories of stressful procedures play a role in their experience of distress, and some survivors of childhood cancer recall disturbing memories of the medical procedures many years later (Stuber & Shemesh, 2006).

Families affect the behavior of children with chronic health problems, as they do the behavior of the healthy children. No one type of chronic illness poses a significantly greater risk of adjustment than another. Thus, factors associated with children's situations—such as family stress and resources—may be more critical to their adaptation than the challenges posed by the illness alone (Peterson & Drotar, 2006). The degree to which parents can assist their older children in developing more autonomy and control over their treatment regimens in a nonconflictual manner predicts the likelihood that the teen will adhere to the treatment regimen. The normal conflict observed in parent–teenager relationships is heightened in families in which the teen is trying to incorporate a treatment regimen into a changing lifestyle. For example, drinking alcohol is a significant risk for teens with diabetes; therefore, conversations and parental expectations regarding experimentation with substance use often are heightened because alcohol use is more deleterious (Jaser & White, 2011).

The amount of concordance between parent and teen perceptions of who is making decisions about treatment is not what predicts adherence to treatments—it is the degree of conflict in the parent–teen relationship (Drotar, 2013). Thus, parents who can help their teen in a nonconfrontational manner to maintain adherence (regardless of whether they agree with their child about who is in fact making treatment decisions) will increase their teen's health and adaptation. In general, the following stress factors that parents face are quite similar across all types of pediatric chronic illness: financial and physical burdens, changes in parenting roles, sibling resentment, child adjustment problems, social isolation, frequent hospitalizations, and grief (Alriksson-Schmidt, Wallander, & Biasini, 2007). It comes as no surprise, therefore, that couples with chronically ill children report more marital conflict, poor communication, role incongruity, and a lack of intimacy and positive affect (Rodrigues & Patterson, 2007).

The point is worth repeating: Despite these psychological and tangible repercussions, many children with chronic illness adapt favorably to these challenges, as do their families (Long & Marsland, 2011). Perceived social support and parental adaptation are key components aiding the child's adaptation, since primary caregivers play an important role in their children's stress and coping abilities. Specifically, mothers who perceive lower levels of illness-related stress, use more adaptive and active ways to cope with stress and problems, and perceive their families as more supportive than conflictual are more likely to show normal adjustment levels themselves (Thompson & Gustafson, 1996). Regardless of the circumstances, we often see this connection: When maternal abilities remain intact, child and family functioning is less impaired. This illustrates the reciprocal relationship between children's adjustment and parental stress and distress—healthy parental adjustment is related to healthy child adjustment, and vice versa. (Most research has considered only the role of mothers on child adjustment, but the specific influence of fathers on children's coping and adaptation to chronic illness is being recognized [Ware & Raval, 2007].) Thus, parental adjustment is one of the important correlates of children's adjustment to chronic illness.

Siblings of children with a chronic illness also experience heightened social and mental health problems.

They tend to have more internalizing symptoms, such as depression and anxiety, lower cognitive scores, and fewer peer activities (Bellin & Kovacs, 2006). These outcomes are worse for chronic illnesses that require daily treatment regimens, which suggests that the increased caregiving demands faced by parents and the subsequent decreased amounts of parental attention for siblings contribute to their maladjustment. Despite these problems, many children with a chronic illness benefit from sibling relationships, and vice versa, because of the positive bond that is often formed between them (Havermans et al., 2011; Long & Marsland, 2011).

Social Adjustment and School Performance

Children's adjustment to chronic illness is reflected not only in terms of psychological distress, but also through developmental accomplishments in social adjustment, peer relationships, and school performance. Because chronic illness results in lifestyle interruptions that interfere with opportunities for social interaction, children with more severe, disruptive illnesses tend to suffer in social adjustment (La Greca, Bearman, & Moore, 2002). This maladjustment often is expressed by children displaying more submissive behavior with their peers and engaging in fewer social activities overall (Meijer et al., 2002).

Consider the peer relationships of children with cancer. Chen explained how the other children did not understand why he could not join in or behave the same as they did—to them he looked normal, so he must be okay. Negative or ill-informed reactions from peers and others are, unfortunately, a fact of life for some children with chronic illness. In a longitudinal study of children with cancer, adolescents were perceived by their teachers as less sociable, less prone toward leadership, and more socially isolated and withdrawn than their peers (Noll et al., 1991). Similar problems in social adjustment are evident among children with illnesses that affect primarily the CNS—cerebral palsy, spina bifida, and brain tumors—because of the impact of these disorders on cognitive abilities such as social judgment (Hysing et al., 2009).

School adjustment and performance is another domain in which children and adolescents with chronic illness are at increased risk for adjustment difficulties. Risk may stem from two sources: primary effects of the illness or its treatment, and secondary consequences of the illness, such as fatigue, absenteeism, or psychological stress (Witt, Riley, & Coiro, 2003). Primary effects of the illness on school performance are especially evident among children with brain-related illnesses. They must undergo aggressive treatment regimens that put a heavy toll on the CNS, especially for younger children (Brown et al., 2007). The most common neurocognitive effects appear in nonverbal abilities and attention or concentration functions (Mulhern et al., 2004; Reeves et al., 2006). Short-term memory, speed of processing, visuomotor coordination, and sequencing ability also frequently are affected (Reeves et al., 2006). Thus, about half of the children with brain-related illnesses are placed in special education settings or do not attend school. In contrast, children with physical, non-brain-related illnesses tend to have normal educational placements; however, they continue to have problems with reading, which may be one indirect effect of chronic illness and school absence (Witt et al., 2003).

How Children Adapt: A Biopsychosocial Model

We have described the adjustment difficulties of children with chronic illness in general terms, but we know that each child's illness and family situation is different. Some children, like Amanda and Chen, have supportive families with adequate resources, but others may not. Countless events can influence children's adaptation to chronic illness; no single factor explains why some children adjust more readily than others.

How do we make sense of the numerous factors influencing children's adjustment? When a single-factor theory is not a sufficient explanation, researchers often develop multifactorial theories that link the most important variables in conceptual and meaningful ways. The *transactional stress and coping model* explains how children's adaptation to chronic illness is influenced not only by the nature of the illness itself, but also by personal and family resources (Gustafson et al., 2006; Thompson et al., 1994). This model helps make sense of the complicated processes that shape children's outcomes.

The transactional stress and coping model emphasizes the stressful nature of chronic illness, which compels the child and family members to adapt. How they accomplish the adaptation is a key factor in children's outcomes.

Illness parameters encompass the type of illness and the severity of the illness, including visible disfigurement and functional impairment. Demographic parameters include the gender, age, and SES of the child, which also can affect the impact of the illness. The model then proposes that important child and family processes mediate the illness–outcome relationship, beyond the illness and demographic factors. Important psychological mediators involve parental adjustment, child adjustment, and their interrelationship, as described next.

Family support plays a crucial role in helping children cope with chronic illness.

Illness Parameters

One would expect that children's psychosocial adjustment varies as a function of their medical condition. Some illnesses have an uncertain course and others have dire effects on everyday activities, adding stress along the way. Different chronic illnesses have many features in common, though, so it often makes sense to study children's adjustment in relation to illness-related dimensions, or parameters, rather than their adjustment to specific illnesses. The common dimensions that vary among different illnesses include things such as the extent to which the illness:

▶ Is visible to others, or involves physical deformity.

▶ Is severe and life-threatening.

▶ Has a worsening or fatal prognosis versus a stable or improving prognosis.

▶ Requires intrusive or painful procedures.

▶ Affects the child's functional status, such as physical or cognitive impairments that affect performance of everyday tasks. (Thompson & Gustafson, 1996)

Children with chronic illness face different challenges along each of these dimensions, so naturally their adjustment may be affected accordingly. Across all medical conditions, the illness parameters that play the most significant role in children's adjustment are *severity*, *prognosis*, and *functional status* (Lavigne & Faier-Routman, 1993). Functional status seems to be especially important in terms of cognitive impairments, such as conditions that involve the brain and CNS.

Personal Characteristics

Chronic medical conditions require both children and family members to accept and cope with considerable stress and uncertainty. Which child characteristics and resources might favor successful adaptation? A child's sex is one consideration: Boys with chronic illness show more adjustment problems overall than girls. However, this sex difference depends on the dimension of adjustment and who is reporting the information. Boys are described by parents and teachers as having more behavior problems than girls; however, girls are more likely than boys to self-report anxiety, depression, and negative perceptions of physical appearance (Miller & La Greca, 2005).

Although children's overall adjustment seldom differs as a function of current age or age at the onset of the illness, economic and health disparities that exist among ethnic minority children and their families play a contributing role. These disparities not only affect the course and treatment of chronic illnesses, but also have a pronounced effect on quality of life and risk of disease and disability. Being poor is a risk factor for many stressful life events, but being poor and having a health problem greatly increases distress and adjustment problems (Greenberg, Raymond, & Leeder, 2011). Similarly, treatment studies on chronic illness in children and adolescents have not addressed important cultural issues that affect treatment outcome, especially compliance with the treatment regimen (Clay, Mordhorst, & Lend, 2002; Elkin & Stoppelbein, 2008).

Not surprisingly, children with greater intellectual ability and acquired strengths in their self-concept and coping skills also show more positive psychological adjustment, regardless of their medical condition. Specifically, children's accurate appraisal of perceived stress—how they interpret and react to daily events and hassles associated with illness management—leads to a better sense of well-being and fewer symptoms of distress and maladjustment (Pai et al., 2006). Chen states this well:

> I now realize that life is full of a series of tests. You never know what is around the corner, but you have to take it as it comes. A positive attitude, and remembering that I have friends and family for support, helps me get through some of the rough days.

Family Adaptation and Functioning

If chronic illness is considered a stressor affecting all family members to some extent, then child adjustment depends in part on the degree of stress and symptoms experienced by other family members, especially the primary caregiver. Undeniably, the family environment assumes greater importance in the lives of children with a chronic illness, in part because a closer parent–child interaction often is necessary to manage the disease.

The transactional model considers parental adaptation to be a key mediator of the relationship between child illness and adjustment for both child and parent. How does a parent "adapt" in a way that favors healthy outcomes? According to the model, parental adaptation is a function of three major processes: (1) how they manage daily stress and view their self-efficacy, as seen with Chen's mother; (2) whether they use active, solution-focused coping; and (3) family functioning and perceived support. Successful parental adaptation, in turn, leads to better parental adjustment and healthier family communication and conflict-resolution skills (Wysocki et al., 2008). Ultimately, of course, parents' positive adjustment greatly increases the likelihood of more positive child outcomes. Parents' perceptions of illness are one aspect of parental adaptation that plays a key role in promoting their child's health. Perceptions of child vulnerability are related to increased social anxiety in their children and more school absences (Long & Marsland, 2011).

Family functioning often is defined in terms of the availability of two types of primary family resources: *utilitarian* and *psychological*. Utilitarian family resources relate to the practical demands of caring for a child with a disability, such as financial resources and parental education, which influence their ability to understand the illness and seek beneficial assistance for their child. Psychological resources are less tangible but often are considered far more important—how family members support one another, relate to each other and to persons outside the family, and resolve conflicts. Together these two types of family resources account for considerable variance in the behavioral and social adjustment of chronically ill children (Robinson et al., 2007).

Intervention

The psychological impact of chronic illness occurs through the disruption of normal processes of child development and family functioning. Fortunately, this impact can be lessened and adaptation can be strengthened by the use of psychosocial interventions that reduce stress, enhance social problem-solving skills, and promote effective child-rearing methods. These various methods often entail stress-management and skill-building components to assist children and family members in their continuous process of adaptation.

The basic goal of intervention is to enhance the quality of life for the children and their families. Ways to achieve this goal have taken a dramatic shift over the past four decades, given the strong interest of pediatric and health psychologists. Prior to the mid-1970s, intervention efforts primarily were based on a child-centered, medically based model. The health professional was the expert, the child was the patient, and parents were passive observers. Today, parents are expected to participate in the decision-making process and their child's educational planning, which has led to family-centered interventions. In effect, families are now recognized as important resources, and they are seen as part of the solution; they are kept in the forefront of children's intervention needs, not in the background.

Empowering Families

This underlying philosophy of family empowerment reduces stress and dependency and enables families to obtain the necessary information to make informed decisions and take competent actions. Chen's family members, for example, took an active role in enhancing his quality of life and were not frightened away or uninformed about his needs and their opportunities. His mother explains:

> Physiotherapy has helped Chen be less dependent on mom and dad. The goal is for him to think ahead and be prepared to do things on his own. An example is at bedtime getting his clothes out and onto the bed for the following morning. Then in the morning he can get himself dressed and transferred into his chair by himself.

Support groups and educational programs of various types offer considerable benefits to children and other family members. Helping families connect with one another and share their common experiences and concerns generates both personal power and important resources for change (Barakat et al., 2013; Drotar, 2006). Participation is the active agent in empowerment, and a cooperative health professional–family model encourages individuals to support one another while providing a venue for modeling positive attitudes and values. Similarly, educational programs that provide information and skills training to family members often are beneficial. The most beneficial programs promote knowledge and self-management of the illness, reintegration of children into the school setting, and support and coordination of care among parents of children with chronic illness (Canter & Roberts, 2012; Drotar & Bonner, 2009). Gaining more knowledge

about their child's disease promotes greater parental understanding of the child and the overall effect of the disease on the family.

In short, treatment-related activities for children with chronic illness often are based on the needs of the entire family. However, these efforts must fit the degree to which parents want to be—and realistically can be—involved in their child's overall care. Intervention methods that favor these adaptive processes adhere to medical regimens and psychologically based approaches to help children cope with the pain that is associated with invasive medical procedures and illness, as described in the next section.

Helping Children Cope

Throughout our discussion of children with chronic illness, we have seen how they must cope with numerous stressful circumstances, ranging from painful medical procedures to peer rejection and functional limitations. For this reason, considerable effort has been placed on ways to enhance their successful coping through support groups (see A Closer Look 13.1) and recreational activities (see A Closer Look 13.2). Much of this work focuses on coping with painful medical procedures, yet these methods also apply to other settings and circumstances, including at school or during home routines. Parental involvement and adaptation are, once again, key components in children's coping; to effectively assist their children, parents must maximize their sense of control over the outcome and progress of their children's health (Robinson et al., 2007).

Enhancing adaptation and quality of life of children with chronic illness similarly requires that children comply as much as possible with medical regimens, both inside and outside the doctor's office. Since children often do not comply with even simpler tasks—like following directions, eating what they should, or getting ready for school—how can we expect them to comply with the unpleasant demands of medical procedures? The significance of these procedures has caused the emphasis in pediatric health psychology to shift to helping children and their parents cope with necessary protocols, rather than developing ways to make them comply.

Evidence suggests that most children and adults do best if a stressful medical procedure is explained first and they are given an opportunity to see what is going to happen. Accordingly, interventions for reducing stress and managing pain during pediatric procedures have applied behavioral and cognitive approaches that emphasize *coping and stress management* (Hermann, 2011). Children who actively seek information about impending painful events show improved adjustment and less distress (Williams, Blount, & Walker, 2011).

Virtual Support Groups

In her private room at New York City's Mount Sinai Medical Center, 12-year-old Lauren peers intently into the colorful screen of a computer monitor. Lauren was diagnosed with a malignant tumor in her right wrist; 9 months of chemotherapy followed, and the radius bone in her right forearm was replaced with a metal rod. But today her mischievous brown eyes and smile light up the room as she plays. Finally tiring of the game, she clicks her way out and uses the computer to place a video call to one of her friends. "I've had bothersome moments," Lauren says after completing the call. "Like when I was in intensive care, and I wasn't allowed to do anything or see anyone. But this system lets me talk to kids from other hospitals who have the same thing as I do. I realized I'm not alone, and that made me feel better."

The system that cheers Lauren and children like her is an interactive network called STARBRIGHT World (SBW). For some of the children, SBW helps speed their recovery; for those less fortunate, it helps provide a measure of pleasure, comfort, diversion, and solace in their last months and weeks. SBW is a safe and secure online community where kids and teens living with serious illnesses can connect with each other. Kids on SBW can chat, read and post to bulletin boards, email, search

Child with chronic illness can speak to others who are going through the same thing via Web technology.

for friends with similar illnesses, participate in fun events and contests, surf pre-screened Web sites, and play games.

Source: The Starbright Foundation.

A Summer Retreat

Promoting social adjustment among children with a chronic illness can be difficult, but enrolling them in summer camps for children with similar illnesses is one way of encouraging social interaction with peers. Camp Oochigeas, the first residential camp for pediatric cancer patients in Canada, is an example of a place where children with similar medical issues can come together and share their experiences. Campers come for a free 2-week stay and participate in a number of camping activities with rest hours and medical regimens built in to their schedule.

Going away to summer camp provides these children with a chance to interact with their peers and be accepted, and to realize they are not the only ones coping with a chronic illness. It boosts their confidence and self-esteem and provides them with a social network that is often missing because of being out of school or feeling different from everyone else. "At a camp like Oochigeas, no one really pays attention to the fact that you have cancer because everyone does." It also gives their families a much needed break from the responsibility of caring for a child with a chronic illness, and it encourages the child to develop some independence and self-care skills. Often, the developmental task of gaining self-care skills and autonomy from parents is delayed for these children because of

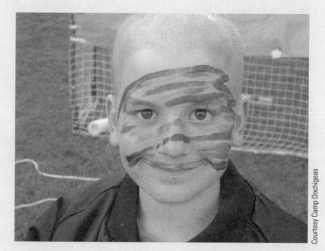

A child with chronic illness attending summer camp.

the nature of their illness. Camp is a way for both the child and parents to have a positive separation experience (in contrast to hospital visits), and to recognize the need for appropriate levels of independence (Odar, Canter, & Roberts, 2013).

Source: Camp OOCHIGEAS (2006).

In addition, parental and family functioning, effective child-rearing strategies to reinforce desired behaviors, and a positive doctor–patient relationship all contribute to children's improved adherence to the requirements of monitoring and treating their illness (Drotar, 2013).

In general, there are two main psychological approaches to helping children cope with stressful medical procedures and chronic and recurrent pain: providing information and training them in coping skills (Thompson & Gustafson, 1996). Information strategies offer verbal explanations and demonstrations as well as modeling the procedure, which reduce distress because this makes the medical procedure more predictable (Jaaniste, Hayes, & von Baeyer, 2007). Coping strategies involve teaching the various coping skills of deep breathing, attention distraction, muscle relaxation, relaxing imagery, emotive imagery, and behavioral rehearsal (e.g., children may be asked to imagine themselves as superheroes undergoing a test of their powers) (Dahlquist, 1999). Children are encouraged to identify specific stressors associated with their illness (e.g., giving themselves an injection) and to learn ways to handle those stressors and prevent distress or failure. Amanda, for instance, coped with having to administer injections by thinking of positive things in her life.

Parents can serve as coaches during the stress and coping procedures and help their children rehearse coping skills both at home and in the clinic (Walker et al., 2007). Not only does using these coping skills lead to the reduction of pain and physical symptoms, but using them also leads to a wide range of benefits that include fewer health-care contacts and school absences, and less interference with family functioning (Bromberg, Gil, & Schanberg, 2011). To help children cope with invasive medical procedures, parents are encouraged to use distraction, contingent praise, and active directives ("take a deep breath now"), but they should avoid explanations, vague commands, or criticism (Hermann, 2011; Wohlheiter & Dahlquist, 2013). Because of its demonstrated benefit, cognitive–behavioral therapy for children with chronic medical conditions that require painful medical procedures has become routine (Elkin & Stoppelbein, 2008).

Section Summary

Chronic Illness

- Children with chronic illness are at increased risk for psychosocial problems, which generally reflect their attempts to cope with stress.
- Children respond to the stress of chronic conditions in many different ways, and adjustment problems are more likely among children with increased disability. Adjustment problems may appear in the form of behavioral and emotional distress symptoms, such as low self-esteem, lack of social competence, poor school performance, and, sometimes, psychiatric disorders.
- Many children and their families adapt favorably to the challenges associated with chronic illness. Perceived social support and maternal adaptation are key components aiding their adaptation.
- Recent shifts to greater family empowerment and parental involvement have resulted in innovative ways to help children cope with the challenges of chronic illness. Psychosocial interventions assist children's adaptation to chronic illness by enhancing their social problem-solving skills and coping skills, and by reinforcing effective child-rearing methods.

ADOLESCENT SUBSTANCE-USE DISORDERS

Drugs are a waste of time. They destroy your memory and your self-respect and everything that goes along with your self-esteem.

—Kurt Cobain

Let's begin this section with a short quiz. Many of us believe we have a good understanding of the nature and extent of substance use in our peer culture, so please look at A Closer Look 13.3 before reading this section to see if you know the facts! As you probably will discover, many myths remain about substance use that merit greater education and awareness, especially among the most vulnerable youths. Although most adolescents experiment with substances ranging from cigarettes to street drugs without experiencing adverse effects, the risks include increased mortality and morbidity related to impaired driving, unsafe sexual practices, aggression, and similar concerns (Earleywine, 2009; Williams, Holmbeck, & Greenley, 2002). Frequent and prolonged consumption not only increases their risk of developing a substance-use disorder, but it also interferes with the development of important psychosocial skills in young adulthood (Haller et al., 2010).

The use and abuse of substances (e.g., nicotine, alcohol, marijuana, and other drugs) is an increasing area of concern, particularly in adolescents. Substance abuse has physical implications for the developing child or adolescent, and it may produce symptoms that mimic other psychopathological behaviors. Substance abuse is also related to a wide variety of psychological disorders.

Substance-related and addictive disorders in DSM-5 encompasses 10 separate classes of drugs, including alcohol, caffeine, cannabis, hallucinogens, inhalants, opioids, sedatives, stimulants, tobacco, and other (or unknown) substances. Gambling has been added in DSM-5 as an addictive disorder. **Substance-use disorders (SUDS)** during adolescence involve self-administration of any of these substances that alters mood, perception, or brain functioning, resulting in **substance abuse** or

substance dependence (Brown, Tomlinson, & Winward, 2013). Whereas almost all abused substances can lead to psychological dependence, some also extend to physical dependence. *Psychological dependence* refers to the subjective feeling of needing the substance to adequately function. *Physical dependence* occurs when the body adapts to the substance's constant presence, and *tolerance* refers to requiring more of the substance to experience an effect once obtained at a lower dose. Another aspect of physical dependence is the experience of withdrawal, an adverse physiological symptom that occurs when consumption of an abused substance is ended abruptly and is thus removed from the body.

The common DSM-5 diagnostic criteria for all SUDs are shown in Table 13.6 (APA, 2013). The central diagnostic feature is straightforward: a problematic pattern of substance use leading to significant impairment or distress. To meet this criterion, an adolescent (or adult) must show two or more significant clinical signs of distress for at least 12 months. The 11 possible signs of distress shown in Table 13.6 reflect four groupings of

TABLE 13.6 | **Diagnostic Criteria for Substance-Use Disorder**

(A) A problematic pattern of substance use leading to clinically significant impairment or distress, as manifested by at least two of the following, occurring within a 12-month period: **DSM-5**

(1) Substance is often taken in larger amounts or over a longer period than was intended.

(2) There is a persistent desire or unsuccessful effort to cut down or control substance use.

(3) A great deal of time is spent in activities necessary to obtain substance, use the substance, or recover from its effects.

(4) There is a craving or a strong desire or urge to use the substance.

(5) Recurrent substance use results in failure to fulfill major role obligations at work, school, or home (e.g., repeated absences or poor work performance related to substance use; substance-related absences, suspensions, or expulsions from school; neglect of children or household).

(6) Continued substance use despite having persistent or recurrent social or interpersonal problems caused or exacerbated by the effects of the substance.

(7) Important social, occupational, or recreational activities are given up or reduced because of substance use.

(8) There is recurrent substance use in situations in which it is physically hazardous (e.g., driving an automobile or operating a machine when impaired by substance use.

(9) Substance use is continued despite knowledge of having a persistent or recurrent physical or psychological

(continues)

TABLE 13.6 | **Diagnostic Criteria for** Substance-Use Disorder *(continued)*

problem that is likely to have been caused or exacerbated by the substance.

(10) Tolerance, as defined by either or both of the following:

  a. A need for markedly increased amounts of substance to achieve intoxication or desired effect.

  b. Markedly diminished effect with continued use of the same amount of the substance.

(11) Withdrawal, as manifested by either of the following:

  a. The characteristic withdrawal syndrome for a substance.

  b. The same (or a closely related) substance is taken to relieve or avoid withdrawal symptoms.

Specify if:

In early remission: None of the criteria have been met for at least 3 months but for less than 12 months (with the exception of "craving")

In sustained remission: None of the criteria have been met at any time during a period of 12 months or longer (with the exception of "craving")

Specify if:

In a controlled environment: This additional specifier is used if the individual is in an environment where access to substance is restricted.

Specify current severity:

Mild: Presence of two to three symptoms

Moderate: Presence of four to five symptoms

Severe: Presence of six or more symptoms

Source: *Diagnostic and Statistical Manual of Mental Disorders*, 5th ed. (Copyright © 2013). American Psychiatric Association.

symptoms that capture the core features of this diagnosis (APA, 2013): *impaired control* (Criteria 1 to 4); *social impairment* (Criteria 5 to 7); *risky use* (Criteria 8 and 9); and *pharmacological criteria* (Criteria 10 and 11).

As with other disorders described in this textbook, these criteria do not adequately consider important developmental differences between adults and adolescents. Substance-abusing adolescents experience withdrawal symptoms, but their physiological dependence and symptoms are less common than the withdrawal symptoms experienced by adults. Adolescents are more likely to show cognitive and affective features associated with substance abuse and/or withdrawal, such as disorientation or mood swings (Brown et al., 2013; Kenneson, Funderburk, & Maisto, 2013).

SUDs among youths also differ from those of adults in terms of their pattern of use, which is likely a function of the restrictions on availability. For example, adolescents tend to drink less often, but drink larger amounts at any one time than adults drink (i.e., binge drinking), which is associated with acute health and social risks (Chassin et al., 2013). Adolescents' substance use also is strongly influenced by peers, their desire for autonomy and experimentation with adult "privileges," and the level of parental supervision they receive (Branstetter, Low, & Furman, 2011; Lippold, Greenberg, & Collins, 2013). These influences affect the expression and features of the SUDs in ways that differ from those of adults.

Prevalence and Course

It should come as little surprise that alcohol remains the most prevalent substance used, and abused, by adolescents. As shown in ● Figure 13.2, two-thirds of high school seniors, over half of 10th-graders, and a third of those in 8th grade report that they have used alcohol over the past year, based on 2012 survey data from over 45,000´students (Johnston et al., 2013a). About one-quarter of these teens report a history of binge drinking, defined as episodic heavy drinking of five or more drinks in a row (inexplicably, recent rates of binge drinking in Canada fall closer to 50% [Young et al., 2011]).

Cigarette smoking has been on the decline, perhaps because of significant prevention efforts and health warnings; in the month leading up to the survey, one in six high school seniors had smoked cigarettes (the lowest levels since surveys started being conducted over 30 years ago). As daily cigarette smoking has decreased,

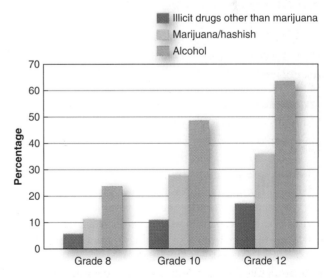

● **FIGURE 13.2** | Trends in annual prevalence of use of various drugs for 8th-, 10th-, and 12th-graders.

Data from *Monitoring the Future*, by Johnston et al. 2013a.

daily marijuana use is increasing among adolescents (daily use now stands at 1.1%, 3.5%, and 6.5% in grades 8, 10, and 12; Johnston et al., 2013a). The number of adolescents who have used MDMA (i.e., ecstasy), opiates, cocaine, and crack had also been increasing, but more recent findings suggest that the use of these drugs is now in decline, as is the number of adolescents using hallucinogens and inhalants (Johnston et al., 2013a).

Given the relatively high levels of substance use among adolescents, it is not surprising that a significant portion meet criteria for a diagnosis of substance abuse or substance dependence. Community-based samples of youths estimate that about 12% of American adolescents met criteria for substance abuse or dependence (National Center on Addiction and Substance Abuse at Columbia University, 2011). Not surprisingly, much higher rates of these disorders (about one in three) are reported among youths with histories of other mental health problems, or with involvement in the child welfare or juvenile justice systems (Colder et al., 2013; Fidalgo, da Silveira, & da Silveira, 2008; Wright, Fagan, & Pinchevsky, 2013).

Age at Onset

A certain amount of substance use during adolescence is normative behavior; therefore, researchers have looked at several factors that may differentiate trajectories of use that are relatively benign from those that have lasting significance. Age at first use is one of the most widely supported risk factors for the onset of substance-use problems and subsequent disorders (Brown et al., 2013). The Canadian National Longitudinal Survey of Youth (NLSY), for example, found that the odds of developing alcohol dependence decreased by 9% for each year that the onset of drinking was delayed (Grant, Stinson, & Harford, 2001). In general, researchers find that alcohol use before age 14 is a strong predictor of subsequent alcohol abuse or dependence, especially when early drinking is followed by rapid escalation in the quantity of alcohol consumption (Chassin et al., 2013).

Sex and Ethnicity

Although past surveys have found that girls typically use fewer types of drugs and use them less often than boys, sex differences in the lifetime prevalence rates of substance use are converging, due mostly to increased substance use among girls. By 2005, girls caught up to boys by the 10th grade and the rates have remained equivalent ever since. Similarly, rates of diagnoses for SUDs no longer differ significantly between boys and girls (Johnston et al., 2013a).

Ethnic differences in rates of substance use and abuse in the 30 days leading up to a survey are shown in ● Figure 13.3. For many years black or African American youths had substantially lower rates of use of any illicit

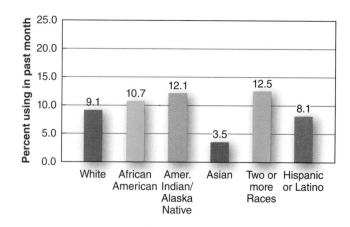

● **FIGURE 13.3** | Past month illicit drug use among persons aged 12 or older, by race/ethnicity: 2010.

Source: Substance Abuse and Mental Health Services Administration (2011).

drug than did whites, but the differences have narrowed in recent years, mostly due to increasing marijuana use among African American students. Hispanics rates of use for many drugs tend to fall near or below rates for whites and African Americans. However, Hispanic seniors have the highest rate of lifetime usage for powder cocaine, crack cocaine, heroin with and without a needle, methamphetamine, and crystal methamphetamine (Substance Abuse and Mental Health Services Administration [SAMHSA], 2011; Johnston et al., 2013b).

Course

Typically, rates of substance use peak around late adolescence and then begin to decline during young adulthood, in conjunction with adult roles of work, marriage, and parenthood (Lee, Chassin, & Villalta, 2013). However, for some youths, a pronounced pattern of early-onset risk taking may signal a more troublesome course that can threaten their well-being in both the short term and long term. As we note in Chapter 9 on conduct disorders, concern is particularly warranted when high-risk behaviors begin well before adolescence, are ongoing rather than occasional, and occur among a group of peers who engage in the same activities (Dick et al., 2013; Hersh, Curry, & Becker, 2013). Indeed, most adolescent risk and problem behaviors co-occur, so an indication of one problem is often a signal that others may be happening or on their way (Wolfe, Jaffe, & Crooks, 2006).

Although experimentation with substances is commonplace among teenagers, it is not harmless; substance use lowers inhibitions, reduces judgment, and increases the risk of physical harm and sexual assault (Oshri et al., 2013; Thompson et al., 2008). A survey of Canadian high school students found that alcohol use influenced the practice of, or involvement in, many other high-risk behaviors (Feldman et al, 1999), most notably unsafe sexual activity, smoking, and drinking and driving. Moreover, girls who report dating aggression are 5 times more likely to use alcohol than girls in nonviolent relationships, whereas boys are 2.5 times more likely to be in such relationships (Pepler et al., 2002). Teens who use alcohol and drugs are more likely to have sexual intercourse at an earlier age, have more sexual partners, and are at greater risk for sexually transmitted diseases (Connolly, Furman, & Konarski, 2000). Substance use is also a risk factor for unhealthy weight control (such as taking diet pills or laxatives), suicidality, and mood and anxiety disorders (Swahn, Bossarte, & Sullivent, 2008).

Associated Characteristics

Among adolescents who fit criteria for substance-use disorder, many related symptoms and behaviors have been noted. These youths tend to use more than one drug simultaneously, with marijuana and alcohol the most common combination, followed by alcohol and hallucinogens (Conway et al., 2013). They also have problems related to poor academic achievement, higher rates of academic failure, higher rates of delinquency, and more parental conflict (Chassin et al., 2013).

Emerging research also suggests that heavy drinking may be physically more dangerous at 15 years of age than a few years later at age 20, because it may disrupt or disturb ongoing neurodevelopmental processes of myelination and synaptic pruning (Luciana et al., 2013; Welch, Carson, & Lawrie, 2013). As compared with teens with lower substance-use levels, teens with histories of heavy drinking performed poorly on tests of memory and attention, in addition to exhibiting other signs of abnormal neurological development (Clark, Thatcher, & Tapert, 2008; Welch et al., 2013). The adolescent hippocampus may be particularly susceptible to alcohol, potentially because of an interaction between adolescent brain development and alcohol exposure (Silveri, 2012).

Causes

Similar to conduct disorders, several pathways and various risk factors have been associated with problematic substance use in adolescents, including personality and developmental factors, family history, family functioning, and peer involvement. Given the causes and associated characteristics associated with SUDs, it comes as no surprise that there is high comorbidity with many disorders covered in this textbook, especially ADHD and conduct problems (Brown et al., 2013).

Personality and Developmental Factors

Let's begin with a reminder of adolescent brain development and how it may underlie substance-use disorders and related personality factors. Some studies have shown a link between developmental changes in sleep and circadian rhythms during adolescence, discussed previously, and the risk of alcohol-use disorders (Hasler & Clark, 2013). The significant adjustments in the sleep–wake cycle that occur during adolescence can lead to a misalignment between teens' sleep–wake schedules and their internal circadian timing. This misalignment, in turn, alters the adolescent's reward-related brain functions. Specifically, critical neurocognitive abilities, such as executive functioning and inhibitory control, are impaired by sleep problems, which lead to an imbalance within the reward circuit.

This circadian imbalance and its related effects on brain development may explain the increased risk-taking and sensation-seeking during adolescence, which accelerates the transition from alcohol and drug experimentation to alcohol-use disorders among teens (Oshri et al., 2013; Stautz & Cooper, 2013). Sensation seeking has been described as a preference for novel, complex, and ambiguous stimuli, and it has been linked to a range of high-risk behaviors, including adolescent substance use (Martin et al., 2008). A longitudinal study looking at two samples of adolescents between grades 8 and 10 found that sensation seeking had a strong predictive value for both current and future marijuana and alcohol use (Crawford et al., 2003). The relationship between sensation seeking and substance use was strongest for predicting marijuana use, followed by alcohol use, and to a lesser extent, cigarette use. Furthermore, there were both sex and ethnicity differences in levels of sensation seeking—males tended to score higher than females, and white adolescents tended to score higher than adolescents with other ethnic backgrounds. However, sensation seeking was not stable over time, suggesting that a window of opportunity may exist to intervene and prevent sensation seeking.

There are also many attitudes that predict substance use; some relate directly to substance use and others are more general attitudes. Having positive attitudes about substance use (i.e., high perceived benefit and acceptability, low perceived risk) and having friends who hold similar views are attitudes and beliefs associated with substance use (Brooks-Russell et al., 2013; SAMSHA, 2003). Perceiving oneself to be physically older than same-age peers and striving for adult social roles are also risky attitudes. Finally, how highly positive adolescents feel about school—in particular, how connected they feel to their school community—is associated with a lower risk for use of substances (Holmbeck et al., 2006). This concept of school connectedness is a nonspecific risk factor; that is, adolescents who feel engaged with and supported by their school tend to exhibit lower levels of risk behavior in a variety of domains (e.g., substance use, violence, sexual behavior, suicidality). In contrast, youths who are more alienated and not involved in school tend to report higher levels of these behaviors.

Family Background

Adolescents with a positive family history for alcoholism may inherit certain brain structures and functional abilities from one or both parents. In particular, they show greater activation in the frontolimbic areas of the brain, as compared with teens without such family histories (Silveri et al., 2011). Such activation is associated with poor inhibition, suggesting they may have a neurobiological vulnerability that reduces their ability to inhibit risk-taking behaviors such as substance use (Silveri, 2012).

Part of the picture for youths with histories of parental alcohol abuse lies not only in neurobiological factors but also in child-rearing and family functioning more generally. The lack of parental involvement and parent–child affection, inconsistent parenting and poor monitoring, and negative parent–child and interparent interactions are all factors that increase the risk of substance use (Brown et al., 2013). An investigation of drinking initiation among sixth-graders found that low parental expectations for abstaining from alcohol not only predicted earlier onset of drinking but also interacted with adolescents' own expectations. That is, if teens held positive expectancies about alcohol use and believed their parents did not hold strong expectations for them not to drink, they were much more likely to initiate alcohol use during grade 6. If they held positive expectancies about alcohol use, but thought that their parents had clear expectations for them not to use alcohol, they were not as likely to initiate such use (Simons-Morton & Chen, 2006). This finding was present for both males and females and for both white and African American youths. It demonstrates that even at a time when youths are turning to their peers for cues about acceptable behavior, parent attitudes and parental drinking patterns still play an important role (Dick et al., 2013; Hummel et al., 2013).

Low parental monitoring—or the extent to which parents do not know "where their adolescents are and who they are with"—has consistently emerged as a predictor of adolescent substance use (DiClemente et al., 2001; Shorey et al., 2013). Interestingly, it seems to be the teens' perception of parental monitoring that is important. (Presumably, there is a correlation between adolescent perceptions of parental monitoring and actual parental practices.) For example, research with six cross-sectional, culturally diverse data sets found a significant protective effect of perceived parental monitoring in predicting lower levels of substance use in each of the six cohorts (Rai et al., 2003).

Rates of substance use among adolescent girls have increased over the past decade to a level similar to that for boys.

Some researchers have found sex differences in the relationship between parental monitoring and substance use. For example, a study of 700 9th- and 10th-graders found that higher levels of parental monitoring were associated with less alcohol use in males, but had no effect on females' behavior (Borawski et al., 2003). In this same study, trust between adolescent females (but not males) and their parents was a strong deterrent for risk behaviors. Related family characteristics that have been linked to adolescent substance use include poor parent–teen communication, poor family values, and family conflict (Handley & Chassin, 2013; Hussong et al., 2008; Telzer, Gonzales, & Fuligni, 2014).

Peers and Culture

Given the importance that peer culture generally plays in adolescents' lives, it is not surprising that peer influences play a large role in determining substance use. The role of peers seems to operate in more than one way. For example, associating with deviant and substance-using peers likely causes youths to adopt beliefs supporting drug use (we tend to have beliefs similar to those of our friends). At the same time, affiliation with these peers also increases access to substances. In addition, the idea of a false consensus (i.e., the belief that everyone is doing it) exerts pressure on youths to engage in substance use. The extent to which individual teens think that their peer group is using substances is related to the individual's decision to use or not use substances (Branstetter et al., 2011). Peer culture also glamorizes substance use, encouraging teens to use alcohol and drugs as a way of "fitting in." About one-third of hit songs, including three-quarters of rap songs, have some form of explicit reference to drug, alcohol, or tobacco use (Primack et al., 2008).

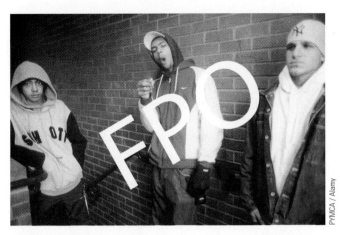

Associating with deviant and substance-using peers increases access to, and adoption of, beliefs supporting drug use.

Treatment and Prevention

Treatment outcomes for adolescents with SUDs have been mixed. Approximately half of adolescents receiving treatment for substance-use disorders (SUDs) relapse within the first 3 months after treatment, and only 20% to 30% remain abstinent at 1 year (Cornelius et al., 2003; Karki et al., 2012). Despite limitations, among the more promising treatments for adolescent substance abuse are those that involve the larger systems affecting the adolescent's behavior, such as peers, family, and school climate (Godley et al., 2014; Waldron & Turner, 2008). Other effective methods focus on personality factors linked to alcohol abuse, such as hopelessness, anxiety sensitivity, impulsivity, and sensation seeking (Conrod, Castellanos-Ryan, & Mackie, 2011).

Derived from interventions for conduct disorders, family-based approaches seek to modify negative interactions between family members, improve communication between members, and develop effective problem-solving skills to address areas of conflict (Anderson et al., 2007; Spoth et al., 2012). Multisystemic therapy (MST), for example, involves intensive intervention that targets family, peer, school, and community systems; it has been especially effective in the treatment of SUDs among delinquent adolescents (Henggeler et al., 2008). Parents or other care providers are provided with step-by-step guidelines for implementing contingency management to control adolescent substance abuse. These steps include familiar cognitive–behavioral interventions such as behavioral contacts and contingencies to reinforce abstinence, as well as ways to overcome common roadblocks to treatment (Henggeler et al., 2012).

The effectiveness of motivational interviewing (MI) with this population has also been supported (Jensen et al., 2011). Motivational interviewing uses a patient-centered and directive approach that addresses the ambivalence and discrepancies between a person's current values and behaviors and their future goals. In general, the type of treatment indicated depends on levels of use and the individual's home environment. Adolescents with low to moderate levels of substance abuse and a more stable home environment are reasonable candidates for outpatient treatment, whereas those with more severe levels of substance abuse, an unstable living situation, or comorbid psychopathology may require an inpatient or residential setting (Brown et al., 2013).

Because adolescence is a time of rapid, major transitions and changes in physical, emotional, and social domains, prevention efforts related to substance use increasingly are being introduced at the elementary and secondary school levels. Facilitating successful transitions—for example, in the areas of romantic and peer relationships, sexual behavior, and healthy lifestyle choices—has the added major benefit of reducing multiple problematic outcomes in later life. Critical health-damaging behaviors that are preventable include substance use and abuse, unsafe sexual practices, and abusive behavior, which all have a common context of peer and dating relationships (Wolfe et al., 2006). These prevention efforts are being recognized as having important payoffs in terms of reductions in future health problems and enhancement of personal goals (Brown et al., 2013).

Effective approaches to adolescent substance-abuse prevention have addressed multiple influences on the individual from peers, family, school, and community. Life skills training, a detailed and well-evaluated program, emphasizes building drug-resistance skills, personal and social competence, and altering cognitive expectancies around substance use (Griffin & Botvin, 2010). Because adolescents must receive consistent messages and reinforcement regarding pressures to use alcohol and drugs, as well as develop effective refusal skills, societal messages about responsible use are emphasized to influence students' behavior. Prevention programs also target the social environment through community and school norms and their efficacy to enact change, and they often include some level of parent involvement and education to improve parent–child communication about substance use (Domitrovich et al., 2010; O'Leary-Barrett et al., 2010).

Section Summary

Adolescent Substance-Use Disorders

- Adolescent substance abuse is related to a wide variety of psychological disorders.
- The central diagnostic feature of substance-use disorder is a problematic pattern of substance use leading to significant impairment or distress.
- A significant proportion of youths (about 12%) meet criteria for a diagnosis of substance abuse or substance dependence.
- A positive family history for alcoholism and peer influences play a large role in determining substance use.
- Among the more promising treatments for adolescent substance abuse are those that involve the larger systems affecting the adolescent's behavior, such as peers, family, and school climate.

Study Resources

14

Feeding and Eating Disorders

I feel like I'm disappearing, getting smaller every day but I look in the mirror—I'm bigger in every way.

—Lyrics from "Tunic (Song for Karen)" by Sonic Youth, written in memory of singer Karen Carpenter, who died of anorexia

ALTHOUGH SERIOUS EATING PROBLEMS have only recently been considered mental disorders, bizarre and unusual eating habits have been documented for many centuries. The ancient Egyptians believed that illness could be avoided through monthly purges. The ancient Romans built the aptly described "vomitorium," where men purged their stomachs after overindulging in a heavy banquet—before returning to eat more. For centuries, voluntary as well as forced starvation has had both saintly and evil guises, whether as religious fasting or as a way to put an end to individuals who seemed possessed and bewitched. Today, as always, overeating and starvation are connected to mental health problems and to unusual cultural practices.

This chapter addresses several eating disorders and their related conditions that affect children and youths. We begin with a discussion of risk factors that affect eating habits among infants and children, followed by discussion of the developmental significance of childhood obesity. Obesity is not a psychiatric disorder, nor is it associated with greater psychopathology. However, children with obesity are at risk of establishing unhealthy dieting patterns, often caused by social discrimination, that sometimes lead to chronic health problems and eating disorders (Puhl & Latner, 2007; Puhl, Luedicke, & Heuer, 2011). We then turn our attention to feeding and eating disorders first occurring during infancy or early childhood.

The last section of the chapter addresses the three major eating disorders of adolescence and young adulthood: anorexia nervosa, bulimia nervosa, and binge eating disorder. Anorexia nervosa (anorexia for short) emerges primarily among adolescent girls and may continue into young adulthood. It often is marked by an obsession with food and a drive for thinness that causes the person to lose sight of what is healthy. Bulimia nervosa (bulimia for short) is characterized by binge eating followed by an effort to compensate, usually through self-induced vomiting, but sometimes by fasting; by misusing laxatives, diuretics, or other medications; or by exercising excessively. Individuals with bulimia are also obsessed with food and with losing weight, but they do not experience the excessive weight loss associated with anorexia. Most persons with bulimia are within 10% of their normal weight, whereas individuals with anorexia refuse to maintain even a minimally normal weight. Binge eating disorder (BED) is a new diagnosis in the *Diagnostic and Statistical Manual of Mental Disorders,* 5th edition (DSM-5), involving periods of excessive eating, accompanied by a feeling of a loss of control. It differs from bulimia primarily because of the absence of compensatory behaviors.

Eating disorders have traditionally been only a medical concern. Studies of their etiology and treatment have focused on physiological mechanisms and the serious biological consequences associated with these disorders. Over the past quarter century, as mental health professionals began to study psychosocial factors—genetic makeup, cognitive and social development, and everyday experiences between infant and caregivers—they discovered that many of the same factors underlying other major childhood disorders significantly influence early feeding and eating disorders.

Unlike most disorders of childhood and adolescence described in this text, however, the causes of major eating disorders seem to be disproportionately related to sociocultural influences, rather than psychological and biological influences. What makes these disorders particularly unusual is that they are so closely linked to Western culture, where food is plentiful and a person's appearance, especially for young women, is so highly valued. Eating disorders have increasingly become a problem for adolescents in Western society: collectively, they are the third most common illness in adolescent females (Hudson et al., 2007; Swanson et al. 2011).

HOW EATING PATTERNS DEVELOP

Anyone who has ever watched a 2-year-old eat spaghetti knows that learning to feed oneself is not a simple process. In fact, feeding and eating problems are a normal part of development for most children as they learn through gradual approximations.

Normal Development

Troublesome eating habits and limited food preferences are among the most distinguishing characteristics of early childhood. Approximately one in four children (under age 12) are described as picky eaters by their parents (Mascola, Bryson, & Agras, 2010). Picky eating is more common among girls than boys (Rydell & Dahl, 2005), but its relationship to the emergence of eating disorders during adolescence or adulthood is unclear (Jacobi et al., 2004). Beginning around age 9, girls are more anxious than boys about losing weight (Philipsen & Brooks-Gunn, 2008).

Societal norms and media's focus on thinness and attractiveness is partly to blame for weight-consciousness among pre-teen girls. (Bell & Dittmar, 2011; Nouri, Hill, & Orrell-Valente, 2011). In addition, normal concerns about weight and appearance can either be reduced or increased by the comments of parents, friends, and romantic partners. The effects of the early parent–child relationship on fundamental biological processes such as eating and growth patterns are of paramount importance (Corning et al., 2010).

Courtesy of David Wolfe

Eating disorders should not be confused with disorderly eating, which is a normal part of early development.

Entering school is the next significant developmental landmark because of increasing social pressure to conform to narrow perceptions of desirable body type. Significantly, the desire to achieve an ideal image can turn into an obsession during adolescence.

Developmental Risk Factors

A developmental perspective of eating problems and eating disorders raises the intriguing possibility of a continuum of "eating pathology" that ranges from dieting to clinical syndromes, across all developmental periods (Attie & Brooks-Gunn, 1995). ● Figure 14.1

illustrates how problem eating from a young age may contribute to being overweight or obese during childhood. Overweight children are often teased or rejected by their peers in elementary school, which in turn may cause a drive for thinness with the intention of improving negative body image and acceptance (Lawler & Nixon, 2011; Puhl et al., 2011). **Drive for thinness** is a key motivational variable that underlies dieting and body image, among young females in particular, whereby the individual believes that losing more weight is the answer to overcoming her troubles and to achieving success (Philipsen & Brooks-Gunn, 2008). However, such behavior creates the negative side effects of weight preoccupation, concern with appearance, and restrained eating, which increase the risk of an eating disorder (Touyz, Polivy, & Hay, 2008).

Early Eating Habits, Attitudes, and Behaviors

Disturbed eating attitudes describe a person's belief that cultural standards for attractiveness, body image, and social acceptance are closely tied to one's ability to control diet and weight gain. Even among 7- to 10-year-olds, concerns about weight, dieting, and physique are common, suggesting that Western sociocultural values and preoccupation with body weight and dieting—factors that lead to eating disorders among vulnerable adolescents—may be internalized and expressed at a very early age (Thompson, Rafiroiu, & Sargent, 2003).

Researchers following sample groups of children and adolescents over several years have documented the continuity between eating problems during childhood (such as struggles at mealtime or disinterest in food) and the subsequent onset of a disorder. Examining patterns of eating problems over 8 years among

Eating Problems

Problem eating

Teasing

Drive for thinness,
Negative body image,
dieting, weight concerns

© iStockphoto.com/PicturePartners

BananaStock/Jupiterimages

© Elena Elisseeva/Dreamstime.com

Early childhood

Middle childhood

Adolescence

Developmental Periods

● **FIGURE 14.1** | A developmental continuum of eating habits and disorders.

normal adolescent girls, Graber and colleagues (1994) discovered that about 25% of them showed signs of a serious eating problem at each assessment. These teens had earlier pubertal maturation, higher percentages of body fat, concurrent psychological problems (especially depression), and poorer body image than teens without eating problems (Tyrka et al., 2003).

Weight concerns (such as fear of weight gain, worry about weight and body shape, diet history, and perceived fatness) and body image, in particular, appear to be significantly related to the onset of eating problems and eating disorders during adolescence (Juarascio et al., 2011). This constellation of physical and psychological factors, linked to early eating problems and distorted beliefs, signifies a considerable risk pattern for the development of persistent and possibly severe eating problems (Jacobi et al., 2004; Striegel-Moore & Bulik, 2007). The desire to appear thin may be responsible for the near-epidemic rates of referral of young people with eating disorders, especially bulimia, since the mid-1970s throughout Western society. In contrast, regular family meals may function as a protective factor against eating disorders (Bauer et al., 2011).

Transition into Adolescence

Passage from childhood to early adolescence is full of unexpected challenges, not the least of which is undergoing the significant changes in body shape that require considerable adjustments in self-image. Research has consistently shown that anorexia and bulimia typically occur during adolescence and that onset thereafter is rare (Stice & Bohon, 2013; Striegel-Moore et al., 2005). The timing of maturation also affects dieting behavior, because girls who mature early are likely to be heavier than their late-maturing peers (Derose et al., 2011).

As we saw with younger children, girls report feeling worse about themselves than do boys, most likely because girls place greater emphasis on self-perceptions of physical appearance (Paxton, Eisenberg, & Neumark-Sztainer, 2006). Although they readily acknowledge their interpersonal and social abilities, many postpubescent girls say they frequently feel fat and unattractive. In contrast, boys see themselves in a more positive light with respect to achievement, academic aspirations, self-assertion, and body image (O'Dea, 2006, 2008). Contradictory societal messages implying that women must be successful both in traditionally feminine and traditionally masculine roles place added pressure on young women to aspire to some elusive superwoman caricature (Cash & Smolak, 2011). Female adolescents who describe themselves in superwoman terms are more likely to associate thinness with autonomy, success, and recognition for their independent achievements; however, they also are significantly more at risk for eating disorders (Levine & Smolak, 2010).

The all-too-familiar interaction of pubertal weight gain, the beginning of social dating, and threats to achievement status often promote body dissatisfaction, distress, and perceived loss of control in young adolescents, especially because they occur cumulatively over a relatively short period (Philipsen & Brooks-Gunn, 2008). Weight-based harassment by peers is strongly connected to adolescent low body satisfaction and lower self-esteem for boys as well as girls (Bucchianeri et al., 2013). As you might expect, these changes also encourage smoking and other substance use among teenage girls, who feel that these activities protect them from the impulse to binge eat and the consequences of weight gain. The importance of one's perceived body image is discussed later in the sections on anorexia and bulimia.

Dieting and Weight Concerns

Restrictive dieting has become a North American pastime, especially among youths who choose to diet at very young ages. A large-scale survey of students in grades 5 through 8 found that approximately 60% had tried to lose weight in the past 7 days (Thompson et al., 2003), which is consistent with the notion that these concerns often begin as early as elementary school and increase steadily throughout adolescence (Neumark-Sztainer et al., 2011). A significant number of these students report feeling depressed after overeating and then choosing strict dieting as a form of weight control (Stice et al., 2008).

Chronic dieting seems strongly related to both gender and developmental factors. By midadolescence, about two-thirds of girls report being on a diet during the previous year, which is a twofold increase over elementary school. Among those who diet, about 10% of girls are chronic dieters—that is, someone who continuously remains on a diet or who diets sporadically more than 10 times during the year (French et al., 1995). In contrast, only 2% of boys are chronic dieters.

Why does dieting sometimes lead to overeating? Decreasing caloric intake reduces a person's metabolic rate, which allows fat to remain in the cells so that weight loss is, in fact, impeded. This failure to lose weight sets the stage for a vicious cycle of increased commitment to dieting and vulnerability to binge eating. Psychological consequences also contribute to this cycle by creating what some researchers call the "false hope syndrome"—an initial commitment to change one's appearance leads to short-term improvements in mood and self-image, but this hope declines as feelings of failure and loss of control increase (Polivy & Herman, 2005). Loss of control may lead to binge eating, and purging is seen as a way to counteract the perceived effects of binge eating on weight gain. **Purging** is the voluntary use of vomiting, laxatives, or other methods to rid the body of food. Invariably, purging is followed by disgust and self-recrimination, which prompts renewed vows of abstinence and sets the stage for the whole cycle of dieting, overeating, dietary failure, and affective distress to begin again, as shown in ● Figure 14.2 (Polivy & Herman, 2005).

Although dieting is clearly a risk factor in relation to the onset of eating disorders, it should be viewed in perspective: Many young persons diet in order to influence body weight and shape, yet only a small minority develop eating disorders. Dieting can be harmful or beneficial, depending on the individual and the conditions. It is important to distinguish between dieting in individuals (especially children) who are not overweight and dieting in individuals whose excess weight increases medical or psychological risk (Brownell & Rodin, 1994; Isomaa et al., 2010). There is a critical difference between watching your weight as part of a health-conscious lifestyle and chronic, unrealistic dieting that upsets your body's natural rhythm and balance.

A developmental approach to researching and treating eating disorders in youths is essential, yet few researchers have adopted a developmental perspective in their studies. While many of the symptoms exhibited are similar to those of adults, the effects of those symptoms may have lasting and significant effects on adolescents' growth and development. Adolescents with an eating disorder may be deprived of key social,

emotional, and biological developmental processes that normally develop during this period.

Biological Regulators

How do we know when to eat and how much to eat? For most of us, eating, like sleeping, is a natural process, controlled by biorhythms that have adapted successfully over time to the stress and strain of our individual lives. However, normal patterns of eating and growth, as well as the disorders based on disturbances in these patterns, are influenced by physical and psychological processes that continuously interact. In essence, your particular growth and weight pattern is based on the relation between your genes and your constitution, which governs your ability from early infancy to self-regulate your sleep and elimination patterns, appetite, and past and current nutritional patterns.

Metabolic rate, or balance of energy expenditure, is established based on individual genetic and physiological makeup, as well as eating and exercise habits. Individual metabolism, in turn, serves to self-monitor and self-regulate behavior, which is why we may have trouble maintaining changes in weight or exercise. If you burn more energy than you take in, a state of chronic negative energy balance, or hypocaloric malnutrition, can occur. Malnutrition, even for brief periods, is followed by physical attempts to adapt that can produce significant biological, behavioral, and psychological effects, including loss of circadian rhythm; increase in the release of growth hormones; dermatological changes with the loss of fatty tissue or hair pigmentation; and emotional and behavioral changes such as lethargy, depression, and apathy (Woolston, 1991). These changes can have long-term consequences if they occur during crucial developmental stages, or during the acquisition of fundamental cognitive abilities. Feeding and eating disorders thus merit careful study, because these problems can be overlooked when they are accompanied by more pronounced emotional and behavioral problems.

Body Weight

Anyone who has tried dieting knows how hard it is to lose weight and keep it off. Weight loss is rapid for the first few weeks, but most of the lost weight returns with time. In fact, 90% to 95% of those who lose weight regain it within several years (Agras, 2010). Why is body weight so resistant to change? For years, the blame was primarily placed on the dieter's weak resolve or lack of willpower, but today researchers place more credence in the view that each person is biologically and genetically programmed to weigh within a certain natural weight range. A person's natural weight is regulated around his or her own **set point**, which is a comfortable

● **FIGURE 14.2** | The binge–purge cycle.

© Cengage Learning 2013

range of body weight that the body tries to "defend" and maintain (Levin, 2010).

In effect, people who gain or lose weight will experience metabolic changes that strive to bring the body back to its natural weight. If fat levels decrease below our body's normal range, the brain (specifically, the hypothalamus) compensates by slowing metabolism. We begin to feel lethargic, we increase our sleep, and our body temperature decreases slightly to conserve energy (which is why many persons with anorexia complain of being cold). In this state of relative deprivation, uncontrollable urges to binge are common because our bodies are telling us that they need more food than they are getting to function properly.

Similarly, the body fights against weight gain by increasing metabolism and raising body temperature in an effort to burn off extra calories. (Admittedly, this valiant effort is seldom enough to conquer the force of holidays and other feasts.) Because of its responsivity to change, researchers often compare the body's set point to the setting on a thermostat that regulates room temperature. When room temperature falls below a certain range, the thermostat automatically sends a signal to the heating system to increase the heat level until it again reaches the established temperature setting. Human bodies respond similarly to deviations in body weight by turning their metabolic "furnace" up or down (Wilkin, 2010).

Growth

Under normal conditions, the biological mechanisms of growth are like the well-orchestrated ecosystem of a forest or a lake—a system of feedback loops, messenger signals, and major organs that work together to maintain a healthy balance. For humans, the biology of growth fundamentally involves the manner in which circulating hormones interact with available nutritional resources to produce changes throughout the skeletal system. The most significant hormonal determinants of growth rate during childhood are the *growth hormone* (GH) and the *thyroid hormone,* with additional gonadal steroids kicking in during adolescence to produce a further growth spurt and skeletal maturation. From 50% to 75% of growth hormone production occurs after the onset of deep sleep in children and young adults (Woolston, 1991), which may explain why eating and sleep disorders coexist in some younger children (Lyons-Ruth et al., 2014).

Individual growth depends on GH circulating throughout the body. The release of GH from the pituitary gland is determined by the hypothalamus and the higher brain structures that affect it (the limbic cortex and amygdala). These higher brain structures are involved in emotional sensation and response, which may account for the connection between eating and emotional disorders (discussed in the following section). Just as a thermostat determines the need to increase or decrease temperature, the hypothalamus senses the need to release more or less GH throughout the body. To accomplish this task, the hypothalamus releases two controlling hormones that exert opposite effects. The *growth hormone–inhibiting factor* (i.e., somatostatin) essentially inhibits the GH response to internal signals of hunger, so we stop eating. In contrast, the *growth hormone–releasing factor* has the specific function of telling our body when, how, and where to grow by releasing growth hormone from the pituitary.

Familiarity with these biological processes makes it easier to understand how the biological substrates of growth and metabolism can be thrown off balance by many factors that cause behavioral and physiological changes in children or young adults. Although we do not know whether the majority of eating disorders are caused by biological abnormalities or whether the disorder itself creates a biological disruption, these underlying biological mechanisms influencing weight regulation are important to the understanding of eating disorders discussed in the remainder of this chapter.

Section Summary

How Eating Patterns Develop

- Eating problems are common among children.
- Normal concerns about weight and appearance can be influenced unduly by parents and peers, sometimes resulting in eating disturbances.
- Early eating habits, attitudes, and behaviors that place undue concern on body image and a drive for thinness increase the risk of eating disorders.
- Increased dieting and weight concerns often accompany the transition into adolescence, especially for girls, which can lead to the emergence of unhealthy eating patterns.
- Attempts to reduce weight by dieting can lead to a vicious cycle of weight loss and weight gain. Chronic dieting is associated with the onset of adolescent eating disorders.
- Normal patterns of eating and growth, as well as the later emergence of eating disorders, are influenced by biological processes such as one's metabolic rate and set point.

OBESITY

Approximately 1 in 6 children and adolescents (2 to 19 years of age) in North America are obese (Centers for Disease Control and Prevention [CDC], 2014). **Childhood obesity** is a chronic medical condition similar to hypertension or diabetes; it is characterized by excessive body fat. Persons with obesity regulate their weight appropriately, but their set point is elevated. Obesity usually is defined in terms of a *body mass index* (BMI), essentially a height-to-weight ratio, that is above the 95th percentile, based on norms for the child's age and sex. A childhood BMI between the 85th and 95th percentiles is considered overweight.

● Figure 14.3 shows how the BMI is calculated and plotted. Note how the BMIs of overweight and "at risk" children increase more rapidly than the normal BMIs for boys and girls, both of which increase with age, especially during adolescence. The exponential increase in eating at fast-food restaurants and eating convenient junk foods can also contribute to the rise in obesity rates. On any given day, 30% of American children eat fast food (Bowman et al., 2004), and half of the caloric intake of youths in the United States comes from added sugar and fat (CDC, 2014a). The size of meal portions makes a huge difference in caloric intake. For example, a traditional McDonald's burger with a 16-ounce Coke and a small order of fries carries 627 calories and 19 grams of fat. That same meal with cheese and "supersized" carries 1,805 calories and 84 grams of fat. These increases in caloric and fat intake may account for the jump in the percentages of boys and girls who are overweight.

As we have seen, more and more children and adolescents are caught up in a dieting cycle, and the reasons for wanting to lose weight are compelling. Obesity is severely stigmatized in North American society and carries many social and health hazards (Puhl & Latner, 2007). Herein lies a fundamental conflict: The mass media powerfully promote the thin ideal in a land where fast food is widely available and accessible. Although obesity clearly is not a mental disorder, it can affect a child's psychological and physical development significantly. Obese children and adolescents are 5 times more likely than healthy children to experience an impaired quality of life, similar to children with cancer (Phillips et al., 2012; Schwimmer, Burwinkle, & Varni, 2003). Yet, researchers are undecided as to whether psychiatric comorbidity among children is a cause or a consequence of obesity or whether common factors cause both conditions in at-risk children (Kalarchian & Marcus, 2012)

ELLEN

Self-Image and Self-Esteem

It does matter to me what people say and think about my size. I guess the whole self-esteem thing began when I was little and other kids made fun of me for being fat—which basically I feel has continued until about a year ago.

OK, fine, that is other people's rudeness and lack of sensitivity about someone's problem. Because of these a__holes, I have always had to try harder at everything to prove I wasn't just a fat blob—there was a person living, breathing, caring inside that has to be dealt with. . . .

. . . I fell into the trap from about age 5 of letting others' images of a fat me be my own self-image. I have now let myself get to the point of only accepting others' concept of my new getting-thin person and don't allow

(continues)

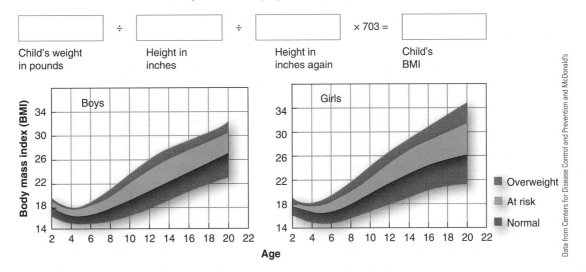

● **FIGURE 14.3** | How to calculate and plot a child's BMI by age and sex.

(continued)

myself to think thin. There are times when I get what I need—either trying a smaller-sized outfit, having a total stranger compliment me or a friend tell me I'm looking nice that day—I get high on those compliments and I can be fueled on them for a day or so and then I'm back to square one—who is this person in the picture?

I am scared. All my life I have wanted to be thin. . . .

I know the day I weigh 170 . . . the number isn't going to make my mind snap into line and make me happy with my accomplishment.

The whole self-esteem thing seems as difficult if not more so than the actual weight loss. To lose weight you eat the right foods and exercise—the weight falls off—but to change how you feel about yourself is a whole different ball of wax. How do you change approximately 18 years of thinking about yourself one way when you are really no longer that person? How do I convince myself—do I write 500 times a day I am thin, worthwhile, nice, organized, good worker, pleasant personality, pretty, smart, logical mind, good advice giver? I know all these things about myself, but they are shadows of the tower of this whole f__ing weight thing. I need a bulldozer to knock over that tower. Where does the bulldozer come from—from inside? But where is it buried, where are the good feelings, the easiness with myself, the self-confidence that I do look nice and desirable?

From "Obesity," by J. P. Foreyt and J. H. Cousins, 1987, pp. 502–503. In M. Hersen and V. B. Van Hasselt (Eds.), *Behavior Therapy with Children and Adolescents.* Copyright © 1987 by John Wiley & Sons, Inc. Reprinted by permission of John Wiley & Sons, Inc.

Ellen, an 18-year-old who first became aware of her obesity when she was 9, describes her thoughts and feelings with respect to her weight: Ellen's self-disclosure captures the social and emotional dilemma that overweight children and adolescents so often face, which she characterizes as "the self-esteem thing." Many obese children and adults suffer the consequences of Western cultural attitudes that equate attractiveness and competence with thinness. As early as first grade, children are less likely to befriend overweight peers, and these attitudes intensify during adolescence (Striegel-Moore & Bulik, 2007). Although her weight losses were slow, with the help of group and individual therapy, Ellen defeated the critical messages that had plagued her since childhood, allowing her to reach and maintain her realistic goal of 170 pounds.

Prevalence and Development

For the past three decades, alarm bells have been sounding over the fact that the number of children who are overweight or obese is increasing. As shown in ● Figure 14.4, obesity rates for all age groups of

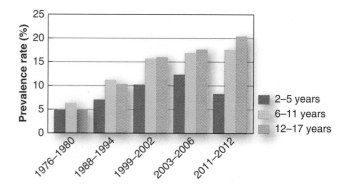

● **FIGURE 14.4** | Prevalence of obese children and adolescents in the United States 1976–2012.

Sources: Hedley et al., 2004; Ogden et al., 2002, 2008, 2014.

children and adolescents have increased from 5% to 17% since the mid-1970s. In the United States and Canada, the obesity rate among boys age 7 to 13 nearly tripled between the early 1980s and the mid-2000s, while the prevalence of obesity among girls of the same age more than doubled (Ogden et al., 2010; Roberts et al., 2012). This trend has emerged worldwide as well, although not to the same degree—the prevalence of childhood overweight and obesity has increased from 4.2% in 1990 to 6.7% in 2010 (de Onis, Blössner, & Borghi, 2010). Although there is some evidence that this trend is stabilizing among children and teens (and has been reduced for preschoolers), rates of childhood obesity and overweight remain high and pose a significant public health issue worldwide (Ogden et al., 2014; Olds et al., 2011).

Obesity during infancy and obesity during later childhood are not strongly related, but *childhood-onset* obesity is more likely to persist into adolescence and adulthood (Wilkin, 2010). Even during their youth, individuals with obesity risk many health concerns, such as cardiovascular problems, diabetes, and elevated cholesterol and triglycerides (Power & Thomas, 2011; Wang et al., 2011). Obesity during childhood may have long-term effects, in that many lifestyle and behavioral choices associated with obesity develop during the school-age years. In fact, obesity is a major factor in reducing life expectancy in North America (Katzmarzyk & Ardern, 2004; Preston & Stokes, 2011).

One troubling finding is that preadolescent obesity is a risk factor in the later emergence of eating disorders, especially for females, primarily because of the manner in which peers ignore or tease children who are obese. Obesity is strongly correlated with teasing by age-mates at an early age; teasing, in turn, predicts overall dissatisfaction with appearance and body image and sets in motion a chain of restrictive and high-risk eating practices (Eisenberg, Neumark-Sztainer,

& Story, 2003). Overweight children and adolescents may require assistance at an early age in developing a healthy, acceptable body image and eating patterns to resist the harmful and cruel pressures of early adolescence (Menzel et al., 2010; Mond et al., 2011).

Overweight students in middle and high schools use fewer healthy weight-control strategies (e.g., physical activity, healthier eating) and more unhealthy strategies (e.g., vomiting, diet pills, laxatives) than nonoverweight students (Boutelle et al., 2002). Thus, a childhood pattern of being overweight may make it more difficult during adolescence and adulthood to achieve or maintain the culturally valued degree of thinness. The individual then may engage in the more extreme weight-control measures that may lead to an eating disorder.

Culture and Socioeconomic Status

There are significant racial and ethnic disparities in obesity prevalence. Among U.S. children and adolescents, Hispanic boys are significantly more likely to be obese than non-Hispanic white boys, and non-Hispanic black girls were significantly more likely to be obese than non-Hispanic white girls (CDC, 2011b). Although reasons for such disparities are many, mothers identify pressures of familial and cultural influences favoring chubbier children (Lindsay et al., 2011; Ramirez et al., 2011). Researchers also point to the problem of "food deserts" that make healthier eating a challenge. In many inner cities and rural communities children and families are unable to access healthy, affordable food because of the lack of transportation and the preponderance of cheap processed foods (Davis et al., 2011).

Minorities make up a significant proportion of low-income populations in North America. Fast food and junk food tends to be relatively inexpensive and more available than healthy foods; thus, rates of consumption of these foods are higher in low-income families (Davis et al., 2011; Swinburn et al., 2011). An additional problem for low-income families is that many of their neighborhoods are unsafe, and parents may keep their children at home because of concern for their safety, which severely limits a child's opportunities for physical activities.

Based on data from 15 industrialized countries, the United States holds the dubious distinction of having the highest percentage of overweight children, whether compared by age (13 vs. 15 years) or gender (Lissau et al., 2004). While the cultural factors that may account for this high rate are unclear, they seem to be transmittable: rates of obesity and eating disorders increase upon exposure to Western culture (O'Dea, 2008). It could be that the massive Western influence and globalization of the fast-food industries continue to fuel the rapid rise in obesity rates. Other countries, however, have obesity rates that are catching up. For example, there has been a dramatic increase in overweight Chinese children in recent years, believed to be due to an increasingly urban lifestyle (Lobstein, 2010).

Causes

Body weight, like height and hair color, is to a large extent a function of pedigree. By age 17, a child of two obese parents has 3 times the chance of being obese as a child of lean parents; moreover, if one sibling is obese, there is a 40% chance that a second sibling also will be obese (Garn et al., 1976; Kral & Faith, 2009). Although heritability may account for a substantial proportion of the variance in obesity, other individual and family-related factors, such as dietary and lifestyle preferences, also play a role.

Leptin has been identified as a hormone that carries instructions to the brain to regulate energy and appetite (Kanoski et al., 2011). Leptin deficiencies have been found among children with severe obesity (Cole, 2007; Montague et al., 1997). Persons with obesity are somehow resistant to leptin's effect—a situation similar to that of adult diabetes, in which a person usually produces insulin but it fails to work properly, causing sugar levels to go out of control. Leptin levels decrease with dieting, so leptin is less likely to provide feedback to the hypothalamus. Paradoxically, this connection between dieting and lower leptin levels may explain why dieting increases hunger and slows metabolism and results in gaining back the lost weight (Cornier, 2011; Moran & Ladenheim, 2011). Similar studies on reward pathways in the brain help to understand obesity in terms of common mechanisms underlying drug addiction and maladaptive eating patterns (Stice et al., 2013).

Despite strong biological forces, proper diet and exercise still play a critical role in determining a child's level of obesity. We not only inherit our biochemical makeup from our parents, but we also look to them as routine instructors and role models as we develop our attitudes toward food and eating. Parents determine what food is available, and they model an approach to exercise and diet. However, inexperienced or highly pressured parents may respond to any sign of distress in the infant or toddler by attempts to feed, by neglect, or by both reactions. Moreover, parents of obese children sometimes have greater difficulty setting limits, which has obvious implications for the child's tendency to overeat (Schuetzmann et al., 2008). Like many other childhood disorders, obesity and poor eating habits are related to the degree of family disorganization, ranging from poor communication and a lack of perceived family support to sexual and physical abuse (Brooke & Mussap, 2013; Neumark-Sztainer et al., 2008).

Treatment

Childhood obesity prevention and intervention efforts consider not only the child's health but also the family's resources. In children with no serious medical complications, pediatricians often recommend proper nutrition to arrest weight gain until the child's height and weight are proportional. Note, however, that this nutrition program does not involve putting the child on a diet, since energy-restricted or unbalanced diets can place a child in jeopardy of medical or learning problems.

Family functioning not only influences eating patterns and obesity, it also can be instrumental in its prevention and treatment. To no one's surprise, any decrease in physical activity relative to food intake, such as eating while viewing television, can result in increased weight. Thus, efforts to curb childhood obesity often focus on addressing parents' knowledge of nutrition and increasing children's physical activity (Gortmaker & Story, 2012; Kitzmann & Beech, 2011).

Treatment should instill active, less sedentary routines. Obese and overweight children need parental encouragement, so many effective weight-loss programs teach parents and children ways to be more active. Children and youth who are taught to be active and are reinforced for being less sedentary (such as playing outdoors rather than watching television) increase their liking for high-intensity activity, which in turn reduces weight (Kitzman et al., 2010; Steele et al., 2012; Theim et al., 2013). Similarly, parents must anticipate problems with weight-control plans and address them by altering the child's environment and daily routines as needed. For example, parents may be advised not to bring high-calorie snack foods into the house and to monitor what they eat in front of their children, as obese children are highly sensitive to food cues in their environments (Temple et al., 2008).

Other behavioral interventions focus on the goal of making the child's eating behaviors and physical activity patterns more adaptive and self-managed. Self-control procedures encourage children to set their own goals for diet, weight, and exercise and teach them the necessary skills to achieve these goals with minimal outside directives from parents or therapists. For example, children may be taught to monitor the quantity and nature of their food, when they eat it, and who shared the meal; similar self-monitoring is encouraged for exercise goals (Wilfley et al., 2007). Even if some children are unable to reach or maintain their intended goal of weight loss, self-control training encourages a greater sense of perceived control among children with obesity (Munsch et al., 2008).

In recent years, schools have done more to help young children develop a healthy body image and promote healthy eating habits. This increase in the involvement of educators was sparked by the alarming number of overweight children over the past decades, as well as by their concern that children may be inundated by cultural forces that place undue value on dieting and appearance. Given the greater awareness of the importance of early eating habits and the influence of cultural expectations, school-based programs now address children's and teens' desire for knowledge and support in developing a healthy body image and eating attitudes. As shown in A Closer Look 14.1, schools have been active in developing a range of educational strategies that involve the whole school environment, including classroom education, cafeteria and vending machine selections, and educating staff and parents to recognize signs of disordered eating and promote healthy eating attitudes and activities (Safron, Cislak, Gaspar, & Luszczynska, 2011).

A CLOSER LOOK 14.1

Junk Food Corporations in Schools

As education resources have decreased in recent years, schools boards have increasingly felt the need to seek funding elsewhere. Corporate sponsors have been quick to jump on board and sign contracts with school districts, allowing their products exclusive rights to be sold within the schools. In 2002, there were 240 U.S. school districts that had exclusive contracts with soft drink companies, and 60% of U.S. middle and high schools had soft-drink vending machines (Fried & Nestle, 2002). Junk food is readily available in most school cafeterias and vending machines, and it is often cheaper than healthy foods.

The plethora of junk food and rising obesity rates have led to criticisms of corporate contracts, and some districts are starting to take action. For example, as of September 2011, students in Ontario, Canada, were no longer able to buy candy, chocolate, pop, fries, and energy drinks on school property. While certainly a step in the right direction, more needs to be done to reduce overweight and obesity among school children. (Based on authors' case material.)

Section Summary

Obesity

- Childhood obesity is defined by a body mass index (BMI) above the 95th percentile for children of the same age and sex.

- Obesity is not a mental disorder, but it can affect a child's psychological and physical development in significant ways.

- Obesity poses a risk for unhealthy dieting patterns, chronic health problems, and later-onset eating disorders.
- Obesity rates have increased dramatically in the past few decades, with a steeper increase in U.S. minority populations.
- The causes of obesity include genetic predisposition as well as family and community influences, such as poor knowledge of nutrition, cultural patterns, and limited access to healthy food choices.
- Treatment and prevention efforts often are aimed at helping parents take an active role in children's proper nutrition and activity level. Schools contribute to this effort by educating children in nutrition, exercise, and awareness of healthy eating attitudes and body image.

FEEDING AND EATING DISORDERS FIRST OCCURRING IN INFANCY AND EARLY CHILDHOOD

Feeding and eating disorders stem from developmental and behavioral problems associated with eating and growth. We discuss those that first occur during infancy or early childhood in this section, followed by adolescent eating disorders.

Avoidant/Restrictive Food Intake Disorder

Avoidant/restrictive food intake disorder is characterized by avoidance or restriction of food intake, leading to significant weight loss (or failure to maintain normal growth) and/or nutritional deficiency. One or more of four key features must be present: significant weight loss, significant nutritional deficiency, dependence on enteral feeding (i.e., use of a feeding tube) or oral nutritional supplements, or marked interference with psychosocial functioning (APA, 2013). In severe cases, especially with infants, malnutrition can lead to health-compromising problems and even death. This disorder does not apply to children who lack adequate food or to children who lack food because of cultural practices. Some children manifest this disorder by avoiding or restricting food based on its sensory characteristics, such as appearance, color, taste, smell, or temperature. (Yes, all kids do this at times, but if it leads to weight loss or nutritional deficiency this disorder may be present.)

Prevalence and Development

Although prevalence rates of avoidant/restrictive food intake disorder are unknown, feeding problems are considered common based on parental reports (Lyons-Ruth et al., 2014). If not identified early, this disorder can be particularly troublesome because it can have lasting effects on growth and development. The disorder is equally common among males and females.

Food avoidance and restriction can arise at any age, but it usually begins in childhood. There is no typical developmental outcome among children with avoidant/restrictive food intake disorder, probably because many of the factors that initially led to the problem in the first place also affect the course of the illness. However, if the onset occurs during the first 2 years of life, it can lead to malnutrition and have serious developmental consequences. If there is no medical reason for the failure to gain weight, such early onset often is associated with poor caregiving, which may include abuse and neglect (APA, 2013). Thus, feeding disorders can lead to, or be the result of, a failure to thrive. **Failure to thrive (FTT)** is a term used to describe serious growth and nutritional problems in infants, subsumed under avoidant/restrictive food intake disorder. FTT can have severe consequences for a child's physical and psychological development. It is embedded in social and economic disadvantage and often is connected to inadequate or abusive caregiving that originates during early infancy. FTT is considered the final common pathway for multiple biological, psychological, and social factors that influence growth and viability of the infant or toddler (Benoit, 2009). As expected, the factors that lead to more serious problems over time include the degree and chronicity of malnutrition, the degree and chronicity of developmental delay, and the severity and duration of the problems in the infant–caregiver relationship (Benoit, 2009; Blissett, Meyer, & Haycraft, 2007).

Causes and Treatment

The etiology of avoidant/restrictive food intake disorder has been studied from both biological and psychosocial perspectives, and the best conclusion at present is that many interacting risk factors influence how a child adapts to a certain level of caloric intake and influence whether the child shows normal or abnormal behavioral development. Because feeding and eating disorders have long been associated with family disadvantage, poverty, unemployment, social isolation, and parental mental illness, considerable attention has been focused on those concerns.

A prominent controversy concerns the significance of emotional deprivation (lack of love) and malnutrition (lack of food), especially for failure to thrive. Investigators have argued that the infant with FTT, for example, has been deprived of maternal stimulation and love, which results in emotional misery, developmental delays, and eventually, physiological changes. In one study, mothers of infants diagnosed with FTT were found to be more insecurely attached than mothers of normal

This young child stopped gaining weight and developed failure to thrive.

infants. These mothers also were more passive and confused and either became intensely angry when discussing past and current attachment relationships or dismissed the attachments as unimportant and non-influential (Benoit, Zeanah, & Barton, 1989). Children who have suffered from FTT as a result of early abuse exhibit poorer outcomes 20 years later than children whose failure to thrive resulted from neglect, lack of parenting, or feeding difficulties (Iwaniec, Sheddon, & Allen, 2003).

Avoidant/restrictive food intake disorder and FTT during early infancy can be related to the poor quality of the caregiver–child attachment, which is likely to reflect the insensitive treatment the caregiver received as a child. Poverty, family disorganization, and limited social support contribute to the likelihood of malnutrition and growth failure; infants who are difficult to feed and nurture because of temperament and acute physical illnesses also may become malnourished and have growth failure (Olsen et al., 2007). Hospitalization to achieve weight gain, without considering ways to improve the parent–child relationship, is often insufficient to protect the child from further harm (Black, Dubowitz, Krishnakumar, & Starr, 2007).

What is striking about FTT, in particular, is that a child's developmental outcome is highly related to the child's home environment. Significant changes in quality of care and in the emotional environment results in better adjustment 20 years later, even for children who failed to thrive because of abuse (Iwaniec et al., 2003). Moreover, early FTT may affect physical growth in childhood, but there is no evidence that it affects future cognitive functioning (Black et al., 2007). For these reasons, much of the etiology of FTT has focused on parental psychopathology that results in maltreatment of the child.

Mothers who have a history of disturbed eating habits and attitudes have also been identified as a specific risk factor for avoidant/restrictive food intake disorder (Blissett et al., 2007). Because the mother–child relationship during the early stages of attachment is critical, eating disorders shown by infants and young children may be symptomatic of a fundamental problem in this relationship (Lyons-Ruth et al., 2015). Thus, treatment regimens involve a detailed assessment of feeding behavior and parent–child interactions, such as smiling, talking, and soothing, while allowing the parents to play a role in the infant's recovery (Atalay & McCord, 2011; Linscheid, 2006).

Pica

Pica (rhymes with mica) is the ingestion of inedible substances, such as hair, insects, or chips of paint; it primarily affects very young children and those with intellectual disability. Infants and toddlers typically put things into their mouths, since taste and smell are their preferred ways of exploring the physical world. This disorder is one of the more common and usually less serious eating disorders found among very young children, yet an infant or young child who eats inedible, nonnutritive substances for a period of 1 month or longer may have a more serious problem (Bryant-Waugh, Markham, Kreipe, & Walsh, 2010).

Although children with pica also are interested in eating normal foods, they persist in consuming inedible items as well. In most reported cases, the disorder begins during infancy and lasts for several months, at which time it remits on its own or in conjunction with added infant stimulation and improved environmental conditions. For individuals with intellectual disability, however, pica may become more serious and life-threatening if it continues into adolescence (Matson et al., 2011).

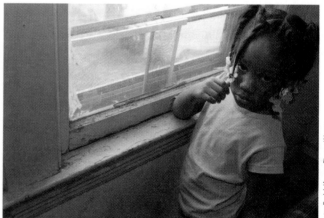

Infants and toddlers with pica may develop the disorder as a result of poor stimulation and supervision. They are at considerable risk of lead poisoning or intestinal obstruction.

Prevalence and Development

Pica is more prevalent among institutionalized children and adults, especially persons with more severe impairments and intellectual disability (de Koning et al., 2007). Among children and adults with intellectual disabilities, the prevalence of pica ranges from 0.3% to 14.4% in the community and from 9% to 25% in institutions (Ali, 2001). The degree of severity often is related to the degree of environmental deprivation and intellectual disability in individuals suffering from the more extreme forms of pica.

Causes and Treatment

Historically, pica was sometimes encouraged by fashions and social pressures that are similar to those that affect body image and appearance today. During the 18th and 19th centuries, for example, young girls sometimes ate lime, coal, vinegar, and chalk because these substances were believed to produce a fashionably pale complexion (Parry-Jones & Parry-Jones, 1994).

Specific causes of pica have not been isolated. Pica may appear during the first and second years of life, even among otherwise normally developing infants and toddlers. The only distinguishing characteristic of these children is that they typically have poor stimulation in their home environment and may be poorly supervised. Because of the risk of lead poisoning or of obstruction in their intestine, pica can become a very serious and substantial problem for this group of infants or toddlers (Bryant-Waugh et al., 2010).

Researchers also have suspected, and in some cases discovered, vitamin or mineral deficiencies among persons with pica, although no specific biological abnormalities have shown a causal link to the disorder (de Koning et al., 2007). There is no evidence, except in cases of intellectual disability, that genetic factors play a role in the etiology of the disorder.

Because of the limited number of treatment studies, no conclusions can be drawn about the relative success of any treatment for pica. Most clinical interventions for children with pica emphasize operant conditioning procedures, in which caregivers are shown how to reinforce the child for desirable behaviors such as exploring the room or playing with objects. Positive forms of attention, including smiling, laughing, and tickling, provide additional stimulation and are especially beneficial, because the disorder often is related to inadequate interaction with caregivers (Linscheid, 2006). Caregivers are also taught to keep the child's environment tidy and to remove or safely store dangerous substances.

Section Summary

Feeding and Eating Disorders First Occurring in Infancy and Early Childhood

- Avoidant/restrictive food intake disorder is characterized by avoidance or restriction of food intake and/or a sudden or rapid deceleration of weight gain.
- Avoidant/restrictive food intake disorder can lead to or result from failure to thrive (FTT), characterized by weight below the fifth percentile for age.
- Pica is the eating of inedible substances. It affects mostly infants, toddlers, and some children with intellectual disability.

EATING DISORDERS OF ADOLESCENCE

Eating disorders (EDs), as well as eating-related problems such as dieting and bingeing, are most likely to appear during two important periods of adolescent development: the early passage into adolescence and the movement from later adolescence to young adulthood (Stice & Bohon, 2013). Early- and middle-childhood risk factors, such as eating problems, dieting patterns, and negative body image, clash with the ongoing challenges that confront adolescents. This clash leads some teens, particularly girls, to exert excessive control over their eating in a misguided effort to manage stress and physical changes. In some instances, this controlled pattern of eating, coupled with other ill-conceived efforts to overcompensate for eating and weight changes (such as excessive exercise), leads to major eating disorders such as anorexia nervosa and bulimia nervosa.

Anorexia nervosa gained medical attention in 1873, when two doctors first described the disorder. Sir William Gull, an English physician, named the malady and described it for the first time as a specific disease. About the same time, in Paris, psychiatrist Charles Lasègue described anorexia from a social and psychological standpoint. Both investigators observed that the disease was most prevalent in the wealthiest social classes, which prompted Lasègue to propose a connection between a lack of parental affection (believed to be relatively common among wealthy families) and a preoccupation with food. Conflict between parents and children could drive some teenage girls to refuse food as an expression of their feelings of rejection. Accordingly, by the turn of the century, the prescribed treatment for anorexia was a "parentectomy," the removal of the child from the family home, which was combined with force-feeding by any means necessary (Munn, Smeltzer, Smeltzer, & Westin, 2010).

References to the disorder now called "bulimia" date back to 6th-century descriptions of more than 40 individuals who displayed symptoms described as "insatiable voracity, morbid or canine appetite, with or without vomiting" (Parry-Jones & Parry-Jones, 1994, p. 288). Interestingly, almost all of these historical cases described males, perhaps because overeating was socially accepted as a sign of wealth or success. Ideal body sizes change with the times and with cultural preferences. Rubenesque figures were considered highly attractive and desirable until the late 19th century, when body image preferences were usurped by major cultural changes. During the Victorian period, refusing food was in keeping with prevailing social pressures. A hearty appetite was considered a wanton expression of sexuality and lack of self-restraint; women were expected to be passively uninterested in both sex and food. Thus, it became morally, spiritually, and socially desirable for women to refuse food, in response to shifting cultural norms for women's appearance and behavior (Brumberg, 1988).

According to physicians around the turn of the 20th century, anorexia nervosa was a symptom of inappropriate romantic choices, blocked educational or social opportunities, and conflicts with parents. Slimness symbolized asexuality and gentility, which implied a respectable amount of social distance from the working classes (Attie & Brooks-Gunn, 1995). Since the 1930s, attitudes and beliefs about women's ideal body size and appearance have been shaped by advertisers, film stars, clothing designers, and similar forces, resulting in a prevailing cultural preference for slimness.

The meaning of food and eating for gender identity, the role of family and social class in determining body image and food choices, and the use of weight regulation as a substitute for self-regulation and control in adolescence remain salient causes of eating disorders to this day. Within the past quarter century, additional aspects of eating disorders, such as the chronic refusal of food, emphasis on overactivity, and bulimic symptoms of bingeing and purging, have gained recognition as significant and potentially dangerous complications (von Ranson & Wallace, 2014).

Anorexia Nervosa

SOOKI

Obsessed with Food and Weight

Sooki is a 19-year old Asian-American college student who is 5 feet 4 inches tall and weighs 90.3 pounds. Friends have not noticed that Sooki has lost so much weight over the past year (25 pounds!) because she wears baggy clothes. About a year ago, Sooki became extremely afraid of becoming fat. She was convinced that weight gain would be the worst thing possible and that her college life would be ruined if she gained weight. Sooki began skipping meals and, when she did eat once or twice a day, consumed only a "salad" of small items. Her salad consists of four lettuce leaves, part of a carrot, an apple slice, and no dressing. Sooki is preoccupied with food and calories. Every bite of food she eats is carefully considered, and she carries charts that list calories per serving of many different foods. She drinks only water and diet soda.

Sooki is obsessed with how much she weighs and how she looks. She owns two scales: one is near her bed and one is in her bathroom. She weighs herself 10 or more times a day. Sooki has told others her butt is too big and her stomach is "poochy." Sooki is markedly underweight but frequently checks her body in the mirror to make sure she is not becoming fat. Her self-esteem depends heavily on her body weight. When Sooki weighs more than 90 pounds she feels bad about herself; when she weighs less than 90 pounds she is perkier. Sooki views weight loss as an impressive achievement in self-discipline. Family members have noticed her weight change and have told Sooki she is underweight. Sooki has not had her menstrual period for 6 months. Still, Sooki does not see her eating and low weight as a problem. She hopes to lose more weight by eliminating "fattening" foods from her diet such as apple slices and diet soda. Sooki has kept to herself recently and leaves her room only to attend class.

From Kearney/Trull. Cengage Advantage Books: Abnormal Psychology and Life, 1E. © 2012 Wadsworth, a part of Cengage Learning, Inc. Reproduced by permission. www.cengage.com/permissions)

Sooki is suffering from **anorexia nervosa**, an eating disorder characterized by:

▶ the refusal to maintain a minimally normal body weight.

▶ an intense fear of gaining weight.

▶ a significant disturbance in the individual's perception and experiences of his or her own size.

As Sooki's story shows, anorexia is a severe eating disorder with serious physical and mental health consequences if left untreated. One of the most notable features of the psychopathology of the disease is that persons who have it deny that they are too thin or that they have a weight problem. As a result, friends or family members often must insist on taking them to see a physician. Diagnostic criteria for anorexia are shown in Table 14.1.

Although the word *anorexia* literally means "loss of appetite," that definition is misleading because the

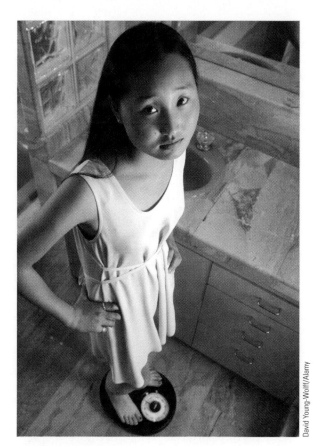

19 year-old Sooki worries about being fat and weighs herself 10 or more times a day.

David Young-Wolff/Alamy

TABLE 14.1 | **Diagnostic Criteria for Anorexia Nervosa**

DSM-5

(A) Restriction of energy intake relative to requirements, leading to a significantly low body weight in the context of age, sex, developmental trajectory, and physical health. *Significantly low weight* is defined as a weight that is less than minimally normal or, for children and adolescents, less than that minimally expected.

(B) Intense fear of gaining weight or of becoming fat, or persistent behavior that interferes with weight gain, even though at a significantly low weight.

(C) Disturbance in the way in which one's body weight or shape is experienced, undue influence of body weight or shape on self-evaluation, or persistent lack of recognition of the seriousness of the current low body weight.

Specify if:

Restricting type: During the past 3 months, the individual has not engaged in recurrent episodes of binge eating or purging behavior (i.e., self-induced vomiting or the misuse of laxatives, diuretics, or enemas). This subtype describes presentations in which weight loss is accomplished primarily through dieting, fasting, and/or excessive exercise.

Binge eating/purging type: During the past 3 months, the individual has engaged in recurrent episodes of binge eating or purging behavior (i.e., self-induced vomiting or the misuse of laxatives, diuretics, or enemas).

Specify if:

In partial remission: After full criteria for anorexia nervosa were previously met, Criteria A (low body weight) has not been met for a sustained period, but either Criterion B (intense fear of gaining weight or becoming fat or behavior that interferes with weight gain) or Criterion C (disturbances in self-perception of weight and shape) is still met.

Specify current severity:

For children and adolescents the minimum level of severity is based on current body mass index (BMI; the weight in kilograms divided by the square of the height in meters) percentile. The level of severity may be increased to reflect clinical symptoms, the degree of functional disability, and the need for supervision.

Mild: BMI ≥17
Moderate: BMI 16 to 16.99
Severe: BMI 15 to 15.99
Extreme: BMI <15

Source: *Diagnostic and Statistical Manual of Mental Disorders,* 5th ed. (Copyright © 2013). American Psychiatric Association.

person with this disorder rarely suffers appetite loss. Weight loss is accomplished deliberately through a very restricted diet, purging, and/or exercise. Although many persons occasionally use these methods to lose weight, the individual with anorexia intensely fears obesity and pursues thinness relentlessly.

Young persons who suffer from anorexia show a major distortion in how they experience their weight and shape. They may become obsessed with measuring themselves to see whether the "fat" has been eliminated. Thus, how they see themselves and how they relate to others is often a function of their perceived shape and weight. To such an individual, weight loss is a triumph of self-discipline. But with anorexia there is never enough weight loss: The person always wants to lose more weight to be on the safe side, and if not enough weight is lost one day, the person may panic and work extra hard to lose weight the next day.

The DSM-5 specifies two subtypes of anorexia based on the methods used to limit caloric intake. In the **restricting type,** individuals seek to lose weight primarily through diet, fasting, or excessive exercise;

in the **binge eating/purging type**, the individual regularly engages in episodes of binge eating or purging, or both. Compared with persons with bulimia, those with the binge eating/purging type of anorexia eat relatively small amounts of food and commonly purge more consistently and thoroughly. Because studies have failed to find significant evidence of the differences between the binge–purge and restricting subtypes of anorexia, subtypes are used mostly to describe current symptoms rather than a distinctive pattern or course (Eddy et al., 2009; Forbush et al., 2010).

Bulimia Nervosa

PHILLIPA

A Well-Kept Secret

Phillipa developed bulimia nervosa at 18. Her strange eating behavior began when she started to diet. Phillipa began gaining weight because she was eating a lot at night. With the extra weight came self-loathing. "I felt like my body was in the way of me being successful at school, and getting dates. I looked in the mirror several times a day, thinking 'I don't even want to be in this body.' There wasn't a minute in my life that I didn't think about some aspect of how I looked."

Although Phillipa dieted and exercised to lose weight, she regularly ate huge amounts of food and maintained her normal weight by forcing herself to vomit. Phillipa often felt like an emotional powder keg—angry, frightened, and depressed. Unable to understand her own behavior, Phillipa thought no one else would either. She felt isolated and lonely. Typically, when things were not going well, she would be overcome with an uncontrollable desire for sweets. She would eat pounds of candy and cake at a time and often not stop until she was exhausted or in severe pain. Then, overwhelmed with guilt and disgust, she would make herself vomit.

Her eating habits so embarrassed her that she kept them secret until, depressed by her mounting problems, she attempted suicide. Fortunately, she didn't succeed. While recuperating in the hospital, Phillipa was referred to an eating disorders clinic where she became involved in group therapy. There she received medications to treat the illness and the understanding and help she so desperately needed from others who had the same problem. With a smile, Phillipa explains: "It taught me that my self-worth is not absolutely correlated with my appearance or what others may think of me."

National Institute of Mental Health [NIMH], 1994b.

Of the two major forms of eating disorders afflicting adolescents and young adults, **bulimia nervosa** is far more common than anorexia. The DSM-5 diagnostic criteria listed in Table 14.2 note that the primary hallmark of bulimia is binge eating. Because most of us overeat certain foods at certain times, you may ask "What exactly is a binge?" As noted in the criteria, a **binge** is an episode of overeating that must involve: (1) an objectively large amount of food (more than most people would eat under the circumstances), and (2) lack of control over what or how much food is eaten.

TABLE 14.2 | **Diagnostic Criteria for Bulimia Nervosa**

DSM-5

(A) Recurrent episodes of binge eating. An episode of binge eating is characterized by both of the following:

(1) Eating, in a discrete period of time (e.g., within any 2-hour period), an amount of food that is definitely larger than most people would eat during a similar period of time and under similar circumstances

(2) A sense of lack of control over eating during the episode (e.g., a feeling that one cannot stop eating or control what or how much one is eating)

(B) Recurrent inappropriate compensatory behavior in order to prevent weight gain, such as self-induced vomiting; the misuse of laxatives, diuretics or enemas, or other medications; fasting; or excessive exercise.

(C) The binge eating and inappropriate compensatory behaviors both occur, on average, at least once a week for 3 months.

(D) Self-evaluation is unduly influenced by body shape and weight.

(E) The disturbance does not occur exclusively during episodes of anorexia nervosa.

Specify if:

In partial remission: After full criteria for bulimia nervosa were previously met, some, but not all, of the criteria have been met for a sustained period of time.

In full remission: After full criteria for bulimia nervosa were previously met, none of the criteria have been met for a sustained period of time.

Specify current severity:

The minimum level of severity is based on the frequency of inappropriate compensatory behaviors (see below). The level of severity may be increased to reflect other symptoms and the degree of functional disability.

Mild: an average of 1 to 3 episodes of inappropriate compensatory behaviors per week.

(continues)

TABLE 14.2 | Diagnostic Criteria for
Bulimia Nervosa (continued)

Moderate: an average of 4 to 7 episodes of inappropriate compensatory behaviors per week.

Severe: an average of 8 to 13 episodes of inappropriate compensatory behaviors per week.

Extreme: an average of 14 or more episodes of inappropriate compensatory behaviors per week.

Source: Diagnostic and Statistical Manual of Mental Disorders, 5th ed. (Copyright © 2013). American Psychiatric Association.

No specific quantity of food constitutes a binge—the context of the behavior that must also be considered. Overeating at celebrations or holiday feasts, for example, is not considered bingeing. Although most binge eaters report overeating junk food rather than fresh fruits and vegetables, the amounts of food they consider a binge vary widely. On average, binge episodes range from 1000 to 4,500 calories, (Wolfe et al., 2009).

Persons with bulimia attempt to conceal binge eating out of shame. Although binges are not planned, a ritual may form wherein the person, sensing no one around, makes a split-second decision (on the way home from a late-night party, for example) to stop, purchase, and consume massive quantities of food. Typically, binge eating follows changes in mood or interpersonal stress, but it also may be related to intense hunger from dieting or to feelings about personal appearance or body shape. Although these feelings may dissipate for awhile, the depressed mood and self-criticism usually return (Smyth et al., 2007).

The second important part of the diagnostic criteria involves the individual's attempts to compensate somehow for a binge. **Compensatory behaviors** are intended to prevent weight gain following a binge episode, and include self-induced vomiting, fasting, exercising, and the misuse of diuretics, laxatives, enemas, or diet pills. By far the most common compensatory technique after an episode of binge eating is induced vomiting—stimulating the gag reflex with the fingers or another instrument. Vomiting produces immediate relief from physical discomfort and reduces fear of gaining weight.

Research with community (nonclinical) samples has not identified any significant differences between persons with bulimia who purge and those who do not (Tanofsky-Kraff et al., 2004). Dietary symptoms (e.g., restraint, purging) are central features of bulimia, but a subset of people with bulimia exhibit both dietary restraint and depressive affect. Young women who have the dietary–depressive pattern exhibit more eating pathology, social impairment, psychiatric comorbidity, and persistence of bulimic symptoms over 5 years than women with only the dietary subtype (Stice & Fairburn, 2003).

Like those with anorexia, adolescents and adults with bulimia often are described as rigid and absolutistic (displaying an all-or-nothing attitude) in their thinking (Joiner, Katz, & Heatherton, 2000; Thompson-Brenner et al., 2008). They see themselves as either completely in control or completely out of control and view everyday events in extremes of either black or white. Phillipa expressed absolutistic thinking, attributing her woes to one thing and one thing only: "I felt like my body was in the way of me being successful at school, and getting dates." These beliefs relate to the DSM-5 criteria, which stress the importance of body shape and weight to self-evaluation. Young women with bulimia, as well as those with anorexia, have greater dissatisfaction with their body proportions and distort their true body size, behaviors that are more strongly connected to cognitive factors, such as biases in attention and memory, and selective interpretation or judgment, than with any actual problem with perceptual ability (Striegel-Moore & Bulik, 2007).

The medical consequences of chronic bulimia can be significant, although they are not as severe as the consequences that can result from anorexia. Common physical symptoms include fatigue, headaches,

<Caption TBD>z

David J. Green - lifestyle themes/Alamy

and puffy cheeks (due to enlarged salivary glands). The permanent or significant loss of dental enamel, especially from the inside surface of the front teeth, is due to the contact of the acidic stomach contents with the teeth. Among females, menstrual irregularity or amenorrhea may occur, although it is not clear whether these disturbances are related to weight fluctuations, other nutritional deficiencies, or stress. Electrolyte imbalances due to purging behavior are sometimes severe enough to cause significant medical problems.

Binge Eating Disorder

Binge eating disorder (BED) has become increasingly widespread during this age of abundant fast food and obesity. Although similar to the binge eating found in bulimia, BED does not include the compensatory behaviors (see Table 14.3). It involves periods of eating more than other people would, accompanied by a feeling of a loss of control (APA, 2013). Researchers differ about whether binge episodes are objective overeating (e.g., over 1,000 calories) or an individual, subjective feeling of losing control (e.g., eating two cookies on a strict diet). Youths define overeating in a variety of ways, including the amount and types of food eaten, emotional consequences after the binge (e.g., feeling guilty), and the individual's reasons for overeating (Neumark-Sztainer et al., 2006). In contrast to individuals with bulimia nervosa, who tend

(C) Marked distress regarding binge eating is present.

(D) The binge eating occurs, on average, at least once a week for 3 months.

(E) The binge eating is not associated with the recurrent use of inappropriate compensatory behavior as in bulimia nervosa and does not occur exclusively during the course of bulimia nervosa or anorexia nervosa.

Specify if:

> **In partial remission:** After full criteria for binge eating disorder were previously met, binge eating occurs at an average frequency of less than one episode per week for a sustained period of time.

> **In full remission:** After full criteria for binge eating disorder were previously met, none of the criteria have been met for a sustained period of time.

Specify current severity:

The minimum level of severity is based on the frequency of episodes of binge eating (see below). The level of severity may be increased to reflect other symptoms and the degree of functional disability.

> **Mild:** 1 to 3 binge eating episodes per week.
> **Moderate:** 4 to 7 binge eating episodes per week.
> **Severe:** 8 to 13 binge eating episodes per week.
> **Extreme:** 14 or more binge eating episodes per week.

Source: Diagnostic and Statistical Manual of Mental Disorders, 5th ed. (Copyright © 2013). American Psychiatric Association.

TABLE 14.3 | Diagnostic Criteria for Binge Eating Disorder

DSM-5

(A) Recurrent episodes of binge eating. An episode of binge eating is characterized by both of the following:

(1) Eating, in a discrete period of time (e.g., within any 2-hour period), an amount of food that is definitely larger than what most people would eat in a similar period of time under similar circumstances.

(2) A sense of lack of control over eating during the episode (e.g., a feeling that one cannot stop eating or control what or how much one is eating).

(B) The binge eating episodes are associated with three (or more) of the following:

(1) Eating much more rapidly than normal

(2) Eating until feeling uncomfortably full

(3) Eating large amounts of food when not feeling physically hungry

(4) Eating alone because of feeling embarrassed by how much one is eating

(5) Feeling disgusted with oneself, depressed, or very guilty afterward.

to be normal weight to overweight, individuals with BED are often overweight or obese (von Ranson & Wallace, 2014).

The mounting concern over BED is justified not only by the higher rates of obesity and weight loss attempts, but also by the negative mental health correlates. Youths with BED score lower on body satisfaction and self-esteem, score higher on depressive mood, and are more likely to report that weight and shape are very important to their overall feelings about themselves (Stice et al., 2009; Stice et al., 2013).

Diagnosing eating disorders is especially difficult among youths, who are still maturing physically, cognitively, and emotionally. As a result, criteria for eating disorders may not be fully met (Eddy et al., 2009; Eddy, Doyle et al., 2008). To accommodate this disparity, DSM-5 includes the categories Other Specified Feeding or Eating Disorder and Other Unspecified Feeding or Eating Disorder. These categories of eating disorders are used for individuals who are deemed to have a clinically significant eating disorder but who do not meet the full criteria for anorexia, bulimia, or BED (sometimes termed *subthreshold*). These "other" categories are less stringent, and therefore are sometimes more appropriate for adolescents (Keel et al., 2010). Because the majority of adolescents with eating problems do not meet the diagnostic criteria for bulimia, anorexia, or BED, professional organizations such as the Society for Adolescent Medicine have advised clinicians to set lower thresholds for diagnosing adolescents with eating disorders (i.e., not requiring that they meet all the DSM-5 criteria).

An overview of key features of anorexia, bulimia, and binge eating disorder is shown in Table 14.4 for ease of comparison.

Prevalence and Development

A large nationwide U.S. sample showed that the lifetime prevalence of anorexia and bulimia among adolescents is 0.3% and 0.9%, respectively (Swanson et al., 2011). Although BED is more prevalent in young adulthood, it affects about 1.5% to 3% of adolescents (Stice, Marti, & Rohde, 2013; Swanson et al., 2011). Distinguishing between the major eating disorders of adolescence and young adulthood can be difficult because anorexia, bulimia, and BED share many features. Adolescents with anorexia or bulimia

TABLE 14.4 | Overview of Anorexia, Bulimia, and Binge Eating Disorders

	Anorexia	Bulimia	Binge Eating Disorder
Key Diagnostic Criteria	• Food restriction leading to significantly low body weight • Fear of or interference with weight gain • Disturbance in self-perceived weight or shape (distorted body perception)	• Recurrent binge eating • Recurrent compensatory behaviors to prevent weight gain • View of self unduly influenced by body shape and weight	• Recurrent episodes of binge eating (similar to bulimia but differs in terms of eating more rapidly, eating alone, eating large amounts when not hungry, and feeling disgusted or guilty afterward) • Marked distress regarding binge eating • Binge eating not associated with compensatory behaviors, as in bulimia
Prevalence in Adolescents and Young Adults	~0.3%	~1%	~1.5–3%
Sex Ratio	Girls affected significantly more than boys (~90%)	Girls affected significantly more than boys (~90%)	Girls more than boys (to a lesser degree than anorexia and bulimia)
Mortality	~5% per decade	~2% per decade	Unknown (overlaps with complications of obesity)
Weight	Markedly reduced	Usually normal	Can be normal, overweight, or obese
Onset	Early to mid-adolescence	Mid- to late adolescence	Late adolescence
Menstrual Irregularity or Amenorrhea	Common	Common	Not present
Comorbidity	Common: bipolar; depression; anxiety; suicide risk Less common: obsessive–compulsive disorder, substance-use disorder	Common: mood disturbance and depression; anxiety Less common: substance-use disorder; suicide risk	Comparable to anorexia and bulimia
Remission	Majority in remission after 5 years	Can be chronic or intermittent, with periods of remission	Similar to bulimia in severity and duration

have distorted body images and nervous feelings after eating. However, persons with anorexia are 15% or more below normal weight, whereas persons with bulimia are within 10% of normal weight and those with BED are often above normal. Also, persons with anorexia engage in binge eating only occasionally and typically avoid forbidden food, whereas those with bulimia and BED binge frequently on forbidden food and then purge to control their weight (bulimia) or feel distressed or upset but do not purge (BED).

Eating disorders can overlap with other mental disorders, such as depression and schizophrenia, obscuring some features and leading to misdiagnosis (Herzog & Eddy, 2007). However, in terms of cognitive beliefs and self-image, only patients with anorexia show an intense drive for thinness and a disturbance in their perception of body image.

Eating Disorders among Young Men

There is increased recognition that eating disorders are more common among young men than was originally believed. Males also are subjected to powerful media images, although perhaps not to the same extent as females. The increasingly muscular male body ideal may be contributing to body dissatisfaction, disordered eating, and harmful weight-control or body-building behaviors (Smolak & Stein, 2010). Young men with eating disorders show some of the same clinical features as young women with eating disorders. However, young men show less of a preoccupation with food or a drive for thinness; rather, they want to be more muscular than they actually are and more muscular than the average male body (Olivardia et al., 2004). In addition, young men and boys are more likely to engage in excessive exercising and overeating, whereas young women and girls are more likely to engage in purging behaviors, to report loss of control while eating, and to try to reduce their caloric intake (von Ranson & Wallace, 2014).

The developmental trajectories and periods of greatest risk for the onset of problem eating symptoms vary between girls and boys as well. In a prospective study of over 3,000 adolescents, symptoms of bulimia among girls increased in mid-adolescence (ages 14 to 16) and then declined slowly, whereas for boys they decreased in mid-adolescence and then started to increase by their early 20s (Abebe, Lien, & von Soest, 2012). This difference in the development and course of eating disorders for girls and boys may be due in part to the predominance of young men's growing fascination with muscularity and thinness, which starts a bit later than girls' interest in feminine ideals. Emerging evidence shows that male interest in muscle development and thinness is related to depressed mood, similar to findings for young girls with early-onset eating

problems (Grossbard et al., 2013). Eating disorders have long been considered a problem affecting primarily women; therefore, young men may be underdiagnosed (Grossbard et al., 2013; Strother et al., 2014).

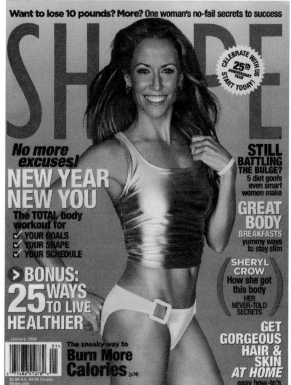

<Caption TBD>z

Sexual Orientation and Eating Disorders

Since the early 1980s, the relationship between sexual orientation and eating disorders has attracted increasing attention from researchers. Gay men appear to be at greater risk for behavioral symptoms of eating disorders than heterosexual men (Brown & Keel, 2013; Jones & Morgan, 2010). Gay men also are more susceptible than heterosexual men to media images promoting thinness (Carper, Negy, & Tantleff-Dunn, 2010) and are more likely than heterosexual men to experience poor body image and body dissatisfaction and symptoms of related eating disorders (Martins, Tiggemann, & Kirkbride, 2007; Smith et al., 2011).

While these studies suggest that gay men may be more susceptible to developing eating disorders and negative body image, the research examining the etiology of body dissatisfaction and eating problems in gay men is sparse. In a survey of 4,374 adolescent boys, those who described themselves as gay or bisexual reported making more efforts to look like boys or men in magazines than did heterosexual boys (Austin et al., 2004). While this study does not necessarily suggest a causal relationship to eating disorders, it does add to the body of literature suggesting that homosexuality is a possible risk factor for the development of eating disorders in male adolescents. Further research into the risk factors that may influence the trajectory of eating problems in gay men will focus our clinical and intervention efforts more efficiently.

Ethnic, Cross-Cultural, and Socioeconomic Considerations

Anorexia has been observed in Western countries as well as every non-Western region of the world, suggesting that anorexia may not be a "culture-bound" syndrome as once believed (Sohl, Touyzl, & Surgenor, 2006). It is becoming increasingly clear that eating disorders do not always manifest the same way in different cultures. In Hong Kong, for example, studies suggest that anorexia may be divided into fat-phobic and non-fat-phobic subtypes and that questionnaires used in Western countries to assess eating disorders may not be sufficiently sensitive to detect the Chinese non-fat-phobic subtype (Lee, Lee, & Leung, 1998).

However, the cross-cultural evidence for bulimia and BED outside of a Western context tells a different story. Keel and Klump's (2003) review of culture and eating disorders found no studies reporting the presence of bulimia in individuals who have not been exposed to Western ideals. Epidemiological data for bulimia in non-Western nations suggest that bulimia has a lower prevalence than anorexia in these countries, and even when it is found in non-Western nations, it is not found in the absence of Western influence. A meta-analysis examining the role of ethnicity and culture in the development of eating disturbances found few differences across ethnic groups for bulimia (Wildes & Emery, 2001). These findings seem to suggest that bulimia is a culture-bound syndrome, arising predominantly in Western regions of the world or in places where individuals probably or definitely have been exposed to Western ideals and culture (Anderson-Fye, 2009).

Socioeconomic status (SES) has long been considered a risk factor for eating disorders among adults, with women of higher SES more likely to diet and have a lower body weight (Nevonen & Norring, 2004). It is plausible that as populations in non-Western nations become more affluent, the risk of developing an eating disorder will increase, regardless of culture or ethnicity. African American women from higher SES backgrounds report levels of body dissatisfaction similar to those of white American women, suggesting that body dissatisfaction is associated more strongly with SES than with ethnicity (Polivy & Herman, 2002). But wealth itself does not automatically lead to an increased prevalence of eating disorders. Once a certain level of affluence has been achieved in a particular society, the association of high SES with eating disorders may no longer exist, owing to the globalization of the boundaries between the socioeconomic classes in modern times (Sohl et al., 2006).

The cross-cultural evidence for eating disorders is further complicated by what some researchers see as a failure of a diagnostic system to adequately capture disorders of eating experienced by members of different ethnic and cultural groups (Wonderlich, Joiner, et al., 2007). This may have deleterious effects for these individuals, who may be suffering from an eating disorder and not receiving proper treatment.

Understanding the role that culture, ethnicity, and SES play in the etiology of eating disorders is challenging. Most of the studies on eating pathology and body image disturbances in non-Western subjects have been undertaken in Western nations rather than in the country of origin. The question of whether or not exposure to Western culture induces eating disorders is complicated further by cultural differences in family environments and socioeconomic levels. Few studies have measured the degree to which an individual has retained his or her traditional cultural values or absorbed the mainstream values. Further complicating the study of ethnicity and eating disorders is that most of the cross-cultural research has focused on the disorders as they have been defined by earlier versions of the DSM. Thus, it is much more difficult to comment on eating disorders such as binge eating disorder outside of a Western context. Further scientific inquiry into all these areas hopefully will contribute to understanding and managing eating disorders, which now are increasingly recognized in individuals from all cultural and ethnic backgrounds (Pike, Dunne, & Addai, 2013).

Developmental Course

Anorexia usually appears during adolescence, between the ages of 14 and 18, although it occasionally does affect older women, men, and prepubertal children. It often begins insidiously, with dieting that gradually leads to life-threatening starvation (Lock & Le Grange, 2006). Sometimes the onset of this dieting and starvation pattern is linked to stressful events, such as being teased about weight, onset of menses, school transitions, and so forth.

Although the symptoms of anorexia are quite specific and well defined, its developmental course and outcome are highly variable. Findings averaged across 119 studies of persons with anorexia show that the rate of mortality is significant (5%); of the survivors, fewer than one-half show full recovery, one-third show fair improvement, and one-fifth continue on a chronic course (Franko et al., 2013; Steinhausen, 2009).

Most common is a fluctuating pattern that involves a restoration of normal weight followed by relapse (Fichter, Quadflieg, & Hedlund, 2006). Although the majority of young persons with anorexia go into remission in 5 years (APA, 2013), those with worse outcomes show more bingeing and purging, and comorbid affective or anxiety disorders (Steinhausen, 2009). Once an individual loses weight and becomes dangerously malnourished, she is hospitalized and begins to show signs of improvement. Nonetheless, a significant number of patients—between 6% and 10%—die from medical complications or suicide (Arcelus et al., 2011; Bulik et al., 2008). Although anorexia is rare, it has the highest mortality rate of any psychiatric disorder and is a leading cause of death for females 15 to 24 years old in the general population (Preti et al., 2011; Striegel-Moore & Bulik, 2007).

Full-blown symptoms of bulimia usually emerge in late adolescence and young adulthood, although episodes of bingeing and purging and a preoccupation with weight begin much earlier (Lock & Le Grange, 2006). A noteworthy aspect of bulimia is that binge eating often develops during or after a period of restrictive dieting (Treasure, Claudino, & Zucker, 2010). Because of the guilt and discomfort caused by binge eating, purging follows as compensation. Bulimia either can follow a chronic course or occur intermittently, with periods of remission alternating with binge eating and purging (Fairburn et al., 2000). However, it is not easy to reverse the developmental course. Because the habits and cultural influences that led to the disorder are so powerful, a chronic pattern of disturbed eating may be established, such as secretive bingeing at social gatherings, which in turn leads to further problems.

Follow-up studies of patients with bulimia indicate that they have a greater chance of recovery than patients with anorexia—between 50% and 75% show full recovery or significant improvement over several years (Chavez & Insel, 2007; Steinhausen & Weber, 2009). The best predictors of a more favorable outcome were younger age at onset and higher social class. Importantly, bulimia responds favorably to treatment that disrupts its cyclical course (Keel et al., 2010).

Similar to the study of long-term outcomes of persons with bulimia, studies of eating behaviors and attitudes among populations of college students suggest that maturing into adulthood and getting away from powerful social pressures that emphasize thinness help many women escape from chronic dieting and abnormal eating. A 20-year follow-up study of body weight, dieting, and symptoms of eating disorders among male and female college students found both encouraging and discouraging results (Keel et al., 2007). On a positive note, women reduced their eating disorder behaviors and increased their body satisfaction ratings. However, body dissatisfaction and desires to lose weight still remained relatively high. Men, on the other hand, were prone to weight gain after college, and many reported increased dieting or disordered eating in the 20 years following college. Although disordered eating tends to decline during the transition to early adulthood, body dissatisfaction remains an issue for many young adults (Keel et al., 2007).

Causes

Why would people starve themselves to near emaciation or eat to the point of illness? The dramatic effects on physical and psychological well-being that can result from eating disorders have inspired many theories. No single factor has been isolated as the major cause of any type of eating disorder, and searching for causes is complicated by the "chicken and egg" problem of causation: Do neurobiological processes disrupt eating patterns, or do eating problems lead to changes in neurobiology?

The single best predictor of risk for developing an eating disorder is being female, and adolescence marks the period of the greatest risk for onset (Striegel-Moore & Bulik, 2007). But not all women or all adolescents develop eating disorders. Thus, explaining the gradual degenerative process of developing an eating disorder requires acknowledging the contribution of all three major etiological domains—biological, sociocultural (including family and peers), and psychological—which can operate singly or in combination to disturb self-regulation in any given individual. Too often, discussions of the etiology of eating disorders become polarized into "cultural" versus "biological" explanations that often ignore the fact that biological and environmental variables are inextricably linked (Striegel-Moore & Bulik, 2007). While the field has made great leaps in understanding the risk factors for the "prototypical" eating disorder case, which is often a young, white, middle- or upper-class North American woman, our knowledge about risk factors unique to diverse cultural populations remains incomplete.

The Biological Dimension

There is reasonable agreement that neurobiological factors play only a minor role in precipitating anorexia and bulimia. However, these factors may contribute to the maintenance of the disorder because of their effects on appetite, mood, perception, and energy regulation (Lock & Le Grange, 2006).

It makes sense to suspect that biological mechanisms (a gene? a neurochemical process?) acting together or alone are responsible for corrupting normal regulatory functions. A slight twist of this scenario places the problem on the individual who disrupts his or her normal regulatory processes in an ill-conceived attempt to achieve weight or diet goals. This disruption may cause biological changes throughout the central nervous and neuroendocrine systems that, in turn, create more disruption. Thus, it also makes sense that success at controlling important bodily functions such as hunger or appetite may lead to unnatural eating habits, resulting in an abusive eating pattern.

Genetic and Constitutional Factors

Eating disorders tend to run in families. Research has found that relatives of patients with anorexia or bulimia, especially female relatives, are 4 to 5 times more likely than persons in the general population to develop an eating disorder (Strober et al., 2000). A large-scale study of 31,406 Swedish twins born between 1935 and 1956 indicates that anorexia and bulimia moderately overlap in genetic and environmental contributors, with heritability playing the larger role in both disorders (Bulik et al., 2010). In this study, the contribution of the shared environment was found to be negligible, and the remaining variance was primarily attributable to unique environmental factors.

If eating disorders are connected to genetic factors, what exactly is inherited? Some people may have a biological vulnerability that interacts with social and psychological factors to increase their chances of developing an eating disorder (Trace et al., 2013). For example, inherited personality traits, such as emotional instability and poor self-control, would predispose an individual to be emotionally reactive to stress, which, in turn, could lead to impulsive eating in an attempt to relieve the feelings associated with stress (Thompson-Brenner et al., 2008). Genomewide association studies currently under way will likely identify genes and pathways involved in eating disorders in the near future (Scherag, Hebebrand, & Hinney, 2010).

Neurobiological Factors

Because serotonin regulates hunger and appetite, studies have focused on this neurotransmitter as a possible cause of anorexia, bulimia, and BED (Calati et al., 2011). Essentially, the presence of serotonin leads to a feeling of fullness and a desire to decrease food intake, so a decrease in serotonin leads to continuous hunger and greater consumption of food at one time—the perfect condition for bingeing. This explanation stems from a gene–environment interaction: children with a genetic risk factor in a serotonin transporter gene are more susceptible to high parental control, which in turns interferes with the child's ability to regulate stress; by adolescence, life events could more easily trigger the onset of anorexia (Karwautz et al., 2011).

One of the strongest findings in support of the serotonin explanation for bulimia comes from studies investigating the relationship of diet to the availability in the brain of the serotonin precursor *tryptophan*. Meals that are rich in protein or low in carbohydrates decrease tryptophan; carbohydrate-rich meals increase it. Put another way, bingeing on sweet and starchy foods creates conditions in the brain that produce more serotonin, which, eventually, leads to a sense of fullness. Binge eating (which usually involves high-carbohydrate food), especially for women, may increase the availability of tryptophan, thereby temporarily increasing brain serotonin (Scherag et al., 2010). It is still not known, however, whether problems related to the availability of serotonin in the brain are due to dieting or are a premorbid characteristic (Trace et al., 2013).

In addition to connections between depression and eating disorders, scientists have found biochemical similarities between people with eating disorders and people with obsessive–compulsive disorder (OCD). Just as serotonin levels are known to be abnormal in people with depression and people with eating disorders, they also are abnormal in patients with OCD (Lock, Garrett, Beenhakker, & Reiss, 2011). Moreover, many persons with bulimia show obsessive–compulsive behavior as severe as that shown among patients diagnosed with OCD, and patients with OCD often have abnormal eating behaviors (Sallet et al., 2010).

In summary, neurobiological abnormalities are found among persons with eating disorders, although at present we cannot determine whether these problems are the result, rather than the primary cause, of semi-starvation or the binge–purge cycle. Understanding how normal eating patterns may initially become disturbed requires a close look at the cultural and psychological components of eating disorders.

Social Dimension

The features of contemporary Western culture could be considered prerequisites for eating disorders. Personal freedom, an emphasis on instant gratification, the availability of food any time of night or day, lack of supervision, and the cultural ideal of diet and exercise for weight loss add up to powerful influences (Attie & Brooks-Gunn, 1995). These factors contribute to a drive for thinness and an emphasis on body image and appearance as the keys to success. As noted earlier, bulimia, but not anorexia, is related primarily to Western culture. Examination of history and of other cultures reveals instances of anorexic behaviors for physical appearance or control issues; however, this is not the case for bulimia (Keel & Klump, 2003; Pike et al., 2013).

In light of the significant social and cultural changes affecting the North American diet, researchers are examining *orthorexia*—a nondiagnostic term meaning "fixation on righteous eating." In contrast to adolescent eating disorders, people with orthorexia are obsessed with food *quality* rather than *quantity* and are less interested in thinness and weight restriction. Orthorexia may begin as an innocent attempt to eat more healthy foods (which we all try to do), which can turn into an obsession about healthy food and diet for a small minority. Because of the intense effort to maintain a rigid healthy eating style, this syndrome may be a form of obsessive–compulsive disorder that can, ironically become so restrictive that health suffers (Brytek-Matera, 2012). Orthorexia has been identified as a concern among professional athletes, who may become obsessed with diet and nutrition to improve their performance (Segura-García et al., 2012).

Sociocultural Factors

Adolescents' concerns about undereating and overeating are legendary, which causes us to question: What aspects of Western culture drive someone, most likely a young woman, to overcome the body's natural rhythm and force it into a punishing and dangerous routine of semi-starvation or frequent purging?

It is well known that for most young white females in middle- and upper-class society, self-worth, happiness, and success are determined primarily by physical appearance, and most eating disorders represent an attempt to feel good with respect to personal appearance and self-control. In reality, body size itself has little or no long-term correlation with personal happiness and success; one's self-concept and self-efficacy are more important. However, a collision may be occurring between our culture and our physiological boundaries, because today's average North American woman between the ages of 17 and 24 is heavier by 5 to 6 pounds than the same average woman of 20 years ago, and today's woman is not satisfied with her body image (Andreyeva, Puhl, & Brownell, 2008).

It appears that as fashion models and media images of women have gotten smaller, adolescent girls have become unhappier—only 15% of teenage girls feel happy "the way I am," as compared with 29% in the mid-1990s (Clay, Vignoles, & Dittmar, 2005). The pursuit of the thin ideal is so pervasive that girls today consider weight loss and being skinny to be more important than sexual issues, alcohol and drug abuse, mental health, disease, and environmental issues (Clark & Tiggemann, 2007). Not surprisingly, some turn to the Internet to connect with others about their body image and receive group support for weight loss, resulting in the popularity of "pro–eating disorders" websites (Sharpe et al., 2011) (see A Closer Look 14.2).

The influence of mass media on body dissatisfaction also affects younger children. Smolak (2004) pointed out that the observed gender, ethnic, cross-cultural, historical, and age differences in levels of body esteem all suggest that culture and society play a major role in the construction of body image in younger children, as they do in adults. While limited research exists on the influence of mass media on body dissatisfaction in children, sociocultural influences such as the media and peers are all potential contributors to children's body image.

For example, in 9- to 12-year-old girls, exposure to media did not predict body dissatisfaction directly but was predictive of conversations about appearance, which in turn predicted body dissatisfaction (Clark & Tiggemann, 2006). In accord with the sociocultural model, increased exposure to appearance media, such as television and magazines, and taking part in peer conversations about appearances were related to body dissatisfaction and dieting behaviors in young girls in grades 4 to 7 (Clark & Tiggemann, 2007). Although media exposure increases children's awareness that appearance is highly valued in our society, actual conversations about this among peers may be a better predictor of the importance a young girl places on this in her life. These findings may inform intervention or prevention efforts targeted at preadolescent girls and the usefulness of media literacy, as well as targeting self and peer beliefs surrounding appearance.

Few would argue against eating disorders being more common in women because of sex-role identification.

Pro–Eating Disorders Websites

The Internet can be a good source of information, but it also can help people who are isolated by a disorder to seek out similar others for mutual support, and not necessarily in healthy ways. With the advent of widespread Internet use has come a proliferation of pro-anorexia and pro-bulimia websites, or "pro-ana" and "pro-mia" as referred to on these sites. These websites recently have emerged as an online movement supporting the virtues of eating disorders. People on these sites reinforce each other's views, share tips on purging and fooling others, and defend their "lifestyle choice" (Haas et al., 2011). However, some of these websites contain controversial and dangerous content, and unfortunately they are more numerous than pro-recovery or professional services websites (Chesley et al., 2003).

A "Letter from Ana" can be found on most personal websites: "I expect a lot from you. You are not allowed to eat much. I will expect you to drop your caloric intake and increase your exercise. I will push you to the limit. You must take it because you cannot defy me. Pretty soon, I am with you always."

Other excerpts from pro-ana websites:

"You'll be FAT if you eat today. Just put it off one more day.

Guys will want to get to know you, not laugh at you and walk away.

Starve off the parts you don't need. They're ugly and drag you down.

Nothing tastes as good as thin feels."

"What's the nutritional information for the chocolate laxatives? If anyone knows, please let me know. I can't believe I'm obsessing over the calorie and carb[ohydrate] content of a laxative."

"That's the designer's dream size, . . . On their sketches, the body is like a hanger. The smaller the sample, the better it drapes— the natural shape of the body distorts their clothing. . . . It's almost like the body is not present." (*Cosmopolitan*, 2001)

Images of women in the 21st century and assumptions about what it is to be feminine are based largely on the idea that girls must be pretty (i.e., not fat) to draw attention and praise from others, whereas boys are admired for their athletic or academic accomplishments. Body build and self-esteem are correlated for girls—but not for boys—by the time they reach the fourth grade (Striegel-Moore & Bulik, 2007). This finding endorses the view that the relationships on which young women's identity and self-worth depend are overly influenced by physical attractiveness and body image.

Sex-role identification is closely tied to cultural norms and expectations, so it is not surprising that women in different cultures do not share the same perception of ideal body weight. Cogan and colleagues (1996) looked at cross-cultural trends in attitudes on obesity and thinness and how they affect dieting patterns in young women from the United States and Ghana. Ghanaian women, as compared with American women, rated larger body sizes as ideal for both sexes. American women scored higher on measures of eating restraint and eating-disordered behavior, and perceived the experience of being overweight as interfering with social acceptance. A disturbing trend indicates that a greater drive for thinness is emerging among young African American girls in the United States in relation to increased peer criticism about weight and appearance (Gilbert et al., 2009; Striegel-Moore et al., 2000).

The forces of culture, combined with gender-based expectations, are powerful determinants of one's perception of ideal body size and associated eating and dieting patterns. Fortunately, these sociocultural patterns may be shifting gradually toward more healthy norms of eating behaviors and lifestyle choices. Eating disorder symptoms, dieting, and body dissatisfaction have been declining significantly on college campuses over the past 30 years (Keel et al., 2007). The increase in public health advertisements, talk shows, and television shows devoted to discussions of eating disorders and to healthy lifestyles may be responsible for raising awareness and prevention of these various disorders and dieting patterns. Perhaps as a further result of these awareness efforts, sociocultural messages about the importance of proper nutrition and body satisfaction are changing as well.

Family Influences

From the very start, researchers and clinicians have placed considerable importance on the role of the family, and parental psychopathology in particular, in considering causes of eating disorders. They have argued that alliances, conflicts, or interactional patterns within a family may play a causal role in the development of eating disorders among some individuals (Minuchin, Rosman, & Baker, 1978). Accordingly, a teen's eating disorder may be functional in that it directs attention away from basic conflicts in the family to the teen's more obvious (symptomatic) problem. Evidence has confirmed that families with members who have eating disorders report worse family functioning than control families, although a typical pattern of family dysfunction is not evident (Holtom-Viesel & Allan, 2014).

Because of the importance of the family environment in shaping a young adolescent's values, it is understandable that family processes may contribute to an overemphasis on weight and dietary control. For example, a mother who is critical of her daughter's weight, or who diets frequently herself and encourages her daughter to diet, may unintentionally become a co-conspirator in the development of an eating disorder (Eisenberg et al., 2012). Similarly, parents who drink heavily or abuse drugs, or who often are absent, uninterested, demanding, or critical, may lay the groundwork for the emergence of bulimia and other disorders in their children. Young people recovering from an eating disorder also may face scrutiny and criticism by other family members, which can lead to less chance of recovery (Munn et al., 2010).

Early clinical suspicions that child sexual abuse could be a risk factor for eating disorders have been supported by ongoing investigations of this important issue (Jacobi et al., 2004). For example, women with a history of one or more incidents of sexual abuse were 3 to 5 times more likely to have bulimia than women with no history of abuse (Sanci et al., 2008). Childhood sexual abuse may be more highly associated with symptoms of bulimia (such as bingeing or purging) because these behaviors can represent an attempt to regulate negative internal states (such as depression and anxiety) that can be the result of the earlier abuse (Holzer et al., 2008; Smolak, 2011).

Similar findings have been reported among population samples of school-aged youths, whereby youths at risk for disordered eating reported more negative perceptions of their families and parents and more experiences of sexual or physical abuse (Neumark-Sztainer et al., 2000). In addition, sexually abused children report many of the early risk signs of eating disorders, such as higher levels of weight dissatisfaction and purging and dieting behavior (Wonderlich, Rosenfeldt, et al., 2007). Some studies have shown that the association between a history of child abuse and eating disorders also is evident among gay and bisexual men (Feldman & Meyer, 2007).

This connection between abuse and eating disorders should be tempered by the awareness that childhood sexual abuse is a general risk factor for psychopathology, rather than a specific risk factor for eating disorders. Other traumatic events, especially those involving a threat to personal safety and/or security (e.g., witnessing domestic violence, assaults, kidnapping, etc.) are also very common in the backgrounds of men and women with eating disorders, as well as those with other psychiatric disorders ((Mitchell et al., 2012). Presumably, childhood trauma is associated with many undesirable adolescent and adult outcomes, of which eating disorders are prominent.

The importance of family factors has led to valuable treatment approaches, as we will see later in this chapter. Nonetheless, family factors must be considered in conjunction with individual and sociocultural factors to explain why the particular features of eating disorders emerge in some families with such dynamics, but not in others.

Psychological Dimension

Understanding the role of psychological processes in the expression of eating disorders requires keeping in mind the powerful social and cultural forces noted previously. External pressures to look thin and be in control of one's weight and appearance interact with certain psychological characteristics to increase the risk of an eating disorder, especially during important developmental transitions. This is a complex, interactive process embedded in multiple layers of biological, familial, personality, and environmental factors. Understandably, this complexity makes causal connections difficult to pinpoint.

Consideration of the psychological dimensions related to eating disorders grew out of the pioneering efforts of Hilda Bruch (1962, 1973), who was the first to propose that self-starvation among persons with anorexia was related to their struggle for autonomy, competence, control, and self-respect. She linked this struggle most closely to parental failure to recognize and confirm their child's emerging independent needs. This sets in motion further confusion that can lead to the principal symptoms of anorexia: disturbance in body image, the inability to recognize and respond to internal sensations or emotions, and the all-pervasive feelings of ineffectiveness and loss of self-control. Her early work set the stage for the cognitive–behavioral interventions used today. She proposed gradual but deliberate relabeling of misconceptions and errors in thinking resulting from faulty developmental experiences and encouraged patients to learn healthy ways of expressing their thoughts and feelings in a genuine and more direct fashion (Silverman, 1997).

Arthur Crisp, another pioneer in the understanding and treatment of eating disorders, considers anorexia to be a type of phobic avoidance disorder, in which the phobic objects are normal adult body weight and shape. He describes this phobia or fear metaphorically as a flight from growth (Crisp, 1997). A young female may begin to perceive herself as being fat as she reaches puberty and starts to change into a more adult size and weight, as a result of family and cultural influences. In response, she tries to pursue and maintain her prepubertal weight as a way to avoid the unwelcome aspects of her own growth. This pursuit becomes a vicious cycle, of course, because trying to maintain one's prepubertal body weight meets powerful biological resistance, so she continues her pursuit of weight loss as "insurance" against these unrelenting forces of nature. In effect, a person with anorexia fears loss of control over her attempts to avoid growth, which often translates into a fear of weighing above 95 to 100 pounds. Like Hilda Bruch's insights, this explanation has led to important treatment efforts.

Adolescents with anorexia are described clinically as being obsessive and rigid, showing emotional restraint, preferring the familiar, having a high need for approval, and showing poor adaptability to change (Arcelus et al., 2013; Thompson-Brenner et al., 2008). These personality features render persons vulnerable to developmental events, such as puberty, that disrupt their carefully maintained sense of self. In a 10-year follow-up of patients with anorexia, their obsessions, compulsions, and social interactions persisted even among those who had their weight restored, leading the researchers to conclude that these problems may be constitutional rather than a result of the disorder (Nilsson et al., 1999). Moreover, more than four of five persons with adolescent-onset anorexia experienced at least one episode of major depression or dysthymia within 10 years after the onset of anorexia (Ivarsson et al., 2000). The common association between anorexia and depression may be due to poor emotion regulation stemming from environmental or neurobiological factors (Haynos & Fruzzetti, 2011), as well as the effect of malnutrition on mood regulation (Mischoulon et al., 2011). After 18 years, most of the youths in this longitudinal study had recovered from anorexia, but they still showed persistent efforts to restrict their eating (Wentz et al., 2012).

Adolescents with bulimia exhibit somewhat different personality characteristics, involving mood swings, poor impulse control, conflict, and obsessive–compulsive behaviors (Arcelus et al., 2013; Krug et al., 2011). In a large epidemiological study, persons with bulimia had a threefold increase in the lifetime occurrence of major depression and at least a doubling of the rate for anxiety disorders. Specific phobias, agoraphobia, panic disorder, generalized anxiety disorder, and alcohol dependence were all more elevated among bulimic individuals than among non-bulimic community members (Garfinkel et al., 1995). Moreover, abuse of alcohol or stimulants to control appetite is also present in about one-third of the clinical samples of adolescents with bulimia (APA, 2013). Depression, in particular, may co-occur with bulimic symptoms in adolescent girls because they are reciprocally related—each disorder increases the risk for onset of the other (Smyth et al., 2007; Stice, Burton, & Shaw, 2004). Finally, sex differences also emerge in relation to psychological factors. Females with symptoms of chronic bulimia report more drive for thinness than do males with similar chronic symptoms, but these same males report more perfectionism and interpersonal distrust (Joiner et al., 2000; Keel et al., 2007).

Eating disorders almost always are accompanied by other disorders. Community samples in which adolescents are randomly selected and interviewed for psychiatric disorders reveal that almost 90% of persons fitting the criteria for an eating disorder also have other clinical disorders—usually depression, anxiety, or OCD (Herzog & Eddy, 2007; Lewinsohn, Striegel-Moore, & Seeley, 2000). Although genetic links certainly play a role, researchers also have focused on personality characteristics such as perfectionism, rigidness, or neuroticism that may be a common link between these disorders (Thompson-Brenner et al., 2008). For example, persons who have a high need for perfection and who also experience high levels of daily stress are more likely to exhibit symptoms of depression (Smyth et al., 2007). Similarly, individuals who score high on perfectionism and perceive themselves as being overweight have a greater risk of bulimic symptoms that they maintain for many years (Holland, Bodell, & Keel, 2013; Tissot & Crowther, 2008). Simply stated, a discrepancy between one's actual self (in this case, perceived weight) and one's ideal self (striving toward perfection) increases the likelihood of eating problems, especially among women.

Let's look at a practical example of how the preceding information can be put into dynamic perspective. The adolescent with bulimia or anorexia feels that her efforts to restrict her diet and lose weight are ways of gaining control over her life and of becoming a better person, beliefs that are formed during childhood and become operational when she faces the challenges of early adolescence. What develops into the rigidity of anorexia or the battle for control of bulimia may begin as a moderate diet. A teenager unwittingly may begin a dangerous eating pattern because of her dissatisfaction with body weight and shape, and her efforts initially are rewarded by weight loss and a sense of greater control and self-worth, such as former gymnast Erica Stokes describes in A Closer Look 14.3.

The transition from dieting to eating disorder may be prompted by the extra attention from peers for what appears to be dramatic willpower and weight loss (Marcos et al., 2013). Therefore, powerful psychological needs may be at the root of the eating disorder, because the disorder itself is a way to cope with strong feelings that the person otherwise does not know how to express or resolve. This dynamic process accounting for the many determinants of eating disorders is depicted visually in ● Figure 14.5.

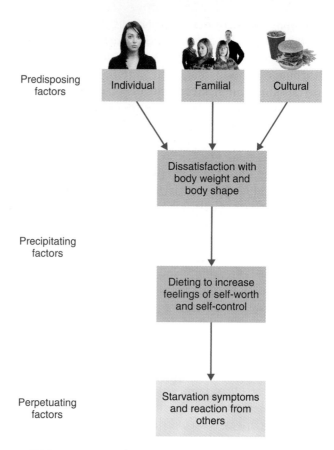

● **FIGURE 14.5** | A dynamic perspective on the determinants of eating disorders.

Reprinted from *The Lancet, 341*, D. M. Garner, Pathogenesis of Anorexia Nervosa, 1631–1635, Copyright 1993, reprinted with permission from Elsevier.

Photo Credits (left to right): © iStockphoto.com/DRB Images, LLC; © Istockphoto.com/ Claudiad; © michelaubryphoto/Fotolia.com

Because of high-profile cases of gymnasts and other performers with eating disorders, the demands of competitive sports, performing arts, and fashion modeling have received much scrutiny. These types of activities emphasize appearance or weight restriction, so involvement in them was cited early on as a risk factor for developing an eating disorder because of the pressure to be thin (Hildebrandt, 2005). Although elevated rates of subclinical symptoms of eating disorders have been found among female dancers and other athletes involved in weight-related sports, the relationship between participation in sports that emphasize thinness and eating disorders is a topic of considerable debate. In a meta-analysis of studies, researchers concluded that there are circumstances when sports participation constitutes a risk factor for eating disorders, as well as situations in which it may be protective (Smolak, Murnen, & Ruble, 2000). That is, different combinations of body focus, sport type, performance level, age, and personality variables may influence risk (Krentz & Warschburger, 2011; Swami & Szmigielska, 2013).

Sports participation has long been known to be associated with higher levels of self-esteem in boys and men, and some research suggests the same is true for girls and women (Schmalz et al., 2007). Thus, sports participation might actually serve to help protect against the development of eating problems, given that high self-esteem generally is associated with lower psychopathology. On the other hand, personality characteristics such as perfectionism and a need for high achievement are found in both patients with eating disorders and athletes (Sassaroli et al., 2008). For some men and women the sporting environment involves an unhealthy mix of pressure to perform that can increase the risk of eating disorders (DiPasquale & Petrie, 2013).

Treatment

Psychological interventions for eating disorders often include some form of individual and/or family-based psychotherapy, sometimes accompanied by medical interventions. While the evidence base for the effectiveness of any form of intervention is still modest, there is increasing support for family-based interventions for adolescents with anorexia (Galsworthy-Francis & Allan, 2014; Watson & Bulik, 2013). The benefits of psychological treatments for bulimia, especially cognitive–behavioral therapy (CBT), are even more encouraging (Hay, 2013; Wilson, Grilo, & Vitousek, 2007). One of many challenges remaining in community-based treatment delivery is that patients often seek (and receive) treatment for weight loss and disguise their eating disorder symptoms, thereby not receiving proper mental health assessment and treatment (Hart et al., 2011).

Most adolescents with anorexia, bulimia, and related eating disorders can be treated on an outpatient basis. Hospitalization usually is required only for a small percentage of adolescents with anorexia who have serious complications due to comorbid diagnoses or who are at high physical and/or psychiatric risk. Inpatient treatment is usually brief, as long as psychological counseling and outpatient psychotherapy are made available (Gowers & Bryant-Waugh, 2004). However, because there is great pressure for psychological treatments to show effectiveness in briefer and briefer periods of time, the growing concern is that high-risk patients are released too soon, before they reach their normal body weight, primarily to reduce costs (Pratt et al., 2003).

Pharmacological

Pharmacological treatments are gaining recognition for assistance in the management of eating disorders, although they are not considered to be the initial treatment of choice (Gowers & Bryant-Waugh, 2004). Because of the strong association between anorexia and bulimia and the affective disorders, selective serotonin reuptake inhibitors (SSRIs) such as fluoxetine (Prozac) have been the most extensively studied and used medications to treat eating disorders, and they are the only treatment approved by the U.S. Food and Drug Administration (Chavez & Insel, 2007). The weight-loss benefits of SSRIs were discovered serendipitously during clinical trials of their ability to regulate mood. Much the same way as bingeing elevates mood in some individuals by increasing carbohydrate levels (Haedt-Matt & Keel, 2011), a sense of well-being could be achieved artificially by regulating serotonin levels.

To date, however, no drug has proved useful or effective for treating symptoms of anorexia among adolescents, and none has consistently improved long-term weight maintenance, changed a distorted self-image, or prevented relapse (Lock & Le Grange, 2006). In contrast, there is a consensus that antidepressants have a useful role in the treatment of bulimia, but probably not as the initial treatment of choice. Persons with bulimia may respond favorably to antidepressants and SSRIs, as long as they are continued for 6 months or so and are accompanied by psychosocial treatments with proven effectiveness, as described in the next section (Touyz, Polivy, & Hay, 2008). Although drug therapy has its usefulness, especially in cases that are not responding to psychological therapy, CBT remains a more effective and often preferred choice than medication alone (McHugh et al., 2013; Wilson et al., 2007).

Psychosocial

The presence of both emotional and physiological problems in eating disorders requires a comprehensive treatment plan, which ideally consists of a treatment team consisting of an internist, a nutritionist, a psychotherapist, and a psychopharmacologist. Once an eating disorder has been diagnosed and other illnesses have been medically ruled out, the clinician determines whether the individual can be treated as an outpatient. Family engagement then may become necessary, to assist family members in managing their fears and worries, as well as to enlist their cooperation. For younger patients, family involvement often is necessary and practical, since parents are responsible for their child's well-being and can offer important directives and guidance that increase successful treatment. In some cases, resolution of family problems—such as parental psychopathology, family isolation, and a poor parent–child relationship—are crucial to recovery from an eating disorder. Recovered patients consider the resolution of family and interpersonal problems to be pivotal to their recovery (Lock & Le Grange, 2006).

The etiology and course of anorexia result in a disorder that is less responsive to treatment than bulimia; nevertheless, inroads certainly are being made. The initial phase of treatment must involve the restoration of weight and the monitoring of any medical complications that might arise. However, restoring a patient's weight may be the easier part of the process. Many patients regain weight initially (especially if hospitalized), but the pattern of weight loss and distorted beliefs returns unless the family and individual factors that initially led to the overemphasis on control of eating are addressed.

The limited empirical support for any treatment for anorexia is due partially to the difficulty of randomly assigning individuals with this life-threatening condition to a control group. Nonetheless, the "best practices" for treating this disorder have evolved based on existing clinical wisdom and modified research designs. One alternative is to randomly assign patients to either "standard care" or to a specific treatment condition to compare their relative effectiveness (without a no-treatment or placebo control group). For example, Touyz et al. (2013) compared CBT and specialist supportive clinical management for adults who had a history of anorexia lasting at least 7 years. Participants received 30 outpatient sessions of either treatment over 8 months. Both interventions led to meaningful improvements in quality of life and social adjustment at 12 months of follow-up, with the CBT intervention showing higher scores on readiness for recovery.

As mentioned, family therapy is the initial treatment of choice for persons with anorexia who are younger and living at home. The facade of togetherness expressed by family members of girls with anorexia often is seen by clinicians as an attempt to disguise covert or overt aggression and avoid conflict. Family-based interventions, therefore, often are required to restore healthy communication patterns (Wilson et al., 2007). By involving the whole family, therapists can deal with the family's attitudes toward body shape and body image that, to an adolescent, can be perceived as subtle but critical judgments. Once weight is restored to within acceptable levels and family support becomes more available, cognitive–behavioral methods similar to the methods described previously can focus more specifically on the patient's rigid beliefs, self-esteem, and self-control processes.

Family therapy does not necessarily mean that all family members are seen at the same time (i.e., conjoint family therapy); in some cases, seeing family members separately is the best approach. For instance, instead of challenging family members' negative interaction patterns, such as conflict avoidance

and alliances (similar to the early work of Minuchin et al., 1978), therapists encourage parents to mobilize the family's resources to take control of their adolescent's eating patterns, raise parents' morale, and engage all members in further therapy. Focusing on the nature of the illness and its treatment helps to avoid both further criticism of the child and placing blame on family members. Working with parents separately from their teenage daughters (which, of course, makes it impossible to challenge interaction patterns and alliances) has been as effective as conjoint methods, and it has been even more beneficial for families with high levels of criticism and hostility (Lock et al., 2010; Retzlaff et al., 2013).

As noted, the most effective current therapies for bulimia involve CBT delivered individually or by involving the family unit (Rutherford & Couturier, 2007; Wilson et al., 2007). Cognitive–behavioral therapists change eating behaviors by rewarding or modeling appropriate behaviors, and by helping patients change distorted or rigid thinking patterns that may contribute to their obsession. CBT has become the standard treatment for bulimia, and it forms the theoretical base for much of the treatment for anorexia (Chavez & Insel, 2007). This evidence-based treatment is appropriate for patients whose age does not mandate family therapy and whose symptoms are moderate to severe.

The clinical application of CBT has been expanded to address specific cues that trigger the urge to binge or to vomit; it also addresses the underlying interpersonal issues that bother some patients, such as body dissatisfaction or distorted drive for thinness (Stice et al., 2008; Stice et al., 2011). The goals of CBT are to modify abnormal cognitions on the importance of body shape and weight and to replace efforts at dietary restraint and purging with more normal eating and activity patterns (Poulsen et al., 2014; Touyz et al., 2008). CBT for the treatment of bulimia includes several components. Patients are first taught to self-monitor their food intake and bingeing and purging episodes, as well as any thoughts and feelings that trigger these episodes. This is combined with regular weighing; specific recommendations on how to achieve desired goals, such as the introduction of avoided foods and meal planning, designed to normalize eating behavior and curb restrictive dieting; cognitive restructuring aimed at habitual reasoning errors and underlying assumptions relevant to the development and maintenance of the eating disorder; and regular review and revision of these procedures to prevent relapse.

Some evidence indicates that psychotherapeutic approaches other than standard CBT also are effective for treating eating disorders. One favored approach is to offer interpersonal therapy that addresses situational and personal issues contributing to the development and maintenance of the disorder (McIntosh et al., 2011). The Internet and community- or school-based educational strategies are also emerging as practical means to reach more individuals before their symptoms become unmanageable. Individuals receive CBT lessons online, and may receive e-mail or social networking support to meet their goals (Beintner, Jacobi, & Schmidt, 2014; Sanchez-Ortiz et al., 2011; Stice, Becker, & Yokum, 2013).

Section Summary

Eating Disorders of Adolescence

- Anorexia nervosa is characterized by a refusal to maintain body weight, an intense fear of gaining weight or becoming fat, a distorted body image, and amenorrhea.
- Bulimia nervosa involves recurrent episodes of binge eating, followed by an effort to compensate by self-induced vomiting or other means of purging. Individuals with bulimia also are unduly influenced by body shape and weight and are obsessed with food.
- Binge eating disorder (BED) involves periods of eating more than other people would, accompanied by a feeling of a loss of control. Unlike bulimia, persons with BED do not show compensatory behaviors.
- Anorexia is less common than bulimia and BED, and it has an earlier onset (ages 14 to 18). These disorders are much more common in girls than in boys.

- If left untreated, eating disorders can become chronic and pose serious threats to health; bulimia and BED have higher rates of recovery than anorexia.
- Biological factors likely do not precipitate eating disorders, but their effects on appetite, mood, perception, and energy regulation contribute to the maintenance of the disorder.
- Features of Western culture and family life play a significant causal role in eating disorders. Emphasis on dieting and physical appearance can lead to a drive for thinness.
- Eating disorders have one of the highest rates of comorbidity. The most common co-existing disorders are depression (including dysthymia) and anxiety (including OCD).
- Adolescents with anorexia are described clinically as being obsessive and rigid, preferring the familiar, having a high need for approval, and showing poor adaptability to change.
- Adolescents with bulimia or BED are more likely to show mood swings, poor impulse control, and obsessive–compulsive behaviors.
- Psychosocial and pharmacological treatments for eating disorders are limited, with no form of intervention particularly beneficial. Clinical approaches often emphasize the importance of changes in family communication patterns.
- Cognitive–behavioral treatments that focus on the attitudes, beliefs, and behaviors supporting dieting, binge eating, or purging are the most effective psychosocial treatments for bulimia. Pharmacological intervention sometimes is used as a corollary treatment for comorbid disorders, such as depression.

Study Resources

SECTION SUMMARIES

KEY TERMS

The Human Brain and Possible Areas Linked to Mental Disorders in Children

The human brain does not reach full cognitive and emotional maturity until a person reaches his or her 30s.

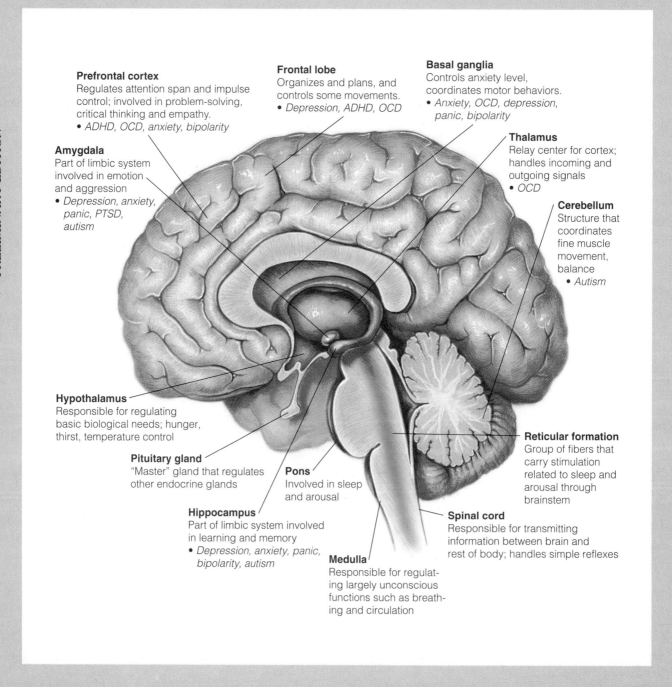

Prefrontal cortex
Regulates attention span and impulse control; involved in problem-solving, critical thinking and empathy.
• *ADHD, OCD, anxiety, bipolarity*

Amygdala
Part of limbic system involved in emotion and aggression
• *Depression, anxiety, panic, PTSD, autism*

Frontal lobe
Organizes and plans, and controls some movements.
• *Depression, ADHD, OCD*

Basal ganglia
Controls anxiety level, coordinates motor behaviors.
• *Anxiety, OCD, depression, panic, bipolarity*

Thalamus
Relay center for cortex; handles incoming and outgoing signals
• *OCD*

Cerebellum
Structure that coordinates fine muscle movement, balance
• *Autism*

Hypothalamus
Responsible for regulating basic biological needs; hunger, thirst, temperature control

Pituitary gland
"Master" gland that regulates other endocrine glands

Pons
Involved in sleep and arousal

Reticular formation
Group of fibers that carry stimulation related to sleep and arousal through brainstem

Hippocampus
Part of limbic system involved in learning and memory
• *Depression, anxiety, panic, bipolarity, autism*

Medulla
Responsible for regulating largely unconscious functions such as breathing and circulation

Spinal cord
Responsible for transmitting information between brain and rest of body; handles simple reflexes

Profile from
Child Behavior Checklist (CBCL):
Syndrome Scales

Hand-scored Syndrome Profile from CBCL completed for Wayne Webster by his mother.

From Achenbach, T. M., & Rescorla, L. A. (2001). *Manual for the ASEBA school-age forms & profiles: An integrated system of multi-informant assessment.* Burlington VT: ASEBA, p. 23.